MODERN SOUTHEAST ASIA SERIES

Steve Maxner, *General Editor*

After the Killing Fields: Lessons from the Cambodian Genocide
by Craig Etcheson

An Loc: The Unfinished War
by General Tran Van Nhut with Christian L. Arevian

The Battle of Ngok Tavak: Allied Valor and Defeat in Vietnam
by Bruce Davies

Military Medicine to Win Hearts and Minds: Aid to Civilians in the Vietnam War
by Robert J. Wilensky

Operation Passage to Freedom: The United States Navy in Vietnam, 1954–1955
by Ronald B. Frankum, Jr.

Vietnam and Beyond: A Diplomat's Cold War Education
by Robert Hopkins Miller

Vietnam Chronicles: The Abrams Tapes, 1968–1972
transcribed and edited by Lewis Sorley

Window on a War: An Anthropologist in the Vietnam Conflict
by Gerald C. Hickey

Vietnam War Memorial (dedicated 27 April 2003) in Westminster, California, by sculptor Tuan Nguyen. *Photograph courtesy of Colonet Ha Mai Viet Collection.*

[The Vietnam War]

AN ASSESSMENT BY
SOUTH VIETNAM'S GENERALS

Edited, and with Introductory and Concluding Essays, by
LEWIS SORLEY

Texas Tech University Press

This book is typeset in Times. The paper used in this book meets the minimum requirements of ANSI/ NISO Z39.48–1992 (R1997). ∞

Library of Congress Cataloging-in-Publication Data

The Vietnam War : an assessment by South Vietnam's generals / edited, and with introductory and concluding essays, by Lewis Sorley.

p. cm. — (Modern Southeast Asia series)

Summary: "Collects seventeen essays by top military leaders of South Vietnam, composed shortly after the end of the Vietnam War. Covers a wide range of topics to present a remarkably candid and self-critical assessment of the war. Contains an introduction and epilogue by Lewis Sorley"—Provided by publisher.

Includes bibliographical references and index.

ISBN 978-0-89672-643-7 (pbk. : alk. paper)

1. Vietnam War, 1961–1975. I. Sorley, Lewis, 1934–

DS557.7.V5664 2010

959.704'3—dc22   2010036094

Printed in the United States of America

10 11 12 13 14 15 16 17 18 / 9 8 7 6 5 4 3 2 1

AUTHOR PHOTO CREDITS: General Cao Van Vien, *U.S. Army Center of Military History*; Lieutenant General Dong Van Khuyen, *Family Collection*; Lieutenant General Ngo Quang Truong, *Family Collection*; Major General Nguyen Duy Hinh, *Family Collection*; Brigadier General Tran Dinh Tho, *Family Collection*; Colonel Hoang Ngoc Lung, *Lt. Gen. William E. Potts Collection*; Lieutenant Colonel Chu Xuan Vien, *Family Collection*.

Texas Tech University Press | Box 41037 | Lubbock, Texas 79409–1037 USA

800.832.4042 | ttup@ttu.edu | www.ttupress.org

For those who served

Long after the war was over, after the fighting had ended, after Bunker was dead, and Abrams too, after the boat people and all the other sad detritus of a lost cause, the eldest of General Abrams's three sons, all Army officers, was on the faculty of the Command & General Staff College at Fort Leavenworth. There someone reminded him of what Robert Shaplen had once said, that his father deserved a better war. "He didn't see it that way," young Creighton responded at once. "He thought the Vietnamese were worth it."

LEWIS SORLEY
A Better War

[Contents]

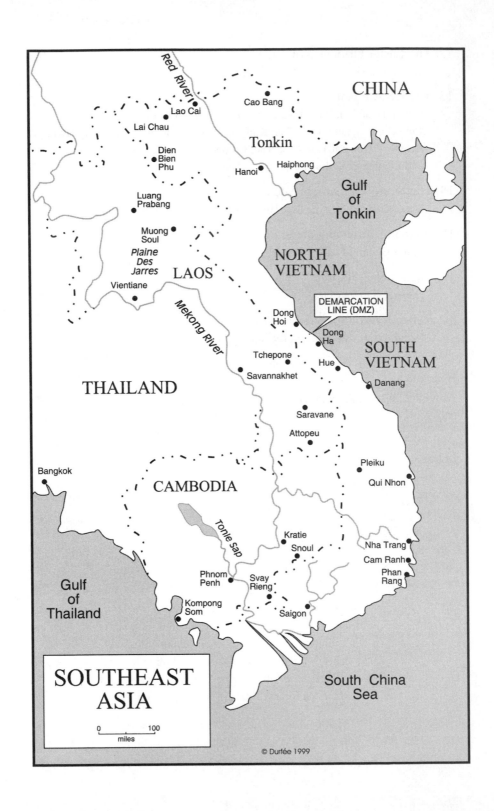

CHINA

Red River

Lao Cai

Cao Bang

Lai Chau

Tonkin

Dien
Bien
Phu

Haiphong

Hanoi

Gulf
of
Tonkin

Luang
Prabang

Muong
Soul

*Plaine
Des
Jarres*

LAOS

NORTH
VIETNAM

Vientiane

Mekong River

DEMARCATION
LINE (DMZ)

Dong
Hoi

Dong
Ha

SOUTH
VIETNAM

THAILAND

Tchepone

Savannakhet

Hue

Danang

Saravane

Attopeu

Pleiku

Bangkok

CAMBODIA

Qui Nhon

Kratie

Tonle Sap

Snoul

Nha Trang

Cam Ranh

Phnom
Penh

Svay
Rieng

Phan
Rang

Gulf
of
Thailand

Kompong
Som

Saigon

SOUTHEAST
ASIA

South China
Sea

0   100
miles

© Durfée 1999

[Introduction]

THE WAR IN BRIEF

To the South Vietnamese involved, it must have seemed as though they had been at war forever. Those who were old enough had gone through the battles of World War II, with the Japanese imposing their rule for a number of years. Then there was the fighting up to 1954 to oust French forces attempting to reimpose their nation's colonial rule. Hardly had that campaign succeeded before those who had rallied to the South found themselves engaged in a bitter and bloody internecine conflict with North Vietnam—and its handmaiden in the South, the Viet Cong—who sought to establish by force of arms their hegemony over the whole of Vietnamese territory.

As early as 1955 American advisors and American military assistance had come to South Vietnam's aid. Over the years the level of this presence grew significantly, providing in addition to advisory input a number of other important kinds of support—military equipment, training, funds, intelligence, communications, and logistics.

By early 1965, however, it was determined that the growing enemy threat was such that deployment of American ground forces would be necessary to keep South Vietnam from succumbing. Over the next four years this commitment continued to grow, reaching by the end of April 1969 a total of 543,400 men, in addition to many thousands more in supporting air and naval units elsewhere in Southeast Asia and contiguous waters.

In the years of the buildup, American forces conducted a war of attrition during which, in large-scale battles often conducted in the deep jungle adjacent to South Vietnam's western borders with Laos and Cambodia, the focus was on killing large numbers of enemy troops. Meanwhile South Vietnam's armed forces were relegated to what was then considered the secondary role of pacification support, a situation in which they were also given low priority when it came to modern weapons and communications equipment.

A new phase began in 1969 when, with a new administration in office in the United States, it was decided to "Vietnamize" the war and, regardless of what the enemy did, progressively withdraw American forces. Thus the buildup of the earlier period was systematically reversed. At the same time, expansion of South Vietnamese armed forces, and in particular their territorial forces, was supported, along with the provision of greatly improved weaponry and other equipment. During this period, pacification was also accorded priority equal to that given military operations. As a result of these initiatives, security of the populace was greatly improved, as was the ability of the South Vietnamese to replace the departing US and other allied forces in providing for their own defense.

In 1973 yet one further phase began with conclusion of the Paris Accords, an agreement that in theory ended the conflict, at the same time providing that allied troops would be withdrawn from South Vietnam and prisoners of war would be exchanged. Ominously, however, no mention was made of the large number of enemy forces deployed in South Vietnam. With practically no surcease, the fighting began again and, so long as the United States continued to provide the necessary military and financial wherewithal, South Vietnam held her own. When, however, the US Congress drastically cut such support, while North Vietnam's patrons dramatically increased support for their client state, South Vietnam was doomed. At the end of April 1975, with the fall of Saigon, the long struggle ended.

THE INDOCHINA MONOGRAPHS

These monographs were written very soon after the end of the Vietnam War, and this context adds pathos and perspective to what the authors have to say. They are still shocked and saddened by the experience of a tragic loss of their country, of their existence there, and of the lives of so many who served under their command, and by beginning new lives for themselves and their families in an adopted county—one for whose succor they are no doubt grateful, but bittersweet largesse nonetheless from a sometime ally who has just abandoned them on the battlefield in their hour of greatest need.

This outlook, with little time to heal from the traumatic events they and their families had so recently undergone, has colored their accounts to no small degree, or so it seems to me. I think, for one, that they are in many instances far too hard on themselves and on the Vietnamese in general, both politically and militarily. They make few excuses, and instead are forthright in assigning, and assuming, blame.

In the three decades or so since these pages were penned, we have learned a great deal about the war in its several stages, including much that explains South Vietnamese failures and incapacity in the early years, when the United States more or less hogged both the best modern weaponry and the bulk of such combat multipliers as close air support, B-52 bombing missions, intra-theater air transport, and helicopters.

Those who opposed the war, or at least their own involvement in it, were at pains—then and now—to portray everything associated with it in as negative terms as possible, and this spilled over onto the reputation of the South Vietnamese armed forces as well. Now we know, however, that when well armed and equipped, and well led, they performed gallantly and with spirit. Repulse of the enemy's massive conventional invasion now recalled as the Easter Offensive of 1972 was perhaps their finest hour. So severely was the enemy punished that it was three years before he could mount another major attack. When that came, the United States had defaulted on its commitments to the South Vietnamese, leaving them hopelessly overmatched against an enemy still robustly supported by his Communist patrons. Thus the outcome was no longer in doubt.

These monographs cover every major aspect of the war. Written by a group of only six authors, men who occupied crucially important positions in South Vietnam's armed forces and performed with great courage and distinction, they represent an impressive intellectual achievement. In most cases a given topic has been addressed by an individual author, although there are several collaborative works as well; on the monograph dealing with American advisors they all took a byline, even the translator. Handicapped to a degree by the loss of the records and archives of their former armed forces, these authors have nevertheless been able to recapture an impressive amount of detail.

Their viewpoints—always interesting, sometimes surprising—add significantly to the literature on the war, a body of work in which the voices of the South Vietnamese themselves have for long been seriously underrepresented. While it is quite apparent that these particular commentators do not, individually or collectively, provide persuasive interpretations of every aspect of the war, especially in view of all that has been learned in the years since the war ended, their outlooks as expressed in the period soon after the loss of their country are valuable, poignant, and ultimately ineffably sad.

The project that produced these monographs, formally designated the Indochina Refugee–Authored Monograph Program, was sponsored by the US Army Center of Military History. The center subsequently contracted with what was then the General Research Corporation to provide facilities and administrative support to the authors. General Andrew J. Goodpaster, who had served in Vietnam as Deputy COMUSMACV, was a member of the panel that chose the contractor. Lieutenant General William E. Potts, for three years during the war the MACV J-2—the senior American intelligence officer in Vietnam—was instrumental in lining up the authors and arranging which topics each would address. Brigadier General James L. Collins Jr. was the distinguished and long-serving U.S. Army Chief of Military History during the entirety of the project.

Work was started at the beginning of 1976 and lasted until the end of 1978, with twenty monographs being completed in total (three of which, dealing with Cambodia and Laos, have been omitted from the present compilation).

The six authors were provided offices and administrative support at a GRC facility in McLean, Virginia. The contractor also put together for use by the authors a small library of basic reference materials such as a chronology and maps and the like. General Potts also maintained an office there, and was often on hand as mentor and facilitator. ARVN Lieutenant Colonel Chu Xuan Vien, who had served in the Republic of Vietnam's embassy in Washington during the final months of the war, was a key participant in the program. During June–December 1975 he had taken part in something called the Quick Reaction Indexing Program, accompanying General Potts to the refugee camps established at Camp Chaffee, Camp Pendleton, and Indiantown Gap Military Reservation. Now Colonel Vien served as translator of the monographs, written in longhand by their authors. His was a very demanding task as each document went through multiple successive drafts.

Each week the authors met with General Potts to discuss the progress of the project and, as drafts became available, to go over the manuscripts and make comments and suggestions. At one such session retired General William C. Westmoreland, former commander of American forces in Vietnam, paid a visit. "It was an honor to receive him," said Colonel Vien. At the end of their discussion, recalled Vien, Westmoreland left the Vietnamese authors with a stark concluding comment: "We betrayed you."

Colonel Vien also noted that at the weekly meetings there were sometimes conflicting opinions between the field commanders and those who had served on high-level staffs, especially when it came to accounts of the closing days of the war. It is clear from the prefatory comments in each monograph, however, that the authors were also very helpful to one another, making this a conspicuously collegial enterprise. When it was over, General Collins hosted a celebratory dinner for the participants at his home.

The completed monographs were published by the US Army Center of Military History in double-spaced typescript, in paperback format with plastic spiral binding, in limited quantities. Most came out in about 1980, several years after the majority of the texts had originally been composed. Copies have over the years become collector's items, with reprints responding to the demand sometimes being available from George Dalley's estimable Dalley Book Service, an invaluable source of materials relating to the Vietnam War.

The current publication in book form—while necessarily representing only a part of the whole, which in the aggregate runs to more than a million words—will make the material available in more permanent form to a wider range of scholars and other interested readers. The included parts, representing nearly half the original material, have been selected on the basis of that content deemed most interesting or most historically significant. Those desiring further detail on such matters as arcane aspects of logistics may consult the original source documents.

Deciding what to include was easy, but choosing those portions to exclude was often very difficult. The monographs cover every conceivable aspect of the war, from combat operations to budgets, from relations with advisors to logistical support, from uniforms to pay to desertions to refugees to bombing to pipelines to prisoners of war to combat rations to family support and even South Vietnamese society. A considerable amount of this material, based on the firsthand observations of these highly placed Vietnamese authors, is to be found nowhere else.

Across the original collection of monographs there was a certain amount of overlapping coverage, since each was formulated as a stand-alone document. Some of that overlap has been retained in this compilation so as to allow each author scope for developing his part of the story as he thought best. Then, too, not all the authors are of one mind on several significant aspects of the war. Those who served as staff officers at the national level, and those who were primarily field commanders, often reflect significantly different perspectives on the same matter. The performance and value of territorial forces provide a dramatic case in point, as do the several assessments of the pacification program. As readers will see, these differences often result in a richer and more nuanced portrayal of the matters discussed.

In other instances, fairly lengthy discussions of a particular aspect of the war have been omitted from a given author's treatment, even though they are very pertinent to his topic, since a compatible view is represented elsewhere in the compilation. An example is the development of territorial forces, the Regional and Popular Forces, which received an extensive treatment (omitted from this collection) in the monograph on Vietnamization, but was also covered in even more detail in the (included) separate discussion devoted exclusively to territorial and again (with a much different assessment, also included) in the discussion of Vietnamese society. Similarly, a consideration of the contributions of American advisors, also found in the original monograph on Vietnamization, has been omitted from this collection in view of the far more extensive and compatible discussion (included) found in the separate monograph on the advisory effort.

Regrettably, the originals of the numerous maps and photographs included in the first editions of the monographs have been lost, and the images in the various published typescript volumes are not of reproduction quality.

Every author has included in the preface to his monograph some words of gratitude for staff support. Since these are very similar in each case, they have been omitted from the individual essays and are represented here by Brigadier General Tran Dinh Tho's comments in his account of "The Cambodian Incursion": "I am also personally indebted to Lieutenant Colonel Chu Xuan Vien and Ms. Pham Thi Bong. Lieutenant Colonel Vien, the last Army attaché serving at the Vietnamese Embassy in Washington DC, has done a highly professional job of translating and editing that helps impart unity of style and organization to the manuscript. Ms. Bong, a former captain in the Republic of Vietnam Armed Forces and also a former member of the Vietnamese Embassy staff, spent long and arduous hours typing, editing, and in the administrative preparation of my manuscript in final form."

Some very minor editorial changes have been made in the texts as originally published—making J2 and J-2 as variously rendered consistent as J-2, for example—and in capitalization and punctuation in certain places. Where variant spellings occurred within a single work or in different monographs—such as "advisor" or "adviser"—one version has been selected for use throughout the collected works. Some very long paragraphs have been broken into smaller segments for ease of reading. Nothing of substance has been changed in any way.

Notes crafted by the original authors are indicated in the usual manner. Brief explanatory notes or emendations added by the editor are enclosed within brackets. Material omitted from the original documents is indicated by ellipses if the omission occurs within a sentence or paragraph. Omissions of a larger section of the manuscript are shown by centered, larger ellipsis points.

In his introduction to the original editions of these works, General Collins noted that "the monographs were not edited or altered and reflect the views of their authors—not necessarily those of the U.S. Army or the Department of Defense. The authors were not attempting to write definitive accounts, but to set down how they saw the war in Southeast Asia." It is hoped that readers will agree that the results constitute a valuable contribution to the literature of a long and complex conflict.

[Acknowledgments]

Over the years my work has been assisted by many people, both those with firsthand knowledge of the events of interest and the indispensable community of archivists, librarians, researchers, and historians upon whom so much depends.

In the case of this work, based on materials originally published by the US Army Center of Military History more than a quarter century ago, I am grateful for the assistance of several current members of the center's staff. I thank Dr. Jeffrey Clarke, Chief of Military History; Dr. Richard Stewart, Chief Historian; Mr. Frank Shirer, Chief of the Historical Resources Branch; Dr. Erik Villard; and Ms. Beth MacKenzie, Chief of the Production Branch.

Once again Albert D. McJoynt has assisted me by preparing excellent maps for which I am most appreciative. Noel Parsons, his successor Robert Mandel, and their colleagues at Texas Tech University Press are rendering a valuable scholarly service in continuing the Modern Southeast Asia Series, and I am grateful to them for bringing this project to completion. I must also record my great respect and admiration for Dr. James Reckner, director emeritus of the Vietnam Center at Texas Tech, for his vision, energy, and commitment to preserving and making available to scholars and general readers alike the history of the Vietnam War in all its complex aspects. Dr. Stephen Maxner, director, and Thomas Reynolds at the Vietnam Center have also been very helpful to this project.

Vietnamese friends living in America have assisted me in many ways on this and earlier projects. I particularly thank the late Lieutenant General Ngo Quang Truong, one of the authors of these monographs, for his generosity with photographs and other materials; Colonel Ha Mai Viet, a fine soldier and author and my classmate at the US Army Armor School many years ago; Michael Do (Do Van Phuc), Nguyen Ky Phong, Nguyen Xuan Phong, Nguyen Tin, Hoi Tran, and Paul Nguyen Van; and Lieutenant Colonel Chu Xuan Vien, translator of the Indochina Monographs, who gave me valuable background on their production. Also thanks to Jackie Bong-Wright, who helped me find Colonel Vien and encouraged me in this project; and to Bill Laurie and Merle Pribbenow, scholars of the Vietnam War who are steeped in its many aspects.

Two scholars widely conversant with the history and lore of the Vietnam War read the entire manuscript on behalf of Texas Tech University Press and made suggestions that served to improve the final product. I am most grateful to Professor Andrew Wiest and Dr. James Willbanks for their diligent work.

Finally, and always, I record my profound gratitude to my wife, Virginia Mezey Sorley, a superb research librarian who has devoted many faithful years to public service.

[The Vietnam War]

AN ASSESSMENT BY
SOUTH VIETNAM'S GENERALS

The RVNAF

Lieutenant General Dong Van Khuyen

PREFACE

The development of the Republic of Vietnam Armed Forces reflected and paralleled the history of the US involvement in the Vietnam War. By the time the last US combat troops departed, this process had taken nearly two decades of advisory effort and billions of US military aid dollars. But what the United States had achieved was well worth all of its efforts and expenditures. For, despite constraints and problems, the RVNAF finally emerged as a strong combat force which even its main adversary, the North Vietnamese Army, held in respect and never underestimated.

To analyze this developmental effort, this monograph focuses on four major aspects: personnel, training, support, and motivation. For each of these areas this work endeavors not only to describe the evolutionary process, but also to discuss pertinent problems and evaluate efforts made to overcome them. In addition, certain issues of particular interest, such as desertions, treatment of prisoners of war, relationships with the people, corruption, and political influence have also been addressed to the extent that they affected the conduct of the war and the RVNAF.

In the preparation of this monograph I have drawn primarily on my personal experience as the last Chief of Staff of the Joint General Staff, RVNAF. I trust that my long career, which encompassed such diverse assignments as combat, training, personnel administration, and logistics, would help impart some insight into the subjects and problems under consideration. . . . [19 December 1978]

I. INTRODUCTION

The Formative Years: A French Legacy

A French colony for almost a century, Vietnam emerged as an independent nation under the Viet Minh regime shortly after the end of World War II. The disarmament of Japanese occupation troops in Indochina—by Nationalist Chinese forces north of the

16th parallel and by British forces in the south—brought about developments which affected the course of this nation for the next decade.

In the north, nationalist parties, some with their own armies, came back from exile and established themselves under the aegis of Nationalist Chinese forces, openly defying the political supremacy of the Viet Minh. Anxious to keep them under control, Ho Chi Minh, the Viet Minh leader and president of the newly created Democratic Republic of Vietnam, invited their leaders to join in a coalition cabinet. But animosity between the nationalists and the Viet Minh continued unabated.

In the south, British troops landed with a French expeditionary force in tow. With British connivance, French forces soon wrested back control from a weak Viet Minh administration, which fought back with machetes and wooden sticks. This was the beginning of a protracted war of resistance which rallied most of the Vietnamese people, ever so ardent to hang on to their newly recovered national independence under the Viet Minh leadership.

The embryonic Viet Minh army, which was formed during the maquis days under Japanese occupation, was evidently no match for the French Expeditionary Corps. After occupying most of former Cochin China, the French pressed Ho Chi Minh for a military presence in the north. To avoid a head-on collision with French forces, Ho Chi Minh agreed to let them establish a foothold in Hanoi and Haiphong. In spite of negotiations, tension continued to rise through skirmishes between French and Viet Minh troops and finally erupted in open warfare on 19 December 1946.

The thin coating of Ho Chi Minh's coalition government for resistance against the French did not sufficiently conceal the Communist nature of the Viet Minh. It began to wear out after 1951. Serious divisions between nationalist parties and the Viet Minh eventually developed into enmity which, further aggravated by bloody purges carried out by the Viet Minh, gradually drove the nationalists to abandon the ranks of resistance fighters and seek shelter in French-controlled areas and wait for more opportune times to join in the national salvation effort. Religions, especially the Roman Catholic Church, no longer saw the Viet Minh as champion of the national cause, but as an atheistic Communist organization with which they could not coexist.

France in the meantime was bogged down in its neocolonialist policy. Her effort to build an autonomous government in Cochin China in mid-1946 failed to attract genuine nationalists, who were either fence sitting or still active in the resistance movement. Both military plans and negotiations with Ho Chi Minh did not produce the desired results. France therefore resigned herself to playing a new political card in the person of ex-emperor Bao Dai, who was living in exile.

Conceived in 1948, this political solution did not officially materialize until 8 March 1949, date of an agreement, signed by French President Auriol and ex-emperor Bao Dai, whereby France officially recognized Vietnam as an independent undivided state. However, it was not until May 1950 that the French National Assembly gave official approval for Vietnam to have its own army.

The Vietnamese Ministry of Defense came into being on 2 July 1949 as a component of the Bao Dai government. This same year a French military mission (Mission Militaire Francaise) was established as a counterpart to the Vietnamese government with the stated purposes of assisting and advising the Vietnamese National Army on the basis of equality and respect for Vietnam's independence and sovereignty. In reality this was an apparatus designed to command and control the Vietnamese National Army. Personnel of this mission were assigned throughout the hierarchy of the Vietnamese National Army, not in an advisory capacity but truly to command and coordinate.

Local guard units formed by the French in previous years, with locally recruited natives under a predominantly French command structure, were transferred to the Vietnamese National Army to become the "National Guard." A number of infantry battalions, designated BVN (Bataillons Vietnamiens), were activated with Vietnamese recruits and French officers and NCOs from the French military mission or Vietnamese officers and NCOs transferred from the French Army.

Both national guard units and the BVN battalions were placed under operational control of the regional French Army commanders. Personnel administration, pay, clothing, equipment, etc., were all handled by directorates. . . . But personnel of these directorates also came from the French Army. Regional military schools and academies were established to train Vietnamese volunteers for officer and NCO duties, but they too were under command and control of French officers and NCOs.

In late 1951 the Thu Duc and Nam Dinh reserve officer schools and a number of local training centers were established to meet mobilization needs. Young men 20 to 30 years old with a baccalaureate degree were mobilized for reserve officer training and subsequent assignment to Vietnamese agencies and units, where they were to serve beside French cadres. Young men 20 years of age and without a baccalaureate degree were inducted into training centers to receive reserve enlisted training.

The General Staff of the Vietnamese National Army was not established until May 1952. Nguyen Van Hinh, a lieutenant colonel in the French Air Force and son of then-premier Nguyen Van Tam, was chief of the military staff of Chief of State Bao Dai when he was promoted to major general to become Chief of the General Staff. His executive officer was a French captain, and his chief of staff a Vietnamese field-grade officer with French citizenship. Other key positions from deputy chief of staff to division and section heads were filled by French majors and captains.

The Vietnamese military region commands were established in July 1952. The territory was divided into four military regions along administrative boundaries: the 1st Military Region for South Vietnam, 2nd Military Region for Central Vietnam, 3rd Military Region for North Vietnam, and 4th Military Region for the Central Highlands. Each military region had a Vietnamese command which paralleled a regional French Army command. The Vietnamese military region command was responsible for organization, administration, supply, and training; operational control and deployment of combat units remained in the hands of the regional French Army commander.

As at the General Staff, only the MR commander and his chief of staff were Vietnamese field-grade officers. Other staff positions were filled by French field-grade or company-grade officers. At the time the MR commands were activated, the 4th Military Region did not even have a Vietnamese command. Responsibility for this region was retained by the commander and staff of the French Army Highlands Regional Command.

Also in 1952, the national guard organization was deactivated and its components absorbed into BVN infantry battalions. At the same time, nearly 60,000 auxiliary troops were transferred from the French Army to be organized into companies.

In 1953, to relieve French units engaged in pacification and territorial security operations and enable the French to reorganize these units into additional mobile battle groups, light infantry battalions (TDKQ) were activated with less strength and a lighter armament than the BVN battalions. To assist French strike forces, a number of BVN battalions were organized into mobile groups (GM) to participate in search and destroy operations initiated by regional French Army commands. Also in 1953, the French-Vietnamese Supreme Council agreed on a program to transfer territorial and operational control to the Vietnamese government according to the following principles: 1) the transfer will take place step by step, with due consideration given to the military situation and development of the Vietnamese armed forces, particularly the new light infantry battalions; 2) the units stationed in areas scheduled for transfer must first be Vietnamized; 3) the Vietnamese military region commander will take control of operations in the transferred area.

To meet the needs of an expanded national army provided for under this early Vietnamization program, the Vietnamese national government proclaimed a general mobilization in April 1953, calling and recalling to active duty all young men 20 to 33 years old. The first transfer of territorial command took place in the 1st Military Region in June 1953. The Vietnamese territory was then divided into military regions, subregions (French subdivisions), sectors (or provinces), and subsectors (or districts).

The Geneva Accords signed on 20 July 1954 between France and the Ho Chi Minh government ended the war and partitioned the state of Vietnam into Communist North Vietnam and nationalist South Vietnam, with the Ben Hai River as the demarcation line.

Prior to the cease-fire, the Vietnamese National Army consisted of 205,500 men (167,700 regulars and 37,800 auxiliary troops) with the following force structure: the army had six mobile group headquarters, one airborne group headquarters, 82 BVN battalions, 81 light infantry battalions, five airborne battalions, six imperial guard battalions, nine 105mm and 155mm artillery battalions, ten reconnaissance squadrons, four engineer battalions, and six transportation battalions; the air force had only one liaison detachment and two observation and combat support detachments; the navy had only three assault squadrons. Agencies and units of the Vietnamese National Army in North Vietnam, along with French forces, were redeployed in South Vietnam after 1954.

• • •

The restoration of Vietnamese sovereignty over territories previously occupied by French forces stretched from August 1954 to April 1955 and was then considered complete except for French positions along QL-15 from Saigon to Vung Tau, the Vung Tau military base, and Tan Son Nhut Air Base. These locations were transferred to Vietnamese control after 28 April 1956, following the deactivation of the French High Command in Indochina. Operations to secure the areas previously under Viet Minh control were initiated between 31 August 1954 and 17 May 1955 according to predetermined plans. Staff positions previously held by French officers were gradually turned over to Vietnamese officers. The Vietnamese defense organization was also reinforced to assume support activities such as postal service, mapping, and railroad operations transferred by French forces.

Reorganization under US Military Advisory Assistance

Following the Geneva Accords of 1954, France gradually restored national sovereignty to the Vietnamese government. On 26 October 1955 South Vietnam became a republic under the leadership of President Ngo Dinh Diem. The United States began to provide direct military aid to the RVNAF. The Military Assistance Advisory Group (MAAG) was established to improve RVNAF capabilities through planning, development, and administration of forces. US advisory teams were successively assigned to central agencies and staffs (Defense Ministry, JGS, corps, and service branch commands), as well as local agencies and units (military schools, training centers, divisions, and military regions).

The term "advisor" sounded very suspicious to the Vietnamese cadre. However, following directives and guidance from the JGS explaining the mission and role of US advisory teams, especially the emphasis on their having "no command authority," confidence in the advisors and the United States developed and flourished. This confidence was supported by the US advisors' conciliatory approach and the new, practical suggestions and advice that they contributed for the benefit of the agencies and units to which they were assigned. Equipment was standardized, uniforms and headgear followed US patterns, insignia of rank were worn on the collar US-style, and training was conducted according to US methods with US manuals and aids. Qualified officers were selected for training in service schools in the United States, while military schooling in France was discontinued. Funds for the operation and maintenance of the Vietnamese army came from US aid. Consequently, the Vietnamese army came to be totally dependent on the US ability to provide aid each year and on the US concept of common defense. The voice of the US advisor and, more generally, of the MAAG mission had a significant impact on Vietnamese officialdom and was usually regarded as a decisive factor.

Following the Geneva Accords of 1954, the Joint General Staff of the Vietnamese National Armed Forces continued to carry out existing force structure development plans in order to consolidate the territorial security structure inherited from the French and build a regular army by upgrading the BVN, light infantry battalions, and mobile groups to regimental and divisional size within the confines of a 200,000-man force. The project was interrupted midway because the peacetime personnel ceiling of the Vietnamese armed forces had yet to be approved by the US government. [The] MAAG made it known that the projected strength for the Vietnamese armed forces in FY 1956 was only 100,000, and subsequently advised the Vietnamese Defense Ministry to reduce its manpower to avoid financial difficulties.

At the historic meeting of 11 December 1954 between Ho Thong Minh, Vietnamese defense minister, and General John W. O'Daniel, Chief MAAG, at the Vietnamese Defense Ministry, the Vietnamese side requested that the pre-armistice ceiling of 200,000 men be maintained because a reduction in force would weaken the nationalist position in the elections provided for by the Geneva Accords. The US side argued that US military aid for FY 1956 might be limited to $200 million, based on a proposed strength of 100,000 men; plans for this strength were already being reviewed in the United States. It was also suggested that the Vietnamese army already had the backing of SEATO forces.

The US government finally approved a force structure of 150,000 men for FY 1956 in July 1955. Both sides then agreed to build this force within the following guidelines: the army would consist of ten infantry divisions, four of which would be conventional (later renamed field divisions, each with 8,600 men), and the remaining six territorial (later renamed light divisions, each with 5,245 men); one airborne group of five battalions; 13 regional regiments; 11 field artillery battalions (ten equipped with 105mm howitzers and one with 155mm howitzers); four armored cavalry regiments; ten divisional signal companies; and 16 light transportation companies. The air force would have 1,150 men and the navy 4,250.

From 1957 to 1959, under MAAG guidance the Vietnamese army was revamped to give it the ability to cope with aggression from North Vietnam. Beginning in October 1957, [the] MAAG and the JGS conducted tests aimed at finding an appropriate standard division-level organization. After two years of research and tests, a standard division-level organization with a strength of 10,450 men was finally approved. In September 1959 the Army of the Republic of Vietnam was reorganized into seven infantry divisions and three corps headquarters. Each infantry division had three regiments (three battalions each), one 105mm artillery battalion, one mortar battalion (4.2-inch), one engineer battalion, and a number of support companies. In addition to divisional artillery, there were eight independent artillery battalions (105mm and 155mm howitzers). There were no changes in airborne and armor troops.

In addition to the three corps headquarters activated for tactical control purposes, the RVNAF already had three military region headquarters established during the second half of 1954 to take charge of territorial security, formerly assumed by the French Army regional commands. [The] MAAG's recommendations for structural changes in the field were easily approved by the JGS, but changes at the central level encountered more difficulties. Central organization retained some purely Vietnamese features. The Joint General Staff continued to be both an interservice staff and an army staff. The Chief/JGS was also Army Chief of Staff. Logistics directorates, though internally reorganized and specialized along the lines of the US Army's technical branches, were still subordinated to the Defense Ministry instead of the JGS, which regarded these directorates merely as support coordinators. On the other hand, engineer, signal, and transportation were classified as corps (such as armor and artillery) and had their own commands under the JGS.

Beginning in 1959, the Communists waged a war of subversion in South Vietnam by terrorizing, assassinating, and abducting members of the government's rural administration infrastructure; inciting and coercing the populace into demonstrating against the administration; and sabotaging public facilities and lines of communications leading to urban centers.

• • •

In the face of this situation, the United States allowed the RVNAF to increase their strength from 150,000 men to 170,000. This was again increased, to 200,000, in FY 1962 and to 225,000 in FY 1963 to make more combat units available and reinforce administrative and support capabilities. In terms of combat units, these successive force structure increases represented 86 ranger companies, 30 infantry battalions, ten regimental headquarters, two divisional headquarters, and one corps command. South Vietnam was reorganized into four corps tactical zones, and the corps commands assumed responsibility for these tactical zones in the place of MR commands, which were deactivated.

• • •

The joint efforts of the US military mission (MAAG and later MACV) and the Vietnamese armed forces produced encouraging results which led many people to believe that Communist insurgency could be defeated in a few years. Unfortunately, the unstable political situation in 1963 led to the military coup of 1 November 1963 which toppled the Ngo Dinh Diem government and ended the First Republic.

Growth and Maturity

Political instability during 1964 drove the Republic of Vietnam to the brink of disaster. The 1 November 1963 coup opened the way for a number of generals and their followers to walk the thorny road of politics. Mutual purges, though causing no bloodshed, deprived the armed forces of a number of highly qualified and experienced personnel, stirred confusion, and affected the morale of the rank and file. The pacification program came to a standstill due to neglect and lack of guidance from the central level. The countryside came under increasing enemy control, which seriously affected recruitment and mobilization efforts. The North Vietnamese Communists seized this opportunity to intensify their infiltration of units and equipment. Estimated Communist strength, which stood at 30,000 men in November 1963, jumped to 212,000 by July 1965. Both NVA and VC troops were now armed with sophisticated AK-47s.

• • •

The direct participation of US forces in mid-1965 pulled the RVN away from the brink of collapse. It also restored confidence to the RVNAF. The presence of US forces was to serve two purposes: 1) to check NVA infiltration and destroy VC/NVA main forces in South Vietnam; and 2) to buy time for the GVN [Government of (South) Vietnam] to achieve political stability, develop a central administration capable of controlling the entire nation, and improve the RVNAF, giving them the ability to cope with the VC in pacification efforts.

Politically, leadership of the nation following the 1 November 1963 coup was entrusted to a military revolutionary council headed by Lieutenant General Duong Van Minh. The countercoup of 30 January 1964 by a group of young generals ended the three-month-old regime of General Minh. The Military Revolutionary Council was replaced by an Armed Forces Council headed by Lieutenant General Nguyen Khanh, who was also chief of state and premier. Under pressure, General Khanh soon turned over two positions to two veteran politicians: Phan Khac Suu became chief of state and Tran Van Huong, premier. Shortly thereafter, because of political dissension between Suu and Huong and disturbances initiated by students, political parties, and religious groups, the Armed Forces Council appointed another seasoned politician, Phan Huy Quat, to replace Huong.

On 6 May 1965 the Armed Forces Council dissolved itself after expressing the desire to return to purely military duties and concentrate efforts on the war. However, because of irreconcilable differences, Suu and Quat later returned leadership of the state to the armed forces.

The Armed Forces Council was therefore reactivated with a broader participation by all general officers holding major command positions and key political roles. Lieutenant General Nguyen Van Thieu was elected council chairman and also chief of state. Air Force Major General Nguyen Cao Ky was appointed chairman of the Central Executive Committee, or prime minister.

Under the Armed Forces Council, the supreme leadership organ of the state, was the National Leadership Committee, which functioned on the principle of collective leadership and individual responsibilities.[1] In mid-April 1966, a committee made up of ten military and ten civilian members was appointed to draft legislation for the election of a constituent assembly.

As a result, a constituent assembly was elected on 11 September 1966. Six months later the new constitution of the Second Republic was promulgated on 1 April 1967. General elections soon followed in September 1967, and Lieutenant General Nguyen Van Thieu was elected president, with Major General Nguyen Cao Ky as vice president. The political situation of South Vietnam began to stabilize.

Militarily, the new government's first priority was to consolidate the national defense structure from national to local levels. Military officers replaced civilian province chiefs while retaining their responsibilities as sector commanders. Corps/CTZ commanders also held the positions of government delegates. Support agencies previously subordinated to the Defense Ministry were placed under the JGS. Technical services such as ordnance, quartermaster, medical, signal, engineer, and transportation were reorganized and placed under the control of the Central Logistics Command. The psychological warfare, chaplain, social welfare, and military security directorates also came under the General Political Warfare Department.

The Civil Defense and Self-Defense Corps became part of the RVNAF under the new designation of Regional and Popular Forces. The RVNAF infantry then consisted of three forces: regular, regional, and popular. At the time of their integration into the RVNAF, the RF/PF totalled 322,187 men organized into approximately 1,000 separate

RF companies and 4,000 PF platoons. Consequently, the RVNAF force structure jumped from 244,749 in FY 1964 to 597,245 in FY 1965, to include 275,058 regulars, 137,187 RF, and 185,000 PF. Under MACV guidance and US DOD approval, the RVNAF force structure was further expanded between FY 1965 and FY 1968 to reach the following composition: infantry—126 battalions, 32 regimental headquarters, and ten divisional commands; airborne—nine battalions, three brigade headquarters, and one divisional command; marines—six battalions and two brigade headquarters; rangers—20 battalions; artillery—24 battalions of 105mm howitzers (including battalions organic to the ten infantry divisions, the airborne division, and the marines) and six battalions of 155mm howitzers organic to corps; armor—11 squadrons equipped with M-113 armored personnel carriers and M-41 tanks; Regional Forces—1,050 companies; Popular Forces—4,560 platoons; Air Force—five squadrons of fighter-bombers (A-1/A-37/F-5), five squadrons of H-34 helicopters, three squadrons of C-47 transports, and four squadrons of O-1/U-17 observation aircraft. During this period US advisory teams were deployed at [the] subsector/district level to advise and assist subsector commanders in the areas of operations, training, and territorial security.

Rural security was substantially improved as a result of search and destroy operations conducted by US and Free World Military Assistance (ROK/Australia/New Zealand/Thailand) forces and the efforts of the RVNAF in improving training, administration, and pacification support operations. The population living in GVN-controlled areas increased from 40 percent in 1965 to 67.2 percent by the end of 1967 as Communist main forces were driven back into their base areas along the border.

Improvement and Modernization under Vietnamization

• • •

The Communist Tet general offensive actually caused the armed forces and people of South Vietnam to strengthen their determination and become more closely united. The number of youths volunteering to serve in the armed forces increased remarkably. The draft age was lowered to 19, then 18, and finally general mobilization was decreed on 19 June 1968. Induction and training centers were all flooded with recruits. The government then launched an accelerated pacification program aimed at reoccupying and consolidating those hamlets lost or destroyed during the enemy's offensive and to expand the GVN territorial control.

As a result of serious losses, North Vietnam agreed to come to Paris for peace talks. The president of the United States ordered a halt to the bombing of North Vietnam and announced his decision not to seek reelection. US forces began to phase out of the RVN while the war was still in progress and no peace settlement was in sight. The RVNAF were hurriedly modernized and expanded to take over tactical and support operations thus far assumed by US forces. This improvement process focused on the RF/PF, which were to take over pacification responsibilities in order to release ARVN infantry divisions for mobile tactical operations. Mobile Advisory Training Teams (MATT) and Mobile Advisory Logistics Teams (MALT) fanned out to give in-place training and guidance to RF companies and PF platoons. The modernization program covered primarily armament, communications, and transportation.

The RVNAF began to receive equipment being used by US forces in the Vietnam theater. The expansion program was designed to balance logistic support, firepower, and mobility with the needs of the combat infantryman, an area previously given low priority because of the availability of US support. Special consideration was also given to the need to support rural pacification efforts. Consequently the increases in force structure between FY 1969 and FY 1973 provided for one-half of the additional strength to go to the RF/PF. The RF were expanded from 1,050 companies in FY 1968 to 1,810 in FY 1973, while the PF grew from 4,560 platoons to 8,166 during the same period.

The buildup in regular army combat forces was extremely modest in comparison with the US forces that they were intended to replace. The infantry received an additional nine battalions, three regimental commands, and one divisional command. The marines were expanded by three battalions, one brigade command, and one divisional command. The rangers increased their forces by 33 border defense battalions and 17 group commands. Combat support elements also saw a significant increase: the Armored Corps grew from 11 squadrons in FY 1968 to 21 in FY 1973, including three new M-48 tank squadrons; artillery units grew from 30 battalions in FY 1968 to 64 in FY 1973, including four 175mm field gun battalions, but excluding 176 territorial artillery sections (105mm howitzers).

The VNAF was expanded from five fighter squadrons to 11 equipped with A-1, A-37, F-37, F-5A, and F-5E aircraft; from five H-34 helicopter squadrons to 21 squadrons consisting of 17 UH-1 and four CH-47 squadrons; and from three C-47 transport squadrons to five squadrons consisting of three C-7 and two C-130A squadrons.

Through joint US-RVNAF efforts, the program designed to improve the combat effectiveness of the RVNAF, modernize their equipment, and expand their force structure progressed annually according to plans. Rural pacification efforts also made steady progress. By the end of 1971, 90 percent of the civilian population lived in areas under GVN control. The RVNAF demonstrated their new capabilities by initiating cross-border operations against Communist sanctuaries in Laos and Cambodia in 1970–1971. Of utmost significance, the RVNAF held fast in the face of the NVA general offensive during 1972 and again showed their resolve during the counterattacks to reoccupy lost territories—with substantial US support in terms of military aid, air and naval firepower, and tactical transportation. The RVNAF were now able to take over the combat responsibilities of US infantry units, allowing them to safely disengage from the war. By cease-fire day there were only 23,515 US troops and 30,449 FWMAF troops left in Vietnam. RVNAF strength by this time had reached the 1.1 million mark.

• • •

II. PERSONNEL ADMINISTRATION

Requirements

• • •

Requirements for replacements were based on average losses incurred during previous years through desertion and combat (MIA, KIA, and unsalvageable WIA), as well as losses resulting from annual discharge involving completion of military service, retirement, disciplinary action, and disability. All three requirements were then divided into officer, NCO, and EM categories.

• • •

Youths enlisting in the RVNAF had to be Vietnamese citizens with good conduct records and of legal age, at least 18 but not yet 32 years old. No youth in the draft or mobilization age group (20–26) was accepted as [a] volunteer. In 1968, when general mobilization was decreed, the volunteer age group was extended to a minimum of 16 and a maximum of 38, and the draft or mobilization age restrictions were dropped. However, youths under 18 years of age required written consent from their parents or guardians.

• • •

Conscription

Based on annual force requirements and related recruitment plans, the JGS worked with the Defense Ministry to establish quarterly procurement programs for draftees, reserve officers, and NCOs. Following the review of these programs and the male resources in each age group, the Mobilization Directorate of the Defense Ministry issued communiqués specifying the age groups to be called for compulsory military service, beginning each year with age 20. If this age group was not sufficient to meet requirements, the next age group was called.

The first mobilization order was issued in July 1951, calling Reserve Officers Class No. 1 and 60,000 draftees in four increments of 15,000 each (6,000 for North Vietnam, 3,000 for Central Vietnam, and 6,000 for South Vietnam) and spaced at two-month intervals. The first increment reported on 16 October 1951. Upon completion of training, the draftees were temporarily sent home, while the reserve officers were assigned to units and agencies of the National Army of Vietnam to work with French officers.

Subsequently, in 1953, to meet the force requirements of a normal expansion plan and a supplementary plan calling for 100,000 men to organize 54 commando battalions (later redesignated light infantry battalions) and 14 artillery batteries designed to relieve French forces committed in pacification operations, general mobilization was declared in April, calling and recalling to active duty all youths 20 to 33 years of age. This general mobilization was conducted in four increments of 10,000 men each, taking effect on 1 July, 1 August, 1 September, and 1 October 1953, respectively, in accordance with approved plans to organize the new units.

By the end of the year, however, only one-half of the quotas had been filled and conscription continued until cease-fire day, 20 July 1954. General mobilization was subsequently discontinued because of reduced manpower requirements. Partial mobilization of eligible youths for officer training was resumed, however, but it affected only those in the 20–22 age group. Two increments of 500 reserve officers were called each year to serve a two-year legal term.

In June 1955 a national policy of compulsory military service was proclaimed, based on the concept of building a strong reserve force for deployment in times of need. The military service policy differed from mobilization in that it affected only youths from 20 to 22 years of age. Compulsory military service being then regarded as a sacred mission, the government launched publicity campaigns in great pomp to promote it. Ceremonies were held to send youths off to induction, and to welcome them at induction or training centers. There were three increments called each year, with 5,000 to 10,000 men in each increment. The duration of service was 12 months, four in training and eight at the unit.

• • •

Individual induction orders were prepared by regional recruitment agencies and delivered to the last known addresses of the individuals concerned through the local administration. Unserved induction orders were returned to recruitment agencies. The number of unserved orders increased with each day because of insecurity in the countryside, lack of zeal and dedication on the part of local administrative and military officials, or failure on the part of the youths concerned to report address changes to local recruitment agencies.

• • •

By 1964 there were an estimated 200,000 cases of draft dodging by youths known to be in the draft age.

To provide improved and efficient administration of national manpower resources, the Mobilization Directorate was created during the second half of 1964 under the Defense Ministry. . . . The primary mission of the Mobilization Directorate at the time was to provide interministerial coordination in stimulating, controlling, and supervising the enforcement of induction orders.

In April 1964, to provide sufficient resources to meet the armed forces' needs, the Vietnamese government issued a new decree governing the military obligations of male citizens which stipulated that all male youths 20 to 25 years of age were required to carry out their obligation in the armed forces or in civil defense. Based on this decree, and to avoid the problems previously encountered in serving individual notices, the Defense Ministry applied collective call-up to individual age groups of EM and NCO resources.

The communiqué of 20 November 1964 specified that all male citizens 20 to 25 years old, whether in a legal or illegal draft status, had to report for induction within a month of the date of the communiqué. It also announced that this was the last chance and that police operations would be launched simultaneously and severe penalties would be given to youths of these age groups who did not comply.

To improve the effectiveness of the armed forces, the legal term of military service was also increased to three years for enlisted men and four years for NCOs and officers. Those NCOs and officers who had completed two years of service by 1964 saw their terms extended by one year and two years, respectively. The RVNAF were thus able to retain a number of experienced cadres who were badly needed in the face of mounting combat requirements. This collective call-up measure, coupled with stepped-up recruitment activities, caused in fact a notable excess in realized strength in late 1964.

By late 1965, however, strength shortages occurred again. The number of recruits, draftees, forced inductees, and re-enlistees was insufficient to meet the needs to organize new units and replace losses suffered through desertion or completion of military service. The government was compelled to extend the draft age from 26 in 1965 to 33 in 1967. Despite this effort, the RVNAF continued to suffer from a shortage of manpower, and their planned expansion during FY 1967 could not be implemented. As the war escalated with each day, the need for combat-experienced cadres and men became more pressing. While US/FWMAF casualties continued to increase, a number of Vietnamese youths were enjoying the good life in the cities. This was an intolerable situation. The policy of systematic discharge upon completion of military obligations also caused the armed forces to lose a substantial number of invaluable experienced cadres and men.

Plans to declare general mobilization in order to concentrate the nation's efforts on building the armed forces, and other projects designed to extend the terms of military service with the objective of retaining combat-experienced cadres and men, were frequently mentioned but could not be carried out because of our unstable political situation. The opportunity came during 1968, after the Communist general offensive pressured the people and the Congress of the United States for a withdrawal of US forces.

Popular consent and the stable domestic political situation prompted the Vietnamese government to lower the draft age to 19 in April 1968 and to 18 a month later. Following this momentum, general mobilization was declared on 19 June 1968. All male citizens 16 to 50 years of age were called to fulfill their military obligations. Males between 18 and 38 were inducted for service in the RVNAF, while 16- and 17-year-olds and men between the ages of 39 [and] 50 were incorporated into the People's Self-Defense Force (PSDF). Male citizens 18 to 38 years of age who were physically unfit to serve in the RVNAF, and those who had received draft deferments, also qualified for PSDF duties. At the same time, reserve components were recalled to active duty.

Since South Vietnam did not have reserve units, this recall to active duty merely applied to individual veterans who had less than 12 years of active duty and were still in the reserve age groups. As a result, 1,055 reserve officers were recalled by the end of 1968 to strengthen the ranks of cadres then suffering from serious shortages. All discharges were suspended, except for reasons of disability. The term of military service was no longer specified, which implied that it was extended indefinitely as long as the war continued.

• • •

The General Mobilization Law caused the number of volunteers to increase significantly. From April to 30 September 1968, the RVNAF strength increased by 98,577, to include 70,519 volunteers and 28,058 draftees.

In January 1969 the Defense Ministry issued a collective call-up of youths born in 1951 (18 years old), requiring them to report between March and December. First to report were those who did not know their exact birthdate. A six-month deferment was granted to those in the last year of secondary education's first cycle or in the first year of secondary education's second cycle in order to allow them to complete their 1968–1969 school year. The procurement of draftees during the first and second quarters of 1969 was very satisfactory. It gave cause for optimism toward our force structure expansion, which was planned within the framework of Vietnamization.

• • •

In 1973, after the Paris Agreement went into effect, many studies were undertaken to deescalate mobilization by lowering draft age limits and specifying a legal term of military service. To make manpower resources available for economic development, the president decided to reduce the RVNAF force structure level from 1,100,000 to 1,000,000. The RVNAF began implementing a gradual reduction in force in June 1973. By July 1974, there were slightly less than 1,000,000 men in the armed forces. But peace did not materialize and heavy fighting soon resumed, which prompted the president to cancel his decision to maintain the force structure level at 1,000,000 men.

To [again] expand the armed forces to a level of 1,100,000 and replace losses estimated over the next 12 months, the JGS determined the requirement for an additional 290,000 men, to include 100,000 to fill the authorized level, 140,000 to replace losses incurred through desertion, and 50,000 to replace other losses. By this time, however, manpower resources in the 19 to 38 age groups were nearly depleted. The primary source of manpower each year was the 18-year-old male population. The Mobilization Directorate estimated this group to number about 200,000, which gave the RVNAF an effective pool of 150,000 to draw from. However, statistics of previous years related to each age group showed that only an estimated 90,000 were drawn into the armed forces through conscription and recruitment. The Defense Ministry therefore recommended that 17-year-olds be called up to meet manpower needs. The domestic political situation of the time probably did not favor such a drastic measure for, by the time of South Vietnam's collapse, the GVN had still not approved the Defense Ministry's recommendation.

• • •

Assignment, Transfer, and Rotation

• • •

Authority to select and appoint personnel to key positions in the RVNAF down to division commanders and service branch chiefs changed with the times. During the First Republic, this authority to select and assign personnel to key positions in the armed forces almost totally rested in the hands of the president and the defense minister. At that time the Chief/JGS had practically no authority over assignments. Even staff division chiefs at the JGS were appointed by the defense minister or the president. This excessive concentration of authority was ridiculed by officers of that period as the "Three D's" system, meaning in Vietnamese "Dang, Dao, and Du." Dang (party) meant a political party or organization sponsored by the government, such as the Can Lao Party, the National Revolutionary Movement, or Women's Solidarity Movement. In order to receive a high appointment, an officer (or his wife) had to be a member of one of these parties or organizations. Dao (religion) was none other than the Roman Catholic Church. The candidate for a high position had to be a member of this church or endorsed by it. Du (damn) was vulgar slang used by natives of Central Vietnam which indicated the president's preference for men of his own native region.

After the November 1963 revolution, the "Three D's" system was replaced by two factors, "Su" and "Tuong," a generalization intended as a joke. Su (Buddhist monk) represented the superior bonzes of the Buddhist Institute for Propagation of the Dharma, who exerted great influence over the government and the armed forces. Tuong (general) meant those generals who took credit for the success of the coup d'etat. RVNAF personnel then believed that important positions were given to those affiliated with one of these two groups. Not until 1965, under the National Leadership Committee, was authority for appointments and promotions in the RVNAF officially defined. Decree No. 205, signed on 12 December 1965 by the chairman of the National Leadership Committee, delegated this authority among the various levels of command.

By this decree the chairman of the National Leadership Committee reserved for himself the authority to appoint the Chief/JGS; the Deputy Chief/JGS; the Chief of Staff/JGS; the commanders of corps/CTZs; the IG; the Commander, VNAF; the Commander, VNN; and the Commander, CMD. The National Leadership Committee member in charge of national defense (defense minister) appointed the heads of CLC [Central Logistics Command], CTC [Central Training Command], and GPWD [General Political Warfare Department]; the chiefs of staff of corps/CTZs; [and] the directors general and directors of the various directorates subordinate to the Defense Ministry. Next in line, the Chief/JGS appointed the commanders of service branches and combat arms; the deputies of the CLC, CTC, and GPWD; the department heads and their deputies; the division commanders; the sector commanders; and the commanders of separate units.[2]

• • •

As for the appointment or transfer of general officers, this was the sole authority of the Chairman, NLC; so was his prerogative in appointing province chiefs. This special rule was deemed appropriate in 1965, when there were but a small number of general officers in the RVNAF. However, over the years that followed, the RVNAF force structure expanded rapidly, creating more positions for general officers and increasing promotions to that grade substantially. In time, especially as of 1967, when General Thieu became president, this special rule virtually deprived the defense minister and the Chief/JGS of the authority to make key appointments, since most of these . . . involved general officers and almost all sector commanders were also province chiefs. Decree No. 205

was therefore left undisturbed, because it conveniently concentrated appointment power in the president where it mattered the most.

• • •

Because of this excessive concentration of powers in the hands of the president, a number of subordinate personnel resorted to influence buying and ignored their immediate commanders, causing extensive obstruction to the efficient working of the military hierarchy. This shortcoming became quite obvious in 1970, when the RVNAF reached their peak strength of 1.1 million, but there were no attempts to amend obsolescent Decree 205, probably because of political dictates or preoccupation with the conduct of the war.

• • •

In order to raise personnel morale and restore justice within the armed forces, the JGS implemented two innovative programs in the area of personnel administration: systematic rotation and career management.

Rotation was first applied in the RVNAF in 1966 to establish impartiality and maximize cadre efficiency. There were four rotation systems: rotation by position in command, staff, or training; rotation by unit from a combat unit to a support unit, an administrative agency, or a school and vice versa; rotation by zone, such as the delta, jungle, coastal lowlands, or highlands; rotation from one CTZ to another or to the central level. Minimum tours of duty were determined on the basis of two years in a combat unit (platoon, company, or battalion), three years in a staff position or in an administrative/support command, and four years in a school or training center. Upon completion of each tour of duty, the serviceman was entitled to request a transfer, and commanders were also required to satisfy these requests.

Although rotation was deemed necessary and mandatory, it was affected by four factors, which often made it impractical, causing results to fall short of expectations and creating discontent, particularly among personnel serving in the Central Highlands, who usually came from other regions. First there was terrain and people. In counterinsurgency warfare, knowledge of the local terrain and people was the essential element of success. It could be obtained only through long exposure to the same environment. Second, there was the socioeconomic factor. In several areas housing was scarce and schooling for military dependents inadequate, while military pay was usually too low in comparison with the cost of living. These hardship areas were apparently not appropriate for longer tours of duty. Then there were also problems of education, background, and family burdens. There was great disparity in backgrounds, both academic and military, among personnel of the armed forces, particularly among the cadres. Many officers in fact had not received sufficient training for their positions and ranks. Finally, the average serviceman had certain private obligations of his own, which could be a large family or old parents. Respect for this traditional attachment to family had always been the hallmark of Vietnamese society.

• • •

Personnel of captain rank and above, who were accustomed to life in combat units, did not like to be transferred to schools or headquarters staffs, where there were too many restrictions and too few opportunities for promotion. Generally only the young officers fresh out of training aspired [to] school or staff positions, but their requests could not be satisfied because they lacked experience and staff background. Officers with large families to support usually preferred long-term assignments in areas where their families had settled to a stable life. Transferring them from one zone to another caused great disruptions in their lives and long-lasting adverse effects on their productivity.

MR-2, especially the Highlands of Darlac-Pleiku-Kontum, was the area most seriously plagued with difficulties. Because of spartan living conditions and virtual isolation, personnel transferred there suffered from the complex that they had fallen out of favor and were being exiled. Local commanders in turn were prejudiced against these men, convinced that to warrant such transfers they had to be undisciplined, incompetent, or undesirable elements. Once they had completed their two years, these men almost always requested transfer to MR-3 or MR-4.

• • •

The JGS did its best to satisfy these requests when resources were available. But resources were meager, while requests for transfer were numerous, which led the JGS to give priority for transfer only to those who had served four years or more in MR-2. On the other hand, there were quite a few servicemen who, over the years, had grown attached to the mountains and forests, the clean fresh air, and the simple, natural life and did not want to leave for any reason.

Despite all the difficulties encountered in its execution, the long-range rotation plan succeeded in building confidence and enthusiasm among the troops. To support this plan and reduce the military expertise disparities within the officer corps, a career management program for RVNAF officers was developed and put into effect in 1966.

Prior to that time, the RVNAF officer had no clear idea of the path he would travel upon leaving Dalat or Thu Duc. Upon graduation, many officers were assigned to staff positions alien to everything they had learned. Others were made instructors in training centers or schools with no experience in combat or unit life. There were no regulations providing for continuing education. Many officers had made it to the rank of lieutenant colonel or colonel with no formal training other than the officer basic training course. Many others held high-level staff positions for which they had never been prepared through formal training. Still others spent their entire military career in only one assignment.

The career management program was designed to correct these discrepancies by supporting rotation plans, helping officers of the infantry—the most vital component of the RVNAF—to be more conscious of the career opportunities available to them so that they would strive harder for success, and making unit commanders aware of the essential criteria required for selection and assignment of officer personnel so that they might be in a better position to contribute to the future of their subordinates. Rank, position, seniority in rank, formal training, and age were the five basic elements that guided the management of an officer's military career.

Under the career management program infantry officers, graduating from the Dalat National Military Academy with the rank of second lieutenant, or from reserve officer courses at the Thu Duc Infantry School with the rank of aspirant, were all required to serve as platoon leaders in combat units on their first assignment. From there they moved on to become company executive officers or company commanders.

After serving a minimum of two years at platoon or company level, with a minimum rank of second lieutenant and a maximum rank of captain, they were transferred to take command of other units within a major unit, within a sector, or within a military region; or they could be assigned to schools to command training platoons or companies or to serve as instructors; or they could be selected to attend advanced infantry training in-country or abroad at Fort Benning, USA.

• • •

In August 1967 the National Defense College was established to train senior leaders for the armed forces and the administration. Elite officers with a minimum rank of lieutenant colonel and a maximum rank of brigadier general were selected to attend this school. Upon graduation these officers were assigned to key positions at the national level or [in] corps and military regions. These courses also prepared them for nomination to general rank in the RVNAF.

• • •

The career management program generated confidence and enthusiasm in the officer ranks, but its application encountered numerous difficulties, particularly during a period of the war when casualties were mounting and the armed forces were expanding at a fast rate. It seemed to require time and determination on the part of all concerned to overcome the obstacles. Above all it required a period to preserve continuity. Despite the difficulties, the RVNAF made a significant step toward training and assigning officer personnel under the career management program, particularly [after] 1971 when the force structure expansion reached its peak.

• • •

Most officer assignments or promotions were subsequently carried out in accordance with the basic criteria of the career management program.

Discharge

There were five types of discharge in the RVNAF: discharge upon completion of legal military obligations; discharge as regulated by career army statutes; discharge for health reasons; discharge for disciplinary reasons; and discharge because of reduction in force structure.

In principle, reserve personnel were automatically discharged upon completion of their legal military obligations. Under the Bao Dai government, from 1951 to 1954, automatic discharge was practically nonexistent. Drafted personnel were retained because of the requirements of the war. However, in 1955, under the Ngo Dinh Diem regime, draftees completing their terms of service were discharged automatically. In 1964, when the draft term was changed to three years for EM and NCOs and four years for officers, under the Nguyen Khanh regime, draftees completing their term were no longer discharged automatically; they had to submit written requests. Those who did not submit requests for discharge were automatically reenlisted. In 1968, under the Second Republic, the discharging of draftees was terminated by virtue of the General Mobilization Law promulgated on 19 June 1968.

• • •

Twice, over the years, there were collective discharges because of reduction in force. These discharges occurred in 1955, following the Geneva Accords, and in 1973 following the Paris Agreement. In the wake of the 1954 Geneva Accords, the Vietnamese National Army strength stood at approximately 200,000. In early December 1954 the US government served notice that South Vietnam had to reduce its armed forces in accordance with peacetime ceilings and the reduction should be completed prior to 1 July 1955 if the Vietnamese government wanted to avoid major financial difficulties. At the time, the United States agreed to only a total force of 100,000 men, which it believed to be adequate for peacetime purposes. The United States also wanted this force to be founded on the concept of fixed-term compulsory military service in order to provide the nation with a reserve force ready on call in times of need.

The Vietnamese desired to maintain their armed forces at their existing level so that they could be reorganized and modernized without conflict with the Geneva Accords. While negotiations were under way, the mandatory reduction in force began as scheduled on 1 January 1955. The reorganized army had to consolidate its command and control structure and technical services, so it needed as many officers and specialists as it could retain. Consequently, priority for discharge went to infantry EM and NCOs. The first to be discharged were the auxiliary forces, whose strength was reported at 33,658. This was done in four increments. Each serviceman received a one-month severance pay upon release, after being notified that he was being returned to civilian life now that peace had been achieved.

• • •

By June 1955, when a force structure of 150,000 men was finally approved by the United States, this mass demobilization had been completed. Nearly 60,000 men had been discharged over the first five months of 1955.

Looking back, everyone agreed that the mass discharge of 1955 was a regrettable action, both cruel and detrimental to the combat effectiveness of the RVNAF. At least 6,000 NCOs, the backbone of the armed forces, had been released during that period. The combat units of 1959–1960 became operationally ineffective, primarily because they lacked qualified and experienced NCOs. The JGS later initiated a drive to recruit former NCOs, but only a very few rejoined. Most had resettled to a stable civilian life or were discouraged by the way they had been handled.

In 1973, following the Paris Agreement, the RVNAF adopted a carefully prepared discharge plan. Drawing on the lesson of 1955, they went at it in a progressive manner. The first step, taken in early 1973, provided for the demobilization of overage reserve and regular army personnel whose service had been extended since 1968; it proceeded smoothly, without incident. The second step, taken in late 1973, provided for the discharge of Type 2 personnel (physically unfit for combat) who had been retained because of war requirements and Type 3 personnel (disabled) temporarily retained for humanitarian reasons, again encountering no adverse reactions. The third step, taken in 1974, involved the discharge of undesirable elements based on a review of disciplinary actions.

• • •

The fourth step, also taken in 1974, provided for the demobilization of personnel with more than 25 years of service based on individual requests and subject to final decision of the defense minister.

• • •

In early 1975, because of the Phuoc Long incident, demobilization was temporarily suspended. Overall, during the two years that followed the cease-fire, more than 40,000 men were discharged as a part of the process of force reduction.

• • •

The Problems of Combat Unit Strength

Maintaining the operational strength of infantry, airborne, ranger, and marine battalions at acceptable levels was a constant concern of the JGS. However, not until 1966 was there any serious effort made to improve the combat strength of these units. During the first half of 1966 the average assigned strength of infantry battalions was 581, or 91 percent of the authorized strength; the present-for-duty strength 472, or 74 percent; and the present-for-combat strength only 437, or 68 percent.

A joint MACV-JGS committee was established to study the causes and devise corrective measures. This committee provided the following reasons why unit strength was so low for combat operations: 1) personnel left at battalion base camps for security and administrative activities were usually higher in number than planned; 2) the number of noneffective personnel was too high, which included those on detached duty outside the battalion, those assigned who had not joined the unit, personnel in school or on leave, personnel confined, MIA and deserters who had not been removed from battalion rosters; 3) the assigned strength of headquarters and support services at regimental, group, brigade, and division level was usually higher than the assigned strength of battalions, not including personnel on detached duty; 4) personnel were shifted internally to special units not included in the authorized force structure, as in the case of assault platoons, special reconnaissance companies ("Black Panthers"), etc.; 5) the assigned strength was usually lower than the authorized strength because assignments and replacements were not made available on a timely basis.

Then there was also the case of the JGS "Honor Guard" Battalion and the "Palace Guard," whose formation was not initially authorized in the RVNAF force structure. The Palace Guard was a regimental-sized unit composed basically of one bodyguard company, two infantry battalions, one armor detachment, and one signal company. Called the "Capital Security Group" during the 1965–1968 period, this organization had the mission of guarding the Independence Palace, the office of the prime minister, and various official guest houses in Saigon, Vung Tau, Dalat, Nha Trang, and Ban Me Thuot.

Deriving its strength chiefly from ARVN personnel on long-term detached duty, this unit was not authorized in the ARVN force structure until 1968.

To improve this situation several corrective actions were taken. First, the detached duty assignments of personnel organic to rifle companies were terminated and individuals concerned were returned to their parent units. Next, unauthorized units were disbanded and their personnel reassigned to rifle companies. Concurrently, stricter personnel administration procedures were enforced. For example, personnel in hospitals or schools for more than one month were transferred out of their parent units and made part of the excess strength of the hospital or school concerned. Confined or MIA personnel were normally transferred out of their parent units and reassigned to regional administrative units. Personnel assigned to a unit were required to report on the exact date specified in the transfer orders. The original unit was held responsible for releasing transferred personnel on schedule.

A "wanted" notice was sent out for AWOL personnel on the 16th day of their absence, and they were removed from strength accounting immediately thereafter. Another corrective action was to minimize exposure to disease, such as dysentery, diarrhea, smallpox, and malaria, by the strict enforcement of preventive medicine. Finally, priority for replacements was given to combat battalions, and quotas for assigned strength, present-for-duty strength, and present-for-combat strength were prescribed to assess the extent of the units' efforts. These quotas required that a battalion maintain an assigned strength of 90 percent of its authorized strength and a present-for-combat ratio of 70 percent, or 450 men for a battalion with an authorized strength of 639 men.

At the rifle company level, it was required that the number of personnel absent from the unit not exceed 10 percent of authorized strength and the number of operationally noneffective personnel be no more than 15 percent of the present-for-duty strength.

After repeated efforts by all levels, actively applying the above measures, the number of infantry battalions conducting tactical operations with a strength of 450 men or more increased significantly, going from 36 battalions in April to 100 in November and stabilizing at 94 in December the same year.

During the following years efforts were continued to maintain the combat strength of battalions at a high level, but results obtained were mixed, for several reasons. However, there was a definite improvement over the period prior to 1966.

There were four problems that the JGS vainly attempted to overcome: 1) the assigned strength at battalion level was always lower than the authorized strength; 2) the number of losses due to desertion remained high despite efforts to prevent it; 3) it was difficult to provide replacements for losses in time, particularly during high peaks of activity and military campaigns; and 4) the infantry, airborne, and marine divisions and the rangers did not have replacement units, nor were they authorized to maintain a pool of replacements. The replacement pipeline provided for in the approved force structure was too small. The total number of personnel being hospitalized, for instance, was never less than 20,000. Personnel undergoing training always numbered not less than 70,000, and those confined awaiting trial not less than 10,000. Combat units therefore suffered their share of these personnel shortages. In 1974 and 1975 the JGS endeavored to reduce noneffective strength as much as possible, but was never able to keep it lower than 90,000 to 95,000 men.

Observations

The RVNAF encountered numerous difficulties in the administration of human resources throughout the war. Controls could not always be performed effectively because of changing security conditions in villages and hamlets; unreported address changes on the part of the population, particularly the youths; Communist pressure and wartime conditions; and Communist seizure of identification papers issued by the government to the civilian population. Statistics on manpower resources used by the Defense Ministry's Mobilization Directorate were derived from estimates rather than based on a population census; they were therefore unreliable.

Partial and progressive mobilization of age groups as applied from 1964 to 1968 was very much consistent with the special conditions of the Vietnam War. The decision to enforce general mobilization in June 1968 was very timely. Nevertheless, implementation was rather lax on the part of local administrative officials at the lower levels. Police operations, although not too successful in rounding up draft dodgers, did contribute to the success of recruitment efforts. Indeed, from 1965 on, when military pays and allowances became lower than civilian standards and civilian employment was readily accessible, the only factor driving youths of draft and mobilization age to enlist was the fear of being hunted by the law. Volunteering also gave them a chance to be assigned to the unit of their choice, while the only alternative to it was to be arrested, stripped of all privileges and benefits, and ultimately forced to serve.

The classification of manpower resource by academic levels to determine the appropriate type of training—as officer, NCO, or EM—was very logical, although this method seemed to favor the rich and the educated urban class. This was true under French rule, when good educational opportunities were limited and available only in the big cities. However, beginning with the Diem administration, and in spite of the war, education facilities at the secondary level expanded considerably and were available in all provincial capitals and district towns. Education and diplomas were no longer inaccessible for most Vietnamese families. The officers of the RVNAF during the last few years of the war indeed came from all walks of life, from both wealthy and poor families.

• • •

Personnel administration in the RVNAF made considerable progress, particularly from 1966 on. Induction procedures were rapidly unified and standardized, and adequate attention was given by all responsible levels to proper completion and timely updating of personnel records. The number of personnel without service numbers or personnel records was greatly reduced in comparison with 1965 and the preceding years.

• • •

Criticisms were directed mainly at the national leadership in the appointment of corps commanders, division commanders, and province chiefs. Many exceptionally qualified personnel were thus relegated to oblivion merely because they did not have the opportunity to serve these leaders in earlier times, or because they chose to ignore the devious methods commonly used to attract the leaders' attention.

Then responsible authorities also seemed to be too submissive to outside influences. This criticism was directed at all levels, from national to local, and from corps to regiments, with particular focus on corps, MR, and province levels. Outside influences included the wives of high-level officials, Buddhist and Catholic leaders, general officers on active duty or retired, congressmen and politicians, who all frequently interfered in the process of transfer and assignment by requesting special considerations for friends and relatives. These interferences annoyed honest commanders, but the less honest ones knew how to turn favors into personal profits. Although the number of personnel benefiting from these favors was small, there were sufficient grounds for a large number of servicemen to feel disenchanted with the system.

Finally, there were commanders who took bribes in exchange for favors. It was fortunate for the RVNAF that these corrupt commanders were but a minority.

III. AWARDS AND PROMOTIONS

• • •

Promotion Authority and Procedure

After the 1 November 1963 coup d'etat, a number of generals, field- and company-grade officers, who were the proteges of junta generals received blanket, special, often double-rank promotions. Among this group were some who deserved this recognition, but others merely rode in on their mentors' coattails. The 1964 countercoup saw another group of underlings of the coup leaders being promoted. It was total chaos. Rumor had it that, in order to earn promotion, one had to be within the orbit of generals; on the outside the situation was hopeless.

However, a development boosted the spirit of the military; it was the enactment of Decree Law 13/64, which, for the first time, established regulations for career military personnel. Such a legislative document had been long desired by military personnel and repeatedly recommended; yet for some obscure reason it was stalled during the entire tenure of the First Republic.

• • •

IV. PERSONNEL SERVICES

The services which the Adjutant General system of the RVNAF rendered to military personnel from induction to discharge were numerous. However, only four vital services will be discussed in this monograph: personnel records, casualty reports, leaves, and postal service.

• • •

Casualty Reporting

Another vital service performed by all units was casualty reporting. Each unit was required to report promptly, accurately, and completely such information concerning its personnel as wounds (light or serious), missing in action, and deaths, whether in combat action or other line of duty.

Casualty reporting took place in two steps. The first consisted of a notification by the fastest means (radio, wire, or messenger) to the unit commander and next of kin, briefly providing the type of casualty and the circumstances under which it occurred. The second step was to confirm the casualty by a detailed narrative report. The major problems most often encountered concerned the notification of next of kin and drafting the narrative report. Notifications were often delayed or even failed to reach their destination. One reason for this was that the addresses recorded in the record booklets were often incomplete and inaccurate. There were instances where the addresses, mostly rural, were located in insecure areas or inaccessible to either the military or the national post office because of unexpected changes in the security situation.

• • •

Another significant problem in casualty reporting resulted from discrepancies usually found in statistics maintained by combat units, medical units, and personnel administration units. The figures reported by combat units were consistently higher than those contained in medical reports. There were several reasons for this. First, the term "casualty" was understood differently by personnel in the two reporting channels. Combat units considered casualties as any individual who was missing, killed, or wounded seriously or lightly, and those cared for at the first aid station, even though they may not have been evacuated.

But, for medical purposes, the term casualty meant only wounded individuals who had been evacuated and treated in medical facilities, whether dispensaries or general hospitals. Individuals with light wounds who had received medical attention and returned to duty were not reported as casualties by medical authorities.

Second, combat units often reported casualty figures without being able to account for them; therefore, they had to make repeated corrections in daily reports which were riddled with errors. Then, also, casualty reports were often filed at least twice by battalion commanders; the first report was a preliminary one and invariably gave lower casualty figures for friendly troops than for the enemy. A few days later, a revised report would be filed to adjust friendly casualty figures previously reported. The readjusted figures were generally higher than the original ones. When asked about this situation, an officer who had served in combat units for a long time confided: "Reporting and rectifying are inevitable on the battlefield. At the beginning of an engagement, a unit must always report on the preliminary outcome to higher echelons. Only much later, after the fighting has declined, does the unit have time to make a headcount of casualties and arrive at accurate statistics. The discrepancy between the two sets of figures is both a fact of life, and a psychological hangup with many field commanders, who are obsessed with the competitive spirit and the kill ratio numbers game. This is an incurable psychological illness prevalent among Vietnamese tactical commanders. I wonder whether it also affects those of other countries."

• • •

Leave of Absence

After a period of service away from home, every fighting man longed for a leave of absence from duty. Two kinds of leaves existed in the RVNAF: the short- and the long-term leave. Short-term leaves included the overnight pass issued to NCOs and EM living off-base, the 24-hour pass issued on weekends and holidays by the primary unit commander, and special leaves granted for weddings, childbirth, or death of parents and parents-in-law. The length of absence in such cases ranged from a few days to a maximum of 15 days and was not deducted from the annual leave. Other types of short-term leaves were graduation leaves on the basis of one day for every month in training granted by schools and training centers upon graduation, and the 30-day annual leaves in peacetime and 15-day annual leaves in wartime, divided into two seven-day increments, granted by the parent unit commander. Annual leaves were regarded as a right and not a privilege and, in peacetime, could be accumulated up to six months. In wartime this regulation was abolished and annual leaves had to be taken within the year or forfeited. The authority to grant annual leaves rested with the JGS.

There were five general types of long-term leaves. The first type was a three-month convalescence leave with pay, which had to be recommended by the medical board of a hospital. This leave was granted by the commander of the hospital concerned. The second type was the six-month leave granted to persons affected by an incurable disease. The term of this leave was renewable, if recommended by the medical board, up to five years if the disease was not attributable to duty or eight years if it was. The third type was a six-month to two-year leave with pay granted in peacetime for educational purposes. Another long-term leave was granted without pay for special reasons such as family problems, education, and candidacy for public office. In wartime this type of leave was abolished for all purposes other than candidacy for public office. Finally, the severance leave of five days for every year in service, up to the maximum of 90 days, was granted by the parent unit commander upon discharge.

• • •

V. DISCIPLINE, MILITARY JUSTICE, AND PROBLEMS OF DESERTION

"Discipline is the strength of the Army." This slogan was the first thing every Vietnamese citizen saw as he walked through the gate of an induction center. It was the most quoted phrase in the RVNAF, and could be seen in the most conspicuous places in billets, classrooms, parade grounds, mess halls, sleeping quarters, and offices. It was the first statement made by cadres and instructors in a course on military conduct and discipline, a commandment to be obeyed by every serviceman, a code to be upheld by every cadre, from corporal to general.

Disciplinary Action and Military Justice

The fabric of the RVNAF was held together by two basic documents: Directive 2121/ TTM/1/PC of the JGS, which specified the authority and sanctions against breach of military conduct and discipline, and Ordinance No. 8 of 1951, which promulgated a Vietnamese military code and the organization of a military justice system.

The RVNAF divided disciplinary infractions into two areas: the area of military conduct, which included attitude and behavior toward self, superiors, inferiors, peers, civil servants, cadres and police, family and the people; and the area of military discipline, which included violation of command channels, AWOL, desertion, malingering, dereliction of duty, and protecting, aiding, or abetting the enemy. As part of its program to improve command and leadership, in 1966 the JGS published a manual for small-unit commanders which contained a summary of infractions, punishments, and authority for punishment.

Punishments, from the lightest to the most severe, included: administrative restriction, disciplinary confinement (with or without pay loss), transfer to hardship posts, demotion, dishonorable discharge, and trial by a court-martial (which usually resulted in a prison term or even dishonorable discharge). For enlisted men, confinement always meant imprisonment in a stockade for periods up to 60 days, including confinement to a solitary cell under guard. For NCOs and officers, confinement was usually less demanding; in many cases it only involved restriction to quarters.

Men incurring punishment during combat operations would serve it when the operations were over. Men incurring punishment while under medical treatment at military hospitals would serve it after recovery. While serving their sentence, EM had to perform labor during duty and off-duty hours and were confined to their cells at night. NCOs and officers were sometimes detained in disciplinary barracks and not allowed visits or freedom of movement. However, in case of service needs they were allowed to go to work, but would be required to go back to confinement for meditation during off-duty hours and at night.

Before 1965 EM under punishment lost their daily base pay, but not their family allowance, for every day they served in the stockade. After 1965, this measure was abolished and EM forfeited their pay only in case of damage or loss of clothing or equipment, embezzlement, AWOL, or an unexcused late in reporting for duty. In case of repeated violations of discipline, the punished serviceman might be transferred to a hardship assignment. For example, he could be transferred from a staff position to combat duty, or from an urban area to the remote backcountry. During the First Indochina War of 1949–1954, several disciplinary companies were formed in each MR to deal with hard-core disciplinary cases, but this measure, considered unnecessarily cruel, was abandoned after 1954.

The authority to impose disciplinary action depended on position and rank. Such an authority conferred by position was always greater than that conferred by rank. For instance, a major had the authority to give an NCO under his command up to 12 days of confinement to quarters. But if he held the position of garrison commander, the number of punishment days he could inflict would increase to 20. Cadres from corporals to full colonels had, besides the authority to punish men under their own command, the authority to recommend disciplinary action against other inferiors who had been caught violating military conduct or discipline. General officers had the authority to punish men of inferior rank, whether under their command or not. When the maximum penalty allowed a cadre had been imposed, and he felt the offense deserved more retribution, he could recommend additional punishment to a higher commander. A man receiving punishment from his superior could appeal to a higher echelon authority if he felt himself [a] victim of injustice or excesses. These appeals would be considered and investigated by the Directorate of the Inspector General or a military security agency.

• • •

The RVNAF military code, which defined criminal cases to be tried by courts-martial, was promulgated by Ordinance No. 8 of 1951, which also established the military justice system. By Decree No. 4/QP/ND of 26 January 1951, the Directorate of Military Justice was created with the responsibility to organize military courts, to recruit and administer personnel for these tribunals, to issue instructions to the military prosecutor, and to research documents from a legal point of view.

During the same year, by Decree No. 138/VP/ND of 23 August 1951, the National Gendarmerie was established to replace the French Gendarmerie in the maintenance of public safety and law and order, and in the enforcement of military law. The activities of this agency were comprehensive because, in addition to its affiliation with the Ministry of Defense, it also operated under the Ministry of Interior in matters of administrative police and national law enforcement, under the Ministry of Justice in matters of judicial police such as the discovery and investigation of felony or misdemeanor or police infractions, and under the Ministry of Economic Affairs in controlling prices and uncovering contraband.

In 1952, to meet the requirements of an expanding national army, the Gendarmerie was supplemented by an adjunct branch called the military police (the Provost Marshal's Office). The Gendarmerie differed from the military police (MP) in that it worked with military authorities and military justice, as well as with civilian authorities in a technical capacity, whereas the MPs worked only within the military under the authority of a garrison commander. The gendarmes had to take an oath of office before the court; the military police did not. Besides the usual military uniforms, gendarmes also wore a red cap, which earned them the popular name of "red-capped policemen."

In 1953, because of their close working relationship, the Military Justice Directorate and the Gendarmerie were fused into one organization, called the Directorate of Military Justice and Gendarmerie, by Decree 70/QP of June 1953. Under the director, a Vietnamese officer, there were two subdirectorates for justice and gendarmerie. Under the subdirectorate of the gendarmerie there was a command to direct and control gendarmerie units. Although part of the organization of the national army, the Gendarmerie was under French command. Not until 1954 were gendarme installations handed over to Vietnamese control. Among them were the Thu Duc and Hanoi Gendarmerie Schools.

In September 1955 both the gendarmerie directorate and command were transferred to Vietnamese control. By this time the gendarmes numbered about 1,000 men, distributed among four companies of various sizes. The South Vietnam Company had two platoons and 29 stations; the North Vietnam Company, two platoons and 11 stations; and the Central Highlands Company, two platoons and five stations. The military police, on the other hand, had just over 100 men deployed in seven stations.

Despite the long years of RVNAF reorganization, and the changing governmental structure under the advisory assistance of the United States since 1955, the military justice and gendarmerie system remained unchanged. Not until 1964 was the Gendarmerie excluded from the organizational structure of the RVNAF. The defense budget for 1965 in fact did not provide any expenditure for it. The Gendarmerie therefore had to disband, and the Directorate of Military Justice and Gendarmerie became just the Directorate of Military Justice. Almost one-half of the gendarmes went to the National Police, and the rest to the military police, but the work the gendarmes had been doing for military tribunals was not clearly assigned to any agency. Neither the civilian nor military police, since they were patterned on the American model, were given the responsibility to carry out the court duties previously performed by the gendarmes. This resulted in thousands of cases which were under investigation being discontinued. The functioning of military courts, too, was interrupted for a considerable time.

In 1966, upon a recommendation by the Directorate of Military Justice to fill this vacuum, the military police command was given the responsibility of carrying out court-martial duties formerly assigned to the Gendarmerie. The military judicial police thus came into being within the RVNAF military police organization, and later became known as the criminal investigation system, which included a head office at the military police command and judicial investigation military police companies at the CTZ or MR echelon. Each company was assigned an area of responsibility and was stationed in squads or teams at crucial points to carry out orders from CTZ military courts under the latter's technical supervision.

The most serious and unsurmountable problem encountered by the investigative military police was the shortage of personnel in the face of an ever-increasing number of cases to be handled and the travel of personnel to conduct investigations or deliver summonses to defendants living in insecure areas. Consequently, investigations took an inordinately long time and were usually left pending, a situation which caused a serious backlog at the prosecutor's office in the regular and field military courts.

Military Courts and Prisons

It was not until ten months after the creation of the Directorate of Military Justice, on 26 January 1951, that a military court was established in Saigon on 22 November 1951. Two other military courts were set up, in Hanoi on 23 March 1953 and in Hue on

21 November 1953. In 1955, after the regroupment of the National Army to the South and the ensuing territorial reorganization, the Nha Trang military court was activated on 13 May 1955. In 1961, along with the organization of South Vietnam into four tactical zones, the Can Tho military court was established to share the burden with the Saigon court. Thus each corps area was served by a military court—the Hue court for I CTZ, the Nha Trang court for II CTZ, the Saigon court for III CTZ, and the Can Tho court for IV CTZ.

The presiding judge of each court was a civilian judge appointed from the local court of appeals. The alternate presiding judge was a field-grade officer from the Military Justice Directorate. Other associate judges were selected from among officers serving in local units and agencies. The prosecutor and his staff were all members of the Military Justice Directorate. Since there were no military defense attorneys, defendants could retain the service of a civilian attorney or, in case of financial hardship, they were assigned a lawyer appointed by the lawyers' council. The jurisdiction of a military court was usually very broad. It had the authority to try any individual from the regular armed forces, RF/PF, or paramilitary forces who had committed an offense against military or civilian criminal law. The court could hand down any sentence, including a death sentence, but the defendant could always appeal to higher authority.

In 1962, to meet the security situation, field military courts came into being in each CTZ by virtue of Decree Law 11/62 of 21 May 1962. The objective was to speed up and simplify the trial of flagrante delicto cases where the evidence was so obvious as to require no extensive investigation. As the GVN saw it, flagrante delicto cases included not only individuals caught in the act, but also those caught in possession of any objects, weapons, instruments, or documents that led authorities to believe that they were party to a crime. Four years later, Decree Law 4/66 extended the jurisdiction of the field military court, in response to the war situation, to include the authority to try cases involving bribery, embezzlement, illegal speculation, and hoarding, whether committed by civilians or uniformed men. Another legislation, Decree Law 15/66, further gave field military courts the authority to try desertion cases, individuals who incited desertion, or protected and harbored deserters. Finally, Decree Law 6/70, promulgated in 1970, endowed field military courts with the authority to try not only deserters and accomplices, but also military, civilian, and police personnel caught in flagrante delicto criminal acts, as well as civilians who were parties to, and accomplices in, felonies or misdemeanors as spelled out in the criminal code and regulations currently in effect.

Each court session was presided over by a military judge, selected from among local senior military officers and assisted by four military jury members. Decisions reached were final and effective immediately, except for the death sentence. Because of their all-military nature, field military courts acted quickly. These courts also met more frequently, and sometimes in the area where the crime had been committed, so as to make their decisions an example to both the military and the civilian populace. Sentences handed down by these courts were often very severe.

In 1970 the Supreme Court decided that the process of law in field military courts was unconstitutional. As a consequence, the court membership was revised to include at each trial a presiding judge, who could be civilian or military, and four associate judges. If the presiding judge was a civilian, he had to be the president or an associate judge of the local civilian court of appeals. If he was a military man, the presiding judge had to be an officer with the rank of major or above, selected from among military justice personnel. Associate judges of field military courts were also required to be professional military judges. Both presiding and associate judges were to be nominated by the Supreme Court. In addition, defendants brought to trial by field military courts had the right to appeal to the Supreme Court, except in case of desertion.

The professional composition of field military courts, although an improvement from a legal standpoint, lost its cutting edge so necessary in wartime. As a result, field military courts unwittingly reverted to the slow and deliberate pace of regular courts. Sentences no longer daunted criminals. Civilian judges were not as eager as their military counterparts had been, perhaps out of fear of retaliation in a troubled war situation. On-the-spot court sessions were also no longer held.

Before 1963, the RVNAF had no separate prisons. Military offenders who were convicted by a court-martial were incarcerated by gendarme companies along with civilian convicts in national or provincial civilian jails. In 1964, in order to relieve overcrowded civilian jails, and to make administrative work simpler, four military prisons were built next to military court buildings in Hue, Nha Trang, Saigon, and Can Tho. The Hue military prison, heavily damaged during the 1968 Communist offensive, was moved to Danang in 1970 for greater security and to be in close proximity of regular and field courts which had been moved there two years earlier. Upon conviction, military personnel were sent directly to combat units as field work gangs if they were deserters condemned to forced labor, or to the nearest military prison to serve their sentences if they were other types of offenders. Civilians being prosecuted before a military court, and insubordinate men who resisted the draft, were also detained in these institutions pending court proceedings.

The shortcomings of military jails were lack of basic comforts, bad food, overcrowding, and delayed trials. There were few conveniences in these facilities because prisons had low construction priority. Most improvement programs were of the self-help type, initiated by prison commanders with building materials provided by US advisors. Compared with [South Vietnam's] Communist POW camps, military prisons had far fewer conveniences. In spite of this awareness, the RVNAF could do little for lack of resources. In the way of food, for example, per capita food allowances were so low that poor nutrition was the inevitable result. A program to increase food intake through vegetable farming and animal raising could not materialize because all military prisons were located in crowded cities where there was insufficient land for either activity.

Frequent visits by families were a reluctantly accepted source of increased food supply for inmates. The number of inmates also varied unexpectedly; at times it increased by 50 percent of capacity, especially after a police operation to locate deserters. There was a protracted delay before trial, usually about three months for deserters and more

than a year for other offenders. A backlog of cases was normal occurrence. Acts of leniency by the Defense Ministry, such as dropping of charges or temporary release to
allow offenders to serve in combat units, coupled with the urging for prompter action by
military courts to bring desertion cases to trial (deserters being the main inmate population of military jails), helped to alleviate this congestion to some extent.

Absence without Leave and Desertion

The most prevalent offense against military discipline, one that directly affected the
capability of units, particularly combat units, was absence without leave. An individual
was considered AWOL when he left his unit without a pass, or failed to report back to
his unit after the expiration of an authorized leave or on completion of temporary duty.

Personnel charged with AWOL received punishments amounting to a jail term for
EM and confinement to an MP house for NCOs and officers. The jail or confinement
term was equal to twice the number of days absent if it was the first such offense of the
year, and three times that number if it was the second such offense of the year. In addition, the culprits suffered a pay forfeit equal to the number of days on AWOL. A three-
time offender within two consecutive years would, besides jail or confinement and for-
feiture of pay, be brought to trial by a disciplinary board for demotion, denied attendance
at military schools, and disqualified for promotion for one year.

After a grace period, anyone on AWOL who failed to return to his unit became a deserter. Before 1964, this grace period was fixed at six days for draftees with 90 days in
the service and 15 days if the service was longer. In 1965 the grace period was changed
to be 30 days for all personnel. However, in 1966 Decree Law 15/66 reduced this period
to be 15 days for all servicemen. On the 16th day, therefore, an AWOL became a deserter.
His parent unit then prepared a search warrant, Form QD-828, and dispatched it to military and civilian police agencies with request for action. If the offender reported to his unit
after the search warrant had gone out, his parent unit would reconsider his case to determine whether he should be pardoned or turned over to the military police. He might be
pardoned if he could produce written evidence to justify the overstaying of his grace period. Such evidence could be based on the inability to secure transportation, an accident,
or any other incident beyond his control. If proper justification was presented, the parent
unit would draft a stop-search notice . . . and send it to responsible agencies. . . .

Desertion was the greatest loss borne by the RVNAF over the years. It constantly
threatened the JGS efforts to implement force structure expansion plans. From 1965 to
1972 desertions averaged about 120,000 per year, and the average monthly desertion
rate was 12 per thousand.

In the ARVN, a breakdown of the monthly desertion rate by combat and noncombat
units during 1968–1972 indicated that desertion was about four to seven times higher in
combat units, especially infantry. The desertion rate among territorial forces was much
lower compared to regular forces. There were about twice as many deserters in the RF [as]
in the PF, which in fact had the lowest desertion rate of all (except noncombat units).

A further analysis showed that, even though the desertion rate among noncombat units was low, this rate was steadily rising every year, climbing from 4.6 per thousand in 1968 to 12.9 per thousand in late 1972. The same rising trend affected ARVN combat units over the same period. Desertion seemed to be worst among the rangers, followed in decreasing order by the infantry, the paratroopers, and the marines. Among infantry divisions, desertion was highest in MR-4, less in MR-2, and least in MR-1. In any event, the ARVN always led in desertion rate among the three services, but this rate abated significantly during the post-cease-fire period.

In an attempt to arrive at a practical solution to the desertion problem, the General Political Warfare Department/JGS conducted interviews with deserters who had been arrested or surrendered themselves, and held extensive consultation with leaders of small units. Five causes were cited by deserters to justify their action: 1) homesickness brought about by separation from families; 2) dislike of units to which assigned; 3) dislike of military service, abhorrence of killings; 4) discontent with commanders; 5) poverty and inadequacy of military pay to support families.

In addition, small-unit commanders believed that there were other factors contributing to desertion. Deserters, they thought, had not been dealt with harshly enough by the law to serve as examples. Also, most of those who deserted had not been ideologically motivated enough in civilian life; they had harbored the intent to desert from the moment they arrived in draft centers. Finally, they could have been incited, or threatened to desert, by the enemy.

As for the most opportune time for desertion, it was learned that many made the attempt during travels from induction centers to military schools or from schools to assigned units, during annual or graduation leaves after they had drawn the enlistment bonus, and during R&R time, especially after an operation in which their unit had suffered heavy losses. The first year in military service was also the most likely time for desertion; so were occasions such as the beginning of the harvest season and Tet holidays. After one year in service, the soldier was much less inclined to desert for any reason.

Areas near population centers, served by lines of communication, had better job opportunities and were [more] propitious for deserters than sparsely populated jungled or mountainous areas. The areas fringing the capital city, and the entire IV Corps Tactical Zone, were most favorable for deserters. Dense population in these areas made for difficult control. If there was less desertion among RF and PF units, it was because they served in their home areas and the war was usually not as severe as it was for the regular army.

A common and most significant trait among deserters was that they almost never took weapons along or went to the other side. This was strong evidence that desertion had always been a socioeconomical problem, never a political one.

• • •

The RVNAF Efforts to Control Desertion

• • •

To combat desertion the JGS initiated several measures. The first and foremost among them was to improve command and leadership in small units. The JGS was convinced that the command and leadership skills of squad and platoon leaders, and of company and battalion commanders, had much to do with desertion. A noted shortcoming involved unit leadership during bivouacs or rest periods in barracks. Attention to the men during these periods was far more lax than during combat operations. Yet it was during these rest periods and idle moments that men needed the most attention and care about their physical and mental well-being from commanders. It was during these moments that men felt homesick, missed their wives and children, and mulled over death and destruction on the battlefield. The intent and act of desertion more frequently occurred then than in combat, when all thoughts were about the enemy.

To assist small-unit commanders in improving their command and leadership abilities, political warfare officers were assigned as assistants to battalion and company commanders throughout the army. In a certain sense, these officers acted as big brothers in an extended family who coordinated personnel, supply, and political warfare activities to assist commanders in meeting their men's material and moral needs. This was part of the New Horizon program of 1966 and the "unit building" program of 1970, both of which provided guidance to small units in carrying out a uniform program of action.

• • •

The second measure the JGS took to combat desertion was to improve personnel management procedures. Three areas singled out for specific attention were assignment, transfer, and leaves. Draftees in recruitment and induction centers received first priority for training at a training center nearest to their hometowns, and maximum care was exercised to avoid sending them to training centers in another military region. Training centers were directed to assign trainees to the platoon or company that came from the same village, district, or province in order to foster an at-home feeling, minimize the effects of homesickness and disorientation, and extend friendship in moments of sorrow. When draftees had finished training, maximum effort was made to assign whole platoons or companies to the MR of origin whenever possible to preserve the valuable esprit de corps that had developed during training.

Units from combat arms and technical services that took in new recruits were required to send a party to the training center to welcome them, arrange for transportation, and care for them throughout the trip back. Efforts were also made by infantry divisions to arrange for new arrivals to spend a few days at the division's training center for orientation purposes and, if possible, to assign entire teams, squads, or platoons to divisional units. Draftees who initially could not be assigned to their home MR would have the right to request a transfer after two years of service, and responsible authorities were under obligation to grant such requests. But this right was to be forfeited if a man had been AWOL during the year. Finally, freshly trained recruits were to be placed in the right jobs according to their MOS and health status.

• • •

Besides measures taken with respect to assignments, transfers, and leaves, the JGS also announced a maximum desertion rate for each division, each ranger group, and each sector. If a unit exceeded this rate, punishment was meted out to the commander concerned after each review of the desertion situation during the monthly meetings of the desertion control committees.

• • •

All of these measures assisted in reducing desertion, but never solved the problem effectively. As a result, active control was always necessary to prevent and deter men from leaving their units without permission. Fixed and mobile control posts, manned by the military and national police, were deployed along axes of communication and at blocking positions to check papers of draft-age men, whether in civilian clothes or in military uniform. More elaborate were police operations conducted to arrest deserters hiding in villages or urban areas, along with draft dodgers and underground Communist agents.

All of these fugitives employed similar methods to deceive government authorities and escape arrest—tunnels, identity change and disguise, and forged or illegally procured papers. Police operations were useful in several respects. First, they helped verify residence status and arrest criminals, deserters, draft dodgers, thieves, hooligans, and underground Communist agents. Then they also created a sense of insecurity among these people which sometimes forced them to surrender.

• • •

Before 1966 desertion was an offense which was tried by a regular military court. Court procedures often took a long time, which reduced the impact of the punishment. To support desertion control measures, the GVN promulgated Decree Law 15/66 in April 1966 conferring authority to try deserters at the CTZ field military court. Sentences passed by these courts ranged from five years of imprisonment to the death penalty in case a serviceman joined the enemy or deserted for the third time. In an effort to deter desertion, the Military Justice Directorate and courts increased their activities and court sessions were held at an accelerated pace. Convicted deserters served their time as hard-labor gangs for companies and battalions in operations, during which time they would do the heavy work such as carrying ammunition or felling trees, working in the midst of fighting hazards like all other soldiers, but carrying no weapons. Their food rations were reduced and their nights spent in confinement. If they were wounded, captured, or killed, they or their survivors received no benefits.

In general, the measures taken by the GVN and the RVNAF to control desertion were fairly adequate, but the results still left much to be desired because of several difficulties. First, our troops were continually exposed to Communist proselytizing action. Dissolving the ranks of the RVNAF had always been a major Communist effort of equal importance with military and political activities. Our enemy employed all kinds of techniques under any conditions to induce or coerce RVNAF servicemen to desert their posts or simply to leave the service. The relatives, wives, children, and parents of our servicemen were the Communists' most prized targets in this effort.

Next there was the problem of forged identification papers which made detection extremely difficult. For control purposes, every serviceman away from his unit had to have three kinds of documents—a plastic military ID card, a certificate of active service issued by the unit commander and valid for one quarter, [and] a pass, leave of absence, or movement order justifying his whereabouts. Similar papers were also required of every male citizen—a plastic ID card issued by the National Police, a voter registration card, and a certificate of draft status issued by appropriate authorities. These were considered sufficient for control purposes. However, with today's sophisticated equipment and know-how, the forging of papers was easy. Resourceful deserters could always obtain all the necessary papers that would help them past control stations and government authorities. Several paper-forging organizations had been uncovered, with complete equipment, in the very heart of Saigon. The problem of forged papers resulted in regrettable incidents between the police and servicemen and reduced the efficiency of the control system. There were instances of genuine papers that policemen took for false ones, and the suspected serviceman was taken to a police station for investigation. Such incidents caused irritation and resentment for both sides.

Then the uninvolved attitude of civilian authorities also made it difficult to uncover deserters. As long as deserters could find a shelter, the desertion problem would not melt away. Local authorities at the block, ward, hamlet, [and] village level and the police usually looked the other way and failed to enforce search orders correctly because of ineptitude, deference, fear of reprisal, or venality. Deserters were also frequently harbored by religious groups, either out of charity, brotherly love, or self-interest. A few religious groups in South Vietnam even kept their doors wide open to all draft-age male citizens, including deserters. Whether by accident or by design, many sacred pagodas and temples had become safe havens for deserters to elude the police dragnet. Searches of these sacred places to uncover deserters often met with opposition and slander in the name of religious freedom. As a result, local authorities usually left them alone.

Over the years, the GVN's treatment of Communist cadres and troops under its Open Arms policy had given servicemen standing trial for desertion, and judges hearing desertion cases, ample food for thought. If the Communists, who killed our people and soldiers, were treated with clemency and forgiveness, they reasoned, why should the government be too harsh toward the men who, during the performance of their duties, committed the error of desertion? It was probably for this reason that our courts usually punished desertion with leniency, giving sentences ranging from just six months to a few years of imprisonment, rarely imposing the maximum-security cell, and virtually never passing death sentences, although the penalties were in the books. The lenient attitude of trial judges toward deserters prompted complaints from unit commandeers. One was heard saying, "Dealing with deserters that way is like putting the horse in the barn and leaving the door open. The courts tolerate and encourage desertion. The courts should give the men a clear-cut choice between two deaths, a glorious death on the battlefield commemorated and compensated by the government and the nation, or the ignoble death of a cowardly, fugitive deserter." How right those remarks were, especially for a field commander beset by the problem of desertion and depleted ranks! But for a judge who administered justice, what a difficult situation it must have been.

The amnesty policy proclaimed by the GVN in 1964, in the wake of the 1 November

1963 revolution that toppled President Ngo Dinh Diem, opened up rehabilitation opportunities for the deserters, but also set a barrier to future desertion control efforts. Deserters still at large, under arrest, and awaiting trial, or serving their time in field work gangs, were all reinstated, if within draft age, and assigned to combat units as required. Though it helped the RVNAF to regain a number of personnel and alleviate troop shortages, this humane and clement policy set a harmful precedent. Believing that there would be other pardoning acts attendant upon some future big event, servicemen kept deserting and went into hiding. Indeed, during the years of greatest military activity this leniency program created huge dents among combat ranks. During the 1968 Communist Tet Offensive, and during the 1972 Easter Offensive, the ARVN desertion rate was at its highest level.

During the years of critical troop shortage the JGS implemented the policy of reinstating not only deserters, but also men in military jails awaiting trial and those serving in civilian correctional institutions. These men had their charges dropped, received a parole or a stay on their sentence, and were taken to regional administrative units for reprocessing into the service. Because of the pressing needs of combat units, the overworked administrative units and careless authorities hastily turned these men over to combat battalions totally deprived physically and unsettled mentally after their time in jail. Desertion under such circumstances was an inevitable outcome.

The inevitability of desertion was also a product of the General Mobilization Law. If this law had helped to replenish the ranks of the RVNAF, it also made desertion unavoidable. It brought into the military service all kinds of people, including the worst elements of a society which had been divided and rotted by a quarter-century war. Uncertain about their own beliefs in a war of ideologies, they were impressed into service. Whether undergoing training or serving in the field, these men were not ideologically prepared for the struggle.

The less ideologically determined a man was, the greater the material incentive had to be. It must be admitted that the government and armed forces of South Vietnam had endeavored to provide servicemen with every material incentive possible. Unfortunately, the benefits were always inadequate. Even while doing their service, most men could not support their families with their salary; after they reached old age and retirement, the situation naturally became worse. Most servicemen saw nothing bright about their future in the military.

Observations

The code of military conduct and discipline for the RVNAF was clear and comprehensive. The law was also adequate and strict, in keeping with the requirements of the war. The training in conduct and discipline, and their application in schools and training centers, was exemplary, especially at the Dalat National Military Academy, the Thu Duc Reserve Officer School, and the Nha Trang NCO School. In these institutions trainees, cadets, instructors, and staff members not only comported themselves in an exemplary manner, but also insisted that their subordinates and fellow soldiers do the same.

However, once assigned to units and in touch with reality, their attitude toward discipline began to relax, especially with regard to military deportment. For example, many commanders let the men under their command grow long hair. To justify their breach of discipline, they argued that a short haircut was irrelevant to valor in combat, and that short hair was a distinctive mark that helped the enemy identify our servicemen easily. Many men were seen on the streets in soiled, rumpled combat uniforms instead of correct street wear. The mere appearance of these unkempt soldiers indicated the lamentable state of discipline prevailing in the RVNAF, especially during the later stages of war.

There were leaders of small units who failed to maintain close control of their troops while operating through villages and who sometimes even condoned larceny or looting, even though they realized that such acts seriously violated military conduct and discipline. Could it be that their hearts had grown weak from witnessing the tremendous hardship that men under their command were experiencing through long days of operating in the jungles and swamps? There were high-ranking cadres and staff officers who used military vehicles, especially the quarter-ton liaison vehicles, for private purposes, knowing that such abuse was forbidden yet persisting in it. Was it because of the high cost of living, the low pay, and the privation of their families? There were commanders, tyrannical disciplinarians, who insulted their men and kept those they punished in tiny barbed-wire cages exposed to the elements. No military law or discipline allowed such treatment. Then there were cadres who chastised their men but failed to record any punishment in individual records, or who punished them on paper without requiring them to serve. Such acts ruined the effectiveness and meaning of a punishment order.

Most notable was the period after the 1 November 1963 revolution in which RVNAF generals overthrew Ngo Dinh Diem and set up a military government. Military disciplinary action was so lax that it failed to deter any serviceman. A case in point was the disciplinary action against the men who participated in the aborted coup of 1965 under the Nguyen Khanh administration, and those who supported the Buddhist struggle of 1966 in [the] I Corps areas under the rule of the National Leadership Committee. These disciplinary actions were woefully inadequate, being merely light punishments, transfers out of home areas, and discharges. There were no trials by court-martial. Severe as a discharge was for a serviceman, it also proved to be a blessing, allowing the man to live safely during the war and to engage in lucrative business. In addition, those high-ranking commanders who the people and troops believed had violated military discipline never came under investigation to receive their just retribution, but were quietly transferred to another key position or removed from office. They continued to enjoy their privileges intact, waiting for a glorious comeback or a discharge. Over the years, there were only two division commanders who had been investigated for their offenses and tried by a field court-martial. They were both demoted and dishonorably discharged. However, these disciplinary actions were far from being prompt and timely. The word got around among the people and military that these actions had been taken not out of a desire to maintain discipline but because of rising adverse popular sentiment.

Except for a tiny minority of servicemen who were fed up with the war, and some

narrow-minded personnel who cared for nothing but their self-interests, the great majority of RVNAF servicemen tried to stay within the bounds of military propriety and discipline. They voluntarily curtained their own personal freedom and material needs to
serve as examples to subordinates and peers alike. Silent, [persevering], patient, they
fought on, and induced subordinates and comrades in arms to fight, with the hope that
peace would soon be restored and that the nation could bind the wounds of war in order
to gain strength for the long-term ideological struggle with the Communists.

VI. THE RVNAF TRAINING BASE

Organization and Development

> The more sweat you shed on a training field,
> the less blood you shed on a battlefield.

Inscribed in big red letters at the entrance of every military school and training center, the above RVNAF training motto stressed a simple truth. It served as a constant reminder for every serviceman undergoing training that, while training might be painful,
it could save his life in combat.

Until 1954, the Vietnamese National Armed Forces' organization for training was
under heavy French influence. The first school for officers was established at Hue in
1948 on the initiative of Mr. Phan Van Giao, governor of Central Vietnam, and sanctioned by the French high commissioner. Vietnam was yet to emerge officially as an independent state.

After graduating two classes, this officers' school was relocated to Dalat where Bao
Dai, the chief of state, established his home and headquarters.[3] Bao Dai took a special
interest in the school and renamed it "Ecole Militaire Inter-Armes de Dalat" (Dalat
Inter-Arms Military School), known under the French acronym EMIAD.

In the fall of 1950 three regional military schools were created to train noncommissioned officers: Nam Dinh (MR-3, or North Vietnam), Hue (MR-2, or Central Vietnam),
and Trung Chanh (MR-1, or South Vietnam). Then, in 1951, to meet growing training
requirements occasioned by partial mobilization, the following schools and training
centers were established in rapid succession: the Thu Duc and Nam Dinh reserve officer
schools; three training centers: Cay Diep (MR-1), Mang Ca (MR-2), and Bac Ninh
(MR-3) for the training of draftees and recruits; the medical college in Hanoi (MR-3)
for the training of career medical officers; the School of Gendarmerie (Military Police)
at Thu Duc; and two training centers for drivers and auto mechanics, one at Hue and the
other at Dalat.[4]

In 1952, as the General Staff and military region headquarters were established, the
Vietnamese National Armed Forces studied plans for the activation of infantry divisions.
Four division training centers were thus established, one in each region, for the purpose

of training infantry personnel. However, a short time later these facilities were redesignated "regional technical training centers" in order to accommodate diverse training requirements occasioned by force development, such as artillery, engineer, and even administration.[5] At the same time, four signal training centers were established, one in each region, for the training of radio operators and second-echelon signal maintenance personnel. In Hanoi, a French-controlled Centre de Formation Tactique (Tactical Training Center) was also created for the training of company, battalion, and regimental commanders. This center was eventually redesignated "Centre d'Etudes Militaires" (Center for Military Studies) and assigned the additional responsibility of training staff officers.

Also during 1952 a regional military school for Montagnards was created in the Central Highlands for the training of noncommissioned officers assigned to Montagnard battalions. Concurrently, an Air Force Training Center and a Naval Training Center were established at Nha Trang to train specialized personnel for each service.

In 1953 the training base was expanded at an accelerated pace to accommodate growing training requirements occasioned by the influx of draftees and the creation of commando (light) battalions. Several new recruit training centers were established: at Quang Yen (MR-3), Suoi Dau (Nha Trang, MR-2), My Tho and Soc Trang (both in MR-1), in addition to existing facilities. The Reserve Officer School at Thu Duc also expanded to increase its capacity from 500 to 1,300 cadets.

During these formative years, the Vietnamese training base was complemented as required by the French school system, both in-country and in France.

• • •

All military schools and training centers were placed under the control of the Direction des Ecoles (School Directorate) until 1953, when this control was taken over by the Military Training Bureau of the General Staff. Although part of the Vietnamese National Armed Forces, these schools and training centers were commanded and staffed by French officers and NCOs. During this period, Vietnamese instructors were few. Despite a gradual increase in numbers, Vietnamese instructors only played a secondary role; they were either assistants or orientation briefers. French was the principal language used in the training process. In units, training did not receive enough emphasis during this period; it was occasionally conducted by French officers and NCOs.

After the 1954 Geneva Accords, all training facilities in North Vietnam were evacuated to the South. At the same time, the training process underwent a great transformation, in keeping with the reorganization of the Vietnamese National Armed Forces, which was undertaken with the training assistance of the joint US-French Training Relations and Instruction Mission (TRIM) on 19 January 1955. As the French withdrew from South Vietnam, the training and reorganization assistance task was taken over by [the] MAAG's Combat Arms Training Organization (CATO) as of 28 April 1956. Eventually all training assistance for the RVNAF was provided by the Training Directorate, MACV, as of 26 April 1965.

At the time [the] MAAG assumed reorganizing and retraining responsibilities in early 1956, the Vietnamese National Armed Forces were besieged with several problems.

There was a definite shortage of experienced officers trained for high command and staff positions; there was also a shortage of officers and NCOs trained in service branch specialties, particularly in logistics. The existing school and training center system was still undeveloped; it did not have enough facilities, training aids, qualified instructors, and adequate training programs, particularly at the regimental and divisional level. Above all, there were no unified training policies and regulations.

To remedy these shortcomings, a joint Vietnamese-US School Planning Board was established on 8 October 1956.

• • •

All . . . schools and training centers were now commanded and staffed by Vietnamese officers, with the assistance of US advisors. Vietnamese also replaced French as the principal language used in training.

• • •

In 1965, the Civil Guard and Self-Defense Corps were integrated with the RVNAF under the respective names of Regional [Forces] and Popular Forces; the Central Training Command was given additional responsibilities to supervise training activities at RF and PF training centers and provide staff assistance to corps commanders in their exercise of command and control over these training centers. Also in 1965, to meet increased requirements, the Political Warfare Training Center was upgraded into a school and relocated to Dalat, where it occupied the premises of the former French School of Gendarmerie.

• • •

In 1967, in order to meet the requirements for leadership cadre at the national level and to conduct studies beyond the competence of the Command and Staff College, the National Defense College (NDC) was established. . . . The NDC was responsible to "educate outstanding and high-ranking military officers and career government civilians to become better qualified in the performance of important duties related to national security; and to study, plan, and develop national defense policies." The first class of the NDC included 15 colonels and lieutenant colonels and six high-ranking civil servants who graduated in April 1969 after a year of study.

• • •

Another large construction project was initiated in the second half of 1968 to improve and modernize the National Military Academy in Dalat. The project, which was heartily endorsed by General Westmoreland, COMUSMACV, was undertaken by the RMK contracting firm at a cost of VN $800 million (or US $6,729,661).

• • •

The RVNAF were extremely proud of their new military academy, which had become a showcase for visiting foreign dignitaries. Its modern laboratory ranked first in the country in terms of equipment and facilities.

• • •

Unit Training

During the period of force structure reorganization beginning in July 1955, which saw the activation of ARVN infantry divisions, a standard unit training program was developed with the assistance of US advisors.

• • •

Phase 1 of unit training was highlighted by movement exercises. During this period, all units were required to practice movements during day and night over increasing distances up to 30 kilometers, and on every type of terrain. A backpack of 12 to 15 kilograms was mandatory for every soldier in movement practice. Field exercises of regimental level during Phase 2 were essentially command post-type exercises, but divisional exercises during Phase 3 involved both CP and field maneuvers. Although this last phase of training began in the fall of 1956 for all divisions, it did not terminate until 1959 because of interruptions caused by enemy-initiated activities.

As the fighting escalated, ARVN units were increasingly committed in counterinsurgency operations. Field exercises of regimental and divisional levels, therefore, were temporarily suspended, beginning in 1960. At the same time, unit training programs were revised to involve only the battalion and smaller units.

• • •

VII. METHODS OF TRAINING

Formal Instruction

By far the most fundamental and effective method of training the individual soldier and the unit was formal instruction conducted at training centers and service schools.

• • •

In-Place Training

In-place training was the second most effective approach to training, after formal instruction at a school or training center. Conducted by the unit itself, in-place training was a commander's responsibility, a continuous process of self-improvement by which the unit endeavored to overcome its weaknesses and develop its strengths in every area.

• • •

In-place training was usually conducted under five different forms. First there were short-duration courses organized by the parent headquarters—corps, division, sector, service branch, or combat arms—and devoted to subjects related to intelligence, counterintelligence, political warfare, ambush, counterambush, raid, patrol, reconnaissance, weapon effectiveness, mine and booby traps, artillery fire adjustment, request for air or naval support, fire coordination, and equipment maintenance. Second there were field exercises, conducted separately by the infantry or in combination with armor, artillery, and helicopter elements. Third, a commander might choose to give lectures or to hold seminars with his subordinates on selected subjects. Fourth, a parent headquarters might deploy mobile training teams to subordinate units to assist in the in-place training process. Finally, a parent headquarters might organize briefings or seminars concerning after-action reports and lessons learned, during which the enemy's, as well as our, strengths and weaknesses were analyzed and discussed.

On-the-Job Training

As an alternative to formal instruction, on-the-job training was widely practiced in the RVNAF, beginning in 1968. Its objective was to accelerate the training and qualification of specialists required by the expansion and modernization of the RVNAF, a process occasioned by the Vietnamization program. On-the-job training supplemented the formal training of specialists conducted at in-country or offshore service schools, which usually required a long time.

• • •

The most popular on-the-job training program was perhaps the "buddy" project undertaken by the US 1st Logistical Command under Major General Joseph M. Heiser Jr. This project was designed to train ARVN logistic personnel in the use, maintenance, and supply of modern equipment items which were being or would be delivered to the RVNAF. Depending on the scope and program, the duration of this training might vary from two days to six months. If the US and ARVN units were in close proximity, ARVN students reported daily to the US unit for training as scheduled. If the training involved widely separated units, then designated ARVN students were detached on a TDY basis to the US unit for the training period, during which they were also administratively supported by the training unit. Upon completion of training, students were returned to their units for appropriate assignment. By the end of 1970 there were in excess of 9,300 ARVN specialists trained on the job by the buddy program.

Another form of OJT involved the transfer of US equipment or facilities to ARVN use; hence, it was designed to train ARVN personnel until they were qualified to take over the operation and maintenance of the US facility being transferred. In this training process, ARVN students were first detached to a US facility to learn their jobs through a period of OJT. At the end of this period the students remained with the US facility instead of returning to their units. They continued working side by side with US specialists, who were gradually phased out. When the transfer of responsibility took place, ARVN personnel were ready to take over and assume complete control.

This form of OJT was most extensively used by US naval, engineer, signal, and transportation units during 1970 for the purpose of transferring assets, facilities, and operational responsibilities to RVNAF counterpart units under several ACTOV [accelerated turnover] programs. It was by far the most successful type of training; not only did it qualify a great number of ARVN specialists in a relatively short time, it also provided for a smooth transition which enabled US units to redeploy without causing any interruption in support operations. The inventory, safeguard, and transfer of US assets were also rapidly and accurately carried out, precluding regrettable losses and pilferages.

On-the-job training was occasionally conducted in ARVN units by US mobile training teams, especially when a new weapon system was introduced for immediate ARVN use and there was no time for formal instruction. Such occasions arose in 1968 during a crash program to equip ARVN units with the M-16 rifle and M-72 rocket launcher, and again in 1972 when the TOW missile was hastily introduced in the midst of the enemy's Easter Offensive. Mobile OJT was an especially effective approach to refresher training for RF and PF units.

Finally, during the cease-fire period, when US military advisors were no longer available, an extensive OJT program was conducted by US Army civilian specialists on TDY and US civilian contractors. Under this program US specialists were assigned to work with ARVN units, assisting them in supply, maintenance, and rebuild operations and training Vietnamese personnel at the same time. The Vietnamese Army Arsenal and General Depot at Long Binh, for example, was assisted by civilian specialists assigned by the US Army Materiel Command. While assisting both agencies in daily operations, these specialists also conducted OJT for Vietnamese military and civilian personnel.

Several companies on contract with the US Army also contributed to this program. Pacific Architects and Engineers and Vinnell Corporation, for example, assisted and trained ARVN engineer personnel in the management of large bases, particularly in the operation, maintenance, and rebuild of high-power generators and air-conditioning systems. Dynalectron Inc. provided assistance to ARVN engineers in the operation of industrial sites while training ARVN specialists in the production of quarry rock and asphalt and in maintaining road-building machinery in support of the LOC program. AAEO Inc. helped operate the ARVN calibration program and trained ARVN calibration specialists at the same time. Finally, Computer Sciences Corporation assisted ARVN logistic organizations such as the National Materiel Management Agency and the Logistic Data Processing Center in their computer operations and trained managers, programmers, and analysts for both agencies.

Combined Operations

Combined US-ARVN operations constituted a special form of on-the-job training for ARVN combat units which was both effective and unique. The basic concept derived from the belief that, by operating alongside US units, ARVN personnel would be able to learn valuable practices in a combat situation that were not always available in formal school training. When participating in combined operations with US units, not only were ARVN commanders and staffs able to observe US operational methods, use of firepower and mobility assets, and leadership in every tactical situation, ARVN units also benefited from US support, especially in firepower, mobility, and medical evacuation, which were not always available through the ARVN system.

• • •

Offshore Training

• • •

Over the years the US-sponsored offshore training program contributed significantly to the improvement of the RVNAF. From FY 1955 to FY 1962, as many as 5,442 Vietnamese servicemen completed courses at various US service schools; among them, the infantry accounted for 1,649 and the logistic branch 2,278. The number of students declined afterwards to a mere 241 during FY 1964. However, as the RVNAF force structure expanded, offshore training also increased to 505 students in FY 1967 and kept growing at a steady pace. After Vietnamization was implemented to improve and modernize the RVNAF, the number of students rose sharply from 752 during FY 1968 to 1,599 during FY 1970, about one-half of which consisted of helicopter pilots.

Beginning with FY 1972, as the RVNAF service school and training center system developed and improved, the requirements for offshore training also gradually decreased. During 1972 there were only 847 students attending US service schools. This number was reduced to 404 for FY 1972, 502 for FY 1974, and finally 159 for FY 1975.

Observations

Under the US Military Assistance Program and advisory efforts successively undertaken by [the] MAAG and MACV, the RVNAF training base constantly developed and improved over the years. When this military assistance program began in 1955, the Vietnamese armed forces had only one training center for recruits and ten service schools, which were enough to support a 150,000-man military force. As the RVNAF force structure increased, especially beginning in 1965, the RVNAF training base also expanded, to 33 training centers and 25 schools in 1970. The total student capacity of recruit training centers and service schools, therefore, increased significantly every year. In terms of recruit training, in particular, this capacity rose from 159,138 in 1966 to 333,777 in 1968 and, ultimately, to an all-time record of 503,740 recruits in 1970. The service schools meanwhile increased their total capacity from 59,826 students in 1966 to 102,126 in 1969.

For all this expansion in capacity, the RVNAF training base did not improve significantly until 1970, when US Army military construction funds were made available for the rehabilitation of classrooms, sleeping quarters, firing ranges, and water and electrical systems. This improvement in facilities brought about a very positive increase in training efficiency. Despite this, training centers frequently ran into problems of overcrowding or underuse which were caused by unregulated inputs of trainees from the recruitment and draft system.

• • •

After US combat forces entered the ground war in 1965 with their impressive array of helilift assets and powerful air and naval firepower, the ARVN training programs were further enriched with new tactics of heliborne operations, eagle flights, and combined arms. Then, when pacification became a national endeavor in 1967, they were also complemented by subjects related to territorial security and rural development. In brief, what had been accomplished by the MACV Training Directorate and CTC to update POIs as required was indeed a most commendable effort.

• • •

Our inability to formulate a military doctrine tailored to the specific conditions of the Vietnam conflict and our national ideology, goals, and resources was a constant source of disappointment. The CTC was at a great loss when, in late 1974, in the face of US military aid cutbacks, it was ordered by President Thieu to formulate a doctrine and tactics designed to fight a "poor man's war." The rush of subsequent events made this undertaking impossible, but this certainly was not a task that could be accomplished overnight.

• • •

In an effort to improve the quality of instructors, the JGS devised a rotation plan which would automatically reassign all officers and NCOs having held an instructor's job for more than four years to combat units and assign those with combat experience to schools, but somehow this plan did not work as expected. There were several reasons for this. For one thing, no field or tactical commander was cooperative enough to release his best officers, for obvious reasons of self-interest. For another, very few competent and combat-experienced officers ever desired to be assigned to schools as instructors, even though this implied [fewer] hazards. Indeed, the majority of young and ambitious officers never considered a school assignment as a stepping stone for career advancement. Most of them rather despised the instructor's job, which they regarded as "unrewarding" or simply "downhill."

• • •

Despite several shortcomings, over the years the RVNAF training efforts produced remarkable achievements. This was largely due to the contributions of US advisors and the US Military Assistance Program.

VIII. PAY AND WELFARE

The RVNAF Pay System

The General Directorate of Finance and Audit, Ministry of National Defense, was the agency responsible for all matters concerning pay and expenditures for the RVNAF. Under its control, there were nine regional finance and administration services located throughout the country, each responsible for a defined area. In its area of responsibility, a finance and administration service managed pay and financial transactions with finance offices organic to infantry regiments, self-administered units, and sector administration and logistic support center. There were in total over 300 such finance offices in the RVNAF; 44 among them were responsible for the RF and PF.

• • •

Paying subordinate servicemen in the unit was a commander's responsibility. The unit commander determined which day of the month payments should begin, but as a rule payday was usually on the 20th (prior to 1968, it was on the 29th or 30th) of the month. Since payments in the RVNAF were usually made in cash, it was the unit finance officer's duty to draw cash from the province treasurer's office against the unit's account. This was usually done one or two days before payday. On this trip to the treasurer's office the finance officer was always escorted by a security element, provided by the unit commander, whose responsibility it was to ensure that the money in transit would not be stolen, lost, or misappropriated.

On payday the disbursing officer or NCO made payments to individual servicemen in the unit based on the blank payroll and under the close supervision of the finance officer. When receiving his pay, each serviceman was required to sign his name or ngerprint on the payroll. In case subordinate elements of the unit were scattered, such as during an operation, payments were disbursed through pay agents. A pay agent was usually a company commander or a battalion staff officer who was given the responsibility to draw cash from the regimental finance office, sign for it on the payroll, then bring it back to make payments. After all payments had been made, the signed payroll and the amount of money left undisbursed because of absentees (AWOL, desertion, or missing in action) were returned to the finance officer, who deposited the leftover cash in the unit account at the province treasurer's office for future payments or disposal.

On a prolonged operation a secondary unit (battalion or company) usually received in advance a food allowance in cash, based on the duration of the operation, the unit payroll, and the current rate of food allowance. The unit commander used this money either to operate a field mess service or make cash payments to each soldier to subsist by himself for the entire duration of the operation.

• • •

In the case of hospitalization, a serviceman continued to draw pay from his unit if hospitalization time was less than one month. Beyond one month, he was nominally transferred to the hospital and received pay from it for the duration of his hospitalization. Prior to 1966, hospitalization was free of charge if the illness or injury was attributable to official business. Otherwise the hospitalized serviceman was required to pay for hospital fees (usually token) at a daily rate determined by his rank. After 1966, however, hospitalization was free for every serviceman, regardless of the cause for it.

• • •

Those servicemen who had been missing in action or captured by the enemy were entitled to all back pays and allowances during their absence after they came back and were reintegrated into the service.

Pay Structure

The monthly payment a Vietnamese serviceman received was for the most part made up of basic pay and four common allowances: technical supplement, cost of living, family, and food. There were also special allowances paid to certain categories of personnel on the basis of their duties or function or as a special incentive bonus.

BASIC PAY

The military basic pay was aligned on a national pay scale with the index number 100 as base. This index number increased with rank (or grade) and rank seniority (echelon). Every three years of rank seniority entitled the serviceman to a higher pay index or pay echelon, but the number of echelons allowable for each grade was limited. For each new grade, the basic pay was always Echelon 1. Basic pay was computed by multiplying the index number by a pay rate, then deducting 6 percent from the total.

Up to 1964 this pay rate was VN $12.24, as determined by Decree No. 28/VN in 1954. The basic pay for index number 100 was considered then the vital minimum of subsistence for a lowest-ranking civil servant. The 6 percent deduction was for pension contribution. As the cost of living kept increasing, in 1967 the GVN authorized an across-the-board increase of 30 for every index number.

In late 1971 a new pay system was introduced which greatly simplified computations of basic pay. The index system was discontinued in favor of a pay scale structured on rank and echelon (rank seniority). A second lieutenant just commissioned earned a basic pay of VN $14,500 (first echelon) and a colonel with three years of seniority in rank VN $28,400 (second echelon). While the seniority required to move up one echelon was three years for all grades, the cash value of each echelon varied according to grade. Basic pay, of course, was but a part of the total payment each serviceman received every month.

FAMILY ALLOWANCE

A family allowance was paid to married servicemen based on number of dependents. The age limit for children was 16, extended to 21 if a child attended school or was unable to work because of physical infirmities or health reasons.

• • •

Family allowance was limited to the first or legitimate wife, but not to the number of children, including adopted children. Prior to 1964 there were different rates of family allowance, which varied according to grade groups: general officers, field-grade officers, company-grade officers, and enlisted men. The rate of child allowance increased from the first through the fifth, but leveled off beginning with the sixth child.[6] In 1964, to bring some measure of equality, only two rates of family allowance were enforced: one for officers and NCOs and the other, slightly lower, for corporals and privates.

In 1971, with the institution of the new pay system, the rates of family allowance were also substantially increased. At the same time, to encourage family planning and to cut down on family allowance payments, the GVN made plans to limit allowance to the fourth child, effective in 1974, a move recommended by US advisory authorities. But these plans were never implemented in view of the economic plight faced by the RVNAF serviceman and the need to maintain troop morale.

COST-OF-LIVING ALLOWANCE

In addition to basic pay and family allowance, the RVNAF serviceman also received [a] cost-of-living allowance, which was in essence a form of compensation for increasing inflation. The cost-of-living allowance was paid to the serviceman himself, his wife, and all eligible children. Beginning in 1964, however, payment was limited to the fifth child. In 1971 plans were made to further limit payment to the fourth child, but were never enforced.

The amount of cost-of-living allowance paid depended on rank and location. There were two rates, one applicable to officers and NCOs and the other to corporals and privates. As to location, South Vietnam was divided into two economic zones for the purpose of allowance computation. The "high" cost-of-living zone comprised all provinces of MR-1 and MR-2, the provinces of Phuoc Long, Phuoc Thanh, and Binh Long of MR-3, and four cities: Hue, Danang, Dalat, and Cam Ranh. The rest of the country made up the "low" cost-of-living zone. Popular Forces were not eligible for this cost-of-living allowance.

• • •

All single corporals and privates were required to take their regular meals at the unit's mess. The cost of these meals was deducted from their monthly pay at a fixed daily rate which, in 1964, was VN $26.50 and VN $33 for low and high cost-of-living zones respectively. This money was used by the unit food service to purchase administrative food (rice, salt, sugar, tea) from a quartermaster depot and fresh food from the local market. All the money that was left after purchases contributed toward a food surplus fund. The unit commander might use this fund either to purchase cooking utensils or to improve food rations for special occasions such as national holidays or the unit commemorative day. Such expenditures were tightly controlled by the regional finance and administration service.

In addition to food allowance, which was built into each serviceman's basic pay, the GVN also authorized a firewood allowance for each unit for the cooking of meals. This allowance was VN $1 per man/day, but was increased to VN $4 after 1967.

• • •

The Lost Battle against Inflation

For the majority of RVNAF servicemen, monthly pay was the unique source of income. The average serviceman therefore depended almost exclusively on this income for his living. Over the years he had found his and his family's prospects for the future increasingly darkened by the rising cost of living.

The real economic plight of the RVNAF serviceman began in 1960 when prices started to go up as a result of deteriorating security in rural areas. Military pay, meanwhile, remained the same as it had been six years earlier. To help the serviceman meet the steadily rising cost of living, in 1964 the GVN gave him a 10 percent raise on his basic pay. This seemed to feed inflation and gave rise to speculatory price fixing, because within just one year the retail price index of rice had risen to 124 and the average consumer price index to 119 over the base index of 100 in 1964. During 1966 the retail price of rice rose another 108 index points, while the consumer price index rose 80 points. Again a provisional pay increase was authorized, averaging from 20 to 30 percent.

• • •

The following year, 1967, the price of rice rose another 303 index points. To help the serviceman offset the rising price of rice, which was the basic food staple, the GVN instituted a rice allowance as a new pay component. This rice allowance was worth VN $200 for the serviceman himself and each of his dependents.[7]

Also during 1967, to assist the serviceman in stretching his monthly pay, the GVN authorized free distribution of combat rations worth VN $35 each for those who participated in operations. This helped the combatant save a little money for his dependents' use. In addition, the RVNAF commissary service sold basic commodities for the serviceman and his dependents at below market prices. This was made possible by a US grant of $42 million for the import of sugar, cooking oil, canned food, and condensed milk. These items were resold to the serviceman at prices 20 to 30 percent below market. To keep supplies replenished after US-provided items had been exhausted, the commissary service was authorized to purchase, free of taxes, some local products such as cigarettes, sugar, and condensed milk and import other basic food items such as canned meat and fish, cooking oil, and instant noodles.

All of these measures helped the serviceman to some extent. However, inflation was rampaging and prices kept rising. In 1969 the retail price of rice rose 536 index points compared to 1964, or 233 points compared to 1967. Rice was becoming not only more expensive but also scarce in local markets, especially in I and II Corps areas. Paper currency was shrinking in value, to the point that most servicemen became weary of pay increases which only seemed to feed inflation. Aware of this predicament, the GVN authorized the free supply of rice to enlisted men on the monthly basis of 21 kilos per man. This came as a tremendous boost in morale for the underprivileged private soldiers, who were thus made immune from the inflationary cost of rice and guaranteed a steady supply. The equally hard-pressed officers and NCOs asked for the same benefit, but their request could not be met because this would cause a prohibitive budget drain, in addition to problems of distribution.

Joining forces with the GVN to combat inflation and ensure an adequate food intake for the RVNAF serviceman, the United States extended a most helping hand when it authorized a three-year free supplementary food program worth US $42.7 million. This program provided 100 percent of basic requirements for the first year, 70 percent for the second year, and 30 percent for the third year. As a result, each serviceman received a free monthly supply of 7.7 pounds of cooking oil and canned meat and fish during the program's first year.

In conjunction with the free rice and canned food programs, the JGS initiated the military farming program to promote private food production by military units and dependents. Designed to improve food intake and provide an additional income for the serviceman and his dependents, the program became an instant success as vegetable planting and chicken and pig raising gained popularity among military households.

Despite its success, the military farming program did not solve the serviceman's economic plight, as prices kept skyrocketing. According to official figures compiled and published by the National Institute of Statistics (which many people believed did not truly reflect the actual cost of living), the price of rice in 1971 rose 833 index points compared to the base year of 1964, or 297 points compared to 1969. Consumer prices in the meantime were up 591 index points compared to 1964 or 263 points compared to 1969. Again the GVN resorted to raising pay by authorizing a daily allowance of VN $100 for combat troops and increasing the serviceman's family allowance by VN $100 for each dependent.

In August 1971 MACV recommended a 28 percent raise in basic pay for each serviceman and a fixed allowance of VN $4,500 for each of the combat troops serving in infantry, ranger, marine, and airborne battalions, or VN $2,000 for an RF trooper serving in a mobile battalion. Three months later the GVN chose to raise the monthly cost-of-living allowance by VN $1,300 for each serviceman and allowed the additional VN $4,500/month for each combatant of the regular forces or VN $2,000 for each RF soldier, as recommended. To further adjust military pay to the ever-increasing cost of living, in 1972 the GVN increased both basic pay and allowances by approximately 30 percent.

In spite of these increases, the RVNAF servicemen's income always lagged far behind the cost of living. The fact was, as revealed by statistics, income rose less than three times for officers and five times for enlisted men during the period from 1964 to 1972, while consumer prices rose 8.5 times and the price of rice 14 times.

• • •

The Veterans

The Ministry of War Veterans was created as a separate governmental department in 1965 in order to alleviate increasing burdens placed on the Ministry of Defense by the administration of veterans affairs. This ministry managed two vital long-range programs designed to provide care and welfare for the veterans: the Veteran Pension and Allowance Program and the Rehabilitation and Job Program.

The Veteran Pension and Allowance Program sought to achieve two basic objectives: to adjust veteran pension and allowance payments to the rising cost of living every year, and to simplify and speed up the process of reviewing and issuing individual retired pension books.

Beginning in 1966, all retired servicemen benefited from the same raises and rice or cost-of-living allowances as authorized RVNAF personnel on active duty. As a result, the basic disability and other allowances for veterans increased substantially from 1966 to 1970.

In addition to raises in pension and allowances, veterans also benefited from commissary services and medical care, just as when they were on active duty. Despite this and other GVN efforts, the lot of veterans, especially those who were disabled, was one of hardship and privations because they were afflicted by the same economic predicament that plagued the serviceman.

• • •

The second major program undertaken by the Ministry of War Veterans was to rehabilitate the disabled veterans and provide them with vocational training and jobs. Prior to 1966, all disabled servicemen who were classified as Category 3 by a medical board, after treatment were automatically discharged from service. After discharge, these servicemen had to apply for orthopedic rehabilitation or vocational training at the National Rehabilitation Institute, like other citizens. Waiting periods were long and years might have passed before the disabled veterans received any treatment or care.

Because of this poignant situation, the disabled servicemen who were likely to be classified as Category 3 all feared the day of final judgment and discharge. They sought ways to procrastinate, or simply went into hiding when called before a medical board, attempting to prolong the time they remained in the service as long as they could. Commanders of administrative units which took them in charge usually looked the other way and never forced them into discharge, anxious not to affect the morale of other servicemen. The RVNAF actual strength was therefore depleted by thousands of such disabled servicemen. The strength of combat units, as a result, suffered from these living casualties because they could not be replaced until removed from the unit's control list.

To solve this thorny problem, in 1966 the Ministry of Defense implemented a new policy concerning the administration of Category 3 servicemen which suspended their discharge until they were rehabilitated and vocationally trained. Under this policy, disabled servicemen were transferred to recuperation centers to undergo an orthopedic rehabilitation period at one of the several rehabilitation centers operated by the Ministry of War Veterans in Saigon, Danang, and Can Tho. While undergoing rehabilitation, they also received vocational orientation and training for a skill commensurate with their physical and mental abilities.

• • •

Observations

The management of pay and allowances in the RVNAF was well organized and efficient. It enabled all administrative units to disburse pay and allowances to the individual serviceman efficiently and timely. Our system of fund custody, control, and audit effectively prevented misappropriations by finance officers. Only neglect on the part of unit commanders ever made it possible, but there were only a few such instances over the years.

The biggest difficulty in our pay administration was to make payments to servicemen serving in secondary units—infantry battalions, RF companies, PF platoons—who, for reasons of security and transportation, were unable to personally come to an administrative unit (regiment or ALS center) to draw their pays. The solution that we adopted, which called on the intermediary of a pay agent from the recipient unit, was logical and expedient. However, it was difficult to control the pay agent's integrity with regard to unclaimed pays—those belonging to personnel listed as AWOL, deserters, and MIAs. During 1974, for example, a joint strength and pay control committee set up by the AG/ JGS and General Directorate of Finance and Audit discovered many payrolls with signatures of servicemen who had been reported as missing or deserters.

The structure of salary, which was built on basic pay and several different allowances, was indeed a complex system of pay computation, but, in view of social traditions and continued inflation, it perhaps afforded us some measure of flexibility, incentive, and justice. Over the years there were several attempts to reform this pay structure—primarily by removing family allowances and modifying certain special allowances—with a view to simplify pay computation and bring about egality and fairness, but no reform project was ever implemented. This was because the GVN was deeply convinced that, as long as income kept lagging far behind the cost of living and no substantial pay raise was possible, any change in the system would adversely affect the morale of troops and upset the established social order.

With regard to welfare and other forms of benefits that the RVNAF servicemen, the disabled veterans, and their families received over the years, it had to be admitted that the GVN and the US government did make serious and laudable efforts. From pay raises and rice allowances to free distribution of combat rations and canned food, commissary services, and free housing, every affordable measure had been taken to provide a decent living for the average soldier and his dependents. Unfortunately, all this was not enough.

The poignant fact was that monthly salary payments, the only source of income for the majority of servicemen, rapidly decreased in purchasing power, beginning in 1963, to the point that, ten years later, no serviceman was able to subsist on his salary alone. From 1964 to 1972, the serviceman's salary increased only by a modest margin, to a maximum of 500 index points for a private. In the meantime the price of rice, the basic food staple for every Vietnamese and a fair indication of the cost of living, increased 14 times and consumer prices almost nine times. But these were only official figures which many people believed were far below the actual cost of living. How could a serviceman make ends meet in such a situation?

To illustrate the economic plight of the RVNAF serviceman, dollar values are perhaps more indicative. In 1964 a colonel, for example, made approximately US $400 a month (at the official exchange rate of 1 US dollar to 35 VN piasters); in 1972 he only made US $82 (rate: 1 US dollar = 465 VN piasters). During the same period an army captain found his monthly salary shrinking from US $287 to US $61 and a private from US $77 to US $30. If we compared a private's pay with that of a minimum-wage earner, we found that he made only about half as much as a laborer in 1969 (VN $4,594 versus VN $9,113).

As an inevitable result, most RVNAF servicemen and their families had to live in privation and hardship. To make ends meet, they had to cut down on everything from food to clothing; many of them did not eat meat for months and did not go to a movie in years. The economic grip was such that many soldiers in combat units ate only a small part of their daily combat rations, just enough to live. They saved these rations and sent them home for their wives and children. I saw several instructors at the Thu Duc Infantry School pack a piece of plain bread or a ball of sticky rice in their sacks at the start of a long day of field exercise. That was all they could afford for breakfast and lunch with a lieutenant's salary. I knew of major and lieutenant colonel households buying rice by the kilo after the 10th of each month when all salary was gone. Many went into heavy debts just to keep their families fed. The common anxiety among officers and enlisted men alike was how long they could go on like that before collapse.

Those who worked in Saigon and other cities managed to earn some extra income by driving taxicabs, riding taxi motorbikes, teaching school, and doing other moonlighting odd jobs during off-duty hours. Their spouses, the traditional housewives, also took jobs or did some peddling business to supplement the family income. Those households living in suburban areas raised chickens and planted vegetables, eking out a meager living off their tiny gardens. By all possible means the RVNAF servicemen struggled for a living, but very few were able to make ends meet. Many felt humiliated when they had to ask for financial support from their parents or relatives. Others were ashamed when they had to misappropriate some military supplies or use military vehicles for their private purposes. They knew that it was wrong, yet their quest for survival seemed to be stronger than any sense of moral uprightness.

Because of economic hardship, many servicemen took to desertion, changing their names in the process, to get lucrative jobs in the private sector. Some [engaged in] illegal businesses or became corrupt, stealing or taking bribes. But the majority remained honest or struggled with themselves to remain incorruptible. They were resigned to their fate and fought on with high hopes for a better future.

Strange as it may seem, the RVNAF servicemen in general never felt envious or jealous of their American, South Korean, or Thai comrades-in-arms whom they knew had much higher salaries and a much better life. They did not feel embittered by this economic disparity, but rather looked on it as an incentive to keep struggling for a better future. This reminds me of a visit I made to the 5th Ranger Group during which I asked some of its troops how they felt about the days they lived with American troops of the 199th Infantry Brigade during combined operations. Without exception, they all said: "If we had a standard of living comparable to that of our American comrades, we would fight until death without a single worry about our families."

Then, during the seminars I held in 1968–1970 on how to develop the RVNAF combat effectiveness, I heard many officers and NCOs from different infantry divisions express their views like this: "We know that the government and our superiors have done many things to help us and our families alleviate our miseries, but that was not enough. We have been tightening our belts to make ends meet, but there is only a limit to what we can do. We thoroughly understand the government's difficulties and the cause for which we keep fighting, but how can we fight with an empty stomach? As our centuries-old wisdom has it: To be able to practice the 'Correct Way,' one must have enough to eat first."

IX. MEDICAL SUPPORT AND COMBAT EQUIPMENT

The RVNAF Medical Treatment System

The RVNAF medical service was created in February 1951 as a technical branch of service directly controlled by the Ministry of National Defense. When the Medical Directorate began to function, the General Staff of the Vietnamese National Armed Forces was yet to be created. In August the next year, three regional medical services were activated in Saigon, Hue, and Hanoi, each with the mission to exercise control over field medical treatment and evacuation facilities and to provide medical support services to Vietnamese units and organizations located in a military region. Both functions were performed in coordination with counterpart regional medical services of the French Expeditionary Corps. A fourth regional medical service was established in Ban Me Thuot at the same time as Headquarters, 4th Military Region, in 1953.

As the Vietnamese armed forces went through reorganization under direct US military advisory assistance, the four regional medical services were deactivated in 1957 and control of field hospitals and medical units came under military region headquarters. When Area Logistics Commands (ALC) were activated in 1961, they not only took over this control but also coordinated medical support for combat units within their areas of responsibility.

• • •

In 1969, in an effort to make medical support coordination and supervision more effective at the field level, four corps medical groups were activated, one for each corps area, relieving the ALCs from this responsibility. With command responsibility over field hospitals, field medical depots, and sector hospitals in the corps area, each medical group provided all medical services in support of corps and other units, to include medical evacuation and preventive medicine. Also in 1969, divisional medical elements were grouped into medical battalions to provide consolidated medical support for all divisional units. This organization of the RVNAF medical service was to remain unchanged until the collapse of South Vietnam.

HOSPITALS

Prior to 1954, the Vietnamese armed forces had only three military hospitals, each with a capacity of about 400 beds: Vo Tanh in Hanoi, Duy Tan in Danang, and Phan Thanh Gian in Can Tho. These were supplemented by garrison dispensaries or station hospitals of 50–150 bed capacity each, generally located in large cities. During that period, the modest Vietnamese medical treatment facilities were substantially augmented by the larger French counterpart system.

After 1955, French forces gradually turned over their medical facilities to the Vietnamese armed forces. Part of these facilities was turned into civilian hospitals and the remaining integrated into the military medical treatment system.

• • •

Despite the addition of new hospitals, the aggregated bed capacity seemed to lag behind growing requirements as the war intensified. The integration of the RF and PF into the RVNAF also placed added support burdens on the medical service, whose treatment facilities were taxed to the limit of their capabilities. As a result, in 1967 an effort was made to expand the bed capacities of major hospitals.

• • •

During the three years beginning in 1967, to facilitate the accommodation of RF and PF troopers, a total of 27 sector hospitals of 100 beds each and 193 district dispensaries of 20 beds each were added to the RVNAF medical treatment system. At the same time, a civilian-military medical cooperation program was initiated to fully utilize provincial medical facilities for the support of both military and civilian patients. Under this program, ARVN doctors, nurses, and technicians joined in the operation of ten provincial hospitals and 86 district dispensaries, with the support of the Ministry of Public Health in medicine, supplies, and equipment. At these jointly operated facilities, RVNAF servicemen were hospitalized or treated entirely free of charge.

• • •

Over the years the total bed capacity of the RVNAF hospitalization system increased at a steady pace. From a mere 2,500 beds in 1955, this capacity rose to 11,400 beds a decade later. In 1968 it nearly doubled, to 21,000 beds, and ultimately reached 24,547 beds by the time of the cease-fire. Bed occupancy over the entire period was continually at a high level, varying from 95 to 98 percent of total capacity. During periods of intense fighting, such as enemy offensives or cross-border operations, hospitals had to install additional cots to handle the great influx of patients. The Easter Offensive of 1972, in particular, kept the three RVNAF major hospitals—Duy Tan (Danang), Cong Hoa (Saigon), and Phan Thanh Gian (Can Tho)—constantly overflowed with patients. At one time during that year a record high of 31,000 fully occupied beds was reached. To provide the extra space required, these hospitals had to release recovering patients for temporary 29-day periods of treatment at home.

In 1973, US $1,796,000 from MASF/MILCON funds [was] made available for the construction of a model 450-bed hospital, intended as a gift-souvenir to the RVNAF from US forces. This hospital was half-completed when the RVN collapsed in late April 1975.

• • •

Not authorized by the MAP-supported force structure, the Paraplegic Hospital at Vung Tau was an unusual institution set up by the ARVN Medical [Directorate] for humanitarian and expedient reasons. The fact was that at all times there were from 400 to 500 paraplegic patients occupying beds in permanence at military hospitals who needed perhaps more care than treatment. Although most had been discharged from service, for several reasons these paraplegic ex-servicemen had nowhere to turn to but military medical facilities which had provided them treatment. Despite continued persuasion, they did not want to leave the hospitals; they [clung] to the beds they considered the last hope of their lives. Many had tried to leave, but most invariably returned after just a few weeks. The tragic fact was that they did not know where to go. The Ministry of War

Veterans, which was responsible for their care and well-being, had no facilities to accommodate them. It was under these circumstances that the Paraplegic Hospital came into being in 1972.

The hospital had an initial capacity of 200 beds and began to take in paraplegic patients in mid-1972. This was a time when the Cong Hoa General Hospital, with well over 100 beds permanently occupied by these patients, and other facilities in MR-3 needed to clear their paraplegics for more urgent cases. Their removal by ambulance trucks from these hospitals, despite explanations by medical authorities, provoked a truly empathetic commotion. Most paraplegic patients being transferred cried in desperation, thinking that perhaps authorities would dump them somewhere en route to get rid of them.

The 200 beds at Vung Tau were fully occupied almost overnight, a clear indication that more beds would be needed. But, since the Medical [Directorate] had about exhausted its capabilities, it was decided by mutual consent to turn over the facility to the Ministry of War Veterans in 1974. This was done with the hope that, as a civilian institution, the paraplegic hospital could obtain humanitarian aid more readily from allied countries. Although officially transferred, the hospital continued to be staffed by ARVN medical personnel and received support from the Medical [Directorate] in medicine. In early 1975, the Republic of China and West Germany indicated their willingness to provide aid for the hospital.

• • •

Enemy troops detained or wounded during combat were evacuated to RVNAF or US medical facilities, where they underwent treatment until recovery. During the period of treatment, they received the same care and food rations as RVNAF or US troops, with the only exception that they were confined to a separate ward under heavy guard because of security reasons.

For normal treatment, enemy prisoners in detention camps were supported by the nearest RVNAF hospital. On Phu Quoc Island, where over 30,000 prisoners were detained, medical support was provided by a 100-bed hospital, built in 1968 at the same time as the prisoner camp. This facility was operated by the ARVN Medical [Directorate].

• • •

Medical Evacuation

• • •

Indeed, US helicopters performed most of the medical evacuation missions for the RVNAF after 1965, accounting for 70–80 percent of daytime and 100 percent of nighttime missions. It was a period during which the incipient VNAF helicopter fleet could not cope with the requirements of stepped-up fighting. Reliance on US medical evacuation, however, caused some administrative drawbacks. Because US helicopter pilots were not familiar with RVNAF hospitals, they frequently brought ARVN patients directly to US medical facilities, making it difficult for units to keep track of their personnel. Occasionally patients even ended up in some US hospital offshore and their whereabouts remained unknown for some time.

Beginning in 1969, Vietnamization trends brought about some modernization and expansion to the VNAF helicopter fleet, whose obsolescent H-34s were gradually replaced by the UH-1s. Each year saw new helicopters added to this fleet, which eventually expanded to 16 squadrons. And increasingly, despite their mixed use, VNAF helicopters took over medical evacuation missions in replacement of redeploying US units.

• • •

During the five months following the outbreak of the 1972 Easter Offensive, VNAF helicopters evacuated a total of 31,600 patients, compared with 1,200 patients evacuated by US helicopters. This was a remarkable achievement, highlighting the coming of age of RVNAF aeromedical evacuation.

The drastic cutback in US military aid in 1974 seriously affected the operation of VNAF helicopters. Flight time during the second half of the year was reduced to a mere 20 percent of the first half. Medical evacuation, which depended largely on the VNAF helicopter fleet, suffered accordingly, despite the high priority assigned to it by field commanders. The impact was most acutely felt by combat units in the Mekong Delta, which depended almost entirely on helicopters for medical evacuation. In remote areas, therefore, units reverted to the old evacuation means of the mid-1950s—litters, hammocks, boats, and vehicles—which were slow and unreliable. Troop morale sank perceptibly as a result. In addition to their being grounded by limited operating funds, helicopters on medevac missions also ran into greater hazards posed by the enemy's expanding antiaircraft system, which included the deadly SA-7 missile. Many evacuation missions were therefore aborted, giving rise to all sorts of harsh criticism against VNAF helicopter pilots.

• • •

During 1972 the enemy's Easter Offensive forced three instances of patient evacuation; one among them ended in tragic failure. This occurred during the process of evacuating patients from the Quang Tri Hospital to Hue city. From 30 March to mid-April, the evacuation took place by 1/4-ton and 3/4-ton ambulance trucks with the purpose of clearing this hospital for the combat wounded. When road traffic became hazardous during the last week of April, the evacuation continued by helicopters and fixed-wing aircraft. On 28 April the remaining patients, about 300 in total, boarded the return convoy of the 1st ALC toward Hue. As the defense of Quang Tri City collapsed, the convoy was stranded on Route QL-1 amid other military vehicles, battered troops, and refugees fleeing south. During the slaughter by enemy artillery fire that followed, the entire contingent of patients perished, along with hundreds of civilian refugees. The other two evacuations of patients, however, took place without any incident. From Hue, 350 patients were successfully airlifted to Danang, while another 400 from Pleiku also made it safely to Qui Nhon and Nha Trang during a period of most intense fighting around Hue and Kontum.

In early 1975 the rapid unfolding of events engulfed the majority of patients and left most of them stranded. The fall of Ban Me Thuot on 11 March occasioned the helpless loss of a 400-bed hospital with patients. It was followed by the 2nd Field Hospital in

Kontum and the 600-bed Pleiku Hospital, whose patients were unable to evacuate in time with the hasty redeployment of II Corps forces toward Tuy Hoa. After these unexpected setbacks, expedient measures were taken to evacuate the three major hospitals along the coast—Nguyen Tri Phuong in Hue, Duy Tan in Danang, and Qui Nhon—in keeping with President Thieu's strategic redeployment plans. On 20 March, all patients from Qui Nhon were evacuated uneventfully toward Nha Trang, Saigon, and Vung Tau. Then the majority of patients in Hue were directed toward Danang, due to reasons of family attachment. When Hue city was hastily evacuated on 25 March, however, no one knew exactly what happened to the Nguyen Tri Phuong Hospital staff and those patients still remaining there. How many finally made it to Danang, along with the 1st Infantry Division troops, it was impossible to ascertain.

In Danang city, which became increasingly crowded with refugees after the evacuation of Hue, about 1,000 litter-case patients at the Duy Tan General Hospital awaited evacuation toward Saigon on 26 March. Only 300 were successfully picked up by four VNAF C-130 flights, because not only was the airport mobbed by panicky refugees, it was also impossible to move the patients through the jammed roads leading to the airport. Over 5,000 patients and staff personnel of the Duy Tan General Hospital therefore became stranded when I Corps forces boarded naval ships to withdraw south during the night of 28 March.

Other military hospitals south of the main resistance line drawn at Nha Trang eventually met with the same fate as this city, and others successively fell after 2 April.

Medical and Blood Supply

ARVN units were all authorized a 30-day supply of medicine, but the types of medicine a unit was authorized to stock were limited if there was no medical doctor in charge. Hospitals and general hospitals were authorized a 60-day supply of medicine, which was replenished by field depots on request.

• • •

Whole blood, which was essential for the life-saving process, was provided by the RVNAF Blood Supply Center, which adjoined the Cong Hoa General Hospital in Saigon. This center was the sole agency supplying blood for the RVNAF medical treatment system. Prior to 1965, because of difficulties in transportation, most of the whole blood collected, processed, and stored at the center was primarily used for transfusions at the Cong Hoa General Hospital and certain other civilian hospitals in the Saigon area. As requirements for whole blood rose after 1965, the center expanded its facilities and equipment with US assistance to increase its capabilities to collect, process, store, and distribute whole blood to military hospitals in the field. Helicopters and fixed-wing aircraft were normally used for the transportation of preserved blood.

In 1967 the RVNAF Blood Supply Center established an annex in Danang, close to the Duy Tan General Hospital, for the collection and distribution of blood in I Corps area. In Saigon, as well as in Danang, blood was collected from volunteer donors, most of them local servicemen, students of service schools and training centers, civilian personnel, and military dependents. All of these donors were not motivated by profit, since they gave their blood free. There was also no coercion, and any publicity was kept in low profile. Still, the number of donors always seemed to exceed the center's capability to handle [them].

• • •

During the 1972 Easter Offensive, nearly 44,000 wounded servicemen received blood transfusion within a five-month period, and there was not a single death caused by shortage of blood. During that period, an average of 8,000 blood units was collected each month.

• • •

Observations

Over the years of its existence, particularly during the years of intense fighting, the RVNAF medical service performed its duties well and with distinction. During the initial period after the hasty departure of the French, this service was plagued by personnel and administration problems. But these shortcomings were gradually overcome with the assistance provided by the United States, the mobilization of civilian medical personnel, and the training process.

In addition to well-equipped hospitals, the ample availability of medicine and medical supplies from US resources kept medical treatment in the RVNAF on a high standard of performance. The well-regulated medical supply system also excelled over other technical services in operating standards. Medical evacuation was timely and effective most of the time, owing to the support provided by US ambulance helicopters and, subsequently, by the VNAF helicopter fleet. Speed and the courage of helicopter crews accounted for thousands of lives saved. The adequate supply of whole blood never impeded the lifesaving process and rarely had to rely on US resources.

• • •

Combat Equipment and Supplies

Being an underdeveloped country with an economy ravaged by continuous war, South Vietnam almost totally depended on US military aid to equip, supply, and maintain its armed forces. Despite conscious efforts to achieve some degree of self-sufficiency, the RVN had never been able to provide the RVNAF with supplies other than food, clothing, and some expendable items. US military aid, therefore, was the lifeline that sustained the RVNAF in combat throughout the war.

Since their inception in 1949 under French control, the Vietnamese National Armed Forces had been equipped with a mixture of French and American MDAP [Mutual Defense Aid Program] materiel. During these formative years, infantry armament consisted basically of French-made weapons such as the MAS-36 rifle, the MAT-49 submachinegun, and the 24–29 automatic rifle, and small quantities of US-made weapons such as the Garand M-1 rifle, the caliber .45 "Thompson" submachinegun, the M-1 carbine, and the Browning automatic rifle (BAR).

Beginning in 1957, under the Military Assistance Program, the RVNAF standardized their equipment with US-made and supplied materiel, all of World War II vintage. In armament, the RVNAF continued to use the same types of US infantry weapons as before, and communicated with radio sets such as the SCR-300, SCR-694, and SCR-399. Their vehicles consisted of the 1/4-ton Willys Jeep truck, the 3/4-ton Dodge truck, and the 2–1/2-ton GMC truck. Names such as Jeep, Dodge, and GMC popularly stood for different categories of truck. The RVNAF armament then proved adequate and powerful enough to subdue bands of Communist insurgents.

During 1959–1960 the RVNAF received the new AN series of radio equipment such as the AN/PRC-10, AN/GRC-34, and AN/GRC-26 field radio sets in replacement of the obsolescent SCR series. These radio sets provided more effective and longer-range communications, which tremendously helped in counterinsurgency operations. During the same period, the World War II vintage vehicle fleet was completely replaced by a new series of Japanese-made trucks which became popularized in the RVNAF as the OSPJ (Off-Shore Procurement, Japan) trucks.

The counterinsurgency war in South Vietnam entered a new phase in 1964 with the introduction of North Vietnamese Army (NVA) regular units and the Communist-bloc-produced AK-47 assault rifle, which proved more powerful and effective than our Garand M-1, M-2 carbine, and caliber .45 submachinegun combined. The AK-47 was soon followed by the deadly RPG (rocket-propelled grenade) light antitank weapon, known as the B-40 and B-41. All RVNAF field commanders agreed that Communist small arms were superior to ours and they pressed the JGS for an improvement.

As a result of MACV intercession, the RVNAF began to receive two new weapons: the antipersonnel Claymore mine, which was light, portable, and extremely effective in defense; and the M-79 grenade launcher, which was both light and easy to maintain. The M-79 also provided an effective range in excess of 400 meters and enabled an infantry soldier to carry as many as 35 grenades in combat. At the same time, a few hundred new ArmaLite AR-15 automatic rifles were made available to ARVN paratroopers for test purposes. The AR-15 proved perhaps the ideal individual weapon for the short and lightly built ARVN soldier. It was light, accurate, and effective. In the hands of the combat-proven and audacious ARVN paratrooper, it was indeed a deadly weapon. Understandably enough, the Airborne Brigade insisted on keeping the AR-15 after the test period.

In the fall of 1965, General Westmoreland, COMUSMACV, informed the JGS that an emergency request for 170,000, later adjusted to 100,000, AR-15s—now officially designated M-16—had been approved by the US Department of Defense. This news brought about an excitement among ARVN soldiers; every combat unit longed for the day the M-16 arrived in-country. The M-16 did arrive finally, but in the hands of US combat troops, because the buildup of US forces in South Vietnam had preempted all priorities for RVNAF equipment. The decision to postpone delivery of the M-16 stemmed from the fact that, by mutual agreement, the RVNAF were to assume the lesser role of supporting pacification against local enemy forces while US units conducted search and destroy operations against enemy main forces. The ARVN desire for the M-16 persisted, however; it was perhaps more ardent than ever now that even enemy local forces were uniformly equipped with the AK-47.

Not until March 1967 were the 100,000 M-16s earmarked for ARVN combat battalions reinstated for delivery, and the first shipment arrived a few months later. But, by year's end, quantities delivered were just enough to equip airborne and marine battalions. Then the enemy's 1968 Tet Offensive broke out in Saigon and across South Vietnam, during which the sharp automatic bursts of the AK-47 seemed to overpower the feeble single shots of the Garand M-1 or M-1 carbine. To face the critical situation, MACV made an emergency effort to airlift M-16 rifles to Saigon and Danang around the clock. ARVN logistic units stood vigil day and night, receiving, processing, and issuing. Hastily assembled mobile training teams, both American and Vietnamese, went into ARVN combat units to provide crash training in the use and maintenance of the new rifle. At the same time, ARVN personnel queued up around the clock at US ammunition depots, drawing initial issues for combat units. In rapid succession all infantry battalions in III, I, IV, and II Corps areas, and ranger units, completed their reception of and initiation to the M-16 rifle by mid-1968.

The speed with which US and ARVN authorities moved to put the M-16 into the hands of the ARVN combat soldier stunned the enemy. When Communist forces in Quang Ngai initiated a second phase of the offensive by attacking the provincial city, they were completely surprised—and overwhelmed—by the deadly firepower put up by defenders of the ARVN 2nd Division. It was only the day before that this unit had taken delivery of the M-16s; several battalions did not even have the time to zero them for accuracy.

During this same period, ARVN infantry battalions also received the new M-60 machinegun in replacement of the BAR and caliber .30 machinegun. Then they were further reinforced with new issues of the LAW antitank rocket and the 90mm recoilless rifle, both of which proved extremely effective against enemy fortifications. By mid-1968, therefore, the new family of weapons had placed ARVN divisions on an equal basis with US combat units in terms of infantry firepower. Soon additional new armored vehicles such as the M-41A1 tank, the M-113 APC, and the V-100 commando car arrived to further modernize ARVN armor units, which were becoming obsolete with their M-24s and M-8s. Field radio communications were also improved after the introduction of the AN/PRC-74 and the AN/PRC-25 radio set, which replaced the trouble-ridden AN/PRC-10. Finally, the entire OSPJ truck fleet was phased out and replaced by the newer and better M-600 series of trucks.

The US decision to Vietnamize the war in 1969 resulted in several improvement and modernization programs intended to enable the RVNAF to gradually assume the major combat role. These programs provided the necessary equipment both to activate new units and to modernize the existing force structure. During 1969–1970 most of this new equipment came partly from US stocks in South Vietnam and partly from turnovers by departing US units. With this bonus, the JGS was able to equip Regional and Popular

Forces with the same modern infantry weapons and communications gear as their ARVN counterparts.

In the fall of 1971, after the conclusion of the lower Laos cross-border operation, the United States added extra punch power to ARVN artillery and armor units by making the self-propelled 175mm gun and the M-48A3 tank available for the first time. Then, in May 1972, it followed up the RVNAF improvement and modernization process with the "Enhance" program, intended to boost South Vietnam's capabilities to resist the enemy's Easter onslaught. Since the objectives of this program were to accelerate the delivery of FY 1972 and FY 1973 equipment and to replace the unusual losses incurred by ARVN forces during 1972, an uninterrupted airlift by C-130s, C-141s, and C-5As kept pouring equipment, day and night, into the three major airports at Saigon, Danang, and Pleiku. During this period of combat emergency, ARVN forces also received the sophisticated TOW antitank missile to cope with enemy T-54 tanks. At the same time, twin 40mm antiaircraft guns, M-102 howitzers, radar sets such as the AN/MPQ-4, and modern tactical vehicles such as the 1/4-ton M-151 and the 2–1/2-ton M-35A2, came to expand and modernize the RVNAF equipment inventory.

The Enhance program was being implemented when prospects of an imminent cease-fire in October 1972 hastily ushered in the "Enhance Plus" project. Seeking to preempt the limitations of a peace agreement which was in the making, the United States quickly set about to bring the RVNAF firepower and mobility up to such a level that they could defend themselves effectively against an enemy offensive of 1972 proportions. The Enhance Plus program, therefore, provided for the filling of TO&Es up to the authorized level, an acceptable attrition and maintenance float, and a high inventory of assets which would turn the one-for-one replacement provision into a South Vietnamese advantage.

The last quarter of 1972 thus saw the hectic shipments of war materiel proceed at an accelerated pace, an effort designed to beat the cease-fire deadline. Most significant among the new arrivals were the necessary assets to equip two M-48 squadrons, three SP 175mm artillery battalions, and two C-130 squadrons (32 aircraft), and enough F-5As to both equip new fighter squadrons and exchange for the more advanced F-5Es later on. On the eve of the cease-fire day, therefore, the RVNAF found themselves in possession of a substantial inventory of war materiel and equipment.

The Impact of Reduced Aid

Peace never came to South Vietnam on 28 January 1973 as provided for by the Paris Agreement. Never for an instant did North Vietnam renounce . . . its ultimate conquest of the South. Repeated and increasingly blatant violations of the cease-fire by the Communists compelled the RVNAF to react in self-defense for the protection of the South Vietnamese people and to ensure territorial integrity. In spite of the ICCS [International Commission of Control and Supervision], and all appearances of self-control by both sides, fighting continued as viciously as ever.

With funds remaining from FY 1973 appropriations, the RVNAF were able to replace expendable items of equipment as war losses. The one-for-one basis was enforced, as required by the Paris Agreement. For the fiscal year ahead, however, it was not clear whether military aid would continue to be dispensed as MASF appropriations or revert to the MAP system. Months passed amid uncertainty but high expectations. In the meantime, the JGS and the US Defense Attaché Office, which replaced MACV in the management of the Security Assistance Program, continued to process requisitions for supplies and equipment within provisions of the FY 1974 program, which had been submitted for approval in early 1973. It was expected that final appropriations would be in the acceptable range of US $1.4–1.6 billion.

Not until January 1974 did the JGS learn from Major General Murray, the US Defense Attaché, that the FY 1974 program was running into difficulties and that the US Congress would most likely reduce appropriations to $1 billion or $900 million. General Murray also advised the JGS to cut back on consumption of supplies, especially in ammunition, in order to keep expenditures within expected appropriations, although the US Department of Defense continued to push for the original $1.4 to 1.6 billion.

By this time, however, US $820.5 million had been expended. With the final appropriations eventually set at $945 million, there was not much the RVNAF could do except to tighten their belt. Since 51 percent of expenditures went for ammunition, this meant that the RVNAF no longer afforded harassment or interdiction fire, even in the face of stepped-up enemy violations and infiltration. A drastically reduced ammunition supply rate was imposed but, in spite of voluntary curtailment in consumption, the available stocks of certain critical items at the end of FY 1974 reached a dangerously low level compared to that of cease-fire day.

The significance of all this lay in the fact that, if the RVNAF were forced in July 1974 to battle the enemy at the 1972 offensive level, they would have expended all their ammunition within less than ten weeks without resupply. By July 1974 there was also a considerable accumulation of war-damaged major items of equipment which could not be replaced for lack of funds.

In anticipation of further cutbacks for the fiscal year ahead, in May 1974 the US Department of Defense requested that an analysis be made of the impacts on RVNAF operational effectiveness at various funding levels, from $1,126,000,000 to $600,000,000.

• • •

From this analysis it was evident that, if FY 1975 appropriations were kept at the $1,126,000,000 level, the RVNAF would be able to defend South Vietnam against Communist activities at the 1974 scale and level of fighting, to include "high points," but in no way could they contain a sustained major offensive. Any level below the $1,126,000,000 mark, therefore, would seriously affect both the capabilities and morale of the RVNAF. It was estimated that at the $750,000,000 funding level, for example, the RVNAF would no longer have the capabilities to defend the entire territory under GVN control, even if fighting continued at the same level of the previous twelve months. At that level of military aid, there was no doubt that the GVN would be compelled to reduce substantially the extent of its territorial control, which, in terms of bargaining power, would represent a serious setback. Both the JGS and the US DAO therefore advised the US Department of Defense that $1,450,000,000 was the funding level required for South Vietnam to defend itself effectively.

During the first quarter of FY 1975, pending approval by the US Congress, the RVNAF subsisted on a continuing resolution authority (CRA) which disbursed funds based on $1 billion for the entire year. At the end of September 1974, however, the JGS was notified by the US DAO that only $700 million had been approved for FY 1975.

News of US military aid cutbacks propagated through the RVNAF hierarchy with the effect of a gigantic concussion bomb. Fears and doubts began to set in as JGS and US DAO authorities sat down to figure out how to make the most of what was available. All agreed that priority should be placed on the RVNAF ability to "move, shoot, and communicate." Of the $700 million available, nearly $120 million had been set aside to meet obligations: $74 million for PCH&T, $36.2 million for US DAO's operating funds, $2.3 million for the carried-over FY 1975 training program, and $3.3 million for pay-back to South Korea on F-5As already transferred.

Less than $580 million was thus left for the entire RVNAF, barely enough just for operation and maintenance. This meant that, except for ammunition, no war losses could ever be replaced on a one-for-one basis as authorized by the Paris Agreement.

The VNAF not only saw its F-5E program shattered beyond any hope, but also found its operating funds so drastically reduced that it had to ground a total of 224 aircraft. This included 61 A-1 fighter-bombers, the entire C-7 fleet (52 aircraft), all of its O-2 observation planes, 31 UH-1 helicopters, and 34 AC-47 and AC-119 gunships. To operate the remaining fleet of aircraft, the VNAF found that the only alternative to grounding was to cut back on flight time. Compared to FY 1974, therefore, flight time was reduced 30 percent for fighter-bombers, 50 percent for transports, and 80 percent for helicopters, which critically affected medical evacuation. The VNN also found itself in the same predicament, having to remove 21 out of 44 river groups from active duty.

Despite restrictions placed on the consumption of ammunition, the ARVN saw to its dismay that ammunition expenditures alone ($239.2 million) accounted for over one-half of its available funds ($407.1 million). More critical was the fact that ARVN corps's monthly requests for additional ammunition above the reduced ASR could only be filled up to an average of 41.4 percent, and that the overall ammunition stock level was constantly far below the cease-fire mark.

As a result of the RVNAF inability to replace expended ammunition, combat units found their initial issues increasingly depleted. The situation was far worse among RF/PF units of the Mekong Delta, where in late 1974 no soldier participated in an operation with an adequate issue of ammunition. Critical items of ammunition such as hand and M-79 grenades became trade commodities, changing hands between territorial and regular forces, which prompted Communist propaganda to dwell on the subject of US abandonment and call for RF and PF units at remote places to desert or surrender.

Other areas of activity were equally affected, which drastically reduced the RVNAF ability to move and to communicate. In addition to grounding aircraft, the RVNAF were also compelled to mothball about 50 percent of their 1/4-ton and 3/4-ton trucks for lack of gasoline, despite curtailed consumption and tight control. In February 1975, the entire RVNAF gasoline stock level stood at 443,962 barrels, to include 250,400 barrels on hand. This meant that, at the intense combat rate, this level would drop to zero sometime in May, and even at the actual consumption rate of 84,000 barrels per month it would dwindle to a mere seven-day supply by the end of FY 1975. The same situation affected diesel fuel, which, given a stock level of 1,301,523 barrels in February 1975 (of which 504,100 barrels were on hand), would be exhausted at the same time as gasoline at the intense combat rate, or reduced to four days of supply by the end of June if expended at the actual rate of consumption (254,000 barrels per month). In any event, even if they had been able to stall the NVA 1975 invasion, the RVNAF would have found themselves completely immobilized sometime in May if no additional appropriations were available.

In early 1975 the supply of dry batteries for the basic infantry radio set AN/PRC-25 was also reduced by one-half as compared to 1972. Communications were therefore affected by this reduction. Because of this and other cutbacks, the RVNAF eventually became an underdog in the face of an ever-stronger enemy. To redress this desperate situation, in January 1975 the GVN requested an additional $241.7 million to supplement the RVNAF needs in ammunition, fuels, medicine, and spare parts. But the US Congress voted down this request in late April 1975.

Observations

Issued from a poor and small country, the RVNAF had always been totally reliant on US military aid for their fight against the Communists. To accomplish their mission, the RVNAF naturally expected to have good weapons and equipment and adequate supplies.

Over the years coordination between the JGS and the US military assistance advisory organization—MAAG-V or MACV—for the purpose of aid programming had been good. There were constant efforts to improve US-supplied materiel, especially weapons, vehicles, and communications equipment. This was done through yearly military assistance programming. With resignation, the RVNAF always accepted what had been programmed for them and fought with whatever the United States chose to supply, never asking for what the United States could not make available because of its global obligations.

There was no other choice. For the RVNAF, it was simply a matter of more or [fewer] sacrifices, depending on the quality or adequacy of their instruments of defense. At no other time was this fact of life more revealing than during the early phase of the 1968 Tet Offensive. As a partner in war, the RVNAF never envied their American counterparts for their more sophisticated and powerful weapon systems, because they realized that US forces had a heavier combat burden. They were only concerned with the types of weapon that the enemy used and how to match him and fight him on equal terms. After all, they could always rely on the support of the powerful US forces. This was the reason why the RVNAF fought with determination and effectively stalled the NVA 1972 Easter invasion.

Without US backing, the morale of RVNAF troops began to waver in 1974. They fought on uneasily, stunned by the complete US indifference in the face of flagrant enemy violations. Their will to resist was finally shattered by the US unwillingness to continue supporting their efforts, no matter how hard they had tried to tighten their belts.

X. DEPORTMENT AND CONDUCT

Since their inception, the Vietnamese armed forces always had an organization devoted to troop morale. This organization evolved throughout the war, and its role eventually expanded to include efforts to win over the people and the enemy.

During the early years responsibility for troop motivation was delegated to a staff organization composed of G-5 divisions at the General Staff and military region headquarters and S-5 sections at recruit training centers. This staff organization produced and disseminated information for use by units and service branches. It also organized and supervised troop entertainment festivities performed by professional artists. However, these activities were incohesive and not very effective.

Not until 1955 did the national cause gain prominence with the establishment of the First Republic; concurrently, motivation efforts developed significantly. After the activation of the Psychological Warfare Directorate under the Ministry of Defense in 1956, the RVNAF received advisory assistance from Nationalist China and expanded the psywar organization throughout the hierarchy, down to the sector and regimental level. Under the ideological influence of Nationalist Chinese advisors, this organization developed into a separate service branch in 1964 with the creation of a General Political Warfare Department (GPWD) under the Joint General Staff.

The political warfare branch had three missions: 1) to create and maintain the loyalty of the RVNAF toward their leaders, nation, and national ideology; 2) to gain and maintain the support of the civilian populace in both friendly and enemy-controlled areas; and 3) to break down the loyalty of enemy soldiers toward their leaders, nation, and national ideology.

To achieve these objectives, the GPWD patterned its organization after the Nationalist Chinese. It consisted of five functional departments: Psychological Warfare, Political Indoctrination, Military Security, Social Welfare, and Commissary; and three chaplain directorates: Roman Catholic, Buddhist, and Protestant. Under its control and supervision there were the Political Warfare College and five polwar battalions, one for the JGS and one for each corps area. Polwar staffs were also incorporated into service commands, technical services, and corps, divisions, and sector headquarters.

In 1966 the polwar system reached further down the hierarchy, to the squad level. At the regimental, battalion, company, and platoon levels, the assistant commander or leader also served as polwar officer or NCO. At the squad level, the leader was assisted by a polwar cadre who was elected by fellow soldiers in the squad.

The RVNAF political warfare organization employed several techniques for the conduct of its activities, including face-to-face contact, leaflets, posters, magazines, radio, and TV. Its efforts were devoted to winning the hearts and minds of the RVNAF soldiers, the civilian population, and the enemy. . . .

Relations with the People

For many generations Vietnamese rulers had been taught to hold the general populace in high esteem and respect. Almost all leaders of Vietnamese history upheld the Confucian principle of "People First, Government Second," and their policies were accordingly devoted to the welfare and peace of the populace. The people were a major force that enabled Vietnam to survive as a nation despite foreign invasions and domination.

It was the Vietnamese people who helped the Viet Minh win the War of Resistance against the French. In fact, their strategy was built on a popular base and, with the solid backing of this base, guerrilla warfare thrived and developed until conditions for victory were finally attained in 1954.

With the same strategy of people's war, the Vietnamese Communists set out to conquer South Vietnam in 1959. The conflict was basically ideological, and both sides realized that the ultimate victor would be the one who won over the people to his side.

But winning over the people of South Vietnam was not an easy mission for either side. The fact was, having lived and suffered in war for over a quarter of a century, most of the people became war weary and noncommittal. They just wanted to live in peace and recover from the ravages of the past. They feared and loathed whoever brought trouble to their villages. In the contest between the Nationalists and Communists, many desired a neutral stance, taking no sides and giving neither support. To be left alone, however, they accommodated both, waiting on the sideline to see who would be victorious. Years of listening to the attractive but hollow lines from both sides had made them sober, wary, suspicious.

To gain popular sympathy, therefore, both sides took precautions not to antagonize the people. This was the preliminary but important step, because both sides knew that their soldiers and cadres were being closely watched and any misstep in their deportment or relations could cause adverse repercussions.

For the South Vietnamese government soldiers, winning popular sympathy was an uphill task because, in the people's eyes, they were the successors of the French Union forces. And the people's memory still agonized over mischievous acts such as looting, arson, [and] rape that these forces had committed not very long ago.

For the Communists, this task was somewhat easier, since they were still identified with the "Resistance" who vindicated [*sic*] the French and liberated the country. But the same slogans with which they waged this war—"national liberation," "stop American aggression"—somehow sounded hollow and misleading. The magic of old-line propaganda, which once worked, seemed to be deteriorating.

In this contest to win popular sympathy and, eventually, support, the RVNAF developed a code of conduct which was mandatory for every soldier to memorize and recite. It consisted of six precepts, four of them related to personal behavior and relations with the people:

1. I pledge to accept every sacrifice and hardship in the fight for the survival of the nation, of my family, and of my own person;
2. I pledge to always obey and execute my commander's orders, and to be vigilant of the enemy's scheme to divide us;
3. I love my compatriots and will always endeavor to protect their lives and properties and respect their religious faith. I respect elders, love children, and behave correctly toward women;
4. I am aware that unpopular acts will push the people toward the Communist side and this amounts to giving a hand to our enemy and destroying ourselves.

To carry the battle of the hearts and minds a step further, in May 1969 the General Political Warfare Department initiated a "For the People" campaign designed to achieve three objectives: 1) to remind servicemen of all ranks that the RVNAF are responsible for protecting the people; 2) to promote civic action activities; and 3) to improve military deportment and discipline.

During a four-month campaign the GPWD employed almost every resource and technique to inform and educate the troops. RVNAF units competed among themselves in conducting civil action programs, giving medical care and dispensing medicine to civilians, and assisting them in community development projects such as building schools, digging drainage and irrigation ditches, and improving public sanitation. "Discipline Weeks" were periodically observed to minimize discipline violations and improve military deportment, with particular emphasis on military courtesy, uniform, personal appearance, and behavior in public places. These were coupled with "Traffic Weeks" which sought to correct bad driving habits, punish recklessness, and reduce accidents and traffic congestions. Encouraged by remarkable results, the JGS extended the campaign until year's end and occasionally revived it during the following years.

One of the dilemmas of the Vietnam War faced by every field commander was how to destroy the enemy without causing casualties or damage to the civilian population. In many situations the choice was not a happy one, but justifiable, because destroying the enemy and protecting our own forces seemed to be imperative, especially in contested areas. But our quest for popular sympathy and support dictated that certain rules should be observed and field commanders should exercise restraint and caution to minimize losses caused to the local population, even when their loyalty was uncertain.

In search and destroy or pacification operations, therefore, several procedures were emphasized. The use of artillery or airstrikes, for example, was authorized only after clearance by local authorities and if this support was absolutely necessary. For cordon and search operations, preparatory fire was usually banned, even though the target might be under enemy control. During search activities, our troops were strictly forbidden from confiscating people's personal properties, even if this only involved a lettuce head or a chicken. If it was necessary to procure food, our troops were instructed to purchase at a fair market price. Many tactical commanders took additional precautions by banning purchases altogether during operations and never allowed their troops to enter villages. As a result, night bivouacs usually took place far from villages and food purchases were made only by mess service personnel. Another strictly enforced rule required that every item borrowed from the people for expedient use should be returned after proper maintenance. Obviously the enforcement of these rules depended on strict control by each unit commander.

To deter mischievous acts, the RVNAF military code imposed severe punishments against violators. Military courts were instructed to expedite criminal cases by holding on-the-spot trials. In 1969 an RF trooper convicted of rape was sentenced to death by a mobile military court held in Hau Nghia Province, where the crime was committed. As a reminder to all servicemen, the JGS published a monthly pamphlet in which all offenses and punishments were publicized, although the names of the culprits were withheld.

Damage to civilian properties was a subject of concern for all field commanders, who usually exercised caution to prevent or minimize it. But damage was frequently inevitable because of tactical requirements or heavy fighting. Destruction of crops caused by defoliation operations around bases or of habitations caused by artillery fire or air-dropped bombs were two frequent types of damage. In such cases, the property owners received compensatory payments from a civic action fund earmarked for that purpose and managed by the General Political Warfare Department.

• • •

The requisition of private land for military use was another delicate problem of public relations faced by the RVNAF during the war. Because of its litigable nature, the RVNAF only resorted to requisitioning as the last measure after public land had been fully utilized. The buildup of US forces beginning in 1965, however, required the requisition of a sizable amount of private land for the construction of airfields and military bases. All such uses of land were subjected to compensatory payments to owners. The price of land was determined by the local province chief and compensations included all crops or habitations located on that land.

The laws and regulations established by the GVN to protect the lives and properties of the civilian population were comprehensive and fair. The RVNAF also drove hard their efforts of educating and motivating personnel of all ranks to maintain discipline and abide by the laws. However, some shortcomings and mischiefs were inevitable in a war situation, which made the GVN endeavor to win the support of the population even more difficult.

Complaints occasionally arose concerning mischievous acts committed by combat troops during operations. Petty larceny, threats, or extortions indeed occurred sometimes, but they were primarily confined to contested areas or areas under enemy control. More often than not, these were individual acts committed by mobile troops who were in the area for only a short time. Local troops operating in areas under GVN control were rarely involved. There were several reasons that accounted for these acts of improper conduct. First, few ARVN soldiers made a distinction between the enemy and the people who lived under his control. Their conduct toward these people was therefore driven either by indiscriminate hatred or the instinct of survival. During long operations, there was also a longing for fresh food and, either because the owners were not there or the soldiers did not have the money, petty larceny of chickens, fruit, or vegetables sometimes occurred. But these acts happened only when control was lax or when the platoon leader chose to look the other way. Over the years, however, very few cases of improper conduct were prosecuted and brought to trial by military courts unless flagrant crimes were involved. While cover-ups were possible, this absence of indictment was perhaps an indication of indifference or passivity on the part of a population so accustomed to abuses and injustices of times past.

Although compensatory payments were mandatory in case of property damage or land requisition, they were not always satisfactory or timely because of the rigid procedures involved. For one thing, confirmation of the damage or actual land use, which involved investigation by several military and civilian agencies, was usually a time-consuming process that might take months or even years. In many instances investigation and confirmation could not be made because either evidence no longer existed or the unit had redeployed or the unit commander involved was deceased. Information provided by the local population, on the other hand, was sketchy and usually unreliable. Many compensation cases, therefore, remained insoluble.

• • •

The people who lived under GVN control seldom saw the true face of the enemy; they rarely realized how deceitful and conceited the Communists could be. When an enemy unit prepared for an attack against one of our military installations, it usually selected avenues of approach far removed from the civilian population. Because the target was always well defined, the enemy's fire on it was accurate, hence losses to the population were minimized. This was a definite advantage that the enemy enjoyed over our troops, who usually found their targets in villages or hamlets where enemy troops hid among the local population. Also, the United States and RVNAF often employed air and indirect-fire weapons.

However, when the objective was a city or a provincial capital, the enemy faced the same situation. He could not hit our troops without also causing losses to the local population. The 1968 Tet Offensive was a case in point. During the various phases of this offensive, the enemy's inaccurate 122mm and 107mm rockets caused considerable damage and losses to the urban population, especially in Saigon. This indiscriminate shelling, coupled with the impressment of people into hazardous chores such as road digging, ammunition carrying, or even laying siege on outposts, eventually backlashed against our enemy's efforts to win popular sympathy. The final popular verdict was rendered against the enemy when thousands of civilians were murdered in Hue city during his thirty-day occupation. Since then, the South Vietnamese people were well immunized against enemy propaganda and there was little doubt as to which side they preferred. "Don't listen to what the Communists say," they repeated among themselves. "Just look at what they did."

• • •

Treatment of Prisoners of War

Even though the United States brought combat troops into South Vietnam in 1965 to fight the Communists alongside the RVNAF, it also never declared war with North Vietnam. As fighting escalated, with the eventual commitment of 192 US and ARVN combat battalions, the number of detained enemy personnel also increased significantly. In the meantime, there were also US personnel, both military and civilian, listed as missing in action but presumably taken prisoners, especially US pilots shot down over North Vietnam. As the problem became more pressing, the United States began to apply [the provisions of] the Geneva International Convention [to] prisoners of war for purposes of classification and treatment.

In 1965 the United States decided to turn over to the RVNAF custody of all enemy personnel detained by its forces during operations. This was an action sanctioned by the Geneva Convention, which authorized such transfers of custody responsibility, provided that certain binding provisions concerning the prisoners' welfare would be observed.

The GVN was faced immediately with three major problems, however. First, it always considered the VC as criminals who should be prosecuted under national laws, although their treatment was as fair as required by Article 3 of the Geneva Convention. The GVN, therefore, continued with this policy, but made public all verdicts rendered. Second, the RVNAF never had any facilities constructed specifically as prisoner camps; they kept only military jails for their own convicts. Consequently all enemy personnel captured by US forces and turned over to RVNAF custody were detained in ordinary prisons, which was a violation of Article 22 of the Geneva Convention. Third, according to Article 12 of the same convention, US forces were still responsible for those enemy personnel captured, even though the RVNAF kept them in custody.

But the United States seemed to be most concerned about the American pilots [and] military and civilian personnel who were captured and detained by the Communists, both in North and South Vietnam. The United States was concerned that, given the GVN's policy of denying the status of prisoners of war to Communist personnel, the VC and North Vietnam might take retaliatory measures against US personnel. Indeed, Hanoi publicly threatened several times to prosecute captured US pilots under its own laws, maintaining that as "war criminals" they were not entitled to protection by the Geneva provisos. The United States, as a result, pressed the GVN for strict observance of the Geneva Convention in the hope that North Vietnam and the VC would be bound to do the same to US prisoners.

At first the GVN was reluctant to yield to pressure, claiming as Hanoi did that, as aggressors and assassins, Communists did not earn the status of prisoners of war defined by the Geneva Convention. The main reason for this attitude was that the GVN, ever suspicious of Communist foul play and intransigence, did not feel assured that North Vietnam and the VC would strictly apply Geneva standards to US and allied personnel under detention. Gradually, in sympathy with the US concern, the GVN softened its stance and finally notified the International Red Cross in August 1965 that the

RVN was respecting and would continue to respect the Geneva Convention on prisoners of war.

In June 1965 a combined JGS-MACV committee was formed to study the detailed implementation of the Geneva Convention. Five months later the committee set in motion a program which included, among other things, efforts to educate combat troops in the subject of prisoners of war and the building of four POW camps, each capable of accommodating initially 1,000 prisoners, for each corps area. Training aids used for this educational purpose included bilingual 3 × 5 cards on the subject "The Enemy in Your Hands" and other materials designed to explain how prisoners of war should be treated according to the Geneva Convention of 12 August 1949. For the first time also RVNAF individual and unit training programs began to include basic subjects on the detention, confirmation, classification, and transfer of prisoners of war. Combat units were held responsible for them from the time they were captured until transferred to POW camps. In addition to combat troops, training also focused on Military Police battalions, which were responsible for the administration and security of POW camps. To further emphasize the effort, the GPWD made the good treatment of prisoners one of the six basic precepts of the RVNAF soldier's code of conduct: "I, soldier of the RVN, absolutely pledge to treat well captured and surrendered enemy prisoners. I will not mistreat them, beat them, or misappropriate their personal belongings."

The building of POW camps began in early 1966 as a crash program. It picked up momentum after a slow start due to material shortages. In May 1966 the first POW camp was completed in Bien Hoa, followed by two others in Pleiku and Danang. By year's end these camps reached a total capacity of 3,000 prisoners, expandable to 4,500 in an emergency.

• • •

By the end of 1967, the RVNAF had increased their total handling capacity to 13,000 prisoners. This was made possible by the construction in midyear of a central POW camp on Phu Quoc Island, the largest ever built. When it was completed in 1969, the Phu Quoc POW camp had ten enclosures, each capable of accommodating 2,000 prisoners.

• • •

During 1973, in full implementation of the Paris Agreement, the GVN released a total of 26,508 Communist POWs. In return, it received only 4,608 of its own POWs, 588 US, and nine from third countries. All former POW camps across South Vietnam were completely deserted and prepared to close down or convert to other uses. But, because peace never came and war resumed in earnest, these camps were reactivated to accommodate newly captured enemy personnel. Subsequent proposals by the GVN to exchange prisoners during Two-Party Joint Military Commission meetings were all turned down by the Communists.

In summary, the GVN always adopted a lenient policy toward the enemy, who was considered a blood relative with a different ideology. It always opened wide its arms to welcome those who returned, and endeavored to induce this rally by persuasive appeals. Consequently, the RVNAF forbade all inhuman actions against enemy personnel after they had been captured or surrendered, and subjected violators to prosecution and punishment. However, it was inevitable that, driven by anger and vindication for the casualties suffered by their comrades, a few RVNAF soldiers did commit atrocious acts against enemy POWs and such stories were reported by the press.

•••

XI. INDOCTRINATION AND MOTIVATION

Indoctrination

Indoctrination or political education was an undertaking of major importance for the RVNAF during our protracted fight against the Communists. A soldier would fight with more dedication if he was ideologically motivated. This tenet held true in the Vietnam War.

Important as it was, ideological indoctrination began only after South Vietnam became a republic. Before that, it was almost nonexistent. The Vietnamese soldier in the pre-Diem era fought without conviction, without knowing why he fought. He merely carried out the orders of his superior.

The French then held both political and military powers. Under their tutelage and domination, Vietnam hardly had a true national cause to motivate its incipient military force. Even Bao Dai had second thoughts about developing the Vietnamese National Army, confiding that "such an undertaking would be detrimental to our nation as long as we do not have an ideal for our men to fight." His conviction was well founded because, as he admitted: "As long as we fail to inspire confidence among the populace, how can we impart enthusiasm and a fighting spirit on our troops? If we say that this is our army, when it is commanded and used by the French, then we admit its mercenary character. How can a mercenary army have any cause to enlist the support of the people?"[8]

As South Vietnam became an independent nation under President Ngo Dinh Diem in 1955, its national cause began to take shape. Under the US military advisory assistance program, the Vietnamese armed forces went through a complete reorganization process built on the concept of mandatory military service. The Diem administration realized that, to defend against Communist aggression, South Vietnam had to derive its power not from an all-volunteer, professional military force, but one composed primarily of reserve elements politically motivated against Communism. It was believed that ideological awareness, once inculcated and firmly held as a cause, would greatly enhance the effectiveness of weapons.

•••

To consolidate a political base for the military, President Diem successively appointed to key command positions officers affiliated with the Can Lao Party, a political monolith created by his brother, Mr. Ngo Dinh Nhu, whose ideology was antithetical to Communism. In addition to political education and ideological immunization against Communism, the GVN felt that ranking officers should also be thoroughly conversant with national goals and defense policies. Therefore, when the Strategic Hamlet program became a national endeavor in 1961, all RVNAF field-grade officers were compelled to attend a seven-day course on the subject conducted by the presidency at the Lo O training center in Bien Hoa Province. Gradually the strategic hamlet, as an ideological subject, was also introduced in political indoctrination programs of instruction at military schools and in units.

Developing the servicemen's knowledge on national policies, while guarding them against the evils of Communism, was imperative in an ideological conflict. This was recognized by almost every RVNAF serviceman. However, very few agreed on the practice of appointing members of the Can Lo Party to key positions in the RVNAF and the GVN tendency to force political affiliation on servicemen. Most RVNAF servicemen believed that, in a free democracy, the military should stay away from party politics in order to be professionally effective. Because of its own interests, no politically involved army would be capable of taking orders, which sometimes gave rise to dissension and bloody coups. Politics, therefore, weakened the military, making them oblivious to defense duties.

• • •

During the period of political instability that followed the overthrow of President Diem, indoctrination was suspended altogether because it was identified with the [defunct] regime. The Strategic Hamlet program fell into neglect, which gave the enemy an opportunity to expand and consolidate his foothold in rural areas. At the grassroots level, GVN control was shaky, and there were indications that the Self-Defense Corps had become incapacitated because of widespread desertion.

Not until 1965, when South Vietnam regained some measure of stability, was indoctrination revived in the RVNAF. The political education process focused on the Popular Forces, whose morale suffered the most during the 1963–1964 period, and was aptly called the "morale rearmament program." Under the guidance of the Indoctrination Division of the RF-PF Command, this program sought to impart anti-Communist ideology on PF troopers, teaching them the art and techniques of winning popular support and appealing for the enemy to rally. During the same year, two new subjects were brought into the RVNAF indoctrination program: North Vietnam's aggressive design in infiltrating regular units into the South and the presence of US combat troops in South Vietnam. This was warranted by the need to counter enemy propaganda directed against US "imperialist aggression" on the one hand and to denounce overt aggression by Hanoi on the other.

In 1966, to test a new and better approach to indoctrination, the GPWD initiated the "New Horizon" project in three different areas and units: the 7th Division in the Mekong Delta, an RF company in Long An Province, and the 23rd Division in the Central Highlands. The New Horizon program was a political warfare campaign designed primarily to improve small-unit leadership and prevent desertion in the RVNAF. Its primary tool was informal troop education and the concomitant implementation of programs seeking to improve the material and moral welfare of the RVNAF soldier.

• • •

Indoctrination subjects included basic issues like why and for whom do we fight; the heroic struggle of our forebears against the Chinese and the French; what is Communism; why do we have to fight the Communists; the cruelty and design of the Communists in South Vietnam; the presence of US troops and the enemy's [slanted] propaganda about it. Various techniques of learning these subjects were employed: storytelling, conversation, questions and answers, etc., which encouraged active participation by every serviceman and attracted his interest. . . .

Encouraged by the excellent results of the pilot project, in 1967 the JGS instituted the New Horizon program in the RVNAF as part of an overall improvement plan. During the year pacification and development also became a national endeavor and a subject of extensive indoctrination in every unit. The objective was to explain to RVNAF soldiers the reasons why pacification was required as a national policy and what the rural population could expect to enjoy in the near future in terms of security, freedom, and prosperity.

The enemy's Tet Offensive during 1968 resulted in a psychological setback for our side, despite his military defeat. The US decision to cease all aerial bombings against North Vietnam, coupled with peace overtures, confused the RVNAF rank and file. Although the South Vietnamese people became more determined than ever in their anti-Communist stance, there prevailed a feeling of uncertainty as to prospects for the future.

• • •

As US forces continued their [re]deployment and peace talks bogged down in futile polemics, new uncertainties and problems surfaced to affect troop morale, particularly as a result of the new US policy of irreversible disengagement. The RVNAF rapidly expanded their force structure and modernized their weapons, but apparently needed more than that to fill in the void of US redeployment and face NVA divisions. The cost of living was skyrocketing, and inflation [was] so rampant that the fixed-salaried serviceman was gradually edged into destitution and hardship. Complaints surfaced everywhere about the RVNAF soldier's plight.

To meet this complex challenge, the JGS embarked on an extensive program designed to improve the RVNAF effectiveness in all areas of activity. To support this program, a JGS delegation visited all corps headquarters and military schools, explaining the new US policy and presenting the various efforts that the GVN was undertaking to improve the lot of the RVNAF serviceman. Audiences thus came to understand that the US troop disengagement did not mean an abandonment of South Vietnam, but was dictated by domestic pressures, and that the United States would continue to support South Vietnam in the fight against the Communists. As to the economic plight of the RVNAF soldier, the JGS delegation assured everyone that the national leaders thoroughly understood the problem and were trying to solve it.

• • •

During the post-cease-fire period, as the RVNAF reverted to a defensive posture and limited their efforts to counteracting enemy violations, the indoctrination program emphasized unit self-improvement in the areas of maintenance, preservation, and economy of materiel. RVNAF servicemen were briefed on the reasons why economy was mandatory, given the national need to devote its limited resources to reconstruction instead of war. They were also educated on measures designed to fight wastage and misuse, to moderate requirements, and to operate within a limited budget. The problem was thoroughly understood as the RVNAF prepared for self-moderation and austerity in the years ahead.

The resumption of the war by the enemy, however, upset all of these efforts. Enemy-initiated activities escalated to such intensity and scale that fighting was the same as in previous years. Despite self-imposed austerity, our units soon found themselves low on ammunition and fuels, the inevitable result of US military aid cutbacks. The RVNAF soldier feared he would not receive adequate supplies to sustain the fight and doubted the future of US support. To allay fears and suspicions, the GPWD and the Central Logistics Command combined efforts to conduct an education campaign, dwelling on the US pledge to continue backing and supporting South Vietnam. In spite of these efforts, suspicion persisted about an eventual abandonment by the United States.

Soon this suspicion became a reality. Phuoc Long fell into enemy hands in early January without the United States taking positive action. Less than three months later, Ban Me Thuot succumbed, which led to the hasty evacuation of Pleiku and Kontum and the tragic disintegration of II Corps forces. Confusion and uncertainty pervaded the mind of every RVNAF serviceman, including the polwar cadre. Rumors spread about [an] American sell-out and territorial concessions in secret agreement with North Vietnam. Polwar cadres were confused; lacking guidance and directives, they themselves became impotent and helpless, unable to make out what was going on. Like other servicemen, they were longing for some explanation and guidance or assurance from the national leadership. But this never came, and the morale of RVNAF troops deteriorated rapidly afterwards.

Other Motivation Methods

• • •

During the 1972 Easter Offensive, a cash award program was instituted to reward enemy tank killers. This was a realistic effort to encourage the destruction of the deadly T-54 (and their Chinese-made version T-59) tanks that the enemy employed during attacks against Quang Tri, Kontum, and An Loc. Cash prizes were given by GVN officials, civilian personalities, or associations, and raised from an initial VN $50,000 to VN $200,000 for each tank destroyed. This greatly stimulated frontline soldiers, who competed among themselves for tank kills. Awards were paid on the spot whenever the situation permitted the visit of prize sponsors. Several units thus earned millions of piasters, which they spent for useful purposes. For the RVNAF soldier of 1972, a cash award was perhaps one of the best stimulants.

Over the years most RVNAF servicemen were also mesmerized by the voice of a girl named Da Lan over the waves of the RVNAF radio broadcast stations. Programs broadcast by Da Lan proved most popular and effective. Her voice flattered, titillated, encouraged, and stimulated the RVNAF soldier and made him feel a hero. She constantly reminded him of his manly mission on the battlefield and assured him that back home everything was all right. Occasionally she sent out gifts or souvenirs to the frontline soldiers, who usually cherished them with jealous favor.

• • •

XII. REGIONAL AND POPULAR FORCES

Accounting for over one-half the total strength of the RVNAF, the Regional [Forces] and Popular Forces played a major counterinsurgency role during the Vietnam War.

• • •

In an effort to unify command and to muster all available military forces to fight the war, in 1964 the CG [Civil Guard] and SDC [Self-Defense Corps] were integrated into the regular army and placed under the command of the JGS. The SDC changed its name to Popular Forces (PF), a designation signifying that the people themselves took up arms and rose to fight the enemy for the national cause, like the patriots who had revolted against French rule. The CG was also given a new name, Regional Forces (RF), which identified them as a local army operating within the boundaries of military regions. The RVNAF consisted, therefore, of three kinds of forces. At the rice-roots level of hamlets and villages, there were the PF, whose targets were Communist guerrillas; at the district and province level, there were the RF, who grappled with Communist local forces; and there was the ARVN, whose opponent was the Communist main-force units.

• • •

To improve command and control, company group headquarters were authorized beginning in 1969. . . . In the wake of this success, RF battalions were employed as the main pacification force in replacement of infantry divisions.

• • •

Observations

It must be admitted that territorial security had not received proper attention since the beginning. During the years from 1955 to 1961, therefore, the main effort and the bulk of resources were devoted to building up defense against invasion. Valuable time had thus been lost during which security at the hamlet and village level, the chief domain of Communist insurgency activities, could have been strengthened.

Not until 1961 did the idea catch on that an effective defense of South Vietnam entailed not only capabilities to meet external aggression, but also the maintenance of internal security as well. Although the MAP program was extended to territorial forces, these forces continued to have a low priority, when compared to the RVNAF, for South Vietnam's elite manpower and material resources.

Even in 1967, when rural pacification became a national policy, the RF and PF continued to play a secondary role, since regular ARVN troops assumed territorial security as their primary mission. In 1969, when US forces began their withdrawal and ARVN infantry divisions were compelled to relinquish their role of pacification support, the RF and PF were given the opportunity to expand and develop, but continued to be poor cousins when it came to receiving their share of logistic support and manpower resources.

With regard to the organization of territorial forces, both the GVN and the US mission had no clear-cut concept, but operated largely on expediency through the painful process of trial and error. The original idea of President Ngo Dinh Diem concerning a village defense based on voluntary participation by the people was both correct and conformed to the age-old Vietnamese tradition of village self-government. Had it been fully developed and implemented, the enemy would have been beaten at his own game. Since the Communist infrastructure and guerrillas could operate only if supported and sheltered by the people, then only the people could single them out and destroy them. The people should be motivated to organize the defense of their own families and communities.

The role of the government was to support them with organizational skills and means, such as weapons and ammunition. Under Mr. Diem's properly conceived self-defense system, the entire village population should alternate between defense duties and normal activities; and the responsibility of defending the village should lie not just with the group on duty but with every villager. In case of alert, for example, not only the people on duty but the whole village should respond and take action.

Despite this, village defense during the period 1955–1961 was not very effective and the Communist infrastructure and the number of guerrillas continued to grow. The main reason was that villagers lacked organization guidance, motivation, and training in defensive tactics, which left them vulnerable to attacks or retaliation by better-trained enemies. At the national level, the weakness seemed to derive from the lack of capable administrative cadres, and the absence of a cohesive party structure capable of organizing villagers and galvanizing them into a strong, fully controlled, and thoroughly motivated combat force. Instead of committing cadres and means to consolidate people's organizations in the village, motivating, and making them all combat effective, the government and the US mission were simply concerned with organizing and training a small group of professional men called Self-Defense Corps.

This policy, while producing a good number of men trained to shoot, unwittingly restricted the people's participation in and capacity for the fight. The enemy therefore had simply to contend with a small force instead of having to deal with every man, woman, and child. Unwittingly, too, this approach induced villagers to rely on these professional fighters for their defense, which they no longer regarded as an obligation or duty.

Making the Popular Forces part of the armed forces in 1964 was a serious mistake of the military government. In all honesty, this move failed to result in greater efficiency in the task of maintaining village security. For all practical purposes, it was the same old concept, the same organization, and the same system of force utilization. But the idea cost the defense budget more, placed an additional administrative burden on RVNAF, and made control all but impossible because the military command structure could not reach down to the level where the PF was so thinly deployed. The move made the RVNAF look impressive in numbers, but not in substance. It wasted a valuable part of the human resources that was sorely needed for the regular force and RF units.

The most serious damage resulted from its fostering among villagers the mentality of dependence upon the army and the tendency to regard the defense of villages against the local enemy as a governmental responsibility and not their own. The people therefore stood on the sidelines, uninvolved and uncommitted.

In 1968, taking advantage of the rising popular hatred of Communists after the Tet Offensive, the government of the Second Republic organized the People's Self-Defense Force (PSDF), whose duties and structure, although larger, were similar to those of the SDC under the First Republic. With the birth of the PSDF, the Popular Forces became a sort of mongrel, neither completely military nor completely popular. Their original purpose having been taken away, they no longer fit in any clear-cut defense concept except to serve as tutors for the PSDF.

It is my opinion that, in the Vietnam War, the maintenance of community security should have been left to the people, with the government's loyal and committed political and military cadres acting as a lever. To fight Communist insurgency, every citizen should have been turned into a militiaman. The government and the armed forces should only provide support and assistance as required beyond the capability of villagers and proportionate to the population and terrain of each community, but not to exceed the limits of the nation's resources. The armed forces should maintain security outside the boundaries of rural communities by using regional forces. The full integration of the RF into the regular army, therefore, was a logical, if belated, move.

• • •

In summary, RF and PF troops were basically good combat soldiers with excellent war records. But their capabilities were not fully developed and employed because of their loose organization, their unimaginative employment, and the lack of an effective command and control system.

XIII. CORRUPTION

Corruption was a media issue of the Vietnam War. It made headlines, both in local and foreign press. It was hotly debated in the RVN National Assembly and in the US Congress. Public opinion suggested that corruption was rampant among South Vietnamese armed forces and government agencies and that it weakened their resolve to fight. There was also the opinion that corruption was just a pretext for character assassination growing out of dark political motives and that it was not as bad as people believed.

The broad issue of corruption is discussed in this monograph only to the extent that it affected the Vietnamese armed forces and the conduct of the war. It is my hope that it will help shed some light on this turbid affair.

Forms and Causes of Corruption

The term "corruption" was traditionally used among Vietnamese to designate shady, dishonest, and devious acts of bureaucrats, in the exercise of national laws, which resulted in the furtherance of their self-interest at the expense of the nation and the people. Bribery and abuse of power came most readily to mind when Vietnamese talked about corruption. A gift became bribery when the gift-bearer gave not out of social or human obligation but out of a desire to gain something in return, to "trade a crawfish for a lobster," so to speak, and when the receiver accepted it with the understanding that it was a form of payment for some favor he had done for the giver. The line drawn between gift and payoff was tenuous indeed.

• • •

The materialistic-minded serviceman was not the exception in the RVNAF. Also, some were power hungry and greedy. There were those who spent a modest fortune to buy high ranks and exalted positions in order to acquire even greater wealth at the first opportunity. Our protracted war spawned two more types of people in the Vietnamese society, one cowardly and death-fearing who spent fortunes to buy safety through draft exemption or a soft, noncombat job if inducted into the military; the other type lived as if each day was the last, fully enjoying himself. The General Mobilization Law drew both of these kinds of people into the RVNAF. The pressing need for expanding the armed forces and combat requirements made it difficult to eliminate such undesirable types from the military.

On the other hand, the nation's dwindling resources did not permit commensurate pay for the servicemen. Low pay, compounded by inflation, put the average serviceman in a pathetic predicament, forcing him to struggle with himself between moral uprightness (which meant poverty and a life of penury for his wife and children) and corruption (which jeopardized combat effectiveness and perhaps the survival of the nation). Because of their chosen probity, a number of officers had to live off their parents' incomes, moonlight during off-duty hours in such jobs as carrying passengers on Honda mopeds, reduce their material needs to a minimum, and be content with a life of frugality and destitution. It was because of this honesty that a number of dependent families were forced to have children live with parents on both sides and wives seek jobs; this resulted in many broken marriages.

Even though some parents, wives, and children had assisted in keeping our men honest, the same people—namely wives and children—were also the very motivating force that often led servicemen into corruption. Both men and wives used each other's clout, with the aid of an entourage of military henchmen, to engage in corrupt practices they could get away with within the husband's authority. If a wife had been accustomed to luxuries, a comfortable house and car, it was difficult for the husband to resist corruption.

• • •

The RVNAF Anticorruption Efforts

In the years before 1965, corruption was not yet an issue in the RVNAF. Most efforts were, therefore, directed toward checking embezzlement by treasury officers or NCOs in self-administrative units such as infantry battalions, artillery battalions, armored squadrons, and headquarters companies. Investigations revealed that embezzling occurred most frequently during periods when commanders were busy with combat operations. In order to ensure cash availability for daily expenses and payroll disbursement on payday while [they] had to be present with operating units and away from base areas, commanders often signed blank authorizations to withdraw cash from the local treasury for the convenient use of treasury officers. Besides, their preoccupation with operations, security, and defense matters, and their lack of understanding of financial regulations caused unit commanders to neglect their function of supervising administrative and financial operations within their units. Unconsciously, they let fraud and deception occur at the expense of public funds and their men's interests.

• • •

After 1965 corruption rapidly became a matter of concern for the RVNAF. The grumblings and whisperings heard among the public and servicemen about corruption within the armed forces were no longer confined to the area of finances, but had spread to personnel and logistics. More detrimental still was the common belief that acts of corruption had the blessings of higher authorities.

• • •

Thanks to improved food programs carried out with the help of the unit's food preparation committee and farming committee, the men's food allowances were no longer diverted, and their meals became more nutritious in spite of meager allowances and skyrocketing prices. A uniform program was also implemented which ensured adequate and timely issuance of correct-size clothing. Subsequently a leave program was adopted with the objective of ensuring that men received leaves when authorized and in accordance with a predetermined schedule. With every passing week, one or two problems were being solved. Gradually the situation in the units was improved enough to remove most causes which contributed to corruption. Indeed, as observed by political warfare cadres and unit commanders, the New Horizon program was the proper remedy for petty corruption problems in units. The success of this program could be attributed to the commitment of individual unit commanders and the concern on the part of higher echelons of command.

• • •

Achievements of the New Horizon Campaign

The New Horizon program, which had been initiated in 1966 in the 44th Regiment, 23rd Infantry Division; the 46th Regiment, 25th Division; and the provinces of Long An and Dinh Tuong on an experimental basis, brought about encouraging results in the units concerned. The troops witnessed a clear change of attitude in their commanders, who showed genuine solicitude for them. Now that they had a clear idea of their rights and benefits, they began to appreciate the efforts made by their commanders and responsible personnel to protect these privileges. After the initial wariness had vanished, they also enjoyed the education sessions. The meetings held by GPWD mobile information teams succeeded in generating a great deal of good feeling among combat troops toward central authorities. The difficulties encountered by the GVN in its attempt to raise the troops' standard of living were received with understanding, and the JGS determination to improve the armed forces' efficiency was well known by all.

• • •

In late 1966 and early 1967 three instances of corruption were unmasked which created quite a sensation in the armed forces. The first case involved the commandant of the Quang Trung Training Center, who had used draftee labor and military real estate and materials to build himself an ice-making plant. Having served under President . . . Thieu, this officer was respected and feared by many. Acting on the information contained in a sealed envelope sent to the AG/JGS, and on orders of the Chief/JGS, the Inspector General made an unexpected visit to determine the truth and later ordered an official investigation. Since the results bore out the allegations, the JGS imposed severe punishment on the offender (60 days of confinement and demotion to lieutenant colonel from full colonel) and his accomplices.

The second case involved an attempt to bribe and acceptance of bribes by a lieutenant colonel who served as chief of the Finance and Budget Office/JGS. Functioning on the principle of separation of responsibility regarding contract bidding for RVNAF, the Chief of Staff/JGS reserved the authority to approve all contracts submitted through public bidding which amounted to 30 million Vietnamese piasters or more. The results of bids were usually submitted by the Engineer Department and the Purchasing Agency to the Finance and Budget Office/JGS for review prior to approval by the Chief of Staff/JGS. One afternoon the Chief of [the] Finance and Budget Office came to see the Chief of Staff and asked him to approve a contract for the construction of an additional 400-bed ward to the Cong Hoa General Hospital. Casually he insinuated to the Chief of Staff that the contractor "would never forget his debt of gratitude."

Angered by this offense to his self-respect, the Chief of Staff immediately ordered the arrest of the Chief of [the] Finance and Budget Office and subjected the whole affair to a thorough investigation. The outcome revealed that, although the bidding had been conducted according to regulations, there was bribery by the winning contractor and acceptance of bribes by the Chief of the Finance and Budget Office. Both men were prosecuted by a military court and received prison terms. After that, the JGS ordered a new bid and the contract offer amounted to 10 percent less than the previous contract.

The last case was a payoff by a reserve officer candidate at Thu Duc who wanted to get an assignment to the Commissary Department. One day, while calling on the AG/JGS, a Catholic priest from Ho Nai, Duc Tu District, Bien Hoa Province, mentioned that his nephew, a Thu Duc reserve officer, had to pay money in order to get an assignment with the Commissary Department. Since this was a good opportunity to obtain the truth, the AG/JGS eagerly pressed the priest for further details. After a moment's hesitation, the priest said he knew nothing more than his nephew's complaint and had no idea who had asked for the money and to whom the money had been paid. The AG insisted and, after promising to protect the priest's nephew and not to impose severe sanctions on the perpetrator, asserted that he just wanted to help in the fight against a social ill which had caused so many problems for the RVNAF. Finally the priest gave the AG his nephew's name and asked him to keep his word.

In the end, the AG had to call the priest's nephew to his office, reiterated his promise, and requested help. The young officer said his mother had given an aspirant named Thuat, who lived in Saigon, 50,000 piasters to take care of the assignment. A check of individual records revealed that Aspirant Thuat was working at the clothing production center of the Quartermaster Corps. Under questioning, the suspect admitted to having accepted 50,000 piasters from the officer to support a poor but large family, that he had not shared the money with anyone else, and he had acted alone on the knowledge that the officer would be assigned to a sedentary position for family reasons. He had just gambled and won. True to his word to the priest, the AG gave Aspirant Thuat only 50 days of confinement and transferred him to a combat unit in II CTZ.

Based on lessons learned from these cases, during the first quarter of 1967 the JGS undertook a vigorous shakeup with the RVNAF, which resulted in the removal from office and discharge of more than half a dozen general officers and over forty field-grade officers. Many had held key positions, such as corps and division commander, chief of central departments, and province chief.[9] This purge had taken place not because of proven corruption charges, but only on the strength of widespread military and popular rumors that these officers had been involved in corrupt practices. It restored faith among servicemen in the JGS's resolve to clean up the armed forces and enjoined other key cadres to stay pure. To avoid JGS action, which was sure to come sooner or later, a number of military personnel who had enriched themselves through devious means took advantage of election laws under the Second Republic and ran for seats in the National Assembly. Some succeeded and gained immunity as representatives or senators. Others, less lucky, were allowed to leave the armed forces for good.

• • •

Corruption as a National Problem

Not until the end of 1970 did anticorruption become a national concern. Vice President Tran Van Huong was then assigned the job of fighting corruption nationwide. The entrusting of such a vital task to the vice president initially revived hopes among the RVNAF ranks. It sounded the alarm for those who were involved in or tempted toward corruption. There was no doubt that Mr. Huong, with his record of probity, his frugal living, his resolve, his welcoming all kinds of information on corrupt acts, and especially his instructions for all civil and military cadres to make public their assets every year, earned the respect and admiration of all. The only matter of concern for the Vietnamese people and armed forces was his advanced age and failing health and the honesty of his entourage. "He is uncorruptible, but is his entourage?" everybody seemed to ask.

For the RVNAF, the effort to combat corruption was once again resumed. Planning, coordination, and supervision were entrusted to a committee composed of commanders of services, combat arms, and technical services, under Lieutenant General Nguyen Van La, Deputy Chief/JGS, serving as chairman, and the Assistant Chief of Staff/J-5 as secretary.

• • •

As a result of its efforts, during 1970–1972 the JGS succeeded in uncovering several important cases of corruption through the process of inspections and investigations. The 2nd Recruitment and Induction Center was found guilty of defrauding draftees of their food allowances. The 16th Armored Squadron in Dinh Tuong Province sold fuel allocated for combat operations. The 47th Regiment wangled equipment from a US camp in Pleiku being turned over to ARVN control. The committee in charge of receiving Camp Radcliff from the 4th US Infantry Division in An Khe was guilty of dereliction of duty, which resulted in robbery of materials and of complicity with military and civilian groups in the removal of equipment for private use. An artillery battalion of the 18th Division, stationed in Bien Hoa, loaned space in its rear base for the storage of goods spirited from the Saigon docks. Rear base personnel of the 3rd Ranger Brigade near Camp Long Binh rented out military vehicles to transport rice for a businessman in Long Khanh Province. However, there was not a single case of corruption involving the transfer and reassignment of personnel.

Strong actions were subsequently taken against the commanders of units found guilty of charges, to include severe disciplinary punishment, removal from office, demotion, and court-martial. Despite this, both the public and the military believed that this anticorruption campaign had struck only the poor small fry, leaving quite intact the big sharks in higher places.

The Corruption Upheaval of 1974–1975

While the campaign was making great progress, the NVA launched an all-out invasion across the Ben Hai River in the spring of 1972. All efforts were, therefore, devoted to stopping the enemy and regaining the territory lost during this offensive.

• • •

The campaign to prevent and fight corruption in the RVNAF, therefore, was relegated to an obscure background, only to resume in 1974, when conditions for corruption had virtually evaporated. Supplies for US forces were no longer available, commodities for the American PX system had tapered off, US camps had been turned over, and all new properties had been properly accounted for. Meanwhile, commodities of the Vietnamese commissary system consisted mostly of domestic and less attractive products; the canned food program and the monthly allowance of rice as a supplemental food allocation had been cut off; and fuels, building materials, and other supplies were no longer as abundant as they had been before aid cutbacks. As a result, the RVNAF anticorruption campaign, during the post-cease-fire period, focused on only four key areas: ghost and ornamental troops, transfers and assignments, contract bidding, and military property.

The most infamous corrupt activity during this period involved ghost and ornamental soldiers. Ghost soldiers referred primarily to those KIA, MIA, or deserters who somehow managed to sign for their pay; although their names had been removed from personnel rosters, they still figured on the payrolls. Ghost soldiers also included those whose names were carried on the unit personnel roster but who were not normally present in the unit because they had been loaned out on official or unofficial duty or authorized to stay at home to practice their private professions. Ornamental troops were used for just that purpose, as decorations for offices and nothing else. Most of these troops were not authorized by TO&E and had been transferred or [were] on loan from combat units.

The evil of ghost and ornamental soldiers had surfaced years before in MR-4, chiefly among RF and PF units. It had been a major target for Lieutenant General Ngo Quang Truong, then MR-4 commander, who succeeded in keeping it under control. By 1974, however, it was a common belief that the scourge of ghost and ornamental troops had broken out again among Regional and Popular Forces of the Mekong Delta. There were good indications that the actual combat strength of RF companies was much lower than reported. A JGS delegation, under the leadership of the J-3/JGS, was formed to determine why the RF and PF in MR-4 had suffered so many casualties as reported. During its one-month mission, this fact-finding delegation made unannounced visits to a number of outposts and RF companies located throughout the 16 provinces of the Mekong Delta. It found hard evidence that the shortage of combat troops had been due, among other things, to the "ghost" and "ornamental" group problem and to insufficient replacements, both of which boosted casualty figures to an abnormally high level.

To secure the president's support for a vital enterprise which would surely affect the interests, pride, and honor of certain influential military and government officials, the JGS recommended and received presidential approval for a program designed to improve territorial forces, including a nationwide campaign against "ghost" and "ornamental" troops. This effort would start with the RF and PF in MR-4. Lieutenant General Nguyen Vinh Nghi, IV Corps commander, was appointed by the president to lead the campaign in MR-4, with the assistance provided by the JGS; he was to report results every three months.

The campaign started by granting a seven-day grace period, during which every unit within the region was to reexamine its ghost and ornamental troops problem, recall all personnel on loan within or outside the unit, and put an end to the practice. The grace period over, the MR-4 commander launched a campaign to combat the problems of ghost and ornamental troops and indiscriminate personnel loan, inform and educate the troops about it, call for everyone's cooperation, and inflict severe and immediate punishments in case of recidivism. Apart from its own resources, MR-4 headquarters received substantial assistance from the JGS. Two hundred officer students from the

Political Warfare College, organized into teams and cells, went out to RF companies and battalions to help commanders set up activities programs and to report to the General Political Warfare Department on the actual state of these units with respect to morale, personnel, supply, administration, and pay in order to facilitate future project planning. Ten personnel and finance teams—representing the AG/JGS, the Data Processing Center, and the General Directorate of Finance and Audit—were simultaneously sent to sectors, particularly those with high personnel strength. Each team was responsible for checking individual records against personnel reports, verifying desertion reports and personnel absent from the unit, and comparing personnel on rosters against those on the payroll. In case of doubt, the team made an unexpected head count against the strength reported to be present.

In addition, the MR-4 commander formed 16 inspection teams with personnel under his command, each headed by a field-grade officer. Each team worked with one sector and was responsible for checking into the problems of personnel administration handled by the sector's AG section, and payroll disbursement by the administrative and logistic support center.

After three months, the MR-4 commander and the assistance teams provided by the JGS and GPWD discovered and accomplished several things. The problem of ghost and ornamental troops was found to be prevalent in most sectors under MR-4 command. Loaning personnel to outside agencies, granting personnel permission to pursue private occupations at home, and delay in removing deserters from payroll were the three most common irregularities. This campaign brought new hopes to RF and PF commanders, who expected to receive more combat troops because all personnel on loan were recalled, and the problem virtually solved. In addition, deserters were promptly reported, removed from unit rosters, and their pay immediately stopped. As a result of this action alone, the amount of payroll money returned to the Treasury exceeded 600 million piasters.

• • •

At the time this campaign was making excellent progress, the Inspector General's Directorate was concluding its painful and drawn-out inquiry into corruption charges involving ghost and ornamental soldiers, position buying and selling, contributions to commanders, [and] illegal use of military vehicles and building materials in the 5th and 25th Infantry Divisions. Because the charges involved two division commanders whose appointment and removal were under presidential authority, the Inspector General's Directorate submitted both cases to the president for decision. This decision took a long time to come. He finally made a severe decision, but when it was publicized the anticorruption movement initiated by opposition political and religious groups had reached such a momentum that his good intent was somewhat eclipsed. Many believed, therefore, that he had made the decision not out of a sincere desire to eradicate corruption, but rather under irresistible pressure from religious groups.

Apart from severe actions, such as maximum disciplinary punishments, removal from office, demotion, discharge, [and] trial by a court-martial against corrupt elements caught in flagrante delicto, the JGS also cleaned its own house through the discharge of a few generals and of more than 4,000 field- and company-grade officers who either had a tainted past or were too old. This clean-up movement restored the faith of many servicemen in the GVN resolve to keep the RVNAF healthy, but it also caused a great deal of resentment and allegations of "ingratitude and dumping" on the part of those discharged.

By that time the anticorruption movement, which had been started by religious groups and later joined by opposition representatives and senators, was gaining intensity. At first the protesters simply asked that the government take concrete actions to clean its own house. The press subsequently carried accusations of corrupt acts by high GVN and military officials, including the MR-4 and MR-2 commanders and the national security advisor to the president. The MR-4 commander countered with a point-by-point defense in the newspaper, but to no avail. The president decided to remove the MR-4 commander and put him in charge of the Infantry School; he also removed the MR-2 commander and made him Chief of Armor Corps without so much as an inquiry, leaving many questions unanswered among the military. As for the national security advisor, the president apparently took no action. Following another turn of the screw, the movement accused the president himself of corrupt practices through news editorials, leaflets, and sermons which seemed to be pushing things to [a] tragic showdown. According to the RVN laws, only the president had the authority to act in cleaning up the government and the armed forces, especially with regard to the removal of generals and officers whom he had appointed to hold key positions in the GVN, RVNAF, and police. Now that his personal integrity was being questioned, whether justly or unjustly, how could he correct anyone?

Corruption was a burning issue not only in South Vietnamese politics, but in American politics as well. Congressman Aspin, for example, brought the problem of RVNAF corruption to the House floor, citing a case in point known among Vietnamese logistic circles as the Hoc Mon case. In early 1975 . . . the US Defense Attaché handed me a telegram from the US Defense Department asking for details about an alleged sale by the RVNAF to businessmen of helicopter rotor blades and parts that were still stocked in Hoc Mon, Gia Dinh Province. The charge had been made by Congressman Aspin. I was shocked, and could hardly speak. I was filled with wrath for the unscrupulous perpetrators, and with pity for the country, which must have reached its ignoble end to have produced such rotten children.

Fortunately, we were able to lay our hands on the heaps of scrap metal in Hoc Mon during our inquiry. We quickly gathered a team of US DAO personnel, VNAF, judicial MP, and National Police to locate these heaps of metal. It wasn't hard to locate them and their owner, who presented completed sales papers from PDO [Property Disposal Office] in Long Binh. VNAF and US DAO specialists, after some digging into the heaps, were able to find helicopter rotor blades and parts, but they were all scraps. The truth was that simple. And the RVNAF emerged from it all, fully vindicated of the corruption allegations.

Scarcely had the political storm subsided when the Communist hurricane arose.

Phuoc Long . . . fell under NVA massive attacks in early 1975. Then Tay Ninh . . . and the provincial capital of Kien Tuong in MR-4 came under attack. Next came the fall of the provincial capital of Ban Me Thuot on 10 March 1975. Both the campaign designed to fight corruption in the RVNAF and the movement to demand a government clean-up gave place to an all-out effort to resist outside Communist invaders who were a thousand times more dangerous than the corrupt enemy from within.

Observations

Corruption did exist in the RVNAF, beginning with the area of finance and subsequently spreading to other areas. The opportunities for corruption proliferated with the escalation of the war, the division of decadence in society, and the impoverishment of servicemen of all ranks. It was not easy to determine the exact number of corrupt servicemen or the effect of corruption on the RVNAF performance. We only knew for certain that opinion in the military and civilian population focused on a small number of general officers in high military and government positions. We also found that an MR which had an honest, just, and impartial commander was least affected by corruption. Conversely, a unit or organization which was unfortunate enough to have a dishonest and greedy commander was certainly plagued by widespread corruption involving almost everyone from the top to the lowest level. In such a case, the troops were discontented, morale was low, equipment became unserviceable, and finally the unit's performance suffered. Cases in point were the 5th and 25th Infantry Divisions under the command of Brigadier General Tran Quoc Lich and Brigadier General Le Van Tu, respectively. Of course, even a unit or organization with an honest commander also had problems with corruption; however, it was usually detected, occurred only surreptitiously, and was perpetrated only by subordinates.

The effort to control and stamp out corruption in the RVNAF was made in all areas and by all echelons of command. It did deter corruption-minded servicemen, but did not eradicate the evil. Indeed, controlling and stamping out corruption while fighting a hot war was an indescribably complex and difficult undertaking.

• • •

The practice of transferring some personnel who had been charged with corruption in the news media to higher positions made bad men contemptuous, discouraged good and well-meaning men, and deterred investigative agencies.

The South Vietnamese press, generally unfaithful to the common cause, had poisoned the public and servicemen alike. After the gate was opened for the flood of complaints and charges to flow in from the military and the populace, the Inspector General's Directorate estimated that only 15 to 20 percent of the charges were substantiated, the rest being mere hearsay.

• • •

XIV. OBSERVATIONS AND CONCLUSIONS

During the twenty years of direct US military aid and advisory assistance, the Vietnamese armed forces expanded rapidly and matured. This was especially true during the eight years of fighting alongside US and FWMA forces.

To reach the force structure level of 1.1 million, the RVNAF had practically absorbed all manpower available. In fact, through partial and finally general mobilization, South Vietnam had scraped the bottom of its manpower resources. Every household, therefore, had at least one member in the military service. To maintain that force structure level, the RVNAF depended primarily on 18-year-old draftees, since most men between 19 and 38 years of age were already in the military service. During 1974 even that resource was drying up, and the ability to provide the personnel required was becoming more problematic each day for the GVN.

• • •

The most debilitating effect on our ability to strike back was the permanent commitment of our strategic reserve forces—the Airborne and the Marine Division—in MR-1 for static defense, beginning in mid-1972. The JGS was fully aware of this weakness and tried to recover them in vain. The same predicament affected our corps commanders, who saw themselves unable to use one of their divisions as a strike reserve for each MR. We therefore fought a war without a strategic reserve force, simply because the "hold all" policy espoused by our president had so dictated.

All this seemed to derive from our inability to adapt our force structure organization to the strategic requirements of each period. During the early years, and until 1961, the organization of our forces had been founded on the US concept of mutual defense, which relied on SEATO and the US protective shield. The ARVN was thus shaped into a conventional force with corps and divisions and a field command for operational control, ready to engage an invasion from the north. Concern for territorial security was relegated to a lower priority, as seen through the disbandment of MR headquarters and the low regard for territorial forces. This was a sound organizational concept if the assumption of a Korean-style invasion had been [correct]. But the war broke out not with a bang but with a whimper. It materialized stealthily, through the disruption of security with subversive activities by guerrillas and local forces.

• • •

In spite of our shortcomings in organization and command and control, the RVNAF did earn the respect of their archenemy, the NVA. An editorial published by North Vietnam's "People's Army" in late 1972 indeed gave high marks to the RVNAF and attributed the survival of South Vietnam to their existence. The RVNAF, the editorial remarked, were a powerful, ultra anti-Communist force made up of cadres of the petit bourgeois class. To crush the South Vietnamese regime, therefore, it was mandatory that this force should be destroyed first.

North Vietnam's three-pronged offensive strategy therefore focused on weakening (by proselytizing actions) and destroying (by military action) the RVNAF. Almost all enemy offensive campaigns during the war were conducted with the objective of destroying, attriting, disrupting, or weakening the RVNAF. Our enemy even predetermined quotas of casualties to be inflicted on the RVNAF during each campaign.

Thus, despite individual acts of misconduct or mischief, and regardless of the damage caused to the population, the RVNAF continued to earn the confidence and trust of the South Vietnamese people, who relied on them for protection against Communist violence. This could be readily seen in the pattern of population distribution. People always aggregated in productive communities around or near military bases [or] outposts, where they were sure they enjoyed security and protection. When a military unit relocated, they became concerned, worried, and usually chose to move to another area where they could find protection again. Because of this coexistence and mutual dependence, the people gradually developed a deep attachment toward RVNAF units and shared with them moments of joy or grief over the years.

The RVNAF had always been regarded by political parties, religious and other social groups, as a tightly knit, powerful organization grouping all elite elements of South Vietnamese society. The confidence people placed in the RVNAF was always unswerving, because they could depend on them for protection and owed them the freedom and security they enjoyed. The effectiveness and prestige of the RVNAF was such that every pressure group would look on them for assistance or for the achievement of certain goals, including designs to change the regime.

• • •

But, although engaged in war, the United States only endeavored to defeat the enemy in South Vietnam. It never sought to defeat North Vietnam, the very source of aggression.

The GVN anti-Communist stance proved to be too extreme, too inflexible. It failed to detect and follow the US trend toward accommodation and negotiation. US policy made a turnabout with the Nixon Doctrine, which deescalated the war, negotiated with the enemy for a solution to the war, extricated troops from South Vietnam, and turned over combat responsibility to the RVNAF—in other words, a total disengagement from the war. Despite this, the GVN held fast to its old strategy and did not place enough emphasis on the Vietnamization process in order to revise its national policies accordingly.

Under the Vietnamization program, the United States provided South Vietnam with just enough military aid required for self-defense. The Paris Agreement, therefore, caught South Vietnam in an utterly disadvantageous position, militarily and politically. Even after President Nixon had resigned and the US Congress's attitude toward the war in South Vietnam had become clear, our president still clung to his inflexible war strategy, building his hopes on continued US military aid and support.

Because of this blind trust in the United States, our leaders had become shortsighted. They regarded the US troop withdrawal simply as a strategic redeployment dictated by political needs. They reasoned that, since this redeployment helped the United States cut down on expenditures, the United States could afford to provide more military aid to South Vietnam. Under no condition did they believe that the United States would abandon South Vietnam, for reasons of honor, credibility, and past investment with US blood and money. All of these arguments became themes of indoctrination, and the RVNAF troops believed what their leaders said.

Sincere confidence that the United States would intervene forcefully in retaliation of Communist violations reassured our leaders after the Paris Agreement. The JGS in fact worked out a secret plan with the US 7th Air Force and briefed all corps commanders on procedures to call for this intervention. Our leaders continued to believe in US air intervention, even after the US Congress had expressly forbidden it. They deluded themselves into thinking that perhaps this simply meant that US intervention would take a longer time to come because of the complex procedures involved.

Another delusion entertained by national leadership was that US military aid would continue at the pre-cease-fire level. So, when FY 1975 appropriations were drastically cut back to a level that might adversely affect the RVNAF combat capabilities, President Thieu blamed the JGS for it. In a staff meeting held at the Independence Palace, he said that the United States was always prepared to provide the RVNAF with whatever they needed. The reason for the cutback, he explained, was that the JGS had not come up with proper justifications for our requirements. And he attributed this to the austerity measures enforced by the JGS to save ammunition and fuels.

The loss of Phuoc Long in early January 1975 was perhaps the beginning of suspicion and disillusion. After having met with a fact-finding US congressional delegation in February, our president should have had second thoughts about the future of US military aid. And, when Ban Me Thuot fell into enemy hands in March without the United States even reacting, he found his last hopes completely shattered. And he decided on a new course of action to save what he could within his means.

But it was already too late. For his new strategy to work, it should have been implemented right after the United States decided to disengage from the war in mid-1969. Then, if we had fully realized what Vietnamization really implied for the future and directed all our efforts to its objectives, perhaps we could have developed a new national policy and a new military strategy more in line with our own situation. While there was no guarantee that this new strategy would have changed the final outcome of the war, at least it would have afforded us more time for preparing to meet the ultimate challenge and spared us the disastrous events of 1975 that led to South Vietnam's collapse.

Then the conduct of the war after the cease-fire agreement, under President Thieu's leadership, also puzzled many people because he held all powers for decisions. It seemed that, when the situation got serious, no tactical move could be made without his approval. The impression he gave was that every military action, however small, would affect the domestic political situation, hence it was imperative that he make the decision. This was particularly true concerning the employment of our general reserve forces.

The JGS attempted in vain to extricate the Marine and Airborne Divisions from their static defense role in MR-1; President Thieu was simply not amenable to such a vital move. During inspection trips, he usually gave direct orders to corps commanders; on other occasions he wrote to them personally. Several important actions, therefore, were undertaken without JGS knowledge or control. The unfortunate skirmish with Red Chinese warships in the Paracels in early 1974 was a case in point. He made the decision to take on the Chinese after listening to a briefing by the naval commander of MR-1 without even informing the JGS. Only when the affair turned sour was the JGS informed and asked to provide support. He did not understand or consider that the area of contest lay beyond the effective range of our tactical jet fighters.

Even though he had a substantial staff of aides and advisors, including the JGS, President Thieu seldom fully utilized their services. In the face of difficult decisions, he preferred to think them over, make decisions by himself instead of having the JGS study the course of action available, and give orders directly to field commanders, bypassing the JGS completely. In the case of the Communist attack on Phuoc Long . . . , for example, he maintained direct contact with the III Corps commander to monitor the situation. Then he called the latter and the Chief of the JGS to his office where, after summary discussions, he decided on reinforcing the besieged garrison.

The events that subsequently unfolded during the final months of the RVN shed a clear light on the way President Thieu handled the conduct of the war. In early March, apparently because of the political turmoil in the nation's capital, he decided to redeploy the Airborne Division from MR-1 to Saigon. To fill that void, he ordered that three newly activated marine brigades and one ranger group of the general reserves be moved to MR-1. But when this ranger group was preparing for movement, he decided to assign it to II Corps in Pleiku after Ban Me Thuot fell on 10 March.

Two days after this momentous setback, he invited the prime minister, the Chief of the JGS, and his own assistant for security to a working breakfast, during which he gave them directives about a new strategy. "Hold our prosperous and populated areas," he explained, pointing to the phase lines he had himself drawn across a map of South Vietnam. It was an idea that he had personally conceived and presented as an irreversible decision. He made no attempt to have the JGS study the implications of this new strategic move or develop plans to implement it. Instead, he chose to do everything alone.

On 14 March, therefore, he flew to Cam Ranh with the same entourage and gave orders to the II Corps commander to "redeploy" his forces from Pleiku-Kontum and use these forces to reoccupy Ban Me Thuot at all costs and hold the line there. It is still a matter of debate whether, after this meeting, General Pham Van Phu, the II Corps commander, received any other directives from the president. In any event, the way he implemented President Thieu's orders clearly indicated that the redeployment of forces really meant an abandonment of Pleiku and Kontum.

The same personal touch also affected the events in MR-1 during the following days. President Thieu again summoned the I Corps commander to his office to expound his new strategy and gave him the directives to carry it out. On 19 March he again called General Truong to his palace. During this meeting Truong presented his own plans, which centered on holding three enclaves: Hue, Danang, and Chu Lai. But President Thieu listened without making any decisions. Apparently he was having second thoughts about his new strategy, the way it had been implemented so far, and the panic it was causing among the population of MR-1. A few days later he directed the JGS to inform the I Corps commander that he could not support the defense of Hue and Chu Lai and it was up to the I Corps commander to redeploy his forces for the defense of Danang.

It was obvious from these events that the JGS no longer had any control over the course of the war. This evidently annoyed the US Army Chief of Staff, General Fred C. Weyand, who visited South Vietnam at that time. During the last meeting he attended at the Independence Palace on 26 March, he bluntly asked: "Who runs the war?" and recommended that the JGS be given more authority in the conduct of the war.

But, even if the JGS had been given more authority, there was perhaps little it could have done to tilt the balance of force to our favor. The fact was that the RVNAF were hardly organized and equipped to handle the post-cease-fire situation. It was true that they had been expanded and modernized through the Vietnamization process, but it had never been assumed that they could defeat the North Vietnamese Army without US air support. So, as soon as the last US troop and plane had left, and particularly after the US Congress had tied the US president's hands in the use of the US Air Force in South Vietnam, the RVNAF found themselves in desperate need of the kind of tactical air support that had helped them win so many battles. Then even our supplies, which had been promised by the United States, dwindled with each fiscal year.

This became so critical in 1974 that our Chief of the JGS, when briefing all US visitors, likened our position to that of a boxer fighting with a hand tied behind him against a fierce opponent who became stronger and stronger after each round.

Indeed, with greatly reduced supplies and the uncertain future of military aid, our forces fought on without much self-assurance. Appeals by our president to fight a "poor man's war" did little to help improve things. Their only effect was to confuse our troops and raise more doubts about the prospects of continued US support, from which our strength derived.

Our enemy, in the meantime, made the most of the cease-fire agreement. Now immune from US airstrikes, he brought more troops and equipment into the South, not only to replace losses but also to augment and modernize his forces. His infiltration route became a highway system on which convoys rolled around the clock from the 17th parallel to Tay Ninh. His supply storage system along this route was modernized with prefabricated warehouses built in the open and a long fuel pipeline that enabled his trucks to keep rolling. The RVNAF remained impotent in the face of all these war preparations. The task of interdicting or destroying this lifeline was simply beyond our capabilities. As 1974 drew to an end, therefore, it was very clear that the balance of power had changed and South Vietnam was crippled by shortages in supply.

The final collapse of South Vietnam was primarily a disintegration of morale that had been accelerated by a panicky population and undispelled rumors of an American sellout. For years the RVNAF had built their strength and morale on military aid and the support of the United States. Evidently only the United States could have saved South Vietnam from this terrible collapse of 1975.

NOTES

1. The National Leadership Committee consisted of ten members: Lieutenant General Nguyen Van Thieu, Chairman and chief of state; Major General Nguyen Cao Ky, vice chairman and prime minister; Lieutenant General Nguyen Duc Thang, secretary; Lieutenant General Nguyen Huu Co, minister of war and development; General Cao Van Vien, Chief, JGS; four corps commanders; and the CMD commander.

2. Province chiefs concurrently serving as sector commanders were appointed by the Chairman of the NLC, and district chiefs serving as subsector commanders were appointed by the chairman of the Central Executive Committee (prime minister).

3. President Nguyen Van Thieu was among the graduates of this school's first class.

4. After graduating the first class of reserve officers (among them Vice President Nguyen Cao Ky), Nam Dinh was merged with the Thu Duc Reserve Officer School in 1952.

5. The Regional Technical Training Center of MR-1 had also the additional responsibility of training paratroopers.

6. Prior to 1964 the RF and PF were not eligible for family allowance.

7. At 1967 prices VN $200 bought 21 kilos of rice, the average monthly consumption of an adult.

8. *Vietnamese Military History,* vol. IV (Saigon: Military History Division, J-5/JGS, 1972).

9. Among those discharged there were Lieutenant General Nguyen Huu Co, then deputy prime minister and minister of war (formerly a corps commander); Major General Bui Huu Nhon, Deputy Chief of Staff, JGS for Logistics (formerly a division commander); Brigadier General Nguyen Thanh Xang, commander of the 25th Infantry Division; Brigadier General Pham Dang Lan, chief of the Engineer Department; and Colonel Xam Tan Phuoc, chief of Kien Giang Province.

2

Strategy and Tactics

Colonel Hoang Ngoc Lung

PREFACE

During the war years, the Republic of Vietnam and the United States pursued a common goal; their armed forces fought against the same enemy, under the same campaign plan, with the same weapon systems, and in the same environment.

The strategic approaches to fighting this war, however, evolved through several stages, depending on the enemy's kind of warfare and force structure; so did the tactics designed to counter his large-unit and guerrilla activities. This monograph endeavors, therefore, to trace back and evaluate our strategic alternatives at each stage of the war and the evolving tactics employed, with particular emphasis on the period of American withdrawal and reduced support.

In the preparation of this monograph, I have expressly confined my discussions of strategy to its military aspect. While this conforms to the limited scope of a military subject, the encompassing nature of strategy, especially one conceived to face the enemy's approach to total war, implies that for a better understanding of military strategy the interplay of social, political, and economic factors should also be brought in as a backdrop. Therefore, wherever appropriate I have found it necessary to place strategic discussions in the total war context. . . . [10 July 1978]

I. INTRODUCTION

North Vietnam's National Objectives and Basic Strategy

The Geneva Accords concluded on 20 July 1954 divided Vietnam into two zones clearly demarcated along the 17th parallel. The North adopted a single-party, totalitarian, socialist regime, while the South had a nationalist government in which pluralism and free enterprise were encouraged. The war that lasted from 1946 to 1954 had come to an end, and the political solution provided for by the Geneva Accords called for a general election to be held two years later to reunify the country.

Peace was necessary for North Vietnam to rebuild its society and heal the wounds of war; in the preceding years the North was the scene of the heaviest fighting of the war. The economy was a shambles; agricultural production fell short of the people's requirements (the annual shortage amounted to approximately 250 thousand tons of rice) and created a need for imports. Highways, bridges, and railroads were in bad condition. Light industries, still in their infancy, were dispersed throughout the country. North Vietnam's military forces, which had so decisively defeated the French at Dien Bien Phu, were strong but in urgent need of reorganization; they had been expanded greatly but irregularly during the war.

The task of rebuilding the country and consolidating its political power required more than two years for the northern leadership to accomplish. This is why South Vietnam's rejection of the 1956 general election occasioned only a diplomatic, though strong, protest from the North.[1]

• • •

Meanwhile, the situation was deteriorating day by day for the Communists in South Vietnam. Out of 50,000 Communist cadres left behind in the South, only 10,000 members were still active by 1959. The remaining 40,000 either rallied to the South Vietnamese government or simply vanished; that is, moved away and quietly stopped operating for the Communists. It came to a point where a district-level Communist cadre, for example, had to serve both as district and village commissar. Sometimes there were no officers at all.

The growing South Vietnamese strength eventually forced the North to reexamine its strategy. In May 1959, at a general meeting of its Central Executive Committee, the Workers' (Communist) Party of North Vietnam decided upon the liberation of South Vietnam. The first step would be to infiltrate the South with cadres that had gone north in 1954. In order to do this, a logistics system would be required. Consequently the North Vietnamese Army established Group 559 with the mission of directing and supporting the infiltration of men, weapons, ammunition, and explosives into the South.

In September 1960, during its Third General Assembly, North Vietnam's Workers' Party officially decided that the twofold strategic goal of the North would be 1) to carry on the building of socialism in the North, and 2) to start the revolutionary war of liberation in the South. The liberation of the South was perceived as a long-term arduous struggle at all levels. The aim was to establish, strengthen, and develop a popular front in the South that gave the appearance of a spontaneous movement by the people to overthrow the government. For that purpose, the National Liberation Front of South Vietnam officially came into being on 20 December 1960.

• • •

The leaders and soldiers who were to carry out the strategy in the South were former Communist cadres and soldiers who had gone north in 1954. Travelling in small groups of 40 to 50, and later in larger groups of 300 to 500, they began infiltrating in 1959, following land routes leading from North Vietnam's Military Region 4 through lower Laos into Quang Tri and Quang Nam in the 1st Military Region and Kontum in the 2nd Military Region of the Republic of Vietnam.

• • •

Once in the South, these infiltrators were sent to Communist-organized areas in accordance with needs and priorities, where they began to assemble regular armed units. In time these units grew from company size to battalions, and in 1961 the first two Communist regiments were organized in South Vietnam. At the same time, Communist guerrillas and their supporting infrastructure were developed, reaching a strength of 20,000 personnel in 1961. By 1963 nearly all of the southern cadres had been returned to the South and North Vietnam began to infiltrate northern cadres and troops.

At the end of 1964, taking advantage of the deterioration of the military and security situation caused by a period of political turmoil in the South, North Vietnam dispatched entire main-force regiments southward.

• • •

South Vietnamese National Objectives and Basic Strategy

Although North Vietnam in the post–Geneva [Accords] era encountered numerous difficulties, South Vietnam was beset with even greater political problems as internal struggles wrecked the country. The situation was serious enough to prompt foreign observers to predict the demise of South Vietnam within two years after Geneva.

The National Army of Vietnam was in the hands of a chief of the General Staff, Major General Nguyen Van Hinh, who was in open and hostile opposition to the government. The military units of the Hoa Hao and Cao Dai religious sects, as well as the National Police Force which was controlled by the Binh Xuyen, carved out their own fiefdoms and enjoyed near autonomy in their regions.[2]

After restoring the authority of the government and regaining control of the armed forces (Major General Hinh was replaced by Major General Le Van Ty), the government of Ngo Dinh Diem proclaimed the founding of the First Republic of South Vietnam on 26 October 1955. President Diem espoused the doctrine of personalism as a response to Communist dogma and embarked on a reorganization of the forces to meet the threat of invasion from the North.

• • •

While the period from 1954 to 1959 was sufficient for the North to strengthen its internal political system and armed forces, the same period saw the South torn by dissension and weakened by political instability. The aborted coup of 11 November 1960, attempted by three paratroop battalions, set a precedent for the repeated use of the armed forces to seize power. Such attempts were successful twice—during the revolution of 11 November 1963 and the coup of 30 January 1964—and forced South Vietnamese leaders to keep a close watch over the armed forces [and] to personally appoint and supervise the commanders of elite general reserve units such as the Airborne and Marine Divisions, as well as the commanders of the key infantry divisions stationed in the 3rd and 4th Military Regions.

The fear of coups affected the attitudes and methods of control used by all presidents and chiefs of state (except for the civilian chief of state Phan Khac Suu, who enjoyed no real authority); they insisted on the power to appoint commanders of corps and divisions, mainly on the basis of personal loyalty, and required that direct orders from the Independence Palace were necessary for any significant deployments of units, especially those from the general reserve and those stationed around the city of Saigon.

The pervasive presidential distrust of the military eroded the armed forces' efficiency and created factionalism in the RVNAF. Military leaders at all levels were frequently preoccupied with internal problems and consequently had little time to study the enemy situation. Politics invaded the military, and it was not the kind of beneficial political consciousness that all patriotic soldiers should have, but the politics of survival of the particular regime in power at the time. The true mission of the armed forces, to defeat Communist aggression, was repeatedly neglected in favor of the unspoken concern to prevent an overthrow of the government.

Building political strength through motivating the people's participation in national defense, originated during the First Republic, was pursued as a national goal by every subsequent South Vietnamese administration. The concept of popular self-defense, aided by military and paramilitary forces, was aimed at establishing and maintaining security, which was the basic condition for realizing political, economic, and social objectives. This concept, the implementation of which kept changing with new experiences and increased American support, emerged under various guises: Strategic Hamlets, New Life Hamlets, Pacification, and Rural Construction and Development. But the end always remained popular participation in and support of the national policy to confront the Communists in military, political, economic, and social areas; to confront the enemy in two fundamental aspects of the people's war waged in the South by the Communists: a popular war and a total war.

• • •

II. EARLY STRATEGIES

Pacification

• • •

It was not until after the Geneva Accords were signed in 1954 that a new political consciousness was crystallized in the South with the establishment of the First Republic, and this political entity took its rightful place in the pacification planning and execution in South Vietnam.

Strategy under the First Republic of South Vietnam

The central characteristic of the South Vietnamese strategy was that it was defensive. This reflected the status of the South, born under difficult political circumstances after the 1954 Geneva Accords and whose national goal was nothing more than to build a free democracy with genuine sovereignty and protection from the aggressive designs of the Communists from the North. From a military point of view, North Vietnam, having trained, grown, and tested its forces and military commanders up to division level in the battles of the war of 1946–1954, had clear military superiority over the South.

The military threat from the North was envisaged by President Ngo Dinh Diem as appearing in two forms. The first was the threat of subversion created in the South by Communist military forces and Communist Party members who stayed behind instead of going north as stipulated in the 1954 Geneva Accords. The second was the threat of invasion by regular North Vietnamese troops. To face this dual threat, the South's military strategy was designed to protect the territory against an invasion across its borders and to counter subversive activities within. The two key elements of the strategy called for 1) reorganizing the army to protect the frontiers, and 2) gaining the support of the people through the Strategic Hamlet program. The task of defending national territory devolved mainly on the regular forces, aided by paramilitary forces. The regular forces were responsible for defending the borders against invasion and served as the general reserve; the paramilitary forces provided area defense, maintained law and order, and carried out pacification and antisubversive operations.

• • •

Improving Communications and Control

When North Vietnam made plans to conquer the South in 1958, one of its major considerations was the introduction of men and weapons. Securing a safe infiltration route for this purpose was therefore a [fundamental] task to be achieved above everything else. During the survey process, Hanoi's agents reconnoitered all access roads along the Laotian panhandle's eastern area and the western border strip of upper South Vietnam. The major task of putting this infiltration road system together and testing its practicability was eventually assigned to a team led by an elderly southern-born cadre who had reputed knowledge of local road communications. This man made a long journey in the reverse direction, departing from South Vietnam and consulting as he progressed north with local Viet Minh agents to select the best practicable route. In time, this famous infiltration route became known to the West as the Ho Chi Minh Trail, an old name dating from the days of the First Indochina War. Many Communist cadres, however, called it the "Old Man Trail" as a special tribute to the man who had pioneered it.

• • •

A study of the provincial organization and boundaries revealed that antiguerrilla operations were rarely undertaken in the border areas between provinces, and coordination between adjacent provinces was poor. The Viet Cong recognized this weakness and exploited it by locating their bases and liaison routes in the boundary regions. President Diem decided to rectify this situation by creating new provinces and boundaries that would centralize the responsibility in the hands of a single province chief for operations against some of the most important Viet Cong installations.

In Military Region 1, Quang Tin Province was created out of parts of Quang Nam and Quang Ngai in order to provide for better operations against the VC Bong Hong secret zone.

Phu Bon Province in Military Region 2 was carved out of four provinces: Pleiku, Binh Dinh, Ban Me Thuot, and Phu Yen. Highway 7B ran through Phu Bon Province and provided one more link between the Highlands (Highway 14) and the coast (Highway 1). By creating Phu Bon, the responsibility for security of this route was centralized.

The vast forested region along the Cambodian border with Ban Me Thuot and Binh Long Provinces could not be adequately covered from the capitals of these two provinces. Infiltration of Communists across the border from Cambodia was occurring unchecked. To deal with this problem, two new provinces, Quang Duc and Phuoc Long, were created.

North of Saigon, in Military Region 3, where the provinces of Binh Duong, Bien Hoa, and Long Khanh met, President Diem created the new province of Phuoc Thanh. This was done to facilitate better control over operations against the VC liaison routes between War Zones C and D that passed through this area, and better coordinate operations in the VC secret zones west of National Route 13, the Boi Loi Woods, Ho Bo Woods, and the Long Nguyen secret zone. (This was the only province created by President Diem that did not survive his demise; it was eliminated when the new government determined that it was unnecessary.)

Another new province was created in Military Region 3: Hau Nghia. This province was constructed from parts of Tay Ninh, Binh Duong, and Long An in order to provide better security along the Cambodian border west of Saigon in the region of the Parrot's Beak and Ba Thu.

Moc Hoa District of Long An Province became a province in Military Region 4, Kien Tuong. It was created to provide better control of Communist infiltration from Svay Rieng Province of Cambodia in the area of the Elephant's Foot. Two other new provinces established in Military Region 4 were Kien Phong and Sa Dec. Together with Kien Tuong, these new provinces provided better coordination for operations against the VC's famous Dong Thap Muoi secret zone, which they boasted was impregnable.

Finally the rich rice-growing region of the lower Mekong Delta, between the provinces of Kien Giang, An Xuyen, Can Tho, and Ba Xuyen, where VC activities were very hard to control, became Chuong Thien Province.

This entire territorial reorganization resulted in positioning provincial centers in key areas where there was intense enemy activity. The results were greater government control of all resources, better defined areas of responsibility, more economical distribution of forces, and greater opportunities for commanders to conduct better surveillance of and operations against the enemy.

Strategic Hamlets

In conjunction with the concepts of the strategic highway network and territorial reorganization, a social problem with important economic and military aspects cried out for attention. South Vietnam had over 800,000 refugees who had moved south after the 1954 treaty and thousands of other destitute people from poverty-stricken Central Vietnam. All these people would have to be resettled and provided opportunities to become self-supporting. Influenced more by military than by humanitarian, political, or economic considerations, the resettlement program, which located the people in areas of military significance such as along strategic highways and in defensive belts around cities, revealed that the leaders of the First Republic recognized that the population was a strategic resource in itself that could be used in the national defense effort, a concept which they developed until it became a national strategy: the strategy of the Strategic Hamlets.

• • •

Agrovilles [fortified communities intended to isolate the rural populace from the enemy] were conceived with two objectives in mind: first, to create conditions favorable to economic and social development in rural areas; and second, to contribute to the maintenance of local security.

As a rule, agrovilles were built in areas formerly controlled by the enemy and along main arteries of communication in order to form secure corridors for the flow of traffic and commerce and for rescue missions to arrive from other areas. As incentives to encourage people to settle in agrovilles, and to facilitate economic and social development, electricity and water, health and educational facilities, and marketplaces were provided by the government. . . . A total of 23 agrovilles were built in 11 provinces, involving 32,000 people and 6,000 hectares of land, strung along highways connecting cities such as Saigon, Dalat, Hue, and Danang.

The Agroville program was flawed in that it created a completely new basic administrative unit. The people, raised in and accustomed to the hamlet as the basic social and administrative unit, had difficulty identifying with the agroville. Further, because each agroville assembled a large population of three to four thousand in a comparatively large area, defense and internal control became extremely difficult and were thus neglected.

With the demise of the Agroville program in 1961, another idea went through a test in various localities and was finally proclaimed as a national policy in March 1962: the strategic hamlets. Hamlets were called strategic because they were the basic administrative units of the country and the very foundation of the program. They were to be built on a plan whose objective was to make changes in four areas: defense, politics, economics, and [culture].

• • •

The revolution of 1 November 1963 toppled the First Republic. Immediately after the coup, Lieutenant General Ton That Dinh, the minister of interior for the new government, declared to newsmen that the Strategic Hamlet program of the house of Ngo had to be abolished. This statement was later denied by other members of the Revolutionary Committee, but a large number of strategic hamlets were dismantled by the Communists, who took advantage of the troubled situation. Nevertheless, the Strategic Hamlet program was regarded by all subsequent governments as having strategic value, and with certain improvements and American aid the South still considered pacification and rural development as the basis of a grand national strategy.

III. STRATEGY DURING THE PERIOD
OF US PARTICIPATION

The demise of the First Republic was followed by a period of political instability. This political instability eroded military security because high-ranking military leaders were more preoccupied with internal fighting. Communist strength grew apace and there were indications that the third strategic stage, a general offensive, was imminent.

• • •

The South's strategy during the period of participation by American forces in the Vietnam War, from March 1965 to 27 January 1973, could be encapsulated in three main tasks: 1) continue the effort of pacification and rural development; 2) dismantle the enemy infrastructure through Operation Phoenix; and 3) expand and modernize the armed forces in accordance with Vietnamization.

Pacification and Rural Development

The Strategic Hamlet program of the First Republic, though severely criticized, was regarded by succeeding leaders of the South as the basic strategy to counter the North's plan to take over South Vietnam. Modifications in the techniques of execution were required, however, to correct weaknesses and to profit by the experiences of the First Republic. The Plan for Victory (Chien Thang), made official in March 1964, required some modifications, the first of which was renaming strategic hamlets; they became "New Life" hamlets.

The Victory Plan was based on the oil slick principle, implementing pacification first in heavily populated and prosperous areas, and gradually spreading to less populated and less prosperous ones.

• • •

Until the mission of the RVNAF was clearly defined as being primarily pacification, the RVNAF had to split its resources between military operations and pacification support. In 1965 this mission was defined as pacification support, but it was not until 1966 that the RVNAF was really ready to assume the mission. Units had to be trained in the pacification effort, in civic action, and in techniques to gain the support of the people.

• • •

The mission of the RVNAF, in their supporting role [in] the pacification and rural development, consisted of conducting mopping-up operations of areas chosen for pacification; establishing, improving, and maintaining security in those areas at a high level until the revolutionary development project had been achieved; and, at the same time, protecting developed areas against relapsing into enemy control.

From 1969 on, as the RVNAF gradually regained operational responsibilities, Regional Forces and Popular Forces replaced regular infantry battalions, and infantry divisions would reinforce RF and PF only on order from division tactical zone commanders and in vital areas which RF and PF were incapable of handling. Thus the principal forces that supported the pacification effort were Regional and Popular Forces. RF units provided mobile defense in the areas lying between hamlets and villages, along enemy routes of communication, and set up a distant security belt for PF units. The main objective of RF was VC provincial guerrilla units. PF units served in their own village or hamlet [and] protected the people, the resources, and fixed installations. PF operated in the hamlets and not far away from them; their main targets were local guerrilla units.

Compared with the pacification effort of the years 1962 to 1967, the pacification and rural development effort of the years after 1967 registered marked improvement on several fronts. In terms of commitment, greater determination was evident in the utilization of regular forces, thus avoiding the criticism that military operations had no connection with pacification.

• • •

An annual combined military plan called Plan AB was developed by the Joint General Staff and the Military Assistance Command, Vietnam (MACV). It spelled out missions and tasks for the RVNAF and US forces, and Free World Military Assistance Forces, in support of pacification and rural development. Serious weaknesses appeared in the plan, however. One was the selection of priority objectives within areas under pacification. Priority objectives were assigned at the provincial level. Priorities were dictated by the security situation, the need for support, the progress of programs, local capabilities, and so on. Though reasonable in principle, this resulted in 44 priority target areas in as many provinces, and no overall priority areas on the national or military region level. The organizational principle of national planning which calls for priorities to be established at the highest level, priorities that correlate to the national strategy, had been reversed. The result was that no two plans for adjacent provinces were mutually compatible, and provincial border areas were ignored. The Communists, capitalizing on the neglect, set up their base areas in these border regions. Each province and district chief looked to the neighboring jurisdiction to handle the problem, but few did.

Another weakness lay in the fact that local authorities frequently selected priority target areas that would lend themselves to easy success so that favorable reports might later be filed with the Central Development Council and favorable evaluations would be made by inspectors.

Another weakness resided in the fact that infantry battalions and regiments were assigned to sector commands in support of the pacification and rural development effort. This meant that division commanders were unable to control their units and divisional staffs had few opportunities to plan operations at the divisional level. Moreover, battalions and regiments assigned to local military authorities were further split into company-sized units so that ultimately it was only at the company level that action was actually performed and experience gained. A serious command and control problem was the result. Although the division commander relinquished control of battalions to sector commanders, the sector commanders actually assumed little control. The battalions still reported to and received orders from their regiments, and all activities and operations by the battalions in support of pacification depended on cooperation and such good will [as] the sector commander could achieve with the battalion commander.

•••

But the most important weakness in the pacification strategy was, up to this point, not even recognized. This was the fact that no concerted action was being taken to destroy the Viet Cong infrastructure (VCI), that complex, widespread apparatus that provided essential support to the military arm of the Viet Cong and directed the entire insurgency effort.

It was true that the government of the First Republic had correctly regarded the VCI as a dangerous force to contend with. As early as 1958, therefore, efforts to eliminate it were carried out in secret under orders from the Independence Palace. President Diem's campaign against the VCI was effective but indiscriminate. By authorizing province chiefs to execute suspects without a hearing, or even a police record, he in effect encouraged abuses. There is little doubt that many political enemies—who were not actually VC—disappeared as a result of the anti-VCI campaign. In any event, Mr. Diem's efforts ended with his overthrow in late 1963.

The successive South Vietnamese governments after him were too beset by power struggles to take any interest in combating the VCI. Lacking direction and guidance, no GVN organization took this task seriously or was equipped to monitor and take action against it.

The armed forces believed that they had no responsibility for action against the VCI; that was the exclusive responsibility of the National Police. The National Police meanwhile were undermanned for the task and ineffective. Therefore, despite suffering heavy losses on the battlefields, the enemy continued his terror and sabotage campaign right in the Saigon metropolitan areas, collected taxes, recruited personnel, and gathered supplies under the very noses of the police.

Not until 1967 was the vital role of the enemy infrastructure perceived, [that it functioned] as the political and administrative arms of the Viet Cong. Its vital missions were to provide support to VC military forces by supplying them with money, food, equipment, medicines, manpower, and services; to prepare for the eventual takeover of the government by securing the allegiance of the people of the South; and to prepare a cadre capable of playing leading roles in a future coalition government.

The importance of the enemy infrastructure was finally realized by the United States. The plan to eliminate the enemy infrastructure, proposed by the United States and approved by the Vietnam government, was put into effect in 1967 and made public under the appellation of Operation Phoenix in August of 1968.

•••

Vietnamization as a term and as a concept was far more important in American politics than it was to the average Vietnamese. In fact, if it hadn't received a great deal of publicity, promoted by the Americans, few Vietnamese would have even heard of it. So far as the Joint General Staff was concerned, which was never briefed on the concept or given guidance by the president, the important event was the expansion and modernization of the RVNAF to meet the growing threat from the North. If the Americans wanted to call that Vietnamization, it was all right, and any senior Vietnamese official was happy to participate in any well-publicized top-level conference with the Americans to discuss this or any other concept. He would gladly put his name to American-drafted proclamations of great purpose because this would serve to enhance his prestige in the eyes of the people and diminish the power of his political opposition.

The trouble with these Vietnamese attitudes was that they missed the vital point: a new strategy had been announced by the Americans. Vietnamization was more than modernization and expansion of the RVNAF; it was essentially a strategy that would require the Vietnamese to survive with greatly reduced American participation. Had President Thieu and the Joint General Staff fully realized this fact, perhaps they would have begun then to build a strategy to cope with it. Instead, the RVNAF made no adjustments in doctrine, organization, or training to compensate for the departure of American troops and firepower.

As a matter of fact, the North Vietnamese reacted much more positively to Vietnamization than did the Southerners. They feared that it would succeed to the extent that a Northern military victory would become increasingly more difficult. Largely for this reason, they launched the 1972 offensive to preempt such success.

The 1972 offensive was followed by the Paris Agreement, which required the absolute withdrawal of American forces, leaving the Republic of Vietnam struggling to find a strategy for survival under new and forbidding circumstances.

The Problem of Survival

The Communist general offensive of the summer of [1972] closed with a cease-fire treaty, a peace agreement. No responsible leader in the South believed, however, that this peace was permanent; war would sooner or later break out again. This peace treaty brought about the withdrawal of all US and allied forces from Vietnam, but did not even discuss the North Vietnamese troops in the South. From then on the balance of military power gradually tipped in favor of North Vietnam. The South Vietnamese leadership knew this, but was comforted by the expectation that strong support from the United States—in terms of military and economic aid and, if necessary, the application of American airpower—would be forthcoming to redress the imbalance if North Vietnam resumed hostilities.

On President Thieu's order, a delegation from the JGS, headed by Lieutenant General Le Nguyen Khang, Chief of Operations, visited each military region to relay to each corps commander instructions to draw up contingency military plans in case of renewed hostilities. These plans were drafted on the assumption that American air support and intervention would be available, especially B-52 bombers, two to three weeks after the war resumed.

National objectives remained unchanged. The RVNAF was charged to regain control of territory that the Communists had captured soon after the cease-fire, to defend occupied territories, and to protect the people. In the confrontations with the NVA that arose, the RVNAF methods of fighting until February 1974 were unchanged; great reliance was placed on fire superiority and mobility. Losses in materiel and expenditures of ammunition had not yet become a matter of concern, because of the promise of one-for-one replacement by the United States, as authorized by the Paris Agreement. The JGS expected American aid to diminish over time, but clung to the belief—based on American assurances—that significant aid cuts would not occur until a genuine peace had been achieved.

• • •

The US decision to reduce military aid to Vietnam during the 1974 fiscal year was made known to the Defense Attaché Office, Saigon (DAO) by the end of September 1973 and was relayed by [the] DAO to [the] JGS in January 1974. By February the JGS had directed combat units to economize on ammunition expenditures, but no strict restrictions were imposed. The reluctance to apply drastic measures was in part due to the abiding faith in the ability of the US administration to sway Congress, and in part to the desire to avert a shock wave from engulfing the armed forces and spreading to the general population.

• • •

In order to live with the cut in military assistance and the plan to develop the nation's economy, the government projected a troop reduction of 100,000. This reduction was to begin in July 1974, affecting first all noncombat units, which could fill only to 85 percent of their authorized strength. No soldiers were ever discharged under the plan because authorized strengths were below the ceiling already. Since the military situation kept worsening day by day, the 100,000 troop slash was abandoned in September 1974.

Now that reduction in personnel could not be carried out, consumption and use of equipment had to be restricted. The Air Force received orders to bring the number of active squadrons from 66 down to 56, and 224 airplanes of all kinds were inactivated. Flying time was reduced; fuel and spare parts supplies were at 65 percent of 1973 levels. The Navy took a cut from 44 to 24 boat units. The artillery could no longer fire harassment and interdiction fire, and daily allowances for 105mm artillery came to eight rounds per tube as compared to 30 rounds in 1972; for 175mm guns the allowance was one round per piece per day. Mortars in outposts could fire no more than three rounds. Soldiers who used to be issued six grenades on each operation now received two. Stories of RF and PF units in IV Corps buying grenades out of their pocket money were, though incredible, nevertheless true.

Such conditions prompted President Thieu to say that the RVNAF had to learn to fight a "poor man's war"; what this poor man's war should entail, however, was never made clear. Its meaning could be reduction in fuel and ammunition consumption, fewer large-scale operations, more small-scale action in their place, and more commando-type actions. But President Thieu never issued such guidance. Old combat tactics were no longer suitable to the new situation.

• • •

These tough problems forced President Thieu into rethinking his strategic position and contemplating territorial defense more commensurate with capabilities. This he once briefly revealed in a meeting of the National Security Council called to review the military situation at the beginning of 1974. In that meeting President Thieu instructed the military region commanders to have ready a plan to abandon part of their territory should it become indefensible, and to determine which part of the territory to relinquish should the need arise. Despite their utmost importance, these instructions were never officially renewed or confirmed and no military region commander obeyed them.

IV. UNITED STATES INFLUENCE ON REPUBLIC OF VIETNAM STRATEGY

Many observers of the Vietnam War have assumed that, because South Vietnam was totally dependent on the United States for the necessary means to defend itself, and because US forces from 1965 to 1968 assumed direct operational responsibilities, the military strategy of the Republic of Vietnam must have closely paralleled that of the United States. It is true that, under these circumstances, US influence could not help but be pervasive. In fact, a survey of the situation in the South from 1954 to 1975 reveals that American influence on the South's strategy varied in direct ratio to the nature and extent of American involvement and assistance in Vietnam.

American Influence in the Pre-Intervention Period

As the leaders of the First Republic assumed the reins of government and the responsibilities for defense, one fact was paramount in their minds: the various factions and sects that each controlled a segment of the nation's military force had to be subdued and the direction of the military effort had to be centralized in the office of the president.

Secondly, the Vietnamese leadership realized that the peace just concluded at Geneva could be temporary; that a future war was possible and that the conflict would be either an invasion from the North, or an insurgency in the South, or a combination of both. If the country were to be adequately prepared, something had to be done immediately to fill the vacuum left by the departure of the French forces, which numbered 235,000 men. The government believed that a national army of 216,000—its strength in 1954—would be required for the defense tasks facing the First Republic.

It was at this point that the first American influence was exerted on the shaping of South Vietnam's military strategy. This influence is recorded in detail in the *Understanding on Development and Training of Autonomous Vietnam Armed Forces,* executed between General J. Lawton Collins and the Government of Vietnam in December 1954.[3] The American view expressed in this document was that South Vietnam needed only the forces required to defeat insurgency; the army would be required to delay an invasion from the North only until SEATO could come to its assistance. For this mission, the Americans would fund a defense establishment of up to 100,000 men.

The Americans also suggested the structure of the Republic's armed forces in some detail. There would be three territorial divisions with a total of 13 security regiments, each with three security battalions. These divisions were the core of the antiguerrilla force. They would also authorize three field divisions, the force that would delay the

North Vietnamese until SEATO would intervene. The general reserve would be one airborne regimental combat team.

• • •

Another American concept promoted by the MAAG during this period was that only a small regular army was required, one that could be rapidly expanded in time of war through a draft of trained reservists. The Vietnamese had no experience with this system and preferred a large standing army of volunteers. The government of Vietnam held that it needed a largely voluntary standing army with few draftees, and conceived of national defense as requiring capabilities to secure areas as well as engaging in mobile defense. Area security, in the government's view, required the activation of regional regiments recruited in local communities and operating in local areas; local recruits would be familiar with the terrain, loyal to their native region, and would give the fullest measure of devotion to their duties. The American view was that the army needed a great deal of mobility, a large number of specialists, and draftees. The MAAG opposed the idea of regional units because regional units would not be strategically mobile. A compromise was finally reached whereby each province would have at least one territorial battalion. The United States also approved three territorial divisions, but while the discussions were going on Vietnam put together the fourth division, presenting the United States with a fait accompli.

• • •

In 1958 all light divisions were disbanded because, in the judgment of General Samuel Williams, chief of the MAAG, they would be no match for regular NVA divisions. Out of the ten divisions, seven identical infantry divisions were formed.

General Williams may have been correct with regard to the inability of the light divisions to handle conventional combat against North Vietnamese regular divisions, but his insistence on forming heavy infantry divisions to deal with them made it apparent that the Americans estimated that SEATO would not be capable of intervening in time if there was an invasion from the North. If not, why should the South organize to repel an invasion rather than simply delay until SEATO forces could be deployed? In any case, while the new infantry divisions might eventually be capable of the mission they were being designed for, there were no light mobile units to move rapidly into remote, difficult terrain against the guerrillas. And, by 1959, the guerrilla threat was growing serious and was, in fact, the only active threat to the nation's security.

President Diem recognized this problem and his administration did something about it. In early 1960 the government ordered each infantry battalion in [the] ARVN to organize one additional company to use in the war against the insurgents. The companies consisted of battle-experienced tough troopers who were lightly equipped and dressed, much the same as their VC adversaries. They wore the black pajamas and Binh Tri Thien sandals and could move quickly and quietly into battle against the VC.[4] These companies, formed without MAAG approval, were the origin of the Vietnamese rangers whose support was picked up by the MAAG in 1961, when the training mission was assigned to the US 5th Special Forces.

Besides the differences in views on regular forces, the MAAG and the government of the First Republic differed on how the Civil Guard and Self-Defense Corps should be organized and controlled. The US concept was manifested in the training program conducted by the Michigan State University Group (MSUG) in Vietnam; the Civil Guard was to be a kind of rural police, equipped with nothing heavier than submachine guns, and organized into small units. The Vietnamese wanted this organization to be a paramilitary force with the capability to assist regular forces and to be organized into large units strong enough to handle actions against local insurgent units.

The desire to strengthen the Civil Guard (and US reluctance to do so) prompted President Diem to negotiate for assistance with Malaysian Prime Minister Tunku Abdul Rahman. The result was a 1960 Malaysian gift to Vietnam of about 600 armored cars of the Ford Lynx and Scout car types for highway security, and 60 Wickham Trolley cars for railroad security. All went to equip the Civil Guard. Additionally, 200,000 shotguns were supplied to the Self-Defense Corps. President Diem was also able to obtain from the Colombo Plan a number of Land Rover jeeps and signal equipment for the Civil Guard.

The Americans eventually came around to the Vietnamese view with regard to the missions and organization of the Civil Guard and the Self-Defense Corps, but the matter of authority over these forces was still an issue in 1960 when the training and equipping of the Civil Guard was transferred by the Americans from the economic aid mission (USOM) to the MAAG. According to the Americans, the Civil Guard and Self-Defense Corps should be transferred from the Ministry of Interior to the Ministry of Defense so that they would respond better to military command. President Diem did not subscribe to this theory. His pragmatic position was that he could better control the internal affairs of the country by placing the Civil Guard and Self-Defense Forces under his minister of interior. He foresaw a potentially unstable condition if he centered too much power and authority in his generals.

Furthermore, Counselor Ngo Dinh Nhu had made it clear on many occasions—during his periodic meetings with the Joint General Staff—that he considered the country's military leadership to be weak, lacking in leadership, and unschooled in strategy and tactics. In short, the military was not capable of assuming responsibility for the paramilitary forces. Nevertheless, responding to pressure from the MAAG, President Diem signed an order in 1961 placing the Civil Guard and Self-Defense Corps under the Ministry of Defense. In fact, however, nothing had changed. The province chiefs, who controlled the local forces as sector commanders and through their subsector commanders, still responded to the minister of interior.

During the years of the First Republic, while the influence of American ideas and American systems was strong in Vietnam, the Vietnamese also looked elsewhere for inspiration and assistance; witness President Diem's contacts with the Colombo Plan and Tunku Abdul Rahman. Another source of influence came out of Malaysia in the person of Sir Robert Thompson. Sir Robert had had considerable experience in the successful British antiguerrilla campaign in Malaysia, and, at the request of President Diem, he brought a small team of advisors to Vietnam. He became the government's police, security, and political warfare advisor.

• • •

Despite such attempts to preserve its independence, however, the imitation of American ways became a fad with many ranking Vietnamese officers. A case in point was the adoption of American-style uniforms.

• • •

US Army training methods and concepts came in with the US Army advisors in 1955 and were adopted by the ARVN. Command and leadership courses were held to retrain officers and noncommissioned officers in everything from the US Army's manual of arms for the rifle to combat tactics and marksmanship with American weapons. These matters were not too difficult for Vietnamese soldiers to accept, but the rigid, harsh American-style discipline of the training camp went down hard. It was just not the Vietnamese way to punish officers and soldiers with pushups for minor infractions of discipline or poor performance.

Two other concepts of training brought by the Americans to Vietnam also caused some difficulties. One was the American insistence that 20-mile marches for soldiers carrying battle gear weighing 30 pounds or more was good training. The painful fact was that the average Vietnamese soldier wasn't built for that kind of exertion in the tropics. The other was the idea that unit training cycles should conclude with regimental- and division-level maneuvers in order to fully exercise the commanders and staffs at different echelons. The trouble was that the war was being fought at that time against small guerrilla bands, and these maneuvers were not only irrelevant but they diverted the troops from active combat responsibilities.

In summary, the American advisors during the First Republic greatly influenced the strategies and methods adopted by the Vietnamese armed forces, but were always ready to compromise and defer to the Vietnamese viewpoint when it became necessary. Perhaps this was a reflection of President Kennedy's stated philosophy to the effect that the United States would provide the means, but the Vietnamese should fight their war in their own way.

Americanization

With time American influence became deeper, especially after the replacement of the First Republic by a succession of governments between 1964 and 1966. The Vietnamese leadership had practically nothing new to propose, while the strategy, except for modifications of the First Republic's Strategic Hamlet program, became Americanized.

In the years from 1965 to 1969, when US forces assumed an active fighting role in Vietnam, military strategy originated at MACV. The RVNAF accepted the responsibility for pacification of populated areas, while American forces carried out search and destroy missions in Communist base areas and along their lines of communication. This strategy of dividing the tasks between the US forces and the RVNAF resulted in heavy Communist losses, but the VCI remained very active and effective.

The destruction of the VCI had been high on the Diem government's priorities, but largely escaped American attention during that period. The reactivation of the effort in the Phoenix program by the Americans was another instance of Americanization, at least as seen by Vietnamese.

• • •

Besides the effect of Americanization on the appearance of the RVNAF and on its equipment and methods of fighting, another effect was much more subtle but of far greater strategic importance: the Americans had designed a purely defensive strategy for Vietnam. It was a strategy that was based on attrition of the enemy through a prolonged defense and made no allowance for decisive offensive action.

• • •

Vo Nguyen Giap observed that the reason the United States imposed restrictions on targets in the North was to prevent the Vietnam War from adversely affecting political, economic, social, and diplomatic objectives of the United States. In other words, the American strategy, according to Giap, was designed to accomplish American objectives. If those objectives happened to coincide with the best interests of South Vietnam, the US-Vietnam alliance was a fortunate one. If not, it was not at all clear that the American strategy was the best for South Vietnam. Nevertheless, given that US support and intervention were at that time critical to the survival of South Vietnam, the leaders of the South had no rational alternative but to accept American leadership in strategy. But this did not mean that there were no voices in dissent offering other strategic ideas.

In 1965, when US forces started pouring into the South, the minister of defense, General Cao Van Vien, wrote a paper entitled "The Strategy of Isolation" in which he likened the task of stopping infiltration to that of turning off the faucet of a water tank. General Vien advocated turning off the faucet through the isolation of North Vietnam. He would fortify a zone along the 17th parallel, from Dong Ha to Savannakhet, and follow this with a landing operation at Vinh or Ha Tinh, just north of the 18th parallel, cutting off the North's front from its rear. In 1972 General Vien published the original paper with the following added conclusions: "In her alliance with the United States, Vietnam was hamstrung in her action, causing her strategy to be confined to the defensive."[5]

• • •

The American defensive–gradual escalation strategy was not only clearly stated by American leaders, it was demonstrated in concrete terms to the South Vietnamese through the Military Assistance Program. In 1974, for example, the most modern planes available to the Vietnamese Air Force were F-5As and A-37s. Although the RVNAF had, in their modernization plans for the years 1969–1972, requested F-104 and F-105 jet fighters, these requests were refused with the explanation that the US Air Force would always be present to provide this sort of capability for South Vietnam.

The RVNAF was equipped with modern weapons only after comparable ones had been employed by the enemy. M-16 rifles were supplied to all RVNAF units only after the 1968 Tet Offensive, when the enemy employed Communist AK-47s in large numbers. Only after the 1971 operation in Laos (Lam Son 719) were M-48 tanks supplied to meet the enemy's T-54s, and 175mm self-propelled guns were furnished to counterbalance the Communist 130mm guns. Following the 1972 Summer Offensive, TOW antitank missiles were supplied after the Communists had employed AT-3 antitank missiles. These modern American weapons were furnished only after the Communists had used theirs on a large scale and had gained military and psychological advantages in doing so.

The Americans, as we have seen, eventually dictated the grand strategy of the conflict. With their monopoly over weaponry and equipment, they also shaped how that strategy would be executed, what tactics and techniques would be employed. It was only a small step to providing the actual impetus and direction to major RVNAF and joint military operations. The Cambodian foray in 1970 and the Laos operation to Tchepone in 1971 came into being only because MACV originated them, promoted them, and supported them.

When the Laos operation ran into difficulty because the North Vietnamese committed their general reserve divisions, MACV proposed throwing an additional Vietnamese infantry division into the fray. The commander of the 2nd ARVN Division was even told by his American advisor to prepare for deployment. President Thieu, however, after meeting with his military staff, decided that the commitment of one more division not only would not improve the situation but would result in heavier losses. Thereupon, he issued orders that this division would not deploy to Laos.

This and other incidents illustrated the fact that, despite the strong American influence during the period of American participation in the war, the allies had a few areas of disagreement. One of the issues of most serious conflict involved the fundamental organization of the armed forces. Whereas MACV always advocated expanding Regional Forces at the expense of the regular forces, the government held to the opposite view and wanted the regular army enlarged and modernized. The American argument was that the cost of an RF unit was considerably less than that of a comparable regular unit. The government conceded that, but thought that the added effectiveness of the regular unit was worth it.

American Influence after Withdrawal

After the Paris Agreement was signed on 28 January 1973, the actual presence of US forces ceased, but US influence persisted almost intact with its impact on the strategy and its execution. In national defense, from organization to operations, from training to combat methods and the utilization of resources and ammunition, nothing much changed until July 1974. Then, confronted by the stark and obvious realities of the decrease in US military assistance, the South sought to find a new strategy to face the deteriorating military situation and the austere budgetary limits.

This matter of dealing with the priorities of a defense budget was a new experience for the RVNAF staff. During the years before the withdrawal of MACV, the RVNAF involvement with the defense budget ended with the presentation of its military requirements. MACV took it from there and determined the priorities and unilaterally managed the execution of the budget.

• • •

In fact, the attempt to adopt new tactics and techniques had only begun when the Communists attacked Ban Me Thuot. The loss of Ban Me Thuot impelled a change in strategy. From the policy and slogan of "Hold All," President Thieu switched to that of "Hold the Southern Half," leaving the northern half of the country undefended. This unexpected change in strategy was never publicly explained by President Thieu and was thought of by the great majority of the people, by the armed forces, and even by high-ranking military officers as the implementation of a secret agreement worked out at the Paris peace talks between the United States and North Vietnam which the government of the South, under tremendous US pressure, had to carry out. Others speculated that it was President Thieu's ploy to force the United States into continuing the commitment it had contracted toward Vietnam. If so, the move failed and the result of this astounding miscalculation was the downfall of the republican form of government and freedom in South Vietnam.

V. THE TACTICS OF THE REPUBLIC OF VIETNAM ARMED FORCES

• • •

A New Direction

In April 1955 the MAAG assumed [responsibility for] the training of the RVNAF infantry. Courses were offered at Fort Benning and Fort Leavenworth for Vietnamese officers. The majority of ranking generals of the RVNAF, including President . . . Thieu and General Cao Van Vien, were trained at Fort Leavenworth after 1956. Vietnamese military schools began to receive US advisors and field manuals. Vietnamese tactics and techniques began to be influenced by American concepts. Up to 1960, however, enemy military activity was insignificant and Vietnamese techniques changed little in practice. Operations conducted to assume control of and pacify areas vacated by Communist troops in accordance with the 1954 Geneva Accords were more political than military. Units had orders to display strength, to win hearts and minds of the people, and to use their weapons only as a last resort. The few military operations that were conducted were opposed by poorly trained, ill-equipped private armies of bandit and religious groups such as the Binh Xuyen in the Rung Sat campaign and the Hoa Hao in the Dinh Tien Hoang and Thoai Ngoc Hau campaigns.

In the meantime, military theory was an area of dispute between two divergent schools of thought, in military schools as well as in the training exercises: one being held by officers still under the influence of French practice and previous battlefield experience, the other by those who had been trained in US military schools. The latter began to gain ascendancy when the RVNAF began receiving armored personnel carriers and helicopters. The employment of these pieces of equipment necessarily entailed the adoption of US techniques and tactics and the help of US advisors.

Armored personnel transport was not new to [the] RVNAF, but heliborne operations constituted a genuinely new dimension in combat. The enemy reacted with surprise and confusion when the RVNAF first used helicopters against him, and this reinforced the confidence of Vietnamese leaders in this tactic. Helicopter assaults eclipsed the parachute assault as the tactic of choice in the RVNAF, although between 1945 and 1954 airborne operations produced brilliant results in audacious raids behind enemy lines. Vietnamese airborne units were the most combat effective in the National Army and had the most fighting experience.

After the treaty of Paris, airborne units continued to play a prominent role as general reserve and strike forces. Even when enemy activities were still weak, paratroopers were used in small operations, most often to rescue outposts or district seats under attacks or pressure. The headquarters of the airborne brigade kept a book containing data on all outposts, district headquarters, and key areas throughout the country. Upon receipt of an order for a rescue mission, the brigade staff would consult the book and select the most favorable drop zone in the area. Assembly time was 45 minutes after issuance of the order; the unit was usually airborne in C-47s an hour later. Normally these missions employed a single company or a company group, but rarely battalion task forces. The largest airborne mission was the last one and involved the commitment of two battalions. They jumped east of National Highway 13 in support of the road-clearing mission to resupply Phuoc Long in June 1965.

• • •

The switch to US tactics and techniques occurred progressively between 1954 and 1964, but it was not until US forces were actively involved in combat in 1965 that ARVN tactics were brought firmly into line with those of the United States. As US forces gained more experience and new equipment, techniques and tactical concepts continued to develop; the RVNAF followed along in these developments.

Modified Tactics and Their Effects

Faced with the tremendous prestige of the US Army's well-organized military establishment, with its solid staff procedures [and] its tactics and techniques that improved constantly as new weapons and equipment were introduced, the RVNAF yielded to total adoption of US doctrine. In a memorandum issued in 1967, the Joint General Staff instructed military schools and units to adopt US field manuals as official operating procedures pending the development of new manuals by the RVNAF. That memorandum recognized a fait accompli.

American field manuals and military schools were not the prime sources of instruction for ARVN units on US Army methods of operation. Practical experience in the field, in close cooperation with American units, was the best teacher. In fact, some of the techniques were not yet written down in the manuals or taught in the schools. An example was the Eagle Flight operation. Particularly suited to relatively flat and open terrain, the Eagle Flight technique employed aerial search to find the enemy, pursuit and fixing of the enemy by gunships, vigorous heliborne assault, and rapid withdrawal in order to stage the next operation.

New techniques for road-clearing and counterambush operations also were developed. Before 1965 ambushes occurred frequently and rarely failed. Many counterambush measures were tried, but were largely ineffective. But from 1966 onward enemy ambushes were sharply reduced. Security and counterambush concepts did not change much, but the abundant means and fast-moving forces rendered the old measures effective. For instance, observation flights conducted while road convoys were in motion could uncover ambushes and bring new, more powerful artillery and bombing strikes on them much more rapidly than before. Reinforcements could be brought to the fight by helicopter to relieve, reinforce, or block the enemy withdrawal. The ambushed units were more confident and better equipped to defend themselves while waiting for help, which they knew would be available immediately.

Reconnaissance patrols were also improved. Formerly reconnaissance patrols had to walk into their objective area and walk out with their reports. Consequently their range was limited and the information was often stale by the time they returned with their reports. With helicopter transport, reconnaissance teams could conduct long-range forays into enemy sanctuaries and along enemy avenues of infiltration and lines of communication. Combat rations, lighter and more nutritious, also allowed longer missions. Improved signal communications enabled the patrols to maintain contact with helicopters and observation airplanes.

ARVN reconnaissance and combat operations were generally restricted to supporting artillery range. Knowledge of this fact helped the enemy to define ARVN's area of operations and objectives. When helicopters became available to move artillery, the enemy could no longer rely with confidence on artillery deployments as indicators of ARVN intentions.

• • •

The most frequent deficiency in combined operations was that operational commanders tended to assign lighter and less dangerous missions to their own units and the harder ones to attached units. Furthermore, difficulties often arose because task force units still responded to direction from their parent units, even though attached or under operational control of another unit. One major reason for failure in the defense of Quang Tri in April 1972 was that the ranger and marine brigades and armored groups placed under control of the 3rd Infantry Division failed to cooperate with or respond to orders of the 3rd Division commander.

• • •

The experience of Operation Lam Son 719 into Laos in 1971, and in the loss of Quang Tri during the Communist 1972 Summer Offensive, revealed [the] inability of I Corps headquarters to execute corps-level operations. The other corps headquarters were similarly inexperienced and ill-equipped to handle multidivision operations. On the other hand, most ARVN staffs and the appropriate commanders could manage division and lower-level operations effectively. In March 1975 the 22nd Division in Binh Dinh and the 18th Division in Long Khanh proved the abilities of these two divisions and their commanders against great odds.

• • •

Solving Difficult Tactical Problems

Throughout the Vietnam War, despite the abundant US support and modern tactics, four tactical problems remained not fully solved. Two of them had existed ever since the beginning of the war, and two developed since 1968. The two old problems were how to conduct effective night operations and how to execute successful cordon and search operations. The two more recent problems were how to counter enemy sapper actions and to reduce the effectiveness of enemy shelling of the cities and airbases.

The Vietnam War pitted the adversaries against each other in every sense. The opposition existed between ideologies: free society versus Communism; and between strategies: immediate solution versus long-term struggle; and day versus night actions.

Night Operations

The allies almost invariably conducted offensive operations during the day, while nearly all Communist activities took place under starlight. This almost exclusive preference—day for the allies and night for the enemy—indeed corresponded to the nature of life and activities of the opposing sides. In Communist-controlled areas, all facets of civilian life—commerce, trade, markets—were conducted before dawn and ceased at sunrise when [the] RVNAF began to operate. Enemy units took advantage of darkness to move personnel and supplies; to mount harassment and offensive sabotage actions against outposts, bridges, and roads; to start shelling; to conduct propaganda activities, collect taxes, and carry out assassinations and kidnappings.

Darkness was a Communist tool and it created two important advantages: security and surprise. Security was achieved because of immunity from detection and hence from destruction by airstrikes. Surprise was gained because it gave the ability to vanish into the landscape and into the populace, or to emerge unexpectedly from these to initiate offensive action. The Communists became thoroughly familiar with night life and nature, whether it was in the jungles, mountains, or lowlands, in the swamps, or along the rivers of trails. Guides and liaison agents played important roles in night movement. They were not only familiar with the terrain, but also with habits of RVNAF outpost troops and their nightly routines such as periodic firing schedules.

The RVNAF leadership fully understood the advantages any attacker should be able to exploit in night operations and constantly encouraged ARVN units to execute a greater share of their offensive actions under the cover of darkness. But the ARVN suffered a number of handicaps which degraded the effectiveness of its night operations. One of these was the elusiveness of suitable enemy targets for night attacks. While the enemy could emerge at night from the cover of forests or swamps to attack fixed RVNAF bases and population centers, the ARVN task was just the opposite: to depart from prominent, well-known bases or from conspicuous field operating sites and enter the deep jungles or treacherous swamps in search of an almost invisible enemy.

Secondly, only country people had a natural affinity for night operations. ARVN officers and noncommissioned officers were all urban dwellers. They were chosen for their educational backgrounds; high school graduates were sent to officer candidate schools and junior high school certificate holders to noncommissioned officer schools. To achieve these degrees, students had to go to schools in district or province capitals. Rural peasants almost never had this opportunity. Even most enlisted men in the National Army were not rural peasants but urbanized peasants and workers who had had contacts with the machine age.

Thirdly, the life and activities of the people on the government side were geared to the day; night was habitually devoted to sleep. The switch from diurnal to nocturnal activities, though logical, was not easy to make. Furthermore, the scattered posts manned by squads, platoons, and companies did not have enough people to perform normal duties such as road clearing and search operations, let alone conduct night operations as well, and when the busy harvest time came around, many PF personnel had to work in the fields during the day; placed on a night ambush position, they would use the time to rest.

• • •

The infrequency of night operations remained a long-standing weakness with ARVN units.

Cordon and Search

Cordon and search was a technique to trap and destroy enemy regional units, scattered guerrillas, and VCI members who had entered hamlets to operate or take refuge. Two coordinated operations were involved: cordon the hamlet, then search it.

• • •

The search was conducted in two steps: an initial search and a thorough search. The initial stage began with a rapid and unexpected entry into the objective, leaving no time for enemy reaction such as hiding materials and weapons, taking cover in secret hideouts, laying mines and booby traps, or launching a counterattack. Entrance into the hamlet would be made from several directions if possible. Once the objective was secured and under control, the thorough search would begin.

The thorough search was conducted methodically. If the hamlet was in a contested area, the people would be interviewed to obtain initial information needed for the search. The calm, alarmed, or anxious attitude of the people being interviewed would indicate whether the targets being sought were present. Children were a reliable source of information because they rarely lied, or if they did their lies would be transparent. The people were encouraged to reveal the locations of mines and booby traps, but, regardless of tip-offs, mines and booby traps had to be carefully sought, detected, marked, and neutralized or destroyed.

• • •

Inside dwellings, hideouts might have been made in double walls; these could be detected by tapping on the outer walls. Brick houses might have hiding space under the roof. Indoor shelters were usually small, consisting of a froghole type of chamber with an opening barely large enough for one person to squeeze through and with an underground room large enough to allow for movement and to store emergency water and supplies. These holes were covered over with a jar of water, a jar of rice, a chaff pile, or some other customary object.

Supplies and document caches were also searched for in dwellings. Because they were used daily, they were likely to be hidden close at hand and where they would be protected from rain. Caches of these supplies were usually found in bamboo sections telescoped together as fake rafters, in hollowed-out and carefully closed house pillars, or in religious altars or ancestor altars which searchers as a rule would not touch out of reverence. Floors, too, were good candidates for caches. The most effective way to detect them was to pour water over the dirt floor. Places that had been excavated would absorb more water at a faster rate than those that hadn't. Fireplaces and kitchen hearths were also suspect.

• • •

It was difficult to conduct effective cordon and search operations without inciting considerable resentment among the people toward the government. The discontent that the populace already felt when their houses were being subjected to a thorough search would, when aggravated by any inconsiderate act by an individual or team, severely undermine the people's good will toward the government. The problem was that few villagers believed that searching was necessary for their own security, and virtually all of them considered it a nuisance and an invasion of their homes.

Defense against Sappers

Sapper action was a special method of combat which employed a small force to achieve major results. In an address delivered on 19 March 1967 at the Sapper Training School in North Vietnam, located at the headquarters of the 305th Sapper Group, Ho Chi Minh said: "Sapper action is a special action which requires special effort and special skills to perform." This statement was found in the records of every major Communist sapper unit. The Sapper Corps was a special combat arm that was trained to oppose a greater force with lesser strength and to move in complete silence. It was created after the pattern of successful guerrilla units of the Viet Minh and raised to an exceptionally high degree of sophistication. The Sapper Corps originated in 1946 when the Viet Minh imaginatively employed professional thieves with special skills and competencies—such as martial arts, swimming, climbing, and housebreaking—to penetrate French installations and bases and steal weapons, ammunition, explosives, [and] documents or carry out assassinations or sabotage.

• • •

From 1969 onward, realizing that the commitment of major units to confront the US Army and ARVN was a costly failure, COSVN [Central Office for South Vietnam (Communist)] converted several infantry battalions to sapper battalions and gave sapper training to all infantry units.

• • •

The sapper threat was recognized and given high priority by security units. Small outposts took inexpensive measures for detecting infiltration which were nevertheless effective, such as raising dogs, geese, and ducks on the outer perimeter of their positions. However, sappers tried to erase their human scent by lying in the night dew for a long time; then they would calmly walk up to the dogs and stroke their heads and pet them. If chased, they would jump into a mud hole to obliterate the scent and lead the dogs astray. But the crudest countermeasure was to eliminate the dogs with food mixed with a tranquilizer or poison.

To deal with geese and ducks, they attached a stalk of blackened water potato plant to the end of a walking stick and dangled it upwind in front of the birds. Thinking they saw snakes, the birds did not dare make a sound. Another way they distracted the ducks and geese was to rub green onion leaves on the sappers' bodies. The smell frightened the birds because they thought they smelled vipers.

• • •

In summary, enemy sapper action was a very effective tactic in the war of attrition and annihilation in terms of material damage and psychological and propaganda impact. The success of sapper action depended on courage, cleverness, and resourcefulness.

Antisapper action had to be based on continuous vigilance, elimination of routine patterns, and, most important, cleverness and resourcefulness to combat the enemy's cleverness and resourcefulness.

Defense against Shelling

Shelling was the most frequent Communist tactic. They used it extensively in guerrilla as well as conventional operations. Shelling was appropriate to guerrilla actions because it harassed and exhausted the enemy, and fought more with less.

When, in 1968, Communist forces began to be equipped with artillery rockets and several kinds of field artillery, preparation shelling was used before infantry assaults. The tactic of "first shelling, then assault" became routine after that time. For a number of enemy military leaders, artillery was a substitute for the airpower which they could not employ in the South. In battles such as that of Quang Tri during the 1972 Summer Offensive, the enemy's 130mm artillery was so successful in pounding ARVN outposts in the DMZ that defensive troops were pinned down while enemy infantry was closing in with impunity.

Such large-scale utilization of artillery occurred only in large engagements, but sporadic shelling occurred everywhere. This kind of shelling was often conducted by three-man teams with artillery rockets or a single mortar. The targets were usually small posts, garrisons, or villages, and were easy to hit with a few rounds. The effect on the people in the target area was often greatly out of proportion to the number of rounds fired or the damage inflicted. It was a matter of personal survival to them, while a 1,000-round concentration of fire on a remote ARVN unit was just something they might read about in the paper. Take the first rocket shelling on 19 March 1968 against Saigon—a total of 22 rockets fell in the center of the city, causing 150 houses to burn; three policemen and two civilians were killed and 32 people were wounded. After this incident, shelling became virtually the only topic of conversation among the population. Materials for the construction of shelters—sandbags and sand—rose sharply in price, then disappeared from the market, and the press demanded that [the] government take immediate measures to protect the population from shelling.

A shelling security belt was devised for Saigon and other important cities. This belt was to reach beyond the effective range of rockets, from eight to ten kilometers. (Though subsequently Communist troops used booster charges to reach a range of 18 kilometers. With this extended capability, enemy rockets were able to hit Danang Air Base from the foot of the mountains at Hai Van Pass.)

• • •

Rockets were easy to smuggle in, to conceal, and to fire. They were usually transported to the firing sites days before, concealed underwater in rice paddies or camouflaged. Launching ramps were simple; they could be two logs tied together at one end or small dirt ramps. They were very inaccurate, but the objective of the firing was terror rather than military destruction, so that did not matter to the enemy.

In cities such as Saigon and Danang special task forces were formed to handle defense against shelling.

• • •

For all their deficiencies, the measures worked out and implemented by the task forces were as effective as could be expected. Take, for example, the case of Saigon city. From late May to late June 1968 the enemy shelled Saigon eight times. After the task force began to work, the enemy was unable to launch another shelling until mid-August, and only two additional until the end of that year.

Patrols in the security belt proved effective in capturing rockets that had not been used, and in preventing transportation of additional rockets from enemy bases into the security zone. In mid-September 1968 an ARVN unit captured a battery of 12 tubes of 107mm rockets in Can Giuoc, Long An Province, south of Saigon. Effective patrolling also caused the enemy to delay firings. A number of rockets, buried too long, failed to explode on impact. In shelling of Saigon on 31 October 1968, four out of eight rockets fired were duds. All units, however, did not perform their patrol duties with zeal or integrity. There was the time when the enemy firing position was in the ambush site supposedly occupied by friendly troops. An investigation revealed that the RVNAF unit had neglected, out of laziness, to move far enough and had instead set up a kilometer short of its objective. After this, commanders were punished when the enemy succeeded in firing from the commander's sector of responsibility. Cash awards were given to units that captured rockets or caught shelling teams in ambush. Eight rockets were once captured in Tan Uyen District, Bien Hoa Province. A patrol uncovered the battery of 122mm rockets timed to go off by a clockwork. Other similar instances of capture occurred, such as where rockets were timed to fire by ingenious mechanical timers. These instances showed that enemy shelling teams were afraid of discovery and counterbattery fire.

• • •

Many attempts were aborted through the combined investigation and intelligence effort of US and Vietnamese forces. Nevertheless it was easier for the enemy to shell than it was for [the] RVNAF to prevent it, and counteraction required many resources, much coordination, and great determination. When these were mustered in sufficient degree to minimize the shelling threat, the RVNAF . . . involved tended to lose the initiative for other operations, they exhausted resources needed for other high-priority tasks, and became tied to the defense of a limited area.

VI. SPECIAL US COMBAT TECHNIQUES

US forces found that the tactics and techniques that were generally employed during World War II and the Korean War were largely inadequate to cope with the battlefield conditions they found in Vietnam. Furthermore, the Vietnam War presented the American military leadership with opportunities to develop new weapons and devices and to test concepts of employment of equipment designed after the end of World War II. The wide use of helicopters, for example, spawned numerous new applications of these versatile machines. The more routine of these applications, such as battlefield reconnaissance, command and control, combat assault, logistic support, and medical evacuation, were gradually adopted by [the] RVNAF as the equipment became available, but other more sophisticated applications remained exclusively in the US arsenal. Examples of these were helicopters specially equipped with night vision and illumination devices and odor-detecting "people sniffer" equipment. The VNAF was equipped with gunships for the support of ground troops, but these were the familiar Huey helicopters and not the more modern Cobras introduced by the US Army later in the war.

• • •

Besides the extensive use of helicopters in virtually every possible military application, four other major battlefield techniques were developed to a high degree of expertise by the Americans in Vietnam. The most prominent of these was the employment of massed B-52 strategic bombers in a tactical role. . . . As used in South Vietnam, these heavy bombers were the most destructive of all weapons, and the psychological and political effects of their strikes were great.

Second only to the B-52s in the psychological and political repercussions caused was the use of defoliants to eliminate the enemy's concealment in the jungles of Vietnam and his food crops in remote areas.

Closely related to the use of chemical defoliants, but lacking the political and psychological effects, was the employment of huge crawler tractors—Rome plows—to remove vegetation that could hide enemy activities.

Finally, chemical warfare (not involving the use of lethal agents as in World War I, but incapacitating types of tear gas) made its appearance on the battlefields of Vietnam and also caused some adverse political reactions.

B-52 Bombers

On 18 June 1965 a news report on the war situation in Vietnam commanded the special attention of war watchers. For the first time B-52 bombers were committed to bomb in War Zone D, forty miles northeast of Saigon. The people of Bien Hoa, the province capital on the southern fringe of War Zone D, were stunned by the violent vibrations and series of explosions and woke up to discover a new word: "B-52." It was rumored that no living thing, large or small, in an area hit by B-52s could survive.

Vietnamese army troops first looked upon the B-52 strikes as a curious American phenomenon, but later learned to appreciate their tremendous destructive effects. This appreciation grew into a feeling of confidence; if the B-52s were in support, all would be well for the ARVN units.

• • •

The enemy was faced with a serious morale problem. The nearly silent approach of the horrendous violence carried by the B-52s was creating great anxiety among his troops. Defectors and prisoners of war attested to this frequently. They told of the sudden destruction of an entire battalion, and once even a complete regiment. Tunnels and caves collapsed and buried the soldiers alive. There was no escape from the power of these heavy bombs; even near misses would cause internal hemorrhages.

In July 1967 Hanoi Radio announced the death of General Nguyen Chi Thanh, commander of all Viet Cong forces in the South. A report spread throughout the Communist ranks that General Thanh had been killed in a B-52 raid on the Tay Ninh–Cambodian border. This was probably a true report, but its validity didn't matter; it was enough that the troops believed it. The fear of the B-52 spread throughout the Viet Cong ranks like a wave.

• • •

The B-52 really proved its worth as a close-support weapon during the 1972 Communist offensive. An Loc and the ARVN units defending it were saved by the timely and accurate B-52 attacks on the three enemy divisions laying siege to the town. The precision with which the B-52s struck on the northern edge of An Loc undoubtedly saved the 81st Airborne Rangers from being overrun in that sector.

After years of fruitless discussions, North Vietnam's agreement finally to accept the terms of the 1973 cease-fire has been attributed by many as a direct result of the heavy B-52 strikes against North Vietnam in December 1972. There is little doubt that these devastating air raids were an important factor in the Communists' decision.

One half hour before the Paris [Agreement] became effective in South Vietnam— 0800 on 28 January 1973—the last B-52 mission was flown against enemy units on the Cua Viet line, where the last major battle of the war had taken place between the South Vietnamese marines and the NVA 325th Division. This strike ended the nine-year involvement of the B-52s in the Vietnam War and, coming as it did in the last minutes before the cease-fire, illustrated the fondness for and reliance on the great bombers that had developed over the years among the RVNAF commanders.

• • •

There is little doubt in the minds of senior South Vietnamese military leaders that, had B-52s been used during the battle for Phuoc Long in December 1974, the success at An Loc would have been repeated. The two NVA divisions that converged on the outnumbered, outgunned little garrison at Song Be–Phuoc Binh would have presented lucrative massed targets for destruction by B-52s. Had B-52s been used in Phuoc Long, the enemy would not have gone ahead with his plans to attack Ban Me Thuot with three divisions and Darlac would not have fallen. The entire chain of events that led to the defeats and evacuation of Military Regions 1 and 2 would have been averted.

Their pleas for B-52 support in the hour of peril unheeded, South Vietnamese leaders—with the technical assistance of a few Americans brought in for the purpose—had clusters of 32 bombs improvised and dropped on enemy units in Tay Ninh Province, hoping to cause the enemy to believe that the B-52s had returned. They caused violent explosions and fires, but did not save Tay Ninh. Such were the flickering flames of a dying lamp.

Defoliation

Defoliation was introduced into the Vietnam War at the end of 1960. This was the time when Communist military activities in the South had begun to intensify. Each passing day saw more snipings, minings, ambushes, and assaults on outposts. Most of these incidents occurred in areas where dense vegetation provided excellent concealment for the enemy.

Also during this period, the Communists began to reorganize their bases where they grew rice and vegetables for their troops. ARVN operations into enemy zones such as the famed Do Xa Zone in Military Region 2 uncovered vast farms, but the ARVN units had no way to destroy the crops. In consultation with US advisors, South Vietnamese military leaders then in 1959 conceived a plan for employing chemical defoliants for this purpose. The United States supplied the chemicals and the delivery means.

Until 1965 defoliation was largely unnoticed, although the National Liberation Front protested for the first time in 1963. When US forces began participating in combat operations in 1965, defoliation increased by leaps and bounds, partly because of the need to establish new military bases and airfields in densely vegetated areas.

Defoliation became a household word in Vietnamese homes in Saigon and neighboring provinces for the first time in July 1965, when defoliants were used to clear the Long Binh area, which was to be the home of US Army, Vietnam, and US II Field Force. Unfortunately, the defoliants sprayed on the brushlands at Long Binh drifted over to the plantations, orchards, and farms of Bien Hoa and neighboring Lai Thieu and took a heavy toll on the rich crops of custard apple, mango, jackfruit, pineapple, and other fruits. The effects appeared overnight. Fruit fell from the trees, and the rubber trees in the large nearby plantations turned brown and lost their leaves. The people were stunned by the results, but didn't know at the time what had caused such devastation. When they finally learned about the defoliants, they became worried lest the chemicals also be dangerous to human and animal life. They remained skeptical of the government's [explanation], even after a member of the government's panel at a press conference tasted the defoliation agent. The farmers, worried about ruined crops and bankruptcy, were not much comforted by the official word that the effects would not last for more than a year.

The government had to establish boards chaired by the provincial agricultural directors to assess damages and set compensation for the farmers.

From then on defoliation became a source of constant anxiety for the growers. In 1966 and 1967, the births of a number of defective babies in Saigon and Tay Ninh were blamed by many people on the defoliants.

In an experiment in 1961 defoliants were issued to [the] VNAF and tried out on jungles. It was discovered that the agents were as effective against jungles as they were against crops and brushland. Soon afterwards, defoliation was carried out to remove vegetation from the roadsides along lines of communication throughout the country [and] to uncover infiltration routes from southern Laos into the 1st and 2nd Military Regions, as well as to wipe out the enemy's crops. The latter effort was part of the plan to deny the enemy his food supply in conjunction with the Strategic Hamlet program which was then being extensively implemented.

The Vietnamese Air Force was incapable of executing the expanding defoliation program, so the USAF took over many of the missions.

• • •

The government of Vietnam approved no defoliation with crop-destructive effects in the IV Corps area, the rice basket of the South. Crop destruction missions would be approved for the I, II, and III Corps areas if the purpose was to deny the enemy and his sympathizers food, forcing them to devote more manpower to farming and less to military activities. Well intentioned as it might have been, this exclusion of most of the Mekong Delta from crop destruction missions was illogical and inappropriate. A case in point was the way the exclusion operated in Dinh Tuong Province, Military Region 4, where the enemy's farming and military activities were consistently more extensive than they were in Long An Province, Military Region 3, where the exclusion did not apply. An even more serious effect of this discrimination showed up in the Central Highlands of Military Region 2. Because there were no absolute bars against crop destruction there, local officials ignored the vulnerability of the Montagnard farms to defoliants used in the jungles. Consequently many of the farms of these semi-migrant people were destroyed. This exacerbated the general ill feeling of the Montagnards toward the government and was exploited by the Communists to good effect. The disaffection generated was one of the main reasons behind the Montagnard separatist movement.

• • •

In the final analysis, the crop interdiction program, although it affected the enemy's food supply to the point of creating shortages in a few units, had only short-lived effects. Units in short supply were resupplied by rear base service troops with rice from Cambodia, the Mekong Delta, or, if they were in Military Region 1, North Vietnam.

Crop destruction by defoliation thus caused popular opposition to the government without any demonstrable advantage; this opposition far eclipsed any real military gain. This fact was eventually recognized by MACV and the government, and, from 1971 on, defoliation of crops was prohibited.

Defoliation of jungled areas was a different matter. Several dense areas which had been enemy bases for many years no longer provided him sufficient concealment. One such region was the Rung Sat, the delta of the Saigon River through which all oceangoing vessels had to pass to reach the port of Saigon. Defoliated in 1968, this dense mangrove swamp was turned bare for easy observation. It ceased to be dangerous except for the infrequent mining incidents. Seven years after defoliation, the forest showed no sign of revival.

In many formerly dense areas that had been hit by defoliants, enemy activity sharply decreased because of the exposure. Ambushes and minings along lines of communication abruptly decreased after dense vegetation had been killed by herbicides. Military bases enjoyed greater security as defensive belts were cleared. Defoliants were spread by helicopter in these belts to reduce contamination of adjacent areas.

• • •

The Rome Plow

Few in Vietnam ever heard the term "Rome plow." For the few Vietnamese who were familiar with US military activities, the term initially conjured up the image of some secret device or weapon rather than that of a bulldozer, equipped with a special blade, manufactured by Rome Caterpillar Company of Rome, Georgia.

• • •

In 1966 Rome plows were first tested by American units to clear jungles, to build helicopter landing zones in wooded areas, and to clear sites for military bases. When they were employed in Cu Chi to clear sites for the US 25th Division, Rome plows won the admiration of Vietnamese logistical and engineer units. Trees three feet in diameter were easily sliced through. No trees could fall on the operators, who were protected by overhead "headache bars." Old, sturdy bamboo clumps were cleanly cut and uprooted by the blades. Underground rooms and tunnels that had been concealed in dense vegetation were uncovered and destroyed by the bulldozers. Small mines and spiked traps were no obstacles for these mighty machines.

• • •

The 1970 Cambodian invasion in the Fishhook area showed the efficiency of Rome plows in finding and demolishing enemy underground shelters and tunnels. These results led to the activation, in late 1970, of the first of three ARVN ground-clearing companies which became operational in 1971. These companies were employed by platoons in support of divisional pacification operations.

• • •

Units in combat operations liked to have the support of Rome plows to destroy booby traps and detonate mines. Only antitank mines could damage Rome plows; smaller mines were ineffectual. Since Rome plows were vulnerable to enemy infantry with antitank grenades (B-40 and B-41), they had to be protected by infantry. The two problems with Rome plows were their huge consumption of diesel fuel (about 600 gallons a day) and the heavy maintenance service required to keep them running.

• • •

Riot Control Agents

Among the weapons employed during the Vietnam War, riot control agents were the only ones that were used on the civilian populace before they were used on the enemy. To control the Buddhist demonstrations in 1963, President Diem's government authorized the use of tear gas grenades for the first time. The people of Saigon became very familiar with these agents.

Riot control agents made their debut in combat operations in 1964, when they were employed by ARVN troops in an attempt to free US prisoners of war held in An Xuyen Province. From then on the tactical employment of riot control agents increased, and, after the initial adverse reaction from the foreign press in 1965, the reporters paid less and less attention to it.

In combat operations, tear gas was introduced into underground hideouts and tunnels. Before being supplied this chemical irritant, ARVN troops used the old-fashioned technique of smoking out the occupants. The technique worked fairly well for underground rooms, but against tunnels it merely exposed other entrances or vents as the smoke billowed from them.

To counter the smoke, Communist troops maintained a supply of water in their underground shelters. When the smoke entered, they covered their faces with wet towels. Against the chemical agents, lime juice squeezed into wet towels had the effect of reducing tearing. Communist troops were also issued plastic gas masks, but they were not very effective. Many prisoners of war said that, when hit by tear gas, they were nauseated, their heads ached, their eyes and noses started running, and their eyes were unable to open for fifteen minutes, during which time they were unable to react to the attack.

Tear gas also proved to be effective in city fighting. In 1968, in the Saigon-Cholon metropolitan area, during which riot control agents were used against the enemy, he suffered a distinct disadvantage because he had no gas masks. He had to give up positions he had meant to hold when confronted with the advance of masked ARVN troops.

• • •

There is no doubt that the sophisticated weapons systems and the new methods of employing the more ordinary weapons and equipment introduced into the Vietnam War by the Americans gave the American forces and the RVNAF some needed advantages over the enemy. While the United States was still in the war, these new techniques could be used to great effect by the RVNAF. When the US forces left the scene and American military assistance funds diminished drastically, the advantages [the] RVNAF enjoyed by virtue of its sharing in these American combat techniques disappeared and even turned into disadvantages.

• • •

In short, the RVNAF had to return to simpler, less costly methods for fighting the war, and success in fighting a defensive war for survival against an aggressive, dedicated enemy requires decisive strategic or tactical advantages. The RVNAF no longer enjoyed the advantages provided by American combat power, and could not afford to provide them for themselves.

VII. STRATEGIES AND TACTICS OF NORTH VIETNAM

• • •

In the long run, however, it was not the distinctive and ingenious Communist set of tactics that brought them the ultimate victory. Rather it was the coherent, long-term, immutable devotion to a strategy that assumed, without question, that victory would come eventually to their side. Total war, people's war; it was one and the same. Their adversaries could not match this concept with any theory of war that they were prepared or willing to follow.

VIII. OBSERVATIONS AND CONCLUSIONS

• • •

During more than twenty years of war between the North and South, each side appeared to have the advantage from time to time. The South faced critical periods and tactical setbacks in 1964, 1968, and 1972, but each time its armed forces rebounded from the brink of defeat and caused the enemy to pull back and regroup. The Communist side suffered serious reverses in 1959, 1967, 1969, 1970, and 1971, but was able to recover to pursue its goal of conquest.

• • •

From a purely military point of view, South Vietnamese leaders improved their tactics and adapted them well to the operational requirements of the war. In contrast to the enemy, however, they failed to coordinate their tactics with their political goals. South Vietnamese units in combat usually were concerned only with military matters: the mission, means, enemy, and terrain. The mission nearly always referred to purely military objectives; little thought was given to the political results or side effects of any operation. This insensitivity to political considerations at times resulted in actions condoned during combat operations which had adverse political effects, such as activities that resulted in the unnecessary loss of civilian lives or damage to their property. This was in stark contrast to Communist practice. Before embarking on an offensive, Communist cadres and troops studied and discussed the political aspects of the military operation, and the tactics employed were designed with this in mind.

Nevertheless, throughout the war RVNAF and US tactics enjoyed some remarkable successes and forced the enemy to make adjustments, devise countermeasures, and delayed his timetable for victory. For example, RVNAF and US raids on the enemy's supply and infiltration routes compelled him to devote considerable combat resources to food production, route security, protection and reconnaissance for night movements, and alternate route construction. Likewise, with their helicopter mobility and heavy firepower, including the B-52s, the RVNAF and Americans conducted many successful attacks on the enemy's previously secure base areas, compelling him to defend in these rear areas and to use men and other resources to repair damage, replace losses, and relocate facilities. Remarkable US advances in communications intelligence means, some of which were also effectively employed by the RVNAF, forced the enemy to adopt communications systems much less efficient than radio and to keep his command posts moving lest they be accurately targeted for destruction.

The modern tactics and techniques introduced into Vietnam by the United States also had some significant effects on the way RVNAF soldiers and their units functioned in combat. The use of helicopters in the infantry assault spelled the end of the parachute assault, which had been developed to a high degree of professionalism by the ARVN airborne units.

But another more serious loss in overall combat efficiency and flexibility was directly caused by the reliance infantry units learned to place on externally provided heavy fire support. They became accustomed to the strikes of fighter-bombers, gunships, B-52s, and divisional artillery that would pound the objective before the assault. They forgot how to take an objective by stealth. They forgot how to use their own mortars, machineguns, and recoilless rifles in close and continuous support of assaulting infantry. They forgot how to maneuver for advantageous terrain in order to breach the weakest points of the enemy position.

After years of reliance on helicopters and trucks to move infantry to battle, units neglected the art of marching and, with this neglect, the troops became lazy; they were tough soldiers, but they didn't really know the extent of their physical capabilities because they were so rarely tested.

The ARVN units fell into some other bad habits, too. As field radios proliferated, few units bothered to use messengers or wire communications. Field encoding systems were either too much trouble to use—if they were relatively secure—or were too easily broken if they were easy to use. Consequently, great amounts of valuable, sensitive operational information were carelessly transmitted for the enemy to intercept. And he became quite good at it.

Eventually, after 1972, there was an end to the bountiful resources RVNAF commanders could call upon. Not only were they suddenly deprived of the heavy American fire support that was critical to the survival of the nation's armed forces in the enemy's recent (1972) great offensive, but restrictions began to be placed on [the] RVNAF's own mobility and firepower because of the decline in the American Military Assistance Program. RVNAF commanders were not prepared to cope with this new austere environment.

• • •

As one reviews and analyzes the South's search for a strategy to defeat the North's strategy, one is struck [by] the fact that the search was inhibited, perhaps fatally, by the factor of time. Time, the importance attached to quick solutions, and the limited time successive regimes—American as well as South Vietnamese—had available to find these solutions, pervaded all aspects of strategic thinking and planning.

A successful strategy must have continuity in time. This was never a problem in North Vietnam. Its leadership, military and civilian, was in office to stay until the strategy was pursued to its conclusive victory, much as America's and Great Britain's leadership remained in office all during World War II. This was not the case in South Vietnam. Its constitution required a presidential election every four years—as did America's—but its president was limited to only two successive terms (as America's was not in its great war). Furthermore, the institutions of republican government were not only undeveloped in South Vietnam when the war started, but were constantly under enemy attack. Governmental stability was denied the Republic of Vietnam, and governmental stability is a sine qua non for a coherent national strategy.

This perennial instability had another deleterious effect: it impelled the political leadership to develop personal followings and loyalties among the armed forces leadership, giving rise to factionalism, division of effort, coup plotting and rumors of the same, all of which contributed to wasteful and sometimes corrupt practices in the employment of military resources. Furthermore, military leaders often rose to positions of great responsibility because of political loyalty rather than because of military qualifications. Some of these leaders were militarily inept.

Another thing happened to South Vietnam's strategy: it became inseparable from the strategies the United States devised for the war. And the US strategies were flawed by the same defect as [that of the] the South Vietnamese: lack of continuity. Furthermore, US policy prohibited a strategy shaped to achieve a real victory over the North. Some critics called it a "no win" strategy, but, whatever it was, the US strategy did not provide for a decisive defeat of the enemy.

South Vietnam's strategy did not begin that way. It started as an original, independent concept, quite removed from American influence. Until about 1963, South Vietnam's leaders were attempting to build a strong base of popular support upon which to form an effective military strategy that could defeat the enemy's broadly based, multifaceted campaign. Certainly the Americans influenced the structure of the South's armed forces during this period, because the support for the entire effort was appropriated by the US Congress and administered by the US Defense Department. It seems regrettable that, as early as 1954, the US Military Assistance Advisory Group failed to understand or appreciate the government's strategy; the MAAG opposed the force structure the government thought best suited for the execution of that strategy. With the Americans holding the purse strings, neither the Vietnamese president nor the RVNAF general staff could exert any significant influence on the military force structure or the military strategy from that time on.

The United States imposed a strategic limitation upon itself, and consequently upon South Vietnam. Its strategic objective was to defeat the Communists in the South, but not those in the North. Consistent with this strategic distinction, the United States provided South Vietnam with the means to defend its own territory, but not to carry the war to the North. This limitation was, to the Communist theoreticians, a strategic absurdity.

The Americans entered the war with awesome power and advanced technology. It seemed that a happy division of labor could be arrived at. The US forces would drive deep into the enemy zones and destroy his main forces, while the RVNAF would confine [their] efforts to pacifying the populated areas. Despite the logic of this strategic decision, it had some serious faults. In the first place, the spectacular battles the Americans fought so well and with so much firepower and such large formations caught the eyes of all elements of the press. These battles became worldwide news. The tough, grinding, and largely successful pacification campaign the RVNAF were waging went largely unnoticed and unreported. The result was the unavoidable but erroneous impression that the Americans were doing all the fighting for the Vietnamese. This gave the Communists more propaganda ammunition for their political war: "The Viet Cong were fighting the Americans to save Vietnam." It was a very effective line; it even convinced a lot of Americans.

Just as it appeared that the Americans had taken over the entire burden of the war from the South Vietnamese, so it appeared that the Vietnamese had abdicated all responsibility for strategic planning. Then came Vietnamization. All this would change and the Vietnamese would assume the primary role for the prosecution of their own war. But it did not quite work out that way. Vietnamization really meant Americanization. The Vietnamese armed forces were deluged with new American war equipment in great quantities, from 175mm guns and 90mm-gunned tanks to F-5 fighter-bombers. It was not possible to return (or revert) to a Vietnamese-style war. It was going to have to be fought the American way. This meant that firepower was the dominant element of the strategy. That was all right—for as long as the firepower was available and applied in the appropriate places at the right time.

The trouble was that the weight of the combat potential could never be brought to bear. After December 1972 the off-again, on-again American bombing strategy against North Vietnam ended for good and the strategy reverted to a South-only strategy. It shortly also became clear to all participants in the struggle that the crucial elements of the South's firepower advantage—US air and naval power—would not be used. But South Vietnamese leaders were too slow to perceive these permutations in the overall strategy. The United States was gone. Left on their own, the Vietnamese leadership had no strategic alternatives available. Perhaps, if they had better understood the workings of the American political system, they would have been better prepared to deal with the new set of circumstances. But they mistakenly believed that the American president could keep his promises against the will of the American Congress. It was too late when they discovered the folly of this assumption.

Belatedly, President Thieu, in late 1974, began talking about fighting a "poor man's war." It was too late to ask for this. There was no base of support for it. The political element of the national strategy had been ignored for too long in favor of the massive firepower and technological advantages that made politics almost irrelevant.

Another of Sun Tzu's maxims was "know yourself and know your enemy, and you will win victories in a hundred battles." The leadership of the Republic of Vietnam knew its enemy, but it knew neither itself nor its ally.

NOTES

1. A communiqué issued by the South Vietnamese government on 6 April 1956 stated "the Government of the RVN respects the present state of peace. As has been stated many times, the Government of RVN desires to seek reunification of the country through peaceful means, especially through truly democratic and free elections when such free conditions obtain."

2. Binh Xuyen was a society of organized crime that gained exceptional power under the French, who permitted it to operate without serious opposition in the Saigon area in exchange for its support against the Viet Minh.

3. File 204–58 (281–45) Org. Planning Files. Functions, Missions and Command Relationships (1963).

4. Binh Tri Thien sandals were the traditional footwear of the VC. Made of sections of rubber tires with inner-tube thongs, their name came from three provinces where the VC were originally strong: Quang *Binh,* Quang *Tri,* and Thua *Thien.*

5. "The Strategy of Isolation," *Military Review*, April 1972, p. 23.

3

RVNAF and US Operational Cooperation and Coordination

Lieutenant General Ngo Quang Truong

PREFACE

Over half a million US combat troops fought in South Vietnam at the height of the war. The indigenous troops they came to assist—the Republic of Vietnam Armed Forces—numbered nearly one million overall, but much less than that in first-line combat-effective troops. In contrast to the Korean War, there was no unified command to direct the common war effort. The nature of the war itself and the environment in which it was fought were also much different from those that made up American military experience. These and other peculiarities of the Vietnam War made the effort of cooperation and coordination between American and Vietnamese combat forces an unusually complex and challenging, though rewarding, venture.

This monograph analyzes the problem areas of operational cooperation and coordination, conceived both as a command and control device to prosecute the common war effort and as a means to improve the combat effectiveness of the RVNAF. It also attempts to evaluate the successes and failures of this combined effort. As author, I am fortunate enough to be able to draw on my personal combat experience, which began as a platoon leader, continued through the intermediate echelons, and culminated in a corps command. Throughout my military career, I was also privileged to be associated with several distinguished US advisors with whom I enjoyed a productive working relationship and whose devoted friendship I greatly value. This has enabled me to gain insight into the subject at hand. Where my memory is short on data and statistics, I have found the documentation available particularly helpful. All the comments that I make—particularly with regard to RVNAF capabilities and leadership—reflect my own point of view as a field commander and for which I am solely responsible. . . . [30 September 1976]

I. INTRODUCTION

The war in South Vietnam took a momentous step forward in March 1965 when US combat troops were committed to the land war. This occurred just five months after the first US airstrike was unleashed against North Vietnam as a result of the *Maddox* incident in the Gulf of Tonkin and other escalated actions by the enemy in the South. By this time the American effort to help the shaky government of South Vietnam to meet the increasing Communist military threat had been built up to approximately 23,000 men, mostly assigned to field advisory teams and combat support units. The decision that President Johnson and the US Congress made to reaffirm US commitment to the Republic of Vietnam was a bold and fateful step. For the first time in the war US ground troops were sent to Vietnam, not only to advise and support their Vietnamese ally, but also to destroy the enemy. A new era was about to open which saw the American and Vietnamese combat troops fight hand in hand in a succession of campaigns designed not only to destroy the enemy, but also to bolster the capabilities of the faltering Republic of Vietnam Armed Forces (RVNAF) as well.

This radical departure of US policy toward South Vietnam did not stem from an expansionist design. Rather it was forced on the United States by the gravity of a deteriorating situation. For one thing, the five-year-old counterinsurgency war had definitely escalated to a new level, and its nature had changed with the introduction of full-strength regimental units from the North Vietnamese regular army (NVA) and the activation of division-sized units in the South, such as the CT-9. The Viet Cong forces, increasingly replenished with North Vietnamese troops, began to receive modern weapons from the Communist bloc such as the AK-47 assault rifle and the RPG-2 rocket launcher.

From all indications, the enemy seemed to be entering an important phase of his strategy, and was on the verge of winning the war, after his resounding victory at Binh Gia. Military strategists—American and Vietnamese alike—were concerned about the possibility of a Communist wedge being driven across the country from the Pleiku-Kontum area to Qui Nhon. This action, if successful, would effectively cut South Vietnam into two parts along QL-19 and create favorable conditions for the enemy to achieve further victories. The whole process, it was feared, could eventually lead to the disruption of the RVNAF and the consequent collapse of South Vietnam. In addition, the overall political and military situation of the Republic of Vietnam (RVN) was deteriorating at an alarming rate.

Only one year and a half had elapsed since President Ngo Dinh Diem was overthrown on 1 November 1963. His overthrow ushered in a period of turmoil marked by internal power struggles, factionalism, and divisiveness. The armed forces lost essential unity of purpose and solidarity which took months, if not years, to restore. The reign of the Military Revolutionary Council led by General Duong Van Minh lasted only three ephemeral months; it ended with the arrest of the Council key members in a bloodless coup staged by General Nguyen Khanh, who installed himself as prime minister. His first act was a wholesale purge to consolidate his power.

Still unable to rally support for his one-man rule, Khanh maneuvered to establish a "triumvirate" military leadership including himself, General Minh, and General Tran Thien Khiem, and appointed a civilian prime minister. To give credibility to a form of "democratic" rule, an assembly of politicians and notables was created under the name of "National High Council" whose given role was half-legislative, half-consultative. But the true political power still lay in the hands of the "Armed Forces Council" composed of a select group of emerging, young, and ambitious men. It was this collective military leadership that replaced the ineffective triumvirate, appointed the chief of state, and later dissolved the National High Council, which had begun to infringe on the generals' power.[1]

The whole period in retrospect seemed to tear the country apart and turn the army into an arena of power struggle and political intrigues. The machinations and upheavals in Saigon made their rippling effect felt throughout the hierarchy. Unit commanders no longer dedicated themselves to the task of fighting the enemy; they spent their time and energy switching loyalty to save their own skins. Plagued by distrust and petty bickering, the military leadership failed to rally popular support and impart sense and direction to the war effort. In the countryside, the Strategic Hamlet system, which heretofore had provided some measure of territorial security, almost completely fell apart due to neglect. Its impetus was gone and many outlying areas relapsed into the grips of the enemy infrastructure.

In several instances Regional and Popular Forces (RF and PF) commanders struck a tacit "live and let live" arrangement with local Communists. The total RVNAF force structure was 500,000 by the end of 1964, but this was just a nominal figure not indicative of real combat strength. By any standards, overall effectiveness of the RVNAF was markedly on the decline. Poorly motivated and poorly led, RVNAF units were hardly a match for their determined and better-disciplined foes.

All in all, this was a dark period of time whose events threatened the very survival of the RVN and, as a direct consequence, brought about the increasing commitment of US combat troops to the land war, which was to be carried [to] new heights over the next few years.

The Buildup

Upon recommendation of General William C. Westmoreland, commander of the US Military Assistance [Command], Vietnam (USMACV), the US government agreed to deploy combat forces to South Vietnam to ward off the imminent disaster faced by the RVN.

• • •

June and July 1965 were the months of most significant events. The four-month-old civilian government under Chief of State Phan Khac Suu and Prime Minister Phan Huy Quat resigned as a result of irreconcilable differences between the two leaders. It was decided that the Armed Forces Council would take over. Apparently leaderless since its chairman, General Khanh, was ousted and expatriated in February as a result of his dictatorial actions, the Council voted to install Lieutenant General Nguyen Van Thieu, then minister of defense, as chairman of the National Leadership Committee (chief of state, or president) and Major General Nguyen Cao Ky, commander of the Vietnamese Air Force, as chairman of the Central Executive Committee (prime minister).

The inauguration of the Thieu-Ky government brought back some measure of political stability and ended the period of turmoil. General Ky's high-handed methods, however, gradually eroded the relationship between himself and General Thieu and led to their ultimate split in 1971.

• • •

The Phasing Down of US Combat Activities

The political impact of the enemy Tet Offensive in 1968 brought about far-reaching developments in US policy concerning the war in Vietnam. While President Johnson emphasized in Honolulu in July 1968 that the US would pursue the war at the current pace if North Vietnam did not curtail its aggression, there were indications that he was inclined toward bringing about peace through negotiations. The stop-and-go bombing orders frequently issued by the US president constituted an effort toward this end, but did not succeed in bringing the Communists to the negotiating table until he decided to step down. As soon as President Nixon took office, he entered into secret negotiations with North Vietnam toward what he had promised: ending the war and bringing home US troops. At the same time, in keeping with his doctrine of self-determination and emphasis on the role the allies were to play in common defense, which he formulated in the Midway Conference on 8 June 1969, he also ordered the initial redeployment of 25,000 US troops as the first step of the withdrawal process. This action, in concert with other US efforts to accelerate the turnover of equipment and the RVNAF Improvement and Modernization Plan, including the building up of [the] RVNAF force level, was part of a preconceived program conveniently called "Vietnamization" and aimed at disengaging US combat troops from Vietnam and turning over combat responsibilities to the RVNAF. Thus, from a peak of 549,500 [authorized; 543,400 deployed] on April 30, total US troop strength in South Vietnam began to decrease in preplanned increments until, by the end of 1969, it had been reduced by 110,000 men. Over the next year—1970—each successive announcement to the effect that the RVNAF had markedly improved was accompanied by a parallel reduction in US force so that, by year end, total US strength stood at only 335,000. Then, over the next two years, the unilateral withdrawal of US troops was kept up at a continuous pace, diminishing US strength by half at the end of 1971 until it was reduced to a token figure of 24,000 a month before the Paris Agreement was signed.

The redeployment of US forces from Vietnam during this period of time was also paralleled by substantial reductions in B-52 sorties, tactical air, and naval support, and the gradual transfer of US bases and other facilities to the RVNAF. Thus, in a sense, US combat operations were progressively reduced, beginning in 1969 and, as far as US forces were concerned, appeared to be just delaying actions pending redeployment.

• • •

Summary of Major Events and Comments

The US active involvement in the Vietnam War was a relatively short but highly effective venture. By the time it ended, the major objectives it set about to accomplish had been reached; there was no doubt about it. In the first place, US engagement in both the air and ground wars had averted the almost certain loss of South Vietnam and set back North Vietnam's plan to conquer the South for several years. Second, US direct intervention had helped stabilize the political turmoil and restore constitutional government and democracy to South Vietnam, thus creating favorable conditions for self-determination, a principle the United States always advocated. Finally, the effectiveness of US airpower, the combat performance of US ground troops, and the availability of US logistical facilities helped consolidate, improve, and expand the capabilities of the RVNAF to the extent that they finally emerged as a viable force capable—under certain conditions—of defending the nation.

Throughout the years of US involvement, several events of far-reaching importance came to affect the course of the war, the tactics used to fight it, and eventually the outcome of the war itself.

The buildup of US combat forces was a quick-reaction move designed to avert an imminent danger rather than to win the war. The United States sent troops to South Vietnam with the reservation that they would be withdrawn as soon as the enemy showed signs of relenting on his aggression. Although US troop strength reached a peak of 549,500 in April 1969, this peak was never maintained for any length of time. Like a perfect parabolic curve, the buildup came down just as soon as it reached its apex, and the curve downward was just as unrelenting as the curve upward. One might speculate, from hindsight, what would have been the course of the war had US strength been maintained for a few years longer. Then the withdrawal of US troops could have been carried out more slowly, thus affording the RVNAF the chance to fill in the void, in terms of combat units, firepower, mobility, and psychological conditioning.

The use of B-52 bombers to support ground troops was a marvelous tactical innovation that helped turn around the outcome of many battles. The fact that it had been used for so long and so unfailingly in every case turned it into a major psychological factor that sustained the morale of the RVNAF in the field. In time, it became a central tactical factor on which our field commanders relied, perhaps unduly, in their battle plans. The same could be said of US firepower in general, whether provided by jet fighters, artillery, or naval guns. It was unfortunate that this firepower support was also reduced along with ground troops, whereas it could have been selectively maintained to keep the tactical balance unimpaired.

Over the period of US involvement, the RVNAF almost doubled in size, if not in capabilities. This rapid expansion and modernization was made possible by general mobilization and the several improvement and modernization plans implemented. While it was true that this was an impressive increase of the overall force structure, figures might be misleading. For one thing, the number of combat units did not increase in any substantial way. The 18th Infantry Division, which was activated in 1966, was largely a consolidation of independent regiments, and the 3rd Division was only created as late as 1971. Several additional ranger groups were organized indeed, but they lacked the firepower and combat footing of divisions, which constitute the true backbone of any army.

For another, the strength of the regular forces was only less than half of the RVNAF total strength. Even then the ratio of logistics and support troops to combat troops was such that the RVNAF in the end did not enjoy any significant increase in overall combat strength. Also, the rapid numerical buildup could only have been achieved [to] the detriment of the quality of troops and lower-echelon leaders, for no amount of training could, in a relatively short time, turn out experienced leaders and combat-tested troops.

Finally, the advent of combined operations conceived and carried out under the tutelage concept, although salutary in its overall effect, hardly helped to enhance Vietnamese planning capabilities. In the planning stage, US commanders usually tended to keep it all to themselves, thus relegating their Vietnamese counterparts to the role of blindfolded executors. This was understandable enough, given the possible leaks on the part of the Vietnamese and the fact that combat assets were largely under US control. Operational plans on the Vietnamese side were sometimes merely translations of US orders. In addition, the tactical role played by RVNAF units was largely a secondary one and only became a major one when US troops redeployed. Then there were other difficulties arising from the mere fact that US troops were total strangers, racially, culturally, and mentally different from the indigenous people they had come to help.

These and other facets of the problem, US operational cooperation and coordination, their successes and failure, strengths and weaknesses, are the things this monograph proposes to elucidate.

II. THE JOINT STAFF AND MACV

The introduction of US combat and other allied forces in the Vietnam ground war to fight alongside the Republic of Vietnam Armed Forces gave rise to problems of coordination and control. Given the size and diversity of forces committed, military leaders at first were inclined toward some form of unified command of the multinational United Nations or NATO type. In April 1965 General Westmoreland, Commander USMACV, suggested the idea of a combined US-RVN command with an American general in charge, assisted by a Vietnamese deputy or chief of staff. For political reasons, however, the USMACV commander thought that this combined command should be gradually and quietly introduced.

The idea of a combined command appeared to receive wide acceptance among top Vietnamese leaders when it was first suggested. They felt that this arrangement offered an ideal arrangement for prosecuting the war, which somehow was going to be the primary responsibility of US forces. The divisiveness amid the Vietnamese military leadership and the deteriorating situation at the time also seemed to favor this arrangement. In time, however, this attitude became less enthusiastic as Vietnamese leaders grew more aware of their role and responsibility and, most particularly, of the attitudes among the population whom they were trying to rally to the national cause. Sensing this changing attitude, the United States dropped the matter altogether and withdrew the recommendation concerning the US-RVN combined command.

• • •

Opting for cooperation and coordination instead of a unified command, General Westmoreland must have carefully balanced the pros and cons. The intimate coopera- tion between MACV and the JGS and his close relationship with his counterpart, and the fact that the United States was providing the RVNAF with equipment and logistical support notwithstanding a substantial increase in the MACV budget, all these could ex- ercise as many direct influences on the RVNAF and the conduct of the war as would a combined command, and without its disadvantages. Under a combined command, in ad- dition to the political and psychological handicaps mentioned earlier, US forces might run the risk of losing some freedom of action, and the pressure exerted through such a command might well lead to an even more extensive American participation in the war. This was not what the United States had set about to do in Vietnam.

And so the concept of cooperation and coordination took over. It was based on the principle of equal partnership and a harmonious division of tasks. US forces were to as- sume the primary burden of the war—searching out and destroying enemy main forces— while the RVN Armed Forces concentrated on supporting pacification and eliminating the enemy infrastructure. Paradoxical as it might seem to traditionalists, the concept of coop- eration and coordination proved to be sound and effective for immediate purposes as well as for the ultimate goal of developing the RVNAF capabilities to defend their country.

At the national level, this concept worked well between MACV and the Joint Gen- eral Staff due to the harmonious relationship between their commanders. Anxious on its part to assume the war role on equal terms and to give new sense and direction to the command and control of the RVNAF, the RVN government designated Lieutenant Gen- eral Cao Van Vien as Chairman of the Joint General Staff in October 1965, and later el- evated him to four-star rank. The affable personality of General Vien, his professional competence, and his apolitical attitude were qualities that made him a fine counterpart of General Westmoreland, a dedicated professional soldier and diplomat. To ensure even closer coordination, General Westmoreland designated as his personal representative to the JGS Brigadier General James L. Collins Jr., who was senior advisor of the RVNAF territorial forces. This close relationship was to produce excellent results in the com- bined effort of prosecuting the war and greatly inspired subordinate commanders and staffs of both countries.

Role of the Joint General Staff

As command body of the RVN Armed Forces, the Joint General Staff was the focus of cooperation and coordination between the RVN and the US forces in South Vietnam.

• • •

Operational Coordination

The JGS and MACV were not responsible for organizing and conducting tactical operations. Their role was to monitor, supervise, and support operations initiated and conducted by ARVN corps and US field forces. As a result, the bulk of staff work performed by the JGS and MACV in operational matters focused on technical and support problems.

As usual, based on joint assessment of the situation, the JGS and MACV advised commanders of ARVN corps and US field forces of the military efforts to be conducted in their areas of responsibility, which generally fell into two major categories: search and destroy, and pacification support. The JGS and MACV also advised them of additional support resources they might expect to receive and how long and where these resources would be provided.

• • •

The 1970 cross-border operation into Cambodia and [the] Lam Son 719 operation into lower Laos were outstanding examples of combined planning effort. In a few cases, however, operational planning was entirely done by the US field forces involved, with little participation by the counterpart ARVN corps staff and never submitted to the JGS for discussion. The JGS operational staff, for example, knew absolutely nothing about Operation Junction City until it was launched, although the operation plan had been published by II FFORCEV a month in advance.[2] It was learned, however, that strict security measures were enforced to prevent compromise, and the planning group was held to a minimum, even within II Field Force. It was doubtful, then, that III ARVN Corps had advance knowledge about this operation at all, despite the fact that the mission assigned the planners of II Field Force read: "On order, II FFORCEV, in coordination and cooperation with the III ARVN Corps, conducts a major offensive into War Zone C, etc."[3]

• • •

Combined Intelligence Activities

Among the various areas of operational cooperation and coordination, none was more concrete and more successful than intelligence. This was because the combined intelligence effort was characterized by mutual support and had a common objective. Both American intelligence and its Vietnamese counterpart had [their] own strengths and weaknesses. The US was endowed with superior technology, sophisticated gadgets, abundant resources, and a vast, competent organization, but lacked profound knowledge about the enemy. In contrast, the RVN had none of the US material advantages, but it enjoyed a vast, intimate knowledge about the enemy, his psychology, his technique, and his culture and language. So the two intelligence counterpart organizations complemented each other very well.

• • •

Logistical Support of the RVNAF

The RVNAF and US forces fighting the war in South Vietnam had their own logistical system[s] and were generally self-supporting. There was, as a result, no combined logistical agency as was the case with intelligence, either at the central echelon or in the field, to provide direct support for units of both forces. Since materiel and equipment were separately managed, the principle set forth for the support of the RVNAF was maximum utilization of Vietnamese assets. Lateral coordination with the US logistical system was made only when RVNAF assets were exhausted. Provisions of additional equipment and supplies for the RVNAF were made on the basis of reimbursement.

• • •

In summary, logistical coordination and cooperation between US forces and the RVNAF brought about excellent results. The RVNAF obtained adequate support from US forces in addition to regular military aid. One of the backlashes of this generosity was the overdependence of Vietnamese consumers on this unlimited support and a certain prejudice against the Vietnamese logistical system. ARVN unit commanders, for example, usually turned to American units nearby to obtain quick and abundant supplies of artillery munitions, grenades, fuel, and construction and barrier material instead of requisitioning through the normal ARVN supply channel. This practice resulted in two drawbacks. First, ARVN units developed a spendthrift habit, making wasteful use of available supplies. Second, the ARVN logistical system was unable to record true requirement experiences.

An outstanding example was the consumption experience pertaining to 105 ammunition. Experiences recorded during the period from 1967 to 1969 showed a consumption rate of only 12–16 rounds per day. This rate shot up to 28–32 rounds per day during the period from 1970 to 1971. When an investigation was made into firing logs, it was found that the consumption rate was the same for both periods. The balance, of course, was provided by US units whose records were unknown to the RVNAF logistical system. It's no wonder that no complaints were ever heard about shortages in munitions and other supplies during the period of US participation in Vietnam.

III. ARVN CORPS AND US FIELD FORCES

Deployment of RVN and US Forces

When the United States initiated its buildup of combat units, South Vietnam was militarily organized into four Corps Tactical Zones (CTZ) and the Capital Military Region (CMR) for the purposes of command, administration, and logistics.[4] Each corps tactical zone was placed under the command of a corps commander, who also assumed the administrative and political duties of a government delegate. Similarly, the Capital Military Region commander was also military governor of Saigon–Gia Dinh.

The I CTZ comprised the five northernmost provinces of South Vietnam; its northern boundary was separated from North Vietnam by the Demilitarized Zone (DMZ). The II CTZ encompassed 12 provinces of the Central Highlands and the coastal area. This was the largest and most sparsely populated zone. The III CTZ covered ten provinces surrounding Saigon and was considered the most important. The IV CTZ was made up of 16 provinces of the Mekong Delta, the rice bowl of South Vietnam. The CMR comprised the metropolitan area of Saigon-Cholon and Gia Dinh Province, whose districts surrounded Saigon like a cocoon.

Each corps tactical zone was, in its turn, divided into Division Tactical Areas (DTA), each DTA being the tactical area of responsibility assigned to an infantry division. There were, as a matter of fact, as many DTAs as there were infantry divisions. In addition to DTAs, a corps tactical zone might include a "special zone" assigned to a separate subordinate command such as the 24th Special Zone of the II CTZ, which was responsible for Kontum and Pleiku Provinces. Each DTA encompassed several provinces which, under the military territorial organization system, were called sectors. In most cases the province chief, usually a field-grade army officer, was also sector commander.

• • •

Due to the nature and proportions of the war, which was mostly fought at the division level and rarely at corps level, corps commanders were delegated authority for operational planning and execution under the supervision of the JGS.

In view of the severe enemy pressure in South Vietnam, the buildup of US and other combat forces of the Free World Military Assistance Organization (FWMAO) was effected rather rapidly. By March 1966, US field forces had been deployed throughout the country. At that time the aggregate strength of the Republic of Vietnam Armed Forces (RVNAF), US, and FWMA forces stood at 816,000 men, including 581,000 of the RVNAF, 22,400 of the FWMAF, and 213,000 of the US forces. The FWMAF represented contributions made by the Republic of Korea, Thailand, Australia, New Zealand, the Republic of China, and the Philippines, in decreasing order of importance. [The Royal Thai Army also contributed troops.]

During this period of US buildup, the RVNAF force structure was made up of: 1) Regular Forces: Army, 273,000; Navy, 15,000; Air Force, 13,000; Marines, 7,100; 2) Territorial Forces: Regional, 135,000; Popular, 137,000; or a total of 580,000 men under arms.

The Army of the Republic of Vietnam (ARVN) was composed primarily of ten infantry divisions deployed to all four CTZs.[5] The 1st and 2nd Infantry Divisions were deployed to the I CTZ; the 22nd and 23rd Infantry Divisions to the II CTZ; the 5th, 10th, and 25th to the III CTZ; and the 7th, 9th, and 21st Infantry Divisions to the IV CTZ.[6] In addition to infantry divisions and separate regiments, which were all under operational control of corps, there were 20 ranger battalions which were usually employed as corps reserves and assigned to them accordingly. An Airborne Division and a Marine Division constituted the general reserve under direct control of the JGS. In total, there were 141 maneuver battalions of the RVN regular forces operating throughout South Vietnam.

• • •

Free World Military Assistance combat forces included: the 1st Battalion, Royal Australian Regiment, and a 105mm howitzer battery of the Royal New Zealand Artillery, totalling 1,400 men and operating in the III CTZ under operational control of the US 173rd Airborne Brigade (Separate); and the Republic of Korea forces, which were mainly deployed in the II CTZ and comprised the "Capital" Infantry Division and the 2nd Marine Brigade, with an aggregate strength of over 20,000 men. In total there were ten maneuver battalions of the FWMAF in South Vietnam.

• • •

Organizational Arrangements for Command and Control

Following the accelerated buildup of US combat troops, command and control organizations were also rapidly developed, and, by March 1966, US field commands were
already in place throughout the country. It was from this time on that large-scale offensive operations began and initiative was gradually regained on all battlefields.

• • •

The realignment of the US advisory system in view of the presence of the US field
forces was a shrewd and suave arrangement which paid off handsomely in a psychological sense insofar as Vietnamese commanders were concerned. Operationally, however, it
brought about practically no change. The day-to-day advisory activities were carried on
as dutifully as ever by the corps advisory group, no matter who became the nominal
chief. The senior advisors, meanwhile, seemed to be more concerned with their own
troops than with advisory duties, which was perfectly natural. In retrospect, if the US
field force commander could have given more time to his role of senior advisor—i.e.,
cooperation and coordination on a daily basis—then perhaps the combined military effort in each corps tactical zone would have been much better.

Mission Relationships

At the corps tactical zone (military region) level, the three US field forces and their
Vietnamese counterparts, the ARVN corps, were on a par with each other. They operated on the basis of cooperation and mutual assistance, being equal partners working
toward a common goal. That this working relationship could be maintained and bring
about excellent results throughout the years could only be ascribed to a commendable
spirit of willingness and self-effacement on the part of the field commanders involved.

Beginning [in] 1966, with a view to expand and coordinate offensive military operations, MACV and the JGS jointly developed a comprehensive "Combined Campaign
Plan," which set forth the objectives, policies, relationships, and the various areas of
coordination required for a harmonious effort of both RVN and US forces in all the
corps tactical zones.

The basic objectives, as determined by the first Combined Campaign Plan, were
to clear, protect, and assist in the development of heavily populated areas around
Saigon, in the Mekong Delta, and in selected portions of the coastal plain. These were
called national objectives. In addition, in each corps tactical zone there were certain
key areas, generally populated and of political and economic importance, to be secured
and protected, which constituted CTZ objectives. Both national and CTZ objectives
were selected on the basis of a strategic concept—sometimes metaphorically called the
"oil stain" strategy—which called for the consolidation of several nuclei in the first
stage, then the outward expansion of government control from these nuclei at a later
stage. Outside of these objective areas, existing governmental centers of political and
demographic importance, such as provincial capitals and district towns, were also to be
protected. Finally, to eliminate the enemy main force, search and destroy operations

were to be conducted in those outlying areas located outside of national and CTZ objectives.

• • •

Despite the fact that the tactical aspect of the situation varied according to the periodic enemy pressure and the terrain and weather of each particular corps tactical zone, operations generally fell into one of three major categories: search and destroy, clearing, and securing. Search and destroy operations were aimed primarily at locating enemy forces and bases, and destroying them without holding terrain. Clearing operations were of the longer-term offensive type, conducted in coordination with territorial forces for the purpose of driving enemy forces away from a target area and holding it for an indefinite period of time. In these operations, the continuing presence of friendly forces was deemed necessary to provide security and instill confidence among the local population. Security operations were generally conducted by territorial forces, frequently augmented by a regular ARVN or US reaction force if necessary. They were mostly saturation patrolling activities conducted on a permanent basis to provide security for lines of communication and important localities within a particular tactical area of responsibility (TAOR).

In keeping with . . . directives and policy, large-unit offensive operations at brigade and higher level were conducted on a regular basis—mostly by US forces and on their initiative—in all CTZs except the Mekong Delta. With abundant firepower and mobility, US units usually focused their efforts in searching out and destroying major enemy units and logistical bases, or reacted in response to the situation and intelligence recorded. The RVNAF, meanwhile, were stretched over the entire national territory for which they were responsible. With only limited firepower and mobility, Vietnamese units usually operated in populated areas near the major axes of communications and concentrated their primary effort on the support of pacification and rural development.

Combined operations, which integrated or paired off ARVN and US units, were sometimes conducted, depending on the tactical situation or as a response to the force requirement of certain types of effort, provided that both sides could muster enough forces for the operation.

• • •

In general the joint concept of force employment during this period tended toward assigning ARVN units more responsibility for territorial security than for mobile combat operations. Lacking substantially in combat support facilities, ARVN units were yet to prove their combat effectiveness and reliability. So the primary effort of seeking out and destroying the enemy was taken up by US forces who, in view of their substantial firepower and mobility assets, enjoyed a great tactical advantage and usually held the initiative in large-scale operations. It was assumed that, for these reasons, US forces were better suited to the task of eliminating enemy main-force units and destroying enemy bases, which were usually located in jungle and mountain areas.

This division of tasks between US and ARVN forces no doubt spared the ARVN corps commanders the major war burden. It was also a reflection of the prevalent political situation in which corps commanders played a preeminent role. Still affected by an undercurrent of instability, the RVN military government found it prudent to entrust political power to corps commanders, who were selected [from] among members of the ruling Armed Forces Council. As a result, ARVN field commanders were sometimes more preoccupied with politics than combat operations. The I Corps commander, Lieutenant General Nguyen Chanh Thi, for example, was deeply involved in politics because of the close relationship he enjoyed with military rulers. His controversial role in the Buddhist uprising in 1966, however, led to his dismissal.

A corps commander was usually assigned many positions of key importance. Lieutenant General Le Nguyen Khang, III Corps commander, for example, retained five additional positions for himself.[7] Because of these burdensome duties, corps commanders were hardly able to devote themselves to the military effort. Hardly, if ever, could they spare time to visit subordinate field units, provide them guidance, and follow up on their actions. As a direct consequence, command and control, morale, and discipline were adversely affected. This situation gradually improved after 1967, when democratic rule was established and more and more professionals were assigned to key commands and positions. Still, to ensure that the common effort would succeed as directed, US field force commanders usually played the preponderant role in the conduct of combat operations. As a result of this role, and of their capacity as senior advisors, they exerted a certain influence on their ARVN counterparts.

• • •

There were some US commanders who contended that, in view of the tremendous military power and superiority enjoyed by US forces, searching out and destroying enemy units hidden in outlying areas was not really a big challenge. This idea was shared by many ARVN commanders. It was true that the United States had more military might than required to win the war in South Vietnam if it had been willing to. But American policy was apparently constrained by its gradual response approach and failed to bring all US military might to bear on the war at the appropriate time.

Various programs of combined action aimed at upgrading the RVNAF combat effectiveness and complementing the effort of US forces at the same time were suggested, but few were implemented. In fact, US units were somewhat chary of the complexities involved in coordination and the additional burden of providing all kinds of support for ARVN units. Only rarely did they suggest combined action. The reason for this reluctance was simple enough: US commanders had varying degrees of skepticism as to the effectiveness of ARVN units as combat companions. They apparently did not always think it worthwhile to cooperate with ARVN units, although any ARVN unit, regardless of its size, could in fact make useful contributions to the fulfillment of their common tasks.

In addition, US field force and unit commanders, having to cope with several duties and obligations at the same time, and trying to perform them in a totally strange and complex environment, seldom demanded or advanced initiatives of their own concerning combined activities with Vietnamese units. As senior advisors, however, they felt obliged to take some interest in ARVN units. But the periodic visits they paid to their counterparts were largely courtesy calls or official tours characterized by all the pomp, civility, and reserve of diplomatic encounters. Ever guarded and courteous, US commanders seldom offended their counterparts by critical remarks which could well have been beneficial for the success of a common enterprise. For the most part, therefore, US commanders stuck to their own business, leaving the day-to-day working contact to US advisors and liaison officers.

ARVN forces deployed in the CTZs were usually bound by their territorial security mission, and constrained by territorial responsibilities. This was a complex mission that finally absorbed and held back the great majority of regular army units. An adverse consequence was that, after a long period of operating from fixed positions, the combat spirit and effectiveness of a unit was greatly reduced. Once adapted to a certain familiar environment, troops tended to become careless and soft and more disposed toward personal comfort; combat aggressiveness either decreased markedly or was completely gone. And, in time, they became just another kind of territorial force.

Cooperation and coordination, as a compromise between military and political considerations, were certainly not an ideal way to prosecute a war, much less the war in Vietnam. But cooperation and coordination did work and did succeed to some extent. It was only regrettable that it had not begun earlier. If, in the initial stage of US participation, US field force commanders had initiated extensive combined action programs and taken advantage of their preeminent positions as senior advisors to demand more of their counterparts, then ARVN units would have certainly benefited more from the presence of and cooperation with US forces. Their combat effectiveness would have [been] upgraded more quickly and more substantially. At the very least, their performance and discipline would have been much better. Finally, if US field force and RVN corps commanders had had the opportunity and willingness to cooperate and coordinate on a daily basis, to see for themselves problems as they arose, and jointly decided on the spot how to solve them, then the combined effort to utilize every available asset to prosecute the war would have been more productive and more successful. These observations were substantiated by the remarkable progress achieved by the RVNAF after the 1968 Tet Offensive through the years of intensive cooperation and coordination with US forces, and as a result of more determined efforts by the United States to help the RVNAF gradually take over the primary war burden.

IV. RVNAF-US JOINT COMBAT OPERATIONS

• • •

Intelligence

• • •

This was an area of vital interest to MACV and the JGS. At the beginning of US participation in the ground war in 1965, ARVN combat intelligence capabilities were still undeveloped. Knowledge about the enemy was scant and not subjected to systematic collection and analysis. ARVN combat intelligence came of age and became the effective instrument it was largely due to cooperation and coordination with US intelligence agencies.

A major step forward was taken by MACV and the JGS when Combined Intelligence Centers, staffed by US and RVNAF personnel, were established to operate the four key intelligence functions: interrogation of enemy prisoners, exploitation of enemy documents and materiel, and establishment of intelligence reports for both US and RVN command systems.

• • •

Operational Planning

In many cases, planning for long-duration campaign[s] or large-scale operations was initiated by Americans. Vietnamese staffs usually played only a marginal role, and their contribution was somewhat pro forma. Vietnamese field commanders had little interest in planning. This was because they did not control the combat support assets required and also, frequently, because they did not have a good grasp of the situation involved. Most of the time the Vietnamese field commanders would only offer a few comments on US-drafted plans or would just uncritically approve the recommendations made by US advisors. They seldom involved their staffs in the planning process.

• • •

Generally ARVN unit commanders at all levels made tactical decisions without a basis of formal planning. An adequate and timely operational plan was a rare thing in ARVN field units. Planning activities were generally confined to the top level, with minimal participation of staff officers and performed only on a daily basis. Partial or segmental orders, which changed with every passing day, were the usual practice for conducting operations. These orders usually allowed very little time for maneuver and support units to complete preparations. The orders were also frequently given at the very last minute. The result was confusion, loose coordination between maneuver units, and ineffective employment of combat support assets. Also intelligence directives were seldom issued along with combat orders. Subordinate units, as a result, rarely concerned themselves with the execution of intelligence plans.

In practice such deficiencies in staff planning did not affect the operational coordination effort seriously. This was because, through US advisors, the ARVN units usually maintained lateral coordination, at every tactical level, with US units. To function effectively they depended primarily on this lateral coordination instead of directives and guidance given through the ARVN channel which, if ever made available, merely reiterated, rather belatedly, what the unit had already learned from US advisors. And, because operational coordination never ran into trouble, there appeared to be no need for combined planning, which unfortunately was seldom made a subject of common interest or concern at the tactical level.

There was no question that US units always operated according to plans which were usually detailed and timely. Planning was an American inherent forte. Not only did American field commanders have a total grasp of the tactical situation, they also enjoyed tremendous support assets. In planning, they were particularly security-minded; and, because of the constant fear of leaks, they tended to do the bulk of the planning unilaterally when combined operations were to be conducted. There was, of course, the usual coordination with, and some contribution from, Vietnamese counterparts at the beginning of the planning process. However, this was apparently just a formality. By having the Vietnamese make an initial contribution, the Americans undoubtedly wanted to spare them the embarrassment of being dependent on American initiative and blindly following what had been laid out. Therefore, when the Americans departed, they left behind a critical weakness in the ARVN operational command process. Now ARVN field commanders had to make do with poor planning and, as a result, usually made haphazard tactical decisions which were never based on careful study and analysis.

Over the years of fighting alongside US units and working with US advisors, it was true that ARVN units had learned a lot and matured in every aspect: technique, staff work, and tactics. Cooperation and coordination did give ARVN tactical commanders excellent opportunities to develop their leadership and assume the combat responsibility. It was unfortunate, however, that, once left to themselves, most of them usually reverted to their old habits, the habits they had acquired well before the advent of US-RVN cooperation. Very few of them, indeed, took any interest in correcting themselves to keep abreast of new trends in warfare and to adjust to the requirements of the tactical situation. As a result, staff planning remained one of the gravest deficiencies among several ARVN field commands up to the final days.

Assignment of Objectives, Operational Areas, and Free-Fire Zones

• • •

In the context of a war without clearly defined front lines, operational efforts usually concentrated on destroying the enemy and expanding the government-controlled area instead of pushing forward a physical front line or occupying more enemy-held territory, as is the case with conventional warfare. In keeping with this warfare aspect, corps tactical zone commands usually determined the areas on which friendly efforts should be concentrated in order to provide security for the population, drive off the enemy main-force units, and interdict enemy infiltrations.

• • •

Secure areas consisted of populous centers where the local government was well established and operating effectively. Movements were free within these areas, day and night. In such areas, there were in general no major enemy actions save for occasional sabotage or random shellings. Consolidation areas were sandwiched between secure areas and clearing zones. These areas were usually under government control and subjected to intense pacification. In such areas, the control of resources and population were strictly enforced. Enemy actions in these areas were usually not conducted on a large scale. They were limited and took place most often in the form of shellings and sabotage. The primary responsibility of friendly forces assigned to consolidation areas was to prevent the enemy from making inroads into secure areas.

Next in the security scale were clearing zones, which were in effect contested areas placed under the control of field commanders. These clearing zones were usually divided into tactical areas of responsibility assigned to combat units whose mission was to destroy enemy units and bases. Clearing zones, in general, included friendly operational bases, unpopulated areas, and areas under enemy control.

Finally, adjoining the national boundary, were border surveillance zones. These were areas in which tactical unit commanders were responsible for detecting enemy troop concentrations and taking necessary security measures.

• • •

Beyond friendly areas of operation, there were zones in which firing could be freely applied. In these free-fire zones, firing, strafing, or bombing could be instantly called whenever the enemy was detected, without fear of confusing him with the local population and without having to obtain time-consuming clearances from local military and civilian authorities. Like interdiction coastal zones, free-fire zones were areas through which the enemy usually moved his troops and supplies, or which he used as safe havens from which to launch shellings or ground attacks against friendly units. These free-fire zones were of course off limits to the local population; and movements to and from these zones were severely limited. While the civilian population generally stayed out of these areas, there were exceptions. Sometimes the civilian population chose to enter prohibited areas where they could find some productive farmland or a fish-yielding canal or coastal lagoon, despite the dangers that might shower on them at any given time. As a matter of fact, the local population knew that friendly control over these areas was not entirely tight or permanent, particularly at night. Consequently, the application of fire on those free-fire zones sometimes inflicted losses on the local populace. There was no way to tell, at night, whether the prowling people were enemy troops or just some fishermen taking in their catch.

Another device for facilitating operations against the enemy while avoiding harm to the civilian population was the imposition of curfews. Briefly speaking, curfews were imposed in insecure areas during the hours of darkness, generally from midnight or sometimes earlier till dawn. During this period, the friendly population was required to remain in their houses. Accordingly, any movement at night could be automatically considered inimical and engaged at once.

The only problem which arose was the imposition of overrestrictive curfew hours—almost always by an overzealous province chief—which interfered unduly with civilian pursuits. As an area became secure, curfews were progressively relaxed and eventually lifted completely. In areas where the authorities and the people were in rapport and communicated freely, the curfew hours could be adjusted readily. In some areas, however, the curfew was a source of friction, particularly where fishermen were concerned, since fishing was conducted most productively at night.

In general, free-fire zones were theoretically a sound idea. In trackless jungle, mountainous areas, and swamps, where the Communists would establish base areas and there was no friendly population, the free-fire zones allowed friendly troops to conduct operations freely without time-consuming requests for political clearance. They did create problems in the boundary areas around the populated centers. Sometimes, in these areas, the farmers, fishermen, or woodcutters would infiltrate the free-fire zone without permission and without the knowledge of the local authorities. As a result, they were sometimes the target of attacks by fire. This obviously caused resentment, regardless of the legalities involved.

In retrospect, the free-fire zone concept, for all its advantages, had some undesirable side effects. In the first place, it encouraged indiscriminate use of unobserved harassment and interdiction fire. This increased the expenditure of artillery ammunition, and the actual effect on the enemy was often rather insignificant. In addition, some commanders would take the easy way out and try to control a free-fire zone by fire, to the detriment of active ground operations. Thus the free-fire zone sometimes encouraged a lack of activity and aggressiveness in low-level commanders.

• • •

Allocation of Resources

• • •

Logistics were usually considered as a limiting factor in combined operations. Their limitations were responsible for the short duration of combat operations conducted by ARVN units. Although the ARVN logistics system was well established at every echelon, it operated on an area basis and was not responsive enough to support ARVN units conducting protracted operations away from their rear bases. This was particularly true during the post-1968 Tet Offensive period.

Certain categories of supply, especially barriers and other materials required for the construction of fire support bases, were usually not available in adequate amounts to meet operational requirements. ARVN logistics staffs were often not thoroughly conversant with the tactical situation. They were usually busy going through rigid, complicated procedures instead of providing direct and timely support for combat units. In general, they were accustomed to conducting business "as usual" and befitting a policy of normal or short-duration support. Logistics was not given its necessary attention by field commanders at any echelon; it did not play its proper role in operational planning.

During the initial period of US participation, ARVN combat units had to depend almost entirely on US units for every kind of supplies, including barrier and construction materials for fire support bases, ammunition, and frequently even food. These supplies were lavishly dispensed by US units, for a certain time. Later on, particularly after the Vietnamization program was formalized, US forces provided supplies for ARVN units only on an emergency basis and if the requested items could not be provided by the Vietnamese logistics system. This was done on purpose to stimulate the development of a self-supporting ARVN logistics system and efficient logistics operation.

• • •

There was no question that ARVN units usually relied on the devoted and adequate support provided by US units, which generally treated them without discrimination. This reliable support was largely instrumental in improving combat morale. Adequately supported ARVN units never faltered when participating in offensive operations against outlying enemy bases. On the contrary, they appeared to enjoy the challenge and become self-confident when authorized to participate in such operations. They certainly preferred them over the tepid pacification support activities.

• • •

Use of Firepower

When large-scale operational efforts were begun in late 1966, artillery and tactical air support made available to ARVN combat units were still limited. Each ARVN infantry division at that time had only two organic 105mm howitzer battalions, with occasional support provided by from two sections to a battery of corps 155mm artillery, depending on tactical requirements. In the absence of organic heavy artillery, ARVN field units usually depended on long-range fire support provided by American 8-inch and 175mm artillery.

It was apparent that, given the high level of enemy activity and the sizable operational areas, such an artillery support structure was not commensurate with tactical requirements. The practice of using only organic artillery also limited the amount of firepower that could effectively be brought to bear in a certain offensive operation. Moreover, in addition to providing support for operational units, corps and divisional artillery units were also responsible for supporting Regional and Popular Forces. Artillery missions, therefore, ranged from providing direct support for regular ARVN units to attachments and direct support for sectors (provinces) and subsectors (districts). To support territorial forces in their mission, ARVN artillery units were usually broken down into sections scattered throughout a corps tactical zone in order to provide coverage for important axes of communication and populous centers.

When they were required to conduct operations well beyond bases and axes of communication, ARVN field units were usually unable to obtain adequate fire support. First, not every ARVN unit had organic artillery. Second, the ARVN artillery unit might be reluctant to deploy, or be proscribed from deploying, in view of its permanent territorial support mission. Third, the tactical situation might demand the helilift of artillery, whereas ARVN artillery units during that time were not capable of this type of mobility. As a result, wherever US artillery units happened to be available for support, they usually did almost all the things normally required of a direct support unit.

• • •

The shortage of artillery assets required for the simultaneous support of different missions generated the need for tactical air to provide support for operational units. Since tactical air invariably achieved excellent results, ARVN unit commanders and certain US advisors developed the tendency to rely entirely on tactical air for support, even when both tactical air and artillery were available and both were equally effective for their purpose. During that period of time, the Vietnamese Air Force was capable of providing only a little over ten sorties per day for each corps tactical zone. Operational units, as a result, depended mostly on the powerful firepower of US tactical air when there was a requirement to level solid enemy fortifications or bases, especially if these objectives were located in jungle or mountainous areas. ARVN operational units also depended on US gunships for immediate support after initial contact with the enemy. In general, coordination and control of tactical air support was smoothly operated through the US advisory communications system.

The powerful US tactical air and artillery firepower provided ARVN combat units with . . . most effective and accurate support and assisted them in winning several major battles. Vietnamese commanders and troops alike were entirely confident of this support effectiveness. This confidence, in turn, enhanced their morale and remarkably improved unit combat effectiveness. The lavish use of firepower, however, became ingrained in Vietnamese tactics and became a bad habit. Whenever contact was made with the enemy, regardless of size or firepower, ARVN units invariably requested all-out fire support by artillery and tactical air; they took less interest in the unit organic weapons, light or heavy. This overreliance on heavy firepower more often than not amounted to sheer waste and overkill, and resulted in much human loss and property damage to the local population living in the area of operation.

To minimize human loss and property damage to the population, MACV and the Joint General Staff jointly published operational procedures regulating the use of firepower which were binding on both US and ARVN units when they conducted operations in populated areas. . . . Given the nature of the Vietnam War, however, it was usually difficult, if not impossible, for operational units to accurately estimate the size and potential of enemy forces before contact was made, and before the objective had been liquidated. There were times when a whole hamlet was leveled and only a dozen or so enemy troops were destroyed with it. In contrast, there were also times when friendly units incurred heavy losses because of inadequate fire support. Save for the few cases of negligence, no unit commander ever wanted to cause losses or injuries to his innocent countrymen. His natural inclination as troop commander, however, was to minimize losses to his men, even when this was apt to cause damage and casualties to the populace. Only the most experienced field commanders could effectively employ firepower with accuracy and tailor it to the size and nature of the objective.

In addition to tactical support, artillery, naval, and tactical and strategic air firepower were also employed in unusual, and unobservable, fire missions to attack and destroy enemy bases and those areas where an enemy troop concentration or movement was reported. There was also the nightly interdiction and harassment artillery fire. These types of fire were effective when they were carefully planned. Artillery interdiction and harassment fire, however, was not carefully planned. It was usually applied in a haphazard and unruly manner, particularly in the Mekong Delta, chiefly for the purpose of enhancing the morale of RF and PF troops in isolated outposts.

Civilian Evacuation, Casualties, and Property Damage

After 1959, when the war entered a more active phase in South Vietnam, many innocent civilians, caught in cross fire between opposing sides, were killed or wounded. Most of these casualties occurred among the rural population. The civilian casualty rate increased proportionately with the fighting level and reached an all-time high in early 1968, when the Communists launched the Tet Offensive against cities and major population centers throughout the country.

Civilian casualties had many causes, but most frequently were due to enemy booby traps or to mortar and rocket fires. Civilians also died from stray fire during battles, or from friendly aerial bombings, and occasionally from the deliberate use of terror by Communist forces. The most worrisome problem in this regard was the deliberate Communist tactic of precipitating a battle in a populated area. If the friendly forces declined to fight in order to avoid casualties and damage to the friendly population, the Communist[s] would strengthen their control of the area. On the other hand, if a battle ensued by choice or was unavoidable, the civilian population suffered casualties and damage. This not only caused resentment against both the GVN and the Communists, but required an extensive and time-consuming rebuilding process to restore the physical damage and for the people to regain their morale and confidence.

• • •

As of late 1968, however, civilian casualties were gradually reduced as a result of improved security, which was achieved throughout most of the countryside by the pacification effort. Regulations for the use of firepower were constantly updated by MACV and the JGS, and their strict application was enforced by both US and ARVN forces when conducting operations in populated areas. Operational techniques such as the soft cordon,[8] for example, which was characterized by a maximum limitation of firepower with a view to minimizing casualties and property damages to the civilian population, were especially encouraged.

So were plans to neutralize the enemy "mini-bases," which were thoroughly rigged with mines and booby traps, especially in IV Corps Tactical Zone. It was also recommended that artillery harassment and interdiction fire be cut to a minimum. Violations of fire employment regulations which caused casualties to the local population were carefully studied to determine those responsible, and also served as a basis for equitable compensation and relief to the victims.

• • •

Skirmishes between the two sides constituted a major source of danger for the civilians and their families who resided in the area. To them, friendly aerial bombings and strafings were as deadly as the enemy rockets, mortar shells, mines, and booby traps. The big difference was that US units always looked after the victims with care and swiftness, regardless of who caused the injuries. This instilled comfort and confidence among the population. By nature, the Vietnamese peasant is resilient and accustomed to hardship. As a matter of fact, he never expected to receive so much help from US units if anything happened to him, his family, or his property. This help was a necessary effort which was both humanitarian and psychologically advantageous insofar as the Vietnamese people were concerned. If all civilian casualties and property damages could have been compensated or repaired as swiftly and as fairly, it would have been a great source of comfort for the unfortunate civilian[s] living in the midst of a war.

• • •

Operation Delaware/Lam Son 216

• • •

Delaware/Lam Son 216 was the first large-scale combined operation conducted by forces of the US 1st Air Cavalry Division and the ARVN 1st Infantry Division against an enemy base located deep in the jungle and mountains. Its success required a close and constant coordination and a mutual trust between the participating forces. Since it was a difficult and hazardous mission, the US 1st Air Cavalry Division at first was not enthusiastic about cooperating with ARVN forces. The combat effectiveness of the ARVN 3rd Regiment was held in serious doubt by US forces. What they were unaware of was the high morale and discipline of this unit. Troops and commanders of the 3rd Regiment were particularly proud when they were given the chance to operate alongside the 1st Air Cavalry Division, a unit whose combat prowess and firepower they held in high regard.

• • •

A great benefit of combined operations of this type was the rapid improvement of ARVN combat effectiveness. The 3rd Regiment, until Operation Delaware/Lam Son 216, was generally considered mediocre among ARVN regiments. But after a few months operating alongside the US 3rd Air Cavalry Brigade in enemy Base Area 114, the 3rd Regiment achieved marked progress and became one of the best ARVN combat units.

• • •

V. COMBINED OPERATIONS AS A MEANS OF IMPROVING ARVN COMBAT EFFECTIVENESS

Objectives and Procedures

One of the major goals of MACV in South Vietnam was to help the RVNAF improve their combat effectiveness so that they would eventually be capable of defending their country unaided. The combat situation in South Vietnam offered excellent opportunities to put this policy to work, since both the RVNAF and US forces fought the same enemy on the same battlefield. The theory espoused by MACV was that, by participating in combat operations hand in hand with American units, Vietnamese forces—regular and territorial—would acquire valuable and practical experience which could hardly be acquired in a training center. Thus combined and joint operations offered ARVN units not only the chance to observe American methods of operation, American use of firepower and mobility assets, and American leadership in action, but also offered the fringe benefits of additional combat support which could not otherwise be made available from Vietnamese resources.

• • •

During the period of US active participation in Vietnam, this training concept was put to use at different levels and at different times. In late 1965 the III Marine Amphibious Force in I Corps Tactical Zone took up the most extensive organized effort of upgrading Popular Forces in a program called "Combined Action" which eventually absorbed a considerable amount of marine manpower. Under the Combined Action Program (CAP), marine rifle squads were sent into hamlets where they lived and operated with the local Popular Forces platoons for a period of several months until the PF platoons were considered effective enough to defend the hamlets by themselves. The program was initiated at first around US bases and along National Route 1, then expanded outward until local security had improved to the degree that the marines were no longer needed.

At this level, the program was tremendously beneficial to the GVN pacification effort. As a matter of fact, it was the district chiefs who designated target hamlets for the CAP in accordance with pacification objectives and local conditions. Despite the fact that the program achieved remarkable success, it was not pursued on a countrywide basis since, unfortunately, it required considerable US manpower. Considering its achievements, one may wonder what the CAP would have contributed to the overall pacification effort had the program been made a systematic and continuous combined US-RVN endeavor throughout the country. It was understandable that US forces were primarily concerned with destroying enemy main forces, but it was also important to eliminate the enemy infrastructure which was at the root of insecurity. The commitment of US forces in this effort would have been entirely justifiable. Similar types of effort were made by US Army units elsewhere since 1965, but were not systematically continued due to the priority given to combat operations.

General Westmoreland felt that Saigon, the national capital, and its surrounding districts should be given priority in the common military effort since they involved the prestige of the GVN. The ARVN and territorial units which were assigned for the defense of this important area, therefore, should also be made effective. As a result he directed, in late 1966, the initiation of Operation Fairfax, the first large-scale combined effort ever attempted, in which American and Vietnamese battalions were paired and tasked to support pacification in three key districts of Gia Dinh Province surrounding Saigon. It was General Westmoreland's desire that US battalions, by participating in combat operations in a populated center, would inspire ARVN regular and territorial units and instill confidence among the population. The three participating US battalions were able to provide considerable combat support resources for the operation, since they were subordinate to three different US infantry divisions.

Operation Fairfax, which lasted the entire year of 1967, was initially troubled by coordination and control problems. US and ARVN units, as a matter of fact, operated more on the basis of cooperation and mutual respect under the control of the district chiefs involved. Since the district chiefs, who were company-grade officers, were outranked by both US and ARVN unit commanders, and not usually held in high regard by the latter, problems were bound to occur. In the absence of higher command directives, minor issues frequently developed into major problems. This situation changed for the better, however, when the 5th ARVN Ranger Group and the US 199th Light Infantry Brigade took over and assumed responsibility for the conduct of the combined effort. Coordination and control became more effective, and the operation was termed a success when the US 199th Light Infantry Brigade was redeployed in November 1967, leaving only ranger and territorial forces in charge.

After the enemy Tet Offensive in 1968, combined operations of this type became more common. In principle, ARVN units remained under Vietnamese commanders, although their headquarters were frequently collocated in the same base with US counterpart units. There were many cases, however, where small units such as platoons or squads were exchanged or cross-attached between US and Vietnamese units. In I Corps Tactical Zone, Lieutenant General Richard G. Stilwell, the new XXIV Corps commander, went a step further when he suggested the integration of all US and ARVN tactical operations in his area of responsibility. His idea highly inspired me who, as commander of the 1st ARVN Infantry Division at that time, was his counterpart. Jointly we began to conceive operations, and each of us contributed his share of the forces. Our units acted in concert under a virtual unified command, since both of us were always in perfect harmony. We also encouraged the collocation of US brigade and ARVN regimental command posts in the same fire support base, since we were agreed that this provided closer and better coordination in tactical matters.

General Stilwell was an indefatigable, energetic, and devoted field commander. He and I usually worked very closely together and spent most of our days in the same helicopter visiting our units. It was my privilege to have been afforded the opportunity to cooperate with him and earn his trust. Our association was truly a working relationship inspired by the professional interest shared with each other and was in contrast to the superficial politeness that characterized so many other similar relationships. And I think that our joint efforts brought about results which highly benefited the common cause we pursued.

The practice that we adopted was fully supported by Major General Melvin Zais, commander of the 101st Airborne Division, who succeeded General Stilwell in 1969. He applied similar methods along the same line in the 1st Marine and . . . Americal Divisions. The Americal Division, however, had for some time conducted combined operations with the ARVN 2nd Infantry Division. The marked improvement of this unit's effectiveness was largely due to these combined operations. The success achieved by the Americal Division could be ascribed to its practice of establishing common tactical areas of responsibility for both US brigades and ARVN regiments and collocating their command posts at the same base camp.

In II Corps Tactical Zone, a combined operations program was initiated by Lieutenant

General William R. Peers, commander of US I Field Force, in early 1968, with the co-operation of his counterpart, Lieutenant General Lu Lan, commander of ARVN II Corps. With the US 4th Infantry Division guarding the Central Highland approaches, Generals Peers and Lu Lan began the "Pair Off" program which combined forces of the US 173rd Airborne Brigade and the ARVN 22nd and 23rd Infantry Divisions. This concept was later expanded to include Vietnamese artillery and other combat support units. There were some drawbacks, however, in operational coordination and cooperation due to the considerable separation of the headquarters of II Corps and I US Field Force and the relative lukewarmness of participating ARVN field commanders.

In III Corps Tactical Zone, similar efforts were later made by the commander of US II Field Force, Lieutenant General Julian J. Ewell. In mid-1969 General Ewell, in cooper-ation with Lieutenant General Do Cao Tri, commander of III Corps, initiated the Dong Tien (Progress Together) program, which paired the 1st and 25th US Infantry Divisions and the 199th Light Infantry Brigade with the ARVN 5th, 25th, and 18th Infantry Divi-sions, respectively. Combined operations were most extensively conducted by the 1st US and 5th ARVN Divisions, and prepared ARVN units to assume almost all of the 1st US Division area of operation when it was redeployed in 1970. On the border areas, II Field Force paired Vietnamese airborne brigades with those of the 1st US Cavalry Divi-sion (Airmobile). In time, the ARVN airborne units became proficient in heliborne op-erations, thanks to the large resources and modern methods used by US units. The Dong Tien program proved invaluable training for ARVN units which later successfully con-ducted the cross-border operation into Cambodia without significant US support.

Combined operations programs, conceived as a means of improving ARVN combat effectiveness, were a successful training vehicle. Not only did ARVN units improve markedly and become more proficient in modern warfare methods, but ARVN leader-ship also became more aggressive as a result of the fine examples displayed by US field commanders. In retrospect, these programs truly paved the way for Vietnamese com-manders to assume new responsibilities as US forces began to withdraw. In contrast, combined operations certainly were not all crowned with success. There were difficul-ties and problems generated by human and procedural factors. The association of US units and their abundant resources also developed certain psychological conditioning and habits among ARVN unit troops and commanders which proved to be adverse in the long run. For the purpose of this monograph, the author proposes to examine in detail each of the four above-mentioned programs.

The Combined Action Program

Shortly after their landing in I Corps Tactical Zone, the marines began a pacification program in the populated area near Danang. The key to this program was the combined action concept, whose basic premise was that rapport with the local population was both a military necessity and a prerequisite for permanent security. The problem of winning over the allegiance of the rural population was one of the most difficult challenges of the war, not only for the government of South Vietnam, but also for the US forces who came to its assistance. This was a unique and unprecedented problem for American tactical commanders. Traditionally American military doctrine, tactics, and training were geared to fight a conventional war; and little thought had been given to the political and psychological aspects of the type of war fought in South Vietnam, where many battles took place in the very midst of the rural populace. To overcome this problem, the approach employed by the marines was to seek rapport with the rural population through the Popular Forces . . . who were stationed throughout the villages and hamlets. Because these PF units were locally recruited, they enjoyed the advantage of knowing the local area and people, including the local enemy. In contrast, they were in general poorly equipped and deficient in leadership and training. These were deficiencies which could be overcome by US resources, leadership, and know-how.

The method used by US marines was to train by example, and the principle applied was to integrate a number of marines at the lowest levels with PF units. The combined action concept thus was a happy marriage between two different elements who mutually reinforced and compensated for each other's weaknesses. In such an arrangement, PF units benefited from US firepower, communications with larger units, and medical evacuation. Conversely, US marines were able to overcome some of the disadvantages of being foreigners.

The Combined Action Program started in August 1965 with a combined action company . . . composed of from three to 12 combined action platoons . . . initially assigned to the area around Hue city. It grew to 79 platoons grouped into 14 companies in 1967 and, by November 1969, reached a total of 114 platoons grouped into 20 companies spread throughout the populated lowlands of all five provinces of I CTZ. These CAPs provided security for some 350 hamlets and protection for about 135,000 villagers. In manpower, the program involved about 2,000 marines and navy corpsmen and approximately 3,000 PF troops.

• • •

Almost all marines participating in the Combined Action Program were volunteers assigned directly from the United States.

• • •

Perhaps the foremost requirements for adaptability to the [program] were the willingness to undergo hardship and, above all, an affection for the Vietnamese people. In all frankness, we had to admit the cold fact that not all marines—and US troops, by extension—understood and warmed to the local Vietnamese people. While it appears doubtful that as many as 40 percent of the marines disliked the Vietnamese, as claimed by a knowledgeable author, the fact was a marine could not live and work with them unless he sympathized with and came to like them.[9] After all, this was a volunteer, not an assigned job, and a CAP marine could quit any time he chose. The turnover rate, happily, was rather small throughout the entire duration of the program. There were even some CAP marines who extended their tour of duty voluntarily for a period of three or more months.

A Combined Action Platoon [CAP] was assigned to work with a village. Marines lived and worked with the PF in the village itself. They trained the PF in the daytime and, together with the PF, conducted patrols and ambushes at night. The headquarters of each CAP was a fortified compound consisting of several barbed-wire fences, heavily sandbagged bunkers, and a network of trenches. This was where the marines and PF ate and slept, and worked in the daytime. The CAP headquarters was also a safe haven where the village chief and RD cadres sometimes spent their night. By any standards, living conditions in the compound were Spartan; there was no electricity and no running water. At night about six marines and 10 PFs guarded the compound, normally at 50 percent alert. The rest of the CAP was out patrolling and laying ambushes. Patrols usually started at dusk and were conducted only as a means to drop off ambush squads or teams, generally two or three each night.

Tactics employed by the CAPs were founded on three basic principles: tactical mobility, economy of force, and credible permanence. Although a CAP did man and guard a headquarters compound, it did not defend the village or hamlet from behind bunkers and barricades. The basic tactical idea was to lay out a screen of ambushes on the approaches to the hamlet instead of putting up a static defense wall around it. The hamlet was usually manned by Popular Self-Defense Forces (PSDF).

This kind of mobility was also used most effectively by the enemy. It instilled a psychology of offense, not of defense, and embodied, in practice, the precept of "defense through offensive." Coupled with stealth, the kind of mobility practiced by the CAP provided not only offensive striking power but also the protection afforded by elusiveness. By virtue of this quality of elusive mobility, the CAP seemed to be everywhere but never predictably anywhere. The unpredictability of CAP ambushes was the basis of CAP security against surprise attacks by overwhelming enemy forces, and, what was more important, it ensured that the enemy would never feel safe anywhere in a CAP area of operations.

• • •

Being a small element, the CAP, of necessity, had to apply the principle of economy of force. Its tactic was to combine a minimum of personnel with a maximum of firepower. In the presence of an enemy force, the CAP exposed only a small target, yet was able to bring down the firepower of a marine battalion in terms of air and artillery support.

• • •

The third principle of CAP tactics was that of credible permanence. The PF, being recruited from the local area, were villagers by nature. Like the PF, the CAP marines were also villagers in that they lived with the PF and among the local population long enough to become known and befriended by the villagers. Their stay partook of permanence, since they would remain as long as they were needed. In a sense the CAP was practically "married" to the people, the village administrative structure, and the land. This quality of permanence was one of the characteristics that set the CAP apart from regular infantry units and accounted for its success among the local population.

• • •

There was no question that the Combined Action Program had a generally good record. US marines were fond of saying that no village under a CAP ever reverted to enemy control. That was true as long as the US protective shield was nearby. More meaningful, however, was the number of villages that ultimately no longer needed marine protection. As a matter of fact, when marines began to withdraw, late in 1969, the security picture in I Corps rural areas was never so bright. The advantages of the CAP were obvious. It provided continuous protection to the village; it trained and motivated a local self-defense force; and it was a potential source for the type of intelligence that would ultimately break the enemy infrastructure.

The presence of the CAP was a source of frustration to the enemy, who attempted unsuccessfully to counter it. As a matter of fact, the enemy was able to destroy some of the CAP headquarters compounds by means of surprise attacks in force. But he never destroyed a mobile CAP. The effectiveness of the CAPs was demonstrated by the fact that, wherever they were located, the enemy was denied his source of manpower because he was denied a free hand in recruiting and intimidation. The enemy was also denied his source of food, since he found it too risky to run rice parties through the ubiquitous CAP ambushes. He was no longer able to collect his taxes of money or rice, or enlist the support of the villagers. His source of intelligence gradually dried up as the villagers cooperated more fully with their PF and marine protectors. Finally, the stability and credibility of the GVN was greatly enhanced when village officials could safely stay in their homes at night and the common people no longer feared reprisals from the enemy.

On the minus side, the CAP was costly in terms of American manpower. The marines and the GVN wanted to expand the CAP, but MACV could not spare the manpower and instead developed the concept of Mobile Training Teams (MTT) to replace the CAPs. There were also difficulties in command relationship in some instances between the CAP and the local district chief. In one case, two village chiefs were summarily removed because they had received favorable publicity and eminence from close cooperation with US marines. I Corps Tactical Zone was an area where local politics played a great role, chiefly at the district and village levels. The VNQDD (Vietnam Nationalist Party) and the Dai Viet Party had ramifications and influence among the population. Many able PF platoon leaders were dismissed or transferred because of their political affiliation, much to the chagrin of the marines, who only knew the military and professional aspect of the problem.

• • •

Operation Fairfax/Rang Dong

In late 1966, while the major American effort in III Corps Tactical Zone continued to focus on enemy main-force units and American operations were typically large-scale efforts such as Operations Cedar Falls and Junction City, General Westmoreland . . . decided to commit an American infantry brigade on a long-term basis to the Capital Military District, which comprised Saigon and Gia Dinh Province around it. This effort became known as Operation Fairfax, which was initiated on 1 December 1966 and terminated on 14 December 1967. At the time of the decision, the security situation in Gia

Dinh Province was deteriorating rapidly and the enemy infrastructure and his 165A Regiment became a major problem. Many villages came under enemy control. The most troublesome areas were the districts of Thu Duc, Nha Be, and Binh Chanh, located directly east, southeast, and south of Saigon, respectively.

According to General Westmoreland, the GVN was reluctant to put regular ARVN forces in the vicinity of Saigon and attempted to solve the security problem by increasing RF-PF strength. At his urging, the JGS assigned two airborne battalions to CMD, but their operations were ineffective. It was clear that ARVN forces could not cope with the situation. The GVN government, meanwhile, was just beginning its program of elections and its political stakes were understandably high. In the face of this situation, the USMACV commander recommended that US troops be committed as a catalyst for ARVN and RF-PF action. He advised the JGS that MACV would match one for one the three ARVN battalions to be committed.

In essence, Operation Fairfax was a combined operation conducted jointly by US II FFV and CMD. "Rang Dong" was its Vietnamese counterpart code name. Forces deployed were three US battalions and three ARVN battalions.

The mission of Operation Fairfax stated that II Field Force, Vietnam, in cooperation with ARVN/GVN, would conduct operations in Binh Chanh, Thu Duc, and Nha Be Districts of the Capital Military District to destroy the Viet Cong forces, guerrillas, and infrastructure. The underlying objective behind this mission was the restoration of security in these areas to a level that could be maintained by ARVN, RF-PF, and the National Police. The US battalions were also assigned the additional mission of training and improving the local RF-PF units to the extent that they would be able to provide continuing security after Fairfax ended.

Initial US forces committed to the operation were three infantry battalions, one from each of three US divisions: the 2–16 Infantry, 1st Division; the 3–22 Infantry, 4th Division; and the 4–9 Infantry, 25th Division. They were replaced in January 1967 by the US 199th Light Infantry Brigade. On the ARVN side, the JGS committed two airborne battalions of the general reserve, the 3rd and 5th, and the 30th Ranger Battalion. These units were subsequently replaced by the 5th Ranger Group.

• • •

Since Fairfax was essentially a pacification operation, US and ARVN battalions were instructed to support the district chief and work for him. The rationale behind this was that operations would be no better than the intelligence provided by the district chief, and he was in fact the government representative in the area. This cooperation was achieved through the establishment of an Area Security Coordination Council (ASCC) which was composed of the American and Vietnamese battalion commanders and the district chief. These principals met every few days to plan and coordinate the overall effort.

• • •

Other innovations in cooperation and coordination were the creation of a Combined Intelligence Center (CIC) and a Civic Action Coordination Center (CACC), which were in fact subcommittees of the ASCC and assisted the latter in matters concerning intelligence and civic actions.

• • •

The entire effort relied on voluntary cooperation. The CIC was in effect an attempt to organize a clearing house for the flow of various intelligence inputs. Its product was distributed to all members involved. Two helpful by-products of this effort were the creation of a combined interrogation section and a combined intelligence reaction force whose success greatly enhanced cooperation and enthusiasm.

The method of operation was a mixture of cross-attachment, pair-off, and integration. Since both battalions had four organic rifle companies, a company from each battalion was placed in direct support of the other battalion, and vice versa. The attached company was further broken down by exchanging platoons with the remaining two companies of the battalion. On many occasions ARVN, RF, PF and US squads worked together. An additional area of emphasis was the requirement to provide maximum training to the district RF and PF units. This was accomplished by placing at least two PF soldiers in every American squad on a continuing basis.

The size of operations varied greatly. Several operations each month involved all eight rifle companies. On the other hand, combined platoons often conducted independent missions away from their parent units. Movement was by foot, helicopter, and boat. While daylight operations were not normally smaller than platoon size, the basic unit for night ambushes was the combined squad. Under this system, the two battalions could saturate the district with over 40 ambushes on a given night.

Specialized operations were also a part of the overall effort. Each week the intermixed units carefully cordoned and searched various villages, in cooperation with district police forces. After several months' experience, and after the enemy main-force units suffered heavy casualties, Fairfax forces shifted emphasis to small-unit antiguerrilla tactics. This effort was a marked success. By breaking down into many small units, and by moving constantly, the combined unit practically saturated the area of operation and effectively deterred enemy movement and resupply throughout the districts. Another tactic contributing to the success of Fairfax operation was the concentration of both day and night operations around selected villages identified as main sources of enemy subsistence. Also coordinated with saturation patrols and selective operations was the use of around-the-clock harassment and interdiction artillery fire and airstrikes on the inaccessible enemy base areas, which in fact drove the enemy either away from or into the area of infantry operations or into ambushes.

A movement control system was also initiated which designated certain key areas off limits, either to all movement, movement by sampans or motorized sampans, or movement without a special pass during curfew hours or even during daytime. Despite its military effectiveness, this movement control sometimes had to be suspended or modified in the interests of the local people, who were in general farmers, workers, or merchants.

• • •

Judged from the results obtained, there was no doubt that Fairfax operation was a success. It was the result of extensive planning, and it received direct attention from the USMACV commander himself. The overall objective was achieved, since security in Gia Dinh Province improved remarkably. Over a thousand enemy were killed, and 40 chose to return to our side. Enemy activity in general was severely disrupted, although his infrastructure was not affected in any serious way. His efforts to reestablish his once-strong influence in the area surrounding Saigon, especially in Binh Chanh District, were largely negated.

• • •

In short, the Fairfax approach was not as permanent as the marine CAP, and the relocation of US units was deemed somewhat premature. Here again, as elsewhere, American presence, initiative, drive, and resources were instrumental in gaining success for a time. The permanent danger was that the ARVN had become psychologically and materially too dependent on Americans.

The Pair-Off Concept

The pair-off concept was instituted in II Corps Tactical Zone in the wake of the enemy 1968 Tet Offensive as an offspring of the "One War" concept then embraced by MACV. Prior to this time, cooperation and coordination in II CTZ, in particular during the enemy offensive, was rather spasmodic and ineffective. The US I Field Force and ARVN II Corps usually operated separately, each concerned with and confined to its own responsibilities. While US forces sought out and fought enemy main-force units in outlying areas of the Central Highlands, II Corps forces generally limited their activities to pacification support in the lowland coastal areas and populated centers. This was a reasonable division of tasks, given the rugged and sprawling terrain and the relative ineffectiveness of ARVN units at that time.

It was then decided that, since enemy forces, whether regular or local, were but one, the war effort should also be one. The key to success was now to exploit effectively the advantages of each national force while minimizing its disadvantages. To US forces, it was like fighting with blindfolds, because the enemy was hard to distinguish. Hence they preferred to keep to their own areas of operation. ARVN units, by contrast, knew the enemy and the terrain well, but could not sustain combat for a lengthy duration, nor could they effectively plan and employ US combat support assets. Besides, accustomed as they were to the brushfire actions of pacification support, there was no way they could get off the ground and look the enemy main-force units squarely in the face.

The pair-off concept thus came about as a means to upgrade ARVN combat effectiveness and prepare ARVN units for a larger share of the combat burden. It was decided that each ARVN unit was to be closely and continually affiliated with a US counterpart unit, and that operations were to be conducted jointly, regardless of the size each force could commit. Coordination and cooperation were effected throughout the hierarchy from corps to battalions and districts. Each month the commanders of II Corps, IFFV, and ROK forces and their staffs convened in a tripartite meeting during which the military situation was reviewed, problems discussed and resolved, and the objectives laid out for the following month in accordance with the MACV-JGS Combined Campaign Plan.

The three commanders took turns in chairing the meetings. Despite the great distance between II Corps and IFFV headquarters, located at Pleiku and Nha Trang respectively, Lieutenant General W. R. Peers, commander of IFFV, made almost daily trips to II Corps headquarters. In addition, there were also periodic meetings of the various staff agencies of the three nations and daily contact and communications between them. Lieutenant General Lu Lan, commander of II Corps, and Major General Chae, then deputy, ROK Field Forces, were in total accord with the pair-off concept. The "One War" concept pervaded the thinking and actions of all commanders and forces within II CTZ.

• • •

The strategic objective of II Corps during that period was to expand government control of the population. Its efforts achieved spectacular gains by October 1968, when 95 percent of the population were reported living in A, B, or C, i.e. secure, hamlets.

• • •

There was no doubt that the pair-off concept . . . brought about some measure of improvement and confidence among ARVN units. It was unfortunate that the program could not be sustained beyond 1969. Despite the temporary achievements, the fundamental, persistent, and most debilitating weakness of ARVN was the lack of strong leadership at all levels. US efforts to help ARVN forces overcome this problem were, in general, not too successful. Another weakness was poor and haphazard staff work, particularly at division and lower levels. This obviously stemmed from poor training and lack of demanding leaders. Coordination and cooperation, finally, depended on the examples set by higher levels of command. The problem was best summed up by Lieutenant General Lu Lan, commander of II Corps, when he said: "If, at the top level, we don't coordinate, how do we expect coordination at lower levels?"

The Dong Tien (Progress Together) Program

Operation Dong Tien was a short-term test program which called for the close association of ARVN III Corps and US II Field Force units on a continuing basis in specific areas of III CTZ. It was a program jointly initiated by the commander of III Corps and the commander of II Field Force. The program began on 1 July and lasted through the rainy season of 1969. Actually, it was somewhat open-ended, with an underlying concept that as an ARVN battalion reached a satisfactory level of combat effectiveness, it was phased out of the program and returned to independent operations.

• • •

In actual implementation of the Dong Tien program, a number of methods of operations were devised and tested at each level. In the area of the ARVN 5th and US 1st Divisions (Binh Duong Province), for example, an area Combined Coordination Center was established at Ben Cat to receive reports from both ARVN and US units and act as the catalyst for the lateral flow of information between US brigades and ARVN regiments. Every evening a combined staff briefing was given to both ARVN and US commanders, with counterpart staff briefings following each other. These mutual brief-ings ultimately led to jointly conceived operations. The two divisions also organized a Combined Strike Force (CSF) at Phu Van consisting of one US and one ARVN company under the command of a US major. But the concept did not work and the CSF was dis-banded.

• • •

The Dong Tien program definitely improved the combat effectiveness of ARVN units throughout III Corps, although it was short-lived. The 8th Regiment, 5th Infantry Division, for example, eliminated over 100 enemy per month in its area of operation, a threefold increase over the pre-Dong Tien period. As an ARVN unit showed definite signs of improvement, it was taken out of the program and assigned a separate AO of its own. The program's most eloquent result lay in the fact that, during 1970, III Corps units were able to successfully conduct independent operations, striking into enemy base areas, and most particularly into Cambodia, with relatively little assistance from US forces. Many basic problems still plagued the ARVN at low-level units, such as weak leadership, lack of planning know-how, and the inability to effectively use combat support assets. In general, the better commanders benefited most; some of the others, while making progress, did not do as well. On balance, however, there was a general improvement in aggressiveness, better coordination, and more sustained combat effort.

Summary and Evaluation

Four different concepts and programs have been presented as approaches attempted by US forces to improve the regular ARVN combat effectiveness and upgrade the local RF-PF units. They have been selected over others for the reason that each effort was conducted in a different corps tactical zone. Two of these efforts focused on low-level territorial units and took place in relatively populated areas. The two others, meanwhile, concentrated on regular ARVN units and took place in outlying areas. Perhaps the over-all objective attempted by MACV when it directed and encouraged these efforts also encompassed a variety of purposes. This objective was reflected in its "One War" con-cept, which purported, in effect, to be the answer to the enemy's "total war" and which was in line with the RVN strategy.

One of the key aspects of the Vietnam War that frequently escaped the minds of some military leaders was that it was a double war, one that was fought by main forces in a conventional manner, and the other waged at the grassroots level with local forces and guerrillas. The enemy was but one, whether one may choose to label him Viet Cong or NVA; he was the Vietnamese Communist, regardless of where he was born or trained. The arbitrary distinction between VC and NVA, however academically justified, was just a fallacy; and it served the myth perpetuated by the enemy that none of the NVA troops was in South Vietnam. The response to this double war was obvious: a double effort was to be made to eliminate the enemy at two different levels, in two different environments, and by two different approaches.

This was the rationale behind pacification and the upgrading of territorial forces, on the one hand, and the sharpening and strengthening of regular ARVN forces on the other. The strategy was both sound and necessary. All programs seemed to work for a certain time; their limited goals were all achieved, sometimes beyond expectations.

The Combined Action Program, for example, gave as good results as anyone could expect. It operated on the same tactical mobility principle of elusiveness that the enemy used so effectively. It presented a credible permanence that fostered the kind of popular rapport and allegiance that was needed to defeat the enemy's own kind of "people's war." It was finally instrumental in bringing about a strengthening of our own infrastructure while denying the enemy the very environment in which he usually prospered.

Discontinuing the program in favor of the less expensive MAT program seemed not to be well justified. What did two or three thousand marines, or even more, really cost in terms of manpower as compared to the hundreds of thousands committed? There is little doubt that the CAP program was a positive influence and that the MAT program was less effective. One can only assume that US authorities felt they could not afford the personnel resources to implement CAP on a nationwide basis.

The Fairfax operation achieved practically the same results as the CAP program, although on a smaller scale. Its success was made possible perhaps due to the personal attention of COMUSMACV himself. Besides, Saigon was an area of great importance to everyone concerned. "It must succeed," was the only explanation the COMUSMACV gave.

The pair-off concept in II Corps CTZ, meanwhile, was not as successful as expected, perhaps because it came about too belatedly and was not sustained for a longer period. The terrain was rugged and too large even for the combined forces of three nations. Cooperation at lower levels was lukewarm at best, given the lack of interest at division level.

The Dong Tien program, by contrast, was a more complex enterprise which succeeded remarkably despite its few months of existence. The dual and cross-attachment arrangement at lower levels seemed to be the answer to the problem of effective cooperation and coordination. But it attested to the infeasibility of joint command at these levels, given the natural tendency of every ARVN leader to be his own boss.

Association with and exposure to US methods and initiative, however, brought to the surface many ARVN inherent weaknesses and deficiencies. Some of them were just differences in methods, culture, or way of life. Others were either technical or procedural problems that could easily be disposed of by more specialized and intensive training. Still others were human and difficult to resolve in the short term. The key to success in every human endeavor is of course people. In coordination and cooperation, personalities played the dominant role. Unless both commanders were willing to play the game and forsake their interest to a degree, there was no way to foster a genuine working relationship. Americans were usually impatient with ARVN lethargic work habits. Given their one-year tour, it was understandable that they always tried to get the most out of it. Vietnamese, meanwhile, felt they had all the time they needed. After all, they might well spend the rest of their lives with this war.

Poor planning was one of the most glaring ARVN deficiencies. It was even more acute at regiment and battalion levels. Perhaps lack of training was responsible for it;

perhaps the quality and limited number of personnel available at these levels did not permit effectiveness in staff work. But the primary reason, however, seemed to be the lack of aggressive and demanding commanders. ARVN commanders at these levels, it was usually admitted, fought battles without tactics, relying primarily on their own personal methods. In addition, the ARVN commander was everything in the unit. His staff had little, if anything, to say. It was the commander who decided everything, told them what to do, where and when to go, and how to run the complete operation. And, when he was absent, very little could be accomplished.

Finally, it was widely accepted that leadership was a perennial problem for [the] ARVN at every level of its hierarchy. This problem was so extensive and so deeply rooted that it is difficult to explain thoroughly within the scope of this monograph. Suffice it to say that, unless a commander or leader had professional competence, devotion, and moral rectitude, he certainly could not expect his subordinates to be dedicated and aggressive. The basic ingredients that were usually found lacking were motivation and aggressiveness. Perhaps the passive and resilient nature of the Vietnamese could not produce the all-pervasive, gung-ho type of tigers of whom Westerners were so proud. In the context of an ideological conflict, there were certain other qualities that perhaps counted more in the eyes of the Vietnamese, qualities that were more ethical, more spiritual, in nature. Perhaps lack of political awareness, and the social and economic degeneration due to the war, were at the root of the problem too. Whatever the causes, the problem certainly could not be solved in a year or two. There was, finally, the will and determination to fight which again depended on motivation and leadership, and without which there was no sense in upgrading mere physical capabilities.

VI. SOME CONSIDERATIONS AFFECTING RVNAF PERFORMANCE

Expansion of the US Territorial Advisory System

As the pace of the US combat force buildup quickened after 1965, the advisory effort also expanded and developed at a rapid tempo. It was a dual effort by the United States to help build stronger regular forces to combat enemy main-force units, on the one hand, and to assist South Vietnam to consolidate its governmental base so that effective control could be exercised throughout the national territory on the other. These two objectives were closely related. As has been said . . . , the war in Vietnam was a dual war which had to be fought on two different levels by two different approaches. While the destruction of enemy main-force units required large-scale operations and the deployment of sizable units and resources, the task of helping South Vietnam consolidate its government demanded that security be provided at the village and hamlet level. Concurrently, as security improved, an expansion of the RVN influence and control was deemed necessary. These are areas where US advisory and assistance contribution[s] were most beneficial.

The US involvement in South Vietnam began soon after the 1954 Geneva Accords with an advisory effort, but this effort existed only at the highest level, in training centers and in major units. It emphasized primarily training and helping the ARVN reorganize its units. In 1959, when the military situation began to deteriorate, advisory teams were sent to infantry regiments and separate battalions in the combat arms of the army, such as artillery and armor, and in the marines. The mission of these teams was to provide immediate assistance, and also to evaluate the effectiveness of the advisory effort. Infantry battalions were assigned advisory teams for the first time in 1961. Also at that time each province was assigned a US advisor whose mission was to assist the province chief and sector commander in administrative as well as tactical duties.

This new interest in territorial matters was perhaps due to the fact that the Civil Guard and Self-Defense Corps began to develop substantially during that time. Then, in 196[?], in an effort to effectively help the government of South Vietnam exercise control over the entire national territory, provincial advisory teams were increased and a limited effort was made to expand the advisory system down to subsector or district level during April and May 1964. This expansion was not systematic, however; it was designed to test the feasibility and efficiency of the advisory effort at that level. In the initial stage, MACV assigned only 13 advisory teams, each composed of an officer and an enlisted man, to districts surrounding Saigon. After just one month of trial, there were definitely encouraging signs of success. As a result, 100 additional teams of five men each, including two officers, were rapidly deployed to selected districts during the period from September to December of the same year. During the next two years, 1965 and 1966, additional advisory teams were made available, and, by the end of 1966, almost all districts throughout the country enjoyed the presence of an advisory team.[10]

As of 1966, in view of the rapid expansion of territorial forces, MACV organized Mobile Advisory Teams (MAT) to work with RF and PF units at the village and hamlet level. By 1968, the US territorial advisory system was well established and functioning as a comprehensive and elaborate organization at the province level.

• • •

Contrary to the usual uneasiness that Americans felt, the presence of US advisors in provinces, and particularly in districts, caused little adverse psychological impact among the population. Conversely, it was this American presence that created confidence in and prestige for the local government.

• • •

In general, US territorial advisory teams were tremendously useful and efficient in problem-solving and rooting out inertia and complacency at sectors and subsectors. Particularly, in view of the language barrier and relative unfamiliarity of US personnel with local problems, the expansion of the US territorial advisory effort was a step in the right direction. Its achievements spoke for themselves. The improvement of RF and PF combat effectiveness, however, was an enormous task which required still more advisory effort and attention.

The Mobile Assistance Concept

The RF and PF were a sizable military force which made up approximately one-half of the total RVNAF strength. They consisted mostly of companies and platoons scattered throughout the national territory with the difficult and important mission of providing and maintaining territorial security. The RF and PF soldier served in or near the hamlet where he was born and grew up. He was familiar with the natural and social environment and the situation in the locality where he was assigned to work, and took an active interest in improving its situation. Basically he was a good soldier endowed with resiliency and endurance. However, being part of the territorial organization, he was placed under an intricate command and control system which generally inhibited his full development. As the lowest echelon in the military hierarchy, RF and PF units did not receive adequate training, equipment, and support.

• • •

During 1967 US field force commands initiated an upgrading program for RF and PF units, based on the mobile training concept. US Mobile Training Teams (MTT), each consisting of from three to ten members, were used in rotation among RF and PF units. The MTT mission was to organize, train, and supervise these units until their performance was deemed satisfactory. . . . The advantage of this mobile training concept was the ability to provide training for a large number of units within a reasonable time.

• • •

Finally, in late 1967, drawing from previous experience, MACV initiated an extensive improvement program for territorial forces, based on the mobile advisory concept which had been successfully adopted by II Field Force. This effort aimed at improving territorial forces in all aspects: tactical operation, administration, and logistic support. In addition to mobile advisory teams, MACV also created Mobile Advisory Logistical Teams (MALT) whose mission was to help upgrade the territorial logistic organization and operation.

This large-scale improvement program was implemented in early 1968. A total of 353 mobile advisory teams was planned, and by year end they had been deployed to all four corps areas. Before their field deployment, these teams received training at the US Army, Vietnam (USARV), advisor school. Upon completion of training, they were assigned to provinces with the mission of upgrading RF and PF units by directly advising and assisting their commanders.

Each MAT consisted of two officers (team chief and deputy), three EM (one light weapons infantryman, one heavy weapons infantryman, and one medic), and one Vietnamese interpreter. The team usually lived with an RF and PF unit if the situation permitted. Its members helped train the unit and accompanied it on operations. Emphasis was placed on command and control; the conduct of operations, particularly night operations; marksmanship; the use of mines and booby traps; and the planning and control of fire support. After achieving its goal of upgrading the territorial unit—which was usually done within 30 days—the MAT moved to another unit and started the training process again. From time to time the team also revisited an old unit to evaluate its progress and to provide assistance as required in order to prevent the unit from deteriorating. A MAT sometimes worked with an RF company and several PF units nearby at the same time. The success of mobile advisory teams could be measured by the improved capability of the territorial forces to conduct independent operations with a minimum of support from the outside.

• • •

By 1970, when almost all RF company group headquarters and companies had achieved substantial improvement, the MATs were redeployed to areas where village and hamlet security needed to be improved, and where the local government control required consolidation. Their new mission focused on upgrading the Popular Forces, training and deploying the People's Self-Defense Forces, and coordinating activities of rural development cadres and the National Police. The MATs also assisted in developing village defense systems which were realistically tailored to local requirements. . . .

After several tests and trials covering a long period of time, the MAT program was found to be the most effective and realistic instrument for upgrading the combat capabilities of territorial forces. An outstanding example of its success was the marked improvement brought to the great mass of RF and PF units in the Mekong Delta, a sizable but ineffective territorial force which had been plagued by lethargy and indolence. Although the task was enormous and complex, MAT members quickly adapted themselves to each situation, strove for innovative ideas, and unfailingly fulfilled their responsibility. Their presence and assistance in the improvement of rural security brought confidence to the population and prestige to the RVN government.

The role of territorial advisors was challenging and interesting. In time, it became one of the most important contributions made by US forces in South Vietnam. As long as the advisory effort lasted, it helped improve the image of the RF and PF trooper who, like his Communist adversary, could fight like a tiger if properly motivated and led, but seldom did because he was not.

Attitude of RVNAF Troops toward Americans

The presence of Americans in South Vietnam no doubt accounted for the pervasive confidence among the population and RVNAF troops that final victory would eventually be theirs. As far as the RVNAF were concerned, Americans were either advisors, samaritans, or comrades in arms. This American standing prevailed no matter how ugly the Americans were painted by Communist propaganda. Very few people in South Vietnam were suspicious of American goodwill and altruism.

• • •

The power and influence of US advisors in the field did tend to overshadow the role of Vietnamese unit commanders. For example, activities of a unit tended to follow along the lines recommended by the advisor. In many instances it was the advisor who won the battle by calling in effective tactical air or firepower support from US resources. This gradually produced overreliance and sometimes total dependence on US advisors.

As a consequence, the initiative, responsibility, and prestige that the unit commander usually wielded were greatly affected and, over the long run, the presence of advisors resulted in reduced opportunity for ARVN cadres to develop their command capabilities and leadership.

When US combat units were introduced into South Vietnam to fight the war, their role overshadowed the advisory effort because they held the initiative on the battlefield and coordinated all military efforts. As of this time, ARVN units began to keep close contact with US units through the intermediary of advisors. Their purpose was to obtain additional support from US resources to meet operational requirements, and, almost unfailingly, US units obliged by giving all that had been requested. Because of the plentiful and sometimes lavish support provided by US units, the morale and combat effectiveness of ARVN units were very high. Later, when called upon to participate in combined operations with US forces, ARVN units appeared to enjoy the opportunity, if only because of the dependable support they could always expect. In time, they came to regard Americans as protectors and providers instead of advisors and comrades-in-arms.

The consequence of overreliance on material assets as substitutes for initiative and prowess was a failure to develop the infantryman's capabilities to the full—the very qualities that distinguished the Vietnamese soldier: endurance, perseverance, resiliency, and manual dexterity. Because they were organized and trained by US standards, and exposed for a long time to US warfare methods, ARVN units inevitably became accustomed to conducting operations with an abundance of supporting material resources. The result was that, when American presence and assistance were no longer available, the morale and combat effectiveness of ARVN units became uncertain.

The Tendency to Let Americans Do It All

The American military presence in South Vietnam, with its powerful combat forces, its impressive array of resources, and its gigantic bases, really overshadowed the Republic of Vietnam Armed Forces. The Vietnamese people suddenly found their own military forces shrunken to the size of a midget. There was nothing in the RVNAF comparable to the awesome might and modern assets which symbolized the "omnipotent" posture of the United States. Soon, they were convinced, Americans would deal the insurgency a resounding defeat. Those were the first impressions engendered by the initial buildup of US combat forces and their successful offensive campaigns to retake the areas that had been lost to the enemy. At that time the Vietnamese were reassured, and, by staking total confidence in US might, they took little interest in the efforts of the RVNAF, which appeared in their eyes as insignificant and superficial.

It was true that even the highest field commands, the ARVN corps, had only limited resources and limited capability. At best they were just capable of controlling territorial security activities and implementing short-term plans such as dry season or rainy season campaign plans and plans for the protection of rice crops, national resources, etc. Those were routine and undramatic plans which looked more important in form than in substance and which were renewed and repeated every year. Small wonder that nothing substantial had ever been achieved through such operations.

Corps commands almost never deployed and operated in the field as tactical headquarters. They never had the opportunity, nor the requirement, to operate in the field because operations were usually conducted at the battalion or regiment level, or at the most, and only rarely, at division level. And most operations lasted only a short time to allow units to return to their territorial duties, to which they were permanently tied.

When US field forces began operation in corps tactical zones, their capabilities and combat posture practically turned each of them into a key tactical command for the initiation and coordination of all military efforts within its area of interest. For one thing, field forces had a better grasp of the military situation, and, for another, almost all support resources were under their control. This operational practice reflected and befitted the realities of this period and was deemed vital for the integration of all military efforts to effectively counteract an emergency situation.

From a temporary arrangement dictated by expediency, US field forces gradually became permanent. Their initiative, responsiveness, and all-pervasive efficiency soon stifled the development of ARVN operational capabilities at the tactical level. Soon ARVN tactical commanders began to lose their combat initiative and became overly dependent on US forces for meeting major enemy initiatives. Gradually they lost interest in the combat situation outside of pacification areas. It was as if the war was being fought in a distant and alien world. ARVN commanders had little idea of what US forces were doing; US activities were, after all, none of their business. The passivity and lack of enthusiasm on the part of ARVN tactical commanders resulted in a greater freedom of action for US forces, first of all because ARVN units would not get in their way, and second [because] if they were called upon to cooperate there was not much they could contribute to the joint effort.

During the period from 1965 to 1968 ARVN units performed only a secondary role which was mostly confined to the support of pacification. US units, meanwhile, were responsible for nearly all combat operations throughout the corps areas. The less spectacular operations of ARVN units earned them the unjustified criticism that they were not too concerned with the combat situation. In fact, there was little they could do about it. ARVN units had indeed improved a great deal in combat effectiveness by this time, but they were still considered not up to the task of taking on major enemy units.

In general, they were inadequately equipped to respond effectively to operational requirements. It was during this period that combined operations were initiated, but the idea of cooperating with ARVN units was not widely welcomed by US forces. In the eyes of some US commanders ARVN units were but an additional burden they had to take in tow and that were apt to cause more problems during than they were worth. Moreover, the feeling among some US commanders during that period was that US forces alone could defeat the insurgency without ARVN participation.

The strategy then adopted by MACV and the JGS concerning the prosecution of the war placed equal emphasis on three major tasks: combat operations, pacification, and territorial security, which were all equally important. The division of tasks, as outlined by the Combined Campaign Plan, was a judicious distribution of responsibilities in which each force, Vietnamese or American, was employed according to its capabilities or where its advantages could be best exploited. The attempted goal was to achieve a balance of tasks which could eventually bring about maximum contribution to the joint effort. Hence it was agreed that US forces, with their plentiful resources, would tackle the hardest part by conducting search and destroy operations, while the lesser endowed ARVN forces focused their efforts on pacification and security. ARVN units accepted this division of tasks with some reluctance, since most of them would have welcomed the opportunity to conduct mobile operations, especially when reinforced by American firepower and mobility support.

ARVN units at that time were seldom given the opportunity to develop their combat effectiveness, bound as they were to the tedious task of pacification support and territorial security responsibility. Boredom and routine gradually eroded their combat skill and spirit to the point that they became almost as passive and as lethargic as the territorial forces. But the enemy 1968 Tet Offensive came in time to offer ARVN units the much-welcomed chance of undertaking active combat operations once again. Starting with the battles fought during this offensive, ARVN units really took the big leap forward and contributed a larger and larger share to the combat burden heretofore almost exclusively borne by US forces.

• • •

The conclusion that has to be drawn from the foregoing is that, if there really was a tendency to let Americans do it all, it was not the natural and common inclination of all ARVN commanders. But it did exist to some extent. Thus, either it could be attributed to undue reliance [on] and uncritical confidence in US capabilities and resources, or it stemmed from a common desire shared by both sides to meet emergency requirements.

Effect of One-Year Tour and Six-Month Rotation

Hundreds of thousands of American servicemen contributed to the American effort in Vietnam over the years of involvement and direct participation. They either served in US units or as advisors to the RVNAF; there were many among them who volunteered for more than one tour of duty; some served two or even three tours. Except for the top positions, the usual tour of duty for the American serviceman in Vietnam was one year. It was a short time indeed, but for all practical purposes one year seemed reasonable enough and was suitable to most of them.

The continuous exposure of US troops to field conditions and war risks, however, made the one-year tour of combat duties a long one, particularly in the Vietnamese environment. Hence a six-month tour rotation policy was adopted to alleviate trauma and risks. Since the American participation in the ground war was not designed to last for a long time, it was a reasonable policy to allocate the hardship so that nobody had to endure more than his fair share. This policy proved beneficial for the upkeep of morale and effectiveness as far as US forces were concerned. For the advisory program, however, the one-year tour obviously had its drawbacks.

Among ARVN units the change of personnel, particularly in command positions, greatly affected the performance of the unit. Because of the lack of a solid foundation, and despite formal standing operating procedures, all activities of the unit depended almost entirely on the personality and capabilities of the commanding officer. If he was a good commander, the unit performed well. But if he was ineffective, the unit was apt to deteriorate rapidly.

In contrast, US units appeared not to be affected much by personnel change. This was due to established traditions, a solid foundation, and well-honed operating procedures from the top to the bottom level. A good US commander could only make his unit a little better, whereas the worst that a bad commander could do to his unit was a slight decrease in overall efficiency which in most cases was hardly perceptible.

• • •

Over the years of association with the US presence, each Vietnamese commander worked with several American advisors; they lived with each other and fought side by side, like a man and his shadow. An ARVN commander usually stayed in his position for many years, but every year he had to work with a different advisor. At the battalion level, this change in relationship occurred every six months. The relatively rapid turnover of advisors at battalion level had a definite adverse effect on the advisory program. While an advisor did not command the unit, his prestige and standing among ARVN troops were considerable. He was understood to be in a position of power and authority with regard to his counterpart. As a result, every change of advisor disturbed the atmosphere of the unit.

• • •

VII. SUMMARY AND CONCLUSIONS

The introduction of US combat forces in early 1965 saved the Republic of Vietnam from military defeat and helped it restore stability and consolidate a more viable regime. The short-term goals that the United States set about to accomplish were successfully achieved within a relatively short time. Despite obstacles, the Americans also finally succeeded in developing and improving the Vietnamese armed forces on which the Republic of Vietnam depended for its survival.

Resorting to the use of combat force meant that the US advisory effort and level of military assistance up to that time had either fallen short of their goal or were not enough. Then three and a half years of intensive fighting also failed to bring the enemy to his knees. Entering the war with the posture and disposition of a fire brigade, the Americans rushed about to save the Vietnamese house from destruction, but took little interest in caring for the victims. Only after they realized that the victims, too, should be made firefighters to save their own houses did Americans set about to really care for them. Valuable time was lost, and, by the time the victims could get onto their feet and began to move forward a few steps after recovery, the fire brigade was called back to home station.

Throughout the years of participation, the American presence greatly bolstered the RVNAF performance and morale. There could be no doubt about it. The position enjoyed by Americans with regard to the RVNAF was either advisor or comrade-in-arms. Well established, and with carefully selected personnel whose devotion and abilities were undeniable, the US advisory system admirably performed its difficult and complex role. American combat units also made substantial contributions to this effort.

• • •

It is difficult to make an assessment of the US advisory effort. Suffice it to say that it was instrumental in transforming a disorganized, poorly led, and unschooled army of some 150,000 into a modern and highly organized tri-service military force, nearly ten times as large, which successfully held and pushed back the NVA invasion of 1972.

During the first few years the effort of US advisors met with considerable obstacles, particularly in the area of training. Several years of hard fighting on all battlefields from north to south, and of living close to French forces—and undoubtedly under their influence—had instilled a certain psychology of intractability, unruliness, and complacency among the Vietnamese military cadre. Their adjustment to the American way of doing things was painful and slow. They found American training and warfare methods too inflexible, too mechanical, and not realistically adapted to the Vietnamese battlefield. The language barrier and cultural difference also formed a wide and seeming unbridgeable gap. To a certain extent, the Vietnamese were not interested in training and did not think it was necessary. After all, they felt they were experienced enough and knew how to fight this kind of war. American tactical advice was something they thought they could do without.

During the early 1960s most US Army company-grade officers that were assigned to field advisory duties—except for a few Korean War veterans—had no combat experience. They were in a truly awkward position vis-à-vis the Vietnamese regimental and battalion commanders who had gone through so many battles during the First Indochina War. Their role and effectiveness, as a consequence, were greatly reduced. The advisor's duties were mostly limited to end-use inspections, maintenance of weapons and materiel, and assisting the unit in military techniques and logistics, but seldom in operational matters.

This situation changed when US combat support assets—airlift, helicopters, and, later, tactical air—were made available. For the first time ARVN unit commanders felt vulnerable and helpless without advisors who controlled and provided the support assets. The role of advisors began to grow in importance and their effectiveness increased markedly with the advent of airmobile operations and US tactical air support. This new aspect and level of the war had changed the advisory relationship for the better.

• • •

The US advisory effort suffered a setback during the first few years of active US participation in the war. The role of advisors was overshadowed by the presence of US combat forces on whom the success or failure of the war effort depended. ARVN units began to turn to US field commanders for operational guidance and support, since it was they who wielded true military power, not the regular advisors who during this time acted mostly in a liaison role. Because of their reduced role, and the priority of personnel assignment given to US combat forces, the selection of advisors was no longer subject to exacting criteria and the advisory effectiveness suffered accordingly.

• • •

The task of upgrading RF and PF combat effectiveness through the device of mobile assistance teams was only reasonably successful. This was due less to the limitations of advisory personnel than to constraints of the territorial command and control system. Conceived and operating as part of the RVNAF, the RF and PF were nevertheless placed under a different command channel and more often than not were employed in a haphazard and unorthodox manner by a province or district chief who was always too busy with his administrative or political duties. Lacking strong and effective main force backing and adequate combat support, RF and PF were usually exposed to piecemeal defeat and seldom had the offensive spirit or the motivation required to accomplish their difficult mission.

On their part, the ARVN regular units did not fare much better, bound as they were to their territorial security and pacification support duties. Only rarely did they have the opportunity to evade the debilitating effect of routine activities and participate in mobile operations. Not until after 1968 was there any systematic effort to improve their combat effectiveness through intensive programs of combined operations. But by the time ARVN units really got off to a good start US forces were already standing down to redeploy.

• • •

It was the US forces that held the initiative in combat operations, because they were assigned this mission and controlled all vital support assets. The division of tasks thus determined by the Combined Campaign Plan reflected the status of the RVNAF during this period. Their combat effectiveness was marginal and their combat support assets were still very limited.

• • •

As has been said earlier, ARVN corps commanders were usually deeply involved in administration and political matters, and could not spare enough time or energy to devote to the tactical problems, which, fortunately, were cared for by US field forces. The rare visits they made to subordinate units were always solemn, formal, and time-consuming occasions that practically stopped all activities of the unit being visited. An ARVN corps commander never casually dropped in for a visit or for a working session with the unit commander. . . . Corps commanders were not interested in what US forces were doing, either. There were occasional visits to US forces, of course, but they were more in the nature of ceremonial or official functions. Although some claimed that US field forces withheld information concerning US plans and activities—which was probably true in a few instances—corps commanders were never fully informed about the tactical situation and friendly activities, either Vietnamese or American. They depended totally on US initiative and efforts.

• • •

At lower echelons, brigade or battalion, US unit commanders were generally reluctant to participate in combined operations with ARVN units. At these levels there existed no advisor-counterpart relationship between US and ARVN unit commanders. When they participated in combined operations, their relationship was usually one of mutual support—for the duration of the common effort. The reluctance to cooperate on the part of US brigade or battalion commanders derived chiefly from a prejudice against the combat effectiveness of ARVN units. They appeared not to realize that perseverance, determination, and tolerance were the ingredients that were required from both sides to arrive at genuine cooperation.

• • •

A major impediment for the RVNAF was the continuing lack of combat support assets and the perennial shortage of forces available for combined operations. Almost all assets required for the support of ARVN units were provided by US forces, from a command and liaison ship to airlift or helilift facilities, firepower, engineers, supplies, medical evacuation, etc. In large measure, therefore, combined operations depended on the availability of resources. This explained why they were usually initiated and planned by US forces. Then, in order to muster enough forces for the combined effort, it was usually necessary to redeploy ARVN units committed to pacification support. This was a step that neither the US field force commander nor the corps commander took lightly, given the emphasis the RVN government placed on pacification and rural development at the time.

Not until after the successful counterattack by US and ARVN forces in the wake of the enemy 1968 Tet Offensive did operational cooperation and coordination develop into a systematic and purposeful effort. This was basically due to a drastic change in American policy toward the war. The United States was more and more inclined to curtail US participation and was turning over more combat responsibility to the RVNAF. Programs were initiated to quickly expand and modernize the RVNAF on the one hand and upgrade Vietnamese combat effectiveness on the other. This preparatory work was to pave the way for the Vietnamization program and the disengagement of US forces from South Vietnam.

The task of improving the RVNAF combat effectiveness became the major concern of MACV and US field forces. . . . In contrast to the earlier period, combined operations involved an increasing number of ARVN units and were conducted more regularly within preconceived programs. At the same time, more modern weapons and equipment were made available to ARVN infantry divisions.

• • •

One may wonder what these programs could have done to the RVNAF had they been initiated at the very beginning of the US participation in the war. Then, perhaps, Vietnamization could have begun much earlier. And if, instead of a gradual response approach, the United States had fully and resolutely brought its entire military might to bear on the war effort, then surely the outcome of the war would have been different.

• • •

In general, despite shortcomings and drawbacks, the US presence and effort truly helped the RVNAF to improve in most aspects. In return, US commanders, and advisors in particular, learned something about the complex nature of the Vietnam War and acquired invaluable experience that might be helpful to them in some future conflict. Why was there a failure to produce strong leadership and motivation? This was, in the final analysis, what plagued the RVNAF the most. To be able to answer this question requires a thorough knowledge of the nature of the war, the kind of political system that directed the war effort, and the circumstances that affected leadership and motivation. A full answer to why there was such a profound lack of strong leadership and adequate motivation lies in these characteristics of the war, its politics, and its circumstances. It can be said, though, that good leadership and motivation were definitely not developed to an adequate extent and that this failure had a disastrous effect on the eventual outcome of the war.

NOTES

1. This high-handed coup prompted US Ambassador Maxwell D. Taylor to use the rather undiplomatic method of dressing down the Vietnamese generals for their unsettling action. The United States was striving during this time to restore political stability in South Vietnam.

2. Lieutenant General Bernard William Rogers, *Cedar Falls–Junction City: A Turning Point* (Washington, DC: DA, 1974), p. 85.

3. Ibid., p. 87.

4. In 1970 the designation Corps Tactical Zone was changed into Military Region (MR), and the Capital Military Region became Capital Military District (CMD) under operational control of MR-3. DTAs were abolished. Presidential Decree No. 614a-TT/SL, 1 July 1970.

5. The total number of ARVN infantry divisions increased to 11 when the 3rd Infantry Division was activated in October 1971 to replace the US 3rd Marine Division.

6. In 1967, upon recommendation of the 10th Division Commander, Brigadier General Do Ke Giai, who believed that number 10 was a bad number, the 10th Division was changed into the 18th, presumably a luckier number.

7. In addition to his political positions as member, National Leadership Committee, and government delegate to III Corps Tactical Zone, General Khang was also Commander, CMD; military governor of Saigon–Gia Dinh; and Commander, Marine Division, a position he held for 12 years.

8. The soft cordon is characterized by limited use of firepower, resulting in minimum property damages and injury to civilians, and slow, painstaking searches of villages and suspicious areas by the sweeping and cordon forces. The cordon force serves a dual purpose: it blocks, and at the same time searches. The so-called blocking positions are not static defensive positions, but are moving, searching troops who make detailed searches. They occupy and serve as a "noose" around the cordoned area. The protracted occupation of an area causes the concealed enemy to become impatient and hungry, forcing them to reveal their hiding places. . . .

9. F. J. West Jr., *The Village* (New York: Harper and Row, 1972), p. 11.

10. In some provinces and districts US Special Forces teams acted as advisors.

4

Territorial Forces

Lieutenant General Ngo Quang Truong

PREFACE

A significant aspect of the South Vietnamese counterinsurgency effort was the employment of several differently organized military and paramilitary forces, each in a different role. Among them the territorial forces, which made up more than one-half of the total RVNAF strength, deserved particular interest because of their vital role in pacification.

Pitted against Communist local force and guerrilla units, the territorial forces fought a low-key warfare of their own at the grassroots level, far removed from the war's limelight. Their exploits were rarely sung, their shortcomings often unjustly criticized. But, without their contribution, pacification could hardly have succeeded as it did.

To evaluate the performance of the territorial forces, this monograph seeks to present the Vietnamese point of view on their roles and missions, development, training, employment, and support as they evolved during the war. More emphatically, it also attempts to analyze their problems and to determine if, in their actual condition, the territorial forces were effective enough as antithesis to Communist insurgency warfare.

Although I have drawn primarily from my own experience in the preparation of this monograph, several distinguished colleagues of mine have also contributed to it. . . . [28 July 1978]

I. INTRODUCTION

An Abstract of Communist Insurgency in South Vietnam

The end of the First Indochina War in 1954 left the Democratic Republic of Vietnam (DRV or Viet Minh) with a well-developed political and military organization potentially capable of carrying on the fight with combined guerrilla-conventional warfare.

In the South, this organization consisted of about 90,000 troops who controlled several war zones . . . and guerrilla bases. . . . After the partition, the majority of this force was regrouped and evacuated to north of the 17th parallel in accordance with the Geneva Accords. In the process, the Viet Minh left behind an estimated five to ten thousand men, mostly selected from among well-trained, disciplined, and loyal party members. This fifth column was ordered to put away weapons and ammunition in secret storage, mostly in areas of difficult access along the border or in the Mekong Delta. They and other political elements were to mix in the stream of normal life and wait for orders to resume action. It was these men who made up the initial nucleus of insurgency after the South Vietnamese government refused to take part in the 1956 reunification elections.

During 1956 and 1957 the Viet Minh spent most of their efforts recruiting and reactivating former base areas. In the meantime those who had regrouped to the North and received insurgency training there began to reinfiltrate into the South. This movement of Communist insurgency was thus building up force in earnest while South Vietnam complacently went about its task of nation building. Gradually the underground Viet Minh forces gained in strength and organization, ready to exploit the unsettled conditions which characterized the first few years of the Republic of Vietnam. By the end of 1957 a campaign of terror and assassination was in progress and the first signs of security deterioration began to [be] manifest in rural areas.

Insurgency as a concerted effort did not begin until 1959. By this time subversive activities by the Communist Viet Minh, now known as Viet Cong, had taken on alarming proportions, especially in the Mekong Delta, and soon spread all over the country. Infiltration from North Vietnam through lower Laos and the DMZ, and from the sea, also increased by the month and in time became an established pattern for the years ahead.

North Vietnam's design for the South, which was decided during the Third Congress of the Communist Party in September 1960, was to concentrate every effort on what it called "the primary strategic mission to prosecute a revolution for national liberation" in South Vietnam. As Hanoi leaders saw it, this mission was going to be a tough and protracted process requiring several different forms of struggle, from the lowest to the highest. The objective was to build, consolidate, and develop a popular front in the South which would appear as if the South Vietnamese population was revolting to overthrow their own government. This was how the National Liberation Front (NLF) for South Vietnam came into being when its creation was officially proclaimed on 20 December 1960. In early 1962, Hanoi took a further step toward full control of the insurgency war when it upgraded its southern Political Commissariat into the Central Office for South Vietnam (COSVN), the party's politburo in the South.

• • •

With large infusions of men and weapons from North Vietnam, the Viet Cong were therefore able to upgrade their terrorist activities to full-fledged guerrilla warfare. During 1960 the first battalion-sized attacks were initiated against outlying towns and outposts, to include a few conducted against ARVN forces. Most significant were the attacks in early 1960 against an element of the 32nd Regiment in the Mekong Delta and the headquarters, 12th Light Division, in Tay Ninh Province, which created quite a tremor across the country. Soon these attacks gained in tempo and reached multibattalion size during 1961; as a result, several outlying areas succumbed [to] Communist control.[1] In the meantime, the flow of infiltration from the North kept increasing in size, and local recruiting efforts by the VC also became more successful as enemy control expanded.

By 1962 the Viet Cong guerrilla force structure had increased to over 75,000. This force consisted of three categories: full-time guerrillas, part-time guerrillas, and rural support elements. Full-time guerrillas were estimated at 18,000 and organized into companies and battalions which operated at the provincial level; they were considered the VC military. Part-time guerrillas, estimated at about 40,000, were organized at the district level into platoons and companies. Summarily trained, they were equipped with small weapons, mines, and explosives. The rural support elements numbered about 17,000 and constituted a reserve force at the village level. During the daytime, they went about their normal business, but at night participated in activities under the local guerrilla chief's orders. Usually equipped with knives or machetes, they sometimes operated with firearms. These support elements played an important role in guerrilla operations, providing new recruits, supplying food, and collecting information concerning village defense, local government officials, and security forces.

From these three categories of guerrilla forces, the VC eventually built up their main, local, and guerrilla units, which all increased in size and structure to keep up with intensified war efforts. By the end of 1963 the VC main force had reached a level of 35,000, a figure which kept expanding every year with the flow of weapons infiltrated from the North, especially those supplied by Russia and Red China.

As their forces grew in strength, the VC stepped up attacks, terror, and sabotage, despite governmental countermeasures. Between 1963 and 1965 the level of armed conflict in South Vietnam grew to alarming proportions. The VC also benefited from the domestic political difficulties faced by the GVN during this period, which they exploited to their advantage by expanding the range and scale of their activities. During 1964 alone they assassinated 436 hamlet chiefs or other officials and abducted 1,131 others. More than 1,350 civilians were killed by VC mines or terrorist activities, and at least 8,400 were kidnapped. This level of activity continued into 1965.

With their growing military posture, during 1964–1965 the VC gradually expanded their control over rural areas and upgraded their force structure to division size. From all indications it was apparent that they were evolving into the final or mobile warfare phase.

THE RVN'S COUNTERINSURGENCY EFFORTS

Born amid tumultuous political events that marked the aftermath of the 1954 Geneva Accords, the Republic of Vietnam endeavored to develop a free, democratic, fully sovereign country that could resist Communist aggression from the North.

The threat of a military conquest by North Vietnam was genuine, especially after 1956. South Vietnam's leaders estimated then that this conquest could materialize either under the form of a subversive war waged by Hanoi-directed Communist elements remaining in the South or through an outright invasion from the North conducted by NVA regular forces.

In the face of this double threat, South Vietnam planned its defense structure to cope with either or both possibilities. This, in essence, consisted of defending the national territory against a possible invasion from across the borders and eliminating subversive activities within the national boundaries. The objective was to ensure territorial integrity and pacify the whole country.

Toward that objective, the force structure of South Vietnam was organized into two principal components: the regular forces and the territorial forces.

• • •

Territorial forces were made up of the Regional Forces and the Popular Forces, formerly known as the Civil Guard and the Self-Defense Corps, respectively. Their organization was local in nature, being kept mostly at the small-unit level (platoon and company), lightly equipped, and tasked for pacification and the maintenance of territorial security.

The first significant pacification effort made under the First Republic to counter Communist insurgency was the Agroville program. Launched by President Ngo Dinh Diem in July 1959, after the Communists began to step up disruptive activities, the program was designed to assemble those rural people who lived in scattered isolation into farming agglomerations for better governmental control and protection. Called "agrovilles," these farming agglomerations were to serve a double purpose: maintenance of local security and socioeconomical development. Despite sound planning and a promising start, the few pilot agrovilles carved out of the Mekong Delta's wilderness did not live up to expectations. Too large for effective defense, they proved to be vulnerable and unrealistic.

Drawing from this unsuccessful experiment, the Diem administration worked on another pacification concept and put it to [the] test in a few areas during 1961. The concept, which became known as the "strategic hamlet," was officially declared a national policy in March 1962.

Considered the most important pacification effort under the First Republic, the Strategic Hamlet program was essentially based on the British counterinsurgency experience in Malaya. Designed to counter Communist people's war and neutralize its frontless effect, the guiding concept of the program was to turn each individual hamlet, the natural geographic and demographic unit of South Vietnam, into a defense fortification. Hamlet defense was deemed basic and easier to organize and control than the village, the administrative unit. Under the vision of Mr. Nhu, who devised the concept to neutralize the effect of a war without front lines, we had to create interconnected lines of defense. These lines of defense were to be made up of strategic hamlets linked together in a mutual support system and, when interconnected, would create large secure areas which made it easier to detect the enemy and facilitated mutual security support among the hamlets.

• • •

When implemented, the Strategic Hamlet program revealed certain intrinsic weaknesses. A major weakness, which derived basically from the initial concept, was the forced displacement of a substantial number of farmers, which eventually generated an undercurrent of discontent. In addition to uprooting them from their lands and ancestral graveyards to which they felt intimately attached by tradition, the transplanting of farming people to an unfamiliar environment also tended to make their living standards somewhat lower.

Another basic difficulty was physical protection. Although in theory the strategic hamlets should receive support not only among themselves but also from territorial and regular forces, there was seldom close coordination in local defense plans. Many hamlets under attack, therefore, found themselves isolated with no one to depend on for support but their own people.

As for training and equipment, they proved totally inadequate for the purposes intended. The VC, in fact, encountered no significant difficulties when they mounted attacks against strategic hamlets, of which a good number were destroyed. By the end of 1963 the program fell into disfavor and neglect after President Diem was overthrown.

The new military government which took over did not have any plans, nor was any significant effort made, to pacify the rural areas. The objective then was simply to destroy the VC. After General Nguyen Khanh came to power in March 1964 the government initiated the "Victory Plan," the [essence] of which was to pacify the countryside on the "oil stain" concept. Pacification was to progress slowly but firmly, gaining ground from secure areas and expanding outward as it proceeded.

Despite the comprehensiveness of the Victory Plan, which sought to implement pacification in several aspects and required close military-civilian cooperation, in reality it turned out to be primarily a military campaign endeavoring not so much to obtain the lasting results of pacification as to destroy the enemy. Therefore South Vietnam's pacification efforts to counter Communist insurgency up to that time achieved very little indeed. It was possible that each attempt had been undermined by unfavorable circumstances prevailing in that particular period. But, basically, these efforts still fell far short of the objective intended, which was to bring about and maintain local security, a prerequisite of pacification.

• • •

To save South Vietnam from the danger of collapse and to stop Communist aggression, the United States introduced combat troops in 1965. The next period saw the war intensified by US-conducted large-scale operations which achieved substantial results. Enemy forces were soundly defeated and their combat potential markedly reduced. All important populous centers were successively cleared from enemy pressure and the situation improved remarkably as a result.

All of these achievements, however, in spite of their magnitude, represented temporary success rather than lasting progress. The key issue in territorial security remained unsolved as long as the VC guerrilla and local forces, with the support of their political infrastructure, were still intact. Experience indicated that pacification would not produce lasting results until these elements were discovered and eliminated.

Therefore the efforts to fight the insurgency war in South Vietnam were twofold. In

addition to destroying enemy main-force units and defending the borders against infiltration, the government had also to deal with the VC infrastructure and guerrillas, the
enemy's insurgent component. This was precisely the role to be performed by the territorial forces.

II. SOUTH VIETNAM'S ORGANIZATION
FOR TERRITORIAL DEFENSE

• • •

Military Organization and Control

Up to 1957, South Vietnam retained its military territorial organization as it had been
under French control. There were then only three military regions: MR-1, which comprised the provinces of former Cochin China and was headquartered at Thu Duc in Gia
Dinh Province; MR-2, which encompassed all the provinces of former Central Vietnam
and whose headquarters was located in Hue; MR-4, which was headquartered at Ban
Me Thuot and encompassed the Central Highlands.[2] Under the control of military region headquarters there were sectors defined by provincial boundaries. During this period the sector commander served as deputy for security for the province chief, who was
usually a civilian. Infantry divisions were deployed to military regions as required by
defense requirements; they were subordinated to military region headquarters only in
matters concerning territorial security.

In late 1958, in keeping with ARVN reorganization trends which saw the activation
of field and light infantry divisions, three corps headquarters were created: I Corps at
Danang; II Corps at Pleiku; and III Corps in Saigon. These corps headquarters were organized with the purpose of controlling infantry divisions assigned to them to fight a
hypothetical large-scale invasion by the North Vietnamese Army.

But large-scale or conventional warfare at the division or corps level did not materialize at the outbreak of Communist insurgency. The war began instead at the grassroots
level with small VC guerrilla units which, through the use of hit-and-run tactics, gradually gained control in rural areas, especially in former MR-1. To alleviate the territorial
control and combat burdens for MR-1, an area teeming with Communist insurgents who
lived either among the popular masses or in the jungle, the government created a new
military region, called MR-5, with headquarters in Can Tho.

In 1961 several significant reorganization efforts were made in order to achieve unity
of command and place particular emphasis on pacification. South Vietnam was divided
into four Corps Tactical Zones (CTZ), each placed under the control of an army corps.
Each CTZ was in turn divided into Division Tactical Areas (DTA), for which subordinate infantry divisions were responsible. The 1st CTZ or I Corps area encompassed the
five northernmost provinces, which made up two DTAs. The 2nd CTZ or II Corps area
included 12 provinces of the Central Highlands and coastal lowlands, which were distributed between two DTAs. The 3rd CTZ or III Corps area comprised the ten provinces

that surrounded Saigon and the Capital Military District (CMD), which encompassed Saigon city and Gia Dinh Province. The 4th CTZ or IV Corps area was divided into three DTAs and included all 16 provinces of the Mekong Delta.

To achieve unity of command, the three former military region headquarters were deactivated and a new IV Corps headquarters was activated at Can Tho. Corps commanders were also CTZ commanders; likewise, division commanders were also DTA commanders. Both the CTZ and DTA were responsible not only for mobile operations but also for territorial security in their zones and areas of responsibility. At the same time, civilian province chiefs were gradually replaced by military officers, especially in those areas where security deteriorated. When a military officer was appointed province chief, he also served as sector commander at the same time. This practice soon became firmly established and eventually all province chiefs were military officers, especially following the overthrow of Mr. Diem.[3] It was believed that, in a country at war, a military province chief was better suited to the task of pacification, since he could coordinate military and civilian activities. This practice also applied to district chiefs, who served as subsector commanders at the same time.

In 1970, in order to provide more combat forces for mobile operations in replacement of US units, the formal DTAs were disbanded, theoretically freeing infantry divisions from their territorial responsibilities. Divisions were assigned informal areas of tactical responsibility instead, whose configurations depended on the local security situation. South Vietnam was still divided into four corps areas which retained former boundaries, but were called military regions in place of CTZ. Corps commanders, as military region commanders, exercised direct control over sectors as far as territorial security was concerned. Sectors remained the same, as did subsectors.

This organization was maintained until late 1973. In early 1974, to improve the maintenance of security at the grassroots level and in preparation for a political contest with the Communists, South Vietnam's military territorial organization was extended to the village level through the activation of sub-subsector headquarters. A sub-subsector commander, usually a junior officer, performed the role of assistant village chief for security, responsible for the control and coordination of village security forces, to include Popular Forces, People's Self-Defense Forces, and the National Police. This was the last effort to improve territorial command and control made by the GVN.

In spite of complexities and shortcomings which inevitably came as a result of several changes in territorial organization and control, the efforts made by the GVN in that direction represented perhaps the best compromise between dictates of the growing politico-military war and available resources. South Vietnam's organization for territorial control was also a compromise between centralization and efforts of decentralization which were made during the later stages of the war.

At the corps/military region level, the most serious shortcoming was undoubtedly the fact that the corps commander and his staff were constantly overburdened by innumerable tasks and responsibilities. The span of control was simply too much for a corps headquarters to handle, such as in the case[s] of MR-2 and MR-3, each of which consisted of more than ten provinces. In the extreme case of MR-4, which encompassed 16 provinces, obviously every basic principle of command and control was seriously violated. MR-1 was relatively better off with only five provinces, but here I Corps had to shoulder heavier combat responsibilities occasioned by large-scale threats and attacks by the majority of NVA divisions.

• • •

The abolition of DTAs, on the other hand, did not bring about any of the desired results. Whether DTAs now became tactical areas of interest (TAOI), tactical areas of responsibility (TAOR), or areas of operation (AO), the ARVN infantry divisions continued to be bound by territorial responsibilities. The primary reason why they could not be extricated from their territorial security mission was that the military region headquarters could not militarily control the territory for which it was responsible. Besides, the evolving security situation in certain areas did not allow the redeployment of divisional units if security was to be maintained.

• • •

To be sure, I [as IV Corps commander] found it impossible to extricate infantry divisions from territorial missions because they were the primary forces that kept territorial security from deteriorating. Aside from their resources which could be used to effectively support territorial activities, infantry divisions also performed certain critically needed services such as inspecting and supervising fixed installations [and] the defense of outposts and bridges, especially in outlying areas, services that required highly professional expertise. The role played by infantry divisions therefore became indispensable for the maintenance of territorial security. This indicates why our 11 ARVN infantry divisions were never entirely mobile in a true sense, regardless of their efforts. The only exception came during the 1972 Easter Offensive, when the 21st and 23rd Divisions were temporarily extracted from territorial missions, but then it was just a case of force majeure. To be freed from territorial responsibilities in order to conduct mobile operations—like the Airborne and Marine Divisions—was a major desire of division commanders. Unfortunately, they were never able to escape the tedious chores demanded by territorial security.

At the province or sector level, the fact that the province chief doubled as a military commander also caused many problems. A province chief usually found himself overburdened by military and civilian duties. As a military commander, he was in charge of a territorial force whose strength might be the equivalent of two divisions, such as in the case of Dinh Tuong and Binh Dinh, two of the largest provinces. In addition, as province chief he had to direct and supervise his provincial administration, including those activities originated by ministries of the central government. But his role was an integrated one, and, even though overburdened, he could operate much more effectively than if his responsibilities were divided, as during the First Republic. For the task of pacification implied that every effort should be an integration or detailed coordination of military-civilian activities, and this requirement could not be achieved by having a province chief looking after administrative affairs while a sector commander was solely responsible for military operations. For the purposes of unity of command and pacification, the dual role of the province chief was essential. After all, like the corps commander, he could always delegate authority to his deputy for administration and deputy sector commander.

In general, South Vietnam had gone through several trials and errors in the quest for the best approach to fighting a war which was devoid of conventional front lines and rear areas. Under such circumstances, and given the environment of South Vietnam, it was hard indeed to find any simple solution which would be better than the prevailing arrangement for territorial command and control.

III. THE REGIONAL AND POPULAR FORCES

Evolution of a Concept

During the first few years of its existence South Vietnam wanted to maintain a military force composed primarily of volunteers. From the lessons learned during the 1946–1954 war, South Vietnamese military leaders believed that, for the defense of their new nation to be effective, this military force should have the capabilities to maintain territorial security and fight a mobile war at the same time. Therefore, in addition to regular forces which were upgraded from mobile groups to infantry divisions in early 1955, they advocated the activation of local-force regiments with men recruited locally. This concept was based on the simple logic that these men were intimately familiar with the geographical and social environment of their locality, and, attached as they were by tradition to their native villages, they would be more dedicated to fight for their defense if the necessity should arise.

This concept was not shared by US advisors of the Military Assistance and Advisory Group (MAAG), who maintained that the Army of the Republic of Vietnam (ARVN) should be a mobile ground force consisting primarily of draftees. They also disapproved of the local recruitment principle, fearing that this would make the ARVN less mobile. Our army, as a result, was reorganized along American conventional guidelines into four field divisions and, as a measure of compromise, six light divisions, totalling 30 regular infantry regiments after ridding itself of all auxiliary force units. The four 8,600-man field divisions would be employed to confront an invasion from the North, conventional-style. The light divisions, with a strength of 5,245 each, were designed primarily to conduct mobile operations to suppress rebels and guerrillas and to support the field divisions. By 1958, however, the light divisions were disbanded, for, as the Chief MAAG, Lieutenant General Samuel T. Williams, observed, they were not capable of confronting regular North Vietnamese divisions.

At that time, it appeared that South Vietnam's defense was based on the concept that the ARVN needed only to fight a delaying action during the initial stage of an invasion pending eventual intervention by the US and SEATO forces. As a result, our ten divisions were transformed into seven standardized infantry divisions, conventionally organized, trained, and equipped to fight a conventional war. Preoccupied as it was with the task of preparing the ARVN for an eventual showdown with the North Vietnamese Army, [the] MAAG took some interest in the problem of territorial security, but, in its view, this was a matter that the GVN should and could handle with its own resources.

When fighting finally broke out, it did not take the form of a conventional, Korean-style invasion. It rather began as a brushfire war fought with subversive activities and guerrillas tactics away from the urban centers. Waged day and night, this small war gradually gained in tempo, nipping away at the secure fabric of rural areas. In the face of growing insurgency, ARVN units found themselves ill-fitted to fight this type of war, for which they had not been trained.

In mid-1959, to meet the immediate requirements of beating Communist insurgents in their own game, the GVN activated 65 "special action" companies which later became known as rangers. Acting without MAAG concurrence, the GVN was compelled to take away one company from each four-company infantry battalion to provide the necessary manpower for the ranger forces. By June the next year, however, [the] MAAG was sold on the special warfare concept and agreed to support and train the ranger companies.

To assist South Vietnam in meeting the growing Communist threat, a counterinsurgency plan was prepared for study in September 1960 under the supervision of Lieutenant General Lionel C. McGarr, the new Chief, MAAG. The objective of this plan was to check the expansion of insurgency by increasing South Vietnam's force structure. For the conduct of the war, the plan's basic concept advocated the division of South Vietnam's territory into tactical areas placed under military commands appropriately structured and sufficiently strong to exercise effective control and supervision. Security in individual areas was to be maintained by ARVN units, rangers, and territorial forces acting in close coordination and cooperation. In February 1961 the completed counterinsurgency plan was approved. It provided basic guidelines for all subsequent planning and actions in the years ahead.

The territorial forces, whose employment figures in this counterinsurgency plan, were military organizations placed under the direct control of sector and subsector commanders to assure territorial security. Two principal components made up the territorial forces: the Civil Guard and the Self-Defense Corps, which eventually became the Regional and Popular Forces in 1964. The Regional Forces (RF) were basically organized into rifle companies, augmented as required by a number of river boat companies, mechanized platoons, heavy weapons platoons, reconnaissance units, administration and logistic support companies, and elements of command and control. Although normally operating at the company level, the RF were capable of conducting multicompany operations. The Popular Forces, on the other hand, never progressed beyond the platoon, their basic unit of organization, which was conceived for combat in villages and hamlets. These forces were essentially infantry; their equipment and mode of subsistence were more austere than those of the RF.

The rules were thus established: the RF served the province and the PF the district, but their goals remained essentially the same. There was no standard distribution of RF companies for each province. Their assigned number varied according to the size and population of the individual province and the priority placed on it. The same principle applied to the distribution of PF platoons for individual districts.

Background and Missions

In their role as guardians of territorial security, the RF primary mission was to conduct operations against enemy local forces. The RF supported the PF in maintaining security for villages and hamlets and protecting axes of communication, governmental installations, and the economic infrastructure. Placed under the control of the sector commander, the RF occasionally performed operational missions at the multicompany level during relatively long periods of time. In many instances, the RF also served as a provincial reaction force. In addition, the RF were employed in the defense of outposts or combat bases located in relatively insecure areas.

• • •

To help defray equipment costs, the GVN turned to some allied countries besides the United States, such as Malaysia and Australia, for assistance. As a result, in addition to a hodgepodge of old weapons left behind by French forces, the Civil Guard was also equipped with vintage Ford Lynx armored vehicles and scout cars provided by Malaysia and Land Rover trucks and radio equipment donated by Australia.

The Popular Forces were primarily employed as security forces for villages and hamlets to defend against local enemy guerrillas. They were also deployed to guard axes of communication and fixed installations, man outposts, conduct patrols, gather intelligence, and lay ambushes within the boundaries of the district. They were controlled either by the district or the village chief.

• • •

Organization and Force Development

From their inception to 1960 both the Civil Guard and Self-Defense Corps were neither adequately equipped nor organized and controlled to accomplish their missions in a satisfactory manner. This derived in good part from the lack of US support. South Vietnamese and US viewpoints differed greatly as to the role and significance assigned to these forces. It was South Vietnam's desire to turn the Civil Guard and Self-Defense Corps into strong territorial forces capable of assisting the regular ARVN in defense missions. Therefore the Civil Guard in particular should be organized into battalions and regimental-sized units, sufficiently equipped and armed to defeat enemy local forces. The United States saw it differently, however. As expressed through the Civil Guard training program developed by the Michigan State University (MSU) group, the United States considered the CG nothing more than a rural police force, and neither the CG nor the SDC was supported by the Military Assistance Program (MAP).

Beginning in 1960, however, as insurgent activities became a serious threat for South Vietnam, the United States expended significant efforts to develop and increase the combat effectiveness of these forces. To facilitate US support procedures, in December

1960 the GVN promulgated a decree placing the Civil Guard and the Self-Defense Corps under the Ministry of Defense. On this legal ground, the MAAG began to provide advisors to work with the Civil Guard Directorate in matters concerning training and equipment. Expenditures for the CG, however, were funded by the US International Cooperation Administration (ICA). In 1961 MAAG funding covered both forces.

• • •

Despite the fact that the CG and SDC now operated under the Ministry of Defense and benefited from the US Military Assistance Program, they were not part of the Republic of Vietnam Armed Forces (RVNAF). The CG and SDC forces therefore received no support from the RVNAF, although they performed increasingly difficult missions combating the Viet Cong and suffered the same hardship and dangers as the regular ARVN. As a consequence, they fared very poorly by comparison, especially in training, logistic support, and command and leadership. Still, with MAAG support, the CG and SDC made substantial progress. There were no objective criteria for measuring the improvements in the territorial forces, but regional commanders and other officials noted greater efficiency in the performance of SDC and CG daily activities, and in the discipline and morale of the troops.

• • •

By late 1966 the RF organization was standardized at the separate company level . . . and the Popular Forces were organized into standard platoons. This standardization and consolidation process was also enforced in other aspects. In each province there was only a single consolidated company responsible for all support activities for the RF and PF. The PF black uniform was discarded in favor of the standard olive green and khaki uniforms of the ARVN infantry. Gradually, in their outlook, deportment, and combat performance, the RF and PF troopers shed their paramilitary origins and increasingly became full-fledged soldiers.

These advances in the status and capabilities of the RF and PF were not without American interest, assistance and support. In fact, in October 1967 General Abrams, then Deputy Commander, MACV, directed a MACV staff and US field command study to find ways to improve the combat effectiveness of the territorial forces. In the summer of that year the advisory responsibility for RF and PF had already been consolidated in the office of the MACV deputy for Civil Operations and Revolutionary Development Support (CORDS). This was a change that greatly improved the coordination of all US efforts in pacification support and had a direct beneficial effect on territorial forces.

As a consequence of the MACV and CORDS interest in the territorials, and a result of General Abrams' study, mobile training teams were organized and, by mid-1968, were engaged in training territorials in the field.

With American support, the RF force structure constantly expanded, from 888 companies in 1967 to 1,119 in 1968 and 1,471 in 1969. This expansion, coupled with stepped-up combat activities, brought about problems for the sector and subsector headquarters as far as operational control was concerned. To improve this control, RF company group headquarters were activated beginning in 1969. Each group headquarters was capable of exercising operational control over two to five RF companies in combat missions.

During 1969 RF companies were also experimentally grouped into battalions for the purpose of testing their capabilities for mobile operations within a province. This effort was occasioned by the fact that enemy local forces had upgraded their activities to battalion and, occasionally, regimental level. By the end of June 1970 there were a total of 31 RF battalions and 232 RF company groups thus formed.

• • •

Encouraged by the performance of RF battalions in mobile combat operations, the JGS gradually transformed company group headquarters into full-fledged battalion headquarters. By 1973 a total of 360 RF battalions had thus been formed and fully employed. The success of this plan, and the necessity of freeing ARVN infantry divisions for mobile combat missions in replacement of US major units, which by this time had been withdrawn, urged the JGS to take a further step in upgrading the RF. In the JGS's view, if RF battalions could be grouped into regiments or brigades, they would certainly be able to take over the major responsibility of supporting pacification which ARVN infantry divisions now assumed. Strategically, this would make the conduct of the war much more effective, since the type of warfare now being fought had become increasingly large scale and conventional.

The idea was subjected to extensive debates, but finally it was deemed unfeasible for two reasons: lack of competent cadre and lack of funds for additional equipment.

• • •

By late 1974 stepped-up war activities by NVA main-force units, especially in MR-2, and the GVN policy dictates of maintaining territorial integrity had edged our ARVN infantry divisions into a situation of overextension for static defense from which they could hardly extricate [themselves] without replacement forces. The protracted commitment in MR-1 of our only two general reserve divisions made South Vietnam's defense posture look even worse in the face of the constant enemy buildup along the western border. Within each province there was an urgent need for a strong mobile strike force to confront local enemy forces, because regular reinforcements from MR headquarters were difficult and often impossible to obtain. Each of our ARVN corps, with all of its units committed and overextended, also felt the need for a mobile reserve force which could be used to assist infantry divisions in facing serious tactical situations and, in case of heavy losses, as replacement units.

These requirements led to the activation of RF mobile groups, still a makeshift solution in view of US aid constraints, but responsive enough to warrant their expedient formation. Each RF mobile group was nothing more than a permanent assemblage of the existing sector tactical headquarters and RF battalions, plus some organic artillery support. Oddly enough, its composition very nearly matched the old French Groupe Mobile (GM) of the First Indochina War: a tactical headquarters with the same support units (except for the polwar platoon), three infantry battalions (RF), and a battery of four 105mm howitzers. The RF mobile group was thus made capable of self-sustained combat operations and, since it was not bound by sector boundaries, could be used to reinforce infantry divisions as required within the MR.

The JGS planning called for 27 such RF mobile groups to be activated, beginning in January 1975. By 30 April, seven had become operational and employed extensively in MR-3 and MR-4. The process of RF organization and force development ended with this final concept.

From their inception to the very last days of the war, the RF and PF almost always made up more than one-half of the total RVNAF strength. Their combined strength naturally exceeded that of all regular infantry forces. At their latest stage of development, the RF numbered about 312,000, distributed among 1,810 rifle companies, 24 river boat companies, 51 mechanized platoons (V-100), and logistic support and staff elements. The PF numbered somewhat less, 220,800 in total, broken down into 7,968 platoons. Over the years these territorial forces had become the subject of constant study and exchanges between the JGS and MACV.

In terms of unit organizations, the RF progressed from separate companies to company groups, battalions, and finally mobile groups. This gradual upgrading into larger units somehow deprived the RF of their local character, but it was dictated by South Vietnam's growing force requirements and the changing nature of the war, especially during the later stages.

Almost every military authority, especially South Vietnamese, agreed that these trends in RF organizational and force development responded to the requirements of the war. While agreeing, some thought that the activation of RF regimental-sized units came rather belatedly. They believed that this should have been done in 1971, when most US infantry divisions had been withdrawn and the enemy was grouping his local forces into battalions and regiments and preparing for mobile conventional warfare. I agree with this opinion. If we had achieved this at that time, then ARVN infantry divisions would not have found themselves overextended when replacing US units being redeployed. They could have become more mobile and would have constituted a formidable deterrent to invasion. Then the problem of general reserves and corps reserves would have been solved, or at least been less acute. If such had been our military posture, I believe that North Vietnam would have been less inclined to conduct a full-scale invasion as in 1972 and 1975, even without US military presence.

• • •

Recruitment and Administration

From their inception the RF and PF procured their manpower through recruitment and conscription. This manpower came primarily from two sources: discharged RVNAF servicemen, and civilian youths not falling into the draft age class (20–22 for the period prior to 1964). Those in this age class were obligated to do their military service for a mandatory period of time (usually two years) and could volunteer to serve in the RF or PF only after discharge.

Until 1960, recruitment for the RF and PF did not have any significant difficulties.

But, beginning in 1961, it ran into increasing competition with recruiting efforts of the regular forces, which sought to complement their quotas of draftees to meet expansion requirements. The RF and PF lost in this competition; their lower pay and enlistment bonus did not attract enough volunteers. To provide the manpower required by the RF-PF force structure expansion, many province chiefs resorted to recruiting outsiders, people from other provinces. They found that personnel resources were usually abundant in Vinh Binh and Ba Xuyen Provinces, with their large Khmer communities, or those provinces with large numbers of Hoa Hao and Cao Dai followers (Chau Doc, Long Xuyen, Phong Dinh, Tay Ninh).

• • •

By 1964 the extended draft age (20–25) made it seemingly harder for the RF and PF to recruit. However, their recruitment was assisted by police operations which sought to track down draft evaders and deserters. Volunteers for service in the RF and PF also became more numerous, especially among those youths 23, 24, and 25 years of age who made up the standby draft age classes. Their incentive for enlistment came from an ardent desire to stay near their hometowns and families; service in the RF or PF was their only chance. At the same time, draft evaders and deserters, fearful of being convicted if caught or weary of living as fugitives, sought ways to enlist in the RF and PF. They did this by procuring for themselves new identification papers, legally or illegally.[4]

Beginning in 1965, RF and PF recruitment became more successful, primarily because of readjusted pay scales and other newly instituted allowances. The RF soldier now earned about the same as an ARVN soldier, including family allowances. The PF soldier's contractual pay, usually a fixed indemnity, also doubled. In addition, both the RF and PF soldiers enjoyed the privilege of serving in their hometowns or villages. Enlistment in the RF and PF received a further boost when, in September 1966, new recruits were awarded the same enlistment or reenlistment bonus that only ARVN recruits had enjoyed.

From 1965 to 1967 the government of Vietnam was too unstable to attempt a general mobilization—the opposition to such a move was strong and vocal—but the government did manage to promulgate several incremental steps to extend the upper limit of draft age to 30. This again benefited the RF and PF, as those youths likely to be called up next usually beat the draft by enlisting in the territorial forces.

Following the Communist offensive of Tet 1968, the climate was right for general mobilization. Not only were the Americans pushing for it, but the country's politicians and people were ready for it.

• • •

With the promulgation of the General Mobilization Law in June 1968, every male citizen between 18 and 38 became eligible for mandatory service in the RVNAF, including RF and PF troopers. An exception was made, however, for those between 31 and 38 who volunteered to serve in the RF or PF. It was this measure which helped boost RF and PF recruitment to unprecedented levels. By the end of 1968 total RF strength had exceeded its authorized level by a large margin (219,000 against 185,873). The same was also true of PF strength, although the excess margin was smaller (173,500 against 167,640). As a result, the activation of additional RF companies and PF platoons to meet expanding pacification requirements went smoothly according to plans during the following years.

Still, in some provinces, RF and PF recruitment among the age classes of 17 and from 31 to 38 did not fare as well as in others. It was as though manpower resources in these provinces had dried up. To assist them with manpower problems, beginning in 1970 the JGS approved a special measure allowing these sectors to recruit among the draft age classes (from 18 to 30) within a limited time, based on recommendations from MR headquarters. As a last resort, this measure was reluctantly taken because the JGS was fully aware that, by doing so, it tacitly condoned draft evasion and desertion. In fact experience revealed that almost all of those recruited in the RF and PF who fell between these draft age limits were either draft evaders, illegal deferments and [exemptions], or deserters. As such, they should have all been arrested and prosecuted by military tribunals. But somehow they managed to stay free in defiance of the law. Obviously this was possible only because local authorities had chosen to look the other way. Bribery was apparently one of the causes for this irregularity, but, in the final analysis, perhaps local authorities believed it not worthwhile to enforce a law which meted out only a few months of imprisonment for those convicted. After all, convicted or not, they would eventually end up either in the military or in enemy hands. It was much better to accept them in the service and have additional combatants than lose them to the enemy.

This was the rationale for recruiting draft evaders and deserters instead of prosecuting them as criminals. Still, for the whole affair to look legal, the JGS always insisted on their having "legal draft status" as a matter of formality when it authorized recruitment. As a matter of expediency, sector recruitment offices obliged by giving recruits hints on how to obtain "legal" papers, which were readily accepted for recruitment purposes until the day such papers were detected as illegal. In practice, the illegality of these papers was almost never challenged, because local authorities believed that it would serve no useful purpose. Usually only when claims were filed by inheritors to collect death gratuities did this illegality surface, but then—for humanitarian reasons—the Ministry of Defense always authorized a "readjustment" to legal status.

• • •

The RF promotion system, long a stumbling block for the career advancement of RF cadres, was radically changed in 1966 when it instituted annual (regular) and battle (special) promotions, which had only been available to our regular forces. Despite this, and continued training, RF ranks were unable to produce enough cadres to meet increasing requirements, especially beginning in 1967 when pacification received national emphasis.

There was, therefore, an increasing demand for regular force officers and NCOs to be transferred to the RF on an extended, attached basis, and this trend was growing every year. During 1965, only 878 ARVN officers were attached to the RF; this number increased to 3,376 by 1968. The next two years saw unprecedented numbers of ARVN officers transferred to the RF; the transfer was in effect so extensive that, by 1970, they outnumbered RF officers by a large margin (10,800 against 8,592). NCO transfers also increased by leaps and bounds. . . . Most of this transferred cadre consisted of reserve officers and NCOs who graduated from Thu Duc and the NCO Academy at Nha Trang, respectively, and whose origins represented a fair regional balance, to include a substantial percentage of those born in North Vietnam.

• • •

The local character of the RF, who were always considered "hometown soldiers," therefore gradually disappeared at the officer and NCO level. It was retained only among the rank and file and those of Montagnard origins. By inclination, most of the transferred officers and NCOs preferred duty in the ARVN if given a free choice. They regarded duty in the RF as lowly and degrading, unbecoming of their regular force status. This feeling arose partly from a long prejudice which viewed the RF as a "poor cousin" and partly from the fact that opportunities for self-achievement in the usually neglected RF, particularly in terms of promotion and awards, were not as good as in the ARVN.

The Popular Forces, by contrast, did not have a rank system like the RF or the ARVN. There were only cadre functions: team leader, assistant squad leader, squad leader, assistant platoon leader, and platoon leader, which was the highest position in the PF. Consequently a PF cadre was promoted to the next higher position only when there was a vacancy.

PF cadres were usually selected from among volunteer youths who had a smattering of military training or combat experience, especially those who had fought alongside or against French forces. Their appointments were recommended by the village chief, endorsed by the district chief, then approved and made official by the province chief's decision.

• • •

Training

From the day the territorial forces came into being up to 1960, formal training was almost nonexistent. During that period they operated in a hodgepodge manner, almost like posses of volunteers. Those with some combat experience by virtue of their former service in French forces informally trained and guided the green troopers.

Not until 1961, when they benefited directly from the US military assistance and advisory program, did the territorial forces begin to receive formal training under the auspices of MAAG advisors. Supervised by the General Directorate of Civil Guard and Self-Defense Corps, training was then focused on the unit level. Each CG company went through a 12-week unit training program, while each SDC platoon or squad was trained only for six weeks. Initially this training was conducted in the field by mobile MAAG advisory training teams which rotated among units. Subsequently it was taken over by training centers as these facilities were constructed and became available on the basis of one SDC (PF) training center for each province and one CG (RF) training center per military region.

Up to 1964, however, basic individual training of recruits for the replacement pipeline was not available on a systematic basis. Training provided either by US mobile training teams or training centers was primarily of the unit type, designed to improve poorly performing units or to initiate the newly activated ones.

Beginning in 1965, as the RF and PF began to operate as components of the RVNAF and training responsibilities were taken over by the Central Training Command/JGS, training for the RF and PF became more comprehensive and systematic, including both basic and refresher for individuals as well as for units. A standardized program of basic and refresher individual training was enforced for both the regular and territorial forces.

• • •

Left to themselves, units rarely conducted any training between operations, primarily because of the lack of interest on the part of unit commanders. They spent most of their idle time [in] rest and recuperation. Finally, sector and subsector commanders seldom made serious efforts to enforce unit training among the RF and PF, knowing that this would tax these units to the limit of their endurance.

IV. THE PARAMILITARY FORCES

While the role of the RF and PF was a [fundamental] one in the maintenance of territorial security, other forces of a paramilitary nature also participated in it, and their role was no less significant. These were the Rural Development (RD) cadres, the People's Self-Defense Corps, and the National Police, which all operated in permanence in villages and hamlets.

As far as village and hamlet security was concerned, these paramilitary forces had a direct working relationship with the RF and PF, and together they formed a mutually supporting defense system. In general, the territorial forces made up the outer protective shield; their role was to prevent VC forces from penetrating the village or hamlet perimeter. Internal security, law, and order were maintained by paramilitary forces who guarded against VC intruders [and] detected and neutralized VCI elements and supporters.

This division of tasks was deemed important for the pacification process because, even though enemy main- or local-force units were kept at bay, village and hamlet security might still be jeopardized by enemy elements living undetected among the population. The Viet Cong infrastructure (VCI), the underground political and supporting arm of Communist insurgency, was pervasive, invisible, and resilient. As long as its political, economic, and intelligence cells were alive, the threat of insurgency still persisted, either through subversive activities or the resurrection of armed rebels.

In a certain sense, therefore, paramilitary forces were unique organizations conceived solely for the purpose of fighting Communist insurgency in South Vietnam. Important as they were, these forces came into being only during the middle stages of the war, for their requirements arose with experience gained in combating insurgency and during pacification efforts. The National Police existed long before the advent of insurgency, but their commitment to a rural role began only with pacification. And, as was the case with the RF and PF, the initial concept on paramilitary forces also evolved through arduous debates and controversy.

• • •

V. RF-PF EMPLOYMENT AND PERFORMANCE

Role and Responsibilities

The employment of territorial forces in South Vietnam evolved with time and the changing war situation. During the initial stage, RF companies were primarily deployed to man the countrywide outpost system which was designed to provide security for rural areas, populated centers, and strategically important places. From these outposts, which served as their operational bases, the RF conducted small-scale operations, usually reconnaissance and patrols, to interdict the penetration of enemy guerrilla or local-force units into areas under their protection. RF units were also employed for the defense of critical points along strategic lines of communication such as important bridges and ferries. Confined to a province, the main realm of RF activity was the district.

The PF, which were made up of rural youths, were initially used to protect their home villages and hamlets against underground VCI elements living illegally among the population and from guerrillas intruding from the outside. The most usual forms of PF activity were to man a squad- or half-squad-sized outpost at the village headquarters and watchtowers on road and waterway accesses to the village, conduct patrols and reconnaissance in the near vicinity of the village, and to employ night ambushes on village approaches. In addition, the PF also searched households for suspects and inspected properties, performing these police functions because there were usually no police stationed in the village. Occasionally platoons might be assembled into a company-sized strike force to assist outposts under enemy attack.

Beginning in 1965, when the GVN initiated the policy of pacification and rural development, and after US combat forces took charge of the main-force war, regular ARVN units took the primary responsibility of supporting pacification. As a result, about 60 percent of ARVN infantry battalions were placed under the sectors' operational control to provide direct support to the pacification program, assisting and augmenting the RF and PF in the maintenance of territorial security. During that period the role of the RF and PF was an obscure one; their equipment was rudimentary and their combat capabilities marginal.

The RF and PF played this secondary role for four years, supporting ARVN, until 1969. Then, as ARVN forces again became involved in the main-force war, the territorials took over as the primary pacification forces. By that time the RF and PF had expanded and improved in several aspects. With more modern equipment and systematic training they had become increasingly combat effective. In secure areas the PF took over the responsibilities normally assigned to the RF; the RF, now freed from static missions, increased their mobile operations. In secure villages and hamlets the PF missions were turned over to the PSDF and National Police.

In 1970 selected RF battalions were committed to missions outside their home provinces. This deployment took place at first in MR-4 and was soon repeated in other military regions. Some RF units now became mobile forces which could be deployed in any province within a military region. The PF were also affected by this trend toward mobility and flexibility. In several instances PF responsibilities were extended into adjacent areas. RF or PF units were increasingly employed attached to regular ARVN units in search and destroy operations or in combat missions such as destroying guerrilla bases and mopping up.

By 1972, after the majority of US and FWMAF combat units had been redeployed from South Vietnam, the RF and PF found their roles expanded even more. For, in addition to their normal duties of territorial security and pacification support, RF and PF units were also deployed, in conjunction with infantry divisions, to defend important combat bases, including several in the DMZ area such as A2, A1, Anne, and Barbara, replacing withdrawn US units. Although they were not prepared by training or experience for this assignment, territorial forces did their best to accomplish it. When NVA units invaded South Vietnam in force in early 1972, many RF-PF made significant contributions in repelling NVA units on the front lines. Ever since that experience military region commanders regularly assigned territorial security and mobile combat operational missions to the RF.

Created primarily to maintain local security and defend their home villages and hamlets against Communist insurgents, the RF and PF were organized, equipped, trained, and supported for this purpose. When called upon to accomplish other missions or to be redeployed from their home villages or provinces, they naturally became less effective because they lost their primary advantage, familiarity with the local environment. Another disadvantage was that, when assigned to fight as regular forces in a conventional manner, they did not have the organic firepower and mobility that the regular ARVN enjoyed. Their performance therefore was contingent to a great extent on the support given them by the regular ARVN forces.

Deployment of Forces

Because of their responsibilities for territorial security, RF and PF units were deployed all over South Vietnam. From cities to the most remote rural areas the RF and PF were as ubiquitous as the outposts and watchtowers they manned: one company here, one platoon there, sometimes just a few men. The total number of these fixed positions was approximately 9,000, over half of which were in the Mekong Delta. This dispersion of forces created numerous difficulties for the territorial commanders who commanded and controlled them. One of the most challenging problems was how to deploy and use them effectively to meet security requirements.

The deployment of the RF and PF was largely predicated on the local security situation.

As a rule, when security improved and governmental control was stabilized in an area, the territorial forces assigned there would be redeployed to a less secure area. This was the working principle of the oil stain which kept spreading as the situation permitted. Guided by this principle, territorial commanders could, depending on the local situation and local manpower, redistribute their forces for the purpose of expanding security by redeployment. They could move a unit from one tactical position to another, or from one assigned area to another; they could also transfer responsibilities among forces by turning over secure areas to paramilitary forces and redeploying RF and PF units to areas where security needed to be consolidated.

In spite of principles which had been established for the effective deployment and employment of the RF and PF, many units were permanently rooted in static duties, performing routine chores in urban areas with which they had become familiar, such as guarding governmental buildings and escorting VIPs, while elsewhere the expanding pacification process in rural areas was short of required forces. The reasons for this inefficient employment of territorials could be traced to inefficient local leadership and the inability of the central authority, the JGS, to make its influence felt at the local level.

• • •

Of the many examples of erroneous employment of territorial forces, overextension was the most common mistake committed by sector chiefs, especially in provinces permanently under heavy enemy pressure, such as Quang Ngai, Binh Dinh, Kien Hoa, and Chuong Thien. In some areas of Chuong Thien Province, PF outposts were even surrounded by enemy flags and propaganda posters. The PF troops inside these outposts never dared venture outside.

Effective employment of territorial forces was the subject of constant concern for territorial commanders at all levels, from military region to district. Despite their efforts, few succeeded in managing and employing effectively such a large and widely dispersed force. As of June 1970, for example, there were as many as 1,640 RF companies and 6,969 PF platoons deployed. Even during the period when US helilift assets were still abundant and available for their use on a priority basis, many sector and district commanders were unable to visit all of their units. Several outposts therefore spent a whole year without being visited by the sector or the district commander. When helicopters were few and priority for their use given to tactical missions, inspection and supervision of RF and PF units were even more curtailed. The use of roads or waterways for inspection purposes was not only a time-consuming process, but also required escort and itinerary security for visiting parties. As a result, territorial commanders usually monitored the activities of their RF and PF units through reports. Whether these units performed as effectively as reported depended almost entirely on the leadership of RF company commanders and PF platoon and squad leaders. The upgrading of RF companies into groups and battalions in 1970 and the establishment of sector tactical commands in 1972 proved useful in controlling the employment of such a large and widely dispersed force.

Outposts and Strongpoints

• • •

The general configuration of the outpost system provided a good indication as to which areas were under GVN control and which were not. The concept of constructing outposts for the defense of villages and hamlets dated far back in time. Most recently, during the First Indochina War, the French also adopted this concept and constructed some large-scale outpost systems such as the famous "De Lattre Line" in North Vietnam. The basic idea was to control rural areas through these outposts and to prevent enemy penetrations into populous centers. The concept of the outpost was, therefore, deeply ingrained, not only in military minds but also in the daily life of our citizens. To the population, the outpost was the symbol of governmental authority, an indication of the government's determination to stay with them and provide protection. As a result, the construction of new outposts, or the loss of outposts to the enemy, or even their evacuation for military purposes, affected the morale and life of the local population. Territorial commanders were therefore frequently caught between military requirements and the need to maintain the people's morale. The enemy was undoubtedly aware of this psychological factor, and he consequently devoted his efforts to attacking or isolating outposts.

The outpost system by itself had several shortcomings. In the first place it absorbed a large military force in static defense. Secondly, its construction required not only large budgetary outlays but also contributions in labor. Such a system also naturally dispersed combat and combat support assets. Therefore, as pacification expanded, our forces and their resources became more diluted, providing good targets for enemy attacks. Another inevitable shortcoming inherent in the system was that, when a unit remained long rooted in one place, its activities turned into predictable routines and all initiative became blunted with time.

It was hard under those circumstances to avoid negligence of duties. In many instances the unit tended to be passive and preferred to remain inside the outpost after dark. This gave the enemy freedom to move about, collecting taxes and food, making propaganda, recruiting, or simply terrorizing the villagers. By being passive or inactive, the unit which manned the outpost not only became a good target for enemy attack at any time but also, when such an attack occurred, wrought upon itself sure destruction and heavy losses. Over the years the losses and casualties suffered by the RF and PF resulted more from enemy attacks against outposts than from their activities on the outside.

In spite of these shortcomings, South Vietnamese military authorities were never able to dispense with the outpost system, nor could they develop a satisfactory alternative. In 1964 the province of Long An experimented with the concept of mobile defense, employing RF and PF units in mobile activities, instead of in outposts, for the defense of villages. After a month of activity, provincial authorities realized that the RF and PF units still required a point of support, a place to rest. The outpost system therefore proved indispensable. But many of its weaknesses were subsequently overcome by

strong support from the outside in terms of firepower or reinforcements, whenever required, and by increased inspections conducted by territorial commanders.

• • •

Pacification

Operating inside the screen provided by ARVN and US forces, the territorial forces
provided security for the pacification program. Their essential task was to keep the territory free from attacks by enemy forces in insecure areas and to prevent enemy disruptive activities from undermining progress in economic, political, and social development
in secure areas.

Even though ARVN units were also employed for this task in great numbers, such
as during 1967–1968, and augmented by US forces in many instances, the primary responsibility for territorial security and pacification support remained with the RF and
PF. The ARVN forces were naturally stronger, their combat assets more abundant, and
they had more firepower and mobility, but the security problem involved in the pacification process was not just a tactical mission that a combat unit could carry out successfully under normal circumstances. Territorial security required the ability to recognize
and identify the enemy among the masses, a familiarity with all accesses [and] hiding
places in the hamlets, a working relationship and close touch with the population, and,
above all, the people's cooperation and support. All of these requirements could hardly
be met with satisfaction by regular ARVN units, whose strengths were conventional in
nature and whose primary target was the enemy's main force, not his local or guerrilla
units.

Pacification forces were therefore local, hometown forces. They operated in and out
of the hamlets at night, preventing the local guerillas, the propagandists, the tax collec-
tors, and other repressive elements from penetrating their communities, and, during the
daytime, they lived among the population. The local population was close to them. If
they were not locally born themselves, at least they were combatants who were well
known by the local people.

They usually operated at the small-unit level—squad, platoon, or company. Their
normal tactics were ambushes, patrols, guerrilla-type raids, and small-scale cordon and
search operations. Unlike the typical cordon and search operations conducted by regular
ARVN forces, theirs were of low profile and characterized by the absence or minimum
use of large-caliber firepower. This was intended to prevent human losses and property
damage. During the search, they also progressed slowly and methodically, taking time
and pains to flush out the suspects from their hideouts.

• • •

Experience . . . indicated that when the shield or screen provided by ARVN and US
units on the outside was solid and reliable, allowing no chance for enemy main-force
units to penetrate, then the RF and PF were most effective.

An example that fully demonstrated this point was the performance of the RF and PF
in Quang Tri and Thua Thien, the two northernmost provinces of South Vietnam. Prior

to 1968 the RF and PF in these two provinces rarely conducted any significant activities. Their passivity allowed the Viet Cong to gradually gain footholds in the population centers. However, as ARVN and US forces were brought in to clear out enemy base areas along the foothills, and after they created an effective shield for the protection of the lowland coastal area, the RF and PF suddenly recovered from their stupor. Along with ARVN and US forces, and riding on the crest of successive victories, they helped clear the Viet Cong·from the coastal area which was between QL-1 and the coastline. There was no enemy stronghold, large or small, in the area, including the famous "Street without Joy," that escaped their search, despite limitations in mobility and firepower. This constant pressure by the RF and PF soon drove enemy local forces away, since they no longer had access to a safe haven. At the same time, the VCI was also gradually wiped out. As a result, the coastal lowlands of Quang Tri and Thua Thien Provinces, the site of some of the fiercest battles of the war, gradually regained vitality, and, as of mid-1969, the local population began to enjoy life peacefully under the protection of the territorial forces and behind the shield provided by regular forces.

• • •

Dong Khoi Operations

One of the most effective techniques for the employment of our forces in support of security and pacification was to launch several cordon and search operations concurrently throughout a military region. These Dong Khoi, or "synchronized," operations (another translation would be "spontaneous uprising") were periodically conducted by MR-4, beginning in 1970, their concept being based on a successful series of operations called "Hiep Dong" (Joining Forces) initiated earlier by the province of Quang Tin. They were remarkably effective and employed only Vietnamese forces, no Americans.

The concept of synchronous operations consisted essentially of employing territorial forces in coordination with local paramilitary forces to conduct uninterrupted short-duration operations (three to five days) simultaneously over the entire area of the military region. The objective of these operations was to discover, eliminate, or neutralize all enemy local-force and guerrilla units and the VCI. To achieve this, friendly forces endeavored to destroy all enemy organizations and facilities in the area of operations, to include lines of communication and mini (guerrilla) bases, by thoroughly coordinating combat efforts with intelligence activities, and by exploiting instantaneously all intelligence data gathered on the spot, especially those provided by ralliers. Offensive in nature, these operations also sought to preempt all enemy actions, whether known or pre-planned, at the very beginning of their preparations.

• • •

The results achieved through each surge of synchronous operations usually exceeded those obtained by daily activities by a large margin. The total number of enemy personnel killed and detained throughout the military region often reached an average of several hundreds for each surge, while friendly losses were usually minimal. A major element of this success was the fact that all territorial and paramilitary forces and intelligence units were required to commit at least 75 percent of their combat strength, and they usually participated at full strength.

• • •

In addition to providing integration of forces and unity of action, the technique of synchronous operations also proved to be an excellent way to mobilize the huge masses of armed men, to include the People's Self-Defense Force, into action, giving them initiative and developing a pervasive spirit of teamwork and emulation among the elements that had never previously existed.

Combat Support

From their inception to 1961, the period when the RF and PF had not yet benefited from the US Military Assistance Program, our territorial forces were equipped only with obsolescent weapons of different makes, some dating back to World War I. They were short of ammunition, and much of what they had was long outdated. When participating in any operation, therefore, they were uneasy and unsure of themselves, fearful that, having engaged the enemy, their ammunition might not be replenished. However, as soon as the US Military Assistance Program was extended to territorial forces, the RF and PF began to receive infantry weapons identical to those of ARVN units, such as the M-1 Garand, the M-1 carbine, submachineguns, the BAR, and the 60mm mortar, all of World War II vintage. This improvement in armament enhanced the RF and PF self-assurance and partly increased their combat effectiveness.

By 1964, however, when VC units began to receive modern weapons supplied by the Communist bloc, such as the AK-47, the RPG-7, and especially B-40 and B-41 grenade launchers, the firepower of the RF and PF became inadequate and much inferior to the enemy's. This created an adverse psychological effect which greatly undermined self-assurance among the RF and PF ranks.

• • •

During the 1968 Tet Offensive, the RF and PF were clearly outgunned and overwhelmed by the fierce firepower of enemy local-force units, all equipped with AK-47s and B-40s. As many as 477 outposts were forced to evacuate under enemy pressure during the first month of the offensive. To overcome this weakness in firepower, beginning in 1969 the RF and PF gradually received, under the RVNAF improvement and modernization program, such modern US weapons as the M-16 rifle, the M-60 machinegun, the M-79 grenade launcher, and the LAW rocket launcher, in replacement of all obsolescent World War II items. In addition to modern armament, the RF and PF were also equipped with improved field radios such as the AN/PRC-25, which replaced the obsolescent SCR-300 or the trouble-ridden AN/PRC-10. As a result of improved firepower and communications, the morale of the RF and PF received a remarkable boost, and this substantially enhanced their enthusiasm as well as their capabilities for defense.

• • •

[The] inadequacy of fire support received by the RF and PF during combat naturally affected their performance and partly accounted for their high losses. As the RF and PF expanded and improved, however, there was a critical need to provide them with adequate fire support, and this could be achieved only when they had their own artillery. In late 1970, therefore, a total of 176 territorial artillery sections were created to provide direct support for the RF and PF throughout the country. Placed under the operational control of sector headquarters, these artillery units offered territorial commanders much more flexibility in providing fire support for the RF and PF during combat operations; this was especially true when outposts came under enemy attacks or during "high points" of enemy activity.

Among all the resources used to support RF and PF activities, perhaps the most popular was the bulldozer. Each military region (except for MR-4) was provided with a bulldozer company of 35 machines each. Bulldozers were truly the most valuable and effective instrument to improve territorial security. A scaled-down version of US Rome plows, these bulldozers were used to clear bushes and heavy vegetation along axes of communication, enlarge fields of fire around important military bases, and, most particularly, to level the enemy's mini-bases near populated areas.

• • •

VI. EFFORTS TO IMPROVE RF AND PF COMBAT EFFECTIVENESS

In addition to the normal process of expanding and improving the territorial forces in terms of organization, force structure, training, equipment, command and control . . . , South Vietnamese and American authorities also made determined efforts to improve their combat effectiveness. These efforts, which ranged from bettering the lot of the common soldier to motivating and training him for actual combat, were undertaken as circumstances and resources permitted, and as required by the specific situation of each period.

The problem of improving combat effectiveness was much more difficult with the RF and PF than with the ARVN for the simple reason that they consisted primarily of small units which operated separately and were deployed to almost every corner of South Vietnam. However, the various approaches and techniques used to meet this challenge were responsive enough to make the entire undertaking a worthwhile effort.

• • •

In spite of . . . apparent lack of adequate indoctrination, the RF and PF continued to fight valiantly and without remiss until the final days of the drawn-out war. This was because their lack of formal indoctrination was more than compensated for by natural motivation. As local combatants, they fought to protect their home villages where they were born and where their ancestors were buried.

• • •

On-the-Spot Training

• • •

In addition to the marines' Combined Action Program in I Corps area, in 1967 US field forces elsewhere also initiated training programs for the RF and PF by employing mobile training teams. Composed of from three to ten members, each mobile training team was assigned an area where it visited RF and PF units in rotation to conduct training. Despite the common approach, several different names were used for these mobile training teams: Combined Mobile Training Teams, Combined Mobile Improvement Teams, "Red Catchers" and "Impact" Teams, and RF Company Training Teams. Their duties ranged from conducting single-day training sessions for PF platoons to five-week unit refresher courses for RF companies.

• • •

In mid-1967, to maintain the improvement momentum, the Military Assistance Command, Vietnam, experimented with the Regional Forces Company Training Team concept on a countrywide basis. This concept was essentially based on the Marine Combined Action Program being conducted in I Corps area. Each team, which consisted of three officers and three NCOs, was assigned to an RF company undergoing training at a training center. During this time it provided assistance in the completion of the training program. When the unit left the training center, the team accompanied it to the home province, where it continued to provide on-the-spot training and assist the unit in combat activities until the unit developed a full capability for independent operations. This usually took from six to nine months.

RF company training teams played a more assertive role than advisory duties usually required, but they did not enjoy command prerogatives, which remained with the RF company commanders. Because of the extended time involved and close cooperation, however, both the RF company commander and the US training team chief usually had a good harmonious working relationship based on mutual respect and understanding. Most RF companies that took this training displayed significant progress, as demonstrated by better performance in combat operations, improved security conditions, and higher morale. There was also discernible enthusiasm on the part of RF company commanders and their subordinates, who all appreciated the effort being expended for their benefit. They usually regretted the day when the US training team left the unit. Although the achievement[s] of RF company training teams were not the same in every area where they were assigned, this concept proved an excellent approach to improving territorial forces.

• • •

Mobile Advisory Teams

• • •

The mobile advisory program was launched in early 1968 with 353 teams deployed to all four corps areas. Before their deployment team members attended a training course of one or two months at the US Army Advisory School at Di An. Each team consisted of two officers (team chief and his deputy), three enlisted men (one light weapon advisor, one heavy weapon advisor, one medic), and one Vietnamese interpreter.

Whenever the situation permitted, mobile advisory teams usually lived and worked with RF and PF units, assisting in unit training and accompanying them in combat operations. Training emphasis was placed on leadership, the conduct of operations, night operations, marksmanship, the use of mines and booby traps, and the planning and control of firepower support. The duration of training was usually about 30 days. After the training objectives had been achieved and the unit under tutelage had demonstrated self-assurance, initiative, and effectiveness, the advisory team moved to another unit, where the same training cycle began anew.

• • •

In spite of heavy burdens and the complexities of the work involved, mobile advisory teams in general managed to adapt themselves to the local situation, displayed a capacity for initiative, and accomplished their mission with excellent results. Their success could be directly measured by the significant increase in RF and PF operations, beginning in 1968, and the remarkable performance that these forces frequently displayed during operations conducted separately with minimum support. Indirectly, therefore, mobile advisory teams contributed a great deal to the progress achieved in pacification. As a complementary effort, mobile advisory logistic teams (MALT) were activated at the same time to help improve administrative and logistic support for the RF and PF.

• • •

In retrospect, the employment of mobile advisory teams proved very effective in improving the combat effectiveness of the RF and PF. To a significant extent, this program filled the gaps caused in the formal training process by the reluctance of sectors to rotate RF and PF units into the refresher training cycle in the face of tactical requirements and by the uninterrupted involvement of RF and PF units in the pacification program. Mobile advisory teams not only succeeded in developing a close rapport with RF and PF units they came to assist, but also inspired sympathy and confidence among the rural population during the time they carried out their duties in villages and hamlets. More than a civic action effort, US advisory teams conveyed to the majority of the rural people the true meaning and significance of the American presence in South Vietnam and by their action[s] and behavior effectively disproved all enemy propaganda claims of American aggression.

• • •

VII. OBSERVATIONS AND CONCLUSIONS

The Importance of Territorial Security

In spite of their low profile and the absence of front-page press reports, activities designed to maintain territorial security proved no less important than the large-scale search and destroy operations conducted during the Vietnam War. These activities contributed significantly to the joint RVN-US war effort.

From hindsight, to counter the kind of warfare purported by the enemy to be a "people's war," the conventional search and destroy approach was not enough to ensure durable success and to solve the problems of insurgency. The dual nature of the Vietnam conflict, which combined subversive activities with outright aggression, apparently required that territorial security be established and maintained as a [fundamental] condition for stabilization and national viability. To achieve this, it was essential that we suppress terrorism, sabotage, and other disruptive activities that enemy guerrillas and infrastructure elements waged at the grassroots level, the village and hamlet.

The Communist approach to warfare sought first and foremost to cripple our ability to resist by inflicting damage and losses to the people living under our control and destroying our national resources. Their method of "liberating" the rural areas, one of the major goals of Communist strategy, was to sabotage our lines of communication and wreck our bridges, interdicting our access and denying our control. Then they gained control by dissolving our social and administrative structure, using violence and terror to reduce our people to silence and submission. They turned villages and hamlets thus subdued into fortifications and constantly strived to expand control into populated areas by the same process. To regain control, we were forced to employ military strength, which further wrought havoc to civilian properties and local resources and thus played into the enemy's scheme.

Against this putrefying process it was obvious that South Vietnam should have had a strong organization for territorial security and control from the very beginning. Even though this organization might not have been able to eradicate insurgency, at least it could have limited its expansion and devastating effect. The sad fact was that, once their houses, gardens, and ricefields—most of which had been inherited through generations of hard toil—had been destroyed, there was absolutely nothing that could attract or attach the people to a new village, much less to cause them to defend it. The GVN did make significant efforts to rebuild or rehabilitate the villages ravaged by war, but somehow the lost faith was hard to restore. In the process, our country also incurred heavy expenditures, not to mention the great sacrifice in human lives and lost time.

From the onset of insurgency in 1959 until 1966–1967, when the American force buildup helped regain some measure of stability, about half of South Vietnam's rural areas were severely devastated. During that time countless prosperous villages and fertile lands were turned into guerrilla bases which nurtured and sheltered the enemy, making security and pacification difficult and sometimes almost hopeless.

A strong, effective territorial control system therefore would have served a double purpose: it would have protected the population against subversion and provided support for military activities. To a significant degree, the performance of our tactical units depended on the efficiency of that support. Without local intelligence, guides, traffic security, etc., it would be difficult for combat units to achieve success in the accomplishment of their missions. While regular units—the divisions, regiments, battalions—could always rest and recuperate during periods of relative lull, the territorial forces could not afford that luxury. They were perennially engaged in the small war with round-the-clock search operations, security patrols, and the task of protecting urban centers and lines of communication within their areas of responsibility.

As counterinsurgency grew into total, all-out war, beginning in 1968, and pacification efforts gained in momentum, our territorial security system played an even more important role. It was this system that provided the means for the effective use and coordination of national resources for the implementation of military, political, economic, and social programs designed to fight the total war. Throughout the major periods of the Vietnam conflict, therefore, the territorial system always performed a [fundamental] role and was aptly regarded as the mainstay of the war machinery.

The RF and PF Soldier

The forces that constituted the backbone of this territorial security system were the RF and PF, both locally recruited and employed, although differently organized, trained, and equipped. The men who made up these forces were, for the most part, rural peasants accustomed to hard manual labor, enduring and resilient to hardship, pragmatic, and possessing an extensive knowledge about life and work in nature.

As individuals, the RF and PF soldiers were basically good-natured, decent, kind, and well disposed toward other people. In a deterministic sense, they accepted war as their fate and were resigned to hardship and even death, which they faced with unequalled impassivity. They fought the war with patience and perseverance, meeting each challenge and facing the enemy with self-control. As a result, during the war years they always suffered considerably more losses than the regular forces, even during the periods when ARVN conducted large-scale operations such as the cross-border campaigns of 1970 and 1971. During 1970, for example, the RF and PF incurred 15,783 losses compared to the ARVN's 5,602; during 1971, RF and PF losses reached 17,750 against 4,232 for the ARVN. For the period of most intense fighting, 1968–1972, the aggregate total of RF and PF losses was 69,291, or about twice the ARVN total of 36,932.

In spite of these terrible losses, the RF and PF still accounted for the largest number of volunteers serving in the RVNAF during the entire war. Within their ranks many were senior citizens, one, PF trooper Nguyen Van Moi of Duc Lang District in Chuong Thien Province, reaching the incredible age of 70. In 1971, Mr. Moi was awarded two medals (one was American) for gallantry in combat action. He was cited as one of MR-4's outstanding combatants for that year.

Because of their scattered deployment to remote rural areas, the RF and PF soldiers were always in a position to be [poisoned] by enemy propaganda. In fact, the VC proved particularly adept at proselytizing South Vietnamese servicemen, which was one of their three major strategic efforts. This effort was generally directed against the RF and PF, but the enemy did not succeed in subverting these forces. The single instance of unit disintegration ever reported among the RF and PF occurred in Hoai An District of Binh Dinh Province—a long-established Communist stronghold—during the 1972 Easter invasion, but it was an unconfirmed report since this area was never retaken afterwards. However, individual cases of desertion or defection did occur, sometimes involving two or three or even five in one unit at the same time. RF and PF deserters amounted to only one-fifth of the ARVN total, and most of them rejoined their families rather than enemy ranks, for obvious reasons of deep attachment or economic demands.

The enemy had only one way to subvert the RF and PF. He constantly tried to plant his own agents by infiltration through recruitment channels. Working inside an RF or PF unit, these agents sought to destroy the organization, combining their actions with an attack from the outside. They would furnish intelligence information to the VC before the attack; they might also prepare the way by killing sentries and would often throw explosives or grenades into the command and weapons bunkers during the attack. They rarely succeeded in proselytizing their fellow troopers or making them turncoats through persuasion alone. Fifth columnist actions worked for some time, especially among isolated outposts of the Mekong Delta, but they became rare after a new ID card system was instituted for all citizens of South Vietnam, military and civilian alike.

In a war situation in which agents of the enemy infrastructure lived mixed with the people, identification was a difficult problem, especially for members of regular units which did not stay in the same geographical area very long. The presence of the RF and PF soldiers in rural areas therefore became a necessity. Recruited and trained to serve in his hometown or home village, he was naturally entirely familiar with the local environment. His detailed knowledge of the local terrain and people was even better than that of a VC agent operating in the area. The RF or PF soldier knew in detail all the back alleys of the hamlet, every household living in it, even individual members of each household, and the pattern of their lives. He knew who lived in each house, who owned the rice-fields, how much rice each household consumed, and which household had a relative working for the VC. He also knew who among the villagers to ask for information, and what kind of information to be expected from each.

What would have passed unnoticed by a regular soldier could be of particular interest to the RF or PF soldier. He could even instinctively open fire on an enemy or group of enemy passing by who would otherwise not appear much different from other people. A regular soldier might have let them pass out of indifference or, if the strangers were suspicious enough to warrant an identity check, would have noticed nothing peculiar to confirm them as enemy. Such insights were the hallmark of the RF and PF soldier. Living in close proximity to nature, he was extremely sensitive to minute changes in the environment, changes that only he knew to have occurred because they upset the natural order. As a consequence, well-concealed mines, booby traps, or enemy hideouts usually could not escape the sharp eye of the RF and PF soldier.

The general evaluation of RF and PF effectiveness was usually good. This was the consensus among US units which had the opportunity to associate with both regular and territorial forces. Usually US commanders much preferred to work with RF and PF units, whose virtues and special abilities they also extolled. In terms of missions, command structure, training, and equipment, there was a marked disparity between the regular and territorial forces, a disparity caused by priorities. Yet, in terms of performance and achievements, the underdog RF and PF seemed to fare much better. The major advantage enjoyed by the RF and PF, an advantage that more than compensated for their inferiority in training and armament, was their undisputed knowledge of the local environment and local people. The ARVN units, which were unattached to any particular area, did not have that knowledge. More importantly, motivation was what contributed most to the effectiveness of the RF and PF and accounted for their high achievements. This motivation was not artificial; it was a matter of life or death for someone who had to defend his own family and his own village.

The local character of the territorial forces made them particularly fit for the maintenance of security and pacification tasks. Their methods of operation also suited the purposes of local governments. In those villages and hamlets whose security and control needed to be restored, no local authorities would want fierce battles fought with artillery and air support. Not only were these actions generally inefficient against local enemy guerrillas, the use of firepower was also a major cause of concern for the villagers. When a conventional approach was used against bands of enemy guerrillas, it tended to multiply their numbers rather than eliminate them effectively; this of course made the pacification task even more difficult. From my experience, I believe that most province or district chiefs would rather have a few additional RF companies than an ARVN battalion for this type of operation.

To fight an insurgency war, it is essential for any government to win the people's support and to enlist their cooperation. Whether this can be achieved depends a great deal on the popular attitude toward the governmental troops who protect the population against insurgents. Therefore rapport with the people was an important yardstick to measure not only the GVN's success, but also the popularity and effectiveness of the RF and PF. If this rapport was good, cooperation would increase, local authorities would benefit from additional intelligence sources, and the villagers would also be reluctant to give the enemy support. Over the years, the attitude of the South Vietnamese people and of local spiritual and political leaders was in general favorable toward the RF and PF. For one thing, in addition to a good rapport with locals, the RF and PF, unlike some unruly ARVN units that occasionally swept through the locality, rarely committed mischievous acts against their own friends and relatives.

Terrain and the people are two decisive factors in an antiguerrilla or counterinsurgency war. In South Vietnam, the terrain was highly diverse; it was made up of well-defined areas, each with its own geographical features. There were mountainous and jungle-covered plateaus, vast alluvial plains, and inundated swamps, each inhabited by different ethnic groups with different customs and manners. All of these people were bound by the same attachment to their own habitats. The Communists took advantage of this terrain diversity to establish numerous mini-bases, dependent on the local people for survival and growth. Under such circumstances, it was not easy for any regular army unit to detect and identify the enemy. Therefore the concept of employing a military force made up of local people who were intimately familiar with the local environment and local population proved to be a truly appropriate response to Communist insurgency.

Evolving Problems

In spite of the importance of territorial security throughout the war, South Vietnamese and American authorities never seemed to place enough emphasis on it. Territorial security was almost neglected during the initial stage. From 1955 to 1960, all efforts and resources were devoted to the buildup of anti-invasion capabilities, with only token concern about security matters. A long and valuable time was thus irretrievably lost in the effort to consolidate territorial security, especially at the infrastructure level, the village and hamlet. During this period, subversion and insurgency were yet to be recognized as a serious threat in the eyes of South Vietnam's political and military leaders and US authorities.

Not until 1961 did they realize that the effective defense of South Vietnam required not only anti-aggression but also anti-insurgency capabilities. And not until then, as a result, was the Military Assistance Program extended to the territorial forces. And, even then, these forces were placed far below regular forces in the order of priorities; they were regarded as auxiliary and less expensive troops. As a matter of fact, the cost of maintaining one regular soldier was two or three times greater than one RF soldier and four times greater than a PF soldier.

By 1967 US forces had made significant gains in driving VC/NVA forces deep into the remote jungles and into their sanctuaries across the border. Regular ARVN units assumed the pacification mission in the cleared areas and the territorials still were relegated to minor security and supporting roles. It was not until the US interest in advising and supporting the territorials began to have an effect in late 1968 that definite improvements in RF/PF performance could be seen.

The RF and PF received more interest in 1968 and 1969 and as US units began to stand down and redeploy. This was in fact dictated by the need to free ARVN forces from their static role so that they could assume the primary combat responsibility in the place of US forces. As the ARVN gradually took over search and destroy operations, the role of the RF and PF was also upgraded to that of pacification support, a role just relinquished by the ARVN. At this time the RF and PF began to expand in force structure with a rather high priority, but still second in terms of manpower and logistic support. Concurrently, more advisory effort was devoted to improving territorial force units. Still, US advisors assigned to work with the territorial system accounted for only 11 percent of the total advisory strength.

The development of the RF and PF was never based on any clear-cut long-range concept. Except for the PF, which remained essentially platoon-based, the RF underwent several organizational changes, progressing by hesitant steps from company to company group, then to battalion, and finally tactical group. Because there was no coherent long-range plan, each of these steps was a creature of the moment, of the particular phase and character of the conflict at the time. As the leadership, American and

Vietnamese alike, perceived new or modified requirements for territorial forces, decisions were made to change organizations and strengths to cope with these requirements. The commanders and staffs responsible for implementing the changes did their best to respond, but the results were often disappointing because sufficient time for recruiting, equipping, and training had not been available. As a consequence, the RF appeared to be constantly in a state of organizational confusion which made command and control very difficult.

A major structural weakness, the RF and PF command and control system, was a loose assemblage of unconnected parts which never functioned cohesively. Their logistic support system also suffered from the same structural problem. Even after consolidation and improvement, sector administrative and logistic support centers were cumbersome, inefficient; their responsibilities were never clearly defined. Rarely, if ever, was an RF or PF soldier or even an officer able to fully understand his own system.

To an army unit, in addition to duty and dedication to the national cause, tradition and uniforms were also significant elements of motivation. Because of their heterogeneous nature, the RF and PF never had a tradition or distinctive uniform which made them look and feel proud like the airborne, marine, or infantry soldiers. Their virtues were seldom extolled and their accomplishments usually slighted. This evaluative misconception seemed to derive basically from prejudice coupled with a nearsighted tendency to measure results only by body count and weapons captured. Most Vietnamese citizens, especially the city dwellers, were unable to realize that such achievements as hamlets pacified, the number of people living under GVN control, or the trafficability on key lines of communication were possible largely due to the unsung feats of the RF and PF.

Compared to search and destroy operations, territorial security activities were immensely more complex. ARVN regular units had a clear-cut mission: to destroy the enemy. The RF and PF, by contrast, were employed to perform a multitude of different tasks, depending on local requirements. These requirements were truly burdensome, and often demanded too much of the RF and PF. Routinely the RF and PF were required to look after security for the village and hamlet, the district, the province, military installations, industrial areas, and for lines of communication. They were also sometimes tasked to conduct search and destroy operations, to serve as quick reaction strike forces against enemy-initiated actions, and to participate in civic action activities. In addition to these tasks, they had to carry out countless chores related to official (and private) business at the discretion and upon orders of local authorities, civilian or military.

In brief, the RF and PF were an instrument that the government used to meet every imaginable kind of requirement, from combat to incidental details. Obviously the overworked RF and PF units became weary and less vigilant, no matter how enduring they might be. And, since demands always seemed to surpass the number of units available, the RF and PF rarely had a chance to rest, recuperate, or undergo refresher training.

In addition to shortcomings caused by an unsound structure and erroneous employment, the territorial forces also had inherent weaknesses. The RF and PF soldier, being locally born, possessed certain innate qualities and a knowledge of local environment that few other soldiers could duplicate. But he was less resourceful and less audacious when faced with the unexpected. Subservient by nature, he submitted himself completely to his superiors. Conditioned by local habits and the local way of life, he was oriented toward rigid "formality" or "procedures" more than expediency or results. The average RF or PF soldier had only a vague notion of emergency, to which he attached neither value nor importance. To him, it hardly mattered whether a task should be performed in 12 instead of 24 hours, or whether it should be done today or tomorrow. When he was tired, rest was the only thing that mattered; what remained to be done could always wait. Three months at a training center did little to change this inherent easy-going manner.

Command and control of the RF and PF were also heavily influenced by local politics. Because of the need to enlist popular support, local governments usually showed obsequious deference to influential religious and political leaders in their areas. In certain provinces of the Mekong Delta's eastern and western zones, the GVN usually appointed province and district chiefs from among the Hao Hoa and Cao Dai followers in order to obtain the support and cooperation of these religious sects. These appointments had to be approved by their leaders. The same practice occurred in those areas of MR-1 where the Dai Viet and VNQDD were influential. It followed that many RF and PF cadres had been promoted or reassigned in this way.

Despite political expediency, this practice degraded the authority of local governments and adversely affected the discipline of RF and PF units. In several instances it was also at the source of corruption and crimes. Such debilitating vices as "ghost" or "ornamental" soldiers, and crimes [such] as harboring deserters or draft evaders, etc., occurred more frequently because of [the] protection available.[5] The law required severe punishment for these vices and crimes, but was rarely enforced appropriately. Local authorities found myriad ways to bypass the law or just looked the other way, anxious not to offend the influential personalities who protected the culprits.

During the period I served as MR-4 commander (1970–1972) I found that the RF and PF were very effective, and they played a [fundamental] role in the maintenance of security and pacification within this region. To appropriately exploit the valuable potential of these forces, I was determined to keep them well disciplined, in addition to providing special care, because I firmly believed that discipline made the strength of any army. As a matter of priority, therefore, I launched successive campaigns to eradicate the vices of "ghost" and "ornamental" soldiers, and to track down deserters and draft evaders. All these efforts were made with determination, without regard to frictions or fear of offending anyone. Unfortunately, while these campaigns were making excellent progress a directive from the office of the prime minister told me to suspend them at once, including the tracking down of deserters. The only explanation offered to me was that, in the view of local personalities, such activities would adversely affect the next rice harvest (and possibly the next presidential election as well).

I have presented some of the typical problems that plagued the territorial system and the forces which constituted its backbone. These problems indicate that, as long as there were too many exceptions and irregularities, the government could not effectively rule by law, and military discipline and control could not be maintained. This was precisely what lay at the root of the weaknesses in our territorial forces.

Conclusions

Although they were besieged by complex problems, the RF and PF did succeed in the performance of their role. Territorial security and pacification constantly improved, and the RF and PF themselves also made remarkable progress. During the last few years of the war the territorial forces proved particularly strong, despite repeated Communist military and proselytizing assaults. They became, eventually, the redoubtable nemesis of enemy local guerrillas and infrastructure cadre.

To the problem of insurgency in South Vietnam, however, the RF and PF alone were not the solution. Given their organization and mission, RF and PF performance depended primarily on the effectiveness of the regular units which provided the protective shield against invading forces. When this shield was solid, the RF and PF could easily defeat adversaries of the same size. But, when enemy main-force units succeeded in penetrating this shield in large numbers, there was no way the RF and PF, with their limited capabilities, could defend themselves. Unfortunately, this happened often in South Vietnam because geographical configuration and terrain were not conducive to effective defense against infiltration.

The people's organization for self-defense also had a direct bearing on RF and PF performance. In villages and hamlets where the people were well organized and paramilitary forces functioned effectively, the task of territorial forces was much easier. However, competent authorities at the grassroots level were few, and the majority of village chiefs did not have strong leadership to coordinate the paramilitary forces and rally the people for the support of local security.

During the war years MACV and the Vietnamese leadership both made constant efforts to make the RF and PF more effective and efficient. Many ideas were suggested and many approaches were tested. The consolidation and simplification of the command structure within the RVNAF, and the centralization of advisory and support activities at CORDS, were both important, beneficial changes. As the war became more and more one of large regular formations opposing each other, the increases in RF/PF strength and the formation of larger RF units were called for. Unfortunately, although the many problems perennially facing the RF and PF soldiers were recognized by most American and Vietnamese military authorities, little could be done to correct them.

In general, the RF and PF soldiers were excellent combatants; they were very effective in the counterinsurgency war. As individuals, they could measure up to any of their regular counterparts. But the problems and influences that surrounded the RF and PF weakened their posture, and the intensity of the war often overshadowed their role. Their responsibilities were truly complex and burdensome. Too much was demanded of the RF and PF, and too little was given them in return. However, I am sure that no other force in South Vietnam, operating under the same conditions and priorities, could have contributed more than our Regional and Popular Forces to the total war effort.

NOTES

1. The first two VC regimental-sized units were activated during 1961.

2. This division was part of the pre-Geneva territorial organization. The [missing] MR-3 happened to be North Vietnam minus the provinces of the panhandle. Its headquarters was in Hanoi.

3. Before the inauguration of the Second Republic in September 1967, a few civilians were still appointed as mayors and province chiefs (Dalat, Danang, Quang Nam, etc.) for local political reasons.

4. Although a criminal act, the changing of personal identification was seldom detectable and inevitable in a country at war. Papers could be lost, destroyed, or confiscated by the enemy. Even official records of birth, usually locally kept, were occasionally destroyed by acts of war. As a result, anyone could petition for and obtain a "writ in lieu of birth certificate" from a court of appeals. Counterfeit identification papers were less common.

5. "Ghost" soldiers were those whose names appeared on the unit's pay ledger and were paid each month, but did not really exist. In general, they were all deserters or deceased. "Ornamental" soldiers were those who did nothing useful for the unit. Most were recommended by local personalities to serve as office boys or house servants for high-ranking officers in cities to avoid combat duties. Coming mostly from wealthy families, they did not care who took their monthly pay.

5

Pacification

Brigadier General Tran Dinh Tho

PREFACE

Pacification is the military, political, economic, and social process of establishing or reestablishing local government responsive to and involving the participation of the people. It includes the provision of sustained, credible territorial security, the destruction of the enemy's underground government, the assertion or reassertion of political control and involvement of the people in government, and the initiation of economic and social activity capable of self-sustenance and expansion.

Defined as such, pacification is a broad and complex strategic concept which encompasses many fields of national endeavor. As a program implemented jointly with the US military effort in South Vietnam, pacification appears to have involved every American serviceman and civilian who served there, many of whom indeed participated in conceiving the idea and helping put it to work.

As they and other responsible Vietnamese officials may have realized, the magnitude and intricacies of pacification problems defy even the most diligent attempt to analyze and present them as cohesive subjects within the limited scope of a monograph. To the general reader, unless he has a comprehensive background of the Vietnamese situation, the implementation of pacification through time and space can also frustrate any effort to arrive at comprehensive generalizations. That fact is—and I am certain that many will share my opinion—there exist but a few authorities on pacification as a total subject. However, there are many Vietnamese and Americans who were highly professional and effective in their areas of responsibility within the overall program.

In an effort to present every relevant aspect of the GVN pacification effort, I have mostly relied on my personal experience as one of the many architects who helped draw [up] part of the blueprint and oversaw its progress, and complemented it by conducting interviews with responsible officials and studying available documentation. . . . [10 October 1977]

I. INTRODUCTION

The war in Vietnam was a continuation of the basic conflict, begun in 1946, which pitted the Communists against the free, nationalistic Vietnamese. Punctuated by a short pause following the Geneva Accords, the Communist-led struggle in the South followed fundamentally consistent policies and strategies aimed at achieving complete political dominance over all of Vietnam.

The Viet Cong insurgents, operating behind a screen of a national liberation movement, were fronts for the Vietnamese Communist Party, whose Politburo in Hanoi directed the total war effort. Although the Viet Cong profited from the Viet Minh experience and knew how to conceal their true identity, they were unable to make the appeal of their cause as strong as the feverish desire for independence was for the Viet Minh in 1949. The Viet Minh had been able to take over the control of the nationalist and anticolonial movements and eliminate most of the nationalist contenders in the process. They had enjoyed an undisputed cause and derived from it great strength and popularity. The Viet Cong also attempted to revive the anticolonial, anti-imperialist issue, but the old magic failed to work because South Vietnam, despite its heavy reliance on US aid, had become a truly independent nation.

The regime of the Republic of Vietnam, under Ngo Dinh Diem and successive military and civilian governments, was thus faced with a double challenge, that of nation building and the threat of insurgency and outright invasion from the North. In many respects the war against the Viet Cong bore the characteristics of a civil war, although both sides received aid and were supported with troops from outside sources.

The cells of the Viet Cong infrastructure, aided by and in concert with local and NVA main forces, acted on the body of South Vietnam like cancerous tumors and sapped the strength of the GVN. The GVN task of nation building stood little chance of success unless these tumors were removed, and the GVN military effort was inextricably entwined with political, social, and economic endeavors. Together, they made up the total effort known as pacification.

Nowhere was this total effort more arduous than in the Vietnamese countryside, the main battleground of the war and pacification. The Vietnamese countryside suffered most from destruction and privations and was the feeding ground for social injustice, crimes, oppressions, and all the vices generated by a colonialist and feudalistic heritage. Land was inequitably distributed, most private land being in the possession of wealthy landlords. The majority of the farmers did not own the land they cultivated, but had to lease it from landlords who charged exorbitant rents. It was also plagued by debilitating diseases, lack of medication and sanitation, shortages of food and clothing, and widespread illiteracy.

Because of the lack of schools and teachers, most rural children were denied an education and forced at an early age to work as farmhands under harsh and difficult conditions. The prospects for the future looked grim and disheartening.

South Vietnam, before the French–Viet Minh war began in 1946, ranked as one of the top rice producers among Southeast Asian countries. And 90 percent of its population lived on rice farming and depended on agriculture as a principal means of subsistence. Yet, during the war, South Vietnam had to import rice in increasing quantities each year. The escalating war forced the peasants to relinquish their land and farming, quit breeding cattle and poultry, and move to urban areas as refugees. Unemployment was widespread and became more serious each year. The national economy deteriorated and functioned only as a result of aid transfusions. As a result of population growth and increasing imports through US aid programs, consumption rose, surpassing production by a five-to-one ratio.

The village and hamlet governmental structure was truly the relic of a feudalistic age. Local leaders, who in most cases inherited their positions, domineered and exploited the peasant by levying high rents and taxes. The farmworker led a miserable life, barely subsisting on what was left of the fruit of his toil after land rents, and going further into debt with each decade. The undercurrent of discontent among the rural people was widespread.

In addition to suffering social vices and economic misfortunes, South Vietnam was also the victim of blatant invasion from Communist North Vietnam, assisted by the Communist bloc. In the face of this situation, the government and people of South Vietnam endeavored on the one hand to defeat the Communist aggressors, and on the other hand to reform their own society. It was a difficult enterprise, because both tasks demanded equal priority. National resources and manpower were utilized to the full, augmented by considerable contributions in combat forces, material resources, and money from the United States and the Free World.

To our side, as well as to the enemy, the rural area of South Vietnam was to be the decisive battlefield. Without it, the enemy would lose his foothold and the opportunities to protract his war, for the rural area was his major source of subsistence and manpower. The countryside was the arena for the ideological struggle between the Free World and Communism. It was where the battle for the hearts and minds of the people was fought, and whoever won their trust, cooperation, and support would be the final victor. Without the rural area, which in Communist doctrine included not only the agricultural lands but also the forests, swamps, and mountains, the nation could hardly survive.

To win the battle for the rural area, the enemy conceived the strategy of "encircling the cities with the rural area," while on the RVN side "all efforts of the nation were to focus on the rural area." In fact, one element of the enemy's strategy in attacking the cities and towns in his general offensive of 1968 was to draw the GVN and allied forces out of the countryside, where they were enjoying considerable success in pacification. The Communists believed control of the rural area was the key to success in a people's war.

• • •

In the ideological struggle, the rural area was also a fecund ground for political indoctrination and for fomenting class hatred and class struggle. The marked inequality between rural life and urban life existed not only in terms of material comfort and basic necessities, but also in the disparity with which law and order were enforced. In many instances, rural life appeared to be governed by a different set of laws and regulations. Too frequently, central government directives were interpreted and manipulated by village authorities to suit their own purposes or merely disregarded in favor of their own rules.

• • •

The RVN government was fully aware of the Communist dependence on the rural area, and the national strategy of "Pacification and Development" was designed to separate the Communists from it. The strategy also sought to establish the GVN presence in less secure, contested areas, with a view of controlling the nation's manpower and resources and denying them to the enemy. Despite its awareness, the RVN initially appeared not to be truly cognizant of the full implications of the problem at hand. Its efforts to implement pacification were not pushed hard enough, and sometimes appeared to be devoid of genuine enthusiasm. These efforts also met with vigorous opposition from the Communists, who persistently sought to thwart or offset whatever achievements the RVN happened to gain.

One of the Communists' first reactions was, characteristically enough, to oppose the establishment of local government at the village and hamlet level, since this was an extension of the prestige, laws, and political influence of the RVN central government. Unable to wreck the RVN governmental infrastructure, the Communists resorted to effective methods of intimidation, repression, and terror. Through machinations and manipulations, they managed to help into office those who were considered "middle-of-the-roaders," men who were too weak and too indifferent to serve in any effective way, and obstructed the nomination of local leaders who enjoyed prestige, affection, and respect among the population. The Communists resorted to kidnapping or outright assassination if intimidation failed to remove those local officials whom they considered too devoted or too zealous. Countless officials at the grassroots level were reduced to silence or became casualties. The enemy's goal was to instill fear, disenchantment, and anxiety among the active GVN cadre and force them into inaction.

In addition to their effort to neutralize or paralyze our local government structure, the Communists also systematically set about to undermine and disrupt every program the RVN initiated at the local level. Such key programs as "Land to the Tiller" and "Farm Credit" met with vicious slander or outright sabotage. For example, Communist cadres instigated the peasants to apply in mass for credits in order to overtax the bureaucracy and exhaust the funds; then they urged the peasants not to make repayments. The fish-breeding program also failed to interest farmers at first because Communist cadres spread the rumor that the type of fish that the GVN had imported from the Philippines would cause leprosy.

The most significant Communist opposition to pacification dated back to the early days of the First Republic's Strategic Hamlet system, which the Communists vilified as a program designed to "repress the population" and to "imprison the population behind the hamlet's barrier." In addition to the vilification campaign, the Communists stepped up attacks and shellings against strategic hamlets.

After their defeat during the 1968 general offensive, Communist main-force units had to withdraw to border base areas, leaving much of the countryside to GVN control. The pacification program subsequently made remarkable progress across the country. This took the Communist command in the South by surprise, and it resolved to wreck the GVN's pacification and development program at all costs. As a matter of fact, almost all directives issued by COSVN during that period focused on a determined effort to defeat the GVN pacification program.[1] A document captured in 1971 admitted that the loss of the rural area would eventually make it impossible for the Communists to gain victory.[2]

To confront the enemy and compete with him in the rural area, the GVN first sought to place all villages and hamlets across the country under military control. In addition to protecting the population, the GVN also strove to regiment it into organizations and arm its able-bodied members. The goal was to turn villages and hamlets into centers of resistance against the enemy and to make him feel unsafe wherever he went. Once this was done, development could take place with more chance of success. Regional and Popular Forces (RF and PF) and People's Self-Defense Forces (PSDF) were employed to defend and protect their own villages. The tactic was based on a guerrilla warfare precept: if the enemy force was small, destroy it; if it was sizable, harass and pin it down, or withdraw to conserve force and call for regular reinforcements to destroy it. ARVN regular units, meanwhile, would concentrate on attacking and destroying the enemy's logistical bases and his main-force units, thus denying him the chance to rest, recuperate, or reorganize.

• • •

In conclusion, in place of the social disruption caused by deliberate sabotage by the Communists, the government and people of South Vietnam were determined, with the assistance provided by the United States and the Free World, to transform South Vietnam into an anti-Communist outpost of the Free World, to heal the social ills inherited from colonialism and feudalism, and to make their country prosperous.

The efforts of the GVN in pacification could be summed up by the three national goals that pacification sought to achieve, namely: 1) to end the war, which implied eliminating Viet Cong infrastructure (VCI), defeating invasion forces, and maintaining security; 2) to develop democracy, which implied the establishment of elective government and democratic institutions and enlisting the participation of the people in national life; and 3) to reform society by eliminating injustice and social vices, and providing every citizen equal opportunities for advancement and equal protection under the law.

II. PACIFICATION STRATEGY AND OBJECTIVES

The Enemy Threat

The war was first waged under the cover of a popular uprising against the South Vietnamese government and not as an outright invasion. The Communists created the National Liberation Front (NLF) on 20 December 1960 to give the war a political cover.

The NLF was in fact just what its name conveyed, a front. The actual authority for conducting the war in South Vietnam remained in the hands of the Politburo in Hanoi, which directed the war in the South through five major commands: the B-5 Front was responsible for the DMZ area; Military Region Tri-Thien-Hue (MRTTH) for the provinces of Quang Tri and Thua Thien; Military Region 5 for the coastal provinces from Quang Nam in the north through Khanh Hoa in the south; B-3 Front generally for the highland area in western GVN MR-2; and COSVN, the Central Office for South Vietnam. COSVN was responsible for South Vietnam's southern half, a geographical area corresponding to GVN MR-3, MR-4, and the southern part of MR-2 of the Republic of Vietnam.

The conflict, according to the Communists, was a "people's war," a war waged by all the people in all aspects: military, political, economic, social, cultural, etc. The enemy used the same strategy it used with success during the First Indochina War, 1949–1954, a three-phased strategy adapted from Mao Tse Tung's theory of protracted war, which was supposed to progress from strategic defensive to strategic offensive. Guerrilla warfare was the form during the first phase. Its purpose was to harass and wear down the opponent. The second phase involved the beginning of mobile warfare and consisted of attacks against enemy fortifications with the purpose of attriting the enemy's military potential and driving him into a strategic defense. The final phase was an all-out offensive employing mobile warfare combined with fortification warfare, aimed at complete destruction of enemy forces.

Communist forces in South Vietnam consisted of three principal components: 1) the infrastructure (political and support) and guerrillas; 2) regional forces; and 3) regular or main forces. There were two types of guerrillas: the paramilitary and the full military or unattached. Guerrilla activities were generally localized and consisted of sabotage, assassination, [and] harassment, which were aimed at sowing confusion, terror, and loss of confidence among the population and forcing the RVN forces to spread thin and lose mobility. Guerrillas also constituted a source of manpower for regional forces, whose scope of activities was more extensive and whose combat effectiveness and armament were better. Regional forces were generally employed in a supporting role when regular forces were committed, and they both used the tactics of mobile warfare.

Guerrillas were organized into squads and platoons, while regional forces consisted of battalions and regiments. Regular forces were initially of battalion or regimental size, but were gradually upgraded into divisions and finally army corps.

By 1959, when the enemy began to rekindle war activities in South Vietnam, Communist forces consisted primarily of Viet Cong elements, or South Vietnamese Communists. Their cadre were mainly former Viet Minh elements regrouped to North Vietnam in 1954 but reintroduced into the South after 1959. In 1962, however, North Vietnam began to infiltrate men into the South to help the Viet Cong build up its multilevel military force, and also as replacements for increasing losses. By 1964 entire NVA regiments were introduced into the South and, after US combat forces entered the war a year later, division-sized NVA units were recorded fighting on southern battlefields.

The infiltration of NVA men and units, together with combat and logistic support elements, continued unabated despite heavy US bombardments. During this period, intelligence reports indicated a constant movement of NVA divisions in and out of South Vietnam. At the time of the 1972 invasion, there were 14 NVA infantry divisions committed to three main fronts in South Vietnam, supported by one sapper division, one artillery division, and one AAA division. These forces remained in the South until the cease-fire in January 1973 and constituted a permanent military threat for the RVN. By this time, 90 percent of Communist combat units in South Vietnam were NVA and only one-third of total Communist strength was Viet Cong.

The enemy infrastructure which existed in South Vietnam from the beginning of the war did not cause grave concern to the GVN until 1967, when its role became prominent in combat support. Despite heavy losses incurred by enemy main-force units, this infrastructure continued its activities such as tax collection, supply, recruitment, etc., even in the areas adjacent to cities and US and RVNAF bases. The war in Vietnam was being fought on two levels: the conspicuous, violent, high level of combat against Communist armed forces, and the silent, ubiquitous, low-key but no less deadly struggle against the enemy infrastructure.

The elimination of the VCI proved to be a task much more difficult than the destruction of enemy combat units because of its cellular, well-dispersed, and well-concealed organization. The VCI was in fact so well woven into the South Vietnamese social fabric that it was almost invulnerable to detection. Even if one VCI cell was discovered, it would be difficult to trace it to others because of airtight compartmentalization.

System Evolution

Under the First Republic (1955–1963), the concept of strategic hamlets took shape in a piecemeal manner in some localities during 1961. It was subsequently expanded and developed into a cohesive, nationwide system.

In the beginning, some local authorities merely duplicated the village defense system as it had been employed with success against the Viet Minh in Bui Chu and Phat Diem, the two oldest Roman Catholic diocesan areas in North Vietnam. In Ninh Thuan Province, for example, Lieutenant Colonel Khanh, the province chief, initiated a village defense program by encouraging villagers to plant a special kind of cactus around their village. Growing rapidly to over a meter in height, the spiny and thorn-bristled cactus hedge formed a difficult barrier which discouraged enemy infiltrators from penetrating the village. Male and female youths were tasked for security and guard duties, using rudimentary weapons such as pointed sticks, lances, and spears.

In Darlac Province, Trung Hoa village was fashioned into a North Vietnam-type village by Father Hoa, a Catholic priest of Chinese origin who fled North Vietnam in 1954. Father Hoa had brought with him a large number of Nung people, a North Vietnamese ethnic group, whom he helped resettle in the village.[3] The Nung resettlement area soon became a tightly stockaded village whose defense enclosure of wooden stakes was reinforced by a system of camouflaged trap holes lined with poison-soaked spikes. The poison would cause hard-to-heal and sometimes fatal infections. For the defense against Viet Cong attacks, villagers were armed with crossbows and arrows, lances, and spears, in addition to a few obsolete rifles.

Despite crude weapons, the defense of the two villages was effective. This success inspired the Vinh Long province chief, Lieutenant Colonel Le Van Phuoc, to establish self-defense systems in a number of villages located along QL-4, patterned after Ninh Thuan and Trung Hoa. Although experimental, these village defense systems proved successful counters to guerrilla activities.

In order to develop a village defense system for the entire country, Counselor Ngo Dinh Nhu developed the concept of strategic hamlets.[4] This concept was an amalgamation of ideas derived from Vietnamese self-defense villages, British anti-Communist tactics successfully used in Malaya, and the Israeli kibbutz defense system. By 1961 Mr. Nhu's concept developed into a cohesive national policy, and its ensuing Strategic Hamlet program, which he himself directed, was initiated on a nationwide basis. Designed to transform villages and hamlets into antiguerrilla bastions, the basic idea was to oppose the Communists with a ubiquitous resistance and defense system whose "main and long front line" was the villages and hamlets themselves. With each village and hamlet fortified and armed, the enemy would find it very difficult to select a weak point to attack. He would find strong resistance everywhere.

According to Mr. Nhu, the enemy enjoyed the advantage of fighting a frontless war. To offset that advantage, he said, we had to turn the rural areas into a "crisscrossed line of defense." The regular army would not be able to spread its troops over this line anyway, so there was no need to greatly expand it. Instead, the army would be kept at a reasonable size and improved in combat effectiveness; it would concentrate primarily on enemy base areas and main-force units. The people would become the primary force in the fight against enemy guerrillas. Toward that end, they would organize the defense of villages and hamlets by themselves and fight the enemy by employing "people's guerrilla tactics."

The Strategic Hamlet program progressed slowly, but proved effective enough in the face of an insurgency still in its embryonic stage. The slow progress could be attributed to the fact that the program did not enjoy such large-scale US support as its successor later did. It was partly funded by the national budget and partly by the Military Assistance Program. Despite this, by the end of 1962 statistics showed that, out of a total of 11,864 hamlets, 3,235 had been completed and about 34 percent of the total population was considered as living under the GVN protection.[5]

The percentage of population under GVN control was computed on the basis of reports submitted through the administrative hierarchy, from village to district to province, and from province to the central government. This reporting procedure was not as accurate as the Hamlet Evaluation System (HES) which the US later initiated in 1967. There was the possibility that Viet Cong infrastructure members were among the population recorded as living in GVN-controlled hamlets.

To ensure tight population control, some local governments adopted stringent measures such as a census file for every household (containing not only names and other particulars of its members, but also a group photograph showing every member of the household). Those households having members or relatives who had regrouped to North Vietnam or were active Viet Cong were identified by red dots, one dot for each such member, painted on a pillar in front of the house. Blue dots were used for other members of the household. Thus, at a glance, local government officials could tell which households had members cooperating with the other side. Naturally, these households were subject to discreet surveillance by the local government.

In 1963 several political upheavals slowed the accomplishment of the objectives of the Strategic Hamlet program and eventually terminated it altogether, but until that year the program was achieving considerable success in neutralizing the local VCI and in organizing effective local defenses. The Buddhist opposition movement in 1963 led to a military coup which overthrew the Ngo Dinh Diem regime and ushered in a period of turmoil and instability. At the same time, the military situation deteriorated markedly through the escalation of attacks by the Viet Cong. The Strategic Hamlet program, as a consequence, came to a complete stop. Those cadre who had managed and directed the program were either arrested or removed for having been part of the old regime. The few cadre who remained free disassociated themselves from the program. Soon after the military junta took over, its president officially announced the abolition of the Strategic Hamlet program in a proclamation that was widely acclaimed by the public and secretly enjoyed by the enemy. In some localities, the gains achieved through two years of hard toil disintegrated almost overnight. The Military Revolutionary Council had acted out of political necessity, but had not foreseen the detrimental consequences.

The countryside was once again left without governmental control, and the enemy at once filled this void with his own apparatus. During the months immediately following the overthrow of President Diem, the overall situation became utterly chaotic, with coups and countercoups, power struggles, and an increased level of enemy attacks.

In the face of the deteriorating situation, the GVN was in a dilemma. On the one hand, there was no way to reinstate the Strategic Hamlet program, since it had been linked with the old regime and officially abolished. On the other hand, the GVN could not give the enemy free reign over the countryside. As a solution, the government instituted a new pacification program, the "New Life Hamlet" program. As a matter of fact, there was nothing that could distinguish this program from its predecessor, only a change in name.

The New Life program began to move unsteadily forward. At first it was a loosely controlled, hesitant, unenthusiastic effort. There were not enough resources to commit to the program, and the new cadre were reluctant to implement it forcefully for fear of being identified with the old regime cadre. Furthermore, the leadership gave it no clear-cut direction, and the organizations that were to operate the program were plagued by ineffectiveness and incompetence. Very few local authorities knew exactly what to do or how to do it.

The year 1965 came as a miracle that saved South Vietnam from probable collapse. US combat troops, followed by Free World Military Assistance forces, were committed to South Vietnam to ward off an imminent Communist victory, and the United States poured in material resources to help the RVN regain its military footing. After initial successes that restored stability and maintained a fair military balance, both the US and the RVN governments could turn their attention to pacification.

Based on lessons learned through the Strategic Hamlet and the New Life Hamlet, the GVN initiated the Rural Development program in 1966. This was followed, in 1967, by the so-called New Model pacification program. To give a good start to this effort, centralized planning was initiated, but there was a clear lack of coordination between the military plan and its civilian counterpart. As a result, the organizational structure for operational control was not effective and there was little mutual support between the military and the civilian efforts. Moreover, there was a shortage of cadre at all levels and the training effort failed to turn them out in sufficient numbers.

The ARVN, meanwhile, considered pacification a responsibility of the civilians; it claimed to have no part in it, since its mission was to conduct mobile operations to destroy the enemy. During this period, the Regional and Popular Forces were still in their nascent stage; they were not yet capable of taking up the pacification responsibilities. In order to provide effective support for the pacification program, the RF and PF (formerly Civil Guard and People's Militia or Self-Defense Corps, respectively) required expansion, reorganization, and more intensive training.

Despite all these constraints, the pacification program seemed to be well on its way to progress. Its chances of success, however, were undermined by the enemy's general offensive in 1968. All the forces that had been committed to the pacification program, regular and territorial alike, had to be redeployed for the defense of provincial capitals and district towns. The countryside was once again left open to enemy control.

After successively defeating the enemy's attack in 1968, the GVN and RVNAF followed up their victories by initiating a three-month pacification plan, called the "Accelerated Pacification Campaign," from November 1968 to January 1969. The campaign was designed to enlarge the extent of GVN control, and this was a most appropriate time for the special pacification effort to succeed, since enemy forces had by then withdrawn to their border base areas for refitting and reorganizing. The RVNAF, with the support of the US and all other allied troops, enjoyed the initiative on all battlefields. As a result, the pacification effort was crowned with success.

In 1969 and 1970, pacification progressed by leaps and bounds. The total number of people and the extent of territory under GVN control surpassed all expectations. The enemy was effectively driven back to his bases over the border, and his units were unable to undertake any major action, preoccupied as they were with refitting and regrouping. Pursuing their military gains, the RVNAF took the initiative and struck across the border, first into enemy bases in Cambodia in 1970 and then into lower Laos. As a result, during 1971 the GVN had time to consolidate the gains achieved during the two previous years without major confrontations with enemy main-force units. In view of the markedly improved situation, the GVN found it appropriate to choose another name for its pacification effort. From 1971 on it was called "Community Defense and Development," the ultimate goal for which the GVN was striving.

During this period the enemy studied the lessons learned from his military defeat in 1968. Meanwhile, in view of the remarkable gains achieved by the GVN in its pacification program, the enemy was in danger of being denied the countryside altogether.

In 1972 the Communists launched a new general offensive, an offensive which was radically different from the 1968 Tet Offensive. Supported by tanks and artillery, nearly five NVA infantry divisions crossed the DMZ and invaded Quang Tri. Simultaneously, three divisions attacked north of Kontum and three others north of Binh Long. This offensive was aimed at forcing a coalition government on South Vietnam, defeating the Vietnamization program so that the RVNAF would be unable to take over the combat role from US forces, and, finally, forcing the RVN to accept terms advantageous to the Communist side at the Paris talks. The GVN and the RVNAF were determined to defend the countryside at all costs, and the RVNAF had, by this time, improved and matured into a formidable fighting force. Furthermore, despite the gradual withdrawal of US combat forces from Vietnam, there still remained in-country sizable US strategic and tactical air, naval firepower, and logistical support to assist the RVNAF.

With effective US support, the RVNAF were able to hold out against the greatly reinforced regular NVA forces and prevent further inroads into the countryside. Following these military achievements, the GVN concentrated on consolidating the pacification gains instead of pushing for further expansion. Rather than renewing another annual effort, the government looked farther ahead and developed a four-year pacification plan. This was known as [the] "1972–1975 Community Defense and Local Development" plan, which was designed, as the name implied, to consolidate territorial security on the one hand and to develop the nation in all aspects on the other.

No sooner had the plan been implemented than it was obstructed by the disadvantages brought about by the Paris Agreement of 28 January 1973. Taking advantage of the agreement, the enemy increased his strength in the countryside through infiltration of weapons, equipment, and manpower from North Vietnam.

Thus, over the long war years, the pacification effort had been revitalized time and again under several different names: Strategic Hamlet, New Life Hamlet, Rural or Revolutionary Development, National Pacification and Development, and finally Community Defense and Local Development. Despite the various names, which changed with each regime in power, the basic national objectives laid out in each plan remained essentially the same. The only differences between early and later plans were some operational procedures, the ever-expanding scale and extent of the effort, and the increasing contributions in financial and material resources made by the United States and other friendly nations.

Strategy and Operational Concept

• • •

To provide security for pacification, the RVNAF and US forces adopted the strategic concept of "clear and hold." In practice, clear and hold operations were designed to destroy the enemy, neutralize his forces, and drive them away from the area to be pacified.

Then, by maintaining a permanent ARVN force in the area to ensure security, a local government could be established and in time elections could be held to institute democracy. When the area reached that stage of development, the enemy would be unable to return to harass and to take revenge on the people.

"Clear and hold" differed greatly from "search and destroy," which was widely employed during the initial stage of active US participation in the war. For, even when Communist units had been effectively defeated or driven away from a certain area, they were still able to return and renew their activities if there were no friendly forces to secure the area. An area was considered "cleared" when the enemy's main or local forces, guerrillas, and infrastructure had been destroyed or neutralized. The principal role in this stage was given to major ARVN units, augmented sometimes by Regional Forces, and often supported and assisted by US or Free World Military Assistance (FWMA) forces. ARVN forces were also assisted by National Police (NP) forces, who provided information concerning the enemy's infrastructure and helped screen and interrogate persons detained.

As the term implied, activities during the "securing" stage were aimed at eliminating remnants of enemy forces or infrastructure, protecting the population, and preventing the enemy from reviving his activities. At the same time, the government tried to establish its presence in villages and hamlets in order to create the conditions for developmental projects to flourish. An area was designated totally secure when the villages and hamlets in it were assigned enough military and police forces to deter all terrorist activities directed against the population. Police field forces were employed in the elimination of the VCI or, in coordination with territorial forces, the maintenance of security in villages and hamlets. ARVN and US forces meanwhile operated in adjacent areas as a shield to divert the enemy's regular forces from the area being pacified, and to relieve any pressure the enemy might exert on it. As soon as the area became secure, Regional Forces began to take over from ARVN forces, thus releasing them for new operations.

• • •

Interim Objectives and Priorities

While the ultimate national goals to be achieved through pacification remained unchanged, the GVN established yearly programs with specific objectives to be met during the year. For example, the pacification effort prior to 1968 focused on populated, prosperous urban areas, those areas bordering on important lines of communication and waterways, and those villages and hamlets surrounding provincial capitals and district towns. The strategic concept then, which was labeled "the spreading oil stain," consisted of consolidating pacified nuclei from which the pacification effort would spread out in all directions. Since urban areas were the hubs of the RVN strategy, the enemy chose to strike directly into them during his general offensive of 1968, although his ultimate goal remained liberating the rural areas.

As soon as the last enemy attacks were driven back, the GVN immediately set about to restore control of the rural areas through a special large-scale and intensive pacification campaign which lasted three months, from 1 November 1968 to 31 January 1969. The goal of this campaign was to retake the hamlets lost and to expand the territory under GVN control. This was a departure from the 1968 pacification effort, which concentrated on populated areas and urban centers. The special campaign was designed to achieve these major objectives: 1) to expand the territory under GVN control, 2) to destroy the enemy infrastructure, 3) to organize and arm the People's Self-Defense Forces, [and] 4) to establish the local governmental structure wherever it had never been established.

As a result of the achievements of the special campaign, the pacification effort was pushed more vigorously during 1969. Under GVN directives, those provinces that met all the objectives of the campaign were to continue adding to the areas under GVN control and consolidating their gains. On the other hand, if a province had not met the objectives, it was required to achieve them before proceeding with the 1969 plan.

• • •

Since the 1969 pacification concept focused on expanding governmental control into contested areas, and on the village as the basic unit (instead of the hamlet), the displacement of the local populace from one hamlet to another for purposes of pacification was deemed unnecessary and disadvantageous. Displacement of land-bound peasants would be an unpopular act that would have adverse consequences on their daily life.

To implement this overall concept, the GVN laid out objectives to be achieved by year's end:

1. An increase in percentage of population under GVN control, up to 90 percent across the country.
2. To destroy, by all means, at least 23,400 enemy infrastructure cadre.
3. To build the PSDF to a strength of two million members, and equip this force with 400,000 individual weapons.
4. To establish local governments for all villages and hamlets over the entire national territory.
5. To secure the defection of at least 36,000 enemy cadre and troops.
6. To reduce the total number of war victims and refugees below the one million mark, and to resettle or return to their home villages 300,000 people.
7. To step up information and propaganda activities.
8. To encourage the development of the local economy.

All the objectives that had been set forth for the previous year were retained in 1970. Like the previous year, the 1970 pacification objectives focused primarily on the protection of the population against Communist terrorism and the maximum destruction of the enemy infrastructure. To achieve this, the GVN pushed the buildup of PSDF to four million, double the 1969 strength, and including 1,500,000 combat members and 2,500,000 support members. At the same time, it made an effort to train and equip this force in order to turn it into a combat-effective force ready to take over from Popular Forces

when required. To expand GVN control, it was required that village and hamlet government and district and provincial councils be established throughout the country. The
Chieu Hoi program meanwhile was aimed at the high- and middle-echelon enemy cadre;
it appealed for their cooperation in the common task of nation building.

• • •

In summary, all hamlets were to be upgraded to A, B, or C category, and at least
90 percent of the people would be living in A or B hamlets.

The Ultimate National Goals

The year 1971 ushered in a period of improved security throughout the nation. The
RVNAF held the initiative on all battlefields, crossed the heretofore inviolable national
border, and struck destructive blows on the enemy's logistical bases and sanctuaries.
Cross-border operations conducted by US-RVNAF units into Cambodia in 1970 and the
Laos incursion in 1971, in addition to the closing of Sihanoukville port by the new
Cambodian government in 1970, effectively upset Communist plans for an early summer offensive against Saigon, a repetition of their 1968 offensive. As a result, the Communists were compelled to reorganize their bases and replace their battle losses. Almost
the entire population of South Vietnam lived under effective protection of the government and the armed forces. The situation was so good that the GVN deemed it a most
appropriate time to pass on to the nation-building phase, particularly economic development and social reform. Pacification was considered an anachronistic term, since its
most important objective had been achieved.

The new pacification plan for 1971 was thus redesignated "Community Defense and
Development." It was designed to destroy whatever was left of the enemy infrastructure,
achieve maximum efficiency in the governmental structure, expand and develop the national economy, and push ahead more vigorously the land reform program. The ARVN
regular forces, which had been partially pinned down by their pacification duties, were
to turn over territorial responsibilities to the RF and PF. The goal was to release ARVN
forces for mobile operations while affording the RF and PF the opportunity to prove
themselves in combating enemy local forces and guerrillas.

The objectives set forth for the 1971 Community Defense and Development Plan
were grouped under three basic national goals, which remained the ultimate goals for
which the RVN was striving. These were called the "Three Selves," namely: Self-Defense,
Self-Management, and Self-Sufficiency.

• • •

The National Police Force, whose primary role was to destroy the enemy infrastructure, was to be increased to 122,000 men by year's end in order to provide every village
with a police force strong enough to maintain law and order.

• • •

Improved security and increased effectiveness of the local government structure and
national cadre would allow the GVN to switch more energy to self-sufficiency, the task of
improving, socially and economically, the living conditions of the population. Toward

that end, the Land to the Tiller program, a bold land reform measure which was initiated late in 1970, had the planned purpose of distributing 400,000 hectares of farmland to landless farmworkers.[6] This was intended both as an incentive to help boost farm production and as a means to achieve social justice and win the peasants over to the RVN cause. Other agricultural improvement programs, such as forestry, fisheries, and farm breeding, were also pushed vigorously forward. At the same time, the GVN also undertook an extensive project of irrigation, encouraged the planting of two or three crops of "miracle rice," and established rural development banks throughout the country to provide needed credit for farmers to plant rice or other supplementary crops and to breed cattle or poultry.

• • •

In summary, the 1972–1975 Community Defense and Local Development Plan was designed to consolidate security and increase development efforts in local communities with the view of achieving the three basic goals of Self-Defense, Self-Management, and Self-Sufficiency.

The war the Communists waged was purported to be a people's war. This was a myth perpetuated by Communist [dogma] and propaganda. The part played by the South Vietnamese people in prosecuting the war on the Communist side was minimal and insignificant. In fact, the South Vietnamese people always chose to flee in the face of Communist incursions.

Winning support, the strategic goal of pacification, was paramount to the RVN cause. Yet the people seemed indifferent to the GVN courtship. If successful, the pacification effort would replace this indifference with a solid commitment on the part of the people, a commitment that would support the defense of the nation and achieve a just peace.

III. OPERATION AND SUPPORT

The GVN Organization for Pacification

Beginning in 1966, when pacification became a cohesively organized effort and was subjected to centralized annual planning, the GVN established a nationwide control and monitoring system designed to coordinate activities of the various organizations and agencies involved in the program. As far as the civilian government was concerned, there was always a shortage of qualified personnel required for key executive positions. Consequently, several high-ranking military officers were appointed cabinet ministers or to highly responsible positions in the pacification program.

• • •

Whether responsible or not for pacification, division commanders were usually overburdened by problems concerning territorial security. Almost 80 percent of their time was spent solving these problems, and, as a consequence, a division commander had little time left for mobile operations. After 1970 a significant effort was made to alleviate division commanders' territorial responsibilities and to permit them to gradually take over combat responsibilities from the departing US forces. This effort was made by releasing divisional units from their static pacification support mission and replacing them gradually with Regional Forces. Thus sectors or provinces were made directly subordinate to the military region as far as territorial security and pacification support were concerned. As of that time, at corps headquarters the position of deputy corps commander for territory was created, and he was placed in charge of territorial security and pacification support within his military region.

The province was the primary level responsible for actually carrying out the pacification program. As chairman of the Provincial Pacification and Development Council . . . he was directly responsible to the corps commander for military affairs and to the central government for administrative affairs and the management of national resources committed to the pacification program.

Province chiefs were appointed by presidential decree upon recommendation of the corps commander and with prior concurrence of the prime minister. They were mostly army officers, usually with the rank of colonel or lieutenant colonel. Within his province, the province chief was responsible for everything—tactical operations, administration, and politics.

A province chief was assisted by two deputies: a deputy for administration, always a civilian, and a deputy for military affairs, who was also called deputy sector commander (since the province chief was the sector commander). The deputy sector commander assisted the province chief in all matters concerning territorial security; tactical operations; the employment, organization, and control of Regional/Popular Forces; and the control of paramilitary forces in the province (National Police, RD cadre, PSDF).

• • •

Employment of Forces in Support of Pacification

• • •

Prior to 1966, the role of the National Police was generally confined to maintaining law and order in urban areas, cities, provincial capitals, and district towns; there was no police force in villages and hamlets. National Police forces were subordinated to the Ministry of Interior and placed under the control of a [National Police] General Directorate. Over the years, the NP expanded considerably, in keeping with its growing role, and finally developed into an authorized 122,000-man-strong paramilitary force. NP forces included uniformed police, special police, combat or field police, and harbor police. In addition to the NP central command, there were four regional commands, one for each military region, and the Saigon command. At the province level, there was an NP service; at district level an NP section; and at village level an NP subsection.

During the period of intensified pacification effort, the NP made significant contributions in the destruction of the enemy infrastructure and maintenance of law and order in villages and hamlets.

Police Field Forces (PFF) were well equipped and organized into companies. PFF companies were deployed in provinces, where they operated in cooperation and coordination with rural development cadre groups.

• • •

While equipped and trained in the same way as other police forces, the PFF specialized in the role of antiviolence and antirebellion and had combat capabilities similar to military forces.

• • •

Rural Development (RD) cadre were organized into groups of 39 men each. In the Central Highlands, RD cadre were called Rural Mountaineers and organized into groups of 70 men each. RD cadre were recruited in each province and sent to the Vung Tau RD Training Center for training. Upon completion of training they were sent back to their provinces of origin. Each RD group was composed of a group headquarters, a military section, and a reconstruction section.[7]

• • •

During the period from 1965 to 1970, RD cadre groups played key roles in the pacification and development effort. As of 1971, however, since the pacification program focused on community defense and community development, it was directly operated by the specialized cadre of various ministries. As a result, RD cadre groups were deactivated and the personnel were absorbed into the ministries, such as Information and Open Arms, Agriculture, etc., depending on their qualifications.

• • •

To provide better security, province and district chiefs were free to employ their forces where, when, and how they deemed best. RF battalions, because of their independent operational capabilities, were usually employed in combined operations with regular ARVN forces or as province reaction forces. Seldom were they broken down into smaller elements to man static defense positions. The deployment of RF battalions into other provinces, however, was the prerogative of the military region commander.

• • •

The case of RF company groups was somewhat different. Because of their limited command and control capabilities, RF company groups were generally employed in well-defined areas of operation, and always confined to the home province. They were mostly employed for local security missions. RF company groups were best suited for providing security for limited areas within a district, supervising National Police forces and the People's Self-Defense Forces, and providing guidance for village and hamlet chiefs in organizing and consolidating their local defense systems. Separate RF companies, which were not organic to any group or battalion, were mostly employed for the protection of public utility installations, roads, and bridges.

Popular Force platoons were assigned to villages and operated according to the village chief's defense plan under the control of his deputy for security. Depending on the situation, PF platoons might be deployed to operate in village boundary areas or in adjacent villages. The long-duration deployment of a PF platoon from its home village was discouraged, and subject to approval by the military region command. When operating away from its home village, a PF platoon received free rations of rice.

People's Self-Defense Forces were not usually employed in a military capacity. Being an auxiliary force, PSDF members assisted Popular Forces in the enforcement of security in the villages and participated in activities involving the villagers and their families. In secure areas, PSDFs were also employed to guard roads and bridges and in mixed patrols with PFs. However, PSDFs were almost never entrusted the task of manning the defense of important GVN installations or vital lines of communication.

The great number of military forces employed in support of pacification never seemed to keep up with the requirements occasioned by the necessity to deploy a permanent occupation force to every hamlet. The situation was such that, when protection forces were deployed from a certain area considered "secure," that area might relapse into insecurity and the local population would lose confidence in the GVN. To ensure a judicious employment of forces, the Central Pacification and Development Council devised certain principles which were embodied in the concept of area security. According to this concept, whenever an area had been pacified and was deemed secure, its military forces would be reduced and partly redeployed to other less secure areas. This redistribution of forces generally occurred within a military region and was a function of the changing situation, and the MR commander made the decisions affecting the redeployment of regular ARVN forces and RF battalions.

US Organization for Pacification Support

• • •

In conjunction with their combat efforts, US forces also performed civic action activities which were highly praiseworthy in view of their effective contributions to the GVN pacification effort. US civic action programs underwent some changes in emphasis; in 1964, for example, US civic action efforts were focused on providing health protection and sanitation for the peasantry in rural areas. They included such programs as well-digging and anti-malaria operations. In 1965, however, in view of the massive US participation, US civic programs emphasized the necessity to reduce casualties and damage to the civilian population, foster good rapport between US forces and the population, and assist the peasants in their farmwork, particularly in those areas adjacent to US bases. US civic action programs also helped the local population to repair roads and build bridges, schools, maternity wards, and dispensaries.

Civic action programs implemented by US forces gained popular sympathy and developed excellent rapport between them and the civilian population. In addition to the building task, US forces took good care of the civilian population whenever casualties and damage occurred. Injured civilians were always immediately evacuated for treatment, and all damages were compensated for with fairness. In this respect, US forces seldom incurred criticism, since they carried out with zeal MACV directives to "limit to the maximum extent casualties and damages to the civilian population."

• • •

The Phoenix Program

The Phoenix program was proposed by US authorities in 1967 as a means to consolidate and unify intelligence activities aimed at the destruction of the VCI. Despite GVN concurrence, it was nearly a year before the government approved Phoenix by executive decree. The delay stemmed from difficulties in defining terms of reference for the program and in selecting the agency responsible for its execution.

To implement the program, Phoenix committees were established from the central government to the districts, with the missions of collecting information on the VCI and planning for [and] organizing operations to neutralize it.

Corps commanders [and] province and district chiefs served as chairmen of the Phoenix committees at their respective levels. . . . Members of a Phoenix committee included representatives of the Police Field Force, the Special Police, the Military Security Service [MSS], the Provincial Reconnaissance Unit (PRU), and Chieu Hoi, RD cadre, sector S-2, and other military organizations.

The coordination of intelligence and operations among various military and civilian agencies included the following tasks: 1) to collect, corroborate, and disseminate information pertaining to key cadre, organization, and plans of the VCI; 2) to exploit information gathered in a timely manner so as to conduct quick reaction military operations; and 3) to classify, interrogate, and recommend the adjudication of suspects temporarily detained.

The task of eliminating the VCI was carried out in close coordination with search and destroy and pacification operations, making full use of propaganda and psywar techniques and resources. The Phoenix effort was supported by military units in combined operations, closely coordinated with police forces. The goal was maximum coordination; Police Field Forces and the PRU joined in the task of eliminating the VCI. RF and PF units participated in operations designed to attack and destroy the VCI. For example, these units provided the information, held or cordoned the target, and protected searching and screening parties made up of the Special Police, Police Field Forces, and military security personnel.

Information on the VCI, collected by intelligence agencies during military operations, or by the provincial interrogation center, was immediately disseminated to related units or agencies, to the DIOCC [District Intelligence and Operations Coordination Committee], and to the provincial permanent center for exploitation.

Provincial Reconnaissance Units . . . conducted special operations to collect or exploit information and participated in combined operations with other forces. Organized and armed by the US Embassy, PRUs were placed under the control of and employed by the provincial police chiefs when the National Police were assigned the responsibility of implementing the Phoenix program. Together with Police Field Force units, PRUs made up the main police striking force in the task of eliminating the VCI.

• • •

Chieu Hoi (Open Arms) cadre, because of their specialized knowledge of the enemy, were particularly useful in the elimination of the VCI. They were most effective in appealing for enemy personnel's return and providing support to intelligence collection activities or reaction operations. Selected returnees were employed in the interrogation of VC suspects or to identify VCI personnel among refugees.

The enemy infrastructure usually conveyed the general impression that its personnel were a special breed of fanatic Communist cadres. In fact, a distinction had to be made between those VCI cadre who were truly indoctrinated party members and the sympathizers or common people who were induced into serving in the VCI. In most cases, the second category of VCI personnel was made up of ordinary poor people who cooperated with the enemy either because of his pressure or for profit. They included smugglers of medicine and other essential commodities plying their trade between GVN-controlled and VC areas.

People detained by police and security forces during military operations were first classified into three categories—VC or NVA soldier, suspected member of the VCI, or undetermined identity. If subsequent interrogation, documentation, police records check, and possibly possession of weapons proved conclusively that the individual was clearly an enemy soldier or a VCI operative, he (or she) was sent to the PW camp (in the first instance) or remanded to trial (if a member of the VCI).

If, on the other hand, no evidence was found to implicate the person as a VCI member, he was released. Those detainees who were suspected of being members of the VCI but could not be convicted as such for lack of evidence were placed under the jurisdiction of the provincial security committee, which had the authority to either release or detain them temporarily pending investigation. This committee was chaired by the province chief and included the provincial judge or prosecutor, the police chief, the MSS representative, the sector S-2, and representatives of operational forces as members.

The role of the MSS representative was particularly significant since the MSS, a counterintelligence agency, collected and provided information on the VCI to the PIOCC and DIOCC. The committee was empowered to release or detain a suspect at the provincial reeducation center (jail) for a period of time ranging from three months to a maximum of two years. The "trial" of suspects took place once a month, and its procedure began with a presentation of records by the police chief. If there were no complications, the committee immediately decided on each case.

This procedure was criticized as unconstitutional and undemocratic because it amounted to a trial without due legal process. However, the GVN contended that it was simply an administrative, not a judicial, act, hence not determined by national laws. And, since it was not a trial process in the legal sense, the suspect could not have legal counsel, nor was his presence required when the committee made its decision.

The reason the GVN resorted to this procedure against the VCI was that it was nearly impossible in most cases to produce enough hard evidence for indictment, yet the suspect's culpability was certain beyond reasonable doubt. Thus, to stay on the safe side (the official reasoning went), it was better to detain the suspect than to free the criminal, even at the expense of incurring some wrath. On the other hand, the GVN authorities were faced with the problem of identifying hard-core VCI members from among the suspects who, for the most part, were just sympathizers or innocent people induced into the VCI service under persuasion, coercion, or threats of blackmail, or simply to earn a living. To provide enough time for thorough research and investigation, temporary detention of the suspects was necessary.

For all the criticism directed against it, the detention power authorized provincial security committees failed to deter the VCI members still at large, since the maximum two years behind bars was not really too high a price for the hard-core VC. Compared to what had been done under the First Republic, which outlawed the Communists altogether, detention appeared mild and even democratic. Under President Diem's secret directives, province chiefs were allowed to "dispose of" VCI members in whatever way they deemed appropriate, including murder, without legal justification. The VCI members were especially fearful of the "Central Vietnam Task Force" organized and directed by Diem's brother, Mr. Ngo Dinh Can, in the early 1960s. The task force members indiscriminately slaughtered every VCI member they hunted down, and this deterred VCI overt activities for some time.

Under the Second Republic, the spirit of democracy was strong and pervasive, precluding the use of harsh measures. Against members of the VCI captured, the strongest measure taken was detention, which, to hard-core elements, could be looked upon as a period of rest pending release and renewed activities. To the innocent people detained because of suspicion, however, detention was apt to alienate them from the GVN cause and, under Communist proselytizing influence, could well turn them into sympathizers and eventually members of the VCI.

The GVN had no choice [but to] proceed with the program of eliminating the VCI, which could be equated with a military force in terms of destructive effectiveness. GVN officials responsible for the program were fond of saying that eliminating a district or province political commissar of the VCI was tantamount to putting a whole VC company out of action. Given the effect of the program on VCI activities, this was not an inflated statement.

The period from the inception of the Phoenix program up to 1971, which was considered the best year of the RVN in terms of security and pacification achievements, saw a marked decline in VCI activities. Out of an estimated total of 40,000 members recorded by 1971, the VCI suffered 15,603 eliminated or neutralized (broken down into 5,615 killed, 4,391 detained, and 5,597 returnees), or more than one-third of its strength. In 1968 the VCI suffered the biggest loss ever in its ranks, because it was pushed into overt military activities in support of the "general offensive-general uprising" campaign.

In retrospect, the Phoenix program can be termed a reasonable success. This success could have been maintained and furthered as long as South Vietnam was free from NVA incursions. Like pacification in general, its achievements could be offset by military reverses. The momentum of the program came to a standstill in 1972, for example, when NVA units launched the Easter Offensive. The same was true of the post-cease-fire period, during which pacification and other programs suffered severe setbacks in the face of stepped-up enemy attacks which the RVNAF alone, thinly spread as they were, and with reduced war supplies, were unable to contain effectively.

The program was also beset by internal problems, among which the most serious was the shortage of capable intelligence personnel at the province and district levels for effective coordination of activities against the VCI. Next came the lack of appropriate support and weight given to the program by province and district chiefs who, either because of their overburdened responsibilities or failure to realize the importance of the program and take proper interest in it, placed its execution squarely into the hands of the National Police. Left to its own initiative, the politically oriented National Police were generally reluctant to take forceful actions and became ineffective against the VCI.

Then there was the problem of identifying and prosecuting VCI members operating under cover and living mixed with the population. Identification was particularly difficult against planted agents in crowded urban and suburban areas, where the mass of working people lived. Very seldom, if ever, was their presence detected by the National Police.

The same problem was even harder in the rural areas where village and hamlet councilmen operated in constant fear of retaliation, which accounted for their lack of enthusiasm or even dereliction in eliminating the VCI. More often than not, they failed to take action, even when they knew there were enemy agents living in the community, for sometimes these agents turned out to be the relatives of certain councilmen themselves. The fear of retaliation led to a propensity toward accommodation and finally developed into a philosophy of "live and let live" which was at the root of passivity and inaction. In a few extreme cases, some councilmen might turn out to be the very VCI that the Phoenix effort set out to eliminate.

IV. RVN-US COOPERATION AND COORDINATION IN PACIFICATION

• • •

An Evaluation

US assistance played a vital role in the total pacification effort, beginning with the top level where the GVN ministries, as planners and supervisors of their own program, seemed to need it the most. They were usually plagued by a shortage of personnel required for the various programs. In addition, there were not always qualified cadre for all specialized fields. Training and qualifying such specialists in sufficient numbers took a long time and close support from various US agencies. Planning for specialist requirements was also a time-consuming task, since it involved the compilation and review of individual requests received from all the provinces. Despite these shortcomings, the assistance provided by CORDS and other US agencies usually satisfied every need in personnel training required by the ministries. This was due to the very close cooperation and coordination between the GVN agencies and CORDS and other US agencies. Every plan and program was subject to careful studies by both sides.

At the CTZ/MR level, however, it seemed that the US side usually held the initiative in planning. For one thing, at this level there was always a substantial US staff with a wide variety of specialists and qualified personnel. Sometimes a plan was subjected to careful studies by the US staff for five or six months before actually being forwarded for the first time. In general, US Army staffs were made up of talented and experienced officers who had become experts in their own right. They were extremely efficient and helpful in assessing and evaluating pacification results. In particular, they proved to be unequalled experts in evaluating hamlets, monitoring and assessing the employment and capabilities of territorial forces, and in monitoring the implementation of such programs as Phoenix, Chieu Hoi, and war refugees. Their contributions of opinions, ideas, and suggestions were always pertinent and valuable for remedying deficiencies; their role in pacification support was particularly valuable, and in many cases indispensable.

On the RVN side, it was admitted that at the field levels, corps and division, staff officers did not always possess a thorough understanding of the pacification concept and its programs. As a result, most of the planning was initiated and undertaken by the US side. At the beginning of the pacification effort, for example, a plan disseminated by the central level to corps was merely duplicated and sent verbatim to provinces, without comments or specific guidance. The corps staff responsible for pacification usually consisted of inexperienced officers who were not familiar with planning or studies, and often they were assigned to pacification because they did not fit into any other staff capability. As a result, corps were unable to make studies or plans that could help improve the pacification effort.

By contrast, at the execution level—i.e., province—there were many talented and experienced province chiefs. Some held their positions for several years and consequently had a full grasp of provincial problems, the local terrain, and the local population. Others had innovative ideas and achieved spectacular gains in pacification. Province senior advisors usually stayed in their jobs only one year, or sometimes a little longer, and as a result they were not entirely knowledgeable about the province and its pacification problems. Nevertheless, they played key roles in providing assistance and support for their counterparts. If a province was well supplied with materiel or received adequate military support, it was invariably due to the province senior advisor's active role. His connections and resourcefulness were invaluable assets that made him extremely useful to the province chief. Through his connections with higher-echelon commands, for example, a province senior advisor could always communicate his counterpart's problems and obtain immediate response and help. Sometimes a province senior advisor even used MACV or the US Embassy leverage to get things done quickly through the ARVN or GVN channel in support of his counterpart; advisors were effective in cutting through red tape.

The role of the district advisor was particularly a difficult and demanding one, even more so than that of the province advisor. To be effective, the district advisor had to assume a dual role: military and political. He advised and assisted the district chief, not only in military and operational matters but also in the use of national resources, the supervision of village and hamlet councils, civic actions, and public relations. In other words, the district advisor had to double as an administrative and political counselor to help his counterpart manage district affairs. Given the relatively young and inexperienced district staff, and the extent of work involved in the management of a district, the advisor's role was an uphill task indeed. To give an example, each district managed an average of 30–40 PF platoons, three to six RF companies, thousands of PSDF, Police Field Force, and the RD cadre.

But, by and large, US district advisors performed extremely well, despite their alien environment. Mostly young army officers at the beginning of their assignment, they usually became inveterate old-timers of the Vietnam War, wiser though not older, and extremely adept at handling counterinsurgency problems by the time their tour of duty was over. Their contributions to the pacification effort were most significant in the areas of security and rural development. As a special breed of politico-military advisors, they were very popular with the local officials and population.

In summary, US senior advisors at the province and district level played very important roles in pacification support and made substantial contributions to the provinces and districts where they were assigned. There were indeed several advisors who were more active and devoted to pacification than their counterparts. Many were seen making visits to villages and hamlets if there was a requirement to know more about the real situation. Finally, there were many who sacrificed their lives in the pursuit of their advisory duties.

V. PACIFICATION TECHNIQUES AND OPERATIONS

The pacification process usually began with a tactical operation which went through three major phases, each involving the employment of different forces.

In the initial phase, regular ARVN or territorial forces or both conducted a security operation in the area targeted for pacification. Their objective was to destroy or drive away enemy main- or local-force units and guerrillas. Since the area to be pacified was usually populated, the use of firepower was subject to limitations to minimize casualties and damage. As soon as the enemy units were destroyed or driven away, friendly forces usually broke down into small elements for a careful search to destroy the remnants of the enemy or those enemy who tried to escape by mixing with the populace. At the same time, psywar and propaganda activities were conducted, first to publicize the victory and secondly to intimidate or proselytize enemy cadre into surrendering or rallying to the GVN side.

• • •

During the second phase, while friendly forces shifted their activities farther away to ensure complete protection for the village, cadre teams and regional forces began to enter the village to take over control, replacing the operational forces. This was time for the true pacification effort to begin. By this time, local guerrillas and the VCI in the village had either been destroyed or neutralized, but there might still be some elements hidden in underground shelters. The mission of the RF was to provide security and protection for the national cadre teams and to conduct searches to root out any remaining enemy. National cadre teams then began the process of separating the enemy from the people. This process consisted of investigation, screening, classification, and checking identification papers. This job was performed by the National Police.

• • •

The goal was to demonstrate to the villager the credible presence of security forces who would stay in the village as long as required to protect them.

The last phase was devoted to developmental works. It began as soon as the village had become secure and free from enemy interference or harassment, either by the VCI or guerrillas. National cadre teams began long-term works such as building a school, a maternity ward, an information office, [or] a marketplace and repairing roads and erecting bridges. All these efforts had the goal of bringing about security and prosperity for the villagers and letting them appreciate the contrast between what the GVN was doing and what the enemy had said they would do.

• • •

Pacification Techniques

First priority in pacification was usually given to populated and economically prosperous areas, urban centers, and villages and hamlets bordering on vital lines of communication and waterways. As soon as these areas were pacified, the effort would shift to adjacent areas. The idea was to spread out as an "oil stain" from secure areas into less secure or semisecure areas, and from there into insecure areas. Areas targeted for pacification which were termed semisecure or insecure were usually selected so that they interconnected with secure areas by convenient communications.

• • •

Coordination in Security Activities

• • •

In 1964, well before the success of Operation Rang Dong/Fairfax, the government began the Hop Tac pacification campaign in the Capital Military District with the purpose of clearing and securing this area. The Hop Tac campaign was conducted by III Corps forces and was operationally controlled by a command post at the CMD headquarters. The staff in charge of the campaign was a joint military-civilian organization which combined III Corps military officers with GVN ministerial and US embassy representatives.

The Hop Tac campaign failed to achieve its objectives because of several difficulties. First, there were not enough police to maintain law and order in all hamlets. Second, there was a shortage of territorial forces to provide protection and maintain security in those areas cleared by regular forces. Third, civilian development projects such as the construction of schools, marketplaces, and maternity wards were unable to make any progress due to political instability in the national capital; this was a period of turmoil during which several governments succeeded each other within a short time. Finally, there was a total lack of guidance and direction from the central government. Without a central pacification control body and specialized cadre, the campaign was doomed to failure and was suspended in September 1965.

• • •

The Hamlet Evaluation System

In January 1967 MACV . . . first used the Hamlet Evaluation System (HES), a computer-based measurement, to discern the status of rural security, the progress of the pacification program, and identify problem areas. The district senior advisor filled in a questionnaire on each hamlet. The hamlet data were forwarded through the chain of command to MACV . . . , where [they were] collated and analyzed. The questionnaire covered two major areas, hamlet security and progress in civil operations.

To ascertain the extent of security, the questionnaire covered all enemy disruptive activities in a hamlet or in adjacent areas, such as harassment fire or shelling, terrorist actions, sabotage, propaganda, proselytizing actions, kidnappings, and assassinations. Other data concerning friendly activities to provide security and protection for the local population were also recorded in the form of answers to such questions as: 1) How effective were those activities? 2) Who actually held the initiative, friendly or enemy forces? 3) Were friendly forces capable of providing security? 4) What results did friendly activities achieve? 5) What casualties and damage were caused to the local population in terms of human lives and property, both by friendly and enemy forces?

In addition to security, the HES also measured the progress of efforts in civil operations. Data for this part included answers to questions about the maintenance of law and order in the hamlet; the behavior and attitude of local government officials; the degree of popular sympathy toward GVN cadre; the elections of village and hamlet councils; the influence of the GVN and that of the enemy on the local population; the extent of development in public health and education; the availability of schools, dispensaries, [and] maternity wards; and the influence of local political parties.

All the questions concerning security and civil operations were printed on a card. The district senior advisor filled out the appropriate answers on the card and submitted it through channels. The data provided in the cards were elaborate and scientifically devised. They were tremendously helpful to higher authorities or field commanders, who were able at a glance to visualize what happened in a certain area and to assess correctly the situation. There were, however, certain shortcomings inherent in the HES, the most readily discernible of which was the relative time lag of the reporting system.

Reports submitted by district senior advisors, for example, took weeks to reach the central echelon, and before MACV/CORDS compiled and sent them to agencies and major units for exploitation at least one month had elapsed. There were other data contained in the HES monthly report concerning actions to be taken by various agencies, for example, which were no longer effective, since by the time the HES report was published these actions had already been taken. A HES report recorded, for example, that the PF unit in a certain village was short of M-79s or M-60s due to combat losses, but in reality these losses had been replaced during the month it took the district senior advisor's report to reach MACV/CORDS and get published. A major cause for the slow reporting system was the delay in the RVNAF postal service or the lack of mail routing facilities, which became especially serious after the redeployment of US forces.

The data recorded by district senior advisors were obtained partly from village and hamlet officials' reports, party from information provided by friendly forces or through the advisory channel, and partly from actual visits to villages and hamlets by the senior advisor and the district chief. A question arose, however, as to the validity and reliability of the reports thus obtained, doubts about accuracy and timeliness. The most reliable way to have accurate data was to make visits to the villages and hamlets and see for oneself. But the truth was that, even if all the time available were devoted to visits, and even if road communication and transportation facilities and helicopters were available at all times, no one could possibly cover all the villages and hamlets of a district in a single month.

The HES was subsequently transferred from MACV/CORDS to Vietnamese authorities. The JGS took over the task of evaluating territorial forces, while the Central Pacification and Development Center took charge of civil operations reporting. The operation of the system became less efficient, partly because at the district level the GVN did not have officials as knowledgeable as the advisors to estimate and record with accuracy HES elements, and partly because of the large costs involved in supporting the system, which the GVN could scarcely afford.

VI. SOCIAL REFORM AND ECONOMIC DEVELOPMENT

Objectives

South Vietnam subsisted on foreign aid, primarily US aid. Its consumption far surpassed its production because of the lack of an extensive industrial base. Due to security improvements after 1970, the GVN set about to achieve long-range goals that can be summarized in a "three selves" policy. All plans and programs were geared to and guided by this policy.

Self-defense meant the people were to defend themselves, their families, and their communities. The PSDF were a means to provide this kind of self-defense, being organized and manned by the people themselves and armed and assisted by the government. The goal to be achieved gradually was to use PSDF for the defense of villages and hamlets in place of territorial forces, who would take over territorial security responsibilities from regular ARVN forces. Then the ARVN could be freed to take over combat responsibilities from US forces.

Self-management was designed to promote democracy and a democratic way of life. The people elected representatives to run their own affairs, administer their own villages, and manage their own budget. The people also participated in groups, associations designed to develop a mutual assistance spirit. Village properties and resources were managed by the people through their representatives, with the technical assistance of the government.

Self-sufficiency was to be achieved through self-help programs and projects in which the people contributed their own capital and labor. The government provided assistance only when required. Self-help projects were initiated and managed by the people, from start to finish. The ultimate goal was not only to bring about a more prosperous life for the people, but also to sustain the war effort for as long as it was required without relying too heavily on foreign aid.

• • •

The Relief and Resettlement of Refugees

• • •

The GVN policy of relief for refugees was a realistic one in that it sought first to provide emergency help and then to resettle the refugees in secure areas where they could find opportunities to make a living by themselves. Depending on the circumstances, the GVN might in a few instances allow refugees to return to their home villages. This home-returning effort was particularly strong during 1969.

• • •

The refugee relief and resettlement program was a gigantic effort that succeeded only because of the great financial assistance provided by the US government and other Free World countries. It was a truly humanitarian program that helped to heal the wounds caused by the war.

US agencies and some other international organizations played key roles in contributing to the success of the program. They provided refugees with medicine, food, and relief necessities. They helped in vocational training, in developing education, and in caring for orphans and the sick and the wounded. Altogether 12 US and international organizations were involved in the refugee relief and resettlement program. Some were responsible for distributing relief items donated by US government or charity organizations. Others, such as the American Red Cross and the International Red Cross, provided personnel and staff to assist in the operation of refugee camps or resettlement centers. In addition, these organizations also helped train refugees in farming techniques, handicraft, construction work, and in cattle and poultry breeding, and assisted them in the settlement or resettlement process. The Community Development Foundation, in particular, conducted training courses in refugee camp operation for personnel of the Ministry of Health, Social Welfare, and Relief. Other vocational training courses were also organized by charity and nonprofit organizations to train refugees in new occupations.

Agricultural Development

Vietnam is basically an agricultural country. Its production output was still low because of its conservative techniques. Agricultural reform therefore became a concern, and the GVN initiated many programs to pursue it within the pacification framework. Such programs as animal husbandry, agricultural affairs, Montagnard agriculture and animal husbandry, and fisheries were designed to contribute to the rural development effort and to improve the national agriculture. In each province these programs were established and implemented by the provincial rural development council with the co-operation of technical services.

• • •

In the New Life hamlets the program was more extensive. It included training farmers and distributing pigs, chickens, ducks, and other kinds of livestock. Farmer training taught new animal husbandry methods, how to build pens and farms, how to choose livestock breeds, the advantages provided by mixed feed to livestock, and how to cure livestock diseases. The purpose of pig distribution was to popularize the improved breeds of pigs and, at the same time, to support to some extent the poor farmers who could not afford animal husbandry. Each needy family willing to raise livestock was allotted two breeding pigs and, on an average, each hamlet was allotted 40 pigs.

The distribution of pigs to hamlet households was implemented on the basis of certain criteria. First, piglets raised for meat should be crossbred from Yorkshire, Berkshire, or Danish breeds weighing more than eight kilos. Sows should be almost of pure Yorkshire, Berkshire, or Danish breeds weighing more than nine kilos. Boars should be of pure Yorkshire, Berkshire, or Danish breeds weighing more than two kilos. Then medicine for the elimination of parasites and preventive shots should be given to the pigs kept for distribution. The procedure used for distribution determined that sows were allotted on the basis of the sharing of litters, but boars were allotted free. The animal husbandry office would take one two-month piglet from the first litter.

Chickens and ducks were only distributed to the hamlets that had not received an allocation of pigs. However, chickens and pigs could be distributed simultaneously to those hamlets having a large population and animal husbandry abilities. Each family was allotted ten breeding chickens or from 40 to 50 ducks, all free of charge. For the province that had requested a distribution of chickens but had not received it in due time, ducks could be provided in lieu of chickens.

As to other kinds of livestock, depending on the local situation the province could provide a distribution of oxen, goats, and rabbits for farmers. This was on the basis of profit-sharing in the case of cows and goats.

• • •

The Fisheries Program

The fisheries program was designed to provide guidance to farmers concerning freshwater fisheries and to fishermen concerning saltwater fisheries, provide support to poor fishermen (such as breeding fish and fishing gear) for the development of fisheries, and to improve fisheries by motorizing fishing boats. In addition, the Ministry of Agriculture also ran a permanent program which provided for activities concerning saltwater fisheries, the survey of lakes and ponds to determine fishing suitability, the compilation of fishing statistics, the digging of fishponds, and the construction of refrigerating rooms.

At the hamlet level, the program provided training for farmers and fishermen in fish culture methods, the use of fishing equipment, the digging of ponds for fish breeding and rearing, the preparation of fish food, etc. To encourage fish breeding and rearing, breeding fish were distributed free to the hamlet people who had the abilities for such activities. Different kinds of fish were provided, depending on the availability of fresh or salt water in the areas. Fish were distributed on the basis of one fish per square meter of lake or pond.

• • •

An Evaluation

The GVN faced a tremendously difficult task in trying to reform a rural society as complex and as backward as South Vietnam's. Despite the trend toward urbanization and the depletion of male population during the most intensive war years, the countryside remained the major ground of contest where the GVN emphasis was placed on restoring the rural economic infrastructure and improving health and education. These efforts were the mainstay of pacification and development.

The hamlet self-help program was a move in the right direction, since the hamlet was the basic communal unit. The range of projects embraced by the program reflected its realistic goal of rebuilding the war-shattered rural infrastructure and bringing about immediate practical benefits for the peasantry. The GVN also hoped that a rebuilt rural area could contribute significantly toward developing the national economy.

A key feature which accounted for its initial acceptance by the local population was the self-help character of the program. Experience showed that, when their own interests were at stake, and when they had a voice in the management of their own affairs, the people volunteered and willingly cooperated.

• • •

Civic actions conducted by US and FWMA forces during the period of their commitment, 1965–1972, gave the program great support, particularly in those areas near operational bases. In addition to providing construction materials, the allied troops frequently contributed labor and turned the finished work over to the local population as gifts. Some overzealous local governments, however, turned the program into a coercive enterprise, requiring the people to meet arbitrarily established deadlines, often at the cost of relinquishing their own business. Despite this, the overall program received wide acceptance by the peasantry.

In health and education, the period from 1969 to 1972 was a period of vigorous development in terms of efforts committed and results achieved. The rural education program virtually eradicated illiteracy among peasant children and youth and effectively increased the elementary student population multifold. More students went up to high schools, because the majority of villages were provided with a first-level middle school (four-year program equivalent to US 7th, 8th, 9th, and 10th grades). This was an unprecedented opportunity for rural students who, during the previous years, had to go to the only middle school at the district town, sometimes at prohibitive distances from their villages. The remarkable progress made in rural education was possible due primarily to aid funds which helped subsidize higher salaries for rural teachers, build new schools or additional classrooms, and provide free textbooks and not infrequently free school supplies as well, for the underprivileged students. But, extensive as it was, the development in rural education was but a part of an outdated educational system based primarily on old French methodology and devoid of a new national spirit. The system belatedly underwent some improvement and modernization in 1974.

Despite the GVN efforts, the benefits the rural population enjoyed in terms of medical care seemed to derive chiefly from programs sponsored by allied countries, international organizations, and, in particular, US forces in Vietnam. The US MEDCAP program was especially beneficial to the local population living in US areas of operation. Allied medical teams and international charity organizations were active in several provinces of the 2nd and 3rd Military Regions. In the Central Highlands, the US Special Forces did a splendid job helping the Montagnards fight diseases and improve sanitation. The GVN rural health program was a laudable effort, but it was inefficiently managed and plagued by problems such as the lack of medical personnel and medicine. Pilferages and illicit traffic in drugs further aggravated the problem by enabling the Viet Cong to purchase large quantities of critical medicine.

By far the heaviest burden the GVN had to shoulder during the war years was the problem of refugees. The highest figure recorded after the 1968 Tet Offensive was about three million, or one-sixth of the total population. The GVN effort was twofold: providing temporary relief and helping in resettlement. Despite the availability of aid funds, which provided up to 80 percent for the refugee resettlement costs, and the humanitarian help of US charity organizations, the task was monumental and the effort an uphill struggle. From 1969 to 1971 the problem was alleviated thanks to improved security, which allowed most refugees to return to their villages. There remained, however, about 300,000 refugees living in camps for whom care and resettlement were constantly needed. Most relief items donated by US charity organizations, such as powdered milk and Western clothes, usually found their way to local markets since they were alien to the Vietnamese rural way of life. Part of them also reached the refugees, but were resold to pad the greedy camp officials' pocketbooks.

The GVN effort to resettle refugees was not very successful, since most resettlement areas were located in insecure areas and became targets of VC harassments. There was also not enough cultivable land and water for irrigation. The result was, after a certain time living under relief, refugees drifted away again and not infrequently ended up in a refugee camp. Several refugees did this five or six times, all at the expense of the GVN. But the resettlement effort greatly improved with Dr. Phan Quang Dan's program of Land Reclamation and Hamlet Resettlement, which began in early 1974. This was a large-scale effort, well planned and well supported, which was welcomed not only by refugees but also by veterans who voluntarily joined the program. The program had a good chance of resolving the refugee problem when it was thrown in utter disarray by events in early 1975.

In keeping with the pacification progress, agricultural development projects also brought about rosy achievements during 1969–1971. This was possible due to the availability of seeds, insecticides, fertilizers, and farm machines purchased through the economic aid program. For a time, at least, the rural area took on a prosperous outlook. Cultivated acreage was expanded and rice production per hectare greatly increased. The fishing industry also improved and expanded, thanks to motorboats and refrigeration technology. Increased production in rice, however, failed to meet consumption demands, with the result that, in 1972, the year of greatest expectations, South Vietnam continued to rely on imports. This did not make sense, however, because estimates of actual production indicated at least a level of self-sufficiency. Most province chiefs did testify in effect that there were no rice shortages except in the MR-1 provinces. The problem therefore seemed to involve speculation by greedy Chinese businessmen in the Mekong Delta and purchases made by the Viet Cong, who always offered to buy at high prices. A belated effort made by GVN authorities in 1974 to control the traffic in rice failed to produce any significant results. The rice problem seemed beyond the GVN capability to solve. This hurt its efforts at rebuilding the national economy and achieving real progress in pacification.

For all its efforts, the GVN was still a long way from solving the social and economic problems that plagued South Vietnam, especially in the context of a war in which the enemy always held the initiative and had the capability to wreck any achievements any time he chose. This happened in 1968 and again in 1972, when a few months of attacks undid years of hard toil. Unless South Vietnam was free from North Vietnam's military threat, pacification or any nation-building task remained a hopeless proposition.

VII. THE GVN POLITICAL, INFORMATION, AND CHIEU HOI EFFORTS

Information and Propaganda

Information and propaganda were designed to exert a favorable influence on the population by publicizing the government policies and programs and eliciting popular trust and support for them. When employed properly, they were sharp-edged tools for the advancement of political and military goals, shattered the enemy's morale, made him feel disenchanted, and incited him to rally.

As they were practiced in South Vietnam, all information and propaganda activities were conducted and coordinated by the GVN Ministry of Information through a system that reached down to the village level. . . . Prior to 1965 the GVN information and propaganda facilities were scant. In each district town there was only a tiny information hall adorned with outdated pictures and magazines. Information personnel were few, because the entire GVN information service was organized as a general directorate and not as a ministry, as it was later under the Second Republic.

After the active participation of US forces in the Vietnam War, however, the GVN information service expanded substantially due to the considerable assistance and support provided by such US agencies as the United States Operations Mission (USOM), United States Information Service (USIS), and Joint US Public Affairs Office (JUSPAO). Each province information service was provided with movie projectors, a film library, and a mobile projection unit using Lambretta van-scooters as vehicles for shows in villages and hamlets. The rural population was given the opportunity to watch film shows at least once a month, a kind of entertainment unavailable to most of them before then. USOM and USIS also provided funds and information equipment for all provinces, and even district information halls were supplied with domestic and foreign newspapers and pictures. The GVN Information Ministry, with the support of JUSPAO, purchased [copies of] 19 out of 24 daily newspapers published in Saigon and distributed them to village information halls.

Additional radio stations were built in major cities, and, to expand radio broadcasts into rural areas, a total of 100,000 JUSPAO-supplied transistorized radios were distributed free to peasant families living in villages and hamlets. In addition, the GVN also imported great quantities of inexpensive radio receivers so that the population could afford to buy them. The voice of the GVN could thus reach the majority of the population across the country. Even in the Central Highlands, a radio transmitting station was build to broadcast programs in several Montagnard languages. Twelve radio stations eventually operated across the nation. In outlying areas not covered by the GVN information service, aircraft were used, again with US support, to drop leaflets or to broadcast messages. These psychological operations were designed both to inform the population and to call upon enemy cadre to surrender or rally.

South Vietnam did not have a TV broadcasting station until 1966. At first, JUSPAO made TV broadcasts through an airborne transmitting station. A TV studio and broadcast station were subsequently built in Saigon, and GVN information personnel were trained by JUSPAO in the operation of the station and the production of TV programs. The TV network was later expanded through additional transmitting and relay stations at Hue, Can Tho, and Nha Trang.

Aided by the United States, the GVN was in command of a vast array of information and propaganda instruments which were more numerous and sophisticated than those that the enemy possessed. The problem was that the information cadre did not properly exploit these instruments to produce the desired effect. Despite his meager resources, the enemy appeared to get more results out of his propaganda efforts. It seemed that the enemy knew how to make better use of his propaganda means, and, by properly exploiting mass psychology, he was also able to arouse popular sympathy more successfully.

For a short period following the Paris Agreement some progress was achieved by the GVN in information and propaganda. It purposefully built up and exploited the people's hatred toward the Communists. For the first time a genuine effort was made to put the arts and literature at the service of propaganda. Songs and plays, for example, no longer displayed languid lyricism as in the old days. But the most extensively read news mediums in the country, the daily newspapers, were left unexploited for propaganda purposes. The majority of them were owned and operated by private entrepreneurs who were more concerned about commercial success than the anti-Communist cause. The GVN was unable to exert any influence on the daily newspapers, except for the ARVN-owned *Tien Tuyen* ("Front Line"). Despite several stringent measures that the GVN imposed on the free press, such as censure, temporary suspension, fines, revocation of license, and legal prosecution, they were all ineffective in rallying the press to the national cause.

The Chieu Hoi (Open Arms) Program

The Chieu Hoi (Open Arms), or Great National Solidarity, program was initiated by the GVN to subvert the morale of enemy cadre and troops and call upon them to leave their ranks and rally to the national cause. The basic theme was that both sides were brothers in the same family and, since both wanted to end the war, the best and least costly way was to renounce internecine bloodletting, forsake hatred, and cooperate with each other to rebuild the shattered nation.

During a decade of implementation, from 1963 to 1973, the Chieu Hoi program produced impressive results: 159,741 enemy troops and cadre rallied to the GVN cause.[8] Most notorious among the ralliers were some high-ranking military cadre such as Tam Ha, Huynh Cu, and Le Xuan Chuyen, who returned to the GVN side well before the cease-fire period, and the political commissar of Lam Dong Province and the personal secretary to the Saigon-Cholon political commissar, both of whom rallied during the post-cease-fire period. The number of ralliers reached an all-time high during 1969, when 47,087 enemy cadre and troops chose to side with the GVN, apparently as a result of Communist setbacks during the previous year.

• • •

During the period of reeducation and readjustment, ralliers were well fed and well treated. They were allowed to correspond with their families and receive visits. They were never roughly treated or compelled to do hard labor, as in enemy-run so-called "reeducation centers." While living in a Chieu Hoi center, ralliers were free to converse, watch TV, listen to radio broadcasts, read books, or just relax. Depending on personal desires, ralliers were given vocational training in such courses as tailoring, embroidering, handicraft, etc. The GVN policy was to help each of them acquire a skill to earn a living when he was returned to normal life. The reeducation period usually lasted from 45 to 60 days, and upon release from Chieu Hoi centers ralliers were permitted, depending on their readjustment and repentance, to apply for public service jobs, enlist in the armed forces, or seek jobs in private industries. Those who wanted to return to their home villages and live a quiet honest life were given transportation allowances.

Another GVN effort to win over ralliers completely—politically and psychologically—and also to make the Chieu Hoi effort more meaningful, was to provide the ralliers with housing facilities once they were released from reeducation centers. The GVN constructed a total of 42 Chieu Hoi villages, one for each province, consisting of housing units which were allocated free of charge to ralliers. This was a most welcomed program which really helped the ralliers begin a new lift without hardship.

In general, ralliers were more extensively employed by US forces and US Embassy

agencies than the GVN. In MR-1, for example, US marine units used ralliers as informants, interrogators, or scouts during operations, especially when US units staged raids
against Communist bases. Because of their intimate knowledge of local terrain, ralliers
were very effective as scouts.

In addition, ralliers were also used in intelligence work against the VCI by US Embassy agencies. Ralliers made up the bulk of Provincial Reconnaissance Units, a paramilitary force organized, armed, and financed by the US Embassy. Later the PRUs were
placed under the control of provincial police chiefs as a striking force for the elimination of the VCI. This was done after the National Police were made responsible for the
implementation of the Phoenix program in 1968.

• • •

All told, the Chieu Hoi program was a meaningful and humanitarian effort which
provided real opportunities for wrongdoers to mend their ways and begin a new life.
The large number of enemy personnel who chose freedom gave some measure of the
effect of the program. The figures differed from year to year; the higher figures were
recorded when the fighting was more intense. Ralliers generally helped our side know
more about the true situation on the other side, and they sometimes provided invaluable
intelligence. It was learned from their stories that, by and large, Communist morale was
low and the troops were confused. Because of protracted fighting, most of them became
disenchanted with the war and longed for reunion with their families. Other ralliers told
of the lack of medical treatment and medicine, spartan living conditions, unbearable
hardships, and human losses that sometimes edged entire enemy units toward despair
and to defection attempts. Had it not been for fears of retaliation against their relatives,
several complete enemy units would have chosen to defect after their 1968 defeat.

Because of the potential of the Chieu Hoi program, the enemy made efforts to counter it. Communist political commissars, for example, told their troops that ralliers were
all killed by the GVN.

For all its merits, the Chieu Hoi program had some shortcomings. For one thing, the
GVN placed no control over those ralliers who had been released to return to their home
villages. The local governments also failed to keep track of the former ralliers. As a result, there occurred several cases of false rallying. Upon release, they conducted subversive activities for a while and then returned to their base areas. The allocation of free
housing for ralliers also caused great animosity and jealousy among ARVN troops and
veterans, many of whom were disabled. The disabled veterans' grievances soon gave rise
to unlawful acts of house squatting in open defiance of the GVN. They felt that, as soldiers who had risked their lives to fight the Communists and had become casualties as a
result, they were not treated as well as the ralliers who only recently had shot at them.

The GVN had pushed the program too far, without due consideration for the sensitivities and welfare of war veterans. In a program such as Chieu Hoi, the pros and cons
of certain benefits should have been carefully weighed in the context of a war-ravaged
society and sounder priorities should have been established. Despite this, however, the
Chieu Hoi program was one of the most effective and least costly ways of ending the

war. After all, the cost of killing an enemy soldier was much greater than the amount spent to induce him to rally.

Relations with Ethnic Minorities

The Central Highlands of South Vietnam occupied an important strategic position, in view of their continuity with Laos, Cambodia, and especially with the enemy north-south infiltration and supply corridor which ran along the entire length of South Vietnam's western border. The area was sparsely populated, mostly inhabited by Montagnards, who numbered nearly one million and consisted of 29 different tribal groups, each having its own language and customs.[9] These tribal groups usually lived in isolation from the Vietnamese and were generally oblivious to the fact that there existed a GVN and national laws.

• • •

Beginning in 1961, the GVN took renewed interest in the Highlands and sought to rally the ethnic minorities by making certain overtures, such as forbidding the use of the derogatory appellation *moi* (savage) by Vietnamese and encouraging the use of the newly coined substitute "new Vietnamese compatriot" when referring to Montagnards. In addition, a special education program was initiated which encouraged them to learn Vietnamese and granted special credits and waivers in all kinds of examinations. Finally, special tribunals were established to provide Montagnards with a fair trial process, based not on Vietnamese laws but on each tribe's customs and manners.

At the same time, with the concurrence of the GVN, the US Special Forces began to make inroads into the Highlands. They initiated civic action programs, such as dispensary service and the distribution of medicine, with the purpose of rallying their support. The Special Forces' objective was to shake off the lingering influence of the French and Viet Minh among the Montagnards and turn them into guerrilla fighters, gradually organizing and arming tribal villages for self-defense. The first of such self-defense villages was Enao in Ban Me Thuot Province. Despite these efforts, the Montagnards were still heavily influenced by the French, and especially by the Viet Minh-instilled idea of an autonomous state which would replace GVN authority and prohibit Vietnamese homesteaders among them.

These feelings were fomented by Montagnards who made up the FULRO (Unified Front of Struggle for the Oppressed Races) movement and erupted into open rebellion in 1964 in Ban Me Thuot. The FULRO, masquerading as representatives of all tribal groups, demanded an autonomous state in the Central Highlands and equal rights with the Vietnamese. Some Civilian Irregular Defense Groups (CIDG), trained by US Special Forces and led by ARVN officers, joined the rebellion on 20 September 1964, killed their commanders, and took hostages to press for their demands.

The rebellion was finally quelled, but this was a sobering experience for the GVN. To deal with the Montagnards' grievances, the GVN initiated a systematic effort designed to improve their political and social standing, beginning in 1965 under the Nguyen Cao Ky administration. The government created a Ministry of Ethnic Minorities, headed by a Montagnard, whose responsibility was to look after all problems concerning the development of tribal groups. Provinces of the Central Highlands, such as Ban Me Thuot, Pleiku, and Kontum, were placed under the control of Montagnard province chiefs; the departmental services in these provinces were also headed by Montagnards. In the ARVN and territorial forces, Montagnards were also promoted to field-grade officers and given commands or responsible positions. Elected officials in villages, city councils, and in the senate and lower house also included Montagnards.

• • •

In general, the GVN strove to improve the Montagnards' lot through the pacification program. But the rate of progress in the Highlands was somehow slower than elsewhere, perhaps because they were still suspicious of the GVN goodwill, and probably because the Montagnards were chary of a newly transplanted culture which was not at all like their way of life.

Land Reform and the Land to the Tiller Program

To the Communists and the GVN alike, the rural area was of strategic importance, and both admitted this fact. The majority of the rural population were peasants who, as a class, could be rallied to any worthy cause if properly motivated. One of the best incentives for their motivation was land ownership, since for generations the Vietnamese peasants who eked out a meager living from the land were mostly landless farmworkers or sharecroppers. At the root of the conflict there were also problems of social injustice, oppressive landlords, and the class struggle, which could all be attributable to the inequality between the haves and the have-nots.

• • •

Under the Second Republic of Vietnam, there were . . . attempts at land reform during the initial years, but not until 1970 were there any significant and purposeful efforts. Land reform was undertaken on a scale extensive enough to take on a revolutionary outlook through the issuance of Presidential Decree No. 3/70, which authorized all peasants to become small landowners. Each peasant was allocated a fair amount of land for farming purposes entirely free of charge. The decree also officially terminated the practice of land rent and determined that the farmer was entitled to all the fruits of his labor and in fact owned the piece of land he actually tilled.

Due to the political significance of the Land to the Tiller program, the date of the presidential decree that initiated it—26 March 1970—was proclaimed as a national holiday. For the rural population, this was truly the greatest and most total revolution ever attempted. For the first time in generations the peasants' aspirations had been realized, and this was indeed the boldest move that any government had ever made in South Vietnam.

During 1970 a total of 210,371 hectares of land was distributed, a figure that surpassed the planned objective by 5 percent. By April 1973 the amount of land which had been planned for free distribution to landless farmers during the period from 1970 to 1973 had all been allocated, a total of one million hectares, or 2.47 million acres.[10] The rapid progress of the program was made possible by the substantial assistance provided by the United States in terms of experts, automatic data processing facilities, land surveying aircraft, and the enormous fund of $500 million which had been earmarked for the entire program.

• • •

The impact of the Land to the Tiller program was profound and far-reaching. Social justice was restored, the GVN prestige grew every day, and it appeared that it was on the way to win the war. The enemy, in the meantime, strove hard to wreck these achievements. By devious means he incited the people to oppose and undermine the program; for example, he forbade them to pay back loans owed the GVN, sabotaged the machinery imported for the farmers, stole farm machines, or took them away from farmers for ransom.

Village and Hamlet Elections

Traditionally the village is the basic political, social, and economic unit of Vietnam. It has its own territorial boundary, a population and its own resources, and usually enjoys administrative autonomy. In the old days, the village was a self-contained microcosm with its own government and laws, and the village chief was not unlike a lord who reigned over his tiny kingdom. In most instances, the village customs prevailed over the laws decreed by the imperial court, and the village was governed by a council of notables which made all the important decisions for the village chief. This system was perpetuated over the generations and, with some modification in organization and name, became what it was in modern times, the village council, with the exception that its members in modern times were chosen through the popular vote.

• • •

As an administrative unit, the village incorporated several hamlets. Hamlets were geographic subdivisions of a village and placed under its administration. Throughout South Vietnam, there were 2,151 villages with a total of 10,522 hamlets.

• • •

With a view to improving the effectiveness of the local government apparatus, the GVN conducted training courses for village and hamlet officials at the National Cadre Training Center at Vung Tau. The purpose was to consolidate the village and hamlet officials' anti-Communist spirit and train them in administrative procedures so that they could serve the people more efficiently. This was also in keeping with the pacification long-range goals that the GVN had set to achieve: self-defense, self-management, and self-sufficiency. Since only a solid infrastructure could bring about the conditions for achieving these national goals, efforts focused on the village and hamlet officials who operated and maintained that infrastructural foundation.

Elections at the village and hamlet level were a political innovation which attempted to institute democracy in a rural society still heavily influenced by traditions. Held within the context of a raging war, these elections met with some serious difficulties. In many villages there were very few youths left and the majority of their population consisted of elderly people, women, and children. As a result, the GVN had to bring in people from other localities and even allowed servicemen on active duty to run for office. When elected, these officials could not function effectively, partly because they were strangers, and partly because the village population would not work with those they did not feel were their own people. Thus, despite their devotedness and hard work, such officials could achieve very little because they did not enjoy [the] trust and support of the villagers.

Despite difficulties, village and hamlet elections proceeded with remarkably good results due to improved security. By 1971, out of a total of 2,151 villages, 2,053 or 95.5 percent had elected village councils.

• • •

People's Self-Defense Forces

The People's Self-Defense Forces were not a political or military organization, or an affiliate of some religion, but a people's organization. With government assistance in armament and training, its members were supposed to defend themselves, their families, and their property against the Communists.

The need for a PSDF organization arose in the wake of the enemy 1968 Tet Offensive as a result of the spontaneous demand from the people. The attacks waged by the Communists during 1968 completely alienated the people who had incurred heavy losses, not so much because of the fighting, but because of Communist atrocities. Several thousands of Vietnamese, among them Catholic refugees from North Vietnam, asked the GVN to give them arms so that they could defend themselves and their communities. In response to this popular demand, the GVN initiated the People's Self-Defense program, which was established by the [General] Mobilization Law of June 1968. The basic objectives of the PSDF program were to provide the people with the means to defend their families, homes, and hamlets or villages in both rural and urban areas; to assist the National Police and RVNAF in maintaining security and order; to promote community development activities for self-help and improvement in both rural and urban areas; and to assist the police in identifying the enemy.

• • •

Under the [General] Mobilization Law, all able-bodied men in the age groups of 16–17 and 39–50, except those joining the RVNAF on a voluntary basis, and males between 18 and 38 (draft age) deferred from military service, were required to be members of the PSDF. Veterans who had served full terms of military service, elderly people, and women who were not physically capable to serve as combat PSDF could join support groups.

Combat PSDF were organized into groups with an authorized strength of 134 and consisted of three inter-teams of 44 members each. Each inter-team was further broken down into three 14-member teams. A team was composed of a team leader, an assistant leader, three cells of three male members each, and one cell of three female members. In case there were no [female] volunteers as combat members, the strength of a group was reduced to 107.

• • •

By the end of 1970, the PSDF had grown into a sizable force which included a total of 1,397,000 combat members out of 1,500,000 planned and 2,400,156 support members out of a planned 2.5 million. Combat PSDF members were armed with 463,752 individual weapons of assorted types. Across the country, 95 percent of villages and hamlets had their own PSDF organizations by this time.

• • •

An Evaluation

The GVN efforts at instituting grassroots democracy, informing and educating the people, winning over their support, rallying the enemy's infrastructure members, and bringing about social and racial justice achieved only mild, superficial successes, except in the case of the Land to the Tiller program. The truth seemed to indicate that the political achievements of a regime could never be better than popular consent. The "soloist performance" during the presidential elections in 1971 reflected the true light of a democracy which existed only for form's sake. Many knowledgeable Vietnamese believed that, as a nation, South Vietnam failed because of bad political leadership.

Through the balloting process, the GVN attempted to institute democracy at the village and hamlet level. The quantitative results obtained by 1971 were impressive, but failed to convey a true picture of real political life. The first truth was that the Vietnamese villages could do without elections if people were allowed to manage their own affairs without interference from the central government. For generations the traditional Vietnamese village had been the most democratic institution, even under the most despotic monarchies.

• • •

As to the problem of ethnic minorities, and the Montagnards in particular, it was more of a political than a socioracial issue. The GVN became more alert to this issue after the FULRO-[instigated] rebellion erupted in 1964. The rebel leader, Y Bham, demanded autonomous status for the Montagnards, which practically amounted to political secession. This was entirely unpalatable to the GVN and to the Vietnamese in general. Racially, the Vietnamese always felt superior to the Montagnards, whom they condescended to treat as equals only for political purposes. But the integration process, like other socioracial problems, was slow and frustrating for both sides. It might take generations, or it might remain a problem forever. But the GVN policy and actions seemed to be consistent with the long-range goal of achieving national unity.

• • •

Among the pacification achievements, only the Land to the Tiller program stood out as a resounding success which might portend considerable political gains in the long range. It might eventually become the model for social justice in backward agrarian countries if sustained and capped by a more popular political regime. In the case of Vietnam, agrarian reform had always been a political instrument. The Viet Minh did it in 1954 in North Vietnam to hasten the process of conversion to socialism. Ngo Dinh Diem tried it to bolster his regime, but his half-hearted, small-scale program failed. The success achieved by the Second Republic in 1970 was possible only because of the availability of American financial and technical aid. It succeeded because it was the right thing to do at the right moment. But, while the peasantry acclaimed it, it also turned a cool back on the regime that sponsored it. Nevertheless, the program was a bold step in the right direction. Its long-range impact, unfortunately, did not have the chance to materialize.

The political experience gained through pacification thus seemed to demonstrate that whatever instrument or ploy the GVN used to gain popular consent and support only worked to the extent of credibility and popularity of the regime. The results expected could in no way be better than the regime itself. In fact, they mirrored accurately the standing of the regime and its acceptance by the citizenship.

VIII. AN ASSESSMENT OF PACIFICATION: SOME ACHIEVEMENTS, DIFFICULTIES, AND SHORTCOMINGS

The Ideological Aspect of Pacification

The war in South Vietnam polarized Vietnamese into Communists and anti-Communists and brought them onto a head-on collision course. Some called this war an ideological conflict. This was true, but only to some extent because, although opposed to Marx[ism]-Leninism, the nationalist cause hardly showed a doctrinary cohesion worthy of being called an ideological rival. Several Vietnamese intellectuals therefore felt the need and actually searched for a codified political doctrine capable of providing ideological guidance and motivation to the nationalist cause. Ngo Dinh Nhu for some time succeeded in selling this syncretistic version of "personalism," from which he also derived certain cohesive concepts as the doctrinal basis for his Strategic Hamlet program. Genuine as his concern was, the complexity of his philosophy enlightened no one, much less the peasantry, and served no useful purposes. Other efforts in general never went beyond "tearoom" chats or magazine articles. The futility with which the search for an ideology met indicated that this was perhaps a pseudo-problem which interested only the educated elite and that the peasantry, faced with the pressing and immediate questions of livelihood and security, would benefit more from a pragmatic approach to pacification and nation building.

The conflict was also termed a civil war, which is probably more appropriate, since the issues at stake had deep roots in the political, social, and economic fabric of Vietnam. The Communists, Viet Minh or Viet Cong, were dedicated revolutionaries in the sense that they wanted to destroy all traditional institutions and values and move toward disciplinarian and collectivized life under socialism. Those who opposed them, by contrast, adhered to a liberal, humanistic way of life sustained by cultural traditions and economic prosperity. Pacification therefore provided the RVN with the opportunities to preserve and develop this way of life which most Vietnamese, I believe, if given a free choice, would certainly prefer over dehumanized coercive collectivization.

It was in this direction that every GVN effort had moved, regardless of the regime or the name assigned to it. The strategy of pacification underwent very little change over the years. The Ngo Dinh Diem government was more ambitious in trying to make its Strategic Hamlet philosophy a national doctrine, but its Communist-inspired methods were harsh and self-serving. The five-family group system, for example, despite its purported goal of "mutual assistance" and protection against Communist penetration, was a Machiavellian scheme, an instrument for control and repression. The dominant role of the village youth leader, who was the sole appointee among elected councilmen and directly responsive to Mr. Nhu's Republican Youth, was another example of the control techniques so common in authoritarian states. It was, in the end, the methods that negated and defeated the doctrine which itself professed to be humanistic.

The next few military governments that succeeded Mr. Diem attempted to improve on and revitalize the Strategic Hamlet program by adopting a new attitude toward pacification, symbolized by a new name: New Life. In essence, the effort amounted to pouring the same old wine into a new bottle, since the center of interest was still the hamlet. It was remarkable not in what it professed to do, but in its efforts to avoid treading the path of abuses and excesses that had led to Mr. Diem's demise. Hesitant and half-hearted, the New Life effort made no new inroads of any significance.

Pacification was greatly aided by the CORDS arrangement, which for the first time provided cohesive support for the GVN effort under Nguyen Cao Ky. Also, Ky attempted to cover pacification with an ideological veneer. He professed that his government was a "poor man's government" and made use of revolutionary terminology to suit his good intent. He called himself "Chairman of the Central Executive Committee" instead of prime minister and addressed his cabinet ministers as "commissioners." He even coined the term "Revolutionary Development" for the pacification effort, although in Vietnamese it was never called that.

The new pacification czar, Major General Nguyen Duc Thang, was his trusted friend, an energetic, hard-driving, gung-ho type of a leader. To boost the image of a revolutionary working for the poor man's cause, Thang usually donned the peasant's black calico pajamas chosen as the uniform for his cadre. He even appointed a former Viet Minh battalion commander, Colonel Nguyen Be, as commandant of the RD Training Center at Vung Tau. In all respects Thang was the perfect match for his new US counterpart, Ambassador Robert Komer, an equally positive leader and hard driver. The remarkable thing about it all was the charismatic effect of the new momentum given to the pacification effort by the Thang-Komer duo. But all these outward manifestations betrayed an obsessive preoccupation with appearances which led to the tendency of substituting statistical results for true achievements.

The only reliable parameter of pacification success was found in the "hearts and minds" of the people, not in self-serving figures. A million propaganda leaflets dropped did not even guarantee that a single soul was won over. This showed to what extent statistical results, even those backed up by the most advanced techniques, could be misleading.

Statistics versus Achievements

If we believe official statistics, in 1963 more than ten million South Vietnamese inhabitants were living in about 9,000 strategic hamlets and in urban centers. Given the total number of hamlets (11,864) and the population at that time (14.4 million), GVN control was fairly well established over approximately 70 percent of the nation. As far as statistics went, that was an encouraging prospect, and the Strategic Hamlet program was anything but a failure. But a quick verification undertaken in 1964 revealed that only 10 percent of these hamlets were really defensible and the remaining were either indefensible or penetrated by the VCI. The lesson here was well learned. It showed how unreliable the reports were from province chiefs (on which these statistics were based).

The scientific measurements used in the Hamlet Evaluation System, however, increased the accuracy of reports and the validity of statistical results. The system, however, had its shortcomings. Apart from the time lag between information gathering and final reports, we were again confronted with the unreliability of the basic data fed by village and hamlet officials. As has been said, the district chief or his advisor had no way of verifying the accuracy of these data unless he personally made spot checks, which was something nearly impossible to do often enough to meet requirements. Thus the final monthly report's reliability was largely a matter of faith, a matter of whether or not we could trust the hamlet officials, and to what extent.

• • •

The lack of adequate data for the entire lifetime of the pacification program, particularly the period after the cease-fire, makes any attempt at assessment difficult. With the amount of data available it is possible, however, to discern certain trends or patterns indicative of both progress and problems. The most discernible pattern in pacification was that progress depended entirely on security, and that it was generally better than during the Strategic Hamlet period. A less obvious but still discernible trend showed that pacification progress was a curve with peaks and troughs. 1967 and 1971 were the years when the best statistical results were gained, but 1971 reached a peak never before attained.

Characteristically enough, these peaks were invariably followed by troughs, which were when security was at a lower ebb: 1968 and 1972, the years of the enemy's big offensives. This pointed toward another significant pattern: a major enemy spoiling action could always be expected when pacification seemed to attain a reasonable degree of success. The last major enemy offensive in early 1975 did not run counter to this pattern. It was attempted at a time when the GVN, despite its difficulties and some territorial losses, seemed to be consolidating its foothold in the rural area.

But statistical results told only part of the story. In 1971, for example, the GVN was apparently in firm control in terms of hamlet security, claiming that 85.3 percent of all hamlets were entirely or relatively secure, while the enemy controlled a mere 3.6 percent and about 11 percent were contested. Population control achieved the same spectacular results; 92.4 percent of South Vietnamese inhabitants were reported living in secure or reasonably secure hamlets, to include urban centers. The Viet Cong, meanwhile, controlled only 1.1 percent. Again about 11 percent were contested. These results were obtained at a time when VCI activities were at their lowest level and when Communist main and local forces were avoiding engagements in preparation for their next big push. The situation then appeared as if the GVN was left alone to go about its nation-building task. But it was only the calm that precedes a big storm.

The security attained was not a guarantee that it would be immune to enemy spoiling actions and that the trend was irreversible. The results only reflected the situation at a certain time; they did not represent the kind of solid, permanent achievements that defied retrogression. Also, to attain these results, the GVN overextended its capabilities and relied heavily on American support. The lesson of 1972 indicated that, without the military protective shield, pacification setbacks could occur any time the enemy chose to strike in force. By 1974, the GVN had run out of strategic reserves to maintain a reasonable degree of security and control in the face of stepped-up enemy attacks. Its strategic options were limited. It was finally reduced to a simple matter of how much control it could afford.

GVN efforts at eliminating the VCI and winning over its members at the same time seemed to be reasonably effective if statistics could be trusted. In fact, reports gave the Phung Hoang (Phoenix) program credit for making a sizable dent in the VCI ranks: 15,603 casualties by 1971, or about one-fourth of total VCI size, estimated at 63,757. But this casualty figure included the VCI greatest losses incurred during 1968, when its members surfaced and actively participated in the Tet Offensive. It also included a number of VC killed in local firefights by ARVN forces. Chieu Hoi results were equally encouraging: by 1971, a total of 159,741 "enemy" personnel had crossed the line to freedom. This included 97,696 military troops and cadres, 45,173 political cadres, and 16,872 undefinable "others."

But, apart from the low caliber of enemy personnel killed or rallied, the statistical results included a substantial number of undefinable "enemy" personnel who were classified as such primarily because they were either innocents caught under suspicion or inhabitants of the other side coming over for safety and a decent livelihood. The fact that several among [the] ralliers switched sides many times over the years was a clear indication that, except for a few enemy agents, they were something besides enemy personnel. One may [ask], if so many enemy personnel had rallied or been eliminated, how could the VCI continue to pose a permanent threat to the pacification effort? Indeed, if statistics were useful, they strongly indicated [that] the enemy's capability to recruit and replace surpassed everything we usually attributed to him.

To ensure security and provide protection for the people living under GVN control, a military shield was indispensable. While US forces did not always participate in pacification operations, their powerful combat support assets and intervention capabilities directly contributed to the clearing of several pacification areas. Their most significant effectiveness was the destruction of enemy bases and lines of communication, which indirectly accounted for the improvement of security in rural areas. But the main re-sponsibility for providing the protective shield remained with the regular and territorial units of the RVNAF. That shield was indispensable, because hamlet security forces—the PF, the PSDF, and the police—could not survive enemy attacks without it. The inter-dependence of forces thus became a key feature of the pacification strategy.

During the period 1967–1972, the RVNAF grew rapidly in strength, reaching a peak of nearly 1.1 million men. More than half that strength was composed of territorial forces, an indication of their maturity and increasing role in pacification. Sheer numeri-cal strength, however, failed to convey the true picture of combat effectiveness. A con-clusion that one may draw is that the RF and PF failed in areas where enemy forces were superior, and that this failure accounted for the continued bogdown of ARVN reg-ular divisions in territorial security missions. One of my constant headaches as J-3/JGS came from requests for reinforcements from field commanders, who always asked for more and never seemed happy to settle for less. This was perhaps another indication of the RF and PF ineffectiveness. Somehow I got the impression that pacification support was like a leaking tank. No matter how much more manpower you put in it, it never seemed to be enough for the task.

Hamlet security forces also increased substantially during this period. The PSDF, for example, reached a total of nearly four million by 1970, of which 1,326,571 were com-bat members, equipped with a total of 463,752 individual weapons. Statistics also showed that 95 percent of secure and relatively secure hamlets were defended by PSDF, and each of these hamlets had from one to several teams (11 men each), depending on its size. What the statistics did not reveal was the high density of PSDF in cities and urban areas, where their role was light, and a much lower distribution in rural areas, where the PSDF role was more critical. This imbalance in distribution reflected the lower male population in rural areas and was one defect that could never be corrected unless the trend of urbanization was reversed. But, even in urban areas, the nominal strength of PSDF was not indicative of their effectiveness. Their notorious trigger-happy unruliness was particularly irritating to the urban people. Some thought that they stood a better chance of being fired on when stopped by a PSDF than by a Viet Cong.

The expansion of police forces to rural areas was also a significant effort to combat the VCI, in addition to maintaining law and order. The modest strength of the police, however, limited its capabilities. There were no police available at the hamlet level, which was the most important natural subdivision of South Vietnamese rural society.

All in all, the statistical results of pacification showed steady progress, particularly after the momentum was gained through the three-month accelerated program in late 1968. They reached an all-high record in 1971, but suffered some setbacks during the 1972 Easter Offensive. Pacification gains were stabilized again after the short, disrup-tive campaign of "Land and Population Grab" that the enemy launched without success immediately after the cease-fire. Despite stepped-up activities during 1974, the Com-munists seemed to have lost their foothold in the rural areas. And the pacification gains were being consolidated when North Vietnam decided to go all out once again in early

1975. South Vietnam was lost, not because pacification had failed, but because its weakened military forces, hampered by the flow of panicky refugees, were unable to hold the entire North Vietnamese Army in check.

The Communist Challenge to Pacification

• • •

An estimated 61,000 village officials and GVN civil servants were reported to be assassinated or executed from 1958 to 1966. During the next three-year period, from 1968 to 1970, casualties caused by the VC to the civilian population more than doubled, even tripled, the yearly rate of the previous period.[11]

The extent of terrorism and sabotage was such that, to save the countryside from Communist control, the GVN initiated the Strategic Hamlet program in 1962. The program produced good effects, despite inflated reports by province chiefs. Its progress prompted the Viet Cong in late 1963 to demand the dismantling of these fortified hamlets, which they denounced as "disguised concentration camps." Profiting from the political unrest and instability in Saigon before and after Mr. Diem's downfall, the Viet Cong systematically wrecked the program by penetration and attacks. They came perilously close to success, with widespread disorder and violence, but the general uprising never came about.

Recognizing the futility of guerrilla warfare as a means of conquest, the Communists decided in early 1964 to shift their strategy toward military violence and began to infiltrate regular NVA units of regimental size into the South. This was the beginning of a force buildup, accompanied by the revival or construction of logistical bases in the border areas. From 1965 to 1967, the war had a predominantly military outlook, with pitched battles between US and Communist forces and large-scale US search and destroy operations against Viet Cong base areas. These military actions completely overshadowed the other war being fought on a lesser scale against the VCI and guerrillas at the grassroots level, the war for the control of the rural area for which the GVN and its forces were primarily responsible.

The Viet Cong sought to wreck the pacification effort by a three-pronged strategy based on offensive tactics, political maneuvers, and proselytizing actions aimed at the RVNAF. This came to be known as the three offensive spearheads: military, political, and proselytizing, which the Viet Cong used selectively or in combination throughout the war.

The offensive tactics most extensively used by the VC were ambush, hit-and-run attack, road interdiction, shelling, and more or less conventional attacks. The GVN recorded these activities as enemy-initiated incidents. During the period from 1968 to 1970, for example, a yearly average of slightly more than 10,000 incidents [was] reported. The ambush was the most important, since it served well the Viet Cong political and psychological purposes. A successful ambush always had repercussions which affected the GVN credibility and the morale of ARVN troops. Enemy ambushes were directed against a variety of targets: GVN officials, ARVN troops, supply convoys, etc., but most notoriously they were laid against reinforcements. This was one favorite Communist tactic called . . . attack the outpost to smash the reinforcement . . . which the Viet Cong used with great success, despite ARVN precautions. With the increasing use of air cover and helicopters, however, large-scale ambushes became less efficient and gradually diminished, especially since the participation of US combat troops.

• • •

In 1968 the Communists unexpectedly launched their Tet Offensive. Its most serious impact was the temporary disruption of pacification efforts in the rural areas, since ARVN forces were redeployed for the defense of major cities, provincial capitals, and district towns. Despite this, the enemy infrastructure was unable to exploit the situation because it was committed to the general offensive effort. A large part of the VCI was thus destroyed during 1968, which accounted for the success of the accelerated pacification campaign late that year. It was also during and after this offensive that the enemy began to make extensive use of a new deadly weapon: the 122mm rocket. Most enemy shellings were conducted against military and airbases, but also against cities and urban areas. The indiscriminate firing of rockets against urban centers caused extensive civilian casualties and a feeling of terror among the population. Saigon was the most heavily struck by rockets during May 1968, and this shelling seemed to work against the Viet Cong psychologically. To the population it was an indication of their desperation in the face of military defeat.

Pacification also suffered setbacks as a result of the 1972 Easter Offensive. Although the enemy offensive was localized in three major areas, the deployment of ARVN forces to meet the challenge created some voids in pacification support. The influx of refugees fleeing the embattled areas also caused additional burdens to the GVN. The most serious effect caused by the offensive was the complete absorption of the RVNAF general reserves in territorial defense, and the ARVN seemed to be immobilized in territorial security missions, gradually losing tactical mobility.

When the cease-fire was announced, the enemy launched a vicious campaign designed to wrest more control. This was known as the Land and Population Grab campaign, during which enemy forces succeeded in penetrating more than 400 villages across the country. But the campaign was short-lived; the enemy's effort met with determined RVNAF counteraction and failed. But, while the enemy was unable to grab more control, the GVN pacification effort also came to a standstill as a result of US aid cutbacks and a preoccupation [with] force conservation. The cease-fire thus ushered in a period during which the GVN strove to hold on to as much geographical area as possible. The deployment of ARVN combat forces for territorial security enabled the enemy to prepare extensively for his ultimate offensive. Border outposts and ranger camps successively fell into enemy hands. By the end of 1974, while the enemy was assured of a military advantage through his force buildup, the GVN seemed barely able to maintain its widely dispersed defensive posture, which by now had become more and more costly. The loss of Phuoc Long, followed by Ban Me Thuot, brought to light the strategic weaknesses of the RVN. The question now was how long the country could survive in the face of all-out invasion.

• • •

Proselytizing actions were mainly directed against the ARVN, and the RF and PF in particular. Their effectiveness on the ARVN was limited, but the RF and PF troopers were less resistant victims. In the Mekong Delta, the VCI was successful in transforming several RF and PF soldiers into turncoats. This accounted for the loss of many outposts that reached a worrisome level in certain provinces such as Chuong Thien and Kien Hoa. Proselytizing actions were usually accompanied by threats, blackmail, or terror, whose purpose was to induce fear, loss of confidence, and the lowering of morale. These actions were usually carried out by planted agents who successfully penetrated into RF and PF ranks.

The enemy's challenge to pacification was multifaceted and persistent. It was a combined political and military effort which fell in line with his overall strategy of conquest. But, as long as this effort was made on a local level, the enemy stood no chance of success. He must have realized this and decided to conquer the South by military invasion instead. This was no proof, however, that pacification had failed as a strategy.

• • •

The Impact of US Policies

The RVN depended almost entirely on the United States for its nation-building effort and defense against Communist subversion and invasion. American policies, therefore, could help make or break that effort.

• • •

During the five years that preceded the outbreak of war, American military policy sought to train and equip the Vietnamese military as a conventional force to face an eventual conventional invasion. However, this invasion first materialized under the unconventional form of subversion, sustained by guerrilla warfare. The RVNAF, tailored to the US Army image, were hard-pressed to fight this kind of war, for which they were ill-prepared. Increased US military aid and the availability of US combat support assets failed to solve the basic problem of the long-term conflict.

On its own initiative, the GVN came up with its Strategic Hamlet program to counter the subversive war. Instead of providing this program with adequate material and technical support, the United States continued with regular military aid. Instead of encouraging this new program, American officials were inclined to find fault with it and criticize its shortcomings. When South Vietnam nearly came apart in late 1964 as a result of political instability and military setbacks, the United States decided to save it the American way. Perhaps this was the only way at the time, but, having regained the military advantage, the United States decided to proceed with the military war and only showed lukewarm interest in the "other war," which was left to the GVN to fight.

Four precious years were thus lost before the United States renewed any interest in the other war. It seemed as if the United States had failed to realize the dual aspect of the war, whose nature was even ignored by some US commanders. That was a regrettable error of strategic proportions that cost human lives, political support, and time. Only after military emphasis failed did the United States become more conscious of the nature of the total conflict and make a truly cohesive effort to help the GVN with its other war. But the years had been lost that could have perhaps radically changed the outcome of the war for rural control had the Strategic Hamlet program received the full weight of US support from the start.

• • •

The US insistence on political stability and elective, democratic government as preconditions to continued aid and support effectively molded the RVN regime into a Western-style democracy that functioned primarily in form, not in substance. The true nature of the regime remained intrigue-ridden, dictatorial, and repressive. Perhaps the Vietnamese peasantry was not yet ready to cope with ballots and senators. In any case, they were more preoccupied with down-to-earth things such as a decent living, social justice, and security that hopefully pacification would bring about. These also happened to be the implied goals of US aid and support.

But, only two years after its first cohesive effort to support pacification, the United States already thought of disengagement. While these intensive two years were enough to [impart] progress and momentum to the pacification effort, the gradual removal of the US military protective shield began to overtax the RVNAF capabilities to fight two wars at the same time, despite force structure increase and modernization. Still, benefiting from the initial momentum, pacification harvested its most abundant results during the following three years, 1969–1971, with continued US support.

The Paris Agreement soon ushered in a most difficult period for the GVN, which had to face, with complete US withdrawal, continued enemy harassment, an eventual resumption of the war, and, most unfortunately, a sizable cutback in US aid. All these events reduced the GVN strategic options to a simple matter of survival; pacification could hardly progress when the nation's survival was at stake. It was finally the US people who repudiated even the last flimsy hope of survival and sealed the fate of South Vietnam as a free nation.

IX. OBSERVATIONS AND CONCLUSIONS

• • •

As to the general population, hardened and disenchanted as they were by the long, destructive war, disillusioned and frustrated by an elusive peace, and ever worried about an uncertain future, many naturally remained uncommitted to the GVN cause and its efforts. Perhaps this was the common syndrome of war weariness and social malaise. But, to most of them, the crucial and immediate concern was how to subsist materially and survive war hazards. Everything else, including political awareness or even democracy, was less significant; and, as long as they lived with privations and hardships and insecurity and uncertainty as to the future, no one could blame them for lack of commitment or apathy.

But the Vietnamese people were inherently alien to Communism and always longed for freedom. The million or so North Vietnamese people who first chose to flee south in 1954 eloquently spoke for their love of freedom above everything else, including careers and personal properties. The people's insurrection at Quynh Luu in Nghe An Province, North Vietnam, in November 1956, and the subsequent movements of refugees fleeing the advance of Communists in South Vietnam during the period from 1968 to 1972 and in 1975 indicated that, given a choice, the Vietnamese always opted for freedom. Even now that South Vietnam has come under Communist control, refugees still escaping from Vietnam report continuing resistance.

• • •

NOTES

1. COSVN: Central Office [for] South Vietnam, the Communist headquarters located near the Cambodian border north of Saigon.

2. Enemy document captured in 1971 and confirmed by J-2/JGS.

3. Another important Nung resettlement area was established at Nam Can, a district of An Xuyen Province in the Mekong Delta.

4. Mr. Ngo Dinh Nhu was the younger brother of President Ngo Dinh Diem. In addition to his official position as political advisor to the president, he was also the founder of the Can Lao Party.

5. A strategic hamlet was considered completed when it met the following criteria: a) The enemy infrastructure had been neutralized. b) The population had been organized for hamlet defense. c) The defense system (barrier, moat, trenches, traps, etc.) had been physically established. d) Secret underground shelters for weapons and personnel had been constructed for the hamlet defense force. e) The hamlet council and administrative body had been elected and [was] functioning. The population of South Vietnam in 1961 was estimated at 14 million.

6. Hectare is a unit of area measurement in the metric system equivalent to 10,000 square meters or approximately 2.47 acres.

7. As of 1970, the military section was removed from the organization of RD cadre teams, thus reducing the authorized strength of each team to 25. This resulted from a marked improvement of the security situation and the sizable expansion of Regional and Popular Forces. In 1971, following the deactivation of the Ministry of Rural Development, RD cadre personnel were reintegrated into various ministries such as Information/Open Arms, Agriculture, and Public Works.

8. This total breaks down into 97,696 military cadre and troops, 45,173 political cadre, and 16,872 others. These ralliers also surrendered 10,699 individual weapons and 545 crew-served weapons to GVN authorities.

9. Among these tribal groups, the Rhade were relatively more numerous and more civilized. Some Rhade tribesmen had enlisted in French Union forces.

10. The basic allocation was three hectares per farmer.

11. 1968: 32,364 total casualties caused by enemy antipacification terrorist activities (10,108 kidnapped, 15,918 wounded, 6,338 killed). 1969: 27,790 total (6,096 kidnapped, 15,603 wounded, 6,090 killed). 1970: 22,720 total (6,245 kidnapped, 11,177 wounded, 5,298 killed).

6

Leadership

General Cao Van Vien

PREFACE

War and politics posed many challenges to South Vietnam's military leadership. Unlike his counterpart in some countries, the Vietnamese military commander was not simply a leader of men in combat. Depending on the level of command, he had to play his part in national politics, be himself a grassroots politician, or engage in political warfare. To achieve success, he was often expected to possess several qualities not always required of a professional military leader. The requirements of leadership therefore sometimes transcended the conventional framework of accepted rules and principles.

Given these requirements, and the fallibility of human nature, it had not always been easy to evaluate the total performance of our leadership. The dilemma we faced was that, while professional competence during actual combat was a critical criterion, we could not tolerate deliberate aberrations in moral and social codes.

In my analysis of the successes and failures of our leadership, I have endeavored to be fair and objective. If I seem to be laudatory of some officers while critical of others, it is not my intention to embarrass any individual. Performance has been the sole basis for all of my evaluations. . . . [7 July 1978]

I. INTRODUCTION

A Millenary Tradition of Military Leadership

• • •

When Japanese forces overthrew the French colonial government in a lightning military coup on 9 March 1945, a great number of Vietnamese officers and NCOs serving in the French colonial infantry chose to return to civilian life. But some followed their units into China and remained with the French Army. The Japanese occupation did not last long, however; it ended with Japan's surrender in August the same year.

The Viet Minh immediately took advantage of this political vacuum to seize power and establish themselves as the legitimate government of independent Vietnam on

2 September 1945. In the meantime, France was also preparing to reconquer her former colony because, in spite of President Roosevelt's strong opposition, the allies had agreed to restore French presence in Indochina. With the help of British forces, who had the mission to disarm the defeated Japanese in Indochina south of the 16th parallel, and tacit American approval, the French first retook the southern part of Vietnam by force against heavy resistance by Viet Minh-led guerrillas. But, to reconquer the North, they had first to negotiate with the new Vietnamese government under Ho Chi Minh. This government had the blessing of Bao Dai, the former emperor who now served as Supreme Counselor, and enjoyed the support of the Vietnamese people.

The weak military posture of Ho Chi Minh's government compelled him to yield to French demands and allow French forces into Hanoi and Haiphong. But when the French threatened, by ruse and by force, to expand their control from these footholds, the Viet Minh leaders had no choice but to fight. Fighting, in fact, had never ceased since the French returned to Indochina and established [their] rule in Saigon. But not until France refused to resume negotiations and decided to take over the North by force did Ho Chi Minh resort to armed resistance. On 19 December 1946 he called on the Vietnamese people to attack and oust the French from Hanoi. And thus officially began the First Indochina War.

Birth of the Vietnamese National Army

During the first few years of the war the French succeeded in occupying most urban areas and key lines of communication. Wherever they established control, they immediately sought collaborators among those Vietnamese who had served under the French colonial regime, such as former mandarins, civil servants, and village officials, to establish a pro-French government. At the same time, they also recruited the veterans of the French colonial infantry and Garde Indigène, assembled them into units called "forces suppletives" (auxiliary forces), and assigned these units service and support missions.

When the French first set about to reconquer Indochina, they were confident they would succeed with the employment of sheer military force. Politically, therefore, they only sought the collaboration of submissive elements and the local intelligentsia through material rewards.

• • •

As the war intensified, and after attempts to negotiate with the Viet Minh had failed, France contacted ex-emperor Bao Dai, who lived in exile in Hong Kong, to put in motion the so-called nationalist solution. This effort produced the Ha Long Agreement of 5 June 1948, signed by French High Commissioner Emile Bollaert and Bao Dai on the French destroyer *Duguay Trouin*. According to this agreement, France recognized Vietnam as an independent state whose eventual reunification was to be freely accomplished by the Vietnamese themselves. In return, Vietnam declared to join the French Union as an "associated state." As a result of the Ha Long Agreement, a provisional central government of Vietnam was established under the premiership of Mr. Nguyen Van Xuan. It was also agreed that French and Vietnamese authorities would cooperate in the organization of various agencies under this government, to include the Vietnamese armed forces. Thus the creation of a Vietnamese National Army was formally decreed by the Ha Long Agreement. But this agreement was only a stepping stone toward a formal treaty between France and Vietnam. Not until 8 March 1949 was this treaty finally signed between Bao Dai and the president of the French Republic, Vincent Auriol. By this treaty, France formally recognized Vietnam as an independent and unified nation.

The Vietnamese National Armed Forces, however, were not officially created until a year later, on 11 May 1950. Initial plans called for the activation of a 60,000-man military force, about half of which consisted of regular troops and the other half of auxiliary troops. The first mission assigned to this national force was to pacify the country and take up part of the combat responsibility heretofore assumed entirely by French forces.

During 1950, therefore, several Vietnamese military schools were established. . . . During the initial stage, the commandants, staff officers, and instructors of these schools were all French. Only much later were they gradually replaced by Vietnamese officers. In order to provide the necessary cadre for this nascent national army, a great number of Vietnamese officers and NCOs serving in French Union forces were detached to the Vietnamese National Armed Forces. These cadres were subsequently fully integrated into the national forces. Also a number of auxiliary and French Union units were redesignated and transferred to the national forces, even though French officers remained in command. Eventually these units were all commanded by Vietnamese officers.

• • •

During the next few years the Vietnamese National Armed Forces set about to improve force structure and territorial organization. In May 1951 the Ministry of National Defense began to function officially, even though its creation had been sanctioned at the time of the first national government two years earlier. The Ministry of Defense initially assumed the duties of the General Staff, which was not created until a year later in May 1952.

• • •

The French defeat at Dien Bien Phu on 7 May 1954 . . . ushered in an emergency situation in northern Vietnam. Desertion was widespread among Vietnamese units. . . . During the month of May alone, some 4,303 regulars and 694 auxiliary troops became deserters. By the end of May 1954, the total strength of the Vietnamese armed forces stood at 249,517, to include 205,613 regular and 43,904 auxiliary troops. By the time the cease-fire was declared, however, this strength had been substantially depleted by desertion, especially among units located in northern Vietnam. This was a result of deteriorating morale and uncertainty. Under the growing pressure of an enemy on the verge of victory, not only had these units been compelled to fight without rest or replacements for long periods of time, they were also critically affected by enemy propaganda and the prospect of having to leave North Vietnam, where most of their troops were born.

A French Legacy

Prior to the Geneva Accords of 1954, French forces assumed all responsibilities for combat operations and territorial security in Vietnam, despite the existence of the

Vietnamese National Armed Forces with their own command and control system. During this period, Vietnamese units operated under the control of French commanders of larger units or territorial commands. Not until much later were a few tactical areas of responsibility placed under Vietnamese authority, and this was done only gradually. As a result, the Vietnamese General Staff and military region commands were merely responsible for the organization, administration, and training of Vietnamese units.

In brief, it seemed that Vietnam always had to obtain what it wanted the hard way. After World War II, for example, political independence was gained only after tremendous difficulties and several challenges. This was also true for our military forces. Initially, after becoming an "independent state," Vietnam was allowed only a few auxiliary units. Not until the military situation had become difficult, with increased losses and slow replacements, and not until she was faced with domestic problems did France resort to the "nationalist solution" and think about creating the Vietnamese National Armed Forces. And this did not occur until four years after France had returned to Indochina.

The Vietnamese National Armed Forces, therefore, suffered some retardation in their growth, progressing hesitantly from companies to battalions and finally to mobile groups only when the war was about to be concluded. Most Vietnamese battalions were originally those transferred from French Union forces, and their cadres were also those who had served in French units. These Vietnamese officers and NCOs, who did not have the same educational background and uniform military training, differed greatly in command abilities. Vietnamese officers who graduated from Saint Cyr, for example, might have perfect command of French and excellent military knowledge, but were qualified only for staff assignments; most of them in fact had very little combat experience. By contrast, the majority of those who graduated from in-country French military schools or came from the enlisted ranks were excellent combatants but bad staff officers. As to those officers who came from auxiliary forces or religious sects, they were usually good in combat but lacked basic military knowledge.

Among the first Vietnamese officers who held important positions, the most notable was perhaps Lieutenant General Nguyen Van Hinh, the first Chief of the General Staff of the Vietnamese National Armed Forces. He was the son of Mr. Nguyen Van Tam, the prime minister. Married to a French woman and of French nationality, General Hinh had served for a long time in the French Air Force. When he came back to Vietnam in 1950, he was a major and assigned the position of secretary general at the Ministry of National Defense. Promoted to lieutenant colonel in 1951, he served as military aide to Chief of State Bao Dai until his appointment as chief of the General Staff. When Hinh was appointed he was immediately promoted to the rank of brigadier general.

In addition to General Hinh, there were two other officers assigned to key positions. They were Major Tran Van Minh, who was appointed chief of staff for General Hinh, and Major Tran Van Don, director of the Military Security Service. Both were of French nationality, graduated from French military schools, and had just completed the command and staff course in Paris.

As part of French Union forces, Vietnamese units also suffered from the same disparity in combat capabilities, primarily because of the purpose for which they were employed and the locality where they were activated. In general, colonial airborne and commando units fought very well, while infantry units were rated as only average. As to auxiliary forces and those belonging to religious sects, they were generally poor in combat (except for a very few units). During combat operations, which were generally of the mopping-up type, Vietnamese units seldom respected the lives and properties of the local population. Unfortunately, this state of things was remedied only during the last few years of the war.

The training of officers and troops was conducted entirely by French military personnel or at French Union military schools. Training materials, therefore, were all prepared in French and published by the French Ministry of War. Even in Vietnamese military schools, which were commanded and staffed by French officers, French training materials were used and French tactics were taught. Additionally, even though the Vietnamese General Staff was created in 1952, French continued to be used as the official language in the Vietnamese armed forces. Not until 1955 was this use terminated and Vietnamese became the official language in all military correspondence.

It is clearly obvious, therefore, that the Vietnamese National Armed Forces were the offspring of the French Union forces, whose image they faithfully mirrored and whose flaws and weaknesses they also inherited.

• • •

Emphasis on discipline was thus the mainstay of French forces, and this led to a concept of command and leadership based solely on the position and authority of the commander. All subordinates were condemned to be blindfolded executors of any order issued by their superior.

Generations of Vietnamese officers were imbued with this concept of leadership, which they accepted as an indisputable maxim and guidance. Working closely together with and under the tutelage of French cadres for several years, Vietnamese officers were also heavily influenced by the way these French cadres actually exercised command and leadership.

• • •

Thus the problem that plagued the Vietnamese National Armed Forces from the beginning was the lack of military leaders. It was the legacy we inherited from nearly one century of French domination, during which our millenary tradition of military leadership was completely lost. It was a serious problem that South Vietnam was able to solve only belatedly, although beginning in 1954 all of our units were commanded by Vietnamese officers. But, even then, national authority was still largely in the hands of the French, who made all the decisions concerning the conduct of the war and politics, this despite the fact that some areas had been placed under Vietnamese military control. This situation was not resolved until the advent of the 1954 Geneva Accords and Mr. Ngo Dinh Diem became prime minister. And only then did Vietnam enjoy genuine independence, complete sovereignty, and an independent army.

Such was the status of military leadership in the Vietnamese National Armed Forces at the eve of Vietnam's partition and before South Vietnam even became a new nation south of the 17th parallel.

• • •

II. LEADERSHIP UNDER PRESIDENT DIEM'S REGIME

Background

On 16 June 1954 Chief of State Bao Dai designated Mr. Ngo Dinh Diem, then living in exile in the United States, as prime minister, after promising him considerable authority in political and military affairs. However, within just a few weeks after he took office on 7 July 1954, Prime Minister Diem realized that he actually had no authority at all. Power in the State of Vietnam remained fractured, as in the past; portions were held by a number of fiercely competing factions. The interests of the groups among whom it was divided were quite compatible with those of the French, whose domination had rested largely on the ancient principle of "divide and rule." In addition to dealing with the chaotic political conditions he inherited from the colonial regime, Diem faced equally discouraging tasks on several other fronts. The country was in ruins. Most bridges had been blown up. Canals, road, railways, telephone and telegraph services had either been destroyed or were in disrepair; vast regions of rice land were uncultivated; countless peasants who had fled the countryside found themselves unemployed in the cities. And Diem's administration, run by an incompetent civil service, politically hostile and disintegrating, had to provide the human and material resources for receiving, feeding, and temporarily settling hundreds of thousands of refugees who had fled from the North to the South, adding enormous burdens to a totally insolvent state and government.

With his aspiration to give the country a unified and strong government, Diem represented the supreme national needs of the hour. But how could he overcome the obstructions of the many forces and factions hostile to or indifferent to his efforts? He was opposed by the army, which was still under French command and headed by Vietnamese officers appointed by Bao Dai and the French. He was disobeyed by the police and the secret service, which Bao Dai had sold to the Binh Xuyen, his closest ally among the sects. Diem's national aims clashed with the "feudal" power structures of the Hoa Hao and Cao Dai sects, which with their private armies ruled most of the country west and south of Saigon. He met the hostility of the French and Chinese circles, who controlled much of the Vietnamese economy and who knew that a strong national regime was bound to limit their powers.

This was true also for the Vietnamese landlords, who feared that Diem's call for national "revolution" implied radical projects of agrarian reform. The old collaborators inside and outside the administration sabotaged Diem's every step to secure control of the existing government apparatus, and the old "fence sitters," the attentists, now more numerous than ever among the intellectuals, refused to support Diem out of fear of an early collapse of his regime and a takeover of the South by the Viet Minh. This possible takeover was indeed the greatest of all dangers that threatened Diem and, together with everything else, was the reason that the chances for the survival of Diem's regime were generally regarded as nil.[1]

This was how bleak the situation of South Vietnam looked when Ngo Dinh Diem took office. In the contemporary history of Vietnam, perhaps Mr. Diem was the only leader to be confronted with the partition of the country as soon as he was appointed and the numerous difficult problems involved that he had to solve.

The Diem administration placed first priority on negotiations with the French for the immediate transfer of military and administrative authorities to the government of South Vietnam. The French agreed only to a gradual transfer. On 27 September 1954, however, an agreement was reached in Washington between the United States and France whereby all military, economic, financial, and commercial powers that France still held would be transferred to the government of South Vietnam beginning on 1 January 1955. By this agreement the United States also agreed to provide aid directly to the independent nation of South Vietnam, and the French Expeditionary Corps would be repatriated upon request of the South Vietnamese government. In reality, French forces redeployed from the Saigon-Cholon area to Vung Tau on 20 May 1955 and withdrew completely from South Vietnam only on 28 April 1956.

In early September 1954 the chief of the Vietnamese General Staff, Lieutenant General Nguyen Van Hinh, openly attacked Prime Minister Diem, who responded by ordering him on a mission to France for six months. General Hinh resisted Diem's orders, arguing that since Chief of State Bao Dai appointed him to his present position, only the Chief of State could remove him from office. The conflict dragged on for three tense months, creating confusion and divisions within the armed forces. Although General Hinh was in control of the armed forces, he did not dare use force to overthrow Prime Minister Diem, fully aware that Mr. Diem had strong American support.

Several army units, repulsed by General Hinh's rebellious and pro-French attitude, manifested their support for the prime minister. Most remarkable was the action taken by Major Thai Quang Hoang (later promoted to lieutenant general), who as commander of the Ninh Thuan sector took to the maquis with 700 of his men in a rebellion against the General Staff. His action was supported by several other units located in the Phan Thiet and Nha Trang areas. Fearing an armywide rebellion, finally Chief of State Bao Dai summoned General Hinh to France and subsequently removed him from office on 29 November 1954. Prime Minister Diem immediately appointed Brigadier General Le Van Ty, then commander of the 1st Military Region, to replace General Hinh as Chief of the General Staff.

• • •

The Vietnamese National Armed Forces meanwhile activated four infantry divisions on 1 January 1955; these were the 6th (Nung) Division, 11th, 21st, and 31st Divisions. But, in contrast to previous years, the General Staff had to interrupt this development trend because of a force structure ceiling imposed by the US Military Assistance Advisory Group (MAAG). The decision to cut back on military assistance came as a surprise for the General Staff, which was informed only at the end of 1954. In early 1955, therefore, the General Staff took emergency measures to bring the total strength down to the imposed ceiling within the prescribed time. At that time, [the] MAAG desired to reduce the total strength by one-half, from over 200,000 to 100,000. In [the] MAAG's view, the Vietnamese armed forces, having no longer to fight a war, should be reorganized and trimmed down to perform a peacetime mission.

In addition, [the] MAAG also advised the General Staff against maintaining a professional army composed entirely of volunteers. Instead, the Vietnamese army should include a draft component and rotate this component in and out of service every 18 months, the legal duration of military service for conscripts. After the 18 months of mandatory service, the draftees would be discharged and become reservists "on call." In brief, the MAAG-conceived force structure plan was designed to maintain an adequate defense force at all times without having to incur big expenditures.

The Vietnamese General Staff meanwhile suggested that a force structure of 150,000 be maintained, which, it argued, was not in violation of the Geneva Accords and would provide for the effective defense of the national territory. But this recommendation was rejected by [the] MAAG, and, as a result, the Vietnamese General Staff was compelled to implement a large-scale discharge program without being prepared for it. The sudden and arbitrary discharge of thousands of NCOs and enlisted men created an emotional shock throughout the ranks.

• • •

To solve the economic and social problems caused by the mandatory discharge, and also to win over these veterans, the Diem government created the Civil Guard on 8 April 1955, which was supported by the national budget and placed under the control of the Ministry of Interior. In mid-June 1955, when [the] MAAG approved the 150,000 force structure plan, the General Staff suspended discharge orders. By that time, however, 58,445 servicemen had already been removed from military payrolls and the strength of the Vietnamese National Armed Forces stood at 167,555.

• • •

On 23 October 1955 a nationwide referendum was held on the issue of whether or not to maintain Bao Dai as chief of state. An overwhelming majority (98.2 percent) of the population voted for his dismissal and expressed confidence in the leadership of Prime Minister Diem. Three days later, on 26 October 1955, Diem became president of the Republic of Vietnam and the National Armed Forces were redesignated the Republic of Vietnam Armed Forces (RVNAF). . . .

Looking back on the first eighteen months of his administration, no one could dispute the fact that President Diem had achieved many important things and overcome seemingly insurmountable obstacles. The difficulties which he had been required to face were so immense, so numerous, that several foreign observers did not think his regime could survive beyond one year. But not only did he survive, he regained complete sovereignty for the new nation, administratively, diplomatically, and militarily. He skillfully maneuvered the withdrawal of the French Expeditionary Corps from South Vietnam, imparted unity and loyalty to the armed forces, and eliminated all armed religious sects that had imposed their control over several areas. At the same time, he effectively reorganized the nation's administrative and military apparatus, and, most importantly, he laid the foundation for a political regime which could confront and compete with the Communist state of North Vietnam and ensure for South Vietnam a position of its own in international affairs. Several people who had criticized him now reversed themselves and heaped praise on him, the man they credited with bringing about a "miracle."

During the following years, under President Diem's leadership South Vietnam confidently [trod] its way toward progress and prosperity. The entire monetary system underwent reorganization, as did budgetary affairs and central banking. There was a dramatic increase in the number of hospitals, dispensaries, maternity clinics, and public health facilities. Progress in the field of education was equally remarkable. During a four-year period, from 1955 to 1959, the number of students attending community elementary schools increased almost threefold. Nearly 10,000 students were enrolled in universities by the end of that period, including about 2,000 who studied abroad. To provide an efficient bureaucracy for his administration, President Diem enlarged the National Institute of Administration, which not only trained future civil servants, but also provided career improvement courses in law and economics.

Sustained by political stability and relative peace, the national economy gradually recovered. In agriculture rice production, which stood at 2.6 million metric tons in 1954, rose to 3.4 million in 1956 and 5 million in 1959. Progress in the production of rubber was even greater, topping prewar levels in 1955. The prewar levels were also reached a few years later in the production of coffee and by the fishing industry, while production figures of all other agricultural crops, although rising considerably, still remained below prewar levels.

• • •

Politically, the Diem government endeavored to strengthen the democratic base of the regime by instituting general elections. Three such elections were organized—in 1956, 1959, and 1963—to elect members of the National Assembly, and one in 1961 to reelect the president. To further strengthen the regime and compete politically with North Vietnam, several political organizations were created, such as the National Revolutionary Movement, the National Movement of Revolutionary Civil Servants, the Republican Youth, and, most notoriously, the Personalist Labor Party (Dang Can Lao Nhan Vi) conceived as a political opponent to the Communist Party of North Vietnam. The party chairman was Ngo Dinh Nhu, the president's younger brother, who was also credited with formulating the doctrine of personalism as an ideological antithesis to Communism.

• • •

Returning from the US Army Command and General Staff College in the summer of 1957, I had the privilege to begin a close professional association with President Diem that lasted for nearly three years. I was assigned to the Presidential Palace as the president's chief of staff. He looked to me for military advice, and all orders he had for the

Joint General Staff he gave to me for transmittal. I saw firsthand the strong talent for leadership President Diem exhibited, his great concern for the people of Vietnam, and the earnest efforts he made on behalf of security for the country.

I also came to appreciate the brilliance of Mr. Nhu, the president's brother. He was an innovative thinker—not a real leader as was Diem, but a man of ideas. The president would sign no paper or utter any prepared speech unless Mr. Nhu had first reviewed and approved it. Indeed, Mr. Nhu personally wrote most of Diem's speeches and was responsible for developing all major aspects of national policy and strategy during this period.

While the Diem government devoted its efforts to nation building, North Vietnam began to initiate disruptive activities following President Diem's rejection of elections toward unification. Former Viet Minh cadres who remained in South Vietnam after 1954 were ordered into action. At the same time, North Vietnam reinfiltrated in[to] the South those cadres who had regrouped to the North. The insurgency thus began and gradually picked up in scope and intensity. From sabotage and assassination, terrorist actions stepped up into small-scale attacks against remote outposts and finally developed into battalion-sized warfare.

• • •

To counter the Communist insurgency, President Diem created the ranger forces, whose concept took after the French Commandos of the 1949–1954 war. His plans initially met with opposition from [the] MAAG, which not only suspected a political motive, but objected to the transferring of the most experienced officers and men from established units to the rangers. In the face of growing insurgency, however, [the] MAAG finally agreed to support the ranger forces by providing Special Forces teams to train them. When they were activated, the Vietnamese ranger forces numbered about 9,000 men, or 65 companies, originally transferred from infantry battalions on the basis of one rifle company per battalion (each battalion had then four rifle companies). Later these companies were increased to 86. . . . Beginning in 1961, [the] MAAG also agreed to increase the RVNAF force structure from 150,000 to 170,000.

Despite President Diem's leadership and his many accomplishments—or perhaps in some cases because of them—he had many enemies within the country besides the Communists. And, despite his brilliance, Mr. Nhu took too little account of the public's animosity toward him as the president's counselor, animosities that were naturally transferred to the president himself. Reflecting the political turmoil that still weakened the country, even though remarkable progress had been made in virtually all aspects of national life, opponents of the regime, not content to follow the constitutional processes, plotted violent means to supplant the elected leadership of the country.

One attempt took place in November 1960 in which Colonel Nguyen Chanh Thi employed his paratroopers to initiate the coup, which ultimately ended in failure. The second attempt took place in February 1962, when two dissident pilots bombed the Independence Palace with their A-1 Skyraiders. This attack caused considerable damage to the old palace, which was later rebuilt. But in 1963 a new group of plotters exploited the riotous situation caused by the dissident Buddhists and gathered enough strength, and American support, to depose the Diem government.

The self-immolation of Reverend Thich Quang Duc and other monks effectively burned the bridge of possible reconciliation between the Diem government and the Buddhists. Mrs. Ngo Dinh Nhu, who derided the Buddhist self-immolation as "a barbecue party," joined her husband in demanding that the Buddhist protesters be crushed, charging that they were Communist-led extremists. The United States, meanwhile, urged the government to make concessions and exile the Nhus. This was a completely impractical idea. It was no more possible for President Diem to banish his brother than to sever his own head. Mr. Nhu was not only the president's brains, he was his most loyal and trusted advisor and supporter.

While President Diem was still undecided, on August 21 elements of the Vietnamese Special Forces attacked the Xa Loi and other pagodas in Saigon, apparently under Mr. Nhu's orders. The monks, and even the nuns, were brutally beaten and apprehended. Thousands of students and teachers who demonstrated for the monks were arrested, and all high schools and universities were ordered closed. This heavy-handed repression enraged many officials, military officers, and professionals whose children were manhandled and jailed. It also ended support for the Diem regime at home and abroad.

The United States seemed to have rushed the unraveling of events by suspending subsidies for imports and support for the Special Forces. Enraged, Nhu acrimoniously accused Americans and other foreign elements of plotting against the Diem government. Encouraged by the American attitude, several army officers began to plot Diem's overthrow. One group was led by Colonel Do Mau, the trusted director of the Military Security Service, and Major General Tran Thien Khiem, Chief of Staff of the JGS. Do Mau and Khiem were joined by other officers, students, and workers. Another group, which included Generals Tran Van Do, Duong Van Minh, and Le Van Kim, enlisted the cooperation of Lieutenant General Do Cao Tri, commander of I Corps, and Lieutenant General Nguyen Khanh, commander of II Corps.

• • •

And so the conspiracy went undetected until the generals decided to strike. On 1 November government troops entered Saigon and seized control. Within hours the president and his brother were both brutally murdered. The First Republic was over and Vietnam had lost a great leader.

Training and Leadership Development in the RVNAF

• • •

A new draft policy which differed radically from the mobilization policy instituted in 1950 was implemented soon after the cease-fire. This new policy called into mandatory service only those youths between 20 and 22 years of age, to the exclusion of all other ages. The Diem government considered this military obligation a sacred mission that every youth of that age had to carry out.

• • •

In addition to training new recruits, Training Center No. 1 also conducted command and leadership courses.

• • •

The impact of the command and leadership course was far-reaching and extremely beneficial to the Vietnamese National Army, whose outlook as a modern military force began to take shape almost immediately. Only a short time following the first few courses, the bearing and appearance of Vietnamese servicemen seemed to change completely. At the General Staff, for example, officers and NCOs were seen neat and elegant in their well-pressed starched khaki uniforms, close crewcuts, and shining black regulation shoes, going about their duties with correct deportment and a disciplined manner. The same was true with field units, the majority of whose personnel displayed the same commendable deportment and manner and were equally smart in their new combat fatigues and boots.

• • •

The training process at divisions continued at an enthusiastic and busy pace until 1959, when it was suspended altogether because of combat operations required to counter increased insurgent activities.

• • •

The selection of officers and NCOs for the Vietnamese National Army was . . . almost entirely based on academic achievements or formal education. Some criticism arose that the armed forces were under the control of the educated urbanites—the rich people—and that such selection lacked a popular base. This criticism was partly true, especially during the formative years of the Vietnamese armed forces. Perhaps during that period academic background was the only criterion available for selective purposes. During the following years, as South Vietnam developed, the educational base was greatly enlarged with the proliferation of schools at all levels, to include higher education, and the number of students with academic achievements also increased manyfold and represented a wide cross section of society. Thus, although education was still the criterion for selection, such criticism no longer held true as far as the lack of popular base was concerned.

• • •

All procurement, accounting, and budgeting, and the management of military properties, were also under the control of the Ministry of Defense. This was a key feature of the Vietnamese defense structure in which the president of the Republic was also minister of defense, assisted by a secretary of state for defense. As a result, the Chief of the General Staff, the military region commanders, and the division commanders were required to report directly to the president for important matters or at his summons. A special radio network installed at the presidential palace provided the president with direct communications with corps and division commanders, from whom he obtained reports and to whom he often gave orders.

The promotion of officers was a responsibility of the Personnel Directorate, operating directly under the secretary of state for defense. Every year this directorate compiled a list of promotion candidates, usually kept strictly confidential, and submitted it to the president for decision. When he reviewed this list, the president usually consulted the director of Military Security or other heads of agencies as required, but he himself decided who should be promoted. Therefore promotion during those years was highly selective and difficult. The same procedure applied to the appointment of military officers in key positions; it was all decided by the president.

The Military Assistance Advisory Group, Vietnam, was fully aware of this state of things. It sought to improve the authority of the Joint General Staff by recommending a different command structure which would have brought the Ministry of Defense and General Staff closer together, both physically and in command relationship. This recommendation was rejected by President Diem, however. True to the nature of an autocratic ruler, he did not want any one individual other than himself to wield too much authority. He preferred to maintain a system of power division in which all subordinates should remain personally loyal to him. Despite objections from the MAAG, President Diem persisted in this practice.

• • •

Operations against the Binh Xuyen and Rebellious Religious Sects

After regaining full control of the armed forces and initiating reorganization plans, the South Vietnamese government turned its attention to the thorny problems of suppressing armed rebellions by religious sects, such as the Hoa Hao in the Mekong Delta, and removing the Binh Xuyen gang from the police organizations. These operations provided the opportunity for emergent field commandeers to prove their tactical resourcefulness and military leadership.

Since early 1948, when he disassociated himself from the Viet Minh and cooperated with the French, Mr. Le Van Vien, alias Bay Vien, had proved extremely effective in the employment of his forces, called the Binh Xuyen, to destroy the Viet Minh's underground organizations in the Saigon-Cholon area. The French trusted him and gave him and the Binh Xuyen complete control over the Saigon-Cholon area, to include the Rung Sat mangrove redoubt and the waterway connecting the sea with the Saigon harbor. The Binh Xuyen thus enjoyed several exclusive privileges in commerce, for example a virtual monopoly to cut timber, to provide river transportation services, and to operate bus lines from Saigon to Vung Tau and provinces of the Mekong Delta. They were also authorized to operate two notorious casinos, "The Great World" in Cholon and Kim Chung, and a big brothel in Saigon. All profits that the Binh Xuyen made in these operations were used to maintain and develop their forces.

Public opinion was greatly concerned, however, when Chief of State Bao Dai made Bay Vien a brigadier general and later appointed Lai Huu Sang, one of the latter's proteges, director general of National Police and Security. Rumors had it that the Binh Xuyen had bribed their way into key governmental positions and that the government, or Prime Minister Buu Loc, had received the hefty sum of 40 million piasters in these transactions.

The Binh Xuyen forces consisted of about 2,000 troops, organized into five battalions;

1,500 crack "assault police" troopers making up two battalions; and approximately 10,000 followers, all members of the so-called Popular Front. The 1,500 crack assault police troops of the Binh Xuyen manned 21 police stations scattered about Saigon-Cholon.

In early 1955 Prime Minister Ngo Dinh Diem decided to crack down on the Binh Xuyen's infamous operations. This was in keeping with his proclaimed policy of uniting the armed forces and eradicating all social vices. He refused to extend the licenses for gambling casinos and brothels, forcing Bay Vien to close them down. After the loss of these lucrative operations, Bay Vien reacted just like any warlord deprived of his privileges. He joined forces with the Cao Dai and Hoa Hao religious sects, which also found themselves in the same position, to form a political alliance seeking to overthrow Diem's government. The Cao Dai and Hoa Hao private armies, which had enjoyed feudal autonomy and financial support from the French, were now ordered to disband and to be incorporated into the national armed forces. This was the last thing they would want to happen.

The alliance of the Binh Xuyen, Cao Dai, and Hoa Hao was manifested by the creation of the "Front for the Unification of All National Forces." On 21 March 1955 this front passed a resolution, which sounded like an ultimatum, demanding Prime Minister Diem . . . form a new cabinet within five days. The resolution was signed by Pham Cong Tac, head of the Cao Dai sect; Lieutenant Generals Tran Van Soai and Nguyen Thanh Phuong; and Major Generals Le Van Vien, Lam Thanh Nguyen, Le Quang Vinh, and Trinh Minh The.

Prime Minister Diem remained undisturbed by this demand. He maintained his position that all political problems should wait until after the national armed forces had been unified. Frustrated by his unyielding stance, all the Cao Dai and Hoa Hao who served as Diem's cabinet members tendered their resignations. Diem's own secretary of state for defense, Ho Thong Minh, whom he had appointed, also resigned in protest.

However, the Binh Xuyen–Cao Dai–Hoa Hao political alliance was not strong and determined enough to overthrow Mr. Diem. In the meantime, attracted by Diem's courage and leadership, several groups of dissident Hoa Hao and Cao Dai rallied to the government. These included 3,500 men under Colonel Nguyen Van Hue and another 1,500 under Major Nguyen Day of the Hoa Hao, and other Cao Dai armed elements under Trinh Minh The. The had rallied to Mr. Diem in late 1954 and served as a major general of the national forces. Lieutenant General Nguyen Thanh Phuong, the spokesman of the front itself, also rallied to the government four weeks after the resolution was passed. Only the Binh Xuyen remained recalcitrant and determined to oppose Mr. Diem.

The Binh Xuyen's opposition soon turned into armed rebellion. The first provocation by the Binh Xuyen took place on midnight 30 March 1955 when a group of assault police attacked a police station and the General Staff headquarters on Tran Hung Dao Boulevard with the support of machineguns and recoilless rifles installed in nearby buildings. This attack was not successful and the Binh Xuyen element was driven away two hours later by governmental forces from the Saigon-Cholon subdivision. Both sides suffered a few casualties and a cease-fire was declared at 2:30 a.m.

After the incident, the French High Command ordered its troops to occupy key areas in the city under the pretext of protecting French nationals and installations. A few areas were declared off-limits to governmental forces, to include the area under the Binh Xuyen's control. At the same time, the governmental forces met with shortages of ammunition and fuel, whose supply was still provided by French forces. The Vietnamese armed forces were also ordered not to provoke the Binh Xuyen.

During the month that followed the incident, the Binh Xuyen reinforced the defenses of their areas and continued to provoke governmental forces by kidnapping individual servicemen and harassing military installations by sniper fire or grenades. The situation became more tense when Prime Minister Diem appointed Colonel Nguyen Loc Le as director general of the National Police in place of Lai Huu Sang, a Binh Xuyen man. On 28 April 1955 a small group of soldiers passing by the Petrus Ky High School were fired upon by the Binh Xuyen's assault police inside. [Angered] by this provocative act, the Vietnamese paratroopers retaliated by attacking the Binh Xuyen position. The fighting lasted throughout the afternoon, and by the next morning the Binh Xuyen had to fall back to their redoubt on the other side of the Y Bridge. During that day, the Vietnamese paratroopers controlled the entire Cholon area and maneuvered into positions facing the Binh Xuyen along the Double Canal. In Saigon, governmental forces also restored complete control after clearing all Binh Xuyen-held positions.

At the height of this crisis, on 29 April 1955 Chief of State Bao Dai summoned Prime Minister Diem and Major General Le Van Ty, Chief of the General Staff, to France for consultation. By the same message, Bao Dao also appointed Major General Nguyen Van Vy as Commander in Chief of the Vietnamese National Armed Forces. Disregarding Bao Dai's orders, Prime Minister Diem decided that he and the Chief of the General Staff could not afford to leave the country, even temporarily, in the midst of this situation. He also ignored Bao Dai's orders to replace General Le Van Ty, an unnecessary change that only added to the present crisis.

On 30 April a group of approximately 200 people, acting on behalf of the "national revolutionary forces," met at the City Hall and passed a resolution urging action to remove Bao Dai. In the afternoon, Major General Nguyen Van Vy, Bao Dai's newly designated Chief of the General Staff, reported to the Independence Palace, accompanied by Colonel Nguyen Tuyen, commander of the Imperial Guard, to officiate his new appointment. At the palace he was overwhelmed and chased away by General Trinh Minh The and members of the National Revolutionary Forces (later called People's Council for Revolution). Fearing for his life, General Vy fled to France the next day.

During the period from 30 April to 3 May 1955, governmental forces—composed primarily of the Airborne Brigade, recruit units of Training Center No. 1, a few battalions of the Saigon-Cholon subdivision, and General Trinh Minh The's Regiment No. 60—attacked the Binh Xuyen stronghold and drove their forces away from Cholon. The Binh Xuyen resisted weakly; some of them surrendered, and the bulk of their forces withdrew into the mangrove area of Rung Sat. During a battle at the Tan Thuan Dong Bridge, Major General Trinh Minh The was killed. Prime Minister Diem promoted him posthumously to the rank of lieutenant general and accorded him the full honors of an official funeral.

From their redoubt in Rung Sat, the Binh Xuyen continued harassing governmental outposts located on the periphery of this area. These activities also impeded shipping movements on the Saigon River. For a short time the Binh Xuyen managed to survive because the government was concentrating its operational efforts against the Hoa Hao in the Mekong Delta. Not until 21 September 1955 did the government take military action to eliminate the Binh Xuyen, when Operation Hoang Dieu was launched under the command of Colonel Duong Van Minh, then commander of the Saigon-Cholon subdivision.

• • •

Demoralized and under constant bombardment by governmental forces, the Binh Xuyen disintegrated rapidly.

• • •

After this victorious campaign, Colonel Duong Van Minh was promoted to major general. Many other officers and troops of the operational units were also promoted or decorated. On 6 November 1955 the victorious force returned to Saigon and paraded amid cheers and jubilations of the population.

At this time, however, the campaign conducted in the Mekong Delta to eliminate the rebellious Hoa Hao elements still fell short of its objectives, even after six months of operation. Code-named Dinh Tien Hoang, this campaign had begun on 23 May 1955 under the command of Colonel Duong Van Duc with the commitment of 12 infantry battalions and territorial forces. The governmental forces achieved some military success after disrupting the opposing units and destroying their installations and combat morale, but at the same time they also alienated the local population with their harsh and undiscriminating methods. It was widely believed then that the government wanted to annihilate all religious sects without discrimination or mercy. As a result, President Diem ordered Major General Duong Van Minh, the victor [over] the Binh Xuyen, to take over the conduct of operations.

As soon as General Minh established his field command post, which was called Headquarters, Combined Western and Dong Thap Combat Zones, in Long Xuyen Province, he initiated a new operational campaign, code-named Nguyen Hue, on 1 January 1956.

• • •

Under General Minh's command, the Nguyen Hue campaign was a complete success after one and a half months of operation. By 17 February 1956 almost all objectives had been achieved and the dissidents practically eliminated. Losses inflicted on the dissidents amounted to 268 killed, 3,750 ralliers, and 2,719 assorted weapons captured. Friendly forces suffered 31 killed, 115 wounded, 7 missing in action, and 11 weapons lost.

At the beginning of the campaign, General Minh believed he could rally the dissidents under Mr. Tran Van Soai without bloodshed. First he directed governmental forces to encircle and isolate Mr. Soai's troops. Then, after showing the dissidents that they had no way of escaping, he began prodding Mr. Soai for a negotiated surrender. After several secret contacts with General Minh's representatives, finally Soai agreed to meet with Mr. Nguyen Ngoc Tho, President Diem's special envoy. He laid down some conditions for his surrender, which were all met by the government. Then, on 17 February 1956, Mr. Soai and his troops officially surrendered and rallied to the government.

The same tactic of pressure and negotiations was used to win over General Le Quang Vinh, alias Ba Cut, who was perhaps the most recalcitrant among the Hoa Hao dissident leaders. Ba Cut also agreed to meet with President Diem's envoy, but set several extravagant conditions for his return. He was finally caught by a Civil Guard reconnaissance squad on 13 April 1956 at Chac Ca Dao in Long Xuyen Province. Convicted by the Criminal Court and a military tribunal of rebellion and treason, Ba Cut was sentenced to death and executed on 13 July 1956 at Can Tho.

Eliminating the dissidents was perhaps not too difficult a problem for the government, since the rebellious forces were no match for the governmental forces. But the same governmental forces who had defeated the Binh Xuyen, the Cao Dai, and the Hoa Hao did not have the same self-assurance when it came time to confront the Communists. The following event proved that defeat was often the result of poor leadership.

Performance of the 7th Division in the Battle of Ap Bac

While in command of the 7th Infantry Division, Major General Huynh Van Cao initiated a pattern of activity which in time became an established routine for the division. He would commemorate every important national event, such as the National Day or President Diem's birthday, by conducting an operation of political significance. When he left the 7th Division to command IV Corps, General Cao was replaced by Colonel Bui Dinh Dam, also a presidential appointee like himself. Both were Roman Catholic, loyal to the regime, and no doubt high-ranking members of the all-powerful Can Lao Party [the political party on which President Diem relied].

Soon after becoming commander of the 7th Division, Colonel Dam thought of a military exploit which could be offered to President Diem as a present on his birthday, 3 January 1963. It so happened that, two days before that, an observation plane had spotted about 100 VC in the village of Ap Bac in Dinh Tuong Province. This surely looked like an easy win, and Colonel Dam decided to launch an operation the next day, 2 January, after some planning. During the previous night, he landed an element of his division in an area north of the Ap Bac village. At the same time, a second element moved south of the village by trucks, while a third element established a screen on the highway east of the village. For this operation, Colonel Dam had committed three battalions of the 12th Regiment, two ranger companies, four Civil Guard companies, 13 M-114 APCs, and six 105mm howitzers.

At 0600 hours, after all ARVN elements had taken up their assigned positions around the village, the operation began with half an hour of intense preparatory fire against the target by the air force and artillery. Then Colonel Dam gave the orders for an infantry assault, which was conducted by two Civil Guard companies. The enemy force inside the village was estimated at about 200, well entrenched in communication trenches, foxholes, and defense positions. This preparedness indicated that perhaps the enemy had advance information on the ARVN operation. Not until our troops had progressed near the village did the enemy open fire.

From the very first minutes of the engagement, 40 of the government troops had been put out of action. Overwhelmed by a heavy fire from the village, the two Civil Guard companies fell back and two others made the assault. The enemy employed the same tactic: he would wait until the troops came [into] close proximity of the village, and only then would he open fire. After the failure of the two initial infantry assaults, the 7th Division commander decided to land new troops in the village by helicopters. Three helicopters with ARVN troops aboard were immediately downed by enemy 37mm anti-aircraft fire; others were forced to a safer altitude. In a second landing attempt, two more helicopters were downed and the landing was aborted.

During the following hour, the 7th Division launched simultaneous attacks from the south, the north, and the east, but they all ended in failure. The next phase of attacks by ARVN forces involved four companies which had not been previously committed; still they made no significant headway.

By this time the IV Corps commander had flown in to observe the battle, and perhaps to give Colonel Dam a helping hand. A new phase of attack began with 20 minutes of artillery preparatory fire on enemy positions; well over 200 rounds were expended. This time, the 7th Division commander employed a total of eight companies for the assault against the village. The ARVN troops attacked desperately but in vain. Finally it was decided to spearhead the attack by armored personnel carriers with infantry troops aboard and following in their wake. The enemy still persisted in employing the same tactic. When the armored personnel carriers came to within range, four of them received direct hits and caught fire; four others were damaged. The final attack thus came to a complete stop.

In the face of continued failure, IV Corps requested the JGS for reinforcements. In the afternoon it was decided to airdrop a battalion of paratroopers over the target area. The battalion was the only reserve force left at that time; the other three airborne battalions and the brigade commander were being committed to an operation in War Zone C in Tay Ninh Province. From the way the enemy reacted to the airdrop operation, there was a possibility that our communications had been intercepted and the enemy had known our airdrop plan, and even the drop zone as well, in advance. As a result, as soon as our paratroopers left the airplanes and were dangling in the air, they were immediately fired upon by the enemy from the ground.

Despite heavy casualties, the airborne battalion succeeded in assembling its troops upon touching ground and made an effort to carry out its mission. But it was dark and the paratroopers' attack was not as successful as planned. Taking advantage of darkness, the enemy force slipped out of the village during the night. The next morning, when the paratroopers went on the attack, they found no enemy resistance at all. Total ARVN casualties during this battle, both killed and wounded, amounted to approximately 400. It was later known that the enemy force inside Ap Bac village was the 512th Mobile Battalion of My Tho Province, whose estimated strength was about 300. It also appeared that the enemy had known about the 7th Division's operational plan against Ap Bac and had brought in reinforcements.

• • •

Observations

These examples I have selected reflect certain aspects of military leadership during President Diem's administration, especially leadership at division and higher levels. During that period, military leadership was molded by the influence of several factors. First, the RVNAF, being an offspring of the French Expeditionary Corps in Indochina, were still very much influenced by French methods of operation and the French approach to command and leadership, despite the fact that they had been reorganized and trained in the American way. Second, for more than a year after they had become fully autonomous, the RVNAF functioned practically as an instrument of the regime, which used them for political purposes.

The use of ARVN forces to eliminate the dissident religious sects was an example, but this challenge did not provide a full measure of military leadership, since the armed rebels did not enjoy popular support and militarily they were no match for the better-equipped and superior governmental forces. The true test of military leadership was evidenced only by a few significant combat engagements, and, although Communist insurgency was still in the developing stage, there were already indications that the command and control system did not lend itself to effective military leadership.

In the first place, the Joint General Staff, which was supposed to function as a command body, did not enjoy true authority in the military hierarchy. It was just an intermediary between the president and field units. Some of the vital functions that were needed for its effective operation and control—such as personnel administration, political warfare, and military security—were all performed by the Ministry of Defense.

By far the most important function to exercise control over the armed forces was the promotion of officers and their assignment to key positions. But this was an authority enjoyed by the Directorate of Personnel of the Ministry of Defense, and all final decisions on promotion or assignment were made by the president himself. Initially, the promotion of general officers was invariably dictated by political motives. President Diem, for example, freely handed out general ranks to several military chieftains of the Hoa Hao and Cao Dai. The assignment of officers to key command positions was also a process of clannish political consideration aimed primarily at strengthening the regime. Usually such appointments were based on three criteria: first, the candidate had to be a native of Central Vietnam who had proved his loyalty to the regime; second, he had to be a Roman Catholic; and finally, a member of the Can Lao Party.[2] There were of course exceptions to this rule, but at least those selected for key positions had to meet one of the three criteria. The same rule applied to promotion, which in addition to these criteria also required that the candidate had some military achievement to show for his records.

This method of assignment and promotion naturally produced an army of sycophants whose primary preoccupation was to please the president and earn his trust and esteem.

Some unit commanders even doctored combat reports, exaggerating enemy losses while minimizing their own, just to impress the president. But, unless they were extremely skillful and adept, it was not always easy to do this, because the president could always check their reports through [the] MAAG or through his own reporting channels, which could be the Can Lao Party or the military security system.

For the elimination of the rebellious sects, the government had committed corps-sized forces, but its success . . . derived partially from the fact that the rebellious forces were both demoralized and ill-equipped. In fact, these operations could be considered as simple field exercises, with the difference that there was a real enemy and real ammunition was fired. However, credit must be given to those operational commanders who had proved their skills and initiative during combat.

• • •

The assignment of major unit commanders based on the three criteria . . . produced another adverse effect on the performance of the armed forces. Those who did not qualify for these positions became disenchanted; they were convinced that they could do better than those who had been selected. And, among those who had been selected, a few certainly did not measure up to their tasks.

The colonel selected for command of the 7th Division, for example, was perhaps an excellent staff officer, but as a tactical commander he had proved inadequate in combat skills and experience. When placed in command of a division he did not know how to use his forces effectively. His most serious mistake in the battle of Ap Bac was the failure to overwhelm the enemy from the very beginning with a superior infantry-armor force. His piecemeal, hesitant commitment of inadequate forces in successive assault attempts gave the enemy ample time for reorganizing and recovering. His second mistake was to select both the landing zone and the drop zone in too close proximity of enemy positions. Also he had directed the main attack against a point where the enemy's defenses appeared to be the strongest. In addition to these tactical blunders, the commander was perhaps not aware of the fact that the shortage of combat-experienced non-commissioned officers in his units also contributed very significantly to his ineffective infantry assaults and the overall performance of his division.

• • •

But, while command and leadership at the top and higher levels of the military hierarchy were to some extent under the influence of political dictates, the lower levels were not affected by it. In several small units, the principles of military leadership were respected and produced magnificent results.

• • •

III. LEADERSHIP DURING THE PERIOD
OF THE DIRECTORATE

Background

Following the successful coup of November 1963 in which both President Diem and his brother Nhu found tragic death, the military junta set about reestablishing order and government with strong popular support and high hopes. Promising elections and a return to civilian rule within twelve months, the junta disbanded the National Assembly and replaced it by a Military Revolutionary Council (MRC) composed mostly of junta members and chaired by General Duong Van Minh, who also became chief of state. A new cabinet was formed, headed by Prime Minister Nguyen Ngoc Tho, Diem's vice president, and key ministries such as Defense, Interior, and Information were taken over by generals.

To erase the image of the old regime, the new government disbanded the secret police, the National Revolutionary Movement, the Can Lao Party, and the Women's Solidarity Movement. A Council of Notables, composed of respected academic and professional personalities, was created to draft a new constitution, but it disintegrated into futile debates. Efforts to strengthen and consolidate political organizations also ended in failure while generals maneuvered for greater power.

In the immediate aftermath of the military coup, and under the new military government, the Republic of Vietnam Armed Forces underwent a radical change and were never the same again. There was a sudden awareness of political power among the officer corps, especially the generals, and anyone ambitious enough could always expect high returns in terms of money and position.

Those who had taken part in the coup, directly or indirectly, were awarded with double, even triple, promotions. Several officers were suddenly promoted simply by being relatives of or connected with junta members. During a nostalgic visit to his former division a high-ranking junta member brought along rank insignia by the bags and distributed them freely, as if they were souvenirs. This promotion spree created quite a crisis in rank value and seriously undermined military discipline and leadership. In the eyes of the uninvolved officers, this was perhaps the most irresponsible act on the part of the victorious generals, a vindication [sic] that betrayed their own ambitions and unruliness.

By comparison, Diem's much criticized promotion criteria looked rather benign, since the recipients were but a selected few. Gradually the military splintered into small "centers of power," each evolving around an original junta member and picking up new loyalties as it grew and expanded.

Before General Minh could implement a reform program, he was pushed aside on 30 January 1964 by General Nguyen Khanh. The pretext was a rumored neutralist coup by other members of the junta following an unpopular French proposal for neutralization of Vietnam. After exiling the suspected generals to Dalat, Khanh persuaded Minh to remain chief of staff while Khanh became premier and chairman of the MRC.

Proclaiming an anti-Communist, anti-neutralist, and anti-French policy, Khanh advanced a program of urban and rural development. He promised a civilian government with a constitution, but dismissed the Council of Notables previously assigned this task. All able-bodied citizens were ordered mobilized for military service or "New Life" hamlet development.[3]

Meanwhile, most of South Vietnam's Buddhist sects and organizations joined the United Buddhist Church (UBC). To appease the Buddhists, Khanh (himself a Buddhist) recognized the UBC and donated land for a national pagoda. Khanh also cancelled the Catholics' favored legal status and authorized a Buddhist chaplain corps for the armed forces. Despite these gestures, Buddhists soon charged Khanh with repression.

Taking advantage of these disruptive forces, the Viet Cong stepped up their activities. Infiltration from North Vietnam of about 2,000 per month was matched by local recruitment. Increasing quantities of Communist-bloc weapons arrived by land and sea. In response, US advisory and combat support personnel increased to over 22,000 by the end of 1964. . . .

General Khanh, apparently considering the moment opportune for establishing a dictatorship, declared a national emergency and assumed total authority. Next came the constitution, the infamous "Vung Tau Charter," which gave nearly absolute powers to the president. To this position the MRC elected Khanh, displacing Minh. Outraged students demonstrated, joined and encouraged by Buddhist monks who charged repression by former Can Lao and Diemists.

Faced with continuing strife and Buddhist intransigence, Khanh withdrew the Vung Tau Charter and resigned. For an interim government the MRC selected a triumvirate—Generals Minh, Khanh, and Khiem. After a rest in Dalat, during which Saigon remained in chaos and Buddhists in Hue and Danang organized "revolutionary committees," Khanh returned to bring temporary order. He promised a civilian government and a national congress, but when he organized an interim cabinet with heavy civilian representation the generals eliminated from power seized Saigon on 13 September 1964. Khanh was in Dalat, but some younger officers, including Air Commodore Nguyen Cao Ky, opposed the dissidents. Ky's support proved decisive, for the armed planes circling over the coup headquarters brought capitulation without bloodshed.

While the young officers exerted a growing political influence, a High National Council (HNC) appointed by Minh completed provisional organization of a civilian government. The transfer took place 26 October, with the HNC's chairman, Phan Khac Suu, replacing General Minh as chief of state. Former Saigon mayor Tran Van Huong became prime minister, with a civilian cabinet of "technicians." Khanh remained commander in chief and head of a new Armed Forces Council, while Minh and Khiem were assigned abroad as ambassadors.

A combination of factors doomed [the] civilian government. Catholic and Buddhist groups, their differences intensified and political ambitions whetted by the summer's riots, demonstrated against Huong, charging that they had not been adequately consulted on political matters. They organized student demonstrations in Danang, Hue, and Saigon, sacked the USIS library and cultural center in Hue, and demonstrated in front of the US Embassy in Saigon. Promising to restore order, Khanh induced the Armed Forces Council to dismiss the Huong government in late January.

In mid-February a joint military-civilian Legislative Council was set up and a new cabinet formed under Dr. Phan Huy Quat, a former foreign minister. Quat's largely civilian cabinet attempted a balanced representation of minority religious groups with a Buddhist majority. Almost immediately a pro-Catholic faction attempted another coup. While it failed to take over the government, the coup did oust General Khanh, who in fifteen months had antagonized every faction. Though "honorably exiled" as an ambassador-at-large, Khanh was later charged with misuse of government funds and took refuge in France.

On 20 May a group of junior officers and civilians was charged with plotting to assassinate the premier. Their arrests increased Catholic agitation and forced a cabinet crisis into the open when Chief of State Phan Khac Suu refused to recognize Premier Quat's right to dismiss cabinet officers. Unable to reconcile their difference, both Suu and Quat turned over power to the "young Turk" generals, who accepted it and installed a war cabinet on 11 June 1965.

Ten of the young generals formed a National Leadership Committee.[4] General Nguyen Van Thieu became chief of state, while Air Vice Marshal Nguyen Cao Ky became prime minister. Ky entered enthusiastically into his duties. He declared war on North Vietnam to put the country on a war footing and broke relations with France. He doubled the soldier's pay, halved that of high officials, and offered a program of austerity and reform. He also attacked war profiteering and graft.

When Ky became premier, the Communists appeared to have raised the insurgency to phase three, the general offensive. Government control of the Delta had declined until the major cities were virtually besieged. North Vietnam's growing infiltration of military and political personnel and supplies, combined with the political chaos in the South, had brought staggering Viet Cong victories during the first half of 1965.

• • •

At the Honolulu Conference in February 1966 Generals Ky and Thieu and other top Vietnamese leaders met with their American counterparts, including President Johnson and four cabinet secretaries. The conference placed US support behind the Ky government, but emphasized not merely military victory but also reconstruction and South Vietnam's social and political reform. The Honolulu Declaration committed the Ky government to encourage national unity and broaden popular participation in nation building by a democratic constitution and an elective government.

After returning from Honolulu, Ky reshuffled his cabinet to emphasize "social revolution" and began plans for constituent assembly elections. But the Honolulu pledges opened the floodgates of political agitation as various groups sought to seize the political initiative. A political-religious confrontation was touched off in March 1966 by the dismissal of General Nguyen Chanh Thi, who treated the I Corps area as a fief and ignored Premier Ky's orders. Militant students and Buddhist leaders in Hue and Danang, led by Thich Tri Quang, organized massive protest demonstrations supporting Thi and demanding the removal of Chief of State Thieu.

Proceeding with his program despite a militant Buddhist boycott, Premier Ky in April convened a representative congress which recommended plans for elections and the time and manner for transfer to civilian rule. An election law drafting committee assembled in May. The Election Law promulgated 19 June created 117 electoral districts, with nine reserved for Montagnards. The new constituent assembly was elected on 11 September 1966 with the mission to draft a new constitution. Then, on 1 April 1967, the government promulgated the new constitution of Vietnam. On 3 September 1967 General Thieu was elected president and Air Vice Marshal Ky vice president.

Manpower and Training

The RVNAF in the meantime had expanded from 395,000 to 643,000, to include 343,000 for the army.

• • •

As the RVNAF force structure increased to meet the requirements of intensified war, the shortage of manpower began to surface as a serious problem which impeded recruitment and replacement. . . .

Limitations in manpower resources were the main obstacle. This stemmed from anachronistic military service laws which were promulgated a decade earlier and included too many loopholes, making deferment and exemption easily obtainable by youths of draft age. Then there was the problem of draft dodgers, which further drained the manpower resources. To remedy these problems, a new mobilization law, called the "Citizen's Duties Act," was promulgated on 6 April 1964. This law determined that all male citizens between the ages of 20 and 25 were required to perform military service duties for a period of two years, either in the armed forces or in civil defense organizations.[5] At the same time, amnesty was given to those youths who had been convicted of insubordination and draft evasion, with the purpose of turning these fugitives into recruits. Still, at the end of 1965, a modest estimate put the number of draft dodgers at large at 200,000.

• • •

But, perhaps because of the prevailing political instability, manpower shortage became a problem again during 1965. As a consequence, the draft age was gradually raised to 26, then 27, and finally 33 in 1967.

Another equally debilitating problem that gave rise to manpower shortages was desertion. In South Vietnam desertion had taken on an unusual dimension and aspect of its own because of the protracted war which seemed to have no end in sight and to increase constantly in intensity. Adding to the hazards of the war, there were economic hardships created by skyrocketing prices which made the life of servicemen increasingly miserable. Those were the major reasons that edged the South Vietnamese soldier into desertion. There were of course other causes for desertion, such as family separation and poor leadership by unit commanders. But it also seemed that a society which was generally indifferent to the war efforts, and practically protected draft evaders and deserters, could be a significant factor that encouraged desertion or at least made it less culpable.

• • •

The selection of officer candidates, which so far had been based primarily on academic achievements, was for some time criticized as being a form of favoritism which impeded the promotion of the less educated but combat-experienced enlisted men. As a remedy, in 1966 the JGS instituted special officer training courses for those enlisted men having the rank of corporal first class or sergeant who had at least two years of service and were rated excellent. By the end of that year, more than 2,000 qualified enlisted men had become officers who, by virtue of their combat records, added tremendously to the effective performance of small units.

• • •

[Thus] within the space of four years the entire training base of the RVNAF was either reorganized or expanded and modernized in order to meet the requirements of a doubling force structure, especially those of command and leadership. During this period several events occurred which fully illustrated the status of military leadership in the RVNAF. The examples I have selected . . . concern the conduct of the I Corps and 1st Infantry Division commanders during the 1966 Buddhist crisis, the performance of certain province chiefs, and the exploits of airborne battalion commanders.

I Corps and the 1st Infantry Division during the 1966 Buddhist Crisis

Under President Diem's regime the minority Roman Catholic Church unquestionably enjoyed several privileges and exclusive rights smacking of favoritism. This was one of the major causes that led to the demise of the regime in late 1963. Consequently Buddhist influence increased and the Buddhists eventually became a major pressure group in the nation's political life by virtue of their new political awareness. But, just like the Roman Catholics of years past, they seemed insatiable in their demands for privileges and a greater say in national affairs. And successive governments of the post-Diem era also seemed eager to give in to their every demand.

General Nguyen Khanh started the buildup of Buddhist influence by allotting public land for the erection of a "National Pagoda," which became the symbol of Buddhist predominance. Then he authorized the activation of the Buddhist chaplain corps in the RVNAF. The Buddhist chaplains, who came under the United Buddhist Church, never confined themselves to religious matters. A few of them acted as spiritual and political leaders of the units to which they were assigned. During that time the influence of the Vien Hoa Dao (Institute for the Propagation of Buddhism), the United Buddhist Church's executive branch, was all-encompassing, reaching into all levels of the military and governmental hierarchy. For all practical purposes it functioned not unlike a super cabinet with powers of appointing cabinet ministers and granting other favors and privileges. It came as no surprise that, after every session of the Armed Forces Council, the Vien Hoa Dao immediately knew what decisions had been made. Several senior officers, to include a few members of the Armed Forces Council, felt no qualms about reporting all they knew—even military secrets—to their spiritual leaders, considering it the duty of a loyal Buddhist.

By the time the Honolulu summit conference was convened on 6 February 1966, the National Leadership Committee had ruled the country for eight months. The political turmoil of the past two years seemed to have run its course, and South Vietnam was apparently heading toward stability. At the Honolulu Conference the US leaders expressed their desire that South Vietnam's political base be broadened so as to allow popular participation and to progress toward elective government and a democratic regime. At home, political parties, and the Buddhists in particular, viewed this patronizing attitude as a tacit agreement by the United States to support the National Leadership Committee. They believed that, in the event of elective government, surely Mr. Thieu and Mr. Ky would come out winners. This, in their eyes, amounted to sanctioning continued military rule and making a mockery of elective government and democracy. The stage was thus set for what was about to unfold in Hue and Danang, the strongholds of militant Buddhists.

Apparently under the influence and perhaps the instigation of political and religious leaders in his corps area, Lieutenant General Nguyen Chanh Thi, I Corps commander and government delegate, who was also a member of the ruling National Leadership Committee, began to manifest his insubordination and unfriendliness toward the central government in Saigon. Rarely did he correctly implement orders received from Saigon, and he made it no secret. He even scribbled derogatory remarks on official papers passing through his desk to accentuate his displeasure with Saigon. Fearing a breakdown in command and control that could be disastrous to the war efforts, the National Leadership Committee decided to remove General Thi on the pretext that he should have his chronic sinusitis treated abroad. He was replaced by Major General Nguyen Van Chuan, commander of the 1st Infantry Division.

Immediately after General Thi's removal, the Buddhists began to press for a civilian government. They held meetings and mass demonstrations in Hue, Danang, and Hoi An, vocally demanding the immediate resignation of Generals Thieu and Ky. Gradually the Buddhist-led opposition picked up momentum and spread to Nha Trang and Saigon. Most disturbing to the central government was that fact that in Danang ARVN personnel, civil servants, and dock workers also took part in antigovernment demonstrations. . . . Masses of followers congregated at Buddhist temples and the National Pagoda to listen to antigovernment harangues by militant bonzes.

At Hue the situation became one of emergency when, at the end of March, students took over the radio station and closed down the university. Increasingly large numbers of RVNAF personnel and civil servants joined in antigovernment activities. Local military authorities and governments, meanwhile, remained passive and took no action against the rebels. In early April, Lieutenant General Pham Xuan Chieu, secretary general of the National Leadership Committee, was sent to Hue to negotiate a modus vivendi with the dissidents. He was besieged by the students, who put him in a "cyclopousse" and paraded him, prisoner-style, through the streets. The mayor of Danang,

Dr. Nguyen Van Man, openly sided with the dissidents, while I Corps and the 1st Infantry Division declared their antigovernment stance on radio.

On 4 April 1966 Prime Minister Ky held a press conference at the JGS officers' club in which he announced that he would deploy troops to the I Corps area to squelch the demonstrations and restore order and security. The dissidents in Danang responded by blocking all accesses from the airport and preparing to resist. They also urged every household to display an altar in the street, hoping to deter the government from taking action. On the next morning an airlift movement brought to Danang airport a governmental force composed of marines, field police, and a squadron of M-48 tanks. However, the force confined itself to the airport and was unable to act. While Major General Chuan, the I Corps commander, was summoned to the airport to report on the situation, Colonel Dam Quang Yeu, commander of the Quang Nam Special Sector, maneuvered his troops and artillery in an apparent move to encircle and threaten the airport. In his report, General Chuan seemed to be sympathetic to the dissidents' cause; it was apparent that he was not willing to act against them. General Chuan was removed and replaced by Lieutenant General Ton That Dinh.

• • •

When he took over as I Corps commander, General Dinh seemed entirely devoted to solving the crisis in his area of responsibility. But, as time went by, he gradually made fewer and fewer contacts with the JGS and the National Leadership Committee. Finally he stopped reporting his activities to Saigon altogether. It was apparent that General Dinh had also succumbed to Buddhist influence, like his two predecessors. Summoned to Saigon for a high-level meeting, he refused to comply.

The National Leadership Committee was thus faced with a dangerous and difficult situation. On the one hand, antigovernment demonstrations continued to grow in fervor and extent. On the other, the corps commanders successively appointed to deal with the situation seemed to disappear from sight and, one after another, openly or tacitly took side with the dissidents and no longer responded to central control. Obviously they had all become co-conspirators, and it was as if they had been entranced into it by some invisible force, a force so strong they could not resist. This overwhelming force was perhaps personified by the Venerable Thich Tri Quang, who, as uncontested leader of the militant Buddhist faction, had been pulling the strings behind the scene for some time.

The situation became one of even greater emergency when reports indicated that the Communists were trying to win over the militant Buddhists and the dissident ARVN units to their side. There was then a real danger of losing the entire I Corps area to Communist control if no action was taken in time. The JGS was well aware of this danger. If the RVNAF were to remain a cohesive military force, then no insubordination, let alone armed rebellion, could be allowed within their ranks, no matter what religious force was behind it. A swift action was decided to subdue the insubordinate I Corps headquarters in Danang as the first priority. To my view, the dissidents' strength derived chiefly from the support of I Corps, and, once this support was removed, the political crisis would resolve itself.

The JGS plan of action centered on a surprise move to take I Corps headquarters under control. But, for this move to succeed, it was imperative that every troop deployment be kept secret. As a routine part of its unit rotation schedule, therefore, the JGS announced the replacement of one marine battalion which had been operating in Quang Ngai Province for some time by a fresh one from Saigon. This was part of a conceived scheme to use both units to take I Corps headquarters by surprise. Orders for the unit rotation were therefore made public, but the deployment of additional troops by the same movement and plans for the occupation of I Corps headquarters were kept secret because of possible leaks to the Vien Hoa Dao.

At 0100 on 14 May 1966 an airlift utilizing both military transports and Air Vietnam commercial flights brought one marine battalion to Danang airport, the first contingent of a larger force deployment which was to follow during the day. When the battalion commander had assembled all of his troops on the tarmac, he still did not know what mission he was going to carry out. Only then was he briefly ordered to proceed to I Corps headquarters and take it, with the support of M-48 tanks. He was instructed to act as if he were bringing his troops to I Corps headquarters to reinforce it on the JGS orders and not to open fire unless there was resistance. The marine and M-48 task force then moved toward I Corps headquarters, which it entered and occupied without any incident. When General Dinh received the report that Saigon troops were installed at his headquarters, he drove to I Corps headquarters, but, seeing that its entrance was being blocked by tanks, he went to the US marine headquarters and remained there.

The uneventful occupation of I Corps headquarters was immediately reported to Saigon. Meanwhile the airlift continued, and, eventually, another marine and two airborne battalions were brought to Danang. At about noontime, Premier Ky arrived in Danang, accompanied by a group of generals and cabinet members. By this time the reoccupation of other military installations in the city had been in full progress. Brigadier General Du Quoc Dong, commander of the Airborne Division, was put in command of the occupation forces, whose orders were to end disorder and anarchy. To avoid unnecessary bloodshed, the governmental forces were instructed to use appeals and persuasion to obtain the surrender of dissident units. If they refused to capitulate, they should be encircled and isolated; and only when they opened fire were governmental troops allowed to fire back.

Soon most of Danang was restored to order and Major General Huynh Van Cao was appointed the new I Corps commander. He seemed pleased with his new job until, during a visit to Hue city, his helicopter was shot at by an ARVN serviceman's pistol while taking off. General Cao escaped uninjured, but upon returning to Danang he became a changed person. After charging General Loan with threatening and attempting to assassinate him, he sought refuge in the US marine headquarters, relinquishing his command. General Cao's sudden change of attitude seemed odd and inexplicable. Perhaps he had feared for his life, or perhaps he had been persuaded into inaction by the Venerable Thich Tri Quang. In any event, as a native of Central Vietnam himself and a Roman Catholic, he probably did not want to go down [in] history as the man who repressed the Buddhists of Central Vietnam.

In the meantime, Danang was being cleared of the last but most recalcitrant group of dissidents. The Tinh Hoi Pagoda, which was their headquarters and located north of the airport, had been effectively encircled and cut off from the outside for some time. From all indications, the dissidents were running short of food and water. One of their leaders, Dr. Man, who had been the mayor of Danang, attempted to slip out by night but was arrested by governmental forces. Shortly after his arrest the dissident forces inside the pagoda capitulated and turned in over 100 weapons of all types. The crisis in Danang was thus resolved after a long and tense week. Major General Hoang Xuan Lam, the 2nd Infantry Division commander, became the new I Corps commander.

From the beginning of the crisis the government had been reluctant to use military force against the dissidents in Hue, who enjoyed the support of Brigadier General Phan Xuan Nhuan, commander of the 1st Infantry Division. Actions had been limited to isolating the city and restricting the supply of basic commodities for it. When the dissident problem in Danang had been resolved, the government secretly dispatched some emissaries to Hue to get in touch with military commanders in the area in an effort to dissuade them from giving support to the militant Buddhists. To give weight to its determination to restore order in the city, the government deployed three airborne battalions to the Dong Da Training Center under the command of Colonel Ngo Quang Truong, deputy commander of the Airborne Division. This was intended only as a show of force, because the battalions were committed to combat operations around Hue.

The crisis in Hue proved to be more serious. Being the cradle of the dissident movement, the city was teeming with radical students and extremists. It was also where the rebellion's central headquarters was located. Thus, despite their failure in Danang, the dissidents continued their disruptive rampage in Hue. But here their activities were more violent and took on an unquestionably anti-American appearance. The USIS Library was ransacked and burned down by extremist students and workers. Hundreds of Buddhist monks and nuns staged a fasting sit-in demonstration in front of the US Consulate building; the crisis mounted when one of the nuns immolated herself. The drama reverberated throughout the country and led to other self-immolations. Then the climax was reached when the US Consulate building in Hue was set afire. To the military commanders in Hue, who had been backing the Buddhist demands, it was obvious that the struggle was getting out of hand and becoming hopeless. Disillusioned by this and other excesses, the mayor of Hue, Lieutenant Colonel Pham Van Khoa, and the 1st Division commander, General Phan Xuan Nhuan, returned to the government side. The greatest danger of military confrontation was thus averted, and the dissident movement, now deprived of military support, was doomed to end in failure.

What followed in the days ahead consisted of police actions to clear the city [of] the remnants of the tattered struggle movement. Brigadier General Loan was placed in charge of this task; it did not take him very long to restore order and security. To further strengthen Hue, Colonel Ngo Quang Truong, now promoted to brigadier general, was appointed commander of the 1st Infantry Division.

The generals and officers who had been involved in the Buddhist rebellions were subsequently indicted and tried by the Armed Forces Council. Lieutenant General Nguyen Chanh Thi was exiled abroad under the pretext of medical treatment, while Generals Chuan, Dinh, Cao, and Nhuan were discharged from service. Eventually Generals Chuan, Dinh, and Cao turned to politics and all became senators. The Venerable Thich Tri Quang in the meantime went on a protracted hunger strike after his failure. He was brought to Saigon for medical treatment at a private clinic, where he remained for a long time.

The Buddhist crisis in the I Corps area having been resolved, the National Leadership Committee set about to widen its political base and prepare the groundwork for elective government and a democratic regime, the very things the Buddhists had been demanding.

• • •

Observations

The years from early 1964 to late 1967 can be summarily divided into two distinct periods. The first period, which lasted until mid-1965, was truly one of the bleakest, marked by political instability and military defeats. Within the short span of one year and a half, the country underwent three successive coups and countercoups, and no government lasted even one year. The Military Revolutionary Council under General Minh was ousted after just three months in power. The next administration, under General Nguyen Khanh, lasted only nine months, and the civilian government that took over from him fared no better. Militarily, South Vietnam went from one defeat to another, and the situation so deteriorated that the United States was compelled to participate in the ground war.

During that period of time, military leadership in the RVNAF was influenced by several factors. First, the removal of President Diem from power gave the Communists a valuable chance of winning militarily in South Vietnam. As a result, they began to increase the infiltration of men and weapons into the South to take advantage of a situation deemed favorable for their takeover.

Next, political turmoil and the frequent turnover of governments in Saigon exerted a profound impact on the morale of troops and utterly confused the population. A number of military commanders, who had become addicted to power since the original coup, realized that the shortest way to promotion and important positions was through conspiracy and coups. Therefore they spent most of their time plotting intrigues, switching allegiances, and maneuvering for political prominence.

The RVNAF suffered from all this neglect and irresponsibility. Their command and control became loose, and nonexistent at times, because each commander cared only for his own precarious future. Military hierarchy was upset by uncontrolled promotions, which were handed out to buy allegiance, especially as far as generals and colonels were concerned. General Nguyen Khanh, for example, promoted many generals and colonels to win their support for his Vung Tau Charter. Finally, those who had served under President Diem's administration became passive and uncooperative.

The second period began when the National Leadership Committee took power; it lasted for nearly two and a half years. This was a period during which the JGS was able to play its role correctly and achieve substantial progress in personnel administration, force structure expansion, and unit training. Most importantly, it took a special interest in command and leadership at the unit level. At the same time, the JGS endeavored to solve the problems occasioned by manpower shortages and desertion. This was also a period deemed entirely favorable for the improvement and consolidation of the RVNAF because, with the participation of US and FWMA forces, our forces were responsible primarily for the support of pacification and rural development.

• • •

Despite the political turmoil which affected higher levels of the RVNAF hierarchy, performance at the regimental and battalion levels continued to be good and seemed unaffected by events. The performance of airborne battalions during this period provided a striking example of effective military leadership during combat action. This example seemed to emphasize that, to be effective, military leadership should stay away from politics.

• • •

IV. LEADERSHIP DURING PRESIDENT THIEU'S ERA

Background

The long years between late 1967 and 1975, which spanned two terms of Mr. Thieu's presidency, witnessed several challenges to the RVN's political and military leadership. It was during this period that the enemy launched three major attempts to take South Vietnam by force: the 1968 Tet Offensive, the 1972 Easter Offensive, and the 1975 Final Offensive, which climaxed in the collapse of our nation. In the intervening time between the first two offensives, South Vietnam faced perhaps the biggest challenge of all— Vietnamization, for it implied that South Vietnam's fate now lay in its own hands.

But South Vietnam proved it could survive—with US military aid and support. Twice during 1970 and 1971 the RVNAF demonstrated their coming of age by striking across the national borders, and in 1972 they contained and finally defeated the biggest invasion North Vietnam ever unleashed against the South. Although these exploits testified to the success of Vietnamization, they also placed an unprecedented burden on South Vietnamese military leadership and forced into the open all of its strengths and weaknesses.

To understand the magnitude and implication of these challenges, and the unusual requirements of leadership to meet them, I will examine the major events during this critical period of our history.

By the end of 1967, two years and a half after the United States entered the ground war, the situation in South Vietnam appeared to be improving and pointed toward a bright future. Politically, the nation not only recovered completely from the biggest crisis of the post-Diem era; it also seemed to prosper under a regime founded on constitutional democracy. For the first time in four years civilian rule was restored for South Vietnam.

Militarily, the RVNAF were devoting all efforts to the task of supporting pacification and development.

• • •

The Communist strategic posture had been so weakened that the Communists' chance of a military success in South Vietnam was slim and seemed to recede with each improvement achieved by our side. Because of this, Hanoi decided to change strategy. As long as US troops remained in South Vietnam, there was little hope that insurgency war, which so far had largely sought to dominate the countryside, could ever end in victory. The obvious alternative, as Hanoi saw it, would be to strike at the heart of the regime, i.e., the cities, and, once the cities had been subdued, the rest of the country would fall apart in a matter of time.

• • •

During [the] very first phase of their offensive, which lasted through the month of February, the Communists lost in excess of 45,000 troops killed. Our combined losses amounted to only 5,474, to include 3,557 for the RVNAF, 1,825 for US forces, and 92 for FWMA forces. The countrywide fighting also displaced 599,858 people from their homes and turned them into refugees. Damage to our cities, especially industrial plants and civilian housing, was particularly heavy.

The enemy had planned his campaign to be a general offensive–general uprising, hoping to enlist the support of the people to help him overthrow our government. The mythical uprising never materialized, nor did the population ever give a helping hand to the enemy. In all embattled areas the people were always seen fleeing enemy-held territory toward government-controlled areas, which accounted for the heavy influx of refugees.

Despite its failure, the enemy's countrywide Tet Offensive resulted in unexpected developments which were to affect the course of the war in the years ahead.

For the enemy, this offensive was indisputably a major failure. His strategy had been shattered, and he had lost a considerable amount of manpower and weapons. Most critically, a major part of his infrastructure, which had taken years to build and was committed to the attacks, had been destroyed.

For South Vietnam, the Communist defeat came about as a major source for added confidence and encouragement. Aroused by Communist perfidy and the wreckage the Communists had wrought, increasing numbers of youth volunteered for military service, responded enthusiastically to draft calls, or joined local self-defense organizations. This upsurge of patriotism greatly facilitated the calling up of reserves and made partial mobilization an unprecedented success. Stimulated by this trend, the national congress passed a general mobilization bill which was signed into law on 19 June 1968. The RVNAF, meanwhile, expanded their force structure by 135,000 and began implementing a multiyear modernization and improvement program.

• • •

In the meantime, the RVNAF set about to exploit the gains they had obtained during the first offensive, pushing the enemy farther and farther away from [population] centers. Simultaneously, the JGS strongly interceded with MACV for an increase in force structure and new weapons. An initial 820,000 force structure plan was approved, together with an equipment modernization program which provided the RVNAF with new M-16 rifles, M-2 carbines, M-60 machineguns, and LAW rocket launchers on a large scale. In keeping with the modernization trend, war-worn and obsolete equipment was also to be replaced by newer types.

As a result, the RVNAF received replacement items such as the M-41 tank, the M-113 APC, the V-100 scout car, and the M-600 jeep, in addition to a new series of field radio equipment. This increase in force structure was implemented without problems; the majority of the population responded favorably to the new General Mobilization Law. During 1968 alone, more than 80,000 youths of draft age entered military service. Concurrently, to regain control over those villages which had been disrupted by enemy activities during the year-long offensive, the GVN initiated an accelerated program of pacification beginning in November. The program ended in spectacular success after three months of intense effort.

• • •

The Challenge of Vietnamization

The Vietnamization program, which sought to expand and improve the RVNAF to the point that they would be capable of taking over combat responsibilities from departing US units, had in fact started as early as 1968. It consisted of various annual plans which, during the course of their implementation, had been modified several times to adjust to the changing situation and in an effort to meet the RVNAF requirements. The "Midway Package," which resulted from the June summit conference, represented a major step in that direction. Approved by the US Department of Defense, this set of plans provided for a graduated increase in RVNAF force structure—953,673 for FY 1970 and 992,837 for FY 1971. All of these plans were designed to develop the RVNAF into a modernly equipped, structurally balanced military force capable of self-control, self-management, and self-support. As viewed by the United States, this force was destined to become a war deterrent in the event of peace and total US withdrawal.

Toward that objective, Vietnamization progressed rapidly. Most conspicuous among its achievements were the developments of the Vietnamese Navy and Air Force, the modernization of the RVNAF logistics system, and the expansion of the territorial forces, which provided the mainstay of security and pacification. Despite a marginal increase in force structure, the Vietnamese army kept in good pace with the withdrawal of US units, taking over their areas of responsibility and some of their equipment.

By early 1972 most of this improvement plan had been completed. The biggest achievement that the plan brought about was the activation of the 3rd Infantry Division, whose requirement was dictated by the withdrawal of US combat units from northern

MR-1. The activation of this major ARVN unit had met with initial MACV opposition, but it was subsequently validated to fall within authorized levels of MAP support.

Thus, within the space of less than four years, the RVNAF had expanded considerably in strength, from 820,000 in 1968 to 1,100,000 by 1972. The backbone of this combat force consisted of 11 infantry divisions—comprising 120 battalions and supported by 58 artillery battalions, 19 armored cavalry squadrons, and engineer and signal units—one airborne division, one marine division, and 21 ranger battalions. The ARVN had a total strength of 429,000; the navy 43,000, with 1,680 ships and craft of all tonnages; and the air force 51,000, with well over 1,000 planes of all types, to include about 500 helicopters. The territorial forces, meanwhile, almost doubled in total strength, with approximately 300,000 for the Regional Forces (1,679 companies) and 250,000 for the Popular Forces (8,356 platoons).

• • •

[After 30 April 1975] South Vietnam . . . ceased to exist as a nation. As the events which precipitated its early demise had proven, the nation's ultimate failure was also one of leadership. Throughout the years of its existence, South Vietnam always depended on its armed forces for survival. This dependence was particularly pronounced during and after the withdrawal of US troops. In some respects, the matter of national survival then became a question of whether or not military leadership could measure up to its historical role.

The successes and failures of this leadership are many. For the purpose of this monograph, I believe that the examples I have selected from among them amply illustrate the status of military leadership under President Thieu's regime, the most critical period in our history. These examples will be presented in the following order: The challenge of corruption. Leadership at the corps level. Leadership at the division level. Leadership at the province level. Leadership at the battalion level.

The Challenge of Corruption

• • •

But corruption in MR-4 was not solely confined to the problem of "ghost and ornamental" soldiers among the territorial forces. It was in fact much more widespread and involved several province chiefs and a corps commander as well. As a result, an anti-corruption campaign, which was initiated by religious factions and political opposition elements, soon turned into a strong movement. This movement at first demanded that President Thieu take action to purify the governmental apparatus. In subsequent developments, the movement expanded and publicly charged several high-ranking officials and general officers [with] corruption, including especially Lieutenant General Nguyen Vinh Nghi, IV Corps commander; Lieutenant General Nguyen Van Toan, II Corps commander; and Lieutenant General Dang Van Quang, presidential assistant for security. To ease pressure, President Thieu temporarily removed Generals Nghi and Toan from command, but chose to ignore the case concerning General Quang.[6] This anti-corruption movement reached its climax when President Thieu himself was publicly charged with corruption. This was a period during which President Thieu's authority was jeopardized and his integrity seriously questioned, a dark cloud indicating still darker days ahead.

Corruption was a topic much talked about in the RVNAF, particularly during the later stages of the war. Under President Diem's administration, little was heard about it. Then there were only sporadic "misappropriations of funds" or purloin [sic] cases involving primarily personnel responsible for the management of unit funds. Pilfering and larceny were also committed by some involved in the management of military properties and materiel. By 1965, kickback and bribery were rumored to be practiced by some connected with personnel administration and logistics. But corruption did not become a subject of common discussion and concern until 1967, when the RVNAF initiated a program of development and improvement. It finally took the JGS concentrated effort during 1971 to curtail and counter corruption activities, which by [then] had become widespread in the RVNAF.

• • •

In short, as far as South Vietnam was concerned, corruption could be said to be a social vice generated by the war and by the insecure psychology which prevailed among those elements who cared little about the war or its outcome.

The impact of corruption on the RVNAF combat potential and troop morale was debilitating. Combat effectiveness was greatly reduced because the manpower which could otherwise be allotted to field units found its way into staffs and noncombat units. Troop morale, especially in combat units, was often low because no one was happy to fight and die when others were exempt from these dangers. To combat corruption and remedy its damaging effect, the JGS initiated two major programs in 1967.

• • •

These anticorruption activities brought about substantial and sometimes spectacular results. Two of the most spectacular cases involved the 5th and 25th Infantry Divisions, where our Inspector General conducted a long and difficult investigation on charges of corruption involving "ghost and ornamental soldiers," bribery for promotions, contribution of money to unit commanders, and illicit use of military vehicles and construction materials. Since the charges involved general officers, the reports of the investigation were submitted to President Thieu for decisions and appropriate action. In the light of incriminating evidence, the president removed both division commanders, Brigadier General Le Van Tu and Brigadier General Tran Quang Lich, who were subsequently arrested and prosecuted by a military court.

The RVNAF anticorruption activities conducted by the Inspector General Directorate also brought to light many other lesser cases of corruption. Those convicted were all punished appropriately. Punishments ranged from disciplinary confinement, removal from office, demotion, and discharge to prosecution by a military court. In addition, efforts to purify the officer corps led to the discharge of a few generals and in excess of 4,000 field- and company-grade officers who were either found too old for their ranks or convicted of wrongdoing.

Corruption was inevitable in a society ravaged by war. Debilitating as it was, the worst that corruption could do to South Vietnam was to weaken its combat capabilities and potential. The collapse of South Vietnam as a nation did not result from corruption, but primarily from a change in strategy, which not only came too late but was also badly implemented, and the great reduction in logistic support.

Leadership at the Corps Level: III and IV Corps during the Cambodian Incursion

At the request of the Cambodian government, on 23 May 1970 III Corps initiated Toan Thang, Phase 5, for the relief of Kompong Cham. Kompong Cham was the second largest city in Cambodia, after Phnom Penh, and the seat of the FANK MR-1 headquarters. The city's garrison consisted of four infantry battalions, totalling approximately 1,000 men, supported by four pieces of 105mm artillery with 1,000 rounds of ammunition. On 12 May 1970 units of the NVA 9th Division occupied the Chup Plantation, east of Kompong Cham. Since that day, the city was constantly under enemy pressure. Both the city and its airfield were shelled day and night, and the eastern part of the city was attacked several times by enemy sappers. Kompong Cham was practically isolated since the Mekong River, the major link between the city and Phnom Penh, and Route No. 7 had [both] been interdicted by the enemy. The Cambodian forces defending the city suffered from low morale and shortages of food and ammunition.

To accomplish its mission III Corps formed two task forces, TF 318 and TF 333.

• • •

On the morning of 1 June 1970 the Chup Plantation was finally cleared of the enemy. Our forces continued searching for enemy caches in the area and expanded their activities northwestward in an effort to relieve pressure on the east of Kompong Cham.

Their mission accomplished, ARVN forces withdrew from Cambodia for rest and rehabilitation. Taking advantage of the ARVN withdrawal, the NVA 9th Division returned to the Chup Plantation and again took Kompong Cham under siege and initiated round-the-clock shelling. Once again the city had to be relieved, and III Corps was assigned this task. For this second relief operation III Corps employed three task forces and took six days to clear the enemy.

The cross-border operations that III Corps conducted in Cambodia produced important results. The enemy's heretofore inviolable sanctuaries had been severely disrupted and important quantities of weapons, ammunition, and foodstuffs discovered and captured. Enemy forces were also driven back deeper inside Cambodia.

One of the important factors that contributed to these successes was the initiative enjoyed by our forces in an area which had long been under enemy control. The RVNAF also felt a certain pride in coming to the help of a neighbor country in distress. But the most important factor was excellent command and leadership, especially at the corps level.

The III Corps commander obviously had a talent for organization. He had judiciously tailored his forces to satisfy tactical requirements by creating armor-infantry task forces.

Depending on the composition, III Corps might assign the command of each task force to a regimental commander, an armor squadron commander, or the corps ranger commander. This eventually ensured unity of command and tactical flexibility, which brought out the best from each combat arm. Each task force was also a balanced combination of infantry, armor, and artillery, generally comprising two or three infantry battalions (to include ranger or airborne), an armored cavalry squadron, and one or two artillery batteries. This combination afforded maneuver, shock, and firepower in all operations.

During these operations, the task forces were always directly commanded by Lieutenant General Do Cao Tri, the III Corps commander, assisted by an assistant for operations who was selected from among his division commanders. This arrangement for command and control provided for responsiveness and better support of all participating elements. General Tri was aboard his command ship all day and every day during these operations, making contacts, receiving reports, giving orders, and stimulating his unit commanders on the ground into action. The minute an objective was occupied, he arrived to survey the situation. When any of his units ran into difficulties or clashed violently with the enemy, he invariably landed on friendly positions, personally assisted the unit commander, and encouraged the men. His ubiquitous presence on all battlefields greatly stimulated his troops and kept their morale and determination high.

American reporters who accompanied General Tri into combat operations dubbed him "Vietnam's Patton." His combat prowess, personal courage, and command ability became legendary and widely recognized. But, occasionally, people thought that some of his gestures were ostentatious and calculated to convey an image of himself as a legendary hero. For example, in the battle for the Chup Plantation he landed the minute it was taken by our forces and inspected their positions. Then, while the battle was still fiercely raging nearby, he took a dip in the plantation's swimming pool and quietly lunched in the plantation's clubhouse, as if nothing had happened. This was a peculiar trait of the man that few others possessed, including Major General Nguyen Viet Thanh, the IV Corps commander, who was as courageous and almost as audacious.

Major General Thanh provides another fine example of effective military leadership among our senior officers. As IV Corps commander he personally contributed to the success that his forces achieved during cross-border operations, especially Operation Cuu Long I.

On 2 May 1970 IV Corps initiated this operation in the Parrot's Beak area, in coordination with III Corps. Major General Thanh personally commanded his forces, which consisted of the 9th Division, the 5th Armored Cavalry Squadron, and the 4th Ranger Group.

These units were organized into four infantry-armor task forces which moved out from Kien Tuong Province on three axes and progressed northward to link up with III Corps forces in the Parrot's Beak. This operation was perhaps the largest conducted to date by the RVNAF, and the best coordinated. All infantry and armor elements progressed rapidly on their assigned axes; they divided the objective into several areas in order to facilitate search and destroy activities. In addition to its organic artillery, IV Corps forces were supported by the US 23rd Artillery Group.

For two days our forces made heavy contacts and inflicted severe losses on the enemy in human lives and weapons. On 5 May, IV Corps forces withdrew from the combined area of operation to prepare for the next phase. The results of this operation were impressive and indicated a high standard of military proficiency: friendly: 66 killed and 330 wounded; enemy: 1,010 killed, 204 detained, and 19 rallied; 1,166 individual weapons, 160 crew-served weapons, 100 tons of assorted ammunition seized and destroyed.

This resounding success was directly attributed to IV Corps command and leadership. A poised and silent man, Major General Nguyen Viet Thanh had distinguished himself as a courageous and calm leader since the days when he commanded small units. He always studied the terrain, personally encouraged his men, and directed every major operation. As a result, he was greatly admired and respected by his subordinates. During the next phase of the operation, his command ship unfortunately collided with a US Cobra gunship in bad weather. Both helicopters dropped to the ground in flames, and Major General Thanh found tragic death.

About one year later, Lieutenant General Do Cao Tri, III Corps commander, was also killed in a helicopter accident in Tay Ninh Province. The loss of two experienced and eminent corps commanders, both respectable leaders, in less than a year came as a great shock to the RVNAF. The war had definitely taken a heavy toll with this loss of two of the best military talents South Vietnam ever produced. The RVNAF death list during our extended war was certainly long, with countless other young talents, perhaps not as celebrated as Generals Tri and Thanh, but equally courageous and devoted, who had sacrificed their lives so that our nation could survive. This was perhaps one reason why the RVNAF seemed to lack talented leaders at all levels, a void which became more acute when the nation had to face subsequently even bigger challenges such as the 1972 Easter Offensive.

Leadership at the Corps Level: I Corps during the 1972 Easter Offensive

The enemy initiated his 1972 Easter Offensive by a frontal assault across the DMZ on 30 March. Within less than two days, all ARVN firebases north of the Cam Lo River fell into enemy hands. This blitzkrieg-type action placed a new challenge on RVNAF leadership at all echelons.

On 2 April the 56th Regiment, which defended Camp Carroll, surrendered after being encircled and heavily attacked several times by NVA infantry and artillery. Fifteen hundred men and 22 artillery pieces, to include four 175mm guns, were captured by the enemy. Mai Loc Base, held by the marines, was evacuated shortly thereafter. Despite these initial setbacks, on the fourth day of the offensive the 3rd ARVN Division, which was responsible for the defense of Quang Tri Province, succeeded in establishing a firm defense line along the Cam Lo and Cua Viet Rivers and temporarily stalled the NVA drive, following orders issued by the JGS.

• • •

On 9 April NVA forces launched a coordinated attack with major elements of the 304th and 308th Divisions and two armor regiments. This attack was driven back by ARVN forces, supported by strong US tactical air, and the enemy suffered heavy losses, especially in armor vehicles. Because the terrain was flat and uncovered, most enemy tanks were easy targets for our tactical aircraft and infantry LAW antitank rockets.

In the meantime, farther south, the 1st ARVN Infantry Division effectively stopped all attempts by the NVA 324B Division and two other regiments to move toward Hue from [the] A Shau Valley.

After repelling the enemy attack on 9 April, I Corps planned a counterattack to regain the lost territory in Quang Tri Province. An initial plan, which called for an attack across the Cua Viet River to retake the district of Gio Linh and the northern part of Quang Tri Province south of the DMZ, was discarded in favor of a drive westward. General Hoang Xuan Lam, the I Corps commander, decided to reestablish his former line of defense to the west by launching an all-out counterattack in that direction. Cam Lo, Carroll, and Mai Loc were the major objectives to be retaken.

Orders for the counterattack were immediately relayed by the 3rd Division commander to all of his subordinate units, but none of them seemed enthusiastic to move out. It was apparent that inadequate command and control, and the low morale among units, contributed to this general inertia and, eventually, to the failure of the counterattack. Most unit commanders hid behind pretexts to justify their inaction: high losses or preoccupation with clearing activities in their own areas of responsibility. This general state of inertia lasted until the end of April, during which time no unit made any progress. The counterattack simply failed to materialize, and neither the I Corps commander nor the 3rd Division commander seemed too concerned.

In addition to a loose and overextended command and control system, I Corps performance was beset by the personal approach to command of its commander. General Lam usually bypassed the 3rd Division commander, giving orders directly to the brigades under the latter's control. This was especially true in the case of the 1st Armor Brigade, whose commander was an armor officer, the same branch of service in which General Lam had received most of his experience as a junior officer. The authority of the 3rd Division commander suffered accordingly, which eventually resulted in distrust and even insubordination among the many units attached to his command.

On 18 April a second major enemy attack was driven against the ARVN defense line. All units on this line reported heavy contact with the enemy. But the attack was repelled three hours later by the forceful intervention of US tactical air and B-52s.

During the week that followed this attack, the ARVN line of defense along the Cam Lo and Cua Viet Rivers collapsed for unwarranted reasons. It began when the 20th Tank Squadron left its positions on the Cua Viet line and moved south on QL-1 to destroy an enemy element which was threatening the axis of supply between Dong Ha and Quang Tri City. This was done without the commander concerned even reporting his plan of action to the 3rd Division commander or to adjacent units on the line. Seeing that armor support was being redeployed, and thinking that this was perhaps a withdrawal, ARVN infantry units left their positions and followed suit. By the time the 3rd Division commander personally succeeded in stopping them, the Cua Viet line no longer existed. The ARVN defense line now shrank to the immediate vicinity of Quang Tri City.

• • •

On 30 April the 3rd Division commander summoned his subordinate commanders and briefed them on his plan to withdraw south of the Thach Han River and establish a new line of defense on the southern bank of this river with ranger and infantry units, leaving the defense of Quang Tri City to a marine brigade. This redeployment of forces was designed to release enough armor strength for the clearing of QL-1, which continued to be interdicted. On orders, the units were to move out and take up new positions on the morning of 1 May.

General Hoang Xuan Lam was informed of this plan and appeared to approve by his silence. In any event, he neither confirmed his approval nor issued any instructions to the contrary. On the morning of 1 May, however, he called the 3rd Division commander to inform him that the plan was not approved. He also instructed that all units were to hold their present positions "at all costs" and not to withdraw unless he personally approved.

General Lam was only reiterating the instructions he had just received from President Thieu in Saigon. But these orders immediately resulted in confusion and disorder the minute the 3rd Division commander relayed them to his subordinate units. In vain, he tried to countermand his own orders and issue new ones on the division command radio net. It was too late. Some units had already moved out, others pretended to be moving, and still others simply refused to comply with the new orders. One by one, ARVN units fell back from their original positions in disorder, and it appeared that no force or orders could hold them back. Even the marine brigade, which was left to defend Quang Tri City, also followed suit without command authority. In utter despair, the 3rd Division commander and his staff jumped aboard three armored personnel carriers and tried to catch up with the retreating column of ARVN troops. But on QL-1, the only lifeline to the rear, no movement was possible. It was clogged with vehicles, soldiers, and refugees, and all of them eventually became targets for the merciless poundings of enemy artillery. Despondent, the 3rd Division commander and his staff returned to their CP in the Quang Tri Citadel and were later evacuated by US helicopters.

• • •

When news of unruly rangers ransacking and setting fire to the Dong Ba marketplace in Hue city reached President Thieu through a civilian source, he immediately summoned the National Security Council. In the face of this tragic situation, the council decided to remove General Hoang Xuan Lam from command of I Corps and appoint Major General Ngo Quang Truong in his place. The appointment of General Truong, a Southerner by origin, as I Corps commander was a departure from the normal practice of assigning that position to natives of Central Vietnam only.

The task that faced the new I Corps commander was monumental. He was expected not only to stabilize a chaotic situation of defeat, but also to restore faith and confidence to the population and troops of MR-1. The first thing he did after assuming command was to strengthen I Corps command and control. Toward this goal, he established I Corps Forward at Hue with a select staff composed of able and combat-experienced officers. He placed particular emphasis on the development of a fire support coordination center to better employ all fire support resources available, and a target acquisition element to judiciously exploit the enormous firepower provided by the US Air Force and naval guns.

General Truong then initiated a new defense plan whose concept was simple but effective. It consisted of a clear-cut division of tasks and judicious assignment of responsibilities among subordinate units. Following this plan, he launched a special offensive by fire, called "Thunder Hurricane," which concentrated all types of conventional firepower available, to include B-52s, on enemy targets in MR-1, especially those columns of enemy troops and supplies moving toward Hue. . . .

In a matter of just a few days, as if by miracle, the situation in MR-1 visibly improved and stabilized as General Truong's defense plan went into effect. And, just as soon, stability on the front line brought back law and order to Hue. The city was cleared of all stray soldiers, who were given care and sent back to their units. The improvement in Hue was such that, even though the danger of enemy attacks still persisted, the people who had fled the city began to return in increasing numbers. And soon Hue came alive again with the normal activities of a city in peace.

• • •

On the Armed Forces Day, 19 June 1972, President Thieu visited Hue and reviewed I Corps troops. On this occasion he declared that the enemy Easter Offensive was a complete failure and ordered the RVNAF to take back the lost territories within three months.

His orders were swiftly carried out by I Corps. On 28 June it launched Operation Lam Son 72, a counteroffensive designed to retake Quang Tri. For this effort I Corps employed both the Airborne and Marine Divisions. The Airborne Division conducted the major effort, attacking toward La Vang–Quang Tri on an axis west of QL-1. This effort was supported by the Marine Division, which attacked along Route No. 555 toward Trieu Phong. Meanwhile, west of Hue, the 1st Division held back the enemy who attempted to push toward the city in force.

• • •

The enemy's resistance in Quang Tri Province became heavier as I Corps forces moved nearer the Thach Han River. When the first airborne elements reached into the outskirts of Quang Tri City, the battle turned hellish. The enemy stuck to his position and fought back in desperation, accurately employing concentrated artillery and mortar fire. As the fighting increased, the enemy moved in more reinforcements and, by early September, had assembled a force of six divisions in Quang Tri Province alone.

In the face of this impasse, I Corps decided to switch units and the direction of attack, giving the Marine Division the primary effort. At the same time, frontline units were rotated and given a chance to rest and recuperate. To support the effort to reoccupy Quang Tri City, I Corps also launched secondary attacks to dilute enemy resistance.

Eventually, softened by the massive and sustained firepower of B-52s, tactical air, artillery, and naval gunfire, the enemy resistance weakened after severe losses. Finally, on 16 September [1972], the Marine Division took the Old Citadel and regained control of Quang Tri City.

• • •

One thing was clear, however. General Lam, as I Corps commander, certainly committed several blunders in his exercise of command and tactics. An armor officer who had attended service schools in Vietnam and overseas, General Lam had once been an instructor [in] and then director of our command and staff college. He had also climbed the military hierarchy as a unit commander. Therefore he should have had sufficient professional competence and command ability to assume his role as corps commander with ease. In retrospect, however, his combat experience was limited to counterinsurgency warfare, and, even as division commander, he had conducted only small-unit operations for the purpose of maintaining territorial security. Therefore, when he was confronted with conventional warfare which involved the coordinated employment of major units and fire support resources, he was at a loss. He could have overcome this shortcoming if he had practiced all he had learned and been taught in school, especially modern warfare tactics and principles of leadership, but he had failed to remember his teachings.

His major failure was to overburden the 3rd Division with a span of control so large that it was impossible for the division commander to exercise command effectively. With nine brigades, the division had virtually become a corps, and under these circumstances I Corps should have established additional divisional control headquarters by utilizing, for example, the Marine Division Tactical CP and the Ranger Tactical CP. When initiating his counterattack in April, the I Corps commander also failed to follow up and take appropriate action when units under the 3rd Division procrastinated. This inertia obviously resulted from the lack of positive leadership and combat fatigue, which could have been remedied by a rotation of units. The command and control of the 3rd Division was most difficult when the I Corps commander gave direct orders to the 1st Armor Brigade, maneuvering its units without informing the division commander.

• • •

In general, under the command of General Lam I Corps units seldom received clear-cut orders, nor were they assigned well-defined responsibilities. This could be a result of the I Corps staff's ineffectiveness or its not being properly directed or utilized. In any event, staff coordination was rarely effective when the commander himself was indecisive or failed to take appropriate action when required.

There was also another characteristic about General Lam which should be avoided by leaders at every level. He would not report bad news, or was very slow to do so. When the enemy offensive first started, he failed to report accurately on the DMZ situation, and, as a result, the JGS had no way of knowing that it was a large-scale invasion. As Chief of the JGS, I did not fully grasp the real situation until General Abrams, COMUSMACV, informed me of what was happening.

• • •

Looking back on that difficult period of time, I can now see that it was perhaps unrealistic to expect perfection from a corps commander. The kind of training and experience, the influence of politics on officers of General Lam's generation, and their very background perhaps did not contribute to the cultivation of military leadership required by the circumstances. The very nature of the war, and our tasks at hand, seemed to demand that a corps commander be not only a skilled administrator, a shrewd politician, a leader of men, but also a good field commander well versed in both anti-insurgency and modern warfare tactics and able to employ the vast array of combat support assets in defense as well as in offense. Such omnipotent [*sic*] corps commanders were rare. But rare does not mean that the RVNAF did not have any.

One such corps commander was Lieutenant General Ngo Quang Truong, a career airborne officer who served with the Airborne Division until he became its deputy commander. His combat exploits during this earlier period were many, but what distinguished him most was his innate and unique qualities as a leader of men. I don't think I need to dwell at length on his exploits. . . . Suffice it to say that Truong was one of the best commanders at every echelon the Airborne Division ever had. The only regrettable thing about his early career was that he did not have the opportunity to further his military schooling. Combat duties were so demanding that he hardly had time to attend the advanced courses designed for career officers like himself. However, this lack of advanced training certainly did not affect his military knowledge or professionalism. And he fully proved it when, as I Corps commander, he successfully met the biggest challenge any ARVN field commander ever had to face. Not only did he restore morale and confidence to the troops and population of MR-1, he also quickly stabilized a despondent, chaotic situation and eventually retook that part of MR-1 territory most prized by the enemy. During the counteroffensive he was credited with several tactical initiatives that enabled I Corps forces to neutralize the NVA superiority in strength and artillery and finally destroy even the enemy's will and determination to resist. General Truong's success in accomplishing the almost impossible can be attributed to several factors, but one thing was certain—his outstanding leadership had made him one of the most capable military leaders South Vietnam had ever produced.

Leadership at the Corps Level: II Corps during the Redeployment from Kontum-Pleiku

The redeployment of II Corps forces from the Central Highlands in mid-March 1975 was perhaps a most ignominious example of leadership failure in the history of the RVNAF. It resulted in the tragic loss of this ARVN corps as a major combat force and eventually precipitated the chain of events leading to the final collapse of South Vietnam.

II Corps was under the command of Major General Pham Van Phu, a presidential appointee like other corps commanders. Small and fragile, Phu did not look like a man for sustained or critical actions. His combat record, however, was good. He performed quite well during Lam Son 719 as commander of the 1st Infantry Division. As a junior officer serving in French Union forces, Phu had seen combat action at Dien Bien Phu.

Just four months into his job as II Corps commander, he was about to face the biggest challenge of his military career.

On 14 March [1975], two days after the loss of Ban Me Thuot city, President Thieu summoned General Phu to Cam Ranh for an exclusive meeting. During this meeting, the president ordered him to reoccupy Ban Me Thuot with II Corps forces still available. Since the 23rd Division had been battered during the battle of Ban Me Thuot, and the 22nd Division was engaging the enemy at Binh Khe on Route 19, this implied that, in order to carry out his mission, Phu had to withdraw all of his combat and support units from the Kontum-Pleiku area, bring them down to the coast, and launch a counterattack on Ban Me Thuot from there.

• • •

On the military side, the redeployment operation was deemed a tragic failure. Almost all units withdrawn from the Kontum-Pleiku area incurred losses amounting to 75 percent of their original strength.[7]

• • •

However well justified he was with his concept of tactical surprise, the II Corps commander could not be spared the censure of having failed to establish a detailed plan with his staff and to exercise his direct control over the entire operation. Whatever planning he had done, it was limited, and only a few trusted subordinate commanders had contributed to it and knew about it. Staff work was entirely nonexistent. Colonel Le Khac Ly, the Chief of Staff of II Corps, himself admitted he was totally in the dark.

• • •

The II Corps commander's blind trust in his two trusted subordinates to carry out his orders had been misplaced. The entire redeployment operation lacked unified and effective control from the start. General Tat only looked after his ranger troops. General Cam took no active part in the whole process. His remote supervision was ineffective. The overall control of the movement turned out to be actually exercised by the II Corps Chief of Staff, but only up to Phu Bon, although he had not been given this responsibility. The province chiefs of Phu Bon and Phu Yen had failed to provide road security and protection. They were unable to control their RF and PF units in performing this task. If they had, if the itinerary had been protected, and if river-crossing facilities had been provided in time, the outcome of the redeployment would certainly have been different. But excessive preoccupation with a false sense of secrecy had precluded such vital prearrangements.

• • •

Finally, the failure was also one of leadership at all corps echelons. Troops had not been informed about the operation and what [was] expected of them. Discipline had not been exercised, and constraints had not been imposed in order to avoid disorder and chaos. In particular, they had not been motivated enough to take on the difficult task of destroying enemy blocks, the final obstacles on their way to survival. This failure of leadership had resulted in a rout of strategic proportions. At least 75 percent of II Corps combat strength, to include the 23rd Infantry Division, rangers, armor, artillery, engineer, and signal, had been tragically expended within ten days. The operation intended to reoccupy Ban Me Thuot never materialized, simply because II Corps no longer had any combat troops. And Communist forces had taken the Central Highlands without a fight.

Leadership at the Division Level: The 23rd Division's Defense of Kontum

During the NVA Easter Offensive of 1972 one of the major battles was fought in the Central Highlands of Military Region 2. The enemy had carefully planned and prepared and was determined to seize Kontum City. To meet this challenge, the 23rd ARVN Division was moved during early May approximately 160 kilometers from Ban Me Thuot to Kontum. The division commander, Colonel Ly Tong Ba, was given the mission of assuming command of all ARVN forces in the area and reorganizing them for defense. Even though he was a new and of course inexperienced division commander, occupying the TO&E position of a major general, Colonel Ba demonstrated outstanding leadership ability during a most critical period.

• • •

At this time the 23rd Division was still untried in large-scale combat and had yet to show that it was superior to its vanquished sister, the 22nd Division, which had been soundly defeated during the Dak To–Tan Canh battle just three weeks earlier. But the division commander seemed to make a big difference. Colonel Ba personally inspected the defense perimeter with his staff, encouraged and provided guidance for his troops on tactical details, and demonstrated great care for them. The defense, fire support, and counterattack plans were coordinated and rehearsed daily, drawing from the painful lessons learned by the 22nd Division. All units were given the opportunity to practice-fire the LAW antitank rocket until their troops became confident. More importantly, Colonel Ba's daily round of visits to his units greatly inspired his subordinates, stimulated his commanders, and instilled self-assurance among divisional troops.

Finally, in the early morning of 14 May, the enemy began his attack on Kontum. But the defending forces had been alerted since midnight and were ready.

• • •

Despite its combined force, this initial attack was quickly broken up after several leading enemy tanks were disabled by our artillery, LAW [rockets,] and TOW missiles. The reactions of friendly forces had been quick, decisive, and successful, and the support of tactical air and gunships most effective. ARVN armored elements, although at greatly reduced strength and purposely kept in reserve, had quickly maneuvered to fill in gaps in the defense perimeter.

• • •

The enemy's continued attrition by airstrikes and gunships finally allowed ARVN forces to counterattack and regain the initiative. To dislodge the enemy, they had to resort to bunker-to-bunker fighting and hand grenades. Shortly before noon on 30 May, ARVN forces had regained control of the entire hospital complex, and, although there still remained other scattered pockets of resistance in the northeastern area, the city was clearly out of danger. In the afternoon, President Nguyen Van Thieu flew into Kontum City, despite sporadic rocket and mortar fire. He praised the endurance and fighting spirit of all ARVN forces defending the city and, there on the battlefield, he pinned the brigadier general star on Colonel Ly Tong Ba, the defender of Kontum, for "special frontline merits."

Then, slowly but surely, during the remainder of the day all the enemy positions were taken back. By midday of 31 May, the battle was practically over, since NVA main forces had retreated. Thousands of NVA bodies lay scattered over the battlefield with dozens of T-54 tanks, some intact, but most reduced to charred hulks awkwardly perched among ruins. The enemy's final attempt to take Kontum had ended in utter defeat.

During the battle of Kontum, the 23rd Division commander had proved to be a resourceful commander and fine troop leader. Realizing that unity of command was essential for his task, he had asked for his own regiments to be brought into Kontum to replace the ranger groups. This greatly facilitated his exercise of command and control. Then he provided detailed guidance for his regimental commanders on defense and counterattack plans and ensured that divisional troops practiced the effective use of anti-tank weapons. His daily rounds of visits to all defending units were also an important factor that contributed to the high combat spirit of his troops. After the enemy's first attack, the 23rd Division commander had the good initiative to reduce and consolidate the city's defense perimeter, although the enemy had been driven back. The enemy had several times attempted to break through this perimeter, but failed because Colonel Ba skillfully used and personally commanded his armor and infantry reserve forces to counterattack and effectively seal the breaches. He again proved to be resourceful when he decided to further reduce the defense perimeter after the second attack, when the situation had become critical. But, most importantly, he had fought hand-in-hand with his troops and shared dangers and difficulties with them. His fine and strong leadership made it possible for the 23rd Division to hold and win the final battle for Kontum.

The Leadership of the Province Chiefs of Binh Dinh, Thua Thien, and Khanh Hoa

The years 1969, 1970, and 1971 were the best years for South Vietnam during President Thieu's administration. The country was not only militarily secure, it was well on its way toward full-scale development as a result of spectacular achievements in pacification. This was the main reason why the GVN embarked on an ambitious four-year plan, beginning in 1972, setting high goals for community defense and local development.

The success of pacification during this period naturally depended on province chiefs, most of whom were also military officers. With a few exceptions, they had contributed a great deal to this success. One reason for this was their high caliber, the result of careful selection.

The position of province chief was unique among the assignments that a field-grade officer might have during his career. It was also a unique challenge that taxed his leadership to the extreme of its requirements. Because of the dual aspect of the war, a province chief had to be first and foremost a good tactical commander, well versed not only in counterinsurgency tactics but also in modern warfare. More often than not, he was required to participate in combined operations with major ARVN and US units, and to earn the respect of these units' commanders he had to show he was an equal. The command and control of RF and PF units in a province was not an easy exercise. Not only were they scattered throughout the province, [but] their aggregated strength sometimes exceeded that of an infantry division.

To govern a province effectively, a province chief had to be an able administrator also. He had to supervise a large bureaucracy, prepare and execute the provincial budget, regulate trade and commerce, and protect national resources under his custody. With the advent of pacification, he had to plan for and meet the objectives set forth for security and development, and this required his involvement in countless programs and projects whose implementation needed his constant supervision and guidance. Toward the people he governed, a province chief had to show he was a sensitive leader who listened to their demands and grievances, cared for their lives and welfare, and responded to their aspirations.

Finally, in the exercise of his duties a province chief was usually required to be a public relations man and a politician. He had to receive guests, brief visitors, and escort dignitaries on tours. He had to juggle among political factions and endeavor not to antagonize any. Whatever his creed, he had to show equal regard for all religious groups and sects, whether they be Roman Catholics, Protestants, Buddhists, Cao Dai, or Hoa Hao. In brief, a province chief had to be many things combined in one.

As a result, the province chief was overburdened by his responsibilities. No matter how devoted he was, he simply could not perform all of his duties effectively. So large were the province chief's responsibilities that many had suggested that they be divided between a province chief, who would be solely in charge of administration and development, and a sector commander who would be responsible for security and operational matters. Perhaps this arrangement would have been more responsive to the dual nature of the war.

The three examples that I have selected emphasize a simple fact of life, that if there are good men there are also bad ones, and this is also true of South Vietnamese province chiefs. But, by and large, the military officers who also served as province chiefs had acquitted themselves [in] their role in a most commendable way.

The first example involves a lieutenant colonel in the J-5 Division of the JGS. As a plans officer he proved to be an excellent staff officer. With an analytical mind and a talent for organization, he performed his staff duties extremely well. He was also combat experienced, having served successfully as chief of staff of Thua Thien sector and chief of staff of an infantry regiment. So, when he was appointed province chief of Binh Dinh, everybody expected that he would be a successful one by virtue of his ability and experience.

Binh Dinh was one of the most difficult provinces of MR-2. The enemy pressure here was strong, and the majority of the local population had been subjected to Communist influence for a long time. But the provincial territorial forces under the province chief's control were also strong; there were in fact more RF and PF units here than in any other province. During the first few months in office this officer did quite well. Subsequently, however, there arose charges that he allowed his wife to run a gambling den and favored his relatives with many commercial and business privileges, to the detriment of local businessmen. There were also reports of selling and buying lucrative positions in the provincial military and administrative systems.

These abuses of power were investigated by the GVN Office of Control and Supervision. The colonel was removed from office pending investigation and possible prosecution. Subsequently his promotion was delayed for several years, and he was finally assigned to an immaterial job in MR-4. This was a typical example of a capable military officer who would otherwise have succeeded in his duties of province chief had he not been tempted by money and material rewards. This type of weakness in character was often impossible to detect during the selection process for responsible positions.

Not all province chiefs were corrupt, however. There were many who distinguished themselves, not only by their integrity but also by their devotedness and fine performance. One among them was Colonel Le Van Than, province chief of Thua Thien and mayor of Hue city, who once served as deputy director of the Joint Operations Center, JGS. At first he had a special challenge, since he was a native of North Vietnam and not expected by some to fit well into a slot usually earmarked for natives of Central Vietnam. But Colonel Than proved to be an exception to this rule, and he became one of our finest and most successful province chiefs. A resourceful, hardworking, and highly devoted officer, he learned very quickly the intricacies of local politics and managed to carry out his duties with distinction without offending any political faction.

That he succeeded where others might have failed could be attributed to his adroitness and flexibility, the qualities found only in a shrewd politician. But he was also an excellent tactical commander. . . . In close cooperation with the US 101st Airborne Division and ARVN units, Colonel Than greatly improved security in his province and achieved outstanding results in pacification and development. Because of his distinguished service, he was subsequently placed in command of the 1st ARVN Division and promoted to brigadier general.

Many other province chiefs were less successful than Colonel Than. In fact, several among them produced only medium results in their jobs; for example, Lieutenant Colonel Le Khanh, province chief of Khanh Hoa. Originally a Special Forces officer, Colonel Khanh was a man of tact and gentle manners. Perhaps because of this, he remained province chief for several years. His performance was just about average, and he served without distinction, although Khanh Hoa was a relatively secure province compared to others. Despite this, he continued his career as province chief for several more years, being subsequently nominated province chief of Kien Tuong and then Kien Giang. People said he was a man of luck. In retrospect, however, it is clearly obvious that Colonel Khanh was completely loyal to his superiors, dependable, conscientious, and devoted in the performance of his duties, but did not possess the strong leadership ability required for the more critical areas of South Vietnam.

• • •

V. SUMMARY AND CONCLUSIONS

Military leadership was not a continuous Vietnamese tradition. Interrupted and lost during the century of French domination, this tradition was not born again until we regained our national independence.

Traditional Vietnamese society under French colonialism regarded the military as a lowly profession which it associated with servility and collaborationism. As a menial group serving the occupation forces, the Vietnamese military did not even count as a social class; they were the outcast[s] of society. This contempt for the military, which reflected the passive opposition of the Vietnamese people toward French rule, still lingered until the Vietnamese National Army was formed in 1950. Even Bao Dai meekly admitted this as a fact.

The French presence, therefore, not only served to perpetuate this negative attitude, it also accounted for the complete void in military leadership upon their departure. This was a legacy whose consequences South Vietnam had to bear during its formative years. And the product of that legacy—the infant Vietnamese Armed Forces—grew up and matured only after severing all ties with it.

• • •

High-ranking Vietnamese officers who served in key staff and command positions were all graduates of French military schools or reassigned from French Union forces. Several among them even had French nationality and comported themselves in the manner of French colonels from whom they inherited the major traits of leadership: haughtiness, authoritativeness [sic], and lack of empathy.

But it was during this period that a new generation of Vietnamese officers was born. Those were the graduates of the first classes of reserve officer schools, Nam Dinh and Thu Duc, and the Dalat Inter-Arms Military School. They were to become the backbone of military leadership in the RVNAF. In fact, most of the high-level commanders discussed in the examples, and Thieu and Ky, belonged to this group. The most distinctive traits that set this emerging generation of leaders apart from their predecessors were strong anti-French feelings, political awareness, and dedication to the national cause.

• • •

Military authority . . . was concentrated in the presidency despite the existence of the Joint General Staff. The president exercised this authority either directly or through the Ministry of Defense. Promotions and appointments, especially to key command positions, all came from the palace. As the regime sought to consolidate itself through a monolithic political party, cronyism became the practice of personnel selection, which was based not so much on professional competence as on personal loyalty and political affiliation. Cronyism eventually turned the most trusted but less competent officers of the regime into courtiers who fawned their way up the military hierarchy and created dissension among the RVNAF ranks.

For all its flaws, the Diem administration must be credited with strong national leadership and laudable achievements. It restored national authority, developed the economy, reorganized the armed forces, and turned South Vietnam into a nation of world stature in Southeast Asia. To combat Communist insurgency activities, which increasingly threatened the nation's survival [after] 1959, the GVN instituted an antithetic national ideology culminating in the Strategic Hamlet program. Despite criticisms and excesses, this strategic concept was sound enough to provide the foundation for pacification and development in the years ahead.

As an individual, President Diem was widely recognized as a deeply patriotic, highly ethical, honest, and rather austere national leader who abhorred luxury and devoted all of his time and energy to state affairs. The "éminence grise" of the regime, however, was his younger brother, Mr. Nhu. A silent and meditative scholar, Mr. Nhu distinguished himself by his vast knowledge, sharp intelligence, and innovative ideas. He helped President Diem overcome serious challenges and solve thorny problems of national importance. He was consulted on every aspect of government, and no important decision was ever made without his participation. His influence was such that all cabinet ministers sought his guidance before taking action. It was also Mr. Nhu who gave birth to personalism and the Strategic Hamlet program. During indoctrination sessions, he gave lectures to cabinet ministers and high-ranking military and civilian officials on subjects relating to strategy and even tactics. With the death of the Ngo brothers, South Vietnam had lost two prominent leaders whose stature and capabilities had enabled the nation to face its Communist foes with self-assurance.

But, because of their towering authority, military leadership in the RVNAF had no chance to develop, especially at the higher levels. The military situation also posed no major challenges as the RVNAF devoted all their efforts to reorganization and training. The RVNAF commanders, therefore, did not have good opportunities to assert their leadership qualities and talents.

The period of the National Leadership Committee can be viewed as a period of crisis in leadership. The death of President Diem resulted in such a void in leadership that no one among the victorious generals could take his place. National leadership, therefore, broke down into factions that fought among themselves for ascendancy. The crisis was resolved by instituting collective leadership and a division of power and authority among the generals. But this seemed to satisfy no one, especially the more ambitious. Furthermore, collective leadership weakened the RVNAF command and control, and for some time confusion reigned throughout the military hierarchy, because no military commander was sure to whom he could give orders and from whom he would take orders.

• • •

The Second Republic was a period of big challenges that thoroughly tested both national and military leadership. The advent of elective democracy removed politics from the RVNAF and strengthened military command and control. Therefore, despite an inflationary economy, social vices, and internal dissent, the period saw the emergence of aggressive and strong military leadership from corps down to small units. This leadership seemed to grow and mature professionally despite great adversity. Throughout the major challenges they had to face, RVNAF commanders successfully carried out increasingly difficult tasks in a most commendable manner.

• • •

The RVNAF leadership . . . proved it had come of age, especially during the 1970 Cambodian incursion, the first major test of Vietnamization. Strong and dedicated leadership enabled III and IV Corps to achieve great success during the operation and set an example in which the RVNAF could take pride. It was only unfortunate that such excellent leaders as Generals Tri and Thanh had found their promising careers cut short by accidental death. I Corps, however, fared less well during the cross-border operation into lower Laos. The apparent lack of strong leadership deprived this major ARVN command of a chance to prove its full capabilities.

The same lack of strong and effective leadership led to the initial setback of I Corps during the 1972 Easter Offensive. Had I Corps had a better arrangement for command and control, perhaps Quang Tri would not have been lost despite the ferocity of enemy attacks. The example I have provided concerning I Corps during its counteroffensive amply proves that leadership did make a difference. Why else would a corps commander succeed where another had failed if not because of superior leadership? But men like General Truong were rather the exception among ARVN commanders. In fact, during its entire existence, South Vietnam did not produce very many leaders like him. I believe that, if II Corps had been led by someone like General Truong, perhaps it would not have met with such a tragic fate at the time of its redeployment during the final enemy offensive in 1975.

As a challenge to RVNAF leadership, the 1972 offensive also provided the opportunity for other commanders to prove their talents. An Loc had held against extreme odds, partly due to US air support, but also because its commander refused to yield to overwhelming pressure. And this inspired his men to fight on despite privations and hardship. Kontum was another example of resourceful and dedicated leadership at the division level. The merit of its successful defender lay in the fact that he was an aggressive commander who knew how to use his resources and trained his subordinates well.

The cease-fire agreement of January 1973 ushered South Vietnam into an unfavorable situation which demanded flexibility and resourcefulness in dealing with an archenemy. But the RVN leadership failed to come to grips with reality and maintained a position which proved untenable as soon as US military aid was cut back. During this period the RVNAF overextended themselves and found it hard to counter intensifying enemy violations effectively without US support. In spite of their dedication, ARVN commanders felt less self-assured in the absence of US advisors and support. The prevailing mood was one of uncertainty and false hope in the face of mounting enemy buildup.

Internal dissension and growing demands for the elimination of corruption cornered

President Thieu into removing some of the better field commanders and replacing them with those of dubious courage and dedication. The choice he made was indeed a hard one and perhaps against his will. It proved disastrous in mid-March 1975 when a troop redeployment of strategic proportions, on which he had relied to save the situation, ended in failure because of poor and unreliable leadership. The ensuing collapse of South Vietnam, in the final analysis, was also the accumulated failure of a leadership which did not see for itself all the implications of changing policies and take action in time.

In retrospect, we have to admit that, despite this failure, both the national and military leadership of South Vietnam did make serious efforts in the performance of their roles. But these efforts were impeded, not only by the debilitating effect of a protracted war and a divisive society, but also by certain external factors beyond their control. To survive, the nation certainly needed unlimited resources and superior leadership. Unfortunately, the ill fate of South Vietnam had wanted [sic] that it should have neither.

Of the flaws and vulnerabilities that military leadership in the RVNAF might have demonstrated, the most detrimental were perhaps political-mindedness and corruption. The November coup of 1963 had changed military leadership so completely that the RVNAF were never the same again. Its effect could still be felt even after elective democracy had been institutionalized. Politics had been so ingrained among senior commanders that it was impossible for them to relinquish it and return to military professionalism. The Thieu regime, in fact, feared not so much the enemy from the outside as those who had once been partners and comrades-in-arms. And that explained why, one by one, the politically ambitious ones had to go, but potential rivalry still persisted.

As to corruption, although it was not directly accountable for the collapse of the nation, its effect certainly debilitated professional competency and, by extension, the war effort. The regime eventually accepted corruption as an inevitable vice because, as Vice President Huong had tragically admitted, "we would be left with practically no one to fight the war if all corrupt commanders were to be prosecuted and relieved."

• • •

During the decade I served as chairman of the RVNAF Joint General Staff, I had witnessed all the successes and failures of our leadership. Even though this leadership had done its best, it still proved inadequate for this most difficult period of our nation's history. And this explains to some extent the final failure of South Vietnam. Perhaps the survival of our nation would have required someone like a latter-day Tran Hung Dao or Nguyen Hue. The lack of such outstanding leadership indicates how destructive the long war had been in its heavy toll [on] young and promising leaders, and how ravaging the French repressions against Vietnamese nationalists.

That one generation of leaders had failed does not necessarily mean that the way to success had been irretrievably blocked. Looking ahead into the future, there seems to be less cause for pessimism and despair. According to press reports and refugee accounts, the armed resistance against the new Communist regime in South Vietnam is gaining momentum. Although it is a long and uphill struggle, the resistance has earned the respect and admiration of all Vietnamese living in exile. But, for this armed struggle to succeed, there is an obvious and urgent need for outside assistance and support in every aspect, in addition to the resistance movement's efforts to survive, fight, and expand on its own. Whoever the leaders of that movement may be, they certainly represent a new generation of emergent leadership of unprecedented self-abnegation, sacrifice, and devotion. From the lessons learned during the lost war, and with support from the outside, this emergent leadership has all the chances to succeed where the old one had failed. In this perspective, perhaps the resistance is not a utopia at all, despite some arguments to the contrary.

I conclude this monograph on a note of hope and with prayers for the reemergence of a free South Vietnam in the not too distant future, a South Vietnam led by men of talent and high morals—the truly great leaders of Vietnamese history.

NOTES

1. Joseph Buttinger, *Vietnam: A Dragon Embattled* (New York: Praeger, 1967), pp. 852–853.

2. Vietnamese officers jokingly called this the "Three-D system": Dao (religion), Du (obscene word used by natives of Central Vietnam), and Dang (party).

3. New Life, or Tan Sinh, was the new name used for the former strategic hamlets. The basic concept and organization of the system remained unchanged.

4. Members of the National Leadership Committee or Directorate included: chairman: Lieutenant General Nguyen Van Thieu; deputy: Air Marshal Nguyen Cao Ky; secretary general: Lieutenant General Pham Xuan Chieu; members: Lieutenant General Nguyen Huu Co, General Cao Van Vien, and the four corps commanders.

5. Mandatory military service was subsequently increased to three years for enlisted men and four years for officers and NCOs.

6. In terms of military professionalism, both Generals Nghi and Toan were good field commanders. General Nghi, in particular, excelled in staff work and exercised his command duties with methodical and calculated care. In March 1975, when serving as commandant of the Infantry School, he volunteered to assist the III Corps commander in defending the southern provinces of MR-2. As for General Toan, he was appointed to replace General Ngo Dzu as II Corps commander at a time when MR-2 was heavily threatened by the enemy's 1972 Easter Offensive. He succeeded in defeating the enemy offensive in the Central Highlands and improving the situation in MR-2 thereafter. Subsequently serving as Armor commander and III Corps commander, General Toan was a courageous and professionally competent commander.

7. According to an estimate by the II Corps Chief of Staff, Colonel Le Khac Ly, 5,000 out of 20,000 logistic and support troops were finally retrieved.

7

Intelligence

Colonel Hoang Ngoc Lung

PREFACE

The war in Vietnam was often called an intelligence war. The challenges and responsibilities placed on the South Vietnam–United States–Free World intelligence community were great and constant.

During this long war the entire intelligence program improved each day as our data base expanded, as more was learned about the elusive enemy, personnel were trained, and new procedures and techniques were tested and found effective.

The most rewarding experience in intelligence activities during the Vietnam War was the very close cooperation and coordination between American and Vietnamese military intelligence personnel and systems. It was this cooperation that helped RVNAF military intelligence upgrade and become self-reliant during the post-cease-fire period.

This monograph attempts to record all the facts concerning intelligence activities, its organizations and coordination procedures, its successes and failures during the period from 1965 to the final days of the Republic of Vietnam. In this attempt, one of the difficulties I faced was the lack of documentation to make my work more accurate and more substantial. To overcome this shortcoming, I have interviewed several former colleagues of mine, American and Vietnamese, all of them highly experienced with intelligence activities in Vietnam. Apart from their invaluable contributions, most of the writing is based on my personal knowledge and experience.

I am indebted to General Cao Van Vien, Chairman of the Joint General Staff, Lieutenant General Dong Van Khuyen, Chief of Staff—under whom I served several years as Assistant Chief of Staff J-2/JGS—and Brigadier General Tranh Dinh Tho, Assistant Chief of Staff J-3/JGS, for their valuable comments. Lieutenant General Ngo Quang Truong, Commanding General of I Corps, and Major General Nguyen Duy Hinh, Commander of the 3rd Infantry Division, contributed thoughtful remarks and the practical view of field commanders. [31 October 1976]

I. INTRODUCTION

During the Vietnam War, there was a constant improvement of intelligence as each day passed. It is usually recognized that during the final years of cooperation between the Republic of Vietnam and United States combat forces, the commanders at most echelons were better informed about the enemy than in any war in the histories of these two nations.

This was made possible because of the close coordination and cooperation between RVN and US military intelligence personnel and activities. This cooperation of joint planning, execution, and exchange of information was essential because the RVN and the United States were faced with an elusive enemy who, justifiably enough, earned such rhetorical qualifications as "unknown" or "mythical." Knowledge about the enemy, as we confronted him in Vietnam, was not an easy proposition. But it was not an unattainable goal, nor did it elude our success altogether.

• • •

Role of Intelligence in the Vietnam War

The US intelligence apparatus in Vietnam was part of and within the framework of the total US intelligence establishment. Thus it relied primarily on advancements in science and technology. It reflected the characteristics of a great power which could afford a multiplicity of big organizations, each having its own collection apparatus and often competing with one another in collection, analysis, and production of knowledge about the enemy. The contributions made by US intelligence, particularly in collection, were so effective that they created an abnormal reliance on US intelligence. The reliance was so great that many Vietnamese officials, including some military commanders, took it for granted that every piece of information coming from an American agency was valid regardless of the professional competence of the reporter or the authority of the source. Others even believed that no enemy move or scheme could ever go undetected by US collection networks and that if it did it was only because the United States, for political reasons, wanted it to happen that way.

• • •

The first coherent South Vietnamese military intelligence organization was the J-2 element of the General Staff, with 32 men commanded by a Vietnamese captain. The Military Security Service (counterintelligence), activated at about the same time, was commanded by a Vietnamese major. In early 1953, a counterintelligence element was added to the General Staff as a separate staff component designated J-6. By July 1955, the authorized strength of J-2, General Staff, had been augmented to 46 with the activation of the Imagery Interpretation Center. But, up until the day the Geneva Accords were signed in 1954, South Vietnamese military intelligence activities were performed by the French forces' "Deuxieme Bureau," which functioned as a separate organization and acted on its own initiative. Unfortunately, but characteristically, when the French forces withdrew from Vietnam they took with them all their experience and systems of collection as well as their intelligence files.

The Vietnamese officers who manned the J-2 section of the General Staff at that time were not career intelligence men. Only a handful of them had taken a basic, battalion-level intelligence course conducted by a French officer at the Thu Duc Reserve Officer School. As required by the activation of new units, or the upgrading of existing ones, there was an urgent need to train intelligence officers.

• • •

From 1954 to 1963, military intelligence efforts were largely oriented toward collecting domestic political intelligence. It was the period of political turmoil during which leaders of the First Republic were faced with armed rebellions of religious sects in 1955–1956 and later with the Buddhist opposition movement in 1963. The South Vietnamese intelligence structure during that time was an agglomeration of separate agencies each directly or indirectly controlled by the presidency, but all serving the same political goal of consolidating the new regime. Under the presidency, the Social and Political Studies Service was responsible for domestic political intelligence collection, while the Liaison Service was charged with foreign intelligence, directed primarily toward North Vietnam and, later on, with security protection for the president and his closest advisors, Mr. and Mrs. Ngo Dinh Nhu. When the Buddhist opposition movement reached its climax in 1963 with the active participation of students, all intelligence agencies, both on the civilian side and the military side, focused their activities on gathering domestic political information. The J-2 of the Joint General Staff thus found himself performing a task [which] went beyond his intended mission and authority.

The November Revolution of 1963 brought about a complete reversal of the process of decentralizing the intelligence structure and making its constituent organizations separate and responsible to various authorities. Thus, from a situation of complete centralization in the office of the presidency, the national organization for intelligence went to the opposite extreme.

• • •

The domestic political situation made its impact on military intelligence. Lacking centralization and unified guidance, intelligence efforts became diffused and of little value. Adding to the problems, during this embryonic stage intelligence facilities were woefully inadequate and intelligence personnel still lacked technical know-how and professional experience. The military intelligence organizations operated independently of each other and the collection effort was limited geographically to South Vietnam. Intelligence pertaining to North Vietnam or eastern Laos was produced only occasionally and did not constitute a systematic effort under centralized planning and direction.

• • •

South Vietnamese military intelligence came of age in 1965 when, as a result of the increased tempo of war, the national leadership began to appreciate its importance. The active participation of US forces in the war brought about close intelligence coordination with RVN forces, and it was this coordination that gave the greatest impetus to

Vietnamese military intelligence. The most remarkable progress was achieved in combat intelligence. A tremendous amount of information was collected about the enemy.

• • •

Denied the capability to collect adequate information about the enemy outside South Vietnam and forced by internal political circumstances to operate a fragmented intelligence apparatus, South Vietnam intelligence agencies were ill equipped to perform their crucial tasks. In fact one might wonder, as in the other aspects of the war, whether internal rather than external factors most influenced the course of the war and brought about its tragic conclusion.

II. INTELLIGENCE, CULTURE, AND LANGUAGE

• • •

Language, Translation, and Cultural Interpretation

• • •

The most important feature of the Vietnam War is that it was a conflict between North Vietnam and South Vietnam, [and] hence a civil war in some of its aspects. What people usually failed to recognize or took rather lightly was the deep-seated cultural and linguistic difference between the warring adversaries, and this was precisely what caused so many failures and setbacks. A Communist plan of attack which was coordinated with actions by traitors within our ranks was defeated simply because of the difference in launching time. The Communist planners apparently failed to realize that their own official time, aligned on Hanoi time, was one hour later than Saigon time. When the traitors starting firing one hour too soon, they exposed themselves and were all arrested. The attack from the outside never materialized because of this initial setback.

Another case of failure occurred when a Communist cadre was arrested while visiting his family, who lived in a government-controlled rural area. To neighbors who dropped in to see him, he was introduced by his parents as a city-dwelling visitor. While they were chatting, a jet fighter happened to fly by at low altitude and creat[ed] supersonic booms. Through conditioned reflex the Communist cadre sought cover by crawling under the bed. This took everybody present aback. He had unknowingly given himself away simply by failing to adapt to a new cultural environment.

When they chose the Tet holidays to launch their 1968 general offensive campaign, the Communists were primarily interested in its surprise and totally disregarded its adverse psychological effect. This was understandable, because to North Vietnam Tet was merely a custom that needed to be changed because it was both the manifestation of a feudalistic heritage and an occasion for wasteful, luxurious spending. Accordingly, the traditional importance of Tet in North Vietnam was downplayed by Communist authorities. But to South Vietnam, which revered traditions, Tet was as sacred as always because people regarded Tet less as a celebration than a spiritual tie between man and the universe, between the living and the dead, and also between the living people themselves. As a result, the South Vietnamese troops were angrily determined to eliminate the violators of sacred Tet and, in the aftermath of the offensive, recruiting was never so successful.

South Vietnam's basic weakness in the war was taking too lightly the enemy's will to carry out his plans. We tended to liken our adversaries to ourselves and assess them according to our subjective thinking. For example, if a Communist plan was disclosed, we usually believed that our enemy would discard it, since we always considered everything that had been leaked as too risky. But, to the Communists, it was not always so, because their goal always outweighed the risks to be incurred, and, if the political requirement so dictated, a plan once worked out was usually implemented regardless of the risks caused by disclosure.

• • •

III. REPUBLIC OF VIETNAM AND US INTELLIGENCE ORGANIZATIONS IN SOUTH VIETNAM

The RVN National and Local Intelligence Coordination Committees

Robert Thompson, a Vietnam specialist, wrote that in 1966, in Saigon, he had been able to identify 17 different US and Republic of Vietnam intelligence agencies.[1] He did not name them. However, if we were to take into account all intelligence agencies in the entire Republic, Vietnamese agencies alone actually exceeded this number but fluctuated with time. As of 1965, on the civilian side, there were at one time or another:

1. The Central Intelligence Office (CIO).
2. The National Police (NP).
3. The Directorate of North Vietnamese Affairs of the Office of the Chairman, Central Executive Committee.
4. The Intelligence Directorate of the Ministry of Foreign Affairs.[2]
5. The Directorate General of Administrative Security.
6. The Rural Development (RD) cadre group.
7. The Civil Affairs cadre group.
8. Armed propaganda teams of the Chieu Hoi (Open Arms) Ministry.
9. Census and grievance teams.

Military intelligence agencies included the following:

1. The Military Security Directorate (better known as MSS).
2. J-7 of the Joint General Staff (J-7/JGS).
3. The Strategic Technical Directorate (STRATDAT).
4. The Liaison Service.

5. The Research and Documentation Office of the National Defense Ministry.
6. G-2, Special Forces.
7. The Intelligence Directorate of the General Political Warfare Department.
8. J-2/JGS, and subordinate service intelligence staff and units such as A-2 of the Vietnam Air Force (A-2/VNAF); N-2 of the Vietnam Navy (VNN); Special Collection Detachment/VNAF; Special Collection Detachment/VNN (Unit 701); G-2s of Army corps, infantry divisions, and general reserve divisions; corps and division military intelligence detachments; division long-range reconnaissance companies; S-2s of sectors and subsectors with their respective intelligence/security platoons and squads; and the 924th Support Group, J-2/JGS (later renamed Unit 101).

There were also two kinds of Vietnamese intelligence units which came under direct US operational control: the Provincial Reconnaissance Units (PRU) and the Kit Carson Scouts (units made up of Communist defectors).[3]

Though some of the intelligence organizations were later disbanded (North Vietnamese Affairs Directorate, civil affairs cadre, G-2/Special Forces) or merged (the Liaison Service became subordinated to STRATDAT) or disappeared with the withdrawal of US forces (Kit Carson Scouts), there remained a significant number of them.

• • •

Nevertheless, in 1967 it was realized for the first time that intelligence in Vietnam focused solely on enemy military forces and ignored a no less important force, the Communist political force, also known as Viet Cong infrastructure (VCI). As a result, a new effort was initiated on a national scale to root out the VCI, and the NP was allowed to expand in order to cope with this extensive task.

The need for a concerted intelligence effort led to the establishment of the Phoenix program in 1968 (Decree 280a/TT/SL, 1 July 1968). This program, originally being an American idea endorsed by the GVN, was administered through existing Provincial and District Intelligence and Operations Coordination Committees (PIOCC and DIOCC, respectively). The Phoenix program sought further coordination than was effected at the old intelligence coordination committees. It provided for coordination between intelligence and tactical operations with the aim of permitting immediate tactical response that would lead to destruction of the VCI.

Many government officials felt that this program, though upgraded to a national policy and enjoying total US support from its inception to cease-fire day, did not live up to expectations. In organization the program's shortcoming was that, while theoretically the concept of entrusting eradication of the VCI to police forces was sound, in reality police personnel in charge of the program at provincial and district levels did not have the qualifications, prestige, or experience for such an assignment. Chiefs of NP services and subservices were all fresh out of training. They were second lieutenants at provincial level and noncommissioned officers at district level, while their counterparts in military intelligence or military security were captains or first lieutenants at provincial level and warrant officers or second lieutenants at district level. The military officers were also better qualified and more experienced than their police counterparts.

• • •

When the NP became a command in 1971 and its strength was increased to 121,000, it filled 13,000 slots with Republic of Vietnam Armed Forces (RVNAF) personnel who had volunteered to transfer to police status. A number of high-ranking military intelligence and military security officers were also detached to the NP Command to take over key positions and facilitate coordination between this civilian authority and the armed forces. This greatly enhanced the spirit of cooperation between the civilians and the armed forces on the one hand and improved the NP collection capabilities on the other.

In summary, having numerous intelligence agencies does not necessarily guarantee good intelligence. It has been known to produce adverse results.

• • •

Vietnamese intelligence agencies which operated jointly with US intelligence organizations were somewhat influenced by the latter. US military intelligence includes intelligence agencies of the Army, Air Force, Navy, and Marine Corps. These agencies are independent from one another. This was not feasible in the RVNAF because [the] VNAF and VNN were but small services. Because they were directly supported by their US counterpart agencies and were able to observe the independence enjoyed by the latter, A-2/VNAF and N-2/VNN during 1965–1967 wanted to demonstrate their own independence from other Vietnamese services by having their own concepts of organization and operations, their own training programs, their own collection plans and operations, etc.

The organizational concept as applied to Vietnamese intelligence reflected an indiscriminate combination of US, French, and Chinese concepts, whereas only the strong points of each system should have been selected and reconciled with the others in keeping with the context of the Vietnam situation. This would have been the best way to arrive at an appropriate organizational concept.

• • •

Vietnamese Civilian Intelligence Agencies

THE CENTRAL INTELLIGENCE OFFICE

The CIO was established in May 1961. It was given authority to control and coordinate the operation of intelligence organizations in the country to ensure that requirements for intelligence of national scope would be adequately met.[4] This included military and nonmilitary organizations, as well as the NP. It had by then become evident that the various intelligence agencies in Vietnam were too self-centered and no agency had access to another's resources. The stated objectives of the CIO were never reached because of the ever-changing internal political situation and the complex nature of the intelligence agencies involved.

• • •

The foreign intelligence division operated numerous stations. These stations were the eyes and ears of the CIO in foreign countries. They collected intelligence on both North Vietnam and South Vietnam. They were positioned in friendly countries where there were reasonable prospects for developing collection activities.

• • •

These stations were not successful in their efforts to collect information on North Vietnam because of tight control exercised by its regime over activities of overseas Vietnamese visiting home. Personnel of the embassies of East European countries, some of them indirect CIO sources, were subjected to similar controls in North Vietnam.

At home, the CIO's primary effort was counterespionage. Counterespionage by the CIO differed from counterespionage by the NP or MSS in scope, nature, and sensitivity, and mostly involved cases over which neither of the latter two had jurisdiction. Those were cases involving constitutional institutions like the Upper House and Lower House of the National Assembly, the Inspectorate, and the Supreme Court; executive institutions like the Office of the President and the Office of the Premier; or influential personalities of domestic political movements and parties.

• • •

The interrogation division of the CIO worked with sources of information considered to be of a strategic nature, politically and militarily. In principle, military prisoners of war were first interrogated by military intelligence personnel, then transferred to CIO control upon request by the latter. However, beginning in 1971, the CIO obtained first choice over all sources of strategic intelligence, even if their knowledge was limited to purely military matters. Those selected were evacuated immediately for CIO interrogation, and no military agency, even J-2/JGS, was allowed access to these sources.[5]

• • •

The CIO's real responsibility remained a political one. In particular, it was responsible for ensuring the security of the regime by watching out for plots against it from within or without.

• • •

THE NATIONAL POLICE AND OTHER CIVILIAN AGENCIES

The [Police Special Branch] (PSB) deployed intelligence nets to collect information on the VCI. The Police Field Forces [PFF] conducted raids or operations against VCI personnel or targets identified by the PSB. The PFF also served as a reserve for the NP for intervention where needed, such as to quell antigovernment demonstrations.

• • •

In the fields of intelligence and security, the NP Command was the principal agency responsible for identifying and detaining VCI personnel.

• • •

In its efforts to identify VCI personnel, the NP relied on police-organized informants' nets, information provided by volunteers and by such forces or groups as the Popular Self-Defense Forces (PSDF), information disclosed by VCI prisoners, information acquired from human or document sources by uniformed policy or the PFF, and information received from friendly sources such as civilian groups, rural development cadre, or civil affairs cadre.

• • •

The VCI, already deemed to be a large and effective Communist force which provided supplies, hiding places, guides and propaganda resources, was thought by many to be made up of fanatics with something undefinable in them. In reality, there were two categories: the real VCI personnel imbued with Communist ideology; and those who had been persuaded, bought, or coerced into working for the former. The second category consisted of civilians that were like other civilians except that most of them were indigent. Many became part of the VCI out of greed. For example, they purchased drugs and other necessities in government-controlled areas and resold them to the Communists. Some made a living out of this; others did it because of Communist pressure.

• • •

The VCI suffered a devastating blow in 1968 when its forces came out [into] the open during the Tet general offensive. The resulting losses were such that it never again matched the magnitude and performances of the past.

• • •

Vietnamese Military Intelligence Organizations

When attempting to define responsibility for military intelligence operations in the RVN Armed Forces, attention is always directed at the role of J-2/JGS, thought by many to be the highest authority in military intelligence and enjoying the sole prerogative for planning, coordinating, and controlling all intelligence efforts in the armed forces. Nothing is farther from the truth. This misconception of the role of J-2/JGS apparently derives from knowledge of the organization and mission of the earlier French Deuxieme Bureau and of American military intelligence.

In reality, J-2/JGS was but a military intelligence agency among others. With regard to authority, it was on a par with MSS, J-7/JGS, and STRATDAT. MSS was responsible for counterintelligence (CI), while J-7/JGS was responsible for signal intelligence and communications security.

• • •

The organization of military intelligence in the RVN Armed Forces lacked a principal agency which would normally prepare a common military intelligence plan, establish common intelligence requirements, and act as the only authority responsible for reporting on the enemy situation. The intricacies of internal politics had defeated efforts to unify military intelligence organizations. As a result, coordination and cooperation among these agencies were based on personal concepts and convenience of the agency heads involved rather than on established staff policies.

THE MILITARY SECURITY DEPARTMENT

Contrary to US organizational policies, responsibility for counterintelligence in the Vietnamese armed forces was entrusted to the Military Security Department (better known as Military Security Service, or MSS), not to J-2/JGS. The Republic of China's influence was evident in the subordination of MSS to the General Political Warfare Department (GPWD), which came under JGS. However, this subordination was only theoretical because for all practical purposes the MSS usually reported directly to the president or the premier, from whom it received its directives.

While other Vietnamese intelligence agencies were patterned after US intelligence, the organization of the MSS was entirely the product of self-formulated concepts. Though counterintelligence was its avowed mission, one of the MSS's unofficial but most critical efforts—which was performed only at headquarters level—was to detect and prevent military coups against the regime. With such a politically oriented real mission, MSS was organized to became an agency vested with power, authority, and influence. It was fully funded by the national budget without need for US assistance. MSS was the only military agency empowered to apprehend, detain, and investigate civilians and military personnel alike without due legal process. MSS commented on appointments within the armed forces, granted security clearances, cleared applications for exit visas or overseas training, and was the key member of annual military promotion boards.

• • •

In summary, MSS was well and strongly organized and was able to retain its independence. It was credited with many successful counterintelligence feats. Had all Vietnamese military intelligence agencies been organized like the MSS, military intelligence as a whole would have earned more respect and consideration.

J-7/JGS AND THE SPECIAL TECHNICAL AND SECURITY BRANCH

J-7 was a general staff division of the JGS responsible for planning, supervising, and controlling signal intelligence and communications security activities performed by units and organizations making up the Special Technical and Security Branch. In addition to J-7/JGS, the Special Technical and Security Branch consisted of Unit 15, Unit 16, Unit 17, and field organizations and units such as signal intelligence centers assigned to corps and divisional technical detachments.

The mission of the Special Technical and Security Branch was to collect and produce signal intelligence and communications-electronics intelligence and ensure communications security for the entire RVNAF and certain key governmental agencies.

• • •

Of the four signal intelligence centers, three were established at I, II, and IV Corps Headquarters in Danang, Pleiku, and Can Tho, respectively, and the fourth was established in Saigon to support III Corps. Each center collected information through radio intercept, radio direction finding, and transcribing. To provide support for these centers, there were, in addition, four fixed radio intercept stations located at Phu Bai (MR-1), Song Mao (MR-2), Vung Tau (MR-3), and Con Son Island.

• • •

Signal intelligence centers and divisional technical detachments reported directly to corps and division commanders (or their chiefs of staff), respectively. Their reporting channel did not go through corps or division G-2s. However, copies of their special reports were always made available to G-2. The major shortcoming of this direct reporting system lies in the fact that intelligence data submitted to field commanders were usually raw and not interpreted. This shortcoming became a real danger when communications specialists tried to analyze and interpret data by themselves, as they sometimes did. The Signal Intelligence Center at Danang, for example, once submitted a report predicting that an enemy military "high point" was going to occur at a certain precise date. But the expected event never materialized. An investigation later revealed that a communications specialist had taken the liberty to analyze and interpret the raw data collected all by himself.

• • •

High-frequency radio direction finding was not very effective in Vietnam because the length and narrowness of the country did not lend themselves to accurate cross-bearings. This technique only helped determine target areas for ARDF [airborne radio direction finding].

Airborne communications intercept was performed in conjunction with ground intercept to produce communications intelligence (COMINT) and electronic intelligence (ELINT) data. This technique was very effective in providing accurate and timely information. However, J-7/JGS only had EC-47 aircraft at its service, while US forces used sophisticated aircraft such as C-130F, RC-135, RU-21D, JU-21A, etc.

Information provided by communications intelligence at the beginning of the US direct participation in the Vietnam War enraptured ARVN unit commanders with its accuracy and timeliness.

• • •

Following the 28 January 1973 Paris Agreement, the most significant loss was in ARDF resources, as EC-47 aircraft were unable to operate over areas heavily defended by enemy antiaircraft artillery; they were confined, therefore, to operating over the lowlands and coastal areas. Still, with the expansion of SIGINT and COMINT efforts, signal and communications intelligence contributed substantially to supplementing combat intelligence collected from other sources.

J-2/JGS AND THE RVNAF MILITARY INTELLIGENCE BRANCH

J-2/JGS, as a general staff division of the JGS and command body of the Military Intelligence Branch, was primarily responsible for military intelligence activities in the RVNAF. Its duties were generally limited to combat intelligence, and its span of control confined to South Vietnam.

J-2/JGS exercised no control over foreign intelligence activities, which were performed by Vietnamese military attachés under the direct control of the minister of defense; nor had J-2/JGS any connection with political warfare intelligence activities, which were under direct control of the General Political Warfare Department (GPWD). Since war was the primary national effort, the role of J-2/JGS, and the military intelligence branch by extension, became more and more preeminent over the years. Its position and authority with regard to other intelligence agencies, however, remained unchanged.

• • •

The principal human intelligence (HUMINT) collection agency of J-2/JGS was Unit 101. In addition, the Military Intelligence Center under J-2/JGS control provided technical support in the areas of imagery interpretation, order of battle, targeting, documents, interrogation of prisoners of war and defectors, and exploitation of enemy weapons and equipment.

• • •

Because of the lack of real power over subordinate levels and the lack of a sole-user communications system, intelligence information collected by Vietnamese agencies and units during this period was routed to J-2/JGS through MACV (Military Assistance Command, Vietnam) channels rather than through local communication facilities. Information sent through RVNAF channels came in very late. This situation was gradually improved as more operational responsibilities were shifted to the RVNAF and JGS intelligence support to the local levels became more effective. From the time of the 1972 summer general offensive onward, military intelligence operational activities proved to be very effective and the only obstacles encountered were caused by insufficient resources.

• • •

During the period from 1967 to the cease-fire, J-2/JGS exercised operational control over four combined US-Vietnamese intelligence centers in addition to Unit 101 and the MI Center. Depending on its functions, each staff division of J-2/JGS was responsible for coordinating and supervising the activities of one or many centers and/or agencies.

ARVN COMBAT AND TERRITORIAL
INTELLIGENCE ORGANIZATION

• • •

As an additional tool for intelligence collection, G-2/Division [had] attached a long-range reconnaissance or special reconnaissance company whose main mission was to carry out intelligence plans prepared by G-2. The tactical conduct of these intelligence operations was planned by G-3. Reconnaissance companies received special training at the Ranger Training Center in Duc My and proved to be daring, combat-experienced units. Because of their combat audacity they were gradually used more as a reserve or reaction unit for special combat situations rather than for intelligence-gathering purposes.

Division G-2 was the key level in combat intelligence, constantly monitoring the situation, pressing the units to report and turn in captured documents, new weapons, and preliminary information from interrogation of prisoners of war and defectors. The main obstacle that hampered its effectiveness remained the lack of facilities to ensure expeditious movement of materials from the field to base camp and from there on to corps and above.

• • •

VIETNAMESE AIR FORCE INTELLIGENCE ORGANIZATION

A-2's mission was to collect information on the organization, equipment, and capabilities of the North Vietnamese Air Force, the conditions of airfields in North Vietnam and of those in South Vietnam susceptible to use by the Communists, and North Vietnam's air defense and radar systems. A-2 was also responsible for providing bomb damage assessments (BDA). A-2 had a collection section, a targeting section, an imagery interpretation center, and a special collection detachment.

• • •

The collection section assigned collection missions and monitored the enemy situation nationwide, with special emphasis on locations of friendly airbases and areas of intense enemy air defense activities. The collection section also kept track of the various types of air defense armament used by the enemy, with special priority being given to such weapons as the heat-seeking SA-7 missile.

• • •

The targeting section conducted briefings and debriefings for bombing missions whose targets were designated at the national level, and coordinated with air support squadrons in the conduct of photographic or observation flights.

Once a photo mission was completed, films were delivered to the Imagery Center for processing and interpretation. Results were then forwarded to the users, J-2/JGS, and the air division concerned. This process took three days, and therefore on many occasions results were no longer consistent with tactical developments.

Air reconnaissance support was limited to Military Regions 2, 3, and 4. In MR-1, the highlands of MR-2, and the joint boundary area of MR-2 and MR-3, air reconnaissance support could not be provided due to the intensity of enemy air defenses. As a result, [the] VNAF had to depend on the US "Buffalo Hunter" program for air reconnaissance over these areas.

The Imagery Center was capable of producing selected prints and duplicating positives of aerial photos provided by the USAF as well as making mosaics of photos obtained by VNAF RC-47s, despite the obsolescence of its equipment and the scarcity of print paper. In June 1974, a fire broke out at the center because of deteriorating electrical wiring and its activities were subsequently curtailed.

Because of the extremely limited number of photo reconnaissance aircraft at its disposal (four RF-5s and four RC-47s), the inadequacy and obsolescence of camera equipment, [and] the threat of enemy air defenses, the Vietnamese Air Force had to depend on US support for 95% of in-country aerial photographs during the period following the cease-fire.

VIETNAMESE NAVY INTELLIGENCE ORGANIZATION

The VNN's primary mission was to detect Communist seaborne infiltration. This infiltration took on more magnitude and significance beginning in March 1970, after Sihanoukville had ceased to be an entry point for logistical supplies shipped from North Vietnam. After the Paris Agreement, the US Navy discontinued its patrolling off Vietnamese territorial waters, while [the] VNN was only capable of coastal patrols and interception and riverine missions. N-2 scope of activity was subjected to the same limitations.

• • •

N-2 had a mobile interrogation team which provided interrogation support to naval intelligence units when needed, as in the case of interception of North Vietnamese fishermen lost in MR-1, or foreign fishing vessels violating Vietnamese territorial waters.

• • •

In July 1970, the special collection detachment was redesignated Unit 701. Its collection operations were also reorganized to involve personnel of the unit disguised as civilians who operated fishing craft or in fishing villages to monitor Communist seaborne infiltration and smuggling activities.

In general, both [the] VNN and VNAF were not capable of conducting sea reconnaissance, either by air or by naval craft; nor were they equipped with telephoto cameras to photograph and identify the various types of vessels. Naval craft at sea provided information on Soviet or Chicom ships loaded with bulky cargoes.

VNN repeatedly reported sightings of Soviet ships in territorial waters off MR-1 and MR-2 after the cease-fire, but no infiltrations were detected. Apparently, since expanded logistical roadways in-country and in lower Laos more than adequately supported the needs of Communist units, sea infiltration was no longer as much needed as before.

• • •

IV. INTELLIGENCE COOPERATION AND COORDINATION

Concepts and Problems

There is general agreement that, in the Vietnam War, though US-Vietnamese cooperation and coordination existed in every field and sector, they were nowhere as concrete and distinctive as in the area of intelligence. A common mission, common objectives, common efforts, and similarity in organization and operational procedures all contributed to this cooperation and coordination. US and Vietnamese intelligence organizations had their own assets and liabilities.

The United States had sophisticated equipment, lavish means, effective techniques and management, and large-scale organizations. However, they lacked basic knowledge of the enemy, the language, and the culture; furthermore, personnel were often replaced after a year's tour of duty.

Vietnam didn't have sophisticated assets, but Vietnamese intelligence personnel were more experienced and knowledgeable about the Vietnam War, about the enemy and his psychology and techniques, and, especially important, they shared a common language with the enemy.

• • •

Weapons and equipment were classified as either common or sophisticated, with sophisticated weapons being those seized for the first time in the Vietnam theater. The common types were resolved according to status of forces agreements which provided for the capturing forces to keep what they had captured.

The sophisticated weapons, that is, those captured for the first time in the Vietnam theater, were Vietnamese property. On the second capture, these items might go to the US side. On subsequent captures either side might keep the items. In reality, the Vietnamese side did not have the capability to test really sophisticated pieces of equipment, and the US side was allowed to keep them for testing before returning or transferring them to Vietnamese custody.

To facilitate the testing process, no time limits were set. Test results were to be made available to the Vietnamese side. Actually, the agreement was carried out in a looser manner, as in the case of the SA-7 heat-seeking missile used for the first time in the Vietnam War during the 1972 general attack. Because of testing needs, all captured SA-7s were turned over to the US side, and the Vietnamese had only a plastic mock-up of the weapon.

There were no problems in the area of captured documents because they were easily reproduced. All handwritten, printed, typewritten, drawn or engraved materials, tape recordings, photographs, films, and seals were considered to be documents.

The US side transferred all prisoners of war and Hoi Chanh (defectors) to Vietnamese control. Though the United States never officially declared war on the Vietnamese Communists, the 1949 Geneva Convention [provision] on prisoners of war provided for a country to be allowed to entrust custody of its PW to another country as long as both fulfilled their obligations concerning good treatment of these prisoners. Consequently, PW of US or Free World Military Assistance Forces (US/FWMAF) were evacuated through US channels to the central Combined Military Interrogation Center (CMIC) in Saigon or CMICs at corps or division level, or [to] RVN-operated PW camps.

On the RVN side, the difficulty was not in making secret or top secret documents available to the United States. Problems were frequently occasioned by US requests to downgrade materials, mostly Communist documents, for distribution to US information agencies or the US press corps. Vietnamese laws prohibited the distribution of Communist documents. Once downgraded, the documents were exploited by the US press and were eventually published by the Vietnamese newspapers as translations, which frequently led to criticism of the Vietnamese press and US journalistic privileges.

Combined Intelligence Activities

In military intelligence, cooperation and coordination were conducted in one of two modes. The first mode provided for US personnel to function both as advisors and colleagues. The second mode gave them a strictly advisory capacity. The first type of relationship was established at Joint General Staff (JGS) level, the four combined intelligence centers, Collection Unit 101, J-7/JGS and subordinate elements, and the Military Security Department (better known as MSS). The second type of relationship existed at corps and division G-2s, sector and subsector S-2s, and local MSS services.

• • •

J-2/JGS and J-2/USMACV

During the initial period of US participation in the Vietnam War, cooperation and coordination between J-2/MACV and J-2/JGS were performed through a US liaison team permanently installed at J-2/JGS and consisting of four officers (two army and one each from the navy and air force) and a noncommissioned officer.

The task of this liaison team was more administrative than professional, and little was accomplished in terms of information exchange or situation estimates. This situation improved during the next period when Major General Joseph A. McChristian was assigned as Chief J-2/MACV. For the first time, there were initiated weekly intelligence briefings conducted by US and ARVN staff officers. During these briefings, both parties compared and exchanged information received during the week and presented their respective assessments and estimates concerning enemy capabilities for the following week.

Still, coordination was generally limited to staff officers. There were occasional consultations between the two J-2 chiefs, but these meetings were not part of any established procedure, nor did they relate to anything other than work policies and administration. As a matter of fact, the Chief J-2/JGS and his US counterpart met only when needed and generally with the purpose of acquainting themselves with [the] organization, operation, and training of each side.

The exchange of information, as a result, lacked spontaneity and timeliness. But it was also during this period that the idea of combined activities took shape and was implemented with the activation of combined intelligence centers whose operations were intended to benefit both MACV and the JGS.

Not until 1969, however, did intelligence cooperation and coordination between MACV and the JGS become really close and effective. This was due to the professional interest given to the combined intelligence effort by the Chief J-2/MACV, Major General William E. Potts. In addition to weekly combined staff meetings, the Chief J-2/MACV also took the unprecedented step of discussing the situation and exchanging professional viewpoints with his counterpart and generally made himself available for every worthy discussion. It was also due to his dedicated and untiring effort that combined intelligence activities were greatly enhanced and became instrumental in improving the effectiveness of Vietnamese military intelligence.

At the combined intelligence centers and Collection Unit 101, coordination and collaboration materialized in the form of bilateral US/Vietnamese activities. There were four combined intelligence centers: Combined Intelligence Center, Vietnam (CICV); Combined Document Exploitation Center (CDEC); Combined Military Interrogation Center (CMIC); and Combined Materiel Exploitation Center (CMEC).

Each center had two elements, one Vietnamese, the other US, each with its own director. These two elements shared the same installations and facilities. Personnel were integrated in individual sections. Documents were compiled bilingually.

• • •

COMBINED INTELLIGENCE CENTER, VIETNAM (CICV)

This center was conceived in 1965 and its building inaugurated on 17 January 1967, although the various US/Vietnamese sections of the center had previously and individually initiated coordination of activities. The center operated around the clock with permanent and rotating teams.

The mission of CICV was to compile and provide intelligence data to the J-2s. These data were related to terrain, weather, lines of communication (LOCs), bridges and culverts, and local area features; Vietnamese Communist order of battle (OB), Communist base areas, infiltration corridors, bombing targets, bomb damage assessment (BDA); [and] imagery interpretation (II).

• • •

In the area of OB [order of battle], though close bilateral coordination was effected right on the spot, the two sides differed on enemy strength figures, with RVN-computed figures always the higher. The reason for the discrepancy was that authority to accept enemy strength and forces rested on J-2/JGS on the Vietnamese side, while on the US side acceptance had to come from [the] Commander in Chief, Pacific (CINCPAC), [and] the DIA, and the acceptance procedure on the RVN side almost proved, in a few instances, more flexible.

In OB considerations, strength figures on guerrilla and VCI forces were usually not very accurate, especially after the general offensive of Tet 1968, when most of the heavy losses sustained by the enemy were actually borne by the guerrillas and the VCI. Efforts to keep a close count of the VCI ran into difficulties because sectors and subsectors did not have accurate figures or did not report them objectively. This reporting depended on each commander's personal appraisal of the local situation. A sector maintained a steady 100 in its count of the local VCI while submitting monthly reports on the number put out of action.

In reality, even the Communists did not have these figures. This was precisely why in 1969 they sent inspection groups to each locality to conduct an on-the-spot census. Communist documents admitted that even their own provincial and district officials were unable to keep count of their membership.

As regards enemy units, it was conceived that they must be categorized into Main Force, Local Force, guerrillas or VCI, and identified as Viet Cong (VC) or North Vietnam Army (NVA). This second classification was very important because, on the one hand, North Vietnam always denied it had any forces in the South, and on the other [the]

RVN was endeavoring to prove that the war efforts originated in the North. Classification was based upon the following definitions:

North Vietnamese Army (NVA) units: a unit formed, trained, and designated by North Vietnam as an NVA unit and composed completely or primarily of North Vietnamese. Depending on their subordination, these units may be categorized as Local Force or Main Force.

Viet Cong (VC) units: a unit formed and trained in South Vietnam (or in some instances Cambodia and Laos) whose original composition consisted primarily of people residing in South Vietnam. Depending upon their subordination, these units may be categorized as guerrilla, Local Force, or Main Force.

Main Force (MF) units: those VC or NVA military units which are directly subordinate to the Central Office for South Vietnam (COSVN) [or] a Viet Cong military region, military subregion, or front.

Local Force (LF) units: those VC or NVA military units which are directly subordinate to province and district party committees and normally operating within the territorial jurisdiction of their respective control headquarters.

Guerrillas: guerrillas are fighting forces, usually organized into platoons and squads, directly subordinate to the party apparatus at village and hamlet level. Although they form a full-time part of the enemy's offensive threat, the amount of time devoted to guerrilla duties by the individual guerrilla varies. At times guerrillas operate outside their home villages and hamlets, often with LF and MF units. Typical missions include limited offensive operations, harassment, sabotage, propaganda, protection of party committees, collection of taxes, and also security and reconnaissance for MF and LF units.

Vietnamese Communist infrastructure (VCI): the VCI is the political and administrative organization through which the VC seek control of the people of the RVN. It embodies the Communist Party control structure and the leadership and administration of front organizations from the national through the hamlet level. The VCI include[d] individuals who [were] members or probationary members of the Vietnamese Communist Party, also known as the People's Revolutionary Party, and those non-Communist members who perform[ed] an enemy cadre function described in the "Current Breakout of VCI Executive and Significant Cadre" (also known as the "Green Book") published by the Government of Vietnam (GVN). The VCI [did] not include members of the enemy military forces who would qualify as PW according to the Geneva Convention rules.

Another aspect of the OB problem was that, when referring to enemy strength and forces, everyone usually implied those physically present on South Vietnam (SVN) territory, with no consideration given to those positioned in border areas of Cambodia, Laos, or North Vietnam (NVN). Such limited thinking led to misconceptions as to the status of conflicting forces. For instance, it was believed that the Communists had only

300,000 men against the combined 1,500,000 US/RVNAF troops. These 300,000 Communist troops in the South were trained, supplied, and replenished by units stationed across the border. In Laos, Rear Service Group 559 alone had 50,000 men to move supplies from NVN to SVN by way of the Ho Chi Minh Trail.

In 1970, when the tactical situation compelled major Communist units in Military Regions 3 and 4 (MR-3 and MR-4) of the RVN to seek refuge in Cambodia, the overall Communist strength in SVN dropped, but this very same fact created an illusory situation, as Communist divisions could reinfiltrate within a day or two, with their combat capabilities reinforced through rest, training, and replenishment received while [in] Cambodian territory. Misconceptions could not be dispelled despite the fact that these units were carried in OB holdings as "units in border areas."

Disagreements over enemy strength and forces occurred right within the RVNAF between J-2/JGS and the corps, divisions, and sectors, though authority for acceptance of enemy units had been clearly defined, with the JGS level handling units of battalion size and higher, and military regions/corps assuming responsibility for companies and smaller units. Quarterly OB discussions with the various units involved accomplished nothing more than reducing the discrepancies.

In late 1972, as the drafting of the Paris Agreement was nearing completion, the RVN side felt the need to demonstrate the presence of the NVA in the South and subsequently insisted that an OB book be compiled that would identify by composition all NVA units in the South. The need was justified, but realization was not that easy. Finally, based on all information gathered over a period of three years, from 1970 through 1972, rosters of NVA personnel in each unit were compiled and those thus identified numbered up to 115,000.

• • •

Aerial photos were one of the favorite sources of intelligence for briefings, debriefings, and intelligence studies. Around June 1972, after Quang Tri City had fallen, enemy 130mm and 122mm field guns continually pounded on Hue city. Enemy gun positions had to be located, but direction-finding radars could not help determine these positions. Aircraft were finally called in to continually photograph the suspected positions in an attempt to catch the guns as they were being pulled out of their camouflaged positions or when they opened fire.

Films taken by aircraft from the 460th Tactical Reconnaissance Wing were processed for immediate photo readouts and Hot and Immediate Photo Interpretation Reports (HOPIRs and IPIRs). Results were immediately relayed to the Tactical Air Command and the artillery for firing on them before the enemy was able to move the guns out of the identified positions. This procedure proved more effective in reducing enemy attacks by fire than B-52 strikes.

• • •

The VN Targets Section focused mainly on observing the status of enemy base areas and infiltration routes. Each base area (BA) was given a three-digit number designation for identification purposes, as opposed to the Communists' own designations. Base areas in MR-1 were given a 100 series [number], MR-2 a 200 series, MR-3 a 300 series, and MR-4 a 400 series. Base areas in Laos received a 600 series and those in Cambodia a 700 series.

Factors considered in observing and determining the status of an enemy BA were US-established. The same technique was used in conducting pattern analyses. Vietnamese corps and division commanders appreciated this technique very much because the thorough recapitulation of information on a specific area (with up to 30 different types of information) was in itself a factual assessment and needed no further explanations.

This information was categorized and normally presented in eight different overlays placed on a master map and with the following information plotted: enemy units and their movements in the areas as indicated in ARDF reports; information obtained by SLAR [side-looking airborne radar] or Red Haze; information derived from aerial photos and aerial reconnaissance; information derived from PWs, Hoi Chanh, and documents; information reported by agents; types of incidents recorded in the area; enemy air defenses; and information resulting from intelligence studies of the area. These overlays were updated every three months.

• • •

COMBINED DOCUMENT EXPLOITATION CENTER (CDEC)

This center was organized on 1 October 1965. Prior to that the United States had a liaison element and a team of Vietnamese civilian translators. As a combined MI center, it had both VN and US elements, each with its own director.

• • •

The VN element did not have a translation team, but the US element had the capability to translate Vietnamese, English, French, Chinese, Cambodian, and Japanese. Documents were always considered to be a very valuable source of information. However, prior to the establishment of CDEC the evacuation of documents from the capturing unit to the Document Exploitation Section sometimes took up to six months. During this time documents were exploited at numerous levels prior to reaching the national level. This caused delays, inability to verify circumstances of acquisition, losses or mix-ups, and inconsistencies. Also, analysts along the way tampered with the originals. After exploitation, the results were late in reaching the affected areas or the capturing units because they were forwarded through military postal channels and the recipient units might have been on tactical operations in remote areas. In this case the mail ended up at their rear base camps.

• • •

To overcome this problem, intelligence advisors to RVNAF units and J-2/JGS met the TO&E needs of corps and divisions by providing each with a document copier, but after a while difficulties occurred because the machines broke down and there were no qualified personnel to repair them, or the units had no funds to purchase the fluid and paper necessary for the copying process. Coordination with US agencies to whom lavish means were available helped to solve the problem. When there were important documents to examine, go-teams were dispatched to do the job right on the spot or [to] photograph the documents for the units, while the originals would be taken back to CDEC for exploitation.

At the center, information was exploited within 12 to 24 hours and the units received feedback within 48 hours thanks to daily or special flights. Routine documents were forwarded to CDEC in the same timely manner. Expeditious and professional exploitation boosted the unit commanders' confidence and made them more willing to urge their subordinates to send the documents in instead of keeping them for a long time as they had previously done.

• • •

In 1968, captured documents numbered 900,000 pages. Exploitation results showed that only an estimated 10 percent had intelligence value. This center was restricted to exploiting documents captured in the field and thus did not have access to reference or Communist publications commercially available in such countries as France or Hong Kong. This latter type of material was processed by the US Document Exploitation Center in Japan.

• • •

Most available documents had been captured by US forces, primarily because in the first years of their involvement they were responsible for tactical operations while RVNAF units worked in pacification. Moreover, the US military were trained to focus maximum attention on documents. The documents were all in the Vietnamese language, and, since US personnel could not tell the value of each, they turned in all captured documents.

• • •

RVNAF units paid minimum attention to capturing documents and immediately discarded those they came upon which they considered to be propaganda. In 1971, a unit of the 7th Infantry Division, RVNAF, staged an ambush in My Tho. The reported results were that two enemy junks had been sunk, five enemy troops [were] killed in action (KIA), and seven K54 pistols [were] captured. When the guns arrived at division headquarters, the division G-2 observed they were of the latest model and that the holsters bore a gold star, all indicative of the high ranks of the users. However, no documents were found. Preliminary investigations showed that the ambushing unit did capture a number of documents, but did not give them any consideration because they were too busy searching for additional weapons in the river. Finally the 7th Division's G-2 had the unit return to the site and a few remaining documents were found. These indicated the Communist team ambushed was made up of battalion and provincial unit cadre.

In this particular case the psychology of the troops was such that they believed capturing documents was not as important as other combat achievements and would cause the operation to be prolonged, pending the exploitation of the documents. Therefore they were not too eager to turn in documents. Still, the Vietnam War did demonstrate that knowledge of Communist strategic courses of action was gained through captured documents. Through lavish means of communication, transportation, and operation, and through expeditious and professional exploitation, CDEC made documents an abundant and accurate source of information and the most trusted in the area of combat intelligence.

COMBINED MILITARY INTERROGATION CENTER (CMIC)

• • •

The Interrogation Section had several teams, some in charge of geographical areas such as MRs 1, 2, 3, and 4, others specializing in political, military, or economic affairs, or infiltration, etc. Reports prepared by the interrogation teams were forwarded to the Editing Division, which synthesized them for clarity, prepared sketch maps of bases from the information obtained, etc. Technical information was submitted to specialists from the engineer, signal, artillery, ordnance, etc. corps for review. This activity on the US side was the responsibility of its Reporting Section. This section also translated Vietnamese interrogation reports into English.

• • •

When sources arrived at CMIC they were divided into two groups. One group was interrogated by the VN element, the other by the US element. If there were only one source, the VN element usually interrogated him on the first day and the US element had access to him on the second day. This procedure was changed in April 1971 after it had been determined that a day was not sufficient for any one side to complete its assignment. Subsequently, the Vietnamese were given three days and the Americans two. If the source was deemed to have information which responded to the special needs of the VN or the US element, that element was given priority for interrogation. Interrogation results were exchanged for corroboration and complementing.

Originally, US personnel selected for interrogation assignments were those who could speak Vietnamese, of whom there were very few. Those who spoke fluently enough to debate with the sources were even fewer. Gradually, US element interrogation had to be conducted through Vietnamese male or female interpreters, all noncommissioned officers, and could not be as effective as the VN element interrogation.

The VN element had interrogation specialists who were all officers with long experience in interrogation, with facility in the Communists' language and with knowledge of Communist organization and OB. Thus these VN interrogators were able to immediately detect any attempts to make false statements.

Many of the sources did lie, because the common psychology of PW and Hoi Chanh was a mixture of suspicion, fear, and a desire to receive better treatment. It prompted some to lie about their positions or ranks or to exaggerate in their reporting. All sources who came to CMIC were subjected to fingerprinting, photographing, and haircutting, and received a towel, soap, toothbrush, toothpaste, mat, and a blue uniform. Each source received a daily food ration worth VN $36.50, later increased to VN $49.00, which was equivalent to the daily ration of an RVNAF enlisted man. There were daily sick calls, a physician to care for them, and a dispensary with medics on duty 24 hours a day. The more seriously ill were hospitalized. The International Red Cross occasionally requested to visit or contact the PW, and the requests were granted. Reports made upon completion of these visits were very positive.

• • •

When speaking of interrogation matters, it was often believed, and more so by the PW, that they involved torture and inhumane treatment. These conditions existed only in the remote past. The Vietnam War was determined to be a war for the hearts and minds, a war of ideologies, and this concept extended to interrogation activities. The interrogator was trained to believe in the hearts-and-minds approach, and this belief was reinforced with each day on the job.

Interrogation by psychological methods produced more and better results and brought the interrogator decent satisfaction and a sense of self-confidence. Communist troops and their cadré were extensively indoctrinated on [the] RVN, society, the RVNAF, abuses, classes, savage torture, etc.

A Communist political cadre at provincial party committee level, captured on his way back from attending a regional-level discussion on the 1968 general attack, stated that he was firmly determined not to disclose any information and was prepared to cope with torture. This torture did not take place. The interrogator maintained an extremely decent attitude, and the subject was detained in a room with a window which allowed him to observe all the activities of the interrogation unit. Another surprise came to him when he noted the democratic activities of the officers, noncommissioned officers, and enlisted men of the RVNAF, and the very close and nondiscriminatory rapport between them, particularly after work.

The Communist attack right inside the capital failed to cause these servicemen to panic, and they continued to perform their duties in a dedicated and cheerful manner, prompting the cadre to ponder and to wonder if, after all, SVN did not have a righteous cause. Even the presence of US advisors in the unit did not provide him with an indication that there was something abnormal in the relations between US and VN personnel or in their daily activities. All these observations finally led him to decide to cooperate with the interrogator.

Decent treatment came as a surprise to all PW and Hoi Chanh. One Hoi Chanh recalled he had turned himself in at a military base, bringing along a K54 pistol. He expected to be harassed with questions for information of military value. He was surprised to find that the officer in command treated him in a very friendly manner, asking about his family, and about life in Communist ranks, as if they were two friends reunited after a long separation and eager to learn about each other's families. No mention was made of military information. The pistol he had brought with him lay on the table, by his side, when it should have been put away as a precaution.

Facing realities which totally contradicted prejudices gained through indoctrination was the principal motivating force that prompted interrogated personnel to cooperate. This cooperation became even more sincere as the treatment of the source improved. On one occasion, a high-ranking defector who had returned from regroupment to NVN indicated, in the course of a conversation, that he missed his family very much. With the lavish means available to the US side, the family was brought in to be reunited with the source, who never thought this could ever be done.

Information provided by PW and Hoi Chanh was often of high value. It would have been a real mistake to determine validity of information solely on the basis of rank and position. This only applied to the US and RVNAF people, since they were subjected to need-to-know restrictions. On the Communist side, the policy of group study and discussion of assignments enabled the individual private to gain some insight on strategic intentions and requirements behind the campaign to come.

• • •

COMBINED MATERIEL EXPLOITATION CENTER (CMEC)

Of the four combined centers, CMEC was the last established. Prior to that, the VN element was a materiel exploitation section of the MI Center/J-2/JGS, whose productivity in terms of in-depth exploitation of war trophies was negligible. Its primary concern with captured materiel was to use [it] as a basis for protests with the International Control Commission or for displays.

The Vietnam theater frequently saw the introduction of sophisticated arms and equipment from the Communist bloc. New weapons, in particular, were used in every general attack to reinforce enemy troop confidence as well as to surprise the RVNAF with unexpected enemy firepower. In intelligence collection, the appearance of new types of arms and equipment at the front line was always a telltale sign of a Communist general attack in the making. The Communists were cunning in that, despite being supplied with sophisticated materiel from abroad, they pursued their efforts to make some locally for propaganda and motivation purposes.

• • •

CMEC's most useful role was the publication of handbooks on Communist war materiel used or likely to be used in Vietnam. These handbooks helped tactical units identify and report captured materiel and equipment. In Vietnam, however, the units often proved untruthful in their reporting of new Communist armament, particularly individual weapons identified by the handbooks as sophisticated. Many unit commanders kept those trophies as souvenirs or gave them away as gifts to personalities in the administration. The best that technical intelligence personnel could do was to photograph these items. Later, as the units were given authority to set up unit displays, many commanders found ways to retain numerous types of crew-served weapons that were captured for the first time.

Communist forces sometimes received arms from the Communist bloc that were not even featured in the handbooks. In 1972, when they used SA-7 heat-seeking missiles for the first time, these weapons were unknown to CMEC. Characteristics of the US Redeye missile had to be invoked when attempting to describe the SA-7. The first SA-7 missile to be captured, in Quang Tri Province, was turned over to the United States, and so were subsequent catches, in order for examination and testing to be thorough. Later, in faithful implementation of a section of the bipartite agreement which dealt with war trophies, a plastic replica of the SA-7 was made for display in lieu of the real thing.

Another weapon that the Communists used for the first time in Kontum in 1972, and [which] caused serious psychological impact on RVNAF armored and infantry troops, was the AT-3 Sagger missile, designed for use against tanks, boats, or bunkers. At Tan Canh, Kontum, in MR-2, RVNAF armored units described the zigzagging flights of the projectiles in pursuit of armored vehicles and the subsequent destruction of the latter as in uncanny, deific battles of ancient mythology.

• • •

This missile was rigged with wiring and the gunner had to steer it. Because of its jumbled wires it was first nicknamed "bach tuoc" (octopus). Firing from an exposed position while the battle was raging frequently made the gunner lose control and miss the targets. This prompted Communist troops to play with words and call the missile "bach truot" (ever-missing). . . .

The psychological effect that sophisticated arms and equipment of the Communist bloc initially [had] cannot be refuted. In this regard, enemy tanks and armored vehicles are not to be ignored. The RVNAF soldiers were used to fighting with tanks and armored vehicles supporting them from the rear. For a period of time they were rudely shocked when facing enemy tanks and armored vehicles for the first time. Later, as they received more advanced antitank weapons, gained more experience, and learned from CMEC of the vulnerabilities of each type of vehicle, the tactical units competed to destroy enemy tanks for rewards. Foremost of the tank-killer units were those defending An Loc.

• • •

Cooperation and Coordination in Human Intelligence

RVNAF Human Intelligence (HUMINT) units included Unit 101 of J-2/JGS, the collection sections of corps and division G-2s, and the collection subsections of sector and subsector S-2s. The Vietnam Navy (VNN) had Unit 701, and the Vietnam Air Force (VNAF) had its own, undesignated, collection detachment. Human sources were the oldest and most basic form of intelligence collection, but to the Vietnamese armed forces it was not until 1962 that this concept began to materialize and develop. At this time the 300th Special Detachment was activated with a strength of 388 men. Its mission was to collect strategic intelligence on the Communists, but its operations were limited to SVN territory. From the very beginning it conducted bilateral operations with US elements.

• • •

Though effecting very close coordination in their collection efforts on common targets, each side gradually developed unilateral operations in response to its own needs. On the VN side, for instance, the internal political situation in 1963 grew tense with the Buddhist movement opposing the government and thus generated new, unilateral, collection needs. This was precisely why the 300th Special Detachment became too well known after the 1 November 1963 revolution. Therefore its designation was changed to the 924th Support Group, and it was placed under the operational control of the Chief of Staff/JGS, although technical supervision was provided by J-2/JGS.

• • •

No longer constrained to its original mission as the 924th Support Group, Unit 101 now reached into Cambodia to support RVNAF cross-border operations conducted in 1970. Unit 101 teams dispatched officers, under the cover of representatives of J-2/JGS and corps G-2s, to the Cambodian military region G-2s and to some important provinces of Cambodia to exchange information on the enemy situation and monitor the tactical situation.

In South Vietnam, because collection operations were conducted covertly, facilities and personnel were placed under civilian cover. Agent handlers were given civilian occupations compatible with their own skills and consistent with the environment in their respective target areas. These occupations included teaching in private schools, operating small businesses, selling hogs, driving cargo trucks, etc. Resources had to be provided to build the cover. The United States provided operational funds which helped purchase civilian vehicles and motorcycles, rent safehouses, pay agents, and provide for other expenditures related to collection operations.

• • •

Though supported devotedly by the 525th MI Group in funds, resources, and technical advice, the Vietnamese collection effort met with two major difficulties which seriously hampered its operations. The first one was not unique to Unit 101. As a matter of fact all other HUMINT collection organizations experienced the same problem. It involved cooperation from the sources and the civilian population.

In Vietnam a longstanding question was why our side was unable to set up a "people's intelligence" system, i.e., use the populace in an intelligence capacity as the Communists did. The answer to this question was very simple except for an unwillingness to face the truth. One had to motivate the Vietnamese civilian to perform intelligence duties or to cooperate with intelligence agencies.

The motivation on the Communist side was that failure to comply meant harsh punishment. However, on the RVN side incentives were hard to find, and there even was a motivating force which produced adverse effects. The people in SVN who lived under the nationalist regime were still very much influenced by Confucian ethics, which asserts that reporting on someone else's activity is not chivalrous if the report brings that person harm. Noninterference with another person's actions might also be derived from the Confucian philosophy of "not doing unto others what one shalt not have others do unto oneself." This led the Vietnamese civilian to adopt the oft-condemned attitude of "not lifting a finger while the neighbor's house is burning."

These views, added to prejudices against the activities of the old French Deuxieme Bureau in Vietnam, caused people to look down on those connected with security and intelligence, or those providing information to these agencies.

Prejudices against security and intelligence were gradually washed away with time, but collaboration continued to be ignored by the populace, and most agents cooperated for subsistence rather than ideals. Even in this case the earned income hardly justified the risks encountered, particularly when going deep into enemy-controlled zones. The

Communists were merciless against those they considered spies, to whom they meted out harsh punishment. Many people were assassinated and notes were found on their bodies accusing them of acting as agents for the SVN government, which in many cases was not true. This was why the bona fide agents program designed to induce popular collaboration in return for rewards also failed. The only agents available were mostly professionals who worked simultaneously for several agencies or doctored known information for their own reporting.

An agent once provided Unit 101 with information on enemy forces in an entire MR, complete with extremely accurate details on their cover designators, cover numbers, letter box numbers, organization charts, etc. The accuracy caused such bewilderment among intelligence officers that J-2/JGS had to check with Unit 101 to ascertain the reliability and capability of the source. Later the source slipped up and was found to be in possession of an MR-prepared document on Communist OB which he had used to write reports on real units but imaginary activities.

This is not to say there were no outstanding agents or those with extremely promising potential. However, where such sources were found, active competition developed among the collection agencies and the winner was always the one with the most means and power. Unit 101 frequently saw extremely good prospective sources unexpectedly terminate their services just as they were about to be officially recruited.

The second difficulty encountered in HUMINT was the state of general mobilization which caused all male citizens from 18 to 37 years of age to be conscripted. Personnel of the various intelligence nets of Unit 101 operating under cover were required to have papers certifying the legality of their draft status, draft exemption, or military discharge. As far as agents were concerned, failure to obtain draft deferment for them negated all the efforts to develop them as sources.

The agency which had authority to issue such documentation was the Mobilization Directorate. It refused to do so because it considered such action to be illegal, though the JGS and the Defense Ministry had both approved it for intelligence purposes. Finally the Directorate approved draft deferment for no more than 30 agents a year, and no more than three times each. To fulfill the need for legal documents for the agent handlers, Unit 101 had to resort to forging discharge papers. This, however, was legal forgery in that J-2/JGS and the Mobilization Directorate were given rosters identifying those to whom such papers had been issued.

• • •

Generally speaking, though bilateral collection efforts helped resolve the problem of collection means and techniques, they failed to upgrade the quality of information acquired, and collection through agent sources enjoyed but a modest position with regard to other collection techniques, even when the 525th MI Group was always there to support these activities during the period from 1965 to 1973. In 1972, this support was gradually reduced until after the Paris Agreement went into effect on 28 January 1973, when there was but a single representative of the 500th MI Group, which was beginning to replace the 525th.

Cooperation and Coordination in Aerial Photo Reconnaissance

During World War II, it was estimated that 80 percent of intelligence information acquired came from aerial photo reconnaissance. This percentage remained the same during the Korean conflict. In the Vietnam War, although no official statistics are available to this date, aerial photo reconnaissance probably accounted for 65 to 70 percent of the intelligence information acquired.

Unlike the cooperation and coordination in other fields such as combat intelligence or special collection, in aerial photo reconnaissance the VN side's contribution was rather modest. This was because the United States, with its air superiority and abundant assets, bore the brunt of the photo missions throughout the Vietnam War.

By 1960, [the] VNAF had only two C-45 aircraft for air photo missions, both with extremely limited capabilities. In 1965, [the] VNAF was able to organize a reconnaissance squadron, and in 1967 this was increased to two squadrons. However, the total number of aircraft was only 13, of where there were three RC-47s, one EC-47, and nine U-6As.[6]

Aircraft such as the T-28 were modified to become RT-28s for photo missions over areas defended by enemy antiaircraft guns. Later this program was terminated because the equipment was too old and photos taken could not be used for mapping purposes. Not until after the Vietnamization plan had been implemented did the VNAF get to activate a squadron of 12 RC-47s (716th Squadron) and another squadron of six RF-5s (522nd Squadron).

• • •

From 1965 to 1969, the RVNAF were responsible only for supporting pacification and rural development; thus there was not much need for air photo reconnaissance. Besides, the photos taken by the US side on its own were sufficient to meet the needs on the VN side.

• • •

By cease-fire day the air photo program had fulfilled all the needs of the requesting units, with the United States providing 97 percent of the coverage and [the] VNAF credited with the remainder. The Vietnam Air Force's participation in visual reconnaissance was greater, but this program was restricted by the weather, nocturnal conditions, terrain concealment (particularly in mountainous areas), and enemy antiaircraft firepower. The Vietnam Air Force's ability to fill the gaps caused by the withdrawal of effective US support following the Paris Agreement was minimal, particularly in the face of continued requests by the units which had become overly dependent on aerial photographs.

Signal Intelligence

In the RVNAF, J-7/JGS was responsible for the acquisition of signal intelligence (SIGINT). Prior to 1961, signal intelligence was unknown in the RVNAF. However, the First Republic did give consideration to applying this technique in intelligence activities.

The nucleus of a center for radio intercept was established in Saigon in 1955 under the RVNAF Telecommunications Command with a staff of approximately 80 military and civilian personnel who had had basic radio intercept experience with the French Army. This center had a branch in Danang. At that time, the mission was to monitor broadcasts from Communist radio stations in Peking, Moscow, and Hanoi, as well as free-world stations such as the BBC and the VOA.[7]

In 1961, when SIGINT materialized, the unit which first came into being was designated 1st Signal Research and Exploitation Company and placed under technical supervision of the commander, ARVN Telecommunications Command. Another agency was established which took the name of Special Technical Exploitation Agency and became subordinate to the Chief of Staff/JGS.

After repeated political upheavals such as revolution and successive coups, the agency in charge of radio intercept at the CIO, which in turn reported directly to the Chief of Staff and Commander in Chief, was transferred to the JGS, and J-7 thus came into being.

• • •

With the increasing need, detachments were activated to provide direct support to Vietnamese infantry divisions. In late September 1967 the first three detachments were organized to support the 2nd, 22nd, and 5th Divisions, respectively. Other detachments were subsequently formed for the remaining divisions and they became operational in 1968. Radio direction finding (RDF) stations were also established in Danang to support MR-1; in Pleiku to support MR-2; in Vung Tau to support MR-3; in Can Tho to support MR-4; and in Con Son to support MR-4.

J-7/JGS personnel were trained in airborne radio directing finding (ARDF) from U-6A aircraft in early 1968. In 1970, as the Vietnamization program began, J-7 personnel were trained by the 694th Air Force Security Force in ARDF from ED-47 aircraft.

• • •

Between 1965 and 1968 the United States was the sole provider of ARDF information. . . . J-7/JGS gradually gained credit for up to 90 percent of ARDF and MRDF information acquired in-country.

• • •

Signal intelligence proved to be a valuable source of information and was very well appreciated by tactical unit commanders, since it provided early warning of enemy troop movements and allowed time to devise countermeasures. This confidence was reflected in the designation of ARDF information as A2 information, and everyone but the intelligence specialists swore by A2 information but had no idea what ARDF was.[8]

• • •

V. MILITARY INTELLIGENCE COOPERATION AND COORDINATION IN VIETNAM FOLLOWING US MILITARY DISENGAGEMENT

Defense Attaché Office, Intelligence Branch

The Paris Agreement of 27 January 1973 called for withdrawal of all US forces from Vietnam except 50 servicemen assigned to the Defense Attaché Office (DAO). This also applied to US intelligence organizations. They left, taking home their sophisticated equipment, lavish means, and numerous technicians. The US intelligence apparatus which remained in Vietnam after cease-fire day consisted of OSA and the DAO Intelligence Branch.

The DAO Intelligence Branch was an entirely new organization with extremely limited personnel allocations—by previous standards—of ten military and 97 civilian personnel. Later, the number of military personnel was further reduced to three. The mission of the DAO Intelligence Branch was to collect, evaluate, and disseminate information on North Vietnam and the Viet Cong in response to intelligence information requirements levied by the US Army Support Activities Group in Thailand; Commander in Chief, Pacific, in Hawaii; DIA; and other national intelligence agencies.

• • •

Intelligence data supplied by the J-2/JGS to the DAO Intelligence Branch were intelligence data acquired within the scope of its responsibilities and pertaining to South Vietnamese territory. Intelligence data furnished by the DAO Intelligence Branch to J-2/JGS was information pertaining to the areas outside South Vietnam, information on North Vietnam, and information related to infiltration from North Vietnam to South Vietnam.

Difficulties Encountered

Under the new situation, after US forces had left and the Paris Agreement went into effect, intelligence data could be classified [into] two categories: 1) totally lost, or 2) limited and reduced. Those data in the first category included information obtained through SLAR (side-looking airborne radar), Red Haze, and People Sniffer techniques; information derived from sensors; and weather indicators from satellites.

Data of the second category included aerial photographs of North Vietnam and Laos; information from in-country air photo reconnaissance; information from combat intelligence sources; information from agent sources; and special intelligence studies.

• • •

It was precisely at this time when intelligence was confronted with numerous obstacles and challenges that the need for intelligence information became more pressing and important, more imperative even, than during the war. The Paris Agreement brought no peace of mind to the leaders of South Vietnam. There was a continuing strategic intelligence requirement to determine the changes in North Vietnam's conduct of the war in the wake of the agreement, the state of rehabilitation of military and economic potentials in

North Vietnam and Communist-controlled portions of South Vietnam, and the level of infiltration of personnel and logistics from the North to the South.

Other less important but much needed information pertained to negotiating strategies and the four- and two-party commissions, the composition and activities of the Communist delegations, etc.

The standstill cease-fire had brought the Communists an advantage in that they now had buffer leopard-spot zones. These were considered by the Communists to be access points to the zones effectively controlled by each side. The Communist objective was to prevent infiltration by RVN intelligence into their zones through these points while using the same points as bridgeheads for their own infiltration into nationalist zones to gather intelligence.

The Paris Agreement gave birth to a new political element, the Third Force, which encompassed the left-oriented political forces opposing the government. Civilian intelligence agencies and the Military Security Department . . . virtually diverted their entire efforts to cope with this threat.

None of the armed forces intelligence agencies, J-2 or J-7/JGS, received any additional means to cope with their new difficulties. STRATDAT (Strategic Technical Directorate), too, was deprived of all the means that had given it mobility, and it was reduced to reassigning its teams to the military regions to assist them in a tactical capacity.

The combined intelligence centers of the past were ordered merged into a single center, designated Unit 306, of J-2/JGS. This reorganization created additional difficulties for J-2/JGS because the TO&E was subsequently revised to reflect a reduction by one rank for all job titles, while the missions required more effort than in the past.

• • •

Combat intelligence data acquired were substantially reduced. In 1973, for instance, the enemy targeted his attacks against isolated outposts near infiltration routes and, by concentrating large forces, was always assured of victory. Such battles yielded no PW or documents to help identify the enemy units involved. Hoi Chanh now came in smaller numbers, and there were no high-ranking ones. The psychology was such that defections came when the fighting was fierce, when the enemy's tactical position was weak, and [when] the RVN had the upper hand. In the seesaw situation of semi-war and semi-peace only the most determined defected, and there was a high rate of false defections.

Fewer documents were captured, not only because there were fewer contacts with the enemy but also because the enemy had applied stricter secrecy control measures, forbidding his troops to carry documents during an operational mission. This prohibition occurred after the RVN had repeatedly used captured documents to substantiate its protests of Communist crimes and deliberate violations of the cease-fire.

Intelligence previously acquired through communications means was substantially reduced because the Communists had identified the communications intelligence reliance on overflights. To contain friendly air activities, an additional 20 Communist air defense regiments infiltrated after the cease-fire with sophisticated armament never before observed in the Vietnam theater.

Among this new arsenal were SA-2 missiles; modified SA-7 heat-seeking missiles; radar-guided 100mm, 57mm, and 37mm antiaircraft guns; and self-propelled, multiple-barreled antiaircraft artillery. The air defense perimeter expanded daily and proportionately reduced aircraft operational ranges. Typically in MR-3 enemy 37mm antiaircraft guns were positioned in Ben Cat, Binh Duong, 15 miles northwest of Saigon. The antiaircraft missile which caused the strongest psychological impact was the modified SA-7 missile. Its effective altitude and speed had been increased, the altitude being increased from 9,000 feet to 15,000 feet, forcing VNAF pilots to fly above 15,000 feet. However, RC-47 and EC-47 aircraft could not fly above 10,000 feet. Moreover, photos taken by RF-5s flying above 4,500 or 5,000 feet were not usable because of the type of cameras mounted on the aircraft. . . .

Areas denied to aerial photo reconnaissance were MR-1, the tri-border area and the highlands of MR-2, and the northern part of MR-3. Missions over these areas were very difficult because [the] VNAF had no long-range rescue teams.

• • •

Beginning on 1 September 1974, reductions in military aid caused fuel allocations and replacement parts to [the] VNAF to drop to 65 percent of the year 1973. This, in turn, led to a drop of air photo reconnaissance performance to 52 percent of the previous year. Total flight time for RC-47s was reduced to 150 hours a month, [and] for RF-5s to 45 hours a month. To meet an essential air photo reconnaissance need, J-2/JGS interceded with J-3/JGS to either borrow flight time from the following month or reduce other flights, but this was virtually impossible. These situations occurred when the Communists launched large-scale attacks, as in Ban Me Thuot. In other cases, air photo reconnaissance needs conflicted with the need to fly tactical air or logistical support.

The Vietnam Air Force could not conduct night reconnaissance, as it did not have sophisticated aircraft such as the RF-101C Voodoo, RB-57F Canberra, RF-4C Phantom, or OV-1 Mohawk. After Communist forces had overrun Ban Me Thuot, the requirement was to detect enemy armored and vehicular movements from Ban Me Thuot toward MR-3 or the coastal areas of MR-2. Monitoring the lines of communication was possible for a maximum of only eight hours a day, which meant enemy forces had 16 hours a day to move undetected.

US-ARVN Intelligence Cooperation and Coordination in the Face of New Difficulties

In air photo reconnaissance [the] VNAF could meet only 7–10 percent of the in-country requirements, which meant that 90 percent of these requirements were still dependent on USAF air photo reconnaissance capabilities called upon through the DAO Intelligence Branch.

Most US aircraft took off from Thailand. Reconnaissance flights were conducted over North Vietnam, Laos, and South Vietnam by SR-71s and U-2s. RF-4s provided coverage of Cambodia and a 25-nautical-mile-wide corridor along the Vietnamese-Cambodian border. Unmanned aircraft, or Buffalo Hunters, were also used in South Vietnam.

In order to ensure secrecy and avoid North Vietnamese protests, information obtained from SR-71 and U-2 missions was not passed to the RVN. Exceptions were made in only very special cases and with DIA approval. Photographs and information obtained by RF-4s were passed to the Vietnamese upon special request and with adequate justification of the need. Unmanned aircraft . . . were the only source of information that the Vietnamese were totally entitled to. These aircraft were launched from DC-130s at an altitude of 20,000 feet, but this was not allowed over Laotian territory after June 1974. Thirty to forty flights were performed per month, especially over areas inaccessible to [the] VNAF. Photos thus taken were very sharp and clear. The overflights were programmed four days in advance. . . . In some areas Buffalo Hunters were used in a tactical reconnaissance capacity to provide information in support of battlefield requirements. This occurred, for instance, in July 1974 during the battles of Thuong Duc and Duc Duc in MR-1.

In mid-1974, Buffalo Hunter and RF-4 flights were stopped in Laos. When the situation in the RVN began to pick up in intensity, the US reinforced drone overflights with RF-4 missions in South Vietnam, but such flights were conducted at very high altitudes to avoid complications which might develop should any be shot down.

The two Vietnamese Army and Air Force Imagery Interpretation Centers usually reinterpreted and reprinted the duplicate positives for distribution to the areas concerned. Reinterpretation served a purpose. A photo, for instance, was interpreted by Nakhon Phanom as showing NVA T-60 medium tanks on RVN territory. Verification of this information was of utmost significance, as North Vietnam had not been known to have such tanks. Reinterpretation indicated these were only T-54 or T-59 tanks. Finally, another overflight was conducted over the target area and DIA interpreters identified the tanks as T-54s and T-59s. . . .

In urgent cases, a method commonly used for delivery was to carefully package the prints and take them to a civilian terminal. There they were entrusted to passengers on Air Vietnam's domestic flights who were deemed reliable, such as high-ranking military officers on TDY or leave, or members of the clergy. Identification of these passengers, the flight number, flight time, etc., were then transmitted to the local agency, which sent personnel out to meet the plane. This became the prime method used by RVN military intelligence to ensure expeditious delivery of documents.

• • •

Communist countermeasures were another obstacle to ARDF. Once an EC-47 entered a target zone, it took five to ten minutes to pick up radio signals, and three lines of bearing had to be obtained for a target fix. In the wake of the cease-fire the Communists frequently used 2- to 5-watt radios with very short ranges which, added to the rugged features of mountain and forest terrain, made intercept very difficult. In addition, they used FM voice communications which the EC-47 could not pick up, as it was not equipped for DF/FM voice intercept. The Communists also used landlines whenever they could.

A comparison in 1974 based strictly on the number of aircraft dedicated to ARDF would show that the capability for this type of mission had dropped to about one-third of the 1972 capability. Moreover, each flight was reduced from eight hours to five. Furthermore, a situation which received very little attention prevailed during the period from late 1973 onward. In the face of increasing costs of living, military pay remained stationary and therefore military personnel had to reduce their consumption of nutrients. As a result, their productivity dropped markedly after three flight hours.

• • •

While PHOTINT [photo intelligence] encountered numerous obstacles resulting from US troop withdrawals, the obstacles were minimal in the area of HUMINT. Before leaving, the 525th Military Intelligence Group had transferred to Unit 101 and MSS all transferable equipment, including 17 radio-teletypes. It has also trained 50 NCOs for five weeks to replace personnel of the 504th Signal Detachment in operating these radio sets. . . . After the cease-fire the US representative was a member of the 500th MI Group's Special Activities in Thailand. This group continued to fund Unit 101's operations. Bilateral operations of the past were now conducted solely by Unit 101 personnel. However, from a technical point of view the personnel had by then become extremely proficient and the results showed no negative effects of a change to unilateral operation. . . .

Generally speaking, the cease-fire entailed a substantial reduction of intelligence sources and collection means, particularly PHOTINT means. Those difficulties of a financial nature could not be resolved because funds were just not available. This was why efforts to overcome PHOTINT limitations could not succeed, though many projects had been formulated. . . .

In mid-1973, pilot sector intercept teams were set up in Binh Dinh, MR-2, and Quang Tin, MR-1. Personnel of these teams were selected from the sectors and their S-2 staffs, and equipment consisted of AN/PRC-25s or captured enemy radios. Thanks to enemy codes previously captured in their local areas, these teams gradually succeeded in intercepting and decoding most radio communications between enemy local-force units, and in some cases between enemy main forces. This experiment was very successful and the equipment required no additional costs.

• • •

Conclusions

• • •

At JGS and DAO headquarters, coordination was extremely good because it was based on practical considerations, openness, and mutual trust. Credit for successful cooperation must be given to Colonel William E. LeGro, DAO Chief, Intelligence Branch, a true professional with broad experience and a very dedicated man.

Daily meetings between the two sides were held to exchange information, discuss the situation, coordinate requirements, and divide responsibilities, particularly in the area of PHOTINT. Though data were picked up by J-7, the interpretation of Communist unit relationships and subordination required assistance from the US side because J-7 could not relate call signs to specific Communist units, particularly those in North Vietnam or those recently infiltrated from North Vietnam.

Daily and weekly intelligence summaries were exchanged regularly between J-2/JGS and the DAO Intelligence Branch. Every month the DAO Intelligence Branch conducted situation briefings, which were of special interest to the Vietnamese side, particularly in terms of information on North Vietnam and infiltration-related activities. Because it did not have enough personnel, the DAO Intelligence Branch limited its own activities to current intelligence and situation estimates and did not compile intelligence studies. In contrast, J-2/JGS made it a special effort to conduct studies on the enemy and was noted for its achievements in the areas of Communist military doctrine, Communist strategic and tactical courses of action, artillery, communications, engineers, armor, messenger services, sappers, and Communist base areas.

In summary, the cease-fire saw the US side drastically reduce field collection activities, since direct needs no longer existed. DAO intelligence requirements had to compete for priority with intelligence requirements in other areas of Southeast Asia. On the Vietnamese side, PHOTINT was substantially reduced, but this was compensated in part by increased efforts in COMINT. Quantitative reduction of combat intelligence was offset by qualitative improvements and revamping of collection agent networks. Close coordination between Vietnamese and US intelligence agencies also helped intelligence respond effectively to the needs of the situation from the cease-fire to the very last day.

VI. SUCCESSES AND FAILURES OF ARVN INTELLIGENCE

The 1968 General Offensive

When the Communists launched their general offensive against cities across South Vietnam in 1968, including Saigon and Hue, almost everybody agreed that it was a total surprise. The general populace of South Vietnam felt that the intelligence establishment had failed to discover the enemy scheme. Moreover, casting the blame on intelligence was partially justified. Any military offensive must be preceded by preparations. There was no reason why an offensive of such proportions should have entirely escaped the prying eyes and ears of every intelligence agent.

Strange as it may seem, no one reproved US intelligence for this common failure, but they did reprove the United States. One widespread popular Vietnamese belief at that time was that the United States had entered into a tacit agreement with the Communists to let them proceed with a military action designed to bring about a quick political solution for the war.

On the RVN side, no timely warnings were issued, nor was there any indication that an enemy action was imminent. Two days before the outbreak of the offensive, there was a decision to reduce the Tet truce from 48 to 36 hours and to confine 50 percent of troops to barracks. However, at the time the Communists began their attacks, on the second day of Tet, most ARVN garrison units were left with only a scant 10 to 20 percent of their combat strength. The majority of the troops were absent to celebrate Tet with their families. President Thieu himself was not in Saigon; he was quietly celebrating Tet in My Tho, home of his wife's family. Intelligence had failed; there was no question about it. What concerned many people in retrospect was to what extent intelligence had failed, and how the Communists had gone about preparing for their general offensive.

To put the event in its proper perspective, an examination of the military situation in 1967 is deemed necessary. This was a period of relative stability; the security picture displayed throughout rural areas was truly bright. Our two-pronged strategy of "pacification and search-and-destroy" inflicted important losses on the enemy. On the battlefield, major engagements took place only in border areas such as south of the DMZ, west of the Central Highlands, and the northeast of MR-3.

The first indicator of a general offensive was an enemy document captured from the CT-5 Division in March 1967 which revealed a planned attack against Saigon. This plan of attack was so primitive and so ingenuous that intelligence experts simply disregarded it as utopian. Then, sometime in early October, the RVN intelligence establishment learned about the content of Resolution No. 13, issued by North Vietnam's Labor Party Central Committee.

The resolution called for large-scale offensive attacks designed to bring about victory within a short time. At about the same time, another captured enemy document belonging to the Armor Section of COSVN, code-named Detachment 16, mentioned an enemy effort to train his troops in sapper techniques and the use of captured ARVN tanks. Then, later in November, another captured document dated 1 September 1967 and bearing the title "New Mission, New Tasks" revealed among other things that the new objectives now coveted were to terminate the American presence in Vietnam and [bring about] a coalition government. The document also disclosed that the conduct of the offensive was basically a triple effort: military, political, and proselytizing action, to be launched in conjunction with a general popular uprising, hence its code name TCK-TCN (abbreviations used in the document for "general offensive—general uprising").

Two other captured documents again pointed specifically toward a general offensive. The first one, a document of the B-3 Front headquarters captured in Dak To (MR-2) in October 1967 spoke about large-scale preparations being made for the 1968 Winter–Spring Campaign. The second document, captured in Quang Tin during the same month, was most specific of all. It said, in effect: "It is about time we proceeded with the general offensive and general uprising. By utilizing military units in coordination with the uprising movement of the popular mass, we will attack all provincial capitals and district towns and eventually liberate the capital."

Thus, during 1967, the number of captured documents was substantial and indicated a large military move. In addition to the documents specified above, there were several other piecemeal documents mentioning combat tactics in cities, a kind of tactic heretofore never subjected to discussion by the enemy.

Aside from documents, our intelligence also learned about an enemy effort to reorganize his territorial command and control, particularly in his MR-4 or Saigon-Cholon

MR and his Tri-Thien-Hue MR. As of September 1967, the enemy MR-4 was reorganized into five subregions centered on Saigon, which in turn was divided into five areas or sectors. At that time the significance of this enemy reorganization effort was unclear. Only after the offensive was launched did we know that it was part of the attack plan. Each of the five subregions was responsible for the offensive effort against a related target area of Saigon.

On 17 November 1967 the National Liberation Front of South Vietnam proposed a seven-day truce for the Tet holidays, which began in late January 1968. This was advanced at the same time with the three-day truce proposed for Christmas and New Year's. The truce proposal was immediately interpreted by our intelligence officers as an enemy move to take advantage of the truce to increase his logistic movements prior to a major offensive. With all the intelligence data gathered, it was evident that the enemy was preparing for a major offensive campaign.

Our intelligence apparatus correctly estimated this move, but its attention was directed toward the areas usually considered strategically important, such as Khe Sanh. The probability of Khe Sanh becoming a decisive contest objective like Dien Bien Phu in 1954 was foremost in the minds of our intelligence analysts. Little attention, if any, was given to the cities as probable objectives. The timing of the enemy offensive was also estimated as more likely to occur sometime after Tet [rather] than before.

In early January 1968 another enemy document was captured in II CTZ. This was Combat Order No. 1, detailing a plan of attack on Pleiku City sometime before Tet.

On 28 January 1968, during a raid conducted in Qui Nhon City, the local MSS arrested 11 Communist cadres of the city local forces, together with two prerecorded tapes. The tapes contained a proclamation inciting the population to rise up against the government and announcing that, in addition to the occupation of Binh Dinh Province, the "Vietnamese forces struggling for Peace and Unification" were also in control of Saigon, Hue, and Danang. The captured cadres declared that Communist forces were going to launch an attack against Qui Nhon city and certain others during the Tet period.

On the same day G-2 of III Corps discovered the concentration of an enemy force consisting of one artillery and two infantry regiments in an area north of Bien Hoa. Then the next day, 29 January, the local population of Ho Nai District, Bien Hoa Province, reported the appearance of a Communist unit in an area adjacent to the district headquarters itself. During the night, guards on duty at III Corps Headquarters discovered an enemy armed reconnaissance team and shot down one team member at the gate. In Can Tho, Communist sappers disguised as tourists were apprehended by the police while they were looking for rooms in a hotel.

At 2100 hours on 30 January 1968 troops of an RF battalion manning positions on the defense belt of Saigon captured an enemy soldier armed with an AK-47 rifle. He disclosed that Communist forces were going to attack Saigon city, Tan Son Nhut airport, the Joint General Staff, and the Saigon radio station at 0300 hours on 31 January. Then, at 2130 hours, another Communist soldier was captured at Phu Nhuan (in Saigon) with two AK-47s of the collapsible stock model.

At exactly 0300 hours on 31 January 1968, or the second day of Tet (Year of the Monkey in the lunar calendar), the enemy general offensive broke out.

Those were the intelligence data collected in a chronological sequence that pertained to the 1968 general offensive. Through these data alone the enemy scheme of a general offensive was evident.

Other data of significance could have proved helpful in intelligence analysis and situation estimates during that time, but they were overlooked or not given proper attention. There was, for example, the appearance of new Communist weapons such as the modern AK-47 rifle and RPG-2 (B-40) rocket launcher. The existence of such weapons was regarded by our intelligence experts as part of a normal modernization progress and not particularly significant.

Then a rapid succession of enemy attacks against district towns in III and IV CTZs, to include an attack on the city of My Tho, failed to raise any suspicion of an abnormal effort by the enemy. The attack on Loc Ninh district town in Binh Long Province, north of Saigon, on 29 October 1967 was particularly significant, since it was conducted by forces of the CT-9 Division, reinforced by two regiments of the CT-7 Division and artillery units. The enemy succeeded, despite heavy losses, in occupying this district town, which they held for some time. The significance of these enemy actions was somehow lost to our intelligence experts. Only some time after the Tet general offensive had begun did it dawn on them that all these attacks were conducted with the purpose of testing the effectiveness of combat tactics used against cities and towns and probing the reaction of the United States and the RVN.

The "Happy Tet" poem by Ho Chi Minh that Radio Hanoi repeatedly broadcast for some time before Tet was also a significant indicator that failed to draw the attention of our intelligence experts. For one thing, it had become a habit of the North Vietnamese leader to address happy Tet wishes to the North Vietnamese population every year. For another, words of exhortation to victory were nothing new in Communist propaganda jargon. [What] our intelligence experts failed to detect was the meaning that something new would happen this coming Tet, and that it was going to be entirely different from previous years. The significance of Ho's short poem as a signal for preparations and attack was later confirmed by several enemy prisoners and returnees.

In brief, the information on hand was clear enough. There could be no mistake about its implication and meaning. It is much easier in retrospect to see the enemy general offensive coming out loud and clear against city targets. What made our intelligence experts ignore the enemy plan was simply that they were all convinced, out of prejudice and pride, that the enemy did not possess the capability, and that it would be sheer foolishness for the enemy to attempt to attack our cities. Such reasoning is understandable. Clearly, it is in line with the military intelligence theory that only capabilities are real and valid for estimate purposes; intentions are vague at best, hence not valid.

It was precisely because of this theory that our intelligence experts overlooked the most basic thing in the analysis procedure, a synthesis of all pertinent data, in this case of the data in hand on offensives against cities. Such a synthesis could have been used to see if the threat of a general offensive was real, or how probable it was. At the very least, there would have been requirements for additional intelligence data or some advance warnings to the military leadership.

However, our military leaders would not have believed such a probability if they had been warned. Given the optimistic mood prevailing in domestic and American politics at the time, they were all elated about military gains and generally held the view that a military victory would materialize in the not-too-distant future. The intelligence establishment was heavily influenced by such optimistic prospects, and its tendency to echo the official line was understandable. . . .

As a matter of fact, there did exist some intelligence analysts who were really concerned about [the] information available. However, they persisted in thinking in a Phase I-II-III manner. During 1967 the general tendency of enemy activities was still confined to Phase I of Communist strategy, which was essentially defensive. To pass on to Phase III, which was the general offensive phase, they thought that the enemy had to proceed through Phase II, which was a holding phase characterized by limited contested actions. But our error was the assumption that the enemy military effort at the end of 1967 was still in Phase I. In reality, judging by the mobile form of warfare which the enemy had been conducting for some time, he had already passed on to Phase II, although this transition had been gradual.

A major shortcoming of Vietnamese intelligence during this pre-Tet period, which contributed to its failure to predict the Tet Offensive, was the total lack of coordination among its multifarious agencies. Each . . . seemed to be interested only in its own activities as an independent organization. The exchange of information was formal, if any, and generally untimely. No one agency had real authority in intelligence or was qualified to serve as a clearing house uniquely responsible for intelligence production.

The coordination between RVN and US intelligence agencies was also slack and piecemeal. Forty-eight hours before the general offensive began, US forces were placed on general alert. It was apparent that US intelligence was concerned and took no chances. On the RVN side, ARVN corps commands were also issued a warning by JGS as to the possibility of an enemy offensive, but apparently the warning came too late for any effective preparations. It was in fact issued on New Year Day, barely sixteen hours before the outbreak of the first attack.

The 1968 Tet general offensive was a sobering event for the Vietnamese intelligence establishment. Many of its deficiencies were exposed and it was able to learn many invaluable lessons. First, it was learned that in an ideological war such as the Vietnamese conflict political considerations almost always outweighed tactical considerations. Experience shows that even though the enemy might sometimes lack the military capabilities for an offensive, he still went ahead with this offensive against all odds if there was a certain political goal to be achieved.

One lesson was that the search for enemy intentions was also important. Second, it was learned that the enemy always tried to achieve the element of tactical surprise for each new major effort by the employment of new weapons or weapon systems. The tactic to be used was also usually tested prior to launching the offensive. Another invaluable lesson learned by the intelligence officer was [that] he should be truthful, unbiased, and should never try to please his superiors by interpreting facts [in] a light they favored or in the way they wished.

The first phase of the 1968 general offensive also helped the RVN intelligence establishment to learn more about the enemy. Unprecedented numbers of prisoners, returnees, and important captured documents contributed toward deepening our knowledge on the enemy's strategy and policies. As a result, we knew well in advance every detail about the follow-up phase of his offensive, even the exact time of the first attack, which began on 5 May 1968. This was due to our agent sources within enemy ranks. In addition to information on the enemy campaign, these sources also divulged the difficulties that COSVN was facing, particularly the deteriorating morale of Communist units. At the same time, high-ranking returnees contributed much invaluable information on the enemy's internal situation.

The general offensive of 1968 resulted in a very significant military defeat for the enemy. He had thought that he could achieve a quick military victory by going all out against our major cities and population centers. He had hoped that the population would rise up and give him a hand, but none of these things had happened. At the cost of thousands of lives, he must have realized that his strategy did not work. Within just a few months after the defeat, COSVN felt compelled to issue in rapid succession three major policy documents—Resolution No. 8, Addendum to Resolution No. 8, and Resolution No. 9—justifying the military defeat and explaining the need for a change in strategy, all in self-serving propagandistic style.

If anything, these documents showed to what extent the morale of enemy troops had been shattered and revealed the disarray of his units. But the political gains the enemy obtained through his general offensive apparently led to the disengagement of US forces and the initiation of the Vietnamization program. Operations which revealed progress in Vietnamization, such as the cross-border incursions into Cambodia in 1970 and into lower Laos in 1971, were among the many causes that compelled the enemy to launch his general offensive of summer 1972.

The 1972 Easter Offensive

In early December 1971 information concerning a Communist general offensive during 1972 was already being obtained and recorded. In contrast to the previous experience of 1968, the first information gathered on the enemy preparations in North Vietnam was detected and made available to me by the J-2 of MACV. It was learned that North Vietnamese general reserve divisions, after a prolonged campaign in lower Laos during 1971, were redirected to North Vietnam, where they went through a process of replenishment and refitting and were preparing to move south.

From a strategic standpoint, the probability of an enemy general offensive during 1972 made sense, since it was a presidential election year in the United States. The enemy apparently anticipated the internal difficulties that the United States was going to face during the election year.

He surmised that these difficulties would give him favorable opportunities. During 1971 foreign aid to North Vietnam had increased substantially and its level was only a little less than during 1967. Based on lessons learned during 1968, this increase in foreign aid level was unmistakably an indication of a general offensive.

Battles fought in lower Laos early in 1971 confirmed the fact that Communist forces had received quantities of deadly new weapons such as artillery field guns and howitzers of 100mm, 130mm, and 152mm, T-34 and T-54 tanks, SA-2 antiair missiles, etc. With the new deployment and disposition of NVA general reserve divisions in South Vietnam, it was estimated that the general offensive would take place in three specific areas: Tri-Thien-Hue in MR-1, Kontum-Pleiku in MR-2, and Tay Ninh in MR-3. It was estimated that the enemy's tactical approach would be concentrated on a few key objectives in each military region instead of encompassing all objectives throughout the country. The timing for the offensive was estimated to be sometime during March 1972.

Such was, in general terms, the intelligence estimate concerning the enemy 1972 general offensive which was issued in mid-January 1972 as a result of an ever-increasing flow of data. The exact time frame for this offensive was still under debate at that time. It was estimated that March would be the best time as far as the enemy was concerned because during the dry season, which had begun in October the previous year, enemy supplies were moved in great quantities into South Vietnam. By the end of February, it was estimated, these supplies would have reached COSVN and been distributed to units under its control in MR-3 and MR-4. Since the 1968 memory was still fresh, the assumption was that the enemy would choose not to strike during the Tet holidays, but probably before or after.

Late in February 1972 President Thieu paid a visit to ARVN major units, during which he presented his Happy Tet greetings to the troops. The places that he visited almost coincided with the probable objectives of the enemy offensive. It appeared as if his itinerary had been selected on purpose—Dong Ha and Hue in MR-1 and Dak To, Tan Canh, Le Minh, and Binh Dinh in MR-2. The visit was also intended to provide the president an opportunity to review the military situation with his field commanders in the face of the coming general offensive, and particularly to assess the concern of our troops regarding the use of 130mm artillery by the enemy against the area south of the DMZ. But enemy tanks and their probable use in the offensive did not give rise to any appreciable concern among our field commanders. Apparently they thought that, with the US tremendous firepower, enemy tanks would be sitting ducks.

On 19 February 1972 information was obtained concerning instructions passed from High Command Hanoi to Headquarters, B-3 Front. Subsequently, some of these instructions were passed on by this headquarters to its subordinate divisions and provinces. The indications were clear enough and led both US and the RVN intelligence authorities to the conclusion that the enemy was going to launch his general offensive immediately after the truce, probably on the fifth day of Tet. In Vietnamese intelligence eyes, this date was of particular significance, since it was the day selected by Emperor Quang Trung to launch his famous military march north to defeat the Chiang in 1788.

As a result, a general alert was issued to units throughout the country. But the enemy changed his plans and chose not to strike on that date. It was unclear to the RVN intelligence as to why there was such a countermand order. It was possible, however, to surmise that the postponement had some connection with President Nixon's visit to mainland China from 21 to 28 February 1972. It was probable that China asked for such a postponement because it did not want any misstep to spoil the nascent US-China relationship.

Late in March 1972 information was obtained by J-7 of the JGS that 29 March was to be the D-Day of the general offensive. This information was disseminated to all ARVN units as a measure of precaution.

The 1972 Summer Offensive, as it became known to our side, broke out at first in the DMZ area on 30 March 1972. Enemy 130mm artillery pieces positioned north of the DMZ concentrated their fire on all ARVN outposts in the DMZ area. In a subsequent action, NVA general reserve units moved across the Ben Hai River with the support of tanks. The direction of attack during the enemy offensive in MR-1 was a surprise to our field command. As a matter of fact, we had failed to predict that the enemy would cross the DMZ and mount a frontal attack against Gio Linh, Cam Lo, and other outposts. It had been our assumption that the enemy attack would be from the west instead of the north, because crossing the DMZ would be a blatant violation of the Geneva Accords.

The enemy firepower and forceful, all-out drive across the DMZ so overwhelmed our advance positions that they were unable to report accurately the situation to the headquarters of the 3rd Division and I Corps. As it turned out, up to three days after it was launched the enemy general offensive in MR-1 still failed to arouse any major concern in Saigon.

The situation became serious when Communist forces infiltrated into MR-3 from Cambodia and overran Loc Ninh on 4 April. Intelligence data collected from a returnee and communication sources had pointed toward Binh Long Province as a major target area, but our own attention was directed more toward Tay Ninh than Loc Ninh (a northernmost district town of Binh Long Province) because of Tay Ninh's political importance. The enemy chose to attack Binh Long with two divisions, the CT-5 and CT-9, with the support of tanks and with the CT-7 division establishing blocking positions on QL-13 between Chon Thanh and An Loc.

The appearance of Communist tanks on the Binh Long front was claimed by the III Corps commander to be a complete surprise. The tanks were instrumental in the quick overrunning of Loc Ninh district town and the encirclement of An Loc, provincial capital of Binh Long Province. Information on enemy tanks, however, had been reported by agent sources during the ARVN operation at Krek and Chup in Cambodia as early as in December 1971. Those reports disclosed that there was a concentration of about 30 tanks, including PT-76s, T-34s, and T-54s, in the area of the Chup Plantation. Reports made at that time by the Cambodian local population to G-2, Republic of Khmer Forces General Staff, also indicated the same thing. But still our aerial photo reconnaissance failed to produce any positive evidence. These reports on enemy tanks had been disseminated three times to the III Corps commander and his subordinate division commanders. His claim of surprise was therefore unfounded. When enemy tanks moved toward An Loc, two new types among them were discovered—Chicom-made T-59s and some other models of the Russian-made BTR.

In MR-2 the enemy general offensive had already begun during March by drives against military strongpoints in the Truong Son mountain range northwest of Kontum. The enemy main force conducting those attacks was the 320th and NT-2 Divisions, whose presence had been detected by American sources. Two ARVN airborne brigades, deployed as reinforcement for II Corps, had been engaged by enemy forces several times, but it was not ascertained whether these forces were part of the 320th Division. Finally the II Corps commander promised to give a big reward to whichever unit succeeded in capturing enemy prisoners needed to corroborate intelligence reports and identify enemy forces.

One day later, an airborne battalion captured five enemy troops of the 320th Division, and the next day another four prisoners of the same division. The enemy pressure was particularly heavy at Dak To and Tan Canh, where the 22nd ARVN Infantry Division headquarters was located. On 21 April, based on intelligence reports, the enemy intention to attack the division headquarters became evident. In the light of synthesized data on enemy movements, the division G-2 warned of an imminent tank-supported attack against the division headquarters, probably during the next two or three days. But this enemy capability was rejected by the II Corps commander and his American advisor. On 23 April, enemy PT-76 tanks moved in to attack the 22nd Division headquarters and overran it during the day.

During the first three months of the general offensive, which broke out almost simultaneously on three separate fronts, it was difficult to know which front was the enemy main effort. On all three fronts, intelligence collection was provided effectively by information derived from all sources available, such as aerial photos, communications intercept, and radio direction finding, in addition to combat intelligence and agent sources. In fact, US-RVNAF intelligence forces were so effective during this time that the movement of the 271st Regiment was accurately followed from the DMZ area to Tay Ninh. After the 271st Regiment was engaged by our forces in Tay Ninh, its identity and other particulars were confirmed by prisoners and documents captured.

The loss of Quang Tri City on 1 May 1972 and the heavy casualties suffered by forces of the 3rd Division while retreating on what became [known] as the "Boulevard of Horror" toward Hue aggravated the situation and endangered this city. The question pondered by intelligence experts at that time was when Hue would be attacked. It had become evident that should the enemy choose to attack Hue immediately, this city stood no chance of holding out, given the shattered morale of ARVN troops and the local population.

The enemy's failure to advance onto Hue after Quang Tri was regarded by many from hindsight as one of his major blunders, for he had squandered an invaluable opportunity to overrun this city. The simple truth was that he had run out of his capabilities after taking Quang Tri, although he was fully aware of the situation in Hue and [was] willing to take advantage of it. Through reports made by enemy units to higher commands, it was learned that two regiments of the NVA 304th Division were almost totally annihilated.

During the months that followed, battles continued to rage with fierceness despite a decrease in their number. In the meantime, at the conference table in Paris, the positions held by the United States and North Vietnam were still light years away from each other. Based on a synthesis of intelligence data in mid-July 1972, JGS nevertheless predicted quite accurately that a cease-fire was in the making and would probably materialize sometime during November 1972. The cease-fire, it was also foreseen, would be a standstill arrangement leading to a situation of "leopard skin" troop disposition and calling for the creation of a national council of reconciliation and concord, the transitional step toward an eventual coalition government.

The fact that a cease-fire was in the making became evident in the light of stepped-up orders issued by the enemy to make a census of RVNAF prisoners, and to search for detailed information on his own personnel that were detained by the RVN, including names. Information on the date of the cease-fire became clearer in early October 1972, and up to one month before it actually became effective our intelligence had gathered much data on an enemy scheme to take advantage of the cease-fire. The cease-fire of 28 January 1973 was a new page in the history of the Vietnam War, and brought about new challenges for the RVN.

The Post-Cease-Fire Period

Whatever the viewpoint, the Paris Agreement of 28 January 1973 came about as a real turning point of the war in Vietnam. It brought about a temporary and uncertain peace. But how long would this peace last, and how soon would the war resume, and under what form? Was it going to be a conventional general offensive of the 1972 type, or was it to be a combined military-political effort in which military pressure was used as a leverage to force the RVN to comply with political solutions conceived and advanced by the Communists? Those were the questions that arose, because resumption of the war was foreseen as inevitable, regardless of its form. But the vital question that preoccupied the RVN was the matter of time—when?

The first information that helped confirm the eventuality of war resumption was provided by our own prisoners, who had been released by North Vietnam and gathered the information on their way south. In North Vietnam, they reported, the mandatory military service was still as effective as ever and North Vietnamese cadres never believed that there would be true peace.

The official party line was particularly clear as to the meaning of peace and the Paris Agreement. As it was explained by Van Tien Dung and To Huu during their visits to Communist units in South Vietnam in March 1973, and later reported by enemy prisoners and returnees, the Paris Agreement was but a pause, a stopover rest on the long journey toward conquering the South. The idea of a stopover rest stemmed from a practical policy espoused by Truong Chinh which . . . was aimed at buying time for North Vietnam to reorganize and refit its own forces while continuing to attrite the adversary forces by military action.

As a matter of fact, two plans were implemented simultaneously by the Communists during that time. The first plan pertained to the implementation of the Paris Agreement whereby, based on and taking advantage of the legalistic aspect of the agreement, the Communists would take up a political struggle to achieve political gains. This amounted to demanding 12 basic freedom rights for the people of South Vietnam, to include the right of movement.

To achieve this goal, the Communists felt they should demonstrate to the Vietnamese people, particularly the South Vietnamese populace, the attractiveness of life under their regime. Among other things, they believed they ought to show that Communist living conditions under a Communist regime were adequately comfortable and not in any way inferior to those found in South Vietnam.

As a result Dong Ha, formerly an RVN district town, was transformed into a modern city intended both as an unofficial capital for the PRG and a model of Communist-run cities. It mushroomed overnight with prefabricated buildings, was provided with electricity and running water, and was even adorned with a public transportation system of some 30 brand-new buses. The first aerial photo taken of Dong Ha, which revealed the presence of these buses, took our intelligence experts by surprise because, even in Hanoi, the capital of North Vietnam, there were no buses of this type. Our conjecture at first was that the buses were needed to meet increasing demands in logistics transportation. But subsequent information obtained from Dong Ha indicated otherwise. The buses were used to transport civilian passengers, which was something highly unusual but required to make up a showcase of Communist modern living. The significance of the whole show became evident when we learned about a Communist plan to induce people to return to their home villages in the areas under their control and to attract those living under government control to go over to their side. In the Dong Ha marketplace, Red Chinese consumer goods were plentiful and conspicuously displayed.

At the same time, North Vietnam also introduced teachers, public health workers, and administrative cadre into enemy-controlled areas in order to assist in running those places. In MR-3, according to agent sources, about 5,000 Vietnamese living in Cambodia had been coaxed by the Communists to repatriate and settle in an area near Tay Ninh; this information was later confirmed by enemy prisoners. For a long time the NLF of South Vietnam had contemplated Tay Ninh as the future capital for a Communist-controlled nation, because geographically it was adjacent to War Zone C and the Cambodian border and, politically, it was an important area where the Cao Dai temple was located.

The enemy's plan of "returning people to their home villages" was initiated at about the same time with the Land and Population Grab plan, which was designed to wrest more control away from the RVN government. Those were the objectives contained in Directive No. 2/73 that COSVN issued about one week before cease-fire day. One month after the Paris Agreement went into effect, COSVN issued another directive, No. 3/73, whose aim was to reassert the five plans and objectives of struggle earmarked for the post-cease-fire period—military struggle, political struggle, proselytizing of RVNAF troops, deployment of combat forces and expansions of territory, and legalistic implementation of the Paris Agreement. Through this directive, the Communists still considered political struggle as the main effort, but they also strove to achieve a military balance in their favor by developing a combat force larger and more powerful than the RVNAF.

Directive No. 3/73 was known to us only partially, however. Most of the information came from various agent sources and piecemeal documents. We came into possession of the complete text of the directive only after a raid conducted by the sector of Binh Thuan into an enemy base in May 1973.

During this period, two enemy troop movements took place simultaneously. On the one hand, general reserve units such as the 304th, 308th, and 312th Divisions withdrew into North Vietnam to undergo refitting. On the other hand, troop infiltrations continued their movement into South Vietnam, intended as local replacements and replenishments.

In logistics, the enemy initiated a campaign called "logistic general offensive" to increase movement of supplies into South Vietnam, particularly into the northern area of MR-1. Intelligence sources indicated that the first campaign lasted 45 days. Later, aerial photos taken to confirm those reports revealed that the amount of supplies brought south was so great that much had to be stored in the open. Apparently additional warehouses had not been built in time to store the increased influx of supplies.

The Joint Communiqué signed in Paris on 13 June 1973 did not bring about any concrete results. Neither side was willing to make concessions, and only paid lip service to enforcing a true cease-fire. Internationally, meanwhile, several events of importance occurred, the most significant of which, as far as the RVN was concerned, was the termination of US involvement in Cambodia.

Domestically, some opposition movements came into the open and were particularly active, such as the national reconciliation movement, the anticorruption movement, the famine relief movement, etc. All these events spurred COSVN into issuing Directive No. 4 in September 1973. The entire text of this document was provided by an agent working with the enemy. Its genuineness was recognized after being collated with other sources. The purpose of COSVN Directive No. 4 was "to provide guidance for military and political cadres, people's organizations, and party members in mobilizing the popular mass for a three-front struggle against the South Vietnamese government, with particular attention given to the violent force of the popular mass."

Also during this time, the sector of Lam Dong succeeded in enlisting the collaboration of an enemy provincial commissar. This political commissar, who later returned to our side, gave us a most important revelation—the Communists were preparing a "strategic raid" type offensive in MR-1 whose objectives were Hue and Danang. North Vietnam's Air Force, it was disclosed, would also be employed during this offensive. The purpose of the enemy plan was to strike a forceful military blow to achieve some accomplished facts and exert pressure for political demands related to the implementation of the Paris Agreement.

By chance, an aerial photo taken over Laos revealed a reduced model of an airfield constructed on the ground, complete with airplanes parked in revetments, landing strips, and control tower. Our intelligence experts tried to match this model with configurations of airfields in Vietnam, Laos, and Cambodia, and discovered that the airfield model represented exactly the structural configuration of Danang airfield.

As to the enemy's plan to employ the North Vietnamese Air Force in an offensive in South Vietnam, it was learned as early as during the first week of the 1972 Summer Offensive that North Vietnam had plans to conduct air raids against Carroll Base and Quang Tri City, despite the absolute air superiority enjoyed by both the US and the RVN Air Force over South Vietnamese battlefields. The enemy strategic raid plan was later made public by the RVN government in an effort both to denounce the Communist scheme of making a mockery of the Paris Agreement and to forestall an enemy military action that could result in grave consequences.

At the end of 1973, several Communist leaders openly hinted at a strategy shift in South Vietnam. The new Communist strategy, it was disclosed, purported to push hard with military activities and escalate attacks in terms of target importance and forces committed. Communist forces would concentrate now on more important targets such as district towns and subsector headquarters instead of isolated outposts, and would increase the size of their attacks to regimental level and above, with combined use of artillery, armor, and antiaircraft weapons. This strategy was affirmed by Resolution No. 21 of the North Vietnamese Labor Party as a result of a session held in October 1973. Based on this guidance, COSVN developed Resolution No. 12 of its own, whose existence became known to us in early 1974 (but its entire text was not available until March).

According to this resolution, the Communists admitted that never before in the war had their military forces in South Vietnam been so strong and [they] were in fact stronger than the RVNAF. The resolution also indicated that military activities to be conducted in the future would all be large-scale actions, but they would be consistent with a policy of flexibility, or skillful coordination between military and political-diplomatic efforts. In other words, the Communists contended that military actions should result in political and diplomatic gains.

North Vietnam's assessment of its military might was not entirely subjective or self-serving. On the contrary, it reflected quite accurately the balance of forces between the two warring sides. For, in addition to replacing losses incurred during the 1972 Summer Offensive, the enemy also succeeded in increasing substantially his military potential, particularly in terms of antiaircraft weapons, armor, and artillery.

At Khe Sanh, for example, SAM-2 antiaircraft missiles were installed as soon as the cease-fire went into effect. Other radar-controlled antiaircraft weapons, such as 37mm and 57mm guns, were deployed as far south as in MR-3. There were more than 400 enemy tanks and armored vehicles after replacements were received. Heavy artillery, such as 130mm and 122mm field guns, was introduced into the tri-border area in MR-2 and the north of MR-3 in great quantities. Despite serious limitations in aerial photo reconnaissance, our intelligence was able to detect enemy tanks, either camouflaged under thatched roofs or while moving, and . . . to detect the movements of 130mm artillery guns from outside the border into MR-3. This information constituted evidence of tremendous infiltrations and logistical buildup during the post-cease-fire period.

Information provided by the US Defense Attaché Office revealed that Logistics Corps 559 and three of its subordinate units—Logistics Divisions 470, 471, and 473, formerly operating on Laotian territory along the old Ho Chi Minh Trail—had moved inside South Vietnam to construct roads and transport supplies along the newly opened Truong Son corridor. Other logistical divisions of Corps 559 meanwhile still continued operating outside South Vietnam—Division 472 in lower Laos, and Division 571 at Ban Karai and Mu Gia Pass.

The Truong Son corridor, or new Route 14, was now extended from North to South Vietnam, and major targets of enemy attacks all lay in those areas bearing upon the extension work on this new road system. In addition, the enemy installed two separate fuel pipeline systems, one leading from North Vietnam across the DMZ into MR-1 and terminating in Quang Nam Province, the other running south from Laos into South Vietnam along the Cambodian border and reaching into Quang Duc Province in MR-3. Data gathered on the characteristics of these pipelines were carefully studied by our intelligence experts, who found that they carried diesel oil. This fact was confirmed by the end of 1974 when a long-range reconnaissance team was sent into Quang Duc Province to destroy part of the pipeline system.

Implementing Resolution No. 21 of North Vietnam's Labor Party and Resolution No. 12 of COSVN, enemy forces attacked and overran their first target of importance, the Dak Pek district town in Kontum Province, which was in effect the first district town lost to the enemy since the cease-fire. The enemy attack took place on 17 May 1974 and was an instant success. The lack of forceful reaction on the part of ARVN forces appeared to stimulate and encourage the enemy to overrun in rapid succession a series of other district towns.

The most significant enemy action was his attack on the Thuong Duc district town in Quang Nam Province in July 1974. This attack was significant not so much because of the economic and demographic importance of the target areas, which included the Nong Son coal mine and a population of 20,000, but primarily because of a new tactic employed by the enemy, a form of conventional, combined-arms mobile warfare.

The enemy unit conducting this attack was the NVA 304th Division (-), which had been directly deployed from Quang Tri and joined forces with the 29/324B Regiment, which had moved north from Dak Pek in Kontum Province. The combined movements of these two units came about as a complete surprise for the local field command because, in contrast with the previous period, we were unable to detect them. In addition to these infantry formations, the enemy employed one artillery regiment and one armor regiment.

• • •

The new mobile, combined-arms tactic was recorded as the first instance of its employment by the enemy on a South Vietnamese battlefield. In the eyes of Vietnamese intelligence experts, it was reminiscent of a lesson learned previously from the enemy's practice of testing a tactic before actually using it in a major offensive. This mobile tactic was also characteristic of the maneuvering concept espoused by Van Tien Dung, NVA Chief of Staff. It obviously bore his personal mark. As a result, it was surmised that he, instead of Vo Nguyen Giap, would be tasked to direct a future general offensive effort in South Vietnam.

In October 1974 a returnee, who belonged to a reconnaissance unit of the CT-7 Division, disclosed that the enemy was planning to attack the district towns of Phuoc Long Province which lay along QL-14, such as Don Luan, Duc Phong, and even the provincial capital itself. He also revealed that the CT-7 Division was tasked to conduct this offensive campaign with the support of tanks and artillery. This information proved correct and reliable, being later confirmed by communications intercept and agent sources. It was also consistent with the enemy's advocated strategy of escalating his military effort from attacks against isolated outposts to attacks against district towns and then provincial capitals. The enemy launched his initial efforts against Don Luan and Duc Phong on 14 December 1974 and finally overran the Phuoc Long provincial capital on 6 January 1975.

The 1975 General Offensive

The enemy's preparation to reinfiltrate his general reserve divisions from the North into South Vietnam was first made available to [the] JGS by [the] DAO. It was revealed in November 1974 that the NVA 316th Division, after its withdrawal from the Plain of Jars in Laos, and after undergoing refitting and indoctrination in North Vietnam's MR-4, was the first one ordered to move into South Vietnam. Another NVA division, the 341st, which had been disbanded since 1968, was now reactivated and received the same orders. The NVA 312th, 338th, and 320th Divisions followed suit at a later time.

• • •

In logistics activities, there were increased movements of supplies and personnel into South Vietnam at the outset of the 1974–1975 dry season, which began in October. Long convoys, sometimes numbering more than 200 vehicles, were sighted moving along the new infiltration route, which began in North Vietnam, extended along QL-9 into lower Laos via Khe Sanh, then veered south toward the tri-border area in MR-2 and from there toward COSVN headquarters. In addition, other vehicle movements were also seen bringing men and supplies from the A Shau–A Luoi area into Quang Nam, Quang Tin, and Quang Ngai Provinces in MR-1 and into northern Binh Dinh Province in MR-2.

• • •

The year-end estimate of the situation in 1974, issued by J-2/JGS, observed that the Communists had the capabilities to launch a general offensive of a scale and intensity comparable to those of the 1972 Summer Offensive and that this offensive could be sustained for as long as 18 months. The scope of the general offensive, it was forecast, would be a compromise between the 1968 and 1972 campaigns, that is, an effort encompassing both frontline offensives and attacks against cities and provincial capitals. The most appropriate time frame for this effort was estimated [to be from] 25 March 1975 onward.

Not everybody believed this prediction. While there was general agreement on the facts presented, a few people were of the opinion that during 1975 there would be attacks of a major scale but short of a general offensive. These individuals thought the general offensive would probably take place in 1976, a US presidential election year. The RVN military intelligence nevertheless stuck to the estimate that 1975 would be the year, especially after several additional enemy documents advocated the need to launch decisive attacks against major cities such as Hue, Danang, Saigon, and Can Tho. The enemy reasoned that once these important cities were taken, others would follow suit.

By now in the Mekong Delta, an intelligence synthesis indicated that the enemy's main effort was to attack and occupy Moc Hoa, provincial capital of Kien Tuong, open an infiltration corridor leading from outside the Cambodian border into his base in the Plain of Reeds, and interdict movement on QL-4 between Saigon and Can Tho. But the CT-5 Division, which was to carry out this scheme, was defeated by the ARVN 7th and 9th Infantry Divisions.

With an aim to coordinate its general military effort, COSVN made plans to attack Tay Ninh City with the CT-9 division and elements of the CT-5 Division, to be augmented in time by newly infiltrated units. This piece of intelligence was provided by an enemy agent and duly confirmed by other sources. Politically, Tay Ninh was an important province because it was the seat of the Cao Dai sect, and militarily it was a key buffer zone between the Cambodian border and War Zone C and the Iron Triangle. It had been coveted by the enemy for a long time.

To counteract this move, III Corps deployed the entire 25th Infantry Division, reinforced by one infantry regiment, the 81st Airborne Ranger Group, and an armor brigade, into Tay Ninh. The engagement broke out on 10 March 1975 and led to the loss of a string of outposts located along the western bank of the East Vam Co River, west of Tay Ninh Province. But the 6th Regiment of the enemy CT-5 Division suffered heavy losses during this battle.

Southeast of Tay Ninh, Tri Tam district town and the Michelin plantation were also attacked and overrun by the CT-9 Division. The CT-9 Division then joined forces with three local battalions in a subsequent move to cut off QL-22 and interdict traffic between Tay Ninh and Saigon. The CT-9 Division failed in this effort, however, and QL-22 was finally cleared by friendly forces.

North of Tay Ninh, enemy pressure was particularly threatening after Ba Den Mountain had been occupied. The enemy then moved his artillery pieces into mountain caves which had been transformed into invulnerable firing positions by his engineers. Tay Ninh city was thus directly threatened by enemy artillery fire. The mounting enemy pressure was such that the Cao Dai Church was compelled to issue a statement declaring that its temple was a neutral zone and asking both sides to stop military actions in this area.

The enemy's main effort, however, was directed toward MR-2. Since early February 1975 contact had been lost with the NVA 320th Division, which usually operated in the Duc Co area west of Pleiku. While efforts were being made to search for the whereabouts of this major enemy unit, an enemy cadre division was preparing to move south to launch an attack against Ban Me Thuot, to interdict QL-14 at the joint boundary of Pleiku and Ban Me Thuot Provinces by attacking the district town of Thuan Man, and to mount ambushes at the Buon Blech Pass to interdict our relief efforts from Pleiku. The returnee also disclosed that this attack would be supported by tanks and artillery and that the 320th Division was under strict orders to conceal its movement toward Ban Me Thuot. Among other things reported by this returnee, it was learned that enemy troops and cadres were not informed of the geographical names of transit locations and that movements were to be made only during hours of darkness. The 320th Division also exercised complete radio silence while moving.

After the loss of Ban Me Thuot, an enemy prisoner disclosed an interesting detail concerning the enemy's attempt at deceiving our intelligence effort. To keep its movement secret, the 320th Division left behind its command radio station at Duc Co, which continued to transmit while the division was slipping away. In fact, this deception served no useful purpose. For a long time our EC-47 airplanes had not dared to venture in this area because of heavy enemy antiaircraft fire. The objective thus selected by the enemy for this offensive—Ban Me Thuot—turned out to be an entirely new one, since his usual objectives in MR-2 were Kontum and Pleiku.

Despite efforts by several reconnaissance units injected in the area between Pleiku and Ban Me Thuot to look for the 320th Division, its whereabouts were still unknown. But through many interrogation sessions, our returnees proved to be sincere. As a result, G-2/II Corps concluded . . . that Ban Me Thuot was going to be the target of the new enemy offensive.

At about this time, in Binh Dinh Province, intelligence sources of the 22nd Infantry Division revealed that the entire enemy NT-3 (Gold Star) Division was concentrating its forces in an attempt to interdict QL-19 at Binh Khe and An Tuc, and that this effort might last up to three months. Other sources from Nha Trang reported that QL-21 would be interdicted between Nha Trang and Ban Me Thuot. All these data clearly pointed toward an enemy plan of offensive [action] whose initial move was to cut off all lines of communication around Ban Me Thuot in order to isolate it before conducting the main attack.

This was the intelligence estimate presented to the II Corps commander, but for some reason he did not believe the enemy would attack Ban Me Thuot. The defense of Ban Me Thuot was nevertheless reinforced by the 53rd Infantry Regiment and the tactical command post of the 23rd Infantry Division. The city, up to that time, had been defended only by territorial forces.

In the meantime, our intelligence lost track of the NVA 316th Division, whose presence in North Vietnam had been reported. Our guess was that this division was moving south. A warning was then issued to all corps and division commands to watch for the 316th Division, but all efforts failed to locate this elusive unit.

Late in February 1975, intelligence sources in Binh Dinh Province reported continuing movement of the NVA 3rd Division toward QL-19, and, on 3 March, it was confirmed that this axis of communication was being interdicted. The 22nd Division reacted immediately by deploying two regiments to Binh Khe and An Tuc. Although friendly troops held firm their positions at these two places, they were unable to clear QL-19.

At the same time, the enemy 95B Regiment attacked QL-19 at Le Trung, making the interdiction of this vital road more serious. At Khanh Duong, the enemy 25B [*sic*] Regiment established blocking positions on QL-14 and effectively cut off all traffic from Ban Me Thuot to Nha Trang. On 7 March, during an engagement with enemy forces at Duc Lap, southeast of Ban Me Thuot, our troops captured a document which revealed the presence of the F-10 Division in this area. So this division, too, had moved away from the Kontum area into the vicinity of Ban Me Thuot. Another captured document, which was the enemy plan of attack against the city, disclosed that the main effort would be driven from the southwest; it was to be preceded by sapper penetrations, artillery preparatory fire, and an initial assault by tanks.

On 8 March Thuon Nam district town was attacked; QL-14 was thus interdicted midway between Pleiku and Ban Me Thuot, exactly as reported previously by the returnee. By this time it had become evident that Ban Me Thuot would be the objective of the enemy offensive.

Preparations for the defense were going on feverishly in Ban Me Thuot as of 9 March. The city braced itself for the attack, because red alert orders had been issued. Garrison units established positions on tall buildings in the city and were issued additional anti-tank ammunition. At 0330 on the morning of 10 March 1975, enemy tanks began to move into Ban Me Thuot. But, according to an enemy document captured later in Ban Me Thuot, the attack took place at least two days earlier than planned. The enemy had advanced the attack date because he knew his plan had been leaked. He rushed the attack before our forces had a chance to consolidate their defenses.

As the battle unfolded, it was learned that the 320th Division attacked the city and the Phuong Duc airfield from the north. The F-10 Division moved in from the southwest, while the 316th Division stayed back as reserve and did not participate in the attack until 11 March. Enemy prisoners captured from the 316th Division disclosed that their unit had moved from North Vietnam by trucks, using the Ho Chi Minh Trail in Laotian territory, and only crossed into South Vietnam at Duc Lap in Quang Duc Province in order to avoid detection by our intelligence. Orders given to the 316th Division were strict—its movement was to be kept absolutely secret. No radio contact between elements was allowed, and on arrival at destination no contact was permitted, even with local Communist authorities.

The enemy's basic objective when launching his offensive in the Central Highlands of MR-2 in early March 1975, as developed from a captured enemy document, was to occupy two out of its three provinces by the end of the dry season. Then, at the outset of the rainy season, he would stop his military activities and offer to negotiate with the

RVN government. In all probability he would demand the establishment of the National Council of Reconciliation and Concord, and perhaps a coalition government as well. If the RVN should refuse this demand, then he would have the justification to resume the offensive.

In any case, the offensive was intended to force the RVN government into making political concessions. Since the Central Highlands was composed of only three provinces (Kontum, Pleiku, Darlac), according to Communist territorial organization the next target of enemy attack after Ban Me Thuot was expected to be Pleiku.

The RVN decision to withdraw from Kontum and Pleiku must have been a total surprise for the enemy. As a matter of fact, a report from the B-3 Front on 18 March disclosed that the enemy was completely stunned by this move.

• • •

In Saigon . . . political circles were still desperately clinging to the hopes that a political modus vivendi and a cease-fire could be achieved at the last minute. They did not know that Hanoi had decided to take Saigon by 19 May, [the] anniversary of Ho Chi Minh's birthday. That information was provided by an enemy agent on 17 April. The enemy final offensive, according to this source, was code-named the "Ho Chi Minh Campaign," and its final objective, Saigon, had already been renamed as Ho Chi Minh City.

• • •

In the morning of 29 April, the Communists began to shell Tan Son Nhut, the JGS, and other places in Saigon. At the same time, enemy infantry units also launched probing attacks in the suburbs of Saigon. At 1000 hours the following day, 30 April 1975, orders for the RVNAF to surrender were proclaimed on Radio Saigon.

A nation had ceased to exist; an armed force had been defeated. Sharing in this national tragic event, intelligence had also been defeated. At least, that was what the leader of the Republic of Vietnam concluded when he scribbled a personal observation on a report submitted to him by the National Intelligence Coordination Committee in mid-April 1975: "Intelligence, beware of information planted by the Communists. They strike Ban Me Thuot when you said Pleiku. And you said Tay Ninh while they attacked Phuoc Long."

• • •

VIII. CONCLUSIONS

Every qualified observer will agree that the RVN had too many intelligence agencies—civilian, paramilitary, and military. These agencies were in different command channels and reported to different authorities. This gave rise to redundancies in tasks and objectives, dilution of effort, and, worst of all, unhealthy competition. An effort was made to offset the handicaps of this situation by establishing intelligence coordination committees, but this solution did not work out as expected. Effective coordination suffered from the fact that it depended upon the willingness to cooperate of the individual members involved.

• • •

South Vietnamese leaders were of course fully aware of the organizational complexity and multiplicity of the intelligence establishment and, consequently, the need for streamlining and unifying the intelligence effort. But the intricate interplay of political powers and interests prevented progress along these lines because it remained the basic desire of each executive authority to have under his personal control an intelligence agency that he could freely use for his own end. Moreover, there was always the danger of creating a new kind of power rivalry if all intelligence agencies were placed under any one authority. No one really wanted an all-powerful intelligence authority.

• • •

Within South Vietnam the primary interests in information and the objectives of intelligence activities focused mostly on the military situation and internal politics. Economic intelligence was largely neglected. The lack of good economic intelligence led to ineffective resource control programs. Rice, the most important national resource, which directly affected the lives of the populace, was not subject to effective control. Production, distribution, and trade in this vital commodity were manipulated by profiteering middlemen who always managed to divert large quantities into enemy-controlled areas. In addition to speculation and pilferage of rice, the RVN government was also plagued by a proliferation of counterfeited banknotes. There were many reasons to believe that the enemy was behind this sabotage of the currency, but this suspicion was never confirmed by hard intelligence.

Despite the emphasis on tactical intelligence—and some considered this emphasis excessive—the resources allotted for tactical intelligence collection were far below requirements. The RVN defense expenditures represented the greatest share of the national budget, but most of the defense budget was earmarked for what were considered priority needs "to move, to shoot, and to communicate." Very little was spent "to see"; the leadership failed to realize that it made little sense to have mobility and firepower if the enemy could not be found and his activities anticipated.

Not only did the RVN political and defense leadership show little interest in military intelligence, field commanders in general did not regard military intelligence as a command responsibility such as operations, logistics, and training. Strange as it may seem, military intelligence was considered a staff responsibility, an activity for which intelligence specialists were primarily responsible. With this attitude, it is not surprising that military intelligence was frequently made the scapegoat for tactical failures, while victories invariably appeared the result of good tactical operation.

• • •

In the Vietnam War, with its strong ideological context, enemy capabilities more often than not did not indicate the probability of attack and therefore did not protect against surprise. Political dictates usually overrode military common sense, and Communist units were often tasked to launch attacks for political gain without having the required capabilities to execute such attacks successfully. "Suicide" was the usual term used to describe surprise attacks; we learned that suicide was one of the enemy's capabilities. It was apparent that intelligence estimates had to take into account both enemy capabilities and intentions, no matter how farfetched his intentions might be.

Intelligence estimates were sometimes erroneous because the analyst tended to see the enemy through the lens of his own culture and experience, and judged the enemy's actions and behavior as if the enemy would react as he would, given certain stimuli. This was a common shortcoming. Intelligence analysts were rare who could reason the way the enemy did. This at least in part accounted for the fact that [the] RVN military intelligence establishment failed to predict the enemy attack across the DMZ in the 1972 Summer Offensive. Such an action, it was thought, would constitute such a blatant violation of the 1954 Geneva Accords that the enemy would certainly never do it, given his usually reverent remarks about the inviolability of the Accords. . . .

In fact, it was not easy to place ourselves in the enemy's position because our imagination, albeit aided by a thorough knowledge of the enemy, usually fell short of reality. For example, although it was common knowledge that the enemy attached importance to the defense of his bases and rural areas, we only discovered how important they were when he resolved to attack our cities, at great cost, just to loosen our grip on the rural areas. To most of us it was a sobering experience that helped us learn more about the enemy.

• • •

Intelligence in Vietnam was truly a complex business because the war itself was complex. It was at the same time a war of ideologies, a civil war between the North and the South, and a war that was half conventional, half unconventional, and finally totally conventional at the end. Furthermore, it was a proving ground for strategies, tactics, and the modern weapon systems of two great contending world blocs.

Intelligence in Vietnam had its share of failures and successes. During the early period of the war it was plagued by instability, dilution of effort, and a lack of professionalism. With the advent of cooperation and coordination with US forces, however, it gradually improved and really attained solid ground after 1968. From that time on, its activities were crowned with successes on a professional point of view.

But its successes could have been more substantial if intelligence had been given its justified status and, more importantly, if its capabilities had been employed more impartially, objectively, and in a more disinterested manner. Intelligence could have reaped more successes if the political system to which it responded could have rallied more popular support and consequently obtained more contributions toward intelligence activities from people in all walks of life. Such assistance to one's own armed forces, after all, was nothing more than a civil obligation which, like paying taxes, was perhaps not pleasant, but nonetheless was vital to the existence of the nation.

• • •

[F]inally, any nation fighting for its existence must make every effort to mobilize its entire population in support of its armed forces, and this support must include intelligence. If it does, the reward could be immeasurable in terms of frustrating the enemy's intelligence and tactical operations, as well as providing to the nation's armed forces a vast resource of information concerning enemy activities.

NOTES

1. Sir Robert Thompson, *Phoenix, Myths and Relevances of the Viet Nam War,* as quoted by James (Paddy) Fitzsimmons, *Lugano Review* 4 (April 1975), p. 61.

2. This organization existed only in name, not in substance.

3. The PRUs were initially created and controlled by CORDS, US Embassy. As of 31 March 1969, they were transferred to the National Police. Each PRU operated under the control of the province chief.

4. First Twelve-Month Report of Chief, MAAG, Vietnam, September 1961, p. 12.

5. By order of the Chairman, National Intelligence Coordination Committee.

6. *Fact Book,* MACV J-3 (August 1967), p. 39.

7. Information obtained from the BBC and VOA was used to cross-check domestic news.

8. The RVN military intelligence evaluation system was the same used by the US Army. Letters A, B, C, D, E, and F are used to indicate the relative reliability of the source, while numbers 1, 2, 3, 4, 5, and 6 are used to indicate the evaluation of the accuracy of the information itself.

8

Logistics

Lieutenant General Dong Van Khuyen

PREFACE

The Republic of Vietnam was basically an agrarian country with a very low level of industrialization. Even in peacetime there was reasonable doubt that its national resources could ever feed a standing military force of one million men, much less equip and support it logistically. An unrelenting war of aggression waged by North Vietnam with modern, sophisticated, Communist-supplied armament made it even more difficult for the beleaguered republic to defend itself without relying on American military aid.

The story of RVNAF logistics was a gradual process of buildup that began virtually from scratch. With the injection of US military aid, and under the tutelage of US advisors, the RVNAF developed an impressive logistical system founded on American doctrine, American equipment, and American money. During the course of its evolution and expansion the RVNAF logistics system adopted and efficiently implemented modern techniques. It eventually became, like a mirror image of its mentor and supplier, structured functionally and automated operationally, a perfect model of sound organization and efficient management. Latter-day ARVN logisticians even thought out their problems and evaluated their programs in terms of cost and effectiveness, substituting modern management criteria for old outdated business practices.

Over the war years, ARVN logisticians successfully met several challenges, some problematical, such as the insufficiency of mobility assets and military aid cutbacks, but none so serious as to question the fundamental soundness of their system. Indeed, they all took pride in it and were gratified by the fact that never, during the entire war, had a battle been lost, nor had an operation ever been delayed, because of the lack of logistic support. True as this may have been, ARVN logistic achievements would never have been possible without the significant support and assistance contributed by US forces and US advisors. In fact, the evolution of RVNAF logistics was a true story of cooperation which culminated in an unprecedented degree of involvement and responsibility-sharing by both partners, up to the very last minute.

Integrity and truthfulness are the principles that have guided me throughout the preparation of this monograph. I have to draw primarily on my personal involvement with the system, which I commanded and helped to shape for several years, almost since its inception. To substantiate some of the key events or major highlights I have relied on personal interviews with the principals involved, both American and Vietnamese. All of the illustrations are from my personal collection and are unavailable elsewhere. . . . [15 December 1976]

I. INTRODUCTION

For twenty-one years, 1955–1975, from its inception to its final collapse, the Republic of Vietnam almost totally depended on United States aid for its nation-building effort. This included aid for economic development as well as that required for defending itself against Communist subversion and invasion.

• • •

By the time the 300-day moratorium [following completion of the 1954 Geneva Accords] was over, the national government agencies, the National Army of Vietnam, and nearly one million freedom-loving North Vietnamese had, with the assistance of the United States, moved south and were determined, together with the people of South Vietnam, to build a new nation south of the Ben Hai River.

The Logistics Environment

It was in those compelling circumstances that the Republic of Vietnam (RVN), or South Vietnam, was born in 1955 and baptized by the United States as a free and independent nation. Saigon, its capital, lies one half of the globe away from Washington DC, or a distance of 12 flight hours by jet [aircraft]. Saigon is 1,800 miles from Okinawa and 7,800 miles from Travis Air Force Base in California. From the east coast of the United States, sea routes take 34 days to reach Vietnam; from San Francisco approximately 19 days are required.

Situated at the southern end and eastern side of the Indochinese peninsula, which protrudes from mainland Asia like a pistol grip, South Vietnam shares a common border with North Vietnam to the north and Laos and Cambodia to the west. Its long coastline extends along the South China Sea to the Gulf of Siam. The national territory of South Vietnam is long and narrow, measuring about 700 miles from the Ben Hai River at the 17th parallel to the tip of the peninsula and the 8th parallel at Ca Mau. It varies in width from 40 to 125 miles. It is approximately as long as California, but is only approximately one-third as wide. The stately Truong Son mountain range (otherwise called Chaine Annamitique or Cordillera) extends along three-fourths of the western portion of South Vietnam, from the northern end to a distance of 60 miles from Saigon. This mountain range is dotted with peaks ranging from 2,000 to 8,000 feet, and its steep eastern slope faces the South China Sea. Thus it forms a natural bulwark protecting the western flank of South Vietnam and, together with the vast Central Highlands which rolls out on its western slope, offers the best avenues of approach to infiltrate into and dominate the lower plains.

The Mekong Delta, which is formed by silt deposits of the Mekong and Saigon

Rivers, covers about one-fourth of the total area of South Vietnam and is called [the] "rice bowl." Its soil is partially dry and partially swampy all year round. Swamp areas such as Ca Mau and Dong Thap (Plain of Reeds) favor rice planting but not construction. In addition to major rivers such as the Tien Giang (Mekong), Hau Giang (Bassac), and the two tributaries of the Saigon River—the Vam Co East and Vam Co West, the Mekong Delta is checkered by over 2,500 miles of crisscrossing irrigation canals.

As a tropical country, South Vietnam has a hot and humid climate which is characterized by two distinct seasons: a dry season and a rainy or monsoon season. Its overall average temperature is 84 degrees F. In Saigon the monthly average for the daily high temperature ranges from 87 degrees to 95 degrees F., the daily low from 70 degrees to 76 degrees F.

The weather varies greatly from one part of South Vietnam to another. In the Mekong Delta and the Central Highlands, the rainy season starts in May and ends in October, with an average annual precipitation of 58 inches. July and August are the hottest months in these areas. North of the Central Highlands, in the area which was Military Region (MR) 1, the weather reverses itself. Here the rainy season begins in September and lasts until February. It is marked by devastating typhoons which every year slash out against Hue and other coastal cities from the South China Sea during the September–November period. Precipitation in Hue averages 116 inches per year, while Saigon enjoys clear and sunny days and dry, cool nights.

There has been no recent official census of South Vietnam's population. However, based on a 1954 figure of 12 million and an estimated annual growth rate of from 2 to 2.3 percent, the 1964 population was about 15 million and the 1974 population was about 19 million. About 80 percent of the population live in rural areas, cities and towns scattered throughout the fertile Mekong Delta and the narrow coastal plains. In addition to Vietnamese, there are ethnic minorities in the large cities, particularly in the Saigon-Cholon metropolitan area, mostly as merchants and business retailers. Also there are the Khmers, who form a farmer community of about 500,000, living in the provinces on both sides of the Bassac River and near the Cambodian border. Finally, there are over one million Montagnards who belong to two basic language stocks, the Mon-Khmer and Malayo-Polynesian. The Montagnards are divided into numerous tribal groups scattered throughout the Central Highlands. Contrary to the other groups in South Vietnam, the Montagnards quite generally engage in slash and burn crop planting.

Every year, prior to 1975, there was a net of approximately 200,000 to 250,000 adults entering the working force, which was mostly made up of farmers and fishermen. Industriousness, amicability, perseverance, and piety are the innate moral qualities of the Vietnamese people. The Vietnamese social unit is the extended family whose members—grandparents, parents, their sons and daughters and their spouses and children—live . . . close [together] and seldom leave their neighborhood or hamlet, which is also the burial place of the family's forebears. The Vietnamese family is essentially patriarchal; males are favored over females. The husband is usually the head and breadwinner of the family, while his wife takes care of the household and rears children. She rarely participates in social activities. Most Vietnamese are Buddhists. There are over two million who are Roman Catholics, but there are relatively few Protestants. In addition, there are the Hoa Hao and the Cao Dai religious sects, each with a sizable number of followers.

• • •

Vietnam is an agricultural country. Rice and rubber are its most important products. Before World War II, Vietnam was one of the world's great rice exporters, after Burma and Thailand. Due to the devastating effects of the 1949–1954 French–Viet Minh war (which came to be known as the First Indochina War), effective rice-planting area in South Vietnam was reduced from 2,464,000 to 1,660,000 hectares, and production from 2.5 million to 2 million metric tons.[1]

• • •

The country's communication system was relatively developed but heavily wrecked by the First Indochina War. The Trans-Vietnam Railway, which connects Saigon with Hue via Phan Thiet, Nha Trang, Qui Nhon, Quang Ngai, and Danang and parallels Route 1, was destroyed by the war and became unusable by 1954. Also about 60 percent of the roads were destroyed by the war. In South Vietnam, there were four categories of roads: National Routes (QL), Inter-Provincial Routes (LTL), Provincial Routes (TL), and Rural Routes (HL).

• • •

The system of national routes converges on Saigon. The more important routes are: QL-1, QL-13, QL-14, QL-19, QL-21, QL-20, and QL-4. QL-1 runs along the coastline, connecting Saigon with coastal cities and provincial capitals to the north, up to Ben Hai. It winds through two spectacular passes, Deo Ca in the Tuy Hoa area and Hai Van, just north of Danang. QL-13 starts from Saigon and runs north, connecting the capital with Cambodia and Laos. QL-14 runs the entire length of the Central Highlands, through Ban Me Thuot, Pleiku, and Kontum, then veers cross-country to connect with QL-1 at Hoa An. QL-19 and QL-21 are the two major routes connecting the Central Highlands cities with those on the coast. QL-19 connects Pleiku with Qui Nhon via [the] Mang Yang and An Khe Passes; farther south, QL-21 links Ban Me Thuot with Nha Trang via the M'Drak (Khanh Duong) Pass. QL-20 connects Dalat, the productive vegetable garden and year-round placid, cool, vacation resort, with the capital. QL-4 is the main supply artery which brings agricultural products, fish, shrimp, and charcoal from the Mekong Delta provinces to Saigon through two major ferries, one at My Thuan across the Mekong River and the other at Can Tho across the Bassac River, and two long bridges at Ben Luc and Tan An which cross the Vam Co East and Vam Co West Rivers, respectively. The Mekong River, meanwhile, together with the vast system of tributaries and canals which connect with it, provides the most vital supply means for Saigon. Convoys of sampans, boats, and barges sail on it day and night in both directions.

The port of Saigon, the RVN's most important harbor, established on the Saigon River about 50 miles inland, is capable of accommodating oceangoing vessels. Other ports, such as Nha Trang, Qui Nhon, and Danang, which are not protected and hence are subject to frequent typhoon devastations, can only dock coastal vessels. Cam Ranh, yet to be developed, is a beautiful, naturally protected port capable of accommodating oceangoing vessels and was used by the United States as a military harbor.

In air communication, at the time of the 1954 Geneva Accords there were two airlines, the government-run Air Vietnam and a privately owned airline, Cosara, which went out of business. Air Vietnam was then equipped with over ten propeller-driven aircraft, mostly DC-3 and DC-4s. Three major airports, Tan Son Nhut (Saigon), Bien Hoa, and Danang, were capable of accommodating jet aircraft. Tan Son Nhut was the most important, being a stopover and refueling station for international flights. Because of expensive airfares, however, few Vietnamese people used commercial air transportation.

Toward Economic Recovery

• • •

With increased US economic aid . . . and technical assistance, the RVN gradually restored economic stability within a few years and became financially secure by 1960. Its large annual budget deficit had been effectively offset by aid, and the GVN treasury no longer had to borrow heavily from the National Bank. Due to security, agriculture also regained full productivity during this period. The total crop-planting surface expanded from 1,660,000 hectares in 1954 to 2.4 million hectares in 1960, and rice production increased rapidly, from 2,080,000 tons in 1954 to 5,092,000 tons by 1960, generating a surplus of 340,000 tons for export in 1960. Industry meanwhile received less attention due to priorities given agricultural development.

From 1961 to 1964 renewed and increasingly escalated sabotage activities by the Communists took the rural areas under their grip. Agricultural development met with serious obstacles and difficulties. Total rice-planting acreage and production increased a mere 10 percent during the period, and rice export was reduced from 323,000 tons in 1963 to 49,000 tons in 1964.

Then the war escalated considerably during 1965 and the following years, with the introduction of NVA forces and the active participation of US and Free World Military Assistance troops. As a result of extensive combat operations (which took place mostly in rural, jungled, and mountainous areas), the absorption of manpower into the services of US troops in Saigon and other urban areas, and the stepped-up enlistment in the expanding RVNAF, over 300,000 hectares of ricefields were left unattended and South Vietnam's rice production declined markedly. Instead of exporting rice, as it had done during the previous years, the RVN had to import it in increasing quantities. During 1967 and 1968, for example, rice imports reached the highest levels, peaking at 765,087 tons for 1968.

• • •

From 1969 to 1972, the GVN pacification program made remarkable progress in the rural areas. Due to its achievements, the rural outlook became bright. The achievements included the resettlement of over a million refugees, the introduction of "miracle rice," and greatly increased use of machinery in farmwork. Thanks to mechanized tilling and irrigation, and chemical fertilizers, the total rice planting acreage was on the rise, increasing from 2,393,800 hectares in 1968 to 2,722,000 hectares in 1972. Rice production also increased, from 4,366,150 tons to 6,690,000 tons during the same period, reducing imports from 765,087 tons in 1968 to 137,000 tons in 1971 and balancing consumption requirements in 1972.

• • •

The enemy's Easter Offensive in 1972 had [a] serious impact on the RVN economic recovery effort. Three cities—Quang Tri, An Loc, and Kontum—were leveled and reduced to heaps of rubble; over 200 bridges and several miles of highways were either destroyed or heavily damaged. About 40 percent of rubber plantations ceased operation and production. In addition to physical destruction, the enemy offensive campaign also displaced 1,320,000 people from their productive jobs and turned them into refugees. Over 900,000 of these were living in relief and resettlement centers hastily built by the GVN.

• • •

Hard-pressed by immediate problems and the prospect of eventual American disengagement, President . . . Thieu made a trip to the United States in April 1973, where he sought President Nixon's commitment to help the RVN to maintain the status quo, rehabilitate war damage and resettle refugees occasioned by the Communist 1972 Easter Offensive, and initiate a long-range economic development program.

The economic aid package proposed by President Thieu called for some increase in the first three years—US $649 million for 1973, US $783 million for 1974, and US $717 million for 1975—to be tapered off during the subsequent years and finally reduced to US $95 million by 1980. The RVN's aid request received negligible support from the US Congress. Actual US economic aid appropriations disbursed for the RVN during this critical three-year period amounted to US $501.7 million, $653.3 million, and $237.8 million for 1973, 1974, and 1975, respectively.

• • •

Overall, during this period, the RVN was hit hard by worldwide inflation. More critically, the price increase affected those commodities needed most by the RVN—rice, fuel, fertilizers, sugar, cement, steel, and iron—which accounted for 34 percent of South Vietnam's imports. From the second half of 1972 until the end of 1973 the prices of these commodities increased a sharp 80 percent, and, from 1973 to 1974, [the] overall price increase in import commodities was estimated at 53 percent.

• • •

Rice production during the 1973–1974 crop period reached 6.6 million tons, an increase of 11 percent over the previous year, and was expected to rise to 7.1 million tons in 1975. While the use of imported fertilizers was effectively cut down by 30 percent, the actual crop-planting acreage expanded by 10 percent. Despite increased production, rice import increased to 305,000 tons in 1973 and 300,500 tons in 1974.

• • •

Despite sizable cuts in expenditures and the implementation of certain austerity measures, the GVN national budget increased every year to meet immediate requirements generated by the rehabilitation of war damage, the resettlement of refugees, and the maintenance of a large military force. The GVN had several times attempted to decrease the military force, but was unable to because of the ever-increasing intensity of enemy activities. Defense expenditures in 1973 were successfully cut down to 55 percent of the total national budget, as compared to 64 percent in 1972.

• • •

The total economic picture of the RVN was unsatisfactory from the day it was born until it collapsed. Endowed with limited economic and financial resources and only embryonic industrial capabilities, the RVN was not capable of subsisting, much less defending itself. The RVNAF depended entirely on US military aid during all these years for their organization, equipment, training, and combat capabilities. The contribution of the GVN defense budget was rather modest as compared to what was provided by the United States and could only cover personnel salaries and a few operating costs.

During the two decades (1955–1975) of US military aid, how were the RVNAF logistically supported, particularly during the eight years 1965–1972, as they fought alongside US and FWMA forces, and the 12 years when they struggled alone for the cause of freedom (1955–1964 and 1973–1975)? How were US equipment and materiel employed and maintained? And how did the RVNAF logistical system cope with the management of huge quantities of modern equipment and the support of combat operations during the presence of US advisors and US logistical facilities and after they were removed? To provide the answers for these encompassing questions, this monograph will present the ARVN logistical structure and activities as they evolved through three significant periods of RVN military history.

[The first period goes] from 1954 to 1968, which includes the 1954–1964 formative years when the RVNAF were fighting alone against the Communist subversion, with US advisory assistance, and the period 1965–1972 when they fought alongside US and FWMA forces.

[The second period goes] from 1969 to the cease-fire of 28 January 1973, which was the period during which the Vietnamization program was implemented.

[The third period is] the post-cease-fire period—the two and a half years during which the RVNAF assumed lone responsibility for combat against Communist invasion forces—which ended tragically when the RVN crumbled and ceased to exist as a nation.

II. LOGISTICAL ORGANIZATION

Background

• • •

The RVNAF Logistics System

Prior to the 1954 Geneva Accords, the logistics system of the Vietnamese National Army (VNA) operated as part of the French Union forces and was skeletal and inefficient.

• • •

In general, the common responsibility of Vietnamese logistical directorates was to function in coordination with and under the assistance of French counterpart directorates which provided appropriate support as required.

• • •

Vietnamese technical services functioned separately and had an organization of their own, but before 1954 they were all commanded by French officers and the majority of their staffs were also French.

The Vietnamese infantry battalion was a self-administered unit. It was usually supported by the nearest French logistical units in its area of operation if Vietnamese logistical units were not available. Besides being responsible for their own logistical support, Vietnamese battalions were also required to provide support to designated paramilitary forces in their areas of operation. Mobile battalions, however, were exempted from this responsibility.

• • •

After Dien Bien Phu in 1954 there was a hasty withdrawal of many French forces, particularly logistical unit commanders and staffs and their logistical assets. This provided both a challenge and an opportunity for the RVNAF logistical cadre, particularly the emerging young officers, to prove their resourcefulness in the face of adverse circumstances and [the] indifferent attitude of their French counterparts.

• • •

In 1954 French logistical units and assets, including their French commanders and staffs, quickly evacuated Vietnam without warning or any prearrangement for turnover. Since the 1954 Geneva Accords authorized the replacement of war materiel on a one-to-one basis, the RVNAF General Staff was particularly concerned about what and how much equipment and materiel the French forces were removing from Vietnam. The RVNAF General Staff kept pressing the French High Command for such data in order to have justification to present to the International Control Commission when the RVN wanted to introduce replacements, but all requests were only partially fulfilled.

To face urgent requirements, and also because of political considerations, the GVN assigned several military officers without logistical experience to key logistical command and staff positions. These officers did their best in the RVNAF logistical system, based on their observations when previously working in various assignments with French forces.

Not until 1 June 1956 was there a significant US effort to help the RVNAF improve their logistical organization and operation. This was when the US Temporary Equipment Recovery Mission (TERM) was established.[2] With advice and assistance provided by TERM, and in view of expanding support and training requirements and the direct military aid received from the United States, the RVNAF logistical system improved rapidly, despite obstruction by a minority of commanders who held key positions in logistical organizations at the central and regional levels.

• • •

In keeping with US logistical organization and operational concepts, the RVNAF logistical system went through a reorganization process which was completed in 1957.

• • •

In 1959 a standard 10,450-man TO&E was adopted for all seven infantry divisions. This provided for a division headquarters, an ordnance company, a quartermaster company, a medical company, a signal company, a transportation company, and an engineer battalion.

Then, in 1961 and 1962, as the RVNAF force structure continued to expand, new direct support units were activated at the field level. Under the new territorial organization, which established four Corps Tactical Zones (CTZ), there was a need to consolidate logistics operational support and control. As a result, three Area Logistical Commands (ALC) were activated: the 1st ALC, located at Danang, provided support for I Corps/I CTZ; the 2nd ALC, located at Qui Nhon, provided support for II Corps/II CTZ, with the exception of the Binh Lam Special Sector (Binh Thuan and Lam Dong Provinces); and the 3rd ALC, located in Saigon, provided support for both the III Corps/III CTZ and IV Corps/IV CTZ, in addition to the Binh Lam Special Sector of II CTZ.

In 1964 a major reorganization effort was made at the central level with the purpose of consolidating command and control and unifying operations and management throughout the RVNAF. As a result, the Office of J-4/JGS was transformed into the Central Logistics Command (CLC), which became a unique agency vested with logistical responsibilities for the entire RVNAF and directly subordinated to the Chief of the JGS.

• • •

In 1965, to meet the urgent requirements in land and buildings for the US and FWMA forces, a ministerial "Real Estate Committee" was created under the CLC supervision. At the same time, the 4th and 5th Area Logistical Commands were activated to alleviate burdens placed on the overtasked 2nd and 3rd ALC. The 4th ALC, located at Can Tho, was responsible for the support of IV Corps/IV CTZ, while the 5th ALC, located at Cam Ranh, provided support for seven provinces of the II CTZ.

• • •

By the end of 1968 the organization responsible for planning, operating, and supervising the entire RVNAF logistics system was the Central Logistics Command. The commander of the CLC acted both as a staff officer (Deputy Chief of Staff [for] Logistics) and a commander.

• • •

Under the direct control of the CLC, the various departments . . . included technical services and their subordinate and field units: Ordnance, Quartermaster, Signal, Engineer, Transportation, Medical, and the Central Purchasing Office and the Commissary Service.

• • •

III. LOGISTICAL OPERATION

Supply Procedures

To facilitate management, the RVNAF in the late 1950s adopted the same classification of supplies as used in the US logistical system in the 1950s. Class I supplies included food items; Class II supplies consisted of Table of Organization and Equipment (TO&E) equipment and replacement parts; Class III supplies consisted of all types of fuel, including wood; Class IV supplies encompassed defense barrier materiel, and other items not provided for by TO&Es; and Class V supplies consisted of all types of ammunition.

Class I supplies, i.e., food items, had three categories: "administrative" food, fresh food, and combat rations. Administrative food consisted of rice, salt, sugar, and tea, which were procured and stored by the Quartermaster Department and issued to units on the basis of the number of troops fed by the unit mess service. The daily rice allocation for each man was 650 grams (one pound nine ounces), and the rice supply level stocked by each unit was 30 days. Units located in outlying mountainous areas in I and II Corps areas were allowed a 90-day supply level, particularly during the rainy season, which adversely affected resupply activities. As prescribed by regulations, all enlisted men, single or married but not living with their families, were required to take meals in the unit-operated mess.

Fresh food was not stored and issued by quartermaster units, but was procured by the consuming unit from the local markets. There was no refrigeration system in the quartermaster service for food storage, except for military hospitals. Combat rations were, in major part, supplied by the Military Assistance Program (MAP) and issued only during tactical operations or field exercises. Combat units participating in operations usually received a two-day supply of combat rations, which were individually kept by soldiers, but combat rations were consumed only when fighting made food preparation impracticable. Remote outposts and border camps were authorized a seven-day storage of combat rations, to be used only in case of inclement weather or enemy encirclement or attack.

• • •

Having inherited assets turned over by French forces, the RVNAF were equipped with many different types of equipment, including French, Japanese, British, and German design. The most urgent task in 1957 and 1958 was standardization on US equipment, which was vigorously implemented unit by unit, region by region. The goal to be achieved was that all units should be equipped with the same type of US equipment, weapons such as the Colt .45 caliber pistol, the Thompson .45 caliber submachinegun, and the .30 caliber Browning automatic rifle (BAR), and vehicles such as the Willys 1/4-ton jeep, the Dodge 3/4-ton truck, and the GMC 2-1/2-ton truck. During 1958 and 1959 the RVNAF received 1/4- and 2-1/2-ton MAP trucks, made in Japan, which were called OSPJ trucks by Vietnamese logisticians and served as substitutes for US-made vehicles, apparently as a result of cost-cutting measures. By 1959, all signal equipment had been standardized and consisted only of US-made SCR-series radio sets.

• • •

Class III supplies, primarily POL (petroleum, oils, and lubricants), were entirely supplied by commercial firms such as Shell, Esso, and Caltex, which had supply contracts with US forces. Within Vietnam, POL were shipped from commercial tank farms at Nha Be or Lien Chieu (Danang) to military depots by naval tankers, chartered commercial ships, or by tank trucks, military or commercial. POL were usually stored in 50-gallon [*sic*] drums and five-gallon cans. The central depot at Go Vap and field depots at Thanh My An (Saigon), Vung Tau, and Danang were each equipped with a few large tanks for fuel storage.

• • •

Class V items, ammunition, were usually shipped to Saigon, unloaded at Cat Lai, near Nha Be, then stored at the central ammunition depot at Thanh Tuy Ha (Bien Hoa Province) for subsequent distribution to field depots as replenishment for their stock level. Units were issued and allowed to keep a basic load equivalent to three days of combat. This basic load of ammunition was carried both by individual soldiers and by unit vehicles while on operation. Ammunition consumed in combat was automatically restored to the unit by the nearest field depot or supply point.

• • •

Requirement Planning

• • •

In early 1966 the grant aid Military Assistance Program was replaced by the Military Assistance, Service-Funded (MASF) program, but requisitioning and programming procedures and techniques remained the same as far as the RVNAF logistical system was concerned. With regard to secondary and expendable items, the requirement planning process began by requisitions submitted to Military Assistance Command, Vietnam (MACV) by RVNAF service base depots. These requisitions were made jointly by depot commanders and their advisors, based on consumption experience and an authorized stock level of 180 days. After approval by MACV, the requisitions were forwarded to the US Army International Logistics Center (USAILC) in New Cumberland, Pennsylvania, in case of continental US items or to the US Army Depot in Japan in case of offshore program items. Requisitions of medical equipment were forwarded to the US Army Medical Depot on Okinawa.

Stock Control

The normal in-country stock level approved was 180 days. Order and shipping time varied from 90 to 120 days.

Equipment Modernization

Modernization of equipment for the Vietnamese armed forces was a constant concern of both RVNAF and US logisticians. After the standardization effort in 1957 and 1958, the RVNAF effectively rid themselves of French, Japanese, and British equipment and became equipped with US weapons and vehicles of World War II vintage. Then old utility vehicles were replaced by Japanese commerically built 1/4-, 3/4-, and 2–1/2-ton trucks, commonly called OSPJ (offshore procurement, Japan) vehicles. In 1964, these OSPJ trucks were again replaced by another array of commercially built trucks called the M-600 series.

By 1964, the problem of weapon modernization had become an urgent matter in view of the substantial increase in modern weapons, mostly Russian-made, used by Communist forces in South Vietnam. The Communist AK-47 rifle proved more effective in combat than the M-1A1 Garand or the M-1 and M-2 carbines which were introduced into the RVNAF in early 1964, and by 1967 all Communist forces in South Vietnam employed the AK-47 as the standard individual weapon.

During that time a limited quantity of the new AR-15 ArmaLite rifles were sent to Vietnam for test purposes. In 1967 the United States approved the M-16 rifle as the standard individual weapon for the RVNAF, but the quantities initially made available were just enough to equip the airborne and marine units of the general reserve. So, during the enemy Tet Offensive of 1968, the crisp, rattling sounds of AK-47s echoing in Saigon and some other cities seemed to make a mockery of the weaker single shots of Garands and carbines fired by stupefied friendly troops.

Emergency measures were taken to airlift quantities of M-16s to Saigon and Danang day and night. RVNAF logistical units worked around the clock to receive, process, and issue, and combat unit supply officers queued up to take delivery for their troops. At the same time, mobile training units, both Vietnamese and American, with the cooperation of US advisors, went into RVNAF combat units, where they conducted crash courses on the M-16. Technical manuals for the operation and maintenance of the M-16 were hastily translated, published, and distributed, along with pocket-sized preventive maintenance instruction cards on the basis of one card per rifle.

Field depot personnel, meanwhile, lined up at US depots day and night to take delivery of basic load ammunition for combat units. First, infantry battalions, then rangers and long-range reconnaissance companies were successively equipped with the new rifle, and, by mid-1968, the crash M-16 program had been successfully completed. Now it was the enemy's turn to be shocked as he was confronted by the overwhelming firepower of the ARVN 2nd Infantry Division, which he attacked in Quang Ngai city during the second phase of the offensive. The enemy did not know that the 2nd Division units had been equipped with M-16s only one day before the attack. Most of the units had not had time even to practice fire or zero their new rifles, but they were very effective anyway. It was also during this time that RVNAF units began to receive, almost as urgently, new M-72 antitank LAW rockets and M-60 machineguns.

In addition to weapons, the modernization program also placed emphasis on armored vehicles, signal equipment, and utility trucks. New types of materiel and equipment gradually entered the RVNAF inventory as replacements. Armored vehicles such as M-41 tanks, M-113/M-114 personnel carriers, and V-100 scout cars came to replace the M-24s, the half-tracks, and the M-8 scout cars. New field radio sets such as the AN/

PRC-25, the AN/VRC series, [and] the AN/GRC-9, 26, 106, and 122 replaced the old SCR series and the trouble-ridden AN/PRC-10.

•••

Support for Regional and Popular Forces

In 1965 the Civil Guard (CG) and People's Militia (PM) became part of the RVNAF, were redesignated Regional Forces (RF) and Popular Forces (PF), respectively, and began to receive direct support from the Military Assistance Program. Regional Forces were organized into separate companies, while Popular Forces were organized into platoons and squads.

•••

As of 1967 the support for RF and PF became streamlined and was entirely funded by US military assistance through MACV Civil Operations and Revolutionary Development Support (CORDS) and the RVN defense budget, just as [was] the RVNAF.

Since the RF and PF were local forces, the sector's Administrative and Logistical Support Company was truly the hub of the RF and PF logistical system. To be able to meet RF and PF requirements, and in the face of road interdiction possibilities, each ALS company was authorized certain levels of supplies: 30 days for "administrative" food, based on mess-fed troop strength; 7 days for POL; 15 days for ammunition; individual clothing items equivalent to 10 percent of troops to be actually supported; and 15 days for repair parts.

•••

In addition to supporting RF and PF units, ALS companies also provided weapons and ammunition support for the People's Self-Defense Forces (PSDF), which were activated in April 1968. Over 400,000 assorted weapons were distributed among the PSDF through ALS companies.

•••

Transportation

•••

Ground transportation facilities, as provided by ARVN light and medium truck companies or chartered commercial trucks, adequately met RVNAF requirements. A major obstruction to ground movements, however, was the trafficability of bridges, ferries, and passes, and road security. The trafficability . . . was gradually improved by 1966 through various road and bridge modernization programs. Bridges were rebuilt to accommodate a minimum load of 35 tons, and important passes such as Hai Van on QL-1, north of Danang, Mang Yang on QL-19 between Qui Nhon and Pleiku, Deo Ca on QL-1 north of Nha Trang, and M'Drak on QL-21 between Nha Trang and Ban Me Thuot were widened and asphalt-surfaced to handle two-way traffic. But road security remained a permanent concern for logisticians.

One of the distinguishing aspects of the Vietnam War was the constant enemy effort to sabotage, mine, ambush, harass, and interdict roads and traffic on all lines of communication. Supplies therefore had to be moved by truck convoys, and the problem of providing road security and protection for supply convoys was always the major concern of tactical and logistical commanders.

• • •

South Vietnam's main railway ran along the coastline from Saigon to Dong Ha. Constantly sabotaged and long neglected, it was in very poor shape when the First Indochina War was over in 1954. Rehabilitation work began on the railways almost immediately after the 1954 Geneva Accords, but progressed very slowly. By 1958 three portions of the railway had been completely rehabilitated: 1) from Saigon to Qui Nhon via Phan Thiet and Nha Trang; 2) from Phan Thiet to Dalat; and 3) from Danang to Dong Ha. By 1960 the Qui Nhon–Danang portion was completed, and, for the first time since the outbreak of hostilities in Vietnam, railway service became continuous from Saigon to Dong Ha. But it did not last long because, by that time, the Communists had considerably stepped up their sabotage activities. Railway service was frequently disrupted and, as a result, did not contribute much to military transportation.

In 1966, in the face of growing military and economic needs, a major effort was undertaken by the combined US-RVN Railway Committee (MACV, USAID, CLC, Ministry of Public Works) to rebuild the railway system. From 1966 to 1969 the US and the RVN government spent in excess of 25 million US dollars on the rebuild task. Two hundred freight cars were also provided by US aid, together with new diesel locomotives. However, security conditions in the areas bordering on the rail track, and the ease and determination with which the enemy carried out his sabotage activities, prevented full use of the railway. Only five short portions could be operated with relative security: 1) Saigon to Xuan Loc, via Bien Hoa and Long Binh; 2) Nha Trang to Tuy Hoa; 3) Nha Trang to Ninh Thuan; 4) Qui Nhon to Phu Cat; and 5) Danang to Hue.

Railway, as a result, was not a significant transportation facility for military purposes in South Vietnam except for the few hundred thousand tons of construction materials, especially crushed rock, that were moved short distances for the RVN program of road, base, and airfield construction.

Sea transportation provided the main supply routes from Saigon harbor to the II Corps area through Nha Trang and Qui Nhon ports and to the I Corps area through the Danang port.

Among the four major commercial ports of South Vietnam (Saigon, Nha Trang, Qui Nhon, and Danang), only the Saigon port was capable of accommodating deep-draft vessels. It could dock six vessels at piers and another eight at buoys at any one time. Farther south, in the Nha Be area, was the POL port which could accommodate three tankers at the same time. A little north of the main piers, across [from] the Saigon City Hall, there was the Nguyen Hue pier, capable of handling four coastal vessels at the same time.

Prior to 1964, all oceangoing vessels transporting military assistance cargoes for the RVNAF were docked at the Saigon commercial port. . . . Ammunition cargo ships were docked at buoys off the Cat Lai pier and unloaded on barges which were subsequently towed away to Thanh Tuy Ha pier for unloading and transportation to the central ammunition depot there or to Binh Trieu pier for unloading and transportation to the 3rd ALC field ammunition depot at Cat Lai. For the shipment of ammunition and other cargoes to field depots at Danang and Qui Nhon, either chartered commercial coastal vessels or VNN ships were used. VNN ships were preferred for the transportation of ammunition and explosives since commercial vessels were not structurally suited for these types of cargo.

• • •

In 1965 the accelerated buildup of US and FWMA forces in South Vietnam, and the RVNAF structure expansion, created an emergency situation for supply requirements and other support needs. US equipment and construction materials were transported in large quantities by fleets of cargo ships which continually arrived at the four tiny and underequipped Vietnamese ports, causing massive and serious congestion of the ports, piers, and dockside warehouses. At times there were well over 100 ships queuing up for a docking space. During those hectic days, the coordination and full utilization of all US, RVNAF, and civilian port facilities became an urgent problem.

By tacit agreement US forces, which had by far the most facilities, experience, and supply requirements, were made responsible for port operation in Saigon, Nha Trang, Qui Nhon, and Danang, in coordination and cooperation with the RVNAF Saigon Transportation Terminal and other transportation units and the GVN port authorities. Dockside military warehouses and storage areas and part of [the] civilian facilities were turned over to US forces for accelerated expansion and modernization.

• • •

In addition to port management improvement and the full utilization of shallow-draft vessels for the relay of cargoes unloaded from cargo ships anchored offshore, a modernization and new construction program was initiated in 1965 to improve handling capabilities of major ports. The Saigon harbor was thoroughly dredged and repair work done on its main piers at Khanh Hoi in order to increase its docking capacity. Storage areas were repaired and additional warehouses constructed to add new storage facilities. About three miles up the Saigon River, near the Saigon–Bien Hoa highway, a new military port was constructed and came to be known as "Saigon Newport." With 7,700 feet of piers, 2,399,000 square feet of roofed warehouses, and 430,000 square yards of open storage, Saigon Newport was capable of handling 11,500 tons of cargo per day.

In the II Corps area, the Cam Ranh peninsula and its white sand dunes and beaches were transformed into a magnificent military port with 6,300 feet of piers, 881,000 square feet of covered warehouses, and 377,000 square yards of open storage space. Cam Ranh was the only port that made possible the direct unloading of ammunition cargoes from docked oceangoing vessels onto its pier. Another military port was also newly built at Qui Nhon. With 4,300 feet of piers, 105,000 square feet of roofed warehouses, and 359,000 square yards of open storage space, Qui Nhon port was capable of handling 6,400 tons of cargo daily.

At Danang in [the] I Corps area, a new port was built at Tien Sa with 7,100 feet of piers, 21,000 square feet of warehouses, and 89,000 square yards of open storage space. It was capable of handling 10,700 tons of cargo daily.

In the Mekong Delta, since rivers were the main supply routes from Saigon, two river ports were built at Dong Tam (Dinh Tuong Province) and Binh Thuy (Phong Dinh Province) to handle river-bound cargoes. The Dong Tam port was capable of handling 1,200 tons of cargo per day, while the Binh Thuy port could only handle 300 tons per day.

• • •

The limited VNAF airlift assets—C-47 and C-119 cargo planes—were placed under the direction and control of the CLC Movement Control [Division] to handle all inter-regional and intraregional air transport requirements. . . .

Helicopters, however, were placed under the control of corps headquarters. By the end of 1968, the VNAF still had only 25 CH-34s and 85 UH-1s to meet all types of tactical requirements, including troop movements, liaison, emergency supply, and medical evacuation.

The need for air transportation became particularly acute during 1968 in the face of continued road insecurity, increased combat operations, and almost daily firefights. The VNAF limited assets were never able to handle daily airlift requirements. Well over 70 percent of interregional air cargo and personnel transportation was provided by US forces through MACV J-4. US Army aviation units were tremendously helpful in providing intraregional air transportation for the RVNAF with their UH-1s, CH-47s, and CH-54s. . . .

Hospitalization and Medical Evacuation

The RVNAF system of medical treatment and hospitalization consisted of: 1) unit and area dispensaries which were responsible for dispensing medicine, administering first aid, and providing limited medical treatment not exceeding seven days; 2) three 400-bed field hospitals with surgical facilities and capable of medical treatment and hospitalization for a period from 15 to 30 days; 3) 11 provincial hospitals, with capacities ranging from 400 to 600 beds, capable of treating sick and wounded soldiers until complete recovery . . . ; and 4) two general hospitals: Cong Hoa in Saigon with a 2,400-bed capacity and Duy Tan in Danang with an 1,800-bed capacity.

In addition, each infantry division, the Airborne Division, and the Marine Division had [its] own medical company and three medical platoons, one for each infantry regiment or brigade, to take care of medical treatment for troops and their dependents. A division medical company was capable of operating a mobile surgical station, which was usually located where the division CP was. The VNAF and VNN, however, did not have hospitalization facilities of their own. Their personnel were treated and hospitalized at the nearest ARVN hospital.

In keeping with the increasing requirements of the RF and PF, which became part of the RVNAF in 1965, 193 subsector dispensaries were established, each with a 20-bed capacity, and 27 sector hospitals, each with a 100-bed capacity.

By the end of 1968, the total hospitalization capacity of the RVNAF medical facilities amounted to 21,000 beds, expandable to 23,000 as required. Most medical treatment facilities were located in old one-story brick buildings or tin-roofed barracks, devoid of modern comfort. The only modern and comfortable medical treatment facility was a new 500-bed ward of the Cong Hoa General Hospital, which was built during 1966–1967.

• • •

During 1968, 10 out of 27 sector hospitals and 86 out of 193 district dispensaries were jointly operated by civilian and military medical personnel under a program which continued to benefit both the public and the armed forces until the very last days of the RVN.

• • •

RVNAF servicemen were treated and hospitalized at these jointly operated facilities entirely free of charge. At other civilian hospitals, not covered by the program, they were accepted for free treatment but had to pay for their food.

In addition to medical treatment facilities, the RVNAF Medical [Directorate] also operated a blood supply center which, during this period of time, was reinforced with additional equipment and facilities for the reception of fresh blood and preparation of dried blood and serum to provide for the battlefield's needs.

• • •

The RVNAF did not possess fixed-wing aircraft or helicopters solely for use in medical evacuation. Their aircraft were employed for all kinds of missions, including medical evacuation.

• • •

As fighting expanded and increased in intensity, roads and waterways became more and more insecure, making medical evacuation all the more difficult. The relative weakness of the VNAF during that time did not help solve the problem, and the morale of combat troops was adversely affected.

The US participation in the ground war brought with it a most helpful asset: the US Army medevac helicopter, which came in great quantities. As of 1965, 70 percent of RVNAF medical evacuation cases were handled by the US Army medevac helicopters, which either belonged to US tactical units or the US 46th Medical Brigade. US medevac helicopters operated around the clock and went almost anywhere to pick up the wounded, from outlying outposts to the hottest battlefield.

• • •

In time, due to close cooperation and coordination between RVNAF and US forces, US medical evacuation became the most appreciated and trusted assistance and earned the respect of all RVNAF servicemen. Thanks to it, the percentage of patients who died as soon as they were brought to a medical facility was cut from 4.0 to 2.5 percent during 1966–1968.

• • •

In general, ARVN patients brought to US medical facilities were treated as if they were US servicemen and returned to the nearest ARVN medical facility as soon as this was medically feasible.

• • •

Operational Support

Tasked primarily for the role of pacification support during this period of time, the ARVN generally conducted operations at the sector level with battalions, companies, or even platoons. The support for such combat operations, therefore, was just a matter of routine with which the sector ASL companies and the ALC direct support units were well familiar. There were, so to speak, no major problems involved in the logistic support for pacification operations. As to combined operations in which ARVN forces of regimental size participated alongside US forces, logistic support was usually provided by US units beyond and above ARVN logistic capabilities, particularly as far as ammunition and POL were concerned.

The most remarkable ARVN logistic activities during this period of time took place during the enemy Tet Offensive of 1968, which came as a surprise for the ARVN and consequently caught its logisticians unaware. Suddenly . . . enemy forces surfaced as if from nowhere and vigorously attacked all key GVN and RVNAF positions in Hue, Saigon, My Tho, Vinh Long, and other cities and towns. At the same time, they cut off all supply routes and isolated all cities and towns under attack. Two of the most notable battles which bore heavily on logistic activities were those at Hue and in Saigon.

At Hue . . . the main ground supply route to the [1st Infantry] Division from Phu Bai, ten miles away, had been cut off. The Truong Tien Bridge was also blown up. The division headquarters was thus practically sealed off. Supply by air, helicopter, or airdrop was impossible; the weather is never so bad as during this period of the year. The cloud ceiling was never tree-top level, and visibility was nil. It was cold and wet, and rain continued unabated.

•••

Supply for the troops and civilian population who were stranded in the Old Citadel was not a problem during the first few days of the fighting. Sixty days of rice supply and combat rations had been stocked in the 1st ALC Quartermaster Depot. All units had seven days of POL in reserve, in addition to the January allocations. A stockage of small arms ammunition equivalent to a regiment's basic load was available. The Nguyen Tri Phuong field hospital, with its 600-bed capacity, was located in the Old Citadel. So, if economy measures and tight control were enforced, infantry units in the Old Citadel would be able to sustain combat for at least one week without resupply, especially as regards ammunition. But the siege could not be lifted. It lasted five, then seven, then ten days, and the weather did not get any better. No air support or supply was feasible.

The 1st Infantry Division CP in the meantime requested a special supply of ammunition, especially fragmentation grenades, Claymore mines, and M-72 rockets. With airlift assistance provided by US C-130 cargo planes, the ammunition was collected at Phu Bai in no time. Airdrop assets were also assembled at Danang, and all types of aircraft stood ready to take off any time the weather . . . lifted. But the fighting could not wait. The ammunition had to get to our troops by some other means. Supply boats could be used, but the usual landing area near the Truong Tien Bridge was in enemy hands. The only alternative was the Bao Vinh landing, located near the northern gate of the Citadel. It was a landing ordinarily used by fishing sampans, but never tried by military boats. However, in view of the situation, Bao Vinh might be the final resort, since it was the only alternative. . . .

The four LCM-8s of the 10th River Boat Group, assembled in Danang one week before the outbreak of the enemy offensive as reinforcements for the 1st ALC, were loaded with 120 tons of ammunition. Braving cold rain and rough seas, off they went, [also carrying] the worries and hopes of ARVN logisticians. It took them two days to reach the Thuan An estuary. Slowly they proceeded upstream on the placid Perfume River and finally made it to the tiny landing of Bao Vinh. The enemy was caught unaware by this move; there was no reaction. Our troops got the ammunition they so desperately needed and fighting continued.

The weather finally cleared and tactical air support became more effective with every passing day. Finally, after 26 days of siege and intense fighting, the Citadel was wrested back under friendly control amid tearful cheers of our die-hard troops.

As CLC commander, the first visit I made in Hue after the siege of the Old Citadel had been lifted was to the Nguyen Tri Phuong field hospital. The hospital commander, a Medical [Directorate] lieutenant colonel, reported to me what had happened during the month-long battle. The hospital had been overcrowded with wounded troops and civilians. To accommodate them, additional cots had to be laid out almost everywhere. Medicine was adequate, but there was not enough fresh blood for transfusions. The hospital had functioned well, thanks to the voluntary help of some civilian doctors who had sought refuge. Very few died of injuries at the hospital, but the Citadel area, he had heard, was strewn with corpses. They had been gathered in heaps and buried collectively in mass graves.

In Saigon, the Communists launched their offensive at about the same time as in Hue. . . . All main supply roads leading into Saigon had been either interdicted or sabotaged. Class I, III, and V base depots in the Go Vap area were effectively sealed off by enemy road blocks.

● ● ●

A makeshift supply point for Class I, II [sic], and V supplies was set up in the parking areas in front of and behind the CLC building. Ten supply trucks, winding their way through unaffected roads and alleys, brought needed materiel and equipment to the JGS supply point from the 230th Ordnance Company, the 20th Ordnance Base Depot, and the 631st Signal Support Battalion in the Phu Tho area. But the road leading to the Go Vap ammunition depot was interdicted. Two H-34 helicopters, each under the control of a CLC staff officer, were used to airlift ammunition from Go Vap to the supply point. The first supply run went well, but in the second run the helicopters were fired upon by enemy troops positioned high on a water tower nearby. The siege was being tightened around the Go Vap depot. Switching direction, the helicopters flew to the Thanh Tuy Ha depot, 20 minutes away, [and] still unaffected by the fighting. Ammunition airlift shuttles were subsequently carried out around the clock.

Critical items such as fragmentation grenades and Claymore mines were collected from the Quang Trung Training Center and the Thu Duc Infantry School and helilifted to the JGS. Three M-41 tanks, then two 105mm howitzers, were sent in as reinforcements, causing additional supply problems since helilift assets were limited. To get them resupplied, two trucks had to be sent through Tan Son Nhut to the Airborne Division's Class V supply point for 105mm ammunition, but 90mm ammunition had to be helilifted from the Thanh Tuy Ha depot. Despite limited supplies, the tanks' accurate fire effectively eliminated all enemy positions on high-rise buildings around the JGS. And, although plagued by difficulties, the JGS makeshift supply point satisfied friendly requirements.

In food supply, the JGS seemed to be in a bad position since the rice depot of the headquarters company was in enemy hands and there was no way to get through enemy blocks to the QM depot at Hanh Thong Tay. Fortunately there was a commissary retail store in the JGS compound, well stocked for Tet business with rice, sugar, instant noodles, and canned food. All its stocks were immediately "requisitioned," and the store served well as a Class I supply point for the first week.

The Cong Hoa General Hospital, north of the JGS compound, was also surrounded by enemy troops who, from the top of water towers nearby, fired upon medevac helicopters, preventing them from landing. For treatment purposes, wounded troops were sent to the US 3rd Field Hospital, across the street from the JGS main gate, and the Do Vinh hospital of the Airborne Division.

• • •

The second phase of the enemy offensive came, as expected, in May. But this time our combat units were well prepared. Fighting broke out in the Binh Trieu area, making the ammunition loading pier there unusable. Supply boats had to unload at the Bach Dang pier in Saigon downtown. The Go Vap ammunition depot was attacked and overrun; over 4,000 tons of ammunition were blown up. Despite this, ammunition resupply for friendly troops in the Capital Military District area encountered no problem, due to the pre-positioning of supplies at many supply points.

In [the] II and IV Corps areas, combat units fared extremely well with their own supply reserves, which had been replenished as required by their respective ALCs. There were practically no significant logistical problems that these ALCs could not solve with their available resources. The CLC intervened only to meet three special requests during the first few days of the offensive: 1) fuel needed for the operation of provincial generator plants which, because of the Tet holidays, the sector ALS companies were unable to draw in time; 2) rice supply for an RF company which, because of enemy encirclement, was not able to buy on the local market, and 3) fuel supply for the 4th ALC field depot, whose stocks the Shell plant at Can Tho had failed to replenish due to its own shortage. The shortage, it was learned, was caused by the failure of chartered commercial boats to deliver fuel at Can Tho for fear of the fighting.

Summary and Evaluation

From a logistical viewpoint, the decade between 1955 and 1964 can be said to be a period during which the foundation of the RVNAF logistical system was laid, based on the US technical service organizational concept. Supply management and maintenance functions were the responsibilities given to five separate technical services: Ordnance, Quartermaster, Medical, Signal, and Engineer. Each technical service had its own system of base depots and field depots. In maintenance, each technical service also had its own facilities, a depot maintenance facility, and field maintenance shops in the corps areas.

• • •

The increase of logistical units during the next period, from 1965 to 1968, responded effectively to the growing support required by an expanding army. But the base depots were largely ignored and improved very little, largely due to the application of the direct shipment method whereby equipment was delivered from the United States directly to field depots, bypassing the base depots. Despite the efficiency of this method, base depots still had functions and deserved more attention.

• • •

The major difficulty encountered during 1965–1968 was the discrepancy between RVNAF and US figures with regard to authorized and on-hand quantities. A reason for this was the lack of inventories, which had not been conducted for several years due to preoccupation with tactical matters and the accelerated expansion of forces.

The improvement and modernization of RVNAF equipment was emphasized during 1965–1968 through various programs. Clean-sweep actions effectively eliminated every foreign-made piece of equipment, and standardization programs gradually equipped the RVNAF with US-made, but vintage, materiel. As of 1968, in the aftermath of the enemy Tet Offensive, there was a serious effort at modernization, especially with regard to armament. M-16 rifles and other modern weapons were brought in to replace World War II armament, and this greatly enhanced the ARVN troop morale. Field radio sets for infantry units were also gradually modernized. With regard to vehicles, there was a steady improvement through three replacement phases, ending with the M-600 series.

• • •

For the medical treatment of RVNAF patients, the ARVN medical system was entirely capable of handling every problem. The only difficulty encountered was the lack of amenities at dispensaries and hospitals, particularly at provincial station hospitals which were in most cases tin-roofed and tin-walled constructions, incapable of handling an upsurge of casualties such as during the 1968 Tet Offensive. Medicine and fresh blood were supplied without difficulties and medical evacuation was generally adequate. However, medical evacuation by helicopters was entirely dependent on US assets.

Logistic support for RF and PF made remarkable progress during this period, ever since they became part of the RVNAF. There were still many weaknesses, however, in the sector and subsector supply systems and in the operation of sector ALS companies, particularly as regards the efficiency of personnel. The prepositioning of Class I, III, and V supplies at these ALS companies at levels ranging from 7 to 30 days proved especially responsive to this type of frontless war, especially in the face of the enemy's strategy of isolation and interdiction. And this responsiveness prevailed despite the expanded volume of supplies and the budget increase involved.

The support for major ARVN combat operations during 1965–1968 was almost nonexistent, because ARVN infantry divisions were only tasked for pacification support. Their activities, therefore, were limited both in size and in duration, requiring no major logistic support effort. Because of this, ARVN logistic units had no chance during this period to put their support capabilities to the test.

Twelve years of receiving direct US aid and assistance resulted in a remarkably big leap forward for the RVNAF logistic system in terms of organization, operation, and management. All loopholes in the system seemed to be effectively filled in by US advisors and US forces. What remained to be seen in 1968 was how the RVNAF set about filling in these loopholes by themselves during the following years under the Vietnamization program.

IV. LOGISTICS IMPROVEMENT PROGRAMS

Background and Objectives

By the time the Tet Offensive faltered, after the third and unsuccessful phase of attacks in August 1968, Communist forces were on the decline while the RVNAF gained confidence. When fighting subsided on all major battlefields, enemy main forces had been driven out of important areas across the country.

On 8 June 1969 the presidents of the United States and the Republic of Vietnam jointly agreed that the RVNAF should replace US forces engaged in combat. President Nixon announced the withdrawal of the first 25,000-man increment, to be followed by others depending on the improvement in training and equipment of the RVNAF, the progress made in the Paris peace talks, and the level of Communist activities. At the same time, President Thieu also declared that the RVNAF would take over combat responsibility for the departing US troops.

This was the beginning of "Vietnamization," a term that left several Vietnamese officials pondering amid doubt and confusion. Strange as it may have seemed, no guidance or explanation was given by the RVN national leaders for a program of such significance. Questions were asked in private, but left unanswered. It had become a fact that US troops would be withdrawn, but how long would it take? Would it be a complete pullout, or would there be a residual peacekeeping force like in South Korea? It was generally understood that, to replace US forces, the RVNAF would be expanded, but no one knew how much. Should the capability be to fight the Viet Cong alone, or the entire North Vietnamese Army? And how would the present inadequacies in the RVNAF be satisfied, particularly with regard to naval and air support?

US combat strength in South Vietnam continued to decrease, year after year. One by one, US infantry divisions and Free World Military Assistance units left the country, and, by 28 January 1973, the day of the cease-fire, only 23,516 US and 30,449 FWMA personnel remained. During this period of time the RVNAF force structure increased steadily to 875,790 during FY 1969, then to 986,360 during FY 1970, and finally to 1,100,000 during the following fiscal years. The force expansion program focused on the Regional and Popular Forces, armor, and artillery units, but also included the addition of the 3rd ARVN Infantry Division. This brought the total number of regular divisions to 13, to include the Airborne and Marine Divisions.

In early 1972 ARVN combat forces consisted of 120 infantry battalions supported by 58 artillery battalions. These forces included one 175mm battalion; 19 armor squadrons, including one M-48 squadron; four combat and four construction engineer groups; 58 ranger battalions, including 37 border surveillance ranger battalions; and two general reserve divisions, the Airborne and Marine. Total ARVN and Marine strength stood at 429,000; the Navy, 43,000 with 1,680 assorted ships and craft; and the Air Force, 51,000 with over 1,000 aircraft, including nearly 500 helicopters. RF companies were consolidated into company groups and battalions to increase operational control efficiency.

In conjunction with force structure expansion, plans were implemented to modernize equipment and improve the logistics system. Modern equipment was gradually made available, both to equip newly activated units and to replaced phased-out items. RVNAF equipment assets increased from 600,000 to over one million weapons, from 36,000 to 65,000 trucks, from 35,000 to over 75,000 communications-electronics sets, and from 2,000 to 5,000 armored vehicles.

ARVN infantry divisions were gradually released from their area security responsibilities to become mobile, and the task of pacification was turned over to territorial forces.

• • •

On 18 October 1972 the Joint General Staff received reports that a cease-fire was imminent and that vital equipment would be delivered soon to the RVNAF before the official day of the cease-fire. This was the beginning of the "Enhance Plus" program, which was to continue until year end at an accelerated pace, with emergency deliveries of materiel and equipment by US cargo planes and ships. The titles for those bases still being used by US forces were expediently transferred to the RVNAF. At the same time, procedures were established for the turnover of materiel and equipment still being used by US units and military agencies and ROK units. Then, on 28 January 1973, the Paris Agreement became effective, being signed on the previous day after five long years of negotiations. US and FWMA forces were required by the agreement to be completely withdrawn within 60 days. What remained of the greatly reduced US military advisory and assistance organization in South Vietnam was incorporated into the Defense Attaché Office (DAO) with a very limited number of military and civilian personnel authorized.

During the period of Vietnamization, the JGS initiated, with the encouragement and support of MACV, several specific programs designed to improve the logistical support for an expanding and modernizing tri-service military force. These programs were undertaken to accomplish several basic objectives that the JGS had set about to achieve in view of the US disengagement from the war.

First and foremost, it was realized that, since the US advisory and support efforts, tactical and logistics, would gradually be removed, there was a requirement for the RVNAF to take over, step by step, all the logistic requirements which had been entirely performed by US units and advisors: planning, programming, requisitioning, handling of deliveries, distribution, storage, issue, maintenance, rebuilding, and salvaging.

• • •

Base Depot Upgrade

• • •

A problem was encountered in recruiting civilian personnel, since ARVN pay scales were much lower than those offered by US agencies and private firms. As an example, only 60 percent of the personnel quotas targeted for 1969 were obtained. Another problem arose from the alarming rate of turnover. Many qualified experienced personnel quit their jobs for more lucrative offers. Pay raises and special allowances, as job incentives to retain personnel, were not authorized by the GVN, which feared a chain-reaction effect on the national civilian payroll which the annual budget could not support. RVN law also forbade the recruitment of civil servants under the age of 18, while all 18-year-olds and older people in good physical condition were serving in the armed forces. Civilian personnel requirements could not be filled by servicemen, since combat units received first priority for manpower.

But the Central Logistics Command kept interceding in favor of the programs, and, finally, the prime minister approved a special measure which allowed the RVNAF to recruit, as of 1970, 17-year-olds as defense civil servants in the service of the army, navy, and air force base depot system. When these employees became draft-eligible at 18, they were authorized to enter the reserve corps and continue to work in base depots. As civil servants of the reserve corps, they were also subject to guard duties, overtime work without pay, and other military obligations. The employment of women, although being encouraged, was not successful because the idea of working women was still too novel to be accepted by Vietnamese traditions. Also a woman's salary was usually much lower than for a man.

By the end of 1972, the number of civilian personnel recruited into service was encouraging. . . . Many of the 17-year-old civilian personnel recruited, however, were high school students with little mechanical knowledge. Under a specially approved program, these youngsters were to be trained to become administrative clerks and skilled workers. A crash program of accelerated training was established, and a small number of 17-year-old civilian personnel attended regular courses conducted by technical service schools, which normally were not authorized to accept civilians. A greater number attended courses conducted in the base depots under the tutorship of Vietnamese and American specialists. The remaining were trained on the job. . . .

In addition to regular salaried personnel, the base depots under the upgrade program also accepted 15- and 16-year-old trainees, selected from among the dependents of servicemen. By the end of 1974 there were well over 300 such youngsters undergoing training at these three base depots.

The base depot upgrade program successfully transformed the old, run-down facilities into modern, well-equipped industrial plants that the RVNAF proudly acquired for the first time. They compared favorably with those in more advanced countries. The ARVN personnel, both civilian and military, in these base depots worked and trained hard under the tutelage of American specialists who knew they would soon depart. They were proud of this valuable association and the modern facilities, which they showed with satisfaction to visiting dignitaries, American and foreign. To them, a whole future opened up.

• • •

Improving RF-PF Logistics Support

The RF and PF, which made up more than half of total RVNAF strength, became the object of a logistics improvement program during this period of time. The improvement program covered both RF-PF units and the Administrative and Logistics Support companies which provided the support.

• • •

Besides reorganization, training, and personnel management, the ALS centers were provided a new two-year construction and rehabilitation program—worth nearly US $10 million—which was undertaken by Pacific Architects and Engineers. This program was designed to improve shop and truck maintenance facilities and storage warehouses for food, clothing, fuel, and ammunition. Each center's transportation assets, which consisted of a 2–1/2-ton truck platoon equipped with from 18 to 40 vehicles, were also augmented as required by chartered commercial transportation facilities such as buses, trucks, boats, and even three-wheeled "Lambrettas" to expedite supplies to districts, outposts, and to PF and RF units wherever they were located. To resupply ALS centers located more than 40 miles from the nearest ARVN field depot, periodic convoys were organized by ALCs. For remote districts and outposts that road and waterway transportation facilities could not safely reach, UH-1 or CH-47 helicopters were employed for their resupply.

Training

As the RVNAF logistics structure expanded and more sophisticated equipment entered the supply inventory, and in view of the eventual takeover from the United States, the requirements for more specialists, more maintenance consciousness, and more skills became increasingly apparent. To meet these requirements, the JGS and MACV stepped up training activities throughout the RVNAF under a system of centralized, combined planning and control.

• • •

In addition to various regular courses conducted by technical service schools, ARVN specialists were also sent to US units or contractors' facilities to undergo on-the-job training. For example, the US 4th Terminal Command helped train ARVN specialists in the operation and servicing of river boats [and] floating cranes, and helped train port managers. US contractors such as Vinnell and Pacific Engineers helped train ARVN engineer personnel in high-power generator depot maintenance; Dynalectron assisted in the training of managers for road construction parks and in training operators, supply specialists, and third- and fourth-echelon repairmen for special road-building machinery employed in the Military Construction, Army, Lines of Communication (MCA/LOC) program . . . ; [and] signal specialists for the newly established calibration systems were trained by AAEO, Inc. Finally, the Computer Sciences Corporation provided training of ADP managers, programmers, and analysts for the RVN Automated Materiel Management System and the ADP Center.

• • •

The Food Program

The efforts of ARVN logisticians during this period of time were not only confined to improving logistics operations and unit support. Their efforts also extended to the living conditions of the individual soldier and his dependents. The soldier, as the lowest fixed income earner, had for some time begun to feel the pinch of inflation and rising prices. The GVN had been slow-moving to initiate effective measures to improve this situation. In the face of worsening prospects that might adversely affect troop morale, the JGS did make some efforts to improve nutrition through a food program for the benefit of servicemen and their dependents. In fact, the food program was an integrated effort consisting of three components: 1) the military commissary system, 2) the food donation program, and 3) the military farming program.

The military commissary system began its operation in 1968 with funds returned from the sale of canned food donated by US forces during 1967. The system was designed to provide servicemen and dependents with food and commodities at prices lower than on the local market. . . . The procurement of cigarettes, sugar, canned milk, and soft drinks for the commissary system was exempt from GVN taxes. The GVN also authorized the direct import of certain essential foods such as cooking oil, canned meat, fish, and instant noodles. As a result, the retail prices of these commodities were from 25 to 30 percent lower than on the local market. While the system benefited the servicemen and enhanced their morale, it was also plagued by selfish abuses of certain greedy personnel and . . . aroused the jealousy of local businessmen and complaints from GVN economic officials.

• • •

By and large, it was estimated that the commissary system helped the average serviceman family save from 5 to 10 percent of his income.

• • •

During 1969, based on a recommendation by the JGS which was approved by MACV and endorsed by USAID, the US Department of Defense approved the donation of US $42.7 million worth of canned food to be distributed free to servicemen. This program was implemented in three years. During the first year it covered 100 percent of salaried servicemen; during the second year, distribution was reduced to 70 percent, and, during the third year, to 30 percent of RVNAF strength, in keeping with progress made in the military farming program and other GVN economic projects. Under the free canned food program each serviceman was issued three monthly coupons, each coupon to be redeemed for one can of fish, one can of meat, and one can of cooking oil or shortening, the total weighing about 7.7 pounds. Canned foods were shipped directly from the United States to quartermaster field depots at Danang, Qui Nhon, Nha Trang, Can Tho, and the 10th Food and Clothing Base Depot in Saigon. Each unit was distributed an advance revolving reserve of canned food equivalent to 10 percent of its payroll troop strength. This reserve was replenished by the local field depot against coupons collected.

The free canned food program brought about comfort and confidence among the servicemen. It testified to the solicitude that the GVN and the US government displayed toward the welfare of the individual ARVN soldier. Beneficial as it was, the program was nonetheless plagued by intricate difficulties and not effectively controlled. Difficulties arose chiefly from personnel and administration problems occasioned by AWOLs, deserters, MIAs, and KIAs, [and] from pilferage in storage and in transition to field depots. A small number of responsible but dishonest personnel found ways to cheat the innocent soldiers and steal from them.

As a contribution to the GVN effort to solve the difficult economic and salary problems, the military farming program was planned and enthusiastically implemented to achieve the following objectives: 1) to increase food intake and nutrition for servicemen and their dependents; 2) to help servicemen, [and] especially their dependents, to be gainfully employed during leisure time; 3) to employ in productive work second- and third-degree disabled servicemen who still remained in service but were not combat-worthy; 4) to reinforce the unit system of self-defense against enemy sappers; 5) to instill a spirit of self-reliance, self-sufficiency, and patience among servicemen and their dependents to sustain a protracted war; and 6) to contribute to the GVN effort of economic development in the areas of agriculture and farm-breeding.

Under the program individual servicemen and their dependents, and entire units, were encouraged to tend small patches of vegetables and to raise pigs and chickens. The basic idea was to help them procure meat and vegetables which they could not afford at market prices. Vegetable growing began initially on unused land in base camps and in dependent housing areas. Then it extended to the areas around camps and bases. Ultimately it was to expand into adjacent areas and into enemy-controlled areas. The basis for farm-breeding was one pig and three chickens for every serviceman's family.

• • •

After more than three years of patience and hard toiling, the results . . . were encouraging. Two animal feed production centers (at Danang and Saigon) and four piglet and young chicken production centers (at Danang, Qui Nhon, Ban Me Thuot, and Saigon) were established. Among them, these centers were capable of supplying 300 tons of feed, 30,000 young chickens, and 200 piglets every month. These were sold to units and individual servicemen at prices 20 to 25 percent lower than on the market. In vegetable planting, by now every unit had its own garden of lettuce, eggplant, pepper, and gourd for daily consumption. . . .

During this period of time the farming program also trained over 5,000 disabled servicemen as agricultural specialists of the local level who were knowledgeable about crop planting techniques, fertilizers, seed selection, and modern farm-breeding methods.

In late 1972, as a result of a misunderstanding among politicians and businessmen, who feared a market monopolization by the armed forces and unfair competition with the private sector, and under their pressure, the GVN gave orders to suspend the program with the explanation that "a military force does not produce." After liquidation of assets in early 1973, there still remained a fund of VN $300 million, which was authorized by the GVN to be spent for improvement work on the RVNAF cemeteries, in particular the cemetery at Bien Hoa, where lay the remains of over 10,000 servicemen.

By mid-1974, in the face of darkening economic [prospects], increasing defense expenditures, and a serious reduction in military aid, all of which happened at a time when it was impossible to reduce RVNAF strength, the GVN ordered a feasibility study of a people's defense concept which would make every soldier a part-time farmer and provide for a pool of reservist farmers. At the same time, it appealed for RVNAF units to participate in farmwork and in farm production. Unfortunately, it was too late for the new policy to produce any effect.

V. THE SUPPLY AND MAINTENANCE IMPROVEMENT PROGRAM

Basic Concept and Objectives

• • •

With the great increase in inventory assets that accompanied the great expansion in force structure during the period of Vietnamization, it became evident that hand entries on accounting ledgers, requisitions, and reports were no longer adequate. To provide quick and accurate data for planning and programming purposes, a computerized management system was indicated. In the technical services situation, it was difficult or impossible to monitor or follow up on requisitions and reconcile due-in data with US agencies because of the radical differences between the RVNAF and US logistics systems. Whereas the US logistics system was thoroughly automated and operated on a functional concept, the RVNAF system, up to early 1969, was manual and based on technical services.

• • •

Supply Activities

MAJOR ITEMS

There was no change in the planning and programming process as regards major items during this period of time, except for the fact that the National Materiel Management

Agency [NMMA] took over the functions performed separately by the Ordnance, Quartermaster, Signal, and Engineer departments as of FY 1973. As usual, based on annual aid appropriations that had been approved, the US International Logistics Center (ILC) automatically forwarded equipment to South Vietnam.

• • •

For several years there had been no inventory conducted for the purpose of reconciling record figures with the amount of assets on hand and arriving at accurate figures which could be reliably used by both sides. Even for high-cost and low-density equipment such as M-48 tanks, 175mm artillery guns, and M-113 APCs, no inventory was ever made. The ESR [Equipment Status Report] discrepancy problem was serious enough that it became the subject of a direct report made by the JGS to General Creighton W. Abrams in late October 1972 when, as Chief of Staff, US Army, he made a visit to South Vietnam to inform the GVN of the coming Enhance Plus program.

In order to provide the US Department of the Army with a relatively accurate set of figures that could be used for the Enhance Plus program, several combined MACV-JGS inventory teams were sent to units and logistic support organizations to take a quick inventory of items considered essential for the US mission. The results of this inventory were temporarily used to reconcile differences between US and ARVN equipment status reports.

• • •

In October 1972 the Enhance Plus project was implemented in the face of an imminent agreement on the cessation of hostilities which would certainly put a ban on the import of war materiel. The project was aimed at helping the RVNAF: 1) increase firepower and mobility, 2) fill present shortages, and 3) acquire an attrition and maintenance float. The goal was to stock up the RVNAF with enough property assets to offset the limitations to be imposed by the eventual cease-fire agreement. Under the project, a quantity of major items was rushed to South Vietnam by air and sea. They included RVNAF equipment rebuilt at US overseas base depots such as M-113 APCs, M-41 tanks, 2–1/2-ton M35A2 trucks, A1E1 fighter-bombers, new tanks, artillery pieces, and airplanes in sufficient quantities to equip two M-48 squadrons, three 175mm artillery battalions, three C-130A [squadrons], and a number of F-5A squadrons. In addition, remaining US and ROK combat units, advisory groups, and US contractors were instructed to transfer their armaments and equipment "as is" to the RVNAF, to include individual and crew-served weapons, 105mm and 155mm howitzers, and standard and nonstandard utility vehicles.

• • •

Class I Supplies

Rice is the basic diet staple of the Vietnamese. During this period the RVN rice production was on the decline due to the ravages of war and could not meet domestic consumption requirements. As a result, rice had to be imported from the United States, Thailand, and Taiwan. Poor control of rice distribution resulted in speculation and price increases which seriously affected the ARVN soldier's life.

As an incentive to enhance troop morale and shield the individual soldiers from the impact of price increases, the GVN decided in 1970 to grant each enlisted man a monthly rice allocation of 21 kilos (46.2 pounds) in addition to his pay. This became known as the 21-kilo rice program.

• • •

In 1973 the program was terminated and rice allocations were replaced by cash allowances. Welcomed by [MR-4] troops, the change caused some frustration among soldiers living in other [military regions] where rice was sold at higher prices. This frustration persisted despite the GVN promise to keep allowances in line with rice price increases.

In addition to regular rice allocations or allowances, the GVN also initiated a special 300-gram/day rice program as a hardship compensation for those soldiers assigned to border camps and outlying outposts. Each man received a monthly rice allocation, based on 300 grams/day, in addition to his pay. Corps commanders were responsible for recommending which outposts were entitled to program benefits and for controlling the distribution of rice.

Each ARVN combat ration consisted of three instant rice bags (for breakfast, lunch, and dinner) and a package containing a meat can, food accessories, and spices. In terms of nutrition and taste, ARVN combat rations were entirely suited to the Vietnamese soldier. Usually combat rations were issued to troops when they participated in an operation and subsequently were reimbursed by pay deductions on the basis of daily food allowance, which was from VN $35 to $50 per day. As a result, many soldiers complained about these deductions. They considered them unjust and preferred to provide their own food. In reality, the cost of a combat ration in 1969 was from VN $250 to $300, which was about six or seven times the daily food allowance deducted.

Because of the high costs involved, the RVNAF had to limit the consumption of combat rations during operations and authorized their use only when fighting made cooking impossible. As a rule, operating units had to depend primarily on fresh food which was either bought from the local market or supplied from the rear.

In 1970, to reward the fighting soldier for his hardship, an agreement was reached between the GVN and MACV whereby combat rations would be issued free to units actually participating in operations on the basis of combat days. Corps headquarters were made responsible for the programming, requisitioning, distribution, and control of combat rations, which were either produced and procured locally or overseas and sometimes included American C-rations. Monthly issues of combat rations increased substantially every year, from an initial 800,000 rations/man/day [*sic*] in 1970 to 1,750,000 in 1971 and then 3,200,000 in 1972. The RVN national budget was capable of financing only one-eighth of the total cost.

The issue of free combat rations greatly gratified the combat soldiers and alleviated a great burden for tactical commanders. Some soldiers even saved some of their combat rations and brought them back to their families as gifts. [From] the logistician's viewpoint, however, this was another cause for concern. Combat rations cost the RVN budget billions of piasters and tens of million US dollars every year. Also, they became in time a profitable commodity which benefited corrupt commanders, as evident from the amount of combat rations sold commercially on the local market.

Class III Supplies

The Quartermaster Department was the sole agency responsible for the management of two types of POL, motor gasoline and diesel fuel, for all three RVNAF services. Aviation fuels such as JP4 and avgas 115/145 were the responsibility of the VNAF.

• • •

The POL storage level determined for the RVNAF was 60 days of supply, but storage capabilities could not effectively meet the requirements, which grew every year. As a result, the principle of "tank filling" was applied instead. During the period from 1965 to 1968 the US Army and Navy built several fixed fuel storage tanks with capacities ranging from 3,000 to 50,000 barrels at Tan My, Danang, Qui Nhon, Cam Ranh, and Long Binh. The aggregated capacity of these tanks amounted to 1.6 million barrels. The US Air Force also built several tank farms at airbases with a total capacity of 350,000 barrels. All these tank farms were gradually turned over to the Quartermaster Department and the VNAF during 1972.

In addition to fixed metal tanks and 55-gallon drums, which were used at field depots and supply points, there were also rubberized collapsible tanks of various capacities, up to 50,000 gallons, used at operational distribution points, and JP4 supply points for helicopters. Several pipeline systems were also built by US forces to facilitate fuel transportation from ports to tank farms and from tank farms to US bases.

• • •

The transportation of fuels from foreign supply sources to South Vietnam was undertaken by SAPOV [South Asia Petroleum Office, Vietnam]-chartered or MSTS [Military Sea Transportation Service] tankers. Upon arrival at Vietnamese major ports at Danang, Qui Nhon, Nha Trang, and Saigon, fuels were pumped directly from tankers to military or civilian tank farms through pipelines. From these tank farms, fuels were subsequently delivered by chartered vessels, by barges to lesser ports, or by commercial and military tank trucks to field depots and supply points throughout South Vietnam. Major tank farms or storage areas were located at Lien Chieu (near Danang), Qui Nhon, Nha Trang, Nha Be (near Saigon), Can Tho, Long Binh, Bien Hoa, Tan Son Nhut, and Go Vap, where the 30th POL Storage Base depot was located. For the emergency resupply of supply points that ordinary road or waterway transportation could not reach because of enemy interdiction or siege, US forces usually provided CH-47 helicopters and "bladder birds" which brought millions of gallons of fuel from Tan Son Nhut and Bien Hoa AFB to wherever resupply was urgently needed.

• • •

Despite tight control measures, the pilferage of fuels was inevitable. A few types of fuel such as gasoline, diesel oil, JP4, etc. were frequently seen displayed in bottles for sale in some cities and around US, ARVN, and FWMA bases. Such fuel losses usually resulted from thefts and gifts or donations in exchange for services rendered by the local population. Control was also impossible at helicopter distribution points, where measuring instruments did not exist, or when fuel supply was made by airdrop or airlift.

Maintenance Activities

The weakest link in the ARVN maintenance system was usually found at the grassroots level, the user units. The objective to be achieved during this period, therefore, was to improve organizational maintenance and to promote maintenance consciousness among unit commanders.

• • •

Preventive maintenance now became a six-day subject which was inserted into regular courses conducted by the Command and Staff College, the Infantry School, the National Military Academy, and was emphasized in service advanced courses. Maintenance awareness was also made the major theme of songs, music pieces, plays, [and] poems that were carried by the CLC monthly maintenance pamphlet and the RVNAF bimonthly *Chien Si Cong Hoa* ("The Republic's Combatant") magazine, and performed on troop entertainment occasions.

• • •

During 1972, as a result of the rapid redeployment of US maintenance support units and the massive turnover of US equipment through the crash Keystone, Enhance, and Enhance Plus projects, ARVN field support units, especially ordnance and engineer, found themselves overwhelmed by excessive workloads required by the reception, storage, classification, evacuation, third-echelon repair, and second-echelon maintenance. They had to perform all these tasks in a short time to provide timely issues to newly activated units, in addition to filling requisitions from existing units. Lack of parts, lack of manpower, and lack of storage space were three major difficulties faced by these units. As a result, there was a backlog of over 5,000 assorted trucks and vehicles lying around unattended in all storage yards in the 1st, 2nd, and 3rd logistical areas as of March 1973.

• • •

Upon completion of the base depot upgrade program, Phase 1, 95 to 99 percent of major items and assemblies were rebuilt in-country. Those few items that still required rebuild at overseas bases were all new equipment such as M-48A3 tanks, 175mm guns, and a number of combat-damaged M-113s whose rebuild, in view of their low density, could not be economically performed by the Army Arsenal.

• • •

VI. SUPPORT ACTIVITIES AND BASE TRANSFER

Ammunition Supply

Ammunition management was a responsibility divided among the ARVN, the VNAF, and the VNN. Each service managed its own ammunition and special ordnance.

•••

Planning and programming for RVNAF ammunition requirements, up to the time of the Paris Agreement in January 1973, were essentially functions performed by MACV J-4 in coordination with US Army, Pacific (USARPAC). The Ordnance Department's role was only a modest one, consisting primarily of providing issue experience data to US advisors. The stock level that the RVNAF were authorized to retain varied greatly from period to period, not only in terms of supply days but also in the way the supply rate was computed. This level was initially set at 90 supply days . . . based on both World War II and the Korean War consumption experiences, with some modifications.

As of 1966, however, the computation of RVNAF ammunition stock levels was based on the US Army "Theater Required Supply Rate for Ammunition, Southeast Asia," prescribed by US Army, Pacific. . . . The required supply rate usually changed after each conference on ammunition held in Hawaii.

After the enemy Tet Offensive of 1968, supply rates were changed again. The computation basis was modified to reflect two rates: Intensive Combat Rate (ICR) and Theater Sustaining Rate (TSR). As a result, the RVNAF stockage level was changed, but remained at 90 days, consisting of 60 days of in-country stockage and 30 days of offshore reserve. In-country stockage was based on both rates, half of it on ICR and the other half on TSR. Offshore reserve was based on ICR.

•••

From 1966 to 1970, the period of most active US participation in the war, the RVNAF were spared the responsibility of receiving and distributing ammunition for consumer units. These tasks were completely taken over by US forces. The Ordnance Department's role was simply to submit replenishment requirements to US advisors who, after coordinating programming actions with MACV and USARV, would notify it of planned actions. Then, based on authorized allocation, the Ordnance Department would instruct field depots either to take deliveries at designated US depots or wait for supplies delivered by US trucks or barges.

Through the entire process the RVNAF acted only as a customer of US logistics units in Vietnam. There were several reasons for this. First, ammunition requirements increased sharply and unexpectedly during this period of intensive combat, from 40,000 tons/month in 1966 to 90,000 tons/month in 1968 and to over 100,000 tons/month during 1970. Second, the limited assets available for unloading, storing, and transporting would be better utilized if placed under a single-manager agency. And finally, given the gigantic amount of ammunition involved, the RVNAF just did not have enough qualified personnel, transportation assets, and storage facilities to handle it by themselves.

As of 1970, with the gradual turnover of US ammunition depots, and as a result of the depot upgrade program and the substantial increase in ordnance personnel and ammunition specialists, the RVNAF were capable of operating a large number of modern depots, including those at Danang, Qui Nhon, Dong Ba Thin, Thanh Tuy Ha, Go Vap, and Long Binh, and of taking deliveries of ammunition cargoes at major harbors after they had been offloaded by US forces.

Ammunition Storage, Transportation, Security, and Disposal Problems

• • •

The changing storage level at depots during the war sometimes seriously violated the minimum safety distance, and, as a result, safety and security became in time mutually exclusive conditions between which the commander had to make a choice and take full responsibility for it if anything went wrong. Most ARVN ammunition depots fell into this category. If they were safe, they were not secure, and if they were secure they were not safe enough. A case in point was the 511th Depot at Tien Sa, near Danang, which, when built by French forces during the early 1950s, was both secure and safe. By 1965, however, it had become entirely unsafe due to the growth of Danang city and the congested logistics facilities built by US forces on this tiny peninsula. Despite its lack of safety, the depot enjoyed more security and was less subject to sabotage and shelling. By contrast, the ARVN field ammunition depot at Phu Thanh, and its USARV sister at Phu Tai nearby, both in Binh Dinh Province, which were built in a foothill area completely isolated from the provincial capital and the local population, were completely safe but were the two depots that suffered the most from enemy attacks and sabotage.

• • •

Storage facilities in most ARVN depots during 1969–1970 consisted of open storage pads, which were usually small, narrow, and humid, inadequately ventilated warehouses which did not permit the use of forklifts. In addition, their internal road systems were generally damaged. Therefore about 90 percent of all ARVN ammunition was stored in open pads, and the separation between them seriously violated safety requirements. This was the case with field depots at Danang, Nha Trang, and Go Vap.

In 1970 an improvement project was jointly undertaken by MACV and the JGS at a cost of US $50 million. The project consisted of: 1) improving the deployment of ARVN ammunition depots and planning for the use of US depots which would shortly be turned over; 2) building new warehouses [and] enlarging and rehabilitating old ones so as to include open pads, roads, and defense systems; and 3) modernizing loading and unloading by the use of electric-powered forklifts. Reinforced concrete bunkers of the Stradley type were selected for new construction.

• • •

All construction works of the first and second phases of the project were performed under contract by Pacific Architect and Engineers and completed during 1971 and 1972. By the time the project entered into its third phase, funds were no longer available and the project had to be cancelled.

• • •

During the period from 1965 to 1972, ammunition was shipped directly to five ports in South Vietnam: Danang, Qui Nhon, Cam Ranh, Vung Tau, and Cat Lai (Saigon). Off-loading from ships was undertaken by American, Vietnamese, and Korean contractors, operating under the control of US forces. At Danang and Qui Nhon, ammunition was unloaded from ships anchored offshore onto barges or LCUs and LCM-8s, then moved to piers from where it was unloaded again and trucked away to field depots. Transportation from Danang to advance depots and supply points located north of Hai Van Pass was effected by LSTs, LCUs, and LCM-8s which unloaded at Tan My (Thua Thien), My Thuy, and Cua Viet (Quang Tri). Ammunition was moved to depots located in the Central Highlands by escorted convoys. At Cam Ranh, unloading was also performed offshore until 1966, when a DeLong pier was built. Ammunition bound for MR-4 was unloaded offshore at Vung Tau, then towed by barges to Dong Tam base for distribution to consumers in the Mekong area, and to Tra Noc (Can Tho) in the Bassac area.

• • •

Fixed-wing aircraft were used sometimes to transport critical items of ammunition, mostly for emergency tactical requirements or when roads were interdicted for a sustained period of time. But CH-47 helicopters proved to be by far the most effective means of moving ammunition to battlefront units and to isolated outposts.

Like POL, ammunition was a major target for Communist sabotage action. During the war, the Communists employed every imaginable form of warfare and tactic against our ammunition depots. The three most dangerous forms of Communist sabotage were planted agents, sapper penetration, and shelling. Each act of sabotage was always the subject of painstaking planning, during which time enemy agents carefully studied depot layout, access, and personnel habits. When the plan was carried out, it usually succeeded.

Severe security measures were taken against planted agents, who usually bribed or pressured ARVN personnel into cooperating with them when a sabotage plan was attempted. In fact, all personnel working at an ammunition depot had to be carefully screened and cleared by the Military Security Department (MSD) and the National Police, then rechecked periodically. Guard personnel, in addition to being security-cleared, were rotated every year, or every six months if necessary. Frequent security checks were conducted by MSD agents throughout all depot areas, usually after duty hours.

Communist sappers were sabotage agents who had been thoroughly trained for their mission. Hence they were particularly effective in crossing minefields, cutting through barbed wire systems, and employing explosives armed with time fuses. Usually their actions were minutely planned, well rehearsed, and swiftly carried out. Sappers thrived on darkness, concealment, and friendly habit patterns. To defend against sapper actions, ARVN ammunition depots were each provided with an illumination system, watchtowers, barbed wire, antipersonnel and illuminated minefields, and a well-cleared area at least 200 yards wide around the depot outer perimeter. A major problem faced by ammunition depots was the lack of organic personnel to man watchtowers and maintain the lighting system, minefields, and the cleared area. The concern and continual support of tactical commanders at all levels were required. A few important depots were reinforced with a sensor system and watchdogs.

To neutralize the enemy capability for shelling ammunition depots, tactical and territorial commanders usually conducted saturation patrol activities around the depots and laid ambushes along the perimeters of effective 82mm mortar range. However, despite ARVN vigilance, the Communists succeeded, during 1972, in conducting 37 sapper penetrations and 13 shellings, causing destruction to 23,903 tons of ammunition worth in excess of US $54 million.

• • •

Transportation and Movement Control

• • •

Due to . . . prearrangement, the transfer of ports progressed harmoniously without a single instance of interruption. By the time of the cease-fire in January 1973, only Newport in Saigon was still operated by US forces.

• • •

The operation of ports and piers, as taken over by the RVNAF, ran smoothly without serious impediments save for a lack of funds for the dredging of channels and pier drafts. This was especially true at Tan My, which required special equipment not available in Vietnam.

• • •

With regard to air transportation, during the period from 1969 to 1972 the VNAF was augmented with two types of cargo aircraft: C-123s and C-7s. The C-123 "Provider" was faster than the C-119 and could carry 12,000 pounds of cargo or 60 troops. The C-7 "Caribou" had the advantage of short takeoff and landing, requiring an airstrip only one-quarter the length of that required by C-119s or C-123s. Its use was very convenient for the supply of outposts and border camps. Each C-7 could carry 4,500 pounds of cargo or 32 troops.

With its three C-123 squadrons and three C-7 squadrons, each equipped with 18 aircraft, the VNAF became the main supplier of air transportation for the RVNAF, replacing gradually the US Air Force. In early 1969, the VNAF's share of air transportation was only 30 percent. During the first ten months of 1972 the VNAF transported a total of 450,000 troops, or 66 percent of troop movement requirements. In supply transportation, however, the VNAF share was smaller, amounting to 45 percent of total supplies moved by air. As a result, prior to April 1972 USAF reinforcement amounted to only one C-130 per day for cargo or personnel transport. During the 1972 Easter Offensive, USAF support in C-130 cargo planes increased manyfold due to increased demands for troop movement.

• • •

During the first three months of the Easter Offensive (April, May, June) . . . the VNAF average share in total supply tonnage airlifted was only 30 percent because of a marked increase in requirements. Its peak performance occurred in May and October, with 3,593 and 3,439 tons, respectively. However, if more efficient management had been provided VNAF performance could have been better.

In general, VNAF airlift capabilities could meet only normal requirements during the pre-Easter Offensive 1968–1972 period. It was unable to handle the big surge in airlift movements occasioned by a major enemy offensive campaign such as the 1972 Easter Offensive.

In October 1972, under the Enhance Plus program, the VNAF received an additional 32 C-130A cargo planes, which were faster and had a much greater capacity. Each C-130A could carry 30,000 pounds of cargo or 100 troops, so the deficiency in airlift capabilities shown during the Easter Offensive stood a good chance of being overcome.

With regard to combat airlift, the VNAF helicopter assets increased significantly, from 85 UH-1s in early 1969 to between 550 and 600 by the time of the cease-fire. The VNAF also had, at the end of 1972, four CH-47 squadrons, each equipped with 18 aircraft. The CH-47 could carry 33 troops or 8,000 pounds of cargo. Since helicopter assets were placed under employment prerogatives of corps commanders for combat support missions, including medical evacuation, it was difficult to evaluate their performance. But, with a helicopter fleet of this size, it was apparent that the void caused by the redeployment of US troops would not be too serious.

The Transfer of US Bases

During their eight years of direct participation in the Vietnam War, 1965 through 1972, US forces had built many bases, large and small, throughout South Vietnam to meet their combat and support requirements. With the rapid pace of redeployment, which began in mid-1969, these bases gradually became superfluous to US needs. Once a base was declared excess by MACV, it was immediately turned over to GVN and RVNAF use, with priority given to the RVNAF.

• • •

It was not required for the RVNAF to take over every base available. The JGS/CLC was responsible for ensuring the judicious use of transferred bases in coordination with ARVN corps and for recommending to the GVN General Directorate of Plans those bases for which the RVNAF had no use.

• • •

There were in general two types of bases: operational bases and logistics support bases. Operational bases usually provided cantonment facilities for US combat battalions, brigades, and divisions. At the battalion and brigade level, operational bases consisted mostly of tin or canvas-roofed wooden barracks and defense positions. These bases were usually destroyed or just left behind unattended by US units when they redeployed. US divisional bases were much better, being composed partially of tin-roofed wooden barracks and partially of prefabricated metallic buildings used for offices and warehouses. These bases had a good, though only partially surfaced, road system; a high-power (generally from 500 to 1,500 KVA) electric generating plant; and a deep-well water supply system. When transferred, they were usually turned over to ARVN infantry divisions or separate tactical units. The advantages offered by these bases were their capacity to accommodate entire large units, thus facilitating coordination and control; their isolation from populous areas; their spaciousness; and their modern facilities. If properly maintained, these bases would provide lasting, magnificent service.

Despite the advantages to the RVNAF, these large operational bases caused certain problems. For example, some of them were too spacious even for an entire ARVN division, and most of the barracks had begun to deteriorate, requiring major rebuilding work. More often than not, the units which took over these bases found themselves short of personnel to fill all the barracks, to man all guardposts and defense positions, and—more critically—to properly maintain all the facilities. As a result, ARVN units gradually shrank their living perimeter and cannibalized those barracks no longer in use in order to repair and rebuild the good ones. The power-generating system, although a vital utility, created an additional operating and maintenance burden that no ARVN infantry division could shoulder easily. Also the elaborate mess and dining complex, with its electric or gas ranges, was totally incompatible with ARVN mess service, hence rarely used.

• • •

In contrast to operational bases, US Army support or logistics bases consisted primarily of more permanent-type construction, with metal buildings used as offices, shops, and warehouses, and with a few wooden barracks. All these bases had a good surfaced road system, in addition to high-voltage power, air conditioning, and water systems. When transferred, these bases were used to accommodate ARVN central logistics agencies and field support units. Although these bases had the same advantages and disadvantages as the operational bases, US logistical bases entirely suited the requirements occasioned by the RVNAF logistics reorganization plan and helped minimize the need for new construction. The only shortcomings found in the use of these bases were their relative isolation from urban areas which were the main source of labor and the complexity of their high-voltage central air conditioning and refrigerated warehouse systems.

• • •

All US bases were title-transferred to RVNAF control as of 18 October 1972 in anticipation of the cease-fire agreement, and especially as a "fait accompli" to preempt the provisions concerning the mandatory dismantling of US bases in South Vietnam. Since they were still operated by US forces at that time, legal formalities required that the GVN sign for their temporary release for US use after the title transfer had been accomplished. The Communist NLF military delegation to the Four-Party Joint Military Commission later found, to their complete dismay, that there were no longer any US bases to be dismantled, as required by the Paris Agreement, since they were all legally owned by the RVNAF. According to an ARVN officer present during the meeting, General Tran Van Tra of the NLF delegation could not conceal his ire and frustration when learning about this.

With regard to war materiel taken over by the RVNAF as a result of the base title transfer, the NMMA kept complete property record books whose entries accounted for every item received. These records were to be presented to the ICCS as documents justifying the extent of RVNAF property assets when required. Strangely, the ICCS never asked for them.

VII. LOGISTIC SUPPORT FOR COMBAT OPERATIONS

General Concept

As the RVNAF gradually took over combat responsibilities from US forces during 1968–1972, a division of tasks became mandatory between regular and territorial forces, and between infantry and the general reserve divisions.

Under the mission realignment, RF and PF units were given the general responsibility for territorial security and pacification support. Their objectives were the Viet Cong infrastructure (VCI) and the Communist local forces. Their assigned areas of operation were hamlets and villages, sometimes districts, for PF units; and provinces and certain interprovincial areas with the military region for RF units. Territorial force activities were generally of squad, platoon, company, or battalion size, and mostly consisted of patrols and ambushes on enemy communication routes, raids against district and village VCI targets, protection of waterways and roads, and police operations.

Since these activities took place within a logistic support area for which the provincial Administrative and Logistic Support (ALS) Center was responsible, support activities became routine matters and were determined by the standing operating procedures of the ALS Center and the sector. When an RF battalion was attached to another sector, its logistic support was implemented through an administrative order issued by the Area Logistical Command. The sector headquarters and the ALS Center of the province where the attached battalion operated were responsible for the supply of food, fuels, ammunition, dry batteries, barrier material, and second-echelon maintenance and medical evacuation for that unit. The RF battalion in this case continued to be supported by the original sector headquarters and ALS Center as regards personnel administration and pay, replacements, and major items of equipment.

ARVN infantry divisions, in the meantime, were released from their territorial responsibilities and gradually increased mobile combat operations against Communist main-force units as US combat forces stood down and departed. Each infantry division was assigned a tactical area of [responsibility] (TAOR) within the military region. Its logistic support was provided by the divisional logistics battalion, assisted and supported by the ALC logistic support units already deployed in the area. In general, during this period of time each infantry division confined its activities within a specified TAOR and never was employed in interregional operations except for a unique circumstance. One exception occurred during the enemy 1972 Easter Offensive, when the 21st Infantry Division was moved from its TAOR (Ca Mau–Bac Lieu) in MR-4 to the Chon Thanh front in MR-3.

The Airborne and Marine Divisions, as general reserve forces of the JGS, were normally located in Saigon and Bien Hoa, but they were apt to be employed anywhere in the country when required. The most vital consideration with regard to these divisions, therefore, was an ability to move them rapidly to where they were needed and to provide them with support on the battlefield. During the period from 1969 to 1972, due to the availability of US Air Force assets, moving the Airborne and Marine Divisions was readily accomplished. Experience showed that the entire Airborne Division could be airlifted from Saigon to Hue in just three days.

• • •

Because the Airborne and Marine Divisions moved so frequently, their transportation and logistic support had become familiar tasks, not only for the divisions themselves but also for all direct support units involved. There was no instance in which these divisions were caught short by a lack of supplies or other kinds of support. As a result, logistic support for combat operations, whether for infantry or general reserve divisions, became in time a routine, uneventful matter. More notable, however, were special support activities performed during offensive campaigns, whether friendly or enemy-initiated, especially during the 1970 Cambodian cross-border operation, the 1971 incursion into lower Laos, and the enemy 1972 Easter Offensive.

The Cambodian Cross-Border Operation

The Cambodian cross-border operation consisted of several offensive activities conducted by the ARVN III and IV Corps in continuous succession, starting 1 May 1970. These activities were designed to destroy the rear service and logistics installations of the enemy and cut off his supply and communication routes. These routes had been operative on Cambodian soil for several years without interference. They were also conducted to help relieve the National Khmer forces from heavy pressure that the Khmer Rouge exerted in the areas of Kompong Trach–Tuk Meas–Takeo, along the Mekong River and QL-1 from the border to Svay Rieng and Neak Luong, and in the Prey Veng–Chup–Dambe region.

• • •

POL was stored at supply points, either in 55-gallon drums or in rubberized collapsible bags of 10,000 or 50,000 gallons. The Thien Ngon supply point in particular was capable of supplying 16 helicopters at any one time. In general the replenishment of POL supply points on both sides of the border encountered no difficulties.

There were some problems, however, in the supply of POL for M-113 and M-41 squadrons operating at great distances from lines of communication. Since there were not enough M-548 cargo carriers to use on land, CH-47 Chinook helicopters had to be employed to sling-carry 55-gallon drums to where the armor elements operated. Supply by airdrop was made only once. Tracked M-548 cargo carriers proved very effective in moving supplies from a supply point to armor units in this type of terrain. Their quantity, however, was much less than had been authorized, and their unserviceability rate was rather high due to overwork and lack of parts.

The requirement for JP4 was by far the greatest. As a result, tank trucks were used primarily to move JP4 for the replenishment of collapsible bags at supply points. There were certain times when the QL-1 stretch between Go Dau Ha and Neak Luong was temporarily interdicted, during which times the refueling for helicopters at the Neak Luong supply point had to be made with hand-operated Japy pumps out of 55-gallon drums, a very slow operation.

• • •

Two most rapidly expended types of ammunition were 105mm and 155mm artillery rounds and .50 caliber cartridges for M-113 APCs. Artillery ammunition averaged 60 percent of all issues. Its average expenditure rate was 50 to 60 rounds/piece/day for a 105mm howitzer and 18 to 25 rounds/piece/day for a 155mm howitzer.

• • •

Medical evacuation from battlefield areas was accomplished entirely by the VNAF throughout the operation. Patients were evacuated toward military hospitals located near the border, such as those at Tay Ninh (400 beds), Kien Tuong (200 beds, a mixed civilian-military facility), Long Xuyen (400 beds), and Kien Giang. . . .

The retrograde of materiel damaged beyond the capability of mobile repair teams toward support bases encountered no great difficulties during the initial phase of the operation. As ARVN units gradually advanced more deeply into Cambodia, they also moved away from major axes of communication. The retrograde of damaged materiel, therefore, became more difficult, especially in the case of M-113 APCs, due to terrain and the shortage of wreckers. The number of XM-801 wreckers, as authorized by TO&Es, was not enough to handle heavy combat wreckage loads. In addition, the swampy ground of battlefield areas quickly took a heavy toll on XM-801s. As a result, several heavily damaged M-113s had to be destroyed on the spot, particularly in the Kampot area, a IV Corps area of operation, and in the Chuplong area under control of III Corps. From forward support bases, damaged materiel and equipment were gradually moved to the rear toward Can Tho and Saigon. The major problem encountered during these movements was a shortage of prime movers and semitrailers.

• • •

In addition to providing support for ARVN operational forces, the RVNAF logistic efforts also benefited Khmer forces during the cross-border operations. As a gesture of goodwill and friendship, the RVNAF provided the FANK[3] substantial services and aid.

Since Khmer forces employed Communist bloc armament during that time, the RVNAF gave to FANK in excess of 30,000 captured weapons, including AK-47 assault rifles, B-40 and B-41 rocket launchers, and 62mm and 82mm mortars, and over 2,000 individual clothing sets, including fatigues and berets. The RVNAF also provided maintenance support and petroleum supply, on a reimbursable basis, for Khmer river boats operating on the Mekong River. During battles, ARVN forces also let FANK units share with them certain critical items of ammunition, helped them with medical evacuation by helicopter, and airlifted supplies for their border outposts.

Finally, the RVNAF also gave the FANK a helping hand by assisting in the reception and shipment of US materiel from Saigon to Phnom Penh, and the transportation of Khmer nationals and recruits from refugee camps along the border to Phnom Penh.

AN EVALUATION

The Cambodian cross-border operation was well supported logistically. There was in fact no single instance in which operational activities were disrupted or cancelled for lack of supplies. The selection of areas of operation was logistically sound, affording good road and waterway communication and security. Both road and river transportation assets adequately accomplished all movement requirements. Advance support bases established in Cambodia at Krek and Neak Luong functioned effectively, without US advisors. Medical evacuation was also accomplished effectively by VNAF helicopters.

There were, however, several shortcomings and areas that needed improvement. In the first place, the activation of advance support bases with separate teams, platoons detached from technical service direct support units, did not lend itself to effective control and coordination. A field support organization of this type was definitely not responsive enough for a sustained operation like the Cambodian incursion. To coordinate efficiently all support activities at each of these advance bases was a difficult requirement which dictated the presence of an ALC staff officer at all times.

Then there was the shortage problem, particularly of petroleum storage facilities, tank trucks, all-terrain cargo carriers, and heavy equipment movers. For example, there were not enough collapsible fuel tanks of the 10,000 and 50,000 gallon types, which were critically needed at helicopter refueling stations. For petroleum resupply movements, there was also a shortage of 5,000-gallon tank trucks, which were perfectly tailored for this task. For the cross-country transportation of supplies, especially for armor units which operated at a great distance from roads, the need for additional M-548 cargo carriers was critically felt. Finally, the recovery of damaged equipment from battlefields was considerably impeded by a shortage of prime movers and flatbed 25-ton semitrailers.

Lam Son 719

Lam Son 719 was a combined RVNAF-US operation conducted into lower Laos from 30 January to 9 April 1971 with the objectives of disrupting North Vietnam infiltration activities on the Ho Chi Minh Trail, and destroying enemy supply bases along the trail and his vital rear service area at Tchepone.

• • •

An outstanding feature of Lam Son 719 was the direct support provided by US logistics units to I Corps forces during the first nine days of the operation, and its gradual phasing out during the next nine days. Lam Son 719 was also a combined corps-level effort in which ARVN combat divisions operated far from their usual TAORs and beyond the 1st ALC normal area of responsibility.

• • •

Strangely, the 1st ALC commander, the man responsible for the success or failure of support activities on the ARVN side, was not among those who were authorized advance knowledge of the operation and a role in its planning. Neither was his US advisor. Whatever the rationale, and however it was justified, planning should have been extended at least to the 1st ALC commander and his advisor and, if possible, three of his key staff officers: ammunition, POL, and transportation. If it had not been acceptable at the beginning, then one or two weeks before D-Day at the latest these responsible

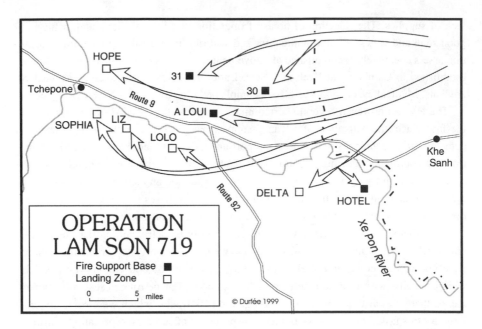

officers should have been involved in the planning just to ensure adequate detail and effective preparations.

Because of the lack of advance planning, the 1st ALC was overwhelmed by the rush of last-minute activities and proceeded with the deployment of its units without careful preparations. The deployment of Class III and V supply points for a special corps-level operation was simply beyond the organic capabilities of the 1st ALC ammunition and POL field depots. Subsequent piecemeal reinforcements in personnel and facilities expediently detached from other ALCs were not responsive enough for an operation of long duration and the tonnage of supplies to be handled. An advance depot with a separate TO&E would have been more appropriate.

• • •

Lieutenant General Hoang Xuan Lam, commanding general of I Corps and Lam Son 719, indeed complained that Colonel Mai Duy Thuong, 1st ALC commander, was not always available at Khe Sanh, and he was right to some extent. In fact, as it was organized the 1st ALC was organically not capable of establishing three forward headquarters at the same time. Colonel Thuong simply could not afford to be at any one place continuously, since there were so many things to coordinate and expedite at other places. What the I Corps commander could have done for the Khe Sanh support base, given its relatively more important role, was to provide an officer and a staff to exercise control over the activities of separate technical service elements and to coordinate with ARVN divisional logistics battalions and FSA 26–2 [US Forward Support Activity 26–2]. It was apparent that either a support battalion or a group, organized along functional lines, would have been more appropriate.

Nevertheless, coordination and cooperation between Major General [Arthur] H. Sweeney, CG, US Army Support Command, Danang, and Colonel Thuong . . . , and between their staffs, was excellent and instrumental in bringing about good results during the execution phase. The lack of early combined planning . . . was partially offset by the exchange of liaison officers between US Army Support Command, Danang, and the 1st ALC. General Sweeney's initiative in establishing a US-ARVN Logistic Control Center at FSA 26–2 was also very helpful, since it enabled its commander to be in full control of the overall supply situation in his area of responsibility and make mutually beneficial decisions in a timely manner. It also helped balance assets between the two sides and made possible the economical use of resupply transportation assets.

• • •

With regard to ammunition, the co-location of US and ARVN depots at the same site was a sound idea, since it facilitated coordination, afforded mutual support, and was economical for security assets. General Lam's unexpected decision to increase the stockage objective from 7 to 15 days, especially for 105mm and 155mm ammunition, however, made the ARVN depot unsafe and forced the US depot to move to another place. Protecting ammunition depots was a responsibility of corps tactical units, but they were always short of troops for guard detail. As a result, to ensure adequate protection depot personnel had to double as guards and this greatly reduced the efficiency of depot operations.

• • •

The issue of ammunition to ARVN tactical units was subjected to drastic variations during this operation. For two or three days in a row the amount issued varied from 500 to 1,000 short tons per day, but on some days there was no issue requirement at all. This made it difficult for depots to keep a balanced stockage objective without violating safety rules or exhausting the safety level, especially as regards the high-explosive 105mm and 155mm ammunition.

• • •

In general, organizational maintenance at ARVN tactical units was largely neglected and ARVN commanders sought every pretext to justify its lack. Maintenance was relatively poor on 105mm and 155mm pieces, M-113 APCs, and M-41 tanks. Contact teams detached to provide maintenance for operational units reported that minor troubles would not have occurred if those units had spent just 20 minutes every day on preventive maintenance and one day every week on second-echelon maintenance control.

• • •

Regular truck convoys from Danang to Hue and Quang Tri were provided by ARVN medium truck companies. ARVN light truck companies were responsible for the Tan My–Quang Tri–Khe Sanh axis. During the first three weeks of the operation the QL-9 stretch from Ca Lu to Khe Sanh, usually a narrow and steep road, became muddy and slippery as a result of steady rain. It was practicable only one way for 2-1/2 and 5-ton cargo trucks and 1,200-gallon tank trucks. Ammunition and POL carried by 5-ton prime movers and 12-ton semitrailer convoys had to be offloaded at Ca Lu and then transported to Khe Sanh by light trucks. With improving weather and special rehabilitation efforts by US engineer units, the Ca Lu–Khe Sanh sector soon became trafficable for two-way medium truck traffic.

Supply convoys shuttled day and night between Tan My or Quang Tri and Khe Sanh to meet stockage objectives. A convoy usually departed from Quang Tri at 0500 hours and arrived at Khe Sanh around 1300 hours, then—after unloading—departed again at 1600 or 1700 hours and was back at Quang Tri by 2100 or 2200 hours. The same pattern and rhythm were kept up day after day, despite personnel and materiel losses caused by frequent enemy attacks, especially at night.

In air transportation, it was initially planned that the Khe Sanh airfield would begin operation on 4 February to handle from 40 to 60 C-130 flights daily, or from 550 to 600 tons of supplies, including petroleum. Due to extensive repairs, especially the need for reinstalling the airstrip matting, the Khe Sanh airfield did not become operational until 14 February. The weather unpredictability, a heavy morning fog, and the lack of runway lighting considerably impeded air movements and permitted only 21 landings and take-offs per day, or a daily average of 264 tons. Throughout the operation, a total of 11,000 short tons of supplies was airlifted to Khe Sanh, of which 9,400 short tons were delivered by the US Army Support Command, Danang, and 1,600 short tons by the ARVN 1st ALC. This tonnage included 1,174,547 gallons of JP4, 3,600 short tons of ammunition, and 2,000 tons of food, all for emergency requirements.

In sea transportation, the Tan My pier, which was the key offloading point for supply ships in the northern part of MR-1, was usable for LSTs and barges. Over 56,000 short tons of supplies were offloaded here for subsequent trucking to Quang Tri and Khe Sanh. A ramp at Dong Ha, which accommodated only LCUs, also received over 18,000 short tons of supplies. Both places were operated by US Army Support Command, Danang, since most supply ships belonged to the US Navy. The RVNAF contribution in sea transportation was modest, consisting of 2 LSTs, 2 LCMs, and a certain number of LCM-8s. Consequently over 70 percent of ARVN cargo bound for Tan My was transported by US ships.

• • •

Medical evacuation was accomplished by helicopters from battlefields to Khe Sanh and from there to Quang Tri, by 3/4-ton ambulance and fixed-wing aircraft from Quang Tri to Hue, and by fixed-wing aircraft directly from Khe Sanh to Duy Tan hospital in Danang if required. During the first two weeks of the operation medical evacuation from areas of operation in Laos to Khe Sanh ran smoothly. It became increasingly difficult as the enemy deployed more antiaircraft weapons. Finally, during the last phase of the operation, when ARVN forces withdrew toward the RVN side of the border, medical evacuation was not always possible. This was the first time that some wounded ARVN soldiers were left behind on the battlefield.

THE WITHDRAWAL PHASE

With regard to most damaged equipment, evacuation toward Danang was no problem, with the exception of 105mm and 155mm artillery pieces. However, heavy engineer equipment and armored vehicles severely damaged during battles fought in Laos were destroyed and left behind. This, according to after-action reports by participant units, was due to tactical expediency, rough terrain, and the lack of evacuation resources.

• • •

AN EVALUATION

Lam Son 719 was effectively supported logistically. In effect no tactical activity was ever cancelled or delayed due to the lack of supplies. The first three weeks of the operation, however, caused much concern among ARVN logisticians because of the ten-day delay in activating the Khe Sanh airfield, the reduced trafficability of the Ca Lu–Khe Sanh axis, and difficulties in offloading activities and pumping of fuel at piers caused by a rough sea.

The area of operation was rough, jungled, and mountainous terrain, alien to regular support activities. QL-9 was the unique supply axis for ARVN forces operating in Laos. It was narrow and precipitous on both sides of the border. The supply of ARVN operational forces in Laos from Khe Sanh, therefore, depended entirely on the powerful US helicopter fleet. This seemed to be the reason why the I Corps commander was not interested in having QL-9 on the other side of the border rehabilitated. The effectiveness of supply helicopters was greatly reduced by the increasingly dense enemy antiaircraft fire. This was very different from the Cambodian cross-border operation.

As far as the RVNAF were concerned, Lam Son 719 exposed certain shortcomings and deficiencies in their field support system. As in the Cambodian cross-border operation, field support was provided through advance bases which consisted of several separate supply and service support elements, making coordination difficult and requiring the constant presence of an ALC element that acted as a control body.

• • •

For the transport of POL there was a definite shortage of 5,000-gallon tank trucks which were tailored for long hauls. As to sea and air transportation, the contributions made by the VNAF and VNN were but minimal. It was the US forces who provided almost everything, from naval ships to port operations and from helicopters at the front line to fixed-wing aircraft at the rear.

The 1972 Easter Offensive

• • •

In MR-2, after QL-19 and QL-14 between Pleiku and Kontum had been interdicted in late April, the resupply of POL for the 23rd Division in Kontum had to be airlifted from Pleiku in 500-gallon rubber bladders and VNAF C-123s. The POL field depot at Pleiku was supplied by tank trucks using the QL-21 Nha Trang–Ban Me Thuot and QL-14 Ban Me Thuot–Pleiku route. On 16 May the Kontum POL supply point and two VNAF C-123s were destroyed by enemy fire. Only then were C-130s used to reestablish this supply point on 21 May. Its primary requirement was JP4 for helicopters.

At An Loc, POL and other supplies were delivered by air. The most needed supply was gasoline for power generators supplying the communications system.

In ammunition, the average monthly expenditure rate during the offensive was about 100,000 to 120,000 short tons. There was a big surge in artillery ammunition expenditure, especially in 105mm, which increased from 18 to 36 rounds/piece/day at the Hue–Quang Tri front. Other types of ammunition, such as 90mm antitank, 106mm recoilless, M-72 rockets, Claymore mines, fragmentation hand grenades, M-79 grenades, and .50 caliber cartridges, were also expended at such abnormally high rates that by the end of the first week of fighting their stockage level had reached the emergency level. An airlift was immediately launched, initially with VNAF C-119s and C-123s and later with USAF C-130s, in order to keep all field depots replenished at appropriate levels. In the meantime, ammunition was urgently transported to South Vietnam by fleets of supply ships which offloaded day and night at Danang, Cam Ranh, and Cat Lai, while USAF C-130s and C-141s directly brought those ammunition items considered critical to Pleiku, Danang, and Saigon.

Requirements for the Hue–Quang Tri front were by far the greatest. As a result, ammunition was offloaded from deep-draft vessels at Danang onto smaller ships—LSTs, LSMs, LCUs, LCM-8s—and onto barges, and was immediately routed to the Tan My pier, where trucks were available to carry it on to Quang Tri. The supply of ammunition for the Quang Tri front ran smoothly until the advance depot at Ai Tu Combat Base was blown up a second time by enemy artillery fire on 29 April. The supply convoy of that day was redirected toward the old depot at La Vang, but was unable to unload because of heavy fighting and was stranded there. I Corps immediately requested air delivery, but did not designate an appropriate dropping zone. Two VNAF C-123s were deployed to Danang on 30 April to make air deliveries on I Corps orders. The first aircraft succeeded in delivering its cargo, but the second was shot down in the afternoon. Air delivery of ammunition was temporarily suspended due to heavy antiaircraft fire and bad weather. During the period of I Corps counterattack, a floating pontoon was established at My Thuy (Vander [*sic:* Wunder?] Beach) as a second pier where ammunition and fuels were unloaded from smaller LCM-8s and transported directly to the Marine Division.

In Kontum, the supply of ammunition followed the same route used for fuels. . . . When drawn-out fighting at the Kontum airfield made it unusable for fixed-wing aircraft, ammunition was delivered by parachute or was sling-carried by CH-47s to the 23rd Division units in the city.

In An Loc, however, from the beginning of the siege until its end, the defenders' ammunition requirements, which consisted chiefly of small arms ammunition, M-72 rockets, Claymore mines, and fragmentation hand grenades, were delivered by air every day.

• • •

The replacement of equipment and materiel that was damaged or lost, especially during the early stage of the offensive, was swift and total, despite the heavy losses. During the month of April alone, total ARVN losses amounted to 18 155mm and 47 105mm howitzers, 21 M-41 and 16 M-48 tanks, 89 M-113 APCs, and over 240 utility vehicles. The JGS/CLC reserves were exhausted after refitting two infantry regiments and one artillery battalion of the 3rd Division, regrouped from the DMZ. In order to expedite the replacement of materiel losses, it was agreed between the JGS/CLC and MACV J-4 that an emergency reporting system be instituted, in addition to normal procedures. Under the emergency . . . system, infantry divisions, separate units, and sectors were authorized to submit daily preliminary loss reports, accompanied by a list of equipment needed for each unit to be combat effective. A compilation of losses and requirements was then communicated by the CLC to MACV J-4, where calls were made to the United States in lieu of regular requisitions. The next step of the emergency . . . system consisted of removing losses from accounting records at reporting units, the JGS, and MACV. After careful verification of losses incurred, regular reports had to be [filed] through normal procedures and not later than 30 days after the losses occurred.

• • •

During the enemy offensive, several ARVN troop movements were accomplished to respond quickly to tactical requirements on all three battlefronts. These extensive interregional troop movements were by far the most important, and successful, and the swiftest during the war since 1965. In the face of a fast-changing situation in three different military regions, the Airborne and Marine Divisions of the general reserve were airlifted, brigade by brigade, across the country, and each movement took no more than 36 hours. Two of the more memorable troop movements during this period were the deployment of three ranger groups from MR-3 to MR-1 and the deployment of the 21st Infantry Division from MR-4 to MR-3.

The deployment of the 4th, 5th, and 6th Ranger Groups and a Forward CP of the Ranger Command to the DMZ front was decided on 3 April 1972, three days after NVA forces crossed the DMZ. The 4th and 5th Ranger Groups were then conducting an operation in the Tay Ninh area. Planning for their movements was jointly conducted by III Corps, the JGS/J-3, CLC, and VNAF. Their movements were to be completed within one day. The 6th Ranger Group and Ranger Forward CP were to be airlifted from Bien Hoa AFB and the 4th and 5th Ranger Groups from Tay Ninh airfield. All these units had to be at Phu Bai on 5 April.

With the assistance of the US Air Force, the airlift was swiftly and efficiently carried out around the clock for 27 hours. Aircraft embarkings and debarkings were orderly and timely as scheduled. No delays or cancellation of flights occurred. By 5 April, 4,048 troops and 130 vehicles of the entire ranger contingent were at Phu Bai, where they were then supported by the 1st ALC supply and maintenance support elements. . . . On 6 April the 6th Ranger Group was transported by trucks to Quang Tri, where it was placed under the operational control of the 3rd Infantry Division, while the 4th and 5th Ranger Groups constituted I Corps reserves.

The decision to reinforce III Corps with the 21st Infantry Division was made on 7 April, when the division was participating in a pacification operation in the U Minh area of An Xuyen Province. According to the deployment plan, IV Corps was to helilift other forces to replace the 21st Division units at U Minh and assemble the division at the Bac Lieu airfield as of 9 April to be airlifted to Bien Hoa. The bulk of the division's mechanized elements, including infantry vehicles, armor, and artillery units, were to move by road. The troop switching and airlift went smoothly as planned, but during the night of 9 April the Cai Rang Bridge on QL-4 between Soc Trang and Can Tho was sabotaged. Troop movements by road were interrupted for the entire morning of 10 April and resumed only when a pontoon bridge was completed by the 40th Combat Engineer Group. By the afternoon of 11 April the entire 21st Infantry Division had been assembled at Bien Hoa, where its units received predeployment supply and maintenance support by the 3rd ALC units. The next day the division moved out by road and assumed the defense of Lai Khe, blocking a threat of enemy advance toward Saigon.

• • •

With regard to sea transportation, the Tan My pier was undoubtedly the heart of the supply system for northern MR-1 during the enemy offensive. If for some reason port activities had been stopped at Tan My, ARVN military activities on the Hue–Quang Tri front would have been paralyzed. From the beginning of the enemy offensive until September 1972, the Tan My pier was busy day and night receiving oceangoing and coastal vessels and offloading an average of 1,500 to 1,800 short tons of cargo each day. The major trouble with Tan My was its shallow channel, which was usually filled with sand deposits during the rainy season, especially during typhoons. Its maintenance was therefore difficult and expensive. Every year, up to 1971, US forces had used special dredgers to clear the channel.

Port activities at other places such as Danang, Cam Ranh, Newport, Saigon, and Cat Lai were also very hectic during the period of the offensive. This offered a splendid opportunity for personnel of the ARVN Transportation Corps to train on their job. Finally, the JGS/CLC also received substantial assistance and support from MACV/TMA and the Military Sea Transportation Service.

In air transportation, the most remarkable achievement of the USAF and VNAF during the offensive . . . was the air-delivered supply of An Loc and Kontum. This air delivery was in addition to emergency airlifts of ammunition and POL elsewhere. From hindsight it can be said that An Loc held firm against the enemy's repeated onslaughts not only because of ARVN troops' fighting stamina and endurance, but also because of adequate supplies which were delivered to them by air. In a sense, it was the success of air deliveries which defeated the Communist tactic of enveloping and strangling the city.

The supply by helicopters for An Loc, which began on 7 April, was suspended five days later after three US CH-47s were heavily damaged and one VNAF CH-47 [was] destroyed by enemy antiaircraft fire. To keep the besieged city supplied, VNAF C-123 "Providers" were used from 12 to 16 April, employing the low-level paradrop method. Thirty-nine C-123 flights succeeded in this difficult task. Two of them were hit by antiaircraft fire, but managed to return to base. On the fifth day and the fortieth low-altitude run, a C-123 was hit, exploded, and crashed two miles southwest of An Loc. As a result, airdrops had to be temporarily suspended while the battle for An Loc was raging fiercely.

On 15 April, to help meet emergency supply requirements, MACV decided to try the USAF C-130s for low-altitude runs. The C-130 had the advantage of high speed, hence would be harder for the enemy to hit. The C-130s made use of the low-altitude container delivery system, and the dropping zone was the soccer stadium south of the city. It was planned that five daylight flights would be made daily on 16, 17, and 18 April to bring ammunition, food, and medicine for the hard-pressed ARVN troops in the city. The results obtained were most encouraging. The first C-130 was hit but managed to return to base. However, the fifth one crashed as soon as it was hit. Consequently the low-altitude runs were suspended and a new method, the high-altitude, low-opening (HALO) system was tried from 19 to 23 April.

Guided by radar on the target, C-130s dropped their cargoes at an altitude from 6,000 to 9,000 feet. The cargoes dropped freely until 500 to 800 feet, at which altitude their parachutes would open and bring them down over the stadium. This method, while safe for the aircraft that made the delivery, was not very efficient. For example, many parachutes failed to open, while many others did open but too early or too late. As a result, a lot of cargo fell into enemy hands. Tactical aircraft were unable to destroy all wayward cargo, since dense vegetation around the target prevented good observation. The amount of cargo missing the target was such that the enemy had to assign special details for their recovery. The reason for failure, it was learned, was the inexperience of the ARVN 90th Air Drop Storage and Supply Base personnel in packing parachutes for the HALO method, despite previous training in the United States.

While the problem remained unsolved, it was decided to try the low-altitude container delivery method again from 23 to 26 April, with the modification that the aircraft would approach the city from several different directions. The results were as good as expected, but our success led the enemy to position his antiaircraft weapons on trees around the stadium. On 26 April one C-130 was hit, exploded, and crashed. Unflinching in its determination, the USAF changed tactics. Instead of daylight runs, C-130s now made night runs, at different times, using the cover of darkness for aircraft safety. While these night runs eluded enemy watchers, they also posed some problem in marking the dropping zone. Various kinds of lights, such as marker lights and spot lights, were used as a spotter system on the ground, but, because of the congested area of defense, they blended easily with other lights. Although the results were minimal, the airdrops were kept up, sometimes during daytime and sometimes at night, to foster hope among the besieged defenders on the ground. When, on 3 May, the third C-130 was hit and crashed, the low-altitude runs were suspended altogether.

In the meantime, from 23 April to 4 May, 66 packing specialists of the US 549th QM Aerial Resupply Company from Okinawa came to Saigon to help train ARVN personnel in aerial delivery packing and to join USAF specialists in studying proper delivery techniques for An Loc. Several trial drops were conducted in Cu Chi to test two particular delivery methods, the HALO and high-velocity drop, which were both used as of 5 May with excellent results. The HALO method was 90 percent accurate, while the high-velocity drop effectiveness was as high as 98 percent. US and ARVN logisticians were elated by such achievements. The Tan Son Nhut "hot pad" was busy day and night with the movements of prime movers and of semitrailers fully loaded with ammunition, medicine, and food. The food included ready-cooked pork, chicken, and vegetables. Also newspapers from people's organizations, sent out of gratitude, were included as gifts to the defenders of An Loc. An army of US and ARVN specialists labored around the clock, under the scorching sun or stormy rains, to package crates and containers and to load them on the waiting airplanes. The activities were never so feverish nor the feeling so enthusiastic. Thanks to these commendable efforts, the defenders of An Loc had more than they needed to keep on fighting. On 25 May part of the air supply activities were redirected to the supply of Kontum without depriving An Loc of its critical deliveries. . . .

Due to the intensity of fighting, the number of wounded increased considerably. In order to provide enough space for hospitalization and treatment of freshly wounded soldiers from the three raging battlefronts, efforts were made to evacuate those patients who were near recovery. Such patients were moved from general hospitals and sector hospitals to various recuperation centers. A total of 3,500 recovering patients were relocated from the Cong Hoa and Duy Tan general hospitals, and from three station hospitals—Pleiku, Qui Nhon, and Nguyen Hue—into newly relocated recuperation centers at Phuoc Tuong, Vung Tau, and Cam Ranh. The total bed capacity of these hospitals was also increased to 31,000. From the beginning of the enemy offensive to 31 August 1972, a total of 274,000 patients were checked in for treatment, including 44,000 transfusion cases. The death rate stood at a low 2 percent. At the central blood bank in Saigon and its branch banks in Can Tho, Nha Trang, and Danang, the number of blood donors doubled during this period. An average of 8,000 blood units were received per month.

• • •

In An Loc, the situation was by far the worst. No decent treatment facility was available in the city because the sector hospital was totally destroyed by enemy artillery fire. Medical evacuation by helilift took place in conjunction with supply runs from 7 to 12 April, but was not effective due to lack of tight control and determination on the part of field commanders. As a result, only patients who could walk were evacuated, while the seriously wounded were left behind. Disorder usually occurred during embarking. Patients rushed for a place on helicopters, which sometimes could not take off because of overloading. After 12 April, US and VNAF helicopters braved enemy antiaircraft fire on numerous occasions in an effort to land in An Loc, but they failed most of the time. On 3 May, under the guidance of Colonel John Richardson, commander, US 12th Combat Aviation Group, four VNAF helicopters managed to land in An Loc, but they were unable to evacuate the gravely wounded. The same disorder and chaos reigned over embarking, and only those patients who could walk made it out on the helicopters. The tragic result was that many wounded patients died in An Loc for lack of treatment and medicine. They were then summarily buried in collective graves dug near the sector hospital.

From the onset of the enemy offensive until the end of August 1972, VNAF helicopters were used extensively for medical evacuation. The assistance provided by US Army aviation units was minimal. Of a total 32,800 wounded patients evacuated, VNAF helicopters accounted for 31,600.

• • •

Summary and Evaluation

The period from 1969 to the time of the cease-fire, January 1973, saw a substantial expansion and improvement of the RVNAF. This prepared them for taking over combat responsibilities from US and FWMA forces, but continued advisory and assistance support from the United States was needed.

Logistics improvements during this period were brought into the entire system, and did not focus only on the field level, as had been the case during the pre-Vietnamization period. At the central level, the Logistic Data Processing Center and the National Materiel Management Agency were created to improve management and standardize procedures. This made it possible for the Central Logistical Command to control effectively all assets on hand. Rebuild bases were also modernized with a view to increasing in-country capabilities, reducing the need for offshore rebuild, cutting short the time of equipment inactivation, and creating more jobs for civilians. By the end of 1972, about 95 percent of ARVN equipment was rebuilt by in-country facilities.

• • •

The support of RF and PF units also underwent a reorganization which was functionally improved. Each provincial administrative and logistic support center was able to stock up to 30 days of Class I, III, and V supplies. This, and the flexibility afforded by the various sizes of their TO&Es, proved responsive to the deployment of RF and PF units, and particularly to the frontless nature of a war in which lines of communication were frequently interdicted and most actions occurred at the village level.

The efforts of the JGS to improve living standards and food intake for the ARVN soldier through various programs such as commissary retail service, canned food donations, vegetable growing, and poultry breeding, free combat rations, free food during hospitalization, etc., tremendously benefited the underprivileged ARVN soldiers and their dependents. However, beneficial as they were, most of these programs were too short-lived to bring about enduring results, and finally all were defeated by rampant inflation and by the GVN inability to adjust salaries for the servicemen.

• • •

The transfer of bases and the turnover of the responsibility for terminals and port activities to the RVNAF were smooth and uninterrupted. By the end of 1972, all ports and transportation terminals across South Vietnam were operated by Vietnamese personnel except for the unique case of Newport, Saigon.

Area Logistical Commands did a splendid job and proved thoroughly skilled in the support of combat operations. Their effectiveness was thoroughly tested and proven during the three major offensive campaigns of this period: the Cambodian cross-border operation, Lam Son 719, and the Communist 1972 Easter Offensive.

With regard to improvement and modernization, the RVNAF benefited greatly from the Enhance program in terms of equipment, armament, and morale. This was in spite of some initial shortcomings in operation and maintenance caused by the overflow of new and sophisticated equipment into the ARVN supply and support channels. These shortcomings were quickly disposed of through assistance provided by US mobile training teams, by US units, ... by US specialist teams sent over from the continental United States, and above all by the enthusiastic spirit to learn displayed by ARVN students. Then the Enhance Plus program, initiated in October 1972, helped fill the large gap in mobility assets which was so critically brought to light by the enemy Easter Offensive. The 32 C-130A airplanes delivered through the program greatly improved the RVNAF mobility. Mobility would have been even more enhanced if additional LSTs had been made available.

All in all, the Vietnamization program progressed with remarkable speed and instilled enthusiasm and confidence among those ARVN logisticians who were looking forward to the more ambitious goal of self-management. It was under these encouraging circumstances that the Paris Agreement occurred, an occurrence which was to become the ultimate turning point in the RVN military history.

VIII. THE POST-CEASE-FIRE LOGISTIC STRUCTURE

Background

• • •

With regard to military activities, the Paris Agreement required that all armed and police forces of both sides remain in place; end all hostile activities, acts of terrorism, and revenge; and cease all operations, patrols, and reconnaissance on land, in the air, and on the sea into the other side's territory. Mines, booby traps, and obstacles to traffic would be removed within 15 days. The US and Free World units, as well as all military advisors, technicians, and personnel, would be withdrawn from South Vietnam, together with their armament and ammunition, within 60 days. US military installations would also be dismantled within this period. Lost and worn-out war materiel, armament, and ammunition could be replaced on the basis of piece for piece through predetermined ports of entry and under the control of the International Commission of Control and Supervision (ICCS) and the Two-Party Joint Military Commission (JMC).

In compliance with the Paris Agreement, the United States and its allies engaged in the war in the Republic of Vietnam withdrew their military units and turned over to the Republic of Vietnam Armed Forces ... all military bases and equipment. The United States set up a Defense Attaché Office (DAO) with a limited number of military and civilian personnel under the direction of Major General John Murray, a US Army logistician, on the premises of the former MACV compound at Tan Son Nhut. [The] DAO was entrusted with the responsibility of managing the Security Assistance Program for the RVN and cooperating with the RVNAF Joint General Staff to lay out programs and plans designed to make the RVNAF self-supporting in the logistics field.

Under DAO supervision, several US contractors worked directly with the RVNAF logistics agencies and units:

1. The Computer Sciences Corporation (CS) had representatives at the Logistic Data Processing Center and the National Materiel Management Agency.
2. The Pacific Architects and Engineers, Incorporated (PA&E), worked with the Engineer Department to continue maintenance work on the US bases just transferred, particularly on their high-voltage transmission, air-conditioning, and sewage systems, and helped train Vietnamese engineers in base management, supply, and maintenance of these systems. Each Area Logistics Command was assigned a PA&E team who worked closely with its staff.
3. The Dynalectron Corporation cooperated with the Engineer Department in continuing the maintenance of special highway construction equipment transferred to engineer units and the management of industrial zones, which were set up in the LOC construction program, and helped train Vietnamese engineers in the supply and maintenance of the above equipment and the operation of the industrial zones. Dynalectron technicians were assigned to live and work with Vietnamese engineer units participating in the LOC construction program. Its main office was located at Long Binh Base.
4. The Vinnell Corporation operated at both the 40th Engineer base and the Long Binh general depot. At the 40th Engineer base depot the contractors helped rebuild high-power generators and air conditioners, and at the same time trained Vietnamese technicians. At the Long Binh general depot Vinnell personnel were made responsible for the organization and operation of the depot; the movement of the 20th Ordnance Storage Depot from Phu Tho (Saigon) to Long Binh; general engineer equipment and parts, with the exception of those belonging to the rebuild program . . . ; and the training of the Vietnamese personnel who would gradually take over from them.
5. The American Association of Engineers Overseas, Inc. (AAEOI), was responsible for the maintenance and calibration . . . of the peculiar and standard test measurement diagnostic equipment commonly used in the RVN army, and the training of Vietnamese technicians in this field.
6. The Alaskan Barge and Transport Company was responsible for the paperwork related to the reception and transfer of aid equipment at ports, and for the training of Vietnamese personnel in these procedures and methods.

• • •

US military aid, which was the lifeline of the RVNAF, was sharply reduced to $1 billion in FY 1974. This compelled the RVNAF to reduce expenditures to the limit of aid appropriations while waiting for supplemental military aid. It was hoped that the US Congress would change its attitude following the increased Communist violations of the agreement. However, no supplemental military aid ever came. Military aid for FY 1975 was further reduced to $700 million, which in terms of purchasing power was equivalent to $595 million in 1974. Compared with the previous year's level, military aid was thus reduced by nearly 50 percent, while enemy activities increased by 70 percent.

The RVNAF continued to fight under harsher conditions and exercised maximum economy and shrewd management to avoid running out of supplies before deliveries were received.

Concept and Objectives

Even after US forces had totally redeployed from South Vietnam it was always a Vietnamese conviction that the United States would continue its assistance in kind and economic support to help the RVN recover from the war. It was believed that the United States would continue to support the RVNAF for at least a few more years to deter North Vietnam. As a gesture of good will toward peace the United States would perhaps reduce military aid in the first postwar year to an amount deemed sufficient to support the RVNAF in peacetime, help them repair the huge quantity of military equipment turned over by US forces to be used as war reserves, and complete the project of modernizing the army arsenal and the construction of indoor storage facilities for ammunition depots. Later perhaps military aid might decrease or increase, depending on the attitude of North Vietnam and the budgetary capabilities of the RVN. US personnel, it was surmised, would gradually decrease as progress was made by Vietnamese logistics personnel, and, finally, some would remain to serve as military aid managers, auditors, and consultants. Fire support and strategic mobility were two capabilities that could reasonably be expected from the United States if the RVN met with serious difficulties. It was doubtful, however, that US ground forces would come back to Vietnam, whatever the circumstances.

With regard to the Communists, it was believed that they would decrease their military activities without giving up their scheme of annexing South Vietnam by political or military means. Their options would certainly depend on the capabilities of the GVN and RVNAF on the one hand, and on the US attitude toward Vietnam on the other.

• • •

IX. IMPROVING SUPPLY AND MAINTENANCE MANAGEMENT

Replacement of War Materiel and Armaments

• • •

The Paris Agreement terminated all aid in major items of equipment for the purposes of equipping, TO&E filling, or the development of a maintenance float. Article 7 of the agreement reads in fact: "The two South Vietnamese parties shall be permitted to make periodic replacements of armaments, munitions and war materiel which have been destroyed, damaged, worn out or used up after the cease-fire, on the basis of piece for piece of the same characteristics and properties, under supervision of the Joint Military Commission of the two South Vietnamese parties and the International Commission of Control and Supervision."[4]

• • •

The replacement of losses in war materiel and armaments was carried out satisfactorily in FY 1973, but was gradually reduced in FY 1974 and became nonexistent in FY 1975 due to the sudden cut of US military aid.

• • •

In January 1974, when it became known semiofficially that the US House committee had recommended US $1 billion and the two committees (US Senate–House) approved only US $900 million as military aid appropriations for Laos and Vietnam (from these appropriations SVN expected to have $813 million), it was apparent that the RVNAF were left with only US $90 million to spend in the six remaining months of the fiscal year. As a result, NMMA/CLC immediately revised downward all requirements and limited them to the basic necessities required for the support of three major functions, namely to shoot, to move, and to communicate.

• • •

In September, due-in requisitions were sharply reduced again following the US Congress decision to appropriate only US $700 million for FY 1975. On the other hand, supplies actually received through requisitions also decreased sharply, from 24,000 metric tons against 14,092 requisitions in March to 7,000 tons against 2,199 requisitions in May.

• • •

New Management Techniques

MISSION-ESSENTIAL ITEMS

During the first six months of 1973, with the hope that peace would be achieved through the proper implementation of the Paris Agreement, and in the face of a reduction in US military aid and the national defense budget, the RVNAF began to put into effect certain measures to maintain, protect, and conserve the "mission essential" items being used by units. Mission-essential items were defined as those items which were considered vital to maintain the RVNAF capabilities to shoot, to move, and to communicate. All mission-essential equipment had to be lubricated and stored in safe, covered areas. Only 50 percent of vehicles were to be used; the remainder were to be kept as war reserves. Vehicles damaged in traffic accidents were not to be replaced. Abuses and damages due to inadvertence or lack of maintenance were severely punished and the repair costs were to be reimbursed by the culprits.

• • •

In January 1974, when it was learned that military aid for FY 1974 was in difficulty with the US Congress, and that the piece-for-piece replacement of war materiel had little chance to continue, the JGS took steps to reduce the percentage of equipment that units were allowed to keep on hand against their TO&Es, especially armament, vehicles, and radio equipment.

• • •

Petroleum Supply

• • •

To facilitate control of pilferage, fuels for military vehicles were colored blue and drastic measures were taken to stop their retail on the local market. Sales were reduced as a result, but could not be entirely stopped because the poverty-stricken military dependents and petty entrepreneurs always managed to pilfer some for resale. POL consumption was reduced to a minimum for administration support vehicles, but kept at a reasonable rate for combat and combat support vehicles and equipment. Military vehicles in units, and especially in major staffs, were pooled under the commander's control. Strict penalty measures were taken against nonofficial use of vehicles. The administrative use of vehicles was carefully planned to carry proper loads both ways. Maximum economy of energy was enforced in administrative services. Air conditioners were turned off or removed and lights were mandatorily turned off after duty hours. Lamps and bulbs in US-transferred installations were removed for storage. Parts of depot and shop roofing sheets were replaced with transparent roofing to obtain sunlight and save electric power. In US-transferred installations where commercial power was available, all the large generators were removed and shipped back to the United States. Power generators in remote but sensitive areas, such as command posts, POL depots, ammunition depots, [and] bridges on main communication axes operated only six or eight hours nightly. The use of dual generators in the Integrated Communications System was also eliminated in favor of single-generator operation.

• • •

X. AMMUNITION SUPPORT

Ammunition Economy

Ammunition is the most important supply on the battlefield. High troop morale and modern weapons alone cannot defeat the enemy if there is not enough ammunition to fire the weapons. Also, ammunition is a large share of the logistics expenditures. This was particularly true in the Vietnam War. During FY 1974, for example, ammunition required 51 percent of the funds allocated to the ARVN for logistics, or US $301 million.

• • •

Ammunition economy was the first priority in an austerity program designed to reduce defense expenditures, and artillery ammunition became the focus of attention at all ARVN echelons. One month after the Paris Agreement went into effect, CLC/JGS took certain measures to save ammunition throughout the entire RVNAF.

• • •

The results obtained through these measures were encouraging. Monthly issues of ammunition during the post-cease-fire years amounted to 15,707 short tons for 1973,

19,984 for 1974, and even the highest monthly issue of 1975 (24,333 tons) was only about one-third of the average for 1972 (73,356 tons/month).

• • •

As additional requests were not fully satisfied, unit basic loads of ammunition became increasingly depleted during FY 1975. The units' basic loads during 1973 and early 1974 were all above the authorized level by 50 to 150 percent, thanks to accumulated storage before the Paris Agreement and adequate replacement issues during the first half of FY 1974. However, by September 1974 the units' basic loads in 40mm HE, 60mm HE, hand grenades, and Claymore mines were so low they were only 50 percent or less of the authorized level, particularly among RF and PF units. As a result, after inventories and confirmation by inspection teams, the JGS/CLC had to allocate more than US $7 million to bring the basic loads of units up to authorized levels.

• • •

Ammunition Aid Program for FY 1975

The Paris Agreement permitted the replacement of expended ammunition on a piece-for-piece basis. The ARVN stock on hand on the cease-fire day was 178,000 short tons. Every month the RVNAF reported to ICCS the quantity of ammunition they expended and had in stock and requested import authorization. In spite of the cease-fire, ammunition was issued on a continuous basis in order to cope with Communist violations of the agreement. From February to the end of June 1973, nearly 137,000 short tons of ammunition were issued, and, as budget allocations were not available for replacement, the stock on hand dropped to 135,000 short tons at the end of FY 1973. A total of 43,000 short tons was not replaced. In FY 1974 the funds allocated for ammunition were only US $301 million, while Communist violations increased both in tempo and intensity. Despite curtailed consumption, the tonnage of ammunition issued during the fiscal year amounted to 187,000 short tons. With the price increase, $301 million was barely enough to procure 181,000 short tons to replenish the ammunition expended during the fiscal year. By the end of FY 1974 the stock on hand dropped to 129,000 short tons; 40,000 short tons were not replaced due to the lack of funds. The DAO's request for US $180 million in supplemental aid was not approved.

• • •

US military aid for FY 1975 provided only US $239,200,000 for ground ammunition, or 59.8 percent of the requirements. On a monthly average the RVNAF was thus allowed to spend US $19,900,000, while US $37,300,000 was required based on issue experience from July 1974 to February 1975. As a result, by early March 1975, since requisitions had accounted for $224,226,900, only $14,900,000 remained for the last three months of FY 1975.

• • •

The average monthly issue during the first eight months of the fiscal year was 19,808 short tons, or only 27 percent of the monthly issue before the cease-fire (73,356 short tons). The stock on hand in late February 1975 was 121,000 short tons, as compared to

178,000 short tons on the cease-fire day; 57,000 short tons had not been replaced. After the losses in Ban Me Thuot and those incurred during the evacuation of Pleiku and Kontum in March, the stock on hand in late March 1975 was only 75,886 short tons. After the withdrawal from MR-1, the stock on hand in early April 1975 was only 44,238 short tons.

• • •

During the period from December 1974 to February 1975 the stock level started to increase to meet the expected requirements during the lunar new year. Requests submitted in January, February, [and] March 1975 also increased from US $23 to $25 million in order to cope with the spring, or dry season, offensive expected during April through June. . . . The amount of funds remaining for the fiscal year was only US $14,900,000. If no supplemental military aid was received, and assuming that the ammunition previously requested would arrive, and that the issues in April, May, and June would increase by 21 percent as expected (from 19,808 short tons to 24,000 short tons a month), the stock level would drop to a dangerous level of 56,879 short tons, or just 32 days of supply, by 30 June 1975. Furthermore, this stock was dispersed at 19 sites throughout the country, and, if Communist sabotage was successful in just a few areas, the stock level would be exhausted before any shipment of replacement ammunition could possibly reach Vietnam. Consequently, [the] DAO and the JGS requested a supplemental fund of US $178,906,469 to meet the requirements for the three remaining months of FY 1975 and to raise the stock level to 130,000 short tons. The request was never approved.

• • •

Price increases greatly aggravated the ammunition problem. Between December 1973 and June 1974 the cost of 38 types of key ammunition had increased by 29 percent. It again increased by 27.7 percent at the beginning of FY 1975 and by another 14.21 percent by 24 March 1975. The effective purchasing power of FY 1975 funds allocated for ammunition of US $239,900,000 was reduced to 72.3 percent.

To prevent ammunition from running out before the appropriation of supplemental military aid, and to operate within the approved limits, immediately after the Paris Agreement the RVNAF had to take strong control measures to curtail its consumption, in comparison with previous years when US forces were fighting by their side. Economy directives were frequently reiterated by the JGS and corps headquarters and inspections were increased. These actions and measures inadvertently created among the troops and small units an impression that there was not enough ammunition for combat. As a result, malpractices such as trading, buying, and storing M-79 grenades, hand grenades, and Claymore mines were widespread among RF and PF units. The local Communists exploited this situation to propagandize that the United States was abandoning the RVN and, in turn, the RVNAF was letting the RF-PF down; the enemy appealed to RF-PF troops in remote outposts to surrender or to defect.

Indeed the ammunition consumed by RVNAF decreased considerably during the post-cease-fire period. Artillery support for remote outposts under Communist attack, and for harassment of Communist base areas, was sharply curtailed or even stopped. Ammunition stock was indeed lower than before. But combat units never lacked ammunition during an engagement with the enemy and no operation was delayed for lack of ammunition.

XI. SERVICE SUPPORT: TRANSPORTATION AND MEDICAL

Transportation Facilities

• • •

Cutbacks in military aid for FY 1975 considerably affected the capabilities of transportation groups, although priority in supply and maintenance was given to these groups, especially to 2-1/2-ton trucks and 5-ton tractors. Their capabilities, therefore, gradually decreased, despite excellent maintenance, because of extensive use, lack of replacements for unserviceable trucks requiring fourth-echelon repair, and shortage of parts, particularly engines. By February 1975 all six transportation groups had only 80 to 85 percent of their authorized 2-1/2-ton trucks and 50 to 55 percent of their 5-ton tractors on hand. Of these assets, only 75 to 80 percent of the trucks and 45 to 50 percent of the tractors were serviceable.

• • •

In air transportation, the C-47, C-119, and C-123 cargo planes were phased out and replaced by C-7 Caribous and C-130A Hercules. During the post-cease-fire period there were three C-7 squadrons with 18 aircraft each and two C-130 squadrons with 16 aircraft each. While C-123s were turned in, C-47 and C-119 cargo planes were transformed into AC-47 and AC-119 gunships for fire support. The number of UH-1 helicopters meanwhile increased to nearly 600 and CH-47 Chinooks to 72. Between the cease-fire day and the end of FY 1974, thanks to the efforts made by DAO and VNAF technicians and US contractors, aircraft serviceability rates reached an average of 60 to 65 percent for UH-1 helicopters, 20 to 25 percent for CH-47 helicopters, 8 to 10 [percent for] C-7s, and 2 to 4 [percent for] C-130A per day.

In September 1974, due to the reduction of military aid for FY 1975, [the] VNAF had to temporarily ground all three C-7 squadrons in order to devote all its resources to the two C-130A squadrons. But—due to technical reasons such as leaking tanks or dented wings, shortage of parts, and lengthy maintenance checks in Singapore, and despite DAO and US contractors' efforts—the number of daily serviceable C-130A planes was very small, generally 6 to 8, sometimes 10, out of a total of 32.

• • •

Contingency Plans

To readily cope with Communist violations of the cease-fire, CLC/JGS worked out . . . contingency plans:

1. Movement of strategic reserves. The strategic reserves of the JGS/RVNAF were made up of the Airborne Division, the Marine Division, and three ranger groups. These units were often deployed within a short time from one military region to another as reinforcements for important fronts. . . . However, with the reduced number of serviceable aircraft after cease-fire day, [the] VNAF could not airlift these strategic reserves in such a time period. In order to move general reserve units to any area within a minimum time and have them ready for combat, their movements were planned ahead as follows:
   a. Troops, with their individual weapons, signal vehicles, artillery, and tractors—except the basic load of ammunition—would be airlifted.
   b. The heavy equipment of these units, and the division logistics battalion, would be transported by VNN LSTs.
   c. Pending the arrival of the sealifted elements, the local ALC would provide the basic ammunition loads, transportation facilities, and communications and support in supply and maintenance.

Under this plan an airborne brigade would be able to move from Saigon to Danang in MR-1, or to Pleiku in MR-2, or the reverse, and be ready for combat within two or three days. The movement of an entire division would take longer, from six to eight days. For a ranger group, its movement would take from one and a half to two days. This plan was successfully carried out on several occasions during 1972 when airborne and marine brigades assigned to MR-1 were rotated and when ranger groups were sent as reinforcements to MR-2.

• • •

After the cease-fire, the total number of hospital beds remained at 24,547 for the entire RVNAF. When required, this total could be increased to 31,000, as it had been during the 1972 Communist offensive. Despite the cease-fire, the number of occupied beds still fluctuated between 21,500 and 24,200, as it had before the cease-fire.

• • •

Medical Evacuation

Rapid and safe medical evacuation from the battleground to the nearest first aid stations and military hospitals always received special attention. This concern was expressed through the activation of medical groups to work closely with corps headquarters and corps tactical operations centers. Medical evacuation by helicopter was naturally the most effective. During 1971–1972, 83 helicopter pilots, 21 crews, and 28 medical corpsmen were sent to the United States for training at helicopter medical evacuation units. The VNAF did not have such units; helicopters had always been used for other purposes. From 1965 to 1971 most medical evacuations by helicopter were flown by US Army aviation units. As of the second half of 1971, with the growth of [the] VNAF, however, medical evacuation was gradually taken over by Vietnamese pilots.

• • •

It is noteworthy that, during the 1972 offensive from 1 April through 31 August, VNAF helicopters evacuated a total of 31,600 casualties, while US helicopters evacuated only 1,200.

In September 1974 the reduction of military aid for FY 1975 to US $700 million affected seriously VNAF activities. Helicopter flying time was then reduced to a mere 20 percent of that of the first half of 1974. This seriously affected medical evacuation, despite corps commanders' efforts to set a high priority for this type of mission. The most serious impact was felt in MR-4, where the terrain was crisscrossed by many rivers and canals, roads were in poor condition, and medical evacuation had always been dependent on helicopters. Units were forced to use sampans and hammocks to carry the wounded to major roads for evacuation by ambulance trucks. This type of evacuation was of course not satisfactory, and the troops complained bitterly about it.

XII. CONSTRUCTION

The Lines of Communication (LOC) Program

The Republic of Vietnam had more than 12,500 miles of narrow, mostly damaged roads which had not been repaired since World War II and the 1946–1954 war against the French. To support pacification operations and the development of the economy, a program to modernize strategic and tactical lines of communication was outlined in 1967. A total of 2,527 miles (4,075 kilometers) of highways was targeted in the program, including national routes QL-1, connecting Saigon with the coastal towns up to Dong Ha (Quang Tri); QL-19 from Pleiku to Qui Nhon; QL-21 from Nha Trang to Ban Me Thuot, a major route of supply from the sea to the highlands; QL-13 from Saigon to Chon Thanh; QL-14 from Chon Thanh to Ban Me Thuot, Pleiku, and Kontum; QL-20 from Saigon to Dalat; and QL-4 from Saigon to the prosperous provinces of the Mekong Delta. . . . A beltway was built around the capital to divert traffic from the city and to improve its defense. In addition to national routes, the highway improvement program also included lesser roads such as Interprovincial Route 15 that connected the capital with Vung Tau, which was considered as the second port of entry after Saigon. The modernized roads were opened to two-way traffic with bridges of 35-ton capacity and above. The estimated cost of the program was US $463 million, or more than US $180,000 per mile.

• • •

The Lines of Communication Program was expected to end on 30 June 1975, and the remaining 70 miles (112 kilometers) of the 416 miles (671 kilometers) of highways and 6,560 feet of the 36,080 feet of bridges which had been built by ARVN engineer units at a cost of nearly US $15 million was transferred to the National Highways Program financed by USAID. . . .

Role of ARVN Engineers

The LOC program assigned the modernization of 671 kilometers of highway and 11,000 meters of bridge to ARVN engineers. From 1968 to 1970 the participation by ARVN engineers was limited to the construction of bridges and rock-unloading piers for the Delta rock program. The most noteworthy participation was the construction by the 20th Combat Engineer Group of the 3,281-foot-long Tuy Hoa Bridge on QL-1 in Phu Yen Province. In 1971, following a TO&E change in highway construction equipment, construction engineer units were equipped with 150-ton/hour asphalt plants, 35- and later 75-ton/hour rock crushers, and 5-ton dump trucks. Some commercial-type road construction equipment was transferred from MCA/LOC. With this new equipment the 5th Construction Engineer Group started the construction of the road from Gia Rai to QL-1 at the boundary of MR-2 and MR-3. Due to their anxiety to learn and improve, as well as to their zeal, the men of the 5th Engineer Group successfully accomplished this difficult task and the road became the pride of the ARVN Engineer Corps. The reception committee, which included the Ministry of Public Works and US officials, was satisfied, and the quality production rate met US standards.

• • •

In spite of difficulties in the supply of spare parts for the repair of equipment and operation of the work sites, fuel, transportation of crushed rock from quarries to unloading points, and from there to work sites, transportation of long and heavy pre-stressed concrete beams from the DGH production plant in Chau Thoi mountain to the construction site, the modernization of bridges and highways progressed satisfactorily. On 31 July 1974 the remaining work included 146.1 miles (235 kilometers) of highway and 9,295 feet (2,834 meters) of bridge. Also in 1974, due to the closing of exhausted quarries in MR-3 and the difficulties encountered in the Nui Sap (MR-4) quarry, ARVN engineers were entrusted with the mission of supplying crushed rock to the entire military and public works highway modernization program throughout MR-4. Due to ARVN engineers' efforts and the wholehearted assistance from DAO technicians, the Nui Sam quarry was modernized with two rock-crushers with a 250-ton/hour output and other equipment. The Vinh Te canal, running from the quarry to the Mekong River, was dredged by the Surface Transportation Directorate to accommodate tugboats and 500-ton barges. In April 1975 the work remaining to be done included 70 miles (112 kilometers) of highway and 6,562 feet (2,000 meters) of bridge.

Tactical Bridges

In addition to their participation in the strategic highway construction, ARVN engineers also played an important role in the reconstruction of bridges and roads sabotaged by the Communists. Communist sabotage of LOCs in 1972 averaged 820 feet (250 meters) of bridge a week. Engineer units, from tactical bridge companies to combat and construction engineer battalions, were deployed along main LOCs to repair the sabotaged bridges and highways and reopen them to traffic within 24 hours. Reconstruction usually consisted of building M4T6 or Bailey tactical bridges, or temporary repair with wooden beams or steel beams and wooden floor, or opening bypasses. During 1974–1975 Communist sabotage techniques were improved by the use of explosives and mines. Several miles of QL-4 from Saigon to Can Tho were blown up at one time, thus increasing considerably the requirement for rock in MR-4. Rock and dirt were kept in reserve along QL-4 at Cai Be and My Tho for such emergencies. To increase the reserves in tactical bridges, DGH and the Engineer Department started a program to recover the Bailey bridges formerly used by US forces on secondary roads in the pacification program. To replace these Bailey bridges, Eiffel bridges and steel-timber permanent and semipermanent structures were used.

• • •

The Dependents Shelter Program

The problem of military dependents in the Vietnam War was a headache, not only for unit commanders but also for the JGS and national leaders. An old saying is that only when the well-being of the dependents in the rear is assured will the troops at the front devote themselves to defeating the enemy. Several facts affected the solutions employed by the RVNAF to solve the dependents problem.

The RVNAF strength increased from 150,000 men in 1955 to more than 600,000 in 1968 and to 1.1 million men in 1972. Draftees formed the overwhelming majority in the armed forces. Career soldiers were the minority. The length of military service changed from two years during the 1954–1963 period to four years for officers and three years for NCOs and EM from 1964 to 1968 and became indefinite as of 1969. The age limit for military service was also raised from 18 to 33, and then to 39. In compliance with the General Mobilization Law of 1968, all military personnel, either career or drafted, who had reached the age limit but were still able-bodied had to remain in the service. For this reason about 60 percent of military personnel were married, and they usually had large families.

True to Vietnamese customs, the wife usually stayed home to care for the children, did household chores, or helped in farmwork; to raise the children, she relied on her husband's salary. It was . . . common knowledge that on paydays the troops' wives came to the unit to wait for their husbands' salaries. In some cases soldiers went AWOL in order to take their salaries to their families.

The soldiers' pay was too low as compared with the skyrocketing cost of living. The fact that they lived away from their families further aggravated their financial situation. Before 1959, both single and married soldiers received a quarters allowance if they were not provided free army quarters. This allowance was later abolished to simplify pay scales.

The Vietnam War was one without a front and there was no secure rear area. The enemy could be everywhere, ready to sabotage and to kill. The tempo and density of his activities increased or decreased unpredictably, depending on the areas and weather. The scenes of soldiers huddling together with their wives and children in the confines of tin-roofed defense positions were familiar and not easy to forget.

Tactics often changed, too. Units were sometimes thinly deployed for area pacification, sometimes concentrated for mobile operations. The troops were frequently transferred from one location to another, and went on operations month after month. Units were seldom rotated for rest and recuperation, and the soldiers' leaves were often delayed.

As the RVNAF were the strongest anti-Communist institution in South Vietnam, troop proselytizing was one [element] of the Communists' three-pronged (political, military, troop proselytizing) offensive. The Communists subverted our troops through their dependents. By means of bribery, pressure, threat, and propaganda, the enemy employed troop dependents to urge their husbands to desert their units, kill their fellow soldiers, and supply him with weapons, ammunition, and information. The troop dependents living among civilians became easy prey for Communist subversion.

The construction of dependent quarters was the solution opted for by the RVNAF. Due to restrictions in the defense budget, however, the construction of dependent quarters from 1954 to 1961 was entirely assumed by the units and depended on unit commanders' initiatives and good will. In 1962 it became urgently necessary to build dependent quarters because of the deterioration of the situation in rural areas. Considering that the care for troop dependents was a social service, the Ministry of National Defense entrusted the organization of dependent quarters to the Directorate of Social Service.[5]

Every year the Social Service Directorate procured enough cut lumber, tin, and nails for 50 rows of ten units each and issued them to units, which built the quarters with their own labor. Management was poor and resulted in abuses. In 1966, when requirements outgrew the management capabilities of the Social Service [Directorate], the program was transferred to CLC. An inventory of housing units . . . revealed the loss of much material. The number of housing units built did not correspond with the quantity of materials issued. Many units had been issued materials although they had neither the capability nor the land for construction. Also, most quarters lacked sanitation and water and deteriorated rapidly after three years. In some areas units moved to another location, leaving behind newly constructed quarters.

• • •

With the small budget allocated, CLC was able only to build from 100 to 120 rows a year, and each ARVN unit received only one to three rows. Since construction sites were scattered throughout the country where battalions usually operated, sometimes construction was completed just as the battalions moved to another location because security was reestablished. At other times, construction had to be stopped because of the deterioration of security. To raise the troops' morale, in 1969 the JGS requested MACV to study the use of military aid to help the RVN defense budget finance the construction of dependent quarters.

• • •

In the meantime, President Thieu wrote to President Nixon asking for the approval of aid for the construction of ARVN dependent quarters. As a result, approval was obtained for the construction of 100,000 housing units within a period of four years.

• • •

It was the committee's plan to build 100,000 housing units within four years, from 1969 to 1973. In the first year 10,000 to 15,000 units would be built on a trial basis, to be followed by 25,000 units for the second year, 30,000 units for the third year, and the remainder in the fourth year. Of the 100,000 housing units, 10 percent were to be allocated to [the] VNAF and VNN. Priority of construction was given to the 90,000 housing units required by ARVN combat units such as the airborne, marine, and infantry divisions, armor, and mobile RF units. Construction of 1,000 units in Dong Tam Base for the 11th Regiment, 7th Infantry Division, a unit with the highest rate of desertion, was designed to test the counter-desertion effect of the program. . . .

Another major requirement set up by the committee was that the construction sites must be located in the rear base of divisions, regiments, and groups, with the exception of RF battalions. The sites should be neither too far nor too close to the unit cantonments so that the troops would not have to walk a long distance, the unit commander could keep an eye on the quarters, and the defense would not be hindered. The sites must also be large enough to accommodate 300 housing units with a dispensary, a school, and a playground for children, and to allow further development of farming or business activities.

Civilian contractors would be used to the maximum extent allowed by the budget in order to create jobs for the unemployed, whose number increased as a result of the redeployment of US forces. ARVN engineer units would only be employed for the construction of dependent quarters when contractors or funds were not available.

The program started in earnest as corps and infantry divisions searched for land. Division combat troops were particularly happy to see that both the US and RVN governments were caring for the well-being of their families. During this period most divisions had land available from the reception of huge US bases. The 21st Infantry Division in MR-4 was an exception. In addition to the cement-block-making plant transferred by PA&E and set up at the rear base of the 5th Construction Engineer Group in Hoc Mon to produce cement blocks for the program in MR-3, the Engineer Department designed and built 35 manual and electric-operated cement-block-making machines for issue to engineer units in other MRs. The shortage of construction materials was satisfactorily resolved by MACV J-4 and CLC through loans in materials diverted from other projects.

In spite of natural disasters and enemy activities, the construction program progressed satisfactorily until 1972, when the Communist Easter Offensive damaged a number of houses already built or under construction. The program was nearly stopped as contractors abandoned construction sites for lack of security, the supply of materials slowed down, construction and combat engineer units had to devote their efforts to supporting military operations, and transportation means were tied up in the shipment of ammunition and fuel for combat requirements. The program resumed in the third quarter of 1972, but was interrupted again for lack of funds as a result of military aid cuts in the second half of FY 1973 and in FY 1974. The US $11.2 million fund still needed for the program was included by [the] DAO and JGS in FY 1975. But with only US $700 million approved for this fiscal year, the program which had been approved by the

US and RVN presidents for the construction of 100,000 housing units had to be suspended after 75 percent of the task had been completed.

A Lesson Well Learned

In an ideological war of subversion which was fought without a front line, it was very essential to gather the troop dependents in an area near the units' rear bases. The troops were thus assured that their families were safe and well taken care of, and the dependents felt better protected and informed while living near the units. The dependent camp was also an effective anti-Communist weapon because it helped the unit control in part the thoughts of the troops and their dependents and prevent Communist propaganda and subversion. Statistics showed that desertion was almost nil among the troops living with their families in a dependent camp. Living in a dependent camp, the troops were able not only to save the money otherwise spent for the trips they regularly made to visit their families, but also to receive social service benefits provided by the military or the GVN.

The exact number of housing units required was hard to determine over the years because, in addition to strength increases, the military service status changed continually with security, social aspects, and the weather. Families of the killed, missing, disabled, and discharged soldiers continued to live in dependent camps, although they were only authorized to remain there for six to twelve months. For humanitarian reasons, the unit commanders could not evict them, particularly in the face of the adverse effect this might cause to the morale of other soldiers. As a typical case, the dependent quarters of the Airborne and Marine Divisions were always filled, in spite of additional housing construction given to these units. The dependent camps were filled to capacity when the harvest season was over, and when the war spread to villages and hamlets. However, many quarters were vacant during harvest or when security in the unit area was threatened, as was the case with the 7th Division in Dinh Tuong and the 40th Regiment, 22nd Division, in Dak To (Kontum). All major units had to have a fixed rear base, which remained there no matter for how long or where the units operated.

• • •

Support for the GVN Resettlement Program

In January 1974 the RVN president directed the JGS to provide active support for Dr. Phan Quang Dan, deputy prime minister for Land Reclamation and Hamlet Establishment, in his efforts to resettle over 200,000 refugees still living in camps. After studying the problem, the JGS saw a good opportunity to coordinate Dr. Dan's plan with the territorial security plan, or, in a broader sense, to [coordinate] the agricultural-economic plan with the military plan, and to integrate the military discharge plan with the Land Reclamation and Hamlet Establishment (LRHE) plan by creating jobs for the military personnel who had already been or were to be discharged.[6]

• • •

In order to take the refugees to resettlement areas before the rainy season started in May 1974 so that crops could be planted in time, and because the LOC program was interrupted for lack of funds, the Engineer Department mobilized 30 bulldozers to clear the land for housing and cultivation areas and to assist in the work being done by manual labor hired . . . at six locations: Phuoc Tuy, Bien Hoa, and Long Khanh (MR-3) and Lam Dong, Binh Thuan, and Cam Ranh (MR-2). Engineer units also built roads in the housing and cultivation areas, marked the lots, and erected nearly 1,000 housing units with materials provided by Free World countries.

• • •

As regards the veterans' participation in the LRHE program, the JGS received more than 10,000 applications and transported over 1,000 families to resettlement areas in an atmosphere of enthusiasm and confidence. Applications were also received from soldiers on active duty for their dependents' participation in the program in preparation for their eventual discharge. The program was progressing satisfactorily when it was interrupted in March 1975.

The Bien Hoa Military Cemetery

Special cemeteries reserved for the burial of dead soldiers whose families did not wish to bury them in family plots had existed for a long time. Built at the initiative of local authorities, they all lacked uniformity and solemnity. In 1967 steps were taken to build a consolidated and uniform military cemetery in Bien Hoa, along the Saigon–Bien Hoa highway, 20 miles from the capital. The cemetery was designed in the shape of a bee, symbolizing "building" and meaning that soldiers at the end of their lives rested there after having fought for the building of a lasting peace and freedom for future generations. They were like the bees which daily built their hives in spite of obstacles or sabotage. Soldiers were buried side by side, without discrimination of rank or religion, their heads pointing toward the Monument for the Dead built on a hilltop. The design of this monument was selected in a nationwide contest and consisted of a 43-meter tower and a 5-meter high mourning turban. Names of the soldiers resting here were inscribed on the inside wall of the turban. On the outside, 12 sculptures depicted 12 heroic periods of Vietnam history, from the founding of the nation through the resistances against Chinese and French rule to the defense of a free South Vietnam by the RVNAF.

The required 120 tons of copper had been collected by the Army Arsenal from recovered artillery shells and cast into bars. Construction work by the 5th Combat Engineer Group was expected to take 18 months. The 12 copper sculptures were expected to be completed in five years. In February 1975 the tower and 30 percent of the mourning turban, or 70 percent of the total project, were completed. Also by then, the cemetery had accepted the remains of more than 20,000 soldiers, including Lieutenant General Do Cao Tri, former commanding general, III Corps, and other RVNAF generals. The statue of the "Soldier at the End of His Fighting Life" in black copper was erected by the side of the Saigon–Bien Hoa highway at the entrance to the cemetery. About 500 meters behind this statue was the tomb of the Unknown Soldier, which was built in Oriental style on top of a small hill, where incense was burned and wreaths were laid on major national and religious holidays. This was the place where local and foreign dignitaries paid their respects to the dead. The burial grounds started at the foot of the hill, with uniform graves for inexpensive construction and maintenance amid the green lawns maintained for two years by more than 100 Category 2 and 3 soldiers (in poor health and disabled) awaiting discharge, and by the children of ARVN logistics personnel. Farther to the right was the reception and processing ward for the dead, with large refrigeration rooms and funeral rooms which were busy throughout the war years. Next door was the administrative building with dining and waiting rooms for relatives of the dead.

The Bien Hoa Military Cemetery where RVNAF soldiers were laid to rest was also the place where young Vietnamese men and women came to escape the hot afternoons of Saigon.

XIII. FINANCIAL AND BUDGET MANAGEMENT

Planning and Budgeting

The costs of the Vietnam War were borne by two budgets, the Vietnam national budget and the US defense budget, more commonly known as military aid.

The Vietnam national budget, defense section, came from the contributions of Vietnamese citizens and from US civilian aid, commonly known as Joint Support (JS), which was provided through the Commercial Import Program (CIP) and Agricultural Trade Development and Assistance Act of 1954, also known as Public Law 480 (PL-480). Seventy-five percent of the RVN defense budget was used to pay salaries and allowances, the rest to procure locally a few expendable materials and to pay for civilian employees and services.

• • •

The management of military aid was the most important function by far, since it covered all expenditures for equipment and supplies such as ammunition, fuel, medicine, repair parts, etc. US military aid, dispensed to the RVN through the Military Assistance Program (MAP), had increased substantially by US FY 1968 and reached a record high in US FY 1973.

The survival of the RVN depended on US military aid. But, important as this was, the RVNAF had absolutely no management responsibility for military aid from planning to execution. Everything was taken care of by US advisors and by MACV. Vietnamese counterparts were sometimes consulted, but only for form's sake. The RVNAF, as a result, were at the mercy of US advisors and MACV. The RVNAF usually presented their requirements without being able to determine the priorities. Not being responsible for management, the RVNAF common practice was to ask for more than was required and settle for less. In a certain sense this was haggling at its worst.

Whenever I had the opportunity to accompany the US Assistant Secretaries of Defense during their visits to the RVN, I always suggested that the RVNAF be allowed to participate in the management of US military aid and be provided with management information related to it. I was convinced that, if we shared the responsibility, aid would become more effective and more economical. On the other hand, I often discussed the same subject with J-4, MACV, and assured him that CLC would not try to get in his way. On the contrary, CLC would help alleviate the burden placed on him. What I kept wondering at the time was whether my suggestion was in any way against US regulations or caused any embarrassment to J-4, MACV, and the advisors.

• • •

This [supplemental aid for FY 1974 and the aid budget for FY 1975] was the first time in 20 years of US-RVN cooperation that the entire military aid budget lay on the desk of the CLC commander. It was quite a remarkable feat in view of the long time it took before the RVNAF could really participate in the management of [the] US military aid budget.

Then came the time to review the annual military aid budget. There were strong words and demands in favor of military aid from some US congressmen, especially Senators Stennis and McClellan and Representative Mahon. However, the news was that there would be military aid cutbacks for FY 1974 in both the main and the supplemental parts. News of still more reductions in aid for FY 1974 was also relayed to Saigon. Brigadier General John Murray, the US Defense Attaché, found himself in a difficult position, especially in January 1974 when he was informed by the US Department of Defense . . . that only about US $900 million would be approved for US FY 1974. The expenditures, meanwhile, had already amounted to US $813 million. Thus the RVNAF would only have less than US $90 million for the remaining six months of the fiscal year!

• • •

As a result of these additional efforts and responsibilities, CLC managers were gratified with their accomplishments in the management of aid. They had learned much, and had accomplished much, in a short time. It was not known whether RVNAF participation in military aid management and the sharing of its responsibilities with [the] DAO was a consequence of the circumstances, of a new US attitude toward RVNAF capabilities, or of a change in US aid regulations.

The FY 1975 Military Aid Program

As jointly prepared and submitted by [the] DAO and the JGS, the RVNAF budgetary requirements in FY 1975 were estimated at US $890 million for the ARVN, including $123 million earmarked for replenishing TO&E authorizations and for replacing losses in major items of equipment; $559 million for the VNAF, including $252 million to procure the improved F5-Es in replacement of F5-As and to replace losses in C-130As and helicopters; and $80 million for the VNN, including $52 million for the replacement of ship losses. The total requested was US $1.529 billion.

• • •

In August 1974 it was learned that the US Congress approved only US $700 million in military aid for the RVN in FY 1975, $200 million less than the previous year and less than half of the required amount. This came as a complete shock for the entire RVNAF, particularly as the Communists were stepping up their violations of the Paris Agreement in total disregard of world opinion. By all indications, they were well prepared to resume all-out war. Their lines of communications and bases were strengthened and extended. Convoys of materials, weapons, and ammunition were sighted heading south both by day and by night. Intelligence reports also revealed that, for the same fiscal year, North Vietnam received about US $1.2 billion in military aid from the Communists, or nearly twice the FY 1975 US military aid appropriations for the RVN. Furthermore, Communist aid money had a greater purchasing power because of the low cost of equipment and labor and shorter shipment routes.

The purchasing power of the US dollar had been diminishing each year; and $700 million of FY 1975 aid was really worth only $595 million in terms of FY 1974 prices. Why such a disastrous cut in military aid? Why did it have to occur at such juncture? Was it the US Congress showing its displeasure toward President Nixon and demonstrating to the world at large that the United States desired a negotiated peace? Was it because the United States wanted the RVN to be more yielding to Communist demands? Was it because the United States had retracted from its avowed defense strategy? Perhaps, to the United States, Southeast Asia was not as important as the Middle East? Many such questions were asked by the people and soldiers of South Vietnam, but all remained unanswered. Wonder, skepticism, and anxiety began to set in among the Vietnamese. Regardless of how this came about, RVNAF logisticians knew that US $700 million was clearly not enough to support a large modern military force at a time when the enemy had resumed large-scale war, a war that was just short of all-out invasion.

The combat potential of the RVNAF was diminished, and more territory and more people would be lost. In the long term, the RVN would have to face Communist annexation unless an appropriate solution on the national and international plane was found. The immediate task, however, was survival. It was how to use the aid money most efficiently, limit the requirements and expenditures, [and do this] with a minimum of danger to the combat posture and maximum protection of the population. After several soul-searching meetings, all the while nurturing a flimsy hope that the US Congress would favorably vote on supplemental aid, [the] DAO and the JGS outlined certain policies to face the new financial situation. It was decided that:

1. Approximately $120 million was to be set aside for mandatory expenditures, including $74 million for PCH&T, $36.2 million for DAO operating costs, $4.3 million in training funds carried over into FY 1975, $2.3 million for training, and $3.3 million for F-5A reimbursement to South Korea.
2. The remaining funds were devoted to operation and maintenance.
3. The replacement of major items of equipment on a piece-by-piece basis was suspended; so were the modernization programs, including the F-5E program, the LOC program, the third phase of base depot renovation, and the dependent quar-

ters construction program which had previously been approved by President Nixon.

4. Operation expenditures were solely devoted to the three basic requirements: moving, shooting, and communicating.

5. Unit, division, and corps commanders were urged to further step up the preventive maintenance program and the proper use of the facilities on hand. Also they were urged to strictly control consumption and avoid waste, especially in fuel and ammunition.

6. DAO and CLC/NMMA logisticians should carefully weigh all expenditures and allow procurements only when all local resources (substitutes, cannibalization, and improvisation) had been exhausted.

7. Priority of supply was given to the ARVN over other services. It was hoped that under adverse conditions the RVNAF weaknesses in air and naval mobility and firepower could be swiftly reinforced by the US Air Force and Navy, once approval was obtained from the US Congress.

The US $700 million of FY 1975 was distributed as follows by [the] DAO and the JGS: army: $458 million, or 65 percent; air force: $183 million, or 26 percent; navy: $13 million, or 2 percent; set aside: $46 million, or 7 percent.

• • •

With the allocated funds, the VNAF and VNN were unable to operate all the aircraft and ships on hand. As a result, after several staff meetings between [the] DAO and [the] JGS, it was decided that the following measures be taken:

1. For the VNAF: to ground a total of 13 squadrons, including three A-1 fighter squadrons, three O-1 observation squadrons, three C-7 transportation squadrons, and two training squadrons. Flight time would be assigned in priority to fighter-bombers and transport aircraft. The more than 400 VNAF students who were attending schools in the United States would have to be called back.

2. For the VNN: to immobilize 50 percent of the river groups and more than 200 RF river craft. The immobilized craft would be used to fill the TO&Es of remaining river groups and kept in reserve. Priority of support would be given to LSTs in order to keep them at maximum operational capability.

• • •

At the beginning of the fiscal year the Continuing Resolution Authority (CRA) for the first quarter was determined at US $131.4 million for the ARVN in the belief that military aid for FY 1975 would eventually amount to US $1 billion. Most of the funds were expended for ammunition ($75 million), POL ($21 million), and current technical assistance contracts. In the second quarter $75 million was released in October 1974, including $5.5 million for ammo and $14.5 million for POL. The $99 million for the third quarter was released in mid-December 1974, with $54.4 million for ammunition and $16.2 million for POL; the remaining was for other requirements. For the mean-time, due to an emergency requirement to procure $700,000 worth of fire control equip-ment in the third quarter, $300,000 had to be diverted from the spare parts to the defined line items funds, which then stood at $400,000.

During the fourth quarter, to cope with the stepped-up tempo of the war and the daily evolution of the situation, priorities were given to ammunition and to major items of equipment. $11.9 million was thus transferred from the spare parts and POL funds to the ammo funds, increasing them from $239.2 million to $251.1 million. Another $13.7 mil-lion was diverted from the spare parts, food, and navy funds ($1.7 million) to the major item funds, for increase to $14.6 million. Finally, $2.6 million was transferred from the spare parts and food funds to individual equipment funds.

A Reprogramming Effort

It was all too apparent that, no matter what military measures were taken, the ap-proved budget of US $700 million was inadequate to meet the minimum RVNAF re-quirements.

Indeed, the management at all echelons was greatly improved in order to properly use the aid money and the assets that were on hand. Equipment was properly main-tained; waste and abuse were kept at a minimum.

Ammunition and fuel were thriftily expended. The use of individual clothing and jungle boots was extended from six months to nine months for combat troops and to 18 months for combat [support] troops and from 24 to 36 months for other troops. Poncho design was also altered to lower its cost from US $7.58 to $5.25 each. Annual issue of boot socks was reduced from three to two pairs. Helmets, helmet liners, and rucksacks were only issued to combat units. The allocation of BA-4386 batteries for AN/PRC-25 radio sets was reduced from six to four batteries a month and used batteries had to be traded in for new ones on a piece-by-piece basis. Salvage yards were thoroughly searched for materials usable in production, or as spare parts and repair parts. Used sur-gical dressings, bandages, disposable syringes, needles, gloves, and intravenous sets were all sterilized for reuse.

To be able to continue the fighting for survival, the JGS/CLC, with DAO assistance, made a last effort to reprogram the FY 1975 supplemental aid at US $241,700,000. . . .

• • •

In late March 1975, as a result of the disastrous retreats in MR-2 and MR-1, the RVNAF submitted an additional request for US $387,854,500 to procure necessary major items to refit the battered units that were retrieved and to reorganize the RF-PF units.

Both requests were included in the US president's message to the Congress in April 1975 as a final plea for the RVNAF survival. History has it that the US Congress chose to ignore the survival package and opt for humanitarian aid for those who survived.

XIV. THE FINAL DAYS

Impact of the New Strategy

Although the cutbacks in US military aid during the post-cease-fire period had a shocking effect on the entire RVNAF, the cold fact that dwindling aid was becoming a way of life did provide an opportunity for military commanders to prove their resourcefulness and determination for survival. "Fighting a poor man's war" was a slogan often quoted by field commanders who devised innovative ways to fight the enemy with the least material assets, and [persuade their] troops to put up with the new circumstances. Austerity measures became the object of a large-scale troop education program, but political warfare cadre found it difficult to convince troops of the necessity to use sparingly the supplies that they had thought were endless.

To logistics managers, reduced aid meant that they had to be more cost-conscious and make the most economical use of every dollar appropriated.

• • •

The problem they had was how to avoid "scraping the bottom" before supplemental aid arrived.

In the meantime, there was hardly any letup in the logistic support for combat operations across the country. Despite reduced supply rates, ARVN troops fought on with unflinching fierceness in all the major battles of the period: the Thuong Duc front south of Danang in MR-1, the Phuoc Long front, Tay Ninh, La Nga in MR-3, and Kien Tuong in the border area of MR-4. They fought and won most of the battles, although support was a far cry from what they had been accustomed to when fighting alongside US troops.

As a pure coincidence, the dry season—which is the season for military campaigns, "high points," and redoubled efforts for both warring parties—was also the time during which another battle was being fought halfway around the world, the battle on the question of supplemental aid for fiscal year 1975. The dry season of 1975 began with ominous signals for the fate of US military aid and that of the RVN. First there was the rapid loss of Phuoc Long in early January. Then there was the unfavorable, almost indifferent attitude of US congressmen who visited South Vietnam during January and February. Finally there was the multidivision-sized force overrunning of Ban Me Thuot, the second provincial capital to fall under Communist control within a space of two months. And all this stirred no semblance of a reaction from the International Commission of Control and Supervision (ICCS), or from the United States.

These events were perhaps the last straw that pushed President . . . Thieu into changing the RVN strategy with a decision that he made on 11 March 1975. To hold at all costs all the territory that RVN effectively controlled on the cease-fire day had been the sacrosanct commandment that dictated the RVN strategy up to the loss of Ban Me Thuot. Now it was only the populous and relatively prosperous areas that really mattered in his reformed strategical point of view. These included all the territory of MR-3 and MR-4, the irreducible stronghold to be defended at all costs. As to MR-1 and MR-2, their defense was just a matter of "hold as you can" as far as ARVN field commanders were concerned. In more specific terms, however, MR-1 was to be held, depending on I Corps capabilities, through phased lines of defense successively marked across Hue, the Hai Van Pass, and Chu Lai. If I Corps could do it, then Hue should be held; if not, it could retreat to the next line or the next after that. For MR-2, a vague line across Tuy Hoa was indicated as the last-ditch line of defense for II Corps.

On 14 March 1975, during a meeting at Cam Ranh, after reviewing the military situation in MR-2, President Thieu gave orders for II Corps to redeploy its forces presently located in the Pleiku-Kontum area and employ them to reoccupy Ban Me Thuot. Five days later, at the Independence Palace, the I Corps commander presented his own plan for the defense of MR-1, which consisted of redeploying his forces to Hue and Chu Lai in the first place and holding them if possible. If not, the forces that had been redeployed to Hue and Chu Lai would fall back on Danang, the last enclave to be defended, as estimates went, by a four-division plus force. The president simply acquiesced without comment.

As it turned out, the II Corps redeployment from Pleiku-Kontum was a failure due to the lack of planning and preparations. The enemy successfully caught up with the retreating convoys moving toward the coast along Route LRL-7B and inflicted severe losses on them. Most II Corps units were destroyed, including four ranger groups, one M-48 squadron, one 175mm artillery battalion, and logistics direct support units. Total losses in materiel and equipment were estimated at over US $250 million, of which there were 17,885 tons of ammunition (valued at US $36.5 million) and US $2 million worth of petroleum. No destruction was ordered or carried out, despite the existence of emergency plans. On orders from the JGS, [the] VNAF later sent its bombers back to destroy the ammunition and fuel left behind, but the results were minimal.

News of the sudden evacuation of Pleiku and Kontum caused confusion and anxiety among the population and the troops. Adverse rumors spread that the GVN had struck a partition arrangement with the Communists, that the United States had decided to abandon South Vietnam, etc. Soon, in fear and panic, the population of Quang Tri and Hue flowed uncontrollably into Danang, seeking ways to move farther south despite assurances from President Thieu that Hue would be held at all costs.

The Logistics Redeployment Plan

There was little doubt that the switch in strategy would bear heavily on the RVNAF logistic support capabilities. The losses incurred in Ban Me Thuot had been heavy enough. To carry out the troop redeployments involved in the new defense plan, a lot of mobility assets would be required, and, more importantly, efforts should be made to recover to the maximum extent possible all the major items and supplies stocked in depots throughout MR-1 and MR-2. As soon as the presidential decision was learned, the Central Logistics Command/JGS immediately requested USDAO for additional transportation assets while feverishly working on a plan to redeploy logistics units. Caught unaware by the sudden troop redeployment from Pleiku-Kontum, the CLC was unable to salvage anything from that area, but it was hopeful that there was still time to save MR-1 from that situation.

Plans were accordingly made and actions quickly taken. The Danang General Depot was ordered to cease reception of aid equipment and requests were made to redirect all supply shipments bound for it toward the Long Binh General Depot. After completing the evacuation of all Danang stock assets on hand, the Danang General Depot was to merge with the Long Binh General Depot. The 41st Medium Maintenance Center at Danang would also be redeployed, after evacuating its assets, partly to Long Binh, where it would reinforce the 43rd MMC, and partly to Can Tho to augment the 44th MMC. Shipments of ammunition by oceangoing vessels bound for Danang were to be redirected to Saigon, and field depots were to reduce their stock level in keeping with tactical requirements. Their personnel, when evacuated, would be absorbed by the 53rd Ammo Group of the 3rd ALC. Patients undergoing treatment at the Duy Tan General Hospital and the Nguyen Tri Phuong field hospital would be partially evacuated to the Cong Hoa General Hospital in Saigon and to the recuperation center at Vung Tau. Meanwhile, all logistic support units of the 2nd ALC received orders to stand down and gradually move to Cam Ranh, where they would reinforce their counterparts of the 5th ALC.

The evacuation of materiel assets, both major items of equipment and supplies, proved to be difficult due to the scarcity of transportation facilities. A system of evacuation priorities had to be established for various types of materiel and locations.

First priority was given to armament, signal equipment, trucks, and serviceable armored vehicles, and the Hue area. Next came ammunition and POL, and the Danang area. The last to be evacuated were unserviceable equipment, depending on [their] condition, and the Qui Nhon area.

• • •

As the VNN LSTs were all committed to the sealift of the Airborne Division from Danang to Nha Trang and Saigon, and to ammunition transportation, during the period from 18 to 24 March 1975, they would not be available for the evacuation of equipment and supplies. At the CLC request, USDAO agreed to let the ARVN use five tugboats and six barges which had previously been used in Cambodia, and three deep-draft vessels of the Military Sealift Command (MSC). Four tugboats and four 2,0000-ton barges would be available at Danang on 27 March; the remaining tugboat and two 5,000-ton barges would arrive at Qui Nhon on the same day. The MSC deep-draft vessels, meanwhile, would be redirected toward Danang after unloading. The USS *Pioneer Contender* arrived on 28 March, followed by the USS *Pioneer Commander* on 30 March and the USS *Trans-Colorado* on 31 March. In addition, USDAO leased another South Korean LST for the evacuation of ammunition from Qui Nhon.

No sooner had the evacuation of equipment and supplies from Hue to Danang begun than it was suspended. Only a few LCM-8 shiploads and one truck convoy had moved out. It had become painfully difficult by 19 March to continue, because of the onrushing flow of refugees from Quang Tri and Hue. Refugees blocked all other traffic on route QL-1. On 22 March, QL-1 was interdicted by enemy forces. The Tan My pier, piled up with transit cargoes, including those awaiting loading, overflowed with frantic refugees. The refugees soon turned into uncontrollable mobs and commandeered all docked

LCM-8s, LCUs, and barges for Danang, regardless of whether they were loading or off-loading. An entire day was lost in settling this upheaval. To assuage the refugees' plight, and also to clear them from the pier and keep the road back to Hue open for ammunition trucks, it was decided to use all boats and barges then available to pick up refugees from the landing near the Truong Tien Bridge in Hue and at Tan My and ship them directly to Thai Duong Ha. At Thai Duong Ha they could wait for other ships and boats bound for Danang. Port activities resumed immediately at Tan My after this delay and the vital 155mm ammunition kept pouring into Hue, but by this time the evacuation of equipment and supplies had become moot because of orders issued by I Corps to evacuate Hue on 25 March. All ships and barges earmarked for this task were now diverted to carrying troops and their dependents toward Danang.

At Danang, most equipment to be evacuated had been partially transported to the pier to await loading, but no ships were available. The two LSTs slated for this task had been ordered to Tan My to pick up troops and dependents of the 1st Infantry Division and the Hue sector. As scheduled and provided by USDAO, the four tugboats and barges and the USS *Pioneer Contender* arrived in Danang on 27 and 28 March, respectively, but by this time the city had become overcrowded with refugees. All roads leading to the pier were tightly jammed, making it impossible for trucks to move. The 1st ALC estimated that there were 9,000 short tons of ammunition and 34,000 short tons of other supplies and equipment, including vehicles and machinery, awaiting shipment to Saigon. Faced with the unexpected turn of events, both [the] USDAO and the JGS decided to suspend the operation and divert all available facilities to the evacuation of refugees. It had become clear that, for the Danang enclave to hold, all refugees had to be cleared.

From Qui Nhon to Cam Ranh the retreat of equipment was more successful, although it was slowed down by a shortage of facilities. The available LCM-8s busily plied the route, bringing the much-needed weapons, vehicles, and artillery pieces toward Cam Ranh for the refitting of the battered 23rd Infantry Division and other units retrieved from Ban Me Thuot, Pleiku, and Kontum. And, as scheduled, the USDAO-provided tugboat and its two barges arrived at Qui Nhon on 27 March and, after being fully loaded with vehicles, ammunition, and other supplies, returned to Cam Ranh on 29 March. Port activities in Qui Nhon ran smoothly until 30 March, when enemy troops infiltrated into the city. By contrast to Tan My and Danang, the port of Qui Nhon was not besieged by refugees. The refugees moved toward Nha Trang by road. Given the short time available, and the inadequacy of assets, not all equipment and supplies at Qui Nhon were [successfully] evacuated. If only a few more LSTs had been made available, as had been requested, much more could have been retrieved, especially ammunition and POL. Only one million gallons of gasoline and diesel fuel was evacuated to Nha Trang from Danang and Qui Nhon. In general, the equipment retreat operation was unsuccessful because of an initial lack of sealift assets and the rapid deterioration of the situation which materialized well before any outside reinforcements, especially those from the United States, had time to arrive.

The Evacuation of ARVN Units and Refugees from MR-1 and MR-2

Within the space of one week after orders were issued for the evacuation of Hue, almost all of the VNN and Transportation Corps meager assets had to contend with a deluge of troops and dependents from the several divisions and provinces of MR-1. From Cua Thuan they picked up units of the 1st Infantry Division, a marine brigade, and RF and PF troops of the Thua Thien sector and transported them to Danang. From Chu Lai, they picked up over 5,000 troops from the 2nd Infantry Division and from the sectors of Quang Ngai and Quang Tin and evacuated them toward the Ly Son (Re) Island, 20 miles offshore. Finally, during the night of 28 March, they evacuated I Corps forces from Danang.

Over 6,000 marines and 4,000 troops of the 3rd Infantry Division and other units at Danang arrived at Cam Ranh on 31 March. However, only two days later they had to be evacuated again toward Vung Tau after the Khanh Duong line of defense, held by the 3rd Airborne Brigade, had been broken through by the NVA F-10 Division and Tuy Hoa had been overrun by the NVA 320th Division. Then, on 30 March, the VNN evacuated the 2nd Infantry Division from Ly Son Island toward Binh Tuy in MR-3. Finally, during the night of 31 March, VNN ships picked up at Qui Nhon troops of the 22nd Infantry Division, which had retreated from Binh Khe on QL-19, and directed them toward Vung Tau. By 3 April 1975 all retrievable I and II Corps units had arrived at their ports of destination in MR-3. There they immediately went through an accelerated process of regrouping, refitting, reorganization, and retraining.

The problem of refugees, in the meantime, continued to impede the RVNAF activities as it had during the evacuation of Pleiku-Kontum and the later withdrawal from Hue and Danang. It was the refugees who made it impossible to evacuate equipment and supplies from MR-1 . . . , and it was also the refugee rush that accounted for the disruption of several units. In general, it was the refugee predicament that was responsible for the wreckage of well-laid-out defense plans.

Over the years, ever since the war broke out, refugees were a major burden for the GVN in terms of care and relief, and refugees were a plague for tactical commanders. The pattern had become all too familiar. It was like a tidal wave that rose and ebbed with the tempo of the fighting. When fighting erupted in some area, people fled from their villages and came to town to live in makeshift relief centers as refugees. As soon as the enemy was driven away, most would go back, but many elected to make a new life in cities or were resettled elsewhere by the GVN. The relief task in time became a matter of routine for local governments. Each city and each provincial capital had its own relief committee and refugee centers. They were part of a system directed by a central relief committee, an interministerial body usually chaired by the minister of social affairs. The mayor or province chief was chairman of the municipal or provincial relief committee, acting under directives of the central relief committee chairman. Corps commanders were neither responsible for nor took part in the relief and resettlement effort.

There were times when the total number of refugees cared for by the GVN at centers throughout the country reached into the millions. Normal procedures for relief consisted of cash allocations to local committees, who either procured essential subsistence items and distributed them among refugee family units or just gave them the cash. Donations from domestic or foreign charity organizations were usually made in kind and distributed directly to the refugees.

After the cease-fire, a significant effort was undertaken by the GVN to resettle the refugees, particularly those who overcrowded the relief centers in MR-1. This effort was known as the "Wasteland Reclamation and Hamlet Settlement" program, which was under the direction of Dr. Phan Quang Dan, the then deputy prime minister and minister of social affairs. To assist in the program, the JGS occasionally provided interregional sealift support at his request, but only when commercial facilities were not available.

On 19 March 1975, to face the growing refugee problem, the central relief committee convened a meeting under Dr. Dan's chairmanship. The JGS was invited to attend. Since the unexpected turn of military events, which were unfolding in MR-2 as a result of President Thieu's new strategic decision, had taken on a grave importance and a momentous influx of refugees was expected in the next few days, I personally came to the meeting as Chief of Staff/JGS. During the meeting, upon Dr. Dan's request, I gave him a brief rundown of the military situation, focusing on Ban Me Thuot and the redeployment of II Corps from Pleiku-Kontum. I also briefed him on the RVNAF transportation capabilities and concluded that, in the face of new events, the JGS would be unable to provide refugee transportation support for his program as before. Predicting that the influx of refugees would increase manyfold as the war intensified, I suggested that the only way the GVN could cope with it was to ask for outside help.

If the 1954 experience could serve as a useful antecedent, I said, the GVN should begin immediately to do three specific things: 1) to requisition all available commercial vessels for the transportation of refugees; 2) to make an appeal to the Free World countries, especially the United States and those allies who had fought in Vietnam, asking them to provide help in transportation facilities as they had done back in 1954; and 3) to create a movement control body to coordinate the employment of all assets made available.

Dr. Dan found my recommendations reasonably sound and without further discussion he instructed the Ministry of Public Works to issue an executive order requisitioning without delay all Vietnamese vessels presently operating the domestic routes and directing home those presently at foreign ports. All commercial vessels thus requisitioned would be primarily used to support the refugee settlement program and would be placed under the direction of the Movement Control Division, CLC, which Dr. Dan had made the committee's control body [as] I had suggested. Its authority also extended to foreign vessels that would be made available to the RVN as a result of its appeal. As to the new locations for refugee settlement, Dr. Dan informed me that all refugees from MR-1 would be relocated at Cam Ranh, Lam Dong, and Binh Thuan, where new settlement hamlets were being built, and that a committee headed by himself would travel to these areas to arrange for additional settlement sites.

A whole week had passed since the 19 March 1975 meeting was held, but no requisition order had been issued. The minister of public works apparently felt he was not competent enough to sign the order and would rather have Dr. Dan sign it. Dr. Dan, meanwhile, was out of town making necessary arrangements.

The refugee situation in Danang by this time had become increasingly difficult to handle. Relief centers were all overcrowded and control was getting out of hand. Robberies, assaults, and begging for food became common. The piers and wharves overflowed with people waiting in vain for a boat or a ship to go south. The immediate problem facing GVN authorities was to clear the mass of refugees from Danang without delay and direct them toward Cam Ranh and from there to settlement areas. The appeal for help had been made; it was received with compassion and assistance was on its way, or so it seemed. Dr. Dan, in the meantime, spent his time conferring with US Embassy officials asking for help.

A few commercial jets chartered by the US Embassy came to Danang to pick up refugees and move them to Cam Ranh. But the evacuation by air had to be suspended after a few flights because of chaos and disorder during embarking. This was 27 March, two days before the fall of Danang. On the same day 5,000 dependents of the 1st Infantry Division and the Hue sector arrived at Danang on the VNS *Truong Thanh* of Vishipco Lines. This was the first and only Vietnamese commercial ship ever officially used for the evacuation of refugees. The CLC had arranged for its use well before any requisition order was even issued. The other vessels had no chance to serve the public because, by the time the order was finally issued, MR-1 no longer existed.

On the same day, 27 March, . . . four tugboats towing four barges and the USS *Pioneer Contender* also arrived in Danang on USDAO orders, intended for the evacuation of equipment and supplies. They were diverted to carrying refugees to Cam Ranh. Since they were not prepared to accommodate passengers, there was no drinking water on board the barges. The DAO representative, Mr. E. G. Hey, on TDY at Danang from Transportation Section, Army Division, USDAO, since 24 March, and the 1st ALC personnel tried in vain to load 500-gallon water trailers on the barges. The *Pioneer Contender,* anchored offshore, planned to take aboard about 6,000 refugees in view of her modest comfort amenities. Embarking was to take place at the Thong Nhut deep-water pier on lighters towed by tugboats under the direction of the US General Consulate personnel.

At 2100 hours the first lighter came to its berth along the pier. Like a herd of wild buffalo the crowd of refugees—civilian population, troops, and dependents alike—charged forward, stampeding, trampling, elbowing each other, for a place aboard. The US Consulate General security personnel and I Corps military police had a most difficult time restoring order and only reasonably succeeded after several tumultuous ordeals. By the time it was full, the lighter could hardly move. Not only was it overloaded, it was also counterpulled by other refugees onshore who thought they were being left behind. A long pulling match took place between the tugboat and the desperate refugees. Finally the lighter broke off from shore and made it to the *Pioneer Contender* at 1130 hours the next day, 28 March.

Embarking onboard the *Pioneer Contender* was no less hazardous and time-consuming. Children had to be relayed from hand to hand through a line of people precariously perched along a narrow, swaying gangplank. It seemed that the embarking would go on forever, for the lighter was constantly assaulted by small boats which kept pouring still more people onboard. The *Pioneer Contender* had now between 10,000 and 12,000 refugees onboard, twice the load she had planned to take. Unable to take more, she finally lifted anchor at 1800 hours and arrived at Cam Ranh in the morning of 29 March.

At Cam Ranh, local authorities were not prepared to receive the refugees from MR-1. The 5th ALC, with its own resources, took responsibility to take them by truck to the Cam Ranh relief center on the other side of the peninsula. After debarking its human load, the *Pioneer Contender* immediately sailed back to Danang, together with the *Pioneer Commander*. Both arrived offshore Danang at 0700 hours on 30 March and continued loading refugees who arrived by US barges or by small boats. Another contingent of 10,000 to 12,000 hungry, exhausted people, troops and dependents, were shipped to Cam Ranh on 31 March. They were again received by the 5th ALC and driven to the relief center. Accounts of mischief, robberies, murders, rapes, and other crimes during the journey on high seas between Danang and Cam Ranh began to circulate among rumors that enemy agents were planted among refugees to create disorder and difficulties for the GVN. Whatever the real cause of this human depravity, the refugees' odyssey had been full of torment and anguish.

In the meantime the situation in Qui Nhon, Nha Trang, and Cam Ranh was deteriorating rapidly. The human flow of refugees continued unabated on QL-1, moving toward the south. Many refugees took to the high seas by fishing boats and were picked up by US naval ships operating offshore along the coast south of Danang.[7] Like a destructive calamity, the flow of refugees created panic, disruption, and collapse wherever it moved. Vung Tau, the port of entry for Dr. Dan's settlement program, overflowed with troops, dependents, and other refugees from MR-1 and MR-2. Fearing an onset of total morale collapse, President Thieu forbade refugees from entering Vung Tau and directed the central relief committee to divert them to Phu Quoc Island, where a makeshift refugee center was hastily established with facilities of the POW camps. His decision not to let refugees enter Vung Tau gave rise to mutinous actions onboard the refugee ships. Some refugees threatened to blow up the ships or commandeered them not to sail toward Phu Quoc. A long time was spent in explaining before the refugees would listen to reason.

A total of 40,000 refugees were finally shipped to Phu Quoc by US vessels. The makeshift refugee center on the island lacked everything to function properly and provide the essentials for the refugees. ARVN personnel, including medical corpsmen, were hastily sent to the island to man the camp and provide emergency care. The refugees there suffered most from eye infection and a lack of cooking and sleeping facilities.

In addition to sealift, the US Embassy and Air Vietnam also provided sporadic flights for the evacuation of refugees from Danang. On 27 March the JGS was informed by the central relief committee that an emergency airlift by US commercial jets would be undertaken at once, to be augmented later by Australian aircraft. The committee also estimated that the flights could move from 12,000 to 14,000 refugees a day from Danang to Cam Ranh. It was most welcome news, although local authorities and the 5th ALC at

Cam Ranh had some cause for concern in the face of this additional influx. However, the airlift had to be terminated after a few flights due to safety reasons. At Danang airport, local authorities had been unable to exercise control over the mob of refugees and unruly servicemen who fought desperately among themselves to get on board.

The initial lack of transportation facilities seemed to be the major handicap that caused the huge impasse in Danang and defeated subsequent efforts of evacuation. Driven to desperation by a futile long wait, exhausted by hunger and fatigue, the mass of refugees had turned into a herd of trapped animals who defied even death when scrambling for . . . freedom. By the time the facilities arrived, it had become too late.

Confidence could have been restored, impatience would have been soothed, panic would not have occurred, and surely Danang would have held, at least for a much longer time, if there had been adequate sealift and airlift facilities from the start. The influx of refugees had reached such proportions that it simply outgrew the GVN capabilities to provide shelter, food, and medicare. But, even if adequate evacuation facilities had been made available, the millions of people thus displaced would have created such a problem that it would have taken the GVN years to solve in the face of unrelenting invasion threats.

Regrouping and Refitting Efforts

In early 1975, drawing on lessons from the enemy's 1974 offensive campaign in Quang Nam (MR-1) and the loss of Phuoc Long (MR-3), and with the hope that US aid would continue at an adequate level, the JGS felt that, in order to effectively meet the enemy's escalated efforts, adequate reserve forces would have to be reconstituted, not only at the strategic level but also at the field level.

Plans were initiated to strengthen ARVN combat forces and restore reserves. They consisted of:

Priority One: Activating an additional brigade for each airborne and marine division. Activating an additional battalion for each of the three marine brigades and two ranger groups.

Priority Two: Activating a total of 27 Regional Force mobile groups by regrouping RF battalions and area artillery sections. These RF groups would be made operationally self-supporting and could be employed as reinforcements for infantry divisions. Each group would consist of three RF battalions and a four-piece artillery battery.

Priority Three: Activating four ranger divisional headquarters designed to improve the operational control of existing ranger groups and to adapt them to division-sized conventional warfare in the immediate future.

Priority One plans were immediately implemented, with excellent results, due to emergency requirements in strategic reserves and the availability of equipment stocks. Other plans, however, could not be carried out in view of the reduced FY 1975 aid. They would have to wait until supplemental appropriations were approved or until the next fiscal year.

The loss of Ban Me Thuot and the tragic redeployment of II Corps from Pleiku-Kontum during the month of March resulted in losses of such proportions that the existing maintenance float and the FY 1975 aid budget could not replace them, even in part. Reprogramming was possible within FY 1975 appropriations, but only US $13.8 million could be spared. Refitting costs, meanwhile, based on ARVN standards, were estimated at US $18,831,000 for one infantry division, US $11,727,000 for a ranger group, US $22.7 million for an M-48 squadron, and US $8,340,000 for an M-113 squadron. It was obvious that, to refit II Corps units, supplemental FY 1975 aid was a must.

General F. C. Weyand's trip to South Vietnam on 26 March 1975 came as a timely light at the end of a long and dark tunnel. Three projects were presented to him by the JGS, along with hopes that the US Congress [would] favorably consider supplemental aid for FY 1975 and appropriations for FY 1976. Project 1 or Priority One required US $221,579,354 for the replacement of combat force losses incurred at Ban Me Thuot and during the ill-fated redeployments from Pleiku-Kontum, Quang Duc, and Phu Bon in MR-2, plus estimated losses for the sectors of Quang Tri, Thua Thien, Quang Ngai, and Quang Tin of MR-1 during the planned retreat toward the Danang enclave. Project 2 required US $69,635,796 for the regrouping of 81 RF battalions and area artillery sections into 27 RF mobile combat groups. Project 3 envisioned the consolidation of 12 ranger groups into four ranger divisions at a cost of US $96,639,350.

The evacuation of I Corps forces from Danang on 29 March forced the JGS to establish a priority system for the immediate refitting of combat forces. First priority was given to the rehabilitation of the 3rd Airborne Brigade, the Marine Division, and the 2nd, 22nd, and 3rd Infantry Divisions.

• • •

This refitting plan was undertaken with hopes that the United States would provide replacements as quickly as it had done after the enemy Easter invasion of 1972. Equipment and materiel needed for this plan came from several sources. In the first place there were organic weapons retrieved from withdrawn units and individual soldiers; these should be used first. Second, some equipment was to be retrieved from third- and fourth-echelon repair shops in MR-3 and MR-4, rebuild shops, and the maintenance float. Third, military and service schools could provide up to 50 percent of their organic equipment. Last, ARVN logisticians were looking forward to US emergency deliveries.

A few days after General Weyand's visit, some US equipment deliveries did materialize as expected, though not as plentiful as in 1972. They came in rapid succession during the first few days of April, then tapered off and came to an end as of 19 April.

• • •

The refitting process ran into difficulties due to the limited amount of equipment delivered. It was far less than that received in 1972 after the enemy initiated the Easter invasion. Vehicles, for example, consisted only of 1/4-ton and 2–1/2-ton trucks and signal equipment of basic field radio and telephone sets. Its progress was also greatly impeded by the grave deterioration of morale among units and the civilian population.

Support for MR-3 during the Final Days

By the time Nha Trang was evacuated on 2 April 1975, II Corps virtually ceased to exist as a combat force. As a last-ditch effort to stop the enemy advance and save the two remaining provinces of MR-2—Ninh Thuan and Binh Thuan—III Corps was designated to take responsibility on 4 April.

The 2nd Airborne Brigade was airlifted to Phan Rang AFB, together with long-range reconnaissance teams of the Strategic Technical Directorate (STD/JGS) and the III Corps Forward CP under the command of Lieutenant General Nguyen Vinh Nghi. To provide support for these two provinces, the 3rd ALC established two Class III and V supply points at Phan Rang and Phan Thiet. It also moved a forward CP element to Phan Thiet to control and coordinate support activities in the entire area north of Binh Tuy on the one hand and to follow up on the retrieval of equipment discarded by II Corps units during their retreat or by individual soldiers cut off from their units on the other. The recovery task focused particularly on trucks, armored vehicles, weapons, artillery, and signal equipment. Retrieved equipment was retreated toward three points—the Phan Thiet airfield and the fishing ports of Ninh Thuan and Binh Thuan—for shipment toward Long Binh.

Sealift became the major transportation mode, since QL-1 was interdicted between Phan Thiet and Saigon. Fleets of LCM-8s and LCUs . . . shuttled day and night between Vung Tau and Phan Thiet, bringing forward ammunition and fuels and returning with recovered equipment. In addition to the two mobile supply points, the 3rd ALC also established a floating ammunition supply point using barges and tugboats assigned for the task by the CLC/JGS and a floating POL supply point on the American tanker USS *Rincon*, which shuttled back and forth between Phan Rang and Vung Tau.

The enemy pressure on Bien Hoa and Long Khanh increased incessantly in the meantime, forcing III Corps to redeploy the 2nd Airborne Brigade back to Bien Hoa as corps reserves. To replace it, one refitted regiment of the 2nd Infantry Division and another ranger group, just withdrawn from Chon Thanh, were moved to Phan Rang, along with an M-113 troop. The switch was nearly completed on 16 April, when the Phan Rang AFB and the city itself were forcefully attacked and overrun by the NVA F-10 Division and elements of the NVA 3rd . . . Division. The Class V supply point at Phan Rang was hit and blown up. An LCU unloading ammunition at the ramp was also hit and sunk; another vessel, an LCM-8, suffered some damage. Then, in rapid succession, Phan Thiet on 18 April and Binh Tuy on 20 April were lost to the enemy.

On other battlefronts, however, in Tay Ninh, Binh Duong, Long Khanh, and MR-4, logistic support activities progressed with normal smoothness, encountering no major difficulties. The area of support having been greatly reduced, airlift no longer was a problem by this time. The few serviceable C-130A cargo planes which were made available each day, three to four in all, were diverted to a more pressing though unusual use of fire support. Instead of supply cargoes, they now dropped homemade incendiary bombs (50-gallon [sic] drums filled with discarded diesel oil), 250- and 500-pound bombs, and even a few 15,000-pound "daisy cutters" on enemy units, and, strangely, these bomb runs effectively destroyed a major NVA unit and stopped its advance toward Bien Hoa.

Reinforced by the refitted units of MR-1 and MR-2, which were low on both equipment and morale, III Corps made a last-ditch stand to hold the defense line with its three organic divisions. The Long Binh logistics base now lay adjacent to the last line of defense that III Corps was holding to protect Saigon. It was well within artillery range of NVA divisions who were poised to advance toward their final objective. Supplies at the general depot were removed to Saigon. In preparation for the battle for Saigon, which was reminiscent of Tet 1968, an ammunition supply point was reconstituted at Go Vap, next to the Army Arsenal. Other ammunition dispersion points—the JGS, the CMD, the Airborne Division rear base, the Quang Trung Training Center—were well replenished and ready for action.

Major items of equipment which were earmarked for the continuing refitting process were diverted to the 331st DSG at Phu Tho. Other aid equipment and supplies unloaded from US ships were directed toward the 40th Engineer Base Depot at Phu Tho, which now performed processing and storage functions to alleviate partially the Long Binh General Depot's responsibility. Efforts were feverishly made to transform Vung Tau into a major logistics base and substitute port of entry for Newport, Saigon. Another Class V supply point was established at Vung Tau to serve both as a dispersion and a receiving point for ammunition offloaded from oceangoing vessels. This supply point would also relay ammunition to Saigon and to Can Tho directly in case ships could not enter the Saigon channel toward Cat Lai. ARVN engineer troops worked around the clock to rehabilitate the former US ammunition depot at Vung Tau for this purpose. At the same time, the port operation section of the Saigon Transportation Terminal was also directed toward Vung Tau, along with offloading and transportation assets. The Phu Quoc Island was reconnoitered for the possibility of establishing a Class III and V supply point earmarked for aircraft supply and supply dispersion.

The military situation, meanwhile, continued to deteriorate rapidly. It looked as if nothing, except for a US reintervention, could conceivably stop the onrush of the entire North Vietnamese Army—14 infantry divisions in all, complemented by armor and artillery units. To save the loss of valuable assets, and acting on a recommendation by the US Assistant Secretary of Defense who was on a mission in Saigon during its final days, the CLC/JGS agreed to an early evacuation of high-cost equipment and materiel from Saigon for future use. The rapid turn of events never allowed this move to be carried out. On 26 April [the] DAO and the CLC terminated all ammunition and POL offloading activities at Cat Lai and Nha Be. US ships were directed toward Vung Tau.

At 1800 hours on 28 April the Communists bombed Tan Son Nhut AFB with captured VNAF aircraft, just as President Duong Van Minh's inauguration ceremony was over. On 29 April, the new president ordered all US personnel out of Saigon by the next morning. In the morning of 30 April, at 1000 hours, he ordered the surrender of the

RVNAF as Communist tanks and advance units moved toward Saigon. With his order, South Vietnam ceased to exist as a free nation and over 20 million freedom-loving people of South Vietnam became captives of a dictatorial Communist regime. The iron curtain finally closed on Vietnam and ended 21 years of US military aid.

• • •

XV. CONCLUSION

The evolution of the RVNAF logistics system was a slow process of structural and functional adaptation which began with US military aid and ended with it. It was an organization that improved as it progressed, and modernized as it grew, benefiting both from new management concepts and from US technology.

• • •

Staff work, technology, inspection, and training were the four major areas of endeavor in which US advisors daily helped their Vietnamese counterparts improve. During the first few years US advisory teams existed only at the central level: G-4/JGS and technical service directorates. In 1961, in keeping with the stepped-up logistics support for embattled areas, US advisors were gradually assigned to base depots, area logistics commands, and field support units. Regardless of the level or location of units to which they were assigned, US advisory personnel were almost always seated in close proximity to their counterparts, and sometimes even shared the same office.

• • •

The collocation of advisors and counterparts seemed to have created an "esprit de corps" and a commonness in responsibility, since it facilitated contact and discussion, hence mutual understanding, despite a certain uneasiness at the beginning. Thanks to daily personal contacts, US advisors were able to dispense with paperwork almost entirely, save for the monthly end-use inspection report. This spirit of close cooperation [manifested] itself not only at work but also during off-duty hours when they shared the same club and entertainment facilities. During field trips, advisors and their counterparts shared the same transportation, took their meals together, and often stayed at the same place. Most significantly, during critical periods when ARVN personnel were confined to barracks, US advisors usually made a point of spending the night at the unit and helping with the unit's defense, although they were never required to do so. These acts made them popular among ARVN troops and earned their affection and respect.

Then, during the years following 1965 when US combat and logistical units began to be deployed across the country, advisory teams also served as an invaluable link between them and ARVN units. US advisors during this period effectively helped ARVN logistical units overcome their weaknesses and increase their efficiency by providing them such services as transportation, mobile repair teams, contact teams, emergency supply, etc. They also helped coordinate the organization of road or waterway convoys between US and ARVN units and arranged for ARVN personnel to be trained on the job at US support units.

In 1970, as the United States began to redeploy its forces from Vietnam, field logistic advisory personnel were gradually reduced until there remained only a few teams at the central level and at area logistics commands. To fill in the void created by the absence of US advisors at field and direct support units, senior logistics advisors and their staffs made more frequent field visits with ARVN counterparts.

Then came the Paris Agreement in January 1973, and with it the withdrawal of all US advisors. In contrast with MACV, the US Defense Attaché Office . . . was just a co-worker at the Central Logistics Command, responsible for receiving the RVNAF requirements, programming them in terms of dollar value, recommending their approval, managing the funds appropriated, and controlling the end use of equipment.

During 17 years of advisory assistance, 1956–1973, and through approximately two years of close cooperation during 1974 and 1975, ARVN logisticians were able to learn many things from US personnel, military and civilian, whether they served as advisors or coworkers. They came to appreciate and admire such American personal virtues as perseverance, tactfulness, and hard work. They learned a great deal from American leadership, staff work, and modern management techniques. US advisors [were] not only senior, they also had superior professional knowledge and experience. Hence they were always held in high esteem and respected. Up until 1967, . . . [the] US advisory relationship seemed to be rigid and formal. But from 1968 on, i.e., during the Vietnamization period and after the Paris Agreement, this relationship tended to be more relaxed, more open, and more sincerely devoted to genuine cooperation. As a result, during this period the presence of US advisors and coworkers inspired confidence and affection among ARVN logisticians with whom they cooperated. It [was] also during this period that ARVN logisticians benefited the most from learning; they took great pride in their achievements and thought a great deal more about the future.

• • •

Throughout the twenty years of its existence, 1955–1975, the ARVN logistics system evolved incessantly for the better. From a technical organization concept, it progressed toward a fully functional organization. From hand recording of transactions it progressed toward electronic data processing. To meet increasing war demands, it also had to improve its support effectiveness, whether for pacification or for large-scale offensive and counteroffensive operations.

• • •

The RVNAF did not entertain the illusion that they could rely on US military aid forever. Sooner or later they would have to be self-reliant, but how soon? During the post-cease-fire period some criticized the GVN and the JGS for failure to plan ahead and for perpetuating overreliance on US military aid. This criticism was perhaps justified in the face of the Communist invasion threat. US military aid became increasingly uncertain during the last two years. Self-reliance, or the ability to sustain oneself in war without foreign aid, was easier said than done. This was a dream that every aid-receiving nation entertained, but the road toward true [self-]reliance seemed to be a long and tough one.

• • •

The Republic of Vietnam was just a tiny country ravaged by war for over a quarter of a century. With its basically agricultural economy, it could not sustain, by its own means, [defense against] a modern and conventional war waged by North Vietnam and supplied by the Communist bloc. The survival of South Vietnam depended in a large measure on the viability of the RVNAF. The RVNAF performance, their capabilities to win or lose, in the final analysis depended on the level of US financial and materiel aid.

NOTES

1. A hectare (ha) is an area unit of the metric system. A hectare contains 10,000 square meters and is equivalent to 2.47 US acres.

2. TERM was dissolved in 1960 and its personnel absorbed in MAAG.

3. FANK: Forces Armées Nationales Khmer (National Khmer Armed Forces), abbreviation officially used by the Republic of Khmer.

4. *Agreement on Ending the War and Restoring Peace in Vietnam*, Paris: 27 January 1973. English text.

5. The Directorate of Social Service under the Ministry of Defense was later redesignated Social Service Department under the General Political Warfare Department.

6. In compliance with the RVN president's directive to keep the RVNAF strength at the one million level, J-1/JGS set [out] in 1974 to rejuvenate military ranks by discharging military personnel reaching age limits who had completed 25 years of service and discharging those in poor health or undisciplined.

7. Among them there were USNS *Miller*, USNS *Greenville Victory*, and USNS *American Challenger*.

9

The General Offensives of 1968–1969

Colonel Hoang Ngoc Lung

PREFACE

Much has been written about the enemy's 1968 Tet Offensive, a major event in the Vietnam War. However, most publications on this subject, to include books and press accounts of the Western world and South Vietnam's own official military history records, [have] focused primarily on the spectacular aspect of battles fought during early 1968.

This monograph endeavors instead to analyze and compare all four periods of enemy offensive activities, which lasted well into 1969. Seeking to present the Vietnamese point of view, it assesses enemy and friendly strategies, the reactions and combat performance of the RVNAF and Free World Military Assistance Forces, and the impact of the offensive on the conduct of the war with regard to the enemy, South Vietnam, and the United States.

In the preparation of this monograph, I have drawn heavily on my personal experience and recollections. Interviews with involved principals and a review of documentation have also helped establish credibility of facts and depth of insight. The most valuable data, unobtainable anywhere else, are those provided by Lieutenant General William E. Potts, USA (Retired) from his personal files. For this courtesy I certainly owe him a debt of gratitude. . . . [27 June 1978]

I. WAR DURING THE 1965–1967 PERIOD

The Impact of US Search and Destroy Operations

• • •

The year 1968 began with a stream of intelligence reports on the enemy's imminent Winter–Spring Campaign, which bore all the signs of a major offensive. Despite the telltale signs, both the US and RVN commands were still speculating on the probability of the enemy campaign, and neither was certain when it would take place or if it would even be conducted. No evidence obtained so far had ever pointed clearly toward the inevitability.

As early as 19 October 1967 the enemy had announced he would observe a seven-day truce on the Tet occasion. This was the longest truce ever proposed by the Communists. Many, especially US and RVN intelligence analysts, had speculated that the enemy would take advantage of the truce period to move his units and supplies and complete the last stage of his preparations for the Winter–Spring Campaign. Our intelligence also estimated that this campaign would be primarily directed against the Khe Sanh Base, where reports had indicated an enemy force concentration of at least three main force divisions.

To face this mounting pressure around Khe Sanh, the US command deployed the 1st Air Cavalry Division and one brigade of the 101st Airborne Division from II Corps area to I Corps area to strengthen the defense of the two northernmost provinces. Then, on 21 January 1968, two NVA divisions initiated an attack on Khe Sanh Base with the support of artillery. Concurrently, enemy armor made its first appearance during the war when five PT-76s were sighted at Lang Vei, five miles west of Khe Sanh.

As the battle raged on fiercely, Khe Sanh drew most of the US command's attention and concern. The RVN was much less concerned, since no ARVN force had been involved prior to the siege. Not until the fighting had been in full progress did the RVN decide to deploy one ARVN ranger battalion to the base, more for political than tactical reasons, evidently, for the RVN presence was deemed symbolically significant in a battle that eventually would make history.

Despite Khe Sanh and other developments in the military situation, the RVN population and even its leadership still felt reassured. The presence of one-half million US and Free World troops and US air and firepower had convinced everybody that the Communists could hardly conduct anything big, and [that] if they attempted to do so they would surely incur heavy losses and a tragic defeat.

In any event, Tet was approaching and, to most Vietnamese, everything else hardly mattered, including politics and the war. Even those who were deeply concerned about current events seemed carefree enough to join in the feverish pre-Tet shopping spree and preparations.

This year the festive mood among Vietnamese was particularly accentuated. By contrast to previous years, the level of individual income seemed to have risen substantially as a result of increasing business and job opportunities brought about by the presence of US and Free World troops. To add to the expectation of festivities ahead, the GVN removed the long ban on traditional firecrackers during Tet, which set in motion a booming business in manufacturing and imports. The wealthy Vietnamese were particularly fond of firecrackers imported from Hong Kong, whose machinegun-like noise was rhythmically accentuated by big booms that sounded like grenade explosions. The GVN Ministry of Information went all out in its public relations campaign, distributing Tet presents for the troops and the underprivileged. Each gift parcel contained, in addition to the usual toilet articles, a horoscope predicting among other things a bright future for South Vietnam in the Year of the Monkey and, naturally, disaster for the Communists.

On New Year's Day some piecemeal information was circulated among the Saigon population to the effect that the enemy was attacking a few cities across the country. But this information created only a small ripple of concern not strong enough to distract people from celebrating.

Then, during the night, amid the deafening noise and echo of unending firecrackers, there were also heard more distinct, sharper reports of AK-47 and RPM automatic rifle rounds interspersed by B-40 rocket thuds. But no one seemed to recognize these ominous sounds until dawn, when early commuters bumped into strange faces, strange uniforms, and the distinctive "Binh Tri Thien" rubber sandals in some city quarters. Then it was too late; the surprise had been almost total.

• • •

II. NORTH VIETNAM'S CHANGE OF STRATEGY AND PREPARATION FOR THE GENERAL OFFENSIVE– GENERAL UPRISING

Communist Strategy in South Vietnam during the 1965–1966 and 1966–1967 Dry Seasons

The Communists' foremost concern after the rapid buildup of US and Free World troops in South Vietnam was to search for an appropriate strategy to confront the new war situation.

This task was not an easy one. In the first place, Communist military leaders seemed to know very little about US forces. In an article written in 1967 under the pen name of Truong Son, one of the highest-ranking Communist military leaders in South Vietnam admitted that during the summer of 1966, one year after the US had begun its force buildup, COSVN and its key military commanders were still probing desperately to resolve puzzling questions concerning US strategy and total strength, specific capabilities of each major US unit, and American rules of activity.

Nguyen Chi Thanh, commander of all Communist forces in the COSVN area of South Vietnam, analyzed the balance of forces and recognized that US forces enjoyed three advantages: great numerical strength, a powerful air force, and sizable artillery and armor. In his quest for an appropriate strategy to offset the imbalance of forces which was increasingly tilting in favor of the US-RVN side, Thanh strongly advocated the large-scale offensive approach. He believed that his side should take advantage of the offensive momentum gained during the dry season prior to the introduction of US forces and carry it on with major-scale attacks by main force units. This strategic approach naturally called for a bigger commitment of NVA forces.

• • •

[Thus] Thanh concluded that the most effective strategy was to conduct the offensive on all battlefronts continuously and with determination. He believed that this was the only way to gain the initiative in the conduct of the war.

Truong Son also shared this concept. Echoing Thanh's lines, he propounded that to make it impossible for the United States to take advantage of its superiority in air and firepower, the most effective approach would be to launch close-range attacks on head-quarters, bases, and troop cantonments on a massive scale. He was convinced that the Communist side would be much better off with this approach than hesitatingly search-ing for any other strategy which involved no immediate and decisive action. To waver, he argued, would bring forth disastrous consequences.

Successive surges of Communist activities during the 1965–1966 dry season seemed to reflect Nguyen Chi Thanh's strategy of determined confrontation. As these activities eventually ended in failure, especially after the tragic defeat at Plei Me, North Vietnam's military leaders began to voice doubts and criticize Thanh's conduct of the war.

Without directly incriminating Thanh, Vo Nguyen Giap made a cool assessment of the war situation in South Vietnam and advocated a temporary regression to defensive warfare. He believed that Communist forces were not yet ready to confront American superiority in combat strength and firepower. A more appropriate strategy, he argued, would be to focus on small-scale harassment attacks, guerrilla-style, consolidate the de-fense posture, and buy time for the activation, training, and infiltration of additional NVA units. Only then would Communist forces in South Vietnam be prepared for the offensive phase of warfare.

Giap's moderate stance was rejected by Nguyen Chi Thanh. To drive home his dis-pleasure with North Vietnam's minister of defense, Thanh acrimoniously attacked those he considered "conservative and captive of old methods and past experience." "Because these people could not see beyond their past," he charged, "they thought only of me-chanically repeating the past and were incapable of analyzing the concrete local situa-tion which required an entirely new kind of response."

The conflict that broke out between Giap and Thanh remained unresolved. After the 1966–1967 dry season, during which US forces successfully stepped up search-and-destroy operations, the old polemic resumed with rekindled [passion]. Each kept reiter-ating his own arguments, and neither seemed amenable to a reconciled viewpoint. The enemy's quest for a most appropriate strategy to meet the US challenge in South Viet-nam thus remained an issue open to debates.

• • •

In spite of Hanoi's official stance, Nguyen Chi Thanh did not renounce his con-viction. In a last analysis, written in May 1967, in which he made an assessment of the 1966–1967 dry season campaigns, Thanh still maintained his view, although he was more cognizant of the role and value of guerrilla and local forces in South Vietnam.

This polemical impasse among Communist generals on which kind of strategy was best for the prosecution of the war was not resolved until the death of Nguyen Chi Thanh, which was announced on 6 July 1967.[1] What followed in the wake of his death seemed to vindicate Vo Nguyen Giap's viewpoint and took the war on a new course. Giap's viewpoint was thoroughly discussed in a lengthy article published in the *People's*

Army daily on 14 and 16 September 1967 and subsequently broadcast by Hanoi Radio. The article was pompously entitled "Big Victory, Gigantic Task."

Vo Nguyen Giap's Strategic Viewpoint after the 1966–1967 Dry Season

"Big Victory, Gigantic Task" was actually the fourth article Giap wrote during 1967. In terms of content, it was considered the most significant because it accurately expounded North Vietnam's military strategy for the years ahead. More importantly, it seemed to highlight Giap's viewpoints, which were going to provide guidance for Communist forces in South Vietnam. Unlike Nguyen Chi Thanh, Tran Van Tra (his successor) adhered completely [to] the policies and viewpoints of Vo Nguyen Giap.[2]

• • •

Appraising his main opponent, Giap demonstrated how people's war activities had kept them dispersed over vast areas, pointing as examples to the DMZ, where US marines were spread thinly over a defense perimeter 500 to 600 kilometers long, and the Central Highlands, where US Army units had to defend an area of more than 200 square kilometers. Giap recognized that US firepower was strong and considerable, especially B-52s, but this firepower was not effective because, in people's war, objectives were scattered almost everywhere.

Strategically, Giap was convinced that, in its role as the world's fire brigade, the United States could not maintain a large military force in South Vietnam for any long period. He believed that the United States would be worn down by the war and sooner or later would have to negotiate for its end on terms foreseen as advantageous to the Communist side.

As a result, US and Free World troops were the primary targets for attack on the Communist list of priorities, followed by US bases and the US logistic system. The Communist objective was to inflict as many casualties on US troops as possible. Attacks on the RVNAF and the GVN were considered only as third and fourth priorities.

• • •

Predicting the future course of events, Vo Nguyen Giap estimated that the United States would expand the war into Cambodia, Laos, and possibly North Vietnam also, where a major landing of US forces could take place. Giap's concern about a US landing was genuine and [worrisome] enough to prompt him to warn that, in such an event, Red China would probably intervene. In any event, he insinuated that North Vietnam would be well prepared to counter it.

Up to this time Giap had always emphasized that the war in South Vietnam was a protracted one and that it might last five, ten, or twenty years or even longer. This line of thought happened to be a mimic of Ho Chi Minh's declaration of policy made at the outbreak of the war. It was also reiterated by Nguyen Chi Thanh in his last article published in May 1967.

Giap's article, therefore, sounded like a confirmation of North Vietnam's unflinching belief in the doctrine of protracted warfare. His words were unfortunately taken at their face value and completely misled our analysts.

Not knowing that Giap's writing was intended to stimulate South Vietnamese insurgents on the one hand, and to confuse our side as to North Vietnam's true course of action on the other, our analysts hastily concluded, in the light of Giap's article, that North Vietnam was yet to show that it was prepared for a general offensive in the near future. In all likelihood, they estimated, North Vietnam was still pursuing a protracted course of warfare and far from willing to bypass its intermediary phase.

In fact the North Vietnamese leadership had already decided differently. There were several reasons for North Vietnam to make the strategic decision to launch a general offensive in South Vietnam during the 1967–1968 dry season.

Reasons for the 1968 General Offensive and Communist Preparations

Vo Nguyen Giap revealed that he was primarily concerned about two things. First, the United States would probably expand the war beyond South Vietnam's territory, and second the GVN pacification and development program would be successful.[3]

• • •

Despite its advocacy of protracted warfare conceived as antidote to the US strategy of quick victory, North Vietnam began to feel its increasingly debilitating impact. Even while it argued that the ratio of human losses, which stood at one American for every ten North Vietnamese, was more of a concern to the United States, the Hanoi leadership was having second thoughts. In fact, the effect of accumulated damage and casualties that the North Vietnamese population was suffering had generated an undercurrent of bitterness and frustration that might jeopardize the long-term war effort.

• • •

One week before the general offensive actually took place, the RVN suddenly obtained an unprecedented intelligence windfall in the person of a high-ranking enemy prisoner. He was Nam Dong, political commissar of the enemy MR-6 headquarters, captured in an ambush while he was on his way back from a conference at COSVN. After intensive interrogation lasting several weeks, Nam Dong disclosed that North Vietnam was switching its strategy from protracted warfare to general offensive–general uprising, a radical departure from the conduct of the 1946–1954 First Indochina War.

• • •

One strategic opportunity was the US presidential election in November 1968. Hanoi believed that in the event of a Communist victory the Johnson administration, which had already run into difficulties because of strong domestic opposition to the war, would no longer be able to bring more troops to South Vietnam. Eventually, it might even be compelled to reduce US troop strength and seek negotiations on terms advantageous to the Communist side.

The other strategic opportunity, according to Nam Dong, came from increasing opposition, both domestic and international, to US intervention in Vietnam. Therefore a big Communist victory would make this opposition stronger and more widespread, which in all likelihood would force the United States to terminate its involvement in Vietnam against its own will.

As to the tactical advantage, the Communists felt certain they would be able to achieve surprise. Therefore, Nam Dong revealed, Hanoi had decided to launch the general offensive during the Tet holidays.

• • •

The Communists were well aware that they would suffer great losses when attacking the cities. But losses were not North Vietnam's main concern, Nam Dong argued, because its capacities for replacement had been estimated at about three times those of South Vietnam.

There were other advantages which North Vietnam thought would favor the Communist side. It believed that the RVNAF was no longer combat effective, both in defensive and offensive maneuvers. The South Vietnamese people, Hanoi believed, hated Americans and the Thieu government. They had manifested their antipathy through frequent demonstrations and violence and by joining such popular organizations as the National Salvation and Buddhist movements. Hanoi was thus convinced that they were ripe for insurrection and ready to join the Communist side in the event of a general offensive.

In all respects Nam Dong's deposition proved to be reliable. His revelations corroborated several unconfirmed reports, for example Vo Nguyen Giap's interest in the 1968 US presidential election. Even though Giap wrote in his article that such an election was merely a device for the US party in power to reshuffle its ranks, and that the US policy of aggression would remain unchanged regardless of the election outcome, Hanoi in reality was well aware of the fact that in an election year a US president was seldom inclined to make bold policy decisions.

• • •

Hanoi's belief in the support of the South Vietnamese population was further enhanced by the RVN presidential election in the fall of 1967 in which the winning slate of President Nguyen Van Thieu and Vice President Nguyen Cao Ky obtained only 34 percent of the popular vote. Evidence of popular sympathy was obvious when the runner-up candidate, Truong Dinh Dzu, collected 17 percent of the ballots on the basis of his "restoring peace and ending the war" platform, which happened to concur with the NLF political line.[4]

The Communists estimated therefore that a general offensive against South Vietnam's cities would have the inevitable effect of a catalyst which initiated a popular insurrection.

• • •

To prepare for that big event, North Vietnam evidently required special assistance from Russia and Red China, not only in military hardware but also, though not as urgent, in economic aid. The insistent quest for this assistance eventually resulted in a military aid package agreement between Moscow and Hanoi in early September 1967. Russia agreed to provide North Vietnam with additional warplanes, rockets, antiaircraft artillery, armored vehicles, infantry weapons, and ammunition. Then, in October 1967, Hanoi announced that Communist bloc countries, especially Russia and Red China, had agreed to increase military and economic aid to North Vietnam.

This increased military aid eventually found its way into South Vietnam, where Communist infantry forces, with the AK-47 assault rifle and B-40 rocket launcher now becoming standard issues, began to enjoy a marked advantage over the RVNAF in terms of firepower.[5]

• • •

The earliest evidence of preparatory activity dated back to March or April 1967, when North Vietnam confirmed its switch of strategy through the promulgation of Resolution No. 13. A short time later the first instance of political preparation was detected in May [of] the same year, when COSVN summoned the deputy chairman of Saigon–Gia Dinh's Committee for the Proselytizing of Intellectuals and assigned him the mission to contact and keep close touch with those personalities earmarked by the Communists to take part in future coalition government.

• • •

Apparently, however, the Communists foresaw that, even if their offensive was to succeed militarily, they could never actually defeat both the RVNAF and US forces in South Vietnam. Therefore, as enemy ralliers and prisoners later disclosed, the offensive was primarily targeted against RVNAF and GVN installations. US forces did not interest Communist strategists, because the main objective was to destroy the RVNAF and overthrow the RVN government through countrywide popular revolt. In such an event, US bases and installations would become virtually isolated, and US forces would never dare to use firepower indiscriminately against Communist forces hidden behind the popular shield. In the end, as the Communists calculated, the United States would have its hands so tied that it would be compelled to negotiate for troop withdrawal with the new (coalition) government of South Vietnam.

• • •

On the military front, as diversionary actions, Communist forces launched several large-scale attacks against Khe Sanh Base in the DMZ area, Dak To in the Central Highlands, and Phuoc Long and Loc Ninh farther south near the Cambodian border. All of these attacks were aimed at drawing the concern of US and RVN military leaders, forcing them to bring forth reinforcements which would otherwise have been committed to the defense of populous and urban areas, hence at the same time creating favorable conditions for sapper penetrations into cities.

• • •

According to the enemy's concept of operation, infiltrated sapper units were the primary forces employed to attack important targets and headquarters in cities, with the support of local-force battalions. Once these objectives had been occupied, the attacking elements were to hold them at all costs for a period from two to five days to afford main-force units the necessary time to move in as reinforcements.

• • •

The infiltration of weapons and ammunition into cities was subjected to meticulous planning in order to avoid detection. Toward that end, it was coordinated with and took advantage of normal traffic movements of goods and merchandise regularly delivered to urban markets. These movements were accelerated during the busy trade periods such as Christmas, New Year, and particularly during the pre-Tet week when traffic was heaviest and control usually more relaxed.

Although various techniques of infiltration were used, the most common and reliable turned out to be the one practice so familiar to smugglers: double-decked trucks and boats and concealment beneath cargoes. Once the weapons, explosives, and ammunition had been successfully smuggled in, they were to be distributed among the VCI members, who would keep them . . . in their own houses or hide them in such unsuspected areas as cemeteries, drainage ditches, and garbage dumps.

• • •

For those units that were slated to attack first, combat orders were issued only 48 to 72 hours prior to action. And, contrary to usual operational practice, unit missions and terrain studies were simply discussed to an extent considered reasonably compatible with local combat requirements. As a result, no unit commander from the middle level down ever knew that the attack he was going to conduct was part of a countrywide general offensive.

• • •

III. THE RVN AND ENEMY PREPARATIONS

How Much Did We Know?

In March 1967 ARVN units captured an enemy document during an operation in the III Corps area. The document, which belonged to the enemy CT-5 Division, discussed summarily a plan of attack against Saigon. This plan was rudimentary and so amateurishly prepared that both ARVN and US intelligence analysts [dismissed] it as pure fantasy.

Two months later, the National Police apprehended a high-ranking enemy cadre by the name of Ba Tra. He declared being deputy chairman of the Committee for the Proselytizing of Intellectuals for the Saigon-Cholon area. Among documents seized from his possession there was a list naming a few members of the Saigon intelligentsia. Ba Tra disclosed that they were the personalities whom the NLF earmarked as cabinet members of a future coalition government of South Vietnam. His mission was to contact, persuade, and prepare them for selected cabinet-rank positions in that government. This was the first time that information on a Communist-sponsored coalition government in South Vietnam was ever obtained. The motives behind this project, and the objectives contemplated, remained unclear however.

• • •

When North Vietnam made public the text of Vo Nguyen Giap's article "Big Victory, Giant Task," which Hanoi Radio carried from 14 to 16 September 1967 in its daily programs, South Vietnam immediately sensed that something new had been brought into enemy war policies. As usual, Communist rhetoric only made sense if read between the lines. A change in strategy seemed transparent enough, but nobody could decipher exactly what direction it would take.

Not until early October was ARVN intelligence able to obtain, through its agent network, the first lead of that new strategic direction: Resolution No. 13 of North Vietnam's Politburo. In no-nonsense terms Resolution No. 13 called for victory in a short time and prescribed the strategy of large-scale offensive to achieve it.

• • •

On 25 October 1967 still another important enemy document fell into our hands in Tay Ninh Province. Dated 1 September 1967, it contained these introductory remarks: "This is instructional material to help better understand the new situation and our new task." Apparently it was intended for midlevel cadres. The document consisted of two parts, the first part outlining the main objective to be achieved by Communist forces—ending the American presence in South Vietnam. This was to be accomplished by the establishment of a coalition government, and the NLF would be playing a major role in arranging for the American exit. The second part of the document discussed the strategy of [a] "three-pronged offensive" designed to: (1) defeat the RVNAF; (2) destroy US political and military institutions [*sic*]; and (3) instigate a countrywide insurrection of the popular masses. This projected offensive bore the abbreviated designation TCK-TKN, which stood for Tong Cong Kich–Tong Khoi Nghia (General Offensive–General Uprising).

• • •

Another enemy document seized in Quang Tin Province, I Corps area, in November provided substantial detail on the General Offensive–General Uprising that was about to unfold. A passage in the document read, in fact: "This is the time we should proceed with our General Offensive–General Uprising. Through the coordinated use of military forces combined with a countrywide popular uprising, we shall attack every provincial city, and every district town, including the capital, Saigon, which we shall liberate."

• • •

At 2100 hours on 30 January an RF element tending an ambush on the Saigon defense perimeter captured an enemy soldier with an AK-47. The prisoner disclosed that Communist troops were going to attack Saigon, Tan Son Nhut Air Base, the Joint General Staff compound, and [the] Saigon Radio station at 0300 hours on 31 January 1968. This happened to be just a few hours away. And the attack on Saigon, as it turned out, began exactly at 0300 hours on 31 January 1968, in the small hours of the second day of Tet.

The Surprise: Why?

One thing was certain. The enemy had really achieved the element of surprise. The surprise was so total that, even though he was informed of all developments in the enemy situation which I have summarized, President Thieu at the last minute did not take any significant action to counter the enemy's move. Apparently he did not believe that things could develop as indicated by a few intelligence reports. At the time the fighting erupted across the country he was at My Tho for a Tet reunion with his wife's family.

Even after fighting had erupted at several places in Saigon, and despite an announcement made by Vice President Nguyen Cao Ky over Saigon Radio in which he appealed to our population to stay calm, many people still thought that it was simply a coup. Many others said they could not believe their eyes when, in the early morning of 31 January, they saw troops in palm-leafed hats and black rubber sandals, Binh-Tri-Thien style. That these Communist troops could actually establish themselves in some of the city blocks of Saigon was simply an incredible accomplishment.

It was thus obvious that, on our part, nobody was convinced that the Communists would launch a concerted offensive against cities and towns across the country during the Tet holidays.

• • •

With the information available to South Vietnam, it was true that the enemy hardly had the capabilities for such an ambitious action. Most intelligence data collected on the enemy during the period prior to the offensive either indicated that his units were facing difficulties or that the morale of his troops had declined markedly. Furthermore, given the prevailing balance of forces and the deployment and disposition of enemy main-force units at that time, which showed that they were still confined to outlying areas far removed from urban centers, there was little possibility that the enemy could initiate a general offensive, regardless of his intention. Our analysts further argued that, even though the enemy was bold enough to attack and successfully occupy part of a city or a district town, how was he ever capable of holding it for any long period? Besides, it was hardly possible that the enemy would want to incur inevitable heavy losses for something predictably ephemeral.

• • •

Vo Nguyen Giap's article "Big Victory, Giant Task" also contributed its part to the serious error committed by our intelligence analysts. The idea which influenced them most was Giap's contention that the war was going to last many more years. With this clue, they finally concluded that the General Offensive–General Uprising to which enemy documents referred would not materialize in the immediate future.

• • •

But the biggest shortcoming of our intelligence structure was perhaps the almost total lack of coordination between agencies, or the lack of a coordinating agency. This shortcoming came to our attention as early as in 1960–1961, [but] was never remedied and remained a significant weakness until 1968, despite the creation of the Central Intelligence Organization (CIO), which was directly under presidential control.

• • •

As for US military intelligence, there was no doubt that it was highly successful on collecting information through technical facilities. At the time of the 1968 Tet Offensive, however, the United States did not appear to be as capable in the production of intelligence as during the subsequent stages of the war. Additionally it appeared that US intelligence suffered from the same subjectivity that plagued its ARVN counterpart. Obviously US military intelligence also failed to come to any solid conclusion as far as the scope, size, and timing of the enemy offensive were concerned.

• • •

In the light of available information, our RVN intelligence estimated, therefore, that the Communists would launch a major offensive campaign whose principal objectives were the Khe Sanh Base, the strongpoints south of the DMZ, and other friendly bases along the western borders of II and III Corps areas. This estimate coincided with the personal views of our field commanders and national leader.

• • •

On the afternoon of 29 January, contents of . . . two prerecorded tapes seized from the enemy at Qui Nhon by the MSS were transmitted back to II Corps headquarters and the Joint Operations Center, JGS, via hot lines. General Cao Van Vien, Chief of the JGS, immediately ordered his J-3 to call all corps commanders, warn them of the imminent enemy attack, and instruct them to take appropriate defensive measures. Whether all corps commanders took this warning seriously, or how they implemented the J-3 instructions, [was] not clear at the time. In any event, many ARVN commanders later claimed that this warning failed to communicate any true sense of urgency.

• • •

The uninterrupted noise of firecrackers continued to echo throughout the city at all hours, even during the night. And, when the first enemy rounds were fired at 0200 on 1 February, they blended into this noisy background. A few hours earlier, at around midnight, many Saigon people saw groups of armed men moving silently in the dark in some street blocks. Most thought that perhaps a coup was unfolding.

And so the attack of Saigon, which rolled up the curtain for the countrywide 1968 enemy offensive, took place at a time and against objectives our people least expected.

IV. THE GENERAL OFFENSIVE, PHASE I

A Bird's-Eye View

The countrywide attacks that made up the 1968 Tet Offensive did not all occur at the same time. Twenty-four hours before the actual offensive began, five provincial capitals of II Corps area—Nha Trang, Ban Me Thuot, Kontum, Pleiku, and Qui Nhon—and Danang city in I Corps area were already under attack.

• • •

By general consensus, it was agreed that the date of the offensive was 31 January 1968, the day the enemy attacked Saigon, Cholon, and Gia Dinh. Other cities and provincial capitals that came under attack on the same day as Saigon were Quang Tri, Hue, Quang Tin, Quang Ngai in I Corps area; Phan Thiet in II Corps area; and Can Tho and Vinh Long in IV Corps area.

The next day, 1 February, the enemy initiated attacks on Bien Hoa, Long Khanh, Binh Duong in III Corps area; and Kien Hoa, Dinh Tuong, Go Cong, Kien Giang, Vinh Binh, and Kien Tuong in IV Corps area. The latest attack in date, which took place on 10 February, was on Bac Lieu in IV Corps area. In total, 28 out of South Vietnam's 48 cities and provincial capitals had become objectives of the general offensive. The ones that had been spared were regarded by the enemy as insignificant and subjected only to minor harassments.

Regardless of the size and importance of the objective, the enemy followed exactly the same pattern of attack. His primary targets remained without exception the highest local RVNAF headquarters and the radio broadcasting station. The forces that conducted the initial attack were all local units, sappers, and VCI elements. Their mission was to capture and hold designated targets until reinforcements could move in from outside the city. Accompanying the attacking elements were political cadres who had the responsibility to coax the local population into rebellion.

At Danang, the seat of I Corps headquarters and one of the first two objectives to come under attack in this corps area, Colonel Nguyen Duy Hinh, acting Chief of Staff, I Corps, received a phone call from the JGS in Saigon at about 2000 on 29 January. The JGS informed him that the enemy would probably initiate an increased surge of activities and admonished caution and defensive measures. After reporting to Lieutenant General Hoang Xuan Lam, I Corps commander, and acting on his instructions, Colonel Hinh informed all subordinate units and asked them to carry out the JGS orders.

At about 0300 on 30 January the enemy began to attack Hoi An, the provincial capital of Quang Nam, some 30 kilometers south of Danang. Half an hour later Colonel Hinh heard many shots being fired at the I Corps headquarters. From his house, only 500 meters away, he saw brilliant tracers ricocheting upward from the stream of cross fire. "Enemy attack," he thought to himself as he picked up the telephone to inform the I Corps commander. As Colonel Hinh vividly recalled, General Lam's first reaction was an expression of incredulity: "Baloney, baloney," he said, interrupting Colonel Hinh's verbal report.

• • •

In II Corps area, Nha Trang was the first city to be attacked during the 1968 general offensive. The enemy attack took place at 0030 on 31 January, just after the Tet midnight rite had been performed. . . .

• • •

At Kontum, Pleiku, and Ban Me Thuot, the three Central Highlands provincial cities which all came under attack on the day before the offensive began, the enemy pattern of attack was almost identical. At each place, sapper elements would penetrate the city first, to be immediately followed by a main-force regiment.

• • •

In the III Corps area the enemy concentrated his primary effort on Saigon, [Cholon], and Gia Dinh, which made up the Saigon metropolitan area. His effort here was closely coordinated with other attacks throughout the corps area which, according to plans, proceeded at a frenetic pace in Bien Hoa, Binh Duong, Long Khanh, Long An, and Hau Nghia.

In the IV Corps area enemy attacks were conducted against 13 out of 16 provincial cities. The offensive was therefore most extensive, despite the absence of NVA units.

• • •

Despite heavy fighting at some places, in general the enemy's offensive seemed to run out of steam by the end of the first week. In most provincial cities, friendly control was thoroughly regained in less than one week. Two exceptions to this were Saigon and Hue, the current and ancient capitals of the nation, respectively. The political significance of these cities was evident enough. It was where the enemy concentrated most of his determined efforts.

The Attack on Saigon

As the enemy offensive unfolded in Saigon during the night of Tet's first day (31 January 1968), six major objectives became apparent: the RVNAF Joint General Staff, the Independence Palace, the US Embassy, Tan Son Nhut Air Base, the National Broadcasting Station, and the Vietnamese Navy headquarters. . . .

Except for Tan Son Nhut, the primary enemy force that conducted attacks against these objectives was the C-10 City Sapper Battalion. With a strength of 250, the C-10 Battalion consisted entirely of men who were living under a perfect cover within Saigon; they were, therefore, thoroughly familiar with city life and the streets of Saigon. Some of them were cyclopousse or taxicab drivers.

• • •

The attack on Gate No. 5 of the JGS compound took place at 0200. Part of the C-10 sapper platoon which was to conduct the attack arrived on a bus, but several of its members had already taken position in the Long Hoa Pagoda just across the street. When the bus stopped in front of the gate, the sapper contingent jumped out, attempting to run through the gate, usually kept closed, which was just opened to let a general officer in. Precisely at that moment a US MP patrol jeep happened to pass by. As enemy sappers momentarily turned their attention to the jeep and opened fire on it, the ARVN guard closed the gate and fired back from a side bunker. The US jeep under attack was immediately reinforced by US MP personnel from BOQ No. 3 and other US installations nearby. The enemy attack on Gate No. 5 ended in complete failure.

• • •

At noon a US helicopter landed in the JGS compound and out stepped President Thieu. He immediately convened a meeting with several members of his cabinet who, since the enemy attack began, had found their way individually into the JGS compound. The JGS thus temporarily turned into an alternate Independence Palace where measures were being taken to counter the enemy offensive despite the uneasy fact that fighting was no more than one kilometer away.

• • •

The attack on the Independence Palace was also conducted by a 34-man platoon of the C-10 Sapper Battalion. At 0130 on 31 January this platoon placed B-40 fire on the staff entrance gate of the palace on Nguyen Du Street and attempted to crash through. The palace security forces, which were made up of the Presidential Guard, police, MPs, and two tanks, reacted forcefully and immediately stopped the sappers' assault. Driven back, the enemy took refuge in an unfinished high-rise building across the street. During the next two days, except for two of its men captured alive, the entire sapper platoon was killed.

• • •

Three blocks away, a similar suicidal attack was attempted against the US Embassy on Thong Nhat Boulevard. This enemy force consisted of 19 sappers, all from the C-10 Battalion, equipped with B-40 rocket launchers and explosives. A few succeeded in penetrating the front yard but could not get into the locked building. By the next morning, all 19 sappers had been killed.

In the attack against the National Broadcasting Station, enemy sappers disguised themselves as field police troopers. This C-10 sapper element rapidly overwhelmed the field police squad defending the station for broadcasting, because it was just an audio and recording studio. The chief of the transmitter station, which was located at Quan Tre several miles away, was resourceful enough to switch off the remote audio lines from the main studio as soon as it was occupied. He then used a standby studio equipped with tape recorders. Saigon Radio therefore continued to broadcast without interruption, using primarily prerecorded programs. Nobody ever detected anything abnormal on the airwaves.

At 0500 the airborne company, which was assuming alert duties at the MSS compound nearby, deployed its troops to the radio station. After less than two hours of fighting the paratroopers destroyed the entire sapper element and captured the station. By 0700 the main studio was functioning again and started its regular program of the day with Vice President Nguyen Cao Ky's announcement and appeal to the population.

• • •

At Tan Son Nhut, a major attack was driven against the airport by three enemy battalions, two of them local force and one from the 9th Division. This enemy force simultaneously attacked Gates No. 10, No. 51, and No. 2 at 0300.

Approaching the airport from the Vinatexco textile plant located to the west, where the enemy had established a field command post and positioned antiaircraft weapons on the roof of the building, the enemy force broke through Gate No. 51 and advanced about 200 meters inside the fence, moving toward the main runway. But here the enemy met with fierce resistance from airport security forces, which consisted of Vice President Ky's security guard, the National Police, and paratroopers who defended their rear base nearby. Friendly forces were also joined by two USARV platoons.

Almost immediately two companies of the 8th Airborne Battalion, which was waiting for air transportation in the military terminal, arrived as reinforcement. As a result, the enemy suffered substantial losses and was unable to make any progress. At the same time the 3rd Armored [Cavalry] Squadron of the US 25th Infantry Division at Cu Chi began its movement toward Tan Son Nhut after an emergency request for relief by US forces at the airport. On its way to Tan Son Nhut the US armor column was guided by air-dropped flares and took cross-country shortcuts, bypassing the embattled area of Hoc Mon and probably ambush sites. At daybreak, the column entered Tan Son Nhut and inflicted serious losses to the enemy force, which was compelled to fall back to the Vinatexco area.

At 0900 VNAF and USAF tactical air attacked the Vinatexco compound, inflicting further losses to the enemy. Around Gate No. 51, site of the most furious fighting, over 300 enemy troops lay dead. At Gate No. 2, meanwhile, the fierce resistance put up by the ARVN 2nd Service Battalion effectively kept the enemy at bay.

Despite the rapid restoration of friendly control at these major objectives, by daybreak enemy local forces had penetrated several areas in western and southern Saigon. At Cholon, one enemy local-force battalion had penetrated and occupied the Phu Tho Racetrack. As the enemy saw it, the Phu Tho Racetrack was a critical strongpoint for his efforts, because its occupation would deny our forces a large field which they could use to bring in reinforcements by helicopters. This racetrack also lay adjacent to a critical junction of major roads between Saigon and Cholon, and provided an excellent staging area for assembling and dispatching troops. From this area enemy 82mm mortars could also effectively support any combat action or shell any target in Saigon or Cholon, to include the Tan Son Nhut Air Base.

The next mission to be accomplished by the enemy local-force battalion occupying the Phu Tho Racetrack was to attack the Chi Hoa prison complex and free Communist detainees. However, this battalion lost contact with its two local guides and did not know the way to reach Chi Hoa, barely two kilometers away. Since most of the local population in the area had fled, and those who remained tactfully refused to serve as guides, the enemy battalion found itself confined to the racetrack. The Chi Hoa prison complex remained untouched even during the subsequent phases of the offensive.

• • •

The enemy also attacked Camp Phu Dong, which was the headquarters of the ARVN Armor Command. Since the purpose of the attack was to capture ARVN armored vehicles, the enemy force included an element of COSVN's 16th Section, which specialized in armor employment and tactics. Even though the enemy had made careful preparations, his reconnaissance had failed to reveal that all ARVN armored vehicles on the base had been moved elsewhere two months earlier.

• • •

By the end of the first 48 hours, it was obvious that the enemy chance of success had greatly diminished. Not a single major objective in Saigon was in his hands, and the promised reinforcements were nowhere in sight. Hopes of a popular uprising also began to falter.

• • •

During this time the Saigon VCI proved to be extremely active. Many of its members served as guides for the attacking units. A few of them were actually holding jobs in US and GVN agencies. Among those killed during the offensive, one even had a CMD-issued pass authorizing him to circulate during curfew hours. Several others had passes allowing them access to some US civilian installations. When the attack on Saigon began, believing that the offensive and uprising were going to be a success, most of the city's VCI members surfaced and participated in subversive activities. They performed many useful tasks in support of the attacking forces, serving as guides and informants in the areas under Communist control, where they helped search and arrest GVN officials, policemen, and military officers. They acted as propagandists, encouraging the people and inciting them to revolt and demonstrate in support of the "liberation" forces. As a result of these supporting activities, the enemy local forces that attacked Saigon and Cholon were able to move around in a metropolitan area that was obviously too large, too populous, too strange, and whose modern facilities and civilization remained beyond their realm of knowledge.

By this time as many as 15 enemy battalions had been introduced into the general area that comprised Saigon, Cholon, and part of Gia Dinh Province. They had occupied a northern suburb of Saigon, the 7th and 8th Precincts in Cholon, the Phu Tho Racetrack, and part of a few city blocks in Saigon itself. They broke down into small elements, taking shelter in people's homes, organizing defense positions in high-rise buildings, and awaiting the reinforcement of main-force units which were to move in from the outside as planned.

• • •

At Bien Hoa, the enemy 5th Division attacked simultaneously the US Army base at Long Binh, the Bien Hoa Air Base, and III Corps headquarters, but missed the Communist prisoner camp near the city because of confusion. The two companies of the 275th Regiment that received the mission to attack this camp, in coordination with another element, had been instructed to move to a rendezvous point which was formerly a rubber plantation nearby. Unfortunately for the enemy, this rubber plantation had been cleared a month earlier by Rome plows. So, when they arrived at the rendezvous point and found that no rubber plantation was in sight, the two companies moved to another area, missing the attack.

At the Bien Hoa Air Force Base the attack driven by the enemy 274th Regiment was completely stalled by fierce resistance put up by the defending RF battalion after the eastern end of the runway had been penetrated. At III Corps headquarters, meanwhile, even though the attacking enemy local-force battalion had been reinforced by one battalion of the 5th Division, it was unable to break through the defense perimeter. Shortly thereafter, the intervention of the US 11th Armored Cavalry Regiment finally shattered all enemy efforts at both places. At Long Binh, despite detailed planning, the enemy was able only to blow up a few ammunition dumps on the base.

• • •

In general, enemy attacks in the provinces surrounding Saigon were all short-lived, lasting no longer than one day on the average. The enemy not only lacked the capability to hold, he also met with swift and forceful reactions by the local defending forces. As it turned out, most RF battalions performed unexpectedly well, fighting courageously in defense and counterattacking with enthusiastic vigor, aided in their efforts by US infantry units, armor, artillery, and gunships. As a result, targets temporarily overrun by the enemy at the beginning of the attack were all retaken within a short time.

The most sustained enemy effort in III Corps area remained locked in Saigon, his primary objective, where fighting was still raging. After the initial shock of surprise, however, ARVN and US forces began to counterattack and seize the initiative.

Clearing Operations in Saigon

At the time the enemy attacked Saigon, ARVN forces available for the defense of the city consisted of eight infantry battalions. These did not include the three RF battalions, two MP battalions, and two service battalions which were detached piecemeal for guard and security duties at military and governmental installations, checkpoints, and bridges.

The first action taken by the Joint General Staff after the attack on Saigon was to call general reserve units back for the immediate relief of the city. Within 48 hours, therefore, an additional seven infantry battalions had been brought back because of fast transportation facilities available. By the end of the third day of the attack, RVNAF forces in the Saigon area had increased to a total of five airborne battalions, five marine battalions, five ranger battalions, [and] one artillery battalion which had all been withdrawn from their previous commitment in II, III, and IV Corps. The recall of these forces had not been easy. With heavy combat burdens on their own shoulders, the II and IV Corps commanders were particularly reluctant to release them.

With additional forces available, the JGS decided to launch a major relief operation to clear enemy troops from the nation's capital. Lieutenant General Nguyen Duc Thang, then minister of rural development and former J-3 of the JGS, came up with a plan which was quickly approved and code-named after the JGS compound's designation, Tran Hung Dao. Because of the significance of the relief operation, General Cao Van Vien, Chief of the JGS, took personal command.

The concept of operation was based on the idea of organizing Saigon and its suburbs into several areas of operation and assigning each area or zone to a specific service or combat arm. Initially there were five areas of operation or zones, designated A, B, C, D, and E. Zone A was assigned to the Airborne Division, because it was where its headquarters was based. Zone B was assigned to the Marine Division for the same reason. Zone C, which was essentially downtown Saigon and relatively more secure, was made the responsibility of the National Police. At that time total NP strength in Saigon, to include field police forces, numbered in excess of 20,000. Zone D, which included the Chinatown in Cholon, was assigned to the RVNAF Ranger Command. Zone E, which included Tran Hung Dao camp and the MACV compound, was made the responsibility of the JGS Headquarters Commandant. For the defense of this zone the JGS honor guard battalion was reinforced by four makeshift battalions which had been assembled with personnel of the JGS staff divisions and other service agencies located within the JGS compound and totalled 1,928 men, mostly officers and NCOs. The JGS staff divisions retained only about one-third of their personnel, those who were deemed utterly necessary for critical staff work. Zone F was added to the original plan only on 9 February. Since this area comprised mostly outlying suburbs, and the ARVN did not have enough forces to commit there, it was assigned to US forces.

• • •

Clearing activities were most vigorous during the week from 5 to 12 February, especially in Zone D, where it was difficult to uproot enemy elements nested in people's houses in a particularly dense area. In several cases our forces had to ask the people to leave the combat area before moving in. In addition to hit-and-run tactics, the enemy also positioned antiaircraft weapons on high-rise buildings, which seriously impeded support missions flown by gunships. Destroying these antiaircraft weapons was therefore a priority task for our forces.

In some areas in Cholon the enemy occupied several Buddhist temples and hospitals, using them as shelters or operational bases. The An Quang Pagoda, a celebrated Buddhist temple associated with the Buddhist militants of 1966, was used as a high-level headquarters. In their determination to destroy this enemy command post, our forces retook the pagoda with air support, even at the price of causing extensive damage to it. A short distance away, the Children's Hospital was also used as [a] troop cantonment and defense strongpoint.

• • •

The last major battle fought in Saigon took place in the Phu Dinh–Phu Lam area on 11 February. With the support of a US unit, ARVN ranger forces completely wiped out a high-level enemy command post located in the Phu Lam communal temple. Among the 30 enemy bodies found inside, there were six armed with pistols, an evident indication of high ranks. From the documents [found] on them we learned that the place had sheltered a protection element of COSVN's forward command post. Speculations therefore arose and spread about to the effect that Tran Do, the Communist general who directed the attack on Saigon, had been killed. However, a subsequent fingerprint check on the bodies found that Tran Do was not among them. Since the results of this fingerprint check were not made public, rumors of Tran Do's death persisted and accounted for a jubilant mood among the Saigon population and troops.

The fighting in Saigon abated immediately following this battle. On 17 February, however, it resumed with fresh intensity with the onset of a new series of attacks. These attacks began with fierce rocket fire striking at Tan Son Nhut and the MACV headquarters nearby, causing considerable damage to the air passenger terminal. Then enemy infantry troops moved in and pushed hard, primarily against Tan Son Nhut AFB, the area from Hoc Mon to Xom Moi in Go Vap, and the Phu Lam area south of Cholon.

The renewed attack lasted until early March, highlighted by several firefights inside Saigon and Cholon. Its intensity, however, was much less than that of Phase I.

• • •

Countrywide, meanwhile, the military situation improved remarkably. Mopping-up activities effectively cleared most cities and provincial capitals from the encroachment of enemy troops with the exception of Hue, where fighting [had been] raging ferociously since the beginning of the offensive. Here the loss in human lives incurred by the civilian population had reached the proportions of a natural disaster, which was made even more horrible by the mass massacre of approximately 4,000 people, all victims of Communist atrocities committed during the 25 days the city remained under their control.

The Battle of Hue

Hue, the ancient capital of Vietnam, had a population of approximately 140,000 at the time the enemy offensive began. It was the cradle of militant Buddhism, whose confrontation with President Ngo Dinh Diem in 1963 led to his death and the demise of his regime.

• • •

At the time the attack on Hue began, ARVN forces available in the city consisted solely of the headquarters of the 1st Infantry Division, which was located in Mang Ca, a small and isolated camp in the northern corner of the Old Citadel.

The square-shaped Old Citadel occupied an area whose outer perimeter consisted of a solid earth and stone rampart, 20 feet thick and from 25 to 30 feet high, surrounded by a zigzag moat. Inside this rampart, and at a distance varying from 20 to 80 yards from it, there was a brick wall. Both the rampart and the wall were built in 1802 under the reign of Emperor Gia Long, the forefather of the Nguyen dynasty.

Within the Old Citadel there were two areas of particular interest: the Imperial Palace, with its stately Midday Gate topped by a majestic flagpole, all constructed in ancient architectural style, and the Tay Loc Airfield, a product of modern times. South of the Old Citadel ran the River of Perfume, over which two bridges provided access to the more contemporary southern part of the city, Trang Tien and Bach Ho. On this southern bank of the river were located governmental and military installations such as the Thua Thien sector headquarters and the MACV compound.

No US combat unit was based in Hue city. The nearest US base was at Phu Bai, eight kilometers to the southeast, where the US 3rd Marine Division had established its headquarters.

As for ARVN forces, besides the 1st Infantry Division headquarters located inside the Old Citadel, the nearest combat units were the 7th Armored Cavalry Squadron at An Cuu, two kilometers to the southeast; and the 2nd Airborne Battalion, which established a temporary base near QL-1, 17 kilometers northwest of Hue in the vicinity of the "Street without Joy."

• • •

Lunar New Year's Day passed without event amid traditional celebrations. Then, past midnight, at 0340, the enemy struck with a fierce preparatory fire of 122mm rockets and 82mm mortars. The enemy forces which conducted the initial attack on Hue consisted of two infantry regiments, two sapper battalions, and one artillery (rocket) battalion, assisted by sappers already in place inside the city. According to plans, the 6th Regiment was to attack the Old Citadel and push its primary effort against the 1st Infantry Division headquarters, while the 4th Regiment was to attack the MACV compound and the Thua Thien sector headquarters, both located on the southern bank of the river.

• • •

By the morning of the next day . . . Hue city had practically fallen under enemy control, with the exception of key military and governmental headquarters. In the Old Citadel, the NLF flag was hoisted on the Midday Gate flagpole at 0800.

Judging the situation critical, the 1st Division commander ordered the 2nd Airborne Battalion, the 7th Armored Cavalry Squadron, and his own 3rd Regiment back to Hue to reinforce the defense of division headquarters and clear the city. All three units were intercepted and attacked on their way.

• • •

By now it was obvious that, to clear the enemy's foothold in the city, the 1st Division would require more forces. The division commander therefore ordered the 9th Airborne Battalion back from Quang Tri. With US helilift support, the battalion landed in Mang Ca during 2 February. It was followed shortly thereafter by the 4th Battalion, 2nd Regiment, 1st Division, also helilifted in from Dong Ha. With these additional forces, the 1st Division finally retook the Tay Loc Airfield inside the Old Citadel after two days of heavy fighting, during which the enemy lost in excess of 200 killed.

• • •

During that time, enemy forces attacked and overran the municipal prison of Hue, where approximately 2,000 prisoners were detained. After being freed, a large majority of these prisoners were used as local labor, while others were given weapons and joined enemy combat units as replacements. The enemy also began to consolidate his control over the city with the effective help of local VCI members. The local VCI had compiled a blacklist containing the names and addresses of all those who served in the military, in the government, or in US agencies. This list served a double purpose. It enabled enemy forces to search for and arrest those they considered "enemies of the revolution" for immediate elimination. It also helped the enemy in screening and classifying the civilian population of Hue.

According to accounts of survivors, the first thing Communists did after occupying Hue was to divide the city into areas and put each area under the control of a "Revolutionary Committee." All inhabitants were required to report to and register with the Revolutionary Committee of their area. They were also to turn in all weapons, ammunition, and radio receivers in their possession. After registration, everybody was let free to go home. During the days that followed registration, many people were asked to report again and never returned. They were those whose names had been placed on the VCI blacklist. When inquiring about their condition or location, their families were informed that they had to attend a reeducation course.

Information which leaked back gradually revealed the true nature of this reeducation process. According to a few who managed to escape and survive, all those detained for the purpose of "reeducation" were given picks and shovels and ordered to dig shelters. They did not suspect that these shelters were to become their own graves.

Later, after Hue had been liberated, most of these mass graves were found after a diligent and systematic search. We thus discovered many such graves on the campuses of the Gia Long and Gia Hoi high schools and in the vicinity of the Tang Quang Tu Pagoda, all within city limits. But there were several others which would have never been discovered had they not been pinpointed by enemy returnees; they were all located outside the city in such outlying areas as those forests surrounding the Tu Duc and Minh Mang tombs.

This mass murder eventually went down in history as the most abominable and inhuman atrocity ever committed by the Communists during the war. Although they condemned it, many South Vietnamese were at a loss when trying to determine why this was necessary. After all, they reasoned, Hue had always been considered more antigovernment than anywhere else in South Vietnam.

• • •

On 12 February three Vietnamese marine battalions were deployed to Hue. Two among them had participated in battles at My Tho in the Mekong Delta and at Go Vap in Gia Dinh Province. All three battalions were transported by naval craft to the Bao Vinh landing, from where they moved to the 1st Division headquarters compound. And, just as soon as they arrived, the marines launched counterattacks to retake the Citadel, but progress was slow in the absence of direct air and artillery support.

The next day, US marine forces began to join in the effort to clear the Citadel. Even solidly entrenched behind [the] indestructible walls of the old rampart, enemy forces suffered heavy losses caused by the accurate fire of 106mm recoilless rifles mounted on ONTOS vehicles. The weather also began to improve markedly, which made the support provided [to the] US marines by US tactical aircraft more effective and quickened the pace of clearing operations. The enemy was apparently digging in for a long stay. He had strewn substantial obstacles on roadways inside the Citadel, barricading himself behind trucks and other vehicles and heaps of household furniture taken from the population. He also positioned sharpshooters at key points to deter the advance of our troops.

• • •

On 22 February two ARVN ranger battalions arrived in Hue to reinforce the efforts of clearing the Gia Hoi area of Hue city. Then, at 0500 on 24 February, the 2nd Battalion of the 3rd Regiment, 1st ARVN Division, finally retook the Imperial Court inside the Citadel, where its troops immediately brought down the NLF flag, ripped it into tatters, and hoisted the RVN national colors. For the first time in 25 days our yellow and triple-red-striped flag fluttered triumphantly in the early morning air. This also marked the total reoccupation of Hue city, for by that time only one isolated enemy element still remained in Gia Hoi. The next day this element was wiped out.

The battle for Hue lasted only 25 days, but it was by far the fiercest, the bloodiest, and the most destructive. During the battle the enemy had committed a total of 16 battalions, or nearly the equivalent of two infantry divisions; according to our statistics, he had lost in excess of 2,000 killed. An enemy document captured later revealed that in the battle of Hue he had suffered 1,042 killed and several times that amount wounded. It also provided an inventory of troop commanders killed, which amounted to one regimental, eight battalion, and 24 company commanders, and 72 platoon leaders.

• • •

RVNAF casualties . . . amounted to 213 killed and 879 wounded. On the part of the civilian population, however, losses, both material and human, were extremely heavy. Approximately 80 percent of all houses within the Citadel area had been completely destroyed. During the short period of enemy occupation, the people of Hue also lived in agony among horrors and hardships that they had never encountered before. In addition to war hazards, they had suffered from shortages of food, water, and lighting. They also had to move among decaying corpses that could not be buried and whose stink could drive everyone to hysteria.

This brief coexistence with the Communists during the period of their occupation eventually caused the people of Hue to change their minds completely. From an attitude of confrontation, they had learned to accommodate with the national government and, above all, to reject with determination every political inclination smacking of sympathy toward Communists.

V. THE OFFENSIVE, PHASES II, III, AND IV

Phase II, May 1968

Prior to taking part in the General Offensive–General Uprising of Tet 1968, all Communist political and military cadres had received guidance instructions to the effect that this was going to be the biggest, and also the last, offensive. The effort, therefore, demanded [the] highest level of determination on the part of every participant.

However, just a few days after the offensive had been set in motion, an "absolutely secret" memorandum bearing the signature of Bay Hong, code name for Pham Hung, the COSVN leader, began to circulate among the Communist hierarchy. This memorandum, captured in Military Region 3, made an overall assessment of the situation and contained several self-critical remarks. Despite substantial gains, the memorandum admitted, Communist forces still fell short of their objectives. They had not yet occupied as many targets as had been planned, they had not yet wiped out South Vietnam's mobile and defense forces, and they had not yet succeeded in inciting a popular uprising against the government. All of these shortfalls were attributed to the failure to expand proselytizing activities, untimeliness and lack of continuity in propaganda actions, and the delay and interruption of communications.

• • •

In the eyes of the enemy, Phase II of the offensive was particularly significant because of certain political developments that would probably affect the American war effort. First of all, there was the decision, made by President Johnson on 31 March, to cease all bombings north of the 20th parallel, which in effect would spare up to 80 percent of North Vietnamese territory. The decision he also made and announced at the same time, not to run for reelection in November, was surely an indication of severe difficulties in American internal politics. Negotiations, meanwhile, had reached the stage where an appropriate location for peace talks would soon be agreed [on] by all parties concerned. All of these significant events were looked upon as favorable to the Communist side. Therefore, to further enhance his political posture, the enemy considered it mandatory to follow up his first offensive with a second one.

• • •

Information on the enemy's second phase of his offensive was obtained during the first week of April. It was disclosed by a high-ranking enemy rallier, Colonel Tran Van Dac, alias Tam Ha, who was deputy political commissar of the enemy MR-4. Colonel Tam Ha did not believe in the success of the general offensive and was not convinced that the urban population would rise up and join in the offensive, even before the launching of Phase I. After he received orders to prepare for Phase II, he decided to rally to the GVN and disclosed valuable information concerning enemy plans. According to Colonel Tam Ha, Phase II had been planned to take place on 22 April, but owing to delays in preparations it would be most likely postponed for about two weeks. He also disclosed that the main objective of attack for Phase II was Saigon, and that the enemy was going to commit a force equivalent to two infantry divisions in this attack.

• • •

On 3 May, just when American and North Vietnamese negotiators announced that they were progressing toward actual peace talks, which were soon to begin in Paris, III Corps received reliable information from one of its penetration agents that the enemy would launch his second phase of attacks during the night of 4 May.

• • •

As scheduled and indicated by our intelligence reports, Phase II of this offensive was launched during the night of 4 May and began with extensive shellings against 119 targets across the country, to include provincial cities, district towns, villages, and military installations. Apart from Saigon, the main objective, ground attacks were driven only against Bu Dop, an outlying district town in III Corps area, three miles east of the Cambodian border. . . . Enemy ground attacks against Saigon took place at 0400 on 5 May through two primary efforts, west and north, and a secondary effort east of the city. By breaking down into small elements, enemy units had succeeded in penetrating the outlying suburbs of Saigon before the attack. Some of these elements utilized boats and even trucks to infiltrate into the city. At a checkpoint outside Saigon, our forces apprehended some enemy troops hidden in a double-decked truck loaded with bricks; having difficulty breathing, the troops crawled out from the lower deck. In some other areas enemy troops disguised themselves as ARVN troops.

Immediately after an intensive shelling, two enemy local-force battalions attacked the Saigon–Bien Hoa Highway Bridge just east of the city. The Binh Loi Bridge, three kilometers to the northwest, also came under heavy attack by two battalions of the enemy Dong Nai Regiment. Both bridges were major accesses connecting Bien Hoa with Saigon across the Saigon River. But both attacks were driven back by Vietnamese marine units during the day of 5 May.

The next day, 6 May, the enemy launched another effort from the west of Saigon. In this effort, enemy attacks which took place in two villages west and southwest of Tan Son Nhut Air Base were defeated by elements of the US 25th Infantry Division and air cavalry units. The enemy suffered severe losses.

• • •

By 12 May Phase II of the general offensive against Saigon-Cholon had been defeated with an enemy death toll of about 3,000. During this phase the enemy had committed elements of eight regiments and three separate battalions. Actually, however, only 13 enemy battalions had successfully penetrated Saigon and conducted attacks within the city.

The situation remained calm afterwards, and not until 25 May did the enemy come back again with another surge of attacks which, by contrast with the first one, caught us rather unaware. Enemy forces this time had filtered through the Saigon security belt without being detected. The Dong Nai Regiment, for example, had already been in place at An Phu Dong, a guerrilla base just three kilometers north of Saigon, two days before the attack, but its presence was not known. Obviously the vigilance of CMD troops had diminished and their patrol activities had slackened because of the long days of combat during the last few weeks. Not until enemy forces had begun to move into the suburbs did they sound the alert.

• • •

By this time, however, the use of tactical air and artillery to support relief operations in Saigon had begun to incur some adverse opinion among the urban population about their destructive effect. To soothe popular sentiment, the newly designated prime minister, Mr. Tran Van Huong, issued instructions to the effect that our forces had to curtail the use of firepower in the densely populated suburbs.

In the area occupied by the Quyet Thang Regiment, our airborne units, abiding by the new orders, requested the use of riot control agents to dislodge enemy troops from their shelters. But the use of riot control agents in this area proved ineffective because, as soon as it was released by our aircraft, prevailing winds immediately blew it away and sometimes back toward our lines. Our paratroopers, therefore, had to resort to night raids against enemy positions, a tactic which proved effective. Decimated by heavy losses after a few days of fighting, the Quyet Thang Regiment asked for reinforcements from the Dong Nai Regiment. The reinforcements arrived, but were intercepted and destroyed by an ARVN airborne battalion. Faced with the risk of complete annihilation, the Quyet Thang regimental commander left behind a battalion to fight a delaying action while he and the rest of the regiment tried to slip away. When this regiment reached the Bang Ky Bridge, it was intercepted by our marines and was forced to fall back in disorder to the Cay Thi area and lost all chances of breaking through the tightening ARVN ring of troops. On 17 June the deputy commander of the Quyet Thang Regiment, Senior Captain Pham Van Xuong, surrendered. He informed us that his regiment's strength was down to 230, but 110 among them were wounded.

Xuong's surrender was immediately exploited by our psywar units. His appeal for surrender addressed to enemy troops was recorded on tape and broadcast from circling aircraft. One by one, elements of what remained of the shattered Quyet Thang Regiment surfaced and surrendered. By 18 June a total of 152 enemy troops had laid down their weapons and capitulated. This was by far the largest surrender the enemy had made to date. The remnants of this regiment were subsequently either tracked down and killed or captured. The Quyet Thang Regiment no longer existed in the enemy's order of battle. And with it the enemy's offensive effort in northern Saigon also came to an end.

• • •

A major tactical blunder committed by our forces here was their failure to cordon off the area occupied by enemy troops with a continuous security belt. Instead, they just posted a few security guard details around it. This allowed the enemy to move with ease, especially at night. As a result, an entire city block in downtown Cholon, to include its main thoroughfare, Boulevard Tong Doc Phuong, came under enemy control. Enemy troops immediately occupied high-rise buildings in the area and dug in for defense.

The battle for the relief of Cholon became painful and drawn-out. Our forces had to rely on tactical air and gunships to destroy enemy resistance nests lodged on the top floors of several buildings. In addition, they also used M-79 grenade launchers and 57mm recoilless rifles to take on enemy weapon positions one by one and eventually inflicted quite serious losses on the enemy.

On 2 June, amid the raging battle, a fatal accident occurred on our side which caused death to some key Vietnamese commanders making up the command of the relief operation in Cholon. Their headquarters was at the Thuong Phuoc High School. A salvo of rockets fired by a US gunship struck this group of officers while they were observing the progress of the battle. Five among them died immediately, to include Colonel Nguyen Van Luan, Saigon police chief; Colonel Dao Ba Phuoc, commander of the 5th Ranger Group; and the 5th Precinct police chief. The mayor of Saigon, Colonel Van Van Cua, and the military governor of Saigon, Colonel Nguyen Van Giam, also present among the group, were injured.

An investigation conducted by US authorities later revealed that the firing accident was caused by technical mishaps. The rockets obviously misfired, and the fire angle was apparently too narrow to afford a good security margin. (The distance between the real target and where the group of officers stood was merely 200 meters.) The crooked minds of some Saigon politicians, however, refused to believe that it was just an accident. They speculated that it was a deliberate American error designed to provide President Thieu with an opportunity to appoint those loyal to him to the key positions held by the deceased and injured officers, all appointees and confidants of Vice President Ky.

In any event, the accident caused a two-day delay in the progress of relief operations. By the time a new commander was appointed and resumed control of operations, the enemy had been solidly entrenched in a Chinese restaurant, the famous Soai Kinh Lam, and our forces were unable to dislodge him. To quicken the relief, the new commander decided to call for armor support and the use of riot control agents. Equipped with gas masks, ARVN troops assaulted the enemy-occupied building after tear gas canisters had been thrown in. They rapidly overwhelmed enemy troops, who had nothing to protect themselves but wet towels. The Soai Kinh Lam Restaurant was retaken easily.

• • •

A tally of enemy-related activities made after the end of Phase II clearly showed a sharp decline as compared to Phase I. During the first four days of Phase II, for example, there were only 52 enemy-initiated infantry attacks, or just one-half of the total recorded during the same period in Phase I (104). Of these attacks, only six were conducted at battalion level or above, as compared to 29 in Phase I.

In contrast, perhaps to compensate for this waning strength of infantry attacks, the enemy had substantially increased his attacks by fire during Phase II. There were 433 shellings reported across the country, compared to just 268 for Phase I. The quantity of mortar shells and rockets expended during Phase II in these attacks by fire also increased more than twofold (10,369 as compared to 4,185).

Of all infantry attacks the enemy initiated during Phase II, only those driven against Gia Dinh (north of Saigon) and Cholon were significant. In both places enemy actions differed [from] those conducted in Phase I in several aspects.

First, apparently to avoid great losses, enemy forces broke down into small elements and penetrated densely populated areas from which they initiated attacks. This was a marked departure from Phase I, during which the enemy launched direct attacks against definite objectives and incurred heavy losses in the process. The lessons of Phase I were apparently well learned. By adhering to populated areas and moving from one place to another in case they could not hold on to any particular place, enemy forces had hoped to reduce the effectiveness of our tanks, artillery, and tactical air. The effect of this tactic brought about extensive physical damage and casualties to the population, which induced their grievances and helped enemy propaganda.

Second, during Phase II the enemy had considerably stepped up his propaganda activities in those areas he penetrated. Armed propaganda teams used loudspeakers to broadcast appeals to the population to rise up and participate in what they called a movement sponsored by the "National Alliance for Peace and Democracy." Ten different kinds of leaflets were distributed by these teams, making the same kind of appeal. In the Cholon and Phu Dinh areas, VCI members searched houses and looked for GVN officials and military and police officers, whom they arrested and took away.

Third, no US installations came under enemy attack during Phase II. This was perhaps a calculated move intended to achieve two things. By sparing US installations, the enemy conveyed the idea that he was showing an attitude of good will toward peace negotiations and, through this, hoped to gain some American sympathy. This move was also aimed at sowing more suspicion among the South Vietnamese population about a prearranged solution to the war which the United States might conclude with the enemy behind their backs. Speculations on this subject had already poisoned public opinion since the beginning of the offensive and affected even some GVN officials and military officers.

The first surge of attacks in Phase II ended with about 4,000 homes destroyed by fire. Our forces suffered 210 killed, to include 67 Americans, and 979 wounded, to include 333 Americans.

All enemy infantry attacks ended by 12 May, but they were followed by the fiercest rocket attacks the enemy had ever unleashed against Saigon. The rocket attacks began on 19 May, apparently to commemorate Ho Chi Minh's birthday. The heaviest attacks took place in June, when Saigon received incoming rockets for 12 consecutive days. During this period, to impart still more terror on the Saigon population, enemy propaganda announced that the shelling campaign would last 100 days with an intensity of at least 100 rockets per day. But this turned out to be just propaganda. Enemy rocket attacks on Saigon were not selective, because populated areas became frequent targets for such attacks. During the 12 consecutive days of rocket attacks in June, over 100 civilians were killed and in excess of 400 wounded.

The trauma of the Saigon population and the grievances occasioned by these rocket attacks were such that the GVN had to take certain emergency measures aimed at protecting Saigon more effectively. The CMD command, which was responsible for this protection, was separated from III Corps control and placed under a newly appointed military governor, Major General Nguyen Van Minh, who was regarded as thoroughly experienced in antishelling measures during the period he commanded the 21st Infantry Division in the Mekong Delta. General Minh immediately appointed a special committee in charge of protecting Saigon against enemy shellings. To increase patrol and surveillance activities along the Saigon rocket belt, CMD was authorized an additional six RF companies and the employment of the 81st Airborne Ranger Group. Particularly effective in night combat, the airborne rangers were used in night patrol activities and to launch night attacks against enemy mini-bases near the rocket belt. Security measures within the CMD were also strengthened, and the new CMD commander was authorized to use all ARVN units located in the CMD for security purposes up to 50 percent of their strengths. All of these new measures greatly contributed to the improvement of security in Saigon and eventually curtailed enemy rocket attacks to a large extent.

The Offensive, Phase III

After the two phases of the offensive which took place during the first half of 1968, the Communists had incurred total losses amounting to 170,000 casualties and 39,800 weapons of all types.

This heavy toll seriously affected the morale of Communist troops and cadres in almost all units. A substantial number of enemy unit commanders had been killed or wounded; many others chose to rally to the GVN.

• • •

The enemy's propaganda apparatus, which had heretofore been considered effective, fell victim to an unexpected backlash. The outcome of the offensive thus far, and the realities witnessed by enemy troops in South Vietnamese cities, contrasted so much with Communist propaganda lines that the latter became outright lies. Southern enemy troops, for example, had been informed that they would receive an enthusiastic support from the urban population, which never materialized. NVA troops who were sent to the South to participate in the offensive had been led to believe that South Vietnam had been "liberated" and what remained for them to do was just go in and take over. The situation of South Vietnam had been represented to them as one of near-collapse in which the exploited population was chafing under repressions and deprivations, longing for the day of liberation. But what Communist troops really saw for themselves, during the short period they came into contact with South Vietnamese urban civilization, had struck them as beyond imagination. NVA troops in particular could not believe their eyes when confronted with the sophisticated amenities of westernized modern life. Their impression was one of awe and bewilderment.

Gradually they came to suspect and disbelieve their own propaganda apparatus. Just as they were suffering from one defeat after another, for example, this apparatus continued to sing news of victory, along with statistical results on "enemy" losses that had been so excessively falsified that even the most gullible Communist troops had to question their veracity. If it was true that all cities of South Vietnam had been liberated, and if RVN and US forces had been inflicted [with] so many losses, enemy troops wondered why they were still required to participate in unending combat operations. The truth finally dawned on them that what they had been told was simply hollow propaganda. And, for the devout Communist, this affected his morale most seriously.

• • •

[COSVN] Resolution No. 7 was issued for the purpose of reiterating the enemy's view of the General Offensive–General Uprising campaign. This campaign, it was argued, was not a one-time offensive, but consisted of several offensive phases, each phase overlapping with the next one and all conducted with growing intensity. Resolution No. 7 then emphasized the need for a third phase, which was to be initiated in August. The date selected for the initiation of this phase was 19 August, the day the Viet Minh August Revolution took place 23 years earlier.

Despite COSVN's determination to proceed with Phase III, obviously our enemy had lost the capabilities to carry it out. By this time, all major enemy units had been driven out of the CMD. The enemy's 9th Division, the single major unit participating in Phase II attacks in Saigon, Hoc Mon, and Ben Luc, had moved to the west of Tay Ninh Province toward border sanctuaries where it would have to lick its wounds and protect infiltration routes at the same time.

The enemy 7th Division, after several engagements with the 1st Australian Task Force in Binh My, and after withdrawing one of its elements from battles north of Saigon during Phase II, had retreated into Hat Dich base, which straddled the common boundaries of Bien Hoa, Long Khanh, and Phuoc Tuy Provinces. Its sister unit, the 5th Division, had also withdrawn into the Boi Loi area and War Zone D.

• • •

As to RVN and US forces, their primary efforts during this period against enemy rocket attacks had resulted in a combined effort taken up by the CMD and III Corps in cooperation and coordination with the US II Field Force. The RVNAF also took advantage of this opportunity to implement a program of force structure expansion and modernization, which saw the activation of new units and the delivery of new weapons.

Tactically, the protection of Saigon became more and more effective as enemy shelling was sharply reduced. To ensure this protection, our forces conducted round-the-clock ground and air patrols, installed counterbattery radars in conjunction with a system of observation towers which covered the entire perimeter of Saigon and its immediate vicinity, and extensively used military dogs for the detection of enemy infiltrations. As a result of these activities, large numbers of 122mm rockets were seized and the enemy was no longer able to pre-position rockets around Saigon. Rocket attacks, therefore, sharply declined beginning in late June.

•••

Phase III of the enemy general offensive began on 17 August 1968, two days earlier than planned. It was a concerted effort that took place simultaneously in I, II, and III Corps areas, primarily through attacks by fire. Saigon, however, came under a rocket attack only on 22 August. A total of 19 122mm rockets were fired on that day, ten in Saigon, six in Cholon, and three in the harbor area. This delayed attack on Saigon was part of the enemy's plan for Phase III. According to this plan, elements of the enemy 1st and 7th Divisions conducted attacks against Tay Ninh, An Loc, and Loc Ninh on 17 and 19 August with the purpose of drawing our forces away from the CMD, which would leave the ground open for local forces of the five enemy subdivisions to penetrate and launch attacks. But this plan did not work, because ARVN and US forces steadfastly remained around Saigon for its defense.

In addition to Saigon, the enemy also attacked another significant target: the Bu Prang Special Forces Camp in Quang Duc Province, five kilometers from the Cambodian border. The battle here lasted several days, ending with enemy losses of 776 killed and friendly losses of 116, including two Americans. This attack, however, marked the last enemy offensive effort during 1968.

Of the three offensive phases conducted so far, Phase III was definitely the weakest in all respects. The enemy was able to launch 15 infantry attacks across the country, compared to 52 attacks in Phase II. Among these 15 attacks only two were of battalion size or above. Attacks by fire were also sharply reduced: a total of 95 were reported, contrasted with 433 in Phase II.

In some other aspects, Phase III attacks also differed from those of the previous two phases. For one thing, these attacks were no longer accompanied by propaganda activities. The enemy's plan for Phase III did not even call for these activities. Obviously he had realized that inciting the South Vietnamese into rebellion and joining Communist ranks was just a utopian proposition.

Secondly, no main-force units joined in the attack against Saigon; only local forces participated, even though they had suffered severe losses during Phase I. In order to bring his local-force battalions up to combat strength for the attack, the enemy had to deactivate some others. Most significantly, enemy units attacking Saigon in August were no longer required to fight to the last man. In fact, an enemy document captured during

Phase III contained an express order for all attacking units to withdraw after accomplishing their mission and not to become involved in sustained combat. The order also emphasized the need to draw "enemy" forces away from Saigon and destroy them in strategic areas (outside of Saigon). Apparently, the enemy realized he had paid too high a price for trying to hold out in Saigon during Phase II. It was also possible that this new order had been dictated by the need to improve troop morale for those units still capable of attack, because this morale was evidently at a low ebb. A diary captured from an enemy cadre in Phase III recorded these confessions:

"Everybody is tired and confused. Many don't want the unit to break down into small elements because it would be easily destroyed by enemy attacks. Many others are afraid they will get lost in the city, still others will surely run into difficulties because they can't swim. On the other hand, the enemy is more active, more numerous, and enjoys the initiative."

• • •

To Communist leaders, especially COSVN, however, the general offensive continued to bring them victories. They pointed to the fact that the United States and RVN had been edged into a deteriorating defensive posture in which they had to redeploy combat units for the defense of cities. The evacuation of Kham Duc and Khe Sanh Base by US troops was . . . evidence of this deteriorating posture. Other events that took place in the United States, such as the resignation of Secretary McNamara and the replacement of General Westmoreland, also proved that the United States was meeting with increasing difficulties.

As a result, the enemy felt a pressing need to keep the offensive spirit alive, if only for the purpose of taking advantage of political events which he was convinced were working to his advantage.

• • •

The enemy situation after Phase III, therefore, was one of longing for replacements and reduced activities which primarily consisted of shellings, sabotage, and terrorists' actions.

Taking advantage of the enemy's plight, the RVN vigorously pushed its pacification program ahead with the purpose of restoring control over rural areas that had been lost as a result of the enemy offensive. At the same time, with a renewed source of fresh manpower, it endeavored to make up for the losses incurred since Tet. Both the enemy and our side were well aware that the 1968 general offensive was yet to run its final course.

The Offensive, Phase IV, February 1969

Phase III of the general offensive exposed all the weaknesses which caused the enemy to fall far short of his objectives, despite his continued and determined efforts. The dictates of politics and a strong bargaining position for peace negotiations, however, continued to keep him under pressure.

COSVN was therefore so hard pressed that, as soon as Phase III had ended in failure, it immediately issued Resolution No. 8 in September to provide guidance for the next effort. By this decision the enemy committed himself to preparing for what he called the "Winter–Spring" offensive campaign.

In terms of objectives to be achieved, Resolution No. 8 did not differ much from the previous two resolutions. Our enemy was still striving for a complete military victory. The approach to achieving this objective was different, however. Resolution No. 8 in effect prescribed a step-by-step effort toward that end instead of pressing for an immediate victory. Realizing perhaps that victory could not be achieved as long as US forces were still in South Vietnam, COSVN observed that efforts should be devoted to attacking and destroying major US force components to such an extent that the United States would have to concede defeat in South Vietnam and cease all bombings against the North. By the time he issued Resolution No. 8, our enemy had all the reasons to expect a cessation of bombings. He rightly claimed that this would be a big victory for his side.

President Johnson's decision to cease all US bombings, beginning on 1 November 1968, came as the enemy had predicted. The cessation of bombings took effect at a time when the onset of the dry season made it possible for our enemy to set his infiltration machine in motion. As if he had fully prepared for it, the enemy did not seem to lose any time in taking advantage of this momentous decision. Only one day after this decision had gone into effect, a large North Vietnamese labor force was assembled under emergency orders to repair and rehabilitate major roads and bridges destroyed by US bombings. At the same time, a fuel pipeline was hastily installed from Dong Hoi to a point just north of the DMZ, a sure indication of stepped-up truck traffic in this area. As aerial photos gradually made all too evident, stockpiles of supplies and war materiel were being assembled in the north and available to be picked up and delivered to southern battlefields.

South of the DMZ, enemy logistic movements also increased considerably. Evidence of an enemy buildup became visible enough through the several operations conducted by US units in this area. During Operation Dewey Canyon in late February 1969, for example, US forces captured an enemy 122mm field gun, which was the first ever seen deployed in South Vietnam.

• • •

By early 1969, indications of an enemy offensive during spring had become evident through several intelligence sources. Most indicative among them was perhaps Directive No. 71, issued by COSVN on 31 January.

This directive reasserted the enemy's intent to renew his General Offensive–General Uprising campaign of 1968 by an offensive effort in the spring of 1969. Drawing lessons from the three offensive phases in 1968, the enemy now placed first priority on destroying US military forces and war-making capabilities in South Vietnam, to be followed in second priority by the destruction of RVN forces and the dismantling of GVN control. To achieve these basic objectives, Directive No. 71 prescribed a program of activities aimed at interdicting major lines of communication, isolating US and RVNAF military bases, wrecking the GVN pacification program, and keeping both the military offensive momentum and the urban insurrection movement going.

In the face of these enemy plans, both the RVN and US forces stepped up their preparations for counteraction. Also drawing lessons from past enemy activity patterns, our forces expanded patrol and operational activities into outlying areas with the purpose of detecting enemy troop movements and preempting enemy attacks.

As a result, when Phase IV of the offensive came about, as predicted, during the night of 22 February, the enemy could not obtain surprise. However, with the benefit of additional supplies and fresh manpower infiltrated during the dry season, the enemy was able to conduct infantry attacks and attacks by fire against over 100 targets across the country, to include provincial capitals, military installations, and outposts.

These attacks were kept at a significant level only for the first five days. During that time, enemy activities were primarily shellings; the most significant ones were rocket attacks on Saigon, Hue, and Danang.

• • •

A significant feature of Phase IV of the enemy offensive was the conspicuous absence of local forces and the exclusive use of main-force units in all attacks. Obviously, after the severe losses incurred during 1968, no local-force unit was capable enough to participate in the 1969 Spring Offensive.

• • •

Compared to Phase III, Phase IV of the enemy offensive was markedly stronger in terms of both level and intensity. Its significance might even equal that of Phase II as far as the enemy was concerned, and a parallel could be appropriately drawn between the two. The number of attacks by fire during Phase IV even surpassed those of Phase II (433), whereas only 95 such attacks were accounted during Phase III. There were 125 infantry attacks during Phase IV, as compared to 52 during Phase II and 15 during Phase III. Attacks of battalion size or larger numbered 16, compared to six in Phase II and two in Phase III.[6]

However, the most conspicuous decline in enemy capabilities during the last phase was perhaps our enemy's inability to launch any infantry attack against Saigon as he did during Phase II. Politically and psychologically, therefore, it seemed that the effect of the general offensive had reached its climax during the first half of 1968. Whatever efforts our enemy attempted after that, to include Phases III and IV, were just inconsequential ripples that did not even affect our military posture.

• • •

For the first half of 1969, a total of 20,000 enemy personnel had become ralliers, a threefold increase over the entire year of 1968. This high rate of desertion reflected the declining morale in most all units during that period. The pressure kept on enemy troops had been overwhelming at a time when irreplaceable losses were increasing and the constant demand for more sacrifices for the sake of bargaining power in future peace talks was being emphasized.

Fully aware of this deteriorating military posture, enemy leaders opted for a new strategic approach to fight the war. Their new strategy no longer called for all-out effort or big-scale offensives. Instead, it became an economy-of-force warfare emphasizing small-scale attacks by small-level units, evidently to keep losses at a minimum. The goal to be achieved, however, remained the same: however small the attacks, they had to draw public attention, domestically and internationally.

For the first time since Giap's article, COSVN admitted the need to preserve forces when it issued Directive No. 55 in April 1969. The directive stressed in effect: "Never again, and under no circumstances, are we going to risk our entire military force for just an offensive. On the contrary, we should endeavor to preserve our military potential for future campaigns."

However sound and realistic this new approach might be, it represented a radical departure from established policies, and, until directed to do so, COSVN would have to keep it in the conceptual stage. Not until after the North Vietnamese Politburo had voted its approval did COSVN make it an official subject for study and indoctrination when it issued Resolution No. 9 in July 1969. Essentially an embodiment of Hanoi's decision to switch strategy, Resolution No. 9 went into effect immediately. Enemy-initiated activities during the rest of 1969 faithfully followed the policies laid out in the resolution.

• • •

VI. IMPACT OF THE 1968–1969 GENERAL OFFENSIVE

"Talk and Fight"

Like a catalyst, the enemy's unsuccessful attacks during Tet 1968 had brought about peace talks in Paris, barely three months after Hue city was wrested back from among smoldering ruins. It was quite indicative of the enemy's warring policy that peace talks should begin in the midst of his second phase of attacks, for "talk and fight" had become the strategy that dictated our enemy's actions in the years ahead.

• • •

Phase IV of the offensive had ended in failure. Still, to prove that he was utterly serious in his demands, and evidently to incite further pressure from the US antiwar movement which he hoped could cause the United States to give in to those demands, the enemy followed up his peace proposal with a military initiative on 11 and 12 May. Essentially a "high point" of cyclical summer activities, this initiative consisted of 212 shellings conducted on a countrywide basis, of which 105 were relatively significant and still included Saigon as a primary target. In several areas, shellings were followed up by infantry attacks, but none of these attacks exceeded battalion size. Conducted primarily at company level, most ended by the end of the second day.

Then, on 10 June 1969, the enemy announced the inauguration of the Provisional Revolutionary Government (PRG) of South Vietnam, which virtually upgraded the rebellious NLF into a political entity of international stature. This was also a calculated move preparing and paving the way for the NLF's participation in the peace talks, which practically placed it on a political par with the Republic of Vietnam should the latter decide to play the "talk-fight" game.

• • •

COSVN Resolutions No. 9 and 14/DKCT

Disseminated among the high levels of the party hierarchy five months after Phase IV of the general offensive, COSVN Resolution No. 9 was a watershed policy directive that set the Communist conduct of the war in South Vietnam on an entirely new course. Most significantly, it provided a cool analysis of the impact of the 1968 General Offensive–General Uprising on our enemy's war posture and thoroughly justified his actions for the past year and a half.

Besides what he termed as successes, which in view of all the evidence gathered by our side could be attributed to his usual bias, our enemy proved to be more candid and unusually objective when he assessed his own shortcomings. And, although called a COSVN resolution, its scope evidently transcended the authority and decision-making power normally assigned to this southern office of the North Vietnamese Politburo. The preamble of the document, therefore, made it clear that the contents resulted from a "total agreement" with North Vietnam's resolution.

Assessing the general situation, our enemy believed that his general offensive had resulted in significant human and materiel losses to US forces. The incremental withdrawal of US troops from South Vietnam and the de-Americanization of the war were appropriately considered a major turning point in the war which effectively changed the balance of forces to our enemy's favor. This new balance of forces provided a new opportunity which, if effectively seized at the proper time, could lead to still bigger victories.

• • •

The COSVN leadership . . . castigated its cadres for being "near-sighted" in appraising the balance of forces between the two sides, exalting the enemy while debasing their own capabilities, distrusting the Politburo's strategy, and consequently fighting without enthusiasm or conviction. The single most important principle that ensured victory for the General Offensive–General Uprising, therefore, had not been adhered to and was lost.

COSVN criticism was especially harsh against those cadres whom it accused of having mistaken the general offensive for just a one-time action of transient nature. This was the most serious mistake that caused them to lose their sense of audacity and duty required in times of emergency, and, as a result, they had become rightist-minded and fearful of action.

For all that candor, our enemy's self-criticism still fell far short of his true condition by the latter half of 1969. In fact, each of the shortcomings that he had confessed implied much more than he dared admit, for obvious reasons. There were also certain other difficulties that he felt not politically appropriate to discuss. Most serious among them was the severe dent made [in] his infrastructure ranks as a result of the 1968 general offensive. The truth was that about half of his infrastructure had been completely and irretrievably destroyed in the process.

• • •

The severe losses incurred by southern-born insurgents, whether infrastructure or local-force elements, during the offensive was a fact that could not be hidden from the families of the deceased. This was also true of northern-born cadres and troops whose families in the North suddenly ceased to hear from them after the offensive. Even though the COSVN leadership never admitted to it, the fact was amply demonstrated by the many diaries and letters captured and the testimony of prisoners and ralliers.

• • •

To overcome these difficulties and remedy his own shortcomings, the enemy sought ways to keep his military activities alive while trying to keep the commitment of forces and his losses down. He found it effective and economical to fight a kind of "souped up" guerrilla warfare: sapper actions. Essentially a sabotage and hit-and-run tactic, sapper actions were not a military novelty. Their chief advantage, however, was to create head-lines, which suited well our enemy's purpose at this juncture, and to inflict as much damage to our military potential as possible at minimum cost. More significantly, from this time on sapper actions were to become the mainstay of enemy activities.

In a military sense, the impact of the 1968-1969 General Offensive–General Upris-ing [led to] a turnabout in enemy strategy, which curtailed main-force warfare and em-phasized small-scale actions by small local-force units. It was in this strategic direction that COSVN Resolution No. 9 explicitly promoted guerrilla warfare and implicitly maintained that small-scale warfare was but a transition phase in the continuous process of general offensive and general uprising.

To further explain this new warfare direction to his rank and file, the enemy passed and issued Resolution No. 14 on guerrilla warfare, which was immediately used as in-doctrination material in all units. Resolution No. 14 went [on] at great length to explain the reasons why it was necessary to break up main- and local-force units into companies while keeping parent unit designations intact. It also encouraged efforts to turn all main-force elements thus broken up into sapper units.

• • •

Despite these . . . setbacks, which came as an adverse consequence of the 1968 gen-eral offensive, our enemy still felt he had the upper hand in long-term prospects. He saw an indisputable advantage in the withdrawal of US troops and the complete cessation of bombings against North Vietnam which in time might give him the ultimate chance of a final conquest.

A Windfall for South Vietnam

Like a cold breeze, the Communist 1968 Tet Offensive seemed to awaken the South Vietnamese people from a lethargic slumber. Everybody became sober and alert, fully aware of what was at stake.

But the damage was done and the moment of truth had arrived. The initial bewilder-ment and terror gradually disappeared and gave way to consciousness and self-assurance. Even though war had stepped into their heretofore secure habitat, and after meeting face to face with an enemy whom they had so far only heard about through all sorts of myths, the urban people still kept their faith intact and never even thought of the RVN being defeated in this showdown of force.

• • •

And, unconsciously, they made a comparison and came to the conclusion that it was most unlikely that the paratroopers, the marines, the rangers could ever be subdued by those peasants. No, they were convinced that the RVN could not lose this war, especially when the mighty US forces were still there at their side.

• • •

As a result of the mobilization law, 6 percent of the South Vietnamese population had virtually become combatants in one way or another. Transposed to another scale, it was as if 12 million Americans had joined the services at the call of duty.

• • •

In Saigon, especially in some suburban Catholic communities, people . . . began to petition the government for weapons and ammunition. At first the distribution of weapons for self-defense purposes was restricted to Catholic communities. Soon, by popular demand, the GVN overcame its cautiousness and made weapons available for all self-defense organizations. This was how the People's Self-Defense movement came into being, a concept which had been espoused since the days of the First Republic but never was implemented on such a scale owing to the lukewarm response by the people. Taking the cue from the growing popular demand, the GVN stepped in and launched a country-wide campaign to institute self-defense forces, not only in cities but in rural areas. By April, just three months after Tet, the People's Self-Defense Forces had become a reality throughout South Vietnam. Their organization was eventually formalized by the [General] Mobilization Law in June 1968.

Riding on the crest of the self-defense movement, the college students of Saigon, made idle by the closing down of universities to make them available as refugee centers, gathered themselves into a paramilitary organization pompously designated "Capital Defense Student Division." Armed with individual weapons, the students were employed to assist the police and ARVN units in maintaining security for the city. When Communist forces attacked Saigon during Phase II of the offensive, 2,000 college students of the division participated in the defense of the city. They were mostly deployed to man checkpoints and guard accesses to Saigon, particularly in the river-bound southern suburbs. The Student Division did not exist for long, however, for as Saigon came back to normal the students also returned to their books.

During the attacks on Saigon, Communist forces were all equipped with AK-47s and rocket launchers, B-40 or B-41. The superiority of these weapons, especially the AK-47, was immediately recognized by the urban people, even by the teenagers. For one thing, after days of listening to battle sounds, the Saigon people were able to differentiate between the sharper, rounder, and more uniform AK-47 bursts and the dull crackles of our Garand and carbine reports. Therefore they could orient themselves and know exactly where the enemy was. To pass idle time while the fighting was still raging, some even amused themselves with this guessing game by listening to the sounds of gunfire and telling whether they were the enemy's or ours. All agreed that the AK-47 sounds were more impressive.

The inferiority of ARVN troops in individual armament eventually became a major concern, which pressed the JGS into asking for improvement. A modernization plan was initiated and placed under a combined JGS-MACV committee for implementation. By May 1968, the first stage of the plan was completed and the RVNAF began to receive modern infantry equipment such as the M-16 rifle, the M-60 machinegun, the M-79 grenade launcher, and the AN/PRC-25 field radio set.

By the same programming effort the United States also made available more heavy equipment for the RVNAF to keep up with their modernization and force structure expansion trends. By the end of 1969 ARVN armor assets had been brought up to 1,500 vehicles, compared to 600 at the time the offensive began. Artillery pieces also increased substantially, to include the M-102 for the Airborne Division, [and] adding two more artillery battalions to each infantry division. The Airborne Division thus found itself with three artillery battalions, one for each brigade, for better direct support, instead of just one for the entire division, as in early 1968. The VNAF also saw its helicopter armada increased fourfold to 400 ships, in addition to 60 more jet fighter-bombers.

• • •

As if to testify to the success of pacification in 1969, the political commissar of the enemy MR-4 (Saigon-Cholon) admitted, in a document captured from him, that the expansion of GVN control was such that he had to spend nearly four months on long detours to reach the Ba Thu area in Cambodia for a high-level COSVN meeting. It had normally taken him only two weeks to travel to the same area.

• • •

To make a final tally, the enemy 1968 offensive affected South Vietnam in several aspects and placed many burdens on the GVN. Eventually, all obstructions were removed and South Vietnam found everything much better than before the offensive. But progress and achievements would have been much more substantial had the South Vietnamese leadership known how to exploit its advantages of the moment. It was agreed that never before had South Vietnam been in such a privileged position, a position which combined all three basic ingredients of success, namely, "opportunity, advantage, and popular consent," as the famous strategist Sun Tzu saw it centuries ago.

The Limitations of South Vietnam's Efforts

Unquestionably the enemy 1968 offensive came as a windfall for South Vietnam in terms of prospects for long-range success. Among the basic ingredients for success, popular consent was the most important, because up to that time it had been missing. For years the battle of the hearts and minds had been waged but never won. But this time, and most unexpectedly, this battle was won without much effort. The stimulating fact was that, during and after the offensive, every South Vietnamese seemed to have made up his mind as to what side he wanted to live with. This almost universal rejection of Communism came about not as a result of propaganda or coercion, but as a profound conviction, a faith suddenly rediscovered in the face of disaster. As a result, the popular consent to align with nationalism was sincere, almost instinctive. Without a formal referendum, the great majority of the South Vietnamese population had overwhelmingly voted for the nationalist regime by their attitude, by their actions. If this popular mandate was maintained and strengthened, then force of will and solidarity could never be subdued by its Communist archenemy.

It was most unfortunate that, as soon as the perils were gone, this national unity and sense of dedication to the national cause also ebbed away, and everything seemed to downgrade to its former condition, edging the nation back to its old problems of divisiveness, factional rivalry, social malaise, and lethargy.

A cunning politician, President Thieu took advantage of the nation's survival effort to consolidate his power, wresting it back from his political rival, Vice President Ky. He fired Ky's appointees, to include the prime minister, reshuffled the cabinet, reappointed key military commanders, and replaced them with his own men. All of these changes did not help improve leadership or advance the national cause. They were made in the same old pattern of power intrigue, based not on talent, experience, or merits, but on personal loyalty and clannish relations. The administrative machinery, therefore, continued to function with the same lethargic pace, plagued by inefficiency, waste, and corruption. Deluded by perpetuating political intrigues, a divisive national leadership, and the aggravation of social ills, the South Vietnamese people, who were expecting progress and innovation, gradually found their newly rediscovered patriotic ardor and dedication sapped and gone.

Militarily, the conduct of war efforts was affected by the replacement of three out of four corps commanders. This change was publicized as an effort to remove incompetence, but the real motive behind it was entirely different. In fact, since Thieu was elected president he had always felt his constitutional power greatly constrained by the Council of Generals, a kind of military politburo which also propped him and Ky up into power, of which he was simply a member. By removing the three key members of this council, President Thieu effectively used his elective authority to deal it a fatal blow and asserted himself as the unrivaled strongman of the regime.

• • •

For all its implications, Vietnamization did not concern the South Vietnamese leadership, who saw in it just a chance to get more war materiel and economic aid from the United States. It failed to see for itself that, to survive without the presence of American troops, a comprehensive national plan, mobilizing all resources available and obtainable, would be required to enable South Vietnam to take over war responsibilities effectively. Aside from criticizing Vietnamization as an inappropriate term to save pride and face, the Independence Palace did not provide any guidance on how it should be implemented, what other requirements it occasioned (in addition to force structure expansion and equipment modernization), and how the war should be fought without the American presence. The South Vietnamese leadership even failed to alert its people [to] the immediate consequences of the US troop withdrawal and condition popular psychology to self-sufficiency and self-defense. As a result, Vietnamization amounted to just that—a normal process of force expansion and modernization, nothing else.

The complacency and nearsightedness with which the South Vietnamese leadership viewed the process of American disengagement derived perhaps from ignorance and blind trust. It was possible that President Thieu did not sense any cause for alarm because he had been promised continued American support. But, as a national leader, he surely took a chance when he did not even question the future of that support.

• • •

VII. OBSERVATIONS AND CONCLUSIONS

The Communist general offensive of 1968–1969 marked an important turning point in the Vietnam War. Despite its short-lived intensity, which lasted for some time during Phase I, then diminished during Phase II, and finally became insignificant during Phases III and IV, the repercussions and effect caused by it bore heavily on the final outcome of the war.

• • •

Of all the military objectives that the Communists had set about to attain—the major cities, provincial capitals, and district towns of South Vietnam—none was under their control when the offensive ended. For this failure, they had to pay a prohibitively high price in human losses, even if we were able to scale down our own reporting statistics.

Our enemy also publicized what he claimed to be "severe losses" inflicted on our side. Knowing Communist propaganda for what it was, there could hardly be any grain of truth in those figures, which had in fact been so exaggerated that even Communist troops and pro-Communist public opinion refused to believe them as a matter of simple logic.

• • •

Popular uprising and tactical surprise were the two key factors that led to genuine victory as the Communists viewed it. Both had been the objectives set forth in the offensive plan, whose success was predicated on their being achieved.

As the offensive unfolded, everyone could see that the Communists were able to achieve only one of these objectives; the much-expected "general uprising" never materialized. If our side was the victim of military surprise, then the total indifference shown by the South Vietnamese people toward Communist instigations came about perhaps as an even bigger surprise for our enemy, because it was political.

Just as we kept asking ourselves why we were surprised, our enemy must have asked himself the same thing. This surprise of his, like ours, had its own causes. For one thing, he had misread the feelings of the South Vietnam population. It was true that urban unrest had crippled South Vietnam to some extent ever since the Buddhist showdown in 1963. This and the subsequent political turmoil, coupled with antigovernment, anti-US protests and demonstrations which climaxed in disruptive acts of violence, were obviously the manifestations of a frustrated urban populace undergoing a phase of political growth crisis. They never meant, as our enemy had erroneously construed it, an expression of sympathy toward insurgency or Communism.

• • •

Apparently very few Vietnamese, especially those who had some knowledge of US capabilities, could bring themselves to believe that the United States was unable to detect Communist preparations for the general offensive. They suspected that the United States did know, but withheld the information because it had struck an agreement with the Communists to end the war and disengage from South Vietnam. This was how the surprise came about, they concluded. To some senior Vietnamese commanders, it also appeared that the US intelligence system, in spite of its technological prowess, had simply failed to fully predict the objectives, scope, and timing of the enemy offensive.

• • •

The chain of events that successively took place in the aftermath of the offensive, such as President Johnson's noncandidacy, the reshuffle of US military leaders seen through the resignation of Defense Secretary Robert S. McNamara and the reassignment of General William C. Westmoreland, the complete cessation of bombings against North Vietnam, the mounting antiwar movement in the United States, and the eventual US troop redeployment from South Vietnam—all were considered as political victories by the Communists. Certainly, as they viewed it, these were far more important than just military gains.

To put it differently, our enemy believed that he had broken the will and determination of the United States through his general offensive. To his reasoning, the US intervention in Vietnam had reached its peak; from this time on, it had no other way to go but downhill.

• • •

Reports on the enemy's offensive came to the American public only from one side, the South Vietnamese side. Among the words and pictures depicting war, destruction, and death, there was none that suggested and effectively conveyed the fact that those involved on our side, to include the people, never lost their confidence in the survival of South Vietnam. The end result of it all seemed rather weird. While those directly involved in the fight were still confident and hopeful, the spectators detached from it had already felt disheartened and gave up.

In this atmosphere, charged with prejudices, everything seemed to take on a meaning quite different from normal. General Westmoreland, for example, requested an additional 200,000 US troops, which made sense militarily, since this reinforcement was needed not only to deter future offensive attempts by the Communists but also to exploit the gains achieved after they had been defeated.

But this request unfortunately brought about a totally different effect, an effect which was both undesirable and unexpected. It fed more fuel to the antiwar movement, whose most vocal elements vehemently demanded the withdrawal of all US troops from Vietnam and an immediate end to the war. Although it never had any significant effect on our conduct of the war, other than mollifying the will of some ARVN junior officers, this clamor struck at the hearts of some segments of the American public, and US congressmen as well, who had already felt bitterly disappointed with the military solution in Vietnam, in which they no longer took heart. For, at a moment of utmost confidence and optimism, the enemy suddenly pulled out a surprise attack which seemed to turn everything upside down.

From hindsight, one may be tempted to question the wisdom of that request for more US troops. At a time when Americans felt increasingly adverse to the war, perhaps a political move such as recommending a gradual reduction in the level of US troops by that same amount would have helped level off the mounting tension. Not only would this have been more logical, it could even bring our hard-earned military victory and other gains into proper focus. After all, we should have required [fewer], and not more, troops in South Vietnam, since the enemy had been so soundly defeated.

• • •

All this led us to the conclusion that the outcome of the enemy's 1968 General Offensive–General Uprising had self-compensating but opposing effects for both sides of the war. [For] our side, South Vietnam and the United States, it was obviously a military success but a political failure in the long term. As [for] our enemy, he was unquestionably defeated militarily, but politically it was hardly deniable that he had won.

• • •

Unfortunately, political clairvoyance and wisdom were not the forte of our leadership. As a result, what we gained from the 1968 Tet Offensive turned out to be just an ephemeral victory. But from it our enemy was able to shape . . . the favorable conditions that enabled him to win the final victory in 1975.

NOTES

1. General Nguyen Chi Thanh reportedly died of B-52 bomb-inflicted injuries in his headquarters, COSVN, somewhere in Tay Ninh Province.

2. Tran Van Tra was a lieutenant general who served as commander of COSVN until the fall of Saigon in 1975. Additionally, during 1973 he headed the NLF delegation to the Joint Military Commission.

3. North Vietnam had prepared to face a probable US landing by organizing a paramilitary force and an extensive self-defense system. Its concern was such that the number one priority, economic production, had become secondary to national defense.

4. There were a total of ten candidates for the 1967 presidential election.

5. AK-47s were captured in South Vietnam for the first time in 1964. Then, in late 1966, Communist forces began to use B-40 and B-41 rocket launchers. Despite their early appearance, these weapons were only issued piecemeal and did not become standard for all Communist units until the 1968 offensive.

6. All statistical figures have been obtained from the files of Lieutenant General William E. Potts, former Assistant Chief of Staff for Intelligence, J-2, MACV (1969–1973) and Assistant Chief of Staff for Intelligence, G-2, US Army Pacific (1967–1968).

10

The Cambodian Incursion

Brigadier General Tran Dinh Tho

PREFACE

For several years Cambodia, under the leadership of Prince Norodom Sihanouk, had condoned the use of part of its territory by the Vietnamese Communists for infiltration routes and logistic bases. These bases supported enemy activities in South Vietnam's Military Regions 3 and 4 and a significant part of Region 2, but were protected because of Cambodia's declared neutrality.

However, the change in government on 18 March 1970 provided South Vietnam and the United States the opportunity to neutralize and disrupt much of the enemy logistic system across the border. Sanctioned by the new Cambodian government, and approved by the presidents of the Republic of Vietnam and the United States, South Vietnamese and US forces launched combined operations into Cambodia's border area from 30 April to 30 June 1970.

As the Assistant Chief of Staff, J-3, of the Joint General Staff, RVNAF, I participated in the combined planning for these historic operations with military representatives from Cambodia and the United States, and then monitored the operations constantly for the Chairman, JGS. In conducting my analysis I have relied on my personal involvement and observations as J-3 and interviews with former members of the Republic of Vietnam Armed Forces.

To provide desired information concerning Khmer participation and actions taken by military elements of the US Embassy in Phnom Penh during these cross-border operations, I am most fortunate to have contributions from . . . supporting authors. Lieutenant General Sak Sutsakhan, the last chief of state and chief of the Khmer Armed Forces General Staff, has authored [section] VII.

In the preparation of this monograph, I am particularly indebted to General Cao Van Vien, former Chairman of the Joint General Staff, and Lieutenant General Dong Van Khuyen, who commanded the Central Logistics Command at the time of the Cambodian incursion, for their valuable guidance. I am also grateful for the critical remarks and suggestions contributed by Lieutenant General Ngo Quang Truong, former commander of IV and I Corps, and Major General Nguyen Duy Hinh, the last commander of the 3rd ARVN Infantry Division. Finally, Colonel Hoang Ngoc Lung, the former Assistant Chief of Staff for Intelligence of the JGS, provided his authoritative expertise on matters concerning the enemy. . . . [15 September 1978]

I. INTRODUCTION

The Friendly Situation Prior to the Incursion

The situation throughout South Vietnam in the early months of 1970 was one of continuing improvement, dating back to the introduction of US combat troops into the war during 1965. This was in marked contrast to the dismally bleak prospects of the Republic of Vietnam in late 1964 and early 1965, when few believed that the new nation would escape Communist conquest.

To counter the RVN and US battlefield successes, North Vietnam switched strategy in 1967 and conceived a bold strike at the cities in order to liberate the countryside. Executed during the 1968 Tet holidays, this offensive strike at the cities of South Vietnam had unexpected consequences for both sides.

To our enemy it was a tragic military defeat. Not only his General Offensive–General Uprising failed, but he also lost significant amounts of weapons and many human lives. In addition, his infrastructure suffered extensive damage.

On the RVN side, the population felt greatly stimulated by the enemy's defeat; morale and self-assurance grew. The GVN took advantage of this opportunity to call reservists to active duty and decreed partial mobilization. Popular response to military duty was enthusiastic.

The American people, however, reacted adversely to the Vietnam War, apparently under the influence of press, radio, and TV reports.

• • •

In South Vietnam, the RVNAF continued clearing the enemy from all populous areas. At the same time, the Joint General Staff (JGS), RVNAF, requested the US Military Assistance Command, Vietnam (MACV) for an increase in the RVNAF force structure and new equipment. An initial 820,000 force structure plan was approved by the United States, along with projects to equip the RVNAF with new weapons such as the M-16 rifle, M-60 machine gun, and LAW rocket. Additional equipment, such as M-41 tanks, AN/PRC-25 radio sets, and 105mm howitzers, was also made available, partly to replace war-weary items and partly to equip newly activated units.

In early 1969, formal peace talks began in Paris, with the participation of the United States, the Republic of Vietnam, North Vietnam, and the National Liberation Front (NLF). These talks failed to bring about any concrete results because Communist negotiators used the conference table primarily as a forum for propaganda. They persistently demanded complete US withdrawal from South Vietnam, removal of the constitutional government of the RVN, and self-determination by the South Vietnamese people as to their own political regime.

At the Midway Conference of 8 June 1969, therefore, a joint communiqué issued by the US and the RVN presidents emphasized both countries' agreement to the principle of "self-determination without interference." In addition, President Nixon announced the first increment of US withdrawal, involving 25,000 troops, and the US determination to emphasize the expansion, improvement, and modernization of the RVNAF.

• • •

By the start of 1970 the situation had improved to the point where the RVNAF and US forces could increase their efforts on destroying enemy bases inside South Vietnam and pushing ahead the pacification and development program. . . . Major RVNAF units conducted operations in coordination and cooperation with US units in order to learn and exchange experience on tactics and techniques employed in large-scale combat operations.

• • •

[Thus] in early 1970 the RVNAF and US forces clearly held the initiative throughout South Vietnam. This was especially true in the GVN Military Region 2, 3, and 4 areas, where major enemy units had been driven back to the Cambodia border area.

The Enemy Situation Prior to the Incursion

• • •

By the end of 1969, the total military strength of Communist forces in South Vietnam was estimated at 243,000, to include 133,000 combat troops, 58,000 command and support personnel, and 52,000 guerrillas. In addition there were estimated to be 84,000 political cadres of the Viet Cong infrastructure.[1] These forces were organized into eight division headquarters, 57 regiments, 271 combat battalions, and 58 combat support battalions. Communist units operating in South Vietnam were equipped with weapons made in Russia, Red China, and other Communist countries. These included the AK-47 assault rifle, the RPD automatic rifle, the RPG grenade launcher, 12.7mm and 14.5mm machineguns, and the B-40 and B-41 light antitank rocket launchers. After the 1968 general offensive, Communist forces used extensively 107mm and 122mm rockets. . . . In general, the situation throughout South Vietnam during the first quarter of 1970 was marked by a significant decline in enemy-initiated activity.

• • •

In the Mekong Delta enemy activities increased in March in the That Son (Seven Mountains) area of Chau Doc Province and in the U Minh Forest area of An Xuyen Province. A remarkable fact was the transformation of the 273rd Regiment, NVA 9th Division, which formerly operated in MR-3, into the local D2 Regiment now operating in the U Minh area. This upsurge of enemy activity in the Mekong Delta resulted from military action by Cambodian troops in border areas after the political event in Phnom Penh on 18 March 1970. Faced with increased difficulties in these areas, the enemy was moving his supplies and materiel into the That Son area, where rugged terrain afforded him good concealment and protection. To provide security for these movements, the enemy had increased harassment activities to hold back friendly forces.

On top of these typical activities during the first quarter of 1970, enemy prisoners and ralliers disclosed that COSVN had been planning two offensive campaigns for 1970, in May and July respectively, with the objective of pressing the Paris peace talks toward an early settlement. However, the sudden change of government in Phnom Penh had forced our enemy to abandon these plans and turn his efforts toward Cambodia.

Beginning in April 1970, therefore, there was a flurry of enemy activity in Cambodia. This activity indicated that the enemy was hastily dispersing and displacing his most valuable materiel deeper inside Cambodia. At the same time, the enemy was endeavoring to control a corridor east of the Mekong River leading south in an apparent attempt to secure movements of supplies for his units in MR-3 and MR-4. Evidently the closing of Sihanoukville by the new Khmer regime was beginning to have an adverse effect on the enemy supply system. Additionally, the enemy realized that the supplies already in Cambodia would be of even greater significance to his immediate combat plans.

• • •

RVN-Cambodia Relations

The Republic of Vietnam and Cambodia were neighbor countries who had had contacts with each other for a long time, despite a temporary break in diplomatic relations. Phnom Penh, the capital of Cambodia, was only a 40-minute flight from Saigon. Vietnamese of Khmer origin who lived in South Vietnam numbered about half a million, mostly concentrated in the Mekong Delta. In Vinh Binh and Ba Xuyen Provinces, ethnic Khmer made up about 70 percent of the provincial population. Most of them were farmers; as citizens, they all received the same treatment as other Vietnamese from the GVN. Approximately 400,000 Vietnamese lived in Cambodia.

• • •

Relations between Cambodia and the RVN deteriorated even more when Sihanouk allowed the NLF to open a permanent office in Phnom Penh in June 1967. This office was upgraded to an embassy when the NLF transformed itself into the so-called Provisional Revolutionary Government of South Vietnam in September 1969. Cambodia was, indeed, the first country ever to recognize and establish diplomatic relations with a ghost government which was the antagonist of the GVN.

The ice between Cambodia and the RVN began to melt after Sihanouk was overthrown on 18 March 1970. The new Khmer regime adopted a harsh anti-Communist line, demanding that North Vietnam and the Viet Cong withdraw their troops from Cambodia. During March 1970, firefights pitted the Khmer forces against NVA and VC troops. In April 1970, the Khmer government appealed to the United Nations for action against increased infiltration of NVA and VC troops into Cambodia. By the beginning of April, NVA and VC troops had increased their activities in areas south of Phnom Penh, harassing the port of Kompong Som (formerly Sihanoukville) and other provinces along the coast. In mid-April the new Khmer government also appealed to free nations for assistance in protecting Cambodia's independence and territorial integrity. Then, in late May 1970, diplomatic relations were resumed between the RVN and Cambodia.

The overthrow of Sihanouk came as a rare opportunity for the RVN and United

States to dispose of their long concern about enemy activities on the other side of the border. In addition, the Khmer government continued to deny use of the port of Sihanoukville to North Vietnam's supply ships.

II. THE ENEMY USE OF CAMBODIAN TERRITORY AND ORGANIZATION FOR LOGISTIC SUPPORT

To provide logistic support for enemy units operating in South Vietnam, North Vietnam established three major supply routes: 1) the Ho Chi Minh Trail; 2) the Sihanoukville port route; and 3) the sea infiltration route. . . . A system of bases was developed in conjunction with these routes where equipment and supplies were received, processed, and stored prior to distribution to combat units inside South Vietnam.

The Ho Chi Minh Trail

The Ho Chi Minh Trail had existed in fact since the French–Viet Minh war. Then it was a system of jungle trails and mountain paths running along the Laos-Vietnam border, used by North Vietnam primarily to send mail and cadres to South Vietnam. It was trafficable only by bicycle, ox cart, or elephant. In 1959, to expand its war of aggression in South Vietnam, North Vietnam activated the 559th Transportation Group, with a strength of approximately 50,000 troops and assisted by 100,000 laborers.

This group was made up of several service branch units such as engineer, transportation, air defense, signal, and medical. Troops and laborers of the 559th Group widened existing trails, built new roads, and connected them into an uninterrupted road system which ran from north of the Demilitarized Zone (DMZ) into Laotian territory, then continued south through the tri-border area and terminated in the eastern part of Cambodia adjacent to South Vietnam. To protect the Ho Chi Minh Trail against USAF bombings, North Vietnam installed an extensive air defense system equipped with all calibers of antiaircraft weapons, from 37mm to 100mm guns.

The enemy's efforts to keep the Ho Chi Minh Trail open to infiltration traffic despite devastating, round-the-clock US airstrikes were truly extraordinary. Aerial photos revealed that new detours and floating pontoons appeared only a few days later where roads and bridges had been destroyed beyond repair. To avoid detection by US air reconnaissance, the enemy took great care in camouflaging his vehicles and dispersing his antiaircraft weapons. From the air, it was difficult to locate these well-concealed weapons unless they fired upon our aircraft. For the transportation of foodstuffs, the load was distributed among individual laborers, each carrying in his backpack from 40 to 60 kilos. These laborers moved in stages from one station to another, usually separated by a day's march. In this way they continued their long journey south each day, regardless of the vagaries of the weather, until reaching the final station.

To facilitate the movement of supplies, weapons, and personnel into South Vietnam, the 559th Group developed a series of "binh trams," or stations, along the Ho Chi Minh Trail. Each station was a self-contained logistic base, responsible for a certain area. Its major components often included transportation, engineer, medical, maintenance, and security units and a number of storage facilities. All movements of equipment and supplies originated in Vinh, North Vietnam, from where they branched out to various points of access to the trail system either on the Laotian border or in the DMZ area.

The passes at Mu Gia, Ban Karai, and Ban Raving were major points of entry into lower Laos. They were used mostly for the personnel and supplies en route to South Vietnam. Eventually our enemy perfected his transportation system and techniques to the point of reducing infiltration time by two-thirds. Among the binh trams operated by the 559th Group a few were cited periodically for meritorious achievements and earned the distinguished name of "Ten Thousand Tons." These stations had succeeded in moving more than ten thousand tons of merchandise during a selected period, despite adverse weather and US bombings.

The Sihanoukville Port Route

The other major logistic route besides the Ho Chi Minh Trail was through the port of Sihanoukville. It originated in the port of Sihanoukville and led across lower Cambodia toward enemy base areas on the Cambodia–South Vietnam border. As far as the enemy was concerned, this port route was the safest and most secure because it lay entirely on Cambodian soil. By contrast with the Ho Chi Minh Trail, the Sihanoukville port route was not subjected to US bombing. . . .

In February 1968, high-ranking Viet Cong and North Vietnam officials went to Phnom Penh to negotiate the establishment of bases in Cambodia and the movement of supplies and equipment through Cambodia to these bases. In March 1968, Sihanouk himself announced that he had approved these requests because, as he said, Cambodia and North Vietnam and the Viet Cong were facing the same enemy—the imperialist American aggressors. Then, during an inspection trip to Takeo the same year, he openly declared that Cambodian authorities would voluntarily overlook trade activities by the Cambodian population to supply the Viet Cong with food, and he would even authorize the use of Cambodian hospitals by VC and NVA wounded until they were fully recovered.

The port of Sihanoukville was a major point of entry for NVA supplies and materiel. It was estimated that the tonnages moving through Sihanoukville were sufficient to meet 100 percent of the requirements of enemy units in the RVN III and IV Corps areas, and perhaps two-thirds of the requirements for enemy units in the II Corps area of South Vietnam.

By contract arrangements with the Hak Ly trucking firm, Communist supplies and equipment were unloaded from ships at the pier and transported by truck to Svay Rieng and Kompong Rau, two Cambodian towns located north of Kien Tuong Province. From these points, VC troops and laborers picked up the supplies and moved them to border base areas.

Intelligence reports subsequently confirmed that some Cambodian military vehicles and troops even assisted the Viet Cong in transporting weapons, ammunition, and foodstuffs toward base areas along the border. Cambodian troops and officials at outposts and checkpoints along the border were bribed by smuggler groups into letting contra-band merchandise such as rice and medicine pass into Viet Cong base areas. Business was brisk and lucrative because the Viet Cong usually paid higher prices. These smug-gling activities were conducted mostly by Chinese entrepreneurs residing in Cambodia.

The Sea Route

In addition to the land route down the Ho Chi Minh Trail and the combination sea-land route through the Sihanoukville port, North Vietnam also endeavored to deliver supplies by trawlers or smaller craft to the beaches of South Vietnam. . . . Beginning in 1965, North Vietnam had equipped its SL-2, SL-3, and SL-5 trawlers with weapons and radio equipment for use in infiltration runs. These were cargo vessels measuring from 25 to 40 meters in length and capable of hauling from 100 to 400 tons of merchandise. They all belonged to an infiltration flotilla under the control of the 500th Sea Transpor-tation Group.

Usually these infiltration trawlers were loaded at Hai Phong (North Vietnam) or at ports on Hai Nan Island (Red China). From these ports they sailed into international wa-ters in the South China Sea and continued their journey south until reaching their desti-nation points on South Vietnam's coastline. From 1965 to 1969, a total of 17 such boats were detected and sunk by US naval or VNN ships, particularly at Vung Ro in Phu Yen Province, Long Toan in Vinh Binh Province, and Bo De in An Xuyen Province. By 1969 Operation Market Time, a combined VNN and US 7th Fleet effort, had practically elimi-nated this method of infiltrating supplies and equipment from North to South Vietnam.

The Base Area System

Because of the weakness of the Lao and the neutralist, pro-Communist forces of Si-hanouk, the VC/NVA were able to establish a series of some 20 bases along the borders between Laos, Cambodia, and Vietnam, which permitted movement of all types of sup-plies for VC/NVA units in South Vietnam. . . . So extensive and complete was this sys-tem that the border areas, particularly in Cambodia, became almost as useful to the VC/NVA effort as North Vietnam itself.

Base areas located to the west of I Corps were not in the objective area for the incur-sion. Therefore, discussion is limited to Base Area 609 and those located to the south of it, the majority of which were located on Cambodian territory.

Base Area 609 was the most important of all the base areas. Located in the tri-border area, it provided permanent locations for the headquarters of the B-3 Front and the 2nd NVA Division, and it was from here that enemy operations in the three provinces of Kontum, Pleiku, and Darlac were controlled. It was also developed as a general depot where everything coming from the north was placed in stock to be distributed later to units to the south of the II Corps area. The redistribution mission was the responsibility of Transport Unit 250. Because of the difficulty of the terrain in which it was located, the US/RVNAF forces elected not to attempt a ground assault on Base Area 609; it was subjected to airstrikes only during the incursion. To the south, Base Area 702 was a rear base for all units operating in Pleiku and Kontum Provinces. Base Area 701—or Chu Pong, as it was more commonly known—supplied units operating in Darlac Province and the southern portions of Pleiku Province. Base Area 740, known also by the name Nam Lyr, supported units in Darlac Province and also served as a transit point for supplies moving to Base Area 252. Of interest is the fact that Base Areas 701, 702, and 740 received supplies from Cambodia (Stung Treng, Lomphat, Kratie) as well.

The most important base area in the III Corps zone was Base Area 354. Located to the west of Tay Ninh, its two NVA rear service groups, the 82nd and the 100th, moved supplies into War Zone C and to Base Area 367. Known also as Duong Minh Chau, Base Area 354 was the objective of US Operation Junction City in 1967, and COSVN headquarters was located there in the early days of the war. To the north were Base Areas 707, 353, 350, 351, and 352, where were found supply depots, headquarters for units and military regions, radio stations, training camps, rest areas, hospitals, POW camps, and ammunition dumps. They were all well constructed, often underground, with communications trenches, and well camouflaged. After US and allied forces began to operate in large numbers in [the] RVN, much information was received to indicate that enemy units abandoned their practice of locating headquarters permanently in one area and began to move around in order to avoid allied bombing.

Base Area 351, also known as Bo Duc, was a corridor for moving supplies into [the] southern III Corps area and into War Zone D; it was operated by Rear Transportation Unit 86. Base Area 352, located in [the] Fishhook, was the supply base for all enemy units in the provinces of Tay Ninh, Binh Long, and Binh Duong and was operated by Rear Transportation Unit 70. Base Area 367, also known as Mo Vet Ba Thu, supported all enemy units in Hau Nghia and Long An Provinces; it was also the entry point for all personnel replacements for enemy units in III and IV areas. Of Base Areas 704 and 709, the more important was 709 because it ensured the supply of enemy units in the three provinces of Kien Tuong, Kien Hoa, and Dinh Tuong. Base Area 704 was also known as Giong Bau and is remembered as the site of a large battle involving the ARVN Airborne Brigade in 1964. General Cao Van Vien, then a colonel, commanded the Airborne Brigade and was wounded in the battle.

According to enemy prisoners and ralliers, most supplies intended for enemy units operating in the III Corps area came from Snoul and Mimot in Cambodia. Snoul received food from Kratie, Mimot, and . . . Kompong Cham. From these . . . transit points, laborers and VC troops moved supplies into South Vietnam through border base areas. The enemy made extensive use of motorized sampans and boats for the transportation of supplies out of Base Area 354; they usually moved by night along the Vam Co River and were heavily camouflaged to avoid detection. During Operation Birmingham in 1967 elements of the US 1st Cavalry Division discovered many such sampans and boats and a loading ramp in the Lo Go area west of Tay Ninh.

There were five infiltration routes leading into the Mekong Delta, four of them by land. The first land route originated in the Parrot's Beak area and led toward a point on the common boundary of MR-3 and MR-4, then into Go Cong Province. The second route started from the Crow's Nest area, north of Kien Tuong Province, went through the Elephant's Foot, and entered Base Area 470. The third route, originating in Cambodian territory, went through a point on the common boundary of Kien Phong and Kien Tuong Provinces, then led toward the eastern part of Base Area 470. The fourth route followed the Mekong River from Cambodia and ran into Kien Hoa Province. A small boat infiltration route ran from the ports of Ream and Kep through the Three Sisters area (the coastal area south of Ha Tien) into the northwestern part of the U Minh Forest. From Kep, this route might also go to the western part of Phu Quoc Island and to the northwestern area of the U Minh Forest. . . .

In early 1970 enemy resources for his conduct of the war in the south had to come primarily from North Vietnam. The movement of these men and this materiel, in the volume required, was made possible by the existence of the infiltration routes and base area system in Cambodia, and by the active cooperation of the government in Cambodia. It is particularly significant that all of the bases supporting enemy operations in the III and IV Corps areas received their supplies through the Cambodian port of Sihanoukville (Kompong Som), to [which] they were delivered by ships from North Vietnam. If Sihanouk had been truly neutral, such extensive enemy use of Cambodian territory would not have been possible, and the major combat initiated by the enemy in RVN during 1970 would have been very difficult, if not impossible.

III. PLANNING THE COMBINED INCURSION AND EARLY CROSS-BORDER OPERATIONS

From the Vietnamese point of view, the Cambodian incursion was a series of operations commencing shortly after the change in government in Cambodia on 18 March 1970 and continuing after the withdrawal of US forces from Cambodia on 30 June 1970.[2]

Significant Events

On 8 March 1970 several demonstrations took place in the Cambodian provinces along the border. The demonstrators demanded that North Vietnamese Army and auxiliary troops withdraw from Cambodia. Two days later, the same demonstrations resumed in earnest. In Phnom Penh, angry demonstrators marched to the North Vietnamese embassy and smashed its windows with rocks.

Chief of State Sihanouk meanwhile was undergoing medical treatment and vacationing in France. The direction of governmental affairs was assumed by General Lon Nol and Deputy Prime Minister Sirik Matak. On 12 March 1970 General Lon Nol sent an official message to Hanoi asking for the withdrawal of NVA and auxiliary forces within 72 hours; the deadline was set for 15 March. On 16 March, other demonstrations took place with the same demand, that NVA/VC forces immediately vacate Cambodian territory. On 18 March 1970 the Cambodian National Assembly passed a resolution stripping Prince Sihanouk of all governmental powers. General Lon Nol took over as prime minister, and Prince Sirik Matak continued to serve as deputy prime minister.

• • •

Then, beginning in early April, NVA forces openly attacked Khmer outposts along the border and other towns east of the Mekong River. On 20 April they overran Snoul, 16 kilometers north of Binh Long Province. On 23 April NVA troops attacked and seized Mimot after destroying an important bridge on Route 13 connecting Snoul with Kratie. On 24 April they attacked the coastal city of Kep, north of Ha Tien, and on 26 April they opened fire on ships and boats sailing on the Mekong River. On the same day they also took the town of Ang Tassom, northwest of Takeo City, and attacked Chhlong City northeast of Phnom Penh. . . .

While NVA forces were conducting these attacks, Vietnamese residents in Cambodia were ordered by the new Khmer government to assemble into camps and [were] denied freedom of movement. In Phnom Penh, a special curfew was imposed on Vietnamese residents from 6:00 p.m. to 6:00 a.m. The new Khmer government explained that these restrictive measures were necessary to prevent NVA troops from penetrating Vietnamese communities and carrying out terrorist actions against Khmer officials and troops.

On 15 April the local population of Chau Doc and An Giang Provinces discovered many corpses floating on the Mekong River from the direction of Phnom Penh upstream. According to their reports, nearly a thousand such bodies were sighted, all of them with arms tied in the back and exposing firearm wounds, some of them beheaded. Our people identified most of them as being Vietnamese. Next the Saigon press on 16 April reported that approximately 100 Vietnamese residents were killed in the Takeo area. Later the Khmer government explained that these were accidental deaths caused by firefights between Khmer and NVA troops. According to the foreign press, however, these Vietnamese residents were killed by Khmer troops while living in concentration camps.[3]

On 17 April the United States discreetly sent over to Phnom Penh 6,000 AK-47 rifles which had been captured from the enemy by US and RVN forces in South Vietnam. At the same time, approximately 3,000–4,000 CIDG troops of Khmer origin were transported to Phnom Penh by US aircraft to assist the Khmer forces.

On 17 April 1970 the new Khmer regime officially announced to the world that North Vietnamese troops were invading Cambodia. By that time three out of Cambodia's 17 provinces had been occupied by NVA forces, who were also exerting heavy pressure on five others. At the same time, Cambodia appealed to the United States and other nations of the Free World for help in resisting North Vietnam's aggression.

RVN Appraisal of the Changed Situation in Cambodia

The Cambodian appeal for help in resisting NVN aggression came indeed as a most welcomed opportunity for South Vietnam to redress an unjust situation in which it had been victimized by Sihanouk's prejudice. For years Sihanouk had closed his eyes to North Vietnam's freedom of action on Cambodian territory, allowing our enemy to establish supply bases and sanctuaries in order to pursue his war of aggression against South Vietnam. Every Vietnamese serviceman wondered then why we did not have the right of pursuit into Cambodia.

But all this had changed. We were delighted when the new Khmer government asserted a hard-line policy against our enemy, demanding that he withdraw his troops from Cambodia. We welcomed the new Khmer government's appeal for help to which we could certainly respond, because [the] RVN had found in the new Khmer regime not only a friendly neighbor but also a comrade-in-arms who shared our cause and fought against the same enemy.

Surely the United States could not ignore this plea. As the leader of the Free World, the United States could not let Cambodia or any other free country fall into Communist hands. American credibility was at stake.

• • •

If we did not act, Cambodia would rapidly collapse. The Khmer [National] Armed Forces (Forces Armees Nationales Khmeres, or FANK) were only 32,000 strong, made up mostly of infantry battalions which were not only rudimentarily equipped but also lacking in combat experience. For the past 17 years these forces [had] fought no war. Now they were facing an invading army which was numerically stronger, better equipped, and thoroughly combat-experienced. It was the same army that had been fighting American and South Vietnamese forces for the past several years.

• • •

Since the fighting in Cambodia was just an extension of the Vietnam War, US and RVN forces were entirely justified in pursuing the enemy beyond the border, and, by the same action, they could destroy NVA materiel, installations, and bases on Cambodian territory. Thus the enemy's potential for war-making in both countries would be reduced. But this action could not be conducted by RVN or US forces alone, for obvious reasons. It should be a combined effort to take better advantage of ARVN numerical strength and US firepower. Besides, a combined action in which US forces took the lead was entirely consistent with the current policy of developing the RVNAF combat capabilities.

In the final analysis, this was perhaps the only course of action capable of not only further improving security in South Vietnam and enhancing the chances of Vietnamization success, but also conceivably bringing about early peace. For the key to security had always been the enemy's safe havens along the border, and if Vietnamization were to succeed after US forces had been withdrawn, then it was mandatory that this permanent threat from the border be removed once and for all. Furthermore, the destruction of these border bases might induce our enemy to negotiate seriously, hence improving the chances of [an] early peace settlement.

• • •

As far as the United States was concerned, failure to destroy enemy bases in Cambodia when the chance presented itself might even jeopardize the troop withdrawal schedule. An additional 150,000 troops had been scheduled for return home by April 1971. For this withdrawal to proceed smoothly, as scheduled, it was necessary to keep US casualties and American emotions down. To achieve this, the best way would be to strike directly at the enemy's present and future capability for causing US casualties. For, by next year's April deadlines, what remained of US forces in South Vietnam would be just enough to protect US bases and installations. If the enemy's capability for war-making was not destroyed now, then he would enjoy unlimited opportunities for causing US casualties by next year, without fear of US retaliation.

Concept for the Combined Incursion

The destruction of enemy logistic installations in Cambodia had in fact been considered by US and RVN military strategists for a long time. It was a military action that should have been carried out before 1970. Political dictates, however, had prevented such an action as long as Sihanouk was still in power.

In mid-April 1970 General Abrams, COMUSMACV, brought up and discussed the subject of attacking NVA bases in Cambodia with General Cao Van Vien, Chief of the JGS/RVNAF. Immediately after, General Vien reported the subject of his discussions to President Nguyen Van Thieu. The Cambodian incursion remained a top secret, known only to the MACV commander and the Chief/JGS during their private discussions. No staff divisions of the JGS received any directive for planning.

A few days after General Vien reported to President Thieu, the JGS received verbal orders from President Thieu that III Corps was to coordinate with the US II Field Force for the conduct of operations against NVA base areas in Cambodia. These verbal orders were then transmitted to Lieutenant General Do Cao Tri, III Corps commander, without modification by the JGS. Up to this point, the JGS had neither made formal plans nor issued any formal directives to corps commanders concerning operations in Cambodia.

In late April 1970 President Thieu sent a secret directive to the JGS authorizing the RVNAF to conduct operations in Cambodia. This directive was then disseminated by the JGS to ARVN corps commanders. A copy of this directive was also sent by the JGS to MACV for information. . . .

The RVNAF area of operation was determined to be a zone running the length of the RVN-Cambodia border, with a depth varying from 40 to 60 kilometers inside Cambodia. . . . This zone was called the tactical area of interest (TAOI). Within this TAOI, ARVN corps commanders were authorized, to the extent of their capabilities, to conduct offensive operations against NVA bases, installations, and storage points or in coordination and cooperation with US forces which might be conducting operations in the zone.

• • •

The free use of this zone by the RVNAF had been agreed upon by the Cambodian government and the FANK general staff during meetings between Vice President Ky and the new Khmer authorities when he visited Phnom Penh in April and early May 1970.

The zone of activity for US forces extended no further than 30 kilometers inside Cambodia. It is not known who decided this, but it could have reflected a desire on the part of President Nixon to be able to show that the US incursion would be of a limited nature. Most of the enemy bases were located within this 30-kilometer-deep zone. After driving away enemy units from these bases, and after destroying NVA supply storages in this zone, US forces were to withdraw. 2400 hours, 30 June 1970 was the time by which US forces were to be out of Cambodia.

On 30 June 1970 President Nixon declared that the only remaining American activity in Cambodia after 1 July would be air missions to interdict the movement of enemy troops and materiel where necessary to protect the lives and security of US forces in South Vietnam.[4]

Planning

Two important enemy logistic areas that especially interested the JGS and MACV were the Fishhook and the area west of Saigon (Angel's Wing–Parrot's Beak). The Fishhook, about 50 miles from Saigon, was an area teeming with enemy bases and supply points and [also] COSVN, the enemy headquarters which directed war efforts in the lower half of RVN. The other area, located just west of Saigon and the provinces of Long An and Hau Nghia, provided the enemy not only with bases and sanctuaries, but also the shortest avenue of approach to Saigon. It was from this base area that the entire NVA 9th Division had penetrated into the western suburbs of Saigon during the 1968 Tet Offensive. Our intelligence indicated that several enemy troop cantonments, training centers, and prisoner camps were located in this area.

It was the estimate of the JGS and MACV, supported by the commanders in the field, that to clean out these two areas would probably require an operational effort of from two to four weeks, depending on the situation. The two staffs also agreed that US combat-experienced units such as the 1st Cavalry Division, the 25th Infantry Division, the 11th Armored Cavalry Regiment, and similar ARVN units such as the Airborne Division, armor and ranger units, and infantry divisions under the control of III Corps would be appropriate for the effort.

May and June were two months of particularly good weather which definitely favored all ground operations. Beyond June, however, the weather was apt to impede operations to a certain extent. Lieutenant General Do Cao Tri, III Corps commander, and Lieutenant General Michael S. Davison, II Field Force commander, after discussions finally agreed to select an area of operations which was defined by a 30-kilometer-deep zone from the boundary of MR-3/MR-4 to the boundary of MR-3/MR-2, enveloping the areas of Parrot's Beak and Angel's Wing.

It was also agreed that the RVNAF would operate in the western portion of the combined areas of operations because the terrain of this area was relatively flat and uncovered, in close proximity to axes of communication, and was an area [with which] RVNAF forces were already familiar. During a later stage, the RVNAF area of operations was expanded westward to the Mekong River and northward to Kompong Cham. The other portion of the area of operations, which ran from the Dog's Face [Head] area eastward to the MR-3/MR-2 boundary, was the responsibility of US II Field Force. The terrain in this area was rugged, consisting mostly of mountains and jungle.

• • •

Plans were completed on 27 April 1970. A special meeting was convened at III Corps headquarters in Bien Hoa for the distribution of tasks. The main objective of this operation was Base Areas 706 and 367, which were located in the province of Svay Rieng in

Cambodia and west of Hau Nghia Province. III Corps forces available for operations in Cambodia at that time consisted of four armored cavalry squadrons (M-41 + M-113), two ranger groups (of three battalions each), and the 46th Infantry Regiment, 25th Infantry Division. These units were organized into three infantry-armor task forces, designated Task Forces 325 [*sic:* 225?], 318, and 333.[5] Designated as Toan Thang 42, the operation plan was to be implemented in two phases. In Phase 1, beginning on 29 April 1970, III Corps forces were to attack the Angel's Wing area. For Phase 2, whose date was yet to be determined, III Corps units were to be joined by IV Corps forces.

While III Corps was nearly completing its operation plans, US II Field Force received, on 24 April 1970, a directive from MACV directing it to conduct operations into the Fishhook area within 72 hours. Enemy base areas that US II Field Force had selected as objectives were Base Areas 350 and 351 north of Loc Ninh and Bu Dop, Base Areas 352 and 353 in the Fishhook area, Base Area 354 west of Trai Bi in Tay Ninh Province, and Base Area 707 north of Thien Ngon. All these base areas were mountain and jungle redoubts, sheltering many important enemy logistic installations in addition to COSVN headquarters.

Initially conceived plans envisaged only attacks against enemy base areas located in the immediate vicinity of northern MR-3 provinces. However, after the operation had been in progress for some time, and especially after substantial results had been achieved, II Corps and US I Field Force received orders on 2 May 1970 to plan for attacks against enemy base areas located along MR-2's western border, such as 609, 710, 702, and 740. These were important base areas which lay in the provinces of Kratie and Stung Streng, in the northeast of Cambodia and adjacent to the RVN border. It was from these base areas that NVA forces under the B-3 Front, such as the NT-2 Division and the 40th Artillery Regiment, had launched attacks against ARVN units and border camps of MR-2 during the past few years. The planning by II Corps and I Field Force terminated on 5 May 1970, and cross-border operations were actually initiated as of 6 May 1970.

• • •

IV. THE COMBINED INCURSION

During the period 30 April through 30 June 1970, the Republic of Vietnam and [the] United States conducted combined and well-coordinated operations across the border into Cambodia. They were generally divided into three groups, based on the military region from which they were initiated; code names were selected by the ARVN and US Army commanders concerned:

Toan Thang (Total Victory) for operations conducted by III Corps and US II Field Force

Cuu Long (Mekong) for operations conducted by IV Corps and the Delta Military Assistance Command (DMAC)

Binh Tay (Tame the West) for operations conducted by II Corps and US I Field
Force

Toan Thang 42

Toan Thang 42 was a six-phase operation, five phases of which were conducted during the combined incursion. The sixth phase was conducted by the Vietnamese after 30 June 1970. . . .

TOAN THANG 42, PHASE 1

On 14 April 1970 . . . the JGS directed III Corps to coordinate with US II Field Force for the initiation of an operation with the objectives of destroying and neutralizing NVA bases in Svay Rieng Province of Cambodia, securing Route No. 1 for the ground repatriation of Vietnamese residents in Cambodia, clearing enemy pressure, and assisting Khmer forces in this area. . . .

ARVN forces which were to participate in this operation consisted of two armored cavalry squadrons organic to III Corps, augmented by two others organic to the 25th and 5th Infantry Divisions . . . , one infantry regiment of the 25th Division, and four ranger battalions of the 2nd Ranger Group, which was organic to III Corps.

• • •

On the morning of 29 April 1970 the ARVN task forces crossed the border after preparatory bombardments of target areas by tactical aircraft and artillery. TF 318 advanced westward along Route No. 1, while TF 225 and TF 333 moved west and south. During the first two days, all ARVN task forces made heavy contact with the enemy while advancing toward their objectives. Where enemy contact was light, ARVN armor and infantry units made use of their organic firepower to rapidly overwhelm enemy forces and occupy the objectives. Artillery and tactical air were used on targets of heavy enemy resistance. Captured enemy personnel and materiel were immediately transported back to South Vietnam by VNAF helicopters. When large caches were discovered, they were either guarded pending evacuation or destroyed. These procedures were consistently used throughout the operation.

With regard to the enemy, the element of surprise no longer existed as soon as ARVN task forces had occupied their initial objectives. During the first two days of the operation the enemy had put up a fierce resistance, inflicting on friendly forces 16 killed and 157 wounded. For his part, the enemy suffered 84 killed and 65 weapons captured. Friendly casualties were high because the enemy had solid fortifications and resisted stubbornly. At the same time, ARVN armored units lacked aggressiveness and did not move forward when contact was made. They would stay behind and provide support for the more audacious ranger and infantry units, which always charged ahead. Sometimes ARVN armored vehicles were unable to fire in support because of infantry troops moving in front of them. This greatly reduced the effectiveness of armored firepower. But these shortcomings were gradually corrected by task force commanders.

On 1 May 1970 TF 225 and TF 333 were resupplied in preparation for Phase 2 of the operation. TF 318 meanwhile received orders to advance toward Svay Rieng. Its mission was to clear enemy pressure on that provincial capital, protect Route No. 1 from Svay Rieng to Chipu, and assist the voluntary return to South Vietnam of Vietnamese residents living in this area. Route No. 1 also became an important supply route, not only for this operation but also for the entire Cambodian incursion.

•••

TOAN THANG 42, PHASE 2

This was an operation conducted jointly by III Corps and IV Corps forces against Base Area 367. It began on 2 May 1970, when Task Forces 333 and 225, from their positions south of Route No. 1, attacked southward into the Parrot's Beak area, while Task Force 318, which was commanded by Colonel Tran Quang Khoi, received orders to attack westward along Route No. 1 in an effort to clear the southern part of Svay Rieng.

From Kien Tuong Province, farther south, a large ARVN force from IV Corps was pushing north. This force consisted of the 9th Infantry Division, five armored cavalry squadrons, and one ranger group. It was moving northward along three different axes and was to link up with III Corps forces at a point south of the Parrot's Beak.

During the first day, TF 225 made heavy contact with the enemy 12 kilometers south of Chipu. The task force was supported by both RVN and US tactical air and artillery since US forces had been authorized to conduct operations on Cambodian territory beginning 30 April 1970.

•••

On 3 May 1970 III Corps task forces linked up with IV Corps units from the south. The forces from both corps then continued searching for enemy installations and supply caches in this area.

While ARVN forces were conducting attacks against enemy Base Areas 706 and 367 to the west in Svay Rieng Province, the US 1st Air Cavalry Division and 11th Armored Cavalry Regiment, in cooperation with the ARVN Airborne Division, launched another offensive effort into the Fishhook area north of Binh Long Province on 1 May 1970.

Fighting by that time had spread over almost the entire border area. Cambodian refugees fleeing war hazards spilled over the border and came into South Vietnam in increasing numbers, particularly in the provinces of Tay Ninh and Binh Long. To solve this problem, Lieutenant General Do Cao Tri, III Corps commander, met with the Khmer Military Region 1 commander at III Corps Forward in Go Dau Ha on 3 May 1970. During the meeting General Tri requested that a Khmer official with full authority be placed in charge of Khmer people seeking refuge in South Vietnam.

The Khmer commander promised that this official would be made available within two days. At the same time he asked III Corps to provide the Khmer official in charge of refugees with transportation during his stay in South Vietnam. The Khmer commander also asked the RVNAF to assist in clearing Route No. 1 from the north and south, because this task was beyond the FANK capabilities. At that time the portion of Route No. 1 which ran from Svay Rieng to Neak Luong on the Mekong River was being interdicted by NVA forces. As a result, all communications between Cambodia's eastern provinces and Phnom Penh had been interrupted.

All requests by the Khmer Military Region 1 commander were promptly approved by General Tri. In turn, General Tri mentioned the fact that there were about 4,000 Vietnamese residents being detained in Khmer concentration camps in Svay Rieng Province. He informed the Khmer commander that III Corps would send over a representative to take charge of formalities concerning the repatriation of these Vietnamese and that assistance from the Svay Rieng local government would be needed.

After three days of combined operations with III Corps, IV Corps forces began to withdraw from the area of operations on 5 May 1970. Meanwhile, TF 333 and TF 225 also fell back and assembled along Route No. 1 to be resupplied.

After regular ARVN forces had vacated the Parrot's Beak area to prepare for the next phase of the operation, Civilian Irregular Defense Group and Regional Force units of Tay Ninh Province were redeployed from the Angel's Wing to the Parrot's Beak area in order to continue the search for enemy stores and caches. On the same day, the US 6/31 Infantry and the 3rd Brigade, US 9th Division, also moved into the area to prevent the enemy from returning.

• • •

IV CORPS PARTICIPATION WITH III CORPS IN TOAN THANG 42, PHASE 2

On 2 May 1970 a large IV Corps task force composed of the ARVN 9th Infantry Division, five armored cavalry squadrons (each with three M-113 troops), and the 4th Ranger Group participated in Phase 2 of Operation Toan Thang 42 alongside III Corps forces. This IV Corps task force was commanded by Major General Nguyen Viet Thanh, IV Corps commander, assisted by Brigadier General Tran Ba Di, 9th Division commander.

The IV Corps task force was organized into four armor-infantry elements which moved north from Kien Tuong Province into Cambodia on three axes to link up with III Corps forces in the Parrot's Beak area. This was the largest operation conducted by IV Corps after its two previous limited incursions. The IV Corps armor-infantry task force advanced rapidly on predetermined axes in conventional warfare style, taking advantage of its strong firepower and mobility. During its advance, the task force enveloped the objective area, cutting it up into several small pockets to facilitate search and destroy operations.

• • •

During two days of heavy engagement with the enemy the IV Corps task force discovered and seized several important enemy weapon and supply caches. At the conclusion of the three-day operation conducted in cooperation with III Corps, the IV Corps task force had killed 1,010 enemy, captured 204 others, and received 19 ralliers; its own casualties amounted to 66 killed and 330 wounded. In addition, the task force seized a total of over 1,000 individual and 60 crew-served weapons, including seven 120mm mortars and five 75mm recoilless rifles. It also captured and destroyed in excess of 100 tons of assorted ammunition. On 5 May, IV Corps armor-infantry elements withdrew from the area in order to prepare for the next stage of cross-border operations.

TOAN THANG 42, PHASE 3

After destroying enemy installations and stores south of Route No. 1, III Corps forces switched their offensive efforts northward. During this phase of the operation, US naval and VNN units were active along the Kompong Spean River, forming a screen to the east. One element of the US 25th Infantry Division also operated in the northeast.

On the morning of 7 May 1970 Task Force 225 attacked westward from Ben Soi, linking up with Task Force 318, which attacked northward from the Prasot-Chipu area. Task Force 333 remained in reserve. During the day both task forces made contact with the enemy. In particular, TF 318 engaged the enemy at ten kilometers north of Prasot, killing 182 and capturing eight. To the east, in the meantime, TF 225 discovered an enemy hospital with a 200-bed capacity and seized quantities of surgical equipment and medicine.

In the afternoon of 9 May, after both task forces had linked up in an area southwest of Kompong Trach, Task Force 318 pushed northward across the Kompong Spean River. Then both task forces continued searching for enemy installations and stores until 11 May 1970.

On 11 May 1970 President Nguyen Van Thieu made an inspection visit to ARVN units in the field, accompanied by Vice President Nguyen Cao Ky. After being briefed by General Tri on the results of the operation, President Thieu informed him of the general situation throughout Cambodia, which was becoming more serious with every passing day. Our residents in Phnom Penh were being badly mistreated by Khmer authorities and needed to be repatriated as soon as possible. To evacuate them, he ordered that III Corps quickly clear Route No. 1 and be prepared to relieve Kompong Trach when required.

TOAN THANG 42, PHASE 4

As a result of President Thieu's directives, General Tri immediately redeployed his forces. Task Forces 318, 333, and 225 were withdrawn from the Kompong Trach area and assembled along Route No. 1 from Chipu to Svay Rieng the same day in order to prepare for Toan Thang 42, Phase 4. This operation was launched on 13 May 1970 for the purposes of clearing Route No. 1 and making way for the repatriation of Vietnamese residents from Phnom Penh. All three task forces, with TF 318 taking the lead, moved westward along Route No. 1 from Svay Rieng. They were to link up with IV Corps forces at Kompong Trabek (during that time, IV Corps was conducting an operation to clear the Mekong River).

• • •

While directing the operation to clear Route No. 1 . . . General Tri also sought to coordinate an attack by IV Corps forces along the Mekong River toward Kompong

Cham. However, Lieutenant General Ngo Dzu, IV Corps commander, disagreed because he felt it [was] too remote an objective for his corps. At the same time, General Tri also planned to reinforce Kompong Cham with an ARVN ranger battalion as a show of force, but this was never done. Therefore, after clearing Route No. 1, and after III Corps had linked up with IV Corps forces on 14 May, General Tri decided to send a liaison team to Kompong Cham to monitor the situation there. General Tri's interim arrangement would provide for the support of Kompong Cham by tactical air through the liaison team, pending a relief action by ARVN units.

• • •

At about the same time, the Khmer press in Phnom Penh carried front-page stories alleging that RVNAF units, while operating in Cambodia, had been repressive against the Khmer population and had ransacked Khmer properties. The Khmer press also asked the RVNAF to withdraw from Cambodia. General Tri felt hurt and was angered by these press articles. He considered this outcry to be an insult to the RVNAF. He privately ordered an investigation and was determined to provide adequate punishment and enforce strict military discipline in case the stories were proven true. In case they were not, he made the decision to recommend to the JGS and President Thieu that the ARVN liaison team at Kompong Cham should be called back and that all air support missions for the benefit of FANK forces should be terminated.

The Relief of Kompong Cham

Kompong Cham was the third largest city in Cambodia and was the seat of the Khmer Military Region 1 headquarters. The mission of relieving this important Cambodian town, located on the Mekong northwest of the Chup Plantation, was given to the III Corps commander, who designated the operation Toan Thang 42, Phase 5. The city was defended by a garrison of four Khmer infantry battalions. But, because of low strength, these four battalions had only 1,000 men; artillery support was provided by a battery of four 105mm howitzers with approximately 1,000 rounds.

Beginning on 12 May 1970, NVA forces of the 9th Division occupied the Chup Plantation area northeast of Kompong Cham. They shelled the city and mounted sniper attacks against its eastern part. The Kompong Cham airfield, northwest of the city, was rendered unusable, being shelled constantly day and night. Communication, by way of the Mekong River from Phnom Penh to Kompong Cham, was also interdicted. The city was then effectively isolated, increasing the problem of food and ammunition shortage. The garrison's morale was at a low ebb; its troops were wondering for how long they could hold under the siege.

To relieve Kompong Cham from the enemy's siege, IV Corps initiated Operation Toan Thang 42, Phase 5, beginning on 23 May 1970. Task Forces 333 and 318 moved on Route No. 7 from Krek and on Route No. 15 from Prey Veng, respectively, both converging north toward an area in the vicinity of the Chup Plantation. As soon as it moved out from Krek toward Chup, the 7th Airborne Battalion of TF 333 was engaged heavily by the enemy. With effective support from US tactical air and gunships, TF 333 quickly controlled the situation, killing 26 enemy and capturing 16. The enemy force was the 2nd Battalion, 272nd Regiment, NVA 9th Division. Two days later, on 25 May, armor and ranger elements of Task Force 318 clashed violently with the enemy south of Route No. 7. The fighting did not abate until the next morning.

• • •

During the day of 28 May, while continuing to advance toward the Chup Plantation, TF 318 again engaged the enemy in heavy fighting, causing him 73 killed, while we suffered 16 wounded. Task Force 225, which was meanwhile operating south of Route No. 1, found additional enemy supply caches and seized a total of 14 tons of assorted ammunition, seven radio sets, four 60mm mortars, three 82mm mortars, two 120mm mortars, and one 75mm howitzer.

Fighting then raged throughout the next day between TFs 318 and 333 and elements of the NVA 9th Division in the area north of Chup. Meanwhile, TF 225 also engaged the enemy heavily in the Angel's Wing area with the support of friendly artillery and tactical air. Enemy antiaircraft fire was particularly heavy during the fighting, causing one VNAF Skyraider, one US F-100, and one Cobra gunship to be downed.

On 1 June 1970, as the fighting ceased, the clearing of Chup Plantation was considered accomplished. However, ARVN forces continued to search for enemy supply caches in this area and expanded their activities to the northeast in an effort to clear enemy pressure from east of Kompong Cham.

• • •

On 19 June 1970, during a meeting at Independence Palace with the Chairman, Joint General Staff, and the four ARVN corps commanders to reassess the cross-border operations, President Thieu concluded that the RVNAF would continue operations in Cambodia despite the withdrawal of US forces planned for 30 June. He also ordered III Corps to proceed with the relief of Kompong Cham for the second time. Additionally, Cambodians were to be prevented from seeking refuge in South Vietnam because, according to enemy prisoners and reliable sources, NVA troops were attempting to infiltrate by passing as refugees.

To accomplish the relief of Kompong Cham as ordered, III Corps deployed its Task Forces 318, 333, and 225 on 21 June. All three task forces attacked toward Chup along Route No. 7 from Krek. After six days of operations, the Chup area and the area southeast of Kompong Cham were practically cleared of enemy forces. To further clear the area south of Kompong Cham, Route No. 15, and the Prey Veng area, III Corps forces were deployed south from Chup toward Prey Veng. TF 318 left the 33rd Ranger Battalion and 1/18 Armored Cavalry Squadron in positions along Route No. 15 to protect this vital supply line.

This was done in the light of intelligence reports that the 1st Regiment, NVA 9th Division, was attempting to interdict Route No. 15 and ambush TF 318 on its way to relieve Prey Veng. En route, TF 318 was heavily engaged by the enemy on 29 June while it advanced along Route No. 15. (During this phase of the operation, which took place beyond the 30 kilometer limit, ARVN units were not accompanied by US advisors.) The fighting resulted in 165 enemy killed. Friendly forces suffered 34 killed, 204 wounded, and 24 missing in action.

The entire Toan Thang 42 operation was considered the most successful ever conducted by III Corps. According to depositions made by enemy prisoners and ralliers, and in particular judging by the large quantities of enemy supplies and materials captured, the following conclusions were quickly apparent:

1. The operation had effectively upset the enemy's plans to overthrow the Lon Nol regime and, as soon as he succeeded in Phnom Penh, launch an offensive in RVN MR-3. This was first disclosed by enemy Lieutenant Colonel Nguyen Thanh, deputy commander of Sub-Military Region 2, who rallied to the GVN. . . .
2. The morale of enemy troops had been seriously affected by the operation, particularly among troops under Sub-Military Region 2. In a few instances, cadres and troops had refused to go into combat. Many had deserted to avoid fighting.
3. The area of Ba Thu and Angel's Wing, considered invincible, had been heavily damaged. Up to 90 percent of enemy supplies in this area had been destroyed or seized by the RVNAF. Heavy casualties had effectively reduced enemy troop strength by 25 percent, especially among Sub-MR-2 units and the Tay Ninh local-force units. As a result, the enemy met with serious difficulties in replacing human and material losses.

This operation also testified to the remarkable progress made by our ARVN logistic system, whose efforts to keep ARVN combat units adequately supplied were most commendable. A few problem areas still existed, such as the shortage of spare parts for armored personnel carriers, which accounted for their high unserviceable rate despite continuing efforts by US and ARVN repair teams in the field.

Toan Thang 43, 44, 45, and 46

The principal units involved in this series of operations were the ARVN Airborne Division, the US 1st Cavalry Division (Airmobile), the US 25th Infantry Division, and the US 11th Armored Cavalry Regiment. They were conducted in the Fishhook area and against Base Areas 350, 351, 352, 353, 354, and 707.

TOAN THANG 43

On 26 April 1970, Major General Elvy B. Roberts, commanding the US 1st Cavalry Division, received orders from Lieutenant General Michael S. Davison, Commander, US II Field Force, to prepare for an operation designed to destroy COSVN headquarters, located in the Fishhook area on Cambodian territory. The US 1st Cavalry Division was to launch this operation within 72 hours after orders were received.

During three consecutive days, from 26 to 28 April, the US 1st Cavalry Division commander and Lieutenant General Du Quoc Dong, the Airborne Division commander, discussed and developed combat plans for the operation. Both units had been operating together in the northernmost provinces of Military Region 3 since the beginning of 1970, within the framework of the Dong Tien campaign, a combined program undertaken by ARVN III Corps and the US II Field Force designed to improve RVNAF combat effectiveness. In their planning, the two division commanders had to review their force dispositions so as to be able to assemble adequate units for the cross-border operation and at the same time ensure that effective security would be maintained in their areas of responsibility in Military Region 3.

• • •

On 28 April the US 1st Cavalry Division commander received orders to initiate the operation within 48 hours. He immediately met with the ARVN Airborne Division commander to review plans [and] the general enemy situation. Both agreed that a combined task force consisting of air cavalry and airborne elements should be employed for the initial stages of the operation. Command and control of this task force was entrusted to Brigadier General Robert M. Shoemaker, Deputy Commander, US 1st Cavalry Division; this task force therefore was designated Task Force Shoemaker. In the meantime, both division staffs began developing plans for the next stage.

The initial concept of operations, as developed by the task force commander, was to employ a combined force consisting of the 3d US Cavalry Brigade (reinforced by one mechanized infantry battalion and one armor battalion), the 3rd ARVN Airborne Brigade, and the 11th US Armored Cavalry Regiment (11th ACR) in a heliborne assault combined with ground attacks. The plan of operation called for extensive preparatory support by B-52s, tactical air, and artillery, followed by the heliborne insertion of the 3rd Airborne Brigade into three landing zones north of the objective to block the enemy's escape routes. Next, this airborne element would advance south to link up with the task force (-) which, in the meantime, would be attacking northward from their positions in the south, with the 3rd Brigade, 1st US Cavalry Division, to the west and the 11th ACR to the east and southeast.

The 1/9 US Cavalry was to conduct reconnaissance patrols over the northern part of the area of operation to detect and further block enemy escapes. In conjunction with this pincer movement in Cambodia, the 9th Regiment, 5th ARVN Division, and the 1st ARVN Armored Cavalry Squadron were to conduct reconnaissance patrols along the western part of Binh Long Province, opposite the area of operation. After the occupation of preplanned objectives, all units were to continue the search for enemy installations and supply caches in the area of operation.

In the early morning of 1 May 1970, six B-52s began bombing the Fishhook area, their last bomb expended by 0545 hours. Fifteen minutes later, US artillery opened its barrages on the area where the 3rd Airborne Brigade was to be inserted. At 0630 hours, the 1st Armored Cavalry Squadron of III Corps moved northwest of An Loc toward the Cambodian border. It was then that the first 15,000-pound bomb was dropped from a US aircraft to clear a landing zone (LZ East) for the 3rd Airborne Brigade; 15 minutes later, another 15,000-pound bomb was detonated, clearing Landing Zone Center.

•••

Ten minutes after the 1/9 Cavalry completed its reconnaissance mission, the first armada of helicopters arrived and inserted an airborne unit at Landing Zone East. Upon touching ground in total safety, the airborne unit began establishing a fire support base with 105mm and 155mm howitzers. While the helicopter armada was landing troops, the 11th ACR moved into its assembly area and crossed the line of departure toward the northeast to link up with the 3rd Cavalry Brigade (+), which had been airlifted across the border at 0945 hours.

The 5th Airborne Battalion was helicoptered by an armada of 62 helicopters, with escort provided by 22 Cobra gunships, into Objective B at 0945 hours and into Landing Zone Center at 1005 hours. Meanwhile, to the west, the 9th Airborne Battalion also made a heliborne assault on Objective A. Both US and ARVN assault forces were surprised by the relative lack of resistance in the objective area. This seemed to conflict with our intelligence reports, which had indicated the presence of enemy antiaircraft and, possibly, elements of COSVN headquarters. However, our forces met with no significant enemy resistance. No antiaircraft fire was observed, and there was only sporadic, scattered small arms fire.

This was a good indication that the enemy had been caught by surprise. He probably had not believed that US and RVN forces would even be able to land in such rough and heavily covered terrain. Upon landing, both airborne elements, the 5th and 9th Airborne Battalions, saw an enemy force of about 200 fleeing in disorder without fighting. Cobra gunships pursued the escaping enemy troops, killing about 20–30 of them.

By the end of the first day friendly forces had achieved remarkable results. The US 1/9 Cavalry, which covered the northern approaches to the objective area, had detected and attacked several groups of enemy troops attempting to break away, killing a total of 156. US tactical air had flown 185 sorties over the area of operation and accounted for 109 enemy killed. In its assigned area of operation, the 5th Airborne Battalion killed 28 and captured seven enemy troops. The prisoners revealed [that] they belonged to three different organizations: the 250th Rehabilitation Unit, the 50th Rear Security Unit, and the 1st Battalion, 165th Regiment, NVA 7th Division.

The 3rd Airborne Battalion discovered an underground cache containing about 6,000 pounds of medicine and new surgical equipment in original packings. The markings on these boxes indicated that the equipment came from Europe and had been sent to Phnom Penh via Air France. As for the US 11th ACR, its 2/11 [Armored Cavalry Squadron] had engaged and killed 50 enemy while suffering only two dead. It also discovered regimental-level troop cantonment facilities.

On 3 May 1970 Task Force Shoemaker was augmented with the US 2nd Cavalry Brigade. During that day, several enemy supply caches were found. In particular the US 1/9 Cavalry, while patrolling in the north, discovered an enemy truck park. Tactical air was called and destroyed seven 2-1/2-ton, 13 3/4-ton, and three 1/4-ton trucks.

Subsequently, on 4 May, US air cavalry elements discovered several enemy shelters and a truck network in a jungled area northwest of the area of operation. Observation planes which were sent over that area reported sighting enemy thatched huts and houses and, farther to the south, several radio antennas. Continuing their observation coverage to the northeast, the pilots guided infantry troops into the area and thus enabled them to discover many underground shelters full of weapons and ammunition, in addition to several houses. This area contained so many enemy installations and caches that US forces dubbed it "The City."

During an extensive search period from 5 to 13 May, friendly forces discovered a total of 182 weapons and ammunition caches, 18 buildings used as mess halls, a large training base complete with firing range, and a farm to provide chickens and pigs. In addition to weapons and ammunition, the uncovered caches also contained foodstuffs, military clothing, medicine, and medical equipment. Most remarkable was the fact that all supplies and material were new. The area called "The City" extended over three square kilometers and was well organized as a supply base with separate receiving and issuing sections. The general condition of buildings and underground shelters indicated that they had been built about two and a half years previously. But several stronger facilities looked as if they [had] been constructed during the last six months.

The following is a partial list of enemy supplies and material uncovered in "The City":

      1,282 individual weapons
    319,000 rounds of 12.7mm ammunition
     25,200 rounds of 14.5mm antiaircraft ammunition
  1,555,900 rounds of AK-47 ammunition
      2,110 hand grenades
     58,000 pounds of explosives
    400,000 rounds of caliber .30 machine gun ammunition
         22 crates of anti-personnel mines
         30 tons of rice
          8 tons of corn
      1,100 pounds of salt

Judging from the substantial quantities of supplies found, this area was probably one of the most important enemy supply bases in Cambodia.

• • •

The large quantities of stored equipment and supplies found by our forces in this base area, and the enemy's current road system in Cambodia, were indicative of his capability to move several thousand tons of supplies per month. This in turn showed that NVA forces operating along the Cambodian border could always expect to obtain their supplies in a very short time.

While US air cavalry and armor and ARVN airborne units operated with success in the Fishhook area, III Corps and US II Field Force on 6 May 1970 launched three simultaneous attacks against enemy Base Areas 350 of Binh Long Province, 351 north of Phuoc Long Province, and 354 west of Tay Ninh Province.

TOAN THANG 44

Conducted by the US 25th Infantry Division, this operation had the objective of destroying enemy Base Area 354, which was located in Cambodia west of Tay Ninh Province. Forces participating in this operation consisted of the 1st Brigade, US 25th Division, with two mechanized battalions (1/5 and 2/22) and two infantry battalions (2/14 and 3/22).

• • •

TOAN THANG 45

On 6 May 1970, the US 1st Cavalry Division (Airmobile) initiated a second cross-border operation, striking against enemy Base Area 351, which was located in Cambodia northwest of Bu Dop, Phuoc Long Province.

• • •

The US 1st Cavalry Division began withdrawing its forces from Cambodia on 20 June. One after another, US battalion headquarters and fire support bases were dismantled and returned to South Vietnam. By 27 June the last firebase of the division had been removed from Cambodia. During this redeployment period, extensive B-52 strikes were used to destroy enemy forces and prevent them from following in pursuit. The last US unit terminated its activities in Cambodia and returned to South Vietnam on 29 June.

TOAN THANG 46

On 6 May 1970, simultaneously with the initiation of Toan Thang 45 by US forces, the 9th Regiment, ARVN 5th Infantry Division, launched operation Toan Thang 46 against enemy Base Area 350. Two battalions of the 9th Regiment were inserted into the target area by US helicopters. During the first few days contacts with the enemy were scattered, but at every contact point our forces invariably discovered an enemy cache containing either foodstuffs or weapons and ammunition. To reinforce this operational force, the 1st Armored Cavalry Squadron was brought into the area of operations on 11 May.

During the day of 21 May both ARVN battalions were heavily engaged by the enemy. However, they received effective support from US tactical air and gunships. After the dust of the battle had settled, our forces discovered an enemy hospital complex capable of providing medical treatment for 500 men. This hospital was equipped with surgical facilities and had adequate supplies of medicine. . . .

During the last two weeks of the operation the 9th Regiment discovered additional enemy supply caches, mostly weapons and ammunition. By mid-June enemy activity had increased significantly but was conducted mostly against isolated ARVN elements.

• • •

By the evening of 27 June our forces were already in night defensive positions on the RVN side of the border. The 9th Regiment continued operating in this border area until 30 June, when it was returned to its rear base at Chon Thanh.

The following is a recapitulation of the results obtained during the operations conducted by US and RVN forces against the Fishhook and Base Areas 350, 351, 352, 353, 354, and 707:

Toan Thang 42: 3,588 enemy killed or captured. 1,891 individual weapons, 478 crew-served weapons, 380.6 tons of ammunition, 1,041.6 tons of rice seized.

Toan Thang 43: 3,190 enemy killed or captured. 4,693 individual weapons, 731 crew-served weapons, 338.4 tons of ammunition, 2,698 tons of rice seized.

Toan Thang 44: 302 enemy killed or captured. 297 individual and 34 crew-served weapons, 4 tons of ammunition, and 217 tons of rice seized.

Toan Thang 45: 1,527 enemy killed or captured. 3,073 individual and 449 crew-served weapons, 791 tons of ammunition, and 1,583 tons of rice seized.

Toan Thang 46: 79 enemy killed or captured. 325 individual and 41 crew-served weapons, 19.7 tons of ammunition, and 79 tons of rice seized.

The quantities of weapons, ammunition, and rice seized in these areas indicated that they were important enemy rear service bases. Most captured crates bore the markings of Communist bloc countries; these items were new and still wrapped in original packings. In particular, weapon and ammunition caches were found in deep underground shelters, well camouflaged and located in dense jungles. All accesses to these supply caches were mined and rigged with booby traps. Most of our casualties were caused by these mines and booby traps.

Clearing the Mekong and Repatriating Vietnamese

• • •

In response to an appeal by the Khmer government which specifically asked for the clearing of the Mekong River and axes of communication to the south by the RVNAF, IV Corps launched Operation Cuu Long I. In addition to its primary objective of clearing the Mekong River, this operation was also intended to repatriate Vietnamese residents in Phnom Penh.

• • •

Despite its success, Operation Cuu Long I was marred by the accidental death of Major General Nguyen Viet Thanh, IV Corps commander, who had effectively directed the operation during its initial stage. On 12 May 1970, while on a field inspection trip over the areas of Kien Tuong and Kien Phong, his helicopter collided with a gunship and crashed. His death occurred while the clearing operation on the Mekong River was still unaccomplished. He was replaced by Major General Ngo Dzu.

• • •

Binh Tay I, II, and III

Not until two days after III Corps and US II Field Force had begun their cross-border operations into Cambodia did II Corps and US I Field Force receive orders to attack enemy base areas along the western border of MR-2. When these orders were received, on 2 May 1970, units of the US 4th Infantry Division and the ARVN 22nd Infantry Division were conducting operations in enemy Base Area 226 northwest of Binh Dinh Province.

To carry out the JGS and MACV orders, II Corps and US I Field Force quickly extracted the 22nd ARVN Division and US 4th Division forces from their areas of operation to refit and resupply. They were moved to staging areas to prepare for cross-border activities.

While the US 4th Division units were being extracted from Base Area 226, the division staff and its ARVN counterpart of the 22nd Division made plans to attack and destroy enemy Base Area 702, located in Cambodia west of Pleiku. . . . When plans were completed, the participating units of the US 4th Division and the 40th Regiment, 22nd Division, were moved on 4 May to a staging area near Special Forces Camp New Plei D'Jereng, west of Pleiku.

• • •

In the meantime, units of the 40th Regiment, 22nd Division, and the 2nd Ranger Group continued search operations in Base Area 702. . . . Operation Binh Tay I was terminated on 25 May 1970. A tally of results provided the following statistics. On the friendly side, 43 were killed and 118 wounded. The enemy incurred 212 killed and seven detained. Our forces seized 20 crew-served and 859 individual weapons. They also confiscated or destroyed 519 tons of rice and burned down 2,157 huts and other surface installations used by the enemy.

• • •

BINH TAY II

II Corps initiated Binh Tay II on 14 May 1970 against Base Area 701 and B-3 Front units such as the 24th, 28th, or 66th Regiments and the 40th Artillery Regiment. Historically, these units would displace toward this base area and from there launch attacks against our border camps in Darlac and Pleiku Provinces.

According to II Corps plans, the 22nd Infantry Division was assigned to carry out this task. After the landing zones had been extensively bombarded by US tactical air, two regiments of the 22nd Division, the 40th and 47th [Regiments], were inserted by US helicopters into the north of Base Area 701. At the same time, the 3rd Armored Cavalry Squadron and reconnaissance elements of the 22nd Division also crossed the border and attacked from the south in order to link up with the two infantry regiments in the north. Meanwhile, a US air cavalry unit conducted patrols to the west to interdict all enemy evasive efforts.

As soon as they landed, troops of the 40th Regiment discovered an enemy ammunition cache containing about two tons of 82mm mortar rounds and B-40 rockets. Continuing their push southward, ARVN infantry elements discovered two additional enemy caches on 17 May from which they seized 100 AK-47 rifles, six crew-served weapons, 10,000 pounds of rice, and 660 kilos of peanuts. On 18 May elements of the 47th Regiment again found an enemy supply cache and seized 159 assorted weapons. Extending their search, our troops discovered an enemy dispensary where they seized 2,000 pounds of medicine and some surgical equipment still in original packings. The next day, 19 May, all elements of the 47th Regiment reported contact with the enemy. When the fighting abated, friendly forces discovered two enemy caches and seized 87 individual weapons and 17 crew-served weapons, including seven Chicom flamethrowers. On the friendly side, one was killed and four wounded.

• • •

During their two-week foray into Base Area 701, ARVN forces made scattered contact only with enemy elements guarding supply installations or with guerrillas. No contact was ever made with any of the enemy's major force units, which in all probability had displaced deep inside Cambodia to conserve their forces. Despite this, our forces managed to kill 73 enemy and detain six others.

BINH TAY III

This operation was conducted by the ARVN 23rd Infantry Division and consisted of three phases. Phase 1, from 20 May to 3 June 1970, and Phase 2, from 4 to 12 June 1970, were intended to destroy enemy Base Area 740, which was located in Cambodia west of Quang Duc and Darlac Provinces.

• • •

On 20 May 1970 Task Forces 8 and 45 initiated operations against Base Area 740. TF 45 was inserted by US helicopters into the northern part of the base area, while TF 8 advanced toward the southern part. Meanwhile, elements of the 7/17 US Air Cavalry Battalion conducted interdiction patrols over the west and north of the objective area, and CIDG units operated along the border to block enemy evasions into Military Region 2. From the RVN side of the border, 8-inch and 175mm artillery units provided firepower support for ARVN forces in the objective area.

• • •

During Phase 1, our forces suffered 29 killed and 77 wounded while inflicting on the enemy 96 killed, one detained, and one rallier. Phase 1 ended on 3 June as Task Force 8 withdrew from the area of operations but continued security of Route No. 14 from Duc Lap to Bu Prang. Phase 2 began on 4 June. While Task Force 45 continued search activities in the area of the Nam Lyr mountain range, Task Force 44 (-) was inserted north of TF 45, and the US 21st [*sic:* 2/1st?] Cavalry continued its patrols west and northwest of the area of operations.

• • •

After one week of refitting and recuperation, the 23rd Division initiated Phase 3 of the operation. During this phase, all three task forces . . . were committed. On 19 June TFs 44 and 45 made heliborne assaults into an area sandwiched between Base Areas 201 and 740. Two fire support bases were established, one in Cambodia for the support of TF 45 and the other in the RVN for the support of TF 44. Throughout the nine days of Phase 3, ARVN forces only made sporadic contact with the enemy, but discovered an important enemy supply cache.

• • •

Friendly casualties during Phase 3 were light as compared to the enemy's and in proportion to the size of forces committed and the duration of the operation. Our forces suffered 38 killed, 113 wounded, and two missing, while inflicting on the enemy 149 killed, two detained, and one rallier. Our losses thus amounted to only one-fourth of the enemy's. In addition, our forces seized 581 individual and 85 crew-served weapons and 447 tons of rice. Another 81 tons of rice were destroyed on the spot. Most weapons captured in this area were either rusty or in bad condition; the more serviceable weapons had probably been removed prior to the operation.

This was the first division-sized operation ever conducted by the 23rd Infantry Division. As compared to the other ten ARVN divisions, the 23rd had only modest capabilities in terms of combat effectiveness and overall performance.

• • •

V. COOPERATION AND COORDINATION FROM 30 APRIL TO 30 JUNE 1970

US-RVN Cooperation and Coordination

For the JGS, the question of launching ground operations across the national border to destroy NVA and VC logistic bases and supply points was not simply a military question; such an incursion would have important political implications as well. For his part, President Nguyen Van Thieu, being a senior and experienced military officer, understood very well the military value to the RVNAF/US military effort to be derived from destroying the enemy bases in Cambodia. Barely one day after Sihanouk was deposed, President Thieu declared, "If Cambodia and South Vietnam and her allies cooperate along the border, then I believe the Communists would find it impossible to stay."

Therefore when General Abrams, COMUSMACV, consulted with the JGS on this question, General Cao Van Vien, Chief of the JGS, immediately reported to President Thieu for guidance and a decision. Before authorizing the RVNAF to conduct operations into Cambodia, President Thieu certainly would have consulted the US Ambassador in Saigon and obtained his concurrence and support.

• • •

American support became stronger and more direct beginning on 1 May 1970 when US forces received the green light to participate in the Cambodian incursion. As of that date, US advisors were also authorized to accompany ARVN units into Cambodia within the self-imposed limit of 30 kilometers or 21.7 miles.

As a result, ARVN units in Cambodia began to receive artillery support from heavier US 8-inch and 175mm pieces in addition to their own organic 105mm and 155mm howitzers. To each ARVN task force was attached US artillery forward observers from the US 23rd Artillery Group. US tactical air and B-52 sorties were also increased for the benefit of ARVN units. This made quite a difference for these ARVN units, which, prior to 1 May, had only the weaker support of the Vietnam Air Force.

For the better use of combined RVN-US firepower assets, senior US advisors to ARVN task forces initiated the establishment of fire coordination centers (FCC) whose members included the senior advisor, a US artillery officer, an ARVN forward artillery observer, and a VNAF forward air controller team. These FCCs provided for the maximum use of both US and RVN artillery and air firepower.

RVN-Khmer Cooperation and Coordination

Immediately after General Lon Nol took power, GVN Vice President Nguyen Cao Ky made secret trips to Phnom Penh twice during April 1970 and an official visit in early May. During this official visit, he was accompanied by Lieutenant General Nguyen Van Vy, our minister of defense. These visits had the objectives of reestablishing diplomatic relations between the RVN and Cambodia and discussing measures of mutual assistance between the two countries. Since the new Cambodian regime had proved inimical to North Vietnam, in contrast to Sihanouk's policies, its survival was deemed of vital importance to South Vietnam's security.

Following Vice President Ky's shuttles between Saigon and Phnom Penh, Colonel Lon Non, younger brother of General Lon Nol, appeared several times in Saigon at the Independence Palace and had contacts with other GVN high-ranking officials. Also, to solve the problem of Vietnamese residents in Cambodia living in refugee camps, and estimated at between 60,000 and 75,000, a GVN delegation, headed by Tran Nguon Phieu, minister of public health and education, flew to Phnom Penh in April 1970 to negotiate their repatriation with Cambodian authorities.

• • •

In retrospect, from a legal point of view it is clearly evident that the RVNAF incursion into Cambodia was conducted with the consent and authorization of the Cambodian government. President Thieu in effect declared to the foreign and domestic press on 8 May 1970 that between himself and General Lon Nol there had been "agreement in principle" two or three days before the initiation of cross-border operations. To further cement the bonds of friendship between the two countries after the RVNAF had successfully cleared the Mekong River and Kompong Cham, President Thieu flew to Neak Luong, where he paid a courtesy visit to General Lon Nol. This first meeting between the two national leaders was also attended by General Cao Van Vien, Chief of the JGS, and the Vietnamese field commanders who had directed the clearing operations, Lieutenant General Do Cao Tri and Lieutenant General Ngo Dzu. Playing host to the Cambodian guests, President Thieu entertained them with a luncheon catered by the famous Hotel Caravelle in Saigon. The food and drink were flown from Saigon to Neak Luong by VNAF helicopters.

• • •

With regard to manpower and equipment required for the development of the FANK, the RVN was also most helpful. In addition to the 4,000 CIDG troopers of Khmer origin made available to the FANK, the JGS and MACV also eventually shipped more than 10,000 captured AK-47 assault rifles and approximately 7,200 surplus M2 carbines to Phnom Penh. These 4,000 CIDG troops contributed effectively to the defense of Phnom Penh by defeating attacks launched by NVA units into the Cambodian capital's surrounding areas.

• • •

Air support was another major area of close cooperation between the RVNAF and the FANK. After its withdrawal from Cambodia on 30 June 1970, the United States continued to conduct some air activity in Cambodia, especially in the area of Kratie–Stung Treng, northeast of Phnom Penh, in order to interdict NVA infiltration and prevent return of the NVA to its destroyed base areas near the border. Because of political sensitivities, US aircraft were not authorized to land in Cambodia after 30 June 1970, but they could perform overflight support missions. US aircraft were also denied the offensive role. During their support missions, such as flying air cover for river convoys, US gunships were allowed to return fire only when being fired at from the ground.

• • •

The Tripartite Meetings

During the period of the Cambodian incursion, it was the RVNAF that played the most active role in cooperation and coordination with Khmer forces. Rarely, if ever, did the initiative for cooperation come from the Cambodian side. This reluctance or inertia could be attributed perhaps to the traditional suspicion and animosity that Cambodians had always felt toward their Vietnamese neighbors. In addition, at this time when diplomatic relations between the two countries had just been resumed, there was a tendency for each to give its own point of view first priority vis-à-vis the other.

To help dispel this animosity, the US initiated monthly meetings among the participating nations—the RVN, the US, and Cambodia—which came to be known as "tripartite" meetings. The first of these meetings took place in early July 1970, after the United States had terminated its combat activities in Cambodia. Each national delegation to the tripartite meetings was led by a high-ranking military officer. The RVN delegation was usually led by Lieutenant General Nguyen Van Manh, Chief of Staff of the JGS. His Cambodian counterpart was Lieutenant General Sak Sutsakhan, Chief of Staff of the FANK. The United States was represented by the Deputy COMUSMACV, [General Fred Weyand]. These meetings took place every month at MACV headquarters, the JGS headquarters, or the FANK General Staff headquarters in Phnom Penh. The chiefs of delegations served as co-chairmen and took turns presiding over the meetings.

• • •

The US initiative to institute tripartite meetings greatly contributed to the consolidation of cooperation and coordination between Cambodia and the RVN. It also helped dispel deep-rooted animosities and prejudices which had existed to some extent between the two nations but had been unfortunately amplified beyond imagination by a fanatical press. As a matter of fact, relations between the RVN and Cambodia were never better or so close as after the institution of tripartite meetings; they were always conducted in a most cooperative spirit, and all problems of common interest were solved to the satisfaction of the parties concerned. This spirit of cooperation existed not only at the national level or the general staff level; it also pervaded lower tactical and administrative levels as well and every aspect of combined operations. Historically, this close cooperation was an unprecedented development between Vietnam and Cambodia.

RVN-US Plans for Cambodia after 30 June 1970

While the Cambodian incursion was in full progress, Lieutenant General Michael S. Davison, US II Field Force commander, and Lieutenant General Do Cao Tri, III Corps commander, jointly made plans for rainy season activities. . . . According to [their] directives, III Corps forces were to continue operations in the zone along the Cambodian border in order to prevent the enemy from resuming his activities and infiltrating into South Vietnam. By 30 June US forces were to withdraw from Cambodia and operate in South Vietnam in the place of ARVN units committed across the border. In addition to these activities, US artillery, tactical air, and possibly B-52s as well would be employed to interdict enemy infiltration.

• • •

The RVN-US combined plan for the rainy season of 1970 was conceived with ambitious goals. It not only provided for the continuation of ARVN operations in Cambodia and the consolidation of security inside South Vietnam, but enabled the United States to continue withdrawing its forces as well. In terms of pacification and security, the plan placed emphasis on eliminating enemy local-force units and infrastructure, driving them away from populous centers, destroying his remnant main-force units, increasing the combat effectiveness of territorial forces, and pushing pacification and development efforts to success.

• • •

One week after RVN and US forces initiated combined operations in Cambodia, President Nixon announced that the RVNAF would probably withdraw from Cambodia at the same time as US forces. This logic was based on the fact that if US forces terminated combat activities in Cambodia they would also remove all logistic and air support being provided across the border. It was certainly true that RVNAF operations in Cambodia depended to a large extent on the US support in helilift, airpower, and logistics. Consequently, if and when this support was withdrawn, the RVNAF would hardly be able to continue operations alone in Cambodia.

In the meantime, speaking for the RVN, Vice President Nguyen Cao Ky declared to the foreign and domestic press, during an interview on 1 June 1970, that "we have not determined when the RVNAF will withdraw from Cambodia. Cambodia and South Vietnam are like teeth and lips; if the lips are opened the teeth will get cold. On the other hand, we don't want to maintain our forces in Cambodia. Neither do we want to sit tight and watch North Vietnamese Communists use Cambodian territory freely as a staging area to launch attacks against South Vietnam as they have done for the past several years. The RVNAF have had their hands tied long enough. Now that they are enjoying freedom of action, we don't want to tie their hands again." Vice President Ky also emphasized that no outside pressure could take away the RVNAF freedom of action because they were acting for the sake of South Vietnam's security.

On 27 June 1970 President Thieu announced on national TV several important decisions, namely: 1) the RVNAF would continue to operate on some Cambodian territory after the withdrawal of US forces; the objective was to prevent NVA units from returning to the sanctuaries and bases that had just been destroyed; 2) the RVNAF would continue to evacuate from Cambodia those Vietnamese who desired to be repatriated; 3) the RVN was prepared to respond to the new Cambodian government's appeal for help against NVA aggression to the extent of its capabilities and when such a response was absolutely necessary; 4) future activities of the RVNAF would be initiated from South Vietnam and without the participation of US advisors; all support required for these activities, such as tactical air and logistics, would be provided by the RVNAF; 5) the bulk of the RVNAF would be withdrawn from Cambodia; and 6) the main objective of South Vietnam was to improve its own security and push Vietnamization toward success. All remaining activities on Cambodian soil served only to achieve this national GVN objective.

• • •

In mid-1971, during monthly tripartite meetings, the Cambodian government asked for the abrogation of the RVNAF zone of operation in Cambodia. To strike a compromise, the RVN proposed that the zone be reduced in depth to 10–15 kilometers. This was no longer important for the RVN because, after US forces terminated their operations in Cambodia on 30 June 1970, we did not have the capability to make deep incursions. What really concerned the RVN was the total abrogation of its right of access into this zone on Cambodian soil. The RVN was afraid that, without free access to this zone, the RVNAF would run into difficulties whenever they were required to conduct operations in pursuit of the enemy.

• • •

VI. CROSS-BORDER OPERATIONS AFTER 30 JUNE 1970

After 30 June 1970, and the withdrawal of US forces from Cambodia, the RVNAF continued to conduct operations in Cambodia in accordance with the agreements already worked out between the RVN and the Cambodian government. A zone 60 kilometers deep inside Cambodia was established for these future cross-border operations. Within this zone, RVNAF forces could operate on the basis of FANK/RVNAF coordination and without further government-to-government negotiation. These operations went on until the signing of the Paris peace accords in January 1973.

• • •

Toan Thang 42/Dai Bang

In December 1970, following a series of attacks against FANK units located along Routes 6 and 7 west and northwest of Kompong Cham, the enemy cut Route 7 and isolated Kompong Cham from Phnom Penh. At the request of the Cambodian government (passed to Saigon via the RVN Embassy in Phnom Penh), President Thieu ordered the JGS to relieve Kompong Cham once more. This would be its third relief by RVNAF. The JGS passed the mission to the III Corps commander and reinforced him with the Airborne Division from the ARVN general reserve.[6] In addition, III Corps was given first priority on the use of all RVNAF helicopter assets.

The 2nd Airborne Brigade was helilifted from Tay Ninh to the airfield just west of Kompong Cham. It was accompanied by the light CP of the Airborne Division. From this CP, established at the airfield, Colonel Nguyen Trung Hau, deputy division commander, coordinated ARVN activities west of the Mekong and the advance of the task force moving along Route 7 toward Kompong Cham. . . .

There was no significant contact with enemy main-force units. Enemy reaction was limited to attacks by fire west of the Mekong and mining and harassment along Route 7 in the Chup area. After one week, ARVN forces withdrew to South Vietnam by air and along Route 7.

Although this operation did little damage to the enemy, it ended a very real threat to Kompong Cham and was a great encouragement to the FANK. It also demonstrated that the ARVN could mount operations west of the Mekong on very short notice.

VII. KHMER PARTICIPATION

Background

Cambodia's participation—or, to put it more accurately, its being dragged into the Indochinese conflict—dated rather far back in the political history of Cambodia.[7] The dominant personality of this entire period was unquestionably Prince Norodom Sihanouk who, first as reigning king, and then as chief of state, held nearly absolute power for more than 30 years in this tiny kingdom which shares over one-half of its national boundaries with South Vietnam.

• • •

The enemy's spectacular show of force and capabilities during the Tet Offensive of February 1968 in Saigon city itself was, to the Khmer, proof that he already had the very heart of this country under siege. All of these events tended to confirm Sihanouk's thesis as to South Vietnam's fate in the first place and, by way of Cambodia, that of the Indochinese peninsula in general.

One might say, therefore, that this increasingly worsening military situation in favor of the enemy, coupled with difficulties and misunderstandings between Phnom Penh and the Western powers, edged Sihanouk further into the adversary's camp in a decisive manner. During this same period the Communists devoted all of their efforts to winning the esteem and trust of this prince who, it was well understood, was far from desiring a fate such as President Ngo Dinh Diem's.

Communist Use of Cambodian Territory

As a matter of fact, Communist forces began, as early as 1962, to infiltrate into the northern and eastern border areas of Cambodia, particularly in Stung Treng, Ratanakiri, Kratie, Prey Veng, Svay Rieng, Takeo, and Kampot. By 1969, these infiltrated forces were estimated at 50,000 men installed in "sanctuaries" whose importance varied from a simple transit center to all types of bases having complete military, logistic, and rest facilities such as bases in Ratanakiri, Mondolkiri, and Snoul.

Because of his "double game," Prince Sihanouk simply omitted, in all of his public statements, references to the existence of these infiltrations and, most particularly, the sanctuaries. He did this apparently to cover up his complicity with North Vietnam and the Viet Cong, on the one hand, and to reject the pretexts of "enemy pursuit" by US and South Vietnamese forces on the other.

• • •

In early 1969 . . . the NVA/VC troops, by then solidly installed in their sanctuaries, began to exert pressure on the civilian population around them, while conducting subversive activities against the Cambodian government. Skirmishes with local Khmer authorities became increasingly serious and bloody, such as the armed rebellion of Khmer-Loeu (Montagnards) in the Ratanakiri and Mondolkiri area, which resulted in the nearly total loss of local Cambodian control over this ethnic group, many among whom later joined the NVA/VC forces, either of their own will or under coercion.

It was this rebellion that induced Sihanouk to admit for the first time in public the threat posed by Communists. In a political speech he delivered at the inauguration of the 27th National Congress, Sihanouk denounced this threat in these terms: "As to infiltrations, control, and incitement of a segment of our fellow countrymen, which are the doing of certain Communist neighbors, as well as the armed rebellion by the traitorous Khmer Communists (in the Palin region of Battambang Province), they will inevitably result, if they do not stop and recede, in the loss of our independence and neutrality."

By mentioning the loss of neutrality in this statement, perhaps Sihanouk wanted to imply that he would be capable of seeking assistance from a foreign power to counter the Communist intrusion. Diplomatic relations with the United States were resumed on 3 June 1969; it was, perhaps, the United States that Sihanouk was trying to put into his balance of foreign relations, which had already tilted a little too heavily in favor of the East. Although it fell on deaf ears, this famous declaration could be regarded as a warning intended for the NLF[8] and their protectors.

The incorporation of Cambodia into the Communist supply system kept pace with the development of the flow of VC/NVA infiltration into Cambodia, and the development of political relations between Cambodia and the Provisional Revolutionary (Viet Cong) Government (PRG).

From the Communist viewpoint, the Ho Chi Minh Trail constituted in fact the only strategic route leading south. Under constant surveillance and continuous bombing by the USAF and VNAF, this route did not lend itself easily to the transportation of the heavy equipment and materiel which were required for NVA troops in the south. If this route were completely interdicted by US and RVN forces, it would be a real disaster for North Vietnam and the Viet Cong. Therefore it was mandatory for the enemy to find an alternate to this vital lifeline which would be less vulnerable to USAF/VNAF bombing. This explained why he turned toward Cambodia, or more particularly toward its seaport of Kompong Som.

It was a most propitious time for the enemy's diplomatic maneuvers. Since Sihanouk had repudiated US aid, Communist countries, and especially Red China, were rushing in to fill this void. It became just a matter of increasing the volume of aid shipments to Cambodia, then routing the surplus to NVA/VC forces; the process passed almost undetected. This alternate route was deemed even more reliable because it was not exposed to the risks of US bombing.

• • •

The first formal cooperation agreement between Cambodia and the PRG was concluded soon after Nguyen Tan Phat, PRG prime minister, paid a six-day official visit to Phnom Penh on 29 June 1969. Designated "Trade and Payment Agreement," it was signed in Phnom Penh on 25 September 1969. Thus were formalized the illegal activities that Prince Sihanouk had already authorized for several years. The seaport of Kompong Som was now wide open to receive shipments of supplies intended for NVA/VC troops.

These supplies were subsequently moved by truck to their destinations via Route No. 4. Unloading and transportation operations were the exclusive activities of a certain Hak Ly, who owned about 200 cargo trucks. From Kompong Som to Kompong Speu or Phnom Penh, the cargoes were carried on trucks rented by Hak Ly. Then, from those places to the final destination, the transportation was provided by Hak Ly's own trucks, which usually unloaded at Snoul and Mimot.

To rid himself of troublesome witnesses, Sihanouk ordered a blacklisting of undesirable foreign correspondents, especially those of the Free World. Finally, citing financial difficulties and criticizing its inactivity, Sihanouk terminated the mandate of the International Control Commission (ICC) on 6 October 1969. On his official request, all members of this international organization left Cambodia by the end of the year.

Thus it was accomplished that the Communists, by painstaking preparation, took advantage of the political uncertainties in that part of the world, and of the dilemma of Sihanouk.

• • •

From his relations with the Communists, Sihanouk was therefore able to obtain at least something with which to equip his country, such as the Khmer-Russian Hospital, the Institute of Technology, cement, paper, glass, and plywood production plants, and some military equipment as well. With regard to military aid, Cambodia usually received a quota which was allotted in each cargo shipment unloaded at Kompong Som. All this largely explained the passivity and silence of dissident intellectuals.

The Royal Khmer Armed Forces

• • •

In conclusion, it was clear that on 18 March 1970 the FARK were distinctly below acceptable levels for a modern military force. Their equipment was not only obsolescent but also hideously disparate, coming chiefly from the surplus of others. In a certain sense, the FARK depots were not unlike junk yards where everyone had conveniently dumped whatever he found of no further use.

Attacks by NVA/VC Forces against Cambodia after 18 March 1970

Sihanouk was stripped of his powers as chief of state on 18 March 1970. It was a legal action decided unanimously by members of both legislative chambers who, in fact, had been pushed toward this action by the increasing threat posed by NVA/VC forces in Cambodia.

• • •

Since NVA/VC forces continued to exert pressure on the local Khmer population, the inhabitants of Svay Rieng began in early March 1970 to manifest their dissatisfaction toward the intruders. These popular manifestations met with retaliations from the enemy and resulted in casualties. This in turn provoked a widespread feeling of discontent among the population which culminated in destructive rampages against the North Vietnamese and PRG embassies in Phnom Penh on 11 and 12 March 1970.

Amid the gravity of this explosive situation, which pitted the Khmer population against the NVA/VC, the Cambodian government, by a diplomatic note of the Ministry of Foreign Affairs, formally requested the NVA/VC to withdraw all of their troops from Cambodian territory. The deadline set was dusk 15 March 1970.

• • •

Following this stage play, the NVA/VC suddenly began on 29 March 1970 their overt aggression against Cambodia. These enemy forces were known to be NVA/VC regular units whose total strength was estimated at between 45,000 and 60,000. Meanwhile the defending forces, our FANK, numbered merely 35,000.[9]

It was a very sudden and widespread attack conducted along the eastern and southeastern boundaries and coming from the sanctuary areas. The suddenness of these attacks did not cause much of a surprise to the FANK command because it had expected them all along. But the time available for defense preparation was so short (just two days, from 27 to 29 March) that many isolated and weakly manned outposts succumbed under the violence of the first enemy assaults. From the very first days, therefore, the FANK was driven back by the enemy push.

• • •

Khmer Cooperation with the RVN and United States
Prior to the Cambodian Incursion

• • •

In early April 1970 General Lon Nol twice received very discreet night visits by Nguyen Cao Ky, South Vietnam's vice president. Though highly secret, these visits nevertheless can be seen as the first steps toward reestablishing diplomatic relations between South Vietnam and Cambodia on the one hand, and toward the initiation of military cooperation and assistance in the face of a common enemy on the other. It is not known exactly how the first of these visits was arranged. Very few people in Phnom Penh knew of them, and they were attended on the Khmer side by General Lon Nol and Prince Sirik Matak only. It is considered possible, however, that General Lon Nol's younger brother, Lon Non, played a part in the arrangements.[10]

In conjunction with these activities, President Nixon also issued a warning to the enemy when, announcing the next increment of US troops withdrawals from South Vietnam, he referred to the enemy's escalation in Laos and Cambodia and declared, on 20 April 1970: "The enemy would be taking grave risks if they attempted to use American withdrawals to jeopardize remaining US forces in Vietnam by increased military action in Vietnam, in Cambodia, or in Laos; if they were to do so I shall not hesitate to take strong and effective measures to deal with that situation."

Ten days after issuing this warning, President Nixon announced, on 30 April 1970, that US forces, in cooperation with the Republic of Vietnam Armed Forces, were going to launch immediate attacks to destroy enemy sanctuaries along the Khmer-Vietnamese border.

• • •

In May 1970 an RVN delegation headed by Vice President Nguyen Cao Ky, and including the GVN minister of defense, made an official visit to Phnom Penh. At the end of this visit, an agreement was concluded which created a 15-kilometer-deep zone on each side of the Cambodian–South Vietnamese border in which Khmer and Vietnamese military authorities at the province and district level could operate freely without prior clearance from either government. It was further understood that operations which might require a deeper penetration into Cambodia would be the object of special government agreement. However, the FANK never had the opportunity to make use of this agreement.

• • •

The Status of the FANK on 1 May 1970

Up to the eve of 29 March 1970, when the enemy began his surprise attack, the FANK had not expanded in any significant way. From the very beginning, therefore, they had to defend themselves against an enemy who was clearly superior in strength, much better equipped, and more combat experienced. This accounted for the loss of territory from the first days of the attack. Gradually, however, the FANK made significant progress in the implementation of their program of expansion and reinforcement. Tens of thousands of volunteers from all walks of life (peasants, city dwellers, students, and even civil servants) joined the armed forces. They were followed by the reenlistment of retired servicemen who then constituted the cadre of the young republican army. This rally of volunteers, which was so vast and so spontaneous, effectively solved the problem of manpower shortages. But, at the same time, it also burdened the FANK command with difficulties in materiel, logistic support (armament, equipment, food, barracks, transportation, etc.), and training. The FANK were experiencing growing pains of crisis proportions. Young men in civilian clothes and sandals were seen riding in civilian trucks and passenger cars to frontline areas as reinforcements. Only 5 percent of these young recruits had gone through even a few days of basic military training. Nearly all of them went to fight the war with empty hands, armed only with a determination to serve and defend their fatherland.

Not until the first weeks of April 1970 did equipment and weapons begin to arrive. These were Chinese-made weapons that US and RVN forces had captured from the enemy. This worsened the existing disparity of armament in the FANK and complicated the work for logistic services even more. (The AK-47 assault rifle was an exception, since it had been in the FANK inventory in relatively large numbers for several years.)

In any event, it was during this month of April 1970 that the emerging FANK took on a new look and their first major units were established. By 1 May 1970, 12 infantry brigades had been activated and deployed.

• • •

FANK Activities during the Incursion

• • •

Following the incursion, the US Embassy in Phnom Penh was augmented by a new section called Military Equipment Delivery Team, Cambodia (MEDTC), whose chief, Brigadier General [Theodore] Mataxis, worked in close cooperation with the FANK general staff on logistic problems. Meanwhile, US military attachés continued and even increased their contacts with the FANK general staff on operational matters. It was only then that the US Military Assistance Program began to take shape, a program jointly studied and planned by MEDTC and the FANK general staff, based on funds allotted by the United States toward this end.

However, even before MEDTC was installed in Phnom Penh, the FANK had already received a substantial amount of materiel from the United States, especially signal equipment for territorial units and air-ground communications. This materiel assistance, which came through South Vietnam, was the work of the Politico-Military Office (POL/MIL) of the US Embassy in Phnom Penh, created in June 1970 and headed by Mr. Jonathan F. Ladd.

• • •

Critical Analysis and Conclusions

During the first hours of the conflict, the Khmer government, as well as Khmer political and military leaders, entertained the hope of resolving this grave problem by peaceful means, especially those means that could be undertaken by that great international organization, the United Nations. As a full member of the United Nations, Cambodia had in fact hoped that this organization would do for Cambodia what it had done for South Korea and Israel by committing its own security troops for the maintenance of peace. Unfortunately, our hopes did not come true.

Therefore, as soon as President Nixon had announced his decision on 30 April 1970 to commit US combat troops in Cambodia . . . there was reason for the Cambodian leadership to feel immediately relieved and content. Indeed we witnessed, in the wake of this intervention, a marked though temporary decrease in combat capabilities on the part of the enemy. Knowing, however, that this important intervention by US forces was both limited in time and scope, the enemy avoided confrontation and was thus able to conserve his main forces while waiting out the deadline for US withdrawal.

If a careful analysis were made of this aspect of the problem and from an enemy viewpoint, one might say that the enemy made a well-calculated move when his forces took the areas east of the Mekong River (Stung Treng, Kratie, Kompong Cham, Prey Veng, and Svay Rieng) and used them as sanctuaries, firmly established this time deep in Cambodian territory. For friendly troops no longer occupied this part of Cambodia, and in a certain sense intervention operations by US and RVN forces in Cambodia merely pushed these mobile and viable enemy sanctuaries deeper inside this abandoned part of Cambodia.

On the Cambodian side, we observed that these operations consisted of frontal, rather than enveloping, maneuvers. This gave the enemy ample opportunity for seeking refuge deeper inside Cambodia. Therefore this part of Cambodia was effectively cut off and isolated from the rest of the country. The local population who stayed behind were thus caught in the grip and remained under the total control and domination of the enemy.

• • •

If, in fact, this operation was conducted solely within the framework of Vietnamization, as the US command had intended it, then it might be considered a success, because it largely contributed to the achievement of Vietnamization within the time limits imposed by the US government. On the other hand, the withdrawal of US troops would be possible only if the RVNAF were capable of taking over. It was difficult at that time to tell that the RVNAF had that capability. For one thing, the NVA/VC sanctuaries were solidly anchored along the entire western border of South Vietnam. For another, the armed forces of South Vietnam were compelled to extend themselves precariously in order to fill the voids created by the departure of US combat units.

The last major actions undertaken by US forces across South Vietnam and in Cambodia, particularly as far as the Cambodian incursion was concerned, provided a feeling of "self-assurance," both for the RVNAF and the FANK. Perhaps they also imparted a certain feeling of moral satisfaction to our American ally, who was disengaging himself from a part of the world where he had been involved and had fought for more than twenty years.

As far as the FANK command was concerned, however, and within the framework of its war efforts against the NVA/VC forces, the destruction or even occupation of that part of Cambodia which was under enemy control, if only done temporarily, did not end the problem for FANK. For, while these temporary effects were sought by the US command, in view of their absolute necessity for Vietnamization to succeed, their repercussions fell with all their weight onto the FANK, which were from the beginning not sufficiently prepared to confront an enemy of this size. To avoid massive bombings by US and RVN forces, the enemy fell back deeper and deeper into the Cambodian territory. These bombings and attacks by friendly forces also caused the complete evacuation of these areas by the civilian population, into which moved the enemy immediately. The result of all this was that a sizable part of the Cambodian territory was lost to the enemy.

• • •

In addition, we have also to consider the psychological impact created by this operation which marked the last episode of the presence of US combat troops in South Vietnam. The publicity with which the US disengagement was made largely benefited the enemy, who took advantage of it to sap the morale of the civilian population and troops alike in Cambodia, as well as in South Vietnam. As a result, there was a certain lowering of morale on our side; during the same period, the other side, encouraged by ever-increasing support and assistance, became more aggressive and began to prepare for its eventual and final victory.

The US policy of disengagement, and the departure of US troops in the midst of this critical period, during which the last decisive card was to be played, thus resulted in a void so great on the allied side that neither the FANK nor the RVNAF were ever able to fill it.

This void was all the more aggravated by the most unfortunate Watergate scandal, which considerably weakened the prestige of [the] US executive branch of government vis-à-vis the American public. And the departure of President Nixon from the political scene in a certain sense sealed the fate of Indochina, because the cutbacks in and eventual termination of US military assistance to the Khmer Republic and South Vietnam inevitably resulted in a disequilibrium in the balance of forces.

The final outcome of this long Vietnam War, conforming as it did to the will of the enemy and to the desire of certain responsible parties, became known on 17 April 1975. On that date, Cambodia, which had been dragged into the arena of the Indochinese conflict as the last participant, succumbed as the first victim. This brought in its wake the fall of Saigon and Vientiane, thus closing a long chapter that extended over more than a decade in the political and military history of modern times, a history rich in lessons and also in sufferings.

With the fall of Cambodia there died a millennial civilization and—irony of fate—there was reborn in its place a cynical demagoguery. The Khmer Republic had thought to bring Cambodian political institutions up to date by eliminating a monarchy, while at the same time preserving all that was most noble of the long Khmer civilization. The actual results were not only disastrous in terms of human loss, but the so-called democratic regime which came to power is more barbaric than any other in our long history—and it happened in this 20th century.

VIII. OBSERVATIONS AND CONCLUSIONS

The Cambodian cross-border operations were the largest ever conducted by the RVNAF. At certain times the RVNAF committed up to 50,000 troops who fought alongside and in full coordination with such US units as the 1st, 25th, [and] 4th Infantry Divisions, the 1st Cavalry Division, and the 11th Armored Cavalry Regiment. For the RVNAF, this was the first time that our major units had been deployed in such numbers at the same time; the total force committed was equivalent to six divisions—the Airborne Division; the 9th, 21st, 25th (-), 22nd (-), and 23rd (-) Infantry Divisions; five ranger groups (of three battalions each); one marine brigade (of three battalions); and nine armored cavalry squadrons, about one-half of the total ARVN armor force. It was also the first time RVNAF major units operated in such numbers as a single maneuver force. Up to the incursion most of them, until replaced by RF and PF units, had performed only pacification support activities while US forces played the major combat role.

• • •

Although forced to fight on unfamiliar terrain, the RVNAF had proved to be thoroughly combat effective, despite initial shortcomings in the coordination of armor and infantry actions. But with these shortcomings remedied the RVNAF truly held the initiative throughout the entire operation.

• • •

A remarkable thing about the early cross-border operations was the fact that, for the first time in several years, RVNAF units went into combat unaccompanied by US advisors. During the combined operations, however, US advisors did accompany ARVN units into Cambodia as far as the 30-kilometer limit. To operate without US advisors was a source of pride for ARVN tactical commanders of battalion level and above. They felt more self-assured of their command abilities, and, in fact, they all proved that they could manage by themselves. Not only were they able to solve all problems related to the support of ARVN units, they also effectively maintained liaison and coordination with US support units, a function which heretofore had been performed by US advisors only.

Perhaps as a result of South Vietnamese maturity and combat effectiveness, US advisors were removed from a number of ARVN battalions after the incursion. These units had indeed proved that they were capable of doing without advisors. Therefore US advisory teams were greatly reduced in certain ARVN units, and, in some instances, they were replaced by liaison teams.

• • •

I believe that if US units had been authorized more time and more space to maneuver, enemy main-force units would not have been able to hide and would have sustained serious losses in men and supplies to US air and artillery firepower.

General Results

The Cambodian incursion of 1970 inflicted severe losses on the enemy, both in human life and in war materiel. His base areas and storage points along the Cambodian border were practically paralyzed. It was the estimate of the JGS, supported by Head-quarters MACV, that it would take the enemy a minimum of six to nine months to reor-ganize his logistic installations and partially restock them.

Friendly forces captured from the enemy a total of 22,892 individual weapons, ar-mament for the equivalent of 54 enemy main-force battalions of 450 men each. The number of crew-served weapons captured amounted to 2,509, enough to equip 27 infan-try battalions. In addition, friendly forces also captured and destroyed approximately 2,500 tons of assorted ammunition, enough to sustain enemy forces oriented against MR-3 and MR-4 in combat for nine to twelve months; it was equivalent to the amount of ammunition that these enemy forces had expended during the previous year.

NVA forces would also run into serious shortages in food because approximately 14,046,000 pounds of rice, among other foodstuffs, had either been seized or destroyed. It was estimated that this amount of rice could feed enemy forces for a period of from four to six months. In the huge amount of ammunition seized by our forces there were in excess of 143,000 rounds of mortar, rocket, and recoilless rifle [ammunition]. Based on knowledge of past enemy consumption, these rounds were the equivalent of what had been used by the enemy during the past 14 months in attacks by fire against our in-stallations and bases. Another significant enemy loss was our capture or destruction of 435 enemy vehicles of all types.

Although the enemy could always procure rice from local sources, either in Cambo-dia or just across the border in South Vietnam, he could not do the same as far as am-munition and equipment were concerned. With the port at Kompong Som now closed, these latter items would, in the future, have to come down the Ho Chi Minh Trail, a de-velopment which would significantly inhibit the enemy's ability to conduct combat op-erations in South Vietnam, especially in Military Regions 3 and 4.

While the incursion's primary objective was the destruction of enemy bases and sup-plies, the enemy also incurred considerable casualties in manpower. A total of 11,349 enemy troops were killed and another 2,328 were made prisoners or rallied to our side.[11] These casualties alone equalled the strength of an enemy division. To replace these losses, it was the estimate of the JGS, supported by Headquarters MACV, that it would take the enemy at least four to six months to recruit and train new troops.

Among the enemy troops and cadres who rallied to our side, the most important was Lieutenant Colonel Nguyen Thanh, deputy commander of the enemy 2nd Subregion, who surrendered in Tay Ninh on 20 May 1970. He disclosed that the US-RVN cross-border operation had completely upset enemy plans to occupy Kompong Cham and Svay Rieng by 1 May 1970 and then assemble all transportation means locally available to rapidly move the NVA 7th and 9th Divisions to Phnom Penh, which they were to oc-cupy by 3 May. Once in control of the Cambodian capital, the enemy planned to launch a "high point" against Saigon with an intensity comparable to the 1968 Tet Offensive. But all of these plans were preempted by our incursion into Cambodia.

In addition to enemy losses inflicted by our ground combat units, we must also in-clude those inflicted by US tactical air and B-52s. During the operation US tactical air flew a total of 6,017 combat support missions, or an average of 210 missions per day (168 preplanned and 42 on call). Also, during the period of combined US-RVN operations in Cambodia, there was a total of 21 "Commando Vault," or 15,000-pound, bombs dropped from C-130s to clear landing zones and, in a few cases, against special targets such as supply points and vehicle parks.

• • •

The most important result of the Cambodian incursion was perhaps the fact that enemy main-force units were driven away from South Vietnam and from its border areas. The departure of these units caused a disruption of coordination between enemy main, local, and guerrilla forces and between the enemy infrastructure and these forces. Enemy activities inside South Vietnam therefore were no longer as extensive or as effective as they had been.

From a strategic standpoint, this operation caused the enemy to extend and disperse his forces even more, as these forces were forced to spread over Cambodia in addition to their normal deployments in the DMZ area, in South Vietnam, and in Laos. The enemy's requirements for support and coordination therefore multiplied and caused him serious difficulties.

• • •

Conclusions

To the Republic of Vietnam, the Cambodian incursion was a most welcomed opportunity. In addition to the military victories achieved in Cambodia, the situation throughout South Vietnam improved markedly as a result of the incursion. Subsequently, during 1970 and 1971, the RVNAF were able to hold the initiative on all the battlegrounds in South Vietnam; they gained in self-confidence, and the confidence of the South Vietnamese population in the RVNAF grew. Most encouraging as well was [that] from that time forward, in its struggle against the Communists, the RVN had another partner. For Cambodia, which previously had been a potential enemy, became a comrade-in-arms and ceased to be a source of irritation.

As a test of progress of Vietnamization, it showed with great clarity the new maturity of the RVN forces. The RVN, for its part, also seized this favorable opportunity to implement its economic development program. In 1970, the RVN was able to launch one of its most ambitious projects, the "Land to the Tiller" program, to radically improve the lot of the farmer. The security situation across the country was so good that tourists who visited South Vietnam during that period were amazed by the calm and peace that reigned everywhere. One could drive his car alone along Route 1, for example, all the way from the Ben Hai River to Ca Mau without risk of sniper fire or land mines, road hazards so common in previous years.

In addition to military gains, the Cambodian incursion also brought to light some political truths that could be exploited to our advantage. Up to this time, North Vietnam always denied that it maintained troops in South Vietnam or in Cambodia and Laos. To avoid being denounced by world opinion, therefore, NVA forces always tried to keep a low profile in Cambodia and Laos. But the incursion had changed all of that. NVA forces were compelled to surface and commit flagrant acts of violence against Cambodia— occupying the northeastern part of the country; surrounding and threatening Phnom Penh; interdicting the Mekong River and the major land lines of communication, Routes 1, 4, 6, and 7, etc. All of these activities revealed the truth about North Vietnam's claims of innocence as to the presence of NVA troops in Cambodia.

As far as Cambodia was concerned, US and RVN combat activities during the incursion had effectively helped clear the enemy's initial pressure when NVA forces attacked populous areas around Phnom Penh. The incursion also afforded Cambodia more time to expand, equip, and retrain its army, which, in view of its small size and combat inexperience, had been hardly capable of coping with surprise attacks launched by stronger and better-equipped enemy forces.

Despite its spectacular results, and the great contribution it made to the allied war effort, it must be recognized that the Cambodian incursion proved, in the long run, to pose little more than a temporary disruption of North Vietnam's march toward domination of all of Laos, Cambodia, and South Vietnam. In spite of very large losses, the enemy had succeeded in taking control of all of Cambodia's northeastern provinces, and, because of his pressure, about one-fourth of Cambodia was no longer under the control of Phnom Penh. More importantly, the bulk of NVA forces in Cambodia, which was estimated at about 40,000 men, was still intact and free to roam about in this part of Cambodia. As long as this force remained there, Cambodia was still facing a mortal danger in its struggle for survival. In time—and time was on his side—the enemy would readjust his infiltration routes along the Ho Chi Minh Trail to accommodate the necessary larger tonnages. With most of eastern Cambodia under NVA control, the old enemy base areas could be reestablished as well.

In the face of these enemy long-range options, there was no corresponding US/RVN strategy. Having destroyed the enemy base areas along the Cambodian border, the RVNAF had accomplished a long-held objective, following which it concentrated on improving the security situation inside South Vietnam. There was no plan to return to the border areas to conduct operations of value to Cambodia, or to keep the enemy base areas cleared out. In the absence of any such long-range repeat operations, it is not difficult to explain the temporary nature of the advantage accruing to the US/RVNAF war effort from the Cambodian incursion. To incapacitate North Vietnam, and end the war on our terms, it would have been necessary to bring that country completely to it knees. But that was a different and much larger problem.

NOTES

1. RVNAF/US Combined Campaign Plan AB/145 (1969).

2. The term "combined incursion" is used to designate those operations which took place during the period when US forces were also authorized to operate in Cambodia—30 April to 30 June 1970. This [section] will discuss the JGS view of the changed situation in Cambodia, the development of a concept

for the combined incursion, planning for the combined incursion, and those cross-border operations conducted by ARVN forces operating alone in Cambodia prior to 30 April 1970. The RVNAF and US operations conducted during the combined incursion are discussed in [section] IV.

3. "Night of Death at Takeo" and "New Horror in Indochina," *Time,* 27 April 1970.

4. Richard M. Nixon, "Report by the President on the Cambodian Operation," 30 June 1970, as quoted in *U.S. News & World Report,* 13 July 1970.

5. A task force was equivalent to a regiment and consisted of one armored cavalry squadron and two or three infantry or ranger battalions. In terms of vehicles, an ARVN armored cavalry squadron was equivalent to a US armor battalion.

6. "Dai Bang" (Eagle) was incorporated into the name of the operation in view of the participation of the Airborne Division.

7. [Editor: General Tho, author of this account, notes that section VII was written by Lieutenant General Sak Sutsakhan, the last chief of state and Chief of the Khmer Armed Forces General Staff.]

8. [Editor: This is rendered "FNL" in the original text, an apparent typographical error.]

9. Note the change from FARK to FANK following the change in government on 18 March 1970.

10. At the same time as these contacts the Cambodian government was also approached by other countries of the Free World, first Thailand, then the Republic of China (Taiwan), followed by South Korea shortly after. All offered to help in some way.

11. Enemy loss figures and examples are taken from President Nixon's report [previously cited] and are cumulative through 29 June 1970.

11

Lam Son 719

Major General Nguyen Duy Hinh

PREFACE

For several years the eastern part of the Laotian panhandle was used by North Vietnam as a corridor for the infiltration of personnel and materiel required to sustain its war efforts in South Vietnam and Cambodia. In addition to the Ho Chi Minh Trail, the eastern panhandle contained many logistic installations and base areas. After the 18 March 1970 change of government in Cambodia, which closed the port of Sihanoukville to the enemy, this trail-base area complex in lower Laos became even more important to North Vietnam in its prosecution of the war in the South. The real hub of this entire complex, where transportation and storage activities were coordinated, was Base Area 604, located west of the Demilitarized Zone and surrounding the district town of Tchepone.

To disrupt the flow of enemy personnel and supplies into South Vietnam, a ground attack was launched across the Laotian border against this enemy hub of activity on 8 February 1971. Operation Lam Son 719 was conducted by I Corps, with substantial US support in firepower and helilift but without the participation of US advisors with those ARVN units fighting in Laos. As a test of Vietnamization, this operation was to demonstrate also the progress achieved in combat effectiveness by the Republic of Vietnam Armed Forces. Further, Lam Son 719 achieved the objective of forestalling a Communist offensive in the spring of 1971.

This monograph will present a critical analysis of all aspects of Lam Son 719, from the planning stage to the withdrawal from lower Laos. In its preparation I have drawn primarily from my own experience as an ARVN infantry division commander and from interviews with Vietnamese unit commanders and staff officers who participated in the operation. . . . [31 July 1977]

I. INTRODUCTION

• • •

This was a difficult time for the enemy. His system of bases and sanctuaries on both sides of the Cambodian border was apparently paralyzed and continued to be harassed.

The port of Sihanoukville (redesignated Kompong Som) was no longer was a free port of entry for his supplies, and our Operation Market Time on the high seas off the Vietnam coastline was effectively interdicting infiltration by sea. To continue supporting its war in the South, it appeared that North Vietnam would have to rely solely on the Ho Chi Minh Trail, the supply route along the rugged Truong Son mountain range. Therefore an invasion of the Laos panhandle became an attractive idea; such an operation would retain the initiative for the RVNAF, disrupt the flow of enemy personnel and supplies to South Vietnam, and greatly reduce the enemy's capability to launch an offensive in 1971.

II. THE OPERATIONAL ENVIRONMENT

The Ho Chi Minh Trail System

A by-product of the First Indochina War (1946–1954), the footpath system that ran north-south along the Truong Son mountain range of Vietnam became known as the Ho Chi Minh Trail. For a long time it had served the strategic purposes of the Viet Minh. From its jungle redoubt of North Vietnam's highlands, the Viet Minh High Command was faced with the pressing need for a secure communication system that would enable it to direct the war effort in South Vietnam and support its subversive activities in neighboring Laos and Cambodia. National Route No. 1, which ran parallel to the coastline, was not practicable because of French control. Sea routes were available, but the risks of running into French naval patrols and foul weather were forbiddingly high. Besides, the Viet Minh did not have a reliable, organized sea transportation fleet. Considering these circumstances, the heavily jungled mountains . . . lent themselves to the establishment of a secure line of communication generally free from observation and attacks.

It was this footpath system that kept the Viet Minh resistance in South Vietnam alive with fresh troops, weapons, and ammunition. By the end of the First Indochina War, the Ho Chi Minh Trail had been well developed, although it was only a system of jungle paths connected by local secondary roads and suitable only [for] movement by foot, animals, and bicycles. Soldiers moved on foot, but military supplies, although usually carried by manpower, were sometimes transported on bicycles, oxcarts, horses, or elephants. The narrow, steep pathways meandered through dense jungles, across streams and mountains, and a journey on the trail was exhausting and slow.

For a time after the Geneva Accords in 1954, the trail was practically abandoned. . . . Then, when South Vietnam, under the leadership of President Ngo Dinh Diem, began restoring its stability and proving that it could stand on its own after repudiating reunification with North Vietnam, the Central Committee of North Vietnam's Communist Party decided on a new course of action against South Vietnam. In May 1959 the North Vietnamese Army . . . High Command activated Transportation Group 559 under the direct control of its Rear Service (Logistics) Department. Group 559 was to be a special unit in charge of moving men and supplies into the South for the support of the insurgency effort which had just been initiated under the form of a "war of liberation." The trail's old pathways were rehabilitated and widened, and new ones were surveyed and projected. Group 559's task of enlarging this strategic axis of infiltration was pushed ahead with vigor and determination.

The increase of subversive activities against South Vietnam was in almost direct proportion to the development of the Ho Chi Minh Trail, since the Communist war effort in the South was largely sustained by a constant flow of cadre and troops from the North. At this early state the flow was sporadic, because the journey was harsh and long for the men and the means of transporting supplies still primitive. But, as pathways were eventually enlarged into roads, the means of transportation were also improved.

Prior to 1965 the Ho Chi Minh system was close to the Vietnam border, but after the United States became involved in the war and bombings increased, the Communists gradually shifted toward the west, where they found the densely jungled areas of lower Laos and eastern Cambodia perfect sanctuaries for the movement or concentration of troops and the storage of weapons and war materiel.

By the end of the 1960s the Ho Chi Minh Trail had become an elaborate system of nearly 2,000 miles of pathways and roads, including some natural waterways. It started at Vinh, ran through the Mu Gia Pass and other lesser passes such as Ban Karai and Ban Raving, penetrated into lower Laos, and finally came out in northern Cambodia and the tri-border area of South Vietnam. In several areas the trail system was so extensive that it could be compared to a cobweb of crisscrossing roads making up a corridor of from 30 to 50 miles wide, complete with bridges (over or under water), culverts, [and] river-crossing ramps, much of it concealed under dense jungle canopies. With the assistance of Pathet Lao guerrillas, the estimated 50,000 troops of NVA Group 559 and about 100,000 Vietnamese volunteers and forced laborers maintained this vital artery.

To protect the corridor, the Communists established an elaborate defense and security system. The duty of Pathet Lao units was to intensify guerrilla activities and launch periodic attacks in order to keep the Royal Lao Army confined to the cities and towns along the Mekong River. The protection of the trail system and storage areas was performed by Group 559 itself. Augmented by infantry units and unattached militiamen, the group defense forces included antiaircraft units armed with all types of light and medium weapons, from 12.7mm, 14.5mm, and 23mm heavy machineguns to 37mm, 57mm, and 100mm antiaircraft cannon.

Group 559 installed a forward headquarters in the southern panhandle of North Vietnam, from where it controlled many "binh trams" (literally, troop stations). In 1970 there were about 40 such stations, from Vinh to the Cambodian border, under the control of a number of intermediary headquarters. Each binh tram was a self-contained logistical complex responsible for a well-defined area. Its subordinate units usually consisted of engineer troops, surface and waterway transportation elements, maintenance units, quartermaster and medical units, warehouses, and a certain number of way stations to support troop movements.

During the cessation of bombing in North Vietnam, trucks moved by convoy from

Vinh down the trail. Upon reaching the Laotian border, they formed units of five to eight vehicles and usually moved only at night or in foul weather in order to avoid the round-the-clock bombing by US Air Force planes. As a result, binh trams were usually separated from one another by a day's journey, and their parking areas were scattered and well concealed. The vehicles moving on the trail only transported supplies and heavy materials. Light equipment was either carried on men's backs or by animals. Since troops had to march, they moved by day or night, using pathways different from those used by trucks. New recruits or replacements usually entered the system at Vinh in North Vietnam, and often marched over 100 days to reach their final destination in South Vietnam. In view of this long journey, they had to rest and recuperate at way stations, where they received food, medicine, and indoctrination. Combat units usually moved by battalions of 500–600 men each, and they often suffered substantial losses from disease and constant bombing by the US Air Force.

The extensive use of vehicles posed a fuel supply problem for the Communists. Until they built a pipeline system from Vinh to the Mu Gia Pass in 1968, all fuels were transported by trucks, but by February 1969 the main pipeline had been extended to the Muong Nong area in Laos, west of the A Shau Valley. Fuel storage areas along this line became one of the major targets for bombing by American planes.

As the insurgency intensified in South Vietnam, efforts to interdict the Ho Chi Minh supply line increased. As early as the first few years of the First Republic, President Ngo Dinh Diem implemented several plans aimed at controlling the territory adjacent to the Laos border. In Military Region 1, agrovilles were established in such areas as Lao Bao, A Shau, A Luoi, and Nam Dong. ARVN units regularly conducted reconnaissance patrols deep into the border areas adjacent to Laos, particularly in the provinces of Quang Nam, Quang Ngai, and Kontum. The enemy base area of Do Xa, which lay astride the boundary of MR-1 and MR-2, was a target for frequent ARVN attacks. In 1958 repair work began on the abandoned stretch of GVN National Route No. 14 which paralleled the Laotian border and connected Kontum with Hoi An in Quang Nam Province, but the onset of the insurgency interrupted the work, which was never resumed.

During the period from 1960 to 1965, as the fighting escalated, the GVN was unable to do anything against the Laos infiltration route, but the United States made a significant contribution in 1961 when it helped organize the highlands Montagnards into combat units (CIDGs) and develop the Vietnamese Special Forces for the defense of the border areas. Against Communist activities on the Ho Chi Minh Trail, however, neither the US Army Special Forces nor their Vietnamese counterparts ever interdicted the Communist logistics system to a significant degree, even during the period of maximum effort. Also, the idea of building the "McNamara Line" of sensors across the Truong Son mountain range at the southern boundary of the DMZ was never fully implemented as planned.

The surveillance and interdiction of the trail, therefore, lay primarily in the hands of the US Air Force, whose reconnaissance planes covered the trail system around the clock. Ground electronic sensors planted along jungle pathways, river crossings, and mountain passes picked up vehicle and other man-made noises [and] transmitted them to overflying planes, which relayed the information to terminal stations to be analyzed and interpreted. The electronic monitoring of enemy activities on the trail system helped record the number of vehicles and men moving along the trail; consequently, intelligence on Communist infiltration was remarkably reliable.

In addition to surveillance, a major task for the US Air Force was to interdict this infiltration. All types of aircraft were used, including B-52 strategic bombers, sophisticated fighter-bombers, and several types of gunships. The US Air Force claimed that its bombs and improved weapons systems inflicted heavy losses [on] the enemy in terms of personnel, vehicles, and materiel moving down the trail. In fact, in early 1971 the Air Force released the story that this interdiction was so effective that only one ton out of every 32 tons shipped from North Vietnam ever reached its final destination in South Vietnam.[1] Subsequent NVA offensive operations in South Vietnam demonstrated that the US Air Force claim was greatly exaggerated.

Among the targets of intensive bombing were the mountain passes and roads, which were pounded day and night. The enemy's efforts to repair the damage were complicated by his lack of heavy machinery, but he was resilient and stubborn. No sooner was a mountain road destroyed than a detour was completed.

The Ho Chi Minh Trail could supply about 50 percent of the enemy's combat needs; in other words, the trail was capable of sustaining Communist forces in RVN Military Regions 1 and 2. The port of Sihanoukville in Cambodia was used to support forces operating in RVN Military Regions 3 and 4. The coup in Phnom Penh during March 1970, however, closed the port. The Ho Chi Minh Trail then became essential for the enemy to support the entire war in South Vietnam. As a result, the NVA Transportation Group 559 received special reinforcements, and, during the second half of 1970, the enemy made a determined effort to develop logistical Base Area 604, adjacent to Quang Tri Province. Concurrently he improved the existing base and road system in the eastern part of lower Laos. After his seizure of the cities of Attopeu and Saravane in Laos, he widened his trail system to the west in order to increase the flow of supplies and to complicate the US Air Force's interdiction efforts.

At the beginning of 1970, the enemy's plan to rehabilitate Route 1036 was suspended for some time due to extensive US bombing along the Laotian border. Nevertheless he succeeded in opening Route 1039 through the Ban Raving Pass, which connected with Route 913. This gave the enemy an additional route into Tchepone, the communications center for Base Area 604. In the meantime, Route 1032A in North Vietnam allowed him to move his trucks to the western edge of the DMZ. Here his supplies were usually floated on the Houay Nam Xe River, and then on the Xe Bang Hiang River, southwesterly toward Tchepone, where they were picked up before reaching the town.

To the south, the enemy had already completed Route 616, which cut across the Xepon River and deep into South Vietnam. The existence of this east-west infiltration route was detected for the first time on 1 January 1970, but subsequent surveillance indicated that enemy activities on it were light. The heaviest traffic was always reported on the north-south axis, moving from Base Area 604 on Routes 96, 926, and 914 toward Base Area 611.

By January 1971 Route 1032A had been connected with Route 1032B, which gave the enemy an additional roadway into lower Laos from North Vietnam. Recordings made by electronic sensors indicated that, of every four trucks leaving North Vietnam, one always moved on this route, regardless of the bombing by US planes west of the DMZ. Aerial photos also revealed that the enemy had built several alternate bypass routes in this area in order to avoid concentrated bombing and ensure the flow of traffic. Reconnaissance planes further reported that east-west Route 925 had been widened, but terminated approximately two and a half miles from the GVN border. This appeared to indicate that the enemy wanted to project another infiltration route into the Khe Sanh area, west of Quang Tri, but subsequent air reconnaissance showed that the enemy was using Route 616 for truck traffic and his activities were increasing substantially south of Base Area 611.

All of these indications clearly confirmed the enemy's efforts to open additional infiltration roads; develop storage areas, transshipment points, and truck parks; and make the entire area just west of Quang Tri Province an intricate logistical and transportation complex, complete with pipelines and bypass roads. Furthermore, all these activities progressed with little interruption, despite continuous bombing. The efforts were most conspicuous in Base Areas 604 and 611. On the other hand, to increase his protection capabilities the enemy also moved additional antiaircraft and combat units into these areas.

Enemy Situation in Northern Military Region 1

In South Vietnam proper, no significant enemy activities were recorded in northern MR-1 during the entire first half of 1970. Enemy initiatives in this area consisted only of attacks by fire and small-scale sapper attacks. Targets were usually remote, small-sized fire support bases and outposts. The enemy main-force units devoted this entire period to building roads, refitting troops, and storing food and supplies, but intelligence reports revealed that enemy forces were preparing to launch an offensive campaign against the two northernmost provinces of MR-1, probably in January 1971.

• • •

Enemy Situation in the Laos Panhandle

The enemy had a sizable combat force in Laos. Within the Royal Lao MR III area, this force was estimated at 42,000 men, consisting of 13 NVA battalions (5,000 men), 20 Pathet Lao battalions (5,000), and about 32,000 troops and cadres of Transportation Group 559. Further south, in Royal Lao MR IV, enemy strength was estimated at 22,000 troops, who made up 17 NVA battalions (7,000 men), 21 Pathet Lao battalions (4,000 men), and about 10,000 troops and cadres belonging to six binh trams of the 559th. In northern Laos, enemy strength was estimated at 33,000, consisting of 16,000 NVA and 17,000 Pathet Lao troops. However, intelligence estimates precluded the participation of these elements in any engagement west of Quang Tri.

Air reconnaissance and agent reports further confirmed the enemy's stepped-up logistical activities and augmentation of combat forces at Base Areas 604 and 611 since the beginning of the lower Laos dry season. In October 1970 an agent report revealed that a division-sized unit, approximately 10,000 strong, was leaving the Mu Gia Pass and moving south. It was believed at that time that this was the 320th NVA Division with its three organic regiments, the 48th, 52nd, and 64th. Subsequent intelligence reports confirmed that the 52nd Regiment was located west of the DMZ and the 64th Regiment was building roads in Quang Binh Province, north of the DMZ. It was, therefore, probable that the 48th Regiment was the unit which was moving into Base Area 604.[2]

• • •

In addition to Communist combat units reported in the proposed operational area west of Quang Tri Province or in its vicinity, there were eight binh trams that had been recently reinforced with approximately 20 antiaircraft battalions.[3] Not all of these battalions were fully equipped, but since each battalion could have from 2 to 16 antiaircraft weapons, it was estimated that the enemy's medium-caliber antiaircraft artillery deployed in the proposed operational area numbered from 170 to 200 pieces of 23mm to 100mm in caliber.

In summary, enemy forces in the area of operation were estimated at three infantry regiments (Regiments 48/320, 24B/304, and 812/324B), an artillery element, and the binh tram units, whose most important capability was antiaircraft. Total enemy strength in the area was estimated at 22,000, to include 7,000 NVA combat troops, 10,000 men belonging to logistic units, and 5,000 Pathet Lao soldiers.

The enemy's capability to reinforce within a short time (two weeks) was estimated at eight regiments, which were: the 52nd and 64th Regiments of the 320th Division, the 29th and 803rd Regiments of the 324B Division, the 3rd and 1st Regiments of the 2nd Division, and the 141st and 9th Separate Regiments, all supported by artillery elements. Additionally, enemy reinforcement capabilities from North Vietnam were also considered by planning staffs and field commanders.

Finally, in January 1971, agent reports disclosed that Communist units located north of the DMZ had received alert orders. The enemy B-5 Front was reported making preparations to face an attack by allied forces against the provinces of southern North Vietnam. Remembering his losses during the Cambodian incursion of the previous year, it appeared that the enemy was consolidating his general defensive posture and would devote particular attention to the security of his infiltration and supply corridor in lower Laos during the remaining months of the 1971 dry season.

The Area of Operation

To inflict maximum damage on the enemy logistic and infiltration corridor system, all intelligence indicated that Tchepone would be the decisive objective area. This area was unpopulated except for a few Montagnards living in the vicinity of Khe Sanh–Lang Vei and a very sparse population in Tchepone itself. Intelligence revealed that all villages and towns whose names appeared on our maps had been evacuated or largely destroyed by the protracted war.

• • •

The primary line of communication (LOC) in the province was National Route No. 1, which ran north-south close to the coastal plains. A secondary LOC was National Route No. 9, which ran from a junction with Route No. 1 in the vicinity of Dong Ha west to the Laotian border. From Dong Ha to Son Lam hamlet (close to FSB Vandegrift), Route No. 9 was a two-lane, all-weather, hard-surfaced road, occasionally subjected to enemy harassment. West of FSB Vandegrift it became a dirt road usable only in good weather; this stretch was insecure and had several destroyed bridges. The Khe Sanh Airfield, which had been abandoned for a long time, would require extensive repairs to be operational.

• • •

To the west, beyond the Laotian border, the terrain was predominantly mountainous. The area of operation on this side of the border was characterized by three prominent features. The first of these was the Xepon River, which ran south and then parallel to Route No. 9 until it reached Tchepone, where it met the Xe Bang Hiang River, the primary north-south waterway in the area. During the rainy season, when most ground lines of communication were inundated, the enemy used the Xe Bang Hiang River to float supplies downstream.

The second prominent terrain feature was the Co Roc Highland adjacent to the Laotian border and just south of Route No. 9. This highland had several peaks with elevations ranging from 500 to 850 meters which dominated Route No. 9 to the east and west. . . .

The third significant terrain feature was a high escarpment whose ridgeline extended all the way to Tchepone, parallel to and south of Route No. 9 and the Xepon River. Several peaks of this ridgeline were 600 to 700 meters high and offered excellent observation over Route No. 9 and the Tchepone area. . . .

The terrain north of Route No. 9 was hilly and heavily vegetated against a backdrop of relatively high peaks which restricted operations in this area almost entirely to infantry. Around Tchepone, the terrain was much lower, sparsely vegetated, and more appropriate for armor vehicles.

Route No. 9 from Khe Sanh to Tchepone was a one-lane, unevenly surfaced, dirt road with destroyed bridges and culverts. Dominated by the high escarpment to the south, this road was easily interdicted. It also was difficult to prepare bypasses, due to the river to the south and the hilly terrain to the north.

• • •

February in the Tchepone area was the transitional period from the northeast to the southwest monsoons. The northeast monsoon, which brought rains and cloudiness to Central Vietnam above the Hai Van Pass from October to March, was the dominant weather factor. The Truong Son mountain range deflected much of this wet weather on the Laotian side, but in the area of operation the skies were generally covered. The amount of cumulus buildup in this area depended on the strength and depth of the monsoon. Average temperature during February was 22 degrees C. in the lowlands and about 18 degrees C. in mountainous regions.

As of mid-March, the southwest monsoon gradually picked up, resulting in a relative improvement of the weather and higher ceilings. The average temperature was warmer than in February, but this was a period of showers during which the skies were temporarily covered. Beginning in May, however, rainfall became heavier over the Truong Son Range, while in the eastern lowlands the weather was dry and hot.

In general, during the period considered for the operation the weather was fairly good but quite unpredictable. From experience, it was estimated that the areas of operations would be cloudy to hazy in the morning. The weather was favorable for air operations only from 1000–1200 hours until midafternoon. The 2,500-foot ceiling in the lowlands would allow only a 1,000-foot altitude in the area of operation. This was recognized as a major handicap, since all aircraft used in support missions would be located in the lowlands and would have to be flown first to the Khe Sanh Airfield. Low ceilings and hazardous mountains would force helicopters flying frontline support missions to follow natural avenues of approach, such as valleys and rivers, which the enemy could interdict with ease. This handicap was going to be an important factor affecting the course of combat operations.

III. THE PLANNING PHASE

How It All Started

To the South Vietnamese political and military leaders, the Ho Chi Minh Trail had always been like a thorn in the back, to be removed at any cost whenever there was a chance. The possibility that something could be done about it began to take shape as the war intensified and US combat forces helped regain the military initiative in 1966.

One of the leading Vietnamese strategists, General Cao Van Vien, who was both Chairman of the Joint General Staff and minister of defense at that time, was the first to advocate the severance of the Communist lifeline. In a testimony given before members of the National Leadership Committee, who ruled the country from June 1965 to September 1967, General Vien propounded an offensive strategy, called the "strategy of isolation and severance," for the effective defense of South Vietnam. This was in essence a two-pronged strategy aimed at isolating the Communist infrastructure and guerrillas from the population within South Vietnam by pacification on the one hand and severing North Vietnam's umbilical cord with its southern battlegrounds on the other.

To implement this severance action, he proposed to invade North Vietnam's southern panhandle with the objective of seizing the city of Vinh, the northern terminal of the Ho Chi Minh Trail, and at the same time establishing a strong defense line across northern Quang Tri Province to run the entire length of National Route No. 9, from the eastern coast to the Mekong River bank. This operation assumed the participation of US and other Free World Military Assistance Forces. The attack against the two southernmost North Vietnamese provinces—Thanh Hoa and Nghe An—and their eventual occupation would serve as leverage for bargaining in truce negotiations, while the defense line along

Route No. 9 would give the RVN a reasonable chance to defend itself after its forces would have been withdrawn from North Vietnam's panhandle. Such was the general outline of General Vien's strategy, which subsequently became the widely commented subject of several lectures and magazine articles.[4] General Vien's concept remained only that, because South Vietnam was unable to perform this momentous task all by itself.

In early January 1971 General Creighton W. Abrams, COMUSMACV, called on General Vien at the JGS and suggested an operation into lower Laos. With the unrealized concept still nurtured in his mind, General Vien gladly agreed. Meeting with General Vien again a few days later, General Abrams explained his concept of the operation on a map. US forces were to clear the way to the border by conducting an operation inside South Vietnam. The main effort was to be conducted by RVNAF airborne and armor forces along Route No. 9 in coordination with a heliborne assault into Tchepone. The purpose was to search and destroy Base Area 604. Other RVNAF units would be employed to cover the northern and southern flanks of the main effort. For the support of the operation, maximum US assets would be provided. After searching and destroying Base Area 604, ARVN forces would shift their effort toward Base Area 611. At the end of the meeting, both General Abrams and General Vien agreed to have staff officers work out an operational plan.

General Vien then reported his discussions with General Abrams to President Nguyen Van Thieu, because he knew this cross-border operation was going to have international repercussions. Being a military man himself, and well versed in military strategy, President Thieu immediately approved the operation.

Recognizing the political realities, General Vien had long since abandoned the idea of an invasion of North Vietnam as part of an operation to sever the Ho Chi Minh Trail, but still his concept differed somewhat from that presented by General Abrams. General Vien advocated an airborne operation into Tchepone as the first step. Then, after searching, the paratroopers would attack east to link up with an armor-infantry task force moving along Route No. 9. After linkup, the forces could shift their effort southward toward Base Area 611. General Vien conceived the foray into Laos to be a raid, an operation of short duration, and ordered his J-3 to look for drop zones around Tchepone. Later, because he felt he should go along with the MACV concept in order to obtain the necessary US support assets, he abandoned this concept and did not even discuss it with General Abrams.

In mid-January the J-3/JGS, Colonel Tran Dinh Tho, and his MACV counterpart flew to Danang. Colonel Tho's mission was to brief Lieutenant General Hoang Xuan Lam, commander of I Corps and MR-1, on the concept of the operation. The meeting took place discreetly at Headquarters, US XXIV Corps. General Lam was taken to a private briefing room where, in front of a general situation map, Colonel Tho explained how the operation was to be conducted as conceived by the Joint General Staff.[5] The main effort of the operation, he said, was to be launched along National Route No. 9 into Laos with the objective of cutting the Ho Chi Minh Trail in the region of Base Area 604 and destroying all enemy installations and supplies stored there.

After this mission had been accomplished, the operational forces were to move south and sweep through Base Area 611 to further create havoc [in] the enemy's logistic system before returning to South Vietnam. This operation was to be conducted and controlled by the I Corps command, which, in addition to its organic units, would be augmented by the entire Airborne Division and two marine brigades. The third marine brigade and the Marine Division headquarters would be available if required. As to US forces, they were going to conduct operations on the RVN side of the border and provide the ARVN operating forces with artillery, helilift, and tactical air support. This concept of operations thus coincided in near totality with the one initially proposed by COMUSMACV.

After this exclusive briefing, General Lam met in private with Lieutenant General [James W.] Sutherland, Commander, US XXIV Corps. General Sutherland's staff had already begun planning after receiving the MACV directive on 7 January, but now joint planning could begin in earnest. A joint planning committee with strictly limited membership began working on the operational plan at the headquarters compound of US XXIV Corps. The only I Corps staff members involved were the G-3 and the G-2. On the US side, the same restriction on the planning staff was initially observed. Both staffs worked closely together in a specifically arranged area with limited and controlled access.

On 17 January, planning guidance was provided by I Corps and US XXIV Corps to participating units under the guise of "Plans for the 1971 Spring-Summer Campaign," and on 21 January General Lam and General Sutherland flew to Saigon where, during a meeting at MACV headquarters, they submitted the plan to the Chairman of the JGS and the MACV commander.[6] Intelligence estimates on which the detailed operational concept was formulated were also carefully reviewed. Subsequently, on the same day, General Lam personally presented his operational plan to President Thieu.

The Basic Operational Plan

The combined operation was code-named Lam Son 719.[7] It was to be executed in four phases during an indefinite period of time with the objective of destroying enemy forces and stockpiles and cutting enemy lines of communications in Base Areas 604 and 611.[8]

In Phase I, which was to be called Operation Dewey Canyon II, the 1st Brigade, US 5th Infantry Division (Mechanized), reinforced, was to advance on D-Day, occupy the Khe Sanh area, and clear Route No. 9 up to the Laotian border, ARVN troop assembly areas, and forward artillery positions required for support of the operation. In the meantime, the US 101st Airborne Division (Airmobile), while continuing its operations in Thua Thien and Quang Tri Provinces, was to conduct artillery attacks by fire in the A Shau Valley, west of Thua Thien Province, from D-Day to D+4 (a diversionary action) and, in cooperation with the 2nd Regiment, 1st ARVN Infantry Division, to be prepared to defend the areas south of the DMZ. The US 45th Engineer Group was assigned the mission to repair Route No. 9 up to the Laotian border and rehabilitate the Khe Sanh airstrip for C-130 use. Tactical air was to be provided by the US 7th Air Force, B-52 strikes by CINCSAC, and gunships and artillery by units of US XXIV Corps. During

Phase I, ARVN forces were to complete their movements toward assembly areas and be prepared to attack on order across the border into lower Laos.

In Phase II, on D-Day I Corps forces, following intensive preparation fires, were to launch their attack into lower Laos. The major effort was to be conducted along Route No. 9 by the Airborne Division, reinforced by the 1st Armor Brigade, [and] engineer and artillery elements. While the 1st Armor Brigade (with its two squadrons 11 and 17) and engineer troops moved along Route No. 9, repairing it as they progressed, an airborne battalion was to be helilifted into Objective A Luoi (geographical name: Ban Dong), and two other airborne battalions were to establish fire support bases . . . to the north. Battalions of the 1st Infantry Division's 1st and 3rd Regiments were to be inserted by helicopter and establish FSBs on the Co Roc elevation south of Route No. 9 to protect the I Corps southern flank. The 1st Ranger Group, with its three battalions (the 21st, 37th, and 39th), was to be helilifted north of Route No. 9 to occupy blocking positions more than 16 kilometers to the northeast of A Luoi and protect the northern flank of the Airborne Division. After the completion of this troop movement, the armor brigade would attack westward from Objective A Luoi to link up with the third airborne brigade, which was to be helilifted into Tchepone. The 147th and 258th Marine Brigades would serve as I Corps reserves at Khe Sanh.

• • •

Phase III was to be initiated after the successful occupation of Tchepone. It was to be the exploitation phase during which search operations would be expanded to destroy enemy bases and stockpiles. The Airborne Division would search the area of Tchepone, while the 1st Infantry Division would conduct search operations to the south. The 1st Ranger Group meanwhile would continue holding blocking positions to the north.

• • •

Phase IV was the withdrawal phase.

• • •

On 22 January XXIV Corps and I Corps completed preparation of their operational orders. On D-Day, 30 January, the Forward CP of I Corps was to be established at Dong Ha; it was to include a small command element to be located at Ham Nghi FSB south of Khe Sanh. The Forward CP of the US XXIV Corps was to move to Quang Tri Combat Base the day before. The I Corps forces were to cross the border on 8 February. During a combined briefing session held at Dong Ha on 2 February, the I Corps operation orders were disseminated to all participating units.

To assist in the execution of Lam Son 719, MACV planned a diversion in the form of a maneuver involving US naval and marine units off the coast of Thanh Hoa Province (North Vietnam).

Division Planning and Preparations

The main effort of Lam Son 719 was assigned to the Airborne Division, and, on 18 January 1971, during a meeting at I Corps headquarters, the division commander, Lieutenant General Du Quoc Dong, learned this for the first time. He immediately ordered his division, at the Airborne Division rear base in Saigon, to begin preparations for deployment. Meanwhile the US advisory team, on 27 January, visited Headquarters, US XXIV Corps, to receive firsthand briefings and report on airborne preparations. Airborne units deployed on an operation in War Zone C (north of Tay Ninh) were withdrawn to receive additional training by US advisors on communications and the employment of US gunships and supply and medevac helicopters, as well as air-ground communications with supporting US tactical aircraft.

General Dong flew to Dong Ha on 1 February 1971 and was followed during the next few days by his staff, the US Airborne Division advisory team, and combat and support units.

The Airborne Division began its operational planning only after it received detailed guidance from the I Corps commander on 2 February during the combined staff meeting at Dong Ha, where the I Corps Forward CP was now located.

The combat plan developed by the Airborne Division called for successive heliborne operations to occupy Objectives 30, 31, and A Luoi in coordination with an armor-infantry thrust along Route No. 9. Intermediate objectives, on which fire support bases would be established, would be seized in the advance to Tchepone, after which battalion-sized blocking positions would be occupied around Tchepone. The heliborne operations to occupy A Luoi and Tchepone would be conducted as soon as the armor-infantry thrust progressed near the objectives. This was to be a coordinated advance so timed as to provide immediate linkup at the objectives.

Initially the armor-infantry thrust consisted of two squadrons, the 11th and 17th, of the 1st Armor Brigade; the 1st Airborne Brigade (with its three battalions, the 1st, 8th, and 9th); the 44th Artillery Battalion (155mm); and the 101st Engineer Battalion. This task force was to advance along Route No. 9, repair roads as it moved, and link up with heliborne units. The 3rd Airborne Brigade (three battalions, the 2nd, 3rd, and 6th) would be the heliborne force assigned to occupy objectives and establish FSBs north of the road. For the assault on Tchepone, the mission was given to the 2nd Airborne Brigade, which consisted of three battalions (the 5th, 7th, and 11th). The troop pickup point for airborne operations would be Ham Nghi Base. The Airborne Division operation plan was presented to Lieutenant General Hoang Xuan Lam on 3 February; he immediately approved it in principle.

Of the two marine brigades to be provided by the JGS, the 258th Brigade (with one artillery and three infantry battalions) was operating in an area southwest of Quang Tri. The other brigade, the 147th, after regrouping its detached units completed its movement by C-130 to Dong Ha on 3 February. Both brigades were to be employed as I Corps reserves and given the temporary mission of security for ARVN forces on the RVN side of the border.

The I Corps organic forces that participated in the operation were the 1st Infantry Division, 1st Ranger Group, and 1st Armor Brigade, all immediately available. The 1st Armor Brigade, with its two squadrons, was attached to the Airborne Division. The 1st Ranger Group was assigned the security mission on the northern flank of the operational area. Its three lightly equipped battalions would be deployed in screening positions facing north.[9] The 1st Infantry Division meanwhile would deploy its two regiments (the 1st and 3rd) to its area of operation south of Route No. 9 with the mission of blocking enemy forces from the south and simultaneously searching enemy Base Area 611. Its two other regiments (the 2nd and 54th) . . . would not participate in the operation, but would remain where they were, east of the DMZ area and west of Hue respectively.

US Support

It was apparent that, due to the lack of helicopters, tactical air, and long-range artillery, I Corps could not conduct such a large-scale operation away from its support bases without assistance. US support was therefore required, not only to compensate for I Corps's lack of assets, but also to provide the kind of mobility and firepower needed for combat against a heavily defended enemy stronghold in rugged terrain. Therefore the US XXIV Corps was charged with planning for this substantial support.

An outstanding feature of Lam Son 719 was the conspicuous absence of US combat troops and US advisors, who were not authorized to go into lower Laos. US advisors could still provide assistance to ARVN staffs, but only at command posts located on the RVN side of the border. Even division senior advisors were not authorized to fly over lower Laos.[10] To compensate for the absence of advisors, who always helped in communicating with US units for support, it was decided to assign a Vietnamese serviceman-interpreter to each of the FAC teams and to the 7th Air Force airborne command and control center. It was also planned that one member of each division advisory team would be airborne over the AO of their respective units. This was intended to alleviate some of the problems related to language and communications.

• • •

Of prime importance to the entire operation was the mobility support provided by US helicopters of all types. The US 101st Airborne Division . . . was assigned this support responsibility. Having to continue its current missions inside South Vietnam, which were greatly expanded due to the redeployment of a number of ARVN units, and to provide operational support in lower Laos at the same time, the 101st Airborne Division obviously could not meet all the requirements with its organic assets, so the division was augmented with four assault helicopter companies (UH-1H), two assault support helicopter companies (CH-47), two air cavalry troops, and two assault helicopter battalion headquarters, all detached from other US divisions. This reinforcement was to be more substantial on days when special requirements arose.

• • •

The commander of the 101st Aviation Group, 101st Airborne Division, was to exercise operational control over all assault, assault support, and aerial weapons helicopter units. In addition, an assistant commander of the 101st Airborne Division was designated as the aviation support coordinator.

• • •

Solving Logistic Problems

• • •

The most vital consideration in logistic planning was supply routes and transportation. The major axes of road communication available were Routes No. 1 and No. 9. While No. 1 was a two-way all-weather road from Danang to Dong Ha, truck traffic from the Dong Ha junction had to move westward on No. 9. This was possible only to Vandegrift Base. From Vandegrift to the Laotian border, No. 9 was extensively damaged, with many destroyed bridges. Therefore US engineer units were charged with repairing and rehabilitating this stretch of road.

• • •

In air transportation, the two existing airfields at Quang Tri and Dong Ha were ready for immediate use. The abandoned airstrip at Khe Sanh, however, needed extensive repairs by US engineer units and was scheduled to become operational on D+6 to accommodate C-130 cargo planes. Several US C-130 planes were also earmarked for the ARVN to transport emergency supplies directly to Khe Sanh. Due to the sizable quantity of helicopters required to support the operation, the supply of aviation fuel was an important problem. . . .

To move supplies to forward combat units operating along Route No. 9, ground transportation was planned. For those units operating far from the road, helicopters would be used, both for resupply and medical evacuation. As to the movement of heavy items of supply to forward areas, the only means available would be large US cargo helicopters.

Observations

The entire planning process—and the resultant operations plan—for Lam Son 719 indicated a carefully considered decision arrived at by responsible US and GVN political and military authorities. The authorities of each country . . . considered in their decisions the best intelligence available to them at the time, and each approached the problem with the best interests of his own country in mind. Of course, each was influenced by the political and military factors peculiar to his own country. Tchepone, the crossroads of enemy supply routes, appeared to be a well selected objective, since all enemy logistic and infiltration movements south had to go through this area. According to intelligence reports, this was indeed an area where important enemy storage facilities were located. The time had finally arrived to sever by ground attacks the lifeline which had sustained enemy warring capabilities for so many years. This was a sound and bold decision following several years of reconnaissance and interdiction efforts from the air.

The time frame selected for the operation was also appropriate in that the dry season in the Laotian panhandle had begun three months earlier. After his substantial losses in Cambodia during 1970, the enemy was using the dry season to the maximum for the movement of replacements south and to replenish his supplies; the enemy was conducting an aggressive "logistic offensive." The amount of supplies in transit and in these storage facilities was substantial, and, if we succeeded in destroying them, the blow [to] the enemy would be most devastating. He would be in serious trouble, not only from our spoiling actions during the remaining three months of the dry season, but also because time was running out for the movement of supplies for that year.

Despite the continuation of redeployments, US military presence in South Vietnam was still substantial enough to support a large-scale offensive by the ARVN. If this offensive were deferred, US support would no longer be as adequate and as effective. This was another consideration of prime importance which contributed to the decision to conduct Lam Son 719 at this time.

Once the decision was made, the speed with which planning and preparations progressed was amazing. Only two weeks after planning guidance was received, operational orders had been developed by I Corps and XXIV Corps. This was indicative of how close and effective cooperation and coordination between US and ARVN staffs had been.

The exchange of intelligence proved to be particularly beneficial to ARVN forces. Lacking long-range reconnaissance facilities, the ARVN intelligence system could not provide adequate data on the Ho Chi Minh Trail and North Vietnam. It was obvious that almost all information concerning enemy capabilities in the target area had to be supplied by the United States.

Combat support provided by the US XXIV Corps for I Corps was another indication of the outstanding support provided by MACV. The I Corps unit commanders who were to participate in the operation felt encouraged and unusually enthusiastic because of this. To them, this was an opportunity not only to prove I Corps combat effectiveness, but also to compete with their colleagues of III and IV Corps who had participated in the Cambodia incursion the previous year. Finally, the fact that no US combat troops were to cross the border, and that even US advisors were precluded from the operation, made the role of ARVN units even more prominent.

In spite of the sound decision, the effective cooperation and coordination between the RVNAF and MACV, and the support allocated by the United States, several problem areas cropped up during the planning phase which should receive special attention. First, the entire process of planning and operational preparations appeared to have taken place in a great rush. Considering the scale of the operation, and the importance of the objectives, the time involved for planning might have been too short. To ensure utmost secrecy, participating units were given only a short time to prepare. In the face of such a difficult campaign, which was to be conducted over unfamiliar terrain, the question that naturally arose was [whether] I Corps units [were] prepared to meet all the unforeseeable challenges. The events that subsequently occurred during the operation left no doubt as to the answer to this question.

Then there was the questionable wisdom in selecting a single road axis for the major effort of the offensive. Hemmed in by dense jungle and rough mountainous terrain, this type of road did not lend itself readily to heavy logistic activities. In South Vietnam, such difficulties in road transportation could be removed by the alternate use of waterways or US airlift facilities. But in lower Laos, jungles, rough mountains, and steep valleys, added to the stubbornness of the enemy, created serious problems that should have received more attention. While there were plans for infantry units to advance and withdraw using different routes, mechanized and armor units were confined to Route No. 9. The holding of this route required the relative superiority of friendly forces, which was not the case.

Next was the tactic of establishing fire support bases. In view of the single axis available to progress through mountains, the effective control of the area of operation and the conduct of search operations depended on the capability of our forces being deployed on both sides of the road, north and south. In our case, the operational plan called for the advance of infantry forces through a series of fire support bases. Each new leap forward necessarily required an additional number of these bases. The use of fire support bases had been successful in South Vietnam, but this success depended a great deal on the overwhelming firepower and initiative of US forces in the face of a less endowed enemy. To be effective in lower Laos, it was apparent that fire support bases would have to enjoy the same conditions.

• • •

Within a period of from one to two weeks, the enemy was capable of reinforcing with up to a total of eight additional infantry regiments, not to mention artillery and other units from North Vietnam. To defeat these 11 infantry regiments and the defense forces of the binh trams, I Corps committed, according to the original plan, only eight infantry regiments or brigades. Our forces enjoyed the advantage of an armor brigade, but our tanks might be of little value off the main axis. Even if, at the limit of its capabilities, I Corps would bring in two additional regiments (the remaining marine brigade and the third regiment of the 1st Infantry Division), it would only have ten regimental-sized units and the balance would still be in favor of the enemy. Additional reinforcements would be highly improbable, and any such effort to obtain them would certainly meet with difficulties.

In the effort to obtain the tactical advantage in the area of operations, and to compensate for the lack of force superiority, the planners of Lam Son 719 expected too much from the support of US tactical air and air cavalry gunships. The question that should have been asked then was how effective would air power be in support of ground combat troops deep in the Truong Son mountain range? If the bombings of North Vietnam had been an indication of this effectiveness, then were the results to be obtained exactly what we had desired? Over the years, the US Air Force had bombed the Ho Chi Minh Trail heavily. Was the effect of these bombings enough to paralyze the enemy's activities on the battlefields of South Vietnam and Cambodia? Too much was expected from airpower, and this problem should have been weighed with caution by the planners.

Then there was the role to be played by helicopters. With the exception of mechanized forces operating along Route No. 9, which would be resupplied by road transportation according to plans, all other operational units would have to depend on helicopters for movement of troops and artillery, supply, and medical evacuation. This was the only means practicable as long as these forces were required to operate considerable distances from roads and fire support bases. There was no doubt that the United States would provide enough helicopters to satisfy requirements. But there was cause to doubt the effectiveness of helicopters in the expected combat situation, considering the terrain and weather in lower Laos and the enemy's antiaircraft capabilities. This was a serious question which required careful consideration.

As the time approached for D-Day, however, ARVN and US commanders and staffs alike appeared to be confident of success. As a testimony to this confidence, I think it appropriate to excerpt here a passage of the report filed by Colonel Arthur W. Pence, senior advisor of the Airborne Division. In this after-action report, Colonel Pence described the mood that prevailed during a meeting at Headquarters, US XXV Corps, prior to Phase I of Lam Son 719. He wrote: "It was apparent at this time that United States intelligence felt that the operation would be lightly opposed and that a two-day preparation of the area prior to D-Day by tactical air would effectively neutralize the enemy antiaircraft capability, although the enemy was credited with having 170 to 200 antiaircraft weapons of mixed caliber in the operational area. The tank threat was considered minimal and the reinforcement capability was listed as fourteen days for two divisions from north of the DMZ."[11]

The RVN military leaders thought that ARVN forces had a tough mission ahead, but would be able to carry it out with the support of the United States. The decision had been made.

• • •

IV. THE OFFENSIVE PHASE

Preparing to Cross the Border

To assist I Corps in making preparations for their cross-border offensive, XXIV Corps implemented Phase I of Lam Son 719 exactly as scheduled at 0000 hours on 30 January 1971.

• • •

The US 14th Combat Engineer Battalion immediately followed the attacking cavalry forces, restoring 9 of the 18 required bridges and 9 of the 20 required culverts along the road. At Khe Sanh, US Army engineers were to survey a site for an assault airstrip which was to run parallel to the old unserviceable PSP airstrip. This assault airstrip, scheduled to be completed on 3 February, was to be used during the initial phase pending repairs on the main airstrip. Concurrently a company of the US 7th Combat Engineer Battalion, with three D-7 bulldozers, immediately started building a road leading from the Rockpile directly to Khe Sanh.

• • •

On 2 February the first combined operational meeting was held at the headquarters of I Corps Forward, attended by all RVNAF and US commanders, and detailed operational orders were issued. Immediately after this meeting, ARVN units feverishly completed their preparations for the big operation that promised numerous challenges.

• • •

The 2nd ARVN Airborne Brigade arrived at the Dong Ha Airfield on 6 February, while other ARVN units—the 1st Armor Brigade, 1st Airborne Brigade, and 3/1 Infantry Regiment—moved overland to the Ham Nghi (Khe Sanh) area. Upon arrival, the 1st Armor Brigade and the 1st Airborne Brigade, which were both scheduled to move out by way of Route No. 9 on D-Day Phase II, immediately entered the assembly area adjacent to the border. That evening, a regrettable incident occurred. A US Navy aircraft mistakenly attacked the ARVN forward elements, destroying one M-113 armored personnel carrier; additionally, six ARVN personnel were killed and 51 armor and airborne personnel wounded. These were the first ARVN casualties of Operation Lam Son 719.

• • •

Ground transportation soon became difficult because the road section between Vandegrift and Khe Sanh was only trafficable one way. Despite this, US and ARVN convoys, combat and logistic alike, moved day and night.

During the first days, and as originally planned, ARVN units were supported by US logistic facilities. As soon as ARVN units reached the assembly area, they were issued supplies in preparation for action. This activity proceeded smoothly, except for some difficulties in the issue of combat rations. Vietnamese combat rations were not similar to American C-rations. Instead of a self-contained package of individual meals, each Vietnamese ration consisted of three separate items: instant rice, canned meat or fish, and condiments. These were packaged individually, but issued collectively by the carton. American logistics personnel were unfamiliar with these rations and with ARVN issue and accounting procedures, so to solve the problem some Vietnamese specialists were detached to FSA 26–2.

• • •

Probably taken by surprise, enemy troops in Quang Tri reacted very slowly and weakly during the first days. Although some mine explosions occurred along the routes of advance, floating mines appeared on the Cau Viet River, and a few rockets were fired into rear support bases, other activities of Communist units in northern Quang Tri Province showed no significant changes. The northwestern corner of Quang Tri, in particular, remained very quiet.

The weather was favorable during the first few days of the operation, and our air support was effective. On 4 and 5 February, however, the weather turned unfavorable; low clouds, interspersed with rain, delayed some troop landing plans and interfered with the activities of engineer units, particularly road repairs and rehabilitation work being conducted at the Khe Sanh airstrip. Although the weather during 6 and 7 February was better than the preceding two days, it was not adequate for effective preemptive airstrikes by the US Air Force.

Lieutenant General James W. Sutherland, commander of XXIV Corps, communicated this information to Lieutenant General Hoang Xuan Lam, commander of I Corps, who decided that the cross-border operation should go ahead despite the lack of adequate preemptive airstrikes.[12] Apparently General Lam would not modify his orders without consulting President Thieu, who had approved the original plan. To compensate for this, General Lam requested that US air cavalry fly ahead of the ARVN thrust. But, because the air cavalry could not cross the border ahead of ARVN units, the RVNAF and US corps commanders agreed that, at precisely 0700 hours on D-Day Phase II (8 February), the Airborne Division would send a combat team across the border, to be immediately followed by air cavalry.[13] This compromise seemed to satisfy both US political restrictions and the I Corps desire for additional support.

Securing Ban Dong

In the early hours of 8 February, 11 Arc Light sorties were flown against targets in lower Laos, as well as to support troop landing zones. The Airborne Division had positioned artillery batteries at Lao Bao, in the immediate vicinity of the border, to support the main thrust along Route No. 9. Everything seemed to be ready, and at 0700 the first airborne-armored team crossed the border. A moment later it was followed by a flight of US air cavalry helicopters which eventually took the lead to cover the main ARVN task force. The ARVN soldiers, after so many days of waiting, were now cheerfully waving from their armored vehicles at foreign and local press reporters. The press embargo, which had been imposed during the initial stage for security reasons, had been lifted a few days earlier, and a number of reporters were already at the border.

This first task force consisted of the 1st Armor Brigade (11th and 17th Armor Squadrons), reinforced by the 1st and 8th Airborne Battalions, the 101st Combat Engineer Battalion, and a platoon of bulldozers. The road on the Laotian side of the border had been cratered and cut by ditches at many places, and the armored elements provided support for the engineer repair crews. Many parts of the road were destroyed beyond quick repair and the engineers had to build detours. Sporadic enemy fire was received, but it was insignificant in the face of our mighty armored force and the brave airborne troops, and they advanced rapidly. Ahead of the column, and on the mountain slopes north and south of the axis of advance, air cavalry gunships struck at enemy air defense positions.

All supporting firepower provided by US forces was coordinated by the US 108th Artillery Group. The 155mm and 8-inch howitzers and long-range guns hit against deep targets in lower Laos, beginning at 0800 hours. The 108th Group expertly and effectively performed its support mission.

• • •

While armored and infantry forces were progressing into Laos along the road, the northern and southern flank security elements were heliborne. The 4/3 Infantry Battalion was transported into Landing Zone Hotel in the Co Roc area by helicopters at 1100 hours, without enemy contact. The 2nd Airborne Battalion reached Landing Zone 30, ten kilometers north of Route No. 9, unhampered. At 1300 hours, however, near Landing Zone Ranger South, five kilometers northwest of LZ 30, the 21st Ranger Battalion's insertion was met with fire from 12.7mm antiaircraft machineguns; 11 rangers [were] wounded and the troop insertion continued while US air cavalry attacked the gun positions. This US gunship activity resulted in a number of enemy troops killed and several trucks destroyed, but more significantly these attacks caused numerous secondary explosions, from a network of fortifications, which lasted over a period of an hour.

At 1620 hours, the 1st and 2nd Battalions of the 3rd Infantry Regiment were helilifted into two areas in the vicinity of Landing Zone Blue, four kilometers southwest of LZ Hotel. Immediately thereafter, the 2/3 Battalion was engaged by the enemy.

• • •

At 1655 hours US air cavalry gunships attacked a suspected target two kilometers east of Landing Zone 31, causing numerous secondary explosions, with flames reaching 1,500 feet in the air. Reconnaissance aircraft reported the fire lasted until just before daylight the following morning. After the attack on this target, the 3rd Airborne Brigade headquarters and 3rd Airborne Battalion occupied Landing Zone 31 unopposed.

• • •

By nightfall of the first day, the ARVN armored column had moved nine kilometers into Laos. Though enemy resistance was weak, the column could not move more rapidly because of the bad road conditions and the dense jungle on both sides of the road.

• • •

In support of the first day of the cross-border operations, US forces had flown 11 B-52 sorties, expending 719 tons of bombs which caused 40 secondary explosions, and performed 468 helicopter gunship and 52 tactical air missions, destroying 11 gun emplacements and 40 trucks, damaging 18 trucks, and causing 13 secondary explosions and 23 fires. Four huge "Commando Vault" bombs had been used to clear landing zones. During the night C-130 gunships had also destroyed additional enemy trucks moving near Ban Dong, the next objective.

On 9 February the weather suddenly turned very poor. Heavy rain made the road a quagmire, preventing the engineers from working. Heliborne troop insertions were delayed, and logistical buildup efforts were halted. Those units already in Laos endeavored to consolidate their positions or increase the range of their patrols.

• • •

The next day, 10 February, the weather improved but did not permit heliborne operations until late in the afternoon, when the 4th Battalion, 1st Infantry Regiment, completed an assault into Landing Zone Delta, ten kilometers due west of LZ Hotel, at 1630 hours. The armored thrust meanwhile resumed at a stronger pace after a day of marking time. At 1700 hours the 9th Airborne Battalion was inserted into Landing Zone A Luoi (Ban Dong), approximately 20 kilometers from the border. Enemy antiaircraft fire was heavy, but, thanks to the dedicated support of air cavalry teams, the landing was completed at 1720 hours. Two hours later, advance elements of the armored column linked up with the 9th Airborne Battalion at A Luoi. This was the greatest success of the day.

• • •

Meanwhile, near the area of operations of the 21st Ranger Battalion, a flight of four VNAF helicopters bound for Landing Zone Ranger South was hit by enemy 37mm antiaircraft artillery fire at 1300 hours. Two helicopters were downed and all passengers were presumed killed. The first helicopter carried two ARVN colonels, the G-3 and G-4 of I Corps. The second helicopter reportedly carried a number of foreign correspondents. It was suspected that the I Corps G-3 had carried with him an operational map of Lam Son 719, along with signal operating instructions and codes. The loss of these documents to the enemy would be extremely significant. A thorough search of the area for the downed helicopters produced no results.

The linkup on Route No. 9 between the armored and airborne troops at Landing Zone A Luoi (Ban Dong), nearly 20 kilometers deep into enemy territory, was an encouraging achievement. I Corps headquarters therefore decided to push the operation farther westward. Reinforcements were sent on 11 February to increase security on the northern and southern flanks before further advance was made.

• • •

From 11 to 16 February, while I Corps staff in the rear was planning the next moves, ARVN units in the forward area in lower Laos expanded their operations and continued the search for the enemy, increasing the number of contacts and caches uncovered. In the rangers' area, on the northern flank, the 37th Ranger Battalion, operating near Fire Support Base Phu Loc and protecting the northwestern approaches to Khe Sanh, was continuously subjected to enemy attacks by fire and probes.

• • •

Around Fire Support Bases 30 and 31, the 2nd and 3rd Airborne Battalions pushed farther out. Their companies made sporadic contacts and proved superior to enemy forces in the area. In the morning of 12 February, in particular, an element of the 2nd Airborne Battalion engaged the enemy five kilometers southeast of Fire Support Base 30, killing 32 enemy troops, seizing 20 individual weapons, and destroying three crew-served weapons. Friendly forces had only three killed. Other sporadic contacts were all in favor of friendly forces.

• • •

In addition to the big guns of the 108th Artillery Group, US air support was an important factor during the first week of the incursion. Each day from 500 to 800 sorties of air cavalry gunships were flown, in addition to approximately 100 sorties of tactical bombers and, depending upon available targets, a number of missions by B-52 strategic bombers. Losses inflicted on the enemy by these airstrikes were very significant.[14] But, despite the devastating US air and artillery support, enemy antiaircraft gunners took a heavy toll of helicopters; and the US air cavalry, as well as the RVNAF, had to increase their efforts to silence the Communist guns.

By the end of the first week of the invasion of Laos, the I Corps armored-airborne advance along Route No. 9 had become much slower and more cautious. Securing and repairing this road had become vital to guarantee a logistical lifeline for ARVN forces in the event inclement weather precluded the use of helicopters. A network of fire support bases had been established along the road to ensure artillery support, and, while the task force proceeded westward, its flanks were effectively protected. An airborne brigade and a ranger group secured the northern flank, while two regiments of the 1st Infantry Division were deployed along the southern flank.

According to the operational plan, the Airborne Division and the 1st Infantry Division were expected to advance westward, each stop forward to be solidly anchored on a fire support base. The planners of Lam Son 719 apparently believed that this tactic, coordinated with the massive support by the USAF and US Army air cavalry, would help accomplish the mission with minimum losses. But, because of this procedure, the operation progressed slowly and did not exactly meet the expectations of US counterparts. In Saigon, General Abrams, COMUSMACV, in a discussion with General . . . Vien . . . expressed his wish to see the operational units reach Tchepone as quickly as possible.[15]

Then, in the afternoon of 16 February, in the forward command post of I Corps at Dong Ha Airfield, Generals Vien and Abrams met with Generals Lam and Sutherland for two and a half hours. After a review of the general situation, a decision was made to step up the operation by having the 1st Infantry Division quickly occupy the higher mountaintops south of the Xepon River and establish fire support bases there to support the Airborne Division's push toward Tchepone. They estimated that this would take three to five days. But, as later events were to prove, battlefield developments seldom occur exactly as planned. Enemy reactions were becoming stronger with each day and the test of strength more arduous.

The Enemy Counteracted

Nearly a week had passed since Ban Dong was occupied. Except for a few clearing activities conducted by units of the 1st Infantry Division, the forward movement of ARVN forces seemed to have stalled. The heliborne insertion of troops through the fierce enemy air defense screen in the afternoon of 10 February had enabled friendly forces to quickly occupy this objective. The linkup with armored forces had also been made immediately thereafter. Fire Support Base Ban Dong was now well entrenched, with six 105mm and six 155mm howitzers and adequate ammunition and supplies. However, as of 16 February, six days after the capture of Ban Dong, there had been no further progress by ARVN troops toward the objective Tchepone. In the meantime, the enemy had increased his air defense capabilities along the mountain slopes to the south. Enemy attacks by fire, which were initially conducted with assorted mortars and 122mm rockets, were now occasionally augmented by long-range artillery. ARVN armored units had tried to advance, but could not make much progress. The dense forests bordering the road required careful, time-consuming reconnaissance to avoid ambush, and this made the armor column's movement extremely slow.

• • •

All these activities were quickly eclipsed by reports of heavy enemy troop concentrations around the 39th and 21st Ranger Battalions. Both battalions were being subjected to attacks by fire and ground attacks, and the fighting lasted all night while friendly artillery, tactical air, and flareships responded quickly in support of the embattled rangers.

The next morning enemy pressure on the 21st Ranger Battalion gradually diminished, but heavy pressure persisted on the 39th Battalion in the Ranger North area. The battle continued over 19 February. Enemy troops here were confirmed to be elements of the 102nd Regiment of the 308th Division, all with new weapons and clothing. Before launching an assault, the rangers reported, the enemy made extensive use of recoilless rifles and mortars; his fire was very accurate. The strongest enemy attacks were directed at the eastern flank of the rangers, which was their weakest spot. However, the 39th Battalion continued to hold its position, with support from US artillery and tactical air.

• • •

While the firefights were raging in the Ranger North area, on 19 February President Thieu visited I Corps Forward CP at Dong Ha. General Lam reported the critical situation faced by the 39th Rangers and the increasingly powerful enemy reactions which were making the planned push toward Tchepone by the Airborne Division highly questionable. In the presence of ARVN division commanders, President Thieu told him to take his time, and, under the present circumstances, perhaps it would be better to expand search activities toward the southwest to cut off Route 914, which led into Base Area 611.

During the night of 19 February the enemy continued to attack the 39th Battalion while launching uninterrupted attacks by fire to hold the 21st Battalion in check. Seven fixed-wing gunships and six flareships were used in support of the 39th Battalion, and, from 0730 to 1430 hours on 20 February, 32 tactical air sorties were flown in support of the rangers. Efforts to resupply and evacuate their casualties were made with strong support from tactical air, gunships, and artillery. Some helicopters managed to land in the area, ammunition was delivered, and some wounded were evacuated. But upon takeoff two helicopters were damaged by enemy fire. One had to land in the positions of the 21st Ranger Battalion (Ranger South), and the other managed to land at Fire Support Base 30.

In the afternoon, reconnaissance aircraft reported sighting an estimated 400 to 500 enemy troops encircling the 39th Battalion. At 1710 hours on 20 February radio contact with the 39th Ranger Battalion was lost. At 1856 hours, I Corps CP received information that the able-bodied personnel of the battalion had fought their way out and reached the 21st Ranger Battalion positions with most of their wounded and all of their weapons, but with very little ammunition left. Those who reached the 21st Ranger Battalion numbered nearly 200; 107 were still able to fight, but 92 were wounded. Total losses were 178 dead and missing and 148 wounded. Intelligence reports indicated enemy casualties to be 639 killed, with a corresponding number of weapons destroyed (423 AK-47s, 15 B40/B41s, and numerous automatic weapons).

With most of the wounded of the 39th Ranger Battalion still stranded in the 21st Rangers' positions, this unit received intense attacks by fire, including 130mm artillery, on the night of 21 February. Plans were made to evacuate the wounded rangers the following day. Toward noon on 22 February the area around the battalion position was subjected to a heavy barrage of fire involving tactical air, air cavalry, aerial artillery, and ground artillery for nearly an hour, while 13 medical evacuation helicopters were airborne, ready to go in. All of them landed and successfully picked up 122 wounded, as well as one US pilot who had been stranded there since his aircraft was shot down. The ranger force remaining in combat position at Ranger South numbered approximately

400 men, including 100 from the 39th Battalion, but two days later, on 24 February, the battalion was ordered by the I Corps commander to withdraw to FSB 30. From there they were helilifted to FSB Phu Loc.

While the 39th Ranger Battalion was holding out, numerous activities took place in other areas. US air cavalry continued to search for and destroy pipelines. Units of the 1st Infantry Division moved farther south, striking along Route 92 and finding a number of enemy installations, but also making numerous contacts and receiving attacks by fire. The 8th Airborne Battalion and armored elements engaged the enemy two kilometers north of Ban Dong, destroying one T-34 tank and a 23mm gun position. This was another strong indication of enemy armor involvement. On the friendly side, a number of US helicopters were shot down while on supply, medical evacuation, or support missions.

The corps commander had concluded that the position held by the 21st Rangers and the survivors of the 39th was untenable. A maximum effort in air and artillery support was required for each resupply and evacuation mission and he had other pressing demands for this support. The position was not an objective in itself, and there was no military advantage in sacrificing a ranger battalion in a doomed attempt to hold it. The corps commander was looking toward his objectives in the west, and he wished to conserve as much of his combat power as possible for the main mission.

• • •

The Loss of Fire Support Base 31

The withdrawal of the 21st Ranger Battalion left the northern flank of the Airborne Division exposed, and Fire Support Bases 31 and 30 now bore the brunt of enemy attacks. They had been under pressure since the 2nd and 3rd Battalions of the 3rd Airborne Brigade were inserted. Established in the immediate vicinity of the Communist north-south supply line, both bases were able to monitor closely enemy troop movements, as well as signs of enemy armored activities. Each battalion left but a small force to defend the bases, while a larger force fanned out in security and search activities, but this mobile force was not sufficient to prevent the enemy from moving close to the bases and setting up mortars and antiaircraft guns to interdict supply and medical evacuation attempts.[16] Each helicopter landing or departing usually resulted in heavy attacks by fire.

To strengthen the security of Fire Support Base 31, which was a more important position and seemed to be more heavily threatened because it housed the 3rd Airborne Brigade headquarters, plans were made to helilift the 6th Airborne Battalion to a mountain range northwest of the base on 13 February. This mountain range controlled a valley running a southeasterly course to Fire Support Base 31, and the valley was the source for attacks by fire against friendly positions. Although B-52 bombs had cleared the landing zone and its approaches, the fleet of helicopters bringing in the first elements of the 6th Airborne Battalion was subjected to heavy attacks by fire immediately upon landing. The remaining elements of the 6th Battalion were diverted to alternate landing zones nearby. Upon touching the ground, the battalion spread out its troops over nearly a kilometer, but continued to receive enemy artillery fire. The battalion then broke up and withdrew south, to near Fire Support Base 31. It had lost 28 KIA, 50 WIA, and 23 MIA during this short venture. Between that time and its eventual evacuation on 19 February, the 6th Battalion was unable to carry out any significant mission. The northwest mountain range remained under enemy control, and FSB 31 continued to hold under heavy enemy pressure.

A company of the 3rd Airborne Battalion operating southwest of FSB 31 received a rallier who was a sergeant platoon leader in the 24B Regiment of the 304th Division. He reported that the Communists had been preparing to counter the RVNAF-US operation since October 1970. Rear service units of Group 559 had in fact received orders to prepare for combat, and an army corps-sized headquarters called the 70th Front was designated in October 1970 to command the 304th, 308th, and 320th Divisions, a number of artillery regiments, an armored regiment, a number of air defense regiments, and other support units. To counter Operation Lam Son 719, the 70th Front Headquarters was sent to lower Laos, along with NVA combat units. The 24B Regiment, along with advance elements of the 9th and 66th Regiments, had infiltrated the border area west of Quang Tri since 9 February. From all these new revelations it appeared that the enemy would make a determined effort to defend his base areas.

The situation heated up following the evacuation of ranger positions in the north and as a result of heavy enemy attacks. The 31st and 32nd Companies, 3rd Airborne Battalion, operating in the mountain ranges northeast of Fire Support Base 31, received orders from the division to move south and meet an armored task force composed of the 17th Armored Squadron and two companies of the 8th Airborne Battalion coming as reinforcement. Remaining at the base were a 105mm artillery battery, the command section of the 3rd Airborne Artillery Battalion, and the 33rd and 34th Rifle Companies. The 34th Company had suffered heavy combat casualties and was left with only 60 men. Outside the base there was only the 3rd Reconnaissance Company, deployed on a mountain to the west. On the night of 23 February a team of Communist sappers was spotted as it attempted to infiltrate the base from the west. Fifteen Communist troops were killed on the spot. The enemy continued to launch attacks by fire and kept our helicopters from providing support. Many of our dead and wounded were left on the base for three or four days as evacuation was not possible.

At 1100 hours on 25 February Fire Support Base 31 received massive attacks by fire, including fire from 130mm field guns. At 1300 hours the 31st Company to the south reported enemy armored movements. The base responded with artillery fire and called for artillery support from Fire Support Bases 30 and A Luoi. The forward air controller's aircraft (FAC 229) was not in the air because of confusion in grid coordinates and did not arrive until 1400 hours. By that time fire from small weapons was being received from all directions and enemy tanks had reached the southern perimeter of the base. The first flight of fixed-wing tactical aircraft to reach the base destroyed a number of enemy tanks on the spot and held back the armored thrust against the southern perimeter. At 1520 hours an estimated 20 tanks, supported by infantry troops, moved in from the northwest and the east. At precisely the same time, an F-4 aircraft was hit and erupted in flames, but the pilot ejected.

The Hammer FAC aircraft left its position to direct efforts to rescue the US pilot, interrupting air support for Fire Support Base 31. After a fierce artillery barrage, the enemy assaulted. At that time a helicopter of the advisory team for the Airborne Division was the only aircraft flying overhead. It turned its M-60 machinegun fire on the enemy, but it was in vain! Artillery from A Luoi and Fire Support Base 30 continued to fire in support, but could not stop the enemy tanks attacking on the hill slopes. Forty minutes later the base was overrun. It is possible that, had the FAC remained on station above the battle, that US airpower could have been employed to hold the firebase. A number of airborne troops managed to break out, but the commanders of the 3rd Airborne Brigade and 3rd Artillery Battalion were captured by the enemy.[17] The weather thereafter worsened and aircraft could not provide support. ARVN losses at Fire Support Base 31 were 155 killed and missing, with a corresponding number of individual weapons and six 105mm howitzers. The enemy lost an estimated 250 killed and 11 PT-76 and T-54 tanks.

Between 25 February and 1 March, on its way to relieve Fire Support Base 31, the armor-infantry task force (composed of the 17th Armored Squadron, the 8th Airborne Battalion, and remaining elements of the 3rd Airborne Battalion) fought three major battles on 25 February, 27 February, and on the night of 1 March 1971. They lost 27 KIA, 186 WIA, one MIA, three M-41 tanks, and 25 armored vehicles destroyed. The enemy sustained 1,130 killed, two captured, over 300 assorted weapons seized, 17 PT-76 and six T-54 tanks and two Molotova trucks destroyed. The prisoners disclosed that the 24B Regiment and the 36th Regiment of the 308th Division, reinforced by the 202nd Tank Regiment, had taken part in recent battles. The 24B Regiment was the unit which attacked Fire Support Base 31, while the 36th Regiment was operating to the south. Cumulative enemy losses during these battles equaled one-half of the strength he initially committed.

Even before the attack on Fire Support Base 31, Fire Support Base 30 of the 2nd Airborne Battalion had been the target of repeated enemy attacks by fire involving all sizes of ammunition in the Communist inventory. Because of the accurate enemy anti-aircraft fire, helicopter takeoffs and landings were very risky. Each resupply mission was planned and prepared as if it had been a landing of combat troops. On 27 February, resupply efforts were made; smoke cover, artillery, gunships, and tactical air were used, but the enemy still shot down an aircraft, which interrupted the supply attempts. Supplies were running low, while the number of dead and wounded increased but could not be evacuated. The base fought desperately to defend itself.

Up to this point, the direction taken by enemy reactions seemed rather clear. The main forces committed consisted of the 304th, 308th, and 2nd . . . Divisions, along with elements of the 320th and 324B Divisions and armored and artillery units. The NVA strategy appeared to concentrate on massing the infantry, armor, and artillery force necessary to isolate and overwhelm—one by one—the RVNAF fire bases. The enemy took advantage of the rugged terrain to disperse his logistic, engineer, and air defense units into small elements which were well entrenched in fortified positions established throughout the area, and ARVN forces made contact wherever they moved; only by summoning concentrated firepower were they able to overpower the enemy.

The enemy appeared to have coped effectively with friendly mobile forces, heliborne insertions of troops, and artillery positions. His mortar fire, which was sustained by adequate reserves of ammunition, was now supplemented by long-range artillery. This came as a new experience for ARVN forces, who were not fully prepared to cope with massive and sustained attacks by fire, and the conventional armor-supported infantry attack that overran FSB 31 was probably the first Communist large-scale combined arms attack in the Indochina theater.

The difficulties that Fire Support Base 31 had experienced and Fire Support Base 30 was now experiencing showed that enemy reactions largely consisted of attacks by fire and air defense. Attacks by fire were designed to create tension and cause attrition. Anti-aircraft fire was aimed at disrupting communications, supply, and medical evacuation by helicopters, isolating the bases.

On the friendly side, several shortcomings were evident from the very beginning of the operation. First, high-level headquarters were located too far from the combat zone and from each other. As a result, they had difficulties coordinating with each other. The US XXIV Corps Forward, for example, was located in Quang Tri, while I Corps Forward was in Dong Ha. Coordination was thus difficult and often slow. Second, the tactical command post of I Corps at Ham Nghi Base was apparently weak. Officers on duty there were all in the junior grades; key staff officers meanwhile remained at Dong Ha. Though the I Corps commander was frequently at Ham Nghi during the day, staff operations were still hampered by the absence of senior staff personnel with enough authority and competence to provide immediate solutions to battlefield emergencies as they arose. This was a noteworthy shortcoming, and it contributed to the loss of Fire Base 31 and the inadequate coordination between RVNAF commands in the withdrawal.

Third, the US XXIV Corps had no representative in the forward area with authority to coordinate the activities of those units supporting the RVNAF forces, such as the 101st Aviation Group, the 1/5 Mechanized Brigade, and the 108th Artillery Group. All these units communicated directly with the ARVN divisions they supported. As a result, coordinating the allocation of support assets among the ARVN divisions became extremely difficult. The divisional advisory staffs meanwhile had no authority to handle the coordination of support and had to refer every action to Quang Tri. Solutions, therefore, were worked out on the basis of expediency, requirements, and goodwill.

In addition, the Airborne Division complained that there was only one forward air controller aircraft for the entire area covered by the division. Since the Airborne Division was involved in several operations simultaneously conducted in different directions, this represented a major handicap. This problem was quite evident during the battle at Fire Support Base 31.

Counterattacks by the enemy revealed the weakness of ARVN antitank weaponry. The Airborne Division reported that the M-72 light antitank weapon was ineffective against armored vehicles, which continued to move after being hit. Lieutenant General

Lam immediately notified the Central Logistical Command. As a result, over 300 3.5-inch rocket launchers with ammunition, all previously considered obsolescent and placed in storage pending return to the United States, were hastily transported to the front for distribution to combat units. XXIV Corps also gathered a number of 90mm recoilless rifles to help the ARVN airborne forces. However, the M-72 light antitank weapon was later retested at the Quang Trung Training Center and proved to be effective. As regards ARVN armor units, this was their first significant confrontation with enemy tanks. ARVN gunners proved to be confused and hasty, firing from too far away and often too soon, thereby frequently causing deflections. Enemy tanks, moreover, seldom moved in the open, but mostly lay in ambush, well concealed in the jungle.

• • •

Tchepone Was the Objective

After capturing and destroying Fire Support Base 31, Communist forces continued to encircle and harass ARVN firebases. North of Route No. 9, Fire Support Base 30 continued to bear the pressure of heavy artillery attacks each day and was cut off from the rear by an almost impenetrable air defense net. The ARVN armored task force which tried to pick up the survivors of the 3rd Airborne Battalion from Fire Support Base 31 was repeatedly engaged by NVA armor-supported infantry.

South of the road, the targets of enemy encirclement were Fire Support Base Hotel 2, seven kilometers southwest of Landing Zone Don, and the 2/3 and 3/3 Battalions of the 1st Infantry Division on mobile operations along Route 92 nearby. On 27 February, despite heavy air strikes which attempted to silence enemy air defense guns, a big H-53 helicopter was hit and exploded in the air while trying to sling-carry a 105mm howitzer. It was then decided to close Fire Support Base Hotel 2 and send the 3rd Regiment northwestward on a mission to interdict and disrupt Route 914. This plan could not be carried out immediately because there still remained a battery of 105mm howitzers whose extrication proved difficult. During the night I Corps headquarters ordered the destruction of the artillery pieces in the base; the defending unit was then to proceed on foot to join the 3rd Regiment. The 2nd and 3rd Battalions of the regiment were also ordered to move their wounded north to find a more suitable pickup point for medical evacuation helicopters. In the morning of 28 February, while on the way, these units came upon a target hit by B-52s and found the bodies of 157 enemy troops, along with numerous weapons destroyed. During that day, medical evacuation efforts were not successful because of intense enemy fire from 82mm mortars and small arms directed at the pickup zone, and one UH-1H was hit by enemy antiaircraft fire and burst into flames.

The situation by this time was becoming increasingly tense throughout the area of operations. Truck convoys were frequently attacked on Route No. 9 in Laos, and, on the RVN territory, the enemy increased efforts to ambush convoys and attack rear bases. The ARVN westward drive was stalled. In the midst of this situation, I Corps headquarters received a directive from President . . . Thieu to have the Marine Division relieve the Airborne Division. He must have realized that such a relief under the combat conditions on that battlefield would be very hazardous. Besides, the Airborne Division was still a strong unit; it had suffered some losses, but these losses were not yet too serious. What then caused him to order its replacement? The most probable answer could be that he was really worried over the additional losses that the Airborne Division would sustain in protracted combat. He certainly would like to keep this elite unit intact at all costs. In any event, the Marine Division was a poor choice for the relief. Despite the combat worthiness of its individual brigades, it had never fought as a division.

It was probably with this bothering thought that, in the afternoon of 28 February, Lieutenant General Lam flew to Saigon with an alternative to present to the president. During his meeting with President Thieu, Lam's plan was adopted. Instead of the Marine Division, the 1st Infantry Division, with three regiments under its command, was selected to proceed northwest from its present positions to occupy Tchepone. The Airborne Division would provide protection for the northern flank and secure Route No. 9. The Marine Division was to deploy two brigades behind the 1st Division; its remaining brigade would serve as the corps reserve.

Tchepone, a tiny town whose civilian population had fled long ago, now had only scars and ruins left. By this time, it had become more of a political and psychological symbol than an objective of practical military value. There was nothing of military importance in the ruined town; enemy supplies and war materiel were all stored in caches in the forests and mountains. Lines of communication were located east and west of Tchepone, not in the town proper. Despite all this, the Tchepone road junction was near the center of NVA logistics activity in the Laos panhandle, and it was understandable that it became a symbol of great importance. The RVN information agencies [and] the press (both foreign and domestic) all contributed their share in making Tchepone the place to reach at all costs, so the ARVN effort now seemed to be more directed at setting foot in Tchepone than trying to destroy the NVA logistical system, which was the real objective of the offensive.

Meeting with Ambassador Bunker and General Abrams in the afternoon of 1 March, President Thieu made known his plan to relieve the Airborne Division and expressed his desire to helilift two infantry regiments into the areas surrounding Tchepone. He also disclosed that the JGS/RVNAF had been ordered to reinforce I Corps with a number of tanks, and that the Marine Division had been sent to the northern front. General Abrams took this opportunity to defend the US position in the face of Senator Tran Van Huong's complaints that the United States was not providing adequate support to RVNAF forces operating in lower Laos. These complaints had given rise to all sorts of rumors speculating on the difficulties ARVN forces encountered in lower Laos.

President Thieu stated that the change of plan did not result from losses sustained by the Airborne Division, but came about because the 1st Infantry Division was more familiar with the lower Laos terrain and, being an organic unit of I Corps, was more accustomed to working with the corps and would respond better to the I Corps commander during this difficult operation.

• • •

More RVNAF forces were also committed to the new effort. The command section of the 369th Marine Brigade and support elements were airlifted directly to Khe Sanh, beginning on 1 March, and this movement was completed two days later. The 2nd Infantry Regiment was ready. The 4th and 7th Armored Squadrons of the 1st and 2nd Infantry Divisions were brought in to reinforce armored elements in lower Laos. I Corps headquarters also relocated the 77th Border Ranger Battalion (+) from Quang Tin and reassigned it to provide security for Fire Support Base Ham Nghi, freeing other forces for combat, and the corps's tactical control CP there was strengthened.

While these preparations were made for the push into Tchepone, there were increasing reports of enemy armor presence throughout the area of operation. In the early morning of 1 March, C-130 gunships reported sighting an estimated eight enemy tanks moving near Route No. 9, approximately eight kilometers west of A Luoi. The gunships attacked and destroyed some of the tanks. Toward noon, tactical air sighted two T-54 tanks south of the road between A Luoi and the border, attacked, and destroyed one.

Meanwhile, in the north, the 17th Armored Squadron was heavily engaged, and Fire Support Base 30 of the 2nd Airborne Battalion remained under siege. At Fire Support Base 30 fierce fighting took place on 3 March from 0100 to 0900 hours. After heavy attacks by fire, enemy infantry, supported by armor, approached friendly positions. The base was located on a high mountain with steep slopes, and enemy tanks were used only to provide direct fire support. C-130 gunships and two Arc Light strikes diverted at the last minute helped the 2nd Airborne Battalion hold its ground. When the gunfire ended, a search around the base produced 98 enemy bodies, 26 AK-47s, eight B-40s, and two machineguns right on the perimeter of defense. Friendly casualties were one killed and four wounded.

However, as a result of repeated enemy attacks by fire during the preceding days, all 12 artillery pieces (six 105mm and six 155mm) had been damaged. In the afternoon of 3 March, the 2nd Airborne Battalion was ordered to abandon its positions and move out to evacuate its wounded and conduct mobile operations. The damaged artillery pieces at the base were destroyed before the battalion left.

During the night of 3 March the 17th Armored Squadron, reinforced by the 8th Airborne Battalion, engaged a battalion-sized enemy force five kilometers north of Ban Dong. Results of the battle were 383 enemy killed, two detained, [and] 71 individual and 28 crew-served weapons seized. Friendly forces suffered over 100 killed and wounded and ten armored vehicles damaged. In the early morning of 4 March, after two resupply and medical evacuation attempts had proved unsuccessful because of heavy enemy fire, an Arc Light strike was made and, following it, a third attempt succeeded in evacuating 77 airborne wounded. Only one UH-1H helicopter was shot down, and an airborne company was brought in as reinforcement. The next day a column of armor-supported airborne troops linked up with the 17th Armored Squadron to resupply it and evacuate the remaining 43 armored wounded. Cumulative enemy losses for the period from 25 February to 3 March throughout the lower Laos area of operation were 1,536 killed. These losses amounted to about one regiment per week.

While the enemy endeavored to annihilate Fire Support Base 30 and the 17th Armored task force, the relief plan was being carried out, marking the beginning of a new offensive phase. Between Fire Support Base A Luoi (Ban Dong) and the border, the Airborne Division set up two fire support bases, Alpha and Bravo, to consolidate the security of Route No. 9. The 1st Ranger Group, with its remaining two battalions (21st and 37th), was deployed northwest of Khe Sanh and provided security for Fire Support Base Phu Loc. The 369th Brigade, kept in reserve by the corps, conducted security operations south of Khe Sanh.

• • •

On 3 March, in execution of the plan to enter Tchepone, the 1st Battalion of the 1st Infantry Regiment was inserted at Landing Zone Lolo, 13 kilometers southeast of Tchepone. The landing had met with strong enemy opposition and had been postponed twice because of additional preparations required for the landing zone. The 1/1 Battalion finally touched ground at the price of 11 helicopters shot down, 44 others hit by gunfire, and two D-4 bulldozers destroyed after being dropped from the air. The following day the 1st Regiment headquarters, the 2/1 Battalion, and a battery of 105mm howitzers were brought into Landing Zone Lolo. Fire Support Base Lolo was thus established. The 4/1 Battalion meanwhile landed at Landing Zone Liz, six kilometers west-northwest of Lolo.[18] The various units then moved out to search the area, but only a few light contacts were made, with minor results.

In the morning of 5 March, in order to continue its westward push, the 2nd Infantry Regiment of the 1st Division was scheduled to occupy Landing Zone Sophia, four and a half kilometers southwest of Tchepone, at 1100 hours, but unexpected bad weather delayed the operation. After preemptive airstrikes, at exactly 1320 hours five UH-1Hs landed safely. Sporadic gunfire was received, but posed no major threat. By nightfall Landing Zone Sophia had eight 105mm howitzers in position with adequate ammunition. Searching farther out, the 4th and 5th Battalions found the bodies of 124 enemy troops and seized 43 AK-47s, nine 12.7mm machineguns, four RPD automatic rifles, nine B-40 rocket launchers, three radios, military clothing, equipment, and food supplies. After securing Fire Support Base Sophia, the 2nd Regiment was now in a position to control Tchepone from its mountain base and keep the areas surrounding the town within range of its artillery.

For the next two days, throughout the area of operation of the 1st Infantry and the Marine Divisions, friendly units caught the spirit of the new offensive. They fought aggressively, repeatedly engaged the enemy, and defeated him everywhere. In the morning of 5 March, in the area of Objective Alpha, the 4th Marine Battalion killed 130 enemy troops and seized 25 assorted weapons, including two 82mm mortars. Friendly forces sustained six killed and 42 wounded. The 4/1 Battalion made contact near Landing Zone Liz, killing 41 Communist troops and seizing 15 weapons, along with two mortars. By 6 March engagements were increasing and occurring everywhere, but friendly forces suffered only light casualties while inflicting heavy losses on the enemy. More importantly, they were now within easy reach of Tchepone, the final objective that President Thieu had ordered them to take just three days earlier.

• • •

The day selected to enter the ultimate objective, Tchepone, was 6 March. A total of 120 US helicopters were assembled to carry out the assault. In addition to B-52s, US tactical air strikes or air cover sorties were scheduled every ten minutes. Elements of the 2/17 US Air Cavalry reconnoitered targets, prepared landing zones, and covered the assault. An enemy attack by fire on Khe Sanh Base forced the huge assemblage of US helicopters to depart 90 minutes earlier than planned, but preparations for this operation had been so carefully executed that, when the first helicopters carrying the 2/2 Battalion landed at Landing Zone Hope, four kilometers northeast of Tchepone, only sporadic gunfire was received. By 1343 hours both the 2nd and 3rd Battalions, along with an element of the 2nd Reconnaissance Company and the tactical command post of the 2nd Infantry Regiment, had landed safely at Hope. Searching the adjoining areas and occupying key positions, the 2nd Regiment only made light contacts but found the bodies of 102 enemy troops killed by B-52s and seized five 12.7mm machineguns and one antiaircraft artillery gun. Extending its search further south toward Tchepone, the 3/2 Battalion found a cache of an estimated 1,000 tons of rice and 2,000 gas masks, along with 31 enemy bodies and numerous weapons destroyed by B-52s. Nearby, the 2/2 Battalion found an area devastated by B-52s, with nearly 100 enemy bodies and assorted weapons shattered to pieces. After the two reinforced ARVN battalions had made assault landings near the objective and rapidly exploited their success, the district town of Tchepone was practically under ARVN control, dominated as it was by the array of artillery pieces to the south. The most remote terrain objective of Lam Son 719 was attained.

V. THE WITHDRAWAL PHASE

The Disengagement

In the early morning of 7 March, the first enemy reactions to the 1st Division's presence at Tchepone occurred in the form of artillery and mortar fire against Fire Support Base Lolo. The first attack, which was brief and light, caused only five casualties, but the second attack was heavier as indirect fire poured in from all calibers of guns, from 82mm mortars to 152mm artillery. More than 20 soldiers were hit—three were killed—and all of the bulldozers used in the construction of fortifications were damaged. While the troops on Lolo were digging in under this heavy bombardment, Fire Support Base A Luoi was also subjected to a heavy attack by fire. NVA artillery fell on the positions intermittently throughout the day, disrupting the scheduled heliborne supply and evacuation runs.

On the same day the Black Panther (Reconnaissance) Company of the 1st Infantry Division, which had been attached to the US 101st Airborne Division from the beginning of the campaign, landed troops about five kilometers west-southwest of Ban Dong to rescue the crew of a US aircraft which had gone down two days before. The Black Panthers scored a major combat exploit by rescuing all the Americans and subsequently made contact with the enemy, sustaining light casualties but killing more than 60 Communist troops. During this violent action, they also seized 30 NVA automatic rifles, destroyed an antiaircraft gun position, and found another 40 NVA soldiers killed by airstrikes.

The 2nd Battalion, 2nd Infantry, on a mission to assess B-52 bomb damage in an area east of Tchepone, found a smashed weapons supply point that contained 150 rocket launchers (122mm), 43 grenade launchers, 17 heavy machineguns, eight 82mm mortars, and 57 AK-47 rifles, all damaged beyond use. Nearby, the battalion found two Communist tanks destroyed by airstrikes and an ammunition storage area which it marked for future disposal (B-52 strikes conducted later on this target resulted in approximately 2,000 secondary explosions). While the 2nd Battalion, 2nd Infantry, reconnoitered east of Tchepone, the 4th Battalion, 1st Infantry, conducted a similar mission in the heights southeast of Tchepone and found the bodies of 112 enemy troops and seized 32 medium mortars, five 12.7mm machineguns, six grenade launchers, and 18 AK-47 rifles.

Meanwhile the 2nd Regiment launched the first foray into Tchepone, to find only a shambles of the former district seat and no human beings in sight. On their way out, the reconnaissance troops killed a squad of NVA soldiers and found a cache containing eight 82mm mortars, two tons of rice, and other military equipment.

During the morning of 8 March, while marine and airborne units made sporadic contacts with the enemy in all other areas with varying degrees of success, Fire Support Base Lolo continued to receive attacks by fire which caused all planned resupply and evacuation flights into the base to be cancelled.

The 2nd Battalion, 2nd Infantry, continued to search the areas around Tchepone and found 52 dead enemy soldiers, along with three heavy machineguns, 44 rifles, and about 50 heavy artillery rounds destroyed by airstrikes.

Late afternoon found the units of the 2nd Regiment assembled near the banks of the Tchepone River. That night, two battalions of the 2nd Regiment moved past Tchepone on the east and crossed the river to the southern side. On 9 March at 0900 hours, the regiment began to climb the ridge to FSB Sophia. The invasion of Tchepone had been completed.

Meanwhile, Lieutenant General Lam . . . arrived at the Presidential Palace in Saigon to report to President Thieu on the situation. General Vien . . . was present at that meeting and heard General Lam present the rationale for the withdrawal and the outline of how it would be executed. Why did General Lam and General Vien recommend to President Thieu that the apparently successful operation into Laos be terminated so far ahead of schedule? The 2nd Infantry had not nearly completed its mission in the hills east of Tchepone, where great quantities of NVA military supplies were stored, and only a brief reconnaissance had been conducted into the town itself. No ARVN reconnaissance in force had reached the Xe Bang Hiang River, the principal waterway that flows from north to south west of the town, although the ARVN commander in this zone had requested that CBU-42 (time-delay bomblets) be sown on the west bank to make it difficult for the NVA to concentrate there. Coincidentally, of course, this barrier also inhibited any ARVN crossing of the river in this area, although it was the western side of the

Tchepone complex that was suspected of containing numerous supply depots and huge quantities of war materiel. The river would have to be crossed to complete the task.

Why was the river not crossed? The answer is that a careful military estimate was made, based upon all the pertinent information available at the time, and the conclusion was inescapable: it was time to get out. First was the problem of terrain. In a tactical sense, ARVN forces were facing an uphill task, progressing as they did from the low-lands, with which they were familiar, to the highlands where the well-entrenched enemy enjoyed the advantage. The only road available for troop and supply movements ran through steep mountains and dense forests. The enemy had operated in this region for many years, was familiar with it, and knew all the trails. He could cut the road or lay ambushes almost anywhere. To the west, past Ban Dong, this road ran through a range of high mountains. All along the slopes the NVA had positioned a dense array of antiair-craft guns, big and small. These guns not only fired at aircraft, but also at ARVN troop columns and truck convoys moving to and from Tchepone.

• • •

In short, the enemy was thoroughly familiar with the terrain in lower Laos and ARVN troops were not. The terrain and weather favored the defenders and handicapped the at-tackers. The area was especially disadvantageous for our mechanized and armored forces, which were restricted to narrow jungle roads on which two vehicles could not pass and on which entire columns could often be jammed or stalled by one disabled vehicle.

The NVA strength and reinforcement capability was the second factor that influ-enced the decision to initiate the withdrawal. Estimated enemy forces in the immediate area of operations consisted of three infantry regiments, rear service elements capable of local defense, and artillery elements especially notable for their air defense capabil-ity. It was estimated that the NVA could reinforce, within two weeks, with up to eight infantry regiments and the equivalent of an artillery regiment.

Heavy artillery and armor also strengthened the enemy's capabilities. First among these was the enemy's dispersed and well-concealed 130mm and 152mm heavy artillery. ARVN's stationary fire support bases on hilltops, therefore, were easy targets for enemy artillery fire. The second factor in the enemy's capability of deep concern to the leader-ship in Saigon was the enemy armor strength that had become apparent. The planners of Lam Son 719 had failed to give sufficient consideration to the threat of NVA armor, and now this threat had become a reality. Even though enemy armor was under daily attack from the air, Fire Support Base 31 had been lost because of the enemy's effective coordi-nation of armor and infantry forces. In other places the enemy used his tanks as highly mobile field guns, moving them individually over trails to ambush ARVN armored vehi-cles on the roads. The maneuvering of tanks on such a large scale over forest trails known only to the enemy posed a great threat to ARVN armored vehicles, which were confined to congested one-way roads strewn with disabled vehicles. Moreover, NVA tanks had thicker armor and mounted guns of a larger caliber than the ARVN tanks, 100mm versus 76mm, and had a significantly greater armor-defeating capability.

Thirdly, even after a month of intensive attack, the enemy's air defense capabilities showed no signs of being subdued, and he had positioned surface-to-air missiles west of the border or at the Ban Raving Pass. These missiles had Route No. 9 from Khe Sanh to Ban Dong within effective range, a challenge that the US Air Force had to face. Around the ARVN's besieged bases, even after waves of airstrikes, enemy antiaircraft guns would reappear close to their original positions. Also antiaircraft batteries were deployed along helicopter avenues of approach; those positioned on the mountain slopes between Ban Dong and Tchepone seemed impossible to uproot. This enemy capability practically neutralized the ARVN advantage of helicopter mobility and logistic support.

In contrast to the enemy, who had large uncommitted reserves in North Vietnam, our reserves were limited indeed. The Airborne and Marine Divisions constituted the entire general reserve of the RVN, and they were already committed. Committing the 1st Infantry Division and the 1st Ranger Group required an extreme effort made possible only with the help of the US 101st Airborne Division, which replaced these two units in the lowlands of Thua Thien Province. And now, in the light of the enemy's reinforcement and strength on the battlefield, it was becoming apparent that the ARVN force committed to Lam Son 719 was too small for the task. General Abrams recommended that the ARVN 2nd Infantry Division be sent in to reinforce, and the division was preparing plans to turn over its area of responsibility in MR-1 to the US 23rd Infantry Division.[19]

Still, in the view of the RVN leadership, one additional division would be insufficient to ensure total victory and would result in a higher casualty figure for our forces in Laos. Also, removing the 2nd Division from MR-1 would leave more of the vital lowland areas of MR-1 undefended. The only reasonable course of action was an orderly withdrawal to conserve as much of the committed force as possible. Further reinforcing this conclusion was the fact that the political and psychological objective of the campaign had been achieved; the RVNAF had entered Tchepone. It was apparent that President Thieu had decided, at the outset, that once Tchepone had been entered by the RVNAF the withdrawal should begin without delay. The main features of the withdrawal plan were outlined to President Thieu at the 9 March meeting.

• • •

The entire withdrawal, according to Lieutenant General Lam's estimate, was scheduled for completion by 31 March.

• • •

The Valiant ARVN 1st Infantry Division

While the withdrawal plan was being explained to the president, the 1st Infantry Regiment began to move toward objective area Ta Luong. Advance elements reported sighting enemy tanks near the area. Further north, near Route No. 9, at ten kilometers southeast of Tchepone, observation teams of the 1st Regiment also reported sighting a Communist armored group. ARVN artillery opened fire and disabled five enemy tanks. Meanwhile, the marine sector was very active. The battalions received heavy attacks by fire and, searching out ten kilometers south-southeast from their bases, found an NVA camp that had been bombed by B-52s with 5,000 heavy artillery rockets, along with numerous other weapons and substantial volumes of ammunition, all destroyed. In the morning of 10 March, the 1st Marine Battalion engaged the enemy twice, the first time in a light encounter and the second time fighting a battalion-sized unit with the following results: 72 enemy killed and 20 small arms, one recoilless rifle, and four grenade launchers seized. The marine losses were only six killed and 19 wounded.

The 1st Infantry Division continued to search the areas of Ta Luong and Route 914 and was able to assess the substantial damages inflicted by B-52 bombing runs. In two areas approximately ten kilometers south and southeast of FSB Sophia, the 4th Battalion found the bodies of 72 Communist troops, 12 Soviet trucks, eight tracked vehicles, three 122mm towed cannon, two 37mm antiaircraft artillery guns, four 12.7mm machineguns, two 122mm rocket launchers, 400 AK-47 rifles, 32 82mm mortars, 18 B-40s, 60 Chicom radios, and huge quantities of food of all types. Most of these supplies were blown to bits by B-52 bombs. The battalion also captured five prisoners of war.

• • •

US air support was becoming more effective since Vietnamese interpreters flying with forward air controllers had become more familiar with the situation. Resupply operations were conducted throughout the battle area, thanks to the daring and the noble spirit of sacrifice of US Army helicopter crews.

Upon the 2nd Infantry Regiment's withdrawal from the area west of Lolo, NVA forces, probably elements of the 1st and 31st Regiments of the NT-2 Division, began to encircle units of the 3rd Infantry Regiment. Beginning on 13 March, the battalions operating in the Ta Luong area (Objectives Gia Lam and Bach Mai) were gradually forced to withdraw north, and Fire Support Base Lolo began to receive uninterrupted attacks by fire. On 14 March the intensity of these attacks increased. During the day the base received an estimated 200 122mm rockets and 100 152mm artillery rounds. Thanks to their solid shelters and trenches, the regiment had only three killed and two wounded, but one D-4 bulldozer and two 105mm howitzers were seriously damaged.

In the meantime, the enemy had moved up to the base and small arms fire was being directed at supply aircraft, causing medical evacuation and resupply attempts to be called off. On 15 March the base could not be resupplied (nor could Alpha or A Luoi, both of which were under attacks by fire). The various units on and around the base were running out of ammunition, and the number of wounded in need of evacuation was increasing. A withdrawal plan was hastily prepared. The headquarters of the 1st Regiment and the battalions outside the base would move east. The 4th Battalion would serve as the rear guard, protecting the regiment in its effort to break through enemy encirclement. The plan was carried out satisfactorily, but the enemy tightened its hold on the 4th Battalion. Finally this unit fought its way out, with the enemy in pursuit, all the while rejecting the NVA demands for it to surrender.

On 17 March, close to the banks of the Tchepone River, the battalion was intercepted and the fighting lasted all day, with tactical air and gunships providing dedicated support. The battalion commander and his deputy were both killed. Most of the company commanders and officers of the battalion were also killed, and the few survivors managed to escape to an area near Route No. 9. There, in the late afternoon of 18 March, US helicopters with tactical air support conducted a daring rescue. Three helicopters were hit and one fighter-bomber exploded in the air, but the 32 survivors of the 4th Battalion were rescued and flown to the rear.[20] The battalion had accomplished well its rearguard mission and, in the process, had sacrificed nearly every man. The fight put up by Fire Support Base Lolo and the units of the 1st Infantry Regiment had resulted in 1,100 enemy killed, causing severe losses to two main-force regiments of the Communist NT-2 Division.

• • •

In the meantime, in the area of the 2nd Regiment, the 5th Battalion received an intense early morning attack of an estimated 300 rounds of mortar and artillery fire. The battalion continued its search operations and, thanks to intensive air support, scored a major victory in the area near Landing Zone Brown, killing nearly 100 enemy and capturing a large number of weapons and a ton of ammunition. In accordance with the withdrawal plan, the headquarters of the 2nd Infantry Regiment was evacuated to Delta 1, while its battalion proceeded east on foot.

From 18 March on it seemed that the enemy was well aware of the ARVN withdrawal, and there were signs of the enemy concentrating a regimental-sized unit northwest of Fire Support Base A Luoi, while pressure increased around Fire Support Base Delta of the 147th Brigade.

• • •

For four days now, reports [had] flowed into I Corps headquarters of strong attacks that included very heavy bombardments by heavy artillery and tank attacks. Reports of ARVN losses, including the decimation of the 4th Battalion, 1st Infantry, were very disturbing to General Lam, as were the many indications that the enemy was reinforcing and maneuvering to prevent the orderly ARVN withdrawal from Laos. So, on the night of 18 March, General Lam called his division commanders to a conference at Ham Nghi Base (Khe Sanh) to hear their assessments and recommendations. They each recommended that disengagement proceed as quickly as possible; General Phu, commanding the 1st Division, displayed anxiety for the first time in the campaign.

When the conference was over, General Lam ordered that the withdrawal proceed at a quicker pace and that preparations begin immediately for the extraction of the 2nd Regiment from the Brown area and Fire Base Delta 1, where all its battalions were under heavy attack and in danger of being cut off and destroyed.

On the morning of 19 March, abandoning Fire Support Base A Luoi (Ban Dong), ARVN armored elements and attached airborne units moved overland to take positions along a line near Fire Support Base Alpha.

• • •

The armored logistic convoy set out, towing damaged vehicles and guns, under the protection of airborne units and other armored elements, while the enemy continued to exert pressure on the rear of the column. At 0730 hours, approximately two kilometers north of Ban Dong, forward air controller aircraft reported sighting four enemy tanks moving down. Approximately four kilometers east of Ban Dong Base the logistic convoy was ambushed and all 18 vehicles immobilized. Some of the lead vehicles were hit by direct fire and destroyed. The road had only one lane; the vehicles behind were stalled in the ambush zone. While the battle was in progress no reports were received from the convoy commander; his superiors were therefore unaware of what was happening to the convoy.

Losses incurred during the ambush were neither reported nor even analyzed afterwards. According to reports from an observation plane, four M-41 tanks and three M-113 APCs, each towing a 105mm howitzer, were apparently damaged among the 18 stranded vehicles. Road security for the movement of this convoy was the responsibility of armor and airborne units, but during the attack the convoy never initiated any request for air support or gunships. Apparently the ambush caught the convoy by surprise and it ended as quickly as it began. Later the commander of the 1st Armor Brigade requested tactical air to destroy the ambushed vehicles, and his request was immediately granted in order to prevent the enemy from capturing usable equipment.

• • •

Late in the afternoon of 19 March Ambassador Bunker and General Abrams were received by President Thieu. President Thieu disclosed he had directed a cautious withdrawal which would be completed from 5–8 April. When the withdrawal was complete, he planned to have about three battalions launch a raid against Muong Nong, the center of Communist Base Area 611, and wanted strong US air support for this raid.

On 20 March the US Air Force and Army helicopters exerted their maximum effort, with 1,388 gunship sorties, 270 tactical air strikes, and 11 B-52 missions dropping 909 tons of bombs. Around 1300 hours the 3rd Battalion, 2nd Regiment, was extracted from the area west of Sophia East by US Army helicopters, which flew through heavy antiaircraft fire to evacuate it from Ham Nghi Base. In the process, 28 of the 40 helicopters involved were hit. Plans for the extraction of the 4/2 Battalion were subsequently aborted because the first helicopter attempting to land was hit by fire and exploded in the air. Before nightfall the artillery pieces at Fire Support Base Alpha, along with the 2nd and 7th Airborne Battalions, were transported back to Vietnam. Plans provided for the 2nd and 4th Battalions, 2nd Regiment, to be picked up the next day, followed by the regimental headquarters, its artillery, and the 1st Battalion, 3rd Infantry, from Fire Support Base Delta 1. The two 2nd Regiment battalions were ordered to find a more secure pickup zone.

In the meantime, the 1st Armor Brigade, reinforced by the 7th and 8th Airborne Battalions, had arrived at Phase Line Alpha the preceding evening. The armored and airborne elements deployed to provide security for Route No. 9 from Alpha to Base Bravo. At 2100 hours the NVA attacked the 8th Airborne Battalion and 11th Armored Cavalry Squadron south of Alpha, but were repulsed with heavy losses.

• • •

On 21 March at 0300 hours, enemy action became intense in the area to the west, where the 2nd and 4th Battalions of the 2nd Regiment were stranded two kilometers east of Sophia East. The regiments of the NVA 2nd Division were determined to attack and annihilate these two battalions, but they were not successful. In the process the enemy lost 245 killed, 52 B-40s and B-41s, seven machineguns, seven 60mm mortars, five 82mm mortars, eight flamethrowers, nine 12.7mm machineguns, and 65 AK-47s. Friendly losses were 37 killed, 58 wounded, and 15 missing. This ARVN victory caused enemy pressure to relax, and the remaining forces of the 1st Infantry Division were transported by US helicopters to Ham Nghi Base before nightfall.

• • •

The situation in the areas manned by the 1st Infantry and the Airborne Divisions had been resolved, but, over in the marines' area, there was an eruption of fire. The 29th and 803rd Regiments of the 324B Division were determined to destroy Fire Support Base Delta. These two enemy units began attacking fiercely at dawn of 21 March. Mortar and direct artillery fire (the latter believed to come from tank guns) were very accurate. All 175mm guns from the RVN side of the border were mobilized to provide close fire support to the marines. In the morning, 13 tactical air sorties provided additional support. A B-52 mission was diverted to the area and crushed an enemy battalion (a PW later reported this battalion had lost 400 men from this B-52 action). The attack was checked and the base held firm. A casualty count showed that the marines had 85 killed, 238 wounded, and 100 weapons damaged, while enemy forces suffered 600 killed, five detained, and an estimated 200 individual and 60 crew-served weapons seized. After the battle, the 147th Brigade and the 7th Marine Battalion ran short of supplies. Thanks to air support, seven US UH-1H helicopters were able to land, bringing ammunition and evacuating wounded. These helicopters were able to return to their base, but all bore battle scars. An eighth helicopter was shot down.

During this period the enemy greatly increased his interference and jamming of our radio communications. Several frequencies were so badly jammed that communications became impossible. In many instances, enemy radio operators argued and exchanged insults with ours. These heated verbal exchanges occurred most frequently when the enemy intensified his attacks against the marines. To return the courtesy, our operators also intercepted and jammed enemy radio frequencies. During one of these interceptions, marine operators overheard a female voice giving combat orders. In general, South Vietnamese units did not make enough effort to safeguard radio communications security, often using the most rudimentary of self-devised code systems. This episode of reciprocal interference and jamming was perhaps more damaging to our side than to the enemy, who was usually more disciplined. The extent of this damage, if any, could never be ascertained because of the intense fighting.

• • •

During the night of 21 March the 1st Armor Brigade and the 1st and 8th Airborne Battalions left their positions along Route No. 9 and moved east through the jungle in search of a point to cross the Xepon River. Successful in avoiding enemy contact, the convoy of nearly 100 vehicles meandered through the dense jungle until about noon the next day, when it came out near the banks of the river about one kilometer south of Route No. 9.

The brigade was provided with a helicopter to help it find a crossing point, and the commander of the Airborne Division had helicopters prepared to airlift light bulldozers, as well as tree-cutting equipment, to help set up a crossing point for the armored vehicles.

During the dry season the Xepon River is usually shallow, but the current is swift and the banks are steep, in many places ten meters straight down. A crossing point for vehicles was therefore not easy to find. Meanwhile, the 9th Airborne Battalion had crossed the river and secured the eastern bank. In late afternoon two D-2 bulldozers and other pieces of equipment were lifted in by US Army CH-54 helicopters and the river-crossing site was prepared.

• • •

Why did the armored convoy leave Route No. 9 and make a cut through the jungle to find a way to cross the river when there was only a final stretch of five kilometers left to cover until the Lao-Viet border? The reason was never officially explained, but Colonel Nguyen Trong Luat, commander of the 1st Armor Brigade, later told this writer that, had his unit not taken to the jungle to seek a way out, he did not believe a single vehicle could have made it back to Vietnam. Route No. 9 was a one-way road, not only littered with abandoned vehicles and rigged with mines all along, but every section of it could conceal a Communist ambush site. It was so treacherous that no one dared venture on it. The withdrawal along Route No. 9 surely did not proceed as planned, in an orderly and controlled manner.

Early the next morning, 23 March, while Khe Sanh Base was still finishing off Communist sappers who had infiltrated earlier, the ARVN armored column crossed the Xepon River and the lines of the US 1st Mechanized Infantry Brigade, 5th Division. The convoy returned with 98 vehicles left behind, among them 22 M-41 tanks and 54 armored personnel carriers. Aerial and photo reconnaissance showed that the ARVN units had left 21 tanks, 26 armored personnel carriers, 13 bulldozers, two graders, and 51 vehicles at a night bivouac area on Route No. 9.

• • •

In lower Laos, meanwhile, fighting was still fierce around Fire Support Base Delta. The airdropping of supplies on the base was not successful, and ammunition stocks had dropped to an alarming level. Enemy troops had penetrated and established a firm foothold inside the marines' perimeter. Late in the afternoon the enemy launched a new attack, this time supported by ten flame-throwing tanks. The marines blew up the first two tanks with light antitank weapons. The third tank detonated mines, and the fourth was hit by tactical air. But the remaining tanks continued to advance. The headquarters of the 147th Brigade had to move out of its position. The 2nd and 4th Battalions supported the 7th Battalion to break the enemy's encirclement and withdraw toward the 258th Brigade (Fire Support Base Hotel). The enemy seemed to have anticipated this move, and he intercepted the troops of the 147th Brigade in an ambush. A pitched battle ensued with enemy tanks and infantry. The following morning, 23 March, all battalion commanders of the 147th Brigade, though wounded, managed to maneuver their battalions to link up with the 258th Brigade.

• • •

There were initially 134 missing reported, but they gradually came back, leaving the entire brigade with only 37 missing. The battle at FSB Delta had cost the enemy an estimated 2,000 troops, seriously hurting his 29th and 803rd Regiments.

• • •

Black Panther Raids

As I have previously mentioned, about a week earlier, on the afternoon of 19 March, President Thieu informed Ambassador Bunker and General Abrams that he had ordered a cautious pullback of RVNAF forces to South Vietnam. He conceived the possibility of the withdrawal lasting until 5–8 April 1971, to be followed by a surprise raid conducted by a regimental-sized force and directed at Muong Nong, the heart of Communist Base Army 611. Operation Lam Son 719 had the objective of disrupting Communist base areas, one [of which] was Base Area 604, whose heart was Tchepone; the other, Area 611, centered on Muong Nong. All ARVN operations had been confined to Base Area 604. As far as Base Area 611 was concerned, the incursion went only as far as its northern boundary. The idea of further attacks into Muong Nong was, therefore, simply a follow-up action to finish the incomplete operation. But, by 25 March 1971, most ARVN forces had already left lower Laos.

• • •

Although it no longer had any battalions in Laos, I Corps, whose forward command post was still located at Dong Ha, had an outstanding mission: the raid into Muong Nong. At this point the world press, as well as public opinion in South Vietnam and the United States, tended to view Operation Lam Son 719 as an incomplete campaign, being too hastily terminated. Photographs of the battered ARVN forces in retreat, taken by war correspondents, coupled with moving news reports, created unfavorable feelings toward the RVN. The operation had received too much publicity, and its objective had been misinterpreted as being decisive by some reporters. To terminate the operation at this time, well before the lower Laos rainy season, would surely be branded a defeat by public opinion. Moreover, the RVN military spokesman, in his vague style of public announcement, reiterated during a press conference after 25 March that the lower Laos operation was not really over and RVN forces were still attacking Communist logistical routes. To get itself off the hook, the GVN surely had to continue Operation Lam Son 719. The attacks against the Ho Chi Minh Trail complex would continue, but less for military gains than for face-saving purposes, particularly in light of the fact that Communist troops had just launched a series of attacks in Quang Nam, Quang Tin, and even in MR-2.

• • •

In the early morning of 31 March, in the projected area of operation, a wave of B-52 strikes was followed by 22 tactical air sorties, all designed to prepare a landing zone south of the Laotian salient approximately 40 kilometers southeast of Lang Vei. However, at 1030 hours reconnaissance aircraft reported continued heavy enemy antiaircraft fire. Preparations of the landing zone by airstrikes were resumed, and, at 1130 hours, a Black Panther unit of the 1st Infantry Division, about 200 men and supported by the 2/17 Air Cavalry Squadron of the US 101st Airborne Division, landed without problems. In the meantime, a forward air controller aircraft and a communication relay aircraft circled over the area. The Black Panther unit searched the area and found the bodies of 85 enemy troops killed and 18 weapons destroyed by B-52 action. Continuing their search, the troops only made light contacts with the enemy.

• • •

The next afternoon the Black Panthers were picked up by US Army helicopters and transported to Hue, while President . . . Thieu was visiting the operational headquarters of I Corps at Dong Ha and the units which had fought in lower Laos. To foreign and local press reporters gathered there, he expressed his belief that the lower Laos operation had been the greatest victory of all and announced a new phase of attacks against the Ho Chi Minh Trail.

• • •

On 6 April another raid of the Black Panther forces . . . was initiated against another area of the Lao-Viet border salient, approximately 22 kilometers southeast of Lang Vei. At 1000 hours, after preparatory airstrikes, the reinforced . . . company landed unopposed. The search it conducted lasted until late afternoon without making contact with the enemy. At one location the Black Panthers found 15 enemy bodies and 17 weapons, along with large quantities of food and an intricate network of tunnels, trenches, and huts, all destroyed. In the course of the operation US tactical air destroyed three antiaircraft gun positions. The Black Panthers were extracted at 1700 hours the same day.

A few hours before the Black Panther unit ended its second raid into enemy bases on the other side of the border, the last ARVN and US units were on their way out of Khe Sanh. The 5th and 54th Infantry Regiments moved to Cam Lo, where they boarded trucks to return to their respective parent units. The US 1st Battalion, 11th Infantry task force, was the last unit to board helicopters leaving Khe Sanh, thereby ending Operation Lam Son 719.

VI. A CRITICAL ANALYSIS

The Balance Sheet of Lam Son 719

The picture of ARVN soldiers hanging on the skids of a helicopter which evacuated them from lower Laos, and other equally dramatic photographs showing battered I Corps troops returning back across the Laotian border, caused grave concern among South Vietnamese, military and civilian alike. Their concern deepened when they read the tantalizing news articles first carried by American newspapers and magazines, then picked up by the foreign and Vietnamese press, which all reported that the ARVN incursion into lower Laos was being terminated. The GVN military spokesman had a hard time denying these reports. He announced that this was simply an exchange of operational forces, and, for all practical purposes, Lam Son 719 was still under way and that ARVN forces were continuing their destructive forays against Communist logistical bases and infiltration routes on the other side of the border. President . . . Thieu echoed this line during his press conference at Dong Ha on 1 April 1971, but news about raids in lower Laos no longer interested Vietnamese public opinion, which was more concerned about the real outcome of the well-publicized campaign. In the absence of official announcements, rumors and speculations proliferated. Everyone wanted to know the truth about friendly losses. But when official results were later made public, no one seemed to believe that they reflected the truth.

Despite the high figure of ARVN casualties, which the GVN confirmed at nearly 6,000, there was still suspicion that the true figure was being concealed from public view. *Newsweek* magazine correspondents estimated this figure unofficially at nearly 10,000. But their figure was definitely inflated, because the highest level of ARVN strength committed during the entire operation reached only 17,000. It is obvious that, if the casualties had been 10,000 as reported by these correspondents, certainly not very many ARVN units would have been able to make their way back to the border, which was not true. Reports on enemy losses, similarly, were regarded as being inflated. Also the general public believed that more US helicopters had been destroyed than official announcements indicated.

RVNAF and US casualties—including killed, wounded, and missing, as reported through military channels—for all of Lam Son 719 totaled 9,065. Most of the 7,683 RVNAF casualties were incurred by the tactical units that participated in the operations in Laos; the 1st Infantry Division and the Airborne Division absorbed over one-half of this total.

I Corps casualties thus represented about 45 percent of the maximum 17,000 troops that were committed during the most active phase of the operation. For Lam Son 719, I Corps had deployed a total of 42 battalion-sized combat units, of which 34 actually fought in lower Laos. Four ARVN battalions suffered losses so severe that they had to be reconstituted; six others, while suffering losses considered "moderate," still managed to fight as units. As to US casualties, they were incurred partly in combat activities conducted in South Vietnam, partly in helilift and air support activities in Laos. . . .

On the ARVN side, the most noteworthy [equipment and materiel] losses were the 87 combat vehicles (to include M-113 armored personnel carriers and similar vehicles), 54 light tanks (M-41), 96 artillery pieces (of both 105mm and 155mm), 31 bulldozers, and over 1,500 radio sets. Most tanks and armored vehicles were damaged and destroyed during combat, but losses also included those left behind which were not able to maneuver around ambush sites. Among the 96 artillery pieces lost, the majority had been damaged by enemy counterbattery fire before being left behind in evacuated fire support bases; the remaining were destroyed by ARVN artillery troops prior to their withdrawal. No engineer machinery was brought back. In fact, the 101st Combat Engineer Battalion and a platoon of the 118th Engineer Land Clearing Company lost all of their heavy equipment.

As to the enemy, his human losses were considerably higher than those suffered by the RVNAF [19,360 killed and 57 captured].

To counteract the ARVN incursion into his most vital logistic base area, the enemy deployed, and the figures were later confirmed, 12 infantry regiments belonging to five different divisions and at least an armor regiment and an artillery regiment. Total enemy combat strength thus committed in the Lam Son 719 area of operation was estimated at 30,000, not to include reserve elements. In addition, the enemy logistic structure in the general area of operations also had from [10,000] to 20,000 men. Out of this total, the enemy lost an estimated 20,000 men, or about one-half. But, while his losses caused by actual combat engagements could be generally verified, his casualties inflicted by artillery and aerial bombings could only be estimated.

• • •

Enemy equipment losses throughout the campaign were also substantial. . . . [Individual weapons: 5,170. Crew-served weapons: 1,963. Vehicles: 2,001 (reported by USAF). Tanks: 106 (US verified 88). Ammunition: 170,346 tons (US verified 20,000 tons). Rice: 1,250 tons.]

Most enemy vehicles were destroyed by US gunships and tactical air. So were enemy tanks of all types. . . . In addition, the enemy fuel pipeline originating in North Vietnam and running through the Lam Son 719 area of operations was cut in several places.

United States Combat Support

No account of Lam Son 719 would be complete without mentioning the importance of US support. In closing the balance sheet on friendly and enemy losses, credit should be duly given to the role performed by US Army aviation, US Air Force, and US Naval air, for without them Lam Son 719 could hardly have been possible.

Topping the scale, and from the point of view of the ARVN infantryman, US Army aviation units contributed by far the most important kind of support. In total, US Army gunships and other types of helicopters flew over 90,000 sorties for the benefit of ARVN forces, to include nearly 24,000 gunship sorties, over 34,000 trooplift sorties, and nearly 20,000 logistic-related sorties.

To carry out their vital support mission, US Army aviation units suffered losses in Laos amounting to 82 aircraft of all types destroyed and over 600 aircraft damaged but recoverable. US Army pilots and crew members who sacrificed their lives in combat numbered 55, while 178 others were wounded and 34 were listed as missing in action.

The performance of the US Air Force . . . was no less impressive. A total of 9,000 tactical air sorties were flown, to include 7,000 over lower Laos. The highest daily number of sorties reached 277 on 8 March 1971.

• • •

US Naval aircraft also contributed significantly to the support of Lam Son 719 with nearly 1,900 sorties launched from US carriers *Hancock, Kitty Hawk,* and *Ranger.*

A particularly important role in air support was performed by the B-52s in the annihilation of enemy installations, rear bases, and troop concentrations. In Operation Lam

Son 719, B-52 sorties were also used to clear landing zones and to provide close support for ARVN forces in many emergency situations. Several ARVN units learned how to use B-52 strikes in their plans for combat maneuvering with skill. Total B-52 strikes in support of Lam Son 719 amounted to 622, to include 421 for the benefit of ARVN forces and 201 in support of US forces.

• • •

In summary, during their 45-day incursion into lower Laos ARVN forces of I Corps inflicted on the enemy heavy casualties amounting to at least 50 percent of the combat forces he had committed to the area of operation. A sizable dent had thus been made [in] the participating elements of five NVA divisions—the 2nd, 304th, 308th, 320th, and 324B—and the logistical units in Base Areas 604 and 611.

In exchange for these results, I Corps suffered casualties equivalent to 45 percent of the combat strength it had committed in the operation, not to mention substantial losses in equipment. Although not a protracted campaign, Lam Son 719 brought about profound repercussions among the South Vietnamese people. Despite official claims of a "big victory" and mass demonstrations to celebrate the "lower Laos victory," the people still were shocked by the severe losses incurred. Perhaps the greatest emotional shock of all was the unprecedented fact that ARVN forces had to leave behind in Laos a substantial number of their dead and wounded. This came as a horrendous trauma for those unlucky families who, in their traditional devotion to the cult of the dead and their attachment to the living, were condemned to live in perpetual sorrow and doubt. It was a violation of beliefs and familial piety that Vietnamese sentiment would never forget and forgive.

Observations and Evaluation

Operation Lam Son 719 was terminated unexpectedly and in haste. Despite official denials to the contrary by GVN authorities, the fact could not be hidden from the inquisitive media reporters of the Free World. The campaign had lasted only 45 days, much shorter than its intended duration, but it was long enough to create a disquieting impact on the troops and population alike. Much speculation had arisen about the merits of the operation measured against the losses and casualties that I Corps had suffered. Was it worth all the bloodshed and the bodies and wounded left behind? Was it a victory or a defeat? Popular sentiment seemed to be aroused by the dramatic accounts and personal feelings of the I Corps troops who returned from Laos. Almost without exception, they did not believe they were victorious.

• • •

Our intensive study and planning resulted in estimates that bolstered confidence. The enemy's opposition would be initially light. His antiaircraft system would be effectively neutralized by our devastating firepower. Our helilift capabilities and mechanized assets would make short work of the occupation of key objectives. Initially it was thought that Tchepone could be ours after three days of combat.[21] Naturally, after that, our search activities would expand and continue until the enemy's logistical system in the area of

operation was effectively strangled. Although there was no official record of the anticipated duration of the campaign, it could be inferred from public statements and private
comments made by authorities that the operation was to last until the onset of the rainy
season in lower Laos, or about early May 1971. From then on, monsoon rains over the
Truong Son mountain range would inhibit the enemy's infiltration and logistic activities.

• • •

During the initial phase of the campaign, the advance of ARVN units was bold, swift,
and effective. The concept of maneuvering along the ridgelines by helilift, combined
with a series of fire support bases, allowed an audacious progress, well supported by
artillery. Heliborne movements were coordinated with an armor thrust; these forces
linked up at predetermined objectives along the axis of the main effort. Both the northern and southern flanks of this effort were also protected, and, once the final objective
was attained, the actual search of the target area and exploitation of combat gains could
be expanded.

This was a sound concept whose success depended on the superiority enjoyed by
ARVN in terms of heliborne mobility, airpower, and mechanized capabilities. Swift
progress made step by step and from peak to peak, and occupation of dominating terrain
features by a series of mutually supporting fire support bases, was the essence of that
concept. It was in fact the faithful transplant of a combat tactic that had worked for so
many years in South Vietnam and should work in lower Laos, given the considerable
concentration of resources. This also offered the ARVN forces an opportunity to put into
combat practice what they had learned from combined operations with US forces.

The rough, jungled terrain of lower Laos proved particularly difficult for ARVN
forces. In every advance they were apt to be engaged by the enemy in heavy firefights. At
almost all prominent terrain features in the area they met head-on with solid defensive
positions deployed by enemy logistic units. This defense system, consisting of mutually
supporting, well dug in, crescent-shaped, covered trench segments, which the enemy
called "horseshoe blocks," was extremely difficult and time-consuming to break through,
since their destruction would require accurate, highly concentrated artillery fire.

One of the first major problems that our forces had to face, in addition to the enemy's
blocking positions, was his elusive but devastating antiaircraft system. The most common weapon he used against our aircraft was the 12.7mm heavy machinegun, which
constantly switched firing positions. In addition, throughout the area there were about
200 AAA pieces, from 23mm up to 100mm, some of them radar-controlled. Even these
heavy weapons frequently changed firing positions, which were usually well concealed.
In general, the enemy's antiaircraft system seemed to be well coordinated and its fire
controlled with skill and discipline.

• • •

Another enemy weapon that was least expected in view of the adverse terrain in lower
Laos was the tank. Since the very first days of the operation, our troops had detected and
reported traces of tracked vehicles. Then enemy prisoners provided additional information
which pointed to the presence of an armor regiment in the area. It was only later, when

some of these tanks made their appearance, that they were observed and attacked by US aircraft. Then a combined infantry-armor attack against FSB 31 made it all too clear that tanks were being used extensively by the enemy, although in a rather unorthodox manner. In his attack against FSB 30, for example, the enemy used tanks only to provide direct support fire, and at FSB Delta his flame-throwing tanks repulsed a counterattack by our marine troops. The enemy's employment of armor was even more unorthodox in that tanks were used individually to ambush our troops along well-concealed jungle paths, as if they were playing a hide-and-seek game. This tactic worked because the enemy knew well the system of paths that crisscrossed the area. Against our armor or truck convoys, enemy tanks were usually positioned in ambush, then suddenly opened fire and withdrew quickly into jungle paths. In addition to PT-76s, the enemy also employed medium T-54 and T-34 tanks whose 100mm and 85mm guns had greater firepower than our 76mm M-41 light tanks. Confined to a one-way road with little room for cross-country maneuver, ARVN armor units found themselves in an extremely disadvantageous position.

While enemy infantry troops seemed to have excellent antitank capabilities, with their B-40 and B-41 teams and their ambush tactics, our infantrymen were not well prepared against enemy tanks. ARVN airborne troops, for example, complained about the ineffectiveness of the M-72 light antitank weapon.[22] As a result, old 3.5-inch rocket launchers and new 90mm recoilless rifles were quickly brought in as replacements. Even US gunships, during the early stage of the operation, were not armed with HEAT rockets, which were required to knock out tanks. Our head-on collision with enemy tanks, therefore, was obviously a big tactical surprise.

Enemy artillery also posed a challenge that could not be easily met. In the first place, mortars of all calibers formed close rings of fire around our positions. Their continuous firing indicated that the enemy had an ample supply of ammunition, which was probably pre-positioned. Next came recoilless rifles, rockets, and artillery of all types. For the first time in the war, ARVN forces came to grips with the deadly fire of enemy 152mm howitzers and 130mm guns, which had a range far greater than their own 105mm and 155mm howitzers. Enemy artillery was emplaced in scattered individual positions, some dug into mountain slopes to elude our counterbattery fire. In addition, several pieces would open fire at the same time from several directions, making them all the more difficult for our forces to locate. Without field radar, ARVN forces had to rely on their technique of crater analysis, which did not produce accurate results.

• • •

In the face of these difficulties, which ARVN forces were not prepared to meet, Operation Lam Son 719 bogged down as soon as it reached Ban Dong. First the rangers, then the paratroopers, and finally the armor troops all had the chance to prove their gallantry in combat and indeed inflicted severe losses to the enemy. But, by this time, the ARVN forces had lost their initiative, and our vigorous offensive thrust was blunted. The state of inconclusive, see-saw fighting continued until the beginning of March when, with increased US helilift and firepower support, the 2nd Regiment of the 1st Infantry Division succeeded in landing in Tchepone, the major terrain objective of the entire operation. For all its merits, this exploit was more a symbolic gesture than a real achievement. It merely meant that "we were there."

The 2nd Regiment did not stay long in Tchepone. The imbalance of forces by that time precluded any attempt at holding and exploiting this objective. Our success in reaching Tchepone was largely due to a flexibility in plans and the awesome capability of US helicopters. The real prize, however, was not to be found there. It was located further west, where the enemy's more important supply caches still lay unsheltered on the ground. But ARVN forces could not get there, nor could they afford to linger long in Tchepone. As swiftly as they came in, they were extracted in haste before the enemy had time to regroup and react. . . . It was true that US helicopters helped with the maneuvering of our forces, but the overall tactical imbalance that prevailed at that time made it impossible for ARVN forces to hold terrain and exploit the gains. This was a truth that no one could deny.

Throughout the operation the role played by US combat support was particularly illustrious. It was evident that, without this support, no incursion would have been possible, much less on such a large scale. The fact that ARVN forces were able to progress into Laos as far as Tchepone was a measure of the significance of US support. When enemy resistance developed into such proportions that no further progress was possible, it became all the more obvious that without US combat troops in the rear and without US helicopters and tactical air support for the front line, it would have been impossible to withdraw with any satisfactory degree of unit integrity.

US support assets were plentiful, but it appeared that, during the early stage of the operation, their control and coordination were not entirely satisfactory. Part of the problem seemed to derive from the physical separation of major operational headquarters. The US XXIV Corps Forward CP was installed at Quang Tri Base, while its counterpart, I Corps Forward CP, was at Dong Ha, about ten miles to the northwest. Still another important element of I Corps Forward CP, the operational control staff, was located farther west at Ham Nghi Base (Khe Sanh), which was 35 miles southwest of Dong Ha. Operating on the principle of cooperation and coordination, both the US and ARVN staffs found it difficult to work effectively while physically separated.

• • •

Although a combined operation, Lam Son 719 had an unusual character of its own. It was the first large-scale operation undertaken without the direct participation of US advisors. Long accustomed to the presence of advisors, which they found reassuring and invaluable, especially in difficult combat situations, ARVN regimental and battalion commanders went into Laos with apprehensive feelings. They realized that this was going to be a difficult challenge, and they were not too sure they could handle the problem of communications with supporting US units. This had always been an exclusive service provided by their advisors, in addition to regular and routine advisory assistance. But they had to accomplish all requirements by themselves this time, and, despite some apprehensions, they all felt proud and believed they could excel without their advisors.

• • •

The question has often surfaced concerning President Thieu's personal influence on the operation. From the beginning it was obvious that his influence was decisive. It was he who approved the idea of launching an offensive into lower Laos, concurred with the general concept of operation, and decided to augment the forces for I Corps. The JGS only acted with his approval. The attachment of the Airborne and Marine Divisions to I Corps for the offensive effort, for example, could not have been done without President Thieu's personal approval. But the selection of 8 February as D-Day, as far as I can determine, was a recommendation of the combined planning staffs of I Corps and the US XXIV Corps. President Thieu had been briefed on this selected date by the I Corps commander. Therefore, without strong reasons for a change, the I Corps commander apparently felt committed to the decision that he had recommended and obtained from the president.

But President Thieu's role was not confined just to the decision to proceed with the operation. At least on two occasions the directives he gave to the I Corps commander clearly affected the course of the operation itself. During a visit to I Corps on 19 February, in the company of a central government delegation, he received an operational briefing presented by the participating ARVN field commanders. During this briefing they outlined for him the serious difficulties being met by ARVN units in lower Laos, with the implied suggestion that a deeper incursion would be inadvisable. At that time the Ranger 21st and 39th Battalions were being heavily engaged, and FSBs 30 and 31 began to detect strong enemy pressure. President Thieu made a few remarks to the effect that ARVN forces should take their time and should conduct search operations in the vicinities of their present positions while waiting for developments. From that day on the Airborne Division would not make any further advance.

The second time involved the decision to push into Tchepone. On 28 February President Thieu met again with the I Corps commander in Saigon. By this time progress on the ground had been stalled for over two weeks, and the foreign press was publicizing daily [the] ARVN's inability to advance further. During this meeting it was President Thieu who decided that ARVN forces should go into Tchepone. As a result, General Lam produced his plan to occupy Tchepone, and President Thieu ordered the JGS to reinforce I Corps with the entire Marine Division and additional armor elements. The attack against Tchepone was conceived merely as a short-term raid to be conducted primarily for its propaganda and morale value.

Although President Thieu suggested that the Marine Division be used to relieve the Airborne Division in the main effort, General Lam convinced him that the 1st Division would be better in this role, while the marines could be employed to protect the rear and the LOC. The division commanders present also agreed that the advance, except for the raid to Tchepone, should be suspended until the enemy's intentions and capabilities became more clear. The field commanders and General Lam also persuaded President Thieu that reinforcement with the 2nd Division in Laos would not improve the situation. Now that the initiative had been largely assumed by the NVA, a much more potent force than the 2nd Division would be required to recapture it.

Finally, President Thieu's desire to conduct a raid in force into Muong Nong ceased to be a practicable course of action by the time the withdrawal was beginning, and General Lam exercised his command prerogatives by not attempting it. It was clear that President Thieu listened carefully to the recommendations of his field commanders, that he did not arbitrarily impose rigid instructions upon them, but that he allowed them the latitude in the execution of plans and orders that combat commanders must have.

The conduct of the operation was also plagued by dissension verging on insubordination among some ARVN field commanders. Lieutenant General Lam was never able to exercise full control over the commanders of the Airborne and Marine Divisions, who were his equals in rank. Of the two, Lieutenant General Du Quoc Dong, the paratrooper, proved to be more submissive, but he did not always carry out the I Corps commander's orders in a strict manner. Lieutenant General Le Nguyen Khang, commander of the Marine Division, who was more senior in rank than the I Corps commander, delegated his command authority to his deputy, Colonel Bui The Lan, who directly exercised operational control over the entire division. While occasionally present at the Marine Division's rear echelon CP, General Khang never attended any official operational briefings presided over by the I Corps commander. Because of this, the Marine Division acted independently on a few occasions when the odds were against it. For example, it made its own decision to abandon FSB Hotel and withdraw its troops from Laos.

President Thieu and General Vien . . . were probably aware of the discord among their subordinates, but they took no remedial action. Perhaps General Lam did not ask for such an action. Or perhaps the matter was so delicate among these generals, who were all considered pillars of the regime, that it defied any easy solution.

• • •

While the RVN announced that its troops had occupied Tchepone, North Vietnam quickly and loudly [denied] it. The GVN in the meantime received foreign press reporters with a total lack of enthusiasm and did not allow them easy access to battleground visits as it had during other operations. This increased suspicion and speculation. Subsequent press articles and pictures depicting the withdrawal of ARVN troops from Laos further confused attempts at assessing the offensive campaign correctly, particularly by foreign observers. However, with the exception of the minority elite in big cities, the South Vietnamese general public was not influenced by the foreign press. Still, the initial publicity about Lam Son 719 looked embarrassingly hollow in their eyes in view of the hasty termination of the operation. This impression lingered on, despite official announcements of victory and the ribbons and medals awarded to the "victorious" troops of I Corps.

• • •

Regardless of these shortcomings, a substantial number of the objectives had been accomplished, which required ARVN units to fight hard and incur great sacrifices. Topping the honor roll, the 1st ARVN Infantry Division [lived] up to its reputation as the number one ARVN combat unit. The division's organic units maneuvered with skill and were well led; its well disciplined troops fought with gallantry and dedication.

• • •

Long considered as the elite unit of the RVNAF, the Airborne Division did not perform as brilliantly as its reputation would indicate during Lam Son 719. Despite the enemy's superiority in maneuvering forces and his employment of new weapons, the fact that the division was unable to hold FSB 31 seemed to be indicative of its lack of contingency planning for such a situation. But our airborne units fought extremely well as individual elements. One of the division's brigade commanders was missing in action—probably captured by the enemy—and five out of nine of its battalion commanders were either killed or wounded. This testified to the intense fighting that the division had to face, but by and large the division accomplished nothing spectacular in its assigned mission. During the final stage, the division also failed to provide effective flank protection for the major effort and secure Route No. 9, even with the reinforcement of four armor squadrons. This failure greatly complicated the ARVN withdrawal from Laos.

As for the Marine Division, it was the first time it had participated in an operation as a division. Accustomed to operating separately at brigade level, and in view of the traditional autonomy of its brigades, the division seemed to have problems of command and control. The 147th Marine Brigade did not succeed in clearing the enemy pressure around FSB Delta, despite continuous efforts, for several days. Then the division made its own decision to withdraw from FSB Hotel and its positions on the Co Roc promontory, apparently to avoid facing a difficult battle. This action clearly reflected the autonomy enjoyed by the division commander, Lieutenant General . . . Khang, who did not consider himself under the control of the I Corps commander, but still made tactical decisions that affected the latter's conduct of the operation. Despite this, marine units fought extremely well during sustained combat under heavy enemy pressure. Regardless of losses, they always retained unit integrity and cohesiveness.

• • •

As to ARVN armor units, their employment in Lam Son 719 was perhaps one of the very few occasions of any large concentration during the war. The 1st Armor Brigade was committed initially with only two squadrons; this total was later increased to four, in addition to two troops of M-41 light tanks redeployed from MR-2. These reinforcements were introduced to offset some losses, but still the deployment of all these armored forces on a short stretch of narrow jungle road, not even 20 kilometers in length and affording no room for maneuver, represented perhaps one of the unwisest moves on the part of the tactical commanders involved.[23] If this decision was deliberate, then perhaps they had seriously underestimated the enemy's capabilities or the restrictions dictated by the terrain in that area. As a result, the 1st Armor Brigade was at a great disadvantage when faced with enemy tanks deep in the jungle. In those circumstances, ARVN armor officers were naturally unable to make effective use of combat tactics they had learned in Western service schools. The brigade commander was also not resourceful enough to meet this unusual combat challenge. The outcome was evident: only one-third of the total number of armored vehicles committed managed to return home after accomplishing nothing substantial. If someone was to be held responsible for this failure, the question would arise as to whether it should be the commander of the brigade or his superior, who committed this unit to such an undesirable and impossible situation.

In contrast, I Corps artillery performed exceptionally well during the entire operation. Fire coordination between ARVN and US supporting units was extremely flexible and effective. Divisional artillery units providing direct support in Laos fared less well, however. Their deployment was also limited. Each infantry regiment or brigade was supported by only one 105mm battery and one 155mm battery. Given the number of artillery pieces left behind in Laos after the hasty withdrawal, one may wonder whether we should have committed more artillery assets to the battle.

• • •

Lessons Learned

Lam Son 719 reflected quite accurately the strengths and weaknesses of the RVNAF combat effectiveness in almost every area: organization, command, leadership, motivation, operating techniques, planning, and execution. It was impeded by certain significant errors and shortcomings that made the entire effort fall short of its intended goal.

Foremost among the most significant problems of Lam Son 719 was perhaps timely tactical intelligence. To give due credit to the intelligence effort, one must admit that intelligence estimates concerning the operation were definitely accurate or nearly accurate as far as enemy capabilities in antiaircraft weapons and troop reinforcements were concerned. However, they were less accurate in other areas. Enemy artillery and armor capabilities were not listed as significant factors. In addition, reports on the area of concentrated supplies were not entirely accurate. Several enemy prisoners in fact disclosed that most [supply] caches had been evacuated to areas outside the AO. The enemy appeared not to be surprised at all; by contrast, he had been prepared and expecting our forces to come in. This led to the conclusion that several things concerning the enemy had eluded our collection capabilities.

• • •

Planning and preparations for the offensive were another major area that needed improvement. The operational plan for Lam Son 719 was adequate only so long as the operation progressed smoothly and ARVN forces were able to hold the initiative. It should have taken contingencies into full consideration and been able to respond to them with resourcefulness. The extent and intensity of enemy reactions, for example, were one contingency that planners apparently overlooked. Then the enemy could well reinforce his resistance by diversionary actions elsewhere in South Vietnam, too. The absence of contingency planning was a glaring deficiency of Lam Son 719.

• • •

As far as command and control were concerned, the most important problem to be solved was insubordination on the part of general reserve unit commanders who, like many other generals, considered themselves the pillars of the regime. The I Corps commander apparently bowed to the political power of these generals, and this adversely affected his conduct of the operation. The unsubmissive attitude of the Marine and Airborne Division commanders was actually inexcusable in that they placed themselves above the national interest and let their personal pride interfere with the task of defeating the enemy. For the operation to succeed as planned, the problem of effective command had to be satisfactorily solved above everything else, because it affected the relationship between subordinate staffs and the control of the operation itself. At least the I Corps commander should have been given the authority to require that his orders be strictly carried out.

• • •

In the area of combat tactics, a most remarkable feature of Lam Son 719 was the use of semifixed fire support bases installed on high peaks. This tactic was a duplication of the American usage in South Vietnam. But the situation in lower Laos did not favor the installation of these FSBs for the reason that the area of operation had been under enemy control for a long time; the enemy was well entrenched and well organized for defense. The several peaks in the area gave the enemy an advantage in observation, which resulted in accurate indirect fire on our fixed fire [support] bases. The amount of troops deployed for the defense of each FSB was also not adequate. The inevitable result was that our units were immobilized in these FSBs and gradually became fixed targets for enemy encirclement and attacks. Most of the 96 artillery pieces lost in Laos resulted from our system of lame-duck FSBs. This system could have been replaced by other alternatives, such as mobile FSBs, selection of lower more accessible sites, and increased use of mortars to augment artillery firepower.

• • •

In summary, Lam Son 719 was a bloody field exercise for ARVN forces under the command of I Corps. Nearly 8,000 ARVN soldiers and millions of dollars worth of valuable equipment and materiel were sacrificed. The realities of battles fought in Laos certainly taught us many invaluable lessons that the RVNAF would have to learn in order to defend South Vietnam effectively. Many of these lessons—those that were appropriate for such treatment—became subjects of instruction at RVNAF service schools and training centers.

VII. OBSERVATIONS AND CONCLUSIONS

• • •

Despite its short duration, Lam Son 719 effectively disrupted the enemy's north-south supply system. This effect was nearly total in the area of operation, somewhat less west of it. Our intelligence revealed that enemy personnel manning the supply base system sustained about 50 percent casualties, along with sizable materiel losses.

• • •

On the part of the RVN, the offensive it had launched into Laos obviously meant much more in another aspect. Simultaneously with this effort, the RVN also initiated a large sweeping operation through several other Communist bases located in Cambodia.

This conduct of two simultaneous major offensive operations beyond the national border would have been impossible for the RVN just two years earlier. More significantly, while our troops were operating outside the border the military situation at home was quiet, security improved, and the redeployment of US combat troops continued at a steady pace. All these accomplishments would have been impossible without considerable progress in the combat effectiveness of the RVNAF and in the Vietnamization and pacification programs.

• • •

The swiftness and forcefulness with which enemy forces reacted to our incursion gave credence to intelligence reports that the enemy had been preparing to launch an offensive of his own sometime during the year. Had it not been for Lam Son 719, the enemy's planned offensive, which occurred in the spring of 1972, may have come up to a year earlier. At it was, the RVNAF were much further along in the process of Vietnamization by Easter 1972 than they were in early 1971 and better prepared to cope with the great and widespread offensive the NVA eventually launched. This delay forced upon the enemy was one of the most important outcomes of Lam Son 719.

• • •

So, in the final analysis, although Lam Son 719 was not a total tactical success, it certainly helped the RVN and the United States to achieve some of their more important strategic objectives. In return, the RVN had to pay a high price and, in the process, exposed some of its weaknesses in the areas of defense and security.

• • •

Lam Son 719 did not come as a surprise for the enemy as intended. This was a profound disappointment for our side. We had tried to keep the planning and preparation process as leakproof as possible, even at the expense of carefully preparing our units for the challenge. But the enemy had correctly anticipated our possible action five months in advance.[24] To counter it, he had activated a corps-level control headquarters, Front 70B, as early as in October 1970 to exercise control over the 304th, 308th, and 320th Divisions. The battleground had also been carefully prepared. To the dismay of ARVN units, they found that, regardless of their direction of advance in the area of operation, they encountered well-organized defense positions. Enemy artillery was also preregistered to every hilltop susceptible of becoming a landing zone for our helicopters. In addition, enemy prisoners testified that a substantial part of supply caches had been removed to other areas. What we had hoped to be a surprise turned out to be something the enemy had planned for as a contingency ever since the Cambodian incursion was terminated.

On the contrary, the surprise, in some areas, was ours. We did not expect to meet head-on with T-54 tanks and 130mm guns in the jungles of Laos. Neither did we suspect that Route No. 9 would be such a problem, heavily mined and riddled with fire ambushes. We had no idea that the enemy had developed to such an extent his defense of our area of operation.

• • •

It is obvious that our commanders and planners had underestimated the enemy's ability to react. We did so because we viewed the enemy through our own lens and judged him according to our experience. Most of our combat decisions were based on subjective reasoning, with the end result that neither our strategy nor our tactics seemed responsive enough to the kind of warfare the enemy was waging.

• • •

Finally, both the RVN and the United States really missed the chance for a big victory during Lam Son 719 on a battleground which was decisive for the outcome of the war. Because of the significance of the panhandle, the enemy had thrown into combat almost all of his reserve forces—12 regiments confirmed and three others probable, and he seemed determined to go all out, win or lose. On our part, we hesitated, we procrastinated, and we passed up a big chance of winning when the chips were all down. For one thing, we failed to foresee the big stake, plan for it carefully, and commit sufficient forces to ensure success. When we went in, we knew that the objective was important. We believed our firepower was superior enough to destroy the massive concentration of enemy forces which resisted us. But we did not use it fully to our advantage to reach our objective as quickly as possible.

As new enemy units arrived in the area, tilting the balance of forces in his favor, we only considered withdrawing to avoid undue losses. Was it an error in planning, or a lack of planning? The 2nd Infantry Division was available for commitment. It could have been redeployed without risk, because the US 23rd Division (Americal) was in its area to provide security. But we did not commit the 2nd Division, for the simple reason that we were not sure we could win. As to committing more forces to ensure victory, the RVNAF simply did not have them available.

In lower Laos our enemy had once more proved that his war machinery was effective. He also proved he was determined and capable enough to muster his force for the protection of his vital area. As individuals, the enemy troops who were captured or rallied to our side all proved to be weary of the war and utterly demoralized. But, within their own ranks and during combat, under the stimulation of command and Party cadres, they were apt to become fearless. During the operation, their repeated waves of assault were so fierce that some were reported occasionally to have been drugged prior to engagement. Whatever the truth, the fact must be admitted that enemy command and control was effective.

North Vietnam also demonstrated it could see far ahead, plan for its goal realistically, and implement its plans with resolution. In addition to having effective command and control, NVA units were well disciplined, well trained, and exceptionally well indoctrinated. Their obvious advantage was positive and determined leadership, both military and political.

The South Vietnamese soldier was definitely superior to his enemy as an individual. He was more experienced, better trained, and wiser. In general, he had fought with determination and professionalism against a numerically superior enemy who endeavored to protect his vital lifeline. Despite the protractedness of the war and overwhelming hardships and privations, he still fought on and accepted sacrifices. This was evident during Lam Son 719.

The immediate results of Lam Son 719 were impressive indeed. However, the far-reaching impact of this operation only materialized a long time afterwards as the situation in both South Vietnam and Cambodia began to improve. But the repercussions of this imperfect exploit seemed to indicate that the long-term struggle of South Vietnam needed to be forged by sharper tactical skills and guided by an appropriate and more effective strategic leadership. This was perhaps the greatest lesson that we could derive from Lam Son 719.

NOTES

1. "Untold Story of the Ho Chi Minh Trail," *U.S. News & World Report,* 15 February 1971.

2. All enemy units referred to in this monograph are infantry unless otherwise specified.

3. US XXIV Corps Operation Order, Lam Son 719, dated 23 January 1971, Annex B (Intelligence), Appendix 2 (Antiaircraft Capability), p. B-2-1.

4. "Vietnam: What Next? The Strategy of Isolation," *Military Review,* April 1972.

5. After the exclusive briefing for General Lam, Colonel Cao Khac Nhat, G-3 I Corps, took Colonel Tho aside and told him, "Why exclude me from the briefing? I have already completed the operational plan."

6. This date was obtained from US XXIV Corps After Action Report, which records, on p. 3: "21 January: XXIV Corps/I Corps received approval of detailed concept."

7. Lam Son was the birthplace of Le Loi, a national hero second only to Tran Hung Dao in popular reverence. Le Loi ejected the Chinese from Vietnam in the early 15th century.

8. The directive given by US XXIV Corps to the US 101st Airborne Division (Airmobile) and the Danang Support Command stated that these units should be prepared to provide support for I Corps operations forces for at least 90 days, in other words until the onset of the Laotian rainy season in early May 1971.

9. General Lam considered the ranger group adequate for this mission, which was to provide the main body early warning of any enemy force approaching on his flank and to delay and force him to concentrate until heavier combat power could be placed against him. It would have been advantageous to assign this mission to a mobile, armor-equipped force, but not only did the rugged terrain preclude this, but General Lam needed his armor and his 1st Division for the main effort. Furthermore, he wanted to keep the 1st Division available for a sweep through Base Area 611.

10. Colonel Arthur W. Pence, After Action Report on Lam Son 719, 1 April 1971, p. 3.

11. Ibid., p. 2.

12. Ibid., pp. 7–8.

13. Specific instructions from COMUSMACV prohibited any US Army elements from entering Laos in advance of the RVNAF border crossing.

14. Bomb damage assessments were extremely difficult and hazardous to conduct in this dense, heavily defended area. As a consequence, only 10 percent of the B-52 targets struck during Lam Son 719 were reconnoitered later on the ground, and even those that were entered by ground troops were so torn up by craters and splintered trees that accurate assessments were impossible. Nevertheless, by putting together all sources of information—prisoner and rallier interrogations, aerial observation and photography, ground reconnaissance, document exploitation, agent reports, and communications intelligence—analysts concluded that enemy losses to US air attacks were substantial.

15. Message 00843, COMUSMACV to CJCS, 141435Z February 1971.

16. Airborne units routinely secured their fire support bases in this manner. Other ARVN units also employed this technique when the terrain and enemy situation made it appropriate.

17. Colonel Nguyen Van Tho, commander of the 3rd Airborne Brigade, was forced by the Communists to make a radio statement denouncing Lam Son 719 shortly after his capture.

18. English names were chosen for objectives, firebases, and the like primarily to facilitate communications with US support units. During the First Indochina War, the French had followed a parallel practice (at Dien Bien Phu, for example). Perhaps feminine names were selected to bring some softness into the virile world of combatants at war. "Lolo," "Liz," and "Sophia" were chosen by Colonel Vu Van Giai, the very effective deputy commander of the 1st Division, who assisted in maneuvering the division during this period. He had served for several years in the DMZ area, in coordination with US combat units, and he naturally followed their practice in naming firebases. The small return that the NVA might have enjoyed by exploiting these names for propaganda value—as proof that the Americans were still in charge despite Vietnamization—was certainly overridden by the practicality of having words the Americans could understand and pronounce.

19. According to General Cao Van Vien, General Abrams mentioned sending the ARVN 2nd Infantry Division into lower Laos to President Thieu, who countered that a US division should be sent alongside. The matter was dropped because US ground forces were not authorized to enter Laos. The planning done by the ARVN 2nd Division and the US 23rd Division was accomplished without orders or direction from the JGS.

20. The next day additional troops managed to reach safety. The reported strength of the 4th Battalion on 19 March was 82 men.

21. Message No. PT008443, COMUSMACV to CJCS and CINCPAC, 141435Z February 1971.

22. It is possible that one of the problems the troopers experienced with the LAW was related to firing the weapon at very close range, shorter than the minimum arming distance of the projectile.

23. The commanders of ARVN I Corps and US XXIV Corps were both armor officers.

24. Deposition made by a Communist sergeant from the 24B Regiment, NVA 304th Division, who defected to our side. Enemy units had received orders to counteract a possible ARVN offensive along Route No. 9 five months before it was launched.

12

The Easter Offensive of 1972

Lieutenant General Ngo Quang Truong

PREFACE

In 1968, a US presidential election year, Communist North Vietnam initiated the Tet Offensive, striking at almost all major cities and towns of South Vietnam. This general offensive was eventually defeated by the collective efforts of the Republic of Vietnam, [the] United States, and Free World [Military] Assistance forces.

Four years later, in 1972—again a US presidential election year—North Vietnam threw its entire military might behind an invasion to conquer the South. This time, however, South Vietnam had to fight for survival with only logistics and combat support provided by the United States. Almost all US and Free World Military Assistance combat forces had been withdrawn [by the time] the first attacks began on 30 April 1972.

By all standards the Easter Offensive of 1972 was one of North Vietnam's most significant initiatives during the Vietnam War. This all-out effort involved eventually in excess of ten divisions on each side and affected the lives of well over a million South Vietnamese people. During the eight long months of fierce fighting the Republic of Vietnam Armed Forces put Vietnamization to a severe test.

During the period of the Easter Offensive I had the privilege of participating in some of its major battles, first as IV Corps and then as I Corps commander, beginning in early May 1972. I visited many of our combat units as they fought the North Vietnam Army, and commanded the RVNAF counteroffensive to retake Quang Tri City. My critical analysis of the 1972 Easter invasion, therefore, is based almost exclusively on my own personal observations, impressions, and interviews with Vietnamese who were directly involved. . . . [31 August 1977]

I. INTRODUCTION

From Insurgency to Conventional Warfare

On 30 March 1972, following heavy artillery preparations, three North Vietnamese Army (NVA) divisions, spearheaded by tanks, crossed the Demilitarized Zone (DMZ) into South Vietnam. From the north and the west they attacked and overran the thinly defended forward outposts and fire support bases held by the 3rd Infantry Division, Army of the Republic of Vietnam (ARVN). Three days later, farther south in Military Region 3, three other NVA divisions closed in on An Loc, 60 miles north of Saigon, after taking a district town near the Cambodian border. Then, on 14 April, two NVA divisions attacked troops of the 22nd ARVN Infantry Division who manned the defenses of northwestern Kontum in Military Region 2, while directly to the east, in the lowlands of Binh Dinh Province, another NVA division struck at the province's three northern district towns.

And so, within two weeks of beginning on Easter day, large conventional battles were fought simultaneously on three major fronts that pitted a total of ten NVA divisions against an equivalent number of ARVN forces. For the first time, almost the entire armored force of North Vietnam was thrown into the battles, along with a significant increase in heavy artillery support. This was the largest offensive ever launched by the Communists against the Republic of Vietnam since the beginning of the war, and, because of enemy timing, it was quickly called the Easter [Offensive]. Judging from the size of forces committed and the tactics employed, this offensive represented a radical departure from the methods of warfare the Communists had historically used in their attempt to conquer the South.

• • •

After their military defeat during 1968, Communist forces in South Vietnam went through a period of decline. Despite attempts at resurgence which materialized with a countrywide offensive on 23 February 1969, and during the following two years under the form of seasonal "high point" activities, they never recovered enough to engage in large-scale and sustained attacks. As a result of his local-force units being severely decimated during 1968, the enemy also had difficulties reestablishing his system of communication and mutual support between border base areas and feeder zones adjacent to urban centers. Therefore NVA main-force units in the South were virtually cut off from their usual source of supply and local guides, which were considered indispensable for effective operations.

• • •

Following up on their successful exploits in Cambodia, in February 1971 the RVNAF launched a large-scale but limited offensive into lower Laos with substantial support in firepower, airlift, and logistics provided by the United States.

• • •

ARVN forces committed in the operation were all elite, combat-proven units of the RVNAF—the 1st Infantry, the Airborne, and the Marine Divisions. But they could not achieve all of the objectives contemplated, partly due to the forceful reactions of the enemy, who for the first time employed tanks and heavy artillery in battles with success, and partly due to some tactical blunders on our part.

This experience seemed to reinforce the enemy's belief that, with his modern weapons, he could defeat South Vietnam's armed forces and, consequently, the war could be ended by a military victory once US troops had been withdrawn. Further, he believed that military victory could only be achieved by a conventional invasion.

To prepare for his invasion, North Vietnam requested and received huge quantities of modern weapons from Russia and Red China during 1971. These included MIG-21 jets, SAM [antiaircraft] missiles, T-54 medium tanks, 130mm guns, 160mm mortars, 57mm antiaircraft guns, and, for the first time, the heat-seeking, shoulder-fired SA-7 missiles. In addition, other war supplies such as spare parts, ammunition, vehicles, and fuels were shipped to North Vietnam in such amounts as never before reported during the previous years of the war.

Despite this growing military threat, the United States and other Free World allied countries maintained their disengagement policy and continued withdrawing their troops from South Vietnam at an accelerated rate. In the process, combat support assets provided by the United States for the RVNAF were also substantially reduced. As the American military presence diminished, the threat from North Vietnam became more serious. And, at the beginning of 1972, it was obvious that a decisive NVA general offensive, which had been in the making for some time, would surely occur.

General Character of the Easter Offensive

• • •

By the end of 1971, evidence of North Vietnam's preparations for the invasion of the South had appeared from a number of sources. Notably, divisions of the NVA general reserve were moving south and a "logistics offensive" was under way in the southern region of North Vietnam. In early December, the Joint General Staff began sending warnings to military region commanders advising them to be prepared for a major enemy attack during early 1972.

• • •

Although there was general agreement in the intelligence community—Vietnamese as well as American—that an offensive in early 1972 was highly probable, some observers of the Vietnam scene, perhaps those not as well informed as those of us privy to the most reliable estimates, were influenced more by what seemed to them to be the illogic of a major North Vietnamese attack at this time. They reasoned that, to ensure victory, North Vietnam would wait until 1973 when most, if not all, US forces would have been withdrawn according to plans. It would be impossible then for the United States to reintroduce troops, and the chances of US intervention by air would also diminish.

To Hanoi, however, 1972 was apparently just as good an opportunity, since by the end of January US combat strength in South Vietnam would have been reduced to 140,000 and should reach below 70,000 by the end of April. By that time the remainder of US forces would consist merely of three combat battalions and some tactical aircraft and helicopters, a combat force no longer considered significant. In a certain sense this residual force would make 1972 look even more attractive in Hanoi's eyes, because if it could achieve a military victory the United States would certainly have to share in South Vietnam's defeat. Moreover, if the Vietnamization program and RVN pacification efforts were permitted to continue successfully and without interruption throughout the year, the military conquest of South Vietnam might well be much more difficult. To Hanoi, therefore, 1972 was the year for action.

• • •

In any event, Hanoi's ultimate goal was to ensure a military victory. It did not make sense in this case to delay action any longer once preparations had been made. For one thing, a long delay would be costly logistically and morale-sapping when thousands of combat troops lay idle. For another, the assembled units might well become targets for heavy strikes by the US Air Force. It then became obvious that late March or early April was the best time to initiate attacks.

• • •

Although the three areas of the enemy's major concentrations—northern MR-1, Kontum, and north of Saigon—were clear indicators that the heaviest attacks would occur in these regions, it was impossible, on the basis of available intelligence, to determine the priority the enemy assigned to the three objective areas. Neither could we tell which attack would be launched first, or if they would occur simultaneously.

• • •

The enemy's Nguyen Hue campaign finally materialized under the form of an unprecedented conventional invasion with three large spearheads or efforts. The first effort was conducted across the DMZ in northern Quang Tri Province; it was combined with another effort driven eastward in the direction of Hue city. The second effort, initiated a few days later, struck into Binh Long Province in northern MR-3 from the Cambodian border. The third effort, which was conducted after initial successes in Quang Tri and Binh Long, was directed against Kontum Province in northern MR-2 at the same time as attacks in Binh Dinh Province in the coastal lowlands. The Mekong Delta, meanwhile, remained unusually quiet despite a significant increase in enemy activities, especially in some areas adjacent to the Cambodian border and in Chuong Thien Province, which bordered on the U Minh Forest. The enemy's effort in MR-4, however, was neither as concentrated nor as sustained as in the other military regions.

North Vietnam, as it turned out, was committing its entire combat force—14 divisions, 26 separate regiments, and supporting armor and artillery units—into the battles, except the 316th Division, which was operating in Laos. The fierceness of this all-out invasion turned parts of South Vietnam into a blazing inferno. The enemy's classic frontal assaults, which spearheaded these battles, proved tremendously effective, at least during the initial stage. Our strongpoints just south of the DMZ, a responsibility of the ARVN 3rd Infantry Division, were unable to hold more than three days under repeated artillery barrages and vigorous attacks by enemy armor and infantry forces. After a month of resisting, our 3rd Division and the defending forces of northern MR-1 disintegrated; Quang Tri City fell into enemy hands. Areas north of Binh Long and west of Kontum were also under his control, and the cities of An Loc and Kontum were under heavy attack.

It was only three months after the outbreak of the invasion that ARVN forces regained their poise, supported by powerful and effective US tactical air and naval gunfire, and began the counteroffensive.

The ARVN counteroffensive was fairly effective. Not only did it completely stall the NVA invasion on all major fronts, it also succeeded in recovering part of the lost territory, including the provincial capital of Quang Tri, the first ever to fall into enemy hands. This feat alone, notwithstanding the heroic siege of An Loc and the unyielding defense of Kontum, eloquently testified to the combat effectiveness of the Republic of Vietnam Armed Forces and offered proof of the success of the Vietnamization program. The biggest challenge had been met, our combat maturity had been proven, and the South Vietnamese people's self-assurance was growing. This occurred at a time when the Paris peace talks were entering the final stage. Never before had the RVN strategic posture been so good, its bargaining position so strong, and its prospects of national survival so promising.

The battles fought during the blazing-red summer of 1972 marked a turning point in the Vietnam War. For the first time Communist North Vietnam realized it had no chance of a military victory while the United States still provided the South with air support and adequate logistics. It was finally compelled to accept a cease-fire.

• • •

II. THE INVASION OF QUANG TRI

Situation Prior to the Offensive

• • •

The two northern provinces of MR-1, Quang Tri and Thua Thien (where Hue was located), were separated from the three provinces to the south—Quang Nam, Quang Tin, and Quang Ngai, by an escarpment which projected into the sea at the Hai Van Pass. Danang, just south of this pass, was the biggest city of the region and the location of the headquarters for ARVN I Corps. It was also a major port capable of accommodating seagoing vessels. A lesser port, Tan My, northeast of Hue, served as a military transportation terminal for shallow-draft vessels supplying ARVN units in northern MR-1. It was in this area that several major battles of the 1972 Easter invasion were fought.

• • •

By March 1972 almost all US combat units had redeployed from MR-1. The single remaining unit, the 196th Infantry Brigade, was standing down and conducted only defensive operations around Danang and Phu Bai airbases, pending return to the United States. Ground combat responsibilities were entirely assumed by ARVN units, with the support of US tactical air and naval gunfire and the assistance of American advisors. In the area north of the Hai Van Pass, where 80,000 American troops had at one time been deployed, there were now only two ARVN infantry divisions supported by a number of newly activated armor and artillery units. Total troop strength committed to the defense of this area did not exceed 25,000.

The backbone of I Corps forces which were responsible for the defense of MR-1 consisted of three ARVN infantry divisions (the 1st, 2nd, and 3rd), the 51st Infantry Regiment, the 1st Ranger Group (with three mobile and six border defense battalions), and the 1st Armor Brigade. . . . The territorial forces of MR-1, whose key combat components were the six Regional Forces . . . battalions and company groups, also contributed significantly to area security in all five provinces. I Corps, commanded by Lieutenant General Hoang Xuan Lam, exercised control over all regular and territorial forces assigned to MR-1. General Lam, an armor officer, was a native of Hue.

On the eve of the enemy offensive, the general disposition of I Corps forces saw the 3rd Infantry Division, which was activated six months earlier, assigned to secure the northernmost frontiers of South Vietnam. Although the division had never fought a coordinated battle as a division, its battalions were seasoned combat teams with long experience fighting in northern Quang Tri. Most of the 3rd Division soldiers were natives of the region, familiar with its terrain and hardened to the harsh, cold dampness of its weather. The battalions of the 56th and 57th Regiments, in particular, were veterans of the DMZ. They occupied base camps and strongpoints they had been in for years, and their dependents lived in the nearby hamlets. Considering the time and expense that would have been involved, it would not have been practical to even consider replacing the 3rd Division on the DMZ front with another division, simply to gain the advantages that might ensue because of more experience in division-level operations.[1] The plain fact was that the battalions of the 3rd Division were the most experienced in the DMZ area of any in the ARVN, and they were expected to perform better than any others in that environment.

The 3rd Division was generally responsible for the province of Quang Tri. Its headquarters, under the command of Brigadier General Vu Van Giai, former deputy commander of the 1st Division, was located at Quang Tri Combat Base. Two of the division's three regiments, the newly activated 56th and 57th, were deployed over a series of strongpoints and fire support bases dotting the area immediately south of the DMZ, from the coastline to the piedmont area in the west. The 56th Regiment was headquartered at Fire Support Base (FSB) Carroll, while the 57th Regiment was located at FSB C1. The 2nd Regiment, which was formerly a component of the 1st Division, occupied Camp Carroll with two of its battalions at FSB C2. Camp Carroll was a large combat base situated seven kilometers southwest of the district town of Cam Lo on QL-9, which was the main road leading west to the Laotian border. The 11th Armored Cavalry Squadron, organic to the division, was located near Landing Zone (LZ) Sharon. The key firebases which supported the 3rd Division were C1, C2, and Camp Carroll.

In addition to its organic units, the 3rd Division exercised operational control over two marine brigades of the general reserve, the 147th and 258th, which were deployed over an arched ridgeline overlooking QL-9 to the west and the Thach Han River to the south. The 147th Marine Brigade was headquartered at Mai Loc Combat Base, while its sister, the 258th Brigade, was at FSB Nancy. These marine dispositions formed a strong line of defense facing west, the direction of most probable enemy attacks, and provided protection for the population in the lowlands of Quang Tri. Under the supervision of the 3rd Division, but not directly controlled by it, were the Regional Force elements which manned a line of outposts facing the DMZ from QL-1 to the coastline. . . .

South of the Quang Tri–Thua Thien provincial boundary and north of the Hai Van Pass lay the tactical area of responsibility of the 1st Infantry Division, commanded by Major General Pham Van Phu. Its primary mission was to defend the western approaches to Hue. It deployed the 1st Regiment at Camp Evans, the 3rd Regiment at FSB T-Bone, and the 54th Regiment at FSB Bastogne. The division headquarters was located at Camp Eagle, just south of Hue. The 7th Armored Cavalry Squadron, organic to the 1st Division, was located with the 1st Infantry Regiment at Camp Evans.

The three provinces of southern MR-1, all located south of the Hai Van Pass, were the responsibility of the 2nd Infantry Division, commanded by Brigadier General Phan Hoa Hiep. The division headquarters was at Chu Lai in Quang Tin Province, where the 4th Armored Cavalry, organic to the division, was also located. Each of the division's three regiments was assigned to a separate province. The 5th Regiment operated near Hoi An in Quang Nam Province, the 6th Regiment was headquartered at FSB Artillery Hill in Quang Tin Province, and the 4th Regiment at FSB Bronco in Quang Ngai Province. In view of its large territorial responsibilities, the 2nd Division was assisted by six border ranger defense battalions.

Among I Corps forces the 1st Armor Brigade—which was to play an important role in the battle for Quang Tri—had not been involved in actual combat for more than a year. The brigade's last combat action took place during the Lam Son 719 operation in lower Laos from February to April 1971, where it had suffered high combat losses. Despite extensive reorganization and refitting efforts, which included the activation of the 20th Tank Squadron, our only unit equipped with M-48 medium tanks, the combat worthiness of the 1st Armor Brigade was still untested and difficult to evaluate.

While the 1st and 2nd Infantry Divisions were thoroughly combat proven, the 3rd Infantry Division was just organized as a unit on 1 October 1971. Two of its three regiments, the 56th and 57th, had been formed and deployed in forward positions along the DMZ barely three weeks before the invasion took place. At that time, the division did not have its own logistic support units and its artillery was still receiving equipment. But the overall status of the division seemed to be fairly good, the morale of its troops was high, and its unit training programs were on schedule. The division commander was professionally capable and highly dedicated to his job; his leadership inspired confidence among subordinate units. The division was still short of many critical items, especially signal communications. Despite this, the division endeavored to develop its combat capabilities through uninterrupted training which appeared to be quite effective. However, in no way could . . . the 3rd Division be considered as fully prepared to fight a large, conventional action.

The two marine brigades which were placed under the operational control of the 3rd Division were in every respect thoroughly combat effective. They were both at full strength, well equipped and well supplied through their own channels. But while their reputation as elite units of the RVNAF was solid and their combat valor held in high esteem, they were seldom totally responsive to the directives and requirements of the 3rd Division commander. It was an unfortunate fact of life in the RVNAF that the loyalties of marine corps units belonged first to the marine corps commander and only second to the commander of the division or corps to which they were attached or assigned. This idiosyncrasy was illustrated, and caused some serious tactical problems, during the Lam Son 719 operation. . . . The reasons for this attitude were deep-seated and founded in the fact that ARVN infantry divisions had very little experience in multibattalion operations, their commanders and staffs had little training and less interest in assuming the responsibilities that come with attachments, and attached units had to rely upon their parent organizations for all kinds of support. Furthermore, attached units—whether they were airborne, marine, ranger, or armor—often found themselves shunted off to the side or sent on poorly planned and imperfectly executed operations.

As far as I Corps headquarters was concerned, it had never really directed and controlled large, coordinated combat operations except for the unique case of Lam Son 719, during which it operated as a command post in the field for the first time. Although the I Corps staff excelled in procedural and administrative work and was effective in the operation and control of routine territorial security activities, it lacked the experience, professionalism, and initiative required of a field staff during critical times [in] battle.

During the month of January 1972 orders were issued by I Corps to all major subordinate units alerting them to be prepared for a big enemy offensive during the Tet holidays. This was done merely to comply with orders from Saigon, since the I Corps commander saw nothing to indicate an imminent major enemy offensive. Although Saigon had concluded that the preparation for movement and combat that had been detected among the NVA divisions north of the DMZ were reason enough to alert the command, these divisions were still far from the line of contact and General Lam saw no cause for immediate alarm. He took cognizance of the enemy's logistical buildup in the area north and west of the I Corps defenses, but still he believed that the Communist Tet actions would be limited to an increase in shellings and sapper attacks on RVNAF lines of communication. General Lam would reserve his concern for the time when the NVA divisions moved into staging areas on the western flank of Quang Tri Province, in western Thua Thien, and [in] southern MR-1. Indications of these deployments were always seen prior to previous offensives, and they were, so far, absent.

And so appropriate measures were taken by I Corps forces to counteract the enemy's harassment activities rather than fully brace themselves for a major enemy offensive. ARVN units indeed reacted effectively to enemy-initiated activities throughout MR-1, and the Tet holidays passed in relative calm. Intelligence officers and tactical commanders, meanwhile, closely monitored and waited for signs of movement of NVA forces. Their correct prediction of the enemy's scope of activities for the Tet period reinforced their confidence that he would probably not depart from his established pattern of making deliberate deployments, which would be detected, prior to launching the offensive.

By February this assessment of the situation gained further credibility when it was revealed that the NVA 324B Division was moving into the A Shau Valley in western Thua Thien Province. This was a familiar and often used staging area for this enemy division to launch attacks against Hue. The 1st ARVN Infantry Division deployed accordingly to preempt this move and clashed violently with NVA units along Route 547, west of Hue, in early March. What remained to be confirmed as definite indications of the predicted offensive in MR-1 was the movement of elements of the NVA 304th and 308th Divisions into western Quang Tri Province. While there were unconfirmed reports that the 66th Regiment of the 304th Division was in the Ba Long Valley near FSB Sarge, the location[s] of the other two regiments, the 9th and 24th, were unknown at that time. They were believed to be just north of the DMZ, as was the entire 308th Division.

General Lam did not believe in the theory that the NVA might attack across the DMZ, although the danger of such an attack had not been ruled out; this had never happened before. This no-man's-land was mostly flat, exposed terrain, unfavorable for the maneuver of large infantry formations, even with armor support, since they would be under observation and fire from our powerful tactical air, artillery, and armored forces, in addition to our system of solid strongpoints. Additional indications of NVA troop movements into western Quang Tri Province also reinforced his belief that, if the enemy was to strike, he would probably come from the west, his usual avenue of approach. Indeed, enemy efforts to open new roads and bring in more antiaircraft weapons in this area made General Lam's assessment even more convincing. But the offensive was not imminent, he reasoned, since enemy preparations were taking place at an apparently slow pace.

When confronted with the possibility of an NVA drive across the DMZ, General Giai, commander of the 3rd Division, had the same reaction as General Lam. He, too, believed that any large attack would come from the west, although he did not reject completely the possibility of an attack from the north since he knew there were indications that the enemy had brought surface-to-air (SAM) missiles, additional 130mm field guns, ammunition, and armor in the area just north of the DMZ, and beginning on 27 March there was a marked increase in indirect fire attacks against the division's fire support bases in the DMZ area.

But General Giai was facing more pressing problems in his area of operation (AO) at that time. His primary concern was to consolidate his recently occupied defensive positions to the west, [and] train and continue to prepare his division for the enemy offensive. Nevertheless, he and his staff were continually debating the problem of dominant terrain features, the enemy's most probable course of action, the disposition of his units, the configuration of their defense positions, and, above all, how to employ his forces effectively in the event of an enemy offensive.

While his staff was developing comprehensive plans for the defense of the division's area of responsibility, General Giai initiated a program of rotating his units among the regimental areas of operation in order to familiarize them thoroughly with the terrain and to eliminate the "firebase syndrome" among his troops. In accordance with this program, on 30 March the 56th and 57th Regiments began the scheduled exchange of their AOs. The 56th Regiment was to take over the 2nd Regiment's AO, to include Camp Carroll,

FSB Khe Gio, and FSB Fuller; it would be responsible for the northwest defense line. The 57th Regiment was moving into the 56th's AO, which extended from Dong Ha due north to the DMZ and east to the coastline. The 2nd Regiment, meanwhile, was taking over the combat bases north of Cam Lo in the AO just vacated by the 56th. By midday, this exchange of AOs had been about half completed when the enemy struck in force.

• • •

The Initial Battles

The enemy offensive began at noon on 30 March with artillery concentrations directed against strongpoints and firebases of the 3rd Division. This fire was well planned and accurate. It was easy for the enemy to determine the exact locations and dispositions of ARVN troops, since these positions had been used by both US and ARVN forces for many years. Additionally, the enemy's long-range 130mm field guns just north of the DMZ had the key ARVN positions in this area well within their fields of fire. These deadly concentrations pounded Camp Carroll, Mai Loc, Sarge, Holcomb, A4, A2, C1, C2, and Dong Ha Combat Base, while elements of the 56th and 57th Regiments were still displacing toward their new locations, FSBs Carroll and Charlie 1, respectively.

These artillery fires were followed by and coordinated with ground attacks, spearheaded by tanks, and came from the north across the DMZ and from the west through Khe Sanh. From the north the enemy push consisted of four spearheads. Two of them were directed against positions of the 56th Regiment in the vicinity of FSB Fuller and FSB A4. The other two moved along and parallel to QL-1 and were directed against the 57th Regiment's positions at FSB A2 and FSB A1. Meanwhile, from the west, the NVA drive was directed against the 147th Marine Brigade at Nui Ba Ho, FSB Sarge, and FSB Holcomb. As confirmed later, enemy forces conducting these initial attacks included elements of the NVA 304th and 308th Divisions, three separate infantry regiments of the B-5 Front, two armor regiments, five artillery regiments, and at least one sapper battalion.

The unexpected assault across the DMZ caught the forward elements of the 3rd Division in movement, only partially settled into defensive positions they had not been in for some time, locally outnumbered three-to-one, and outgunned by the enemy artillery. The ARVN defenses in the DMZ area were designed to counter infiltration and local attacks. There were no positions prepared to give the depth to the battlefield that would be required to contain an attack of the size and momentum of the one that had now fallen upon them.

Enemy attacks increased in intensity during the next day. All firebases along the perimeter of the 3rd Division received heavy artillery fire. The 56th, 57th, and 2nd Regiments and the marine battalions were all in contact with attacking forces. Nui Ba Ho was evacuated late in the evening, and Sarge was overrun during the early hours of 1 April, forcing the marines to fall back to Mai Loc. Enemy pressure forced elements of the 56th Regiment near FSB Fuller and those of the 2nd Regiment near Khe Gio to withdraw south of the Cam Lo River. By evening of 1 April, all strongpoints along the northern perimeter had been evacuated, including FSB Fuller and FSB Khe Gio. The withdrawal from A1, A4, and other strongpoints, including those manned by RF troops, was orderly and executed in accordance with plans and consistent with the tactical situation. However, serious mistakes were committed at A2 and C1, where two artillery batteries were located. The failure of these two bases to obtain prime movers forced the destruction and abandonment of 12 artillery pieces (six 105mm and six 155mm howitzers). By this time, the 56th Regiment had withdrawn to Camp Carroll and was under attack. The 57th Regiment had fallen back to north of Dong Ha and the 2nd Regiment to Cam Lo. The marine units meanwhile remained at Lai Loc and FSB Pedro. As a result of intense enemy artillery fire on Quang Tri Combat Base, the 3rd Division headquarters was relocated to the citadel in Quang Tri City.

At 1800 hours on 1 April General Giai ordered an immediate reorganization of defensive positions. His concept was to take advantage of natural obstacles such as the Cua Viet and Mieu Giang Rivers and establish a line of defense south of these rivers. All divisional forces north of Dong Ha were ordered to withdraw south. The RF and PF units were to hold a line on the southern bank of the Cua Viet River from the coastline to approximately five kilometers inland; the 57th Regiment would establish its positions westward from that point to Dong Ha. The city and its immediate vicinity were placed under control of the 1st Armor Brigade, whose major component—the 20th Tank Squadron—had been hastily thrown into combat as it was about to complete training at Camp Evans. West from Dong Ha and south of the Mieu Giang River, the 2nd Regiment was given responsibility for a line at Cam Lo, reinforced with an armored cavalry squadron. Next to the 2nd Regiment was the 56th, reinforced with the 11th Armored Cavalry Squadron, which was ordered to hold Camp Carroll. This defensive line then extended southward to join the 147th Marine Brigade's AO around Mai Loc. Marine battalions were also ordered to occupy the high ground along QL-9 between Cam Lo and Mai Loc, secure Quang Tri Combat Base, and continue operations near FSB Pedro.

The 3rd Division's defense on 2 April appeared to be well organized. The disposition of divisional forces was good, and the division had fairly tight control over its subordinate units. General Giai personally supervised the division's organization for defense, and his conspicuous presence at some forward positions restored and greatly stimulated morale and self-assurance among his troops. During the following days, the forces that manned the Cua Viet River line—the 57th Regiment, the 1st Armored Brigade, and particularly the RF and PF—fully demonstrated their combat capabilities and were all up to their assigned tasks. They repeatedly repelled the enemy's attempts to cross the river and inflicted heavy losses. The new 20th Tank Squadron also proved effective in its confrontation with NVA tanks, preventing them from approaching river-crossing points at Dong Ha. To the west and southwest, the marines held firmly their positions at the two major bases, Mai Loc and Pedro. They seemed unaffected by their initial setbacks at Sarge, Nui Ba Ho, and Holcomb.

The day of 2 April was marked by several tragic events. It began with simultaneous enemy attacks against Dong Ha and Camp Carroll. Again bad weather precluded effective use of tactical air throughout most of the day. From morning to late evening enemy tanks and infantry forces repeatedly tried to approach Dong Ha from the north. They were engaged by our 57th Regiment, the 20th Tank Squadron, the 3rd Marine Battalion, [and] US naval gunfire and were repulsed at every attempt to cross the Dong Ha Bridge.

The chaotic stream of refugees fleeing the combat scene along QL-1 since early morning deeply affected the morale of the 57th Regiment's troops, who broke ranks around noon and withdrew south in disorder. If there had been a plan to evacuate civilians from the battle area, and if that plan had been well executed, with suitable control and transportation, the troops of the 57th would have probably remained on position. But when they saw the disorder and panic among these refugees—among whom were their own families and relatives—the panic was contagious. When General Giai received word of what was happening, he immediately flew to the position. His presence there restored the confidence of the soldiers and they returned to their units. To stall the enemy's armor-infantry drive, the Dong Ha Bridge was destroyed by ARVN engineers at 1630 hours.

Camp Carroll to the west, in the meantime, had been surrounded by enemy troops since early morning. Troops of the 56th Regiment at the camp valiantly endured heavy artillery fires and resisted repeated assaults by enemy infantry, but received little effective artillery or air support since fire support coordination was poorly planned. The regimental commander, Colonel Pham Van Dinh, who had often proven his courage and devotion (he was the officer who restored the national colors at the Hue Citadel during the 1968 offensive) was despondent. The division was giving him no support and the corps seemed to have forgotten about him. Seeing that his situation was hopeless and wanting to save as many of his soldiers' lives as possible, he called his staff together and announced that he would surrender the command. He ordered his S-2 to carry a white sheet to the main gate of the compound and hang it there. This done, radio contact was made with the enemy and arrangements for the surrender were made. Fifteen hundred ARVN troops were captured, along with 22 artillery pieces, including a 175mm battery and numerous quad-.50s and twin-40s, the largest artillery assemblage in the entire MR-1. The 56th Regiment no longer existed.

The loss of Camp Carroll made the defense of Mai Loc nearby extremely precarious. The 147th Marine Brigade commander decided that this base could not be held and, upon his request, General Giai authorized its evacuation. The marines fell back to Quang Tri late in the afternoon. And so, repeatedly over the last three days, these marine elements had been forced to withdraw and the 3rd Division's AO was shrinking accordingly from both directions, the north and the west. These withdrawals had been orderly, but the brigade had suffered such heavy losses during the battles of the first few days that, immediately upon reaching Quang Tri, it was ordered to proceed directly to Hue for regrouping and refitting. It was replaced by a fresh unit, the 369th Marine Brigade, which immediately set up a new defense around FSB Nancy.

This rotation had a revitalizing effect on the marine troops in the combat zone. It proved to be a vital factor which contributed to the maintenance of a high level of marine combat effectiveness throughout the enemy offensive. Unfortunately for the ARVN troops of the 3rd Infantry Division, the 1st Armor Brigade, and the ranger groups which came as reinforcement, rotation seldom occurred.

Holding the Line

After four days of arduous fighting and tragic setbacks, the friendly situation on the Quang Tri front remained critical. However, there were high hopes that the new defense line would stand firmly. Despite severe blows, both ARVN regular and territorial forces seemed to hold extremely well along this new line. To their credit, they had stopped the NVA invasion—for the time being. They had performed their task well, not through reliance on US air support but with their own combat support. In fact, prolonged bad weather continued to preclude effective tactical air support and severely curtailed the use of helicopter gunships. But US naval gunfire was helpful; so were B-52 strikes, which were conducted five or six times a day against suspected NVA troop concentrations and avenues of approach.

The loss of Camp Carroll and Mai Loc resulted in heavy personnel and materiel sacrifices and had an adverse psychological impact on South Vietnam, but did not seem to dampen either the morale or the self-assurance of the defending forces. In the week that followed, the feeling of self-assurance among ARVN troops on the firing line increased. Every attempt by the enemy to break through was thoroughly defeated. According to unit reports, several enemy attacking formations were broken up, scattered, and forced to withdraw in utter disorder under the shattering fire of our infantry, armor, and artillery.

The enemy now withdrew to regroup, and only scattered contacts and attacks by fire occurred throughout the 3rd Division's area of responsibility. Although the weather continued to prevent the full use of US tactical air support, the ARVN defense line held.

In the meantime, three ARVN ranger groups—the 1st, 4th, and 5th—arrived to reinforce the defense of Quang Tri. As the weather showed some signs of improving, the I Corps commander gave serious consideration to a counterattack which was to be launched as soon as tactical air could apply its full weight. His preoccupation with plans for a counterattack diverted the I Corps staff from reorganizing the defense in depth, an effort that should have been first priority under the circumstances. His failure to recognize this proved to be a serious error that subsequently led to the loss of Quang Tri City.

Apparently General Lam was overly influenced by the arrival of reinforcements. First to arrive was the 369th Marine Brigade, followed by the Ranger Command with three groups of three battalions each, all freshly arrived from Saigon. General Lam believed that with these additional forces he could not only hold the two northern provinces but also retake the lost territory in a short time.

With this conviction, General Lam repeatedly rejected the 3rd Division commander's requests for reinforcement to consolidate the defense of Quang Tri. But General Giai was insistent, and finally the I Corps commander reluctantly sent him first one ranger group, then another. Eventually all four ranger groups in MR-1 were deployed to Quang Tri and attached to the 3rd Division. The attachments were intended to provide General Giai with full operational control and unity of command.

However, despite its growing span of control, the 3rd Division never received additional support in logistics and signal communications essential for the effective exercise of command and control. This problem was recognized at the time by the I Corps staff, which recommended that the control burden placed on General Giai should be reduced. This could have been accomplished by placing the Marine Division under the command of I Corps, and by giving the Marine Division and the Ranger Command each the responsibility for a separate sector. But, for reasons known only to General Lam, these recommendations were brushed aside. Perhaps General Lam did not feel certain he could handle the Marine Division commander who, during Lam Son 719, had failed to comply with his orders but still came out unscathed. As a result, the headquarters, Ranger Command, under Colonel Tran Cong Lieu, was left in Danang without a specific assignment, while the Marine Division headquarters in Hue was not under I Corps command. This state of things provided additional problems for the 3rd Division commander, who frequently found that the orders he gave to his attached units had no effect until the subordinate commander had checked and received guidance from his parent headquarters. This was especially true if the orders required a difficult operation.

But General Lam seemed oblivious to the 3rd Division commander's problems. His mood was optimistic. He believed that I Corps had enough forces to stop NVA units at the present line of defense while he and his staff were working on a plan to launch a counteroffensive.

General Lam's optimism was justified by the events of 9 April. On that day the enemy launched a second major effort, again from the north and the west. But, once again, the defense succeeded in driving back all attacks. The 1st Armor Brigade, the 258th Marine Brigade, and the 5th Ranger Group all reported success. Several enemy tanks were knocked out by the marines, using LAW rockets, and by the tank guns of the 1st Armor Brigade. FSB Pedro, which had been overrun that day, was retaken the next day after 3rd Division troops had repulsed three major attacks. Once more the enemy had failed to break through the ARVN line of defense, even though he had thrown into his effort major elements of the 304th and 308th NVA Divisions and two armor regiments. At the end of the day the 3rd Division's perimeter, which ran from the coastline along the Cua Viet River westward through Dong Ha, then veered south to join FSB Pedro and the Thach Han River, was still intact.

By this time General Giai's personal responsibilities and span of control had expanded far beyond that normally expected for a division commander. As a division commander, he found himself exercising command over two infantry regiments of his own, [and] operational control over two marine brigades, four ranger groups, [and] one armor brigade, plus all the territorial forces of Quang Tri Province. The 3rd Division commander's span of control thus included nine brigades containing a total of twenty-three battalions in addition to the territorial forces. His responsibilities also included supervising and providing protection for I Corps artillery and logistic units operating at Dong Ha, as well as monitoring the status of the provincial and district governments in Quang Tri. He was pleased and stimulated by the total trust the I Corps commander had vested in him.

Strange as it may seem, General Lam seldom felt the urge to visit his subordinate commanders in the field or the I Corps frontline units. He monitored the progress of battles through reports and he issued directives and orders from his headquarters. He never personally observed the 3rd Division line of defense to determine the problems being faced by unit commanders. Apparently he did not think the situation serious enough to warrant his presence. ARVN success during 9 and 10 April buoyed his optimism even more and led to his conviction that the time had arrived for a counterattack. As conceived by his staff, the plan called for an attack across the Cua Viet River in order to retake the district town of Gio Linh and the entire area north to the DMZ. He was convinced that such an attack was within I Corps capabilities and would halt North Vietnam's invasion. If it succeeded, his counterattack might well force the enemy to withdraw all forces [to positions] north of the DMZ.

Although the counterattack plan was thoroughly discussed and considered, it was finally discarded. For one thing, the amount of forces required for success in the northward drive would greatly weaken the western flank of the defense, where the enemy was stronger. If the western flank should fail to remain intact, then Quang Tri City would be in serious jeopardy. Therefore General Lam, after considerable deliberation, decided that the counteroffensive effort should be directed westward instead of to the north. He planned to reestablish the former line of defense in the west by launching an all-out attack to regain, phase line by phase line, such bases as Cam Lo, Camp Carroll, and Mai Loc. At the same time, he ordered participating units to clear all enemy elements from their zones of advance before moving on to the next phase line. The counteroffensive was called Operation Quang Trung 729 [. . . and] was scheduled to begin on 14 April.

General Giai issued the orders to the 3rd Division and its attached units and Quang Trung 729 began. There was no great surge of infantry and armor crossing the line of departure, however. On the contrary, the weary troops on the western flank were already in close contact with the enemy, as they had been for two weeks, and were unwilling or unable to advance. NVA artillery fire was devastating, and attrition in the ARVN ranks was heavy. By the end of the first week of the operation no unit had advanced more than 500 meters from the line of departure.

With his limited command and control facilities, General Giai found it impossible to coordinate a strong, well-supported attack in any part of the zone. Furthermore, it seemed that by this time he was not aware of the deteriorating state of morale among his subordinate commanders and their troops. These commanders had lost confidence in their ability to carry the attack to the enemy, and, because General Giai was unable to exercise personal command over so many dispersed units, his subordinates were able to delay preparations for the attack by claiming logistic problems, personnel attrition, troop fatigue, and every other possible reason to procrastinate. Although they sent General Giai daily reports of their attempts to advance, the line of contact remained unchanged. The orders they had to clear the zone of all enemy before advancing to the next phase line required a cautious, slow-moving attack in any case, and provided them with ample justification for their inability to move faster.

Along with the reports General Giai received from his commanders describing their efforts to clear the enemy from their zones came many requests for airstrikes against enemy concentrations, strikes that were necessary to soften the enemy before the ARVN battalions could begin the advance to the west. As the days wore on, the battalions in contact also flooded 3rd Division headquarters with reports of heavy enemy attacks by fire and high friendly casualties. Quang Trung 729 did not resemble an offensive, but rather had settled into a costly battle of attrition in place in which the ARVN battalions were steadily reduced in strength and effectiveness by the enemy's deadly artillery fire. Morale continued to deteriorate, and General Giai was unable to restore it; neither was he able to prod his battalions out of their holes and bunkers and into the attack.

It seemed that the subordinate commanders knew that their units lacked the strength to break through the NVA formations facing them, that the enemy's artillery would surely catch them in the open and destroy them, and that the coordinated fire and logistical support they would need to carry the attack was beyond the capability of the 3rd Division or I Corps to provide.

It was during this time that the failure of I Corps to establish an effective command and control system became a serious problem. The Marine Division headquarters and the Ranger Command, which had been sent to I Corps expressly to provide control over their organic units, continued to be left out of combat activities and received no specific assignments or responsibilities. But, as parent headquarters of the marines and rangers committed to the combat zone, they contributed much to the confusion of command and control by elaborating on General Giai's orders or by questioning and commenting on everything concerning their units. They were not the only ones to do this, however. General Lam himself frequently issued directives by telephone or radio to individual brigade commanders, especially to the 1st Armor Brigade commander (who belonged to the same branch and who rarely bothered to inform General Giai about these calls). General Giai often learned of these directives only after they had been implemented, and these incidents seriously degraded his authority. Distrust and insubordination gradually set in and finally resulted in total disruption of command and control at the front line in northern MR-1.

After two weeks of continuous rain and heavy cloud cover, which seriously impeded the use of tactical air support, the weather began to improve. With an accelerated tempo, as if to make up for time lost, US aircraft of all types daily swarmed in the skies over Quang Tri. Air sorties by B-52s, tactical aircraft, [and] gunships increased steadily each day, striking all suspicious targets. This upsurge restored the morale and self-assurance of the ground troops.

On 18 April enemy activity increased substantially, with attacks by fire and infantry-armor probes. This became the enemy's third major effort to take Quang Tri. All ARVN and marine units reported contact and indirect fire. At 1830 hours a coordinated enemy attack was launched against the western sector of the 3rd Division. From all positions, units reported movements of enemy tanks. Within the space of three hours the US Air Force responded with tactical air and B-52 missions (diverted from elsewhere) with such devastating strikes that the enemy attack was completely disrupted. This provided ARVN units with an opportunity to pass to the offensive and fully initiate the counter-offensive, Quang Trung 729. But nothing happened; at daybreak the troops still clung to their trenches and made no significant effort to move forward.

The fact that another major effort by the enemy had been effectively stopped deluded the I Corps commander into thinking once more that the situation in Quang Tri was under control. But the inertia developing among ARVN units should have alerted him to the pressing requirement for reorganizing his positions and rotating weary combat units. This need totally escaped him. The enemy's demonstrated ability to conduct a sustained offensive, on the other hand, should also have stimulated a major ARVN effort to implement a coordinated defense plan if Quang Tri was to be held. But this effort was not made.

The following week saw the defense line at Dong Ha and along the Cua Viet River cave in because of a tactical blunder. This came about when reports were received that the enemy was infiltrating from the west and threatening to cut off the supply route between Dong Ha and Quang Tri Combat Base. On his own initiative the 1st Armor Brigade commander directed his 20th Tank Squadron, on the Cua Viet line, to pull back south along QL-1 in order to clear the enemy elements there. As soon as they saw the tanks move south, ARVN troops were gripped with panic, broke ranks, and streamed along. Before the 3rd Division commander detected what was happening, many of his troops had already arrived at Quang Tri Combat Base—and the Cua Viet defense, which was one of our strongest lines of defense, from which the courageous ARVN troops had repeatedly repelled every enemy attack for nearly a month, had been abandoned. It was virtually handed to the enemy on a platter because a tactical commander had taken it upon himself to initiate a major move without reporting to his superior and without foreseeing the consequences of his actions.

Once again, by sheer physical intercession, the 3rd Division commander succeeded in reestablishing order, although not for long. Much precious time had been lost. By the time he had finally regained control of the situation there was no way to push his units back to Cua Viet to restore the lost positions. He was compelled to regroup them west of Quang Tri City and develop a new defense line north of the Thach Han River. This new line surrounded and protected the Quang Tri Combat Base, whose importance as a logistic support center had greatly diminished in view of the dwindling supplies still available there.

On 23 April the 147th Marine Brigade returned to Quang Tri Base to take over its defense after a rest and refitting period in Hue. The 258th Marine Brigade redeployed to Hue, but its 1st Battalion remained at FSB Pedro and came under operational control of the 147th.

During the days that followed the morale of ARVN troops deteriorated rapidly. They were exposed to the daily poundings of enemy artillery and assaults by enemy tanks. They became vulnerable to the intense tempo of conventional warfare. They had to spend long nights, tense, sleepless, agonizing at the prospect of enemy infantry assaults which could surge forward from the dark at any moment. The near-total inertia of ARVN troops at night made it possible for the enemy to rest and recuperate at almost any time he chose. Therefore short lulls during the fighting were invariably the time enemy troops chose to rest. ARVN troops, in the meantime, were constantly kept on the alert, under tension day and night, their energy sapped by fear and uncertainty while often defending a combat base of dubious tactical value.

Quang Tri Combat Base, north of the Thach Han River, was in fact a bad choice for defense from a tactical point of view. As the month of April was drawing to its end, so were the supplies at this base. Consequently the 3rd Division commander decided then to evacuate this base and withdraw south of the river. He worked on the withdrawal plan by himself; he consulted only the division senior advisor. General Giai feared that, if his subordinate commanders learned of his plan, they were apt to wreck it through hasty actions. He also deliberately withheld this plan from the I Corps commander. He simply wanted to be cautious, to get things done. But it was this action that alienated him from the I Corps commander, and the growing distrust that developed between them added a further dimension to the events which eventually led to the fall of Quang Tri City.

The Fall of Quang Tri City

The final NVA actions that contributed to the fall of Quang Tri City occurred during the last week of April. By this time the effect of strain and shock from four weeks of conventional warfare on ill-prepared ARVN troops had taken its toll on unit discipline and effectiveness. Gone were the last remaining shreds of self-assurance and cohesiveness. Units of the 3rd Division fought on without much conviction and were practically left to fend for themselves. The division's sector was shrinking with every passing day.

During this time enemy attacks from the west, near the boundary of Thua Thien Province, cut off QL-1 to the south and interdicted all friendly vehicular traffic over a seven-kilometer stretch. This isolated I Corps forces in Quang Tri Province and completely severed the lifeline which sustained them in combat. The I Corps commander's first reaction to this situation was a series of directives to ARVN logistic units to push supply convoys through the enemy roadblocks. Next the 3rd Division commander was repeatedly ordered to clear QL-1 from the north. These orders compelled General Giai to divert an armored cavalry squadron from its vital frontline role near Quang Tri to conduct operations to the south. Finally the I Corps commander deployed a fresh marine battalion, which was committed to the defense of Hue, to clear QL-1 from the south. These movements severely exhausted fuel and ammunition supplies so critically needed in Quang Tri, but were unsuccessful in reopening this vital lifeline.

The weather was particularly bad on 27 April, and the enemy took advantage of it. Actions on that day signaled the beginning of the NVA push to capture all remaining territory held by ARVN troops in Quang Tri Province. Along the 3rd Division's new defense line—which had shrunk to the immediate vicinity of Quang Tri City to the east, north, and west—units either reported contact with enemy troops or received enemy artillery fire. Throughout the day all forward elements of the division were under fire and engaged by tank-supported enemy infantry. Most units lost some ground but were holding precariously. At the end of the day, most elements of the 1st Armor Brigade were pushed back to within two to three kilometers of QL-1, while enemy artillery fire concentrated heavily on the Quang Tri Combat Base. In response to the 3rd Division commander's declared tactical emergency, US tactical air and B-52 bombers braved adverse weather to stop the enemy advance on Quang Tri.

The next day, 28 April, enemy tanks approached the Quang Tri Bridge, about two kilometers southwest of Quang Tri City, which was the responsibility of the 2nd Regiment. The armored cavalry squadron, which had been sent to reinforce the 2nd Regiment, was holding the bridge, but it was forced to pull back. Elements of the 1st Armor Brigade also experienced setbacks during the day and had withdrawn to within one kilometer north of Quang Tri Combat Base. The brigade commander meanwhile had been wounded and evacuated. With his departure discipline crumbled, and the 1st Armor Brigade troops fled south along QL-1, passing through a roadblock set up by the 147th Marine Brigade.

The 57th Regiment in the meantime had become ineffective. Its commander had no knowledge of the status of his two battalions that had been near Dong Ha city. The only troops he had with him were those of a reconnaissance platoon. Throughout the night men continued to flow south. The only effective unit still defending Quang Tri Combat Base was the 147th Marine Brigade, and it was under heavy and continuous 130mm gun fire.

By 29 April the situation in Quang Tri Province had become critical. The enemy's renewed initiative pointed toward another major effort. On their part, ARVN unit commanders at this time were extremely concerned about fuel and ammunition shortages. Several howitzers had already been destroyed after all available ammunition was expended. The ARVN effort to reopen QL-1 meanwhile progressed at a snail's pace for lack of coordination and positive effort; its outlook was not promising. Quang Tri was kept resupplied by helicopters, which took extreme risks approaching the city, especially by way of QL-1.

In the face of this pending tactical disaster, on 30 April General Giai summoned subordinate commanders to his headquarters and presented his plan to withdraw south of the Thach Han River. Basically the plan consisted of holding Quang Tri City with a marine brigade, establishing a defense line on the southern bank of the Thach Han River with infantry and ranger troops, and releasing enough tank and armored cavalry units for the pressing task of reopening QL-1 to the south. All units were to move during the morning of the next day, 1 May. Informed of General Giai's withdrawal plan, General Lam tacitly concurred, although he never confirmed his approval. Neither did he issue any directives to the 3rd Division commander.

In the morning of 1 May, however, General Lam called the 3rd Division commander and said that he did not approve the withdrawal plan. He issued orders to General Giai to the effect that all units were to remain where they were and hold their positions "at all costs." He also made it clear to General Giai that no withdrawal of any unit would be permitted unless he personally gave the authorization. General Lam's eleventh-hour countermand turned out to be a reiteration of President Thieu's directive, which had just been received from Saigon. This decision was being taken presumably because the Paris peace talks had just been resumed after being boycotted by the RVN delegation since the beginning of the NVA invasion.

It was easy to pick up the telephone and countermand an order. In the field, and under heavy enemy pressure, these conflicting orders inevitably resulted in a nightmare of confusion and chaos. General Giai did not even have sufficient time to countermand his own orders and at the same time impart the new orders to each of his subordinates through a lengthy series of radio calls. Furthermore, all brigade and regimental commanders were not in a position to carry out the new orders. Some of them claimed that their units had already moved to new positions according to plan; others bluntly refused to change a course of action which had already been initiated. General Giai persisted in convincing them to comply with the new instructions received from I Corps. He reiterated the new orders and emphasized that each unit must comply. He also rescinded a previous order to relocate his command post and remained in Quang Tri City.

And so, within the space of four hours, the ARVN dispositions for defense crumbled completely. Those units to the north manning positions around Quang Tri Combat Base streamed across the Thach Han River and continued their way south with the uncontainable force of a flood over a broken dam. The mechanized elements that reached Quang Tri Bridge were unable to cross; the bridge had already been destroyed. They left behind all vehicles and equipment and forded the river toward the south. On the southern bank of the river infantry units did not remain long in their new positions. As soon as they detected ARVN tanks withdrawing south, they deserted their positions and joined the column. But this column did not progress far. Tanks and armored vehicles began to run out of fuel, and, one by one, they were left behind by their crews along QL-1. The only unit that retained full cohesiveness and control during this time was the 147th Marine Brigade, which was defending Quang Tri City. Finally the brigade commander decided for himself that the situation was hopeless, and he too ordered his unit to move out of Quang Tri at 1430 hours, leaving behind the 3rd Division commander and his skeletal staff all alone in the undefended city's old citadel.

Finally, when he learned what was happening, the 3rd Division commander and his staff officers boarded three armored personnel vehicles in an effort to catch up with his own withdrawing column of troops. This occurred while US helicopters came in to rescue the division's advisory personnel and their Vietnamese employees.

The 3rd Division commander's attempt to join his column failed. QL-1 was clogged by refugees and battered troops and all types of vehicles, military and civilian, frantically finding their way into Hue under the most barbarous barrages of enemy interdiction fire. General Giai was forced to return to the old citadel, [where] later he and his small staff were picked up by US helicopters. When the last [HH-3E] Jolly Green Giant lifted off at 1655 hours with the 3rd Division's senior advisor aboard, it was fired upon by enemy small arms. At that time the first NVA troops had already penetrated the

Quang Tri Citadel. Quang Tri City belonged to the enemy; it was the first RVN provincial capital to fall into Communist hands during the war.

On QL-1 the tidal wave of refugees, intermingled with troops, continued to move south. The roadway became a spectacle of incredible destruction. Burning vehicles of all types—trucks, armored vehicles, civilian buses and cars—jammed the highway and forced all traffic off the road, while the frightened mass of humanity was subjected to enemy artillery concentrations. By late afternoon of the next day the carnage was over. Thousands of innocent civilians thus found tragic death on this long stretch of QL-1, which later was dubbed "Terror Boulevard" by the local press. The shock and trauma of this tragedy, like the 1968 massacre in Hue, were to haunt the population of northern MR-1 for a long, long time.

Several ARVN units and the 147th Marine Brigade meanwhile managed to maintain some order in the midst of chaos and fought their way to the vicinity of Hai Lang. The 5th Ranger Group, followed by the 1st and 4th, moved on south to clear an enemy blocking unit. They were joined by the 1st Armor Brigade, which took up night positions four kilometers southwest of Hai Lang. By late evening remnants of the 3rd Division found their way to the vicinity of Camp Evans, where General Giai had arrived. He was attempting to reestablish his headquarters and reorganize his units.

On 2 May the 1st Armor Brigade attempted to move south on QL-1, but came under heavy and continuous artillery fire. These armor forces finally closed on Camp Evans, approximately 25 kilometers south, during the early afternoon. The 147th Marine Brigade meanwhile was also subjected to the same attack, from the direction of Hai Lang, as it moved southward at dawn. With tactical air support and the assistance of some tanks, this brigade during the late afternoon passed through the 369th Marine Brigade defensive positions on QL-1 at the My Chanh River.

The entire province of Quang Tri was now in enemy hands. This provided North Vietnam with the opportunity to accelerate its push into the province of Thua Thien and toward Hue.

III. STABILIZATION AND COUNTEROFFENSIVE

The Defense of Hue

During the month of April, while the 3rd ARVN Infantry Division and its attached units were battling the NVA 304th and 308th Divisions in Quang Tri Province, the 1st ARVN Infantry Division fought back several attempts by the NVA 324B Division to gain control of the western and southwestern approaches to Hue city in Thua Thien Province. Hue city was undoubtedly the prime target of enemy efforts in this area. But the seesaw battles that in fact had begun in early March, then continued throughout the months of April and May without any solid gains from either side, clearly indicated that this was only a secondary front designed to contain the 1st Infantry Division and support the main effort in Quang Tri.

The 1st Infantry Division and territorial forces of Thua Thien Province acquitted themselves admirably in the performance of their tasks. Although their exploits remained on the fringe of the limelight, which was being focused on Quang Tri and An Loc at that time, and seldom mentioned by the press, their valiance and combat effectiveness enabled I Corps to keep the enemy in check on this western flank and maintain overall tactical balance throughout the most critical weeks of the enemy's Easter Offensive. When this offensive was about to enter its second week, and as ARVN reinforcements were being poured into Quang Tri Province to hold Dong Ha and the Cua Viet line, the 1st Division was maintaining a firm line of defense in the foothills area west of Hue. This line extended from Camp Evans in the north, where the 1st Regiment headquarters was located, continued through FSB Rakkasan, then southeast through FSBs Bastogne and Checkmate, and linked up with FSB Birmingham, the command post of the 54th Regiment. The 3rd Regiment was kept in reserve to add depth to the defense. FSB Veghel meanwhile had been evacuated since the outbreak of the invasion.

• • •

The situation around FSB Bastogne and FSB Checkmate became serious during the last two weeks of April. Enemy attacks by fire and ground attacks had increased considerably, and all five defending battalions were down to 50 percent of combat strength. However, as the weather improved, extensive VNAF and US tactical air support kept the positions from being overrun. The enemy in the meantime had brought heavy artillery to the vicinity of Route 547, and these guns presented an increased threat to Hue city.

On 28 April elements of the 29th and 803rd Regiments, NVA 324B Division, attacked FSB Bastogne. Three hours later they overran this firebase, forcing a withdrawal to the east of FSB Birmingham. Consequently FSB Checkmate became vulnerable and was also ordered evacuated during the night. The loss of these bases exposed Hue city to a direct threat of enemy attack.

• • •

With the fall of Quang Tri City and the major part of the province on 1 May, the enemy's pressure naturally shifted toward Hue. On that day he launched a heavy ground attack against FSB King and rocketed Camp Eagle, location of the 1st Division headquarters. By early evening on 2 May FSB Nancy, the last friendly base in Quang Tri Province, was forced to evacuate under heavy pressure after receiving enemy artillery and ground attacks throughout the day. Marine elements had to fall back to south of the My Chanh River, where they established a new defense line guarding the northern approach to Hue city. This was the last withdrawal during the Easter invasion by the forward edge of the I Corps battle area in MR-1.

The first days of May thus found South Vietnam's strategic posture in one of its bleakest periods during the entire war. North of Saigon, An Loc—the provincial capital of Binh Long Province—was under heavy siege. In the highlands of MR-2 the defense of Kontum City was becoming increasingly precarious. In northern MR-1 all of Quang Tri Province now lay in enemy hands; and Bastogne, the strongest bastion covering the western flank of Hue city, had just caved in.

Since the beginning of the offensive, the enemy's pressure in Thua Thien Province had been relatively light. But the fall of Quang Tri Province was a serious psychological blow that deeply affected the morale of troops and the local population. Confidence in the I Corps's ability to defend and hold Hue was shattered, and on 2 May the exodus of panicky refugees toward Danang began to usher in disorder and chaos. In Hue city, throngs of dispirited troops roamed about, haggard, unruly, and craving . . . food. Driven by their basest instincts into mischief and even crime, their presence added to the atmosphere of terror and chaos that reigned throughout the city.

It was amid this confusion and despondency that I was ordered by President Thieu on 3 May to take command of I Corps. I had served in I Corps under General Lam, and the disaster that occurred there was no surprise to me. Neither General Lam nor his staff were competent to maneuver and support large forces in heavy combat. Now this fact was apparent to President Thieu, and, because my corps area was in a stable condition and enjoyed the president's confidence, he selected me to replace General Lam. I had been following events in I Corps since the offensive began and expected to be called upon. I had already selected the staff I would take with me when the president told me of his decision. From my headquarters in IV Corps in Can Tho I flew to Hue that very afternoon with a few staff officers of my own whose abilities and dedication had earned by respect. My arrival in Hue was not unlike the return of a son among the great family of troops and fellow-countrymen of this city whom I had the privilege of serving not very long ago as commanding general, 1st ARVN Infantry Division. I was gratified to discover that the trust they had always vested in me was still lingering. This reassurance was what I needed most in this bleakest hour of history.

On 4 May I immediately set about to restructure command and control. A forward headquarters for I Corps was established at Hue. It was staffed by senior officers who had solid military backgrounds, both in the field and in staff work, a rare assemblage of talents from all three services and service branches. I had wanted to make sure that they knew how to use sensibly and coordinate effectively all corps combat components and supporting units in a conventional warfare environment. I placed particular emphasis on developing an efficient Fire Support Coordination Center (FSCC) which was to streamline the coordinated, effective use of all US and ARVN fire support. A Target Acquisition Element (TAE) was also organized to exploit the tremendous power of the US Air Force and US naval gunfire.

The establishment of I Corps Forward brought about a restoration of confidence among combat units. They all felt reassured that from now on they would be directed, supported, and cared for in a correct manner. The US First Regional Assistance Command (FRAC), under Major General Frederick J. Kroesen and his successor, Major General Howard H. Cooksey, was most cooperative. Both gentlemen honored me with their esteem and friendship, which I highly valued. Together we worked on outstanding problems of common interest with a pervasive spirit of teamwork, openness, and enthusiasm.

On 5 May I initiated a comprehensive plan for the defense of Hue. The plan was simple in its basics; its merit lay in the clear-cut assignment of missions and responsibilities to each I Corps subordinate unit. By that time the only remaining forces capable of effective combat north of the Hai Van Pass were the Marine Division, with its three brigades, and the 1st Infantry Division, of which only two regiments were left (the 54th Regiment had been seriously mauled in the battles for Bastogne). The Marine Division, under its new commander, Colonel Bui The Lan, was responsible for the area north and northwest of Thua Thien Province; its mission was to block all enemy attempts to penetrate Hue.[2] The 1st Infantry Division, still under Major General Phu, was made responsible for the area south and southwest of Hue, defending the approaches from the A Shau Valley.

• • •

My concern at the time was to provide for a defense in depth, to economize force, to create a realistic chain of command, establish strong reserves for each major unit, and integrate the regular and territorial forces, which so far had operated with little coordination, into the corps defense plan. I believed that my concept for operations would respond to all of these immediate requirements.

Following the implementation of this plan, I also initiated a program called "Loi Phong" (Thunder Hurricane) which, in essence, was a sustained offensive by fire conducted on a large scale. The program scheduled the concentrated use of all available kinds of firepower, artillery, tactical air, Arc Light strikes, [and] naval gunfire for each wave of attack, and with enough intensity as to completely destroy every worthwhile target detected, especially those files of enemy personnel and materiel that were streaming toward staging areas near Hue. We hoped that this program would afford us the time required to complete the process of rebuilding and refitting those units which had disintegrated during the month of April.

By 7 May our dispositions for defense in depth were well in place. Each unit, in the forward area as well as in the intermediate echelons, knew exactly what to do. The stabilization of the battlefield had an immediate effect on Hue city. Discipline and order were restored. Stragglers were picked up, placed under control, and rehabilitated. Although the fighting was still raging and the situation far from secure, the population of Hue felt reassured enough to stay in place; even those who had evacuated began to return to the city. Life in the ancient capital began to return to normalcy.

In the meantime, spirited by their recent gains, NVA forces were endeavoring to build up their combat strength and prepare for an all-out drive against Hue. Probing attacks began in all sectors as our intelligence continued to report movements of enemy tanks, artillery, and antiaircraft weapons converging on Hue. Having lost one division in the defense, I Corps required additional forces to meet the next challenge.

At my request, the Joint General Staff began to attach to my command the airborne forces which were being redeployed from other battle areas in MR-2 and MR-3. The first of these, the 2nd Airborne Brigade, arrived in Hue on 8 May and was immediately deployed to reinforce the northern sector at My Chanh, under the operational control of the Marine Division. Soon, in keeping with the increased tempo of enemy activities, the

JGS committed another airborne brigade, the 3rd, to MR-1 on 22 May. I updated my plan of defense as soon as the Airborne Division headquarters arrived and was placed under my control. I assigned it, minus its 1st Brigade but reinforced with the 4th Regiment of the 2nd Division, an area of responsibility northwest of Hue, sandwiched between the 1st Division and the Marine Division. The division's headquarters, under Lieutenant General Du Quoc Dong, was located at Landing Zone (LZ) Sally. Meanwhile, the Marine Division assumed control of the 1st Ranger Group, which had just been reorganized and refitted in Danang.

The rest of the month of May was a period of holding and refitting for I Corps forces. During this time, both the 1st Division and the Marine Division launched a series of limited but spectacular attacks from their forward positions. The Marine Division took the lead with a heliborne assault on 13 May, during which two battalions of the 369th Brigade landed in the Hai Lang area, ten kilometers southeast of Quang Tri City, using helicopters of the 9th US Marine Amphibious Brigade. After landing, the marines swept through their objectives and returned to their defenses at My Chanh. Caught by tactical surprise in his rear area for the first time, the enemy resisted weakly and incurred extremely heavy losses.

To compete with the marines, on 15 May the 1st Infantry Division helilifted troops into Bastogne, caught the enemy off guard, and retook the firebase, while elements of its two regiments cleared the high ground south of the base and FSB Birmingham. A linkup was made the next day, and ten days later FSB Checkmate was back in friendly hands.

News of the reoccupation of these key strongpoints boosted the morale of ARVN troops and deeply moved an exultant populace. Never before had the solidarity between troops and the population in MR-1 been expressed with such effusion and spontaneity. The morale of I Corps troops rose to a high peak, despite the lack of any organized program of motivation.

The fighting abated for about a week after the recapture of FSB Bastogne, then resumed on 21 May, when the enemy struck in force against the marine sector in an attempt to regain the initiative. With a concentrated armor-infantry force, supported by several calibers of artillery, the enemy succeeded initially in breaking through the northeast line of defense. After intense fighting that lasted throughout the next day, the 3rd and 6th Marine Battalions finally drove back the enemy and by nightfall restored their former positions along the My Chanh River. Even while these battles were being fought the Marine Division completed plans for another major assault. In close coordination with the 9th US Marine Amphibious Brigade, naval gunfire and B-52 strikes, and the support of ARVN and marine artillery units, on 24 May the 147th Marine Brigade conducted an amphibious landing at My Thuy (Wunder Beach), ten kilometers north of the defense line, and simultaneously made a heliborne assault into Co Luy, six kilometers west of the coastline. Both elements swept through the enemy-held area and returned to the My Chanh line after several days of operation. This exploit was truly a historic event for the Marine Division, which planned and executed an assault from the sea for the first time.

During the same period the Airborne Division (-), which shared in the responsibility of defending the northwestern approaches to Hue, made it possible for the Marine Division and the 1st Division to become more and more aggressive. By the end of May the 1st Airborne Brigade arrived in Hue, bringing the Airborne Division up to full combat strength. And so, within the space of less than one month, the defense posture of friendly forces in MR-1 had fully stabilized and became even stronger as May drew to its end.

It was quite a change from the bleakest days of early May, when Hue lay agonized amid chaos, terror, and uncertainty. Now there was cause to believe that Hue would hold firm in spite of the enemy's desperate but unsuccessful efforts to break through the marines' line. On 28 May, in front of the stately Midday Gate which opened on the old Imperial Palace at Hue, President Nguyen Van Thieu affirmed this belief when he crowned the Marine Division's successes with a new star pinned on the shoulder of its commander, Colonel Bui The Lan. General Lan solemnly vowed to take back Quang Tri City from the enemy.

Refitting and Retraining

• • •

ARVN casualties and material losses were severe. Several units had deteriorated to such an extent that they needed to be rebuilt from scratch. The 1st Armor Brigade alone had 1,171 casualties and lost 43 M-48s, 66 M-41s, and 103 M-113s. A total of 140 artillery pieces were either lost or destroyed; this meant that about ten ARVN artillery battalions had been stripped of all their equipment. The 3rd Infantry Division had only a skeletal headquarters staff and the remnants of its 2nd and 57th Regiments. All ranger groups suffered about the same casualties, which amounted to over one-half of their former strength.

• • •

Most equipment and material losses were quickly replaced. Among the most critical items were 105mm howitzers, trucks and armored vehicles, individual and crew-served weapons, gas masks, and other supplies such as artillery ammunition, fuses, and Claymore mines. All of these items were rushed to Danang by US C-141 and C-5A aircraft or by surface ships. As a result, during this critical period no combat unit ever ran out of ammunition, although the rates of expenditure had risen dramatically, especially in 105mm and 155mm HE.

To accelerate the retraining process, programs were shortened. . . . Particular emphasis was placed on the use of antitank weapons, especially the TOW missile, the first issue of which arrived on 21 May. Initially, the training for this missile was conducted by Americans from the 196th Infantry Brigade. Eventually, when this brigade returned to the United States, training was continued at the Hoa Cam Training Center in Danang under ARVN instructors.

• • •

General Giai, who no longer had a command, was in Danang on 5 May when he was placed in arrest. Quite unfairly, but fully consistent with the practice in the ARVN,

General Giai was held personally responsible for the defeat of his division. Although I would have been happy to have had General Giai resume command of the reconstituted 3rd Division, I had no choice in the matter. I was barely able to save the name of the division, for I received many calls from the Chief of Staff, General Manh, who told me that President Thieu wanted the 3rd removed from the rolls—it was "bad luck"—and to call the reconstituted division the 27th.

• • •

In general, the refitting and retraining process produced excellent results which, in a certain sense, were comparable to successes being achieved by our combat units defending Hue. The 3rd Division in particular recovered rapidly under the strong leadership of its new commander, Brigadier General Nguyen Duy Hinh. Its return to the combat scene was truly a phenomenal achievement, according to unbiased comments by the RVN and US military authorities.[3]

As the month of June drew to its end, I Corps forces had regained their former combat strength. They were now fully prepared to take on the challenge of driving the enemy from Quang Tri Province.

Quang Tri Retaken

One of the primordial tasks I Corps had to face immediately after the fall of Quang Tri was to regain the initiative. This was my primary concern when I took command. It was not an easy task, given the heavy losses, the deteriorating morale, and the precarious situation prevailing throughout the country at that time. The enemy was experiencing some problems, too. His rapid success in Quang Tri, which he exploited skillfully, had advanced his forces too far ahead of his logistical capabilities. He needed time to resupply in the forward areas, and meanwhile airstrikes against his supply points and lines of communications were slowing this effort.

Stalling the NVA drive in MR-1 was just the first step. To hold back the onrushing tide, our lines of defense had to be consolidated and our forces redeployed and reorganized to exploit their offensive capabilities. Simultaneously, and of equal importance, our troops had to be motivated by strong leadership not only to recoup their morale but also to become aggressive and imbued with an offensive spirit. This was what I began demanding from subordinate commanders, and, as the situation improved, I encouraged them to plan limited offensive operations to keep the enemy off balance. These operations, which were conducted during the months of May and June with a combination of heliborne assaults and amphibious landings, were well executed and achieved excellent results. Their effect on the enemy, coupled with devastating strikes by the US Air Force and Navy, was astounding. Now off balance and on the defensive, enemy forces were more concerned with their safety than the continuation of the offensive, which was stalled. Our limited offensive operations had bought us enough time to prepare for the long-awaited big push northward.

The I Corps offensive campaign, code-named Lam Son 72, was designed primarily to retake Quang Tri Province. It was conceived not as a blitzkrieg but as a coordinated and phased campaign combining the consolidation of the defense of Hue with successive offensive operations from our forward positions at the My Chanh line, first to destroy enemy forces, then to reoccupy Quang Tri City, and finally to restore the provincial government.

• • •

Lam Son 72 was to be initiated on 28 June with a two-pronged attack northward, coordinated with a supporting effort southwest of Hue. The Airborne Division would make the main effort, attacking on the southwest side of QL-1 toward La Vang, while the Marine Division would make the secondary effort along Route 555, moving toward Trieu Phong. The 1st Division, meanwhile, was to pin down enemy forces southwest of Hue. South of [the] Hai Van Pass, in coordination with the northward push, the 3rd Division was to continue ensuring the defense of Danang by conducting economy-of-force operations concurrent with its training and refitting program. In the meantime, the 2nd ARVN Division was to conduct search and destroy operations in Quang Tin and Quang Ngai Provinces.

The plan was submitted simultaneously to Saigon by I Corps headquarters and FRAC about two weeks before D-Day. A day or so later General Cooksey, my senior advisor, told me that MACV had reviewed my plan and suggested that it would be better if I would continue limited spoiling attacks and consider a counteroffensive at a later date. This disturbed me greatly, for my troops were eager to go. I was ready, and it was a good, carefully worked out plan. I decided to present it personally to the president, feeling confident that he would support it. He needed a victory in MR-1 to strengthen his political support.

I flew to Saigon and explained the plan in detail to the president, the prime minister, General Quang (the president's national security deputy), and General Vien. President Thieu listened, then, taking a purple grease pencil, drew an arrow on my map, suggesting a spoiling attack. The prime minister agreed, commenting on the French attack on the "Street without Joy." Discouraged, I folded my map and flew back to Hue.

I worried about this all night, and very early the following morning called General Quang and told him that I would present no more plans to Saigon. If they wanted me to do anything, they should give me a Vietnamese translation of whatever plan they wanted me to execute and I would comply. The president called me about 0900 and told me that he was concerned about my plan, that he felt it was too ambitious, but that he would like me to return to Saigon and show it to him again. This I did the next day, and, after a brief discussion, the president approved the plan.

Lam Son 72 began on 28 June as planned. Both the airborne and marine spearheads made good progress, but slower than we expected. Enemy resistance was moderate during the first few days, except for a few regimental-sized clashes that occurred when our forces crossed the enemy's first line of defense north of the My Chanh River. However, as the enemy fell back and our forces advanced near the Thach Han River, his resistance became heavier.

On 7 July the first airborne elements reached the outskirts of Quang Tri City, where they clashed violently with the enemy defenders. The enemy was determined to hold fast, and his forces were supported by heavy concentrations of artillery and mortar fire. To relieve the pressure on the paratroopers, and also to interdict the enemy's line of communication with the city, along which he continually brought in more troops, I ordered the Marine Division to helilift a battalion two kilometers northeast of the city. This battalion was unable to make any progress, however; it was stopped by enemy infantry and armored elements.

By this time the enemy's determination was all too clear; he planned to hold Quang Tri City to the last man. The enemy's ferocious resistance was such that Quang Tri City suddenly became a "cause célèbre" that attracted emotionally charged comments by public opinion throughout South Vietnam. Although it had not been a primary objective, it had become a symbol and a major challenge. The enemy continued reinforcing; he was determined to go all out for the defense of this city. The ARVN drive was completely stalled.

I Corps's position at this juncture was a difficult one. Pushed by public opinion on one side and faced with the enemy's determination on the other, it was hard-pressed to seek a satisfactory way out. My final assessment was that we could not withdraw again from Quang Tri without admitting total defeat; our only course was to recapture the city. Therefore I directed a switchover of zones and assigned the primary effort to the Marine Division. The offensive then took on a new concept, but the mission remained the same. I concluded that, if the enemy indeed chose to defend Quang Tri City and concentrated his combat forces there, he would give me the opportunity to accomplish my mission employing the superior firepower of our American ally.

• • •

Because of the enemy's determined defense, the recapture of Quang Tri City became a long, strenuous effort which carried into September. By that time, total enemy forces in Quang Tri and Thua Thien Provinces alone reached the incredible proportions of six infantry divisions—the 304th, 308th, 324B, 325th, 320B, and 312th. The 312th Division had been redeployed from Laos and introduced into Quang Tri, along with troop reinforcements for the other divisions. The showdown was inevitable. But the balance of forces was lopsided; the enemy had more than enough strength to contain South Vietnam's three divisions, even though they were our best ones.

• • •

When the offensive campaign entered its tenth week in early September without a decisive outcome in sight, I decided that the delay had been long enough. Enemy forces by that time had been reduced considerably by the volume of firepower delivered by B-52s, tactical air, artillery, and naval gunfire; I was personally convinced that a new major effort by I Corps stood a good chance for success. A victory at this juncture would not only reinforce the RVN's military posture—the enemy had been defeated at An Loc and Kontum—it could also bring about excellent returns in a political sense.

On 8 September, therefore, I Corps launched three separate operations to support its major objective, retaking Quang Tri City. The Airborne Division advanced and occupied three key military installations formerly under ARVN control at La Vang, south of the Quang Tri old citadel. From these positions, the paratroopers were able to provide excellent protection for the southern flank of the marines. The next day the Marine Division initiated the main effort, attacking the old citadel. At the same time, US and RVN forces conducted an "incomplete" amphibious assault on a beach north of the Cua Viet River; the purpose was diversionary. At first the enemy's determined resistance slowed the marines' progress, but elements of the 6th Marine Battalion penetrated one side of the citadel's walls on 14 September. During the following day more marines were injected into the breach and other marine spearheads repeatedly assaulted the eastern and southern faces of the citadel. During the night of 15 September the marines regained control of the citadel. Finally, in the morning of 16 September, the RVN flag was raised on the citadel, amid the cheers of our troops. This was a day of exalting joy for the entire people of South Vietnam.

By late afternoon of the next day the marines had eliminated the last NVA remnants within the citadel and expanded control over the entire city, which was now reduced to heaps of ruin. During the last ten days of fierce assaults on the citadel, 2,767 enemy troops were killed and 43 captured. Marine casualties during this time averaged 150 a day.

After Quang Tri City was retaken, the level of enemy activities throughout northern MR-1 dropped off markedly, especially in the marines' sector. This low activity level continued until 30 September, when the Airborne Division again launched attacks to reoccupy FSB Barbara and FSB Anne. The paratroopers' attacks met with fierce enemy resistance. Their progress was slowed not only by heavy enemy artillery barrages, but also by drenching monsoon rains. As October drew to its end, however, the Airborne Division finally reoccupied FSB Barbara and shifted its effort toward FSB Anne to the north.

• • •

During July FSB Checkmate was subjected to heavy enemy attacks during which it was overrun and retaken several times. Toward the end of the month, FSB Bastogne also came under enemy control. For the first time in five months of hard fighting, and under constant pressure, the 1st Division began to show some signs of weariness. Still it held on to and maintained its line of defense. To help the division regain its vitality and aggressiveness, I decided to reinforce it with the 51st Regiment. Then, in early August, with the strong support of B-52 strikes and US tactical air, the division successively retook Bastogne and Checkmate. During this month, as the enemy gradually lost his initiative, the 1st Division began to launch attacks to enlarge its control toward the west. Taking advantage of its renewed determination, the division even took back Veghel, the remotest fire support base to the southwest, on 19 September. From then on, the NVA 324B Division completely lost its aggressiveness and avoided serious engagements. When October arrived, uninterrupted monsoon rains forced the 1st Division to revert to the defensive. Activities during this time plunged to the lowest level since the beginning of the enemy's Easter Offensive.

From the time I Corps began offensive operations in Quang Tri Province to the end of

July, the three provinces south of the Hai Van Pass were able to maintain reasonable control, despite the low strength of friendly forces. Although sparsely used, B-52 strikes continued to be directed against a number of selected targets. However, as friendly forces in northern MR-1 approached Quang Tri City and were concentrating their efforts on this objective, the enemy suddenly chose to initiate several heavy attacks, especially in the area of the Que Son Valley, against elements of the 2nd ARVN Infantry Division. This move was in all probability intended to alleviate our pressure on Quang Tri.

• • •

In the face of the enemy's mounting pressure, the 2nd Infantry Division, now under Brigadier General Tran Van Nhut, was directed to concentrate its effort on the southernmost province, Quang Ngai, where the threat posed by the NVA 2nd Division was increasing. Meanwhile, the 3rd Infantry Division was assigned the mission to clear the pressure that the NVA 711th Division was exerting in the Que Son Valley, and also to retake the district town of Tien Phuoc in Quang Tin Province. Despite superior enemy forces, both ARVN divisions were determined to fulfill their missions and performed extremely well. The successful operation conducted by the 3rd Division to retake the district town of Tien Phuoc in particular—its first major engagement since its battered withdrawal from Quang Tri not long ago—truly marked its regained status and restored to some extent the popular confidence vested in it.

• • •

Role of US Air and Naval Support

During the entire period of the enemy's Nguyen Hue offensive campaign in MR-1 the support provided by the Vietnamese Air Force and Navy was marginal, although they were employed to the maximum of their limited capabilities. Therefore, when the fighting broke out with great intensity and on such a large scale, ARVN units had to rely mostly on support from US Air Force and naval units. This support was effective and met all of I Corps's requirements.

• • •

As to naval gunfire, its support was modest during the first day of the invasion since only two destroyers . . . were operating offshore MR-1 during late March. When the offensive broke out, however, all naval gunfire ships in the vicinity were immediately dispatched to the area and began providing support for the beleaguered 3rd Division units. The level of naval gunfire support increased with every passing day. At one time during the month of June there were as many as 38 destroyers and three cruisers on the naval gunline. The limited range of their guns, however, still precluded the bombardment of targets located far to the west of QL-1. After the arrival of the heavy cruiser USS *Newport News,* with her 8-inch guns, during May, however, the destructive power and effective range of US naval gunfire increased considerably.

• • •

IV. DEFENDING KONTUM

The NVA Force Buildup

Adjoining the southern boundary of Military Region 1 lay the vast territory of Military Region 2, an area of sprawling high plateaus, rolling hills, and dense jungle commonly called the Central Highlands, which sloped down toward a long, narrow, and curving strip of coastal land to the east. MR-2 was the largest of our four military regions, occupying almost half of South Vietnam's total land area. But it was also the least populated, with approximately three million people, about one-fifth of them Montagnards.

• • •

By early 1972 all US combat units had departed the Central Highlands, but there still remained some logistic units and security forces at Qui Nhon and Cam Ranh bases on the coast. Two South Korean divisions were still deployed in MR-2, one in the An Khe–Qui Nhon area and the other in the Tuy Hoa–Ninh Hoa area. They were, however, in a drawdown status in preparation for redeployment back to Korea.

• • •

Combat responsibilities in MR-2 therefore lay squarely in the hands of ARVN units, just as in other military regions.

• • •

The combat backbone of II Corps consisted of two infantry divisions and one mobile ranger group. Its combat support elements were similar to those of other ARVN corps. The 22nd Infantry Division—with its four regiments, the 40th, 41st, 42nd, and 47th, and under the command of Colonel Le Duc Dat, an armor officer and former province chief—was responsible for the northern part of MR-2. Its efforts were concentrated on two provinces, Kontum in the highlands and Binh Dinh in the lowlands. The 23rd Infantry Division, under the command of Colonel Ly Tong Ba, also an armor officer, was headquartered at Ban Me Thuot, with its three regiments—the 44th, 45th, and 53rd . . . widely deployed over the division's large AO. For the defense of MR-2's long western flank, 11 border ranger battalions were deployed in camps and bases along the border, from Dak Pek and Ben Het in the north to Duc Lap in Quang Duc Province to the south, all under the operational control of II Corps.

II Corps headquarters, under Lieutenant General Ngo Dzu, was located at Pleiku. In addition to its organic forces, II Corps occasionally received reinforcements from the RVNAF general reserve, usually airborne and ranger, when necessary to cope with increased enemy activities.

• • •

Faced with the impending offensive, whose indications had already become too clear, our II Corps command and the Second Regional Assistance Group (SRAG) under Mr. John Paul Vann stepped up air and ARVN border ranger patrols. These reconnaissance activities were concentrated on enemy Base Area 609, which encompassed the tri-border corridor of infiltration and the Plei Trap Valley, some 55 kilometers due west of Kontum City. In late January and early February VNAF and US air cavalry reconnaissance pilots repeatedly uncovered traces of large-scale enemy personnel and materiel movements in the area.

• • •

Intelligence reports on the enemy's buildup, especially on the presence of enemy tanks and artillery, greatly concerned Lieutenant General Ngo Dzu, II Corps commander. He reassessed all information available, and, after consulting with his advisor, Mr. John Paul Vann, whom he highly regarded and respected, General Ngo Dzu initiated a plan and began to redeploy his forces for the defense of the Central Highlands. He moved the 22nd Infantry Division headquarters, one of its regiments (the 47th), and a substantial logistic element of the division from their rear base in Binh Dinh Province to the Tan Canh–Dak To area. There the division co-located its command post with the 42nd Regiment, another divisional unit which had been deployed there for some time.

• • •

The II Corps commander then delineated command and control responsibilities by assigning areas of operation to each of his principal subordinates, a technique similar to that employed in pacification. The 22nd Division commander was given command responsibility over the Dak To area, to include ranger border camps at Ben Het, Dak Mot, Dak Pek, Dak Seang, and Fire Support Bases 5 and 6. The province chief of Kontum was responsible for Kontum City, while the II Corps assistant for operations, Colonel Le Trung Tuong, was to command defense forces in Pleiku. II Corps was thus fully braced for the enemy attack.

• • •

The ominous NVA buildup in MR-2 attracted the attention and concern of our Joint General Staff in Saigon. At II Corps request, therefore, another airborne brigade and the tactical command post of the Airborne Division—the last available reserves in the entire country—were directed to Kontum during the first week of March to assume the responsibility of defending this city and the southern area of the province. As reinforcements poured in, II Corps became more assured of its defense capabilities and initiated additional aggressive search and patrol activities in the suspected area northwest of Kontum as of mid-March.

• • •

Despite the apparent strain on logistic support for ARVN forces in that area, which arose from a single road situation, General Dzu still made plans to deploy the 22nd Division's remaining two regiments from Binh Dinh to Dak To. If this plan were put into effect, Binh Dinh Province, which was another important target being contemplated by the enemy, would be stripped of all ARVN regular forces. Mr. Vann thought this would be most unwise. Anxious to obtain an overall tactical balance for MR-2 in case of concerted enemy attacks, Mr. Vann persuaded General Dzu to keep two regiments in Binh Dinh for the defense of the coastal area and to move the 23rd Infantry Division's AO northward to southern Kontum Province in order to add depth to the defense of Kontum City. This seemed to lessen, but not dispel, General Dzu's excessive worries.

Thus the northern Central Highlands lay poised for the expected enemy attack which was surely to follow Quang Tri–Hue and An Loc. And if the enemy buildup in that area was . . . any indication, this attack would be at least as forceful as those already conducted on the other two fronts.

The Attacks on Tan Canh and Dak To

By the end of the second week of April, contacts with major NVA units had increased markedly, and the area of Tan Canh–Dak To was virtually surrounded by enemy forces. On 14 April Fire Support Base Charlie, at the northern end of Rocket Ridge and ten kilometers southwest of Dak To, was heavily attacked by elements of the NVA 320th Division. In a classic conventional style, the enemy at first pummeled the base with heavy fire from assorted calibers, to include 130mm and 105mm artillery, 75mm recoilless rifle, mortars, and rockets. Then he launched two Korean-type massive assaults against the base, which was defended by an airborne battalion. In spite of vigorous and accurate support by US tactical air and gunships, the enemy's overpowering pressure did not relent and forced the paratroopers to evacuate the base during the night after inflicting serious losses on the enemy forces. A week later, Fire Support Base Delta, at the southern end of Rocket Ridge and also defended by paratroopers, was overrun by enemy armor and infantry after several days of heavy artillery fire.

• • •

The 22nd ARVN Division commander's lack of determination to hold onto the ridgelines in the north and east, which dominated the base area where his command post was located, made the division's defense posture more vulnerable. His defenses had been practically reduced to the main base compound at Tan Canh.

• • •

The 22nd Division's defenses in Tan Canh, while appearing adequate, were in fact becoming precarious, since the northern and eastern flanks had been left uncovered. The remaining fire support bases on Rocket Ridge appeared to be in the solid hands of the airborne brigade and the rangers, but, being located too far south, these bases were more useful to the defense of Kontum City than to Dak To–Tan Canh. In the immediate vicinity of Dak To–Tan Canh, there was only the 47th Regiment at Dak To II, with a tank troop and an airborne battalion in support. The 42nd Regiment was deployed on defensive positions near the compound occupied by the 22nd Division tactical CP in Tan Canh, and, although the 42nd's reputation was one of the worst in the ARVN, its presence there added to the security of the CP. The 42nd had been deployed at Tan Canh for several weeks, and, although Colonel Dat may have felt more secure with a better combat regiment protecting his headquarters, this was not an appropriate time to shift dispositions. Furthermore, it would have seemed illogical to place his least effective regiment farthest from the CP and in a position where it would be likely to be the first hit by the expected offensive. For two weeks enemy artillery fire against the base complex in the Tan Canh–Dak To area had increased most significantly, averaging about 1,000 rounds daily. This fire was accurate, directed from high ground north and east of the Tan Canh compound, and consisted of assorted calibers from 82mm mortars to 130mm guns.

On 23 April the attack began with a strong enemy force consisting of elements of the NVA 2nd Division combined with B-3 Front units, sappers, and tanks. The target was Tan Canh, which was defended by the 42nd Regiment, two batteries of 155mm and 105mm, one M-41 [troop] and one M-113 troop, and a combat engineer company.

During the attack the enemy made extensive use of the wire-guided AT-3 "Sagger" missile, which disabled our tanks and destroyed our bunkers with deadly accuracy. This was the first time our forces were exposed to this weapon, and its use caught them and their US advisors unprepared. One by one the M-41 tanks positioned in defense of the division CP were hit and disabled, along with several bunkers. Then the division tactical operations center took a direct blast at 1030 hours, burned, and had to be partially evacuated. All communications equipment was destroyed by the explosion. Without control and coordination, ARVN forces inside and outside the compound were left to fend for themselves. Morale and confidence had been dealt a devastating blow and rapidly deteriorated.

By noon a makeshift division TOC was established by US advisors at the 42nd Regiment TOC with US signal equipment. This helped the division command group regain some of its composure, but the division commander was visibly distressed. He declined to join the US advisors at the new TOC and remained at his destroyed CP with his deputy, his aide, and some staff officers.

• • •

A few hours before midnight, Dak To district headquarters reported tanks approaching from the west. A Spectre C-130 gunship was dispatched over the area; it located a column of 18 enemy tanks moving toward the district headquarters and engaged them, [but] with little success. At Tan Canh, reports of approaching tanks occasioned a flurry of defense preparations at the 42nd Regiment; a major attack was apparently developing. At about midnight reports indicated that tanks were moving south toward Tan Canh, but no action was taken to stop their advance except for a short engagement by ARVN artillery fire which was rendered ineffective by heavy enemy counterbattery fire. The two bridges on QL-14 leading south toward Tan Canh were left intact.

When enemy tanks and sappers began attacking the 22nd Division CP compound shortly before daybreak, it was already too late for any effective counteraction. After several days enduring heavy enemy artillery fire and taking many casualties, troops of the 42nd Regiment were deeply shocked by the appearance of enemy tanks at the very gate of their compound. They fought in utter disorder, then broke ranks and fled through the defense perimeter.

Realizing that the situation had become hopeless, the division advisory team fought its way through enemy small arms fire and was extracted by an OH-58 helicopter with Mr. Vann aboard. By then the Tan Canh compound had become defenseless, but Colonel Le Duc Dat, the division commander, and his deputy, Colonel Ton That Hung, still remained within the old CP. They and their staff took time to destroy all radio sets and signal SOIs. In the afternoon, it began raining hard, and they all took advantage of the rain to slip out. Since then, no one has ever learned with certainty what happened to

Colonel Dat and his staff; they were presumably all dead. Only his deputy, Colonel Hung, managed to survive and reached Kontum several days later.[4]

• • •

Without any hope for holding out successfully, the 47th Regimental headquarters and defending troops left the area in isolated groups. Subsequently ARVN resistance faded away and the Tan Canh–Dak To area fell into enemy hands. During the next two days NVA forces consolidated their gains and evacuated the 30 artillery pieces left behind by ARVN troops. They extended their control west of Dak To II and south to Dien Binh on QL-14.

In the meantime the NVA 320th Division continued its pressure on the remaining fire support bases on Rocket Ridge. On 25 April the II Corps commander decided to evacuate FSBs Nos. 5 and 6 because of their untenable positions. With this last protective screen finally removed, the entire area west of the Krong Poko River was abandoned to the enemy and Kontum City lay exposed to direct enemy attacks.

• • •

While the enemy was gaining ground in the Central Highlands and preparing to push toward Kontum, in the coastal lowlands of Binh Dinh Province the NVA 3rd Division and VC local forces cut off QL-1 at Bong Son Pass and attacked the three isolated northern districts—Hoai An, Hoai Nhon, and Tam Quan. This forced the 40th and 41st Regiments of the 22nd ARVN Division to abandon their two major bases, Landing Zones English and Bong Son, and other strong points in the area. Enemy attacks then spread out rapidly northward along QL-1 and southwestward along the Kim Son River, engulfing the district towns of Tam Quan and Hoai An in the process. In the face of the enemy's momentum, all defenses in the area crumbled rapidly.

With [the] loss of Binh Dinh's three northern districts, the narrow coastal lowland of South Vietnam was practically cut in two, and, if the enemy succeeded in taking Kontum City, then the defense posture of the country would look bleak indeed. Therefore all attention now turned toward the Central Highlands, where Kontum City was bracing itself for the inevitable NVA push.

In spite of the strong support of US tactical air and B-52s, many ARVN commanders believed that Kontum could not hold. Lieutenant General Ngo Dzu was one of them. Distressed and demoralized by the loss of Tan Canh–Dak To, he felt remorseful about his refusal to reinforce Colonel Dat with the 22nd Division's remaining two regiments. Had not Colonel Dat offered to resign his command the day before the attack, just because he felt that he had not received adequate support?

General Dzu was doubtful that his remaining forces could contain the NVA multidivision push. He believed that Kontum City and even Pleiku, the seat of his own headquarters, would eventually turn into blazing infernos under the enemy's artillery and finally meet with the same fate as Tan Canh and Dak To. He thought of what had happened to Colonel Dat and he feared for himself. Tense, exhausted, and unable to pull himself together, he spent his time calling President Thieu on the telephone day and night, begging for instructions even on the most trivial things. The big challenge had not come, but the pressure had taken its toll.

To the JGS and President Thieu, General Dzu no longer functioned as a field commander capable of self-asserting command and control. He was finally replaced on 10 May by Major General Nguyen Van Toan, ARVN armor commander, who was also serving as assistant commander for operations, I Corps.

Pressure on Kontum City

During the days that followed the 22nd [ARVN] Division's debacle in Tan Canh, the enemy gradually moved his forces to the southeast toward Kontum City. The pressure he exerted on that city from the north was growing with every passing day. South of the city, the short stretch of QL-14 which connected it with Pleiku was also interdicted by solid enemy road blocks in the Chu Pao area, and every effort to neutralize these blocks only added more casualties to ARVN forces. Kontum was thus isolated and surrounded. The final enemy push to take the city would surely occur as soon as he had built up enough supplies and combat forces in staging areas.

With battles raging in other places throughout the country, reinforcing Kontum City was becoming difficult. It was almost impossible now that all general reserves had been fully committed, here and elsewhere. Under such circumstances, obviously II Corps had to rely on the forces it presently controlled for the defense of Kontum. To meet the challenge, on 28 April the 23rd ARVN Division headquarters was moved approximately 160 kilometers from Ban Me Thuot to Kontum City to command all ARVN forces in the area and reorganize them for defense. Security of southern MR-2 became solely the responsibility of the territorial forces.

• • •

The 53rd Regiment of the 23rd ARVN Division was responsible for the defense of the city itself. Time was pressing, and, to gain enough time for the disposition of defense forces, the 2nd and 6th Ranger Groups were given the mission to delay the enemy on QL-14 north of Kontum. In the meantime, B-52 strikes and tactical air were unleashed on enemy troop concentrations, particularly on the abandoned firebases along Rocket Ridge.

The defense plan appeared to be sound and well conceived, but there was still a problem of command and control. Colonel Ly Tong Ba, the 23rd Division commander and defender of Kontum, was faced with difficulties in his exercise of operational control over various elements and units whose effectiveness had been adversely affected by the debacle at Tan Canh. Molding them into a cohesive defense force required more than his leadership could provide. For one thing, he commanded only one regiment, the 53rd. Other units—such as the ranger groups, the airborne brigade, and territorial forces—although placed under his operational control, tended to maintain their own command channels with parent units.

Colonel Ba's predicament was not unlike what General Giai of the 3rd ARVN Division had faced in MR-1, though to a lesser extent. However, as far as the ARVN was concerned, here or elsewhere, operational control had proved difficult to exercise unless the field commander clearly outranked his subordinates or had an established reputation which commanded respect and submission. Colonel Ba apparently enjoyed neither.[5]

• • •

On 1 May the ranger battalions at Vo Dinh came under attack and were ordered to withdraw by the group commander. The ARVN defense line was thus moved back several kilometers to Ngo Trang, just 13 kilometers northwest of Kontum City.

This setback exposed the weakness of the command structure in Kontum. If this city was to hold, Colonel Ba's control would have to be strengthened. At the suggestion of Mr. John Paul Vann, General Toan agreed in early May to bring in the remaining units of the 23rd ARVN Division, the 44th and 45th Regiments, to replace the 2nd and 6th Ranger Groups, respectively. This helped enhance not only Colonel Ba's command, but also the overall effectiveness of the city's defense. Remnant forces of the 22nd ARVN Division, meanwhile, were sent back to their rear bases in Binh Dinh Province for regrouping and refitting.

• • •

Other ARVN positions of the 45th Regiment, now assigned to delay the enemy on QL-14 north of Kontum, also felt the mounting enemy pressure and gradually withdrew toward the city. At the same time, daily air reconnaissance missions reported new pioneer roads and new supply storage areas in the vicinity of Vo Dinh. Prisoners also confirmed on 10 May that the NVA 320th Division was moving into assembly areas north of the city.

• • •

The First Attack against Kontum

By the end of the second week in May the deployment of the 23rd Division's units into positions in and around the city, and their disposition for defense, was completed. This disposition was essentially a perimeter defense, with infantry and armor units blocking approaches from the north and northwest and territorial forces securing the southern and southeastern approaches, facing the Dak Bla River. The 44th Regiment was astride QL-14, about four kilometers northwest of Kontum, while the 45th Regiment defended the northern side of the city and the 53rd, on the northeastern side, protected Kontum airfield.

In spite of this display of force, these defending units did not look impressive. Untried, their combat capabilities were very similar to those of the 22nd Division. The 23rd Division had yet to show that it was superior to its vanquished sister. But the division commander seemed to make a big difference. He personally inspected the defense perimeter with his staff, encouraged and provided guidance for his troops on tactical details, and showed great care for them. The defense, fire support, and counterattack plans were coordinated and rehearsed daily, drawing on the painful lessons learned at Tan Canh. All units were given the opportunity to practice-fire the LAW antitank rocket until their troops became confident that enemy tanks were not as formidable as they had thought. More importantly, Colonel Ba's daily round of visits to his units greatly inspired his subordinates and instilled self-assurance among the troops.

In the early morning of 14 May the enemy's attack on Kontum began. The defending forces had been alerted since midnight, and they stood ready. ARVN and US military intelligence, in the meantime, had been able to detect every enemy movement and even knew the precise time of the attack. Therefore, as the NVA troop and tank columns moved down QL-14 toward Kontum, US Cobra gunships, some of them armed with the new TOW missile, were already airborne from Pleiku. Unlike [with] the attack on Tan Canh, the enemy did not precede his advance with heavy artillery preparations, except on FSB November.

A total of five enemy regiments converged on the city. . . . Despite its force, the initial attack was quickly broken up after several lead tanks fell easy prey to our artillery, LAW [rockets], and TOW missiles.

Kontum City continued to receive sporadic artillery and rocket fire and ground probes during the day. The reactions of friendly forces had been quick, decisive, and successful, and the support of tactical air and gunships most effective. ARVN armored elements, although at greatly reduced strength and held in reserve, had quickly maneuvered to fill in gaps in the defense perimeter. It seemed that the enemy would have a much more difficult time at Kontum than at Tan Canh just three weeks earlier.

As night approached, however, the enemy renewed his attacks with greater force against the 44th and 53rd Regiments. Due to the confusion of night fighting, which precluded effective coordination, an enemy battalion succeeded in breaking through a gap between the two regiments. This situation became critical when this enemy unit enlarged the gap and exploited its gains with successive waves of mass assaults. Even our concentrated artillery fire failed to stop the assaults, and it looked as if the defense would soon meet with disaster. As the situation was becoming more precarious by the minute, Colonel Ba and his advisors worked feverishly on countermeasures.

The only way to turn back the large and growing penetration seemed to be B-52 strikes, two of which had been preplanned for the night. Safety required, however, that ARVN forces be pulled back one hour before the strikes. To fill this gap in time, increased and sustained artillery fire would be necessary. Both ARVN regiments were instructed to hold in place and move back on order. This was a bold and risky move, but there seemed to be no other alternative to save Kontum from falling before dawn.

The two B-52 strikes came exactly on time, as planned, like thunderbolts unleashed over the masses of enemy troops. The explosions rocked the small city and seemed to cave in the rib cages of ARVN troops not far away. As the roar subsided, a dreadful silence fell over the scene. At dawn, ARVN search elements discovered several hundred enemy bodies, with their weapons scattered all around. Kontum was saved.

Success in this first contest gave the defenders of Kontum added confidence. They believed that enemy forces were no match for the devastating firepower of the South Vietnamese and American planes and tanks. They had seen for themselves how the NVA human wave assault was shattered by B-52 strikes. But it also dawned on ARVN commanders that their first success had really been a close shave and that Kontum might well have been in serious jeopardy had it not been for the two B-52 strikes.

In a postmortem examination of the results, Colonel Ba realized that there existed several weaknesses in his defenses. His units had been stretched too thin over the defense perimeter, leaving gaps between them and making coordination difficult at limiting points. His staff had functioned well under stress, but needed improvement, particularly in the coordination of firepower. So he set about tightening the defense by reducing the perimeter. He added some depth by moving the 44th Regiment back into reserve position and replacing it with the 45th.

The new II Corps commander, General Toan, and his advisor, Mr. John Paul Vann, made a visit to Kontum City on 16 May. They reviewed the situation with Colonel Ba and approved his new disposition for defense. They also realized that, despite his [reversal], the enemy still possessed strong capabilities and . . . would surely launch another major attack in the next few days, perhaps with greater intensity.

• • •

By the end of the week following the first attack, all efforts by NVA forces to seize Kontum city had been defeated. Several times during this period the enemy succeeded in breaking through our defense perimeter by violent assaults against positions held by the 44th and 53rd Regiments and penetrating between the 53rd and 45th Regiments. The dent made [in] the sector of the 53rd Regiment on 20 May was particularly serious and had warranted the commitment of M-41 tanks held by the division in reserve.

Colonel Ba proved especially skillful in the maneuver of tanks, his own specialty for many years. His presence on the sites of battle also inspired his troops and helped them drive the enemy back. Elsewhere the accuracy of ARVN artillery fire, and the effectiveness of US Cobra gunships [and] B-52s, and VNAF Spooky gunships, were instrumental in repulsing enemy assaults and penetrations. These successes enabled the restoration of the Kontum airfield to normal operation and the resupply of ammunition and fuel by US C-130s.

• • •

From Pleiku, in the meantime, General Toan launched a major effort on 21 May to clear QL-14 north to Kontum. This vital supply road had been interdicted at Chu Pao Pass for several weeks by the NVA 95B Regiment. The II Corps relief task force consisted of the 2nd and 6th Ranger Groups, augmented by armored cavalry and combat engineer elements. Despite the vigorous support of tactical air and artillery firepower, to include B-52 strikes and the use of CBU-55 bombs, the attack was slowed by multiple enemy blocking positions on both sides of the highway and finally stopped by a system of strongpoints entrenched on the rocky southern slope of the Chu Pao Mountain. Coordinated with the ferocious fire of concentrated artillery, this ring of enemy blocks inflicted serious losses and . . . continued to prevent road supply from Pleiku.

• • •

In spite of the modest results achieved through its offensive efforts, II Corps had effectively upset the enemy's timetable for a last-ditch attempt to take Kontum. More importantly, II Corps had maintained the initiative and morale of its frontline troops, both of which were most critically needed as the first signs of combat weariness began to show.

The Enemy's Final Attempt

After ten days of preparing his forces, the enemy resumed his attack on Kontum on 25 May. As the 23rd Division commander had accurately predicted, this attack had all the intensity of a decisive, make-or-break effort. It had become imperative for the enemy to either achieve a quick victory or . . . withdraw his forces altogether for refitting. The drenching monsoon was setting in over the Central Highlands, and its first effects had begun to be felt in the Kontum-Pleiku area. Even if he had the resources for replacements, a drawn-out campaign at this time could only spell disaster.

The attack began shortly after midnight with artillery fire pounding all the units of the 23rd Division in the Kontum area. The firing concentrated particularly on positions near the airfield and south of the city. At 0300 hours two enemy sapper battalions, with the assistance of elements already in place, began to infiltrate the southeastern positions held by territorial forces. They moved into an area near the airfield [and] occupied a schoolhouse, the Catholic seminary, and the Kontum diocesan office building. From the north and northeast, enemy infantry and tanks swarmed down and penetrated the city. Throughout the morning, and into early afternoon, the division CP and artillery emplacements received continuous incoming artillery and mortar fire.

By late afternoon the enemy still held the areas within his penetration. The enemy's ferocious artillery fires during the day took a heavy toll. Among the artillery firing into the city were the 155mm and 105mm howitzers captured at Tan Canh. This fire was not only intense, but it was also devastatingly accurate, and it neutralized or destroyed a great number of our artillery pieces. The situation became so bleak that a tactical emergency was declared in order to divert all available tactical air and gunships to the area for the day.

During the next day, 26 May, enemy indirect fire increased and a coordinated attack by enemy tanks and infantry pressed against the 53rd Regiment from the north. Pressure also mounted against territorial forces south of the city. With the support of Cobra gunships, a task force of one battalion of the 44th Regiment and eight tanks counterattacked and successfully contained an enemy penetration between the 45th and 53rd Regiments. Still the enemy could not be ejected from the positions he already held. The situation remained stable for the day, however.

Meanwhile, supply shortages had become critical, since the airfield was closed to fixed-wing aircraft, and the city's soccer field was used to accommodate CH-47 Chinooks hauling in emergency supplies and evacuating the seriously wounded. . . .

At nightfall the NVA 64th Regiment attacked again, penetrating between the 53rd and 45th Regiments and concentrating its effort against the latter. Again B-52 strikes, diverted from scheduled missions, fell on the forces attacking the 45th and helped blunt the attack.

In the early morning of the following day, 27 May, the enemy made a surprise thrust with two regiments and one tank company against the 44th Regiment, held in reserve in the city's hospital complex. Fierce fighting ensued in and around this area, resulting in a melee between enemy infantry and T-54 tanks on one side and ARVN troops and TOW missiles and ARVN LAW rockets. By late morning the enemy advance had been halted, but NVA infantry still held the northernmost compound and continued to harass the airfield.

From these and other positions across the northern part of the city the enemy fanned out and formed pockets of resistance, particularly in areas where friendly use of fire was limited. Despite all the efforts of ARVN troops and the firepower of US tactical air and gunships, and even the commitment of ARVN tanks held in reserve, it was difficult to dislodge the enemy from his positions. He seemed determined to dig in and exploit this foothold in the city.

To prevent further penetrations and consolidate his defense, Colonel Ba decided, with the approval of the II Corps commander, to tighten the perimeter again. He moved the 45th Regiment back from FSB November and positioned it on the reduced defense perimeter. This not only helped strengthen his defenses, but also allowed for better use of B-52 strikes in close support.

By the night of the 28th the situation remained critical. NVA forces were still entrenched in the hospital's northern compound, and territorial forces were being engaged in house-to-house fighting in the southern area of the city, where the enemy still held a school and a few houses near the airfield. By this time, however, the enemy began to run into difficulties in resupply. Hourly B-52 strikes had forced him to store supplies at great distances from the city, and his transportation and communication lines were being disrupted by continuous airstrikes. The critical situation in the city also made friendly resupply and medical evacuation increasingly difficult, but airdrops and CH-47 Chinooks from Pleiku nearby responded adequately to emergency requirements.

The attrition caused by airstrikes and gunships finally allowed ARVN forces to counterattack and regain the initiative. To dislodge the enemy, they had to fight from bunker to bunker, using hand grenades. Shortly before noon on 30 May they regained control of the entire hospital complex, and, although there still remained other scattered pockets of resistance in the northeastern area, the city was clearly out of danger.

In the afternoon, President Thieu flew into Kontum City, despite sporadic rocket and mortar fire. He praised the endurance and fighting spirit of all forces defending the city and, right there, with the battlefield still rumbling, he pinned the brigadier general star on Colonel Ly Tong Ba, the defender of Kontum, for "special frontline merits."

Slowly but surely, during the remainder of the day, all positions held by the enemy were taken back. By midday on 31 May the battle was practically over; the NVA main forces had withdrawn. Thousands of NVA bodies lay scattered all over the battlefield, with dozens of T-54 tanks—some intact, but most reduced to charred hulks—awkwardly perched among the ruins. The enemy's final attempt to take Kontum had ended in utter defeat.

By 10 June the last vestige of enemy resistance in the city had disappeared. But, ironically enough, the man who had contributed so much to the ARVN success in Kontum—Mr. John Paul Vann—did not live long enough to savor the fruits of his labor on this day. A strikingly strong, though controversial, personality, Mr. Vann was the personification of courage, selflessness, and dedication. At Tan Canh, he personally directed, at extreme risks to his own life, the extraction of the 22nd Division advisory team. His helicopter crashed at Dak To II, but he continued his rescue mission undaunted.

During the battles for Kontum, he saved the beleaguered city at least twice by making bold decisions on the use of B-52s. He goaded ARVN commanders on the battleline into action and shuttled almost daily, day and night, in and out of the battle area, with complete disregard for his own safety, to make sure that US support for the defense was adequate. On one of his flights into Kontum City, the night before ARVN regained complete control, his helicopter crashed and he was killed. His replacement as chief of SRAG, now redesignated a command, was Brigadier General Michael D. Healy.

• • •

In the coastal lowlands of Binh Dinh Province, the 22nd ARVN Division slowly regained its combat effectiveness after reorganization and refitting. In late July, in cooperation with territorial forces of the province, the division, now under Brigadier General Phan Dinh Niem, retook Hoai Nhon and Tam Quan district towns and reestablished communications on QL-1 north to the southern boundary of Quang Ngai Province. This accomplishment received little public notice, but in terms of psychological, political, and military impact it equalled other ARVN successes such as the reoccupation of Quang Tri and the defense of Kontum.

V. THE SIEGE OF AN LOC

The Enemy's Offensive Plan in MR-3

• • •

Little attention was being devoted to Military Region 3, . . . although there was always the possibility of [an] enemy offensive against Tay Ninh Province and perhaps Saigon itself. The enemy's disposition and capabilities along the entire western flank of South Vietnam, with his easy access to and from sanctuaries in neighboring Laos and Cambodia, made the problem of deducing the enemy's main effort all the more difficult. His advantage was such that the initial success of any thrust could quickly be reinforced and turned into the main effort; if not, it would serve some tactical purpose in support of other attacks. This flexibility was most likely what he had in mind when the southern arm of his Easter invasion struck Loc Ninh on 2 April.

• • •

The field forces of III Corps consisted of three ARVN infantry divisions—the 5th, 18th, and 25th, and three ranger groups—the 3rd, 5th, and 6th. The 25th Division was assigned an area of operation encompassing the provinces of Tay Ninh, Hau Nghia, and Long An, but the division headquarters and its three subordinate infantry regiments were usually located and operated in Tay Ninh Province. The 5th Division was responsible for the area of operation covering Phuoc Long, Binh Long, and Binh Duong Provinces. Its headquarters was located at Lai Khe in Binh Duong Province. The 18th Division's area of operation extended over the provinces of Bien Hoa, Long Khanh, Phuoc Tuy, and Binh Tuy. It was headquartered at Xuan Loc, the provincial capital of Long Khanh.

• • •

During the period from January to March 1972, ARVN intelligence reported the presence of the NVA 5th Division in Base Area 712, near the Cambodian town of Snoul, about 30 kilometers northwest of Loc Ninh on QL-13. The other two enemy divisions, the 7th and 9th, were located in the Cambodian rubber plantation areas of Dambe and Chup, which were two of III Corps's operational objectives planned for the third quarter of 1971, plans which were suspended after the accidental death of Lieutenant General Do Cao Tri, III Corps commander. General Tri's successor, Lieutenant [General] Nguyen Van Minh, advocated a strategy of standoff defense at the border instead of deep incursions into enemy base areas in Cambodia.

During this period, the ARVN commanders of III and IV Corps had independent authority to conduct operations deep into Cambodia, so long as they coordinated with their counterpart military region commanders in the Cambodian Army. They of course informed Saigon of their plans, but Saigon exercised practically no influence on the strategy each corps commander decided to adopt.

• • •

The training of enemy troops for urban warfare was most significant, because this training had been discontinued since 1969 in the aftermath of the Tet Offensive. Not until late 1971 was this type of training known to be resumed for a few enemy main-force units. . . . Thus this document concerning the 9th NVA Division shed the first light on the enemy's plan of attack in MR-3. The target was to be Binh Long, not Tay Ninh as predicted by ARVN intelligence estimates which, based on data collected up to the time the document was seized, had given weight to the enemy's keen interest in Tay Ninh as the future capital for the PRG. . . .

In spite of these revealing pieces of information, III Corps headquarters still did not focus adequate attention on Binh Long, partly because the enemy had never shown great interest in this province.

• • •

The enemy's offensive in MR-3 began in the early morning of 2 April when his 24th Regiment (Separate), with the support of tanks, attacked Fire Support Base Lac Long, located near the Cambodian border 35 kilometers northwest of Tay Ninh City. This base was defended by one battalion of the 49th Regiment, 25th Division. The enemy's commitment of tanks contributed to the rapid collapse of this base, which was overrun by midday.

The rapid loss of FSB Lac Long prompted III Corps to make a quick decision to evacuate all advance outposts located along the Cambodian border. Since these small, remote outposts were difficult to hold against NVA main forces, it was better to consolidate ARVN defenses deeper inside MR-3 in order to avoid losses in personnel and weapons. In rapid succession all forces defending the border outposts, with the exception of one ranger battalion at Tong Le Chon, were ordered to fall back and establish a defense belt around Tay Ninh City. At the request of the battalion commander, who felt certain that his unit would become easy prey for an enemy ambush if it withdrew, III Corps consented to maintaining this border camp.[6]

• • •

Although the details of the enemy's plan did not become known until after the battle was joined in Binh Long and battlefield intelligence began to accumulate, filling in the gaps, COSVN would commit three divisions and two separate regiments, all with armor reinforcements, to the Binh Long campaign. The first phase was the diversion in Tay Ninh, employing the 24th and 271st COSVN Regiments. The second phase would be the attack on Loc Ninh by the 5th NVA Division. The elite 9th NVA Division would then attack and seize An Loc, which would be turned into the capital for the PRG in South Vietnam. The NVA 7th Division, meanwhile, would block south of An Loc and prevent reinforcements from reaching An Loc. After seizing Loc Ninh, the 5th Division would march to Tay Ninh, isolate the city, and destroy the forces of the ARVN 25th Division defending it.

The Attack on Loc Ninh

The attack on Loc Ninh began with an ambush on QL-13, five kilometers north of the town, on 4 April. Ordered to fall back from the border to reinforce the defense of Loc Ninh, an ARVN armored cavalry squadron (-), attached to the 9th Regiment of the ARVN 5th Division, was ambushed by an infantry regiment of the NVA 5th Division. Very few ARVN survivors managed to reach the district town. Early the next morning the district defense forces reported hearing enemy armor on the move. A few hours later the enemy began to shell heavily, then attacked the Loc Ninh subsector headquarters and the rear base of the ARVN 9th Regiment located in the town.

The defenders resisted fiercely and employed the effective support of US tactical air, which was directed onto enemy targets by the US district advisors. By late afternoon the enemy's attempt to capture the Loc Ninh airstrip was defeated by CBU bombs of the air force. During the early hours of the next morning, 6 April, the enemy attacked again, this time with the addition of an armor battalion estimated at between 25 and 30 tanks. Despite direct fire by ARVN artillery to stop the advancing tanks, Loc Ninh was overrun a few hours later.

• • •

The 52nd Task Force was ordered to fall back by road to An Loc to reinforce its defenses, but it was intercepted and attacked at the same road junction. After incurring heavy losses, the 52nd Task Force withdrew into the jungle and, by using alternate routes, finally reached An Loc. Although disorganized and battered, the task force contributed additional personnel critically needed at that time for the defense.

The Siege and First Attacks

Only after the enemy's attack on Loc Ninh had been initiated was the III Corps commander, General Minh, fully convinced that An Loc city would be the primary objective of the enemy offensive. He also realized that if An Loc were overrun, Saigon would be threatened, because only two major obstacles would remain on QL-13 north of Chon Thanh and Lai Khe. Therefore An Loc was to be reinforced at once and held at all costs.

General Minh acted rapidly. The 5th Division headquarters, with Brigadier General Le Van Hung in command, and two battalions of the 3rd Ranger Group were helilifted into An Loc. This movement was completed without difficulties on 5 April, but by this time III Corps no longer had a reserve.

During a meeting on 6 April at the Independence Palace in Saigon to review the military situation throughout the country, General Minh pleaded his case for more troops for the defense of An Loc. His request was overruled by considerations given to the seriousness of the NVA attacks in MR-1 and the enemy's ominous buildup in MR-2. Most of the JGS general reserve forces had already been committed to these regions. The only alternative left to provide reinforcements for III Corps was to assign to it the remaining airborne brigade and an infantry division which could be redeployed from MR-4. The question arose during the meeting as to which of these units would be most appropriate for III Corps.

At this meeting, attended by all corps commanders, Generals Quang and Vien, as well as the president and prime minister, the requirements of each corps for reinforcements were discussed. When it was suggested that the 21st Division be deployed to reinforce I Corps, General Quang argued that the situation at An Loc was potentially even more serious than the problem in Quang Tri. If the NVA succeeded in establishing a PRG capital at An Loc, the psychological and political damage would be intolerable for the GVN. The president agreed, and the subject of which IV Corps division would reinforce III Corps was discussed. Consideration was first given to using the 9th Division, but as IV Corps commander at the time I suggested the 21st Division for two reasons.[7] First, the 21st Division was conducting successful search and destroy operations in the U Minh Forest, and it was particularly effective in mobile operations. Second, the 21st Division had once been commanded by General Minh; placing it under his control again would not only facilitate employment and control by III Corps, but also bring out the best performance from the division.

On 7 April the 1st Airborne Brigade was ordered to move by road from Lai Khe to Chon Thanh. From there it was to conduct operations northward to clear QL-13 up to An Loc and keep this vital supply line open. When reaching a point only six kilometers north of Chon Thanh, still 15 kilometers short of An Loc, the brigade's advance was stopped by a regiment of the 7th NVA Division in solid blocking positions entrenched in the Tau O area. The enemy was determined to dominate this road and interdict every attempt to reinforce or supply An Loc.

After taking Loc Ninh, the NVA 5th Division began moving south toward An Loc.

Beginning on 7 April, the local population living in the vicinity and workers in rubber plantations nearby reported the presence of NVA regular troops. Very rapidly all food items in local markets around An Loc, especially canned or dried food, began to disappear from display counters. Intelligence reports indicated that the enemy's rear services had preempted these food items to keep the combat units supplied while moving toward the next battlefield.

The city itself was not yet under attack, but the Quan Loi airstrip, three kilometers east, came under fire and infantry assaults during the evening of 7 April. The fierceness of this attack was such that two ARVN companies which defended the airstrip were ordered to destroy their two 105mm howitzers and fall back to the city. Two days later they arrived at the edge of An Loc.

The loss of the Quan Loi airfield edged An Loc into complete isolation, because both air and ground communication with the city had now been cut off. The high ground in the Quan Loi area, which dominated the city from the east, also offered the enemy good artillery emplacements and observation from which he could pound targets in the city with deadly accuracy.

• • •

By 7 April, An Loc was entirely encircled and without a fixed-wing airstrip. Between 7 and 12 April all supply missions were flown by VNAF helicopters and C-123s. The use of helicopters ended on the 12th when a VNAF CH-47 was shot down by anti-aircraft fire. From then until 19 April all supplies were dropped by the C-123s. To achieve accuracy, they had to fly at very low altitudes over the drop zone. On the fortieth such sortie a C-123 was shot down.

In the meantime, reinforced by the 21st ARVN Division under the command of Major General Nguyen Vinh Nghi, III Corps was able to deploy the 8th Regiment, 5th ARVN Division, with its two battalions to augment the defense of An Loc. Movement of this 8th Regiment was completed during 11 and 12 April, all by helicopter. The defending force in the city by this time numbered nearly 3,000 men, including RF and PF troops. Chinook CH-47 helicopters were used extensively to move in more supplies and evacuate the wounded and refugees.

Within the city, the situation became more tense by the hour. ARVN patrols outside the perimeter reported increased and heavy contacts with the enemy in the northeast and southeast. Refugees pouring into the city reported sightings of enemy tanks and artillery. All indications for a large attack on An Loc seemed to have finally fallen into place by nightfall of 12 April.

During the early hours of 13 April the enemy began to shell the city heavily. Then, shortly after daylight, units manning positions northwest of the city reported several enemy tanks and vehicles moving toward the city. An AC-130 Spectre gunship on station engaged the enemy and destroyed one tank and four vehicles. Simultaneously several other tanks were reported on the northern side of the perimeter. By 0600 hours the first major attack had begun against positions held by the 7th Regiment on the west. The main effort seemed to be developing from the north, however, spearheaded by armored vehicles. Overwhelmed by superior enemy forces, the ARVN defenders on this side quickly fell back.

A remarkable highlight during the first few hours of fighting was the effective use of the M-72 LAW rocket. In fact, the first tank killed by the ARVN defenders during the enemy attack on An Loc was scored by an RF soldier. Word of this feat spread rapidly among ARVN troops and their confidence was greatly enhanced. It was as if in just a matter of minutes the long-established fear of enemy tanks had suddenly disappeared.

By this time several enemy tanks had breached the defense and penetrated well into the city, but they remained isolated and no accompanying enemy infantry was in sight. One T-54 tank in particular rolled aimlessly through the city, from north to south, before it was destroyed by M-72 fire. Finally four enemy tanks were knocked out and another one surrendered after its crew ran out of ammunition. Taken prisoner, one of the crew members declared he belonged to the 1st Battalion, 203rd NVA Tank Regiment. His unit had moved from North Vietnam through lower Laos and then took shelter in Cambodia. His unit was ordered only the day before to move into Binh Long Province from the border and participate in the An Loc battle.

The III Corps commander appeared to be surprised by the presence of enemy tanks in Binh Long. He seemed to blame ARVN intelligence unduly for that surprise. However, in fact as early as October 1971 ARVN intelligence reports had indicated the presence of enemy armor in the areas of Kratie, Dambe, and Chup on Cambodia[n] territory. . . .

The enemy probably considered the commitment of his tanks in MR-3 to be the key to success. He was certain that he could take Binh Long in five or ten days. . . . To ensure success, and because neither the 9th NVA Division nor its regimental or unit commanders had any experience with combined arms tactics, COSVN decided that COSVN Military Command would directly control the tank units. The results were disastrous. It was obvious that enemy tanks had led the attack and penetrated the perimeter without any support or protection from infantry units.

During 13 April both the 271st and 272nd Regiments of the 9th NVA Division attacked in force. These attacks were met with strong ARVN resistance and the effective firepower of US tactical air and B-52s. Enemy losses for this day alone amounted to nearly 400, over one-half of which were inflicted by airstrikes. But the enemy was undaunted by these heavy casualties. He kept pressing his attacks during the next day, 14 April, preceding his armor advance in the early morning with heavy artillery fires. One of these tanks came within 500 meters of the 5th Division CP before it was disabled. Eventually, however, all enemy efforts during the day once again ended in failure.

After two days of fighting, the morale of the defenders remained remarkably high. They all seemed pervaded by the spirit of "holding or dying," determined to keep An Loc in friendly hands. This came from their conviction that they would never be left to fight alone, and that they would be kept well supplied and reinforced as required. Their convictions were right throughout the battle for An Loc.

The 1st Airborne Brigade meanwhile had been withdrawn from the Tau O area, quickly refitted, and helilifted during 13 and 14 April into positions on Hill 169 and

Windy Hill, three kilometers southeast of An Loc. The presence of paratroopers in the vicinity of the isolated city greatly encouraged the ARVN defenders and local population. Their confidence received an additional boost when they learned that the 21st Infantry Division from the Mekong Delta had reached Tau O on its way northward to relieve An Loc. So, when the enemy resumed his attacks on 15 April with the support of 11 tanks, these tanks became targets for ARVN troops competing among themselves for quick kills. One of these tanks managed to reach a position where it fired point blank at the 5th Division tactical operations center, wounding the S-3 of Binh Long sector and two other staff officers. When the dust of the battle cleared at day's end, 9 of the 11 tanks committed by the enemy had been destroyed.

The battle of An Loc abated somewhat on 16 April. After three days of combat, the enemy had lost 23 tanks, most of them T-54s and T-59s. However, the northern half of the city remained in his hands and his troops were facing ours, separated only by the main downtown boulevard. Also the encirclement of the city seemed to be tightening.

The first enemy effort to take An Loc resulted in failure, and COSVN modified its plan for the next effort. It decided to support the next major attack with a secondary attack against the ARVN 1st Airborne Brigade on Hill 169 and Windy Hill, southeast of the city. This secondary effort would be conducted by two regiments, the 275th of the 5th Division and the 141st of the 7th Division. The main attack on An Loc would remain the 9th Division's responsibility. To minimize the effectiveness of our tactical air, the enemy also ringed the city with additional antiaircraft weapons.

The enemy's new plan of attack, however, came into our possession on 18 April. On that day, in an ambush laid on an enemy line of communication near Tong Le Chan Base, ARVN rangers killed an enemy and found on his body a handwritten report from the 9th NVA Division's political commissar addressed to COSVN headquarters. This report analyzed the initial failure of the 9th NVA Division and attributed it to two major reasons.

First, the intervention of US tactical air and B-52s had been devastating and most effective. Second, coordination was ineffective between armor and infantry forces. The report also contained plans for the new major attack on An Loc which was to begin on 19 April. With this new plan, the enemy apparently believed An Loc could be seized within a matter of hours. So confident was he of success that on 18 April a Hanoi Radio broadcast announced that An Loc had been liberated and that the PRG would be inaugurated in this city on 20 April.

In the early morning hours on 19 April the enemy's attack proceeded exactly as planned and outlined in the captured document. While An Loc city came under heavy artillery and rocket fire, the NVA 275th and 141st Regiments attacked the ARVN 1st Airborne Brigade . . . with the support of six tanks. This attack was so vigorous that the brigade headquarters on Hill 169 was overwhelmed and the 6th Airborne Battalion was forced to destroy its 105mm battery and withdraw. Two companies of this battalion and the 1st Airborne Brigade headquarters fell back to An Loc City. The remaining two companies were cut off and forced to move south; they were later picked up by VNAF helicopters and carried to Chon Thanh. All six enemy tanks were destroyed during the attack, but the high ground dominating the city from the southeast was now in enemy hands.

Meanwhile the 9th NVA Division's attack on the city itself again ended in failure. Its troops were unable to advance in the face of the determined ARVN defenders who still firmly held the southern half of the city. The enemy then modified his plan of attack, attempting to move southwest to QL-13 and attack An Loc from the south. This plan never materialized, for the enemy discovered that on 21 April his staging area, a rubber plantation just south of the city, had been occupied by two battalions of the 1st Airborne Brigade who were firmly entrenched there. Unable to carry out the new plan, the enemy slackened his pace of attack, which finally came to a halt on 23 April, ending in failure his second attempt to take An Loc.

Within the besieged city, friendly forces did not fare much better than the enemy, however. The northern half of the city remained in enemy hands. The enemy's defense in the northeastern quarter was particularly strong and unbreachable. The city's southern half meanwhile came under increasingly heavy attacks by fire every day. On 25 April the city's hospital was hit and destroyed. As a result, no medical treatment was available for our wounded, military and civilian alike. All casualties had to be treated in the areas where they were wounded. Medical evacuation in the meantime became impossible because of intense antiaircraft fire. The city was littered with bodies, most of them unattended for several days. To avoid a possible epidemic, our troops were forced to bury these bodies in common graves.

Supplies were running low; most critically needed were food, ammunition, and medicine. Keeping the city supplied was becoming increasingly difficult. Because of heavy antiaircraft fire, our helicopters only occasionally succeeded in reaching the city, and then only for emergency resupply missions. Beginning on 20 April all resupply missions were conducted by USAF C-130s.

• • •

During this time our General Political Warfare Department had been especially active in enlisting popular support for the ARVN defenders in An Loc. No resupply missions to the besieged city were conducted which did not contain special gift packages from a grateful Saigon population. These gifts consisted of such delicacies as fresh vegetables and barbecued pork and stimulating personal letters of appreciation from schoolgirls. This solidarity action proved to have an excellent impact on the morale of the besieged defenders.

While resupply from the air proceeded without crippling problems, the recovery and distribution of supplies on the ground remained very difficult. Without coordination and control, it was usually those units nearest to the drop zone that got the most supplies. To solve this problem, the 5th Division commander placed Colonel Le Quang Luong, the tough 1st Airborne Brigade commander, in charge of recovery and distribution of airdrops.

• • •

Food and medicine received by ARVN units were usually shared with the local population. In return, the people of An Loc supplemented the ARVN combat ration diet with occasional fresh food such as fruit, vegetables, and meat they gathered from their own gardens. In addition, they assisted ARVN troops in administering first aid and in medical evacuation and doing laundry for them. Never before throughout South Vietnam had cooperation and mutual support between ARVN troops and the local population been so successfully achieved as in An Loc. Among the ARVN units that earned the most admiration and affection from the city's population were the 81st Airborne Rangers and the 1st Airborne Brigade. Both of these units not only fought well and courageously but also proved particularly adept at winning over the people's hearts and minds.

• • •

The Second Phase of Attack

The enemy's preparations for the second attack on An Loc [were] detected as early as 1 May when the 5th NVA Division headquarters relocated south to Hill 169. The following day two regiments of this division, the E-6 and 174th, also moved south. They took up positions on Windy Hill nearby, where they joined their sister regiment, the 275th, which had been there since 19 April after the withdrawal of our 1st Airborne Brigade. Next the 165th and 141st Regiments of the 7th NVA Division left their blocking positions in the Tau O area and moved to the southern and southwestern sectors of the city. These movements were detected and reported quite accurately by airborne radio direction finding (ARDF).

Together with the remaining units of the 9th NVA Division that continued to hold the northeastern portion of the city, this enemy redeployment was indicative of COSVN's determination to commit its entire combat force into an all-out effort to take An Loc. Facing these seven enemy regiments poised around the city, the ARVN defenders numbered fewer than 4,000. Although most were still combat effective, at least a thousand had been wounded. Morale was low since continuous enemy artillery bombardment kept the VNAF medevac helicopters away most of the time. Meanwhile, enemy deployments and an increase in enemy artillery and rocket fire against the city pointed toward an imminent all-out attack.

The new plan of attack was confirmed and other details were learned on 5 May, when an enemy soldier surrendered to regional forces patrolling on the southern defense perimeter. He was a lieutenant from the 9th NVA Division. Interrogated, this enemy rallier reported that his division commander had been severely reprimanded by COSVN for failure to capture An Loc. In the meantime, COSVN's Military Command had approved the 5th NVA Division commander's request that his unit conduct the primary attack instead of the 9th Division. He promised he would take An Loc within two days, as he had Loc Ninh. The rallier also disclosed that the 5th NVA Division's effort from the southeast was to be coordinated with that of the 7th Division from the southwest and a supporting effort by the 9th from the northeast. He did not know the exact time of the attack, but estimated that it would materialize within one week.

In the face of enemy intentions and known troop dispositions, the J-2 and J-3 at MACV began planning the use of B-52s to break the enemy's decisive effort. General Abrams, COMUSMACV, quickly approved his staff's recommendations and provided III Corps with maximum tactical air support and priority in B-52 strikes for the defense of An Loc. The problem with using B-52s in tactical support, however, was precise timing, and to break the enemy effort the first requirement was to know exactly on what day this attack would begin.

On 9 May the enemy initiated strong ground probes and increased his artillery fire. The ground pressure abated within two hours, but the heavy bombardment continued. To anyone knowledgeable about the pattern of enemy attacks in South Vietnam, this was undoubtedly an indication of imminent attack. The next day the same pattern was repeated. Our US-ARVN intelligence was completely accurate concerning the enemy's attack for 11 May and COMUSMACV adjusted his B-52 plan accordingly.

Early in the morning of 11 May, after several hours of intensified artillery bombardment, the enemy began his ground assault from all sides. During the fierce fighting that followed, enemy forces made extensive use of the SA-7 missile against our gunships and tactical air. They also had better coordination between tank and infantry units, but ARVN soldiers stood their ground and systematically sought to destroy enemy tanks with their proven M-72s.

• • •

In the meantime, VNAF and US tactical air, which had been active since the assault began, methodically attacked enemy positions in both salients to the west and northeast. Their effectiveness was total; they not only helped contain enemy penetrations, they also inflicted heavy casualties on the entrenched enemy troops and forced some of them to abandon their positions and flee. During this day alone, nearly 300 tactical air sorties were used in support of An Loc.

The tide of the battle turned in our favor as B-52s began their strikes at 0900 hours, when the intensity of enemy tank-infantry attacks [was] at a peak. Thirty strikes were conducted during the next 24 hours, and their devastating power was stunning. By noon, the enemy's attack had been completely broken. Fleeing in panic, enemy troops were caught in the open by our tactical air; several tank crews abandoned their vehicles. By early afternoon no enemy tank was seen moving. Those that remained in sight were either destroyed or abandoned, several with motors still running. In one area, an entire enemy regiment which had attacked the 81st Airborne Ranger Group was effectively eliminated as a fighting force.

On 12 May the enemy tried again, but his effort was blunt and weak. A few tanks appeared, but fired on the city only from standoff positions, while infantry troops of both sides exchanged small arms fire around the perimeter. Despite deteriorating weather, US tactical air and regular B-52 strikes continued to keep the enemy off balance around the city. The situation was one of stalemate and continued to be so during 13 May. Our chances of holding out in An Loc were increasing.

In the early morning of 14 May enemy tanks and infantry attacked again from the west and southwest. This attack was broken by decisive B-52 strikes and ended by mid-morning. Taking advantage of the enemy's weakening posture, the ARVN defenders counterattacked and regained most of the territory in the city. By now, most enemy troops had withdrawn except for a few small blocking positions west and north of the city. The battle had not been completely won, but it was obvious that the enemy no longer had the capability to capture An Loc.

This last attempt had cost the enemy dearly. Almost his entire armor force committed in the battle had been destroyed. Forty of these tanks and armored vehicles littered the battleground in and around the city. During the following days the situation stabilized as enemy infantry troops completely withdrew outside the city and indirect fire on the city continued to decrease. There were indications that the enemy was now shifting his effort toward the 21st ARVN Division, which was moving north by road toward the besieged city.

An Loc had held against overwhelming odds. To a certain extent this feat could be attributed to the sheer physical endurance of ARVN defenders and the combat audacity of such elite forces as the 81st Airborne Ranger Group and the paratroopers. Also commendable was the combat effectiveness of the territorial forces who fought under the strong leadership of the province chief, Colonel Tran Van Nhut. But the enemy's back had been broken and An Loc saved only because of timely B-52 strikes.

• • •

On 7 July President Thieu made an unannounced visit to An Loc. From a high-altitude approach his helicopter suddenly dived and landed on the soccer field. He was accompanied by Lieutenant General Nguyen Van Minh, who as III Corps commander visited the city for the first time since it came under siege exactly three months earlier. The president was greeted by an emaciated Brigadier General Le Van Hung, the hero of An Loc, whose eyes blinked incessantly under the glaring sun. Later the president confided jokingly to an aide, "Hung looked deceitful to me. Why do you think he kept constantly squinting and blinking his eyes?" The aide replied most seriously, "Why, Mr. President, General Hung had not seen sunlight for a long, long time."

• • •

VII. A CRITICAL ANALYSIS

North Vietnam's Objectives, Strategy, and Tactics

Since their major defeats during 1968 and 1969, the Communist leaders in Hanoi had the urgent requirement to accomplish two things. First, they needed to improve their deteriorating strategic posture in South Vietnam; and second, to have an ultimate chance to win, they had to defeat the Vietnamization process. Politically, as Viet Cong negotiators later disclosed in Paris, North Vietnam's leaders also strongly believed they needed a leverage to strengthen their demand for a coalition government in the South. To achieve this leverage, it was mandatory that they control through military action as much territory of the Republic of Vietnam as possible. This was the rationale behind North Vietnam's decision, made in mid-1971, to conduct the 1972 invasion.

• • •

The Nguyen Hue campaign failed to accomplish [its] intended objectives. In exchange for some insignificant territorial gains, North Vietnam had virtually exhausted its manpower and materiel resources. Estimates placed its losses at over 100,000 casualties and at least one-half of its large-caliber artillery and tanks. By the end of 1972 it became obvious that Hanoi no longer possessed the capabilities for another general offensive in South Vietnam in the immediate future. At the price of this huge sacrifice, the gains that North Vietnam had achieved looked insignificant indeed. Not one of the 44 provincial capitals of South Vietnam (with the exception of the temporary occupation of Quang Tri) ever fell into enemy hands. Out of the 260 district towns, fewer than ten were occupied, almost all of them located in remote border areas, far removed from centers of population.

• • •

Hanoi made a basic strategic error when it dispersed its main-force units and made major efforts on three widely separated fronts instead of concentrating them in a major thrust against a single objective.

• • •

Hanoi's strategic error was further compounded by tactical blunders; two such blunders were most obvious. First, it appeared that all NVA tactical commanders lacked experience in the employment of armor. After overcoming the many problems of introducing tanks into South Vietnam successfully, they failed to use them properly. Instead of making deep thrusts into our lines, creating shock and confusion and disrupting our rear areas, they employed them with hesitancy, primarily in attacks against targets whose armor defenses had been carefully prepared. Our forces learned that some armor vehicles, especially those with external fuel tanks, could be put out of action even by artillery shell fragments.

The second most remarkable tactical error derived from their own concept of infantry assaults. Having initial numerical advantage in all of the major areas of contest, they squandered it in suicidal, massive assaults whose attrition rate was so great that replacements could not possibly maintain unit strengths.

• • •

Much unduly harsh and unjustified criticism has been directed against the performance of the 3rd ARVN Division during the Easter Offensive. The division was new and untested, and was deployed to a critical, potentially vulnerable area. But it was never proven that the 3rd Division consisted mostly of deserters, pardoned military criminals, and other undesirable elements cast off by other units. The 3rd ARVN Division was no weakling. It was new only in name, not in combat experience. Five out of its nine organic infantry battalions and its armored cavalry squadron were all units with long combat records, having fought NVA forces in the DMZ area for several years. Its other four infantry battalions were transferred as complete units, not piecemeal, from

ARVN and territorial forces of Military Region 1. The great majority of the troops and cadres consisted of local servicemen who were well familiar with the rugged terrain of Military Region 1 and hardened to the cold and wet climate in this part of the country. The division's staff, whose nucleus was the former forward command element of the 1st ARVN Division at Dong Ha, was well versed with operations and knew the enemy in the DMZ area. In addition, a substantial number of divisional unit commanders were those who had operated in this area, hand in hand with US units and on almost every battlefield, for several years. As such, the 3rd Division was anything but a green unit, although it lacked the cohesiveness and efficiency of a division that had fought together as a unit.

What, then, caused the demise of this division? To put it briefly, the 3rd Division failed because it was overburdened. For the defense of the DMZ area, this unit had taken over the combat responsibilities formerly assigned to nearly two US divisions, the reinforced US 3rd Marine Division and the 1/5 Brigade (Mechanized). The 3rd Division was required to replace these US units with just four infantry battalions.

• • •

Some observers have suggested that another ARVN division, one that had long been established, could have done better than the 3rd Division. I don't think so. I am not sure that replacing it with any other division would have been a wise move or would have changed the results.

• • •

Looking back on the ordeal of the 3rd ARVN Division, I believe that not very many ARVN divisions could have held initially against the concentrated and conventional attacks launched by the enemy. I also believe that no other unit could have done anything better under the complicated command and control system which was established by the I Corps command.

At the very least, however, the 3rd Division did make two important contributions during the 1972 offensive. It held the Dong Ha line for a month against the overwhelming pressure of superior NVA forces, gaining enough time for Saigon to make necessary preparations for the deployment of general reserve forces to decisive battle areas. And after recovery, which took less than three months, this same division displayed remarkable combat effectiveness battling the NVA 711th Division west of Danang during the final stages of the 1972 enemy offensive.

RVNAF Performance

In 1972, although a few US combat units were still in Vietnam, they were all committed to the defense and security of US bases and installations; the RVNAF had assumed the primary responsibility for the ground war. The Americans provided advice, logistics, and combat support. When the enemy offensive began, Vietnam's fate was in its own hands. President Thieu, the Joint General Staff, and the corps commanders had to decide where, when, and how to fight. The test of Vietnamization had come, and the United States would share in its outcome.

There was no change in strategy; the concept of securing all national territory continued to be the order of the day. Every area, every strongpoint, no matter how small or remote, had to be held "at all cost." The national leadership asserted its firm determination to resist aggression and protect the integrity of South Vietnam's sovereignty; it announced that "we would not yield even a pebble in Quang Tri or a handful of mud in Ca Mau to the enemy."[8] Obviously this declaration did not take into full account either South Vietnam's defense posture or RVNAF capabilities. A more pragmatic leader would have recognized that the RVNAF simply did not have the resources to carry out such a policy, at least not without the full support of US and FWMA combat forces as in years past.

The early disaster in I Corps—particularly the decimation of the 3rd Division—can be attributed largely to the failure of the corps commander and his staff to provide adequate guidance and support to this frontline division. It was the customary practice at I Corps headquarters to shift all tactical responsibility to the divisions, simply by repeating verbatim—perhaps with a few words added—the general mission guidance received from Saigon, such as "Quang Tri must be held at all costs." It did not matter that the division was ill-equipped or too meagerly supported to accomplish such a mission. If Saigon said that a place must be held at all costs, the fact that the corps repeated these instructions to the division was enough to place all responsibility for execution upon the division commander. No one would later question whether the mission was feasible or whether the operation was well supported by the corps. In I Corps, the commander believed that he had done his job when he had said, pointing to a map, "attack there" or "defend here at all costs." When the 3rd Division failed, this logic dictated that its commander be tried for its failure, convicted, and sent to prison.

• • •

US Support

One of the major factors contributing to the RVNAF success in stalling and eventually defeating the enemy's Easter Offensive was US support. Never before had the American response to the NVA threat been so forceful and determined. Among other things, the United States substantially increased its air and naval fire support and provided South Vietnam with as much equipment and supplies as were required. Furthermore, this support was coordinated with an increased bombing campaign in South Vietnam, increased interdiction of enemy supply lines in Laos, renewed bombing of North Vietnam, and the blockade of major North Vietnamese ports, all in a remarkably successful effort to reduce the effect of the enemy offensive.

The role of the US Air Force was decisive in several instances. The support provided by US tactical air and B-52s on all major fronts was timely and most effective; it not only destroyed many enemy formations, but also sustained the morale of the ARVN soldiers. If laudatory words are used here to describe the US Air Force's contributions to the RVNAF success in repelling the enemy's biggest offensive to date, they certainly should not be construed as flattery; they only serve to convey due credit for a highly professional performance. Quang Tri city certainly could not have been retaken, nor could ARVN forces have held at Kontum and An Loc, had it not been for the support provided by the US Air Force.

• • •

At the corps and division levels, advisors played a most significant role. They assisted corps and division staffs in planning and supervising combat operations and developing procedures for the effective use and coordination of tactical air, naval gunfire, and artillery. These were the areas in which ARVN commanders and their staffs most required assistance. The regional assistance commands, therefore, proved to be timely and most responsive institutions that greatly assisted the ARVN corps during the 1972 Easter Offensive.

VIII. SUMMARY AND CONCLUSIONS

Prior to the invasion of 1972, Hanoi had launched several large-scale campaigns in South Vietnam, . . . but none of these initiatives equaled the 1972 Easter Offensive . . . in scale and importance. Undoubtedly Hanoi had intended it to be a decisive military effort.

• • •

During this time of grave emergency, Saigon also rose to the occasion by quickly replacing the ineffective politically appointed generals with professionals who had combat experience.

By mid-June, the RVNAF had wrested the initiative from the invaders. There was no morale collapse among the South Vietnamese population or among RVNAF troops.

• • •

Many observers believed that Hanoi should have acted more cautiously after NVA forces lost the initial momentum and suffered subsequent defeats. But the Hanoi leadership was stubborn and intransigent, bent as always on the most belligerent course of action. The showdown was inevitable, and Hanoi apparently believed it could win. Hanoi's easy victories during April and May seemed to confirm this belief. Gearing up for the showdown, Hanoi probably continued to think that the RVNAF would collapse and only a final blow would be necessary to hasten the process.

• • •

Furthermore, a military victory during the US presidential election year might inhibit the chances of the incumbent being reelected. Hanoi remembered how its 1968 offensive had affected the course of US internal and international politics. Was it not possible that a Communist victory during 1972 would promote the election of a new president who would repudiate the commitment to support South Vietnam? In the final analysis, I believe this may have been Hanoi's objective for some time. In any event, the bloodiest battles of the war raged on for three months in the northernmost corner of South Vietnam.

But North Vietnam no longer had the forces needed to win. On the contrary, the odds were working against the enemy. As the fighting continued, Hanoi's chances of losing were increasing, not only militarily but also politically. Weakened and finally exhausted, the NVA forces were no match for the bolder South Vietnamese units. Contrary to the assessment of several observers, I believe that the last NVA effort in Quang Tri and Thua Thien failed to provide the enemy with any significant political advantages. Falling back in the wake of their defeat, NVA forces dispersed and switched to a less sanguine course of action: a well-orchestrated Land and Population Grab campaign in preparation for a standstill cease-fire. And thus ended the 1972 NVA offensive.

• • •

The American response during the enemy offensive was timely, forceful, and decisive. This staunch resolve of the United States to stand behind its ally stunned the enemy. Additionally, it brought about a strong feeling of self-assurance among the armed forces and population of South Vietnam.

• • •

Throughout the long months of the enemy offensive, the RVNAF performed like the mature, professional, dedicated fighting force it had become. Although this excellent performance was attributable to several factors, a definite tribute must be given to the US advisors, especially the US regional assistance commands. Even during this period of emergency, the US advisory effort continued to help the RVNAF support machinery run smoothly, whether it was recruiting, equipping, training, or replacing losses.

The constant input of fresh and trained manpower kept the RVNAF revitalized and helped maintain combat effectiveness in the forward areas. The RVNAF logistic system functioned efficiently, keeping all combat units resupplied. Intelligence collection and accurate reporting kept field commanders constantly abreast of the situation and were instrumental in formulating successful battle plans. Improved command and control in the field also resulted in better morale for commanders and troops alike. All of these achievements contributed to the ultimate RVNAF success in containing and defeating the most vigorous offensive North Vietnam had ever unleashed on the South, and, without the assistance of US advisors, it would not have been possible.

The final credit for our victory should go to the individual South Vietnamese soldier, regardless of branch or service. His gallantry, courage, and determination were of the highest standard. No less admirable were the sacrifices and hardships endured by the common South Vietnamese people during this long ordeal. While modern weapons might help turn the tide of a battle, they could never replace the individual soldier on the battlefield. No matter how sound a battle plan, or how good a commander, our success could never have been achieved without courageous soldiers.

The average South Vietnamese soldier, who grew up in war, was not only audacious and devoted to the cause for which he had been fighting, but he always took pride in his career and his heart was filled with love for his family, his comrades-in-arms, and his people. He was indeed a heroic warrior who represented the noblest traditions of the Vietnamese people, a most ardent patriot, and an outstanding soldier. His success during 1972 had helped forge a new national spirit of solidarity and survival that was to prevail in the post-cease-fire years.

NOTES

1. Making a permanent shift in deployment of an ARVN division was a major undertaking, since it involved relocating thousands of families as well as soldiers and equipment. It took seven months to complete the move of the ARVN 25th Division from Quang Ngai to Hau Nghia.

2. The division's former commander, Lieutenant General Le Nguyen Khang, was offered the command of II Corps by President Thieu, but he declined. He was later appointed Assistant Chief of the JGS for Operations.

3. Only a year later, in 1973, the 3rd Infantry Division was rated by the Joint General Staff as the best among ARVN divisions. Its commander was also the only division commander to be promoted to the rank of major general during the year.

4. Colonel Ton That Hung later retold his escape odyssey in a book he published under the title *Nguoi Ve Tu Tan Canh* ("The Man Who Came in from Tan Canh").

5. Although the TO&E called for a major general to command a division, the practice of assigning colonels, brigadiers, and even lieutenant generals to these posts was widespread. This clearly caused serious problems, but the practice persisted. The rationale seemed to be that promising colonels should be given the opportunity to prove themselves, especially if they had powerful political sponsors.

6. Tong Le Chan Base remained under ARVN control until April 1974. Following the cease-fire of January 1973, the base was besieged and repeatedly attacked by elements of the NVA 7th and 9th Divisions for over one year before its final evacuation. It became a prominent case of enemy cease-fire violations and an eloquent testimony to ARVN combat heroism.

7. A decision had been initially made to deploy this division to MR-1 in an effort to retake the lost territory north of the Cam Lo River. But Lieutenant General Dang Van Quang, President Thieu's assistant for security, was afraid the GVN would lose face if the PRG succeeded in installing itself at An Loc. Hence the decision was overturned and the 21st Division assigned to MR-3 instead.

8. President Thieu's statement, reiterated many times during his 1972 visits to MR-1.

13

The US Advisor

General Cao Van Vien et al.

PREFACE

The US advisory mission in South Vietnam encompassed many fields of endeavor and affected almost every level of the Republic of Vietnam Armed Forces. It was a demanding exercise of professional duties and a unique human experience for the American advisor, who had not only to struggle with problems of environment and cultural differences and face the complexities and hazards of the war, but also devote his time and energy to supplement our Vietnamese experience with US Army professionalism. The total effort by US advisors contributed directly and immeasurably to the development and modernization of the Vietnamese armed forces.

To the Vietnamese officers and men who benefited from his expertise and experience, the US advisor was both a mentor and a samaritan. Regardless of his level of assignment or branch of service, he could be [identified] by a common trait: a sincere desire to help and devotion to those he advised. Whatever his approach to advisory duties, he always performed with dedication and competence. For nearly two decades these qualities were the hallmark of the US advisor in South Vietnam.

To analyze and evaluate the US advisory experience in its entirety is not an easy task. It cannot be accomplished thoroughly and effectively by a single author, since there were several types of advisors representing different areas of specialty, but all dedicated to a common goal. Therefore each member of the Control Group for the Indochina Refugee–Authored Monograph Program has made a significant contribution as we presented the Vietnamese point of view.

As the last Chairman of the Joint General Staff/RVNAF, a position I held for a decade, I have contributed the chapter concerning the relationship between the JGS and MACV. As I see it, the advisory effort at that level was largely a matter of personal relationship which set the tone and example for the entire system. I am sure that the tributes I pay to the successive MACV commanders, living or deceased, are but a small part of their towering contributions and achievements. . . . [Cao Van Vien, 31 May 1977]

I. INTRODUCTION   Lieutenant Colonel Chu Xuan Vien

A Brief Comparative Historical Account

To understand and appreciate the full impact of the US advisor on the RVN Armed Forces from the Vietnamese viewpoint, it is desirable first to review briefly the evolution of the advisory system, to include how it was organized, supported, and how it functioned at different echelons.

The United States began providing direct military advisory assistance to the Vietnamese National Army in early 1955. However, American commitment to Indochina had started five years earlier when, coming to the help of a hard-pressed war ally, the United States supplied war materiel to the French Expeditionary Corps, which was fighting a dubious war against the Communist-led Viet Minh, then the champion of a strong cause for national independence.

When the US Military Assistance Advisory Group (MAAG), Indochina, was established in late 1950 under Brigadier General Francis G. Brink to administer this aid, the new state of Vietnam had been born only a year earlier as a result of compromise between ex-emperor Bao Dai, chief of state, and the French, who sought to set up a regime capable of competing with the Viet Minh. The United States had promptly recognized Bao Dai and signed with France and the "Associated States" of Indochina (Vietnam, Cambodia, Laos) in December 1950 what came to be known as the Pentalateral Agreements. These agreements formed the basis of US economic and military aid for Vietnam, the first step toward a growing commitment which terminated only a quarter of a century later.

As an associated state of the French Union, Vietnam was granted some degree of autonomy, but not total independence—which came only in the aftermath of the French defeat at Dien Bien Phu in 1954. It was during this period that the National Army of Vietnam came into being, its creation sanctioned by the French need to Vietnamize the war. The Vietnamese army, which initially consisted of auxiliary elements recruited, trained, and led by French cadre, was gradually upgraded into infantry battalions, then mobile groups, by 1953, all under the command of Vietnamese officers. During 1952 command and control of the new national army was established, first with the General Staff, then four military region headquarters, but these bodies were still heavily staffed by French officers. During all this time the US Military Assistance Advisory Group (MAAG) remained far removed from the scene. Its main function was to make sure that US equipment was delivered and properly maintained through liaison with the French High Command. Most Vietnamese tactical commanders in the field were even unaware of its existence until 1953, when they received the first visits by MAAG officers.

The nature of US commitment in Vietnam radically changed after the 1954 Geneva Accords, to become a true military assistance and advisory role, with the advent of South Vietnam, now a separate nation south of the 17th parallel. This came about as a result of an agreement reached between General J. Lawton Collins, President Eisenhower's special envoy, and General Paul Ely, the French High Commissioner and Commander in Chief of the French Expeditionary Corps in Indochina. Under the terms of the agreement, the Vietnamese armed forces were to receive organization and training assistance from the MAAG as of 1 January 1955 and to become fully autonomous six months later. By this time, the General Staff had become all-Vietnamese under Major General Le Van Ty, and, after the regrouping of the 3rd Military Region units from North Vietnam, the entire Vietnamese armed forces strength stood at 215,997, to include 179,197 regular troops who made up about 168 infantry battalions. The day the Collins-Ely agreement went into effect was also the day that three infantry divisions—the 11th, 21st, and 31st—were activated for the first time.

Such was the status of the Vietnamese army when the MAAG began its organization and training efforts. In cooperation with the French, Lieutenant General John W. O'Daniel, who replaced Major General Thomas J. H. Trapnell as Chief MAAG in April 1954, organized the Training Relations and Instruction Mission (TRIM) on 1 February 1955. TRIM was essentially an American concept, but, for the purpose of political convenience, its staff also included French officers who performed mostly in a consultant's role. The first TRIM advisory training teams, largely composed of US Army officers, began their field assignments in April 1955. They were attached to infantry divisions, the airborne brigade, service schools, and training centers. One month later the first US advisors were placed at military region headquarters.

As defined in a memorandum published by the Vietnamese General Staff on 10 April 1955, the mission of TRIM advisors was "to assist and advise, on strictly technical aspects, Vietnamese military commanders to whom they were assigned, in order to rapidly and effectively rebuild the Vietnamese armed forces on a new basis."[1] The insistence on "strictly technical aspects" set the tone and direction for the US Army advisory effort, which was to remain technically oriented throughout its existence. The "new basis" for reorganization needed no clarification: it was understood to be the doctrine of the US Army.

These combined arrangements for training and reorganizing the Vietnamese army continued for more than a year. When the French High Command in Indochina was deactivated on 28 April 1956, TRIM personnel were immediately reassigned to the MAAG's Combat Arms Training and Organization (CATO) Division. It was only then that the Vietnamese armed forces became fully autonomous after taking over all military responsibilities from the departing French.

• • •

During this period the major difficulties of [the] MAAG stemmed from the ceiling imposed on US military personnel by the Geneva Accords. Faced with an increasing commitment to training activities and growing logistical problems, the MAAG was authorized only 342 spaces, of which about two-thirds were devoted to training. The Vietnamese General Staff was also hard-pressed by the same problem of a ceiling which was imposed, not by the Geneva Accords, but by the MAAG, at the 150,000 level.

With the support of direct US economic and military assistance, South Vietnam confidently began its task of nation building. On 26 October 1955 Prime Minister Ngo Dinh

Diem proclaimed the Republic of Vietnam and installed himself as president and supreme commander of the armed forces. The National Armed Forces of Vietnam became the Republic of Vietnam Armed Forces (RVNAF) and the National Army took on its acronym ARVN, so familiar to US Army advisors. At about the same time [the] MAAG, Indochina, was redesignated MAAG, Vietnam, marking the separation of duties for Vietnam, Laos, and Cambodia.

The final pullout of the French Expeditionary Corps from South Vietnam resulted in logistical problems which plagued both the RVNAF General Staff and the MAAG. Not being adequately organized and trained for the handling of logistic support, the RVNAF found themselves unprepared for it. On his part, the new Chief MAAG-V, Lieutenant General Samuel T. Williams, who succeeded General O'Daniel in November 1955, had to face problems caused by the difficulty in locating, recovering, and shipping out excess MDAP equipment left behind unaccounted for by French forces. The RVNAF did not even know exactly how much equipment there was in the inventory. These requirements led to the creation of the Temporary Equipment Recovery Mission (TERM) in June 1956 to clean up the logistical mess and to assist the RVNAF in establishing a workable logistical support system. TERM personnel were later integrated into MAAG-V, which brought total US advisory strength to 692 by 1960.

In the meantime, the Vietnamese army undertook a long and arduous process of reorganization under the auspices of MAAG advisors. During the first stage, it was agreed that ten infantry divisions (six light and four field) would constitute the ARVN backbone. This was accomplished by the end of 1955. The search for an optimum type division for the ARVN, however, continued to preoccupy the MAAG for the next three years. After discarding hundreds of tentative TOEs, it was decided in 1958 that seven regular infantry divisions of 10,500 men each were required by [the] RVN to defend itself against overt aggression from the North.

• • •

Recognizing the unconventional nature of the war, the GVN successively created a 5,000-man Ranger Command and the Special Forces in 1960. The United States, on its part, began reevaluating its advisory effort, which resulted in a comprehensive Counterinsurgency Plan allowing an increase in the RVNAF strength from 150,000 to 170,000 men, MAP support for a 68,000-man Civil Guard and a 40,000-man People's Militia, and providing more US advisors. As a result, for the first time US advisory teams were assigned to ARVN battalions on a selective basis, and US Special Forces teams initiated the training of ARVN ranger companies.

• • •

By the end of 1961, the US advisory effort had expanded to most ARVN battalions and to provinces as well. In the Central Highlands, US Special Forces teams were organizing, arming, and training Montagnards to fight as units which became known as Civilian Irregular Defense Groups (CIDG). In addition, to direct the increased military commitment effectively, it was decided to establish the US Military Assistance Command, Vietnam (MACV), and General Paul D. Harkins was selected as commander. The

Military Assistance Advisory Group was still retained, however, under Major General Charles J. Timmes, who continued directing the Military Assistance Program and the advisory and training effort for the RVNAF.

• • •

The introduction of US tactical aircraft and helicopters brought total American advisory and support personnel to approximately 11,000 by the end of 1962, including 26 Special Forces teams. ARVN units were initiated to airmobile operations transported in US Army helicopters which were operationally controlled by US advisors.

• • •

By the end of 1964 the situation had so deteriorated that President Johnson had to make the fateful decision in early 1965 to bomb North Vietnam and engage in the ground war in the South. The US advisory system had by now extended to the district level. To streamline command and control, the MAAG was dissolved in May 1964 and the military assistance and advisory effort placed under direct control of MACV. A month later, General William C. Westmoreland took over as commander, USMACV.

The buildup of US forces which started in mid-1965, and the intensification of the war during the next few years, towered above the advisory effort and turned US advisors into liaison officers whose primary role was to maintain coordination between ARVN and US units and to obtain US combat support for the ARVN.

• • •

When Vietnamization was officially proclaimed in mid-1969, total US Army advisory strength stood at about 13,500, half of which was assigned to the CORDS organization. In Saigon, General Creighton W. Abrams had succeeded General Westmoreland as Commander, USMACV, since July 1968.

The advent of Vietnamization radically changed the direction of the US advisory effort. The goal now was to expand and improve the RVNAF combat effectiveness to such an extent that they were capable of taking over combat responsibilities from US forces, which were gradually being withdrawn by increments. As a result of successive force structure increases, total RVNAF strength was brought up to 717,214 for 1968, then jumped quickly to the 1.1 million mark within the space of the next four years. ARVN force structure meanwhile accounted for only a modest increase, from 321,056 in 1968 to 448,953 by the time of the cease-fire. During this period, US advisory strength was gradually reduced in keeping with the phasing out of the US presence in South Vietnam.

• • •

As a result of the stand-down and redeployment of US forces, Regional Assistance Commands (RAC) were activated to replace US field forces in the four corps areas during 1971 and 1972, signifying the end of the US combat role in South Vietnam.

The US advisory effort terminated on the cease-fire day, 28 January 1973. To manage the continuing security assistance program for the RVN, the US Defense Attaché Office (USDAO) was established with a very limited number of military personnel. But its relationship with the RVNAF was essentially one of coworkers, not a relationship between advisors and advisees, as it had been. All CORDS functions were taken over by USAID and its residual personnel absorbed into four US Consulates General, one for each military region. At the province level, US civilian personnel were grouped into 20 area offices responsible for civil operations. But even these offices were subsequently dissolved, and finally the US presence in each province was reduced to a small liaison team.

The US Advisory System

Despite the evolution of the system, the objectives contemplated by the US advisory effort in South Vietnam remained essentially consistent throughout its existence. These objectives were to organize, train, and equip the Vietnamese armed forces and develop their combat effectiveness to such an extent as to enable them to maintain internal security and to defend the nation against outside aggression.

• • •

The scope of MACV's mission . . . transcended the military advisory and training functions previously assigned to MAAG-V during nearly a decade of its existence. It clearly encompassed the civil operations in support of the GVN pacification and development program. The difference in mission between MACV and MAAG-V also stemmed from the fact that MACV also functioned as a US theater-type troop command. As a result, only part of MACV headquarters staff personnel actually served in a true advisory capacity. In 1970, for example, only 397 out of 1,668 authorized spaces in MACV's 15 staff agencies were designed officially as "advisors" to the GVN and the JGS/RVNAF.

• • •

At the province level, the senior advisor (PSA) was either military or civilian, depending on the security situation. Of the 44 province advisors, in 1970 there were 25 military and 19 civilians. If the PSA was military, his deputy was a civilian, and vice versa. The PSA's counterpart was the province chief, usually a military officer who commanded the RF/PF as well as GVN administrative personnel.

• • •

Vietnamese Requirements for Advisory Assistance and Support to the US Advisory Effort

The US advisory effort in South Vietnam was a gradual buildup that responded to the needs of the RVNAF and the military situation. Strange as it may seem, the RVNAF requirements for US advisory assistance were never determined by the Vietnamese themselves. From the beginning to the end of the US advisory effort, the RVNAF never requested a specific quota of advisors, nor were they ever able to determine completely what types of advisors were required for their own needs.

The process of determining the requirements for advisory assistance therefore was largely based on estimates and progress, and it was always a function performed by the US senior military headquarters in South Vietnam.

• • •

The requirements for US Army officers assigned to advisory duties in Vietnam seemed to be based on three major criteria: language ability, branch of service, and training. Some degree of fluency in Vietnamese, for example, was required of officers assigned to the RF/PF, particularly those advising the PF training centers and the district chiefs. Experience, however, showed that this linguistic requirement was seldom restrictive and that these advisors rarely achieved a desirable fluency for effective professional communication. US Army officers selected for staff or technical service advisory duties were usually matched branch for branch, but, here again, this requirement was sometimes not strictly observed, chiefly when the advisory position was classified as branch immaterial. The training criterion applied mostly to key advisory positions or specialized areas of duty. Depending on the level, graduates of the National or Army War Colleges, Command and General Staff College, branch career or advanced courses were required [to fill various positions].

• • •

But, regardless of position or specialization, the one-year tour seemed not conducive to more extensive preparation of US officers for advisory duties other than perfunctory requirements and a brief orientation course prior to field deployment.

• • •

In the field, US advisory teams permanently attached to ARVN units and schools were accommodated in Vietnamese facilities, to include office space, billets, and mess service. These facilities were usually located in the same building complex occupied by the ARVN unit.

• • •

II. THE JGS AND MACV   General Cao Van Vien

A Matter of Personal Relationship

When I assumed the command responsibilities as Chief of the Joint General Staff (JGS) in October 1965, I did not really expect to serve in that capacity for nearly a decade. So eventful was my tenure of office that I hardly noticed the passing of time until the very last days of the Republic. During this period, I had the privilege of being a counterpart to three successive MACV commanders, General William C. Westmoreland, General Creighton W. Abrams, and General Frederick C. Weyand, all distinguished professional soldiers whom I admire and respect not only as military leaders but also as friends and advisors.

The decade of my command saw the Republic of Vietnam Armed Forces truly come of age in every respect. Within the space of eight years they had more than doubled in force structure to become a strong, modern, three-service military organization with 1.1 million men under arms by the time of the cease-fire. In early 1965 they were on the verge of losing the military war. In 1968, they stood up valiantly against a most vicious enemy offensive and turned it into a military victory. Twice, in 1970 and 1971, they crossed the national borders and struck devastatingly against the enemy's inviolable sanctuaries and infiltration corridor. In 1972 they stalled and finally broke up a most ferocious and determined invasion by NVA regular divisions on three different fronts. All these exploits, although achieved with substantial support from American firepower, testified to the success of the US military assistance and advisory program.

The relationship between the JGS and MACV had been purely advisory in nature until US forces started to participate in the ground war. The buildup of US combat forces, beginning in mid-1965, added a new dimension to this relationship by making it one of coordination and cooperation for the conduct of the war since MACV had become a theater-type command. General Westmoreland was genuinely concerned, as all military strategists should [be], about the feasibility of a United Nations-type unified command, and he sketched the idea to my immediate predecessor, Lieutenant General Tran Van Minh, and Lieutenant General Nguyen Van Thieu, then minister of defense who was soon to become chairman of the National Leadership Committee. As military men themselves, both understood his concern, but were disturbed at the idea of sacrificing the national cause for the sake of the military war in the event an American general became supreme commander. After all, this was a Vietnamese conflict, and, national sensitivities aside, there was also the question of how world opinion would react if it was fought under the American banner. The matter was not discussed further, and, when I was appointed chief of the JGS, the coexistence of two separate commands looked like the most natural way to manage the war effectively. Never again did General Westmoreland bring up the subject, at least as far as I was concerned.

I enjoyed the same kind of working relationship with the next MACV commander, General Creighton W. Abrams, whose responsibility was to improve the RVNAF, oversee the gradual US troop pullout, and ensure that the RVNAF had the capabilities to assume the combat burden. His leadership and devotedness helped the RVNAF rapidly develop in strength and fighting ability. It was largely General Abrams's idea of putting them to test. I most welcomed his suggestion of a spoiling attack against the enemy's supply bases and infiltration routes which resulted in the Cambodian incursion of 1970 and Lam Son 719 in lower Laos in 1971. It was he again who, in the confusion of the first few hours after the NVA crossed the DMZ in early April 1972, personally informed me of the critical situation and the debacle of the 3rd ARVN Infantry Division. Had it not been for his insight and solicitude, the JGS would have found itself in an embarrassing position after I Corps had apparently lost effective control. The next and last MACV commander, General Fred C. Weyand, who had served as II Field Force commander, had only a brief tour, but was instrumental in bringing the RVNAF up to the required strength and combat capabilities. His finishing touch, the Enhance Plus program, which gave additional mobility and firepower to the RVNAF, brought the Vietnamization process to a successful conclusion.

Looking back over the years of US advisory assistance and cooperation, I think that success owed a great deal to the personal relationship cultivated between the advisor and his counterpart. At the JGS and MACV level, this relationship was of utmost importance since it reflected on the entire system and could make or break the common war effort. But, since its beginning, the US advisory system had been built on solid ground, as evidenced by the productive decade that preceded my tour of duty as chief of the JGS. My predecessor, the venerated and paternal Marshal Le Van Ty, who presided over that earlier decade, was truly the pioneer who laid a solid foundation for the development of a fruitful US-RVNAF relationship. What I later enjoyed was only the legacy of his exemplary leadership. During his time he faced much less complex but more fundamental problems. What he had accomplished with the advisory assistance of various MAAG chiefs was to remain forever the basic framework on which the RVNAF were later developed.

Reorganization and Development of the RVNAF

It was in late 1954 that the Vietnamese General Staff became all-Vietnamese for the first time, without French officers and NCO cadre.[2] Major General Le Van Ty, then commander of the 1st Military Region, was appointed chief of the General Staff, a position he held until his death in 1964. It was also then that Vietnamese began to be used as the official language in the armed forces in the place of French.

From the beginning the General Staff of the Vietnamese National Armed Forces was predominantly army, despite the existence of service components.

• • •

When assuming its advisory and training role, the MAAG directed its primary effort toward the Vietnamese army, which was in fact the most important and by far the largest service.

• • •

After the November military coup d'etat of 1963, which overthrew President Ngo Dinh Diem, the JGS was transformed into an Armed Forces High Command under General Tran Thien Khiem and, later, General Nguyen [Khanh], but its role and functions remained unchanged. This was a period of political uncertainty which saw several governments come and go in rapid succession. The new MACV commander, General William C. Westmoreland, must have had a hard time dealing with politically ambitious ARVN generals who made up the Armed Forces Council and effectively controlled the RVNAF. After civilian rule was restored in early 1965, with the ousting of General Nguyen Khanh, the Armed Forces High Command was placed under the command of Lieutenant General Tran Van Minh. When the National Leadership Committee was formed in mid-1965 to rule the country under Lieutenant General Nguyen Van Thieu and Air "Vice Marshal" Nguyen Cao Ky, I was called upon to serve as Chief of the Joint General Staff, a position I held until the final days of South Vietnam.

• • •

With the institution of the Second Republic in 1967 under President Nguyen Van Thieu, who also effectively assumed his constitutional powers as commander in chief of the RVNAF, the role of the JGS greatly diminished in importance. Although by official decree it was the command body of the RVNAF, the JGS for all practical purposes was reduced to planning and supervising. The president reserved for himself the prerogative of appointing and promoting senior commanders, to include division commanders, technical service chiefs, and province chiefs, and not infrequently he himself gave direct orders to field commanders. This state of things unfortunately continued until the collapse of the regime in April 1975.

In keeping with the turnabout of US policy toward Vietnam, General Creighton W. Abrams succeeded General Westmoreland as Commander, USMACV, in July 1968, with the mission of overseeing the accelerated program designed to improve the combat effectiveness of the RVNAF, thus preparing groundwork for the Vietnamization program, which was formally announced in mid-1969. General Abrams also presided over the gradual redeployment of US combat forces until he left Vietnam in April [sic] 1972 after accomplishing his difficult mission and reassuring the US president that the RVNAF could "hack it" alone. He was replaced by General Fred C. Weyand, who remained until MACV was disbanded after the cease-fire.

Highlights of a Fruitful Relationship

At the beginning of the US advisory effort in South Vietnam which was initiated under TRIM, most US field advisors were deployed to ARVN infantry division headquarters and major training centers. None of them had a rank higher than lieutenant colonel. An arrangement was made whereby, if an American officer was appointed as senior advisor, he was assisted by a French deputy, and vice versa. At the General Staff and military region levels, the organization for advisory assistance at this [stage] was skeletal and informal. All problems were solved through personal contacts or during meetings between the counterpart staffs.

The major obstacle then was the language barrier. Since most ARVN officers only spoke Vietnamese or French, there was the indispensable need for interpreters during every contact with US advisors. In addition to language, there were also problems of dissimilar military background and training. Most ARVN officers then had only a scant knowledge of US Army doctrine, organization, and operational technique. Added together, these problems complicated the task of reorganizing the ARVN and made it a time-consuming process. During discussions on new tables of organization and equipment, a minor difference in opinion was apt to take days to resolve. For example, while ARVN staff officers of the General Staff maintained that the only individual weapon a company commander ever needed was a caliber .45 pistol, US advisors contended that, since a company commander was also required to fight like anybody else in the company, he had to be equipped with a caliber .30 carbine. This type of problem gave rise to lengthy discussions which took twice as much time to get a point through because translation was required.

It was realized that, for the advisory effort to be really beneficial, the problems of language and military knowledge, particularly about US Army doctrine and organization, should be expediently resolved. Strange as it may have seemed, the subject of teaching Vietnamese or French to US advisors was never brought up. A few advisors took private lessons on their own initiative, but only for personal reasons, and most never progressed beyond the greeting stage. Even later, over the war years, I know of no single instance in which a US advisor effectively discussed professional matters with his counterpart in Vietnamese. The learning and development of a new language seemed to have no appeal for US advisors, who must have found it not really worth the effort because of the short tour of duty in Vietnam. So the effort was directed at giving English lessons to Vietnamese servicemen.

• • •

Procedures for Cooperation

By the time the United States decided to commit combat troops to help fight the war in South Vietnam, the initial language barrier and Vietnamese unfamiliarity with American military doctrine and organization were no longer stumbling blocks for the advisory effort. An Armed Forces Language School had been added to the ARVN school system, and it was expanding. US Army school curricular and instructional materials were extensively used throughout the ARVN school and training center system. Most ARVN officers were now able to communicate in English, and they were well familiar with US military doctrine and organization. The switch to the new system and language had been swift and thorough.

Still, there were no detailed written procedures as to how US-ARVN cooperation should be conducted. Most advisor-counterpart relations were informal and unrestrained, shaped largely by improvisations and personalities. At the MACV-JGS level, for example, the procedures for cooperation were determined by ad hoc verbal agreement between the Commander, USMACV, and me, his counterpart, the Chairman of the JGS. We agreed to meet alone every Monday at 2:30 in the afternoon at the JGS for personal and problem-solving discussions. During the week before the meeting I would make notes as problems or issues arose that I wished to discuss with General Westmoreland or General Abrams at our Monday meeting. Meanwhile, my chief of staff would have the staff preparing fact sheets concerning any matter they thought I should bring up with COMUSMACV. The chief would bring these to me on Friday or Saturday, and I would decide whether or not to include them in our discussion. Sometimes I would direct the staff officer to work out the matter with his counterpart first, before I would broach it to COMUSMACV.

I am sure that General Abrams prepared for our meetings similarly, since he often passed to me fact sheets prepared by his staff. We would settle some of the simpler questions at our meetings, but often we would agree only to direct our staffs to work together and present to us an agreed position at a later date. After each meeting I would inform my chief of staff of any answers or decisions reached and, of course, tell him what was necessary to get the staff working. In other words, the outcome of these meetings was a basis for the combined US-RVN military efforts, and all decisions jointly made by the two commanders were communicated to their chiefs of staff and related staff divisions for execution or further study. In addition to the regularly scheduled weekly meetings, it was also agreed that, in case of an emergency, the two commanders would meet at any time, day or night. Less important problems in the meantime could be always solved by personal phone calls.

• • •

Most problems concerning personnel management were resolved in this way. However, COMUSMACV usually abstained from making specific recommendations concerning assignments, transfers, and promotions of ARVN officers except for a few he had personally observed or his advisors in the field felt strongly should be promoted or assigned to key positions in view of their demonstrated merits. These recommendations were always reviewed carefully before any action was taken in order to avoid favoritism or to prevent insidious manipulations of US advisors by ARVN officers.

With regard to reporting to me about Vietnamese officers that the American advisors considered ineffective, inept, or otherwise unsuited for command, Generals Westmoreland and Abrams operated quite differently one from another. It was General Westmoreland's practice to inform me, in detail, of any case where the US advisor had determined that his counterpart should be relieved, and he reached down as far as battalion commanders with this advice. Invariably I would have my chief of staff or J-1 investigate each case, and, if the situation warranted, I would see that the appropriate changes were made. In the case of General Abrams, however, when he and I travelled together on field inspections he would often comment tersely on the state of the command and the ability of the commanders as he saw it. But he never suggested either the promotion or the relief of anyone.

• • •

Beginning in 1965, with the active participation of US and Free World Military Assistance Forces, . . . annual planning was undertaken jointly by the JGS and MACV and resulted in a Combined Campaign Plan.

• • •

Preparation and coordination usually took from two to three months to complete, and the final draft was then submitted to the Commander, USMACV, and the Chairman, JGS, for approval. Finally a simple ceremony was held at the JGS compound, during which the Commander, USMACV, commanders of other FWMAF, and myself as Chairman of the JGS formally approved the plans and signed the document.

• • •

It was common for me, as the Chairman of the JGS, to devote two days each week for visits to field units, but these visits became sporadic after the cease-fire. Often I was accompanied by the commander, USMACV. During these field trips we made a point of solving unit problems on the spot. Initially every month, and later every quarter, both commanders visited ARVN corps headquarters, where they reviewed together the progress made by ARVN units in each corps area as projected in the Combined Campaign Plan.

To further enhance close coordination and cooperation, General Westmoreland, when serving as COMUSMACV, assigned a general officer as his personal representative and liaison officer to the JGS. This general officer also served as senior advisor to the Assistant Chairman/JGS for Territorial Security and Pacification. Later this position was reduced to a liaison function and assumed by a colonel.

The JGS and MACV never shared the same military compound or any common facilities. Initially the MAAG headquarters was located in Cholon; then, in 1957, it moved to the compound vacated by the JGS on Tran Hung Dao Boulevard in Saigon. When MACV was activated in 1962, its headquarters was first located in a crammed apartment building on Pasteur Street. In 1966 it moved to a newly built modern headquarters complex near Tan Son Nhut, about one mile from the JGS headquarters. Although the two headquarters were physically separated, there was never any problem involved in liaison and communications, which remained very close and effective throughout the war years.

An Evaluation

The Republic of Vietnam depended on US military aid to fight the war against Communist aggression. Its military force, the RVNAF, was organized and operated in accordance with US military doctrine and equipped with US materiel. The presence of US advisors at all echelons of the RVNAF hierarchy therefore was an obvious necessity. Consequently a definite requirement always existed for close coordination, cooperation, and effective US advice at the JGS and MACV echelons.

Throughout the war years the US Military Assistance Command, Vietnam, effectively assisted the JGS in developing its plans and programs and provided the support required to implement them successfully. Its advice, assistance, and material support were most conspicuous in the areas of intelligence and logistics, and made possible the expansion and modernization of ARVN intelligence and logistics agencies. These two accomplishments might be regarded as the most spectacular achievements.

• • •

At the field and unit level, there were of course some inevitable frictions and even head-on collisions between advisors and ARVN commanders. This was human and understandable, given the tremendous pressure placed on each advisor and commander by the tactical situation. But the problem was largely local and highly individual; it was limited to only a few cases of any importance.

• • •

No such problem ever happened at the MACV and JGS level; cooperation between advisors and counterparts constantly remained close and sincere. The success of this productive relationship derived from two cardinal factors: self-respect and mutual respect. Despite differences in culture, language, traditions, customs, and personalities, the relationship remained unaffected because of the common realization that, without cooperation and unity, the combined military effort would stand no chance of success.

The advisory task was an effort involving human relations. To ensure success, it had to be carried out with a full understanding of human psychology, a deep devotion to duty, a knowledge of strengths and weaknesses, and in a tactful and courteous manner. The same rule applied to the indigenous people who received advice and assistance. To achieve this, MACV made commendable efforts in providing advisors with background knowledge on Vietnamese culture, traditions, and customs and manners.

Throughout the years of JGS-MACV association, many Vietnamese officers assigned to the JGS believed that their advisors were unduly restricted and restrained by US security regulations. As a result, and despite the common effort, they never divulged the contents of highly classified US documents to their counterparts, even though the information could be of mutual concern. Perhaps because of these security constraints, MACV never discussed nor [even] informed the JGS of its annual military assistance programming for the RVN. The JGS never knew how much force structure increase, equipment, or money were being programmed for a certain year until after Washington had approved. Even then, whatever information the JGS could obtain from MACV was usually sketchy and did not help very much in making detailed plans for the judicious use of money and assets.

The common practice over the years was that all JGS recommendations and requests regarding military aid were received with due respect, but never completely satisfied. MACV seldom provided an explanation concerning the logic or reasons which resulted in this curtailment of support. This state of things changed only after the Paris Agreement was signed and MACV no longer existed.

• • •

III. ARVN BATTALION TO CORPS AND THE TACTICAL ADVISOR   Lieutenant General Ngo Quang Truong

The Tactical Advisory System

As a result of the expanded US advisory effort to help the RVNAF cope with aggravating insurgency problems, and with the approval of the Vietnamese Joint General Staff, the Military Assistance Advisory Group, Vietnam, began to deploy advisors to selected ARVN battalions around the middle of 1961. The mission given to these tactical advisors was to help Vietnamese battalion commanders in operational, communications, and logistic support matters, with the understanding that they were not to engage in actual combat.

By the end of 1961 the US tactical advisory system was reflected in every ARVN combat arm and service battalion, sometimes down to company level, as in the case of armor units, since they usually operated separately. The battalion was chosen as the lowest tactical level to receive advisors since infantry battalions made up the bulk of ARVN combat forces. The infantry battalion was also the lowest level unit to have a headquarters with planning and control capabilities, and it was also the largest organization to be normally employed as a tactical unit. Therefore the advisory effort, with its emphasis on operational and logistical matters, was directed at the level which, it was believed, would most benefit from it.

• • •

In addition to corps infantry and combat arms units, US advisors were also assigned to other combat forces such as the Airborne and Marine Divisions of the general reserve, ranger and Special Forces units, and Civilian Irregular Defense Groups (CIDG). Advisory personnel assigned to special forces units and CIDGs came from the US Army 5th Special Forces Group. Unlike the regular advisory system, the US Army Special Forces organization for advisory assistance was tailored to the specific missions assigned to each type of unit. Since these missions were predominantly border defense and unconventional warfare, US Special Forces advisory teams were sometimes deployed to platoon level, especially in airborne ranger companies and mobile strike task forces (Mike).

• • •

With regard to territorial security and defense, the US advisory effort became particularly significant with the assignment of advisory teams to districts (subsectors) and the expansion of advisory personnel at province (sector) level in 1965. The buildup of US combat forces and the emphasis placed on pacification made the role of these advisory teams especially important, since it involved providing assistance to province and district chiefs in all matters related to the planning and execution of the pacification program and the employment of territorial forces in support of the military plan.

• • •

The Tactical Advisor's Responsibilities

US Army advisors did not command, nor did they exercise operational control or responsibility for any part of the Army of the Republic of Vietnam (ARVN). Their mission and functions were to provide professional military advice and assistance in those specific areas of endeavor assigned by the Military Assistance Command, Vietnam, namely to advise and assist the counterpart ARVN commanders and their staffs in personnel management, training, combat operations, intelligence, security, logistics, and psychological/civil affairs operations.

• • •

Restrained as it was by limitations in personnel, the US advisory effort was largely instrumental in the gradual improvement of ARVN units. Limitations in personnel did not discourage US advisors from doing all they could and striving constantly to make the units they sponsored better every day. In addition to providing the various assets that they could muster for the support of ARVN operational requirements, the advisor's professional knowledge and skills in planning, operations, tactics, and technology contributed substantially to the performance of units in several instances. Their ARVN counterparts learned a great deal from them. In fact, the presence of advisors acted not only as a catalyst through which changes and improvements were attained, but also provided the incentive that stimulated and spurred actions [by] both the unit and its commander. The results obtained throughout the years of US involvement showed that leadership and the management of units underwent a definite improvement and that combat effectiveness increased remarkably.

On the other hand, the advisor's overriding influence sometimes tended to stifle the

ARVN commander's own initiative and diminish his authority and prestige. Usually the advisor confined himself to his advisory role; his relationship with the counterpart was essentially one built on and limited to mutual trust and respect. There were compelling instances, however, that required the advisor to trespass the line drawn, and, by so doing, he practically acted as a commander—on the latter's behalf, naturally. This was what actually happened in a few ARVN units whose weak commanders wavered and were unable to make decisions under battlefield pressure. The prestige and power of the tactical advisor in such circumstances tended, in the long run, to tarnish the role of the ARVN commander in the eyes of his troops.

• • •

The Advisor's Role in Operational Planning and Combat Intelligence

Poor planning was one of the most glaring deficiencies of ARVN units. This deficiency was most serious at regimental and battalion levels. There was not enough formal training in the ARVN to develop planning skills, and the lack of capable personnel at these levels accounted for the absence of improvement in staff work. Whatever the reasons, the responsibility for this deficiency fell squarely on the unit commander, and if he were not demanding or aggressive, his staff would be less disposed to do acceptable staff work. Most ARVN tactical commanders at these echelons fought their battles without formal detailed plans, but by personal improvisation. The commander was all and everything in the unit; his staff's contributions to the performance of the unit were minimal. It was the commander who decided everything, told them what to do, where and when to go, and how to conduct the operation from the beginning to the end. When he was absent, there was little his staff could do without his specific orders. Unfortunately, more often than not, if the commander was not there his staff simply abstained from taking actions, even if they knew what to do.

Because of these critical shortcomings, US advisors at nearly every level were compelled to participate in, or even initiate, planning for operations. Their contributions became even more important during the active participation of US forces, when almost all combat support assets were provided and controlled by US advisors. In these circumstances there was little the ARVN unit commander could do except make decisions based on his advisor's recommendations, regardless of his own initiative. But, regardless of how hard US advisors would like to push, they usually had to act in a most tactful manner in order to keep the relationship intact and maintain harmony.

• • •

Generally speaking, US advisors contributed a great deal to the operational planning conducted by ARVN units. By and large they proved remarkably adept and knowledgeable in this area of endeavor, and their advice was particularly effective when they had a thorough understanding and appreciation of the situation.

• • •

The relationship between US advisors and US units depended partly on the nature of the effort to be achieved and partly on the individual prestige enjoyed by each advisor.

With regard to tactical advisors, especially at regimental and battalion levels, this relationship was not always a happy one. For one thing, at the same unit level the advisor was usually outranked by the US commander. For another, some advisors had not commanded troops in actual combat, even a unit at a lower level. As a result they became self-conscious of their standing, and therefore were somewhat hampered in their coordination effort. US unit commanders sometimes tended to look down upon the US advisors, whom they did not consider as co-equals. This was similar in some respect[s] to the haughty attitude shown, for example, by an ARVN battalion commander toward a district chief, an attitude wholly unjustified and misleading for the simple reason that a district chief's responsibilities were much more complex and heavier by comparison.

• • •

It was really unfortunate that, despite their heavy responsibilities, US advisors seemed to enjoy less prestige and less opportunities for professional advancement than US unit commanders. This lack of respect toward US advisors, added to certain prejudices against ARVN units in general on the part of some US unit commanders, often hindered effective coordination and cooperation efforts between ARVN and US forces.

• • •

It was obvious that ARVN units relied heavily on US-supplied intelligence data in view of its reliability, validity, and timeliness. Since their trust in these special reports was nearly absolute, the prestige of US advisors was particularly enhanced, not only because of their professional capability or knowledge of the enemy situation, but because they were the providers of accurate information. The high validity that Vietnamese commanders usually attributed to US technical sources led to their inference that US advisors at higher levels should be completely knowledgeable about the enemy's policies and plans. Some ARVN tactical commanders believed, for example, that MACV and US field forces knew well in advance the enemy's plan for the 1968 Tet Offensive, but kept this information to themselves for political reasons and only divulged it to some degree to a few ARVN confidants.

• • •

The language barrier was probably the most obvious limiting factor affecting the US intelligence advisory effort. Language proficiency was not only required for daily contacts and coordination between advisors and counterparts, but was also deemed indispensable for the accurate understanding and dissemination of intelligence data and to avoid misunderstanding or confusion when precise terminology, especially as used by the enemy, was concerned. To offset the language shortcoming, US advisors used indigenous interpreters who, at the tactical levels, were helpful with general ideas, but, when it came time to interpret accurately Communist terminology, they were generally not proficient enough for lack of a sufficient intelligence background. The fact was, although they are Vietnamese, Communists—especially North Vietnamese Communists—use a vocabulary which includes several terms whose connotations entirely escape the South Vietnamese layman's ability to comprehend, much less render it in another language.

US Support and the Problem of Leverage

• • •

As mobile operations were increased in frequency and size during the years following Vietnamization, and with the increased participation of all combat arms, logistical support was hampered by severe limitations, especially when the area of operation was far removed from field depots and lines of communication. In such operations almost all supplies and support assets had to be moved by helicopters, and this was the primary reason why ARVN units had to depend on US advisors and, through them, on the support provided by US forces. This dependence centered chiefly on airlift assets and certain critical operational supplies such as ammunition, fuels, barrier materials for the construction of fire support bases, and other items that the ARVN logistics system either did not carry or could not provide in time to meet requirements.

US advisors were usually solicitous and zealous concerning the logistic support for their units. Naturally no advisor could tolerate watching his unit fail to accomplish a mission merely because of a lack of supplies or equipment. That was why ARVN units could always depend on US advisors for whatever supplies they needed in any combat situation.

• • •

US advisors did not command. Nevertheless, they were in a position to influence their counterparts and make them accept their advice and recommendations. There were several ways a US advisor could exert his leverage. As a provider, he might choose to withhold the assets required by the ARVN unit to accomplish its mission pending satisfactory compliance with what the advisor thought was desirable. This always seemed to work—for whatever immediate purpose—since the advisor controlled most of the support assets. Additionally, the US advisor, in view of his broad professional knowledge, was apt to win over this counterpart by force of reason or logic.

As a result, during the years of intensive combat—from 1966 through 1968—when US advisors provided substantial support their influence was undeniably strong, especially during combat operations. But, when the reduction of US support assets was initiated in early 1969 as a part of the Vietnamization program, whatever leverage US advisors could still use to influence their counterparts became essentially a matter of personal relationship and individuality. Some ARVN commanders genuinely liked Americans and continued to cooperate in a commendable spirit of harmonious teamwork. They felt they still needed the assistance of US advisors, whose professionalism and experience [were] respected and held in high esteem.

Others, however, [sensing a change in the wind], deliberately left US advisors out of the picture and failed to consult them, or even inform them of unit activities. Fully aware of this changing attitude, some advisors became cautious and reluctant to give advice and abstained altogether from critical comments. Obviously they knew that their counterparts, like most ARVN commanders, were extremely sensitive to criticism, and, if there was a need to contribute to the accomplishment of certain tasks, these advisors would only offer, tactfully and suavely, constructive remarks lest the rapport and mutual trust be negated.

Experience showed that the advisor who skillfully utilized his leverage with support assets, in combination with his personal persuasive logic and reasoning, in order to influence his counterpart usually succeeded in improving his working relationship and his counterpart's effectiveness. It was also true that leverage, if based only on the provision of support assets, simply resulted in temporary gains by the advisor, who additionally never learned much from a true working relationship. In this case the advisor ceased to be an advisor and his true role was not being accomplished. On the other hand, the tendency to "let the advisor do it all," in the few cases where it might have existed, seemed to stem from a negative attitude of ARVN commanders reacting to excessive and rough leverage. In general, when an advisor began his second tour of duty he was an artful master of his job and knew how to make things work effectively.

Observations on Tours of Duty and Relationships

With the exception of key positions at the command level, the normal tour of duty for ARVN advisors, as well as for US combat troops in South Vietnam, was one year. But not all US tactical advisors in the field stayed on the same job for the entire year. Advisors in ARVN battalions, for example, were rotated every six months if the combat situation permitted. This limited tour policy seemed to benefit the American servicemen in many respects. Its impact on the effectiveness of the advisory effort, however, is a matter worth discussion.

US advisors assigned to ARVN tactical units, especially battalions and regiments, usually worked hand in hand with their counterparts at all times. They lived and fought in an isolated environment which hardly afforded them any material or physical comfort. The constant mental pressure and physical exertion required were not conducive to their maintaining a high degree of efficiency for sustained periods of time. Had they been required to serve for a long or indefinite period of time, certainly their efficiency would have diminished. But the tour was limited. They all knew exactly when they could go home, and this was not only an incentive that spurred them to devote all their time and energy to their jobs, but also a tremendous psychological boost for their families.

The good performance of a tactical advisor, however, seemed to depend on a certain continuity and stability of effort devoted to a unit. This would require him to stay at least eighteen months with a unit, but two years would have been better. The one-year tour/six-month rotation policy, despite its advantages, did not maintain enough continuity to make the advisory effort as effective as desired.

• • •

This also explained why district advisors, whose tour of duty was eighteen months, were more effective in their efforts to help local units and the local population. The difference was obvious; they had more experience and knew more about the local environment.

• • •

Command is a difficult art. Besides professional competence, a commander must also possess certain qualities to exercise the art of command effectively. It is the same with an advisor. The role of the US advisor, in view of its relative complexity, was not an easy one.

Certainly there were several dissimilarities between the US advisor and the ARVN commander. Some of these could be found in their approach to leadership, their culture and way of life. Other differences were either technical or procedural; these could easily be eliminated. There were, however, certain differences resulting from human nature that were impossible to reconcile within a short time. Naturally the keys to success in every human partnership lie in the character and attitudes of the men themselves. Personality therefore played an important role in the advisor-counterpart relationship. It was obvious that, unless both partners wanted to get involved, and unless they subordinated their personal desires for the good of the unit, there was no chance for them to foster a true relationship. But, once a good relationship had been established, the enthusiasm with which each [strove] to work together toward a common goal was apt to induce better cooperation and coordination between their staffs and subordinates. Over the years this became the rule rather than the exception.

In several instances US advisors grew impatient with the seemingly sluggish approach to work displayed by the Vietnamese in general. This was understandable. Having a relatively short tour of duty, US advisors tended to try to accomplish as much as they possibly could within that time. An advisor was apt to deluge his counterpart with ideas, plans, and programs as fast as he could think of them. To his counterpart, however, it was not always easy to cope with all of them at the same time, because there were certain things the advisor would fail to recognize as difficult or impossible unless he was a Vietnamese commander.

As a result, to enable his counterpart to perform effectively, the advisor would have to assign priorities, to sort out and organize suggestions, and find an appropriate time for consultations. If the advisor kept harassing a counterpart with uninterrupted suggestions, regardless of substance, he was apt to discover that he could accomplish very little and that his effectiveness as an advisor was greatly reduced. On the other hand, if he deluded his counterpart with excessive flattery, or just left him alone and was too easygoing, his advice was apt to be taken lightly, even though it was founded upon experience and professional competence.

In general, achievement depended a great deal on the advisor-counterpart relationship. Whether this relationship worked depended again on several things. However, the keys to success were the advisor's personal attitude and his genuine desire to help his counterpart. Mutual respect and understanding were always required. For, without mutual respect, nothing could be achieved and no advisory technique could help.

An Evaluation

By early 1973, when the last US advisory teams departed South Vietnam, most ARVN commanders had worked closely with several different advisors. On an average, each tactical commander had experienced some relationship with from 20 to 30 different advisors over the war years.

During the initial period of the war, the US advisory role was confined to delivering equipment and training ARVN units. As the war escalated in tempo and intensity, advisors became increasingly involved in tactical training and advising ARVN unit commanders on how to conduct combat operations. In this new tactical role, the efforts of advisors initially met with some inertia on the part of some ARVN commanders. These commanders had long combat records resulting from the years they fought alongside French forces. The habits they had developed under French influence were hard to change or modify overnight. They found American training methods too constraining, too conventional, and ill-suited to the war conditions in Vietnam. Whereas the French emphasized commando tactics, characterized by rapid movement and hasty raids with little or no combat support, the American way was methodical, careful, and thorough, characterized by detailed planning and preparation. In a word, it was "by the book."

• • •

To the combat-experienced Vietnamese, much of the American way of doing things was too slow and too "academic." They were complacent with their war records, thinking that they were adequately experienced, or at least knew how to fight this type of war. American tactical training, they felt, was something they did not require at that time.

In some respects the aversion to accepting US advice on tactical matters was not entirely attributable to pride or self-consciousness. In fact, during the early 1960s most US Army company-grade officers assigned to field advisory duties in South Vietnam had no real combat experience, except for the few career officers who had fought in Korea a decade earlier. In the eyes of experienced ARVN regimental and battalion commanders, the standing and value of these young advisors were not very high. Their role therefore was particularly difficult and the range of their effectiveness greatly limited. During this period US advisors mostly concerned themselves with the utilization of equipment, weapons, and equipment maintenance, and assisting ARVN units in technical or logistical matters, but rarely in combat or tactical matters.

The role of US tactical advisors, however, underwent a radical change during the mid-1960s, when US combat support assets, especially airlift, helilift, and tactical air, were introduced into South Vietnam in increasing quantities each year. For the first time in many years, ARVN unit commanders felt vulnerable because of their reliance on US advisors who provided and controlled these combat support assets. The advisory role definitely became more significant, and its effectiveness increased visibly, when heliborne operations and US tactical air support made their appearance. The outlook and intensity of the war seemed to add more purposefulness and a closer rapprochement to the relationship between advisors and their counterparts.

If the impact of the advisory presence was to be evaluated in terms of the specific contributions it brought to the ARVN war effort, then it can be said that every level of ARVN organization for combat needed advisors for some reason, and the usefulness of advisors varied from level to level. At the battalion level, the role of advisors was particularly important as providers and coordinators of combat support; it was less prominent in intelligence, since battalion advisors were not as well versed in the terrain or the enemy situation as the ARVN commanders.

The critical importance of combat support planning and coordination, and the weakness of ARVN commanders in these skills, were painfully demonstrated in the ARVN operations toward Tchepone in Laos in 1971. US advisors did not accompany their battalions and regiments in this campaign, and the optimum employment of US firepower and helilift could not be achieved without them.

As we moved up the tactical hierarchy, the need for advisors was more acutely felt in two specific areas: planning and leadership. The basic weaknesses of ARVN units at regimental and sometimes at division level in those areas seriously affected the performance of subordinate units. However, the strength of US advisors, whose adeptness in planning and leadership was particularly prominent, played a major part in improving these problem areas.

• • •

The leverage of US advisors, meanwhile, seemed to be more effective at the lower levels than at the higher echelons, where it would have provided better results. At higher levels, the advisory effect tended more toward fostering good rapport than applying leverage to get results. Consequently it was not altogether responsive to the requirement for assisting ARVN to overcome its shortcomings. These major shortcomings were in all phases of staff planning, in the operation of communications systems for effective command and control, and in realistic personnel policies that would permit the timely elimination of incompetent commanders. It is unfortunate that US advisors at the top echelons of the structure did not push hard enough for improvements in these fields. The advisory effort should have endeavored first to bring about an effective command, control, and leadership system for the ARVN before trying to improve the combat effectiveness of small units. If this priority had been established, the entire advisory effort would have been more beneficial.

During the last two years of US advisory presence, 1971–1972, the regional assistance commands seemed to be more suited and more responsive to ARVN tactical requirements. In each corps area the regional assistance command commander and his staff provided direct assistance and support to the ARVN corps, especially in planning and directing its combat efforts. It was the new direction and emphasis of the advisory effort at this level that were responsible for the marked improvement of ARVN performance in the field, despite the fact that US advisors and combat support assets at lower levels were being greatly reduced. The performance of ARVN units during the enemy's 1972 Easter Offensive was eloquent testimony to the effectiveness of the regional assistance command concept. It was this emphasis on cooperation and support provided by regional assistance commands to each ARVN corps that helped the RVNAF hold out and avoid defeat and collapse.

In retrospect, our war experience indicates that at the corps level there should have been a strong advisory system at the beginning to work directly with the corps commanders and help them improve their staffs. Each ARVN corps would have been responsible to produce results with the assistance of a limited field advisory system, consisting of the ablest personnel and reaching down to only a few key positions at lower levels. It could have been augmented by a number of mobile training or assistance teams, under the direct control of the regional assistance command commander, to be used when required to meet ARVN tactical and training needs as they surfaced in each individual unit.

IV. THE INTELLIGENCE ADVISOR   Colonel Hoang Ngoc Lung

A Pioneering Effort

• • •

To help the ARVN intelligence branch . . . , the US Army Training Relations and Instruction Mission (TRIM) set about in early 1955 to organize an accelerated two-month intelligence course for ARVN officers. This course was conducted in the Philippines and was the first intelligence assistance provided by the US Army. Most graduates of this course were assigned as instructors to the ARVN Intelligence School in Cay Mai, in the Cholon District of Saigon, which conducted its first course for ARVN intelligence officers in November 1955. The only training materials available at that time for the instructors and their students were transcriptions of the notes the ARVN instructors had taken during their two-month training. The urgent need for more and better instructional materials led to the assignment of the first US Army intelligence advisor in South Vietnam; the Cay Mai Intelligence School was the first ARVN organization to welcome him.

The first American advisor was regarded with considerable awe by the ARVN officers at the Cay Mai school. Not only was this "first" a novel event, but the word "advisor" itself created some impressions in Vietnamese minds that probably would have greatly surprised the American involved. In Vietnamese minds, "advisor" was associated with the position of "conseiller," which implies some supervisory powers such as [those] enjoyed by former emperor Bai Dai when he served as counselor for the first Viet Minh government in 1945. Some derogatory connotations were also visualized, for it was remembered that in the early 1950s Red Chinese advisors to the Viet Minh were acclaimed by the Communists as their "prodigious advisor comrades." Thus the position of an advisor, as far as intelligence officers of the ARVN were concerned, invariably evoked an aura of authority and of scholarly knowledge, especially since it was compared with Mr. Ngo Dinh Nhu, the then all-powerful political counselor to his brother, President Diem.

At the Cay Mai Intelligence School the man most perplexed by the event was the commandant himself. He had been summarily informed by the Training Bureau/General Staff that a US Army advisor would be assigned to his school to provide assistance in training. Nothing more was learned about his mission, functions, authority, or the scope of his activities. These were the things that the commandant wanted to know in detail, but could not obtain from the General Staff. The first action he took was to order the establishment of a separate office for the advisor in the school headquarters compound, and he issued positive instructions to all school personnel that only the two assistant commandants were permitted to deal with the advisor, and then only in his absence.[3]

Despite the commandant's initial misgivings, the advisor's presence was an instant success, since through his efforts the school immediately obtained US Army intelligence training texts which it needed so desperately. In general, the entire school staff was favorably impressed by the advisor's activities and the way he conducted himself. His suggestions helped solve the problem of training aids, and he tactfully kept an eye on the instruction being given in various classrooms, the performance of ARVN instructors, and how the students reacted and progressed. He [made] a point of jotting down his observations and comments and drafted them into memoranda for the personal attention of the school commandant. He also played an active role in helping the commandant run the administrative aspects of the school by offering suggestions on the maintenance of vehicles, weapons, and other equipment. He accompanied the commandant on the weekly inspections, visiting barracks and student sleeping quarters and even participating in social and ceremonial functions held by the school.

The school commandant was elated. His advisor was truly an advisor; the way he performed his duties left no doubt about his sincere desire to help, to assist. He did not exercise any authority, nor did he encroach on the commandant's command duties. The school staff members were greatly gratified by the free English lessons that he conducted, and they felt no complications when performing their daily work in his presence. On their part, the students remained intensely curious about the American advisor and tried to learn as much as they could about his role and his relationship with and attitude toward the school. They were enlightened and pleased with their findings, which assisted them several years later when they welcomed US advisors into their own units.

Increasing Commitment

• • •

With the concurrence of the RVN government, the United States agreed to deploy US Army advisors to all ARVN intelligence organizations, from the Joint General Staff . . . level to corps, divisions, and sectors (provinces).

At the JGS, the US intelligence advisory team which was assigned to J-2 in April 1962 was a pioneering effort at this level. The team consisted of nine officers, two of whom served as senior and deputy senior advisors to the Chief, J-2. The others were assigned to each of the operating divisions of the J-2: collection, training, interrogation, aerial photo, order of battle, and technical intelligence. The mission assigned to the team was not so much to provide advice to the J-2 personnel, but rather to help keep track of and record intelligence data on the enemy situation throughout South Vietnam, especially information pertaining to the enemy's order of battle and infiltration from North Vietnam as collected by ARVN sources.

•••

What the J-2/JGS needed most from the US advisors at that time was assistance in obtaining modern equipment, especially for imagery interpretation, to replace obsolescent equipment. Another urgent need was for US-produced intelligence information. The US team's failure to respond immediately to these requirements made its advisory effort look suspicious in the eyes of ARVN intelligence officers. But gradually the team's contributions to ARVN intelligence, in terms of agent reports and signal intelligence, became significant.

•••

In general, during the period of the increased US commitment (1962–1965), although US advisors were deployed throughout the ARVN intelligence system, their relationship with ARVN intelligence counterparts seemed to be cautious, especially during the period of political upheavals leading to the military coup of 1963. The Diem government suspected that the US Embassy was supporting the rebellious Buddhists and that US intelligence agents stimulated them into action. As a result, the relationship between Vietnamese intelligence personnel and US advisors was seriously affected. Understandably, no Vietnamese intelligence official would want to incriminate himself by maintaining too close a relationship with US intelligence personnel who were suspected of plotting against the government. The subsequent political turmoil during 1964 did not help improve this relationship, and the Vietnamese continued to be cautious and reluctant to become too closely involved. At the corps, division, and sector levels, however, the US-ARVN intelligence relationship was not affected in any way by political events in Saigon.

•••

The Period of Full-Fledged Cooperation

The role of US Army intelligence advisors and the US-ARVN cooperation and coordination in intelligence activities took a vigorous step forward in 1965, when US combat troops were introduced into South Vietnam. The war had entered a new phase, and, in the face of stepped-up Communist attacks and infiltration, US efforts and capabilities to monitor the enemy situation were inadequate.

•••

Effective as it was in collection through the use of modern technology, the US intelligence effort during these early months seemed to be somewhat deficient in analysis and lacked depth when it attempted to assess the true nature of the war and the determination of the enemy. This was understandable, since never before had the United States faced such a pernicious enemy on terrain which thoroughly favored him and under a form of warfare in which he made the rules. Other constraints in language and culture added to the difficulties faced by US intelligence personnel in South Vietnam. These weaknesses, by contrast, were the very strengths of the Vietnamese, who unfortunately did not have the technological capabilities possessed by the Americans.

• • •

The requirement for cooperation, and the concept of mutual compensation, were recognized by the Vietnamese and the Americans and led to a substantial increase in US advisory personnel in the field, from corps level to the district, and to the establishment of combined intelligence agencies. The number of US Army intelligence advisory personnel at sector level, for example, increased from three to seven. More important, however, was the activation of four combined intelligence agencies: the Combined Intelligence Center, Vietnam (CICV); the Combined Document Exploitation Center (CDEC); the Combined Materiel Exploitation Center (CMEC); and the Combined Military Interrogation Center (CMIC). The operation of these centers by a mixed Vietnamese-American staff with US-provided modern assets and Vietnamese indigenous resourcefulness greatly enhanced collection and analyses activities and provided effective intelligence data for MACV J-2, J-2/JGS, and combat units for all allied forces at all levels.

• • •

During daily working contacts US intelligence advisors seldom made professional remarks concerning their counterparts' way of doing their job. Advisory comments, if any, usually consisted of explaining US techniques and procedures which had been found effective. This nonmeddling attitude reflected a tactful respect toward ARVN intelligence officers, who reciprocated in kind. A mutual respect developed, which helped maintain a good working relationship and rapport between the advisor and the advisee.

• • •

At the four combined intelligence agencies, US personnel usually outnumbered their counterparts. Nonetheless, their working relationship was generally good from the very start and caused no problems over the years. This happy and productive cooperation was possible for two reasons. First, the relationship was based on a formal agreement reached between MACV and the JGS which determined the procedures for cooperation covering a wide range of subjects, such as the sharing of office space and facilities, guard and security duties, the authority of each element commander, and the approach to be used in problem solving. Second, and more important, was the exemplary spirit of cooperation displayed by the top intelligence officers of both sides. . . . On his initiative, for example, Major General William E. Potts, US Army, ACS/J-2 MACV, held regular meetings in which he briefed the MACV commander, the chief of the JGS, and his chief of staff and J-2 on the current enemy situation as viewed from the US side. This innovation in US-ARVN intelligence cooperation set the tone for the pervasive spirit of cooperation at all echelons. It also provided the opportunity for General Abrams, COMUSMACV, and General Vien, Chief of the JGS, to discuss in detail the current enemy situation, trends, and intelligence estimates for the future.

Anatomy of a Relationship

• • •

By and large, the attitude of each Vietnamese commander toward his advisor depended on his own enlightened experience and education. It was largely a matter of personal improvisations, never the subject of formal guidance. By contrast, every US advisor was briefed and aided by handbooks on the role he was going to assume, on the country where he was to live—its geography, history, social customs, and manners—and on the specific branch or unit with which he was going to work.

• • •

Despite the hospitable and accommodating nature of Vietnamese in general, and all the preparatory work that US advisors accomplished prior to their assignment, the relationship between them seemed to be affected by certain unfounded prejudices or misconceptions, especially during the early years of US direct participation, instilled perhaps by superficial reports of the communications media—movies and television in particular. The fact was, due to cultural differences and the language barrier, Vietnamese were generally inhibited and almost never took the first step in dealing with foreigners. Whatever contacts they maintained with US advisors were made primarily by commanders or responsible staff officers, since they were the only persons qualified by both the requirement of their jobs and a certain ability to speak the English language.

The cultural inhibition of ARVN personnel seemed to be a reason why some US advisors complained about the lack of enthusiasm and the apparent lethargic approach to work on the part of the Vietnamese. Whatever their merits, critical remarks along these lines certainly did not improve advisor relationships. In defense, the Vietnamese usually argued that US advisors served only one year, enjoyed a good life, and were not immediately concerned about family affairs or anything other than their jobs. As a result, they reasoned, the Americans were able to devote all their energies to their short tours, while they themselves had to live with the war for all their lives.

One year was indeed short as a tour of duty, since it included the unproductive time spent in familiarization with environment and job, usually about three months. In some instances an advisor would be transferred to another job even before completing his one-year tour. As a result, it was impossible for some ARVN commanders to work with any particular advisor long enough to develop a fruitful relationship. The commander of one combined intelligence agency once observed that during the period of a year he had had six different US counterparts. This high turnover rate for advisors seriously affected the combined effort, especially since it was a long-range effort requiring a certain continuity in job relationship. Some ARVN commanders even found, to their dismay, that what had been agreed previously by a certain advisor was not necessarily palatable to his successor. As a result, both sides often abstained from committing themselves to any long-range undertaking.

In view of the nature of intelligence work, which required steadiness and continuity, a longer tour of duty for those advisors assigned to intelligence duties would have been advisable. Eighteen months would have been reasonable, but two years would have certainly been better for the sake of the combined effort. I was especially fortunate that my counterpart, Major General Potts, who had completed previous tours in Vietnam, was held in his position of MACV J-2 for almost four years. This is a good indication of the emphasis placed on the importance of the intelligence program by General Abrams.

• • •

In general, most US advisors were defeated in their effort to use spoken Vietnamese in work discussions. This was understandable, first because Vietnamese, being a tonal language, was phonetically difficult for most Westerners to master in a short time. Then the eagerness of the Vietnamese to practice their English—which most of the educated spoke with some degree of proficiency—really discouraged the US advisors to carry on his Vietnamese language practice. For an American intelligence officer to be really effective in his job, especially when it required a profound knowledge of the Vietnamese Communists, the mastering of Vietnamese was essential. But then not every US Army officer had the time or inclination to develop this ability, and, in view of the variety of intelligence objectives, only a few truly proficient in the language were required.

Outward appearances were sometimes a matter of importance to ARVN personnel. Experience showed that, in combined intelligence agencies, ARVN personnel usually watched US advisors come and go to see if proper military courtesy was rendered to higher-ranking ARVN officers. To them, this was a way to find out for certain whether US personnel considered their ARVN counterparts as rank-for-rank equals, and whether they had any respect for the ARVN in general. Concerned about equality and discrimination as they were, ARVN personnel usually felt gratified when they could share every facility, whether at work or at rest, with Americans on an equal footing. The examples given by US personnel always worked on their counterparts. For example, in a jointly shared facility, if US troops did housecleaning every morning by themselves, ARVN personnel automatically joined them and usually tried to perform just as well.

In general, in their relations with US advisors or coworkers throughout the years, ARVN personnel usually came to the same generalizations as they judged their counterparts. They were convinced that US personnel were very punctual, always neatly dressed, highly disciplined, and respectful of orders; responsible and professionally competent; sociable and compassionate; tactful for the most part—they were well aware that advisors did not command; very well trained, especially the technicians and specialists.

Other qualities that ARVN personnel found common among US intelligence advisors were: they usually monitored events in minute detail and promptly reported them to superiors; they were also willing to help their counterparts overcome difficulties, especially those related to resources needed in the performance of their tasks, and this assistance was always swift.

The traits that the Vietnamese attributed to intelligence advisors were perhaps similar to those found among all advisors, regardless of their branch or specialty. However, objectively speaking, intelligence advisors were more successful in their role than most others. This was perhaps due to the fact that the intelligence advisory effort was undertaken in a most tactful but very effective manner in which the advisor acted both as a coworker and an advisor. This dual approach to advisory assistance made both advisor and counterpart understand each other better, since they shared a common task and worked toward the same objective in a similar environment. As a result, the advice given was more realistic, more essential to the common task, and apt to be more willingly accepted. This approach also made the advisory effort a two-way, mutually benefiting enterprise, since it compensated for the inherent shortcomings found among advisors such as constraints imposed by culture, language, a short tour of duty, and lack of continuity.

• • •

As a result of this assistance, ARVN intelligence improved markedly with every passing day and proved responsive to the requirements placed on it by the need to know more about the enemy, even during the post-cease-fire period when the US advisory role was terminated. The spirit of cooperation and coordination, despite this, was maintained up to the very last moment when South Vietnam collapsed.

V. THE LOGISTIC AND TECHNICAL ADVISOR
Lieutenant General Dong Van Khuyen

Significant Milestones

When the first US field advisors were deployed to major units and military schools of the Vietnamese National Army in early 1955, the Vietnamese army logistic system still functioned under the aegis of French officers and NCOs, who assumed most of the key command and staff positions. The Vietnamese army logistic system was then at its embryonic stage. It functioned as a separate organization, but its young cadre only served in an assistant capacity.

In 1956 the French High Command was dissolved. In its wake the French Expeditionary Corps and all French cadre of the Vietnamese army logistic system departed in haste. It was only then that the US Temporary Equipment Recovery Mission (TERM) was established and the Vietnamese army logistic system began to receive US advisory assistance through TERM.

A senior US Army colonel of the Quartermaster branch was introduced to the Chief, G-4/General Staff. He was to work with this staff division and assist in developing a workable logistic support system for the Vietnamese army. An office was immediately installed for him within the G-4 compound, staffed by a Vietnamese NCO who spoke good English. The advisor's office became part of the G-4 staff division in all respects, and its occupant became known to the Vietnamese personnel as the "Advisor-Colonel." The advisor-colonel seldom stayed in his office. He came and went with unpredictable irregularity, sometimes showing up every day, sometimes appearing only once every two or three days. But the G-4 staff knew that he was extremely busy and worked with total dedication.

Every time he came to his office, he brought something new and a lot of work for the G-4 staff. At first, there were stacks upon stacks of manuals, pamphlets, and assorted publications. Then came unsigned typewritten memoranda containing certain recommendations that he suggested might improve the organization and operation of the system. Sometimes there were pictures taken of glaring deficiencies in preventive maintenance and storage, accompanied by still more memoranda, usually unsigned, but sometimes bearing his signature. He and Vietnamese logisticians held many discussions, always through the intermediary of the NCO-interpreter.

It was with a deep sense of appreciation that Vietnamese logisticians welcomed the growing pile of manuals and memoranda, because they responded exactly to what they had always sought: a new direction for the Vietnamese logistic effort. Months of hard work for all of us would follow each time he came. We were gratified, but felt greatly frustrated by our own inability to understand the language. He seemed to share our eagerness to learn, not only the new things but also the language through which they were to be learned. He cheerfully gave us English lessons in the afternoon after duty hours. Communication between us therefore improved with every passing day as we progressed. The first difficult steps had been taken; they were in the right direction. With his devoted help, we felt confident we could overcome any obstacles that lay in the way of our new direction toward progress.

• • •

Observations of the US Logistical Advisory Effort

• • •

Could there have been an excess of technical advisors? I doubt it. Being on the receiving end of US military aid and advisory assistance for over twenty years, through periods of relative calm as well as intense fighting, my colleagues and I only found a shortage, never an excess, of advisors.

• • •

The effectiveness of advisors depended in large measure on how long they stayed in their jobs. This was especially true of logistic and technical advisors. The one-year tour was definitely too short for these advisors to acquaint themselves with the environment, the procedures, the human relations aspects of their assignment, in order to effectively contribute their experience and know-how to the task of helping improve the RVNAF logistics system. It is my personal opinion that, no[t] having to face the same harshness and hazards as their tactical colleagues, logistic and technical advisors would have contributed much more to the RVNAF if their tours had been longer, two years at the ALC level and three years at the central level. But perhaps this would have placed too much of a strain on their families. A balance, therefore, should have been struck between the results desired in South Vietnam and the personal sacrifices.

• • •

The subjects of misuse, abuse, or theft of military property were only briefly raised by US advisors, and never discussed at length. US advisors also deliberately avoided using the term "corruption" in conversations. It was as if they felt the allusion to corruption was untactful and might hurt ARVN logisticians' feelings. But it was true that ARVN logisticians were never self-conscious about the subject whenever it was brought up. Indeed, they always admitted, without irascibility, the existence of corruption as an inevitable social vice occasioned by a long, destructive war and general impoverishment. They always appreciated the concern of US advisors about this debilitating vice that they themselves, and the RVNAF in general, tried hard to combat and eradicate. So it was with full cognizance of the problem, with candor and openness that ARVN logisticians discussed corruption with US advisors, and even asked for their cooperation in combating it. During the intensive anticorruption drive, US advisors were always kept informed of investigative results and disciplinary measures being taken. But US advisors seemed to make a point of never making allegations nor helping identify any corrupt individual on the basis of hearsay or rumors. In fact, they abstained altogether from providing names.

• • •

A prerequisite of good management was the adequacy of information. By contrast with US advisors, who were usually supplied with all required information concerning ARVN logistical activities, either by ARVN logistical units or through their own system, ARVN personnel were usually denied management information by the US side. Vietnamese logisticians resented this fact, but could not explain it to themselves except by assuming that the Americans were bound by security regulations which forbade them to disclose certain management data to ARVN counterparts. A case in point was information related to the Military Assistance Program and other special programs of military aid. ARVN logisticians were usually kept in the dark as to annual appropriations and quarterly allocations to each technical service. As a consequence, ARVN logisticians were unable to make timely decisions and take appropriate actions in keeping with authorized capabilities. In time, they developed the idea that US resources were inexhaustible and tended to request far more than was actually needed. They did so with the sure expectation that the advisors would cut the requests to fit the program.

• • •

Some Lessons Learned

• • •

As previously mentioned, during the 20 years of benefiting from the US advisory effort, the RVNAF published only two short memoranda, in 1955 and 1958, concerning the relationship of US advisors and ARVN officers. From 1958 on the US-ARVN relationship was the subject of no further directives or instructions. This was indeed an omission of great consequence which gave rise to many unsettled complaints by both sides. Some ARVN commanders thought that US advisors spied on them, while some US advisors contended that ARVN commanders deliberately withheld information concerning their units. But these complaints would have been infrequent had a comprehensive set of instructions been published by the JGS telling each ARVN officer exactly what to do and how to benefit from the program. It was indeed regrettable that this subject was neglected.

The fact that most US officers selected for advisory assignments had to attend an orientation course in the US prior to reporting overseas was an excellent means to prepare them for advisory duties. But US logistic advisors could have benefited even more if a similar but shorter course had been conducted in Vietnam under the CLC sponsorship. Such a course would have greatly enhanced the US advisor's knowledge in terms of Vietnamese culture, the RVNAF logistic structure, operations, and dissimilarities with the US system. Such a course would have made US advisors thoroughly conversant with current programs and problems and the most effective techniques to be used. It certainly would have made the US advisory effort more successful.

• • •

In conclusion, the logistical advisory system as it was established for the benefit of the RVNAF was extremely effective and entirely responsive to our requirements. Despite a difficult task, logistical advisors always accomplished their missions and duly earned the respect and enthusiastic cooperation of ARVN logisticians. The allegation that US advisors acted as policemen only existed among a few nearsighted ARVN commanders who invariably were either incompetent or lacked confidence. In any case, the major offense of US advisors in the eyes of Vietnamese was perhaps an overanxious propensity for immediate results and overzealousness. US advisors were indeed indispensable to the RVNAF as long as we depended on US war materiel. The quantity and categories of advisors of course could vary according to the progress and experience gained by ARVN logisticians, but the RVNAF could not get along without American military aid budget managers and supply and maintenance managers at the central level whenever new types of equipment entered the RVNAF inventory.

VI. THE PACIFICATION ADVISOR
Major General Nguyen Duy Hinh

The US Response to Insurgency

• • •

By the fall of 1959, the insurgents seemed to have gained the upper hand, despite all security measures taken by the Government of Vietnam; their actions gradually became bolder. In September 1959, they ambushed two companies of the 23rd Infantry Division in the Duc My area, and, in early 1960, they launched attacks against the rear base of another division located in Tay Ninh. It was obvious that GVN control was eroding and the cities were being isolated from the countryside, where the Communists seemed to be able to operate freely.

In the face of this mounting crisis, US officials in Saigon began to show more concern for security in the rural areas and improving GVN representation and control. The US Ambassador, together with the Chief, MAAG, and other senior officials of the

"Country Team," developed a Counterinsurgency Plan outlining the political, military, and economic efforts required to help the GVN combat insurgency. Many reforms, mostly political and social, recommended by the US-conceived plan unfortunately were ignored by the Diem administration. Militarily, however, the GVN was eager to accept an expansion of the US advisory effort and increased military aid. The US Military Assistance Advisory Group immediately placed new emphasis on counterinsurgency training and began attaching field advisors to ARVN battalions on a selective basis. At the end of 1960, the MAAG also initiated training and support for the Civil Guard and People's Militia. In addition, US Special Forces teams undertook the training of the newly created ARVN ranger companies. It was very obvious at that time that the United States was increasing its commitment in South Vietnam.

After President John F. Kennedy took office in January 1961, his new administration increased support for the RVN in the face of stepped-up Communist aggression. The formation of the National Liberation Front (NLF), which was announced in Hanoi in December the previous year, left no doubt as to North Vietnam's ultimate objective in the South. Soon after the visit of Major General Edward G. Lansdale to South Vietnam in January, the US government created an interdepartmental action group known as Task Force, Vietnam, with the mission of studying, planning, and coordinating actions for the support of South Vietnam against the Viet Cong. In Saigon, a corresponding task force was also established; it included all members of the country team.

• • •

[Subsequently] a mission to South Vietnam headed by General Maxwell D. Taylor recommended a further increase in US advisory effort and combat support, continued expansion of the RVNAF, and support of the GVN Strategic Hamlet program. These proposals provided a new direction and emphasis to the US military effort during the following years.

• • •

By far the most important and extensive organizations for pacification support were the US advisory efforts at the province and district level. As early as 1962, following President Kennedy's decision for increased emphasis, US military advisors were deployed to all provinces at the same time as USOM field representatives. The need for increased assistance in restoring security during the following year led MACV to test-assign US advisors to the 13 districts surrounding Saigon in April 1964 as the Hop Tac pacification campaign was launched in this area. Results produced by this pilot program proved so encouraging that, two months later, the US Secretary of Defense, Robert S. McNamara, concluded that more districts should have advisors. By the end of 1965, when the RVNAF assumed the primary role of pacification support, the total number of US advisors had increased substantially in provinces and districts.

With the advent of CORDS in May 1967, the US civilian and military advisory efforts at the province and district levels began to consolidate into a single organization. The province senior advisor could be a military officer or a civilian. If he was a military officer, his deputy would be a civilian, and vice versa. Although he was the senior advisor to the Vietnamese province chief, the specialized advisors who made up his staff were authorized, each in his own area of interest, to make recommendations to the province chief. At the district level, most senior advisors were military officers.

• • •

By the time the CORDS organization was well established throughout South Vietnam, the total US pacification advisory strength included about 4,000 military personnel and 800 civilians. By mid-1967 these figures increased even more, but the additional strength was devoted to the task of advising and training the Regional and Popular Forces (RF and PF, formerly Civil Guard and People's Militia, respectively). Most of the additional advisory spaces were used to create a total of 353 Mobile Advisory Teams (MAT) whose mission was to train RF and PF units.

• • •

At the same time Mobile Advisory Logistics Teams (MALT) were also organized to help improve logistical support for the RF and PF.

• • •

By 1969 total US advisory strength in South Vietnam was about 16,000, including 1,000 civilians. By mid-1969, US Army advisors alone numbered about 13,500, including 6,500 in CORDS organizations; 95 percent of these pacification advisors were assigned to field duties outside Saigon, to provinces and districts and to mobile advisory teams. This was perhaps the greatest emphasis ever devoted by the United States in support of the RVN pacification program.

• • •

Relations and Contributions

• • •

During the years following 1965, while US combat troops were pouring into South Vietnam, US authorities also endeavored to help the GVN solve its pacification problems. But, during the initial period of US buildup and subsequent intensification of the fighting, most resources were devoted to the military effort, which outwardly overshadowed the "other war." However, as the GVN regained political stability when Generals Nguyen Van Thieu and Nguyen Cao Ky were installed in power, pacification became again a matter of national priority with the creation of the Ministry of Rural Construction.

• • •

In retrospect, from the Vietnamese point of view US contributions to pacification in South Vietnam were immense and all-encompassing. They covered all areas of endeavor, and included every aspect of support, from financial and material to ideological and technological. Their impact on the program was far-reaching at all levels, in all areas of effort, and much of this credit must be given to the US pacification advisor.

By far the most important and outstanding among US contributions was the expansion and upgrading of the Regional and Popular Forces, which in time made up over one-half of the RVNAF total strength and became as modernized in armament as the regular forces. This achievement was directly attributable to CORDS authorities, who untiringly worked toward developing the RF and PF and providing them adequate support. Upgrading the combat effectiveness of these forces was also a prominent program conducted with dedication by US advisors at provinces and districts and in RF/PF training centers. For many years US mobile training teams—MATs and MALTs—tenaciously devoted themselves to their difficult task under the most spartan conditions and in the roughest areas of South Vietnam. Other cohesive efforts, such as the marines' Combined Action Program in MR-1 and pair-off or combined activities programs in MR-2 and MR-3, also significantly contributed to the marked improvement of territorial forces, the mainstay of security and pacification.

The next significant US contribution to pacification was the sizable expansion of National Police forces, which ranked among the most important elements of pacification. With USAID support, the national police developed into a formidable force, 121,000 men strong by 1972. Its combat elements, the field police units which were created in 1966, became the main operational force against the enemy infrastructure. Police advisors, who were assigned to practically every aspect of police operations, constantly [strove] to develop this paramilitary force into an effective instrument for the identification and destruction of the VC infrastructure.

Many other contributions made by US advisors directly or indirectly to the pacification effort were equally significant. They included civilian or paramilitary forces that US advisors helped activate, train, and provide operational guidance; RD cadres; Provincial Reconnaissance Units (PRU); Census Grievance Teams; and, more significant, the Civilian Irregular Defense Groups (CIDG).

The idea of forming RD cadres, a Communist-inspired concept, was adopted by US advisors and implemented with the backing of the CIA. The first RD cadre groups, characteristically enough, were activated in late 1965 with locally recruited youths in the province of Binh Dinh, a former stronghold of the Viet Minh for many years. US advisors also helped activate and train the Truong Son, or Montagnard RD cadre. Two RD cadre training centers were established with American funds, support, and advisors, one in Pleiku for the Truong Son cadre and the other in Vung Tau, the bigger of the two. The Vung Tau RD training center later became a national center for the training of village and hamlet administrative cadres.

• • •

Throughout the years of the war in South Vietnam US forces undoubtedly contributed much to the pacification effort, directly or indirectly, through tactical operations on the ground, in the air, or at sea, and by providing combat support to ARVN forces, such as helilift, gunships, medical evacuation, and helping destroy and clear enemy base areas. As to US advisors, although they did not participate significantly in all pacification activities such as the People's Self-Defense Force program, there were specific areas of pacification which could not have been successfully undertaken by the GVN without their assistance and contributions.

The Phoenix program was an excellent example. Eliminating the enemy infrastructure had been a major concern and objective of the GVN since the beginning of insurgency.

But the program had lacked cohesiveness, purposefulness, and an efficient organization. At the instigation of US authorities associated with CORDS, the Phoenix program was initiated with a view to consolidate and provide a more effective effort against the VCI. But, even after Phoenix was established at the central level, it would have been extremely difficult to activate in the provinces and districts had it not been for the contributions made by US pacification advisors in terms of facilities and resources. For the PIOCC and DIOCC, for example, US advisors, in addition to their regular duties, even had to supply the typewriters and typists.

• • •

Other pacification-related programs such as Chieu Hoi and, most particularly, refugee relief and resettlement and land reform, benefited substantially from US support and the work of US advisors. The Chieu Hoi (Open Arms) program was rather a slow starter in the RVN antisubversive effort because of the rigid anti-Communist stand adopted by the Diem administration, which outlawed Communism altogether, and also because of the lack of resources. The program became a full-fledged effort only after 1963 when, through US advisors, the GVN learned that the Philippine amnesty policy had produced handsome dividends. The RVN Chieu Hoi effort made excellent progress after 1967, when a ministry was created to give it cohesive direction. In this effort to win over the enemy, the Joint US Public Affairs Office . . . made substantial material contributions, helped print and drop leaflets, conducted broadcasts, and provided money for the ralliers. The United States also provided funds for the establishment of Chieu Hoi centers and vocational training courses. As a result, the number of enemy personnel rallying to the GVN side increased steadily and reached an all-time high (47,000) in 1969. Over the years of its existence, the program resulted in a total of over 200,000 ralliers, which was a remarkable return for the costs involved.

But US contributions were even greater in the relief and resettlement of refugees and the land reform program. As the fighting intensified in 1965 and during the following years, the number of refugees also increased manyfold. With its meager resources, the GVN was unable to handle this growing influx of refugees in a satisfactory manner without US support. The direct participation of US combat troops in the war led US authorities to take a greater interest in the refugee problem. With increasing financial and material aid from the US government and private US charity organizations, the GVN built camp facilities and brought relief to and helped resettle millions of refugees.

• • •

The land reform program, which was regarded as an unprecedented and most resounding success, was partially the product of studies and research conducted by US experts who advised the GVN. The resulting "Land to the Tiller" act, which was proclaimed on 26 March 1970, sought to distribute about one million hectares (2.47 million acres) of farmland to landless farmers within a period of three years. Three years later, this objective had been met on schedule. The GVN paid out a total of 15 billion piasters in cash and another 82 billion piasters in bonds to land owners. The rapidity with which this ambitious program was successfully implemented was largely attributable to the effective assistance provided by US expert-advisors in the areas of land survey and cost computation. In addition, the United States provided over $500 million for the entire program and, more importantly, made certain that its advisors at the province and district levels helped guide the land distribution and compensation effort to success.

Aside from these conspicuous achievements of pacification attained with US money and advisory assistance, there were imperceptible but no less beneficial contributions that helped the RVN administration and armed forces improve their day-to-day operations and bring more scientific knowledge to bear on the conduct of national affairs. The progressive reforms in management and administration achieved throughout the RVN governmental hierarchy were but one of many examples. By exposure to American methodology and procedures, GVN officials learned how to apply modern management techniques to their own operations. And, to keep up with the rapid pace of American business practice, GVN agencies naturally had to adjust their own routine so as not to be left behind in the race toward common objectives. The constant stimulation and encouragement of US advisors were largely responsible for this marked improvement. As a result, the traditional functionary lethargy of colonial times was deeply shaken and gradually gave way to a much more efficient bureaucracy in every aspect.

The same learning and adaptation process was the major reason for improvement in planning by the military staffs at the JGS and field levels.

• • •

The most notable national-scale product was the Four-Year Community Defense and Local Development plan, 1972–1975, an effort which was entirely Vietnamese but bearing the indelible mark of several years of US contributions.

Another very significant contribution by the CORDS staff and US pacification advisors that radically improved the assessment of pacification progress was the modern evaluation system which used scientific analytical methods and advanced operations research technology. The problem included the requirement to effectively manage and evaluate complex pacification operations conducted under scores of programs and encompassing 44 provinces, 250 districts, over 2,000 villages, and 10,000 hamlets, all with the participation and support of hundreds of thousands of troops, policemen, and cadres. It was obvious that only scientific management methods and timely reporting procedures could help our Vietnamese leaders fully understand the situation throughout South Vietnam and make appropriate decisions.

Responding to this critical requirement, CORDS experts and advisors carefully and methodically developed several evaluation and reporting systems, all in apparent cross-connection with one another and covering almost every area of pacification-related activities: PSDF, Chieu Hoi, National Police, refugees, RD cadre, information, self-help projects, land reform, Communist terrorism, and territorial force management. A pacification data bank was established in Saigon to store the experience of several years of performance. Among the systems used to assist in the evaluation of territorial forces was the MACV-originated Territorial Forces Evaluation System. The advisors furnished the data for this system, which provided ARVN commanders with reasonably valid assessments of progress and shortcomings in the territorial forces. But the most note-worthy and more important was perhaps the Hamlet Evaluation System (HES). Despite some adverse criticism, this system proved the best and most valuable tool ever devised for the purpose of efficiently managing a program as complex as pacification. Not only did it contribute to a better evaluation and management of pacification, it also taught our Vietnamese pacification authorities more about their overall program.

I have presented in general terms and from the Vietnamese point of view some of the most discernible contributions made by US advisors to the pacification program in South Vietnam. Most of these contributions, although made at top levels, had a major impact in the field. But, at the field level, there was another aspect of US contributions, more human and more personal in nature, where the US pacification advisor was per-sonally assisting his counterpart in solving daily problems.

• • •

In general, apart from a very few exceptions, all US advisors assigned to the pacifi-cation program at all levels discharged their responsibilities in a most admirable way. Many were highly respected and well liked. Over the years, several individual relation-ships developed into lasting personal friendships. Taken together, all of these individual performances contributed to the overall success of the US advisory effort, especially with regard to pacification. Credit for much of the success of pacification, in the final analysis, must be given to US advisors, with a special tribute to those at the district and province levels.

VII. THE TRAINING ADVISOR   Brigadier General Tran Dinh Tho

A Monumental Achievement

Lieutenant Colonel Robert Murphy, a crew-cut, dark-tanned tall man with a Texan drawl and in khaki shorts, reported to the Inter-Arms School of Thu Duc in February 1955. A lone figure among the dozen or so French instructors who still remained there, he really did not know where to begin. He did not speak French, and the commandant of the school did not speak English. A young Vietnamese instructor who spoke English well was called upon to help them eliminate the language barrier, but the communica-tion process was slow. However, only a short time later, Colonel Murphy accompanied Vietnamese instructors in the field, where he demonstrated, using sign language, marks-manship techniques and the correct use of the Garand M-1. Thus was the beginning of a long training assistance program which would terminate eighteen years later. Colonel Murphy was one of the first US training advisors assigned to the nascent Vietnamese National Armed Forces, and a pioneer for the many Americans who would subsequently assume similar responsibilities.

• • •

During . . . eighteen years of dramatic development, the RVNAF had been trans-formed into a modern combat force, total strength increased more than fivefold, and new organizations, doctrine, and operational techniques adopted. In terms of human effort and material support, this achievement surpassed anything the United States had contributed to any country since the end of the Korean War. Throughout this period the US training advisor played a major role and made a most significant contribution to the RVN Armed Forces. As a former division G-3, corps G-3, and the last J-3 for the RVNAF Joint General Staff, a position I held for seven years, I was personally involved daily in the improvement and effectiveness of the RVNAF and will present from the Vietnamese point of view an evaluation of the US training advisor as he performed his challenging assignment.

Organization for Training and Training Support

• • •

For the convenience of advising the CTC and coordinating the US training advisory effort with RVNAF training activities, the MACV Training Directorate was located adjacent to the Central Training Command in the Joint General Staff compound, from where it exercised coordinating authority over US advisory teams, fixes and mobile, detached to ARVN service schools and training centers. In full cooperation and coordination, the CTC and MACV Training Directorate jointly developed plans, policies, and programs for the training of both ARVN regular and territorial forces and for the development and improvement of ARVN training facilities. At the schools and training centers, US advisory teams assisted ARVN commandants in preparing and conducting training programs and monitored the progress and results achieved.

Training Advisory Activities

• • •

The period from 1955 to 1969 . . . was devoted primarily to training instructors for the ARVN school system, since it received priority assignment of ARVN officers returning from US schools. During this period, over 5,000 ARVN officers and NCOs received training in the United States, in addition to 952 others who were given short orientation tours.

Next to the need of introducing US Army doctrine and tactics to the ARVN leadership, and training instructors for the ARVN school system, there was a requirement to expand and improve the ARVN school system, which had been established, equipped, and turned over by French forces. When French representation departed in 1956, there were only six major training facilities for the entire Vietnamese armed forces, including the National Military Academy at Dalat and the Inter-Arms School of Thu Duc. With US support and advisor assistance, only two years later the number of ARVN training facilities had increased to 18.

• • •

Programs of instruction were also subjected to extensive revision by US training advisors and the MACV Training Directorate to provide updated curricula for over 650 various courses. Most noteworthy of this combined MACV-JGS effort was the establishment in 1970 of a five-year training program for the entire RVNAF and the joint budgetary planning and programming for its support.

• • •

The US training advisory effort took a vigorous step forward as US forces began to redeploy in accordance with the Vietnamization program. The goal to be achieved, according to General Abrams, was to expand and improve the RVNAF to the extent that they could "hack it" alone. As a result, MACV endeavored on the one hand to increase US advisory strength, and select the best qualified officers for advisory duties on the other. By 1970 advisory strength, especially for the training effort, was filled 100 percent, as compared to 55 percent during the pre-Vietnamization period. Among these training advisors, whose total strength reached 3,500 by the end of 1971, about 90 percent had received combat experience in Vietnam.

• • •

Observations and Comments

In general, from the Vietnamese point of view, US advisors assigned for duty at ARVN service schools and training centers were apparently selected with great care, and they all instilled a good impression on ARVN staffs, faculties, and students. Their outward appearance alone inspired discipline and studiousness. Tall, healthy, invariably handsome in their starched uniforms and shining boots, they conveyed the perfect image of neatness and military elegance, a far cry from the usually carefree French instructor of former times in ill-fitted shorts and civilian shoes. Simply by looking at them, the average ARVN student was struck [with] admiration and an ardent desire to imitate. This alone produced a good effect on the students. Another good habit of US training advisors was their punctuality, which directly accounted for the cutback in tardiness among ARVN instructors.

Most training advisors were endowed with broad professional competence; they were entirely knowledgeable in their special areas of interest. The difficult points in instruction or questions raised by ARVN instructors were all explained carefully by advisors who always made a point of being precise and never ad-libbing. If they were in doubt of something they always took time to consult manuals or associates and invariably came back with the correct answers. This intellectual probity exerted a good influence on our ARVN instructors, who gradually [rid] themselves of the poor habit of improvising answers in classrooms, apparently to save face.

In my opinion the most resourceful and effective training advisors were those of the US Special Forces who developed the CIDGs and advised the ARVN ranger forces. Expedient, organizational-minded, and experts in small-unit tactics, US special force advisors were also highly capable in training and staff work. During over a decade of deployment, they single-handedly organized and trained various groups of Montagnards in the Central Highlands and contributed significantly to the defense and control of the border areas, a perilous and most difficult task.

As US forces began to redeploy from South Vietnam in 1969, MACV increased its emphasis on the quality of US officers assigned to training centers. Since there was no longer a requirement for replacements in US units, more combat-experienced personnel were diverted to advisory duties, many of them having served several combat tours. Being familiar with the war, and having lived in various combat situations, they were thoroughly conversant with problems faced by tactical units. Their assignment to ARVN schools and training centers tremendously benefited not only ARVN students but also our instructors.

• • •

The contributions of training advisors to the enlightenment and improvement of the RVNAF were indeed monumental achievements. Their tenacious efforts spanned two long decades of war and hardship. If there was a proper epitaph dedicated to the US training advisor of the Vietnam War, this epitaph ought to be: "The First to Arrive and the Last to Depart."

VIII. OBSERVATIONS AND CONCLUSIONS
Lieutenant Colonel Chu Xuan Vien

The Paris Agreement of January 1973 ended 18 years of American military advisory effort in South Vietnam. Looking back on the evolution of the system and the achievements of the effort, no one can escape the feeling that this was indeed the most ambitious program the US Army and its sister services had ever undertaken for the benefit of an allied military force. That this effort had been a success, there was no single doubt. By the time the last US advisors departed, the RVNAF had become a formidable instrument of peace enforcement, with its 13 well-equipped, well-trained army divisions; a strong and modern air force; and an efficient logistical support system. Under better leadership and with continued American support, this modern military force could well have been an invincible opponent against any invasion.

In terms of system and mission evolution, the US advisory effort appeared to have developed in four distinct phases or periods, which all reflected the changing US policies toward Vietnam. From 1955 to 1960, this effort was modest but far-reaching in consequence. This was a period of reorganization and retraining during which the nascent Vietnamese army was molded into what could be called the mirror-image of the US Army, structurally and doctrinally. While there appeared to be a strong strategic sense in the creation of a division-based army with ancillary combat and service support units, this conventionally trained and organized military force was ill-prepared for the type of counterinsurgency warfare it was called upon to fight in the late 1950s. If the lessons of the First Indochina War had been of any use, it would have been much better to develop at the same time the kind of territorial forces that were to play such an important role during the latter stages of the war. But support for these forces was late in coming, and not until 1961 was there any conscious effort to expand and train the Civil Guard and People's Militia (later to become Regional and Popular Forces).

The period from 1961 to 1965 was devoted to developing counterinsurgency capabilities on the one hand and to providing combat support assistance to the regular forces on the other. The role of the US Special Forces was most significant at this juncture in the training of the CIDGs and strike forces. Despite the usefulness of these organizations, they were an irritation to the GVN, which did not find its image enhanced by the presence of US-paid and supported auxiliaries. Some RVN leaders even suspected American motives behind the program and, when the Rhade rebellion broke out in 1964, they were convinced that it had been condoned by some Americans. US Special Forces also provided training and advisors for the ARVN ranger forces, whose creation met with initial opposition from the Military Assistance Advisory Group, which apparently suspected a political motive behind it. American concern over counterinsurgency further led to the assignment of US advisors to work with Vietnamese province chiefs and assist them in the training and employment of territorial forces. But this effort was at first viewed by the Diem government as a move to control GVN activities in exchange for extended support. Therefore the expansion of the US advisory effort to the district level in 1964, albeit occasioned by circumstantial needs, would have met with GVN opposition had Mr. Diem survived as president.

• • •

The next period (1965–1969) saw the role of US advisors almost completely overshadowed by the presence of US combat units and their active participation in the ground war. Despite a gradual force structure increase, the RVNAF were relegated to the role of pacification support in view of their limited capabilities. During this period the advisory effort seemed to be reduced to maintaining liaison and obtaining US logistical and tactical support for the benefit of ARVN units.

• • •

The advent of Vietnamization brought back to US advisors their proper role and, to the advisory effort, a new sense of dedication. Improved selection of US field advisors, coupled with various programs to enhance the RVNAF tactical and logistical capabilities, quickly yielded remarkable returns. The RVNAF, on their way to full growth, welcomed the effort, but were overwhelmed by the speed with which the programs accelerated. It appeared as if the United States was more concerned about getting out than willing to take the time for the entire process of Vietnamization to produce solid, lasting results; although it was true that, by the time the last US advisor departed, the RVNAF had been left with substantial amounts of assets and had grown into a military giant.

• • •

In general, except for the first few years, almost all US advisors seemed to have been well prepared for their role, which they usually performed with dedication and effectiveness. Depending on the level and specialized area of interest, there were certain dissimilarities in approach and techniques, but the objectives to be achieved remained essentially the same. In this regard, it was difficult to tell the difference from one advisor to another, for they were all dedicated to a similar cause. However, it appeared that, the higher the echelon, the less emphasis was placed on advising. In fact, only at the division and lower levels did US advisors truly act as advisors in the sense that they directly assisted in day-to-day operations and completely devoted their time and energy to advisory duties.

• • •

Although advisors began operating at the district level in 1964, the pacification support effort really made significant headway only as of 1967 with the advent of CORDS, which gave it more cohesive direction and provided more systematic advisory assistance to the RF and PF, the mainstay of territorial security. The spectacular achievements obtained during the following years were largely attributable to US advisors, military and civilian, who helped push the program to success. Their contributions were monumental and affected every aspect of the program, from planning to execution, monitoring and evaluation. Without their efforts and the sizable American financial and materiel support, the pacification program would have progressed much more slowly.

• • •

The inability of some Americans to adjust to local living conditions naturally led to the re-creation of American environments. This was a cultural trait that distinguished Americans from the French, who mixed more easily with the Vietnamese. It seemed that no American could survive without his PX, his compound, and his daily bath. In time, American compounds and PXs became monumental institutions of American culture in Vietnam. To the underprivileged Vietnamese, these constituted a whole world apart, a world so distant that Vietnamese seldom really felt close to Americans in a cultural sense. Exposure to American material opulence induced envy and greed that led to the practice of illicit business. This, added to the insecure psychology of wartime, the miseries of economic life, and the largesse of American aid, contributed to corruption. "American money corrupts," the Vietnamese press used to say. Although there was some slanting insinuation in it, the fact should be admitted that the presence of Americans and their conspicuous display of materialistic wealth created the conditions for, and not infrequently invited, corruption. There were never any written procedures on how to obtain goods through the advisor, but the good-natured and dedicated advisor was usually eager to assist his counterpart if asked.

• • •

There was no doubt that US Army advisors did an excellent job and the US advisory effort in South Vietnam indeed helped the RVNAF attain remarkable achievements in terms of combat effectiveness and technical and managerial skills, But there was one thing that this effort seemed never able to achieve: the inculcation of motivation and effective leadership. This was, after all, neither the fault of US advisors nor a shortcoming of the advisory effort, but a basic weakness of our political regime. The US advisor, as an individual, did all he could to fulfill his mission, and he did it well.

The majority of US Army advisors came out of their tour of duty with a better, more sober understanding of the problems the RVNAF had to face in the war. More importantly, they invariably came away with profound compassion and a heartfelt affection for their counterparts, with whom they had shared the hazards and spartan conditions of combat. Many such relationships had developed into lasting personal friendships. This was perhaps the least publicized human aspect of the US advisory effort that had brought two entirely different nations together for some period of their histories.

NOTES

1. Memorandum No. 1891/TTM/MG, 10 April 1955, signed by Major General Le Van Ty, Chief of the General Staff.

2. The first Vietnamese officers appointed to key staff positions were: Colonel Tran Van Don, chief of staff; Lieutenant Colonel Tran Thien Khiem, deputy chief of staff; Major Tu Cau, G-1; Major Trang Van Chinh, G-2; Lieutenant Colonel Nguyen Van Manh, G-3; Major Cao Van Vien, G-4; Major Tran Tu Oai, G-5 (Psywar); Lieutenant Colonel Tran Ngoc Tam, Training Bureau.

3. I was one of the two assistant commandants.

14

The South Vietnamese Society

Major General Nguyen Duy Hinh and Brigadier General Tran Dinh Tho

PREFACE

During the Vietnam conflict the long and destructive war, Communist subversion, an unstable economy, several changes in government, and the extended presence of Free World Military Forces combined to accentuate the basic weaknesses of South Vietnamese society: divisiveness and infighting.

To evaluate the effect that South Vietnamese society had on the conduct of the war, this monograph seeks to present the Vietnamese point of view on the joint US-RVN efforts to build a strong and viable South Vietnam, the impact of US aid and the American presence on the South Vietnamese society, the most significant social problems that South Vietnam faced during and as a result of the war, and finally the viability of the US-supported regime and its leadership.

To provide this in-depth analysis we, the authors, have drawn primarily on our own experience as major witnesses of South Vietnam's politico-social tragedy and participants in the war effort. Constructed from the combined vantage points of our positions, one in the field and exposed to the rural scene and the other in the very heart of the urban mainstream, this work thoroughly reflects the insider's viewpoint and [intimate] knowledge of South Vietnamese political and social life. . . . [Nguyen Duy Hinh and Tran Dinh Tho, 15 December 1978]

I. THE VIETNAMESE HERITAGE

Ancient Vietnamese Society and the Chinese Influence

Vietnamese have always prided themselves as a people with four thousand years of civilization, two thousand of which is steeped in legends and the remaining enlightened by recorded history. Chinese historians wrote profusely about the Vietnamese people. One of their works, *Viet Tuyen Thu* ("A Treatise on the Viets"), described our people in these words: "The Viets are disdainful, belligerent, astute in military matters, and not afraid to die. They live in the mountains yet move about on water, using boats as vehicles and oars as horses. When they come, it is like a gentle breeze; when they go, it is hard to catch up with them."[1]

Chinese emperors of every dynasty had always wanted to assimilate the Vietnamese by subjugation and domination. The first period of Chinese rule extended for more than ten centuries, from 111 BC to AD 968, the year the Vietnamese regained their sovereignty. During this long period, which was highlighted by five uprisings of Vietnamese patriots, what surprised historians the most was not the deep Chinese influence on the Vietnamese but their ability to resist complete sinicization.

• • •

The most profound Chinese influence on traditional Vietnamese society was perhaps Confucianism. The practice of Confucianism, which was founded by Confucius 500 years before the birth of Christ and later propagated by his nephew Mencius, was known as the Confucian-Mencian Way. Through the ages Confucian-Mencian philosophy so thoroughly permeated Vietnamese politics, ethics, sociology, and even economics that it could be said to be the Vietnamese nation's religion from its birth to the beginning of French rule in 1883.

• • •

In his study of Confucianism Pham Quynh, a Vietnamese scholar in the early 1930s, asserted: "Our society has two great classes, the common people who are rural peasants and the educated or (Confucianist) scholars. The commoners, always submissive and unenvious, look upon the scholars as teachers and guides. The scholars accept this responsibility obligingly and without arrogance; they consider themselves the missionaries of the Confucian-Mencian Way."[2]

The traditional social hierarchy depicted by Pham Quynh survived through generations and remained immutable until recent times. It included, in descending order, the scholars, the farmers, the craftsmen, and the merchants. Popular sentiment, however, did not always regard this established order as absolute. The supremacy of scholars, who usually shunned economic productivity, was often ridiculed by the more pragmatic common people. A popular saying in fact commented sarcastically: "They tell us that scholars come first and farmers second; all right. But when rice runs out and one is running around looking for it, then who should come first but the farmers?" This irreverent attitude toward scholars reflected the lesser extent of influence Confucianism exerted on the populace. The impact of Buddhism and Taoism, both also introduced by the Chinese, was perhaps much greater among them.

Buddhism came to Vietnam at the end of the second century BC and evolved through three periods, the first of which, the period of propagation, lasted until the sixth century. Buddhist philosophy observes that human beings are continually beset by sufferings from one life to the next. The sufferings that one endures in this life are the result of his doings in a previous life, and actions in this life are the cause of sufferings in the next. The real cause of sufferings is man's greed; to eliminate sufferings, therefore, one must eliminate greed. From the seventh to the 14th century, Buddhism gained ascendancy almost as a national religion in Vietnam. It was during this period that Vietnamese emperors adopted Chinese characters as the national script. Since Chinese Buddhist monks were also great literary scholars, they assumed the teaching of Chinese characters. The influence of Buddhism reached its apogee under the Ly and Tran dynasties, whose emperors led a monastic life after abdicating from their thrones. The 15th century then saw the decline of Buddhism, which increasingly came under attack by Confucianists. Buddhist monks gradually lost their scholarship and their grip on the true Buddhist creed; they eventually strayed into heresy, ritualism, and superstitious practices. Despite this, Buddhism remained a major religion in Vietnam, with an estimated 80 percent of the population claiming to be adherents.

Aside from Buddhism, Vietnamese were also influenced by Taoism, although to a lesser degree. Taoism was founded by a Chinese named Lao-Tzu at about the same time as Confucianism. Just as Mencius did for Confucianism, Chuang-Tzu, a disciple, continued to spread the Taoist philosophy and tradition after his master's death. Introduced in Vietnam under Chinese domination, Taoism had a broad following. However, because of the abstruseness of its ontology, perhaps very few understood it. The essence of Taoism lies in quietism and passivism, which implies that one must absolutely give up all concern and desire and ignore the bodily self in order to achieve spiritual purity and tranquillity, a state of the mind devoid of all wishes and actions. Chuang-Tzu compared life to a dream. He told of a dream in which he was transformed into a butterfly; awake, he wondered whether he was a butterfly dreaming of becoming a man. Distorted interpretations of Taoism eventually degraded this philosophy into a popular creed characterized by superstition, magic, and sorcery and widely practiced by the Vietnamese common populace. Among the educated, the impact of Taoism was more philosophical. In general, it created a certain abhorrence of wealth and fame and the quest for an easy life and total freedom.

In short, the combined philosophies of Buddhism, Confucianism, and Taoism exerted a rather unique influence on traditional Vietnamese society: a steadfast adherence to fatalism, or the belief that everything was predestined or preordained by mysterious causes. This was a trait that seemed to affect the drive for action among Vietnamese, whether as individuals or as a community.

• • •

The Vietnamese Spirit of Struggle in Ancient Times

• • •

Resistance to the North was mainly directed against Chinese domination and aggression. Although, during the thousand years of Chinese rule, the Vietnamese had won back only three brief years of independence—from AD 40 to 43—their insurrection was highlighted by the fact that it was led by two heroines, the Trung sisters. At the command of an ill-trained, ill-equipped army of 60,000 men, the Trung sisters succeeded in throwing out the Chinese administrators and troops of the Eastern Han Dynasty by the sheer force of their patriotism. The return of the Chinese army under Ma Yuan eventually forced the Trung sisters to drown themselves in the Hat River, but, even in defeat, this valorous act demonstrated the invincible Vietnamese spirit. "Rather dead than living in shame" had become the predominant trait of national survival ever since.

•••

Besides resounding feats against foreign aggression, the Vietnamese also distinguished themselves by actions designed to punish belligerent peoples to the south and colonize their territories in the process. These actions were dictated by the need to remove a serious threat posed by Champa and Chenla (Cambodia), whose armies had repeatedly invaded since the second century AD (102). Then, at the turn of the 11th century (in the year 1044) [*sic*], the Vietnamese expansion southward began in earnest. By outright annexation, military conquests, or diplomatic maneuvers, this colonizing process did not end until the 18th century.

Two significant developments emerged during this southward movement. As national territory extended southward, the spirit of regionalism was born. It came as a result of difficulties in interregional communication, years of warfare or crop failure, insurgencies in many localities, and the weakening of royal authority with the concomitant strengthening of recalcitrant local authorities. This division of the country into regions, each with its autonomous power, eventually led to a feudal system with 12 warlords in the tenth century.

The second development was the establishment of villages. As the basic administrative unit, the Vietnamese village was autonomous and self-sufficient. The imperial court never dealt directly with villagers. It enforced laws, levied taxes, and impressed citizens into military service or work gangs through the intermediary of the village's council of notables, who were elected by virtue of their titles, education, age, or wealth. This autonomous spirit led to each village having a separate charter which allowed the villagers to manage their own affairs and govern by themselves. Traditionally, therefore, Vietnamese liked to live in small communities. Their attachment and loyalties went first and foremost to their home villages.

•••

In general, from the time the nation was founded until the advent of French rule in the 19th century, the Vietnamese people had exhibited two remarkable traits: a disposition for endurance, patience, conservatism, and fatalism, which was instilled by Chinese doctrines; and a spirit of survival, independence, and expansion which manifested itself in times of national distress. Under French domination, these traits gradually underwent changes in order to adjust to the new circumstances. Accelerated by new developments in world currents, these changes gained strong momentum during the second half of the 19th century.

Vietnamese Society under French Rule

•••

Under the reign of Emperor Tu Duc, who suspected the missionaries of having political motives, the Vietnamese royal court ordered their persecution, giving France's Emperor Napoleon III an excuse to invade Vietnam in 1857. Eventually this led to French occupation of Vietnam and the establishment of French rule in 1883.

At the time of the first French attack, Vietnam already encompassed all of its present-day territory. The Nguyen dynasty divided the country into three regions—the South, the Center, and the North—and placed a royal governor at the head of each region to ensure a unified administration.

When the French took over, they maintained the same territorial division, [although] apparently not for the same purposes, but gave each region a different administrative status in accordance with their objective of "divide and rule." The South (Cochinchina) became a colony directly governed by the French, while the Center (Annam) and the North (Tonkin) were French "protectorates." The Vietnamese emperor was given some token authority over Annam, but real power remained in the hands of the French resident general at the head of each region.

In a move to further degrade the authority of the imperial court, which was executed through the system of mandarins, the French eliminated the mandarinate by replacing it with a French-trained civil service.

• • •

With their favored treatment of this new rising class, and their effort to win friends among Southerners by favoritist policies, the French managed to reinforce the spirit of regionalism that had been latent among Vietnamese.

• • •

A Society in Transition

• • •

Social stratification and class discrimination, once benign, now became accentuated. This was because the French had always wanted Vietnamese society to be deeply class-conscious. The old social hierarchy of "scholars-farmers-craftsmen-merchants" underwent some change which found the merchants prevailing over the farmers. A new class, the soldiers, had been added to the bottom rung of the social ladder; since they came mostly from the ranks of the illiterate peasantry, the soldiers were the most spurned by society. Men of letters still retained their preeminent rank, although true scholars were becoming rare. During this transitional period, people with an elementary or junior high education were all called educated. That was the educational level required to qualify for a low- or middle-level civil servant job, which was socially quite prestigious. Therefore academic degrees, especially those conferred by French schools in-country or in France, were the criteria by which a person's worth was evaluated, the crown of social success.

• • •

As for religion, Christianity gradually gained ascendancy from the support of French authorities, as well as from its own organizational success. Though much less numerous than Buddhists, the Roman Catholics constituted the most powerful community in Vietnam, especially in the North. For their part, the more numerous Buddhists were losing ground because of their inability to unite into a national religious organization and the fact that Buddhism became increasingly riddled by heresy and superstition.

• • •

In short, Vietnamese society at the end of World War II, after French rule had been suddenly terminated by the Japanese, displayed all the signs of stagnancy and backwardness. Still laboring under traditionalism and the vestiges of Chinese influence, this society was suffering from the half-hearted reforms and colonial policies of French rule. The process of eradicating ancient Chinese influence and reforming society on a modern pattern had just begun, and resulted in many dislocations. This was a transitional period during which the old evil was yet to be replaced by the new good and the new evil had already arrived to add to the old one.

Nationalists who were fighting against the French were all patriotic, but they lacked political shrewdness and experience. Premature emergence from the underground also doomed their activities to failure. They were even betrayed by Vietnamese who shared their anticolonialist stance but not their political ideas, then also by the Communists who sold them out to the French. Finally, those who had allied themselves with the Japanese against the French ended up being betrayed too. This hopeless situation lasted until the Japanese defeat. By that time, nationalist parties had been so depleted of talent and leadership that they were unable to take advantage of the political vacuum and seize power. Their inaction gave the Communist Viet Minh a chance to prevail on the people's patriotism and win national independence. Cunningly concealing their true nature and posing as nationalists, the Communists had managed to win the prime sympathy of the people.

Contact with Communism

The Indochinese Communist Party (ICP) was founded in 1930. When the Viet Minh, its [front] organization, seized power on 19 August 1945, the overwhelming majority of Vietnamese had only a vague idea of Communism. Of particular significance at this juncture, most Vietnamese at heart seemed to consider the Viet Minh as just another nationalist group with a different organization and policy.

The psychology of the Vietnamese people at that time was one of yearning for national independence. At any price, Vietnam had to be returned to Vietnamese rule; political persuasion only came second. Ho Chi Minh's skill was in his ability to exploit popular hatred of French colonialism and his manipulation of nationalists. In late 1945, therefore, he disbanded the Indochinese Communist Party, to the confusion of domestic and world opinion. In fact, he had shrewdly prepared for an eventual showdown with the French that required total popular support for success.

• • •

Even though the American involvement was most opportune, the initial stages of South Vietnam's struggle to stand on its own feet were beset with obstacles. The extent of the nation-building effort and American assistance, the gravity of social problems, and the issues of government and leadership will be the topics of discussion in the following chapters.

II. THE CONSOLIDATION OF SOUTH VIETNAM

The Preliminary Conditions

• • •

The Geneva Agreements of 20 July 1954 eventually resolved the military predicament of the French and provided the people of Vietnam the opportunity of choosing between the two newly divided zones. A moratorium was subsequently implemented during which Communist forces took over areas still under French control. It was also the period of authorized evacuation for the population of both zones; for the Hanoi-Haiphong area, this moratorium was set at 300 days.

During the first few days of this evacuation, the Communists virtually took no action. People from the southern delta of North Vietnam were moving in droves into the Hanoi-Haiphong area. In spite of the impassable roads and bridges, they kept moving by all available means: walking, wading across ricefields and rivulets, and boating down rivers, or along the coast to Haiphong if they lived near the sea.

After a few days had passed, Communist authorities realized the complications that were being caused by these mass movements. They began to interfere, first with mild measures, then with sterner and increasingly violent actions. Many villages and towns were cordoned off and placed under close surveillance; people were allowed to move only if they had special passes. Despite this, the refugees managed to flee under cover of darkness or by other surreptitious ways. Their immediate goal was to reach the Hanoi-Haiphong area; from there evacuation to South Vietnam became almost a certainty.

Among the groups that were leaving, the most cohesive and best organized were perhaps the Roman Catholics; led by determined priests, they would not hesitate to use violence to clear their way. Some, however, were less successful. As commander of an armor unit stationed on Route No. 5 at that time, I personally observed the plight of one such community nearby, the Catholic village of Kim Bich, about ten kilometers north of Hai Duong.[3] All the villagers wanted to leave, but the cordon of Viet Minh guerrillas was too tight. To deliver them, I had to maneuver my armor unit through the cordon. Without my armored vehicles, it would have been impossible for these villagers to break through and leave. This occurred just one week after cease-fire day.

Even in the areas under the control of French and Vietnamese forces, the departure of the people, especially government officials, was not easy. At that time the Communists had their cadres and agents deployed almost everywhere, even in the inner cities. Many households were visited by cadres who advised against leaving or threatened to keep them from leaving. For many people, therefore, the departure from Hanoi or Haiphong had to be carried out discreetly. Properties and houses could not be sold or belongings carried away openly. Preparations for the exodus had to be made to appear as if people were intent on staying. The more discreet the preparations, the better the chance of successful departure.

• • •

Eventually, as a result of American and French relief efforts, nearly a million Vietnamese located in the North had made their way to the South by planes or by ships. Had it not been for the obstructions and ploys of Communist authorities, the exodus would have been considerably larger.

•••

There were several reasons for this mass exodus. The most powerful driving force was obviously the determination to fight Communism, which had been acquired through experience with the Viet Minh. If, during the early years of 1945–1948, the entire Vietnamese people had seemed to be carried away by patriotic ardor, it was because the Viet Minh had carefully concealed their Marxist nature. But in later years, after the Viet Minh nationalistic mask had dropped, many people realized they had been duped by the most blatant scheme of exploitation and deceit. The resistance against the French had given the Vietnamese Communist Party its supreme status. From 1950 on, Vietnamese Communist leaders felt so reassured of popular support that they embarked on a class struggle movement in many areas even though, in Vietnamese society, there were no serious class distinctions or conflicts. The middle class and [petite bourgeoisie], though not rich, felt themselves threatened despite the fact that they had sacrificed a great deal for the cause of the resistance.

•••

In their jockeying for power, the Viet Minh did not hesitate to liquidate any adversaries they deemed dangerous. Bui Quang Chieu, founder of the Constitutionalist Party; Vo Van Nga, leader of the Party for Independence; and Nguyen Van Sam, the Imperial Delegate to Cochinchina, were all assassinated. In Hue, the Viet Minh killed the scholar Pham Quynh and Ngo Dinh Khoi, Ngo Dinh Diem's eldest brother, both from the former Bao Dai government and dignitaries with prestige in their times. The Viet Minh did not even spare their own comrades who happened to have divergent views; they killed Ta Thu Thau, for example, who was leader of the Trotskyist Struggle Group. This reign of terror eventually brought about the collapse of the nationalist movement in the South and gave the Viet Minh the indisputable leadership position in the resistance movement.

•••

When South Vietnam emerged as a nation south of the 17th parallel, it was built on a large anti-Communist base. This base consisted of a million North Vietnamese refugees, to include families of military and civil servants, over three million Cao Dai and Hoa Hao adherents, and other military and paramilitary forces. South Vietnamese society at that time could be divided into three significant categories: a small minority with Communist connection and underground Communist cadres, who were hostile to the Nationalist cause; the urban middle class, whose social status made them incompatible with a Communist regime; and the rural peasantry, which was uncommitted but malleable. The conditions were therefore opportune for the forging of a strong anti-Communist regime. But much seemed to depend on how the South Vietnamese government proceeded, and whether this government could demonstrate its usefulness to the people.

Nationalism, or the Nationalist cause on which the Republic of Vietnam was being built, was conceived as an antithesis to international Communism and as an ideological tool for motivation. The preservation of Vietnamese traditions, the maintenance of what remained of the Vietnamese heritage after nearly a century of French rule and nine years of destructive war, and economic development were promoted as strong incentives for the nation-building effort. South Vietnam certainly was not lacking in natural resources. With time and devotion, it should be able to heal all wounds of the past and become a strong, viable nation.

• • •

Motivation of the People

• • •

From the beginning of the conflict, the Nationalists had felt that need for an ideology of their own to light their path and serve as a basis for all of their programs. To meet this need and provide a doctrinal basis for the regime, the First Republic propounded the Personalist doctrine as an antidote to Communism.

According to Mr. Ngo Dinh Nhu, who developed this doctrine, personalism was a blend of Western and Eastern philosophies designed for the total development of the individual in Vietnam's communal-type democracy. Personalism fostered the development of the individual—morally, spiritually, and physically—in harmony with the social needs of the community and as a step toward building the nation's political life. Each individual was to cultivate himself as a contribution to building society as a whole. Human rights and human dignity derived from hard work, and it was through work that democracy and freedom would be achieved. The advocates of personalism hoped to build a balanced democracy in which law and order would reign; they rejected both the excessive libertarianism of Western bourgeois democracies and the restrictions and deceit of Communism.

After the fall of the First Republic and, with it, the demise of personalism, subsequent nationalist governments advanced no other doctrines. In general they espoused an uncompromising anti-Communist stance embedded in a vague nationalistic ideal. This ideal was to build a free and democratic society, as opposed to human enslavement and regimentation under the control of international Communism.

• • •

President Diem had personal prestige and moral rectitude, the qualities of a good leader. He had devoted all of his efforts to build the nation and motivate the people. Some of his collaborators, however, had committed errors that plunged the nation into chaos and led to the collapse of the regime. Suffering from a lack of prestige and unable to solve internal problems and mobilize the masses to join in the anti-Communist struggle, subsequent governments came to depend heavily on the United States. The advent of US participation in the war brought about far-reaching consequences which affected the entire fabric of South Vietnamese society.

III. AMERICAN INFLUENCE ON SOUTH
VIETNAMESE SOCIETY

Significant Contrasts

The Indochinese conflict brought together the Republic of Vietnam and the United States. Although this marriage of convenience was dictated by a common purpose—to contain Communist expansion, and especially North Vietnam's attempt to annex the South—the alliance brought to the surface certain basic incompatibilities between the two nations. . . . Vietnam and the United States were so dissimilar in origins, background, civilization, and environment that they stood at the very antipodes of the human spectrum. Such differences could only be mitigated or ignored, but never totally nullified.

• • •

A fundamental and most important difference between the two partners during the war was in the concept of time and action. While Americans regarded action as a compulsion and something to be performed aggressively in the shortest possible time, Vietnamese seemed to view time as an eternal commodity, an ingredient of the panacea to all problems. For this reason, inaction in the immediate present might be a form of action and was acceptable; it did not mean laziness, evasion, or passivity, but merely implied waiting for an opportune moment to act.

Vietnamese differed from Americans in the way they solved a problem. While the Americans often arrived at an optimum solution, the Vietnamese usually preferred a multiple approach. This inclination was a trait of the Vietnamese character which probably originated from Buddhist and Confucian influence. Buddha taught us that there is not just one buddha—the Enlightened One—but anyone following the right path can work toward his own enlightenment as a buddha. Confucius taught us to use the golden mean in our daily life. According to him, things are never slanted to one side and are subject to change by the natural order. Thus the right attitude to adopt is toward the middle of every issue.

The experience of Vietnam, with its numerous vicissitudes, its changes of dynasties, its political misfortunes of the 19th and 20th centuries, had probably reinforced among Vietnamese the predilection for a multiple approach to solving problems. This occasionally caused unwitting Americans, especially American advisors, to criticize their Vietnamese counterparts for their indecisiveness, their lack of dynamism and drive.

Family attachment of the Vietnamese was known to Americans, but this loyalty, as well as the extended family obligations, were sometimes beyond American comprehension. Vietnamese society had always been a restricted community. The nuclear family always lay within the limits of the extended family. When members of the extended family got married, loyalty to the extended family was further expanded to encompass the new nuclear families. Thus it was that, in human relations, feelings normally took precedence over reason among Vietnamese, and though many Vietnamese realized this as being a weakness, it was not easily overcome. Unlike Americans, Vietnamese gave little heed to social organizations and seldom regarded social activities as part of the individual's life, the exception being North Vietnamese Communists. No political parties in South Vietnam could be ranked among US parties in terms of the role they played in the lives of their members.

The relation between the people and the national leader in Vietnam was also different from what it is in the United States. While Americans make a distinction between the person of the president and his office, Vietnamese tended to regard the two as being inseparable. Such an attitude must have begun in feudal times, when "being loyal to the king is being loyal to the country," and was fostered by every South Vietnamese leader. These leaders identified themselves with the regimes they were leading so that loyalty to the person of the leader was the only way to be loyal to the political establishment.

The disastrous offshoot of this attitude was that anyone who made positive contributions to the system, the government, or the head of an official organization was regarded as a loyalist, and anyone who did not cooperate was regarded as a member of the opposition.

Another difference between Vietnamese and Americans was perhaps most significant, since it concerned the general attitude toward the war. With the war lasting almost continuously since 1946, most Vietnamese, though considering it a scourge, had come to regard it as part of their lives. Many considered peace and the end of all hostilities as wishful thinking and thus reconciled themselves to living with [the war]. This attitude led many Americans to criticize Vietnamese for negativism, flinching resolve, and defeatism.

Important as these differences were, not all Americans fully recognized them, which resulted in misunderstanding and lost opportunities to bridge the gap when cooperation was at stake.

Major Objectives and Their Impact

Throughout its association with Vietnam, the United States had three primary objectives: to assist South Vietnam in building adequate strength to resist aggression by North Vietnam, to help South Vietnam build a democratic state, and to help South Vietnam develop its economy. Each of these major areas of interest had an impact on South Vietnamese society.

• • •

A most significant impact on South Vietnamese society . . . was the drain on our total manpower caused by the expansion of our armed forces. This had a direct effect on our communities, collective activities and interests, standards of living, conduct, and organized patterns of normal life.

During the process of helping the RVN build adequate military strength, the massive military presence of the United States in South Vietnam had a disadvantage in that it usually eclipsed the role of the RVNAF. The US military presence naturally attracted the attention of the foreign, and especially the US, press. Reports on the war were heavily documented in terms of US performance and enemy activities. Conspicuously, most

RVNAF activities were left out of news coverage, and, when reported on a few occasions, the slant was invariably directed against their shortcomings or worse.

This pattern, which was repeated over and over again, was a constant irritation to RVNAF leaders and infused doubts in the minds of those military men who were suffering from a feeling of inadequacy. It even caused some people of South Vietnam to believe that the RVNAF were incapable of protecting them. As for the enemy, he stood to gain by the reports of the foreign press that unwittingly seemed to be extolling Communist exploits. This unfortunate condition contributed to the complete collapse of faith among RVNAF ranks and throughout our society in general at a time when US aid and apparent interest was dwindling.

• • •

During our evolution toward a true democracy the coup d'etat became a popular tool of power groups. Coups became such a fearful obsession for all South Vietnamese leaders that their main effort was to prevent them by appointing close and loyal friends to sensitive posts such as the CMD [Capital Military District], major units, military regions, and armed services. Every other consideration seemed to be subordinated to this concern. The net result was a reduction in the performance level of the RVNAF, since many of our major activities and units were riddled with factionalism, suspicion, and infighting and the fact that military leaders were contending for power by engaging in politics.

• • •

In addition to the impacts that US objectives exerted on South Vietnam militarily, politically, and economically, there was the significant imprint that US aid and the US presence left on South Vietnamese social life. As was true with the usual effect of Western civilization on traditional oriental life, this imprint had its good and bad marks, and both combined to change South Vietnamese society.

Social Impact of the American Presence

South Vietnamese might have differed on how and to what extent the presence of over one-half of a million US troops and advisors had influenced South Vietnamese society. Most agreed, however, that this presence affected primarily the urban segment and had a lesser effort on the rural people. They also agreed that the American influence was perhaps more pervasive than had been thought, because among the many impacts it had created there were tangible ones in the areas of military, political, and economic behavior, as well as intangible ones such as in cultural and social behavior.

• • •

Despite the ravages of the war, the urban society of South Vietnam seemed to thrive in prosperity. The majority of urban and certain wealthy rural people enjoyed all the amenities of modern life: automobiles, motorcycles, air conditioners, refrigerators, television, radio, etc., which were available on a large scale only to industrially developed Asian countries such as Japan. Most remarkably, even the ordinary working class was often able to share in what had usually been restricted to wealthy elements of society.

• • •

The presence of US troops brought about a marked improvement in land communications. Roads were enlarged, extended, or newly built, along with the rehabilitation of old bridges and the construction of new ones. This improved and extended road system not only facilitated interregional and interprovincial communication; it also brought the cities closer to the countryside and narrowed the urban-rural social gap.

• • •

While middle-aged South Vietnamese naturally tended to be conservative and adhered with nostalgia to traditional Vietnamese and French culture, the young people found American culture fashionable and quickly adapted themselves to it. This was evident in the way they dressed and the kind of music they adored. In many urban homes, people used lively bold colors for the interior, an obvious imitation of American decoration style. More conspicuously, the tall and stylish buildings which were rapidly constructed during the 1965–1970 period for the purpose of leasing to Americans added a modern [look] to major cities, making them more beautiful and impressive. With the buildup of US troops, apartment buildings also began to develop and expand rapidly. This was quite a change in living pattern for many South Vietnamese, who had been familiar only with single-family dwellings or extended family cohabitation within the same house.

As a result of the American buildup, a great number of people turned to activities directly or indirectly connected with services for US units and troops. These were contractors, entrepreneurs, businessmen, and some civilian employees serving in US organizations. Because of lucrative service contracts and business dealings, these people gained sizable incomes and many rapidly amassed great fortunes. High income and quick wealth also turned these people into a new privileged urban class, a class by itself that never existed in Vietnamese society before.

Another emerging social element was the prostitutes and bar girls whose numbers quickly multiplied with the buildup of US troops. Socially considered the basest and most contemptible, these elements seemed to take to the good material life with a [vengeance]. With the good and easy money they made, they spent it [on] far-out fashions and a flashy, abandoned lifestyle which exerted a bad influence on women and led many among them, the gullible and morally loose, to follow in their sinful steps. This unwittingly upset the usually puritan mores of traditional South Vietnamese society.

The next privileged social group consisted of civilian employees serving in US organizations, whose salaries were two or three times larger than those of GVN civil servants or servicemen. This disparity in income, coupled with a most lopsided distribution of wealth, was a major source of frustration and social injustice. The civil servants, servicemen, and policemen, those who received fixed and much lower salaries, considered themselves and were in fact [the] most underprivileged elements of society. They were understandably frustrated because the compensation they were receiving did not measure up to the sacrifices and contributions they made for the sake of the country's survival. By contrast, the people who made the most money were those who practically contributed nothing to the war effort.

• • •

On balance, the net result of the American presence in South Vietnam was that, no matter how well intentioned and dedicated Americans had proved to be, the Vietnamese always felt that their friends were playing the leading role in all fields of endeavor. They also had the impression that the United States was behind everything that ever happened to South Vietnam. The inescapable feeling among some Vietnamese nationalists who gave their allegiance to the Republic of Vietnam was that the South could never have made its just cause prevail and used it effectively as a viable alternative to Communism. Hence there were those who seriously questioned the usefulness of what they were doing, and especially the wisdom of American participation in the war.

• • •

IV. SOCIAL PROBLEMS

Discrimination and Factionalism

• • •

Time and isolation finally combined to accentuate . . . changes in the South. Though essentially the same language, Vietnamese underwent some modifications in its diffusion. In the areas of the Perfume River, alteration came in the form of lower pitches and restricted pitch variations in the tonal contrast; in the Mekong Delta and the Dong Nai River basin, linguistic expression became plainer and more direct.[4] Over the length of Vietnam, not only did the accent change from one province to another, but the vocabulary and modes of expression also differed. The milder climate of the South seemed to favor the pioneers; they did not need heavy clothes as in the North, and their housing could be built less elaborately because of fewer typhoons. The immensity and fertility of the land and abundance of food also made life easier and had a distinctive effect on the character of the southern people. Because of fewer hardships and less competition, there was no need for exertion and aggressiveness.

• • •

Regionalism under the First Republic was further compounded by religious discrimination. President Ngo Dinh Diem's family were devout Catholics of long standing. His eldest living brother, Archbishop Ngo Dinh Thuc, was the senior prelate in South Vietnam. In the Confucian tradition, the eldest brother had tremendous authority over his younger siblings. Father Thuc commanded substantial influence in the Vinh Long diocese, which saw significant developments during his tenure. Here was the seedbed of many a national program which highlighted the regime of the First Republic, such as the Nhan Vi (Personalist) cadre training center, the Republican Youth, and the Strategic Hamlets. Catholic clerics had easy access to the Independence Palace, and this rapport naturally resulted in governmental favors to Catholic organizations.

• • •

The ascendancy of military men to power after President Diem's death raised hopes of eradicating discriminatory practices deemed detrimental to national unity and the war effort. Since the RVNAF had always been regarded as a melting pot where regional and religious harmony prevailed, everyone expected the new leaders to set the example.

But the public soon found with disappointment that regionalist feelings were still strong and persistent. Once holding power, for example, General Duong Van Minh made no secret of his discrimination against non-Southerners, with whom he had no inclination to cooperate. So when General Nguyen Khanh, a native Southerner who was married to a Northern woman, deposed Minh on 30 January 1964, he enjoyed some popularity among the generals. Other civilian leaders who succeeded Khanh in power also seemed unable to avoid this common weakness. Mr. Tran Van Huong, for example, preferred to use only Southerners. His government, which was composed mostly of Southerners, did not last long because of this narrow-mindedness. The subsequent conflict between Chief of State Phan Khac Suu (a Southerner) and Prime Minister Phan Huy Quat (a Northerner) stemmed largely from regional rivalry. Prime Minister Quat had asked a number of cabinet ministers to resign in order for him to reshuffle his cabinet. Two southern cabinet members, supported by Mr. Suu, refused to comply. Compounded by criticisms from religious groups, the open rift finally forced Phan Huy Quat to resign and hand power over to the military in June 1966.

Regional discrimination did not just reign among government and military circles; it prevailed among religious and political groups as well. During the Buddhist struggle of 1966, the rift became evident among Buddhist ranks, which split into the militant An Quang faction led by Central-born monks and the Vien Hoa Dao (Institute for the Propagation of Buddhism) led by moderate Northern monks. On several occasions the schism between the two factions degenerated into bloody confrontation, and this weakened the ranks of military Buddhists. Things were no better for political parties, whose ranks were also split along regional lines. There was no solidarity between the Central and Southern branches of the Dai Viet Party; likewise, there was no harmony among the Northern, Central, and Southern organizations of the VNQDD (Nationalist Party).

• • •

While regional discrimination was a fact of South Vietnamese life, the game had its own rules. These were fairness and openness. Fairness required equal treatment and devotion to the common good and not the selfish interests of any individual or faction. Openness demanded that everything be aboveboard, unhidden. As long as these rules were respected, the problem of regionalism could be surmounted.

But, if religious and regional discrimination could be gradually kept under control through conscious efforts, factionalism continued to reign unchecked in all areas. This acute sectarian attitude tended to consider one's own clique, group, party, family, or religion as the only one worthy of trust and preponderance. Such an attitude caused untold harm and was a tragedy for the Republic of Vietnam.

• • •

Family rule was a charge most widely leveled at President Diem's regime. But, besides the president, only two of his brothers ever held public office: Mr. Ngo Dinh Nhu, who served as political advisor to the president, and Mr. Ngo Dinh Luyen, ambassador at large to some European countries. Mr. Luyen spent most of his time in Europe and contributed little to state affairs. Mr. Nhu, however, was the éminence grise, the mastermind of the regime and the one truly indispensable to the president. It was he who charted the RVN course and devised major policies. In the eyes of the South Vietnamese people, Mr. Nhu and Mr. Diem accomplished exceptionally good things.

• • •

With the fall of the First Republic the RVN witnessed a period of disruptive turmoil and factionalism such as had never occurred before. In the place of one ruling party there was now a proliferation of conflicting, quarrelling parties, factions, and cliques. South Vietnamese society, relieved of the constraints of the previous regime, seemed to explode in an uncontrollable paroxysm of activism.

In the wake of the 1 November 1963 coup, the following factions emerged: the ruling Duong Van Minh clique, which was still dividing among its members the spoils of power; the Nguyen Khanh clique that staged the putsch soon afterwards; and the Buddhist clerics who had become arrogant power brokers. Different university student groups and Dai Viet activists also began to make their impact felt. Along with the Nguyen Khanh clique, the "young Turks" (Nguyen Chanh Thi, Nguyen Cao Ky, Nguyen Huu Co, et al.) made their spectacular debut on the political stage. The Catholics, still nurturing their battered image from their close association with the previous regime, became defensive and reacted only when absolutely necessary. The Cao Dai and Hoa Hao, watching from the sidelines, were content with their quiet little power niches. At the same time, civic groups such as the Caravelle Group, the Inter-School Group, old party leaders, and returned political exiles were emerging tumultuously onto the national scene, all vying for power. The South Vietnamese political arena soon turned into chaos. Individuals were pitted against individuals, students against students, parties against parties, religions against religions, and each against all others. Coups and countercoups came in rapid succession. In the twenty months following 1 November 1963 South Vietnam had no less than nine governments, but none seemed to enjoy any popularity.

When the military government led by Nguyen Van Thieu and Nguyen Cao Ky came to power the situation began to stabilize, but not significantly.

• • •

Civic and religious groups, who had been expecting a return to civilian rule, were clearly discontented. Political leaders, who regarded themselves as intellectuals, professed little respect for the individual worth and ability of the generals; they often had no inclination to collaborate with the military. For their part, military leaders prided themselves on their organizational skill and leadership role in the anti-Communist struggle and looked down on civilian leaders as "armchair politicians" or "tearoom statesmen" who were both unrealistic and weak in leadership. Neither side seemed to understand the other, nor was inclined to sit down with the other in a joint venture except when motivated by self-interest.

In general, the civilian Ngo Dinh Diem government, despite its ability to maintain a high degree of stability, had failed to produce a dynamic national unity. Subsequent military governments failed even more dismally to maintain the social order and achieve popular consent and unity. Apart from discrimination and factionalism, South Vietnam's social and political life was replete with contending pressure groups, among which the influence of major religions seemed to eclipse that of political parties.

• • •

The Problem of Ethnic Minorities

The population of South Vietnam consisted roughly of 80 percent ethnic Vietnamese; the remaining was composed mainly of peoples known collectively as ethnic minorities. Excluding a tiny proportion of Indians, Pakistanis, Malays, and Arabs, who lived in the Saigon area and were engaged in commerce and moneylending, the ethnic minorities included the Chams, the Cambodians, the Chinese, and the Montagnards (mountain tribesmen).

Remnants of the kingdom of Champa, the Chams now numbered about 30,000 and settled mostly in the Phan Rang area, with a smaller group residing near the Cambodian border in Chau Doc Province. Basically rice farmers, slash-and-burn gardeners, and forest product gatherers, the docile Chams eked out a meager living and never posed any ethnic problem.

The Cambodians, about 400,000 strong, settled in the Mekong Delta, mainly in Vinh Binh, Ba Xuyen, and Chau Doc Provinces. Most were peaceful rice farmers; a few served in the military or civil service. Having long lived mixed with the Vietnamese, these Cambodians were not far removed from the mainstream culture; they all seemed well on their way to being fully integrated into Vietnamese life.

The Chinese formed the largest minority group of all. Their population was estimated at around one million, concentrated mainly in Cholon (Saigon's Chinatown) and other sizable communities in the Mekong Delta provinces of Kien Giang (Rach Gia), Bac Lieu, and Ba Xuyen (Soc Trang). They were engaged in commerce, real estate, banking, rice trade, and rice milling. Because of their industriousness, patience, solidarity, and mutual assistance, they had achieved success in all branches of business, and held a vital role in the economy of South Vietnam (just as they [did] in the economy of other Southeast Asian countries). The naturalization law promulgated in 1956 by the First Republic, which made it mandatory for all Chinese residents to become Vietnamese citizens, first met with mild opposition, but finally proved beneficial to the Chinese. With Vietnamese citizenship they were enjoying greater economic privileges, as well as the right to run for office, thus gradually acquiring political representation both on the local and . . . national levels.

Generally speaking the Chams, Cambodians, and Chinese engaged in no dramatic struggles. The Chams did little else than quietly establishing relations with foreign

Muslims. The Cambodians had demonstrated in Saigon a few times, demanding rights as a minority group, but their grievances were all met without difficulty. The Chinese seemed seldom to have involved themselves directly in power politics. They were always paying off authorities and accommodating to every government in power to ensure freedom for their private enterprise; they only mildly protested when confronted with harsh measures taken by the government. The greatest minority problem for the GVN was the Montagnards.

• • •

After World War II, when the Viet Minh Front had succeeded in seizing power, the Ho Chi Minh government proclaimed Vietnam as an independent and indivisible country. Soon afterwards the French returned and waged a war to regain mastery over Vietnam, as well as over all of Indochina. High Commissioner d'Argenlieu once again made the Central Highlands an autonomous territory in late May of 1946. French policy had always been bent on severing Montagnard country from the rest of Vietnam and creating division between Montagnards and Vietnamese.

Thus the ancient suspicion and distance that existed between lowlanders and highlanders were further magnified during French rule and continued until today. In 1950 Bao Dai granted a special status to the highlands, which he called "Royal [Domains]" and placed under his direct administration. This act perpetuated the separation of the Montagnard country from the Vietnamese state.

During the resistance war against the French, the Viet Minh tried to win over ethnic groups of North Vietnam's highlands and those of the Truong Son Cordillera in Central Vietnam. Many Montagnards had joined the Viet Minh ranks as resistance combatants. In 1954, when the country was separated in two parts, five to six thousand Jarai and Rhade cadres and soldiers regrouped to the North. Naturally these people were to receive further training and eventually be returned to their native highlands in the south for subversive action.

President Ngo Dinh Diem soon perceived the importance of the Central Highlands and the role of the Montagnards in his nation-building effort. In contrast to the Communist inclination of granting token autonomy to the highlands minorities, his was a policy of acculturation. This was a euphemism for his effort to assimilate the Montagnards to Vietnamese life. The long-range need for South Vietnam, as he saw it, was total ethnic integration and assimilation into Vietnamese society. But the First Republic's assimilation policy seemed to have been executed precipitously. Vietnamese in droves were sent from the lowlands to settle in the highlands, and overzealous government cadres took a number of untactful measures. The Montagnards, still unfamiliar with the status given them by the Vietnamese government, felt disturbed and threatened by the influx of the aggressive Vietnamese settlers. To add oil to the fire, Communist cadres came along with their propaganda and promises for ethic autonomy.

In 1958 a Montagnard autonomy movement came into being. It was the Ba-Ja-Rha-Ko Movement, an acronym for the tribes that comprised it—Bahnar, Jarai, Rhade, and Koho. It was organized by a former French government functionary named Y' Bham

Enuol. The movement was quickly quelled and some of its leaders arrested. Y'Bih Aleo, a Rhade leader, escaped and joined the Communists, who later appointed him vice president of the National Liberation Front and chairman of the Ethnic Autonomy Movement. Another Rhade leader, Y' Bham, and Paul Nur, a Bahnar leader, were imprisoned and not released until after the coup of 1 November 1963.

After initial experience with the 1958 Montagnard struggle for autonomy, the Diem government became more tactful. Administrative cadres were instructed to study Montagnard languages and to be flexible in dealing with the natives. From 1961 on, US Special Forces began to organize and train Montagnard Civilian Irregular Defense Groups (CIDG). Still the animosity and suspicion that divided the Vietnamese and the Montagnards were hard to eliminate.

In mid-1964 another Montagnard autonomy movement emerged under the name of FULRO (Front Unifié pour la Libération des Races Opprimées, or United Front for the Liberation of Oppressed Races). In a manifesto dated 1 August 1964, professing himself representative for the Chams, Rhade, Jarai, Bru, Raglai, Chauma, Bishrue, Bahnar, Sedang, Hre, Kebuan, Hadrung, Mnong, [Stieng], and other tribes, the FULRO leader Y' Bham proclaimed the struggle to throw off the yoke of domination by the Vietnamese. The FULRO reasoned that, since the Communists had waged war to destroy the Montagnards and the GVN was unable to ensure their security and always victimized them, the Montagnards had to fight for their own liberation.

Less than two months after this manifesto was proclaimed, a Montagnard revolt broke out in Ban Me Thuot which sent shock waves rippling through the highlands. During the night of 19 to 20 September 1964, about 500 Montagnard soldiers from five CIDG camps around Ban Me Thuot rose in mutiny, arrested and killed a number of Vietnamese officers and soldiers; they also kept a number of US advisors as hostages and seized the Ban Me Thuot radio station. Here Y' Bham, the FULRO leader, denounced the Vietnamese for committing genocide and demanded autonomy for the Montagnards.

General Nguyen Khanh, the prime minister, went to Ban Me Thuot to solve the problem. After more than a week of negotiation through the mediation of US advisors, the CIDG rebels surrendered and the hostages were released. Prime Minister Nguyen Khanh had rejected the FULRO demand for autonomous government in seven highland provinces, but he did promise several concessions. Montagnard villages would receive farmland four times as large as the current area they were farming, Montagnard customs courts would be restored, Montagnard languages would be taught in elementary schools, the Vietnamese language would be gradually introduced only in upper grades, and Montagnard youth would be granted favored status in admissions to high schools, the Thu Duc Infantry School, and the Dalat National Military Academy.

At the time when the situation in Ban Me Thuot was returning to normal, the FULRO leader Y' Bham, his staff, and a number of Rhade soldiers suddenly disappeared. They took refuge in Cambodia, perhaps still suspicious of GVN promises. In March 1965 Y' Bham was seen attending the Indochinese Peoples' Conference in Phnom Penh which was sponsored by Sihanouk (South Vietnam did not participate). Here he extolled Cambodian assistance and denounced the RVN.

• • •

When Generals Nguyen Van Thieu and Nguyen Cao Ky took the reins of the government the promises to the Montagnards began to materialize one after another. In July 1965 a decree was enacted that revived the Montagnard customs courts, and a Montagnard Military Training Center was established in Pleiku. But, in September 1965, 400 Montagnards in the Buon Ho CIDG camp (north of Ban Me Thuot) were attempting another mutiny. Only a timely intervention by ARVN units managed to disarm the rebels and avert bloodshed. After this incident Prime Minister Nguyen Cao Ky paid a visit to Ban Me Thuot with another package of promises: the administrative and military responsibilities for Montagnard areas would be turned over to native Montagnards and Montagnard candidates would be given preferential treatment for admission into the National Institute of Administration and military schools. A special office for Montagnard Affairs was promptly set up in Ban Me Thuot and placed under the General Directorate for Montagnard Affairs in Saigon, which was headed by the Montagnard leader Paul Nur.

Nevertheless the Montagnard struggle movement was far from dying away. On 17 December 1965 FULRO groups revolted in the three provinces of Phu Bon, Ban Me Thuot (Darlac), and Quang Duc. They held the provincial capital of Quang Duc for a short time, occupied two CIDG camps in Darlac, and killed 30 Vietnamese, including a district chief. These revolts were short-lived, however. After concessions, the government was now ready for firm action; the rebels were tried and sentenced to hard labor or death.

Soon the upgrading of the General Directorate for Montagnard Affairs into the Ministry of Ethnic Development, the presence of Montagnards in the National Assembly as well as in military and administrative positions, and the stabilized situation all contributed to making armed Montagnard rebellions a thing of the past. Furthermore, the GVN never ceased to extend a conciliatory hand to the FULRO movement.

In August 1968 contact with the FULRO was made. Granted immunity, the FULRO leader Y' Bham and his aides came in total secrecy to Ban Me Thuot for a meeting with government representatives. The talks continued in Saigon and resulted in further agreements. In February 1969 a FULRO group rallied to the GVN. An allegiance oath-taking ceremony was to be held in Ban Me Thuot, under the chairmanship of President Nguyen Van Thieu, but at the last minute the FULRO group appeared without Y' Bham. Reportedly he had been detained in Cambodia by FULRO dissidents.

Since then Y' Bham was no longer heard of, and the FULRO dissidents at large collaborated with the Communists. In late 1974 a series of disturbances occurred in the Ban Me Thuot area. There were assassinations, kidnappings, robberies, and murders around the provincial capital and particularly along the highways, where the situation had become extremely insecure. Leaflets that had been gathered indicated that one Y Kpa Koi, a former Montagnard civil servant who had taken up the rebel cause, was the new FULRO leader. It was also reported that Montagnard groups were antagonistic with each other and they created disturbance to discredit the Montagnard minister of ethnic development, who at that time was Mr. Nay Luet.

The GVN had always recognized the Central Highlands as a vital area lying across the Communist north-south infiltration route and inhabited by a people whose allegiance was still in doubt. President Diem's Montagnard policy would have succeeded if it had been carried out in a stable situation untroubled by Communists. With the advent of subversion and war the Montagnards had become more and more aware of the escalating promises by the competing Communist and Nationalist sides. The Nguyen Van Thieu government had much success in dealing with the Montagnards because it granted them maximum concessions. The new ethnic statute had given the Montagnards preferential treatment, so much so that the Cambodia residents, who had been virtually considered Vietnamese citizens, staged demonstrations to demand equal treatment under the same statute. The war had transformed the Montagnard country into a scene of hot contest. Most Montagnard refugees who fled the Communists had given their allegiance to the GVN, and many Montagnards served in regular as well as territorial forces in the highlands, but the dissidents chose to cooperate with the Communists. The Vietnam conflict had torn the Montagnard population asunder, just as it had the Vietnamese people.

The Impact of Communist Insurgency and Protracted War

The Communist threat to South Vietnam materialized under two forms. One was a war of subversion or insurgency which dragged out endlessly and eroded the fabric of society, and the other an invasion from the outside which supported the enemy within and was designed to seize the first opportunity to deliver its decisive blow.

The enemy's subversion caused a great deal of difficulty. It was like an internal malady that worked its lethal way through the nation's body. Deep inside South Vietnam's society, Communist elements seemed to be gnawing at and demolishing its internal structure as a veritable fifth column. The menace was the more dangerous since the enemy had cunningly used the very RVN themes to achieve his goal. The National Liberation Front and the People's Revolutionary Party called themselves popular organizations speaking for the majority of the South Vietnamese and claimed to be fighting for national independence, for an end to "imperialism" and foreign intervention. Those catch phrases that they used, such as "genuine independence," "fight America to save the country," "peace," and "neutrality" sounded big and attractive and seemed irrefutable to any concerned Vietnamese patriot. Moreover, the enemy's stratagem was so insidious and wily that he succeeded in fooling the naïve South Vietnamese public, along with part of the outside world, including pacifists, leftists, and self-styled liberals who prided themselves for their objectivity and perceptiveness. It was this stratagem which provided the material and cause for a protracted conflict between South Vietnam's militant and nonmilitant factions.

• • •

For the loyal cadres of the nationalist government, the Communists had a simple solution: assassination or kidnapping and elimination. Each year the GVN lost thousands of village officials and rural cadres. The enemy terrorized even teachers and rural medics and naturally hated our information cadres the most.

• • •

Changes in the security situation had taught the people to be smart. The higher the intensity of the war, the more contribution the Communists seemed to exact from the people who, though hating the Communists for it, had to maintain a fence-sitting stance in order to survive, irrespective of which side should eventually prevail. The situation was such that, over a period of time, many village cadres and—according to intelligence reports—even some RF and PF outposts, assumed a neutral position and merely gave a perfunctory performance. There were also double-agent village cadres who worked for the GVN during the day and reported to, and received instructions from, the Communist village commissar at night.

• • •

In the later stages of the war, especially from 1968 onwards, the rural masses seemed to realize which side had a worthy cause and was more constructive. From a psychological point of view, it was clear that they were [favorably] disposed toward the GVN. But the conduct of total war, the tactics, and the strategic posture of the RVN did not allow a reversal of the unfavorable combat situation. After the relatively good years of 1969–1972, the situation was back again to where it had been earlier, especially after the fictitious cease-fire of January 1973. The rural people once again saw that a non-committal attitude was still perhaps the wisest.

• • •

The political and social life of South Vietnamese towns and cities was like a jumbled picture or a concert without a conductor and without symphony. For the enemy, it was not at all hard to infiltrate the intellectual groups, the literary and arts circles, and the press corps. South Vietnamese artists, journalists, and writers prided themselves for their "liberalness"; they opposed and found fault with everything. The regime was consequently besmeared, and every nationalist figure was handicapped by a tainted reputation. In time a true crisis of confidence set in because no one seemed to have the ability to lead. This led to the popular myth that only among the leading personalities of the other side were there any bright stars and heroic figures.

• • •

Besides, the protracted war which the Communists waged in South Vietnam had enormous social consequences. Chief among them was the deep chasm that divided country and city. The countryside of South Vietnam was the major arena of contest and, as such, suffered unspeakable destruction. The rural areas were the warehouse of manpower and material resources, and the jungled mountains offered strategic avenues of approach for the invading NVA. Our opponents regarded the rural areas as a strategic objective to be captured, which was the reason why the RVN and its allies defended them at all costs. The participation of US and FWMA forces, with their tremendous firepower, added to the destruction. Many villages were completely obliterated from the surface of the earth. Throughout the war, it could be said that no corner of the countryside had been spared the destructiveness of bombs and shells; many areas had in fact changed hands many times, and each time destruction was worse. The end result was that houses were reduced to rubble, innocent people were killed, untold numbers became displaced, riceland was abandoned, and as much as one-half of the population of the countryside had fled to the security of cities, province capitals, and district towns at some time during the war. A small minority of rural people with resources adapted themselves quickly to city life, but most languished in abject poverty in refugee camps or as outcasts in city streets. When the situation seemed to have improved, the people returned to their home villages, only to flee again at the next battle. This process was repeated again and again over the war years.

The direct result of it all was that the rural people, destitute as they were, became even more miserable. Their way of life, which was considered as reflecting the traditional values of Vietnamese society, had been shaken to its roots. The ancient order seemed to have disintegrated. The villagers and the Montagnards alike seldom saw materialize the promises of our side and the hollow promises of the other side. Faith in the future dwindled, and the only remaining hope was to be left alone in peace.

On the other hand, the urban way of life was totally different. Before the war there was no great disparity between country and city life, but the war had changed all that. First of all, the cities were safe havens where people's lives were relatively secure. There had been a few enemy attacks against the cities, but they all passed and were quickly forgotten. Then, while the villages suffered destruction, the cities profited directly from the war. The cities grew many times richer because of foreign aid, allied soldiers' spending, and the consumer-oriented economy of the nation. . . . City dwellers made good money and seemed to live well in an aura of superficial affluence. The effect was that such a materialistic way of living always demanded fierce competition and sometimes devious means to stay ahead.

The urban [petite] bourgeoisie was so preoccupied with self-interest that it became too selfish. The urban way of life, which had previously been Europeanized, was now Americanized. Urban citizens, from politicians and professionals to clergymen and artisans, all eagerly clamored for democratic freedoms and freedom of enterprise. This egotistic tendency seemed to sit ill with the need for unity and sacrifice for the national cause. While the villages wanted security and were required to fight and make sacrifices to obtain it, the cities just wanted enjoyment and demanded more freedom. The leadership provided by the cities therefore hardly responded to the aspirations of the villages.

Another feature of the Vietnam conflict was that, as the war escalated and protracted, the cities sank deeper into decadence. The urban society was gradually decomposing for its worship of money, its injustices, and its corruption.

• • •

People who were able to survive economically included those who worked for US firms and agencies, the middlemen, private firm employees, pimps, and prostitutes. The people who hovered at the subsistence level included low-ranked servicemen, civil servants, and policemen, veterans, disabled veterans, and refugee peasants.

The South Vietnamese economy, after ten years of implacable war, was in a desperate situation. Let the facts speak for themselves: the official exchange rate of the US dollar was 35 piasters in 1965 and 725 piasters in early 1975, a twenty-one-fold increase; taking the 1963 consumer index in Saigon as base (100), in 1974 this index became 2,330.9, or twenty-three times higher.[5] In the meantime, during the ten-year period between 1965 and 1975, military and civil servants' pay increased by only 600 percent. In terms of equivalent dollars, an enlisted man made $10 a month, an NCO $20, a field-grade officer $30 to $40, and a general officer $70 to $80, including all allowances.

• • •

The effect of this hard economic life was that government and military personnel, cadres, and the police in the rear had to seek supplementary means of economic survival. Moonlighting, such as offering taxi service on motorcycles, tutoring or peddling, wives turning into bar girls and daughters into prostitutes were a few ways of beating the high cost of living. It was small wonder to see high school teachers and even university professors cramming several schools into their daily schedule, in the same way dancing girls in nightclubs hopped from table to table. They, too, had to try hard to beat inflation. It was therefore problematic whether to label as corrupt those lowly civil servants and policemen who asked small fees for their services in order to buy rice for their hungry families. They surely could not get rich with this small extra income. Meanwhile, combat troops were underfed. Plucking a fruit from its tree or catching a chicken in a remote village to supplement a meager diet was an irresistible temptation. The problem of petty pillaging among combat soldiers defied solution.

• • •

In such a tunnel of endless darkness, everyone was frantically looking for an escape and seemed to find consensus in an "antiwar" stance. Each group, according to its own view, was clamoring for an end to hostilities. The motives for such a position were as varied as the groups that held it: to overthrow the government and seize power; to change leadership; to vent frustration with a meaningless, protracted, and inconclusive conflict; to express revulsion at a fratricidal war; to express painful awareness of social decadence; and to express national pride by refuting the excessive interference of the United States in South Vietnamese affairs.

• • •

These antiwar groups were sometimes articulate in their opposition, sometimes quiet in their maneuvers. Behind some of their activities anti-Communist nationalists saw the hand of the Communist underground.[6] They made little impact, however, because most urban people had no inclination to accommodate the Communists.

Yet, in spite of their fear of Communism, South Vietnam's urban public hated the war because it demanded too many sacrifices. In line with such a psychology, South Vietnam's arts, which had been lyrical, romantic, maudlin, and escapist, took on the overtones of war hatred. Artists and writers were now inclined to depict the sufferings of war and social dislocations and formed a new antiwar subculture. South Vietnamese artists often styled themselves free [and] advocated art for art's sake, not for politics' sake.

In their artful portrayal of society they injected the element of hatred for the war. Most influential of all were perhaps the antiwar songs of Trinh Cong Son, who was imitated by other songwriters. These songs did nothing good to the morale of the troops or to the maintenance of the fighting spirit among the masses.

• • •

V. THE REGIME AND LEADERSHIP

South Vietnam and Democracy

Commenting on the Vietnamese character, many administrators during the French rule used variations of the theme "In every Vietnamese there is a mandarin." It seemed evident that monarchy and the mandarin mentality had a deep influence on Vietnamese society and on the life, psychology, and aspirations of the Vietnamese people.

From the time the nation was formed until 1945, a period of almost twenty centuries, the Vietnamese had known nothing but monarchical rule and had come to regard it as inevitable. Dynasty after dynasty, the ruler remained invariably a king with a heavenly mandate (a mandate to rule in the name of heaven). The mandarins who represented the king in every administrative domain were regarded as "the people's fathers and mothers." In the relationship between king and subjects there were no documents to stipulate the king's authority and duties, but the people's duties, as well as the sanctions to be imposed in case of disobedience or negligence, were clearly prescribed.

• • •

In spite of its predominant monarchical character, in the opinion of many the regime exhibited certain traits not unlike those of a democratic system. For example, the mandarins who governed the people were all chosen from among the educated through fair and competitive examinations. With rare exceptions . . . every citizen, including the poorest and the lowliest, enjoyed the right to take part in the examinations. Extremely fair and strict, these examinations were practically free of fraud and government interference. The second democratic feature of the regime was that the people themselves elected the council of notables to handle local government at the village level. Village affairs were also regulated by a charter co-opted by all villagers. This traditional autonomy of grassroots government was summarized by the Vietnamese dictum, "The law of the king yields to the rules of the village."

• • •

The South Vietnamese government, whether under the First or the Second Republic, always tended to abridge civil rights, especially the freedoms of political activity, of expression, and of the press. Invariably national security was invoked as an excuse to impose such restrictions. However nationalist parties and leaders were unwilling to accept arbitrary and indiscriminate actions for fear these would lead to outright dictatorship, which they abhorred.

• • •

Antigovernment factions in South Vietnam were wont to compare the level of freedom in their country with that enjoyed by Western societies, but they seldom contrasted what our people enjoyed with the bondage in Communist North Vietnam. They appealed to Western opinion to exert pressure on the Vietnamese government for ever greater freedom, oblivious of the fact that even in Western societies freedom had its own price and limitations.

Public opinion in Western nations, especially the United States, also seemed to have the tendency to judge democracy in South Vietnam from the familiar viewpoint of Western people who, with higher and more sophisticated intellectual standards, never failed to note shortcomings in our system. But then they also failed to notice the discrepancy between ours and the Communist system. The criticisms of foreign opinion, especially of the Western press, eventually reinforced the fallacious belief that South Vietnam really lacked freedom.

• • •

Democracy and the Leadership of President Ngo Dinh Diem

• • •

No one could say for sure what South Vietnam's situation would have been like if Mr. Diem had not been overthrown. But an objective assessment of various leaders who succeeded him to power after 1963 indicated that Mr. Diem at least possessed certain invaluable leadership qualities that no one else had. The people's respect for his person was evident in the fact that he was addressed and referred to as Cu (Venerable) Diem or Tong Thong (President) Diem, but not the belittling Ong (Mr.) Diem as some leaders had come to be called later. . . . He had earned this respect or eminence, whether or not one criticized him for his errors or disapproved of his policies. No one, however, dared accuse him of corruption, because he was a man of moral excellence totally impervious to worldly pleasures, and his religiously ascetic life was too well known. Mr. Diem also had certain traits of character which some elderly persons enjoyed comparing with those of Ho Chi Minh. Like Ho, for example, he was imbued with revolutionary ideals, gave up position and wealth, and led a life of celibacy. The personal prestige of a leader was paramount in Vietnamese society, whether North or South. For this reason, Ho Chi Minh had created a number of myths about his person to win the respect and trust of the Northern population. But Mr. Diem hardly needed any myths to win his.

• • •

After Mr. Diem's death, South Vietnam earned the reputation of having too many leaders who came and went too rapidly. This was a flaw in South Vietnamese politics, one that prompted pessimists to believe that Mr. Diem's death foreshadowed the demise of free Vietnam. In the Vietnam context, most people agreed that a political leader had to combine talent, integrity, and moral excellence with achievements and contributions to the country. Replacing or dismantling a regime was not difficult, but building a better government, or finding a better national leader than Mr. Diem, proved to be totally elusive to the efforts of both South Vietnam and the United States in later years.

Democracy and Leadership since November 1963

• • •

Leadership in the South ran into total disarray from November 1963 to 19 June 1965, when the military finally took over. During that period there was no single leader with real power or a background worthy of being the captain of the ship of state. In a short period of eighteen months, therefore, South Vietnam had seen a succession of five cabinets led by Nguyen Ngoc Tho, Nguyen Khanh, Tran Van Huong, Nguyen Xuan Oanh, and Phan Huy Quat. As a result, society went through a period of deep division and confidence crisis. Leading politicians opposed each other on the grounds of religion, which almost degenerated into an open religious conflict between Buddhists and Catholics.

• • •

The presidential and senate elections of September 1967 could be considered honest and democratic. Six hundred foreign observers and correspondents had been invited to witness these elections. Contrary to Diem's election in 1960, servicemen received no orders to vote for any tickets; they were completely free to vote for the candidates of their choice. At the polls located in the Joint General Staff compound, for example, a large number of Thieu-Ky ballots were seen discarded and scattered on the ground.

The 34 percent plurality with which Mr. Thieu and Mr. Ky won the election faithfully reflected the constituents' impartiality and the degree of democracy attained. Later on, however, critics both in the country and in the United States seemed to dwell on this 34 percent plurality to prove how little popular support Thieu and Ky had won, but completely ignored the truly democratic nature of the election. For this reason one obsession of South Vietnamese governments in subsequent years was to achieve a high percentage at the polls at any cost. But such an excessive majority as 99.8 percent, which was once reported, only served to increase suspicion about the government's honesty.

The Second Republic lasted from 1 November 1967 until 30 April 1975. Mr. Thieu was the president almost throughout the period and resigned only one week before the collapse of the South. No matter what defense he could muster, he was responsible for this downfall. What, then, were Mr. Thieu's failures in leadership?

Mr. Thieu had leadership qualities. He was cautious, cunning, persevering, intelligent; he was also a courageous man. His visits to the battlegrounds of Kontum and An Loc in 1972, while the fighting was still raging, prompted admiration for his courage, and his presence bolstered the morale of cadres and soldiers alike. Still there was a common belief that Mr. Thieu's ways to govern were those of an overlord incapable of winning hearts and minds. He was nominated by the Armed Forces Council to run for president after promising to abide by the principle of collective leadership. But, once elected, Mr. Thieu acted counter to the council's wishes and was accused of foul play. He considered himself elected by the people, and, having enjoyed US support, he began to ignore and dismantle the very apparatus that had helped him to power.

• • •

Mr. Thieu's moves to replace key military personnel, as well as his breach of trust against the Armed Forces Council, adversely affected military solidarity, creating schisms that reduced the RVNAF performance. Ironically, the need to combat the Communists, who were the main enemies, seemed to get less attention from Mr. Thieu than political infighting and the consolidation of his power.

• • •

Mr. Thieu began to come under heavy attack when he was preparing for his reelection to a second term in 1971. His opponents were Duong Van Minh and Nguyen Cao Ky. The election law had been revised with the objective of causing them the most difficulty. In May 1971 the Supreme Court accepted the candidacy of Mr. Minh and Mr. Thieu only; it rejected Mr. Ky's candidacy on technical grounds. Finally both Mr. Minh and Mr. Ky withdrew, apparently to undermine the election, despite the fact that Mr. Ky's candidacy was later approved. This withdrawal left the field to Mr. Thieu's lone candidacy, a fact that gave rise to criticisms of a "one-man show" and dictatorship.

The Communists' 1972 general offensive gave Mr. Thieu a chance to further strengthen his rule and weaken the opposition of political parties, the press, and other groups. He asked the legislative branch to grant him emergency powers to make laws for six months in order to handle the Communist general offensive. The senate balked, but the house gave him approval, and finally he got his way. With this power he declared a martial law in July 1972, which banned all strikes and acts, words, or pictures deemed detrimental to national security. The police were given the right to shoot to kill criminals in flight.

Next a press law was promulgated in August 1972 whereby, pending court proceedings, the government could suspend a newspaper that had been seized twice before for carrying articles harmful to national security and law and order. Each newspaper owner was also required to deposit a bond equivalent to US $47,000 to defray court costs and fines in case of litigation. The effect of this law was that 14 out of 41 Saigon newspapers had to close down for failure to meet new requirements; of the remaining ones, only two belonged to the opposition.

In September 1972 an executive order replaced the law for the election of village officials. This order empowered province chiefs to appoint village officials, saying explicitly, "In conclusion, although the administration process at the village and hamlet level has made some progress, it is no longer appropriate and capable of meeting the nation's requirements at the present stage of struggle against the Communists." This move was criticized as a regression from democracy.

• • •

Although indications of a large-scale Communist offensive became apparent toward the end of 1974, the press and political personalities considered it a ploy when President Thieu called the nation's attention to this threat. This produced probably the most disastrous effect, one that led to the collapse of South Vietnam. Mr. Thieu had obviously lost the people's trust, and only the Communists stood to gain by it. For example, at the beginning of 1975, when the police discovered that several Vietnamese journalists were

Communist and detained them, the entire press corps engaged in protests on the grounds of government frame-up and repression. There [had] always been a great deal of bad blood between President Thieu and the press corps, which had criticized him on many counts. While these criticism[s] seemed warranted by genuine opposition, there were also among Saigon newspapers several owned by pro-Communists.

• • •

South Vietnam in the final days prior to the collapse was like a patient going through a political delirium, unable to tell the truth from falsehood, and clamoring for Thieu's resignation without an idea of who would take his place or what would be the future course of the nation. The protesters opposed him on grounds of dictatorship and corruption, but none advanced any appropriate solution to the predicament of South Vietnam. Even if their demands had all been met, the fate of South Vietnam probably would not have fared better, and perhaps would have been far worse than it was, because of anarchy. Clearly no one knew what balance to strike between total freedom and total restraint. This was a real crisis of democracy in the face of imminent threat to its survival.

All things considered, Mr. Thieu's regime was perhaps not as totalitarian as it appeared to be, because what the opposition demanded might not even exist in a true democracy; besides, not everyone agreed that Mr. Thieu was a dictator. On the contrary, many were of the opinion that South Vietnam was a case of excessive democracy and freedom, which bred a breakdown of law and order. Their main argument was that, if South Vietnam was a dictatorship, then what would North Vietnam be called?

Generally speaking, the democratic experiment in South Vietnam was a failure of defining the limits of freedom and democracy for a country at war which had just recently been initiated to the democratic system of government. South Vietnam leaders from 1954 to 1975 seemed to fall into two groups: weak demagogic leaders moved by opportunism and having no solid leadership qualities, such as those emerging between 1963 and 1965, and strong leaders like Diem, Ky, and Thieu, who were opposed for being dictatorial. It must be conceded, however, that in spite of allegations to the contrary, South Vietnam did enjoy some measure of democracy which made possible at least two periods of stability.

• • •

Some argued that leadership was the key to it all and that, with good leadership, South Vietnam would have been able to overcome its problems of political immaturity and lack of democratic experience. However, this ideal leadership was perhaps impossible to achieve. After a long period of French represssions, followed by Communist treachery, South Vietnam no longer had any truly devoted and capable nationalist leader left who was worthier than Mr. Diem. His errors, such as nepotism and favoritism for Catholics, were not irremediable. In him people could at least discern the stature of a genuine leader and unequalled nationalist zeal. Mr. Thieu paled beside Mr. Diem in personal prestige. He did not have the necessary background for a leader of the people. He lacked what was termed as revolutionary virtue which the people in the South or North wanted to see in a national leader. The next flaw in his leadership was his overreliance on the United States, which kept him from planning ahead for the day when South Vietnam had to go it alone. Owing to US policies, he had been protected from coups d'ctat. Yet his excessive trust in the US president's authority had led him astray. He had probably deluded himself in thinking that what the president of the RVN could do the US president should be able to do also. He seemed to ignore the fact that the US Congress could also limit the powers of the US president.

Finally, political infighting in South Vietnam, the internecine fight to the death among men in the same boat, could only benefit the Communists. Those South Vietnamese who had struggled for the implementation of democratic rights in times of war could not bring themselves to think that some of these rights did not even exist in a Western society in times of peace. Now that South Vietnam is suffering under the Communist yoke, these people have an eye-opening chance to see for themselves what democracy is or is not. Most probably they will not live long to see it.

VI. OBSERVATIONS AND CONCLUSIONS

South Vietnamese society was clearly polarized into two segments, the rural and the urban, each with a way of life and attitudes entirely different from the other.

• • •

The First Republic was criticized for three main flaws: family rule or nepotism, monolithic party rule, and discrimination on regional and religious grounds. From hindsight, it was quite understandable that, during the incipient years of his rule, President Diem had to rely on his brothers and other close relatives because of his loneness and unfamiliarity with South Vietnam's politics. In time, however, this gave rise to excesses by some of his family members, which became the source of popular discontent.

• • •

The phenomena of divisiveness, discrimination, and infighting were not . . . confined to religions and political parties; in fact, they existed in every stratum of South Vietnam's social fabric, though in varying degrees. The problem of ethnic minorities, for one, was not as serious as foreign opinion had visualized and depicted.

• • •

Infighting and divisiveness were nowhere as serious and damaging as among the South Vietnamese themselves. Regional discrimination, for one, was latent in every social group, every area of activity. At times it broke out into open consciousness, but most of the time it was contained, repressed.

Factionalism, however, was an all-time scourge that affected the entire fabric of South Vietnamese society. Under the First Republic, factionalism was not too serious because after all there was just one faction—the Ngo clan—that dominated all others. But, after the Ngos, factionalism had become an epidemic that no medicine could ever cure. There were so many clans, so many factions, that any attempt [to bring] them together was just unthinkable. Since every faction was contending for its own interests, it became wary of all others, and each could only trust its own members. Every key office in the government, the military, the religions, or civil organizations turned into a small power nucleus around which revolved a clan, a faction.

Factionalism was also smoldering between the military and the civilians. Civilian leaders tended to consider themselves more educated, and held the military in low regard. They did not want to associate with military leaders, whom they derogatorily called "those martial elements." On their part, the RVNAF leaders were proud of the powers they were holding; they also disassociated themselves from civilian personalities, whom they considered effete, incompetent, and incomprehensible, and slighted as "tearoom politicians." The pairing of civilian and military officials in the political arena of South Vietnam therefore appeared as odd as an uneven pair of chopsticks.

• • •

There remained the military who, under these circumstances, constituted perhaps the only truly cohesive and well-organized force capable of contending successfully with the Communists. Civilian rule, for all its desirability, could not be enforced without endangering the nation's survival.

• • •

That South Vietnam existed at all as a nation, and for that long, was chiefly due to US support.

• • •

However, the involvement of Americans, who represented a dynamic civilization, in a nation whose culture was essentially static seemed not very successful in producing a completely satisfactory relationship. The cultural differences between Americans and Vietnamese are antipodal. Americans are active, impatient, and rationalistic, [in contrast] to Vietnamese, who are quiescent, patient, and sentimental. Joining forces for a common effort, Americans and Vietnamese often saw the same problem differently, had different basic concepts, and acted and reacted in different ways. Under the First Republic American influence was not pervasive, because the regime's leaders were self-assured and strong-minded to the point of becoming obstinate. US assistance then was substantial but restrained. Discordance finally contributed to the downfall of a regime regarded by Americans as irredeemable. After that, US involvement in South Vietnam's own affairs seemed to have no bounds.

• • •

The American experience seems to indicate that small nations fighting against Communism with US aid would have been better off if they had endeavored to do things by themselves. Self-reliance should be a motto worth promoting.

• • •

It came as no surprise, both in the eyes of the public and in the belief in knowledgeable quarters, that every national endeavor and the conduct of the war itself totally conformed to American policies. In time the very survival of South Vietnam came to depend on the will and support of the United States. Having nothing left to decide and to show for its valor, the South Vietnamese leadership gradually lost all prestige and real authority. This void in leadership loomed larger than ever after the United States withdrew all of its troops, settled for a peace arrangement, and reduced its involvement. The ranks of South Vietnamese leadership, who heretofore had proved readily amenable to US wishes, now found themselves hopelessly vulnerable, unable to stand on their own feet, and utterly incapable of pulling the nation together.

• • •

The picture thus depicted of South Vietnamese society was indeed bleak and dark, but it did not imply that all South Vietnamese had lost the will to survive and continue the fight. Certainly not all servicemen, civil servants, and policemen neglected their duties or shunned their responsibilities. There were in fact many segments of the South Vietnamese population which still proved aggressively anti-Communist, and the majority of RVNAF servicemen, national policemen, and civil servants continued to fight and serve with dedication and purpose in the hopes that somehow the situation was going to improve. Indeed, there had been too many shiny examples of heroic sacrifices among their ranks to attempt to prove the contrary. In general, no matter what had happened, the South Vietnamese people had displayed throughout the war a most laudable spirit of endurance and resiliency that few other peoples could match.

• • •

The problem of South Vietnam, after all, was perhaps not democracy versus dictatorship, but essentially a matter of how much democratic freedom we could afford at a certain given time.

Unfortunately, the problem of South Vietnam had not been thoroughly understood and correctly solved. Hampered by shortsightedness and retrogression, the class of leaders had lost its ability to lead. Society was torn asunder by internal strife, and the popular mass no longer had faith in the government. It seemed as if the vicious and drawn-out war had drained South Vietnam of all its vital resources and brought it to the brink of moral and material bankruptcy. So, when the US Congress decided it no longer desired to support a continuing war, most people could readily sense that the fate had been sealed for South Vietnam.

NOTES

1. This book was written during the Han Dynasty, after their conquest of Vietnam that lasted from circa 100 BC to circa AD 102.

2. *Nam Phong Tap Chi,* No. 172 (Hanoi, May 1932).

3. This commander was Nguyen Duy Hinh. In 1972 he was promoted to major general as commander of the 3rd ARVN Division, and is the coauthor of this monograph.

4. The Perfume River flows through the area of Hue. The Dong Nai and Mekong Rivers wind their courses east and west of Saigon respectively.

5. National Bank of Vietnam, USAID.

6. The Nguyen Van Thieu government had repeatedly charged some lawmakers, writers, newsmen, and labor union officials of having maintained relations with the Communists.

15

Vietnamization and the Cease-Fire

Major General Nguyen Duy Hinh

PREFACE

This monograph presents the pertinent facts about Vietnamization and the cease-fire and the impact of these events on the situation in South Vietnam. Although a case can be made that Vietnamization started in 1967, when General Creighton W. Abrams was assigned as Deputy COMUSMACV and given the responsibility for upgrading the Republic of Vietnam Armed Forces, the program was officially initiated by President Nixon on 8 June 1969.

During the period the Vietnamization program was implemented, I was able to observe the problems of transition and the obstacles and challenges that the RVNAF met during the process. When the cease-fire came, I was in command of the 3rd Infantry Division. In my area of responsibility, which encompassed Quang Nam and Quang Tin Provinces of Military Region 1, I had to face cease-fire violations almost daily.

Facts presented in this monograph [are] based primarily on my personal experiences and interviews with responsible officers. To some extent available documentation has also been helpful. Observations and opinions, where appropriate, all reflect my personal point of view, for which I am solely responsible. Most valuable, however, are the contributions and comments that have added to my work and helped refine it. . . . [15 September 1976]

I. BACKGROUND

On 8 June 1969 President Nixon met with President Nguyen Van Thieu of the Republic of Vietnam in Midway and proclaimed the Vietnamization of the war. As far as the United States was concerned, this was a major shift in foreign policy aimed at bringing about peace on both the negotiating front and battlefront. When he reported to the American nation on 3 November the same year, President Nixon explained what the United States would endeavor to achieve through Vietnamization: "We have adopted a plan which we have worked out in cooperation with the South Vietnamese for the complete withdrawal of all US combat ground forces, and their replacement by South

Vietnamese forces on an orderly scheduled timetable. This withdrawal will be made from strength and not from weakness."[1]

This was the beginning of an accelerated effort to strengthen the South Vietnamese armed forces and disengage from the war, an alternative course of action taken in the face of the deadlocked peace negotiations in Paris. The new orders given to General Creighton W. Abrams, Commander, USMACV, were to strengthen and improve the Republic of Vietnam Armed Forces (RVNAF) so that they could assume full responsibility for the security of South Vietnam.

For more than fours years now, the war had escalated in level and intensity. More than 540,000 American troops were battling an enemy who seemed to grow stronger and more determined than ever in his goal to subjugate South Vietnam. The casualty toll had been heavy, and the war was causing deep division in the United States and criticism in other areas of the world. When introducing its combat units in 1965, the US apparently had hoped to bring the war to an end as quickly as possible by using military force. Its gradual buildup during the following years practically overshadowed the RVN role in the war, a war which increasingly bore an American outlook.

With more than eight combat divisions, thousands of helicopters, tanks, and artillery pieces, hundreds of fighter-bombers, and the tremendous airpower of B-52 strategic bombers, the United States practically trampled the enemy down under its sheer military weight. The years 1966 and 1967, it was true, gave many encouraging signs. For the first time in the war, enemy bases in South Vietnam were cleared and destroyed and his major units driven across the border. For a time, the enemy appeared to have lost his balance and initiative.

The RVN government quickly exploited the gains on the battlefront by pushing hard its pacification program and consolidating its political base. Gradually but resolutely, South Vietnam was moving toward elective government and full-fledged democracy, leaving behind crises and instability. A National Assembly and a new president were installed, inaugurating a new era of stability and progress. The situation in general had improved and given rise to confidence and hopes. It was not to last long, however.

The Decisive Year of 1968

Beginning in mid-January 1968, intelligence reports confirmed preparations by two NVA divisions, the 325C and 304th, for an attack on the Khe Sanh base held by one US marine regiment and one ARVN ranger battalion. The siege of Khe Sanh began on 21 January 1968. There were, however, no unusual signs as to the future course of the war. Scattered reports on the enemy's capabilities in other places failed to disclose anything worthy of special note. As was usual, a truce was declared on the occasion of Tet, the Year of the Monkey (Mau Than 1968). All of a sudden, during the period of truce and during the days of traditional celebration, the Communists launched a wave of major-scale attacks on the entire territory of South Vietnam. During the offensive, the enemy committed his units to an extent never before encountered on the Indochina battlefield. During the early days of February 1968, the enemy repeatedly attacked or shelled 36 out of 44 provincial capitals, five out of six cities, and 64 out of 242 district towns of the RVN.[2] The city dwellers, who had never before experienced war, were now exposed to actual combat, destruction, and death. In spite of the initial surprise, the RVNAF succeeded, with the assistance of allied forces, in driving back all enemy attacks and regaining control of the situation in most of the embattled areas. Only in Saigon and Hue . . . did combat last for a week or more.

• • •

As a matter of fact, the surprise initially achieved by the enemy was absolute. Property damage and nearly one million homeless war victims became a tremendous burden for the government. But the general uprising of the population that the enemy had predicted simply did not occur.

• • •

The enemy's 1968 military effort was definitely a failure. But its psychological impact and political repercussions gave him an unexpected advantage. To the American public, and to the world at large, the successive waves of the enemy offensive came as a major shock. After three years of participation by over half a million US and allied troops, the American people naturally expected a quick and favorable outcome of the war so that their men would soon return. But the "light at the end of the tunnel" was no longer visible. On the contrary, General Westmoreland now requested an additional reinforcement of 206,000 troops. Many influential persons began to question the US commitment. The antiwar movement gained in force throughout the United States. Neither the "doves" nor the "hawks" were satisfied with the turn of events. On 31 March 1968, while the first Communist general offensive was still in progress, President Johnson was prompted to halt US bombings above the 19th parallel, declare his noncandidacy in the coming presidential elections, and propose peace negotiations. In contrast with previous occasions, North Vietnam this time agreed to negotiate.

President Johnson's decision and the beginning of peace negotiations were watershed events which portended a profound change in American attitude toward the war and its probable course during the years that followed. So a new course was charted and a new field commander put in charge of carrying it out. To General Creighton W. Abrams, who succeeded General Westmoreland as Commander, USMACV, in July 1968, it must have been a most challenging task. He was soon to preside over the gradual disengagement of his own troops from the war as the Vietnamese assumed more of the combat burden.

Ending the war was now the major concern of the United States. As a matter of fact, this was the very platform that helped earn Mr. Nixon a landslide victory in the US presidential elections of November 1968. Inaugurated as president, he pursued his quest for peace by initiating a dual-track approach to end the inconclusive war. With the collaboration of his advisors—the special assistant for national security, Dr. Henry A. Kissinger, and the defense secretary, Mr. Melvin R. Laird, in particular—President

Nixon developed a new defense and foreign policy which later became known as the Nixon Doctrine and which constituted the rationale behind Vietnamization.

• • •

II. THE NIXON DOCTRINE AND VIETNAMIZATION PROGRAM

The Nixon Doctrine

• • •

What distinguished the Nixon Doctrine most was the greater role to be played by each ally. President Nixon stressed that, "while a major American role remains indispensable, other nations can and should assume greater responsibilities."[3]

• • •

The Vietnamization Program

The situation in South Vietnam at the end of 1968 was truly promising. Communist forces had suffered great human loss in the wake of their offensives during the year. The Republic of Vietnam Armed Forces had gained more confidence. Major battlefields were quieter and enemy forces were driven out of many important areas. Pacification resumed its progress and was yielding excellent returns. In March 1969 the US secretary of defense, Melvin R. Laird, visited Vietnam to review the situation. He returned home convinced that it was time to transfer more of the combat responsibility to the Republic of Vietnam Armed Forces. As a result, President Nixon and President Nguyen Van Thieu agreed to implement the Vietnamization program. A decisive turn of the war had materialized and a new course had been charted. This was the beginning of the Vietnamization process.

• • •

It was planned that the Vietnamization program would be implemented in three phases:

1. The first phase consisted of turning over to the RVNAF the ground combat responsibility against VC and NVA forces. During this phase, the United States would continue to provide air, naval, and logistics support.
2. The second phase consisted of developing combat support capabilities in order to help the RVNAF achieve self-reliance. This involved an increase in artillery, air, naval assets, and other support activities. The second phase proceeded simultaneously with the first phase, but it required more time. Even after the bulk of US combat forces had been withdrawn, there remained certain support and security units involved in training.
3. The third phase consisted of reducing the American presence to a military advisory role. A small security element was still required for protection. It had been planned that the advisory and assistance presence would be gradually reduced as

South Vietnam grew in strength until such military presence was no longer required.

In a speech in 1971, the US secretary of defense emphasized that the Vietnamization program was conceived on the basis of certain critical assumptions. First, it was assumed that if the Paris negotiation were not successful, the conflict in South Vietnam would continue. Second, the process of winding down and ending American combat involvement had to begin in 1969 and go forward steadily. Third, as long as the conflict continued Free World assistance to South Vietnam would be required. Fourth, with appropriate Free World assistance, the RVN and its people could in a relatively short period of time cope effectively with threats to their security from both the Viet Cong and the North Vietnamese.[4]

To attain the goal of Vietnamizing the war, the United States focused on the most important part of the program: modernization and development of the RVNAF. Vietnamese force structure would be increased as new units were activated. Strengthening firepower and mobility was considered a vital necessity; additional air and naval units were required. As a result, the Vietnamization program envisaged turning over to the RVNAF a great quantity of materiel and equipment for the activation of these new units and increasing their capabilities. Concurrently, training and logistics plans were developed to support the overall effort.

• • •

US direct involvement had been long, losses heavy, and expenditures burdensome. No Vietnamese ever expected an indefinite US involvement, especially when that involvement resulted in the loss of many lives. Consequently, as the Vietnamese saw it, Vietnamization was the rational thing to do. It would be an injustice to the American effort if we could not eventually become self-reliant. Not only did the Vietnamization program make sense, it was also consistent with Vietnamese feelings. The Vietnamese leaders and people recognized and greatly appreciated the efforts of the United States. And, deep down in their hearts, the Vietnamese always longed for early self-reliance and to break loose from dependence. This would lessen difficulties for their friends and contribute to their satisfaction. That was, and had always been, the true aspiration of Vietnamese people.

At Midway, President . . . Thieu agreed with President Nixon to launch the Vietnamization program. Although he was agreeable to the objectives of the program, on several occasions after returning home he took exception to the term "Vietnamization."

• • •

In my opinion, "Vietnamization" was not a proper term to be used in Vietnam, especially when propaganda was an important enemy weapon.

• • •

South Vietnam continued to fight as it had always fought. Old plans and programs were kept unchanged, except perhaps for a new sense of urgency and emphasis instilled by the US decision to phase down and eventually withdraw its forces. To the armed forces, the Improvement and Modernization Plan which had been initiated years before, through cooperation between the JGS and MACV, continued to be implemented as if it were a matter of routine. Some new units were activated, and the replacement of [re] deployed US and allied units was planned and implemented as required. The pacification effort, which had been pushed vigorously ahead after 1968, now received more attention in view of the eventual US withdrawal.

• • •

We were confident because everyone believed the United States would continue to help financially, materially, technologically, and even spiritually, if not with manpower. With this assistance, South Vietnam would be able to fight its war without the participation of US combat troops.

• • •

It was simply unimaginable that North Vietnam would unilaterally withdraw its troops from the South, not after it had endured four long years of bombing and sacrificed hundreds of thousands of its youth. Meanwhile, appeasement did not prevent the Communist bloc from providing aid to North Vietnam. As long as the war continued— with or without US participation—that aid would surely keep pouring in, unpretentious yet effective and unabated.

Communist aid to North Vietnam had escalated with the US buildup in the South. It was a response calculated to counteract the tremendous firepower of US forces. Now that the United States was deescalating its war and extracting its troops, South Vietnam would have to face alone the results of enemy escalation. In that sense, South Vietnamese anxiety was not wholly unjustified, nor was it unfounded. But, like a shot having been fired, events simply could not reverse their course. South Vietnam could do little but calmly accept the redeployment of US and allied forces while convincing itself that its friends would remain loyal to their commitments.

Redeployment of US and Allied Forces

The redeployment of the first increment of 25,000 US troops, as announced by President Nixon at the Midway meeting, was accomplished without difficulty. It was completed as scheduled on 27 August 1969. On 16 September the US president ordered a second increment of 35,000 [40,500] US troops to be redeployed by December. Then, on 15 December, the US president ordered a third increment of 50,000 to be redeployed prior to April 1970.

• • •

US troops withdrawn, in terms of combat units, amounted to three infantry divisions and a brigade. However, at the end of 1970 there still remained in-country a US combat force equivalent to six divisions.

Also, on 20 April 1970, the US president publicly announced plans to reduce the remaining US combat troops by 150,000 during the next twelve months. Thus, by 1 May 1971, about half of the total US combat strength in South Vietnam would have returned to the United States. With this accomplished, there would still be 284,000 US troops remaining in South Vietnam.

• • •

The decision to redeploy US troops was based on three criteria: the level of enemy activity, progress in the Paris talks, and the strengthening of the RVNAF. During 1968 the enemy had suffered severe losses. As a result, during the years 1969, 1970, and 1971 enemy initiatives were greatly reduced. Indirect attacks by fire of only a few rounds took the place of ground attacks. If anything, enemy activities only served as a reminder of his presence. Moreover, it was a period the enemy required to lick his wounds and reconstitute units. If the level of enemy activities was one of the criteria for the redeployment of US troops, the few years that followed 1968 were definitely favorable.

Meanwhile, the Paris talks continued to make no progress. The RVNAF were improving and developing. As early as in July 1969, during a surprise visit to South Vietnam, President Nixon said "the primary mission of American troops is to enable the South Vietnamese forces to assume the full responsibility for the security of South Vietnam."[5] True to all expectations, the RVNAF had rapidly assumed additional combat responsibilities and were effectively replacing US troops. By the end of 1970 the RVNAF were firmly in control of the area south of the DMZ and part of the Cambodian border. Meanwhile, US combat support was gradually reduced. Also, as of August 1970, from a monthly average of 1,800 sorties during 1968 B-52 sorties were decreased to about 1,000 a month.

The April 1970 decision made by President Nixon to withdraw 150,000 US troops was carried out in three increments. The first increment of 50,000 troops was completed by 15 October 1970; the second of 40,000 troops on 20 December 1970; and the third of 60,000 troops on 30 April 1971. Moreover, three weeks before all of the third increment was redeployed the US president announced his decision (on 7 April 1971) to further reduce US troops in South Vietnam by 100,000 prior to 1 December 1971. US strength therefore plummeted to the 184,000 mark by the end of 1971.

As scheduled, the US 4th and 25th Infantry Divisions were [re]deployed by the end of 1970. In April 1971 the bulk of the US 1st Cavalry Division (Airmobile) and the US 11th Armored Cavalry Regiment [was] also returned to the United States. As a result, US combat strength in South Vietnam was reduced to an equivalent of three divisions, or about a half of pre-redeployment level. In terms of combat units, 70 percent of maneuver battalions had been withdrawn. The redeployment rate thus amounted to an average of 3,000 men per week, or a full division per month. US losses as a consequence decreased sizably, from a high of about 500 a week to less than 50 a week. As compared with 1968, tactical air sorties were also reduced by more than a half. Meanwhile, war expenditures now stood at less than half of 1968 figures. At the height of US participation, 75 percent of total strength of the US Marine Corps was fighting in MR-1 of Vietnam. In May 1971 only one US marine brigade remained.

On 13 June 1971 Secretary of Defense Melvin R. Laird announced that 90 percent of combat responsibilities had been turned over to the RVNAF. Therefore the first phase of the Vietnamization program could be considered completed by summer 1971. Whatever US units still remained on Vietnamese territory were now only responsible for security.

The headquarters of US field forces were deactivated and became regional assistance commands.

Concurrently with the phasedown of the US Army in South Vietnam, US Air Force and naval units also redeployed and turned over their responsibilities to the Vietnamese Air Force and Navy. Beginning in 1970, the Vietnamese Navy took over the inner barrier of the coastal interdiction operation, "Market Time." Other US naval operations were subsequently turned over to the Vietnamese Navy at an accelerated rate.

The redeployment of US forces from Vietnam involved not only US personnel but also US equipment. Some equipment accompanied redeploying US Army units, but the remainder was either transferred to US units in Vietnam or turned over to the RVNAF for immediate use or as maintenance float. The US marine units, however, retained all of their equipment when redeployed to the West Pacific, undoubtedly to remain combat ready. As early as 1968 the US Navy had initiated a program of turning over bases and ships to the Vietnamese Navy. As a result, the redeployment of US naval units was carried out in a very short time. US Air Force units retained their aircraft when redeployed. However, a number of fixed-wing aircraft and helicopters were turned over to the Vietnamese Air Force.

At the end of 1971 and in early 1972, President Nixon announced that additional increments of personnel would be redeployed. On 12 November 1971 he announced that 45,000 US troops would be withdrawn between December 1971 and the end of January 1972, and that an additional 70,000 would be redeployed prior to the end of April. When completed, the total US strength remaining in Vietnam was 69,000. Thus the last US division-sized units were removed from Vietnam. By now all major offensive operations were being conducted by the RVNAF. US losses decreased significantly as a result. In 1971 these losses amounted to 2,175; in 1972, they were reduced to 367, or just one-sixth of the previous year.

Taking advantage of the US redeployment, on 30 March 1972 the enemy initiated a major offensive on three fronts: Quang Tri, Binh Long, and Kontum. However, RVNAF successfully defeated this Easter invasion. Subsequently, on 26 April 1972, President Nixon announced an additional redeployment of 20,000 men, reducing the total US strength to 49,000. And, as of 18 June 1972, he also made it clear that US conscripts would not be sent to Vietnam unless they volunteered. At the same time, US advisors were withdrawn from RVNAF battalions and reduced at the division and regimental levels. By June 1972 the total strength of US advisors in RVNAF units stood at less than 5,000. By the end of 1972 total US strength in Vietnam was down to a lower level than at any time during the previous ten years.

• • •

After the Paris Agreement went into effect on 28 January 1973, all remaining military advisory or liaison teams of the FWMAF left Vietnam before the 60-day deadline. Thus ended a long period of US and Free World participation in the Vietnam War, a participation which embodied the very spirit of regional cooperation espoused by the Nixon Doctrine, and which had effectively stemmed a great deal of Communist aggression in Southeast Asia.

III. STRENGTHENING THE REPUBLIC OF VIETNAM

• • •

The task of improving and strengthening the RVNAF was not new; in fact, this task had been a major objective since the United States initiated direct assistance and aid to South Vietnam. Throughout the years of direct participation in the ground war, however, this task had been relegated to second rank, overtaken by the priority given to the support and maintenance of US combat forces. Plans to strengthen the RVN were now, however, pursued with new determination and direction.

Force Structure Increase

• • •

Beginning in April 1968, the agreement between the United States and North Vietnam to negotiate an end to the war brought new requirements for the RVNAF. Up until that time, the RVN Armed Forces were structurally army-oriented and most developments were concerned with the army; it was understood that US forces would make up for any deficiencies in air and naval capabilities. Now that peace talks had started which could eventually result in the simultaneous withdrawal of US and NVA forces, it was agreed that a radical change in the structural concept should be attempted regarding the RVNAF.

In early April 1968 the US Department of Defense approved a force structure of 717,214 for the RVNAF, and on the 16th of the same month ordered that a plan be developed to gradually turn over combat responsibility to the RVNAF. The United States would continue to provide effective support for the development, improvement, and modernization of the RVNAF.

At the end of May 1968 a force structure recommendation of 801,215 was approved for FY 1970. This recommendation, called the May 68 plan, provided three goals:

1. To develop the RVNAF into a balanced force with command, administration, and self-support capabilities to continue the fighting successfully after the withdrawal of US and NVA troops. This required the expansion of the air force and navy and additional logistical elements. Some support would continue to be provided by US forces.
2. To modernize the RVNAF by replacing obsolete weapons with M-16 rifles, M-2 carbines, and M-60 machineguns. Obsolete or defective vehicles and signal equipment were to be replaced by the more efficient M-series vehicles and AN/PRC-25 radio sets.
3. To plan for the turnover of US equipment to the RVNAF as US forces were withdrawn from Vietnam.

At the end of June 1968 the US Department of Defense provided guidance to assist with the planning for the Improvement and Modernization Program for the RVN Armed Forces:

1. Phase I was based on the assumption that US forces would continue to participate in the war.
2. Phase II required the self-supporting capability for the RVNAF to fight internal insurgency after the withdrawal of US and NVA troops.

In October 1968 implementation of Phase I of the Improvement and Modernization Program was approved based on a force structure of 801,215 men. It emphasized that the RVNAF were to be organized and equipped to have maximum ground combat capability. Approximately three-fourths of the increased strength (84,000) was earmarked for army combat units. The imbalance among the services, and the increase in some logistic capabilities, [was] not corrected, since this plan assumed the continued participation of US forces.

• • •

On 8 October 1968 MACV submitted a recommendation for the RVNAF to be authorized 855,594 men for Phase II of the Improvement and Modernization Program. This strength ceiling would permit a force balance by increasing the strength of the navy, air force, and the logistics branch. In view of the improved military situation, and hopeful progress at the Paris talks, General Abrams (new commander for the USMACV) recommended that the US Department of Defense quickly approve the Phase II Accelerated Plan in order to increase both training capability and pipeline strength. This recommendation was approved by the US Joint Chiefs of Staff on 18 December, except for the part concerning a naval strength increase. Thus the total strength approved amounted to 866,434 men. . . . Subsequently, when naval strength increase was approved on 12 February 1969, the total RVNAF force structure for FY 1969 was increased to 875,790 men.

• • •

During the Midway Conference of 8 June 1969 the RVN delegation recommended a plan for RVNAF improvement to the US government. This recommendation was approved in part by the US Department of Defense and called the "Midway Package," which increased the RVNAF 1970 force structure to 953,673 and that of 1971 to 992,837. The two increments of strength increase, 77,883 for 1970 and 39,164 for 1971, were in part earmarked for additional RF and PF units. The National Police was also slated for a force increase of 15,000 in FY 1970 and 15,000 in FY 1971. The RVNAF total authorized strength already neared the 900,000 mark when President Nixon officially announced the Vietnamization program and the redeployment of US forces at Midway.

• • •

While the process of redeployment and replacement was taking place, the United States continued to study and review force structure requirements for the RVNAF. As a result, Phase III (or the consolidation phase) of the RVNAF Improvement and Modernization Program was developed. This plan called for a further strength increase to 1,100,000 men by the end of FY 1973. It was intended to bring about an improvement in quality rather than in quantity, and concentrated on combat and service support units and territorial forces. In early June 1970 Phase III was approved in principle. Its implementation was to be carried out year by year and adjusted to the prevalent situation.

By early 1972 the major part of Phase III had been accomplished. The biggest change in RVNAF force structure was the activation of an additional infantry division, the 3rd, in the northern part of MR-1 to replace redeployed US units.

• • •

After the Lam Son 719 operation into Laos, additional units were approved for activation, to include one 175mm self-propelled artillery battalion, one M-48 tank squadron, and one antiaircraft battalion equipped with M-42s and M-55s.

• • •

By early 1973, at the time of the cease-fire, the RVN army strength stood at 450,000. In terms of combat units, the army consisted of 171 infantry battalions, 22 armored cavalry and tank squadrons, 60 artillery battalions (105mm and [155]mm), and four self-propelled 175mm artillery battalions, not including territorial artillery sections and other support units.

• • •

The Vietnamese Navy (VNN) underwent substantial development during the Vietnamization period. Naval strength, which stood at a mere 12,000 in 1965, did not grow much during the next three years (19,000 in 1968), but beginning in 1969 it started to rise rapidly, doubling its 1965 strength by the end of 1969 and reaching 40,000 by 1972.

• • •

The Vietnam Air Force (VNAF), like its sister service the navy, also expanded and improved rapidly during the Vietnamization period. From a strength of 19,000 in late 1968 the air force expanded almost twofold, reaching a strength of 37,000 by the end of 1969. During 1970 air force strength increased to 45,000, then to 50,000 in 1971, and finally to 64,000 in 1973.

• • •

Improvement and Modernization

Developing and modernizing the military force expanding from 650,000 to 1,100,000 men within five years certainly involved a tremendous effort. During this period the problem of modernizing weapon systems became critical, since the enemy was receiving modern weapons from Communist countries. Beginning in 1968, and especially during 1971–1974, the enemy constantly modernized his combat forces. So the RVNAF weapon and equipment modernization plan was initiated and pushed hard in conjunction with the force structure increase.

Beginning in 1965, M-24 tanks were gradually replaced by M-41s, and in mid-1967 a few AR-15s (later redesignated M-16) were brought into South Vietnam. This initial shipment of AR-15s was hastily distributed among the airborne units for operational test. The AR-15 was proven to be a light snug weapon having a higher firing rate and a greater impact than the Communist AK-47. But, by the end of 1967, the quantity available was just enough to arm the general reserve force, i.e., the airborne and marine units.

• • •

By mid-1968, all RVNAF infantry battalions were equipped with the new M-16 rifle and, to a lesser extent, with M-60 machineguns, M-79 grenade launchers, and LAW anti-tank rocket launchers.

Other combat forces, such as the RF and PF, combat support units, and even the CIDG all received the M-16 rifle during 1969. Communications equipment was also modernized with the replacement of AN/PRC-10s by AN/PRC-25s and the new VRC series of FM radio sets.

• • •

By the end of 1972 US-supplied war materiel for the RVNAF had reached monumental proportions: 855,000 individual and crew-served weapons, 1,880 tanks and artillery pieces, 44,000 radio sets, and 778 helicopters and fixed-wing aircraft.

During the enemy 1972 Summer Offensive the RVNAF suffered great losses in equipment and weapons. As a result, MACV urgently initiated the NOW project to replace these losses in the shortest time possible. The reequipping and retraining process was thus completed in record time, and it was a feat made possible only by the huge and effective US logistics system.

In the lower Laos operation, and especially in the 1972 enemy Summer Offensive, the Communists simultaneously employed many new weapons: 130mm long-bore guns, T-54 tanks, AT-3 antitank missiles, and the hand-held SA-7 "Strella" antiaircraft missiles. As a consequence, the RVNAF required additional weapons and equipment to counteract the formidable Communist armament. Through the expedient "Enhance" program, 175mm artillery battalions and additional M-48 tank squadrons were activated. TOW antitank missiles were also brought in, with additional UH-1 and CH-47 helicopters.

At the end of October 1972, with a view of providing the RVNAF with an abundant maintenance float, and a high level of stocked assets in anticipation of the eventual limitations imposed by the Paris Agreement, the US government rapidly initiated the "Enhance Plus" program. This program provided the RVNAF with a great quantity of equipment such as the F-5A fighter-bombers, C-130A and C-7 cargo planes, M-48A3 medium tanks, 175mm self-propelled guns, M-42 antiaircraft cannon, LVT-5 amphibious vehicles, and many other items.

• • •

Beginning in mid-1969, as US and allied increments redeployed, US Army, Air Force, and Navy bases were gradually turned over to the RVNAF. . . . Cam Ranh base, which was the biggest ever built in South Vietnam, was transferred to the RVNAF on 1 May 1972, and the Danang military port was integrated into the commercial harbor on 29 March 1973.

• • •

The titular transfer of US bases to the RVNAF prior to the cease-fire was a major surprise for the Communists, who belatedly discovered to their consternation that there were no longer any US bases to be dismantled as required by the [Paris] Agreement.

Among important installations turned over by departing US forces, the most valuable in my opinion were telecommunications stations and terminals, which included an extensive dial telephone system, multiplexing equipment, and microwave relay stations and terminals. This modern communication system constituted an extremely valuable asset for the future development of South Vietnam. Also noteworthy were the achievements brought about by the Lines of Communications Program that the United States implemented in South Vietnam. A new, modern system of surfaced, all-weather highways linked by solid and high-tonnage (50-ton) bridges provided an integrated communication network composed of national and interprovincial routes which connected major cities of the coastal zone with the Central Highlands. In total, there were more than 4,000 kilometers of highways, and this was probably the most modern road system in Southeast Asia. This again was an extremely valuable asset for future economic development.

• • •

The Training Effort

• • •

From 1968 to 1970 efforts by MACV to help develop the RVNAF training system paid off handsomely. The twenty-six military schools conducted a total of 326 different courses of instruction and were capable of training 24,000 students, and up to 34,000 when required. Thirty-three training centers scattered throughout the country conducted 34 different courses of instruction and were capable of accommodating 65,000 trainees and, if necessary, up to a total of 106,000. In addition, the RVNAF continued to send to US service schools a great number of personnel such as pilots, signal specialists, and students for the advanced officers service course and Command and General Staff College.

With the continued redeployment process, the replacement of officers for US combat units in South Vietnam was no longer required. As a result, MACV began to upgrade advisory personnel, particularly US officers assigned to schools and training centers. In September 1970 US training advisory personnel increased from 55 percent to over 100 percent, and by June 1971 up to 90 percent of training advisors had previously received combat experience in Vietnam. By the end of 1971 US training advisory strength stood at more than 3,500. Thanks to the assistance of these training advisors, all training programs (over 650 separate programs) were revised and constantly updated. A five-year RVNAF training and budgeting program was finally established.

• • •

Assistance provided by the United States for the strengthening of the RVN Armed Forces was not only confined to increasing force structure and improving equipment, logistics, and training. It also extended to other areas such as intelligence, management, administration, planning, and leadership. US civilian and military officials in Vietnam also cooperated very closely with the RVN government in the pacification program. Finally, US aid and assistance encompassed almost all other national activities with a view to create overall balance, stability, and progress for the Republic of Vietnam.

IV MEETING THE OBSTACLES AND CHALLENGES

The task of implementing the Vietnamization program while the war against Communist aggression was still raging created many problems for the RVN. First and foremost was the combat burden. While it was understood that assistance in resources, materiel, equipment, technology, and finances was being provided by the United States, the actual task of driving back the enemy and organizing for the fighting had to be the RVN['s] primary responsibility. The military struggle itself was but a facet of the war. Much more complex was the problem of pacifying the country in order to save the people from Communist domination.

• • •

The Military Challenge

• • •

The RVNAF met the first challenge of Vietnamization in late April 1969, when the US 4th Infantry Division turned over combat responsibility in the Kontum area to the 24th Special Zone command. Barely two weeks later the enemy deployed three regiments threatening the Dak To–Ben Het area and launched "high point" attacks throughout II CTZ. [An] ARVN operation was conducted in the area north of Kontum in which forces equivalent to a division were committed. The battles fought in this operation were attritional actions and lasted two months. Supported by US artillery and air firepower, RVNAF forces inflicted heavy losses on the enemy, who finally broke contact and withdrew in late June 1969. This victory bolstered the growing confidence of RVNAF units.

• • •

Enemy reactions in late 1969 and in early 1970 were largely insignificant.

• • •

In June 1971 US Secretary of Defense Melvin R. Laird declared that 90 percent of combat responsibility had been turned over to the ARVN and, two months later, announced that Phase I, Vietnamization, had been completed. This meant that, from that time on, ground combat responsibility would be entirely assumed by the RVNAF. The VN Air Force and Navy, meanwhile, also gradually took over combat responsibility.

• • •

Problems of Transition

First and foremost was the density of combat forces, which naturally decreased significantly. A few examples suffice to illustrate this problem. During 1968, in the two provinces north of Hai Van Pass (Thua Thien and Quang Tri), MACV deployed the US 3rd Marine Division, 101st Airborne Division, 1st Air Cavalry Division, and about three other brigades or reinforced brigade-sized units, totalling 37 maneuver battalions. The ARVN, meanwhile, committed to the same area the 1st Infantry Division, augmented by airborne and marine units, totalling 19 maneuver battalions. In total, the aggregated US-RVN force consisted of 56 maneuver battalions.

Four years later, in 1972, when all US units had left, ARVN forces in the areas were augmented by the 3rd Infantry Division and, with reinforcements, totalled just 30 maneuver battalions. The reduction in combat forces thus amounted to 26 battalions, or nearly one-half, and this is under the assumption that an RVNAF battalion was the equivalent of a US battalion, which was far from true. Thus the real reduction in combat forces was actually much greater.

In artillery, for example, the aggregated total of pieces deployed by the above US units and US XXIV Corps was 400. In 1972 the total number of ARVN artillery pieces, including reinforcements, was merely 160. This represented a reduction of 60 percent in firepower. Furthermore, this figure did not take into account the fact that US ammunition supply rates were much higher. This rough comparison also omitted other US combat support assets such as helicopters, gunships, armor, and tactical air and naval firepower which were made amply available during the time US forces remained in South Vietnam. Moreover, the NVA divisions which confronted ours in 1968 did not have tanks and artillery. In 1972 they had all these and much more.

• • •

Whereas US forces previously employed up to 5,000 helicopters, the VNAF now had to make do with 500. Also, after the cease-fire, US air and naval activities were completely suspended. But the greatest loss in firepower support was the absence of B-52 sorties, which in 1968 and 1969 reached a total of 20,000. The RVNAF did receive additional air and naval assets, but such an increase was insignificant when compared to the huge quantity of US combat assets employed in the war. In terms of ground combat troops, a bigger proportion of the force structure increase was earmarked for the RF and PF. These were primarily lightly equipped small units which were geared to the protection of villages and hamlets. They constantly needed a larger regular force on which they could depend to back them up. This explains why the ARVN was unable to release its infantry divisions for mobile operations.

The improvement and modernization of the RVNAF, moreover, apparently came about as an after-coup response to the modernization of Communist forces. As early as in 1964 regular enemy units fought the Binh Gia battle with the modern AK-47 assault rifle and the RPG rocket launcher. During the following years, these weapons became standard weapons in all enemy units. In 1967, as substitutes for artillery, the enemy used 122mm and 140mm rockets, and by the time he attacked Lang Vei, near Khe Sanh, in early 1968 his units were supported by tanks.

Our units, by contrast, lagged woefully far behind. During the first wave of enemy attacks in early 1968, only a few elite units were equipped with M-16 rifles and M-60 machineguns. By and large, the RVNAF fought back the enemy offensive with inferior armament. During the Lam Son 719 operation in lower Laos in 1971, the ARVN M-41 tanks were proved no match for the 100mm-gun-equipped T-54 tanks. At the same time, our ground troops began to experience the effect of enemy long-range 130mm guns. Only later did the ARVN receive one M-48 tank squadron and one 175mm self-propelled artillery battalion. But the quantity made available proved to be insufficient during the 1972 enemy Summer Offensive. In addition to tanks and large caliber guns, the enemy still caused further surprise in armament by his use of the AT-3 wire-guided missile and the . . . heat-seeking SA-7 antiaircraft missile. Only after the appearance of these sophisticated weapons during this campaign did the United States deliver to the ARVN the TOW missile, more M-48 tanks, and more long-range 175mm guns.

By and large ARVN requests for new weapons, which were intended to counteract a new but untested enemy capability, were all rejected by the United States. It was even more difficult to obtain any kind of offensive weapons from the United States. While [the] North Vietnam air force was equipped with MIG-21s, all requests for F-4 Phantom fighter-bombers met with US indifference. It was obvious then that the VNAF never had an offensive capability, and neither did the VNN. The WHEC-type ships which were turned over from US Coast Guard inventory were bulky, slow, inadequately armed, and capable only of patrolling. DER-type destroyers were also obsolescent escort ships, inadequately armed and definitely not offensive-type naval ships. As a result, when naval gunfire was required to support ground troops, its effectiveness was minimal. The North Vietnam navy, meanwhile, although modest in size, had the advantage of fast offensive-type PT boats equipped with missiles.

As to force structure components, several JGS recommendations were turned down, especially those concerning the activation of additional infantry divisions to increase reserve forces, even though they did not involve any increase in overall strength. The activation of the ARVN 3rd Infantry Division, which arose from dire needs, was an exception in that the United States was faced with an accomplished fact. The United States also rejected the formation of regional regiments, which the RVNAF conceived as a means to upgrade operational capabilities for sectors and to release regular infantry divisions from territorial confines. The result was that, as of late 1972, the RVN no longer had any general reserve force.

In addition to a sizable reduction in combat support, other facilities also became scarcer after US forces had been withdrawn. Operational effectiveness decreased accordingly. An example in the area of military intelligence illustrates the state of things. To solve the problem of aerial photo[s] under the Vietnamization program, the VNAF was equipped with six RF-5s and six RC-47s for photo reconnaissance missions. But these limited facilities only filled part of the J-2/JGS requirement. There was a serious gap in aerial photo coverage since North Vietnam, Cambodia, and Laos were now out of RVNAF reach. Support provided by the "Buffalo Hunter" program (pilotless aerial photo reconnaissance) also dwindled greatly. During the previous years the RVNAF used to enjoy the marvels of US technology in military intelligence: RF-4s, Mohawks, SLAR (side-looking airborne radar), Red Haze (locator of heat-generating targets), Sniffer, etc. These were no longer made available.

• • •

For all its merits, the Vietnamization process did not last long enough for the RVNAF to fully develop their capabilities. While the training of infantry combat units could be performed in a relatively short time, the training and qualification of service specialists or technicians demanded a much longer time.

• • •

The overall result of these accelerated turnover programs was that the RVNAF technical services did not have enough qualified specialists to operate and maintain US-transferred equipment. As a result, serviceability rates were low for ships, aircraft, and tanks. Meanwhile the backlog of unserviceable items of equipment continued to build up in repair shops.

• • •

Because of these reductions in force and in facilities, the RVNAF inevitably ran into many difficulties when assuming the major combat role.

• • •

Despite increased sacrifices, willingness, and expediency, operations were not the same as they had been. With at least a 40 percent reduction in infantry forces, with the greater part of firepower and mobility lost, now RVNAF units were just capable of protecting national priority areas. Enemy bases and infiltration routes located deep in the Truong Son range became objectives that were out of the RVNAF reach. The VNAF was not even equipped to fly reconnaissance missions along this corridor after the cease-fire, because the enemy antiaircraft network had become so dense. Remote areas such as A Shau, A Luoi, Nam Dong, [and] Kham Duc, and bases such as Do Xa and War Zones C and D, now became impenetrable because the ARVN did not have enough troops.

Within the confines of populated areas, however, the RVNAF performed their task quite well—at the price of greater sacrifices. Population centers were kept pacified and security was well maintained. And, around them, there was the protection belt made up of advanced outposts that were defended. The biggest performance, however, was the containment of enemy advance during his 1972 offensive and the reoccupation of almost all lost territory. During late 1972, when the cease-fire first failed to materialize, and then in early 1973, when it went into effect, ARVN units, regular and territorial alike, outdid themselves by holding firm their defense lines and positions. And, despite the enemy effort, in 1973 he lost more land and population than he first set out to grab. All these things were achieved with losses greater than when there was support by US forces.

• • •

Logistics was the branch of service which faced the most problems in achieving maximum performance at reduced costs. During the year preceding the cease-fire the United States had increased military aid in an effort to equip and support the RVNAF and to implement the Vietnamization program. After the cease-fire, however, this aid was reduced and the logistics branch had to make greater efforts to overcome difficulties. Economy was now the foremost objective, and operational costs were cut down. Ammunition and fuel became scarcer and had to be distributed by fixed allocations. And the price of every cartridge, every item of war materiel, was disseminated to troops with a view to make them conscious of economy.

• • •

With regard to major ARVN field units, the problem was, the author thinks, the commanders themselves. During the period when US advisors and US support assets were still available, III and IV Corps commands performed extremely well in the 1970 cross-border operation. In 1971, with the same assistance and support, I Corps direction of the Lam Son 719 operation . . . failed to offer any exemplary model. Vietnamese high-ranking command cadres were partly selected without reference to real talent and ethics. Others had never been thoroughly tried and tested. In those cases, the absence of the US advisor became a great loss indeed. The improvement in this respect would certainly take the RVN more time, demand more sacrifices, and still more recognition of the problem.

In brief, the RVN made several efforts militarily, overcame many difficulties, and incurred more sacrifices in order to take over the combat burden. The RVN mobilized its manpower; built up morale; endured more sacrifices; perfected organization, training, tactics; and improved administration, logistics, support, and personnel in order to achieve the capabilities required for facilitating a smooth, uneventful US troop withdrawal. But the war being fought was primarily a protracted ideological conflict which pitted the Free World and world Communism against each other. Such being the case, the RVN definitely needed a determined material and spiritual support from the United States, as well as from other free countries.

• • •

Toward Self-Reliance

• • •

In anticipation of the dwindling US military aid, the RVN initiated several measures to fight the war by its own means and resources. Another attempt was made to develop a military doctrine which faithfully reflected Vietnamese purposes, resources, and abilities, as opposed to the one borrowed from Western countries. In the field many units, either on their own initiatives or under JGS instructions, began to concentrate troop training on three combat aspects—march, sniper fire, and close combat. March was going to be needed in case trucks and helicopters were no longer available. Also it was the only combat means the Vietnamese infantryman possessed. Sniper training was aimed at improving marksmanship and instilling the single shot habit so that ammunition consumption would be reduced. Finally, close combat training was a much-needed shot in the arm to enhance combat prowess among troops.

• • •

Wasteful firepower practice, it was felt, should be changed and by all means combat units should learn how to fight a "poor man's war." They should learn how to maneuver to bring about maximum shock effect while firepower was missing. This was the only way an infantry unit could prove its combat value. In the face of diminishing ammunition supply rates, artillerymen should learn how to moderate their fire without reducing effectiveness, and that required firing only when the target could be observed. To destroy an enemy blocking position, only one 105mm or one 155mm piece should be needed—if its fire was accurate. Against other targets that required accurate but lesser fire, the 81mm mortar should be enough. These were things that ARVN troops were taught in the field with a view to bring[ing] the Vietnamization process another step forward.

During the 1972 Summer Offensive the enemy began to make proliferated use of artillery, and in time his artillery was augmented by an extensive and particularly dense network of antiaircraft weapons. Beginning in the summer of 1974, this tremendous firepower made a big difference in battles. VNAF observation planes flew fewer and fewer sorties, and, since they were kept at a high altitude by enemy antiaircraft fire, they no longer proved as effective as they had been. As a result, infantry units were compelled to use field observation posts and small reconnaissance teams for the acquisition of targets.

Also, in the face of a scarcer supply of barrier material, units became ingenious in the exploitation of local resources. Trees and wood were widely used to repair barracks and fortifications; pointed sticks of bamboo, and bamboo hedges, came to replace barbed wire; trenches and underground shelters took the place of surface fortifications. In this respect, the RF and PF were really the pioneers and for all practical purposes became entirely self-sufficient in organizing for defense.

• • •

The Communist Counteraction

When the Vietnamization program was initiated, enemy reaction at first was unclear, partly because he did not fully grasp the scope and content of the plan. Besides, the enemy was in a defensive position, militarily speaking. As a matter of fact, COSVN Resolution No. 9, which was issued in July 1969, confirmed the enemy's renunciation of a quick major military victory and advocated instead "partial victories" to be achieved by a flexible military strategy adapted to the various phases of US troop withdrawal. This strategy concentrated on attriting war-making capabilities of the US and the RVN by extensive employment of small but elite units called "Dac Cong" (Special Action, or Sappers). In keeping with this strategy, the enemy substantially increased his sapper forces. In July 1969 there were 39 sapper battalions; a year later this figure was up to 65.

• • •

Despite their bombast, enemy actions failed to impede the Vietnamization program. And, when the program resulted in remarkable achievements, its success, according to enemy documents, stunned COSVN. Contrary to what the enemy had set about to achieve, his bases and major regular units were destroyed one after another and his supply storages had to be moved across the border. As a result, the enemy provincial and district units, and the guerrilla forces of his infrastructure, completely lost rear support and backing. It now took the enemy about two months to move from Kien Hoa to Ba Thu (enemy base in the Parrot's Beak area) instead of one week. The morale of enemy cadres was also on the decline. Besides, 1972 was a US election year, and the Paris talks were still dragging on inconclusively. Convinced that only a forceful military action could redress the situation to his advantage, the enemy decided to launch a general offensive.

• • •

By pushing its main force divisions overtly across the DMZ, and by employing modern weapons such as the T-54 tank, the 130mm gun, the SAM-2 and SA-7 antiaircraft missiles, and the AT-3 antitank missile, North Vietnam undoubtedly wanted to prove that the Vietnamization program was a failure. But it was the enemy who had failed—both in this regard and in his attempt to use battle gains as pressure on the Paris talks. He had occupied a few remote district towns, but what a price he had paid: 100,000 troops killed and a major part of his Russian and Chinese-supplied weapons and equipment lost. He had really failed indeed, at least on the military front. The RVN had stood firmly, and its forces had succeeded in stopping the enemy. Two basic weaknesses stood out, however. First, it was obvious that the RVNAF still required substantial US air and naval fire support, and, second, by committing the last general reserve to MR-1 the RVNAF were overextended to a near breaking point.

V. PEACE NEGOTIATIONS AND THE CEASE-FIRE

• • •

The signing of the Paris Agreement failed to materialize in late October 1972, as previously agreed. In November and December 1972 Dr. Kissinger and Le Duc Tho met again in Paris to discuss certain modifications, some of them based on . . . RVN recommendations. The North Vietnamese negotiator was irreconcilable, and the meetings went into deadlock on 13 December 1972.

President Nixon then ordered a renewal of bombings, apparently to press North Vietnam into accepting the changes. He also sent a special letter to President Thieu, warning him that, if South Vietnam still persisted in refusing to sign, the United States would go ahead and sign the agreement with North Vietnam. Should this occur, President Nixon emphasized, military and economic aid to South Vietnam would be suspended. On the contrary, he promised, if North Vietnam committed a grave violation, the United States would react vigorously. This was what amounted to a guarantee by the president of the United States. In the prevalent situation of South Vietnam, President Thieu hardly had any choice other than clinging to this promise. He finally gave in, apparently to avoid an immediate crisis.

Gravely wounded by twelve consecutive days of intensive bombings, North Vietnam finally dragged itself to the conference table. Dr. Kissinger met with Le Duc Tho again on 8 January 1973. Six days later, the revised text of the agreement was completed. President Nixon decided to stop all US military actions against North Vietnam as of 15 January. On 23 January, Kissinger and Le Duc Tho met at the Majestic Hotel, went over the agreement text for the last time, and initialed it. On 27 January representatives of the four parties to the Paris talks officially signed the agreement on behalf of their governments. And at 0800 hours, Saigon time, the next day, 28 January 1973, the cease-fire went into effect, in principle. To the United States, at least, the war had ended.

The Paris Agreement

The agreement which was signed in Paris on 27 January 1973 was officially called "Agreement on Ending the War and Restoring Peace in Vietnam."

• • •

The cease-fire took place at midnight, GMT, 27 January 1973, or 0800 hours, Saigon time, 28 January 1973. Armed force units of both sides and police forces were to cease all hostilities, sabotage, and reprisal acts; and end all operations, patrols, reconnaissances on the ground, in the air, or on the sea into the territory of the other side. . . . The United States would cease all military activities on North Vietnam territory and clear the blockade mines. The United States would dismantle, detonate, or neutralize all mines that had been implanted in North Vietnam. Within sixty days after the signing of the agreement, [the] United States and allied countries would withdraw all military forces, advisors, military personnel and technicians, and all weapons and equipment from Vietnam. Military installations would also be dismantled within the same period. Armaments, munitions, and expendable items of war materiel which were destroyed or damaged could be replaced on the basis of piece-for-piece of the same characteristics.

• • •

The Communist Scheme

While drafting the last peace proposal in Paris, the Communists also laid out a detailed plan aimed at taking advantage of the cease-fire. The plan was disseminated to all echelons of the Communist Party and armed force hierarchy with detailed instructions for action.

In mid-October 1972 an ARVN unit operating in Quang Nam Province seized an enemy document which turned out to be the cease-fire plan itself. It gave an accurate description of the agreement and the "leopard skin" cease-fire and prescribed an implementation through three phases.

Phase I: This was the pre-cease-fire or preparatory phase. Cadres were instructed to study the agreement carefully, to memorize its provisions, to learn how to interpret them to their advantage, and to be prepared to present them to the public or to debate them with adversaries. Propaganda teams were to be organized as the basic means for proselytizing actions. All sewing machines were to be requisitioned for the manufacture of NLF flags, which would be planted on the cease-fire day in every house, every hamlet, and on every hill. The enemy was thus prepared to demonstrate his ubiquitous presence to whatever international control body was in place at that time. Major units meanwhile were to conduct attacks in order to pin down RVNAF units. During this time Communist regional forces and the local militia, broken down into small elements, were to penetrate every hamlet and every populated area, block every important axis of communication, and stay in place until international representatives arrived.

Phase II: This was the implementation phase centering around the cease-fire day. The precise date and time of the cease-fire would be announced. Three days before cease-fire day all Communist units were to push military attacks vigorously in order to occupy the maximum amount of territory and number of important objectives. On the cease-fire day they were to hold firmly to the gains thus achieved and simultaneously fly the NLF flags. The population and various organizations would stage demonstrations demanding the RVNAF to implement the cease-fire and to return RVN soldiers to their families. Subsequently there was to be insistence on the exercise of rights of freedom, movement, meeting, abrogation of military service, curfew, etc. All these actions were designed to create maximum trouble for the RVN government. In the meantime, armed propaganda units were to push proselytizing actions vigorously, explain the agreement, [and] exhort ARVN soldiers to stop fighting, go on leave, visit their home villages, and renounce military service altogether.

Phase III: This was the post-cease-fire or consolidation phase. All the gains achieved were to be held and consolidated. Subsequent actions would depend on the situation and the results obtained in the previous phases, but the objective was to press on and dismantle the RVNAF, to enhance Communist prestige while keeping up a propaganda effort to demand the implementation and observance of the agreement.

This was, in summarized form, the content of directives issued to subordinate echelons of the Communist Party and army. They were to be responsible for a face-to-face showdown of force and wits. But the cease-fire, which was supposed to take place at the end of October 1972, never materialized. As a result, certain lower-echelon enemy units, which had not been informed of the delay in time, went ahead according to plan. And the Land and Population Grab campaign, which broke out prematurely during the last few days of October 1972, turned into an important military "high point."

Captured documents, when corroborated with intelligence reports and the depositions of returnees and prisoners of war, provided still more revealing details. Most important was Directive No. 2/73, issued by the Communist Party's Central Office for South Vietnam (COSVN) in January 1973 and intended for the party and army hierarchy. The Paris Agreement, according to the directive, was a decisive, historic victory for the Communist movement in South Vietnam and constituted an important step toward achieving the people's democratic revolution in the South. The agreement did not end the struggle for country reunification, but brought about a status of "half-war, half-peace" in which politics was to have a primary role and military actions a support role. In performing this role, military forces were to provide support for the proselytizing effort directed at enemy troops, to protect the people's struggle movement, and to defend the liberated areas.

• • •

Whatever his final course of action, the enemy had already opted for a decisive military solution to settle the problem of South Vietnam. Thus the long-range political struggle appeared to be relegated to a secondary rank, if not entirely forsaken.

• • •

The Cease-Fire

• • •

Simultaneously with land grab and lines of communication interdiction actions, the enemy staged another form of warfare—the flag-planting campaign, for which he had been well prepared. Several days before the cease-fire, the blue and red NLF flag appeared in the areas under his control and wherever his forces succeeded in penetrating. but the RVN had expected it all along and was equally well prepared to counteract.

On the cease-fire day, suddenly the red-striped yellow flag of the RVN was displayed throughout the country. It was painted on rooftops or in front of houses and on every moving vehicle. The spectacle was phenomenal. Troops were even issued individual flags and they waved them wherever they went. It was impossible for the International Commission of Control and Supervision to find out what was happening and who was in control of various areas. A good effect of this campaign was that all the population appeared to be involved and genuinely displayed a positive anti-Communist spirit. It also resulted in frenzied competition by both sides to "remove enemy flags and plant ours." Only one week after the cease-fire day, nearly all the 400-odd hamlets that had been penetrated by the enemy were back under government control and proudly flew the national flags. An exception was a few outlying hamlets and the Hoai An district town north of Binh Dinh Province.

The cease-fire upheavals gradually calmed down after a few weeks, and both sides desisted from probing each other with provoking actions. The military situation also stabilized in all areas. The enemy proselytizing campaign was a fiasco. No demonstrations materialized and no troops deserted their units, despite ear-shattering exhortations on front lines or quietly whispered friendly persuasions elsewhere. The RVNAF stood firm; they did not disintegrate as the enemy had expected. Outsiders might have expected that, in the wake of the inevitable upheavals and skirmishes in the initial stage of the cease-fire, both sides would take steps to seriously implement what had been agreed upon and that a genuine cease-fire would soon take place. Events that followed proved them wrong, because barely two months after the signature of the agreement the Communists committed two other major violations which were considered the most serious of all: the siege of Tong Le Chan Base and the attack against Hong Ngu district town.

Tong Le Chan was a ranger border camp located in the middle of an enemy-controlled area. It effectively interdicted all enemy liaison and troop movements from War Zone C (north of Tay Ninh) into Binh Long or Binh Duong Province. The presence of Tong Le Chan forced the enemy to make long detours and caused him serious difficulties. So the enemy began to encircle this base on 25 March 1973 with the design to force its evacuation. Friendly patrols and supply routes of the defending garrison, the 92nd Ranger Battalion, were effectively blocked. The base had to be supplied at first by helicopters, but the risks they ran became too great because of the dense antiaircraft network around the base; as a result, supplies were airdropped. During the four following months, the enemy shelled the base nearly 300 times with a total of 10,000 assorted rounds and attacked it by infantry eleven times and by sapper actions nine times. While strangling the base, the enemy also stepped up propaganda activities and coaxed the defenders to evacuate the camp under safe conduct. But, by July 1973, the base still stood firm despite an increasing number of dead and gravely wounded (over 30) and the fact that most of the rangers were either ill or wounded. Forceful protests voiced by the RVN government all fell on deaf ears.

Hong Ngu was a district town north of Kien Phong Province (MR-4) which lay on the eastern bank of the Mekong near the Cambodian border. It was a river port where supply convoys bound for Phnom Penh usually stopped over to pick up escorts. At the end of March 1973 the reinforced NVA 1st Division crossed the border and attacked the Hong Ngu river port. The losses the enemy caused to the local population were severe. The area was inhabited by Buddhists of the Hoa Hao sect, a fiercely anti-Communist group, who enjoyed peacefulness and prosperity during the entire war. Now, for the first time, their haven was destroyed and 300 of their people savagely slaughtered. By mid-April 1973 the ARVN 9th Division, augmented by armored elements, counterattacked and drove the enemy division over the border and back into Cambodia, where its troops were further decimated by extensive US airstrikes.[6]

• • •

On 22 September 1973 the NVA 320th Division suddenly moved one tank-supported regiment against the Le Minh (Plei D'jereng) ranger border camp, 25 miles west of Pleiku. Le Minh Base was located on . . . dominating terrain which effectively controlled a major enemy infiltration route from lower Laos into the Central Highlands and a north-south road system which the enemy was building along the Truong Son corridor. It was also near the enemy Duc Co logistics base that was being developed into a major supply point for future battlefields. This was, in fact, the first time since the cease-fire that the enemy used a regimental-sized unit with tank support in an overt attack. It was a clear sign of a significant change in enemy strategic direction. In view of his effort to develop a new infiltration road system, which ran the entire length of South Vietnam's western border, it had become a necessity for the enemy to get rid of obstacles that lay in the way of his progress. Le Minh Base, as part of the border surveillance system, ought to be disposed of, just like Tong Le Chan. And, as he progressed, the enemy felt other bases in the system should be either forced to evacuate or simply destroyed: Mang Buk, Dak Pek, Dak To, Chuong Nghia, Plei Me, Tieu A Tar, Duc Lap, Dak Son, and Bu Prang, a long chain of border outposts designed to control enemy infiltration and collect intelligence. Most of these outposts held out, but all had become isolated and had to be supplied by air.

Two months after the loss of Le Minh Base, the enemy north-south strategic road system reached down to the boundary of Quang Duc Province. This system picked up from QL-14 in MR-1 down to north of Kontum, then veered westward near this side of the border, ran parallel to it, and bent inside again when it came to Quang Duc. But, to go further inside MR-3, the enemy ran smack into Dak Son and Bu Prang, border camps which were to be removed at all costs. In early November 1973, in a mobile warfare field exercise conducted to test combined arms effectiveness, the enemy repeatedly drove attacks against Bu Prang, Dak Son, and Kien Duc, the district town of Quang Duc Province. The enemy propaganda line used to justify his military action in this case was that, since the RVN mounted pacification operations and established new border outposts in his area of control, it was perfectly appropriate for him to retaliate in kind. Nothing could be further from the truth. Everybody knew that these outposts were former CIDG camps that had been turned over to the RVNAF by the US Special Forces long before the cease-fire. But protestations to the ICCS availed to nothing. The 45th Regiment of the ARVN 23rd Division therefore counterattacked and retook Kien Duc and Dak Son. Bu Prang and Bu Bong border camps nearby remained in enemy hands. As a result, the enemy road system had to make a detour over the border before connecting with MR-3 north of Loc Ninh.

•••

By this time enemy violations had become all too flagrant. The RVN was thus forced to respond with its air advantage. The VNAF conducted several retaliation and punishment airstrikes against enemy-held positions such as Duc Co, Loc Ninh, Thien Ngon, Xa Mat, and Lo Go. Apparently to repay the RVNAF in kind, in November 1973 the enemy began to rocket Bien Hoa Air Base. In late December, he also shelled, and sabotaged by sapper action, the Shell fuel storage plant in Nha Be, south of Saigon. Eighty percent of storage gasoline was destroyed by an intense fire, and this occurred at a time when the Middle East oil crisis made its impact felt throughout the world.

In MR-4 the enemy concentrated on neutralizing the RVN pacification effort. Assassinations, kidnappings, harassments against outposts, small-unit attacks, and ambushes were resumed with renewed ardor, as of old. Major enemy units also increased infiltrations into the That Son area with a design to extend his encroachment corridor into the U Minh base. This action resulted in further security deterioration in Kien Giang, Chuong Thien, and An Xuyen Provinces.

VI. DEVELOPMENTS FOLLOWING THE CEASE-FIRE

Implementing the Agreement

The basic things that the Paris Agreement was supposed to bring about, a standstill cease-fire and peace for South Vietnam, thus turned out to be illusory. Nor did other provisions of the agreement fare any better, except for the exchange of prisoners and the withdrawal of US and allied troops.

The first problem for the Paris Agreement was the international machinery which was instituted to control and supervise the implementation of the agreement itself. The negotiators must have been fully aware of the Geneva antecedent—the impotent ICC of the First Indochina War. Thus a four-member International Commission of Control and Supervision (ICCS) was created, which apparently struck a perfect balance: two from the Free World (Canada and Indonesia) and two from the Communist bloc (Poland and

Hungary). The obstacles that the ICCS ran into from its very inception on the cease-fire day was its basic principle of operations: unanimity and consultations. The four members understandably took sides and, having equal voting power, came invariably to a deadlock almost every time an issue was raised. Hungary and Poland naturally sided with the NLF, whom they protected and whose violations they ignored. Canada and Indonesia, meanwhile, tried their best to be objective, but they also supported the RVN and its cause.

• • •

When his mind was set on preventing the presence of the ICCS, the enemy would not hesitate to shoot down a helicopter, even when his liaison officer was aboard. This was exactly what happened to two ICCS helicopters flying on a mission to Lao Bao on 7 April 1973. One helicopter was shot down with eleven men aboard, including two NLF liaison officers; all were killed. The second helicopter, badly hit, was forced to crash land. The enemy later claimed that the helicopters had deviated from the authorized flight corridor. The fact was the enemy did not want the ICCS to poke its nose into the Lao Bao–Khe Sanh area, which was being developed into a gigantic logistics base complete with SAM antiaircraft missiles. At Duc Co, another major enemy logistics base in MR-2, the ICCS team was forced to leave because life became impossible for its members. Not only did the enemy fail to supply them with basic necessities, but their movements were so limited that they were not free to carry out their mission.

Among the four ICCS members, Canadians were the most objective and dedicated to their work. As a result, they were frequently criticized and mistreated by the Communists, who even went to the extreme of arresting an entire Canadian observation team and releasing them only after a long interval. The investigation concerning the enemy violation at Sa Huynh was also noteworthy. The initial request for it came from the NLF who, after occupying Sa Huynh by force, wanted the ICCS to officiate their control over the port. It so happened that, by the time the ICCS investigation team arrived, Sa Huynh had been reoccupied by the ARVN 2nd Division. Seeing that the investigation could turn to the NLF disadvantage, the Communist representatives backed off. But the RVN kept insisting, and finally the Danang ICCS team arrived at Sa Huynh and confirmed that the NLF had, in fact, violated an RVN-held area. This was perhaps the first and only time that all four ICCS members unanimously agreed with the result of the investigation. The chief of the Polish delegation, however, was relieved soon after the Sa Huynh affair. In July 1973, fed up with the uselessness of its role in the ICCS, Canada withdrew its membership and was replaced by Iran.

• • •

Implementing Article 12 of the agreement, both the RVN and the NLF delegations met at La Celle-Saint-Cloud in suburban Paris on 19 March 1973 to discuss the political future of South Vietnam. The RVN delegation chief, Deputy Prime Minister Dr. Nguyen Luu Vien, was an affable, modest man given to open and friendly talks. His counterpart, Nguyen Van Hieu, was quite the opposite. Their positions were irreconcilable, and the gap between was too great. There were six major issues that invariably came to a deadlock every time they were raised: the cease-fire, the National Council of Reconciliation and Concord, the guarantee of freedom and democratic rights, the civilian prisoners, the reduction of troops, and the elections. By the end of April 1973, when the 90-day delay for settlement of South Vietnam's internal problems had expired, the two delegations had not even agreed on an agenda! And so the talks dragged on futilely.

The implementation of the agreement, despite delays and conflicts, did succeed quite remarkably in three areas: the exchange of prisoners of war, the withdrawal of US and allied forces, and the de-mining of North Vietnam. On the very day the agreement was officially signed, the four signatory parties exchanged lists of prisoners among themselves. It was agreed that US troop withdrawal and the exchange of prisoners take place at the same time and be completed within 60 days. During his 24 January 1973 press conference, Dr. Kissinger announced that the return of US prisoners would be carried out in increments spaced out every two weeks. Subsequent plannings were based on this schedule. From the lists exchanged in Paris, North Vietnam admitted to detaining 594 American prisoners, including 562 servicemen, 24 civilians, and eight third-country nationals.

• • •

On 22 March 1973, when it was apparent that North Vietnam did not want to release American prisoners captured in Laos, the US delegation had to threaten to suspend the third and four withdrawal increments and the de-mining to exact a concession from North Vietnam on 29 March.

At the time of the cease-fire, there were 23,516 US and 30,449 allied troops left in South Vietnam. Their withdrawal was spaced out in four increments 15 days apart. After one delay expressly imposed to exert pressure, and as the last group of American prisoners of war returned, the final withdrawal increment was completed on 29 March 1973.

In Paris, the RVN delegation also handed to the Communist side a list of 27,000 prisoners, both North Vietnamese and NLF. When they were released, 238 among those chose to stay behind and threatened suicide if forced to return. Except for three seriously ill prisoners to be returned at a later date, the total number of prisoners returned to the Communists amounted to 26,508. It is noteworthy to mention here the fact that, prior to handing the 27,000-prisoner list to the other side, the RVN had taken expedient steps to grant returnee status to more than 10,000 cooperating Communist prisoners, thus enabling them to live legally in South Vietnam after release from reeducation centers. In exchange for 27,000 released, the RVN took back a total of 4,608 veterans. North Vietnam held 410 prisoners of the RVN as hostages to demand the return of its 238 turncoats. The RVN had compiled a list of its servicemen missing in action: 31,818 in total. Thus more than 25,000 were still detained by the other side. Even if there had been unverifiable deaths among them, and even if many had chosen to stay within Communist ranks, the remaining total, whose existence the other side preferred to ignore, was sizable indeed.

As to political prisoners, the RVN declared it detained 5,018 and immediately released 1,200 as a gesture of goodwill pending agreement with the NLF on internal issues. Meanwhile, the Communists admitted to detaining only 140 RVN cadres. After several protests and contests, the other side gradually raised the figure to 200, then 400, 429, and finally 637, while the RVN census recorded a total of 67,500 civilians kidnapped or captured by the enemy, including 17,000 cadres of all echelons.

• • •

Upon release, RVN prisoners were given rest and recuperation and then, on request, were discharged from service. By contrast, released Communist prisoners were immediately used to replace losses in enemy combat units. On 10 June 1973 a released Communist prisoner asked to return to our side out of war weariness. He gave the information that, of the 1,000 prisoners the RVN released to the enemy on 10 and 11 March 1973, in Phu Yen Province, 700 men under the age of 30 were assigned to MR-5 units, and the remainder returned to their home villages to replenish local provincial units. All 1,000 had first undergone a 10-day reeducation course. Thus the exchange of prisoners practically gave the enemy all at once 27,000 experienced soldiers, enough to activate three infantry divisions.

• • •

In the meantime, in keeping with the Western tradition of being bound by a signed agreement, the US Navy proceeded with the odious task of mine-clearing in all NVN ports and rivers. The task progressed quite slowly due to technological difficulties and also because of the need for renegotiations. Nevertheless it was accomplished within the last 35-day delay as determined by the Paris Joint Communiqué of 13 June 1973. And so the only American obligation left with regard to North Vietnam was the promised postwar reconstruction aid, which North Vietnam preferred to call "war reparations." This problem necessarily depended on the development of the situation and the outcome of the search for American MIAs and the remains of American KIAs.

Communist Preparations

By the end of 1972, in the wake of the Summer Offensive during which North Vietnam committed the majority of its forces to the battlefields of the South, total enemy strength in South Vietnam was estimated at about 300,000. The bulk of enemy combat forces consisted of 14 regular infantry divisions, 30 separate infantry regiments, and sapper, artillery, armored, antiaircraft regiments, and other support units. In MR-1 alone the enemy maintained seven divisions: five in the DMZ area and north of Hai Van Pass: 304, 308, 312, 320, and 324B; and two south of Hai Van Pass: 711 and NT-2. In MR-2, the enemy deployed three divisions: NT-3, F-10, and 968. In MR-3, major regular enemy units included two divisions: CT-7 and CT-9, and several sapper units. MR-4 was the usual operational area for the enemy 1st and CT-5 Divisions.

The enemy infrastructure and militia were greatly reduced after the Summer Offensive, with their total then estimated at a little over 40,000 men. This reduction in strength was to become a major impediment for the enemy in his Land and Population Grab campaign of the cease-fire period.

At the time the standstill cease-fire was announced, military forces of both sides were supposed to stay where they were. The area under effective enemy control, and the fuzzy contested zone in between, ran from the DMZ, where [it] included the northern half of Quang Tri Province, southward along the Truong Son mountain range, to include almost all mountainous areas of MR-1 and MR-2 and northern MR-3. The remaining consisted of "dents" scattered throughout the GVN-controlled territory, which figuratively looked like spots on a leopard skin. Most important among these were the enemy major bases in MR-4, such as U Minh, Ca Mau, That Son, the areas where Chuong Thien, Kien Giang, and Phong Dinh provincial boundaries met, the boundary area between Vinh Long and Vinh Binh Provinces, and the Tri Phap area (Plain of Reeds). Laos and Cambodia meanwhile remained the sanctuaries where the enemy enjoyed absolute freedom of action.

After 1972 enemy forces were in a state of utter exhaustion. His destroyed equipment and supplies were not replaced on time, and troop replacements hardly filled in the huge human losses. Most of his major units were at best barely capable of defensive actions. In Quang Nam Province, troops from the NVA 711th Division who returned to our side before and after the cease-fire revealed that their units were in such a critical shortage of ammunition that each B-40 or B-41 (RPG) rocket launcher was left with three rounds, and several companies were reduced to a skeletal strength of ten cadres or even less.

To the enemy, the cease-fire was a much-needed rest and recuperation period which came just in time. The Communist precept being violence, he undoubtedly must have realized that to conquer a country with a million-strong armed force, political efforts alone, albeit violent politics, would not suffice. Hence military effort was the only key to success. As a result, from the very first day the cease-fire went into effect the enemy embarked on a program of force development that had never been nor could ever be matched in the entire history of the Indochina War.

Foremost among the problems to be solved was logistics. The enemy was extremely concerned about logistics prior to launching a campaign, big or small. It had become an enemy basic tenet that logistics must be adequate in place before combat orders could be issued. Equipment, ammunition, and supplies of all kinds seemed not to pose any difficulties because of increased aid quantities provided by Russia and China. According to intelligence sources, during 1973 North Vietnam received a total of 2.8 million metric tons of goods from Communist bloc countries, up 50 percent from 1972 aid figures, and in 1974 total imported goods increased to 3.5 million tons. So the major problem for the enemy was to transport this materiel into the South and to store and distribute it to his units.

During the entire course of the US direct participation in the war, despite destructive US bombings, the enemy always managed to keep in motion an effective and well-run logistics system to feed his battlefields in the South. Now that this fire had ceased, the enemy logistics effort became much easier. Group 559, under direct control of the General Directorate of Rear Services, NVA General Staff, in Hanoi, was in charge of supply and transportation support for South Vietnam battlefields. By the end of 1972 Group

559 had under its control a total of five Rear Services divisions which were generally located along the Truong Son corridor.

• • •

Each division had a number of subordinate "binh tram" (military stations, literally) or logistics units, which were self-contained organizations complete with administration, engineers, transportation, depot facilities, and protective forces such as infantry troops and antiaircraft units.

• • •

Throughout the period of US bombings against this infiltration corridor, the enemy had required more stations and way stations in between. Trucks usually moved only at night with blackout lights or when the weather was bad, and they were strictly used for cargoes. Troops or personnel, meanwhile, had to march, and they needed rest stations where they ate and recuperated or received medical treatment. As soon as bombings were suspended, trucks moved night and day and also carried troops and personnel. The number of stations was now reduced, because distance [lengthened] in between. Truck movements took less time to reach destinations. A new recruit, for example, before the cease-fire spent about 100 days on the road to move from Vinh (in North Vietnam) to the boundary of MR-3, a journey of 780 miles. After the cease-fire, it took him only 25 days for the same trip. By the end of 1973, when the road system greatly improved, this movement time was further reduced.

One of the Group 559 priority tasks was to extend and improve the new East Truong Son highway and to build large logistics bases. During the post-cease-fire period, enemy engineers labored day and night to complete a new infiltration road which started from Khe Sanh Base, ran along the Tabat–A Shau Valley into west Quang Nam, and by 1974 connected with QL-14 at Ben Giang. From that point on, the existing QL-14 took over and ran south to the north of Kontum. Obstructed by Dak To and Kontum, which were then under RVNAF control, the enemy new infiltration road veered westward near the border and ran along it southward inside MR-2.

• • •

In conjunction with the building of new roads and new logistical bases along his infiltration corridor, the enemy also installed an extensive network of antiaircraft positions to shield his traffic and logistics operation from aerial observation and bombings. The US bombing cessation allowed the enemy to bring into South Vietnam his antiaircraft assets from North Vietnam to protect his new bases. In Quang Tri Province alone, intelligence experts estimated, there were ten enemy antiaircraft regiments at the end of 1972. By the time of the cease-fire, this figure had increased to 12, then to 13 three months later. These AAA units were equipped with all types of weapons, from 12.7mm and 14.5mm heavy machineguns to 100mm guns. Antiaircraft guns larger than 57mm were almost all controlled by radar. The enemy also employed . . . SA-7 "Strella" heat-seeking antiaircraft missiles, including improved models. As of the beginning of 1973, Khe Sanh Base was protected by the 263rd SAM Regiment. Aerial photos taken in April 1973 revealed eight SAM-2 launching positions around the base. The increase in antiaircraft muscle was equally extensive along the infiltration corridor. As a matter of fact, superfluous military stations were transformed into AAA or combat units.

With the new road system completed, enemy truck convoys moved, unchecked, both by day and by night. VNAF observation planes sometimes spotted convoys of 200 to 300 trucks. Materiel and supplies poured into South Vietnam in very large amounts. To the enemy, the movement of troop replacements and even entire combat units now hardly posed any problems. All losses that he incurred in the previous years were effectively replaced during 1973. Intelligence reports indicated that, during the first half of 1973 alone, the enemy brought 65,000 new recruits into South Vietnam, and the amount of supplies the enemy accumulated by July 1973 was enough to support a 13–18-month offensive campaign of the 1972 type. And, for the first time in the war, the seriously wounded were evacuated to North Vietnam.

The North Vietnamese forces now fighting on South Vietnam battlefields had become a modern, sophisticated army which no longer marched, but was entirely mechanized, with substantial armor and artillery support. Its fuel requirements naturally increased manyfold and could no longer be met by vintage drum-rigged bicycles. So, along with the road-building effort, the enemy also installed a fuel pipeline whose terminal was completed by 1972, in time to support the Thua Thien battlefields. Another pipeline ran from the Mu Gia Pass in North Vietnam to near the DMZ; this supported NVA units in Quang Tri Province. During the post-cease-fire period this pipeline system was extended further south, reaching into the vicinity of Quang Duc Province in MR-3. The fuel supply problem for NVA transportation and mechanized units was thus effectively solved.

• • •

During the month of January 1973 and immediately after the cease-fire, North Vietnam took the greatest advantage of the US bombing cessation. Convoy upon convoy of tanks and artillery guns made their way into the South. The number of enemy tanks, which was estimated at about 100 of all types in the aftermath of the 1972 Summer Offensive, soared to nearly 500 by the end of April 1973. Several armored groups rolling along on the Ho Chi Minh Trail were either visually observed or photographed. Most artillery pieces that the enemy brought into South Vietnam were either 122mm short-barrel or 122mm and 130mm long-barrel guns. Also, by the end of April 1973, the enemy brought in an additional 170 pieces of 122mm and 130mm artillery, raising their total number to 250. All these weapons entries were flagrant violations of the Paris Agreement. They were made possible by a blindfolded and crippled ICCS which completely ignored the RVN repeated protests.

• • •

The Republic of Vietnam after the Cease-Fire

The last US troop contingent departed Saigon on 29 March 1973, marking the end of US participation in the Vietnam War and the beginning of a new era during which the RVN was to take its destiny in its own hands.

• • •

Confident at first that the agreement would be respected, and with the guarantee of US airpower deterrence, the South Vietnamese leadership had thought that a true cease-fire would come about and that an interim peace could be maintained. Then a real political contest would take place, as dictated by the agreement. The standstill cease-fire was certainly not the best solution, but it was acceptable if both sides displayed a genuine concern for reconciliation and concord.

• • •

The Paris Agreement devised certain solutions that simply could not find their place in the South Vietnamese context. The standstill cease-fire was one. In this regard, the 1973 agreement was much worse than the 1954 Geneva Accords, which at least provided two well-defined regrouping areas and a reasonable delay for troop withdrawals. This was not the case with the Paris Agreement, whose standstill modus vivendi was a fuzzy mess at best. How could the contending adversaries arrive at a satisfactory agreement as to where one's control was supposed to extend, if they both claimed the same areas? The standstill idea was the basis for the land grab that occurred before, during, and after the cease-fire, with both sides resorting to mutual denunciations. The territorial problem proved to be the thorniest of the problems and probably could never be settled. After two years of dickering and bickering, the two adversaries remained exactly where they had started. Neither would voluntarily yield an inch to the other, and all holiday truces during the war were marred by violations.

The conclusion was evident that a standstill cease-fire simply would not work in a war without front lines, where troops of both sides could be everywhere and nowhere at any given time, and where the adversaries had built up so great a hatred for each other.

• • •

Besides impossible solutions, the Paris Agreement also gave the Communists tremendous advantages, while it tightly bound the RVN hands. No longer bombed and mined, North Vietnam was now entirely free to construct and develop, and at the same time support its war of conquest in the South. North Vietnam, which enjoyed a greater manpower than South Vietnam, could also devote a bigger proportion of it to the war effort. Nothing prevented North Vietnam from using the territory of Laos and Cambodia, which it actually did. Nevertheless, North Vietnam still claimed it respected the independence, unity, and territorial integrity of these countries.

In South Vietnam, meanwhile, the Communists now had a legal foothold. Not only did they have their own government; they were also entitled to a territory and an army of their own. In all respects the NLF had become, by virtue of the agreement, a partner on equal terms. US and allied troops had to withdraw, but the NVA was allowed to stay behind. Which way the balance of forces was going to tilt was all too apparent. The new road system that the enemy was developing and improving would permit him to infiltrate more men in less time. And, now that US airpower was no longer available, the RVN certainly could not handle the infiltration flow alone, much less contain an all-out offensive if it broke out.

• • •

The war in Vietnam had lasted too long. The middle-aged generation had lived with war since 1945, and the youths who went into the military service knew nothing but war. All of them lived face to face with death every minute. Out of an 18 million population, over one million took up arms and fought. On an average, each Vietnamese family counted at least one or two members on military duty. In contested areas, brothers of the same family occasionally fought each other from opposing sides. The war turned rice-fields into wasteland and villages into charred ruins. Farmers quit their lands and came and lived in cities as refugees. Living under war conditions became increasingly miserable as social vices multiplied every day.

• • •

The endurance of the South Vietnamese people had outstretched its limits. The entire population was truly weary and exhausted. Servicemen and civil servants were more concerned with making ends meet than with duties; they lived under a constant mental stress, fearful of immediate dangers and anxious for their dubious future and that of the nation. North Vietnam was also in a state of exhaustion and its people only had the right to sacrifice, not to complain. News of the cease-fire came as a source of relief and joy, welcomed by everybody, troops and population alike, whether in North or South Vietnam. The South Vietnamese people were particularly elated by the prospect of true peace. But those who understood Communism knew that peace was impossible as long as the enemy was within us. Not only was fighting resumed, it grew worse with every passing day.

The South Vietnamese people did not like Communism; as long as the fighting went on, they had to accept war as a way of life. It was true that they were mentally worn out, but still, as long as they lived, there was no way to escape fighting. The government, people, and armed forces of the RVN thus continued the fighting, confident in their belief that the United States would come to their help if they ran into trouble.

The New Balance of Forces

• • •

By early 1974 enemy battlefield preparations seemed to have been completed. From the East Truong Son corridor lateral roads now meandered into coastal plain areas, pointing toward important objectives or forming an arc enveloping advanced RVN district towns and bases. Enemy-initiated activities became increasingly bolder. During 1972, which was the year of the big Summer Offensive, enemy-initiated activities averaged 2,072 incidents monthly; in 1973, the first year of the cease-fire, this average increased to 2,980 incidents per month, and by 1974 soared to 3,330 incidents per month. Objectives of enemy attacks also grew in importance. In addition to remote outposts and hamlets, which were the usual targets for attacks, major population centers and district towns also began to feel heavy enemy pressure. Intelligence reports meanwhile hinted at attacks against provincial capitals and raids against important cities.

• • •

During the spring of 1974, while the US Congress was tightening its purse on aid to South Vietnam, the enemy started his 1974 offensive campaign in MR-3. His goal was to press on and isolate Tay Ninh and Hau Nghia Provinces and simultaneously drive against Saigon.

• • •

The enemy never planned to put his effort at rest with the Paris Agreement. Even while he signed an agreement designed to restore peace, the directions he gave to his units were to maintain a situation of "half war, half peace." Gradually this concept changed into "war in peace," then, as of October 1973, his guidance to the party hierarchy became "offensive in peace" and finally "war to preserve peace." Although Communist jargon was always ambiguous and there were implied connotations and deductions, its evolution made it clear that, while the enemy talked about peace, reconciliation, and concord, what he really advocated was a victory by military force.

The RVN Armed Forces meanwhile made every effort to confront the new situation. But their capabilities were constrained by three factors: respect for the agreement, aid reduction, and a galloping inflation.

• • •

A few comparisons clearly illustrate the RVNAF's shrinking combat capabilities. Strategic bombings by B-52s, for example, amounted to 20,000 sorties in 1972. In 1973 B-52 sorties plummeted to 1,700, and now nothing. In 1972 total tactical air sorties were 90,000; in 1973 they were reduced to 46,500, then to 30,000 in 1974 as a result of aid cutback. In artillery, our side employed 2,350 pieces in 1970; now the RVNAF were left with 1,550 pieces whose firepower gradually declined because of greatly reduced ammunition supply rates.

These limitations in firepower and mobility certainly decreased overall combat effectiveness. No amount of effort or sacrifices could fill in this big void. As a matter of fact, sacrifices increased significantly without any increase in achievements. From 1970 to 1972, for example, thanks to lavish airpower and other support, every friendly killed in action accounted for five enemy killed. In 1973 the ratio was 1:2, and in 1974, when aid was further reduced, the efficiency was only 1:1.5.

During the summer of 1974, while the US Congress voted the biggest cut in FY 1975 military aid for South Vietnam, the enemy began an offensive in MR-3 with a force of nearly two divisions. III Corps encountered no great difficulties in driving back this offensive, however, because, while military aid was beginning to dwindle, supply reserves were still available. Nevertheless, the III Corps commander at that time, Lieutenant General Pham Quoc Thuan, complained: "In the last quarter of 1973, after I took command of III Corps, fuel and ammunition were cut 30 percent as compared to the first quarter, or 60 percent if compared to the same period of the previous year. This supply was further reduced 30 percent in the first quarter of 1974, and another 20 percent in the next quarter. All in all, within a period of only six months the supply of fuel and ammunition was cut to 70 percent as compared to 1973. At the beginning of 1972, III Corps was allotted 200 tactical air sorties a day; by the end of 1973, only 80 sorties were made available, and during the first half year of 1974 the number of sorties allocated fluctuated between 30 and a maximum of 60. This huge reduction in air sorties stemmed not from a shortage of aircraft but from a shortage of fuel, bombs, and ammunition."[7]

In the summer of 1974, while South Vietnam was still taken aback by the newly appropriated FY 1975 military aid budget—$700 million, or less than 40 percent of the original request—the enemy-initiated "H-9" campaign broke out in MR-1. Up to that time, MR-1 had been relatively quiet, save for a few land grab contests of minor importance. Both sides had avoided major clashes since the Sa Huynh affair ended. During the one and a half years of intervening time, MR-1 made remarkable progress in pacification and had started its development programs. Security in rural areas was good enough to encourage most refugees to return to their home villages and begin to rebuild under RVNAF protection.

• • •

On the friendly side, meanwhile, the greatly reduced military aid began to make its impact felt. The 3rd Division was faced with further supply and support cuts while it fought these battles. Artillery ammunition supply rates were reduced to a heartbreaking level: six rounds per day for a 105mm piece and four rounds for a 155mm piece. The entire division supply in gasoline or diesel oil dwindled to approximately 100,000 liters per month, whereas in 1972 it amounted to 400,000 liters for each type of fuel. Even the division commander's command helicopter was allowed only 15 hours of flight per month, which amounted to a mere four hours of flight each week. And this happened while the 3rd Division was fighting the enemy on two separate fronts. The reductions were so extensive that the division could no longer afford using armored units in combat.

These reductions were devastating to the troops' morale. Faced with an enemy whose firepower and resources were constantly upgraded, our troops had to make do with increasing austerity. They were taught single-shot firing, while the enemy rained on them an outpour of deadly fire. Grenades were used sparingly because resupplies did not come in sufficient quantities. While the enemy moved his troops to combat by trucks, our troops were trained to march. And our air force, too, was no longer the effective support it had been. Its observation planes flew higher and higher and fewer and fewer sorties. Medical evacuation meanwhile was slow and ineffective.

• • •

By the end of 1974 the 3rd Division alone had lost 3,500 troops after six months of heavy combat. These losses were not replaced in full. Its maneuver battalions now went into combat with a strength of 350 each, down from 550 prior to July. It seemed that the RVNAF manpower resources were drying up. To maintain a strength of 1.1 million, the RVNAF needed about 250,000 recruits per year, based on previous yearly losses. But the most that the recruiting and mobilization effort could muster usually amounted to only half of this requirement. Now that the losses mounted even faster and in greater quantities in the wake of intensive enemy attacks, the manpower problem became harder to solve. Combat effectiveness of ARVN units, as a result, decreased markedly for lack of adequate replacements.

• • •

VII. SUMMARY AND CONCLUSIONS

The Vietnam War was the longest war ever fought by the United States. Its genesis was in the aftermath of the 1954 French defeat after eight years of anachronic war waged in Vietnam by the French to preserve their colonial interests. After the 1954 Geneva Accords, in keeping with its policy of containing Communism, the United States came to the assistance of South Vietnam in order to provide it with the material aid necessary to successfully defend itself against Communist aggression. American material aid alone, however, proved to be insufficient, and the United States was compelled to bring in combat troops in 1965. From 1965 to 1968, although the US aid was substantially increased, a successful conclusion of the war was not achieved. Then, in 1969, increasing US public objection to the war, compounded by world constraints, resulted in a change in American policy. Instead of containment and confrontation, the United States was now inclined toward negotiation and dialogue. The United States no longer wanted to be an international fire brigade. It began to turn over the responsibility of fighting national wars to the nations involved. This is how Vietnamization came about.

• • •

The 1968 Tet Offensive can fairly be said to have generated the Vietnamization program.

• • •

An immediate impact of the post-1968 force structure increase was that pacification had progressed with remarkable results during each of the following three years. While rural security increased because the enemy infrastructure was on the decline, major enemy units had been driven across the border. The situation was so encouraging that some people talked about the war fading away. Economic and social developments meanwhile promised a bright future. At last the increased production in rural areas had begun to alleviate the countrywide inflation. For some time the Vietnamization program brought about excellent results and created favorable conditions for the gradual withdrawal of US and allied troops. The strengthening of the RVN, as a matter of fact, came as a surprise to the enemy. He felt that he must do something to redress the situation to his advantage. The 1972 Summer Offensive which followed demonstrated that the RVN was still plagued by many difficulties and troubles. It was apparent that Vietnamization had not solved every problem, not even in military terms.

One problem was the decrease in total force structure. At the beginning of 1969, the aggregated strength on our side was more than 1.5 million. After all US and allied forces had withdrawn, the RVNAF was left with a strength of a little over one million, a reduction of one-third. The reduction in combat units was even greater, decreasing by 40 percent from 22 divisions to 13 divisions. In firepower and other support resources, the reduction was even greater. The RVNAF assets were no match for the pre-Vietnamization abundance.

The enemy, by contrast, continued to grow after 1968. From 1969 to 1972 the enemy increased from 52 to 123 combat regiments, or 352 to 646 maneuver battalions. His armor, artillery, and other combat support assets likewise increased in quantity. Furthermore, there was a pronounced increase in quality. While enemy combat units doubled in number, our combat units were nearly halved.

• • •

The Vietnamization program was implemented in haste. In the first place, efforts at strengthening the RVNAF began rather belatedly. In the initial phase of direct participation, 1965 through 1968, the US tended to do everything by itself, since it strived for a quick victory. But when it became impossible to end the war rapidly, and particularly when President Nixon proclaimed his new foreign policy, the United States began to rush the Vietnamization process. Increments of US troop withdrawal followed each other in rapid succession, apparently dictated by domestic political needs. And, when the timetable had been set, US military authorities were really racing and even tried to beat it. South Vietnam could do little but try to keep pace with that race by overextending its forces and hope for the best. The replacement of combat units simply could not be implemented on a one-to-one basis. To really effectively develop its forces, the RVN certainly would have required more time.

• • •

The strengthening of the RVNAF in some respects was not tailored to true requirements and the actual situation. The RVN found itself always lagging behind the enemy in armament modernization. Most typical was the story of the AK-47 assault rifle and the M-16. Only after three years of being the underdog in firepower did the RVN infantry units, in mid-1968, catch up with the enemy. This occurred when they were equipped with the M-16, which was the equal of the AK-47 in performance. The same lag occurred with other weapons. The RVN received M-48 tanks and self-propelled 175mm artillery pieces only after the enemy had effectively deployed his T-54 tanks and 130mm guns. Our troops were equipped with the TOW antitank missile only after enemy tanks had roamed the battlefields. The enemy therefore always caught us by surprise as a result of this lagging modernization.

• • •

American aid chiefly depended on the power of the US executive branch and on the varying attitude of the US Congress. For South Vietnam, it was hard to adjust to the shift from extreme wealth to extreme poverty within a short time. There was also the mental reverse of a person who felt he was abandoned and found himself unexpectedly deprived of means. The enemy meanwhile basked in the confident posture of a successful man approaching wealth and position. This was another instance of inverse progress. Uncertainty about aid necessarily resulted in a state of insecurity. Doubts about the future became greater and finally edged away the belief in final victory.

Turning over combat responsibility to South Vietnam was not enough for the United

States. It also wanted to end the war and recover its prisoners. This was what President Nixon had promised when he ran for office and, in due time, his promise had to be honored.

• • •

The South Vietnamese people fully backed President Thieu's opposition to the United States in late 1968, and again in October 1972, but they also knew he could not hold out any longer. The great majority of the South Vietnamese population did not like Communism, but, at the same time, they felt heartbroken when realizing that the nationalist cause was not strong enough to instill the confidence which was necessary for continued sacrifices and continued struggling. And so, on the political and psychological front, the RVN found itself in a precarious and disadvantageous position.

• • •

The cease-fire could not be implemented. In a war without front lines which had been dragging on inconclusively for so long between two irreconcilable adversaries, standstill cease-fire stood no chance of success. The RVN had hoped for a respite to organize and develop its forces. Despite US and allied troop withdrawal, the RVN still believed in US aid, and especially the US promise to react vigorously in case of blatant violation. There was, after all, no reason why the United States should renege on its promise after sacrificing more than 50,000 troops and spending over $150 billion throughout the long years of commitment and involvement. So the RVN was somewhat confident when it signed the Paris Agreement, although it knew it was impossible to arrive at a genuine agreement with the Communists and, sooner or later, war would be resumed.

• • •

On its part, the RVN . . . tried to do its best to take over the entire war burden, enabling the United States to withdraw its troops. The achievements obtained from 1969 to 1972 eloquently spoke for themselves. Even during the one and one-half years which followed the cease-fire the RVN proved to be capable of handling the struggle alone and, despite all difficulties, still made progress in every aspect. The enemy effort to grab land and his political offensive to disintegrate the RVN ranks both failed miserably.

• • •

The increase in Communist strength in time became a most serious threat. To intelligence experts on our side, this force strengthening was glaring, even blatant: new weapons, missiles, armor, artillery, road building, bridges, truck convoys, modern logistics facilities, etc. By the end of 1974 total enemy regular forces had been built up to more than 20 divisions, and all of them were capable of mobile warfare. The balance of forces therefore tilted dangerously toward the enemy, and, the more this balance tilted, the more the RVN posture deteriorated.

• • •

In the face of all this, the RVN initiated an economic development plan to achieve self-sufficiency within five years, hoping that the United States would support it by increasing aid during the first few years but phasing it out toward the end. The RVN requested, accordingly, $750 million for FY 1975, but only $250 million was approved by the US Congress. This amounted to only one-third of [the] FY 1974 aid budget.

Military aid meanwhile met with a more tragic fate. From $3.3 billion in 1973 it plummeted to $941 million in 1974. The result was [that] the RVN had to use up most of its reserves in ammunition and fuel to fight the battles during 1974. All reserves now stood at below the emergency level. The JGS, as a result, had to cancel all modernization programs, especially the replacement of F-5As by the improved F-5E models, and the one-for-one replacement of war-damaged materiel. Ammunition supply rates and fuel allowances for all units were at a minimum.

But the FY 1975 aid budget imposed still more hardships: out of the $700 million appropriated, the RVNAF could only effectively use about $500 million, the rest being earmarked to cover US Defense Attaché Office operation and to pay outstanding debts. This amount of aid barely met half of the minimum basic requirements.

• • •

After nearly thirty years of war, South Vietnam was exhausted materially and worn out spiritually. Its inherent weaknesses and difficulties were still not overcome, but its means to carry on the fight were reduced drastically. The enemy, in contrast, had never been so strong. So whether the Republic of Vietnam, which had been supported by a long US commitment, survived or perished almost entirely depended on American will.

NOTES

1. "The War in Vietnam," President Richard M. Nixon's Address to the Nation, 3 November 1969 (Speech File Service, US Army Command Information Unit, Washington DC).

2. South Vietnam was administratively divided into 44 provinces and 6 cities (Saigon, Danang, Hue, Dalat, Vung Tau, and Cam Ranh). District town was the term usually employed to designate a district capital.

3. "The Nixon Doctrine: From Potential Despair to New Opportunities," policy speech delivered by Secretary of Defense Melvin R. Laird.

4. "Vietnamization and Total Force Planning: The Nixon Doctrine in Action," policy speech by Secretary of Defense Melvin R. Laird, 1971.

5. President Nixon's address to the nation, 3 November 1969.

6. At that time US air action was still going on in Cambodia.

7. Interview with Lieutenant General Pham Quoc Thuan, former CG, III Corps.

16

The Final Collapse

General Cao Van Vien

PREFACE

This monograph presents the significant events during the last years and months of the Republic of Vietnam. This was not an easy assignment. For nearly a decade before Saigon fell on 30 April 1975, I had served as chairman of the Joint General Staff of the Republic of Vietnam Armed Forces. During these years, I had overseen their growth and shared their victories as well as their setbacks. I felt what a mother must feel when her child suddenly dies an accidental death. My feeling of loss has been overwhelming.

It is a sad story indeed that the reader will find unfolding chapter after chapter in this monograph. As a principal actor and witness, I find it a moral obligation to tell it as it was, for the sake of history and for all those who died for a cause in which they believed. Events have been reconstructed as far as it is possible from my personal knowledge, interviews with responsible officers, and from available documents. To place my story in its proper historical perspective, I have thought it appropriate to begin with a brief summary of military and political events in the wake of the 1972 Communist offensive, then the circumstances in which the Paris Agreement was signed. As I view it, the agreement was the turning point which set South Vietnam on its inexorable course toward growing weakness and, finally, total collapse.

• • •

I. INTRODUCTION

When the Republic of Vietnam collapsed on 30 April 1975 and ceased to exist as a nation, the world at large—friend and foe alike—was taken aback. The rapidity and relative ease with which the Communists took over South Vietnam struck many people, the enemy included, as something unbelievable. How could it be possible? they asked. Why did South Vietnam go under so readily? What happened to the Vietnamese armed forces and the same army that had withstood so gallantly the two ferocious Communist onslaughts of 1968 and 1972? Why did such a powerful army crumble so easily in a matter of days?

The questions are many, but the answers are difficult to obtain. Indeed, to answer all those questions in depth and objectively is not an easy task. The violent emotions and traumatic experience of such a tragic loss may tend to blur or even distort the true facts. Then, too, feelings of guilt, or the instinct of self-preservation of the principals involved, has made it hard to sort out fact from fiction, truth from pretense. While the most immediate causes of the final collapse can readily be identified in the events that built toward it, there are several other causal factors—some deep-rooted and distant, others untold or merely implied in the various accounts.

• • •

Over the years . . . US military aid and, for some time, the assistance of US combat forces helped the Republic of Vietnam build a viable force for self-defense. From an army of 170,000 equipped with obsolete weapons, the Republic of Vietnam Armed Forces finally emerged as a strong, modernly equipped force with over one million men under arms, second to none among non-Communist Asian countries. Its air force was ranked sixth in the world, and its best combat divisions rated as equal to their American counterparts. It is equally true, unfortunately, that in the process this impressive force had become overly dependent on US money and equipment for its own sustenance and on US airpower for moral support, as well as a shield and deterrent against outright invasion from the North. There is no doubt that the South Vietnamese soldier could fight, and he did fight well! But for years he had learned to do things the easy way, taking it for granted the needed supplies would never cease to flow and that if he were in any kind of trouble "Big Brother" would always be there to "bail him out." Such was the psychological conditioning that helped the armed forces of South Vietnam maintain morale and confidence and comforted the population.

So, when the United States shifted its policy to negotiation and began withdrawing its forces from Vietnam under the expedient program of "Vietnamization," the Republic of Vietnam Armed Forces were not entirely prepared to take over, psychologically or physically. How could they—without a substantial increase in the number of major combat units—effectively replace seven divisions, four brigades, and innumerable support units of the US forces committed in Vietnam, in addition to other non-Communist forces? No amount of training, equipment, or political exhortation could effectively fill the physical void or ease the feeling of insecurity that set in. Our forces began to stretch and soon suffered the consequence.

The enemy's offensive of 1972 dramatically brought to the surface the basic weakness of the Vietnamization process. Without US support in airpower and mobility, the Republic of Vietnam Armed Forces could hardly have held An Loc, defended Kontum, or reoccupied Quang Tri. Most lost areas remained lost, for it was now beyond our capabilities to take them back. But still, as long as US airpower was available, the overall balance of forces could be maintained, and the Republic of Vietnam stood a good chance of pulling through.

Then came the turning point that changed it all. The Paris Agreement was served on South Vietnam like a death warrant. The downhill course was set. Small wonder the enemy claimed it was his victory; he had indeed won the first round. With US forces completely gone, the enemy set about making preparations for the final push. His hands were now completely free; no more US airstrikes, not even the remote chance of token retaliation. The balance of forces, which had been precariously maintained with US airpower, had tilted heavily in his favor.

The question of US intervention was the foremost subject of concern for the Republic of Vietnam when it finally became resigned to accepting the Paris Agreement. It was no ploy of playing "hard to get" when President Nguyen Van Thieu insisted on a guarantee of US intervention as a condition for his endorsement. It was a matter of grave consequence that could spell the difference between life and death for the nation. For probably, more than anyone else, he had come to realize that without such a shield the Republic of Vietnam could hardly defend itself against the onslaught of the better-equipped regular divisions of the North Vietnamese Army (NVA). Not only was intervention indispensable militarily, but its guarantee could also bolster the morale of our armed forces. It was unthinkable to attempt to "hack it" alone without Big Brother's protection.

Confidence returned when President Richard M. Nixon finally and solemnly promised to react vigorously in case of a serious violation of the Paris Agreement. The Republic of Vietnam took it as a national commitment on the part of the United States, far from suspecting that there would be such a thing as Watergate and that an angry Congress could so effectively prevent any US president from honoring a commitment, albeit one given by a predecessor.

In early 1975, the enemy apparently gambled that he could overrun Phuoc Long without provoking any US response. He won and became completely certain that the United States had now chosen to stay away from the conflict for good. The road was thus clear for him to take the next big step toward final victory.

If the 1973 Paris Agreement was the starting point for the demise of South Vietnam, and the absence of US intervention was an encouraging sign to the enemy to proceed with his ultimate plan, it was the cutback in US military aid that accelerated the whole process and made defeat inevitable.

Conditioned as they were to fight a war at a certain level of supply, the Republic of Vietnam Armed Forces suddenly found it difficult to carry on at the greatly reduced level of US appropriations for fiscal year 1975. For the first time in the war, whose intensity increased with every enemy escalation, our armed forces were in the decided position of underdog. Gone were their superior firepower and mobility, the very things that helped maintain tactical balance against an enemy who held the initiative. It now became clear that the most the armed forces could hope to achieve was a delaying action pending restoration of US military aid to its former level. The irony of this uphill struggle was that the US president was compelled to beg the Congress for something that it had willingly appropriated for the previous fiscal year. It failed to come through, perhaps because the aid was termed *supplemental* or *additional* instead of *integral,* which it really was.

The big slash in appropriated funds made its tragic impact felt not only on the battlefield, but also in the minds of South Vietnamese strategists as well. The ability to hold territory, they felt, was a direct function of aid level. With the reduction now in force, perhaps it was no longer possible to maintain "territorial integrity." It might be best, they reasoned, to tailor our defense effort to the aid appropriated. Simplistic as it might sound, the idea reflected the realities of the situation. Whatever the motives behind it, President Thieu's decision early in 1975 to redeploy forces was certainly not taken lightly or without firm grounds. But it was also this fateful decision that set in motion a series of setbacks whose cumulative effect led to the final collapse.

What really hastened South Vietnam's demise was the hasty and neglectful manner in which the redeployment was executed. Even if cautiously and correctly carried out, a withdrawal of this magnitude would only stand a fair chance of success, given enemy strength and capabilities of pursuit. Military history abounds in examples of routs; it is the reason why theater commanders are extremely chary of taking such a dangerous step.

In the context of the Vietnam War, whose political and military aspects were intimately intertwined, such a retreat was predisposed to doom if no consideration were given to the Vietnamese civilians who depended on the troops for protection and for whom the war was being fought. Our armed forces were not operating on foreign soil; their role and mission differed from those of an expeditionary force. Removing them from an area without taking steps to evacuate the population amounted to sheer dereliction. The redeployment fiasco in Military Regions (MRs) II and I demonstrated the tragic fact that the population could not be separated from the troops and that troop movements could be halted by a rushing mass of refugees. These are the facts of the case. They explain the rapid moral and physical disintegration of an army that had fought well until undercut by events beyond its control.

II. THE SITUATION BEFORE THE PARIS AGREEMENT

After the Communist offensive of 1972, the Republic of Vietnam Armed Forces were given the task of reoccupying all lost territory. In MR-1, Operation Lam Son 72 was launched with the participation of the 1st Infantry Division, the Airborne Division, the Marine Division, and other supporting units.[1] By 15 September 1972, the city and greater part of the province of Quang Tri had been retaken. A new line of defense was established along the Thach Han River, extending eastward toward the sea. The enemy's reaction in Quang Tri was violent; at the same time he also launched several unsuccessful attacks against the southern part of MR-1.

In MR-2, operations were conducted to relieve enemy pressure around Kontum and Pleiku, to reoccupy the An Lao Valley in Binh Dinh Province, and to clear all main roads, including Route 14 between Kontum and Pleiku and National Routes 19 and 21. . . . In MR-3, reinforced friendly forces successfully relieved enemy pressure around the city of An Loc. However, National Route 13 linking An Loc with Lai Khe remained closed. In MR-4 the situation was one of firm friendly control. All skirmishes with the enemy were taking place on Cambodian territory, although a number of small hamlets in Chuong Thien Province were still under enemy control.

Generally speaking, the military situation during the second half of 1972 reflected a rough balance of forces confronting each other on the battlefield, while the withdrawal of US forces from Vietnam was in full progress. By 1973, however, the loss of US tactical air support (including naval air) was to tip the balance in favor of the Communists.

To cope politically with the emergency situation during 1972, the central government of the Republic of Vietnam took several forceful actions. A state of martial law was proclaimed countrywide, deferments of draftees were drastically limited, and a ban was put on overseas travel for male citizens from 17 to 43 years of age. The president was delegated full legislative powers by the National Assembly for a period of six months, from July to December 1972, in matters of defense and national economy. A more severe law governing the press was promulgated, and scheduled local elections of village and hamlet authorities were canceled. Instead, province chiefs received instructions to reorganize local administrations and to complete the appointment of village and hamlet chiefs within two months.

Earlier Peace Proposals

In military terms, the 1968 Tet Offensive had been a resounding defeat for the Communists but, politically and insofar as mass psychology was concerned, had given them a tremendous advantage. By and large, the American public became disenchanted with the war. General William C. Westmoreland's request for approximately 200,000 additional American troops had tended to reinforce the views of some that the Vietnam problem was hardly soluble militarily.

• • •

Following the Cambodian cross-border operation and the Laos incursion, the United States made two major concessions: that US forces would withdraw within six months after an agreement was reached, and that President Thieu would step down one month before general elections took place. These proposals were turned down in a [negotiating] session held on 3 May 1971. In June, July, and August, [Dr. Henry] Kissinger and [Le Duc] Tho met five times. During these sessions, all proposals advanced by the United States were rejected by the Communists, no matter how they were modified. Only during the last session, in September 1971, did the United States come to realize fully that the Communists really wanted South Vietnam to be turned over to their control before the withdrawal of US troops. The United States became aware of the Communists' true design only after three long years of secret talks! And it was also during the same session that the North Vietnamese realized that the United States was definitely seeking an arrangement to end the war and not a cover for total surrender![2]

• • •

The military situation in the South during April 1972 was such that the United States feared a total collapse of the Republic of Vietnam. Again, Kissinger met with Tho on 2 May 1972 and, faced with a deteriorating situation, proposed that if North Vietnam agreed to a cease-fire and release of US prisoners of war—only that and nothing else—all US forces would be withdrawn within four months. However, the proposal met with instant rejection, and Le Duc Tho was adamant in demanding the removal of the Republic of Vietnam government and the installation of a coalition. To the United States this demand was equally unpalatable. The United States stepped up considerably the bombing of North Vietnamese military targets and proceeded to mine Haiphong harbor and other waterways. Only after intercessions by Russia and Communist China were secret talks resumed between Kissinger and Le Duc Tho in August. . . . During those sessions, although they still persisted in demanding President Thieu's resignation before a cease-fire, the Communists softened their position and recognized the existence of two governments, two armies, and a third political component as an entity in itself. The Provisional Revolutionary Government of the Communists in the South was ostensibly regarded by North Vietnam as a coequal of the Republic of Vietnam government.

Arranging the Cease-Fire

On 16 August 1972 Dr. Kissinger arrived in Saigon. He met with President Thieu and explained the political pressures in the United States and the influence these pressures might have on the approaching presidential election. He also affirmed President Nixon's determination to seek a solution for the Vietnam War. Then, on 11 September 1972, Kissinger and Le Duc Tho met again in Paris. This time all clauses to which both sides had agreed during the talks in July and August were put on paper. In general terms, the agreements were as follows: Due to the existence of two governments, two armies, and other political forces in South Vietnam, national reconciliation, if it [were] to become a reality, should be achieved through mutual respect, and both sides should stop seeking to eliminate the other. South Vietnam should not be forced to accept either a Communist regime or any pro-American regime. Thus, for the first time, the Communists refrained from demanding removal of the Republic of Vietnam government.

In the next session, on 26 September 1972, North Vietnam added to the agreements the formation of a National Council of Reconciliation and Concord. The prospects were good, and hopes were high that peace would soon come. . . . For the first time, the Communists agreed to treat politics and the fighting separately. North Vietnam and the United States would end the fighting by agreeing to a standstill cease-fire, and a political solution for South Vietnam would be subject to discussions between the two parties concerned. The proposal was prepared by Le Duc Tho as a draft agreement in English. Thus ended a conversation between two deaf men that had lasted too many years.[3]

• • •

I recall clearly that [Dr. Kissinger] arrived in Saigon on 18 October, planning to stay two days. The next morning the US delegation with Dr. Kissinger, Ambassador Ellsworth Bunker, General Creighton W. Abrams, and Mr. [William] Sullivan met at the Independence Palace with President Thieu. On the Vietnamese side there were Vice President Tran Van Huong, Prime Minister Tran Thien Khiem, Foreign Minister Tran Van Lam, Mr. Nguyen Phu Duc, Mr. Hoang Duc Nha, and I.

Dr. Kissinger began the session by handing the text of the agreement, in English, to President Thieu. He then explained with emphasis the points he thought advantageous for South Vietnam. The United States, he stressed, pledged to maintain its air bases in Thailand and to keep the Seventh Fleet off Vietnam to deter any attack by the Communists. Economic and military aid would continue for South Vietnam, while the United States believed that secret understandings with Russia and Communist China would drastically reduce their supply of war materiel to North Vietnam and permit the United States to withdraw its troops and recover its prisoners with honor.

Dr. Kissinger also added that this was a good time to arrive at an agreement with the Communists because, after all, South Vietnam did have an army of over one million men and did control 85 percent of its 19 million population. South Vietnam, he was confident, would develop and prosper in the postwar period.

The agreement, Dr. Kissinger concluded, was good and acceptable. However, he did not go into the details of the things yet to be solved, and above all did not inform the South Vietnamese of the timetable for signing the agreement. President Thieu responded by saying he would study the text of the agreement, which was then given to Hoang Duc Nha, the president's private secretary.

An emergency session of our expanded National Security Council was immediately convened to study the text of the agreement. Mr. Nha was the reporter for the session. Militarily, this was to be a standstill cease-fire. While all US and allied forces were to be withdrawn, and all US bases in South Vietnam were to be dismantled, there was no mention of North Vietnamese troops. (It was estimated that North Vietnamese forces in the South numbered ten divisions. In addition, North Vietnamese troops made up 60 to 80 percent of the strength of Communist local units.)

As chairman of the JGS, I voiced my opinion during the first session of the council that control of the cease-fire would be extremely difficult and that a standstill cease-fire in a "leopard skin" pattern carried with it many dangers. There were to be no areas of regrouping and no lines of demarcation, which meant that the enemy forces would be allowed to stay where they were. But there was no doubt that they would not stay in their current locations. Out of their inherently aggressive nature, the Communists would certainly try, as soon as the cease-fire was announced, to break down into small units and penetrate our villages and hamlets, to make their appearance on our lines of communications, and to mark their presence by displaying their flags. To the proposed ICCS, this would be proof enough of Communist control. In an unconventional war, without clearly defined lines, control of both population and territory is difficult to achieve. It would become many times more difficult and more complex in the prospective circumstances. . . .

There was virtual certainty that the Communists were not going to abide by the standstill cease-fire. Their actions in 1954 had given us a strong indication as to what they would do this time. Also, enemy documents captured on 10 October 1972, in the underground shelter of a district commissar in Quang Tin Province, attested to the fact that Communist troops and cadres had been studying the main issues laid out in the draft text of the agreement and had already received instructions for an appropriate line of action. . . .

By far the most important military issue was the presence of the North Vietnamese Army. The situation in September 1972 reflected a rough balance of forces on the battlefield. Now that all US forces would be redeployed without a reciprocal withdrawal of North Vietnamese forces, that balance would undoubtedly lean toward the enemy.

When the [Vietnamese language] text [of the proposed agreement] came under examination, members of the National Security Council immediately realized that it was the original drafted by the North Vietnamese and definitely not a translated version of the English text. The syntax and vocabulary were specifically and purely Communist, North Vietnamese-style. It contained some rare peculiarities and particularly important but controversial terms. The US forces, for example, were called laconically but contemptuously Quan My, which prompted the Vietnamese to remind the US delegation that it should ask for a change to the more decent term Quan Doi Hue Ky. To all knowledgeable Vietnamese in the South, the term Quan My was derogatory and insolent, although it was literally quite correct.

A more important [semantic] issue was the National Council of Reconciliation and Concord, defined as an "administrative structure" and rendered in Vietnamese, undoubtedly with pernicious design, as *co cau chinh quyen,* meaning "government structure." It was thus entirely clear that the North Vietnamese saw [it] as an agency with full governmental powers and, in view of its composition, nothing less than a coalition government. . . . The Vietnamese text also mentioned three Vietnamese nations. North and South Vietnam were only two. What was that third nation? If South Vietnam were to be two nations, then it meant the suzerainty of the South Vietnamese government would be shared with someone else. These were the major issues.

After careful and minute examination, our government came up with twenty-six changes in the draft agreement. While the discussions with the Americans were proceeding, a report from the Republic of Vietnam Embassy in Washington DC, informed the government that during an interview with the foreign press Prime Minister Pham Van Dong of North Vietnam had declared that peace negotiations in Paris were producing good results and that there would be a three-sided coalition government of transition. The report reinforced suspicions of deception. . . . This was an additional reason for President Thieu to harden his opposition to the agreement during the two sessions that took place on 22 October.

• • •

For his part, President Thieu went on radio and television to make his point that the government of South Vietnam could not accept a coalition. North Vietnam in the meantime did not stand still. In an outburst of propagandistic bombast, North Vietnam made public the text of the agreement, revealed the timetable agreed upon on 8 October, denounced President Thieu for having undermined peace, and demanded that the United States sign the agreement on 31 October 1972. In the face of these new developments, Dr. Kissinger called a press conference to explain the text of the agreement to the American public. In his words, "peace is at hand" and all that was required to wrap up the agreement was one more session with the North Vietnamese representative.

During November, a great deal of correspondence was exchanged between Saigon and Washington, but no major changes were made in the text of the agreement. Also, during the same month US C-5 Galaxy cargo planes and cargo ships brought to Saigon an important amount of war materiel and equipment, including F-5 and A-37 fighters, C-130A cargo planes, helicopters, M-48 tanks, and 175mm artillery pieces. American bases and equipment were also transferred intact to the South Vietnamese armed forces. With this equipment JGS activated additional heavy artillery, armor, and antiaircraft artillery units. New C-130A and F-5A squadrons were also formed. Some of the equipment provided, however, could not be used immediately. It had been delivered for later use as replacement equipment in accordance with the provisions of the cease-fire agreement. This crash supply program, called Enhance Plus, was aimed at both military and political goals. . . .

President Nixon had given serious consideration to the discrepancies brought up by the South Vietnamese government, and credit ought to be paid him here for having ordered the reexamination of these discrepancies.

• • •

On 9 November, Kissinger's deputy, General Alexander M. Haig Jr., arrived in Saigon. He delivered a personal letter from President Nixon and stressed the significance of the Enhance Plus program. Since our government was still adamant in its position, General Haig indicated that if South Vietnam kept refusing to sign, the United States might go ahead and sign separately with the North. A few days earlier, on 5 November, the US State Department had announced that Canada, Hungary, Indonesia, and Poland had agreed in principle to participate in ICCS.

Dr. Kissinger and Le Duc Tho met again in Paris on 20 November. . . . During this session with Le Duc Tho, Dr. Kissinger laid out the demands of the Republic of Vietnam and the United States. The first few days of the talks went well and the mood was receptive. However, on 23 November Tho suddenly became tough. He rejected all US proposals and again demanded the removal of the South Vietnamese government. Apparently he was acting on new instructions from Hanoi.

• • •

On 4 December, Dr. Kissinger met with Le Duc Tho again in Paris and found him as intransigent as he had been in their last meeting. . . . Dr. Kissinger left Paris on 13 December. . . . The deadlock this time . . . was real and ominous.

After meeting with Kissinger . . . President Nixon sent a cable to Hanoi warning that unless serious talks were renewed within seventy-eight [sic] hours, the United States would resume bombing. In the absence of a favorable response, the United States began an intensified bombing campaign above the 20th parallel, where bombing had been halted since late October. The devastating power of B-52s proved too much for North Vietnam and attested to the resoluteness of the US position. In my opinion, North Vietnam was *forced* to return to the negotiating table. As a result, the most intensive of all US bombing campaigns against North Vietnam was halted on 30 December.

Eight days later, on 8 January 1973, Dr. Kissinger met with Le Duc Tho. Things went better this time. . . . On 14 January Dr. Kissinger reported to President Nixon on progress. The next day orders were issued for US forces to halt all military activities against North Vietnam.

On 16 January General Haig arrived in Saigon. The government of South Vietnam still took exception to a few issues raised by the protocols. However, on 19 January our government was informed that no more changes would be made and the agreement was going to be initialed on 23 January and officially signed on 27 January in Paris by the four parties involved. The cease-fire would go into effect at 8:00 a.m., Saigon time, on 28 January 1973.

In addition, President Nixon wrote personally to President Thieu on 21 January. If South Vietnam rejected the agreement, Nixon warned, the United States would sign separately with North Vietnam and, as a consequence, all aid to South Vietnam would be cut off. But if South Vietnam signed the agreement, (1) the president of the United States would intercede more vigorously with the US Congress for continuing aid to South Vietnam, and (2) the US government pledged to "react vigorously" to any serious violation of the cease-fire by the North. After many sessions with the National Security Council, and after consulting various personalities of the government and National Assembly, President Thieu wrote a letter of acceptance to President Nixon in which he also recommended a summit meeting right after the agreement had been signed.

• • •

Objectively speaking, the Paris Agreement was not perfect. The United States obtained a disengagement and recovered its prisoners of war. The Communists were allowed to maintain North Vietnamese forces in South Vietnam, but South Vietnam still functioned as a nation with a government of its own.

South Vietnamese Reactions

• • •

In the light of the enemy's design as made known to us in captured documents and especially from lessons learned from the failure of the 1954 Geneva Accords, JGS had worked out a contingency plan with the code name Tran Hung Dao II. This plan provided in considerable detail all the measures to be taken in the face of any move by the enemy and was disseminated to sector echelon and to all combat battalions. It was because of this plan that South Vietnam was not caught by surprise and was able to anticipate and thwart every attempt by the enemy to "grab the land and the population."

On the political plane, a new five-year rural development program was initiated, and a political party, the Dan Chu [Democratic] Party, was formed in anticipation of the coming political struggle with the Communists. Leaders of the Dan Chu Party were mostly high officials of the South Vietnamese administration. By mid-1973, the government had been partially reorganized. Finally, to improve efficiency and foster a better understanding of national policies, the government embarked on a countrywide training program ambitiously called an administrative revolution. Fifteen thousand South Vietnamese civil servants, representing all echelons, had completed this training by mid-1973.

III. THE MILITARY SITUATION AFTER
THE CEASE-FIRE, 1973–1974

In theory, the Paris Agreement of 27 January 1973 terminated the war in Vietnam. However, while true peace prevailed in the North, military conflict continued in the South. No clause in the Paris Agreement called for the withdrawal of Communist forces, nor was there any understanding about keeping them at bay. North Vietnam maintained its large forces in the South to back an eventual political settlement to its advantage while standing ready to cope with all eventualities. Without effective international control machinery to enforce the cease-fire, enemy violations of the Paris Agreement were committed openly and deliberately.

Communist Policy and Strategy

The protracted war in South Vietnam had inflicted heavy losses on both sides, but the toll was notably heavier for the Communists. In an interview with an Italian reporter, Vo Nguyen Giap acknowledged a casualty figure of more than 500,000 for North Vietnam. The Communist soldier, although hardened by party discipline and tempered by intensive indoctrination and watched closely by political cadres, nonetheless desired a real peace and hoped to be reunited with his family. Information from captured documents, prisoners, and ralliers established the fact that in October 1972, when the cease-fire was almost accomplished, the Communist troops, as well as their cadres, were very excited. They listened to BBC and VOA radio broadcasts every day and openly discussed the possibility of returning to North Vietnam. When the 28 October cease-fire failed to materialize, they could not conceal their despair.

• • •

Intelligence revealed that during a May 1973 meeting of provincial party leaders . . . it was concluded that the South Vietnamese revolution could only be achieved by armed violence through a "blitzkrieg" of the type launched in 1968. (Noticeably absent was any mention of political struggle.) . . . However, [a] rallier stressed that the offensive could come only after the approval of both Russia and China, as had been the case in 1968 and 1972. . . .

• • •

On our side during 1973 we had frustrated the enemy's "land and population grab" tactic on the one hand and pushed ahead with rural pacification on the other. However, insofar as the remote outposts were concerned, President Thieu's instructions forbade their evacuation. At all costs, they were to be defended and held. As it turned out, this policy proved politically but not militarily sound. It was fairly easy for the enemy to concentrate a force five or six times greater than ours at any remote place and, with abundant fire support, overwhelm an outpost at will. To attempt to hold all remote outposts, therefore, amounted to sacrificing a substantial number of troops who could be employed effectively elsewhere. But then our government still hoped the Paris Agreement would be observed to some extent. And the maintenance of these outposts, although costly, was thought of as visible proof of the extent of our control. Besides, abandoning these outposts would be tantamount to turning over to the enemy a sizable part of the national territory.

• • •

IV. PROBLEMS AND POLICIES, 1973–1974

• • •

Our strategy immediately after the cease-fire had four major objectives. First and foremost, we were determined to keep the national territory intact and to maintain full control over the population. If any area were seized by the enemy, the armed forces had to wrest it back at all costs. Second, the armed forces were to complete their reorganization, with particular emphasis on replenishing and reequipping units which had suffered significant losses during the enemy offensive of 1972, restoring a sizable general reserve, and consolidating the territorial forces. Third, the armed forces would seek to improve and modernize all their aspects, but especially their logistics, firepower, and mobility. Fourth, the armed forces would continue to assist in the national pacification and development program and take part in other national projects . . . all geared to achieve the "three-self" goal of national policy (self-defense, self-management, self-sufficiency).

Organization of the Armed Forces

• • •

In a shuffle of senior officers on March 1974, Lieutenant General Nguyen Van Manh, chief of staff of JGS since 1969, was made deputy chairman of JGS for pacification and development in place of Lieutenant General Nguyen Van La, who retired because of old age. General Manh, having served in his position for more than four years, was due for replacement. Lieutenant General Dong Van Khuyen, who was then commanding general of the Central Logistics Command, was designated to replace General Manh as chief of staff of JGS. A devoted and hard worker, General Khuyen was to fill both positions until the final days. . . .

• • •

To counter any large-scale violation of the peace agreement by the Communists, a contingency plan was worked out by JGS and USDAO. It was a top secret arrangement whereby the United States agreed to provide our armed forces with appropriate support when required. A system of hot lines was established between the US Support Command at Nakhon Phanom in Thailand and JGS. Our air force headquarters and all four corps commanders were also given direct access to this system.

Provisions of the plan, which was disseminated to corps commanders as a basis for their operational planning, included: 1) the constant updating of B-52 targets; 2) the activation of forward air control systems equipped with appropriate radios and manned by English-speaking personnel who had previously worked with the US Air Force; 3) in the case of a major offensive, our armed forces were to hold their lines for 7 to 15 days, allowing time for the US Congress to approve the employment of US airpower in South Vietnam. The JGS-DAO plan also provided the procedures for requesting US Air Force support. In spite of its apparent promise, the contingency plan was never put into use because the scale of enemy violations in 1973 and 1974 did not warrant a request for intervention. By the time such intervention was required, US Air Force units were not available.

The Reduction of US Military Aid

Ravaged by war for over a quarter century, South Vietnam had very little to contribute to the war effort except manpower and blood. Financially and materially, South Vietnam had to depend on military aid provided by the United States, the factor that largely decided the outcome of the war.

On 2 April 1973 President Thieu was received by President Nixon in the Western White House at San Clemente. Together the two leaders discussed problems related to economic and military aid to South Vietnam and examined the continuing cease-fire violations and the Communist buildup. The visit shored up our confidence in continuing US aid during the postwar period.

• • •

President Thieu sent me, as chairman of the JGS, to the United States in April 1974 to seek support for our aid request. At the Pentagon, I made a presentation of the military situation in South Vietnam, substantiated by documents and photographic evidence of the enemy's escalating violations and his massive movement of men and arms into the country. Officials of the US Department of Defense heartily assured me of their full support. Unfortunately, the US Congress rejected all supplemental aid requests and merely authorized a fiscal year 1975 ceiling of $1 billion, of which only $700 million was finally appropriated. And this amount included operational expenses for USDAO ($46 million appropriated out of $100 million requested). The final appropriation came as a shock to the army and people of South Vietnam. It was certain that the huge gap between requirements and resources that had just been created could never be closed, no matter how much self-restraint was imposed and how well the budget was managed.

• • •

[Finally], there was the possibility the US Congress might review its decision once the furor against President Nixon had died down. After all, US credibility and prestige were at stake, and it was only reasonable to expect that South Vietnam would be given the wherewithal to defend itself after approximately 45,000 young Americans had given their lives for the same cause. It was to this last hope that the armed forces and people of South Vietnam desperately clung, and it was with the belief that somehow the additional aid would be provided that they stoically endured all privations and willingly shed more blood to make up for the missing rounds of ammunition.

A $300 million supplemental appropriation was requested on 2 January 1975, and this amount was boosted to $722 million by President Ford's last-ditch effort on 11 April 1975. By the time the US Congress finally rejected it, however, it was already too late for any kind of hope. The final verdict had been rendered.

The $700 million appropriated for fiscal year 1975 only met about half of our austere requirements. Enemy-initiated actions in the meantime increased 70 percent as compared with the previous year.

• • •

Forebodings for 1975

• • •

Our government had concluded 1974 with an assessment of the military situation. A top-level meeting was convened on 6 December 1974 at the Independence Palace and was chaired, as usual, by the president. The National Security Council members were there, as was the complete array of service and corps commanders. The estimate was that 1975 would be the year when the Communists would probably launch a general offensive, to coincide with and upset our presidential election, scheduled for October, and the 1976 US presidential campaign. The military balance undoubtedly favored the enemy; he had accumulated enough supplies to sustain a major offensive for an uninterrupted period of eighteen months at a level of intensity comparable to his offensive of 1972.

• • •

In the absence of specific guidance by the president, JGS took on itself the task of preparing for the next enemy move. Our major concern was how to reconstitute some general reserve for immediate use.

• • •

V. THE BEGINNING OF THE END

During 1973 and 1974, the enemy did not succeed in occupying any provincial capital of South Vietnam. At one time or another he had contemplated Kontum or Tay Ninh, but both cities proved to be beyond his reach. So he turned to Phuoc Long, the northernmost provincial capital of MR-3, and prepared to attack it with two infantry divisions augmented by an infantry regiment and supported by one tank regiment, one antiaircraft regiment, one field artillery regiment, and several sapper (assault engineer) units.

As early as October 1974 JGS had gathered enough information about the enemy's preparations and plans through technical intelligence, agents, and prisoners to predict the attack against Phuoc Long. The information had many times been made available to III Corps headquarters and the sector headquarters of Phuoc Long, and each time it was updated with new developments. Thus there was no question of surprise when the attack finally materialized in the latter part of December 1974.

• • •

The supply of Phuoc Long was ordinarily done by truck via Interprovincial Route 1A and National Route 14. Local products went to Saigon by the same route. Only one week after the cease-fire, however, the Communists cut this main supply artery at many places. Airlift by helicopters and propeller-driven planes then became the main supply means for the city and the four district towns. The monthly requirement was 400 to 500 tons, mostly rice, salt, sugar, ammunition, and fuel. Beginning in August 1974, III Corps made a concerted effort with II Corps to open National Route 14. The operation somewhat relieved the burden on airlift resources, which now were needed for the secure delivery of such critical items as ammunition, fuel, and medical supplies. However, on 14 December 1974, the district town of Duc Phong, which lay astride the supply route, was overrun by the Communists, and Phuoc Long again became dependent on airlift. And airlift became increasingly costly and unreliable due to the enemy's antiaircraft fire.

• • •

The battle for Phuoc Long began in the latter part of December 1974 and ended on 6 January 1975. . . . On the night of 30 December 1974 the NVA 7th Division and the newly activated 3rd Division launched an attack against the district town of Phuoc Binh, which was within the city's defense perimeter. The attackers were supported by a tank regiment and corps artillery. The battle raged through the morning and into late afternoon, when the district headquarters was badly hit and its operations center destroyed.

• • •

At 0700 on the 1st the enemy, with the support of tanks, began driving his attack from the south into the city of Phuoc Long, but the advance was stopped at the foot of the hill ascending toward the city. At the same time enemy troops encircled and this time overran Ba Ra Mountain, despite maximum activity by our air force. Upon overrunning Ba Ra Mountain, the enemy immediately installed artillery observation posts, and his 130mm guns began to fire accurately at targets within the city. Eight 105mm pieces and four 155mm pieces were hit by the enemy's accurate fire, and all became inactive by 3 January. Communications with the city were interrupted many times. As the battle developed, enemy antiaircraft batteries were positioned on Ba Ra Mountain, and it became increasingly difficult for our aircraft, especially helicopters, to make their approach.

Backed by advantageous defense positions and the effective support of our air force, troops in the city successfully repelled several assaults by enemy troops and tanks at the southern perimeter. They held firm during the day of 2 January. Fifteen enemy tanks were destroyed by our air force and ground troops. The province chief requested medical evacuation for the wounded and supplies and reinforcements. At 1800, however, our radio relay station on Ba Ra Mountain was finally overrun and that communications link with the city was lost.

The same day, 2 January, an emergency meeting chaired by President Thieu was held at the Independence Palace. Present were Vice President Tran Van Huong; Prime Minister Tran Thien Khiem; Lieutenant General Dang Van Quang, presidential assistant for security; Lieutenant General Tran Van Minh, commander in chief of the air force; Lieutenant General Du Quoc Dong, commander of III Corps; Lieutenant General Dong Van Khuyen, chief of staff of JGS and also commanding general of the Central Logistics Command; and I as chairman of JGS. The subject for discussion was whether or not to reinforce Phuoc Long and, if so, how much reinforcement was needed in terms of troops and other resources.

In his capacity as commander of III Corps, General Dong, after his briefing concerning the situation in MR-3 and at Phuoc Long in particular, asked for at least one infantry division or the Airborne Division. His plan was to mount a relief operation by helilifting the division into the city from the north with maximum support of tactical aircraft and helicopters and air-dropped supplies. General Dong then offered to resign, citing his inability to improve the situation in MR-3 since he assumed its command three months earlier. His offer was immediately rejected by President Thieu, who was apparently more concerned with the question of reinforcement. The plan was thoroughly examined, but rejected.

• • •

It was finally decided to reinforce Phuoc Long with assets available in MR-3. The 81st Airborne Ranger Group, because of its experience in the An Loc battle of 1972 and its ability to fight in jungle areas deep in enemy-controlled territory, was selected for the job. Its missions were to support the defense of the city's southern perimeter, the most advantageous avenue of approach to the city, and to try to reoccupy Ba Ra Mountain.

• • •

On 6 January at 0900 enemy troops, supported by tanks, attacked again. The battle raged all day. At 2300 contact was lost with sector headquarters, but the airborne troops still maintained their communications. At 2400 the rangers disengaged and filtered out of the city. . . . From 9 to 15 January the 81st Ranger Group headquarters conducted a search and rescue operation. . . . After four days of search, 121 airborne rangers were retrieved by helicopters. Thus the airborne force lost about half of its committed personnel. Other troops and civilians from Phuoc Long also managed to find their way to safety at various places. A total of over 1,000 people, to include civilians, police, Regional Force troops, and men of the 2nd Battalion of the 7th Infantry, were thus rescued and returned to Saigon. But the province chief, the district chief of Phuoc Binh, the infantry battalion commander, and over 3,000 troops failed to make it back to our lines.

• • •

Militarily, the capture of Phuoc Long gave the enemy extended control over a very large area. Three of his base areas were now linked together in a continuous arc from the Cambodian border across northern MR-3. . . . Psychologically and politically, the loss of Phuoc Long, the first provincial capital of South Vietnam permanently seized by the Communists, came as a shock to the population and the armed forces. The apparent total indifference with which the United States and other non-Communist countries regarded this tragic loss reinforced the doubt the Vietnamese people held concerning the viability of the Paris Agreement. Almost gone was the hope that the United States would forcibly punish the North Vietnamese for their brazen violations of the cease-fire agreement. The people's belief in the power of the armed forces and the government was also deeply shaken. To the Communists Phuoc Long was not merely a military victory. What they had gained psychologically and politically was more important. It was the first big step toward total military conquest, boldly taken yet apparently without fear of any reaction from the United States. . . .

Ban Me Thuot

Major General Pham Van Phu, who had commanded the 1st Infantry Division from October 1970 to July 1972, replaced Lieutenant General Nguyen Van Toan as commander of II Corps in December 1974 upon the recommendation of Vice President Tran Van Huong, who had insisted on removing General Toan because of charges of corruption. President Thieu apparently gave in to his vice president's insistence with reluctance, because he knew that despite the charges General Toan was a thoroughly competent field commander. General Toan was assigned as chief of armor and on 5 February 1975 was also given command of III Corps. He replaced General Dong, who had resigned a month earlier. The change of command in MR-2 contributed to the events that finally led to the collapse of II Corps.

• • •

The enemy's preparations for a major offensive and plan of attack against Ban Me Thuot became obvious. . . . The II Corps G-2 had correctly compiled this estimate as early as mid-February, but unfortunately his warning was not given serious consideration by the corps commander, who believed that the enemy's moves toward Ban Me Thuot were only diversionary, or at most a secondary effort, and that Pleiku would be the main objective. The disposition of II Corps accordingly reflected its commander's thinking. The entire 23rd Division was deployed in the Pleiku area, leaving the task of defending Ban Me Thuot to a ranger group and provincial . . . units composed mostly of Montagnards. At the beginning of March, when alerted to the NVA 320th Division movement toward Ban Me Thuot, II Corps simply sent a headquarters detachment and a regiment, the 53rd of the 23rd Division, back to Ban Me Thuot. . . .

The enemy in the meantime had effectively blocked National Route 21 from Ban Me Thuot to Nha Trang. An unsuccessful clearing operation was conducted by Khanh Hoa Sector, and the road remained blocked . . . some fifty miles east of Ban Me Thuot. On 5 March 1975 the Communists attacked and overran Thuan Man district town on National Route 14, approximately halfway between Pleiku and Ban Me Thuot. Thus communications from Ban Me Thuot to Pleiku and II Corps headquarters and to Nha Trang on the coast were effectively interdicted, and the isolation of Ban Me Thuot was completed.

The battle of Ban Me Thuot began on 10 March and ended on 18 March 1975. In the early hours of 10 March the F-10 Division, supported by armor and artillery, launched a three-pronged attack into the city.

• • •

During the night of 10 March enemy forces were augmented by the 316th Division. The encirclement tightened around the 23rd Division headquarters complex, and the fierceness of the attack increased by the hour. The deputy commander of the 23rd Division at the detachment CP requested close air support. Our tactical aircraft made very accurate bombing runs and destroyed many enemy tanks. Unfortunately, one bomb struck the division's tactical operations center and destroyed it. Communications with II Corps headquarters were lost from that time.

On 13 March the 7th Ranger Group was airlifted from MR-3 to Pleiku and assigned to II Corps headquarters to replace the 44th and 45th Regiments of the 23rd Division, which had been ordered to Ban Me Thuot in an attempt to save the besieged city, by now under the virtual control of the enemy. The next day, 14 March, a relief force composed of the 45th Regiment and one battalion of the 44th was helilifted to Phuoc An, a district town twenty miles east of Ban Me Thuot, where the battered troops from the city's garrison, their dependents, and much of the civilian population had begun to converge. The advance of the relief column was slow and its counterattack ineffective, owing in part to the troubled morale of the troops, whose dependents were being stranded in the city. A large number of troops of the relief force broke ranks and headed toward the city in search of their dependents.

On 16 March the commander of the 23rd Division was slightly wounded and was evacuated from the combat zone. On 18 March Communist forces overran Phuoc An District town, the last base for a relief effort. All fighting for the city had now ceased, and the entire province of Darlac came under enemy control.

• • •

The loss of Ban Me Thuot resulted primarily from a failure to field a sufficient force for the defense of the city when the attack began. The enemy achieved tactical surprise and, more importantly, a vast numerical superiority in committing three infantry divisions with supporting armor and artillery. The commander of II Corps failed to reassess his situation in the light of hard intelligence concerning the movement of the NVA 320th and F-10 Divisions toward Ban Me Thuot and ignored his G-2's assessment, as well as that of JGS. His preconceived and inflexible opinion convinced him that the enemy would strike Pleiku and Kontum, the usual objectives of the enemy's main effort in the past.

• • •

President Thieu's Fateful Decision

During the first two months of 1975, a number of US congressmen made fact-finding visits to South Vietnam. In the face of the deteriorating military situation and in view of the impending congressional debates on the issue of supplementary aid, our government extended a warm welcome to its influential visitors. Members of the US Congress had been urged to see for themselves how South Vietnam was faring economically, politically, and militarily before they should decide whether to grant what had been requested. Hence the visits were awaited with high expectation.

The first visitor was Senator Sam Nunn, followed by Representative Paul N. "Pete" McCloskey and Senator Dewey Bartlett. Then came the main party, including both senators and representatives. JGS thoroughly briefed the first visitors on the current situation in South Vietnam. The briefing centered on the insurmountable shortages that would result without the $300 million supplemental aid and pointed out the imminent danger of overt aggression, which by now had become an obvious fact. The last visitors were not given any official briefings, but some congressmen took time to visit JGS and the permanent exhibit of captured Communist weapons at JGS headquarters.

The backgrounds of the visiting congressmen were as diverse as their opinions on the issue of US aid. Some were for, others were against it. Some came with open minds, and others appeared heavily prejudiced. Some were courteous and modest; others rude and contemptuous. Still others were completely detached and indifferent. But no matter who they were, or how they behaved, all were received with equal warmth and sincerity. They were completely free to see whatever they wished, [and] to contact anyone— pro-government or opposition groups, detainees or free people.

• • •

In general, the departing visitors left behind a feeling of pessimism. The atmosphere was charged with rumors and speculation, all detrimental to the national cause. In the United Sates, we were induced to believe, our government was considered incorrigibly corrupt, despotic, and repressive. Disenchanted and troubled by its own domestic difficulties, political and economic, the United States was no longer in a position to contribute to the war effort. Aid stood no chance of being increased; on the contrary, it would be trimmed further, for American attention had shifted to the Middle East.

No one read the signs and clues better than President Thieu himself. By the time the last visitor had departed, he knew that there was no longer any hope for the $300 million additional aid. He also came to realize that the only possible future trend for US military aid to South Vietnam was downhill. And apparently he made up his mind on the basis of these readings. What he had adamantly refused to do for the last two years, he was now resigned to accept. That was why the redeployment of our armed forces was attempted.

The forceful attack against Ban Me Thuot, and the relative ineffectiveness of II Corps reactions, seemed to act like a catalyst on the mind of President Thieu, the only man who made all the decisions as to how the war should be conducted. So far it had largely been a matter of holding out against increasingly unfavorable odds. Overextended throughout the entire national territory to the last reserve unit, our armed forces certainly could not do much to alter such odds. Besides, reduced aid had in many ways affected their combat capabilities and, more than usually admitted, their morale as well. Under those circumstances, it had become obvious that something had to be done if South Vietnam were to survive at all.

For some time JGS, in its advisory and supporting role, had thought that the armed forces would stand a better chance of holding if they had less territory to defend. From a military point of view, it was a sound idea, but politically it ran afoul of the publicly avowed "holding at all costs" stance that President Thieu had embraced since the cease-fire. No doubt the president must have had second thoughts in his private moments. The deteriorating situation spoke for itself. First Phuoc Long, now Ban Me Thuot, in just two months. What area would be next? Also, the bitter aftertaste of those American lawmakers' visits was still lingering.

So his mind must have been made up when President Thieu invited his prime minister; Lieutenant General Dang Van Quang, his assistant for security affairs; and me for a working breakfast at the palace on 11 March 1975, the day after Ban Me Thuot was attacked. When coffee and food had been served and the attendants had left, he took out a small-scale map of South Vietnam and started the session by going over the military situation with which we were all completely familiar. Then he said, matter-of-factly: "Given our present strength and capabilities, we certainly cannot hold and defend all the territory we want." Instead we should redeploy our forces to hold and defend only those populous and flourishing areas which were really the most important.

The conclusion struck us as one to which he must have given very careful consideration. It was as if he had been holding it back and wanted now to impart the decision to just the three of us around the breakfast table. He outlined on the map those areas he considered important. They encompassed all of MR-3 and MR-4, plus their territorial waters. Those few areas which happened to be presently under Communist control within this territory ought to be reoccupied at all costs. After all, this territory was where our national resources—rice, rubber, industries, etc.—were concentrated. This was by far our most populous and prosperous land. In addition, its continental shelf had recently yielded oil. This was going to be our untouchable heartland, the irreducible national stronghold: Saigon, its surrounding provinces, and the Mekong Delta.

Continuing his impassioned monologue on geopolitics, President Thieu sounded perhaps a trifle less assured when it came to MR-2 and MR-1. In the Central Highlands, he said, indicating the area by a sweeping motion of his hand, the Ban Me Thuot area was more important than Kontum and Pleiku taken together, because of its economic and demographic preponderance. So were the coastal provinces of MR-2, because they bordered on the potentially rich continental shelf. As to MR-1, it was largely a matter of "hold what you can." Here he sketched his idea by drawing a series of phase lines cutting across the width of MR-1 at different locations of the coastline from the north downward. If we were strong enough, he said, we would hold the territory up to Hue or Danang. If not, then we could redeploy farther south to Chu Lai or even Tuy Hoa. This way, he emphasized, we could redeploy our own capabilities [and] hold a more important part of our national territory with a better chance of surviving and prospering as a nation.

And so, with a few preemptory statements, a momentous decision had been made. Its full implication was still not clear, but it certainly carried wide-ranging problems, militarily speaking. As the senior military advisor, I felt obliged to voice my opinion. I said something to the effect that this redeployment was indeed necessary, and I had embraced such an idea for a long time. But so far I had kept it to myself and considered it an improper proposal. First of all, it conflicted with the prevailing national policy, and, second, it could well have been interpreted as an indication of defeatism. What I refrained from adding, though, was that I believed it was too late for any successful redeployment of such magnitude. Besides, it looked to me like a decision that precluded any unfavorable comment. After all, as commander in chief it was the president's prerogative and responsibility to dictate the conduct of the war. He must have known exactly what he was doing.

However radical a departure from the current strategy this decision may have been, it was certainly the most logical thing any leader could do. It had been well over two years since the Paris Agreement was signed, and the situation was deteriorating at an alarming rate. The only criticism that one could make was to question why President Thieu had waited so long. In the meeting he gave no explanation or any indication of the steps in reaching his decision. It seemed to flow naturally from the facts themselves. Previously, he had hoped it would be possible to hold on to remote and sparsely populated areas. If the Communists should violate the Paris Agreement, then ICCS and the world at large would realize who was the culprit. And if the violations were too flagrant, President Thieu had hoped, and had been led to hope, the United States would justifiably take certain forceful actions in response, as promised by President Nixon.

For two years, however, the Communists had been escalating their violations in number and scale to test the willingness of the United States to react. While he was in office, it was true, President Nixon occasionally issued warnings to Hanoi. But after his resignation on 8 August 1974, the promise of "vigorous reaction" became empty rhetoric. Even the attack on Phuoc Long evoked no response in the United States. The negative attitude of most of the visiting American lawmakers deflated the last hopes. It was almost certain that the US Congress was in no mood to see the war continued, much less appropriate additional money to prosecute it. If anything, its mind and book were closed for good.

There was no other choice for President Thieu if he wanted to save what he could while there was still some chance of success. But it was already too late. A redeployment of our forces should have been carried out by mid-1974. At the latest, such a move should have been taken as soon as President Nixon resigned. As the principal architect of Vietnamization and the Paris Agreement, in our view he was the only American official who bore the moral obligation of enforcing the cease-fire. He was also the only credible man who had the courage to take bold and forceful action when it was required. So it was then or never.

The Communists certainly would have welcomed any territorial gain, and cease-fire boundaries could have been a subject of bargaining. We would have been much better off with a reduced but not infested territory. Such an arrangement would have more closely resembled the 1954 agreement: a new demarcation line, regrouping of troops on both sides, etc.; two clean-cut zones instead of the purulent spots of the "leopard skin." It could have been ideal for our own survival. But there were chances the Communists would have rejected it. Didn't they admit their mistake of agreeing to partitioning at Geneva? There was much less chance they would accept this solution again. After all, they had not gone through twenty years of war and hardship for nothing.

By the time Ban Me Thuot was lost, it was far too late. For one thing, the enemy was on a winning streak. For another, he had finally achieved a substantial numerical superiority. Extended and pressed the way we were, there was little chance we could disengage from any place without being pursued and pressed on farther.

There was also the problem of the local population and military dependents. Evacuating or failing to evacuate them at the appropriate time might be the key to success. No national leader in his right mind would ever think of deliberately abandoning the population to the mercy of the enemy. Yet concern for saving his military forces might compel him to do exactly that. But experience had proved that most South Vietnamese fled the Communists if they could. And "population" also meant military dependents, who were the source of comfort and support for the combat troops. It was unthinkable to try to separate them for any length of time, because they always tended to get together. This was especially true considering the traditional Vietnamese family attachment and the marginal living conditions of the troops and their dependents in general. All this had to be carefully considered whenever an attempt was made to separate troops from their families for any lengthy period.

In retrospect, the question is now raised as to the chance South Vietnam had of surviving if the redeployment had not been attempted. It sounds perhaps presumptuous at this time, but I believe the chances were good. For one thing, the self-generated collapse of morale among the troops and population—the direct consequence of the redeployment fiasco and the true catalyst of rapid disintegration—probably would not have happened, and we would still have had almost all our units intact, except perhaps parts of the 23rd Division.

Even after Ban Me Thuot, the enemy would have had to stop and think twice before pressing on with another offensive of that scale in MR-2. The II Corps still had the 22nd Division and the equivalent of two other combat divisions, plus two air divisions and enough logistical support to continue fighting through the dry season. Without the redeployment, I don't think the enemy would have succeeded in gaining much headway in MR-1, either. Then the situation would have dragged on as before, more precariously in the face of dwindling military aid and difficulties in reconstituting a general reserve. But definitely it would not have deteriorated so rapidly and extensively if the redeployment had not been attempted at all.

That was the military prospect in the short run. After Ban Me Thuot, I think the enemy would have tried to pressure for a coalition, and President Thieu might have been inclined to accept it. But even that would merely have been an interim modus vivendi. The Communists would have sought more military victories, with the objective of gaining still more political concessions. But could South Vietnam have withstood the enemy's mounting pressure in the long run? I believe it all depended on the amount of US military aid. The hard and cold fact was that, without additional appropriations, our armed forces would have run out of fuel and ammunition by June 1975. How could any army stand and fight without the essential things with which to do the fighting?

VI. THE ROUT IN THE HIGHLANDS

Two days after the historic meeting at the Independence Palace, during which the redeployment strategy was discussed, President Thieu expressed his desire to see Major General Pham Van Phu, commander of II Corps, at his headquarters in Pleiku. By now, Ban Me Thuot was under virtual control of the Communists, and frantic efforts of II Corps to reoccupy it had been largely unfruitful. Lest the chance of retaking this important city slip by indefinitely, it was President Thieu's intent to review the situation with the field commander and to try to save it. Pleiku was also under pressure and being shelled sporadically by enemy artillery. This was no place for the president to visit, much less for a presumably important discussion. Concerned about the president's safety, General Phu suggested another place and, after some debate, Cam Ranh was selected. The meeting took place on Friday, 14 March 1975.

The meeting place befitted the occasion perfectly. It was a handsome building perched on the top of a sandhill. The building dated from 1966, when it was erected by US forces to accommodate President Johnson when he stopped over to visit US troops. The same personalities who had attended the palace meeting three days earlier accompanied President Thieu to Cam Ranh: Prime Minister Tran Thien Khiem, Lieutenant General Dang Van Quang, and I.

As was customary for every such meeting, the commander of II Corps began the session by giving a briefing on the friendly and enemy situation in his military region. The turn of events as he described it was definitely grave, and his tone profoundly pessimistic. All the major axes of communication of MR-2, National Routes 14, 19, and 21, had been effectively cut by the enemy and traffic had been stopped. The most important of these arteries, Route 19, which cut across the width of the country and served as a vital link between Pleiku and the coastal city of Qui Nhon, was blocked at Binh Khe by the entire NVA 3rd Division; our 22nd Division, with its four regiments and under the energetic command of Brigadier General Phan Dinh Niem, had tried unsuccessfully to dislodge enemy troops solidly entrenched in their blocking positions.

• • •

When the situation briefing was completed, President Thieu pointedly asked the only and foremost question which had been preoccupying his mind. Was it at all possible for General Phu to retake Ban Me Thuot? As expected, the commander of II Corps did not commit himself to a positive and firm answer. He merely asked for reinforcements. Turning to me, President Thieu wanted to know what reserve force we could muster for the effort. But he must have known already. The last reserve unit, the 7th Ranger Group, had been sent to II Corps at General Phu's request when signs of the enemy offensive were still developing. Nothing really was left.

This was the most critical juncture of the entire war. Down to the last chip, our armed forces now faced a showdown with an adversary who continuously upped his ante. The only major reserve units, the Airborne and Marine Divisions, had been committed in MR-1 since 1972. Well before the attack against Ban Me Thuot, President Thieu, apparently for political reasons, had decided to reassign the Airborne Division to the Saigon area. The newly created and combat-ready 468th Marine Brigade, plus a ranger group, were to replace it. Thus I Corps would eventually gain the equivalent of two brigades in return for the three brigades of the Airborne Division. But deployment of the promised ranger group was countermanded by President Thieu himself in the face of the rapidly changing situation. The first airborne brigade to leave MR-1, the 3rd, was being sealifted to Saigon when it received orders on 17 March to debark at Nha Trang and proceed to Khanh Duong on National Route 21 in an emergency move to stop the enemy's advance toward the coast after Ban Me Thuot was lost. As combat erupted fiercely in the following days, the 3rd Airborne Brigade was decimated and never returned to Saigon as intended.

So, at the very stage when a reserve was most needed, JGS could give General Phu nothing. It was as if, by asking something he had known all along, President Thieu wanted everyone to realize the impasse in which we had found ourselves and what was going to dictate his next move. Again, as during the breakfast working session at the palace on 11 March, President Thieu stood up beside a map of South Vietnam and, with General Phu looking on attentively, launched into his explanation of the new strategy to be adopted. By hand gestures he sketched on the map the general contour of the vital areas which General Phu was supposed to hold. Because of its economic and demographic potential, Ban Me Thuot was more important than Pleiku and Kontum taken together. It was now II Corps's task to redeploy its organic forces in such a manner as to reoccupy Ban Me Thuot at all costs. This was the president's order.

President Thieu then asked General Phu how he proposed to redeploy and which route he had in mind for moving troops toward Ban Me Thuot. According to the II Corps commander, National Route 19, which ran from Pleiku eastward to the coast, was impassable; his best division, the 22nd, had been unable to break through at Binh Khe. National Route 14, which connected Pleiku with Ban Me Thuot in a north-south axis, was also blocked at Thuan Man, north of Ban Me Thuot. There was a chance to clear it, but it would be extremely difficult because our progress would be known to the enemy. So General Phu said he planned to use Interprovincial Route 7B. This was a secondary route which, branching off National Route 14 twenty miles south of Pleiku, ran southeasterly through Hau Bon (Cheo Reo) toward Tuy Hoa on the coast. A narrow, ruggedly surfaced track, Interprovincial Route 7B had long been neglected and was out of use. Except for the immediately usable short stretch from National Route 14 to Hau Bon, no one seemed to know its condition. It was known, however, that one of the major bridges across the Song Ba (Ba River) south of Cung Son had been destroyed beyond repair, and the road's terminal stretch west of Tuy Hoa was unusable because of extensive mining by Korean forces a few years earlier. However, the commander of II Corps seemed to know what he was going to do. Tactical surprise was the critical factor, he said, which weighed heavily in his choice. He simply requested JGS to provide river-crossing facilities. I immediately approved this request.

Moving a corps-sized column of troops, equipment, and vehicles along a largely unknown road some 160 miles through the mountains and jungles of the Highlands was a hazardous task of great magnitude. Surprise would only work if the movement were swift and unimpeded. But even the most optimistic commander could not rule out an enemy presence and should take certain precautions. This, after all, used to be the enemy's favored type of terrain where some of the bloodiest ambushes had been sprung against the French Union forces in the 1946–1954 war.

As chairman of the JGS, I felt it imperative to remind General Phu of the difficulties and hazards to be expected and the security measures to be taken. A troop movement of this magnitude, crossing this terrain and going this distance, required the general to ensure security and protection along the entire route. The column should be organized to afford protection for its lead element and its rear element, as well as for the troops in between. Its commander should also have adequate and appropriate signal communications, and air cover and close air support as required.

Finally there were lessons for which the French had paid a high price during the first Indochina War. I reminded him of the French failure in the attempt to extricate their troops from Lang Son in 1947. I also reminded General Phu of how in October 1950 the two columns of troops and vehicles commanded by Colonels Le Page and Charton—the first moving out of That Khe northward and the latter going from Cao Bang southward—had been annihilated in the foothills around Dong Khe along Colonial Route 4. Last I spoke of how, on the very same type of terrain and road that General Phu's column was to move, the famous French Group GM-100 was slaughtered on National Route 19 near An Khe in June 1954 and its remnants given the final coup de grace at Chu-Drek Pass on National Route 14. Those were bloody and tragic lessons that any commander in the treacherous Central Highlands should have kept in mind.

When the meeting drew to its end, and the participants were preparing to leave, General Phu suddenly made a personal request to President Thieu. In an almost pleading tone, he recommended that his subordinate, Colonel Pham Van Tat, who commanded the ranger forces in MR-2, be promoted to brigadier general. I didn't know Colonel Tat personally. I was told he was an able officer, but as a field commander he had no outstanding credits on his combat record. While I had no outright objection, my opinion was that for his promotion to be justified Colonel Tat should wait until he had accomplished some substantial feat in combat. President Thieu was undecided; he hesitated and agreed with my reasoning. But Phu was insistent and repeatedly pleaded his case with the president, who finally gave his consent. (After being promoted, Colonel Tat was designated to command the forces to be redeployed. This explained the insistence with which General Phu had urged the promotion of his most trusted subordinate. General Phu's two deputies, Brigadier Generals Tran Van Cam and Le Van Than, were not given any responsibilities in the redeployment except that General Cam was assigned the vague job of "supervising" the total effort.)

Arriving back in Saigon, I summoned Brigadier General Tran Dinh Tho, my assistant chief of staff J-3, and told him the details of the meeting. My chief of staff, Lieutenant General Dong Van Khuyen, was out of the country on a visit at the time. My instructions to Tho were to keep track of the redeployment movement and to give General Phu a hand, all in discretion, because this was essentially a top secret operation to be conducted by II Corps and to involve only its organic units. It was also a top secret operational order given directly by the president as commander in chief to a field commander. Hence, JGS was unauthorized to initiate any orders for the redeployment of those army and air force components in the Kontum-Pleiku area not directly involved in the operation.

General Phu's Plan

• • •

The mission assigned to General Phu was to move the bulk of these units [in the Kontum-Pleiku area] to Nha Trang and from there conduct a counterattack to retake Ban Me Thuot.

The basic plan of the II Corps commander, for what really amounted to a withdrawal from the Highlands, was to take the enemy by surprise. According to his chief of staff, after General Phu returned from the meeting with the president at Cam Ranh, he convened a limited staff meeting late in the evening of the same day, during which he reported President Thieu's orders and issued his own. Participants included newly promoted Brigadier General Pham Van Tat; Brigadier General Tran Van Cam, deputy II Corps commander for operations; and Brigadier General Pham Ngoc Sang, commander of the 6th Air Division. A general plan of movement was briefly discussed, and it was decided that General Phu and elements of II Corps Forward CP would move to Nha Trang by air, together with Brigadier General Le Trung Tuong, commander of the 23rd Division, who would proceed to Khanh Duong to take charge of the effort to stop the enemy's advance on National Route 21 and try to reoccupy Ban Me Thuot. . . .

General Tat was put in command of all II Corps troops to be redeployed from the Kontum-Pleiku area to Tuy Hoa along Interprovincial Route 7B. Colonel Le Khac Ly was made responsible for the corps staff and all logistical units. The whole operation was to be supervised by General Cam.

• • •

Since the redeployment was conceived and carried out in secrecy, no word was passed to province chiefs of Kontum, Pleiku, and Phu Bon. On 17 March, the second day, late at night, orders were given to the three ranger groups in Kontum to fall back to Pleiku. Only then did the Kontum province chief, Colonel Phan Dinh Hung, learn about the troop movement. Hastily, he went along, but was killed in an ambush halfway between Pleiku and Kontum.

The Flight

On 16 March the first convoy moved out of Pleiku as planned. But no sooner had the last truck departed than news of the movement reached the city. People soon began to leave the city by every means of transportation available, even on foot, taking whatever belongings they could carry. They were later joined by refugees from Kontum, and together with the troops they came to form a long mass of humans and vehicles flowing along the hazardous Route 7B. The exodus from the Highlands had begun.

The first two days, 16 and 17 March, passed without serious incidents. By the evening of 18 March, II Corps headquarters had reached Hau Bon, Phu Bon Province, where a CP was established. It was in this area that all the convoys of the past three days, and the human mass of refugees, were struck. The advance toward the coast, still some one hundred miles away, was impossible because the engineers had not completed a pontoon bridge across the Ea Pa farther down the road.

During the night enemy troops, presumably local units ordered to intercept the stalled column, began shelling and mounting ground attacks. The Hau Bon airstrip, less than one mile from the II Corps CP, was overrun. Fighting continued into late evening of the next day, 19 March. By this time, wounded soldiers and refugees were lying all around. There was practically no control in town. Some unruly Montagnard Regional Force and Popular Force troops began looting or broke ranks and ran away, creating a chaotic commotion among troops and refugees. The situation became increasingly serious as each hour went by. It was then that General Phu issued orders from Nha Trang for Colonel Dong, commander of the 2nd Armor Brigade, to take command of the column.

The convoy moved out of Hau Bon the next day, 20 March, but could only progress fifteen miles. Phu Tac, ahead on the road, had been overrun by the enemy. Still the convoy kept moving, fighting its way ahead. Air support was called at 1600, but unfortunately a few bombs were dropped by error on the lead elements. Nearly an entire ranger battalion became casualties. This fatal incident further stalled the movement and increased confusion and chaos among the troops and refugees. In a frantic effort to seek cover and escape, several soldiers jumped into the river and were drowned. And, at two river-crossing points, some tanks and vehicles were stuck in quicksand when they tried to bypass the road.

At Cung Son, some forty miles from Tuy Hoa, the convoy had to cross the Song Ba (Ba River) to continue the last leg of its journey on local Route 436 on the southern bank of the river. Beyond Cung Son, Route 7B had been mined extensively by Korean forces. A pontoon bridge had been brought to Tuy Hoa from Nha Trang, but it was impossible to move the bridge to Cung Son by road because of several enemy blocking positions. Finally the bridge was carried to Cung Son piece by piece by CH-47 helicopters.

On 22 March the pontoon bridge was finally completed and the convoy crossed over onto Route 436 and proceeded cautiously toward Tuy Hoa. Because of the tremendous rush at the start, a pontoon soon collapsed, causing further losses in lives and vehicles. But it was quickly repaired, and what remained of the battered column soon made it safely to the other side of the river.

It had taken seven days and innumerable casualties for the column to progress so far, but the . . . final leg of the odyssey proved equally slow and even more hazardous. The distance was relatively short, but enemy blocking positions were hard to dislodge. No sooner had the lead element resumed its march than it was stalled immediately by enemy fire. Efforts to clear enemy blocking positions were slow and difficult. The column became bogged down again. It was raining and cold. And the enemy relentlessly kept up his harassing mortar fire. Because of extremely bad weather, the air force was unable to provide close support. Tuy Hoa sector had run out of reinforcements, and the column had to rely on its own strength. Driven by desperation and compassion for the people who shared their lot, the troops of the 34th Ranger Battalion . . . finally resolved to break through or die. Supported by a few remaining M-113s, they stormed ahead and systematically destroyed roadblock after roadblock. As soon as an enemy position was dis-posed of, the column rushed on, oblivious to all dangers ahead. . . .

On 27 March the final blocking position was destroyed and the column at last moved on freely toward Tuy Hoa. It was 2100 when the first vehicles reached the city. No de-liberate effort was ever made to take stock of the number of vehicles and people that fi-nally made it to Tuy Hoa. How many people in the original column survived the tragic journey no one knew exactly. Over 300 vehicles, both military and civilian, later drove up to the fuel supply station set up by the 2nd Logistic Command and asked for refuel-ing. Also approximately 5,000 people sought shelter at a makeshift refugee center at Tuy Hoa that night. Others either proceeded to Qui Nhon or Nha Trang or went home to families and relatives in town.

From a military point of view the withdrawal was a complete failure. Almost all the units withdrawn from the Kontum-Pleiku area were disrupted. The chief of staff, II Corps, Colonel Le Khac Ly, estimated that 5,000 out of 20,000 logistical and support troops were finally retrieved. From the five ranger groups about 900 men reported to II Corps headquarters at Nha Trang. But the 34th Ranger Battalion, later dubbed "block destruction heroes" by the grateful refugees, lost only 50 percent of its strength. It was retained at Tuy Hoa for the defense of the city.

Causes and Results

• • •

With hindsight it is easy to criticize, but however well justified his concept of se-crecy and tactical surprise, the II Corps commander should have worked out a detailed plan with his staff and exercised direct control over the whole operation. Whatever plan-ning he had done was limited, and only a few trusted subordinate commanders had con-tributed and knew about it. Staff work was nonexistent. . . .

• • •

Finally, the failure was also one of leadership at all echelons. Troops had not been briefed, discipline was not enforced, constraints had not been imposed to avoid disorder and chaos. In particular, troops had not been motivated to take on the difficult task of destroying enemy blocking positions, the final obstacles to their survival.

Militarily, the withdrawal had resulted in a rout of strategic proportions. At least 75 percent of II Corps combat strength, to include the 23rd Infantry Division as well as ranger, armor, artillery, engineer, and signal units, had been tragically expended within ten days. The operation to reoccupy Ban Me Thuot failed to materialize, simply because II Corps no longer had any combat troops. Communist troops had taken over Kontum and Pleiku without a fight. . . .

Psychologically and politically, the self-inflicted defeat of II Corps in the Highlands amounted to a horrible nightmare for the people and armed forces of South Vietnam. Confusion, worries, anxiety, accusations, guilt, and a general feeling of distress began to weigh on everybody's mind. Rumors spread rapidly that territorial concessions were in the making. The immediate impact of the rumors was to unleash an uncontrollable surge of refugees seeking by all means and at all costs to leave whatever provinces remained of MR-2. To the north, MR-1 also felt the repercussions. Its population soon joined the refugees and battered troops streaming south along the coast. First, they rushed into Phan Rang and Phan Thiet, then moved on toward Saigon. In the national capital itself, the opposition increased its activities and irreparably widened the government's credibility gap. Confidence in the armed forces also swung down to its lowest ebb. Demonstrators angrily demanded the replacement of President Thieu; they also vigorously voiced anti-American sentiment. A pervasive hope still lingered, however, for some miraculous thing to happen that could save South Vietnam.

VII. DEFEAT IN THE NORTH

The situation in MR-1 had regained some stability after I Corps had defeated the enemy effort to push into the coastal plain southwest of Danang in late 1974.

• • •

However, the losses incurred during this six-month campaign were heavy and hard to replace. Combat effectiveness of most I Corps units had decreased as a result.

• • •

Thus, to confront an enemy main force of five divisions and many separate regiments, I Corps could muster only three infantry divisions, one marine division, four ranger groups, and an armor brigade. . . .

General Truong's Plans

This was the situation presented by the commander of I Corps, Lieutenant General Ngo Quang Truong, to the president on the morning of 13 March 1975. The occasion was a top-level meeting at the Independence Palace, limited, as usual, to the prime minister; me as chairman of JGS; and the ubiquitous presidential assistant for security affairs, Lieutenant General Dang Van Quang. Lieutenant General Nguyen Van Toan, commander of III Corps, was also brought into the conference room after General Truong had finished his briefing. General Toan, in turn, gave a brief rundown of the situation in his military region. The picture he presented was mildly bright; no significant event had been recorded in the past three days.

The president then addressed the conference in earnest. First he made an analysis of the general situation and pointed out the difficulties we were facing in military aid. He admitted he did not entertain any hope of intervention by the US Air Force in case South Vietnam were subjected to an all-out offensive by North Vietnam. He sympathized with the difficulties and handicaps of the corps commanders. Up to now, he admitted, he had given many instructions that he knew could not possibly be carried out.

The president said there was little he could do under the circumstances except to change strategy, to redeploy our forces to hold those vital areas where our national resources were concentrated. Even if we had to lose the jungle and mountainous areas to hold the remaining resource-rich areas (to include the continental shelf), such losses would be definitely much better than a coalition government with the Communists. The resource-rich areas defined in the president's new strategic plan included the Danang region for MR-1. As part of the redeployment plan, conceived in private by the commander in chief himself, the Airborne Division was slated to leave MR-1. Although this strategy was not mentioned at this meeting, the Airborne Division was to be followed by the Marine Division, if possible without endangering the I Corps defense posture. These moves would allow the reconstitution of a general reserve, which was vital to the success of the president's plan. President Thieu also instructed General Toan to temporarily withdraw his forces from An Loc to employ them wherever they were more needed in MR-2.

When the president completed his instructions, it was my turn, as Chairman of JGS, to remind both corps commanders of the precautions to be taken when they withdrew their forces. On that cautious note, the meeting ended. Even without lengthy comments, the session had lasted exactly three and a half hours.

During the next six days the military posture of MR-1 became increasingly precarious. More and more refugees kept flowing into Danang. It was almost impossible to regulate this human deluge. Important passes on National Route 1 were frequently jammed, delaying the movement of the Marine and the Airborne Division.

It was precisely then that General Truong was called to Saigon for a second meeting at the palace on 19 March 1975. The session began at 1100 with Vice President Tran Van Huong also present. As expected, General Truong briefed the president on his MR-1 withdrawal plan. This was well worked out, presenting a choice between two alternate courses.

Course 1 assumed the use of National Route 1. It prescribed two opposite but simultaneous withdrawals via National Route 1 from Hue to Danang and from Chu Lai to Danang.

Course 2 assumed enemy interdiction of National Route 1 and hence the necessity of withdrawing all troops into three enclaves: Hue, Danang, and Chu Lai. However, Hue and Chu Lai were only to serve as layover stations for troops who would be sealifted to Danang during the final stage. So Danang, the major enclave to be held as part of the redeployment plan, would become a stronghold defended by four divisions and four ranger groups.

Less than a week separated the two meetings at the palace. By the time of the second meeting, it was obvious that only the second course stood any chance of success. Any phased withdrawal along National Route 1 had become almost impossible.

• • •

The balance had been irretrievably lost. Besides, even without enemy pressure, I Corps could hardly conduct any major troop movement on an artery jammed beyond control during the last few days by refugees moving toward Danang.

This was in summary what General Truong told the president. "We have only one choice," he said, and "we had better act before it is too late." The only choice was to withdraw our troops toward Hue and Chu Lai, as well as Danang, and take advantage of existing fortifications in these cities, in particular those scattered in the hilly terrain around Hue, in order to destroy enemy troops to the maximum of our ability. General Truong had also heard unconfirmed reports that the Marine Division was to be redeployed to MR-3. If this should occur, it could affect General Truong's plan, and he accordingly asked for President Thieu's decision.

President Thieu's position was excruciating. It was he who had conceived and ordered the whole thing, and already the redeployment from the Central Highlands had given signs of turning sour. Worst of all was the psychological impact on the civilian population that now threatened to throw his plan into utter disarray.

Understandably enough, when it came to giving specific instructions to his field commander, President Thieu sidestepped the withdrawal plan altogether. Instead, he told General Truong to make an effort to hold onto whatever territory he could with whatever forces he now had, including the Marine Division. Then, turning aside and away from the problem, he asked General Quang to prepare a speech. He was going to address the people on TV, he said, to try to calm their emotions and let them know the government was going to defend Hue at all costs. He also seemed to ignore the refugee problem; neither he nor Prime Minister Khiem said anything about General Truong's headache. But, in contrast with the previous meeting, there was a feeling of encouragement this time, if only because the momentous withdrawal decision had been set aside for the time being.

Northern and Southern MR-1

By 1800 the same day, General Truong was back in Danang. As soon as his plane landed, he received an ominous report from Lieutenant General Lam Quang Thi, his deputy, who called in from the I Corps Forward CP at Hue. General Thi reported that 130mm guns were pounding his headquarters area and that enemy troops had just launched a large-scale attack with substantial armor across the outermost defense line at the Thach Han. The overt, all-out offensive of NVA units in MR-1 had begun.

• • •

General Truong immediately reported to JGS and requested permission to employ the 1st Airborne Brigade—the last brigade scheduled for withdrawal from MR-1—when the situation so warranted. The brigade was being assembled at Danang and was preparing to depart for Saigon. President Thieu agreed to the request with one condition: the brigade could be retained, but it should under no circumstances be employed in combat. So the airborne brigade was only to play the role of a morale anchor. It was a good thing that the president had come to realize its psychological value, but no doubt, in his own mind, he did not think the brigade could do much to help alter the situation. By this time the I Corps commander was most unsure about what was really happening in his northernmost province.

During the night of 19 March, all the forces manning the Thach Han defense line, including three Regional Force groups, one ranger battalion, and armor elements, fell back to the My Chanh River. The entire province of Quang Tri came under enemy control. At the My Chanh, the northern boundary of Thua Thien Province, the retreating troops established a new defense line on the southern bank.

In the early morning of 20 March, General Truong flew to the forward CP of the

Marine Division, five miles from the My Chanh line. There he met all major troop commanders in the I Corps forward area, and together they reviewed the situation and discussed a plan for the defense of Hue, which they had been ordered to hold at all costs. The situation that confronted General Truong and his commanders at that time was not too bad. Regular units and territorial forces were in good shape; discipline was good; and morale was high. The loss of Quang Tri might have some adverse effect on the troops, but it was not a big setback in itself. After all, most of the population had evacuated, and the bulk of the Marine Division had safely withdrawn to Danang. Command and control were excellent, and the troops appeared unanimously resolved to hold Hue.

On his way back to Danang, General Truong dropped by Hue for a visit with his deputy for territorial affairs, Major General Hoang Van Lac. His confidence was enhanced after an inspection tour of the city and its troop dispositions. At 1330 President Thieu's articulate voice was heard on radio Hue. He addressed the people, the population of Hue in particular, and ordered the troops to defend the city at all costs. This was a much-needed, albeit somewhat belated, shot in the arm, General Truong thought, but he was not sure of its effect. He left Hue, however, feeling confident and determined.

Arriving back in Danang late in the afternoon, General Truong received a special delivery flash message classified "Secret." It contained orders from the president, relayed by JGS. Contrary to what he had proclaimed in the broadcast, President Thieu now ordered that, because of inability to simultaneously defend all three enclaves (Hue, Danang, Chu Lai), the I Corps commander was free, depending on the situation and enemy pressure, to redeploy his forces for the defense of Danang only. The last airborne brigade was also directed to proceed immediately to Saigon; it left before midnight.

The situation in MR-1 was becoming more serious each day. President Thieu's address continued to be carried over the air during the following days, but it failed to reassure the wary people of Hue. Their confidence had been deeply shaken; they continued to pour out of the city and made their way toward Danang. On 21 March, with additional units brought from his rear, the enemy intensified pressure in the Phu Loc area and brought it to bear most heavily on a stretch of National Route 1 halfway between Hue and Danang, where the packed column of refugees was shelled. The 1st Infantry Division immediately went into action and, with massive artillery and tactical air support, managed initially to relieve this pressure. But the balance of forces already leaned heavily toward the enemy. The 1st Division held out until noon the next day, 22 March. At 1400 the 15th Ranger Group and elements of the 1st Regiment in the Phu Loc area were overcome by superior enemy force. National Route 1 was effectively cut, and there seemed to be no chance of clearing it again. Both the 15th Ranger Group and the 1st Regiment suffered heavy losses.

In the face of this unexpected setback and the virtual impossibility of reopening National Route 1, the commander of I Corps issued orders to contract and consolidate lines for the defense of Hue. In the meantime, with increased naval transport made available to MR-1, the evacuation of civilian refugees and military dependents toward Danang had begun in earnest. Part of the heavy military equipment was also shipped out with the refugees. In the morning of 23 March, enemy guns began to bombard Hue. The shelling continued throughout the day; it was sparse and ineffective, but its psychological effect on the people who were still stranded in the city was terrible. Terror soon gave way to frenzy and chaos.

• • •

In Quang Ngai Province the enemy effort also began and expanded rapidly the same day. Enemy sappers, provincial main force, and other local elements took advantage of the deteriorating situation and attacked in force the airport, various military installations, and the villages located around the provincial capital. National Route 1 was cut midway between the city of Quang Ngai and Chu Lai; Quang Ngai's access road to the coast was also cut. In brief, within a single day the situation deteriorated beyond control. . . .

The Final Evacuation

By the next day, 25 March, all I Corps forces had been gathered into three strongholds: Danang (including Hoi An), Hue to the north, and Chu Lai to the south. The retreat toward these havens had been painful and costly. Most of the troops were weary and disheartened. For a long time they had been fighting, battle after battle, year in and year out, but never before had they felt as truly discouraged. Gone was the hope that someone would give them a hand and help them to recover enough to confront the enemy again as of old.

During this most dispirited moment, another message was delivered to I Corps. Presidential orders again: I Corps was to redeploy its three organic divisions for the defense of Danang, with the Marine Division as a reserve. During the night General Truong ordered the 1st Infantry Division and other units in the Hue area to withdraw toward Danang. At the same time he instructed the 2nd Infantry Division, along with the Quang Ngai sector troops and their dependents, to proceed to Re Island, some twenty miles offshore from Chu Lai.

• • •

By morning of the following day, 26 March, the sea became rough, and extrication by ship was delayed. Nor was the estuary bridge in place in time to be of any use. By noon the tide had risen enough to prevent any attempt to cross the estuary. By this time the enemy had discovered our movements and began to concentrate his artillery fire upon Tu Hien and other pickup points. Command and control failed miserably. Hardly any discipline remained. Only about one-third of the troops finally made it to Danang. But no sooner had they reached the city than they melted away in search of their dependents and a way out. The only units that retained cohesion were the marines.

• • •

During 27 March the situation in Danang deteriorated by the hour. Inside the city, a wild and maddened population made any defense practically impossible. From the outside the enemy pressed in, inexorably, unrelentingly. . . .

On the morning of 28 March the commander of I Corps held an emergency meeting with all unit commanders at his headquarters. Measures were taken to restore order and hastily to reorganize battered units for the last-ditch defense of the city. But these efforts were undermined by a critical shortage of combat troops.

• • •

General Truong informed me of the situation. He also called the president and recommended immediate evacuation by sea. But during the conversation the president did not commit himself to any clear-cut order. He did not tell General Truong whether to withdraw or to hold and fight. He simply asked how many people could be extricated to safety in case of a withdrawal. Apparently he was apprehensive about the way things had turned out. This redeployment could well turn into another tragedy like the one which just happened in the Central Highlands. He wanted to spare himself the pain of another such order.

As soon as the conversation ended, all communications with Saigon were disrupted by enemy artillery fire. The situation by now had become entirely hopeless. Without hesitation, General Truong decided to withdraw from Danang. . . . Before dawn the next morning, 29 March, a thick fog had set in along the coast. All available naval ships were at the rendezvous points as planned, but the tide was low; the ships could not beach; and the troops had to wade and swim toward the ships. By midmorning the embarkation was going smoothly. Nevertheless, when enemy artillery fire began to zero in on the beaches, and the operation became disorderly, many soldiers drowned; others were killed by enemy fire. When the ships left, over 6,000 marines and 4,000 troops of the 3rd Division and other units were on board.

The Refugee Problem

One of the thorniest problems, which MR-1 could hardly solve by itself, was the influx of refugees. It was not a new problem. Almost every significant enemy offensive had created refugees. The population of MR-1 was genuinely wary of the ups and downs of a situation. The memories of Hue in 1968, Quang Tri in 1972, and numerous lesser hardships in between were still vivid and evoked many nightmares. It was as if the citizens of MR-1 had been condemned to live in constant fear, ready to pack up and leave at all times. . . .

Rumors arose and spread: a partition had been arranged with the Communists; the government would surely abandon MR-1, as it had Pleiku and Kontum. These rumors accelerated the exodus, which was already taking on the speed and magnitude of a deluge. By the time the prime minister and cabinet members flew to Danang on 18 March to examine and try to solve the refugee problem, the city was besieged by over half a million uprooted citizens.

• • •

Before presiding over a session with governmental officials directly concerned with the refugee problem, Prime Minister Khiem was taken aside by General Truong for a briefing on the current military situation and his plan for the withdrawal. In particular, General Truong alerted him to the profound agitation among the population. The prime minister was taken aback. He did not suspect that the situation could have changed so rapidly. He instructed General Truong to present his withdrawal plan to the president before implementing it. Then he stepped into the adjoining main conference room, where his cabinet ministers were waiting.

• • •

Hue was abandoned during the night of 25 March. Troops and the remaining civilians retreated along the coast toward Danang. Tam Ky was overrun on 24 March, and Chu Lai evacuated on the 26th. The population of the two southern provinces, Quang Ngai and Quang Tin, also rushed toward Danang. . . . By this time the city was in utter disorder and chaos. People moved about frantically in search of relief and escape. All streets were packed; vehicles were unable to move. It was impossible to move 340 critically wounded servicemen the few miles between the hospital and the airport. "The mass of people stranded in the city was estimated at approximately one and one-half million. They took over every public building, all the public roads, and the harbor. The chaos and disorder were indescribable. Hunger, looting, and crimes were widespread. Traffic was impossible. To maneuver, tanks had to make headway by crushing people first." That was the spectacle . . . reported by Lieutenant General Le Nguyen Khang . . . after returning from a mission to Danang.

On 27 March came the first US commercial jet chartered for the evacuation. It had been planned to airlift about fourteen thousand people in daily runs between Danang and Cam Ranh. But news of the air evacuation spread rapidly. Soon the airport was besieged by a frantic crowd, deserters included, who trampled the security fence, overwhelmed the guards, swamped the runways, and mobbed the aircraft. There was total chaos at planeside, and it took the guards half a day to restore some order. But, as soon as another jet landed, the same disorderly commotion took hold of the crowd. Finally it became so unsafe for the jets themselves that the airlift had to be suspended altogether. . . .

At the harbor another unruly crowd took over the piers. A number of US oceangoing vessels arriving in Danang were ordered to anchor offshore. Then, by barges and small boats, the refugees were taken to the ships. The operation was slow, but it brought good results. As soon as each ship had taken aboard about 10,000 people it was directed toward Cam Ranh. But soon the ships had to be redirected toward Vung Tau and Phu Quoc Island when Nha Trang was evacuated on 1 April. The long southbound voyage was painful and fatal to some refugees who were victims of crimes and other acts of violence by unruly soldiers and by disguised enemy agents. The elements, hunger, and thirst also took their toll, and a number of exhausted people fainted once put on shore. At Phu Quoc more than ten Communist agents were denounced by the refugees for flagrant acts and were executed on the beaches of the island.

• • •

Wherever it went, the refugee flow brought along chaos and disintegration. The danger was such that President Thieu was compelled to ban refugees from the Mekong Delta and the provinces surrounding Saigon. He himself lamented: "If we brought the refugees to some place, sooner or later that place would be lost."

It was obvious that there was no way for I Corps to stand up to an all-out offensive from North Vietnam, given the balance of forces at the time and the rugged terrain of MR-1, which gave the enemy tremendous tactical advantages. But the rapid deterioration of the situation was more the result of confusion and morale collapse than enemy pressure. The decision to redeploy forces, albeit unavoidable, was not entirely clear and firm in the case of I Corps. President Thieu could not bring himself to give clear-cut orders to the corps commander. Apparently the fiasco in MR-2 weighed heavily on his mind and made him reluctant to play the role of commander in chief again. Instead, being an astute politician, he played on the connotation of words, leaving their interpretation, including implications of his silence, to his confused field commander. President Thieu's order to abandon Hue was issued barely one day after his resolve was made and he had promised in public to hold the "ancient capital city." True to his political instinct, however, President Thieu did not provide a time period for this evacuation.

• • •

The Final Days of MR-2

• • •

The danger of being completely overwhelmed was such that II Corps was compelled to order the 22nd Division, its only coherent combat force, to break contact and fall back to Qui Nhon. On 30 March the 41st and 42nd Regiments disengaged from Binh Khe on orders. The 42nd Regiment commander, Col. Nguyen Huu Thong, was indignant; he pleaded with the division commander not to withdraw. . . . But it was already too late. When the two regiments reached Qui Nhon during the night, they were engaged by enemy troops already entrenched in the city. By this time, most of the population and all local defense forces had fled. The harbor was occupied; so were most of the tall buildings. Qui Nhon was already under virtual control of the NVA 3rd Division. After two days of fighting, the 41st and 42nd Regiments, with naval gunfire support, opened a breach south of the city and assembled on a beach four miles south of the harbor. At 0200 on 1 April three naval ships took aboard what remained of the 22nd Division. The commander of the 42nd Regiment refused to evacuate and committed suicide.

In the meantime, the 47th Regiment had been driven out of Phu Cat Air Base, where it had fallen back only two days earlier. In its withdrawal toward Qui Nhon during the night, it ran into an ambush at Phu Cat district town. Enemy troops had overrun the town just a few hours earlier. The body of the town garrison Regional Force battalion commander still lay in the front yard of the district office; rather than surrender, he had preferred to commit suicide. The 47th lost about half of its troops, and its commander, Colonel Le Cau, also took his life on the very site of the battle. The regiment was totally disrupted. When it was regrouped later at Vung Tau, the 22nd Infantry Division numbered slightly over two thousand men.

• • •

As with other cities and towns of MR-2 during this time, disorder and chaos reigned at Nha Trang. No control existed in the city. The police and local defense forces had begun to disappear into the tide of refugees flowing south. Prisoners broke out of jail and created a chaotic commotion throughout the city by shooting haphazardly with seized weapons. II Corps headquarters was still in Nha Trang on 2 April. Late in the morning, Lieutenant General Pham Quoc Thuan, commandant of the NCO School at Duc My, visited General Phu at corps headquarters. They talked in private for about fifteen minutes, then both went to the Nha Trang Air Base. General Phu boarded his helicopter and flew away in search of his remaining units. He returned to Nha Trang at 1800 and reported to JGS that he was unable to make contact with any unit. Despite JGS orders to organize the defense of the air base in coordination with air force and naval units, General Phu departed by aircraft about thirty minutes later without providing instructions for his staff or the air base commander. He did not return and was admitted to the Cong Hoa General Hospital in Saigon on 4 April. General Phu was by then no longer mentally able to exercise command. Besides, there was practically nothing left for him to command. Disorganized and disheartened by this time, II Corps staff soon evacuated Nha Trang.

• • •

[Then] the entire province of Ninh Thuan fell into Communist hands on 16 April. General Nghi, General Sang of the 6th Air Division, and the commander of the 2nd Airborne Brigade, Colonel Nguyen Thu Luong, were missing in action. The next day the district town of Thien Giao in Binh Thuan Province was overrun, and Phan Thiet fell on 18 April. The entire territory of MR-2 was now under enemy control.

VIII. DEFENSE IN THE SOUTH

On 26 March 1975, General Frederick C. Weyand, US Army chief of staff, arrived in Saigon. General Weyand had served in Vietnam for a long time in many capacities. . . . Because of his long association with our country, he was highly esteemed by Vietnamese military and political leaders. [General Weyand was in Vietnam to evaluate the situation and advise President Ford as to what might be done.]

During his call on JGS there was no formal briefing. General Weyand and I only discussed the situation and exchanged ideas. I told General Weyand about the difficulties we were encountering, and I made a single request: that the US Air Force use its B-52s to bomb enemy troop concentrations and exposed base areas. I thought that if B-52s were made available, the confidence and morale of the population and troops of South Vietnam could be restored. However, General Weyand explained to me that any new US military intervention in Vietnam would have to be authorized by the US Congress, and there was little chance our request would be approved.

General Weyand's delegation and the US ambassador then attended an official meeting with President Thieu at the Independence Palace. During this meeting the US delegation brought up the following points:

- The government should explain the situation to the people so they would not be confused by the falsehoods spread by the enemy. Vietnamese leaders should make more personal appearances on TV.

- JGS should receive greater authority.
- JGS should seek a victory, even a small one, to help facilitate the request for the $300 million additional aid. The Communist 5th Division in the Parrot's Beak area west of Duc Hue offered an excellent target.
- The problem of war refugees should be solved. Particular attention should be given to military dependents. They should be moved out of areas where battles were likely to be fought.

All the problems pertaining to the government and the population were discussed by the president and Prime Minister Khiem on one side and the US delegation on the other. The question of handing over more authority to the JGS, however, was not considered because it was a sensitive subject. Only President Thieu could solve that problem if he desired. From the military point of view, I fully agreed we needed a victory, but, for the time being, there was no unit prepared to launch an operation to destroy the NVA 5th Division. This would have to await an appropriate opportunity. I also reiterated the emphasis we placed on the use of B-52s to destroy concentrations of enemy units. This would have an excellent effect on the morale of Vietnamese troops and the population.

• • •

Evacuating military dependents from embattled areas might boomerang. In the absence of their families, in the 1968 Tet Offensive in particular, and at remote outposts, there were instances when wives and children had given effective support in resupplying ammunition, evacuating the wounded, and even firing machineguns.

• • •

The Situation in MR-3

• • •

The enemy force around Bien Hoa and Saigon during the last days amounted to 15 NVA infantry divisions, augmented and supported by a sapper division, an artillery division, some armor brigades, and SAM antiaircraft units.

The enemy offensive was conducted on four different fronts, on each by a force equivalent to a three-division army corps. To confront this impressive force, III Corps could muster only three organic divisions—the 5th, 25th, and 18th; the 3rd Armor Brigade; three ranger groups; and a brigade of the Airborne Division.

• • •

Intelligence reports indicated that the enemy was pressing toward Saigon from many directions. Each advancing corps included two or three main-force divisions supported by artillery and armor. In the meantime, the friendly military situation deteriorated rapidly in the wake of President Thieu's resignation on 21 April 1975. Profiting from the political upheaval in Saigon and the general confusion and low morale among the population and troops, the enemy launched an all-out effort against Bien Hoa from the south and the southeast on 26 April.

• • •

IX. THE LAST DAYS

The loss of Ban Me Thuot and the failure of the Kontum-Pleiku withdrawal caused a significant political upheaval in Saigon. Elements of the underground political opposition came into the open and held meetings to voice their antigovernment feelings. The government moved in and, on 27 March 1975, arrested a number of people suspected of plotting a coup. About the same time, President Thieu instructed his prime minister to form a new cabinet. Given the deteriorating situation, probings and consultations took a long time and ran into insurmountable obstacles. All political personalities who were willing to join the cabinet demanded impossible conditions. Opposition political circles all held President Thieu personally responsible for the tragic military situation. They believed he was no longer able to lead the country out of its predicament. After more than a week of unfruitful consultations, Prime Minister Khiem finally resigned. He gave as the reason for his action the need to allow broader cabinet participation by other political elements.

On 2 April 1975, during an ordinary session, the Senate adopted a resolution with 42 votes for and about 10 against, holding President Thieu responsible for the deteriorating situation and asking him to take immediate steps to form a broader cabinet. Rumors spread at once about a possible coalition government which Mr. Tran Van Lam and Mr. Tran Van Do were willing to lead. But nothing materialized; presumably the idea was rejected by President Thieu.

Three days later, on 5 April, Mr. Nguyen Ba Can, Speaker of the House of Representatives, was designated as the new prime minister. On 8 April, a South Vietnamese F-5 bomber bombed the Independence Palace. This was the first time the new palace had been bombed. (The old palace was attacked in 1960 by an Air Force A-1 Skyraider during Mr. Ngo Dinh Diem's presidency.) Rumors again circulated that the fate of South Vietnam had been decided and that the great powers had agreed to give North Vietnam a free hand in unifying the country. It was speculated that, to save what we could, the government should send a plenipotentiary to Paris and ask the French government to act as official intermediary in negotiations about to be conducted with the Communists. The deadline for such a move was rumored to be 7 April, later extended to 10 April. Deputy Prime Minister Tran Van Don, back from a liaison mission to the United States, reported the same thing to the president on 5 April. But President Thieu appeared incredulous.

• • •

The military situation deteriorated with every passing day, although JGS made every effort to provide support for the field command and to reorganize and refit all battered units for immediate redeployment.

Demands that President Thieu should resign and transfer his powers at once to General Duong Van Minh were resurrected in earnest. A coalition government led by General Minh, it was contended, stood a good chance of being accepted by the Communists; if so, more bloodshed could be averted. On Monday, 21 April, during a meeting at the Independence Palace, President Thieu announced his decision to step down. He insinuated that the

United States wanted his resignation and that, whether or not he consented, certain generals would press for it. He said he hoped that his move would help bring true peace to the country and military aid for the armed forces. As required by the constitution, he was prepared to transfer the presidency to Vice President Tran Van Huong. Finally, he asked the armed forces and the National Police to fully support the new president.

In the evening of 21 April 1975, the televised transfer ceremony took place at the Independence Palace. In his farewell speech, intended for the government and the population, President Thieu made a detailed analysis of the situation and the reasons for his resignation. For the first time he admitted having ordered the evacuation of Pleiku and Kontum because, he said, it was the inevitable course of action to take in the face of the deteriorating situation; but he also insisted that the generals had failed him.

The question most asked, then and now, concerns possible pressures behind President Thieu's resignation. Was it a decision he had made entirely on his own? In his testimony before the Investigations Subcommittee of the House International Relations Committee on 27 January 1976, Ambassador Graham Martin affirmed that he played no significant role in persuading Mr. Thieu to resign. But he also confirmed that during a conversation with President Thieu on 20 April he gave the president intelligence gathered by USDAO and CIA concerning the balance of forces at the time: "I said it was my conclusion that almost all of his generals, although they would continue to fight, believed defense was hopeless unless a respite could be gained through the beginning of the negotiating process. . . . And they did not believe such a process could begin unless the President left or took steps to see that the process began immediately. . . . I said it was my feelings [sic] that if he did not move soon, his generals would ask him to go."[4]

Ambassador Martin emphasized the personal character of his opinions. He was speaking to President Thieu, as he put it, "only as an individual, not for the President or the Secretary of State, or even as the American Ambassador."

As to the "generals would ask him to go" in Ambassador Martin's opinion, I am certain that on our side there was absolutely no pressure from any general to force him to resign.

• • •

President Huong was intent on seeking General Duong Van Minh's participation in the government. He extended an invitation, which was quickly declined by General Minh, who demanded large powers for himself. General Minh had long been advised by a leftist military and political staff. His ambition had always been to become president himself, and he had hoped to be handed the presidency by President Thieu. Although rumors persisted that the Communists were willing to negotiate a political arrangement only with General Minh, Mr. Huong, a believer in constitutional government, did not choose to transfer his presidency to General Minh without the consent of the Congress.

In the meantime, the military situation became increasingly bad. In the afternoon of Sunday, 27 April 1975, the defense minister, Mr. Tran Van Don, led a military delegation composed of general officers of JGS and the commander of CMD in an appearance before a meeting of both houses of Congress. By 1930 [hours], 138 senators and representatives were present. Mr. Don summarized the military situation: Saigon was now surrounded by 15 enemy divisions under the control of three army corps. The Saigon–Vung Tau highway had been cut, and enemy troops were advancing toward the Long Binh base. At 2020 the General Assembly voted (136–2) to hand over the presidency to General Duong Van Minh. The next day, Monday, 28 April 1975, at 1730, General Minh was sworn in as president.[5]

• • •

On one occasion when he met with me after 21 April 1975, General Minh boasted he used to keep in constant touch with the other side by radio. It was a fact he could not disclose before for fear of arrest, but it was all right to tell me now. So he firmly believed that a government with him at the head would be acceptable to the Communists and that they would be willing to negotiate with him for a political solution. This was also why a large number of military officers and civil servants of all ranks elected to stay behind to work for the new government. With the hope they could play some role in the new administration, some people even came back to Saigon with their families after living in foreign countries for several years. As it turned out, North Vietnam had changed its mind. I understand that by late March the US Embassy in Saigon had received reports from one of its agents who had penetrated the Communist Central Office for South Vietnam that North Vietnam was inclined toward a military victory rather than a political arrangement.

General Minh waited in vain for a favorable word from the other side, but nothing came. The response of the Communists was ominous: they bombed Tan Son Nhut Air Base the moment he was sworn in and shelled Saigon barely twelve hours later. Still a last-ditch effort was attempted by General Minh's people to contact the Communists through their representative at Tan Son Nhut. But the answer was evasive and intimidating. It was then that General Minh realized his hope was gone. He gave in to all Communist demands.

General Minh personally admitted he had been duped by the Communists. He advised his closest aide and his son-in-law, Colonel Nguyen Hong Dai, to leave Vietnam. But General Minh was not the only one to be duped. Several other credulous Vietnamese were unable to leave because it was too late by the time they realized what had happened. Among those who elected to stay, however, a few military officers, civil servants, and artists, writers, etc., were treated well and given good positions in the new Communist government because of their past connections and service to the underground Communists. And so we came to realize how deficient our security services, both military and civilian, had been in their effort to prevent penetration by Communists and their agents.

The Evacuation

The people who advocated appeasement and coalition with the Communists believed that an immediate cease-fire—certainly within twenty-four hours—would follow General Minh's inauguration. But for others who had never compromised with the Communists and for whom a coalition meant certain death, the inauguration was a signal to pack and leave. For these people, the die-hard anti-Communists, a chapter of Vietnamese history had closed. It was a chapter written with the blood shed by hundreds of thousands of soldiers for a cause in which they believed. Even after President Thieu had stepped down, most of these people—among them the military officers and civil servants who had served under his regime and leadership—still hoped to carry on the struggle. They were certainly not Thieu's followers; they simply wanted to serve the cause for which they had been fighting. Now that an entirely new chapter had begun, they felt this was no place for them; it was better to leave it to those who believed they could compromise with the Communists.

The plan for evacuating American personnel and selected Vietnamese citizens must have been thoroughly worked out by the US Embassy in Saigon and based on lessons learned from the disorder and difficulties encountered during the evacuation of refugees from Danang and Nha Trang. Any contingency plans which existed were entirely airtight and were carefully kept that way. On the Vietnamese side, neither the civilian government nor the military knew anything officially about these plans. The details remained secret. No one was told, for instance, how many people the US Embassy planned to evacuate, what means were available to transport them, what procedures would be employed, or where or when the evacuees were supposed to meet for the journey. The military had only personal contacts, chiefly with US counterparts, who almost without exception advised them to evacuate their families ahead of time.

The dilemma then facing the military was that the ban on overseas travel was still being enforced. If a serviceman were to leave the country, he would become a deserter. Civilians who left would be charged with illegal exit. On the other hand, since the evacuation facilities were not under Vietnamese control, no one knew for certain how many refugees would be accommodated, where the final destination would be, and what formalities or papers were needed. As a result, JGS did not issue any instructions concerning the evacuation. It was understood, however, that the number of evacuees was limited and highly selective. Those who were selected would be contacted by US personnel and given proper guidance. This was in general what we on the Vietnamese side learned of the American plans.

Only later did it become known that the contingency plan for the evacuation had been worked out by the US Embassy and DAO with the assistance of CINCPAC. The plan, code-named Talon Vise, was constantly updated to reflect requirements and assets available. It also envisaged the possibility of employing aircraft and a US ground force for protection and security. The main concern, as it was learned from Ambassador Martin's later testimony, was to avoid chaos-causing frenzy. The goal was to extricate all American citizens, Vietnamese nationals related to them, and those Vietnamese citizens whose lives would be endangered if they stayed behind. The total number of evacuees falling into the last category was ultimately fixed at 50,000 on 25 April, as Ambassador Martin later testified.

• • •

This is what actually happened: "High-risk" Vietnamese contacted were to furnish a list of relatives whom they wanted to have evacuated. After approval by the US

Embassy or DAO, a rendezvous point was given and evacuees were told to bring along only a hand bag per person for valuable objects or articles of utmost necessity. At the rendezvous point the evacuees were picked up by a bus and driven to the DAO compound. Here they were assigned to large waiting rooms. The planes used in the evacuation airlift, large cargo types such as C-141s or C-130s, would usually arrive late in the afternoon and park at the end of the runways at Tan Son Nhut, far from the airport facilities. When evening came, usually at about 1900 or 2000, well-screened buses would take those evacuees whose names appeared on a manifest, and who had been waiting in the DAO compound, directly to the planes. The police and military security personnel knew about these movements but did not interfere, since their own families were among the evacuees. So the evacuees simply boarded the waiting planes, without going through the formalities normally required by the Ministry of Interior and without any control whatsoever by airport authorities. In other words, as far as the government was concerned, it was an illegal exit. The airlift would continue throughout the night and stop by early morning, only to be resumed in the evening. It went well until 28 April, and was only suspended for good as of 29 April when Tan Son Nhut Air Base was rendered unusable by heavy shelling and bombing.

During the last two days, 29 and 30 April, the US Embassy managed to evacuate about 11,600 additional people by helicopter and by barge. Also a number of fishermen living in coastal areas, and those refugees who made their way out by ships and boats, were picked up by the US 7th Fleet offshore. Judging from the effectiveness with which the evacuation was carried out, the number of people evacuated could have been much higher if there had been more time and if the circumstances had been different.

But, all in all, the evacuation of 130,000 Vietnamese was an admirable feat in itself, comparable in every respect to a successful military operation. This was a far cry from what had happened at Danang, Nha Trang, and even Phnom Penh.

Saigon

By 25 April the enemy's pressure seemed to be enveloping the entire Capital Military District, and his efforts against Saigon were stepped up from many directions.

• • •

Enemy advance elements had already made probing attacks on the outskirts of Saigon. During the night of 26 April sappers simultaneously attacked the Newport complex, the Bien Hoa highway bridge nearby, and the telecommunications terminal complex at Phu Lam.

• • •

On the following night, 27 April, all Regional Force and Popular Force outposts along the East Vam Co River in Hau Nghia Province were attacked and overrun, thus exposing the entire western flank of Saigon to enemy penetration and attack.

• • •

Saigon was thus completely surrounded and now lay within range of the enemy's 130mm guns.

• • •

From 0400 on 29 April, the JGS compound, Tan Son Nhut Air Base, and the Navy headquarters on Bach Dang Quay were shelled intermittently. The JGS compound and Bach Dang Quay sustained only minor damage, but the destruction at Tan Son Nhut Air Base was extensive. Parking areas, fuel dumps, ammunition dumps were all hit. Fires and explosions occurred at several places. The DAO headquarters (old MACV compound) was also hit but suffered only slight physical damage. Two US Marine guards were fatally wounded.

• • •

At 0900 on 29 April the Tan Son Nhut Air Base was bombarded a second time. Damage was extensive. Aircraft in parking areas, including A-37s and in particular four C-130s already loaded with bombs, were hit and exploded. Fires spread rapidly at every place. The airbase was completely out of operation and in disorder. Over 3,000 people who had been there since the day before (28 April) to wait for US evacuation aircraft in the area behind the DAO compound became terrified and frantically fled the base. By 1000 Air Force headquarters was no longer in control of its personnel. In the air, waves of US helicopters swirled and hovered about tall buildings and in the DAO compound evacuating US personnel. It was hard to distinguish US from South Vietnamese helicopters.

• • •

Meanwhile, the Thanh Tuy Ha ammunition depot was badly hit and disintegrated in violent explosions. Contact with the depot was lost at 1300. Enemy tanks by now had appeared at Cat Lai and were firing at the ammunition unloading pier. Completely surrounded and isolated, left without support and without reinforcement, the Capital Military District was waiting helplessly to be conquered.

President Minh gave twenty-four hours for all US personnel to leave Vietnam. The evacuation proceeded feverishly throughout the night and was over at 0500 on 30 April. At 1000 on 30 April 1975 President Minh ordered our armed forces to stop fighting. And South Vietnam came under Communist control and no longer existed as a free nation.

X. CONCLUSIONS AND OBSERVATIONS

South Vietnam was lost to the Communists. After thirty years of test and trial on the Vietnam battlefield, their kind of war—whether called guerrilla war, revolutionary war, people's war, or war of liberation—finally prevailed. This should be a warning to other countries that more Vietnams are in store for the future. Conquered one by one, non-Communist countries are being gradually reduced in number to the extent that some day, perhaps, there will remain only the United States and three or four other powers surrounded by a much greater number of Communist or Communist-leaning countries. It is a somber prospect that we will probably face in the coming decades if we fail to realize the deficiencies and mistakes of the past and come up with a new line of conduct for the future.

Having read the previous chapters, the thoughtful reader should be able to see for himself some of the reasons for the collapse of South Vietnam. Some causes that this monograph points out, explicitly or implicitly, are, as the author saw them:

1. South Vietnam had to accept an agreement which was much too disadvantageous to its survival: The Paris Agreement tilted the balance of power to the Communist side and gave North Vietnam a free hand to launch its offensive in 1975.
2. The pledge given by a US president to react with vigor and which South Vietnam regarded as a national commitment could not be honored by the administration which succeeded him, even when Communist violations were blatant.
3. The unexpected huge slash in US military aid for South Vietnam seriously affected the combat capability and morale of its troops and population.
4. President Thieu made a strategic decision too late for it to have any chance of success, although he acted out of necessity. The withdrawal of II Corps forces was too hasty and disorderly, resulting in the rapid collapse of I Corps and II Corps.
5. South Vietnamese leaders failed to realize that US policy had shifted toward appeasement and accommodation with the Communists, even at the price of reneging on a commitment to help an ally maintain independence. Therefore, they could not adjust to the realities of the post-agreement period, but continued to stake South Vietnam's fate on the elusive and the impossible.

Finally, after many years of continuous war, South Vietnam was approaching political and economic bankruptcy. National unity no longer existed; no one was able to rally the people behind the national cause. Riddled by corruption and sometimes ineptitude and dereliction, the government hardly responded to the needs of a public which had gradually lost confidence in it. Despite rosy plans and projects, the national economy continued its course downward and appeared doomed short of a miracle. Under these conditions, the South Vietnamese social fabric gradually disintegrated, influenced in part by mistrust, divisiveness, uncertainty, and defeatism, until the whole nation appeared to some to resemble a rotten fruit ready to fall at the first passing breeze.

Aside from these major causes, there were of course other reasons to which the total failure can be attributed, reasons whose interplay in the areas of politics, economics, military action, and diplomacy can be traced far back in time. At the end of World War II, the American leadership of the free world could hardly be contested. But, as far as Vietnam in particular and Southeast Asia in general were concerned, US foreign policy shifted many times after 1945, beginning with a virtual absence of policy, then reaching a climax of involvement in a hot anti-Communist confrontation, and finally receding by installments toward accommodation. This change necessarily affected aid policies and the conduct of the war in this part of the world.

• • •

Defense Secretary Melvin R. Laird was critical of the former administration's policy: "From a standpoint of American defense policy, a real tragedy of Vietnam is that

Vietnamization was not started much earlier than 1969, through a policy of deliberately training and equipping the South Vietnamese forces to fight effectively against North Vietnam as well as to cope with internal security problems caused by Viet Cong activity. Such opportunities existed throughout the 1960's (and not just in Vietnam). Apparently, the opportunities were set aside in favor of decisions to introduce substantial American involvements in all phases of the war."[6]

The basic infantry rifle, AR-15, later called M-16, was a case in point. The AR-15 was tested in Vietnam as early as 1964. The Vietnamese Airborne Brigade considered it an excellent weapon: light, easy to maintain, and accurate. The small cartridge could be carried in greater quantity by the infantryman, and the bullet had great penetrating and devastating power due to its high velocity; in sum, it was a rifle tailored for the Vietnamese soldier and the Vietnamese battlefield. However, only a little over two hundred such rifles were brought over for actual use. The M-16 became the basic individual weapon of Republic of Vietnam Armed Forces (RVNAF) infantry years later, after the Communists had dramatically demonstrated the superiority of their AK-47s during the Tet Offensive of 1968. The same was true of other weapons. Our troops were equipped with M-72 anti-tank rocket launchers and later with TOW missiles only after the Communists had begun to use their highly effective B-40s and B-41s. And only when Communist T-54 tanks and 130mm guns appeared on the battlefield did we receive any M-48 tanks and self-propelled 175mm guns. These were only a few examples concerning army weapons.

• • •

On the South Vietnamese side, the conduct of the war was largely defensive. Our goal was to contain Communist expansion within the national territory, and there was no question of an offensive to carry the war into North Vietnam. Only on two occasions did we cross the border and strike into enemy bases in Cambodia and Laos, but even these operations were merely part of the defense and were never prescribed by a continued and deliberate strategy. The primary mission of our armed forces was always to pacify (that is, control) the national territory, hence a twofold strategy: pacification in populated areas and search-and-destroy operations to eliminate major Communist forces in unpopulated areas. Throughout the war, this defensive strategy kept us constantly striving to catch up with an enemy who always held the initiative, whether in tactics or in weaponry.

• • •

The war in Vietnam . . . ceased to be what many people erroneously called a "civil war." In its final stages it became a conventional war of aggression fought with abundant supplies of modern weapons and equipment provided by the Communist bloc. It was a war conceived, planned, conducted, and led by Communist North Vietnam behind screens labeled National Liberation Front and Provisional Revolutionary Government of South Vietnam.

• • •

Attempts to respect certain democratic principles hampered the war effort of a nation struggling for survival. It was forbidden, for example, to take forceful or "antidemocratic" measures to solve problems of national discipline, mobilization, desertion, or draft evasion, or for that matter problems of political life in general such as defeatist opposition or pro-Communism. There were many deficiencies in our control and neutralization of pro-Communist elements who lived and freely mingled with our own people. Even some relatives and dependents of high-ranking Communist cadres lived in peace and freedom in the areas under governmental control. And, after the collapse, some journalists, artists, politicians, and military officers who stayed behind were given responsible positions by the Communists. To my thinking, in all its actions, decisions, and policies, a nation at war should first strive to deal effectively and conclusively with the war. War is priority number one; all other problems are of lesser importance.

• • •

In general, the Communists enjoyed a solid rear area whose stability and security were maintained through the totalitarian, party-controlled measures of a police state.

• • •

In Vietnam during the period of active American participation . . . we never achieved unity of command and thus violated one of the basic principles of war. . . . The substitute principles of cooperation and coordination through understanding and good will as applied at all levels brought about good results because commanders deliberately avoided clashes. Although certain minor clashes occurred due to personalities, misunderstandings, or complexities, they were largely insignificant. But without a single command, our war effort suffered from inadequate will, delayed decisions, and inefficient use of abilities and resources.

• • •

Beginning in 1968, we started to get more intelligence, and it was more accurate than before. Similarly in logistics, our structure was expanded and modernized to respond more effectively to the requirements of all combat units in supply, maintenance, and other services.

• • •

The Communists clearly realized that, as long as the United States kept its military aid at a certain level, South Vietnam would be able to stand and fight. So they went all out and found effective ways to stop that aid. This was one of their most devastating blows, because it struck at the very foundation of the war itself. All the propaganda machinery of North Vietnam went into motion, echoed and amplified by the press and huge propaganda apparatus of the entire Communist bloc. Their worldwide machinations justified their kind of war, on the one hand, and effectively distorted understanding of our war effort on the other. To the people of the United States and the world at large, the war fought by our side was made to appear as an inhuman and evil war and the government of South Vietnam as an inept and corrupt administration deserving no aid.[7]

The American press, many of whose papers were inclined against the war, did not do much to counter this. The cause for which we fought, therefore, was either largely ignored or falsely portrayed. In addition, very vocal antiwar groups in America helped drown out the voices of reason and truth. One of these groups, the Indochina Resource

Center which Ambassador Martin referred to in his House testimony, was an association of college professors, bishops, pastors, and nuns who circulated the infamous "pastoral letter" appealing for peace in Vietnam by ending all military aid.

Communist propaganda also played to the psychological inclinations and moods of the American public, reinforcing antiwar sentiments and the belief that the Vietnam War was a hopeless [venture] that might drag on forever. Out of disenchantment and desperation, American students and youths were roused into violent antiwar demonstration. Moved and spurred by such actions and feelings, the US Congress took steps to end US military involvement and later to reduce military aid for South Vietnam. After the first Indochina War, people said with conviction that the French lost the war in Paris; we can now say with equal justice that the Vietnam War was lost in America.

Our enemy was determined, persistent, and experienced. This is a fact we cannot in all honesty deny. During his long years of struggle, a single, continuous, and unchanging politico-military strategy dictated his conduct of the war. His constant goal was to "liberate," that is, conquer, South Vietnam and unify the country through phases of a people's or revolutionary war in which his military forces played the decisive role. From time to time resolutions adopted after important party meetings influenced certain war activities and sometimes modified them, but they always pointed in the same general direction, the same conduct for the war.

• • •

The Communists never worried about their losses. Every military objective was as good as any other, provided their political objective could be attained.

• • •

Communist weaknesses and failures were well concealed and never successfully exploited by our side. In general, Communist troops were trained only to fight well-rehearsed battles. They were at a loss when initiative and quick reaction were required to confront a new situation or a surprise. But every mistake they made became an object of systematic self-criticism and was corrected in due course. Their tenacity and willingness to learn paid off handsomely.

By contrast, on our side we never learned enough from past experience and never knew how to exploit our successes and achievements, which often went unrecognized. My own contention is that, given the advantageous military position we enjoyed after the 1968 Tet Offensive, if we had pursued our successes by more forceful exploiting actions and larger-scale counterattacks, the Vietnam War could have been resolved then and there. It was common knowledge that the Communists had by then become entirely exhausted; indeed, it took them four years to recover their combat capability. Once, according to an unverified source, B-52s struck the Central Office for South Vietnam and disrupted this Communist nerve center. Unfortunately, we were not able to exploit this success.

The advantages and disadvantages, strengths and weaknesses of both sides added up to the final collapse of South Vietnam. We can still learn from it and devise a sound policy for the future, but some day it will be too late: the Communist challenge is always there.

NOTES

1. The commitment of the Airborne and the Marine Divisions in MR-1 had left the Joint General Staff . . . without any general reserve for the first time in the war.

2. Bernard Kalb and Marvin Kalb, *Kissinger* (Boston: Little, Brown and Co., 1974), pp. 183–184.

3. Ibid., p. 354.

4. "The Vietnam-Cambodia Emergency, 1975," Part III—Vietnam Evacuation: Testimony of Ambassador Graham A. Martin (Hearing before the Special Subcommittee on Investigations of the Committee on International Relations, House of Representatives, 94th Congress, Second Session, 27 January 1976), pp. 546–547.

5. Before President Huong stepped down, he issued a decree relieving me of my position as Chairman of the Joint General Staff. It was then up to the new president to appoint my replacement. I designated Lieutenant General Don Van Khuyen, my chief of staff, as acting chairman of the JGS and left Vietnam on Monday afternoon, 28 April 1975, for the 7th Fleet.

6. "The Nixon Doctrine: From Potential Despair to New Opportunities," speech delivered by Secretary of Defense Melvin R. Laird.

7. [Note omitted.]

17

Reflections on the Vietnam War

General Cao Van Vien and Lieutenant General Dong Van Khuyen

PREFACE

The Vietnam War was an unusual and complex experience. Directed and sustained by Communist North Vietnam under the label of national liberation, it combined the elements of insurgency and conventional warfare. It began with guerrilla tactics, but developed into and concluded with open invasion. Basically, however, it remained an ideological conflict whose ultimate outcome depended on popular participation and support.

The requirements to fight this war were multiple and challenging. Counterinsurgency demanded that we mobilize our resources to strengthen the regime, protect the people and obtain their allegiance, root out the enemy infrastructure, and extend our armed forces to maintain security over the national territory. All this had to be done in the midst of mounting political dissent and social divisiveness. To meet the threat of large-scale conventional attacks, we had to contend with enemy sanctuaries in neighboring countries, the inhospitable terrain of our extensive borders, and uninterrupted infiltration. However, our efforts were greatly restrained by limited forces and prevailing policies.

To analyze critically the chain of events which shaped the final outcome of the war in order to learn from our failures and successes, we have drawn primarily on our first-hand knowledge of major events and our personal involvement in the conduct of war efforts. We hope that in addressing the salient points raised in all previous monographs of this series with fresh insights, our work will be able to provide a critical, comprehensive view of the war experience on the South Vietnam side. . . . [Cao Van Vien and Dong Van Khuyen, 20 December 1978]

I. NATION BUILDING AND INSURGENCY: 1954–1963

The Geneva Agreements of 1954, which put an end to the French–Viet Minh War in Indochina, split Vietnam into two parts along the Ben Hai River at the 17th parallel, intended as a temporary demarcation line. Close to one million North Vietnamese inhabitants chose to migrate south where, together with the southern-born people and the

National Army of Vietnam, they expected to build a new nation. With the direct support provided by the United States, South Vietnam was to become a free republic devoted to the anti-Communist cause.

Soon after its regrouping from above the 17th parallel, the French Expeditionary Corps began to leave South Vietnam, and French authorities also turned over full sovereignty to the nationalist government led by Mr. Ngo Dinh Diem. The French Military Mission, which advised the Vietnamese National Army, was replaced by a joint US-French training mission (TRIM) until 28 April 1956, when the French High Command in Indochina was disbanded, marking the end of French involvement in South Vietnam. From that day onwards, the US Military Assistance Advisory Group, Vietnam (MAAG-V), took over the mission of training, reorganizing, and advising South Vietnam's armed forces.

Concept of Defense

The US military strategy in Southeast Asia at that juncture was no doubt heavily influenced by the US war experience in Korea during 1951–1953. In helping South Vietnam reorganize its national defense, MAAG-V therefore propounded the concept of deploying conventional infantry forces in depth from the Demilitarized Zone (DMZ) southward to face the eventuality of overt aggression from the North. As conceived by MAAG-V, the primary mission of the Vietnamese National Army in this defense posture was to fight a delaying action in case of invasion pending a direct intervention by SEATO forces.

South Vietnam's military authorities fully concurred with this defense concept. However, they did not regard it as the only strategic approach to meeting the Communist threat. Based on their experience during the early period of the Resistance War, and the subsequent fight against the Viet Minh alongside French forces, South Vietnamese military leaders also advanced the concept of territorial or area defense as a complement to conventional force deployment. This concept envisaged the division of the RVN territory into areas of defense, each to be placed under the control of a territorial command whose responsibility was to coordinate all military activities designed to maintain security within its area of responsibility. To fulfill this mission, each territorial command was given control authority over all military, paramilitary, and police forces assigned, to include mobile intervention units attached to it by the regular army.

MAAG-V authorities concurred in part with this territorial defense concept when they initially approved the RVNAF force structure to be composed of two elements: strike units (field divisions) and area defense units (light divisions and separate territorial regiments). In time, however, they rejected this concept altogether. MAAG-V therefore devoted its advisory efforts and all military assistance resources to organizing, training, and equipping the RVNAF as a conventional, anti-invasion military force.

The conventional war of aggression that MAAG-V strategists had assumed, and for which they had helped South Vietnam build its defense, did not materialize when the first signs of Communist aggression were detected. North Vietnam must have learned a lesson from the Korean War. It had seen how an overt act of aggression had failed in the face of determined and concerted reaction by the Free World under US leadership. Taking advantage of its strong point, which had proved successful against the French, North Vietnam began to wage people's or insurgency warfare with the purpose of seizing control in the South. Toward that end, Hanoi had reactivated the local Viet Minh infrastructure and guerrilla elements which had remained behind in 1954 and, at the same time, reinfiltrated the southern-born Viet Minh cadres and troops who had regrouped to the North and received insurgency training there.

During the initial phase of insurgency, the underground Communists employed every subversive tactic in an attempt to control the resource-rich and populous rural areas. These were precisely the areas which had not received adequate attention in the RVN defense system.

Not until 1961 did MAAG-V realize that, to ensure proper protection for South Vietnam and save it from a Communist takeover, the country's defense should be founded not only on its capability to face an invasion from the outside, but also on its ability to maintain security within the national borders. From this awareness, a compromise concept combining anti-invasion defense and territorial security began to evolve. But six years had elapsed and were irretrievably lost. Had the area defense concept been properly emphasized from the beginning, South Vietnam's defense efforts in terms of training and force structure organization could have been more equitably distributed between anti-invasion and territorial security capabilities. And if, at the start of Communist insurgency, South Vietnam had had adequate territorial forces to maintain effective security, especially in vital areas, then perhaps its general posture by 1961 would have been much better.

Organization and Training

• • •

As security continued to deteriorate, the GVN felt an acute need to improve effectiveness in controlling and coordinating territorial military activities, especially in MR-1 (which encompassed then the territory of former Cochinchina), whose headquarters was overburdened by the increased tempo of insurgency. In 1960, therefore, the GVN decided to reduce MR-1's span of territorial control by creating MR-5—with its headquarters at Can Tho—which was assigned responsibility for the Mekong Delta. As a result, South Vietnam had four military regions, each directly responsible for from 5 to 16 sectors or provinces.

In spite of its leverage in dispensing military aid, MAAG-V did not pressure the GVN into disbanding the territorial control system which it disavowed, apparently because of political sensitivities. In keeping with its original defense concept, MAAG-V concentrated instead on developing the Army of the Republic of Vietnam (ARVN) and consolidating the ARVN command and control system. These efforts resulted successively in the activation of seven infantry divisions by 1957, a field command in 1958, and three corps headquarters in 1959.

According to many South Vietnamese military authorities, however, the ARVN field command was not a MAAG-V-sponsored product. They believed that its activation had been motivated by internal politics. In any event, from its inception to 1964, when it was finally disbanded, the ARVN field command accomplished nothing significant in connection with combat operations. Moreover, it was criticized as being a holding area where military officers who were distrusted by the regime marked their idle time.

The activation of corps headquarters, however, received wide acceptance among the RVNAF. Most authorities regarded it as the hallmark of South Vietnam's coming of age in terms of military growth. Aside from national pride, the GVN also felt gratified by the additional support assets these army corps provided, despite the possibility that their activation would upset and complicate the existing territorial command and control system.

Indeed, this soon proved to be a substantial impediment to effective command and control. The difficulties stemmed from the fact that each corps was assigned the same area of responsibility as a military region, and from the lack of directives defining the respective authority of a corps and a military region commander, and the relationship between them with regard to common problems of defense and security. Both the corps and the military region commander, therefore, seemed to enjoy an equal authority, since both were equally responsible to the JGS. This situation gave rise to duplication of responsibility and overlapping of authority between the corps and the military region commander which inevitably entailed jealousy and conflict. Both felt equally responsible for the maintenance of security and equally empowered to employ military forces assigned to their area for that task. Each also reported directly to the JGS, and even to the commander in chief (president), for every event that occurred within his area of responsibility.

The victims of this confusion were the infantry division commandeers, caught between their direct superior, the corps commander, and the territorial chief; they could not satisfy the demands of one without incurring the wrath of the other. If a division commander failed, for example, to make his units available for territorial security duties at the request of the military region commander, his uncooperativeness could be reported to the president. On the other hand, if he met the military region commander's request, he risked reprimand by the corps commander for insubordination.

The realignment of territorial organization during 1961–1962—which saw the deactivation of military region headquarters and the addition of another corps, each responsible for a corps tactical zone (CTZ)—effectively resolved difficulties in command and control. This was in essence a compromise of defense concepts which offended neither [the] MAAG-V nor the JGS, since it provided for territorial control at the region and subregion level through the creation of division tactical areas (DTA) without impeding unity of command. Still, being a compromise, this solution seemed to please neither, especially the JGS.

To the RVN authorities, the deactivation of military region headquarters and assigning territorial responsibilities to corps, and the half-hearted revival of the old subregion organization by making infantry divisions responsible for it, indicated a certain reluctance on the part of MAAG-V authorities to regard territorial security as a truly [fundamental] task. Indeed, [the] MAAG-V seemed oblivious to the fact that the problem of territorial security encompassed much more than just combat activities. By its permanent nature, the task of maintaining territorial security involved innumerable administrative and support activities designed to sustain combat actions on a continuous basis, which only a permanent territorial organization could provide. Tactical activities were essentially temporary; they flowed and ebbed, and they might even cease altogether during certain periods of lull. While tactical units—corps and divisions—could be redeployed at will, depending on requirements, those forces responsible for territorial security could not. This was both dictated by the nature of a war in which enemy attacks were usually unpredictable and the strategic necessity to exert a constant military pressure on the enemy in order to counterbalance his protracted warfare and guerrilla tactics.

A territorial control system therefore had to be construed as the backbone of the counterinsurgency war machinery, the mainstay of tactical forces on which their performance and effectiveness necessarily depended. Consequently we believe that, in the first place, the importance of territorial security should have been correctly assessed and given proper priority within the framework of counterinsurgency efforts. Once this [fundamental] condition had been met, it ensued that American and South Vietnamese authorities should be able to face the defense problem squarely and explore it in depth in order to take proper, realistic actions. We are convinced that, at that early stage of the war, the activation of army corps was not a real necessity, and that efforts should have been devoted instead to consolidating the territorial defense system and making it effective.

• • •

The deployment of infantry divisions for the defense and protection of populous and resource-rich areas was certainly a logical move. However, the assignment of permanent tactical areas of responsibility (DTAs) to divisions, and burdening division headquarters with territorial duties, appeared to be too much of an expediency to suit a protracted war. Moreover, this affected the mobility of infantry divisions, which were designed to operate as strike forces, and the fact that these mobile units stayed in a certain area for a long time made their extrication extremely painful and damaging because of the physical and psychological void they would leave behind in that area. Definitely, the confinement of all nine ARVN infantry divisions to permanent areas of responsibility was not a satisfactory solution to the problem of territorial security.

• • •

The best solution, in our judgment, would have been to realign our territorial organization into seven or nine military regions, each controlling from five to seven sectors. The best employment of our nine infantry divisions would have been to maintain them in a general reserve status and alternately assign them, as required, to military regions for the conduct of pacification operations within a specific and temporary area of tactical responsibility.

• • •

During this period the double subordination of technical services—to the Ministry of Defense command-wise and to the JGS support-wise—caused numerous difficulties in coordination and combat support, making both slow and ineffective. This situation seemed to be perpetrated by political motives. The directors of these services generally outranked the JGS staff division chiefs; most also enjoyed the trust and esteem of the regime, being themselves affiliates of political organizations loyal to Mr. Diem. As a result, they did not have much respect for the JGS or its authority.

Top-level defense organizations abounded. There were policy-making bodies, such as the National Security Council (NSC) and the Ministry of Defense (MOD) and, under them, the Permanent Secretariat of Defense (PSOD) and the JGS. But no one among them was entrusted with real authority, and their services were seldom appropriately used. As far as defense policies and military matters were concerned, President Diem seemed to trust only himself and his brother-counselor. Between them, they devised policies, studied problems, made plans, and then privately issued directives to the executors, often down to a low level and usually bypassing channels. The conduct of the war therefore suffered from lack of uniform planning and coordination.

• • •

From the day he took power, President Diem never trusted the JGS or made proper use of its planning capabilities. He became even more estranged with the JGS, especially after the paratroopers' abortive coup in 1960 and the aerial bombing of his palace in 1962.

The fact that the JGS always performed the duties of an army command, in addition to its joint responsibilities, clearly violated an important principle of staff planning and operation, in spite of the economy in personnel and facilities. The JGS therefore tended to devote most of its efforts to day-to-day ARVN operations, to the detriment of joint and long-range planning. Despite MAAG-V recommendations, President Diem never fully consented to the idea of a separate ARVN command. When he finally but reluctantly approved its activation in 1962, he failed to give this command organization any terms of reference with regard to its authority and responsibilities vis-à-vis the JGS.

The upgrading of our infantry organization into divisions was definitely a sound and prescient move, even during the incipient stage of insurgency, in view of the North Vietnamese Army development trends. It effectively gave a strong backbone to the developing ARVN, making it a proud and formidable opponent of the NVA and enhancing South Vietnam's self-assurance at the same time. [The] MAAG-V's effort to standardize the organization of ARVN infantry divisions by 1959 facilitated their uniform administration and training. However, the deployment of all seven divisions in an anti-invasion disposition near border areas practically left a force vacuum in the Mekong Delta, the primary target of Communist insurgency in view of its rich resources and dense population. This was an unwise force disposition which obviously contributed little to the GVN effort of keeping insurgent activities under control, since at that time all paramilitary forces—such as the police, the Self-Defense Corps, and the Civil Guard—were still in their formative stage.

The GVN corrective action in deploying the major part of these divisions back to populous centers in 1961 was a timely albeit somewhat expedient move which responded well to the stepped-up tempo of insurgency. The same could be said of efforts to activate two additional divisions, four separate infantry regiments, and 86 ranger companies to reinforce the defense of rural areas. Other efforts to equip ARVN armored cavalry units with M-114s, then M-113 APCs, and the effective support of US helicopter units also contributed to improving significantly the combat effectiveness of ARVN infantry units.

Under MAAG-V sponsorship and instigation, formal tactical training in schools and in units was well organized and progressed smoothly, phase after phase, as scheduled. The nature and purpose of this training effort, however, were purely conventional; it did not help combat units cope with the unconventional requirements of counterinsurgency warfare and fight it effectively. Many unit commanders in effect complained of having to "learn one way and practice another way." Naturally US Army doctrine and field manuals served as the guide and yardstick in developing ARVN combat capabilities.

The year 1961 was perhaps the turning point in our training approach. [The] MAAG-V published . . . guidance on "Tactics and Techniques of Counterinsurgency Operations," designed for ARVN use. Drawn upon lessons learned from the First Indochina War and counterinsurgency campaigns in Malaysia and the Philippines, and adapted to the Vietnam context, the tactics and techniques propounded were appropriately responsive to the flexible requirements of the war at that juncture.

• • •

TERRITORIAL FORCES

In contrast to the ARVN development process, the building of local or territorial forces was entirely a South Vietnamese initiative and undertaking. During this period the defense of villages and hamlets was organized at the GVN discretion, without the benefit of MAAG-V advisory assistance. Basically the close-range defense of villages and hamlets was assumed by armed elements called the Self-Defense Corps (SDC); beyond the boundaries of villages, up to the district level, the Civil Guard (CG) took over. The SDC and CG forces were placed under the operational control of village and province chiefs, respectively. Their activities were coordinated with those of the police for the purpose of maintaining local security.

• • •

The Civil Guard organization derived from the concept of auxiliary force prevalent during the semicolonial period. Basically organized into separate companies, the CG was the principal force employed by sector commanders to maintain local security. Its success frequently depended on intervention or support provided by regular army units. Many believed that the CG would not have existed had it not been for the divergence of defense concepts between South Vietnamese and MAAG-V authorities, and especially the MAAG-V-imposed ceiling of 100,000 men for the National Armed Forces in early

1955. In any event, the existence of this GVN-supported military force proved to be beneficial to counterinsurgency efforts in the years ahead.

Not being the beneficiaries of the US Military Assistance Program (MAP), the CG and SDC had to go through an extremely painful and difficult formative process during their initial stage of organization, especially in terms of equipment and logistic support. Naturally their equipment consisted of nothing else but an assortment of obsolete weapons and long-outdated stocks of ammunition, all discarded and left behind by French forces. The CG or SDC troops participated in combat activities with apprehension; in contact with the enemy, his ammunition often would not go off and was not always resupplied in time. Placed low in national priorities, and not being part of the regular army, both the CG and SDC were denied a fair share of manpower resources and did not receive adequate support in logistics and in training. From their inception, they had never been properly trained, whether individually or as units. As a result, their ineffectiveness in counterinsurgency activities was inevitable.

As the fighting intensified, the Civil Guard in particular was called upon to assume increasingly heavy combat responsibilities not unlike those of the regular army. Yet its organization, pay, and other benefits were much below what the regular army enjoyed. Because of this low standing and indifferent care, a certain complex of inferiority and envy developed among its ranks, which eventually affected the performance of the CG as a combat force.

South Vietnam's territorial defense underwent a radical [improvement], beginning in 1961, when the US Military Assistance Program was extended to the CG and SDC and US advisors were assigned to the sector level. Concomitantly, and working hand in hand with the GVN, [the] MAAG-V initiated a program designed to improve and develop the territorial forces, with particular emphasis on basic organization, equipment, and training. The SDC was uniformly realigned into standard squads and platoons for assignment to hamlets and villages, respectively. This organizational concept was logical and fully compatible with the geographical configuration of the South Vietnamese village, whose hamlets were sometimes several miles removed from one another.

• • •

In the counterinsurgency context of South Vietnam, we believe that the smallest size and best-suited unit was the battalion. Only the battalion had the capabilities and an organization flexible enough to meet the fluid tactical requirements of counterinsurgency warfare. For example, a battalion could break down into small units to conduct saturation patrol activities designed to keep a constant pressure on the enemy. If required, it could also quickly reassemble to cordon and search an insecure village or mount a concerted attack against local enemy forces in coordination with other combat arms.

• • •

In terms of equipment, the replacement of all obsolescent weapons by standardized US armament identical to that used by the RVNAF gave the CG and SDC a substantial edge in combat performance. Logistically, it helped make training, supply, and maintenance uniform; psychologically, it boosted the morale of CG and SDC troopers, who now fought with more self-assurance. MAP budget limitations, however, prevented improvements in communications and transportation.

• • •

Counterinsurgency Strategies and Tactics

"Pioneer farms" and "agrovilles" . . . reflected . . . a long-range strategic concept whose purpose was not only to extend security to outlying rural areas, but also to deny Communist insurgents the use of such areas. President Diem certainly deserved the credit for foresightedness because he had correctly surmised what kind of warfare the Communists would wage in South Vietnam.

• • •

Being a deeply patriotic man and a dedicated anti-French nationalist, President Diem must have carefully studied the Viet Minh resistance movement, especially its staging areas and safe havens throughout Vietnam. If the Viet Minh were to attempt a conquest of the South by using the same warfare strategy, he was almost certain where and how they would begin. As a result, President Diem systematically proceeded to preempt the Viet Minh's return by turning their former strongholds first into pioneer farming areas and later agrovilles. Most of these farms and agrovilles were strategically located throughout South Vietnam's high plateau and swampy areas, from the DMZ to the Ca Mau peninsula. To populate these outlying places he brought in North Vietnamese Catholic refugees, Catholic farmers from Central Vietnam, and retired servicemen and their families, all of whom he knew were staunchly anti-Communist and loyal. His action proved prophetic because, throughout the insurgency war that broke out soon afterwards, the Communists were using the same base areas they had used before against the French.

• • •

Critics of the Strategic Hamlet program alleged that the GVN and its US advisors had transplanted this strategic idea in pacification, which had proved a success in Malaysia a decade earlier, but failed to take heed of an important fact: that British concentration measures only affected the Chinese, who were the source of the insurgency, not the indigenous Malays. In South Vietnam, these critics remarked, those who were forced to live in strategic hamlets were the indigenous peasants whose lives had been deeply rooted in their native villages for generations.

This critical remark was true only as far as forced living was concerned, which caused resentment among those people affected. The strategic hamlet concept itself, however, was not necessarily an adaptation of British strategy in Malaysia, despite apparent similarities. This concept had antecedents in Vietnamese history which dated back to the period of Chinese domination, but the most striking and recent precedent was perhaps the "combat village" defense system established during the 1946–1954 war of resistance against the French. To curtail French control, the Viet Minh government practically turned every village into a resistance nest and used the popular saying "when bandits break into a house, even a woman fights back" as an effective combat motto.

The corral-like configuration of the village, especially in North and Central Vietnam, lent itself to excellent defense against penetration, with its high, thorny, and dense bamboo hedge enveloping the habitation inside like a solid, almost impenetrable rampart whose single opening made access control most convenient.

It was this concept of "combat village" that inspired the strategic hamlet defense system. But, if this concept had successfully worked in North and Central Vietnam because it required no dislocation of the rural population, it posed a big problem in South Vietnam, especially in MR-3 and MR-4. The fact was that, in South Vietnam, the village was much larger and consisted of separate hamlets physically removed from one another and often made up of scattered individual habitations. The GVN concept of village defense, therefore, was based on the hamlet, which alleviated problems of barrier organization but in many cases still involved regrouping of the scattered hamlet population.

Regrouping was indispensable for improved protection and better defense, although painful for the dislocated people involved in the process. However, dislocation and interruption of the normal life pattern were not new to the South Vietnamese rural people, who had voluntarily left their homes vacant and their gardens unattended during the resistance war. Dislocation needed not to be painful if it had been thoroughly explained and understood as a necessity required by the people's own safety and dictated by the national cause.

• • •

Regardless of what had been said about it, the Strategic Hamlet program remained a judicious national policy, a true antidote to Communist subversive and total warfare. Its chief merit lay in the fact that it had been comprehensively designed to improve the people's living standards through socioeconomic development at the rice-roots level. It was a sound strategic concept whose objective was to neutralize and counterbalance the effects of a war without front lines by transforming the countryside into a system of mutually supporting fortifications. It sought to build and consolidate the spirit of self-assurance, self-reliance, and voluntary participation which would sustain the nation's efforts in a protracted war of attrition.

Finally the Strategic Hamlet program should prove to be a less costly defense enterprise in the long run, but its success depended on perseverance and continued popular support. Indeed, only the people could neutralize the subversive effects of insurgency warfare, and only the hamlet residents in particular could identify and eliminate the insurgents. For counterinsurgency purposes, no other motive could be stronger than the need to protect one's own family and property. This was the overriding self-defense principle on which the strategic hamlet concept was built.

The major flaw of this undertaking stemmed primarily from the methods and spirit with which local government officials implemented the program. Driven by overzeal and a desire to please President Diem, these officials failed to work out basic plans de-

signed to prepare the local people psychologically for the event and elicit their voluntary participation.

• • •

The end result was that, instead of voluntary participation, a [fundamental] condition
for this national policy to achieve success, the strategic hamlet people found themselves
living in a state of repressed feelings, suspicion, and frustration. Under such circumstances, enemy propaganda and criticisms directed against the government surely combined to edge these people into confusion and disaffection.

• • •

The fact that the Communists were giving top priority to disruptive efforts designed
to dismantle the strategic hamlets testified to the partial success of this program. Technically, the program had indeed succeeded in controlling the hamlet population and isolating them from parasitic Viet Cong agitprop agents and guerrillas. It also won over a
large segment of rural society to the national cause. The eventual continuation of this
basic strategy with a few modifications under the pacification program, which was undertaken by the Second Republic and fully supported by the United States, further demonstrated its soundness, adaptability, and responsiveness to the war situation at the rice-
roots level. It was a regret that, as an ally in the war, the United States had taken so long
to realize the full impact of Communist insurgency and make the proper move to fight it
effectively. Had the Agroville and Strategic Hamlet programs benefited from the same
kind of support [later] given to pacification, we believe that the turn of events would
have drastically changed.

As early as 1958 the GVN had recognized the important role played by the Communist infrastructure in a war of subversion and sabotage. Elements of the Viet Cong infrastructure (VCI) in effect acted not unlike a shadow government where their influence
was strong. They incited and directed subversive activities in areas being contested or
under GVN control. These activities gave the impression of ubiquitous Communist
presence and consequently impaired popular confidence in the GVN.

We believe therefore that, regardless of adverse political consequences, President
Diem's decision to eliminate the VCI, the active Communist war machinery in South
Vietnam, was perhaps the most clear-sighted offensive move at that early stage of insurgency. Directed against the enemy's most vulnerable point, this move was to achieve
the best results through economy of force, despite its low profile. President Diem had
correctly surmised that, once this nerve system was destroyed or neutralized by GVN
actions, the body limbs (assassination squads, village guerrillas, local forces, etc.) would
either be completely paralyzed or their activities would be disjointed, ineffective.

President Diem began his offensive action by promulgating successively Ordinance
Nos. 6 and 47 during 1956 and the famous 10/59 decree-law which completely outlawed the Communists and any actions deemed detrimental to national security. The
10/59 decree-law in particular drew intense fire from political figures of the opposition,
who regarded it as paving the way for bloody repression against dissenters and dictatorship. The most apprehensive provision of this legislation was the creation of special

military tribunals empowered to impose the death penalty within three days of trial on those defendants convicted of flagrant or premeditated acts of sabotage or in violation of national security.

Despite its harshness, this law was indispensable in that it dealt forcefully and promptly with acts of sabotage or subversion and effectively deterred their perpetration. Experience seemed to dictate that there was no other effective way against Communist violence.

• • •

What mattered most was not the promulgation of a punitive law, but how this law could be correctly implemented.

To their credit, the GVN security and law enforcement agencies under the Diem regime did strike effectively at the VCI, but at the same time they also bore down upon the wrong elements. Their mistakes caused a great apprehension among those who had fought the French in the resistance movement, and among the opposition leadership, feeding dissension and disaffection. More specifically, "special action teams" in MR-1—a virtually private security force owned by Mr. Diem and controlled by his youngest brother, Mr. Can, for purported VCI elimination purposes—became the object of controversial opinion because their actions were also directed against political dissidents. To some extent these repressive actions degraded the anti-Communist cause and alienated the public.

• • •

Significant Lessons Learned

1. The defense of South Vietnam was founded on an inappropriate basis at the start, focusing too much on anti-invasion and too little on internal security. War did not materialize under the form of a conventional invasion across the DMZ by NVA major units, nor did it result in big conventional battles as in Korea during 1951–1953. Our main enemy—Communist North Vietnam—waged instead a people's or insurgency war with the purpose of taking over control in South Vietnam. . . .

2. After the outbreak of insurgency, the countryside of South Vietnam rapidly came under enemy subversion. Our hamlet and village officials, in spite of stringent screening and selection procedures, were not appropriately trained and indoctrinated to have a firm ideological stand and a sufficient knowledge of techniques and tactics to be used for the control and protection of the people against Communist subversive activities. Intelligence-gathering capabilities were almost nonexistent at the village and hamlet level. For the defense of villages and hamlets, the SDC and other militia elements responsible for hamlet security had been hastily activated and placed under the control of the village chief. They were neither trained nor indoctrinated, poorly led, and ineffective. The Civil Guard, the primary territorial force responsible for security beyond the confines of villages and hamlets, was also a heterogeneous assemblage of

different auxiliary force elements formerly employed by the French and servicemen of the National Army who had been discharged for reasons of force structure reduction. CG companies lacked capable cadres, were not properly trained
and indoctrinated, and were poorly equipped. They had only very limited combat capabilities.

3. Province and district chiefs, the local authorities who were primarily responsible for territorial security, did not have sufficient forces for the protection of
vital installations in their areas of responsibility. In particular they lacked reserves for intervention purposes in order to meet emergency requirements of
the situation and enhance popular confidence.

4. The territorial command and control system (military regions, sectors), which
was responsible for coordinating all civilian and military efforts for counterinsurgency purposes, did not receive proper attention. As a result, its capabilities
were very limited. By contrast, the tactical system (corps, divisions) developed
rapidly but did not have the appropriate opportunities to demonstrate its
capabilities.

5. The corrective efforts which had been initiated in 1961 with focus on the village
and hamlet level were a move in the proper direction which greatly improved
security in prosperous and populated rural areas. In the light of documents captured, our enemy had admitted that 1961–1962 was the most retrogressive period of his insurgency efforts.

6. Strategic hamlets proved to be effective in protecting the people against Communist subversive activities. They separated the people from the VCI and
cut off a major source of manpower replacement for enemy guerrilla
forces. . . .

7. Improving the effectiveness of the Self-Defense Corps through reorganization,
training, and equipment modernization was a logical step, but the results would
have been much better if the effort had not been limited to full-time elements
and to counterinsurgency techniques and tactics. Hamlet security would have
been much improved, and the protection of the hamlet people against the VCI
and the elimination of the latter would have been more effective, if the improvement program had been extended to part-time SDC members and village and
hamlet officials and more emphasis had been placed on indoctrination and
intelligence.

8. Our emphasis on training the Civil Guard resulted in increasing to some extent
the effectiveness of this force. But these efforts were not enough to overcome
other problems that affected the CG, such as the shortages of cadres, lack of
care, and the complex of inferiority with regard to the ARVN. . . .

9. The redeployment of ARVN infantry divisions to lowland areas, and their employment in conjunction with the CG to maintain area security, effectively
helped reinforce the people's confidence and enhance the morale of local
government officials and territorial troops. . . .

10. The deactivation of MR headquarters and the transformation of corps headquarters into CTZ commands with territorial responsibilities effectively improved command and control in our counterinsurgency efforts. . . .

11. The Buddhist turbulence in 1963 partially diluted our counterinsurgency efforts. The subsequent change in national leadership had the unfortunate effect of destroying the basic works that the First Republic had so painfully built for these efforts: the constitution, the National Assembly, strategic hamlets, people's organizations, and the anti-VCI machinery. North Vietnam took full advantage of this political turmoil, advocating neutralism (which further divided our ranks) and infiltrating more men and materiel, with an attempt to conquer the South by a general military offensive and thus shorten its protracted guerrilla warfare. Because of these developments, South Vietnam gradually retrogressed to the point of collapse, which resulted in US combat troops being introduced in 1965 to save our nation from Communist domination.

II. AMERICANIZATION OF THE WAR: 1964–1967

Strengthening and Expanding the RVNAF

From 1964 to 1967 the RVNAF force structure expanded rapidly. In addition to the beefed-up ARVN, it also absorbed the Civil Guard and the Self-Defense Corps, which were redesignated Regional (RF) and Popular (PF) Forces, respectively, to suit organizational objectives. Both the Regional and Popular Forces became territorial infantry components, while the infantry divisions remained a major mobile strike force in this new realignment.

The inclusion of the RF and PF into the RVNAF force structure improved South Vietnam's conduct of the war in several ways. It unified command and control; concentrated efforts on defense; solved many problems faced by the RF in terms of morale, support, and care; and created favorable conditions for improving the effectiveness of these vital territorial forces. Despite these advantages, the new force structure realignment brought about additional burdens for the ARVN and some criticisms by certain military authorities and politicians.

• • •

Effective coordination of military and administrative activities was mandatory for the maintenance of security and order in a province. To achieve this, the GVN had taken the logical step of unifying command under the province chief.

• • •

To further streamline command and control, the GVN subsequently appointed military officers as province chiefs with control authority over both the province administration and the sector military organization. At the same time the provincial CG office was disbanded and its personnel absorbed into the sector headquarters.

This solution worked out better and was perhaps more suited to the situation of

South Vietnam, but it also made the province chief's responsibilities extremely burdensome. As a result, he was usually unable to devote proper attention to the command and control, support, and care of RF companies, which were not only numerous but also thinly deployed throughout his province. To discharge part of his responsibilities, the province chief had to delegate his authority to the deputy sector commander, the deputy province chief, and the sector chief of staff, but this also seemed not entirely satisfactory. We believe, therefore, that the best way would have been to group RF companies into autonomous battalions.

During the 1964–1967 period, the top defense structure of the RVN also underwent drastic organizational change. The Ministry of Defense added the Directorate of Mobilization to its organization, and the Joint General Staff activated three new functional commands for training, logistics, and political warfare, in addition to making the Adjutant General system a separate branch of service. This reorganization made the conduct of war efforts smoother because management, administration, and support functioned more efficiently in the RVNAF. The deactivation of the field command was a logical move, but the same could not be said of deactivating the ARVN command. By reverting to the old concept of having the JGS double as an army command, the RVNAF no doubt had saved personnel and equipment, cut down on expenditures, and made administration more effective. In the process, however, the JGS also became burdened with routine operations and could not devote enough efforts to developing long-range plans of national significance.

• • •

From experience, we are convinced that an ARVN Command would have been required to alleviate the heavy burdens shouldered by the JGS in the areas of organization, training, and management, because the ARVN was not only rapidly developing, but also the most important of the three services. This would have enabled the JGS to devote its efforts to long-range planning and the conduct of the war.

Many RVN military authorities thought that the RVNAF force structure expansion during the 1964–1967 period had not been properly planned and was not judiciously balanced between combat and support requirements. They also felt that this program had not benefited from a proper allocation of US priorities. Unbalanced development, these authorities pointed out, made the RVNAF overly dependent on US forces for firepower, combat support, tactical mobility, and logistic support. While we agree that the United States should have placed a high priority on expanding the RVNAF and developing their combat capabilities before thinking of committing its own troops, we do not think that the expansion program had not been properly planned or judiciously balanced.

• • •

As to "unbalanced development," we think that this was inevitable to a certain degree in the ratio of infantry combat and support troops, although we have to admit that this imbalance was rather excessive, not only during the 1964–1967 period but also before that. An ideal equilibrium, in our opinion, was impossible to achieve for an army having to depend on foreign aid even for its subsistence. At the very least, however, there should have been some balanced development in firepower capabilities, primarily artillery and tactical air, which were required to enhance the effectiveness of ground combat forces. We believe that the ARVN artillery corps, experienced and capable as it was, should have encountered no significant difficulties in developing its capabilities for short-range as well as long-range firepower.

• • •

US Participation in the War

The multitudinous intervention of US forces in South Vietnam since 1965 was a timely move that pulled our country away from the brink of disaster. This intervention had helped South Vietnam reverse its checkmate position and made it possible for the free republic to survive for another ten years. The concomitant participation of Free World forces had the effect of enhancing the cause of human freedom for which US troops were committed and removed all misconstruction about American imperialist or colonialist designs. There was no doubt about it, but the large presence of foreign troops also had a profound impact on the South Vietnamese people and armed forces.

As a people burdened by the trauma of a long colonial past, the Vietnamese—North and South—were extremely sensitive about the presence of foreign troops on their soil. This presence was to leave an extensive sociopolitical impact on the hearts and minds of Vietnamese on both sides of the DMZ.

• • •

Not until 1967, and especially 1968, did this majority of the South Vietnamese population come to fully appreciate the value of the US military presence and the fallacy of Communist propaganda. They had seen for themselves how US forces had effectively interdicted and driven major Communist units away from populated areas, which restored security to most villages and hamlets. They had witnessed the rehabilitation and construction of roads and bridges, which made communication between cities and rural areas much easier and faster. This came as a revealing contrast to Communist sabotage activities. The rural people of South Vietnam also began to benefit directly from various US aid programs which sought to rebuild the damaged countryside and restore agricultural production by putting science and technology at the service of rural life. Indeed, the affable image of the American friend, as reflected through diligent engineer teams, solicitous civic action groups, and dedicated district advisors, to name just a few, who made the rounds of villages and hamlets across the country, was to remain ineradicably engraved in the hearts of the rustic peasants of South Vietnam.

• • •

The Communists, in the meantime, exploited the US presence to the hilt psychologically and politically, directing their propaganda not only at domestic opinion but also at world opinion. Of course they blamed all destructiveness and social ills on US troops. To incite traditional patriotism among Vietnamese on both sides, and to obtain aid from the Communist bloc, they vocally denounced US forces as imperialist aggressors. Whatever our feelings, we have to admit that the Communists had been successful in instigating Vietnamese patriotic ardor, especially among the rural peasants of South Vietnam, and as early as 1962. This success was one among several factors which contributed to the rapid subversion of the South Vietnamese countryside and the growth of insurgent forces during the initial stage of the war. By 1967, however, patriotism as a Communist propaganda decoy no longer fooled the majority of the South Vietnamese people.

• • •

Apparently the US participation in the war had preempted all priorities otherwise enjoyed by the RVNAF in terms of equipment modernization and allocation. The delay in equipment deliveries which had been programmed for the modernization of armament, communications, and transportation, to include in particular the replacement of M-1 rifles by M-16s intended to counteract the deadly AK-47 that Communist troops had used since 1964, was the most obvious case in point.

• • •

We don't believe that the South Vietnamese population would have readily accepted an American general at the command of the RVNAF, even though he had all the talent and qualities that they admired and respected. On the other hand, we also think that the American public would have balked at the idea of placing the mighty and internationally reputed US forces under the control of an indigenous general whose country was receiving aid from their tax contributions. Furthermore, the creation of an allied command headed by an American general would have bound the United States more firmly to the fate of South Vietnam, and this would have made it extremely difficult for the United States to extricate itself without damaging its honor and world reputation as long as a military victory was still evasive.

As a result, we think that the concept of cooperation and coordination, predicated on the principles of equal partnership and division of responsibilities according to capabilities, was perhaps the wisest and most appropriate in the Vietnam context. With the support of an extensive advisory system, which functioned in all areas and at all levels down to the battalion and district with a total authority over the management of military aid which was the RVNAF's very lifeline, and given the trust and admiration bestowed on them by almost all South Vietnamese military and civilian authorities by virtue of age, professional experience, and leadership qualities, we believe that the MACV commander, as well as US field force commanders, always had enough information, authority, and resources to coordinate and conduct war efforts effectively and to convince their South Vietnamese counterparts to take heed of their suggestions and recommendations, although they did not directly control the RVNAF.

• • •

The division of tasks and responsibilities between the RVNAF and US and FWMAF, which had been formalized since 1966 by annual "Combined Campaign Plans," was both logical and harmonious in that it judiciously exploited the strengths and weaknesses, the capabilities, and the resources of each force. The RVNAF, which were short in combat support resources but long on familiarity with the environment, concentrated their efforts on supporting the GVN pacification program and maintaining territorial security. Through the conduct of long-duration clearing operations and daily security activities, they endeavored primarily to protect and expand secure areas and keep open all key lines of communications against their main adversary, the Communist local forces, guerrillas, and mini-bases. In other words, the RVNAF were employed to fight the "small" war.

Meanwhile US forces, which enjoyed extremely strong and effective support in fire-power and mobility but were alien to the environment, devoted their efforts to disrupting major enemy bases and sanctuaries in outlying and rugged areas and, at the same time, destroying Communist main-force units which usually took shelter in these base and border areas where the population was sparse. They were called upon to confront the enemy in the "big" war.

• • •

Despite its rationality and flexibility, this employment of forces was not entirely im-mune from critical opinions. Some self-conscious authorities considered the secondary role of the RVNAF detrimental to their value and adverse to their combat spirit and aggressiveness. They argued that in the long term this would affect RVNAF combat ef-fectiveness, especially if someday we were required to fight a big conventional war. More poignantly, it seemed that only US forces were actually fighting the war for South Vietnam.

National pride was undoubtedly at the source of such criticism, laudable yet entirely misplaced. It also reflected an ignorance of the dual nature of the war and the true capa-bilities of the RVNAF at that juncture. Indeed, to confront both the "big" and "small" aspects of the war, entwined as they were and equally instrumental for the enemy to control the countryside and strangle our cities, we could not afford to underestimate ei-ther. Both efforts should have been mutually supportive and conducted hand-in-hand; hence fighting the "small" and "big" war was equally important. Given the intricate po-litical situation of South Vietnam during this period, naturally we could not assign re-sponsibilities for territorial security and pacification support to US and FWMA forces. Likewise, it would have been a folly to throw the RVNAF after enemy bases and main-force units, for the simple reason that they were not yet fully capable [of] this task.

Besides, the assignment of tasks for the RVNAF in yearly combined campaign plans, especially the commitment of ARVN infantry divisions to territorial security, was just a continuation of what these forces had been doing since 1961, when the DTA structure was instituted. It was true that, in order to carry out this mission, each infantry division had to spread out its forces in static defense and frequently lost track of those individual battalions placed under operational control of sector headquarters. In time the tedious routine of security activities conducted within the same environment, year in and year out, made divisional units lethargic, complacent, and much less aggressive; their combat effectiveness also eroded in the process, having been accustomed to small-unit actions for too long. All this indeed did not prepare our divisions for large-scale battles that they were called upon to fight when subsequently confronted with the big war. This constraint, however, could have been avoided in 1961, or 1964 at the latest, when they became part of the RVNAF to take over what our divisions had been doing. . . .

The allegation that only American troops were fighting the war, which issued primarily from American and world opinion, did not necessarily stem from the fact that US forces were assuming the major combat role. Whether founded or unfounded, it seemed to reflect a certain truth: the limited number of RVNAF forces available for big actions and the small proportion of ARVN forces employed in large-scale combined operations. More importantly, this allegation also derived from misinformation or [partiality] on the part of the media, especially in the US press.

The truth was that, during the period of US participation, the RVNAF capabilities for big actions consisted solely of airborne units, which were upgraded to a division only in 1966, and a marine brigade. Also, during major combined operations, the role played by ARVN units seemed virtually a symbolic one, since they were mostly assigned peripheral missions such as blocking, screening, LOC security, and evacuation of the local population. Obviously either US field commanders did not trust ARVN capabilities or their acceptance was only half-hearted. On the other hand, ARVN field commanders were also hard-pressed to produce larger forces for these operations, mainly because of our territorial security commitments; in fact, ARVN forces already deployed for territorial security never seemed sufficient. Although RVNAF casualties resulting from daily skirmishes of the small war were comparable or often larger in size to those incurred by United States in periodic search and destroy operations, they seldom attracted the interest of the foreign media. Most of the headlines, therefore, only referred to large-scale US operations conducted with intense fighting and heavy casualties on both sides. Also, while MACV appeared to enjoy a good rapport with the media, which it wisely exploited to support US activities, the GVN seemed to shun all relations with the local press as far as military operations were concerned. This indifference derived less from distrust in the objectivity of press reporters than their normal penchant for sensational stories which in most cases did not serve the war effort.

Pacification and Rural Development

The pacification and rural development program was a harmonious integration of military and civil action efforts designed to confront the total war of insurgency waged by the Communists. In major aspects, it was a continuation and amalgam of various programs that the First Republic administration had initiated to restore security to rural areas and develop the agricultural base. All these previous programs had suffered from incohesiveness, poor planning, lack of military-civilian coordination, and inadequate support. They were almost totally interrupted and underrated for two years following the 1963 coup for reasons of political instability. Not until 1966 were these efforts resumed and strongly revived under the pacification and rural development (PRD) program, drawing on lessons learned from past efforts.

• • •

Below the central level, and similarly organized, the system of GVN and US coordination existed at every echelon of our territorial structure, down to the district. This system was efficient and entirely responsive to PRD requirements. Most of the achievements during the 1966–1971 period were primarily attributable to this productive coordination effort and US support. In general terms, the PRD program and its coordination system enabled both the GVN and MACV to make full use of every available capability and resource; combined all military and civilian activities for the elimination of the VCI, the guerrillas, the local- and main-force units; expand the areas under GVN control; and bring about popular confidence in South Vietnam's free and democratic regime, as well as the prospects of improved living.

As a concomitant to the PRD effort, the Phung Hoang (Phoenix) program, which was initiated in 1967, embodied a vital strategic concept seeking to protect the South Vietnamese people against Communist terrorism. Its main target was the VCI, the enemy's most vulnerable point, long considered as the foundation of Communist insurgency in South Vietnam. The merit of the Phung Hoang concept lay in the fact that, as long as the VCI continued to exist, total victory could not be achieved. Destroying an enemy unit, whether local or main force, amounted to just a short-term military victory. In that sense, it was not an exaggeration to say that the destruction of an enemy company or battalion did not matter as much as the elimination of a VC district or province commissar. As a matter of fact, the death or arrest of a VC province commissar inevitably disrupted or upset all enemy military and political activities in the province for some time. And, if the elimination effort was sustained and extensive, soon the entire province would become "pacified."

In addition to this strategic objective, the Phung Hoang program also sought to overcome major shortcomings in the area of cooperation and coordination among military and civilian intelligence agencies at all levels, and between intelligence activities and military operations. The establishment of operations and intelligence coordination centers at the province and district level (PIOCC and DIOCC) came about as a particularly bright spot in the Phung Hoang organization. Both the PIOCC and the DIOCC were pivotal agencies in charge of planning collection activities and the conduct of anti-VCI operations.

• • •

Since the day it became a national policy and received financial and material assistance from MACCORDS, the Phung Hoang program achieved significant results in terms of VCI members surrendered, detained, and killed. For those still at large, the program also deterred them psychologically, since the overwhelming pressure it exerted had forced them to change identities and locations frequently to evade the dragnet. In time, members of the VCI became hesitant and their activities declined markedly. During the 1972 Easter Offensive, the role of the VCI was insignificant, especially when compared to the 1968 Tet Offensive.

• • •

Public opinion, especially outside South Vietnam, was particularly harsh against the Phung Hoang program, which it condemned for indiscriminate, cold-blooded killings.

This adverse opinion derived in part, we think, from ignorance and misinformation on the objective of the program; the nature, character, and role of the VCI in the war; and the fact that Communists had been outlawed by the RVN constitution. Most critics had the wrong impression that the Phung Hoang program was a terror campaign in disguise and that the GVN had taken advantage of it to assassinate and kidnap its political opponents as well. However, nothing could be further from the truth; the program had never been designed with such a vicious scheme in mind. Probably these critics were either hostile to the South Vietnamese regime, driven by antiwar sentiments, or simply [poisoned] by Communist propaganda.

We do not deny that the program was riddled with serious errors such as the arrest of wrong suspects, indecent treatment [of] detainees, and accidental killing of suspects during skirmishes. But these errors were far from being deliberate actions condoned by a nefarious policy. They simply reflected the weaknesses and unwittingness on the part of certain elements, which was inevitable in an undertaking as large as the Phung Hoang program. GVN officials and US advisors made every possible effort to prevent these unfortunate incidents.

• • •

Village elections, which were instituted in 1967 to replace the undemocratic appointment practice, came about as a sweeping innovation that should consolidate the popular base of the regime. Provided for by the Second Republic constitution and encouraged by the United States, village elections were implemented where security had been restored. The results achieved, however, did not match expectations. For one thing, the protracted war which was ravaging the rural areas, and the demands of both sides, had dislocated or preempted the majority of village male elite, leaving behind just women, elderly people, and children, whose only concern was to live undisturbed. Therefore village-born candidates for office were few, almost nonexistent. Most of those who [put themselves forward] for candidature did not belong to the class of village elite who commanded popular respect; some were even suspected of being sympathetic to the other side. Those few who enjoyed true popular esteem were hesitant, noncommittal. As a result, we can say that most candidates for village office either belonged to this group of people, sponsored and introduced by province and district governments, or were affiliated with local religious groups. Some came from the same district; some were brought in from other localities. When elected, these officials did not act as representatives of the villagers; they behaved like henchmen of the district or province chief and local religious leaders.

During this period of hot war, therefore, village elections were only valid to the extent that they provided rural areas with a coating of democratic veneer; other than that, they often served no useful purpose as far as the people were concerned. That elected village officials were compelled to undergo training and indoctrination at Vung Tau often caused concern and even suspicion among some of our people about the democratic system. However, this training and indoctrination were necessary if we wanted them to truly serve the people.

The Chieu Hoi (Open Arms) program, another significant pacification effort, embodied the very spirit of national reconciliation by giving amnesty to those enemy personnel who wanted to make amends [for] their mistakes. Given the statistical figures on ralliers, who seemed to have defected en masse, the program was quite a resounding success. A closer look revealed, however, that the program had failed to attract middle- and high-level enemy cadres, military or political. Most of those who rallied were the rank-and-file VC soldiers, and a small number consisted of low-level VCI members. They came over to our side not out of ideological conviction, but primarily for personal reasons such as fear of hardship, war weariness, and family problems. The GVN had gone overboard in welcoming and treating these ralliers as decently as resources permitted. By doing so, it aroused the envy and jealousy of our underprivileged soldiers, particularly those deserters who were serving time in spartan military prisons. This was a dilemma for both the GVN and the RVNAF leadership.

The Ethnic Minority program, especially with regard to Montagnards of the Central Highlands, succeeded only in part in alleviating political and racial problems. It would have taken perhaps a few more generations to solve these problems satisfactorily. Only through prolonged social mixing between Vietnamese and Montagnards, constant exposure of Montagnards to modern civilization, and the introduction of science and technology to the service of their daily life could we ever hope to eradicate ethnic disparities. Even if we had tried to give them some form of autonomy, the way North Vietnam had experimented with its own ethnic minorities, this would only have amounted to nothing more than a political veneer which eventually would have disappeared by force of assimilation. The long history of Vietnam had demonstrated that no ethnic minority was able to resist assimilation if it lived as part of the Vietnamese community for a long time.

• • •

Only by building something with their own hands did the people appreciate its true value and protect it jealously against Communist efforts to destroy it. That was the rationale behind the whole concept which had proved true in many instances. Experience also indicated, however, that no development was possible where there was no security. To maintain security, it was essential for the local government and troops to remain with the people and protect them. But whether or not we could ensure a lasting security depended on how well we did in eliminating the VCI and the effectiveness of the shields provided by RVNAF units. Development and security, therefore, were inseparable from each other.

The basic strategy of pacification—which was built on the concept of the "spreading oil stain," i.e., expanding control from urban or secure areas—led to the division of the territory into secure, consolidation, and clearing zones and the employment of the clear and hold tactic. This strategy had proved sound and effective. The clear and hold tactic, in particular, had brought reassurance to the people living in consolidation zones (who usually believed that our troops just came, then departed, while the Communists might have gone, but they always came back and stayed). This was indeed a great improvement from the period of mopping-up operations, during which most of the mischief that alienated the people in contested areas occurred. The clear and hold pattern had changed all that, especially after the ARVN had undergone an intensive political education program initiated in 1965. Familiarity with the local people through long months of social contact effectively developed rapport, which reduced apathy and indifference on the part of the people and mischievous acts on the part of the soldiers.

The major shortcoming of clear and hold operations was that they inevitably required a long duration, many troops, and substantial support facilities. A minimum of six months to one year was normally needed to eliminate or drive away enemy guerrillas and local forces, screen the population, root out the VCI, consolidate the local security system, establish the local government, and create the favorable conditions for the development process to begin. Time was also necessary to develop mutual trust between the local government and the people; this could only be achieved through the arduous process of trial and error.

There had to be adequate troops and support facilities to accomplish a variety of purposes: an outpost system to interdict enemy accesses into the area under pacification; the protection of government installations, economic resources, and arteries of communication; a system of operational and fire support bases, as well as logistic support installations; and the formation of intervention forces, especially at the district and province level, which were essential to keep small enemy units at bay, support the outposts in case of attack, and put constant pressure on the enemy in the area. These tasks were required not only to gain the military initiative, but also and more importantly to reassure the local people of the government's permanent presence and the determination of governmental troops to stay and protect them, which was a key psychological factor that induced local villagers to cooperate. All of these requirements in troops and support were satisfactorily met by the full commitment of ARVN infantry and ranger units to pacification, the quantitative and qualitative development of regular and territorial forces, and the effective support provided by American firepower, mobility, and logistics. Rural security, as a result, improved and expanded by leaps and bounds during this period, which was the source of optimism among RVN and US authorities.

• • •

Major Operations

During the war the enemy's control headquarters, his main-force units, and those local units driven away by pacification forces all took shelter in major base areas and border sanctuaries which were conveniently located in the most rugged type of terrain. Therefore the US efforts to destroy this war-making machinery from 1966 to 1967 were mostly directed at long-established enemy base areas in South Vietnam.

It was not a disgrace for us to say that only US forces had the capabilities—firepower, mobility, and logistic support—to strike at enemy base areas. Major US operations that made history, such as Cedar Falls, launched against the Iron Triangle, Junction City against War Zone C, and Delaware/Lam Son against the A Shau Valley, had shattered the enemy-publicized myth that these bases were impenetrable. All of these operations had a tremendous psychological impact on both enemy and RVNAF troops. The fact was, in spite of gross exaggerations concocted by the NVA command on US casualties and losses during these operations, our enemy was unable to stop the shock that rippled through his ranks. Enemy documents captured subsequently confirmed this fact; our enemy admitted that these operations were a "disaster" for him. For the RVNAF, the disruption of major enemy bases was a source of tremendous encouragement and satisfaction, because it had been a long-nurtured but hard to attain objective coveted by the JGS and MR commands for several years. Through this feat the RVNAF also felt reassured of the US military might and ultimate victory for our side.

Besides this significant morale boost, US-conducted operations against enemy bases also destroyed large quantities of enemy supplies and a major part of the enemy's fortifications, underground shelters, and tunnels, which would have taken him years to rebuild. As far as the total destruction of major enemy units and the enemy's command headquarters was concerned, US forces fared less well because the enemy was evasive. His constant change of headquarters location often made our intelligence reports outdated, despite their accuracy. US and ARVN forces were usually not numerically strong enough to close a tight ring around a base area and to stay inside long enough to make a thorough search.

The rugged, heavily covered, and immense terrain with which the enemy had long been familiar also made it possible for him to disperse and avoid contact or to regroup and attack at will. For this the enemy seemed to have ample time, since the advance of friendly troops was often slow, and the fact that we were not as familiar with the terrain. Also, it was difficult to keep secret a large-scale operation which usually required troop movements and the pre-positioning of logistics prior to D-Day, despite diversionary efforts. The duration of operations was never long enough for our troops to conduct a thorough and more diligent search; to dispirit the fugitives and force them to surrender; and to build more airstrips, LZs, or pioneer roads to facilitate the rapid subsequent reinsertion of troops. Therefore, as soon as friendly troops withdrew, the enemy always came back, and soon this base was operational again. This was regrettable indeed, but perhaps we could not do otherwise as long as US and ARVN troops were insufficient for long-term commitment in these base areas. Since a permanent troop presence was not feasible, it ensued that, in order to control enemy reinfiltration, frequent operations against the same base area were indispensable.

Some critics of the search and destroy tactic argued that these large-scale operations were "aimless," "destructive," "inhuman"; they suggested that efforts should have been conducted at the small-unit level instead. We totally disagree with this. These arguments not only did not take account of the dual nature of the war and the [fundamental] role played by NVA units, they also reflected misinformation about the objective of search and destroy operations. To fight a war without front lines against an enemy who was continually evasive, what tactic other than search and destroy in areas where our intelligence had revealed his presence would have been more effective? With some variations, the search and destroy tactic had long been used by units of all levels with success. More importantly, it had served our common strategic goal.

• • •

The conduct of major operations certainly entailed substantial casualties, at least in the initial stage, but they saved many lives during the course of this protracted war. Not accepting the inevitable losses incurred during these operations, and failure to keep after major enemy units, only encouraged insurgency, fostered its strength, and prolonged the war. Assassinations, kidnappings, and skirmishes, big and small, would have continued as a tedious routine, given the false impression of insignificant casualties, and eventually far exceeded those we suffered during major operations. Only if we were determined and [persevering] enough to locate and strike enemy main forces in their very sanctuaries could we ever make our enemy realize there was no secure place for him in South Vietnam and no hope for a military victory. We believe that only when our enemy realized this would he perhaps be inclined to accept a negotiated settlement.

Therefore we believe that, in the conduct of the Vietnam War, we could neither devote all-out efforts to small insurgent forces and ignore major enemy units nor concentrate on major operations and neglect small-unit operations in support of pacification. Fully aware of this dual aspect of the war, both the JGS and MACV agreed that efforts should be judiciously divided between both types of operations and conducted in a mutually supporting way. Our force structure organization, training, and force employment were flexible enough to switch from one war to the other as the situation required and in keeping with North Vietnam's reinforcement capabilities.

• • •

Anti-Infiltration

Infiltration was a strategy that North Vietnam initiated in 1955 and increased significantly as of 1959 to gradually build up its forces and war materials in South Vietnam. It was a cunning scheme Hanoi conceived to cover up its bloody involvement in the war and deceive world and domestic opinion as to its true design to conquer South Vietnam by force. North Vietnam never admitted the presence of its army in the South. But the rural security situation, as well as the level of fighting in South Vietnam, depended on the extent and effectiveness of North Vietnam's infiltration.

For infiltration purposes, our enemy took full advantage of South Vietnam's 200-mile [*sic:* 700?] coastline and equally long border winding through mountains and jungles in MR-1, MR-2, and MR-3 and the swamplands in MR-4. Since South Vietnam's terrain definitely favored North Vietnam's infiltration, it made the US and RVN's anti-infiltration efforts most difficult. A completely effective defense against all infiltration would have required a force structure and materiel support that were not available. North Vietnam even used the DMZ and the territories of Laos and Cambodia for infiltration purposes, making a mockery of these countries' declared neutrality. The RVN and United States meanwhile dutifully respected international agreements and the sovereignty of these neighbors, which gave North Vietnam a free hand to build sanctuaries, logistic installations, and transit stations on the other side of the border. Cambodia's major port, Kompong Som, was used as an entry point for the deliveries of weapons and ammunition to Communist forces in MR-3, MR-4, and a considerable part of MR-2.

Both the RVN and United States fully realized that, if our anti-infiltration efforts were successful, they would help reduce the level of fighting in the South. If not, the war could drag on indefinitely. The primary source of all infiltration was North Vietnam, the big base that supported Communist war efforts in South Vietnam and the eventual expansion of Communist domination in Southeast Asia. To strike at North Vietnam therefore appeared most desirable to end the war. However, this move was politically unsound and portended the dangers of war expansion. We believed that only an RVNAF action could minimize these dangers, but the RVNAF was not trained or equipped for an invasion of North Vietnam (which was not a goal of the GVN or the US). We just wanted to be permitted to live in peace and develop South Vietnam into a true democracy.

The strategy of exerting pressure on North Vietnam, and thereby forcing its leaders to abandon their policy of supporting the war in South Vietnam, to our judgment, was the most logical in that it minimized the dangers of expanding the ground war. However, the measures applied by the United States and RVN did not create the required pressure to break the will of North Vietnam's leaders and stop the flow of men and supplies into South Vietnam. It appeared that, the greater the pressure the United States and RVN exerted through the "escalation strategy," the larger and more determined North Vietnam's infiltration seemed to become.

• • •

The US congressional resolution adopted in the fall of 1964, in the wake of the Gulf of Tonkin incident, opened the way for the air war over North Vietnam. Conducted initially on a retaliatory basis, US bombings soon continued with regularity. US authorities had hoped that these bombings would eventually break down North Vietnam's will and help end the war. However, after over two years of bombing our enemy appeared more determined than ever. Perhaps the United States had underestimated the endurance and [resolve] of the North Vietnamese leaders and people; or perhaps it had been constrained by considerations of Chinese intervention and its own complex as a major world power which found it morally improper to "punish" a small and underdeveloped country too harshly. In any event, the United States had refrained from applying its airpower forcefully and rapidly enough against all vulnerable targets in North Vietnam. Its strategy of "gradual escalation," progressing from the 17th parallel northward and responding to Hanoi's attitude, had apparently failed to convey its determination to Hanoi's leaders; on the contrary, it had been misinterpreted as a weakness on the part of US leaders. This air war strategy gave North Vietnam the necessary time to adjust to the circumstances and to motivate the populace in organizing for self-defense and develop their hatred toward the United States. It also accorded North Vietnam enough time in receiving emergency military aid from Russia and China to modernize and strengthen its air defense system. Eventually this improved defense system made the US air war increasingly costly in terms of human and material losses, which in turn divided the ranks of US leadership in policy matters. This division was further compounded by adverse world opinion and the mounting antiwar movement in the United States.

• • •

Although it had brought its superior technology to bear on this problem, the US Air Force was unable to stop the flow of infiltration down the corridor. The enemy had taken full advantage of the limitations of airpower and terrain features to adjust his activities, develop alternate routes, and keep infiltration flowing. It was obvious the Air Force alone could not win this battle without the cooperation of ground forces.

Inside South Vietnam, anti-infiltration efforts had been concentrated on two geographical areas—the DMZ and the long border facing Laos and Cambodia. The defense of the 900-mile border was entrusted to approximately 45,000 CIDG and Special Forces troops deployed in camps at strategic locations. Patrol activities conducted from these camps to control major infiltration accesses into South Vietnam, and quick-reacting operations which combined airpower with helicopter mobility, created many difficulties for NVA units. To overrun some of these border camps, our enemy was compelled to concentrate major units of regimental size or large[r] size. Several camps were thus lost to the enemy because we did not have enough defenders and reinforcements to counteract determined enemy attacks, and because of adverse terrain and weather which were not conducive to resupply or tactical air support. As a result, these lost or evacuated camps were only retaken when conditions permitted and troops were available. The A Shau camp, which controlled the major enemy infiltration access and avenue of approach into the Hue-Danang area, and the Plei Me camp, which controlled the southwestern access into Pleiku, were most representative of this border defense system.

The rugged terrain, combined with the length of the defense line and the shortage of RVNAF and US troops, made our border defense ineffective in certain areas. If, instead of deploying our forces along the long border, we had organized an east-west defense line across the 17th parallel and reaching toward the Mekong River in Laos along Route 9, for example, our border defense would have been perhaps easier, less costly, and would have provided more guarantees of success, tactically and strategically. This of course would have required the combined efforts of both Laos and South Vietnam.

The DMZ area, five miles deep on both sides of the Ben Hai River, was a big constraint for the United States and RVN, which scrupulously respected its demilitarized character. One hundred RVN policemen and an ICC team at Gio Linh were just incapable of monitoring this large zone. In May 1966 the entire NVA 324B Division infiltrated across the DMZ into South Vietnam without being challenged. Still, both the RVN and the US governments were not agreeable to our requests for using artillery or naval guns against enemy troops in the DMZ. Not until late 1966, after several bloody battles had occurred between our forces (US marines and the ARVN 1st Infantry Division) and the NVA south of the DMZ (which was supported by its artillery positioned in the DMZ's northern half) did US and ARVN forces finally receive permission to use counterbattery fire. Not until a year later were our forces authorized to pursue the enemy in the DMZ.

Even then, they were compelled to withdraw from it as soon as contact was lost. How could we defend ourselves effectively under such constraints?

In addition to our constant patrolling, the strongpoint and obstacle system, which was supported by tactical air and airmobile reaction forces, also contributed significantly to our anti-infiltration defense. We think that this tactical approach to a most difficult problem was sound and well founded. Such bases as Gio Linh, Con Thien, Cam Lo, and Khe Sanh had earned a much-deserved place in the glorious history of RVNAF-US defense against North Vietnam's oppression. It was at these very bases that North Vietnam's attempts to duplicate a Dien Bien Phu-type victory were completely shattered. The professionalism, endurance, combat spirit, and sophisticated techniques of firepower coordination also found their highest expression through this strongpoint system. The modern US sensor system, and the [persevering] army of US bulldozers, also made a major contribution. It was just unfortunate that this system was stopped at the Laotian border. Had it reached across the Laotian panhandle toward Tchepone, the very hub of North Vietnam's communication and transportation system in that part of Laos, we believe that enemy infiltration could have been drastically curtailed, which would have had a major impact on the course of the war within South Vietnam.

• • •

In summary, the entire anti-infiltration campaign conducted through the combined efforts of RVN and US forces inflicted many losses in both personnel and materiel on North Vietnam. It also caused North Vietnam to divert additional resources for the defense and maintenance of its infiltration routes down the Laotian panhandle. However, with the exception of our successful "Market Time" operations, which eventually prevented resupply through South Vietnam's national waters, our total efforts failed to stop the flow of men and supplies into the South. Those of us in senior positions [within] the RVNAF believed that it would have been impossible to accomplish all our objectives until this infiltration problem was defeated.

Significant Lessons Learned

1. In retrospect, the regrettable death of President Diem, a leader with enough stature to oppose Ho Chi Minh, was a great disaster for South Vietnam in time of war. The three years of political instability that followed edged South Vietnam toward the brink of collapse, which was averted only when the United States committed its combat troops to fight the ground war. . . .

2. Political turmoil made it impossible for South Vietnam to have a stable government, which was required to prosecute the war efficiently and develop long-range plans, especially as far as manpower was concerned. The RVNAF, therefore, was always short of manpower requirements. . . .

3. Just as during the previous period (1954–1963), the RVNAF were not expanded and developed in a proper and timely manner to counter North Vietnam's stepped-up war efforts and assume the primary combat role. Instead, they found themselves performing a secondary role in their own war. . . .

The JGS and MACV did not have medium-range plans for the RVNAF. All planning was done on a yearly basis to keep up with the progress of the war. Despite this, we think that, even in the annual planning process, priority should have been accorded the RVNAF in those areas which could be developed in the near future without difficulty. The United States and the RVN wasted seven valuable years since 1961 by developing the RVNAF in a half-hearted way. We believe that the RVNAF would have been more combat effective had they been expanded in force structure during this period, despite our difficulties with manpower. We also believe that, had priority been given to this expansion and development, the RVNAF would have been able to assume more combat responsibilities during the 1966–1967 period. This could have reduced the level of US force buildup, helped de-Americanize the war, and alleviated some US domestic problems at the same time. . . .

4. We believe that the US objective during this period was overly predicated on the safeguarding of American honor as a major world power guaranteeing the protection of a small ally, the belief that war could be ended shortly with US military might, and the underestimation of the North Vietnamese leadership's determination. All this resulted in the Americanization of the war and all priorities were given to the US force buildup and conduct of the war in South Vietnam.

5. Bombing North Vietnam, from where the war was being directed and sustained, proved logical and necessary. Striking at the will of the enemy leadership was also wise strategy. We believe that it would have been more logical and desirable if the United States had helped the RVNAF develop the capabilities for this undertaking. The US strategy of gradual response proved ineffective against a resilient enemy whose survival was guaranteed by his Communist sponsors. . . .

6. Despite heavy airstrikes, the USAF failed to disrupt significantly North Vietnam's infiltration corridor in lower Laos. This emphasized that modern airpower alone could not completely interdict ground activities effectively. Only ground troops, especially large units, could control and sever this infiltration system operated by a determined and resourceful enemy. . . .

7. During this period the United States and RVN were excessively cautious concerning Cambodia. We think that the RVN should have reserved the right to legitimate self-defense and conducted pursuits of enemy units into Cambodia where appropriate. . . .

8. The fact that anti-infiltration efforts outside South Vietnam were not effective led to the escalation of war inside South Vietnam in terms of intensity and level. The total buildup of Communist combat forces in the South exceeded that of US forces. But, as the buildup progressed, the United States was able to switch strategy from static base defense to search and destroy operations against major enemy units. These operations were initially conducted in the vicinity of enemy

bases, then against the very heart of these bases. All of these significant efforts not only pulled the RVN farther away from disaster, they also created a shock among enemy troops and forced North Vietnam to employ larger units in the South.

9. The RVN military initiative, which had been utterly lost since the end of 1964, was regained during this period. This was made possible by the presence of a strong strategic strike force (US major units), an acceptable level of DTA tactical reserves, and especially the availability of quick-reacting forces at the sector level (provided by ARVN infantry battalions attached to it). The security situation in rural areas therefore began to improve, which enabled the GVN to concentrate on pacification efforts.

10. The Pacification and Development Program, in our judgment, was the best strategic weapon to counter and defeat the Communist concept of people's warfare in the South. . . .

11. The Americanization of the war failed to produce victory as quickly as expected. Because of this, it fostered divisiveness among the US leadership in matters of military and political strategy and among the US public. The Vietnam War became a subject of debate in the preliminary rounds of US presidential elections. The United States began to waver, and its initial optimism gave way to pessimistic reassessments. This occurred while South Vietnam was beginning to stabilize politically and . . . optimism [spread] among its ranks. The GVN therefore continued to view the US posture with optimism, almost oblivious to political difficulties that the United States was facing because of our war. Perhaps it was because the GVN did not fully appreciate US problems.

• • •

III. VIETNAMIZATION: 1968–1972

The 1968 Tet General Offensive

• • •

Despite stepped-up infiltration, during the dry seasons of 1966 and 1967 Communist forces in South Vietnam gradually lost the initiative. Their large-unit attacks had all ended in defeat, with heavy losses inflicted by superior US firepower and mobility. US offensive operations, meanwhile, kept the enemy constantly off balance and greatly attrited his forces. Operations conducted by the RVNAF in support of pacification also reduced significantly the extent of Communist control in rural areas. The VCI and enemy local forces began to run into difficulties, although they were still strong. The enemy strategy of subverting rural areas to strangle the cities no longer proved effective in the face of combined RVN-US offensive efforts. The continuation of this declining military posture would affect the inability of the Hanoi regime and might even spell defeat in the South. Based on our experience at that time, both the RVN and United States were expecting a major counteraction from the enemy to regain his lost initiative.

In due time North Vietnam indeed changed its strategy by striking at the heart of our cities. But, when the Tet general offensive finally materialized, it came as a big surprise for the GVN. We were surprised not because of the absence of telltale indications, which our intelligence had picked up, but primarily because of our subjectivity and complacency, which totally misled our estimates as to the enemy's intention and calculated boldness.

• • •

The Tet Offensive did not help the enemy attain his strategic objectives. He temporarily regained some initiative, but eventually lost it again and found himself in a military posture much worse than before. The RVNAF did not disintegrate; they became stronger and more aggressive. Popular uprisings, a key to quick victory, never materialized. US forces did not bog down as expected, and finally the enemy's ploy of installing a coalition government was completely shattered.

• • •

The enemy's subjectivity also brought him a big surprise. He had preconceived ideas about the weakness of the RVNAF and the people's hostile attitude toward the United States and the GVN. But the RVNAF had fought gallantly and with confidence; they had fully demonstrated their combat capabilities and aggressiveness. Despite their criticisms of the GVN and noncommittal attitude, the South Vietnamese people had resolutely refused to cooperate with the Communists. They were not deceived by such disguised stratagems of Communist domination as "coalition," "neutrality," and "peace." No wonder some observers had humorously called the South Vietnamese people's attitude during the Tet Offensive "a vote by feet." No other expression could be more appropriate.

Although the enemy Tet Offensive solidified the determination and unity of the South Vietnamese people, armed forces, and government to fight against Communism, the event had shocked US officials and politicians. It created dissension among US policy makers in matters of strategy and current policy toward the Vietnam War. It dealt a serious blow to the steadfast confrontational stance of the United States in this part of the world and put into question the US commitments toward the Free World.

• • •

Apparently the antiwar bias of the US media had imprisoned US public opinion. Eventually the pressure exerted by some members of the US Congress and the vocal antiwar segment had turned President Johnson's policy around. He made several fateful decisions, among them the cessation of US bombings above the 20th parallel, the refusal to give General Westmoreland additional troops, and his noncandidacy for reelection, with a view to seek a negotiated settlement of the war and restore US national unity.

• • •

We believe that the final course of the war could have been determined at that time without additional US troops. It could have turned to our advantage if the United States had been determined and patient enough to continue its military offensive strategy a little longer and accelerated the development of the RVNAF in the way we had suggested. It was most unfortunate for South Vietnam that this did not happen.

• • •

Modernization and Improvement of the RVNAF

The new US war and peace strategy consisted of turning over combat responsibilities to the RVNAF under the Vietnamization program in order to allow the incremental redeployment of US troops and negotiating in Paris for a just and true peace in South Vietnam.

The term "Vietnamization" was perhaps improper as far as the South Vietnamese were concerned because of its controversial effect. Why Vietnamization? Had the Vietnamese nationalists not fought against the Communists well before the United States had any interest in Vietnam? Had the people and armed forces of the RVN not fought the war alongside US forces since 1965? Why make it sound [like] only US forces were fighting the Vietnam War? The amount of blood shed by the South Vietnamese was many times greater than that of gallant US troops; the war itself was a matter of survival for the South Vietnamese people, who did not want to submit to the cruelties of Communist domination. But they could not handle it by themselves and had to appeal to the United States for assistance. In an ideological conflict, where propaganda and psychology proved to be effective weapons, the use of Vietnamization as a term deeply hurt the people and the armed forces of the RVN. We feel it unwittingly admitted the US error in strategy and the failure of US military efforts, a historical repeat of the French debacle years earlier.

• • •

The achievements of the RVNAF improvement and modernization programs could be measured by challenges successfully met after 1969. The greater these challenges were, the more self-assured the RVNAF felt of their combat capabilities, which were effectively supported by US firepower and mobility. The Cambodian incursion, the Laos cross-border operation, and the successful confrontation with NVA units during the 1972 Easter Offensive were three major challenges which demonstrated the success of Vietnamization.

Cross-Border Operations

• • •

THE LOWER LAOS CROSS-BORDER OPERATION

The decision to strike into Laos to sever the enemy's vital lifeline that sustained his war in the South, in our judgment, was a strategic decision of prime importance which greatly influenced the course of the war in South Vietnam and Cambodia. Its importance was perhaps equal in magnitude to the strategic decision of bombing North Vietnam.

• • •

The decision to conduct the Laos cross-border operation in 1971 came rather unexpectedly as far as the RVNAF were concerned, but it was quickly welcomed without hesitation. Several questions, however, remained unanswered as to the speed and suddenness with which the decision had been made. Was President Nixon changing the US anti-infiltration strategy, or was it just a retaliatory action against the Communist "talk and fight" strategy? Perhaps the United States desired to test the progress made by the RVNAF under Vietnamization, or perhaps the operation was intended to press North Vietnam into serious negotiations? In any event, no specific duration had been planned for Lam Son 719.

When Lam Son 719 was finally terminated, it created quite a controversy. Both the Communists and the RVN claimed victory. President Thieu did his best to represent the operation as a military success, but perhaps he recognized that Lam Son 719 had fallen short of expectations, tactically and strategically. In terms of achievements, it was not as impressive as the Cambodian incursion. Perhaps the operation had preempted enemy offensive plans, but his only lifeline remained almost intact after our brief disruption. ARVN units were unable to maintain the initiative for the entire operation. No significant amounts of enemy supplies had been discovered and destroyed that could be comparable to the Cambodian caches. Also it appeared that most enemy casualties resulted from US tactical air strikes and gunships.

The enemy was not surprised by Lam Son 719 and was fully prepared to meet our forces head-on. Most of his supplies had long been displaced farther west, beyond Tchepone. The NVA Rear Service forces had been ready to fight back from a system of mutually supporting "blocks," or sophisticated fortifications, which were difficult to destroy. Route 9, the main avenue of approach to Tchepone, had been closely interdicted. More importantly, the NVA had preplanned artillery fire on most places susceptible of becoming landing zones, and its observation posts had been pre-positioned on almost all dominating terrain features in the area of operation.

The NVA 70B Corps had been activated since late 1970 to control and coordinate the 304th, 308th, and 320th Divisions; it displaced into the area of operations as soon as Lam Son 719 was launched. The enemy's reactions were swift and forceful, because he was determined to protect his supply line to the South, utilizing almost all of his strategic reserves and accepting losses without hesitation. Obviously the enemy had drawn on his experience with our familiar pattern of operational maneuvers in South Vietnam. He had taken full advantage of a familiar terrain to maneuver in close proximity to our forces, thereby neutralizing the effectiveness of our superior firepower.

On the friendly side, the lessons learned from this difficult and complex operation were numerous. First, we had underestimated the speed and determination of enemy reactions. There were no contingency plans to face extraordinary or unfavorable developments. Our superiority in tactical air and heliborne mobility was completely negated, first by weather, then by enemy air defense or artillery and mortar fire. Numerically, our infantry was overwhelmed by the enemy, whose firepower was equally strong, but from carefully prepared positions. Deployed in an unfavorable terrain, our 300-vehicle armored force was impotent against enemy tanks and unable to assist the Airborne Division in breaking the enemy encirclement or regaining the initiative. By contrast, the enemy armor had proved aggressive and dangerous; it had taken advantage of a familiar though unfavorable terrain to lay ambushes or close in on our strongpoints and finally combine with infantry to assault and overrun them.

Our infantry units shunned maneuvers when engaged and failed to use their organic fire to destroy the enemy, relying entirely on supporting firepower. The I Corps and the division commanders involved all had reserves, but they failed to use them to overcome difficulties and regain the initiative. Even our available firepower was not properly used, especially during the first month of the operation, because of poor coordination.

• • •

On the national level, there were also several significant lessons to be learned from Lam Son 719. First, the problem of leadership should have been reviewed, especially at corps and division levels. The appointment of general officers to these key command jobs should have been devoid of political considerations and based entirely on military professionalism and competence. Hierarchy could have been respected only if seniority in rank had been taken into consideration in promotion and appointments. Military discipline should have been strictly enforced, even with general officers, especially when the conduct of a major and decisive operation was at stake.

Second, it was obvious that the RVNAF general reserves were totally inadequate. They were even inadequate for the limited objectives of Lam Son 719. With the Airborne and Marine Divisions both committed, the JGS had no flexibility to influence operations. It was a most serious shortcoming for the RVNAF under such circumstances when they were unable to reconstitute a similar reserve to throw into the operation or to meet another emergency. It had therefore become most pressing to release part if not all of our infantry divisions from their territorial responsibilities and place them in strategic reserve or mobile defense posture.

The fact that President Thieu was unwilling to commit the 2nd Infantry Division in Lam Son 719, as suggested by COMUSMACV, reflected his concern that ARVN divisions were unprepared for a strategic task. Experience indicated that it took a certain time for preparation and exercise and a few challenges for an ARVN division to completely rid itself of the "territorial syndrome" and become fully effective as a mobile combat force. Lack of long-range planning in that direction, and other constraints, had deprived both the RVN and United States of a chance to win a big victory where it might have decided the outcome of the war.

Finally, if Lam Son 719 had been intended as a test of Vietnamization, it should have demonstrated that the RVNAF improvement and modernization program still had much to accomplish. Compared to the NVA, the ARVN was developing too slowly and inadequately, especially in armor and artillery. Counterbattery capabilities were another area requiring attention, especially in view of the long-range NVA artillery.

The VNAF modernization program should also have detected the rapidly developing and effective enemy antiair defense. It was obvious to us that our heliborne capability, tactical air support, and logistics were still dependent on US forces. This included our naval transportation capability, but to a lesser extent.

The 1972 Easter Offensive

The Nguyen Hue campaign of early summer 1972 was the NVA's largest and probably most important offensive. For this all-out effort, Hanoi committed almost the entire NVA, using 14 infantry divisions and 26 separate regiments, plus substantial armor and artillery forces. However, in the end, the NVA failed to achieve its major objectives politically and militarily.

Throughout this entire enemy offensive the RVNAF demonstrated a high degree of professionalism and determination. Consequently, no single provincial capital of the RVN was lost to enemy control. Only 10 out of 260 district towns had been permanently occupied, but they were all located in outlying areas. An Loc, which had been intended as a national capital for the PRG, held firmly and gallantly against concerted attacks by three NVA divisions. The RVNAF had not been crushed as anticipated by our enemy. The people of South Vietnam remained calm, undaunted; they also supported our units during the heaviest fighting.

Exhausted by serious losses, the NVA no longer had any significant offensive capability left to achieve political gains during the last quarter of 1972; its units had to disperse to wait and prepare for the next round of low-key activities. More importantly, the morale of the VCI declined markedly. The enemy offensive also failed to disrupt our pacification program, except in the areas of heavy fighting. The Mekong Delta, as an example, was not affected in any way; the enemy had been unable to achieve a single gain in population control. All of the surface communication in the Delta remained secure during this major enemy offensive, despite the redeployment of almost one-half of IV Corps forces to MR-3.

The enemy 1972 Easter Offensive failed for several reasons. Our enemy became complacent after our venture into Laos in Lam Son 719. He underestimated the RVNAF capabilities and the effectiveness and power of the USAF; he also could not predict President Nixon's firm and swift reaction to the invasion. Strategically and tactically, our enemy committed many errors. Two of his most serious mistakes in strategy had to do with priority of efforts and timing. The NVA had distributed its forces among three distant objective areas instead of concentrating on one to achieve a quick and decisive victory. Consequently it did not have the capability to win in any one area. By improper timing our enemy also lost the chance of exploiting his initial success and gave the RVNAF enough time to regroup and consolidate their defenses.

Two tactical errors added to the enemy's failure. The NVA proved inexperienced in the employment of armor and inefficient in coordinating armor and infantry. Instead of taking advantage of armor's shock effect to break through our defenses, he employed tanks hesitantly, without cohesion or infantry support. His tanks therefore became easy targets for our LAWs and heliborne TOWs. Employing armor without air cover and infantry support, the enemy had sacrificed his tanks. The second error stemmed from the enemy's classic mass assault tactic: . . . the human waves were quickly destroyed by our mass firepower.

On our side, there were also several lessons we learned from our initial setback and subsequent victory. They were command and leadership.

We obviously had not remembered the lessons of Lam Son 719. Our leadership was still weakened by personal animosity and political considerations. However, this problem was solved when the I Corps and the Marine Division commanders were replaced by combat-experienced and professional general officers. This timely change in command and leadership had a most favorable impact on our combat units and staffs. The new I Corps commander's frequent visits to his units in the field helped enhance troop morale tremendously at a most critical juncture; they also boosted confidence on the part of small-unit commanders and enabled the I Corps commander to stay on top of the situation at all times. Reports were never a substitute for field visits, and a staff was only as good as its commander. With the same personnel and resources, the new I Corps commander quickly demonstrated what a professional and experienced leader could accomplish during an emergency.

Military hierarchy functioned effectively only if rank and rank seniority were respected, especially for command and control purposes. This should have been the major consideration when we assigned someone to become part of a command system. The removal of the Marine Division commander was therefore timely and necessary for I Corps command to function effectively. The practice of bypassing a responsible and middle echelon in operational control should have been avoided at all costs, since it only created confusion and fostered animosity. Command and control, to be effective, should be kept as simple as possible. We believe that the span of control should never exceed five subordinate units, especially in a complex combat situation.

Giving the 3rd Division commander command and control over at least nine regimental-level units was a serious violation of sound military doctrine, especially since it was our newest division and [had] yet to be tested as an entire unit in combat. It is obvious why this division command was ineffective. Given the seriousness of the situation, and the resources available, it was totally unacceptable for the I Corps commander not to assign any command and control responsibility to the Marine Division headquarters when two out of three marine brigades had been committed, and to the Ranger Command when four ranger groups were being employed. Our initial command and control in the I Corps area caused confusion, which was the primary reason why no unit carried out the Quang Trung counterattack plan as ordered and eventually led to the loss of Quang Tri and the rout of 3rd Division forces.

The deployment of the 23rd Division headquarters to Kontum City and the replacement of the division commander were accomplished at the right moment. But the defense of Kontum could have faltered if the 23rd Division organic forces had not replaced the heterogeneous defense units in time. This gave the division commander unity of command, absolute discipline authority, and morale cohesiveness, which were the very elements of success at Kontum.

• • •

Both the JGS and MACV knew in advance, and in considerable detail, about the 1972 enemy offensive, except for its exact timing and the place of the enemy's primary effort. It was clear to all of us that the enemy had concentrated his forces and had the capability in three different areas. Despite this knowledge, the RVNAF were unable to take any preemptive action or any course other than being alert and reinforcing their defenses and waiting. Only when the offensive had been launched and the enemy's efforts known were our commanders able to maneuver their forces in defense. The primary reason for this static or passive defense posture was that the RVNAF did not have adequate tactical and strategic reserves. Our defense strategy remained founded on the policy of "hold all and at all costs," despite the fact that for the last three years South Vietnam's defense capabilities had been greatly reduced as a result of the US force redeployment. This policy caused our forces to be overextended and not capable of immediate success against a concentrated enemy attack.

Our infantry divisions meanwhile continued to bog down in their territorial security responsibilities. Accustomed as they were to small-unit operations in support of pacification, most ARVN divisions were not prepared, during the initial stage of this enemy offensive, to fight the kind of [conventional] warfare for which they had been organized and equipped. Their defenses were not properly organized in depth with solid fortifications and alternate lines. There was a definite lack in firepower coordination with the VNAF and VNN. Divisional artillery forces were broken down into small elements at fixed firebases which became good targets for concentrated enemy artillery and mortar fire. Our reactions in general took on a routine pattern, as if to meet ordinary "high points." To counter this enemy offensive, our units were often thrown into combat piecemeal—a battalion here, a brigade there—instead of being committed as major tactical formations in order to regain the initiative. This piecemeal employment of forces unwittingly made command and control more difficult and greatly reduced the effectiveness of our combat units.

Our mobile tactical and strategic reserves, a matter of utmost importance for South Vietnam, were woefully inadequate to counteract the enemy's offensive strategy of primary and secondary efforts. . . . Each corps had only one ranger group as a tactical reserve, since all divisional forces had been extended in static defense. The RVNAF general reserves—the Airborne and Marine Divisions—were insufficient for three large fronts. Their employment was usually subjected to careful planning, but again we could not help deploying them by brigade to each needy area. Also, their mobility depended entirely on the USAF. Because of all this, our counterattack could not be conducted as timely and forcefully as desired, especially after enemy attacks had been stalled in Quang Tri and Kontum. This also explained why our field commanders could not afford to rotate their units between combat and rest.

Military dependents and the civilian population living in areas under attack disrupted our combat operations and were a dilemma for our field commanders. If military dependents were evacuated ahead of time, the local population became anxious and sometimes panicky. And if a panicky population fled in mass, the morale of our troops was seriously affected.

Therefore military dependents and the civilian population were left to fend for themselves. When fighting occurred, they usually fled in the direction of safety toward cities and refugee camps; the minute the fighting abated, they invariably returned to their homes. However, there were also many who preferred not to evacuate. It was these people and the returning refugees who caused many problems for our units; this was especially true when several 3rd Division units unexpectedly withdrew from Quang Tri along Route 1. In An Loc, the great number of military dependents and civilian refugees whose movement to the east was blocked by the enemy became quite a supply burden for our forces. However, they also effectively assisted our troops in first aid or supply, and even served as replacements. In general, the calm attitude of the civilian population and their solidarity with our troops were significant contributions to our success in 1972. However, each commander had to include them in the planning process and always be alert to the problems they could cause.

• • •

RVNAF CAPABILITIES FOR SELF-SUPPORT

• • •

The 1972 Easter Offensive came indeed as a major challenge, a valuable test of RVNAF capabilities. We believe its outcome indicated that ARVN forces were fully capable of confronting the NVA if US support was provided in three vital areas: tactical and strategic air, to include troop transport; sea transport; and the replacement of weapons, materiel, and supplies. In long-range artillery and armor capabilities, the ARVN was still inferior to the NVA. Obviously, at this time, Vietnamization still had a long way to go toward developing the self-supporting capabilities of the RVNAF.

• • •

Peace Initiative and Negotiations

• • •

Finally, at the conference table, the United States was negotiating from a position of weakness. Its unilateral troop withdrawal, coupled with a retrogression to enclave defense strategy to reduce casualties, offered the United States no bargaining power. In its own backyard, antiwar pressure mounted, and, urged on by "dove" politicians and other political dictates, the United States went from one concession to another, seeking impatiently to disengage from the war with honor, even at the cost of South Vietnam's future.

That President Thieu had adamantly refused to submit to US wishes in 1968 was understandable, even laudable. But he could not procrastinate for long, because the United States was holding the key to South Vietnam's survival. In the end, only the United States and North Vietnam came away with what they wanted.

Significant Lessons Learned

1. Many major events of the Vietnam War seemed to have occurred during US presidential election years. . . .

    The 1968 Tet Offensive was a major turning point in South Vietnamese history, similar to those that preceded it in 1960 and 1964. But, unlike the previous years, this time the resolve of the United States concerning the pursuit of war had faltered. From a strategy of quick victory, the United States switched to negotiations and "Vietnamized" the war. This opened the way for the Communists to apply their strategy of "talk and fight," which lasted through the four years of the US president's term and culminated in the fourth major turning point in 1972, leading to the Paris Agreement. . . .

2. The policy of "talk and fight" was not a technique used only by the Communists; it was also adopted by the RVN and the United States. However, on our side this technique did not seem as effective because of the US unilateral troop withdrawal and deescalation and the fact that the RVNAF were not strong enough to provide adequate bargaining power during peace talks.

3. By using the expression "Vietnamization" to explain its new policy to the US Congress and public, the US government had unwittingly disregarded the sacrifices of the South Vietnamese people and armed forces and negated the cause of freedom and survival for which they had been fighting. Therefore, President Thieu and the GVN never used this term. . . .

4. Developing and modernizing the RVNAF to enable them to assume the major combat role in the war was a correct policy. It was the very policy that successive GVNs had pursued since the war broke out through requests of increased military aid. Unfortunately, these requests were not approved at an appropriate level to allow the rapid development and modernization of the RVNAF. This stemmed partly from the fact that our political instability had prevented us from taking the strong measures required to procure the necessary manpower. It also seemed to be influenced by the US policy of using its military might to shorten the war. First priority in resources was therefore given to US combat forces, and military assistance for the RVNAF became secondary. Not until the Vietnamization program was announced did improvement and modernization of the RVNAF resume at an accelerated pace. . . .

5. South Vietnam's population of 18 million could not provide the manpower required for a one million military force fighting a long war. . . .

6. The cross-border operations into Cambodia and Laos, and the 1972 Easter Offensive, were excellent opportunities for the RVNAF to improve their combat effectiveness and for our progress in Vietnamization to be tested. As a result of these experiences, our forces became more self-confident and functioned effectively at every level. However, we realized again that US assistance was still required in the areas of advisors and air, mobility, and logistic support. . . .

7. Strategic reserves and strong leadership at corps and division level in the RVNAF were factors that often provided success in our engagements. Our strategic reserves were not sufficient for South Vietnam's extended defense posture in the face of an enemy who held the offensive initiative. The RVNAF force structure expansion and development programs failed to solve the problem of strategic reserves, which became even more critical after the redeployment of eight US combat divisions. . . .

8. The period from late 1968 to 1972 was the best period of achievement for our pacification program. This resulted from effective coordination between the GVN and CORDS, the participation of the people, the significant contributions of US aid, and improved security in rural areas. The improvement of rural security was made possible by the development of the PSDF, the deployment of police forces to villages, the continued implementation of the Phung Hoang program, and the effective shield provided by ARVN divisions. Finally, this was a period when most major enemy units had withdrawn into sanctuaries across the border and the USAF continued to strike enemy base areas both inside South Vietnam and in the lower Laotian panhandle.

IV. THE STRUGGLE FOR SURVIVAL: 1973–1975

The Paris Agreement

The Paris Agreement of January 1973 served only the immediate purposes of the United States and North Vietnam. It enabled President Nixon to keep his promise to the American people. American prisoners of war were released and reunited with their families, and all US troops left South Vietnam safely and honorably. The United States was pleased that it had brought a "just peace" to the people of South Vietnam and terminated a long and inconclusive war, a war that divided the American people.

The Paris Agreement also offered North Vietnam the favorable conditions to pursue its conquest of South Vietnam with success. No longer constrained by bombings and blockades, Hanoi devoted its efforts to reconstruction and development in order to better support its war efforts in South Vietnam. No obstacle now lay in the way of its continued infiltration through Laos and Cambodia. Hanoi simply ignored the restrictive provisions of the Paris Agreement that did not serve its purposes.

In South Vietnam, the NLF was given a legitimate national status. It now had an official government, an army, and a national territory of its own. In all respects, the NLF had become a political entity equal in power to the GVN. All the major obstructions that had prevented North Vietnam and its South Vietnamese lackeys from winning a military victory were now gone. US and FWMA forces had all left, while nearly 300,000 NVA troops still remained on South Vietnamese soil. Never since 1954 had the Communists enjoyed such a strong political and military posture.

All this had been achieved only at a great cost to South Vietnam, for the advantages gained by North Vietnam through the Paris Agreement were also the disadvantages imposed on South Vietnam. Politically, the GVN had been edged into such a position that it could not explain satisfactorily to its people and armed forces why the NLF, heretofore considered a rebel organization at the service of North Vietnamese Communists, suddenly became an equal partner in governmental politics. To many this was a coalition, which the GVN had vowed it would never accept.

• • •

Cease-Fire and Violations

The Paris Agreement never restored peace to South Vietnam. The reports of gunfire continued to echo throughout the country, even after the cease-fire day had passed. Except for the withdrawal of US troops, the exchange of prisoners, the cessation of all US war activities in Vietnam, and the de-mining of North Vietnam's ports, no other provision of the Paris Agreement could be implemented, especially the cease-fire. This was because of the very ambiguity and impracticability of the agreement and the fact that North Vietnam never renounced . . . aggression.

• • •

The Communists . . . totally disregarded the provisions of the agreement. They continued to move personnel and war materials into South Vietnam to replace not only post-cease-fire losses, but also those incurred during the 1972 offensive. At the same time, they accelerated the modernization of their units with a view to tilt the balance of forces in their favor. Just three months after the cease-fire their armor forces had been augmented by 400 tanks, which brought the total to 500, and their 122mm and 130mm guns also increased to 250 pieces, compared to 80 in 1972. By that time NVA air defense units were being upgraded into regiments and divisions, equipped with radar-controlled 37mm, 57mm, and 100mm guns and even SA-2s.

• • •

South Vietnam's Strategic Alternatives

• • •

The hard-line "four no's" anti-Communist policy espoused by President Thieu represented the wishes of the great majority of South Vietnamese. This policy provided for the protection of the constitution and democratic institutions; it sought to defend that part of South Vietnam's territory which the people and the RVNAF had shed blood to build and to preserve. It also reassured South Vietnamese and stimulated them in the face of the dark prospects provided by the Paris Agreement, including those of an American sellout and rumors of further partition.

However, President Thieu was unable to provide the coalescing force required to hold the South Vietnamese together during a major political and military showdown with the Communists. His leadership failed to foster and strengthen national solidarity. The people, and politicians in particular, suspected him of having dictatorial tendencies. Suspicion was further reinforced by some of the measures President Thieu kept pushing to strengthen his political base.

The press law that he enacted in August 1972, to make the press healthy and encourage it to serve the nation during a period of struggle for survival, in which information played an important role, was unfortunately accused of strangling freedom of speech. The closing down of 24 newspapers which failed to meet requirements eventually led to street demonstrations in Saigon. The same adverse reaction greeted the GVN law of political parties. We think that this law was exactly what South Vietnam needed to coalesce all its political groups into a democratic bipartisan system and muster enough political strength to struggle against the Communists. Unfortunately, the opposition accused him of paving the way for a monolithic system dominated by his Democratic Party.

The amendment of the RVN constitution in January 1974, which allowed President Thieu to run for a third term, led to a political crisis in which antigovernment demonstrators accused him of corruption and clamored for his resignation. The opposition consisted mostly of anti-Communist elements who cared for the future of the nation and sincerely wanted a change in leadership in order to create a favorable condition for national unity. However, it was joined by a small number of Communist agents and sympathizers who were bent on sowing disorder and aggravating divisiveness among nationalist ranks.

In spite of his efforts, President Thieu did not have much success in stabilizing the political situation. By the end of 1974, he had reshuffled his cabinet four times and replaced a large number of province chiefs and division and corps commanders with a view to strengthening his administration. Opposition groups alleged that he was not sincere in correcting the flaws of the regime, pointing to several corrupt and incompetent henchmen who still made up his entourage. Some of the better personnel changes, they said, were not of his choice but dictated by political and public pressures. His lofty procrastination failed to dispirit the opposition. Finally, his use of police power to crack down on the opposition ushered the situation into a political impasse.

• • •

In the state of political divisiveness that beset South Vietnam in the fall of 1974, we believe that there were only two acceptable courses of action. President Thieu could have brought up the issue of confidence and let the people decide whether they still wanted him as their leader through a popular referendum. Or he could have proved his disinterest in personal power by resigning in goodwill and given the nation a chance to experiment with fresh and perhaps better leadership.

President Thieu's policy of holding on to every inch of national territory at all costs was consistent with South Vietnam's anti-Communist policy and entirely responsive to the situation created by a standstill cease-fire. Since our enemy could lay claim to any area where our military presence was nonexistent, it had become imperative to hold on to all outposts, hamlets, and district towns, especially those located in sparsely populated outlying corners or even in the heart of enemy base areas.

• • •

As enemy violations escalated in intensity . . . this policy was eventually no longer responsive to South Vietnam's requirements, especially as of FY 1973, when the United States began to reduce military aid.

• • •

The Final Collapse

The rapid collapse of South Vietnam stunned almost everybody, to include every segment of South Vietnamese society. No one, even our enemy, could imagine that the one-million-man RVNAF could have disintegrated so tragically in only 45 days. This resulted from a near-total morale collapse which engulfed the population and armed forces of South Vietnam, beginning in mid-March 1975.

President Thieu's decision to switch strategy, from "hold all at all costs" to "hold as you can," was inevitable; he had no other alternative. The unfortunate thing was that this alternative was implemented too late and without appropriate planning and preparations. Therefore this sudden decision came as a hard psychological blow, with all the undertones of defeat. It made the implementation task extremely difficult and confusing for field commanders involved, and it instilled anxiety and apprehension among the military and civilian population, whose morale had steadily declined as a result of American and world inaction in the face of blatant Communist violations. Despite the tardiness of its implementation, this strategy was viable and would have been applicable in several areas across the country if President Thieu and the JGS had planned for it ahead of time.

• • •

That President Thieu analyzed the problem and made the decision all by himself, without informing the US ambassador or the USDAO chief, was incomprehensible in view of the importance and implications of this decision. No doubt he was fully aware that South Vietnam was not capable of defending itself without assistance. He also knew that US military aid was indispensable for South Vietnam's survival. Therefore, surprising the United States with a fait accompli was totally detrimental to South Vietnam's future, because it gave US authorities no time to plan and prepare for assistance, especially in emergency situations such as the evacuation of Hue and Danang. It was this failure in solving the refugee evacuation problem in time that caused the paralysis and morale disintegration of our I Corps forces.

The implementation of the "hold as you can" policy began with the evacuation of Kontum and Pleiku, an area so far considered strategically important for the defense of the coastal plains. As a beginning action, this move was too risky, erroneous, and rudimentary. It startled the population and RVNAF units in the area, creating panic among them. Hasty execution, coupled with complete GVN silence, gave credence to rumors that this part of the country had been conceded to the Communists through secret agreements. Believing that they were being made victims and hostages of the Communists, the local population fled toward the coast, along with the troop convoys of II Corps.

The president's official order to "redeploy regular forces from Kontum and Pleiku to

Nha Trang in order to reoccupy Ban Me Thuot" was an impossible mission. Even if this redeployment had succeeded, the reoccupation of Ban Me Thuot would not have been possible with redeployed units alone. It would have taken the commitment of general reserves to accomplish this mission, but the Airborne and Marine Divisions were already deployed in MR-1. The second impossible thing was to leave province chiefs and RF and PF troops behind to fend for themselves. This amounted to abandoning these troops to the mercy of NVA units, a sacrifice too big to accept which might seriously affect the morale of RF and PF troops elsewhere and other paramilitary forces as well. The subsequent disintegration of the police, RF, PF, and territorial commands, which occurred well ahead of events during the final weeks of South Vietnam, was perhaps a tragic consequence of this thoughtless act.

The commander of II Corps/MR-2 was not forthright and sincere when he accepted the mission, apparently to please the president. President Thieu had asked him if he felt he could reoccupy Ban Me Thuot, which implied that he was given some time to think about it. As Chief of the JGS, I [General Cao Van Vien] also suggested that II Corps could not expect any reinforcements from the JGS, which meant that he had to rely upon his own forces for this difficult task. I further insinuated the riskiness of the mission by reminding him of past French failures in such attempts. All this amounted to an excellent opportunity for General Phu to ask the president for some time to study the mission in detail. Had General Phu been forthright and courageous enough to do this, he would have had the opportunity to appreciate the impossibility of his mission and answer the president accordingly. Then perhaps President Thieu would have restudied his redeployment concept, because of its far-reaching psychological and political impact, and considered other solutions.

We believe that, since his immediate goal was to reoccupy Ban Me Thuot, he should have used forces other than those in Kontum and Pleiku for this mission. This was necessary to maintain the morale of troops and the civilian population in MR-2. The next step should have been to plan carefully for the evacuation of Kontum and Pleiku in such a way that its implementation would not create any adverse psychological impact.

The fact that President Thieu had personally given direct orders and guidance to General Phu to carry out what he called a "top secret" mission had placed the JGS in a difficult position. Therefore the JGS had to wait for General Phu's plans in order to provide the necessary support. Unfortunately, General Phu did not contact or submit any plans to the JGS before initiating his withdrawal action. Convinced that he must have the element of surprise to succeed, General Phu did not properly plan his operation.

• • •

General Phu's orders for the sectors of Phu Bon and Tuy Hoa to provide security for Route 7B were an act of irresponsibility. Not only were there not enough RF troops for a task of such magnitude (160 miles), nearly 100 miles of this road had not been explored for a long time. To ensure road security, he should have deployed ranger units to occupy dominating terrain features along this road, thereby reinforcing the sector troops and enabling engineer units to reestablish road trafficability in time. If General Phu had done this, and taken diversionary measures in Pleiku and Kontum, we believe that the redeployment of his forces would have been successful.

The element of secrecy that General Phu had desired and expected to achieve did not last very long. When the first convoy left Pleiku, the people were alerted to a possible evacuation. This was inevitable in the context of the Vietnam War. For years our people had depended on army units for their security. Therefore they monitored the activities of military dependents and units; if troops and their dependents left because of enemy action, so did they. As for the enemy, he was indeed surprised by this sudden redeployment. However, he immediately threw his units into the pursuit.

• • •

We believe at that time South Vietnam no longer had the capability to save its people from the trauma of defeat or restore their confidence. President Thieu's vows to "hold at all costs" had no effect on our people, or even on RVNAF troops. The fact was the RVNAF no longer had any significant reserves left to help II Corps establish an effective line of defense or to launch a few successful counterattacks to restore popular and troop confidence. Although the JGS had a contingency plan to extract one infantry division from MR-4 in case of emergency, this plan could not be implemented because of heavy enemy pressure in the Mekong Delta and the hopeless state of the nation's morale. The RVNAF could no longer expect to receive the same level of US support as they had during 1972 in order to refit units, reorganize defenses, and counterattack.

A few victories such as those achieved by IV Corps in Long An and Can Tho, the effective use of incendiary and CBU bombs and even "daisy cutters" by the VNAF, and the gallant battles fought by the 18th Infantry Division against three NVA divisions in Xuan Loc no longer sufficed to stop the rapidly decaying morale of troops and civilians alike. All were expecting some forceful action by the United States to stop the onslaught of NVA divisions. But hopes were all gone after the visit of General Weyand and the US Congress rejected additional military assistance for South Vietnam.

The negative attitude of the US government toward Communist violations, the US Congress's rejection of additional military aid, and the evacuation of personnel from US consulates in MR-1 and MR-2, and from the US Embassy in Saigon, all contributed to the collapse of morale throughout South Vietnam.

Significant Lessons Learned

1. The Paris Agreement did not end the war and restore peace for the people of South Vietnam because the Communists continued to launch attacks across the country. . . .
2. The attitude of the United States greatly influenced the enforcement of the cease-fire. Among four signatory parties of the Paris Agreement, only the United States had the genuine authority and resources to make others respect the agreement. Therefore, after President Nixon . . . had resigned, the attitude and actions of the US government toward blatant Communist violations, as well as [toward] military aid for South Vietnam, practically enhanced North

Vietnam's confidence in pursuing the conquest of South Vietnam with impunity. . . .

In view of its prestige as a leading world power, its moral obligation toward a longstanding ally, and its responsibilities toward the Paris Agreement in enforcing and making other parties enforce it, we think that the US government should have adopted a resolute stance toward and acted vigorously against Communist cease-fire violations. If this had been done, we believe that these violations would not have reached the level and intensity they did, and perhaps South Vietnam's tragic fate could have been averted.

3. Fighting against Communism was the only course of action that South Vietnam could take to ensure its continued survival in freedom and democracy. There was no other way, and no solution could ever replace victory. Political solidarity and military strength were the two factors that we required to achieve this victory for South Vietnam.

President Thieu did not have the courage and capability to create the favorable conditions for national unity. His political prestige diminished greatly after his "solo performance" in 1971, an event that should have never occurred in a democratic nation. It declined even further after he consented to participate in the peace talks as an equal to the NLF, signed an agreement which legalized the existence of two governments and two armies in South Vietnam, approved a constitution amendment to let him run for a third term, and never sincerely or enthusiastically removed the corrupt and incompetent elements in his government. President Thieu's political prestige was completely gone after President Nixon resigned. If he had had the wisdom then to step down and let the people select a national leader more suited to the circumstances, he would have been acclaimed as a true patriot who sincerely cared about the nation's future. But his procrastination led to political instability which seriously affected national unity and morale.

In the Vietnam conflict both the RVNAF and the NVA depended on foreign military aid. It was a fact that neither South nor North Vietnam was able to provide much for their military forces except manpower. If both had continued to receive aid infusion at an appropriate level, neither side would have been able to prevail militarily and the war would have drawn out inconclusively. However the United States quit too early, even before the Vietnamization program was completed, while the Communist bloc continued to provide North Vietnam with increasing aid. US drastic aid cutbacks, at a time when the Communists were escalating their war of conquest, compelled the RVNAF to fight without adequate supplies of fuel and ammunition, despite their belt-tightening efforts. It was a fact that US FY 1975 military aid appropriations only satisfied about one-half of the RVNAF minimum true requirements. . . .

4. The United States made a complete turnabout in its containment policy in Southeast Asia and ambiguously granted South Vietnam a "decent interval" to fend for its own survival. By overrelying on the US promise of continued

support and assistance, the GVN had become complacent and too shortsighted to develop an acceptable strategy for defending South Vietnam in the long term. As a result, when it came to grip with the realities, it was already too late.

5. The sudden switch in South Vietnam's defense strategy resulted in a hasty decision to abandon Pleiku and Kontum on 16 March 1975. The tragic results of this decision shattered the morale of the RVNAF and the South Vietnamese people, which was already swayed by the apparent US indifferent attitude toward stepped-up Communist aggression and the painful aid cutbacks. Half of South Vietnam quickly fell into enemy hands, not as a result of the force and fierceness of the enemy offensive but primarily because of morale disintegration and the evacuation of regular forces. As it rushed southward, the tide of refugees also caused complete disintegration of some of our military units.

In the final analysis, this was the ultimate outcome of a long nation-building process. The strength of South Vietnam and its armed forces had been built primarily on foreign aid, not on its national resources. The fate of South Vietnam therefore depended on its American friends.

V. CONCLUSIONS

The war that Communist North Vietnam waged in the South five years after the 1954 Geneva armistice sought to achieve two objectives: to reunify Vietnam by force and to defeat "American imperialism." North Vietnam had achieved its first objective after long and determined war efforts which culminated in the ignominious surrender of the RVNAF on 30 April 1975. Despite its claims, however, North Vietnam had failed to attain its second goal because the United States had cunningly terminated its inconclusive war efforts with the 1973 Paris Agreement.

• • •

The Vietnam conflict, in a certain sense, was a contest between force of will and military strength. Knowing that they could not defeat the RVN and United States by military strength, the Communists prevailed on perseverance and determination to outlast us. North Vietnam's resolve to conquer South Vietnam and defeat "US imperialism" was consistent throughout the conflict, from active war to peace negotiations. By comparison, US determination was less strong and gradually evaporated with time.

The US resolve to contain the expansion of Communism in Southeast Asia climaxed in its participation in 1965 and remained unchanged until late 1967, despite growing American antiwar sentiments. But, after three years of intense fighting with half a million troops and selected bombings against North Vietnam, the United States began to waver when military victory was nowhere in sight.

In the wake of the 1968 Tet Offensive, US determination declined further when, from war commitments, the United States switched to peace negotiations and ceased bombing unilaterally, going from one concession to another in order to disengage from the war.

The United States finally gave up when it drastically reduced military aid for South Vietnam and remained indifferent toward escalated Communist war efforts, completely oblivious of its commitment toward the RVN and obligations toward the Paris Agreement. This turnabout in attitude encouraged the Communists and made their resolve even stronger. At the same time it also seriously affected South Vietnam's determination to continue the fight alone.

• • •

The Communists . . . used all kinds of subterfuge and tricky propaganda to break the will of South Vietnamese soldiers. Although this proselytizing effort eventually became a major Communist strategic goal, it failed completely to sway our soldiers. It was the collapse of American will that finally shattered South Vietnamese morale and led to Communist victory. To win in a contest of will, one must either have a stronger will or persevere long enough to dispirit the opponent.

The US military and material might was not used at an appropriate level and in the right place to attain the major objective of shattering North Vietnam's determination to pursue its conquest and the secondary goal of stopping the infiltration of men and materiel into the South. The American strategy of gradual response, which was applied to the air war against North Vietnam, did not succeed with an enemy who was resourceful and resilient though of small size. No quick victory was ever possible with the way the United States approached bombing and selected targets. On the contrary, this strategy eventually worked against the United States for several reasons. First, protracted bombing on a small scale and a familiar pattern could only increase US losses. Second, it gave North Vietnam time to modernize and beef up its air defense, with Russian and Chinese aid, while adjusting itself psychologically. Third, as US losses mounted, they also increased the psychological shock among the American people and fueled antiwar feelings.

We believe that the determination of Hanoi's leaders would have been shattered and the war could have ended within a few years after 1965 if the bombings had been carried out on a total scale and in a resolute manner against North Vietnam's most vulnerable points: its ports, which were taking deliveries of war materiel; and its dike system, which protected North Vietnam's rice bowl. The level and targets of US bombings and mining in late 1972 gave us an indication of what could have been achieved if more drastic measures had been taken. But if, for political and humanitarian reasons, the United States could not bring itself to do that, we think it would have been wiser not to expand the air war to North Vietnam.

• • •

The US failure to disrupt North Vietnam's infiltration system in the Laotian panhandle was an indication that airpower alone was perhaps not suited to the nature of this task, despite advanced technology. To control enemy infiltration through this area effectively, we think that airpower should have been applied in conjunction with the use of infantry forces. The expansion of the ground war into lower Laos, therefore, was a justified and most convenient necessity. Since North Vietnam was using Laotian territory for military purposes, in complete disregard of this country's neutrality, the RVN should have had the legitimate right of self-defense by taking military counteractions to stop infiltration. If this enemy windpipe had been effectively strangled by our infantry forces, we believe that the sanctuary system would have been asphyxiated in due time.

• • •

From the beginning to the end, the Vietnam War had always been an insurgency war sustained by infiltration and supported by offensive attacks from North Vietnam. Because of its ultimate goal—overthrowing the RVN government—insurgency was the most important element of the war, with main-force units playing the supporting role. It was insurgent or subversive activities that affected the people's security and their attitude toward the government, more than fierce battles fought in the DMZ or border areas. As a result, anti-insurgency should have been the foundation and priority of the RVN war efforts.

• • •

It was truly detrimental to the war effort that, at the beginning, we did not have any comprehensive plans that set forth the basis for a common strategy and the establishment of a war control apparatus. Not until 1967 did the JGS and MACV come up with the annual Combined Campaign Plan (CCP) which, though not ideal, was a laudable progress in the common war effort. The CCP was not ideal in that it had not been placed in its due context, and because the war control machinery had not been properly adjusted, for effective coordination and integration of US and RVN efforts. For example, the MACV commander did not have complete control of all US agencies involved in pacification support, although he was responsible for it. Likewise the Chief/JGS had no authority over GVN agencies involved in pacification, despite the fact that several aspects of the CCP required the dedicated performance of these agencies. Despite some of its shortcomings, the CCP would have produced better results if it had been instituted a few years earlier, for instance as soon as MACV was activated. Then military actions would have produced more lasting results in pacification because they were supported and continued by civil operations, which in turn would have taken less time and expenditures with the support of military efforts and a permanent security protection system. The concept of "One War" instead of three separate ones—development, pacification, and military efforts—would also have been developed much earlier as a result.

• • •

Militarily, unity of command over all participating forces should be the key to success. The failure to activate a combine command to achieve this unity was militarily deplorable. Politically and psychologically, however, it enhanced South Vietnam's national cause, helped the GVN exercise its newly recovered sovereignty in full, and gave credence to American anticolonialist tradition. Therefore the principle of cooperation and coordination prevailed throughout the war as an alternative to combined command. It had proved effective for the conduct of the war, causing no significant constraints to combined military efforts between RVN and US forces.

• • •

However, the course of the war would have been different and perhaps more beneficial for South Vietnam in the long run if a combined command had been activated. After all, with a US general in overall command, the war would then be [unmistakably] a US responsibility, involving the United States more deeply. Therefore, even in the case of inconclusive fighting, the United States could not disengage from the war easily because its honor and credibility as a leading world power were at stake. Then maybe its resolve to win the war would have been firmer and more consistent.

• • •

Destroying the Communist political infrastructure, the VCI, should have been a priority strategic task during the initial stage of nation building. It was the VCI, not the guerrillas or local forces, which was the foundation of insurgency. As long as the VCI existed, there was no chance to eliminate the guerrillas whose subsistence, support, and growth depended on it. Evidently, when the VCI was isolated, neutralized, and eliminated, sabotage and terrorist activities would gradually disappear, because guerrillas could not exist without replacements, supplies, and intelligence. They would be compelled to move to other areas and become extremely vulnerable to our security activities. Death of the VCI, therefore, was the primary condition of security for national priority areas.

• • •

As mobile self-supporting combat units, ARVN infantry divisions were perfectly adapted to the role of strategic reserves; we must never lose sight of this. The Airborne and Marine Divisions were used as the RVNAF general reserves more because of their availability and excellent combat tradition than because of tactical requirements. Evidently the advent of the helicopter no longer made airborne operations the exclusivity of paratroopers. Likewise our marines never conducted a major amphibious operation in the entire war. Despite their splendid exploits, their employment also caused some complications in terms of tactical coordination and control.

As to infantry divisions, they should fight as separate forces and be placed under corps control only when required. This does not imply that we should not have corps headquarters but, since corps should be purely tactical formations, they should not be assigned any permanent territorial control responsibility.

• • •

As deterrent forces, ARVN infantry divisions should [have been] used only to deliver the decisive blow against major NVA units whenever they were detected or pinned down by our territorial units. The most important thing, therefore, was never to assign any territorial responsibility to infantry divisions, or long security missions which could be detrimental to their combat mobility and morale. Using them in a tactical and strategic reserve posture does not imply that they should stay idle and wait for assignment. In the context of counterinsurgency warfare, infantry divisions should be employed as strike forces, assisting territorial units in crushing enemy local force and guerrilla units and to isolate them from the VCI by destroying the enemy communication and liaison system.

• • •

In terms of nation building and development, the RVN was like an inverted pyramid. Its base, or the political, military, and economic infrastructure at the grassroots level, was weak and poor in every respect, from resources to leadership. By contrast, the summit was powerful and wealthy.

Villages and hamlets are the solid foundation of the nation. The majority of South Vietnamese population lived in rural areas, which were also the principal ground of contest between Nationalists and Communists. The nation-building process, therefore, should begin in rural areas and should be founded on them, and all national efforts should be devoted to strengthening this foundation. Such efforts as improving the PF and RF in 1961, concentrating pacification and development on national priority areas as of 1967, developing PSDF in 1968, and expanding the National Police to villages in 1970 were all excellent moves in the right direction, but they were too late. If all national efforts and US assistance had been devoted to the grassroots level during the initial stage (1955–1956), the situation would have been different.

This national imbalance existed in all areas. Since the Vietnam conflict was basically an insurgency war, the National Police and the people's organization for self-defense should [have been] the primary counterinsurgency forces; their organization and development should have been a first priority task. It was truly unfortunate that, by 1968, the National Police had only 70,000 members, a size that met perhaps peacetime requirements. Lack of care and a sound organization also plagued the People's Self-Defense Force. Evidently the priority given to developing a too-large military force was the primary cause for perennial imbalance.

As a matter of fact, this military force had attracted almost all the nation's elite manpower. But, in a protracted and total war which required fighting and building at the same time, balancing the distribution of manpower among all areas of endeavor was a necessity. Expedient measures designed to overcome this imbalance, such as transferring servicemen to the civilian sector and allowing deferments and exemptions from military service, only partly helped. We think that balance could have been achieved only if we had limited the RVNAF to a size that the nation could support effectively in the long run.

Protracted war also demanded that we mobilize all manpower resources, male and female, to meet national requirements. It was obvious that South Vietnam's manpower resources could not support a million-man military force, although we had sacrificed balance in other areas of activity. The size of a military force fighting a protracted war, we think, should be based on the nation's capacity to sustain it with the annual draft-age resources (18 to 20 years of age). We think that 600,000 or 700,000 was about all South Vietnam could afford, and our military force should be built on quality rather than quantity. We could achieve quality for this reduced-size force by better leadership and discipline. An average-sized but soundly organized, carefully trained, well-disciplined and well-led force, to our thinking, was much more effective than a large one plagued by all kinds of shortcomings. The manageable size of a military force also helped determine the term of mandatory service and allow normal discharges, thereby reducing mental tension caused by indefinite service, which was the cause of indiscipline and lethargy. If the RVNAF had been reduced in size, we believe that this would have helped reinforce our counterinsurgency forces at the grassroots level and restored balance to other efforts.

• • •

South Vietnam's national course, from the day it became a nation until it no longer existed, was not entirely shaped by the national leadership but, to a great extent—we have to admit it—by US policies toward Vietnam and this part of the world. Consequently the survival of South Vietnam in its long struggle against the Communists depended on our leadership's "knowledge about the United States" and its "ability for compromise," because our policies had to comply with the interests of both nations. Ignoring this reality, or deviating from this course, only led to disaster.

The tragic thing for South Vietnam was that there had been too many turnovers in leadership, both in-country and in the United States. This lack of continuity in leadership greatly affected the common war effort. The deaths of President Diem and President Kennedy, and the resignation of President Nixon, were all tragedies for South Vietnam, for a change in leadership usually entailed a change in policies and the cadres in charge of implementing these policies.

The South Vietnamese ship lacked a talented and capable captain to guide it through the Communist storm, especially after the death of President Diem. This serious deficiency stemmed primarily from the fact that the majority of outstanding nationalist leaders had perished at the hands of French colonialists and Vietnamese Communists and during the long war against both of them. A small number of our Nationalist leaders who had gone into exile to work for the nation's big time eventually found their ardor and energy gone with senility. Infighting among Nationalist ranks also dispirited some and tarnished the reputation of others. This scarcity of leadership talent could be largely attributed to the lack of popular base that beset nationalist political parties. It made the choice of a leader who truly enjoyed popular esteem and support almost a hopeless proposition.

It was important to know that, in that choice, the majority of the Vietnamese people always seemed to trust only those who had proven records in the anti-French struggle, and preferred them over the modern intellectual elite. This was understandable enough, given the trauma our people had gone through under the long French domination. A revolutionary background was therefore indispensable for a leader to enjoy popular trust and support. South Vietnam's short history demonstrated that all those personalities with a pro-French background never had any political success. If the people did not oppose them publicly, they always loathed them in private. Young, foreign-educated talents also did not attract the people, chiefly because of political inexperience and the fact that they never fought for their country. Perhaps they would have had some chance of success after proving their talent and dedication for the national cause.

Another interesting thing to learn was that very few among those who had a revolutionary background were educated. Placing them in a leadership position was therefore risky if they did not have the charisma to attract the people. The factor of regionalism was also to be taken into account; it was a reality about which most South Vietnamese were conscious. Regionalism was the cumulative result of French colonialist policies, differences in geography and customs, and difficulties in interregional communication. The migration of nearly one million North Vietnamese helped the amalgamation process, but could not erase regionalism. Overlooking this factor in the choice of national leadership would be an inadequacy.

• • •

Not until 1966 were there any efforts to improve the executive ranks at the village and hamlet level, the major ground of political contest with the Communists. Although the objective of these efforts was sound, the approach to them was wrong. The GVN seemed to have focused on training new cadre and neglected the existing ones. Also, by activating the RD cadres, it had wasted national resources and created confusion, duplication, and rivalry. But this error was recognized in time and the RD cadre organization dissolved. The GVN approached the problem of the cadre correctly when, during 1972–1973, it conducted training courses for village and hamlet officials.

Training able cadres for the execution of national policies and programs was already a difficult and time-consuming task. But fostering moral integrity, a sense of duty, and discipline among the cadre proved even more difficult in the context of protracted war and social divisiveness. To achieve this, it was necessary to give these cadres the opportunity to be in close touch with their superiors, to control and supervise their actions closely, and to be fair in rewards and punishments. Most important, however, was the example set by the local and national leadership. Experience indicated that cadres usually did not act in line with the leader's words, but with his attitude. The leadership, therefore, had to prove their integrity, fairness, and moral rectitude if they wanted the cadres to follow suit.

Within the RVNAF, the cadre ranks of officers and NCOs were heterogeneous in background and not uniform in competence. This was because the RVNAF had been built from various armed organizations and beset by politics. The lack of uniformity was most obvious in education, military training, and combat experience. Those who were combat-experienced were usually uneducated or lacking in formal training, and those who were educated and formally trained were invariably combat-inexperienced.

• • •

The RVN made serious efforts in improving its national institutions and leadership, and maintaining national and military discipline. In these areas, it had received substantial assistance from the United States. In spite of their shortcomings, it had to be admitted that the RVNAF had made significant progress and proved capable and confident enough to successfully meet the major challenges of the war. Our commanders and troops had learned valuable experiences from friends and foes alike. They had matured in war, fought gallantly, and accomplished their increasingly difficult mission in a laudable manner. It was a real tragedy that our military leadership could not have done better in the face of [onrushing] events in early 1975.

[Epilogue]

On 25 May 2000, during the annual Armor Conference at Fort Knox, Kentucky, a special ceremony was held to dedicate a plaque honoring the 712 South Vietnamese officers who had attended the US Army Armor School during the Vietnam War.

Five former officers of the Army of the Republic of Vietnam were present for the ceremony. Lieutenant General Vinh-Loc, a 1955 graduate of the US Army Command and General Staff College, had in Vietnam at various times been director of the Armor School, commanding general of II Corps, and commandant of the National Defense College.

Colonel Ha Mai Viet, a graduate in 1959 of the US Army Armor School's Company Commander Course and in 1962 of the Armor Officer Advance Course, where we were classmates, was in Vietnam director of instruction of the Armor School, commanded a cavalry troop and a cavalry squadron, and was G-3 of the Armor Command, province chief of Quang Tri Province, and G-3 of I Corps.

Colonel Tran Ngoc Truc, a 1957 graduate of the Communications Officer Course and the Company Commander Course at Fort Knox, in 1969 also completed the Armor Officer Advance Course. He commanded a cavalry troop, a cavalry squadron, and an armor brigade.

Lieutenant Colonel Nguyen Huu An, a 1959 graduate of the Communications Officer Course, commanded a cavalry troop and a cavalry squadron.

Major Hang Phong Cao commanded a cavalry troop, was executive officer of a cavalry squadron, and was a district chief. He was subsequently president of the Vietnamese Armor Veterans Association in the United States.

As many at the ceremony knew, General Donn Starry and Professor George Hofmann had recently edited a book on the history of American armor entitled *Camp Colt to Desert Storm*. As author of the chapter on the Vietnam War, I observed that the armored personnel carrier was the workhorse of that conflict, and that it was the Vietnamese who innovated adding the additional firepower, then protected firepower, then supplemental armor that evolved into the ACAV, the armored cavalry assault vehicle. We learned from them, then institutionalized what they had developed.

Americans, most of them, served a one-year tour in Vietnam, although many professionals returned for second and even third tours. These Vietnamese officers served one tour—for the duration. Colonel Nguyen Huu An commanded a cavalry troop for four years, then a cavalry squadron for four more years. Colonel Tran Ngoc Truc did the same thing, then commanded an armor brigade. General Vinh-Loc commanded a division, then a corps, for two years each, then headed the National Defense College for six years. Many other officers had similar service.

In America, these men and their families, and others like them, have greatly enriched our society and culture by their hard work and good citizenship. They are also sending in the aggregate over a billion dollars a year to their families and friends still in Vietnam, constituting one of that country's largest sources of income.

And in Vietnam today the people in the south, the former Republic of Vietnam, are producing 80 percent of the entire gross national product, even though they constitute only about half the total population.

In short, as was noted at the Fort Knox dedication ceremony, we have every reason to be proud of our South Vietnamese colleagues, both because of their conduct through the long and difficult years of warfare and in how they have dealt with the tragedy of the eventual outcome.

In the final days of the war large numbers of South Vietnamese fled their country rather than live there under Communist domination. The first were evacuated in Operation Frequent Wind, conducted during the last days of April 1975, in which all the Americans remaining in country were lifted out by air or sea, along with some 130,000 South Vietnamese, people who, along with their families, were thought to be most at risk. In succeeding days many others, soon to become known collectively as the "boat people," put to sea in anything that would float and braved the dangers of weather, starvation, even pirates, in desperate attempts to find freedom. An unknown number, believed to be large, perished in the attempt.

Many early refugees made their way to America, where at several military bases—Fort Chaffee, Arkansas; Camp Pendleton, California; Indiantown Gap Military Reservation, Pennsylvania; Eglin Air Force Base, Florida—they were housed and cared for until sponsors could be found and they could be relocated to new homes. Many found shelter and, eventually, new lives in Orange County, California; in and around Houston, Texas; in northern Virginia; and even in Minneapolis and St. Paul, Minnesota. Smaller numbers found their way to places all across America.

Subsequently a series of other contingents—people resettled in America under what was called the Orderly Departure Program—were also accepted as immigrants (and, as negotiated with Vietnam's Communist government, allowed to depart their former country without interference). In the final tranche of this program, nearly a quarter century after the war, Nick Sebastian, a West Point graduate then with the Immigration and Naturalization Service, spent three months in what had once been Saigon interviewing candidates for political asylum in the United States, former "boat people" who had been forcibly returned from refugee camps elsewhere in Southeast Asia. It was for Sebastian a moving and humbling experience, for he found both the country of Vietnam and its people beautiful, persevering with admirable spirit under a repressive regime and terrible economic hardship. "The people I met throughout the country," he reported, "accept their loss and in many cases unbelievable subsequent persecution with an equanimity, fortitude, strength of character, and will to survive that is awe-inspiring."

Altogether, over the years, perhaps a million Vietnamese have found their way to the United States. Here they have acted out the American dream, demonstrating determination, industriousness, thrift, ambition, entrepreneurial skill and business acumen, a thirst for education, and—in the main—remarkably little bitterness. Many have become proud American citizens, and some of the younger generation have served with distinction in American armed forces.

On the twenty-fifth anniversary of the fall of Saigon the US House of Representatives, in a gesture of stunning futility, passed a resolution urging "an end to political repression in Vietnam and request[ing] the President to make clear to Vietnam leaders that the U.S. expects Vietnam to respect the political and religious rights of its citizens." The vote, 413–3 in favor of the measure, came a quarter century too late to affect or reverse, much less mitigate or excuse, the earlier abandonment of our ill-fated allies by the US Congress.

Fortunately, in America and elsewhere, the millions of expatriate Vietnamese who make up a new diaspora, having found liberty, are enriching the cultures and economies of their adopted homelands, in the process demonstrating as well what might have been in their native Vietnam. The victory there ultimately was not won, but the spirit and dedication and courage and determination of those who sought it have found productive new soil here and elsewhere in the free world. We are all the better for it.

[Abbreviations and Acronyms]

AAA antiaircraft artillery
ACAV armored cavalry assault vehicle
ACTOV accelerated turnover
ADCC Area Security Coordination Council
ADP automated data processing
AG Adjutant General
ALC Area Logistics Command
ALSC Administrative and Logistical Support Company; Administrative and Logistical Support Center
AO area of operation
APC armored personnel carrier
APO Army Post Office
ARDF airborne radio direction finding
ARVN Army of the Republic of Vietnam
ASEAN Association of Southeast Asian Nations
ASOC Air Support Operations Center
ASR ammunition supply rate
BA base area
BAR Browning automatic rifle
BBC British Broadcasting Corporation
BDA bomb damage assessment
BEQ bachelor enlisted quarters
BOQ bachelor officers quarters
BTR Soviet-manufactured armored personnel carrier
BVN Bataillons Vietnamiens
CACC Civic Action Coordination Center
CAP Combined Action Program
CATO Combat Arms Training Organization
CBU cluster bomb unit
CCP Combined Campaign Plan
CDEC Combined Document Exploitation Center
CG Civil Guard
CI counterintelligence

CIA Central Intelligence Agency
CIC Combined Intelligence Center
CICV Combined Intelligence Center, Vietnam
CIDG Civilian Irregular Defense Group
CINCPAC Commander in Chief, Pacific
CINCSAC Commander in Chief, Strategic Air Command
CIO Central Intelligence Organization
CIP Commercial Import Program
CLC Central Logistics Command
CMAC Capital Military Assistance Command
CMD Capital Military District
CMEC Combined Materiel Exploitation Center
CMIC Combined Military Interrogation Center
CMR Capital Military Region
COC Combined Operations Center
COMINT communications intelligence
COMUSMACV Commander, US Military Assistance Command, Vietnam
CORDS Civil Operations and Revolutionary Development Support
COSVN Central Office for South Vietnam (Communist)
CP command post
CPDC Central Pacification and Development Council
CRA Continuing Resolution Authority
CT Cong Truong (enemy division designator, as in CT-7)
CTC Central Training Command
CTZ corps tactical zone
DAO Defense Attaché Office
DASC Direct Air Support Center
DER Destroyer Escort Radar Picket

DIA Defense Intelligence Agency
DIOCC District Intelligence and Operations
  Coordination Committee
DMAC Delta Military Assistance Command
DMZ Demilitarized Zone
DOC Department of Commerce
DOD Department of Defense
DRAC Delta Regional Assistance Command
DSG Direct Support Group
DTA division tactical area
EAMC Electric Accounting Machine Center
EEI essential elements of information
ELINT electronic intelligence
EM enlisted man
ESR Equipment Status Report
FAC forward air controller
FANK Forces Armées Nationales Khmères
FCC fire coordination center
FDC fire direction center
FFORCEV Field Force, Vietnam
FFV Field Force, Vietnam
FO forward observer
FRAC First Regional Assistance Command
FSA forward support area
FSB fire support base
FSCC fire support coordination center
FULRO Unified Front of Struggle for the
  Oppressed Races
FWMAF Free World Military Assistance
  Forces
FWMAO Free World Military Assistance
  Organization
GM Groupe Mobile
GPWD General Political Warfare Department
GVN Government of (South) Vietnam
HALO high-altitude, low-opening
HES Hamlet Evaluation System
HNC High National Council
HOPIR Hot Photo Interpretation Report
HUMINT human intelligence
ICA International Cooperation
  Administration
ICC International Control Commission
ICCS International Commission of Control
  and Supervision
ICP Indochinese Communist Party
ICR Intensive Combat Rate
ID identification
IDHS Intelligence Data Handling System

IFFV I Field Force, Vietnam
IG Inspector General
II imagery interpretation
IIFFV II Field Force, Vietnam
IIR intelligence information report
ILC International Logistics Center
IPIR Immediate Photo Interpretation Report
IPW interrogation of prisoners of war
JCS Joint Chiefs of Staff (US)
JGS Joint General Staff (RVNAF)
JMC Joint Military Commission
JOC Joint Operations Center
JS Joint Support
JUSPAO Joint United States Public Affairs
  Office
KIA killed in action
KVA kilovolt-ampere
LAW light antitank weapon
LCM landing craft, medium
LCU landing craft, utility
LDPC Logistic Data Processing Center
LF Local Force
LOB lines of bearing
LOC line of communication
LRHE Land Reclamation and Hamlet
  Establishment
LRRP long-range reconnaissance patrol
LSM landing ship, medium
LST landing ship, tank
LTL Interprovincial Route (Lien Tinh Lo)
LZ landing zone
MAAG Military Assistance Advisory Group
MAAG-V Military Assistance Advisory
  Group, Vietnam
MACCORDS Military Assistance Command
  Civil Operations and Revolutionary
  Development Support; Military
  Assistance Command Civil Operations
  and Rural Development Support
MACV Military Assistance Command,
  Vietnam
MAF Marine Amphibious Force
MALT mobile advisory logistics team
MAP Military Assistance Program
MASF Military Assistance, Service-Funded
MAT mobile advisory team
MATT mobile advisory training team
MCA/LOC Military Construction, Army,
  Lines of Communication

MDAP Mutual Defense Aid Program
MEDCAP Medical Civic Action Program
MEDTC Military Equipment Delivery Team,
   Cambodia
MF main force
MI military intelligence
MIA missing in action
MID Military Intelligence Detachment
MILCON military construction
MMC Medium Maintenance Center
MOD Ministry of Defense
MOS military occupational specialty
MP Military Police
MPOC Military Post Office Center
MR military region
MRC Military Revolutionary Council
MSC Military Sealift Command
MSD Military Security Department; Military
   Security Directorate
MSS Military Security Service
MSTS Military Sea Transportation Service
MSU Michigan State University
MSUG Michigan State University Group
MTT mobile training team
NCO noncommissioned officer
NDC National Defense College
NIC National Interrogation Center
NICC National Intelligence Coordination
   Committee
NILO Naval Intelligence Liaison Officer
NKP Nakhon Phanom (Air Base)
NLC National Leadership Committee
NLF National Liberation Front (Viet Cong)
NMMA National Materiel Management
   Agency
NP National Police
NSC National Security Council
NVA North Vietnamese Army
NVN North Vietnam
OACS Office of the Assistant Chief
   of Staff
OB order of battle
OCO Office of Civil Operations
OJT on-the-job training
ONI Office of Naval Intelligence
ONTOS Marine self-propelled multiple
   106mm recoilless rifle
OSA Office of the Special Assistant (to the
   Ambassador)

OSI Office of Special Intelligence (7th Air
   Force)
OSPJ Off-Shore Procurement, Japan
PA&E Pacific Architects and Engineers
PAVN People's Army of [North] Vietnam
PC patrol craft
PCE patrol craft, escort
PCF patrol craft, fast
PCH&T packing, crating, handling, and
   transportation
PDO Property Disposal Office
PF Popular Forces
PFF Police Field Forces
PHILCAG Philippine Civic Action Group
PHOTINT photo intelligence
PIOCC Province Intelligence and Operations
   Coordination Committee
PM People's Militia
POC Police Operations Center
POI program of instruction
POL petroleum, oils, and lubricants
POL/MIL political-military
POW prisoner of war
PRD Pacification and Rural Development
PRG Provisional Revolutionary Government
   (Viet Cong)
PRU Provincial Reconnaissance Unit
PSA province senior advisor
PSB Police Special Branch
PSDF People's Self-Defense Force; Popular
   Self-Defense Force
PSOD Permanent Secretariat of Defense
PSP pierced steel plank
PW prisoner of war
QL National Route (Quoc Lo)
RAC Regional Assistance Command
RAG River Assault Group
RD Rural Development; Revolutionary
   Development
RDF radio direction finding
RF Regional Forces
RMG Regional Mobile Group
ROK Republic of Korea
RPD enemy automatic rifle
RPDC Regional Pacification and
   Development Council
RPG rocket-propelled grenade
RPM Chinese-made light machinegun
RRU Radio Research Unit

R&R rest and recreation
RVN Republic of Vietnam (South Vietnam)
RVNAF Republic of Vietnam Armed Forces
SAAFO Special Assistant to the Ambassador
　　for Field Operations
SAC Strategic Air Command
SAM surface-to-air missile
SAPOV South Asia Petroleum Office,
　　Vietnam
SDC Self-Defense Corps
SEATO Southeast Asia Treaty Organization
SI security/intelligence
SLAR side-looking airborne radar
SOI signal operating instructions
SRAG Second Regional Assistance Group
STRATDAT Strategic Technical Directorate
STS Special Technical and Security Branch
STZ special tactical zone
SUPIR Supplemental Photo Interpretation
　　Report
SVN South Vietnam
SZ special zone
TAC Tactical Air Command
TAE target acquisition element
TAOI tactical area of interest
TAOR tactical area of responsibility
TDKQ light infantry battalion
TDY temporary duty
TERM Temporary Equipment Recovery
　　Mission
TF task force
TMA Traffic Management Agency
TOC Tactical Operations Center
TO&E Table of Organization and Equipment
TOW tube-launched, optically tracked, wire-
　　guided missile
TRAC Third Regional Assistance Command

TRIM Training Relations and Instruction
　　Mission
TSR theater sustaining rate
UBC United Buddhist Church
UMDC Unités Mobiles pour la Défence de la
　　Chrétienté
US United States
USA United States of America; United States
　　Army
USAF United States Air Force
USAID United States Agency for
　　International Development
USAILC United States Army International
　　Logistics Center
USARPAC United States Army, Pacific
USARV United States Army, Vietnam
USDAO United States Defense Attaché
　　Office
USIS United States Information Service
USMACV United States Military Assistance
　　Command, Vietnam
USN United States Navy
USOM United States Operations Mission
USSR Union of Soviet Socialist Republics
VC Viet Cong
VCI Viet Cong infrastructure
VN Vietnam
VNA Vietnamese National Army
VNAF Vietnam Air Force
VNMC Vietnam Marine Corps
VNN Vietnam Navy
VNQDD Viet Nam Quoc Dan Dang
　　(Vietnam Nationalist Party)
VOA Voice of America
WHEC High Endurance Cutter
WIA wounded in action
WP patrol boat

GENERAL CAO VAN VIEN

General Vien served as Chief of South Vietnam's Joint General Staff for an entire decade, from 1965 through the end of the war in 1975. Earlier he had distinguished himself as

Commander of the Airborne Brigade. He was commissioned in 1949, then as a young officer commanded a battalion and served on the JGS. In 1957 he graduated from the US Army's Command and General Staff College at Fort Leavenworth. Before assuming the position of JGS Chairman he had served as Chief of Staff of the JGS and then as Commander of III Corps.

General William Rosson described Vien as a nonpolitical officer who understood and exemplified the professional military ethic, and who as a consequence "was trusted by both Vietnamese and Americans." Added General Bruce Palmer, "General Vien, with long combat experience in the South Vietnamese Army, was a fine soldier and an extraordinary military leader. He remained loyal to President Thieu, supported American policy to the best of his ability, cooperated willingly with the American high command, MACV, and took care of his soldiers—all together no mean list of accomplishments." When General Vien became an American citizen—in Alexandria, Virginia, in 1982—General Palmer's comment was this: "In my opinion, our country gained a brave, decent man."

LIEUTENANT GENERAL DONG VAN KHUYEN

General Khuyen was South Vietnam's chief logistician, establishing the RVNAF Central Logistics Command and serving for

many years as its commander. He was commissioned in 1952 upon graduation from the Thu Duc Reserve Officer Military Training Academy where, following combat duty, he returned as director of instruction of the Thu Duc Infantry School.

He was assigned to the J-4 element of the Joint General Staff in 1958 and, after long service in that post, took command of the 3rd Area Logistics Command in April 1964. After brief service as Chief of Staff, III Corps, in 1965, he was named assistant director of the cabinet in the Ministry of National Defense.

In 1967 he was again assigned to the Joint General Staff, now as Chief of the Logistics Department, J-4, also creating and taking command of the Central Logistics Command. During the final years of the war he simultaneously held the senior logistics post and the position of Chief of Staff of the Joint General Staff under General Vien, who noted that because Khuyen was "a devoted and hard worker" he was able to fill both positions. General Vien also cited logistician Khuyen's "long experience of a man involved with the system he helped develop from the start." His diverse military background included combat, training, personnel administration, and logistics.

Recalled Barry Shillito, General Abrams "felt that Khuyen was as honest a person as you would find—integrity coming out of every pore." Abrams once told his assembled staff that Khuyen was "one of the most capable officers" in South Vietnam's armed forces. And, noted American war correspondent George McArthur, Khuyen was a man of parts, once having written "a stirring training song" entitled "Hymn to the M-16."

LIEUTENANT GENERAL NGO QUANG TRUONG

General Truong was described by General Vien as "a professional soldier who held command positions at every tactical echelon during his distinguished career." He was commis-sioned from the Thu Duc Infantry School in 1954. His early service was with the Airborne Brigade and then, as it expanded, as Deputy Commander of the Airborne Division. In 1966 he took command of the ARVN 1st Infantry Division. *New York Times* journalist A. J. Langguth described the division under Truong as "the pride of the Vietnamese regular army" and noted that Truong "led his men skillfully, bravely and honestly." Still in command of the division during the 1968 Tet Offensive, Truong distinguished himself by conducting a tenacious defense and eventual recapture of Hue from his headquarters in the Citadel.

In 1970 General Truong took command of IV Corps in South Vietnam's Mekong Delta region. In the midst of South Vietnam's greatest battlefield crisis, the enemy's 1972 Easter Offensive, General Truong was brought from IV Corps to become Commander of I Corps, then seriously embattled in the region south of the Demilitarized Zone. Truong's presence and decisiveness immediately stabilized the situation and, under his leadership, South Vietnam's forces rallied and counterattacked, eventually regaining most of the lost territory.

Said General Vien of the challenge then confronting Truong, "the task that faced the new I Corps commander was monumental."

Then: "In a matter of just a few days, as if by miracle, the situation in MR-1 visibly improved and stabilized as General Truong's defense plan went into effect." Finally, "as I Corps commander he successfully met the biggest challenge any ARVN field commander ever had to face."

General Melvin Zais recalled Truong as "a wonderful man; one of the finest soldiers I have every known. He was a very perceptive, very courageous and incorruptible man." And, added Zais, "We loved the 1st ARVN Division, and by every standard and criteria it was a brilliant division." Colonel Harry Summers described Truong as "the best general in the South Vietnamese military." General Creighton Abrams praised Truong's "intelligence, initiative and resourcefulness" and cited those qualities as responsible for the effectiveness of the 1st ARVN Division, "which stands head and shoulders above the other infantry divisions as the best division in the South Vietnamese Army."

MAJOR GENERAL NGUYEN DUY HINH

General Hinh spent much of his career as a staff officer at senior levels. He was commissioned in 1952 as the top graduate in the first class of reserve officers of Vietnam. His early years of service were in North Vietnam as an armor platoon leader, then a reconnaissance company commander, during the French Indochina War. After the 1954 partition he underwent armor training at Saumur, the French armor and cavalry school, and at the US Army Armor School at Fort Knox, then was successively Commandant of the Vietnamese Armor School, Commander of the 2nd Armored Regiment, and Deputy Chief of the Armor Command. He also attended the US Army Command and General Staff College at Fort Leavenworth.

Returning to Vietnam, he was appointed Chief of Staff of the Thu Duc Reserve Officers School, serving in that post for two years. In the middle 1960s he was Chief of Staff of the Regional Force/Popular Force Command and then Deputy Commander for RF/PF. In October 1966 he was named Commander of the Quang Da Special Zone (Danang and Quang Nam Province), served as III Corps Chief of Staff, then in June 1968 was appointed I Corps Chief of Staff. In May 1969 he became a member of the second class at the National Defense College in Saigon, graduating in May 1970, and subsequently was the first member of that class to be promoted to brigadier.

Following an assignment as Deputy Commander of IV Corps, in June 1972 he became Commander of the 3rd ARVN Infantry Division in I Corps where, observed General Truong, he "successfully rebuilt and shaped this division into a strong combat unit" after it had suffered heavy losses in the early weeks of the 1972 Easter Offensive. The division's return to the combat scene, said Truong, "was truly a phenomenal achievement." A year later Hinh was promoted to major general in recognition of his excellent performance as a division commander.

BRIGADIER GENERAL
TRAN DINH THO

General Tho was a vastly experienced plans and operations officer. He was commissioned in 1952 after graduation from Dalat National Military Academy. Following early war-time service as district chief of Cu Chi District, Binh Duong Province, in III Corps, he was a division G-3, then a corps G-3, and finally became J-3 of the Joint General Staff, a position he held for seven years.

COLONEL HOANG NGOC LUNG

Colonel Lung was, noted General Vien, "our foremost expert in RVNAF intelligence." As such he served a long stint as J-2 of the Joint General Staff. He was commissioned in 1952 after graduating with the first class from the Nam Dinh Reserve Officer School in

 North Vietnam. He served in combat in fighting against the Viet Minh and as a captain was advanced to battalion command. He migrated to South Vietnam after the 1954 treaty. Later he served as a liaison officer to the US Army at Fort Bragg. He holds a master's degree in law from the University of Saigon and was a military member of the Vietnamese delegation to the Paris Peace Conference in 1969.

At a 1971 MACV conference attended by General Abrams, Colonel Lung was described as "a dedicated, competent professional supported by an excellent and continually improving staff." Noted Lieutenant Colonel Chu Xuan Vien, Colonel Lung's "estimates of the enemy's capabilities and intentions were almost always accurate. In early 1975 he did not foresee a Communist general offensive until 1976, which was later recognized as correct by the PAVN high command."

LIEUTENANT COLONEL
CHU XUAN VIEN

Colonel Vien was assigned to the Republic of Vietnam Embassy in Washington as the last Army Attaché, a position he held during the spring of 1975. For the Indochina Monographs project he performed the arduous task of translating into English all the material written in Vietnamese by the six principal authors; he also contributed to the monograph on the advisor. He was, noted General Vien, "a knowledgeable analyst with a keen sense of military history and an author in his own right." General Truong also complimented Vien for his role in the monographs project, saying that he had done "a highly professional job of translating and editing that helps impart unity and cohesiveness to the manuscript."

A journalist before he was a soldier, Vien was with Agence France Presse in Hanoi during 1949–1952. Later he embarked on a long career as an ARVN signal officer, including four years as chief of the Communications Service in the Office of the Prime Minister and, before being posted to Washington late in the war, three years as chief of the Strategic Intelligence Division in the Ministry of Defense. Among his other interesting achievements was translating Jean Lartéguy's great novel *The Centurions* into Vietnamese for serial publication in *Thai Do* magazine.

MS. PHAM THI BONG

Ms. Bong, who had also been assigned to the Republic of Vietnam Embassy in Washington and was a former captain in South Vietnam's armed forces, was the typist for the Indochina Monographs projects. All its authors cited her for, as General Khuyen noted, "long hours typing, editing, and in the administrative preparation" of the various manuscripts.

[Appendix: Maps]

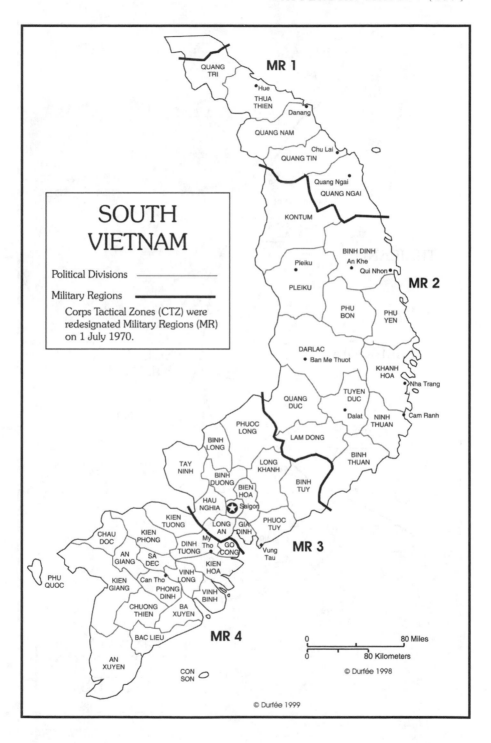

MR 1

QUANG
TRI

•Hue

THUA
THIEN

Danang

QUANG NAM

Chu Lai

QUANG TIN

Quang Ngai
QUANG NGAI

KONTUM

BINH DINH

An Khe
Pleiku   •   •Qui Nhon

PLEIKU

MR 2

PHU
BON

PHU
YEN

DARLAC
• Ban Me Thuot

KHANH
HOA

•Nha Trang

QUANG
DUC

TUYEN
DUC

• Dalat

Cam Ranh

NINH
THUAN

PHUOC
LONG

LAM DONG

BINH
LONG

BINH
THUAN

TAY
NINH

LONG
KHANH

BINH
DUONG

BIEN
HOA

BINH
TUY

HAU
NGHIA   ★ Saigon

KIEN
TUONG   LONG   GIA
AN   DINH

PHUOC
TUY

CHAU
DOC   KIEN
PHONG   My
Tho   GO
CONG

Vung
Tau

MR 3

AN
GIANG   SA
DEC   DINH
TUONG   KIEN
HOA

PHU
QUOC   KIEN
GIANG   Can Tho •   VINH
LONG   VINH
BINH

PHONG
DINH

CHUONG
THIEN   BA
XUYEN

BAC LIEU   MR 4

AN
XUYEN   CON
SON

SOUTH VIETNAM

Political Divisions ————————

Military Regions ————————

Corps Tactical Zones (CTZ) were
redesignated Military Regions (MR)
on 1 July 1970.

0   80 Miles
0   80 Kilometers

© Durfée 1998

© Durfée 1999

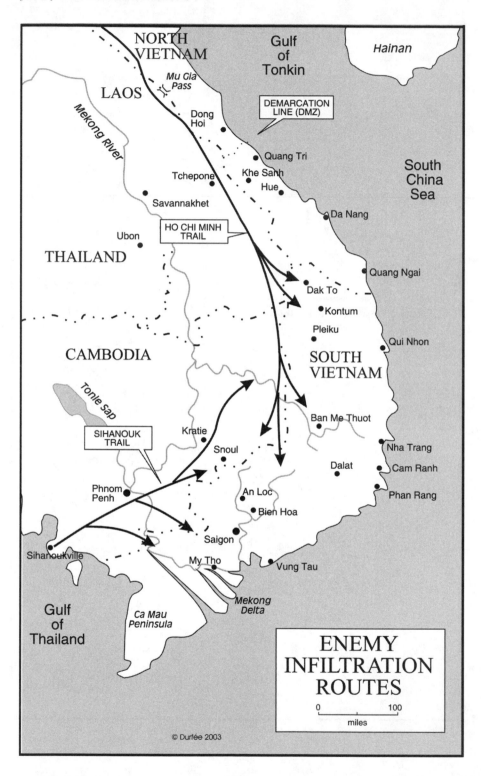

© Durfée 2003

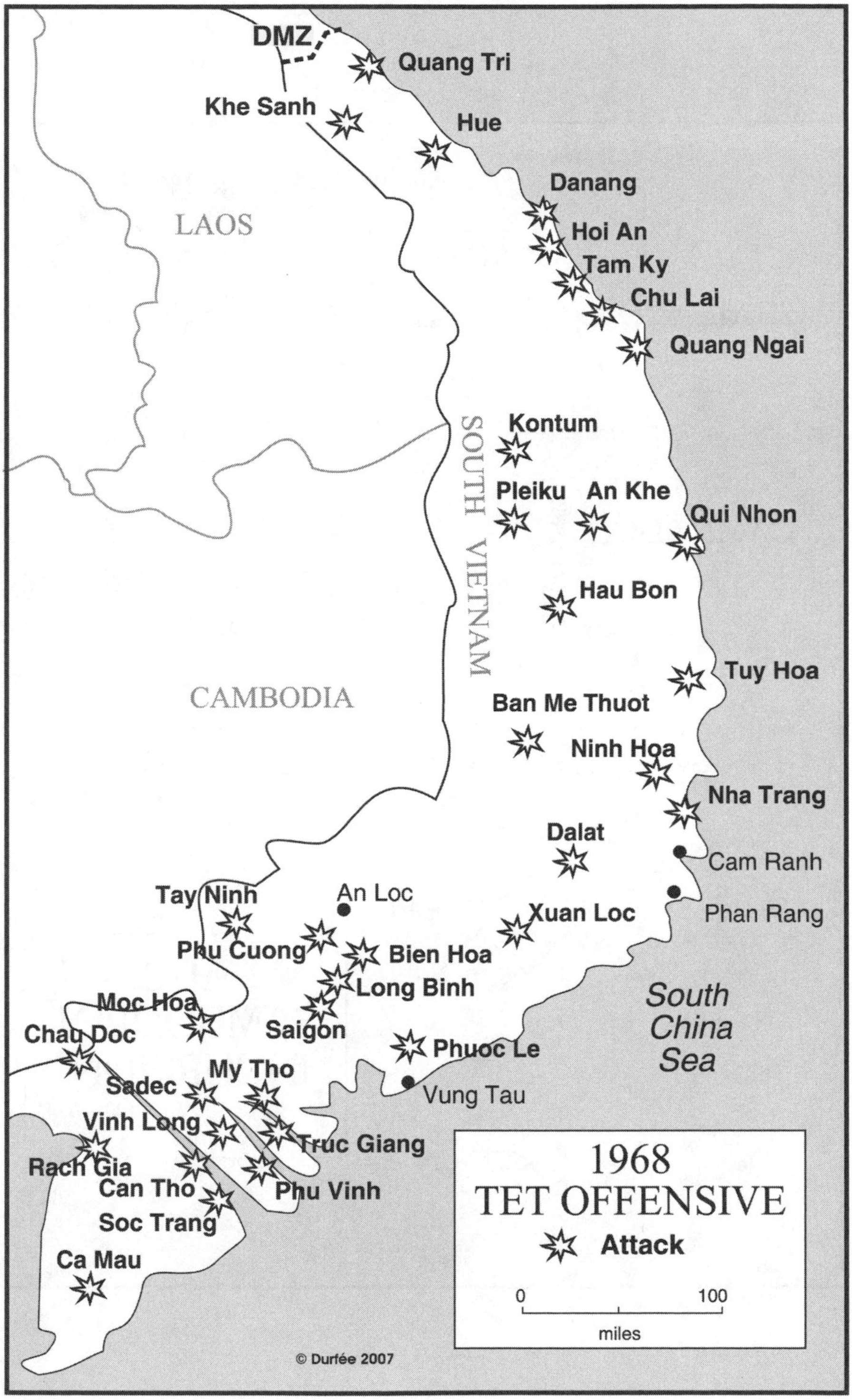
DMZ
Quang Tri
Khe Sanh
Hue
Danang
LAOS
Hoi An
Tam Ky
Chu Lai
Quang Ngai
SOUTH VIETNAM
Kontum
Pleiku
An Khe
Qui Nhon
Hau Bon
Tuy Hoa
CAMBODIA
Ban Me Thuot
Ninh Hoa
Nha Trang
Dalat
Cam Ranh
Tay Ninh
An Loc
Xuan Loc
Phan Rang
Phu Cuong
Bien Hoa
Long Binh
South China Sea
Moc Hoa
Chau Doc
Saigon
Phuoc Le
My Tho
Sadec
Vung Tau
Vinh Long
Truc Giang
Rach Gia
Can Tho
Phu Vinh
Soc Trang
Ca Mau
1968 TET OFFENSIVE
Attack
0
100
miles
© Durfée 2007

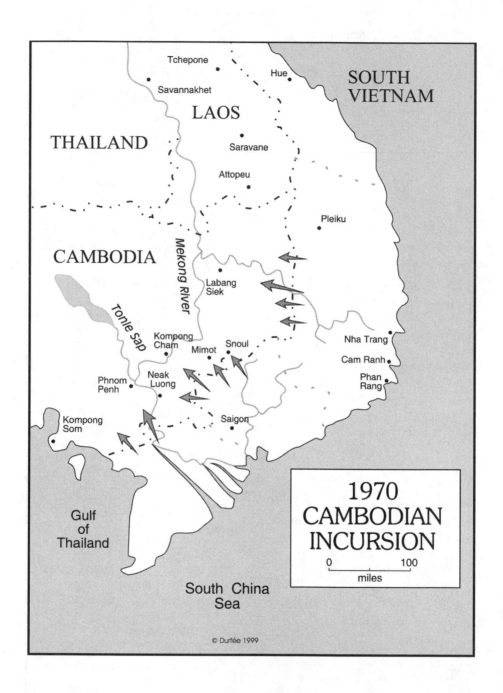

Tchepone

Hue

SOUTH
VIETNAM

Savannakhet

LAOS

THAILAND

Saravane

Attopeu

CAMBODIA

Pleiku

Mekong River

Labang
Siek

Tonle Sap

Kompong
Cham

Mimot

Snoul

Nha Trang

Cam Ranh

Neak
Luong

Phan
Rang

Phnom
Penh

Saigon

Kompong
Som

Gulf
of
Thailand

1970
CAMBODIAN
INCURSION

0   100
miles

South China
Sea

© Durfée 1999

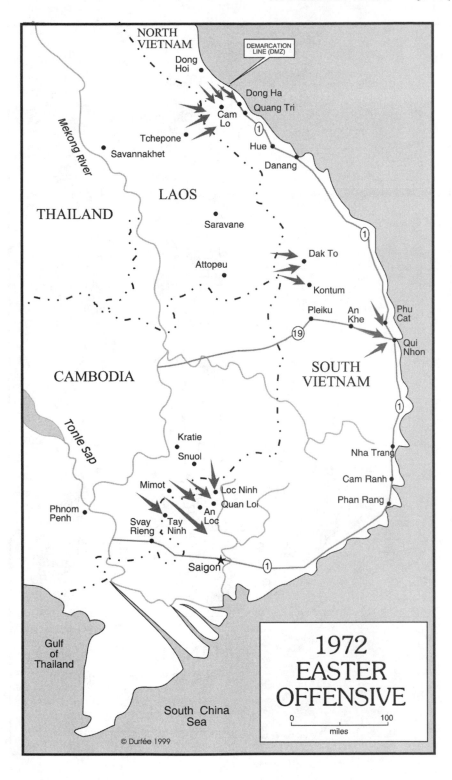

NORTH
VIETNAM

DEMARCATION
LINE (DMZ)

Dong
Hoi

Dong Ha
Quang Tri

Cam
Lo

Tchepone

Savannakhet

Hue

Danang

Mekong River

LAOS

THAILAND

Saravane

Attopeu

Dak To

Kontum

Pleiku

An
Khe

Phu
Cat

19

Qui
Nhon

CAMBODIA

SOUTH
VIETNAM

Tonle Sap

Kratie

Snuol

Nha Trang

Mimot

Loc Ninh
Quan Loi

Cam Ranh

Phan Rang

Phnom
Penh

Svay
Rieng

Tay
Ninh

An
Loc

Saigon

Gulf
of
Thailand

1972
EASTER
OFFENSIVE

0   100
miles

South China
Sea

© Durfée 1999

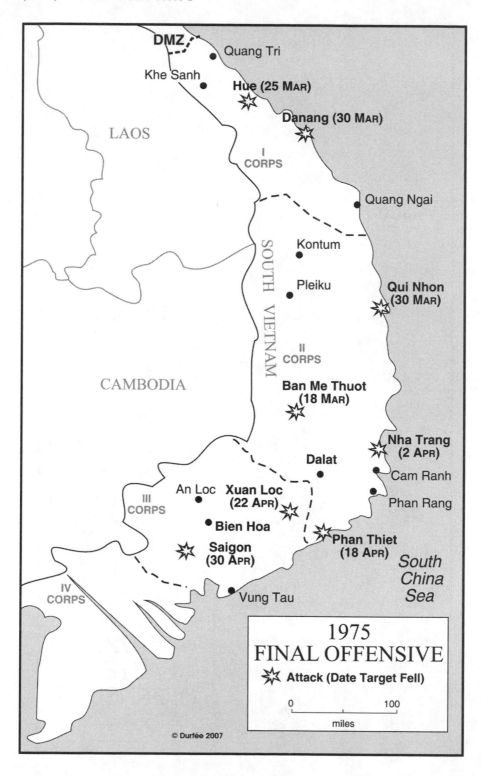

DMZ

Quang Tri

Khe Sanh

Hue (25 MAR)

Danang (30 MAR)

LAOS

I CORPS

Quang Ngai

SOUTH VIETNAM

Kontum

Pleiku

Qui Nhon (30 MAR)

II CORPS

CAMBODIA

Ban Me Thuot (18 MAR)

Nha Trang (2 APR)

Dalat

Cam Ranh

An Loc

Xuan Loc (22 APR)

Phan Rang

III CORPS

Bien Hoa

Saigon (30 APR)

Phan Thiet (18 APR)

South China Sea

IV CORPS

Vung Tau

1975
FINAL OFFENSIVE

Attack (Date Target Fell)

0   100
miles

© Durfée 2007

[About the Editor]

LEWIS SORLEY is a third-generation graduate of the United States Military Academy who also holds a doctorate from Johns Hopkins University. He has served on the faculties at West Point and the Army War College.

His Army service included leadership of tank and armored cavalry units in Germany, Vietnam and the United States, as well as staff positions in the offices of the Secretary of Defense and the Army Chief of Staff. In Vietnam during 1966–1967 he was a plans officer at I Field Force, Vietnam, then executive officer of a tank battalion, 1st Battalion, 69th Armor, operating in the Pleiku area of the Central Highlands.

Dr. Sorley is the author of two biographies, *Thunderbolt: General Creighton Abrams and the Army of His Times* and *Honorable Warrior: General Harold K. Johnson and the Ethics of Command.* The Johnson biography received the Army Historical Foundation's Distinguished Book Award. An excerpt of the Abrams biography was awarded the Peterson Prize as the year's best scholarly article on military history.

His book *A Better War: The Unexamined Victories and Final Tragedy of America's Last Years in Vietnam* was nominated for the Pulitzer Prize. His edited volume entitled *Vietnam Chronicles: The Abrams Tapes, 1968-1972*, also published in Texas Tech University Press's Modern Southeast Asia Series, received the Army Historical Foundation's Trefry Prize, being cited for providing a unique perspective on the art of command. Most recently the American Veterans Center has awarded him the Goodpaster Prize for his devotion to military scholarship.

Dr. Sorley serves as Secretary of the Board of Directors of the Army Historical Foundation and is Executive Director Emeritus of the Association of Military Colleges and Schools of the United States.